SHEPARD'S
McGRAW-HILL

TAX
DICTIONARY
FOR
BUSINESS

SHEPARD'S
McGRAW-HILL

TAX
DICTIONARY
FOR
BUSINESS

DAVID MINARS
RICHARD A. WESTIN

McGraw-Hill, Inc.

New York   San Francisco   Washington, D.C.   Auckland   Bogotá
Caracas   Lisbon   London   Madrid   Mexico City   Milan
· Montreal   New Delhi   San Juan   Singapore
Sydney   Tokyo   Toronto

Library of Congress Catalog Card Number 93-2308

1 2 3 4 5 6 7 8 9 0   DOH/DOH   9 9 8 7 6 5 4 3

ISBN 0-07-042371-7

The sponsoring editor for this book was Caroline Carney, the editing supervisor was Stephen M. Smith, and the production supervisor was Suzanne W. Babeuf. It was set in Times Roman by McGraw-Hill's Professional Book Group composition unit.

Printed and bound by R. R. Donnelley & Sons Company.

 This book is printed on recycled, acid-free paper containing a minimum of 50% recycled de-inked fiber.

To my esteemed colleagues,
Hyman Sardy and Moishe Zelcer

DM

PREFACE

The Internal Revenue Code, with its thousands of complex sections, regulations, and revenue rulings, can create a multitude of problems that can require many hours of serious and time-consuming research to solve, whether you are preparing a tax return or trying to find an answer to a particular tax question. Until now there has not been one reference to which to turn to find clear and concise tax information. That's why we wrote this book.

Shepard's/McGraw-Hill Tax Dictionary for Business provides clear and concise definitions of more than 6000 tax terms. Entries include references to, and quick, yet complete, analysis of, all applicable sections of the Code, regulations, and revenue rulings and procedures, as well as cross-references to any other pertinent terms. This book thus gives you "hands-on" answers to complex tax questions.

The field of federal taxation is based primarily on the disciplines of accounting and law. This book was not written to restate these disciplines, but is aimed at clarifying the interwoven intricacies of federal tax law. It attempts to link the similarities underlying different tax concepts so that a more functional picture of the Code can be understood and utilized when necessary.

You can use the *Dictionary* at home and at work. Whether you are a corporate manager, small business owner, or tax professional, you can use this book's analysis and insights to comply correctly with the increasingly complex areas of taxation. It can help to familiarize you with the array of options for today's tax problems.

This book is an abridged version of a widely used comprehensive text for tax attorneys, *Shepard's 1992–1993 Tax Dictionary* by Richard A. Westin. We took this text and transformed it into a useful and practical book for both professional and personal purposes, one that quickly and efficiently defines puzzling Code terminology.

We believe that this up-to-date and sophisticated, yet practical, dictionary is a unique tool that provides the "tax savvy" needed in today's complicated tax environment.

David Minars
Richard A. Westin

ABOUT THE AUTHORS

David Minars, MBA, CPA, JD, is a tax attorney and deputy chairman of and a professor in the Department of Economics at Brooklyn College of the City University of New York. He has written more than 150 articles in the areas of accounting, law, and federal taxation. Among the many books that he has either authored or coauthored are *The Financial Troubleshooter, Tax Penalties and Interest Handbook*, and *Your Business, Your Money: Strategies for Getting More Cash Out of Your Business*. **Richard A. Westin** is the author of *Shepard's 1992–1993 Tax Dictionary* and is professor of law at the University of Houston Law School. He has written 10 professional books in the field.

SHEPARD'S
McGRAW-HILL

TAX
DICTIONARY
FOR
BUSINESS

A

AAA an acronym for *accumulated adjustments account, which is a corporate account associated with an S corporation*. Essentially, the AAA is a cumulative total of undistributed net income items for S corporation taxable years beginning after 1982.

AAA bypass election an election to sweep out *earnings and profits* of an *S corporation* by means of a *dividend to stockholders*. Section 1368(d)(3) authorizes distributions to be from earnings and profits first. The election and distribution permits the avoidance of a variety of problems, such as the tax on *excess net passive income*.

ACE an acronym for *adjusted current earnings*. The ACE rules are a separate parallel system to both the alternative minimum tax (AMT) and taxable income. S corporations, real estate investment trusts, regulated investment companies, and real estate mortgage investment conduits are not subject to the ACE provisions. The purpose of the ACE adjustment is to ensure that the mismatching of financial statement income and taxable income will not produce inequitable results. The CNEPA of 1992 (Pub. L 102-486) repeals the ACE adjustments for intangible drilling costs and for percentage depletion for years beginning after 1992. §1915.

acq. see *acquiescence*.

ACRS an acronym for *accelerated cost recovery system*. ACRS permits recovery of capital costs for most tangible depreciable property using accelerated methods of cost recovery over predetermined recovery periods generally unrelated to, but shorter than, useful lives.

ADR an abbreviation for *asset depreciation range*. See *class life asset depreciation range system*.

ADS an acronym for the *alternative depreciation system*. Instead of the regular modified accelerated cost recovery system (MACRS), which is based on class life, taxpayers may irrevocably elect to apply the alternative MACRS system to any class of property for any tax year and depreciate assets using the straight-line method or the 150 percent declining-balance method of depreciation. If elected, the alternative system applies to all property in the MACRS class placed in service during the year. Code §168(g).

A.F.T.R. *American Federal Tax Reports*. This Prentice-Hall, Inc., publication contains tax decisions of federal courts other than the *Tax Court*. The second series of A.F.T.R. volumes is referred to as A.F.T.R. 2d.

AICPA American Institute of Certified Public Accountants; the national professional organization of CPAs.

AMT adjustment an adjustment used to increase *alternative minimum taxable income*. This type of adjustment appears in §56. Section 57 contains *items of tax preference* which only increase alternative minimum taxable income (AMTI).

AMT bonds an acronym for *alternative minimum tax bonds*.

ANN. an abbreviation for *an announcement*.

AOD see *actions on decisions*.

abandonment loss a loss resulting from the taxpayer's relinquishment of an interest in worthless property (e.g., a dry well) on property which has lost its utility. Section 165 allows a *deduction* for such losses if they relate to trade or business property or property held for the production of income. See Reg. §1.165-1(b) and -2. The amount of the loss is the adjusted basis of the property at the time of abandonment. The taxpayer must not have acquired the property with a view to its abandonment and must intend to irrevocably discard the asset, with no thought of retrieving it for sale or other disposition. Affirmative behavior is required, mere non-use will not suffice. See *demolition cost and loss*.

abatement reduction of an *assessment* by the IRS. See §6213. Abatement (elimination) of interest or penalties is fairly common. See esp. §6404(e)(1), IRS dilatoriness as basis for abatement. The term is sometimes used descriptively to refer to deductions or other forms of tax relief.

abnormal retirement, asset the retirement of an asset for reasons not contemplated when the *taxpayer fixed the depreciation* rate. Examples include retirement as a result of *casualty or extraordinary obsolescence*. Reg. §1.167(a)-8(b). Abnormal retirement of depreciable property permits *loss deductions* even though the taxpayer does not physically dispose of or abandon the asset. Reg. §1.167(a)-8(a)(3); see also Reg. §1.165-1(b) (nondepreciable property).

above the line another term for *deductions* from *gross income* claimed by *individuals* under §62. The expression arose because early individual *income tax returns (Form 1040)* had a dark line above which such deductions were claimed.

absolute gift see *completed transfer*.

absorption rules, net operating loss carryovers and carrybacks a term used to describe the system under which *net operating losses* (NOLs) are used up. The basic notion is that such losses first may be carried back to the third *taxable year* and used to offset *taxable income* in the third year, the benefit of which is captured by filing a *claim for refund or credit*. The balance moves to the second taxable year; if the balance is not fully used up in that year, then it is applied against taxable income in the first preceding year. Should a balance still remain, it is carried over to the first year following the loss year and forward in the same manner for up to a total of 15 years if still not fully absorbed. The number of years a loss can be carried forward depends on when the loss arose and the character of the *taxpayer* (e.g., *Cuban expropriation losses* are carried forward 20 years). The mechanics of NOL carrybacks and carryovers are complicated because taxable income of the years to which losses are carried must be recomputed, including such items as *charitable contribution deductions*. See, e.g., Reg. §1.172-5(a)(3)(ii). In the case of *individuals*, absorption of NOLs is affected by denying to individual taxpayers the *deduction* for *net capital gains* and *personal* and *dependency exemptions*. §172(b)(2)(A) and (B). Taxpayers can elect not to carry back NOLs, but to carry them forward only.

abuse of discretion   a standard used to determine whether an administrative action taken by the *IRS* (e.g., reallocation of income between related organizations under §482) should be overturned. Generally, abuse of discretion will not be found unless the IRS's actions are at least arbitrary and capricious, a difficult showing to make. The standard may limit the *Commissioner's* discretion to take inconsistent litigating positions. See *discretion*.

abusive tax shelter, penalties, injunctions and crimes an undefined *Code* heading. The implicit reference is to any *partnership* or other *entity*, investment, plan, or arrangement if a *person* participating in its organization (or in the sale of interests in it) makes or furnishes either: (1) a statement as to the availability of any tax benefit to participants which that person knows or has reason to know is false or fraudulent; or (2) a statement indicating that the value of any property or services is more than double the actual value (a *gross valuation overstatement*), provided the value is directly related to the amount of any income tax *deduction* or credit allowable to any participant. §6700. In addition, the *Secretary* may seek injunctive relief to prevent recurrence of abusive tax shelter activity. §7408. Criminal prosecution is possible under §7201 or 18 U.S.C. §371. See *penalty, promoting abusive tax shelters*; *potentially abusive tax shelter*.

accelerated cost recovery   see *accelerated cost recovery system (ACRS)*.

accelerated cost recovery system (ACRS)   a system of *depreciation* applicable to *tangible property*, referred to as cost recovery, which was introduced in the *Economic Recovery Tax Act of 1981*, and is often referred to by its acronym ACRS. The system applies to property *placed in service* by the *taxpayer* on various dates after 1980, except as to certain property in existence before 1981 and which was subject to *churning*. ACRS has been cut back extensively over the years and its present form is often referred to as modified ACRS (or MACRS). Both ACRS and modified ACRS have the simplifying features of presuming a zero *salvage value*, and classifying all tangible property in one of eight *recovery periods*, during which period the property is entirely written off, unless the taxpayer elects to claim a different, longer recovery period. Tabular accelerated write-off methods (generally, the equivalent of 150 percent *declining-balance depreciation*) are applied by ACRS to all *recovery property* over the applicable recovery period or a statutorily designated extended period, absent a prior law election to use the extended *straight-line* method over the same life or an extended life. Certain property is excluded from ACRS, especially overseas property. *Class life asset depreciation range* characterizations are used to classify property under ACRS, and the property must have been a *character subject to depreciation* under §167, the predecessor of ACRS, in order to qualify for so-called cost recovery.

accelerated depreciation   a method of *depreciation* resulting in larger depreciation *deductions* in the earlier years of the life of an asset than would result from application of the *straight-line* (i.e., equal annual depreciation expense) method, but which stops when a *reasonable salvage value* is attained. Illustrations include the *sum-of-the-years' digits* and the *declining-balance* methods of depreciation. These methods may be used for property acquired before 1981 provided the asset is *tangible property* placed in service by the *taxpayer* when new and has a *useful life* of more than three years. §167(c). Section 167(b)(2) and (3) authorize accelerated methods of depreciation.

accepted compromise   see *offer in compromise*.

accident and health insurance, life insurance companies   insurance under which benefits are payable in case of disease, accidental injury, or accidental death. For these purposes, a *life insurance company's* business is separated into two segments: (1) cancellable contracts on which the interest credited to reserves is not allowed; and (2) *noncancellable accident and health policies* on which the interest credit is allowed.

accident and health plan   a written, permanent, enforceable plan as to which *employees* are notified, arranging for the payment, directly or through insurance, of amounts to one or more *employees* in the event of *personal injury or sickness*. §§89(k) (repealed) and 105. It must also be for the exclusive benefit of employees. §89(k). Amounts paid out pursuant to such plans, including sickness and disability funds of the states and the District of Columbia, may be *excluded* from the employee's *gross income*; and contributions and payments may also be *deducted* by the *employer*. §§105(e),

106, 162. Exclusions under accident and health plans extend only to employer-paid or reimbursed *medical care* expenses, payments for disfigurement or loss of a bodily member or function, and certain disability payments. §105(b)–(d). The first two exclusions extend to *dependents* (whether or not a *dependency exemption* can be claimed) and *spouses* of employees. Such plans may be paid directly, reimbursed, or funded through health insurance. These plans are classified as *statutory employee benefit plans* and as such are subject to special *nondiscrimination rules.*

accident or health plan   same as *accident and health plan.*

accommodation transferor   a nontechnical term that describes a party who participates in a transaction under §351 (*transfers to controlled corporations*), involving potentially tax-free incorporations and capital infusions in exchange for *stock* or debt, whose presence satisfies the requirement that the parties to the transaction have 80 percent *control* of the *corporation immediately after the exchange.* Reg. §1.351-1(a)(ii) limits the practice if the transferor's purpose for participating was primarily to qualify other parties' transactions under §351. See Rev. Proc. 76-22, 1976-1 C.B. 562.

account   generally, any fixed bookkeeping entry. In connection with *employee* reporting of reimbursements, the term means an employee's submission to his *employer* of an expense account or other required written statement showing the business nature and the amount of all the employee's expenses (including those charged directly or indirectly to the employer through credit cards or otherwise) broken down into such broad categories as *transportation, meals,* and *lodging* while *away from home overnight, entertainment expenses,* and other *business expenses.* For this purpose, the *Commissioner,* at his discretion, may approve reasonable business practices under which mileage, per diem in lieu of subsistence, and similar allowances providing for *ordinary and necessary business expenses* in accordance with a fixed scale may be regarded as equivalent to an accounting to the employer. Reg. §1.162-17(b)(4). See §274 for related *substantiation* requirements. See *adequate accounting.*

accountable plan   an arrangement established by an *employer* for *employee* expense advances or reimbursements under which: (a) the employee fully accounts to the employer per §§162 and 274; (b) the employee must return any excess funds advanced; and (c) employees do in fact return such funds. Temp. Reg. §1.62-2T contains the term and narrows the definition. Unreimbursed amounts under such plans can be claimed as *deductions* by employees in determining their *adjusted gross incomes.* The other case where such deductions are allowed is where fixed per diem or per use allowances are fully substantiated and the mileage rates and per

diem expense rates for meals and lodging while traveling are used. Where these requirements are not met, the employer must *withhold* on unsubstantiated advances. See *nonaccountable plans; Runzheimer-type plan.*

accountant-client privilege   a privilege against forced disclosure of communications between accountant and client; the privilege is nonexistent under *common* law, and it is rarely recognized in the federal courts. See *Couch v. United States,* 409 U.S. 322 (1973) (no such privilege in federal law). See *United States v. Arthur Young,* 104 S. Ct. 1495 (1984) (rejection of *variant* of the *work product doctrine*). Accountants' papers prepared for lawyers may be privileged under the *attorney-client privilege.* See *tax accrual workpapers.*

accountant's fees, recovery of   a reference to the federal government's reimbursement of fees paid to an accountant either as *reasonable administrative costs* or as *reasonable litigation costs* under §7439. For this purpose, accountants are largely interchangeable with lawyers. See *attorney's fees, recovery of.*

accounting income   see *fiduciary accounting income.*

accounting method   see *method of accounting.*

accounting method, change of   see *change of accounting method.*

accounting period   the period which a *taxpayer* uses to determine *federal income tax* liabilities. Absent a choice to the contrary, *individuals* and entities are automatically relegated to the *calendar year.* §441. *Taxpayers* may generally select other periods, in particular *fiscal years,* such as June 1 to May 30, or in special circumstances, *fifty-two, fifty-three week* taxable *years,* and shorter periods, in cases of changes of accounting periods and taxpayers in existence for less than a 12-month period. §§441(f), 443. *Partnerships* and *S corporations' taxable years* are statutorily controlled and generally preclude adoption of a taxable year for the enterprise different from that of its majority partners, or a noncalendar year, respectively. §§706, 1378(b). Changes in the accounting period call for *IRS* approval. §442.

accounting records   a *taxpayer's* regular books of account and other records and data as may be necessary to support the entries on the taxpayer's books of account and *tax return*; for example, a reconciliation between such books and the return. Reg. §1.446-1(a)(4). Such records are required by §446. The adequacy depends on the *facts and circumstances.*

accounting to employer, employee expenses   see *adequate accounting.*

accounts and notes receivable acquired in the ordinary course of business for services rendered or for the sale of property   a class of *property* generated by sales of *dealer property* or *inventory* or from the rendition of personal services by the *taxpayer*, excluded from *capital asset* status by §1221(4). The term has been extended to include notes held by a savings and loan association in connection with loans made to customers, a seemingly strange result. Rev. Rul. 73-558, 1973-2 C.B. 298.

accounts payable a current liability typically representing a *business* debtor's obligations for merchandise or services bought on open account or for short-term credit. An *accrual method taxpayer* may generally *deduct* accounts payable when the obligation becomes fixed. §61(a).

accounts receivable monies owed typically to a *business* creditor for services rendered or merchandise sold on open account or for short-term credit. *Accrual method taxpayers* generally include such accounts in *gross income* when the accounts arise, and claim *bad debt losses* on a debt's entire or partial *worthlessness*. §§451(a), 166(a). See *business bad debt*.

account stated an account which arises when the *IRS* issues a *certificate of overassessment* to a *taxpayer* for a taxpayer's *overpayment of taxes*. Such an account will arise when the IRS clearly overassessed the tax and the only issue is whether the amount of a deficiency is correct when offset against the overassessment. Such an account does not exist until the balance in favor of the taxpayer is officially relayed to the taxpayer. A taxpayer may sue the IRS for the recovery of such an account. *Id.* See RIA Federal Tax Coordinator 2d paragraph U-4500.

accrual an amount which has been reported under the *accrual method*. See *accrual method*.

accrual method a *method of accounting* pursuant to which items of *income* and *expense* are determined. The method is indifferent to the time of actual receipt and disbursement, requiring instead that amounts be included in *gross income* or be *deducted* when all the events fixing the right to receive, or the duty to pay, respectively, have occurred. This is true even though an immediate, legally enforceable right to receive, or duty to pay, has not yet arisen. No single accrual method is applicable; rather, *taxpayers* adopt the model to their particular economic circumstances. Reg. §1.446-1(c)(1)(ii). The term "accrual basis" is used interchangeably with *accrual method*. See §§446, 451, 461. The Tax Reform Act of 1984 dramatically changed this method of accounting by disallowing *deductions* until *economic performance* (i.e., the delivery of the property or service for which the liability is reported) takes place. See §461(h). See *all events test; claim of right doctrine*.

accrual of benefits see *accrued benefits*.

accrual of bond discount the practice, by the issuer, of claiming current *interest expense deductions* for *original issue discount* under the authority of §163(e)(1) or

Reg. §1.163-4(a), regardless of the *taxpayer's method of accounting*; for the owner of the obligation, the duty under the *original issue discount* rules of §1232 to report the year's ratable share of such discount. Section 1232 was supplemented by §1272.

accrual shipment method a *method of accounting* used by manufacturers and contractors who perform multipart contracts. The revenue is accrued as each segment is completed (e.g., completed and shipped).

accrued benefits those *contributions*, expressed as a dollar figure or as an *annuity* beginning at retirement, which have been earmarked for a particular *participant*, and which that person will receive in whole or in part, but only to the extent he or she has a *vested* right in them. For a *defined benefit plan*, the accrued benefit is stated as an *annual benefit* in the form of an annuity. §411(a)(7)(A)(i). For a *defined contribution plan*, the accrued benefit is simply the balance in the *employee's* account. §411(a)(7)(A)(ii). See Reg. §1.411(a)-7(a)(1) and (2). For example, assume a participant's interest in a plan vests at a rate of 10 percent per year; also assume that the *employee* has been working for three years, during which time the *employer* contributed $1,000 per year to the account. The employee is said to have $3,000 of accrued benefits, but a *vested accrued benefit* of only $900. Thus, if he/she quit at the end of the third year, he/she would forfeit the unvested portion of the accrued benefit (i.e., $2,100). Note that the benefits considered under the accrual rules are only retirement benefits (e.g., not ancillary life insurance coverage). In the interest of fairness to employees, defined benefit plans must, in order to be deemed *qualified plans*, satisfy at least one of three rules dictating minimum accrued benefits: (1) the *three-percent rule*; (2) the *one hundred thirty-three and one-third percent rule*; and (3) the *fractional rule*. §411(b)(1)(A)-(C). The rules are described in Reg. §1.411(b)-1 and relate only to retirement benefits, and not, for example, to disability benefits. See *annual benefit, qualified plans; vesting*.

accumulated adjustments account an account, established for *S corporations*, which consists of the *corporation's taxable income* for the period when the *subchapter S election* was in force, excluding *taxable years* before 1983. *Taxable income* is modified by any adjustments made by *shareholders* to their *bases* in their *stock* while the election is in effect, but adjustments with respect to *tax-exempt income* and *federal income taxes* while a *C corporation* (e.g. *federal income taxes*) are ignored. §1368(e)(1)(A). Before the tax for distributions of *accumulated earnings and profits* is computed, the accumulated adjustments account enables S corporations to make tax-free distributions to shareholders of post-1982 income that has been earned and taxed but not distributed. §1368(c)(1). The part of a *distribution* in excess of the account is treated as a *dividend* to the extent of the corporation's accumulated earnings and profits when it was a *C corporation.* §1368(c)(2). The Tax Reform Act of 1984 provides that only *expenses* in connection with earning *tax-exempt interest* are nondeductible for this purpose, and that the account may be negative. §1361(e)(1)(A), as amended retroactively. Also, a pro rata part of each distribution is deemed made out of the account as distributions are made over the course of the year. §1368(c).

accumulated book depreciation election a nickname for an irrevocable election used for purposes of the *alternative minimum tax* applicable to *corporations.* §56(g)(4)(A)(iv). The election is used for purposes of computing *adjusted current earnings* (ACE). The election permits corporations to *deduct* an amount equal to the amount needed to increase accumulated *depreciation* for ACE purposes on a depreciable property up to the lesser of the year-end accumulated depreciation computed under the *alternative depreciation system* or book system. See *adjusted current earnings.*

accumulated contributions, qualified plans the sum of the *mandatory contributions* of an *employee,* plus *interest* stated under the plan until the plan was affected by the *vesting* rules of §411(a), plus interest on the two foregoing amounts at 5 percent compounded from the date the vesting rules took hold until *normal retirement age.* §411(c)(2)(C); Reg. §1.411(c)-1(c)(3). The term is used to determine whether the *accrued benefit* of mandatory employee contributions is adequate. In the case of *defined benefit plans,* the technique involves multiplying accumulated contributions by an *appropriate conversion factor.* §411(c)(2)(B).

accumulated deductible employee contribution an *employee* contribution to a *qualified plan,* plus *gains,* less *losses* and *expenses.* §72(o)(5)(B). Among other things, monies accrued will be subject to anti*rollover* rules to be promulgated by *regulations* and may not be loaned tax-free to *participants* or beneficiaries. §72(o)(4) and (p)(2)(A)(ii).

accumulated deficit rule jargon for §952(c)(1)(B), which permits a *controlled foreign corporation* to use its accumulated deficits in its *earnings and profits* to offset *subpart F income* that would otherwise be included in the *United States shareholders' gross income.* It calls for the deficit to be a *qualified deficit* and the source of the deficit to be a *qualified activity.* A qualified deficit is one that is attributable to a qualified activity. §952(c)(1)(B)(ii).

accumulated DISC income a category of *earnings and profits* of a *domestic international sales corporation* (DISC). The DISC provisions were largely repealed by the Tax Reform Act of 1984.

accumulated earnings and profits a complex tax bookkeeping account that *corporations* are obligated to maintain to determine the extent to which *distributions* of cash or property to shareholders are taxable as *dividends* under §301. Only post–February 23, 1913 earnings and profits are included in the account. At the close of each *taxable year,* the account is increased in the amount of the undistributed earnings and profits for the current taxable year, and is decreased by the current year's *losses* and distributions allocable to earnings and profits generated in prior years. If a positive balance in *current earnings and profits* exists at the end of the year, the balance is added to the accumulated earnings and profits account (which may be positive or negative), thereby increasing the account (or reducing the deficit) in the next year. Section 312 provides guidance about matters such as the impact of distributions (including tax-free distributions) on earnings and profits, *accelerated depreciation* and cost recovery, *corporate divisions,* and *discharges of indebtedness.* See also *current earnings and profits.*

accumulated earnings credit a *deduction* permitted in determining *accumulated taxable income* for purposes of determining the *accumulated earnings tax.* Section 535(c) grants the so-called credit. (The term "credit" is an obvious misnomer; it is an offset to a base on which a tax is imposed, not a credit against taxes.) The minimum credit for all corporations is $150,000 of aggregate *accumulated earnings and profits* ($250,000 in the case of a nonservice business) and may be much larger if accumulations are "reasonable"; the alternative credit is the portion of *current earnings and profits* which is retained to meet the *reasonable needs of the business,* less *net capital gains,* reduced by associated federal income taxes. *Mere holding and investment companies* are limited to a $250,000 credit.

accumulated earnings tax a *nondeductible excise tax* imposed at a flat 28 percent rate on taxable *corporations* other than *personal holding companies* and *foreign personal holding companies* which accumulate, rather than distribute, earnings beyond the *reasonable needs of the business* in order to avoid federal income taxes at the shareholder level. §§531–537. The retention of income to avoid shareholder taxes must be deliberate, but *tax avoidance* need only be a purpose for the accumulation. The base upon which the tax is imposed is *accumulated taxable income,* as defined in §535, less a *dividends paid deduction* and a substantial *accumulated earnings credit. Certain service corporations* are assured only a $150,000 base and *mere holding or investment companies* are entitled to not over a $250,000 base (inaccurately referred to as a "credit"). See *dividends-paid deduction, corporate.* While the tax does not fall on *foreign* source income, avoidance of the tax on United States source earnings by tiering *foreign corporations* (in particular through interposing a *United States–owned foreign corporation*) is largely prevented. See §535(d)(1), as amended.

accumulated effectively connected earnings and profits the aggregate *effectively connected earnings and profits* for prior years beginning after 1986 minus aggregate *dividend equivalent amounts* from such prior years. §884(b)(2)(B)(ii). This figure caps the increase in the dividend equivalent amount that arises via decreases in *United States net equity.* §884(b)(2)(A). This tends to lessen the burden of the *branch profits tax* because it is based on the dividend equivalent amount. See *dividend equivalent amount.*

accumulated funding deficiency basically, underpayment to a *qualified plan* resulting in a shortfall in the *minimum funding standard account,* the effect of which is to cause the imposition of annual *excise taxes* under §4971(a) and (b) (the tax equals 5 percent of the deficiency determined as of year end, with a 100 percent additional tax for failure to correct the deficiency promptly). Section 412 contains the *full funding limitation* and the *alternative minimum funding standard account* used to determine whether such a deficiency exists. The question is complex and calls for an intensive actuarial inquiry. Shortfalls are subject to waivers for hardship and certain extensions. §412(d) and (e). If, under either test, there is no shortfall, the excise taxes are dissipated. See *minimum funding standards.*

accumulated profits, foreign tax credit the amount of *gains,* profits, or income of any *foreign corporation* computed before the imposition of overseas *income, war profits, and excess profits taxes* (foreign taxes), or with respect to the corporation's profits or income, by any foreign country or *possession* of the United States. §902(c)(1). The definition, which is subject to controversy, calls for the computation of *current earnings and profits* under United States tax rules, adding back foreign taxes, and making various adjustments for foreign accounting rules and currency translations. The adjustments may be made under a *subpart F regulation.* Reg. §1.902-1(g)(1) and (3). See *deemed paid foreign tax credit; foreign tax credit.*

accumulated taxable income the base on which the *accumulated earnings tax* is levied. Essentially, it is the *corporation's taxable income* for the *taxable year,* as adjusted, less the *dividends-paid deduction* and the *accumulated earnings credit* (another credit that actually operates as a deduction). §535(a). Taxable income is adjusted principally to reflect dividend-paying ability. The main adjustments are: (1) disallowance of *net operating loss carryovers, capital loss carryovers,* and *dividends-received deductions* (§535(b)); and (2) reduction of income by *net capital gains* (less associated *federal income taxes* and *net capital losses* from prior years), federal taxes, *charitable contributions* to the extent not already *deducted* (but not contribution *carryovers*), nondeductible *capital losses* (reduced by limited prior net capital gain deductions from ATI), certain foreign

and possessions taxes accrued or deemed paid and used as a *credit,* and certain miscellaneous items. See §§247, 249, 250. The dividends-paid deduction relates to current *dividends, consent dividends,* and dividends paid within 2½ months of the close of the year. §§535(a), 561. See *dividends-paid deduction, corporate.*

accumulation distribution the portion of a *distribution* from a *complex trust* which is allocated to *ordinary income* accumulated in prior years (but not earlier than 1969) pursuant to the *throwback rules* of §§665–668. Section 665(b) defines accumulation distributions as annual distributions that exceed the greater of *distributable net income* or *first-tier distributions,* and then only if such distributions are greater than *fiduciary accounting income.* Further computational rules apply to distributions from *foreign trusts* and distributions to *nonresident aliens* and *foreign corporations.* §§665, 667(c).

accumulation trust an informal term used to describe a *trust* which does not distribute or set aside all its annual *income.* The term is often used in lieu of the technical term, *complex trust.*

accuracy-related penalty a *civil tax penalty* imposed on *underpayment of tax* attributable to any of following: negligence; substantial understatement of income tax; substantial (20 percent penalty) or gross (40 percent penalty) valuation misstatement; substantial overstatement of pension liabilities; or substantial estate or gift tax valuation understatement. §§1.6662-1 to 1.6662-5. The penalty can be waived if the *taxpayer* can show *reasonable cause* and *good faith* and the penalty applies only if a *tax return* has actually been filed. See *penalty, negligence by tax return preparer; penalty, substantial understatement of income tax.*

acquiescence an announcement by the *Commissioner of Internal Revenue* that the *IRS* will abide by a deci-sion (other than a *memorandum decision*) of the *Tax Court* regarding issues decided against the government. Alternatively, the Commissioner may announce a *nonacquiescence.* Acquiescence is generally signalled by "A" or "acq." following a case citation. Nonacquiescence is indicated by "N.A." or "nonacq." following a case citation.

acquiescence in result only a pronouncement that the *Commissioner of Internal Revenue,* although disagreeing with the *Tax Court's* treatment of one or more issues, will not file an appeal in the case.

acquired by bequest, devise, or inheritance received from a *decedent's estate* as a result of a will or, in the absence of a will, as a result of one's status as an *heir,* but not in compensation for services or as payment of a debt. §102(a). See separate headings for the definitions of *bequest* and *inheritance.* The §102(a) *exclusion* from income does not extend to *gross income* from property received from a decedent. §102(b).

acquired obligations   principally, *securities* and obligations allocated to the proceeds of an issue of governmental obligations while such issue is outstanding. The term is defined broadly. *Acquired purpose obligations* are defined as governmental obligations acquired to carry out the purpose of the governmental program for which the obligations are issued (e.g., a note secured by a mortgage or a facility constructed with the proceeds of an *industrial development bond*). Prior law Reg. §1.103-13(b)(4)(iv)(A). *Acquired nonpurpose obligations* are acquired obligations other than acquired purpose obligations. The presence of acquired obligations triggers the possibility that the securities issued to obtain them are *arbitrage bonds*. §143 and former §103(c).

acquiring corporation, survival of tax attributes under pre-1986 Act law, the *corporation* that ultimately, directly or indirectly, acquires the assets of the transferor (i.e., target) corporation pursuant to a *plan of reorganization*. If the assets are fragmented such that any one corporation gets substantially all the assets, the corporation that directly acquires the assets is the acquiring corporation. Reg. §1.381(a)–1(b). The acquiring corporation may inherit the federal income tax characteristics of the transferor corporation as a result of a *corporate reorganization* or *section 332 liquidation*. §381. See *survival of tax attributes*.

acquisition cost, qualified mortgage issue   the cost of acquiring a residence from the seller as a completed residential unit. §143(k)(3) and former §103A(1)(5). The acquisition cost does not include the usual and reasonable costs, such as title, insurance, and transfer costs, survey fees, legal fees, and appraisal expenses. The acquisition cost also does not include the value of services performed by the *mortgagor* or members of the mortgagor's family in completing the residence, or the cost of the land if owned by the mortgagor for at least two years prior to the start of construction of the residence.

acquisition date, preacquisition loss limits   see *preacquisition loss limits*.

acquisition date, section 338 acquisition   the day within the *12-month acquisition period* on which the 80 percent purchase requirement of §338 is met. §338(h)(2). Thereafter, the acquiror has 9 months and 15 days to decide whether to make the *section 338 election*. See *section 338 acquisition*.

acquisition discount   the excess of an obligation's *stated redemption price at maturity* (the amount fixed by the purchase agreement, including interest and other amounts payable at maturity, but not interest based on a fixed rate which is payable unconditionally at fixed one-year or shorter intervals for the obligation's whole term) over the *taxpayer's basis* for the property. §§1283(a)(2) and 1273(a)(2), read together. The *daily portion* of acquisition discount on certain *short-term obligations* is currently includible in the *gross income* of certain *taxpayers*. §1281(a). See *short-term obligation, acquisition discount*.

acquisition indebtedness   *debt* incurred by an *exempt organization* either: (1) in acquiring or improving property; (2) before acquisition or improvement of property, if the debt would not have been incurred were it not for the acquisition or improvement; or (3) after acquisition or improvement, if the debt was reasonably foreseeable at the time of acquisition or improvement and would not have been incurred but for the acquisition or improvement. §514(c). Refinancing the property is considered a continuation of the former debt, plus a new possibly unrelated debt if the refinancing is for more than the original principal amount. §514(c)(3); Reg. §1.514-1(c)(1). In all cases, the property that the debt relates to must be *debt-financed property*. §514(c)(1). For a similar concept arising under §279, see *corporate acquisition indebtedness*.

acquisition indebtedness exception   a provision of §304 (*redemption by affiliated corporations*) to the effect that an acquiring company's assumption of *debt* encumbering the acquired *stock* is not considered a *distribution* of property. See §304(b)(3)(d). The exception is limited to transactions that fall under §351 (tax-free *transfers to controlled corporations*). Thus, the "exception" is quite narrow. Nor does the exception apply if the encumbered stock was acquired from a related (§318) person, unless that *person* entirely withdraws his or her interest in both the issuing and the acquiring corporation. §304(b)(3)(B)(iii). There are exceptions for bank holding companies. See *section 351 transactions*.

acquisition indebtedness, qualified residence interest a form of secured debt that can support a *deduction* for *qualified residence interest paid or accrued*. It is debt secured by a *qualified residence*—a *principal residence* or second residence that was either *used as a residence* for *vacation home rule* purposes (or not at all) during the *taxable year*—and was incurred in acquiring, constructing, or substantially improving the residence. §163(h)(3)(B)(i). Such debt is capped at $1 million ($500,000 for *separate returns*). See *qualified residence interest*.

acquisition premium   a value that arises when a holder acquires a *debt instrument* which has *original issue discount* at a price in excess of its *revised issue price*. §1272(a)(7); Prop. Reg. §1.1272-1(g).

acquisition premium, original issue discount   the excess (e.g., $5) of a price paid for a *debt instrument* (e.g., $95) over its *adjusted issue price* (e.g., $90, being an imaginary original issue price of $90 plus $5 of accrued *original issue discount* (OID)). §1272(a)(6).

Such a premium is amortized and offsets the inclusion of OID in a way that prevents having the holder claim a net *deduction.*

acquisition to evade or avoid taxes   the caption of §269, a provision that denies tax benefits associated with (1) acquiring 50 percent or greater control (by vote or value) of a *corporation,* or (2) a corporation's acquiring some or all of the assets in a nontaxable transaction of another corporation not previously controlled by it or its shareholders, but only if garnering a tax benefit the acquiror would not otherwise enjoy was the principal purpose of the transaction. §269(a).

acquisitive D reorganization   a type of potentially tax-free *corporate reorganization,* in which the basic characteristics are one *corporation's* transfer of all or *substantially all of the assets* of an operating type to a second corporation that is under the *control* of the transferor corporation, its shareholders, (including shareholders immediately before the transfer), or both combined. §§368(a)(1)(D), 354(b)(1)(A). The transfer must be followed by the transferor corporation distributing to its shareholders the *stock, securities,* and other properties received from the transferee. §§368(a)(1)(D), 354(b)(1)(B). The transferor may later be liquidated or left as a husk. In order for these transactions to be tax-free, they must satisfy various judicial criteria (*business purpose, continuity of proprietary interest,* and a greatly softened form of *continuity of business enterprise* requirement) and must be pursuant to a *plan of reorganization.* The Type D reorganization has been used by the *IRS* to show a *reincorporation.* See *divisive reorganization; Type D reorganization.*

action organization   an otherwise exempt *section 501(c)(3) organization* rendered taxable by virtue of its quantitatively excessive political, propaganda, or lobbying activities. The term is defined as an organization otherwise potentially tax-exempt, a substantial part of the activities of which involves trying to influence legislation (whether foreign, federal, state, or local, and whether by referendum, initiative, constitutional amendment, or otherwise). The regulations demand an inquiry into all *facts and circumstances* to determine whether such political activities are excessive. Reg. §1.501(c)(3)-1(c)(3). Other organizations (e.g., §501(c)(4) *social welfare organizations*) can engage in lobbying without loss of exemption, and §501(h) allows limited legislative activities, subject to a modest *excise tax* under §4911. See *lobbying expenditures; tax on lobbying expenditures.*

actions on decisions   the *IRS's Chief Counsel's* Office's recommended actions on adverse decisions and descriptions of reasons behind (1) *nonacquiescence* or *acquiescence* in decisions of the *Tax Court,* and (2) IRS appeals of judicial decisions favorable to *taxpayers.*

Such materials issued after December 24, 1981, are subject to public disclosure.

active business computer software royalties   computer software royalties received by certain *corporations* that: (1) are actively engaged in the *business* of developing computer software; (2) derive at least 50 percent of their *gross income* from such computer software; (3) incur substantial *trade or business expenses*; and (4) distribute the bulk of their passive income other than computer software royalties. See §§543(d) and 553(a)(1). The exception for such royalties extends to *foreign personal holding company income* and *personal holding company income.*

active conduct of a banking, financing, or similar business   a status that arises when a *nonresident alien* or a *foreign corporation* is engaged in the *United States* at any point during a *taxable year* in any one of the following activities: (1) issuing letters of credit to the public and negotiating drafts drawn thereunder; (2) receiving deposits of public funds; (3) purchasing, selling, discounting, or negotiating notes, drafts, bills of exchange, acceptances, or other indebtedness for the public on a regular basis; (4) making loans to the public; (5) financing foreign exchange transactions for the public; or (6) providing trust services for the public. See Reg. §1.864-4(c)(5). The definition does not apply to a foreign corporation which acts merely as a financing vehicle for borrowing funds for its parent corporation or any other person who or which would be a related person within the meaning of §954(d)(3) if the foreign corporation were a *controlled foreign corporation.* Reg. §1.864-4(c)(5). *Dividends, interest,* and securities *gains* and *losses* from sources without the United States may be considered *income from sources within the United States* and are taxed at regular United States tax rates if the *taxpayer* has an office or other fixed place of business in the United States to which the income or loss can be attributed. §§864(c)(4)(B)(ii), 871(b), 882(a).

active conduct of a trade or business   the carrying on of a trade or business. Various *Code* sections add the phrase "active conduct," but it seems without analytical value, except perhaps in the context of *corporate divisions* and *partial liquidations.* See *material participation, passive loss rules; trade or business within the United States.*

active conduct of a trade or business, corporate divisions and partial liquidations   a requirement of §355 (*corporate divisions*) designed to bar *bailouts* of *earnings and profits.* §355(a)(1)(C) and (b). The standard demands that each *corporation* involved in the separation be engaged in the active conduct of a *trade or business* immediately after the distribution, and that the business must have been actively conducted throughout the five-year period ending on the date of *distribution* (§355(b)(2)(B)), and that the business not have been directly or indirectly acquired by the distributee corporation (or members of its *affiliated group*) or the distributing corporation (directly or indirectly) within that period in an entirely or partially taxable transaction. §355(b)(2)(C) and (D). According to Reg. §1.355-1(c), a corporation is considered engaged in the active conduct of a trade or business if it carries on directly, or through a controlled subsidiary, a group of activities for profit-making purposes, usually including the collection of income and the payment of expenses, and including every step in the income-producing process from that group of activities. The question of whether the business is "active" is a factual matter.

active foreign business income *gross income* derived from sources outside the *United States,* which income is attributable to the active conduct of a *trade or business* in a foreign country, or in a *Possession of the United States* by the *individual* or *corporation* (or one or more subsidiaries) in which the upper-tier member has at least half the voting power and value of the lower-tier corporation's subsidiary. §861(c)(1)(A). If at least 80 percent of the *taxpayer's* gross income is such income for a three-year testing period, then payments of *dividends* to foreigners are proportionately exempted from United States *withholding of taxes at source.*

actively engaged in business for purposes of §1551, which allows the *IRS* to deny *accumulated earnings credits* and *graduated taxes* if *tax avoidance* motives prompt transfers of property to new *corporations* or to corporations not actively engaged in *business,* the term refers to more than the winding up of corporate affairs or the maintaining of an office to retain a corporation's existence. Reg. §1.1551-1(d).

active participant, IRA a *participant* in one of the following types of retirement arrangements: a *qualified pension, profit-sharing,* or *stock bonus plan*; a *qualified annuity plan*; a *governmental plan,* except for certain deferred compensation plans; an *annuity contract* or *custodial account* bought by a tax-exempt institution or school; *simplified employee pension plan*; or *trust* maintained by a tax-exempt organization. In the case of *defined benefit plans,* an *individual* is an *active participant* if ineligible for the *plan year* that ends with or within that person's *taxable year.* The person is ineligible even though he or she declined to participate, failed to make the *mandatory contributions* called for under the plan, or did not perform minimum service under the plan. In the case of a *defined contribution plan,* a person is a participant if the *employer* allocated contributions to the person's account for the plan year which ends with or within the person's tax year. §219(g)(5) and Notice 87-16, 1987-5 I.R.B. Active participants, as well as their *spouses,* can generally make only small or no contributions to an *IRA.* The active participant status of one spouse is imputed to the other spouse unless the couple

filed *separate returns* and lived apart throughout the entire taxable year. See §219(g)(1). See *individual retirement arrangement (IRA).*

active participation, lump-sum distributions the period during which a *participant* in a *qualified plan* has not: (1) received a *lump-sum distribution* under the plan; (2) separated from service except in the case of self-employed *individuals*; (3) died; or (4) in the case of a self-employed individual, received a lump-sum distribution on account of disability. Former §402(e)(4)(E); Prop. Reg. §1.402(e)-2(d)(3). The term was important in defining the "ordinary income portion" of a favorably taxed lump-sum distribution. See *lump-sum distribution, qualified plans.*

active participation, passive loss rules sufficient *activity* to cause the *taxpayer* to be deemed engaged in a *trade or business,* but not enough to raise to the level of *material participation* for purposes of the *passive loss rules.* This status can be achieved by participating in management decisions, such as approving new tenants, deciding on rental terms, approving capital or repair disbursements and the like, or arranging for others to provide services in a significant and *bona fide* sense. Instructions for Form 8582 (Passive Activity Loss Limitations). The significance is that there is a special $25,000 *de minimis* rule under which many taxpayers can claim *losses* and *credit equivalents* without suffering the limits imposed by the passive loss rules if they actively participate in rental *real estate* activities. §469(i). Active participation is generally an impossible achievement for *limited partners* or people with an under–10 percent share by value of the interest in real estate, but one *spouse's* participation is attributed to the other. §469(i)(6)(A), (C), and (D). See *passive loss rules.*

active service, military periods of service for the *armed forces* of the United States. Periods of active service also include periods in which military personnel are absent from duty due to sickness, wounds, leave, internment by the enemy, or other lawful causes. Reg. §1.112-1(i) (relating to the definition of favorably taxed *combat pay*).

active solar system, energy investment credit a solar energy system that uses mechanically forced (e.g., fans or pumps) energy transfer to circulate solar generated energy. Reg. §1.48-9(d)(2)(ii). Active solar systems could qualify as *solar energy property.* §48(1)(4); Reg. §1.48-9(d).

activity, hobby loss rules an undertaking (e.g., sheep farming) or series of activities (e.g., sheep and pig farming on the same land) which, in light of all *facts and circumstances,* can be considered a single economic undertaking. Factors that tend to suggest the integration of activities into a single economic undertaking are the organizational and the economic interrelationships of the activities, the business purposes that may be served by aggregating activities in a single trade or business, and the activities' similarity. Reg. §1.181-1(a). Each activity is tested to determine whether it was undertaken with a genuine intention to make a profit; if not, its *losses* are limited by the *hobby loss rules* of §183.

activity not engaged in for profit an *activity* other than one for which *deductions* are allowed under §§162 (*trade or business expenses*) or 212(1)-(2) (*investment*-related expenses); in other words, an activity not undertaken with a genuine *profit motive* and, therefore, subject to the limitations on *losses* imposed by §183. Regulation §1.183-2 awkwardly provides nine objective criteria to test for a genuine profit motive. See *hobby loss rules.*

activity, passive loss rules generally, any *undertaking. Trade or business* undertakings are aggregated if similar and controlled by the same interests. They are similar if more than 50 percent, by value, of their operations are in the same *line of business* or if they are vertically integrated. The presence of common control depends on *all facts and circumstances,* but if not over five *persons* own substantial interests in undertakings, they are rebuttably presumed commonly controlled. Professional service undertakings are parts of the same activity if they are similar, related, or commonly controlled. Common control is evaluated under the same rules as apply to trade or businesses undertakings. Professional service activities are deemed similar if over 20 percent, by value, of their operations are in the same field. Two professional services are related if one of them generates over 20 percent of its *gross income* from customers of the other activity. Aggregation of rental *real estate* undertakings is elective. Taxpayers can treat any combination of activities as a single activity. Alternatively, they can divide their rental real estate activities, or they can recombine them into activities which include parts of different undertakings. There are consistency requirements that limit fragmenting real estate undertakings. First, they must be consistent over the years. Second, they cannot fragment real estate undertakings differently from its treatment by a pass through entity through which the taxpayer holds the property. Nonrental undertakings can be treated as a separate activity for purposes of a *disposition,* even if part of a larger activity under the aggregation provisions. Reg. §1.469-4T. This is helpful in terms of revitalizing suspended *losses.* See *line of business, passive loss rules; undertaking, passive loss rules.*

actual deferral percentage the average of the actual deferral ratios, calculated separately for each *employee* in the group, of the amount of elective contributions, including *qualified nonelective contributions,* and *qualified matching contributions* made on behalf of each

employee for the plan year to the employee's *compensation* for the *plan year.* Reg. §1.401(k)-1(g)(8)(i). If a highly compensated employee participates in two or more *cash or deferred arrangements* (CODAs) sponsored by the employer, all these arrangements are treated as one plan in determining the deferral percentage for that employee. §401(k)(3)(A). See *qualified cash or deferred arrangement.*

actual loss experience a term used for purposes of determining the *minimum tax preference* for *bad debts* of financial institutions, generally determined by using a method similar to the six-year moving average formula (§585(b)(3)), with adjustments. Former Reg. §1.57-1(g)(4)(i).

actuarial margin, separate accounts the amount of money retained by a *life insurance company* operating a *separate account* less the former §804(c) assumed limitation on the amount of investment expenses. Former §801(g)(5)(A).

actuarial statement of valuation a report stating the financial status of a qualified *defined benefit plan,* certified by an *enrolled actuary* and filed by the *plan administrator* for the first and every third *plan year,* or more often, as required by the *IRS.* §6059. The purpose is to assure compliance with *minimum funding standards.* Section 6692 provides penalties for failure to comply.

actuarial tables tables used to determine the life expectancies of *individuals* in order to value property (e.g., *annuities* or *remainders*). The *Treasury Department* has published extensive tables for *estate* and *gift tax* purposes, as well as for determining the taxability of *annuity* payments.

additional assessment a further *assessment* for a *tax* of the same character previously paid in part, including the assessment of a *deficiency* (using the §6211 definition). Reg. §301.6611-1(h)(2)(iv) (*interest* in case of *credits*). The term does not seem to have a unified meaning and seems to be used in its plain meaning of a further assessment. See also Reg. §§1.1311(b)-1(c) and -2(a); 301.6305-1(b) and (h).

additional cost element see *reinvestment element.*

additional depreciation a term used in §1250, relating to *recapture* of *depreciation* as *ordinary income.* Its purpose is to identify the amount of *gain* potentially subject to such recapture. See §1250(b)(1) and (c).

additional first-year depreciation see *bonus expensing; bonus recovery.*

additional member a *corporation* that is considered a member of a *controlled group of corporations* during a *calendar year,* even though it is not a member of the group on December 31 of that year, provided it is a member of the group for one-half or more of the days in the year preceding December 31. §1563(b)(3). An additional member, however, generally cannot be a *tax-exempt organization*, a *foreign corporation* taxable under §881, an *insurance company* taxable under §802, or a *franchised corporation*. §1563(b)(3). The additional-member rule plugs a potential loophole by forming an exception to the general rule that includes only corporations which are members on December 31. See *controlled group of corporations*.

additional standard deductions for the tax year 1993, a $700 additional *standard deduction* for being *age 65* or older and a further $700 for being *blind*. An elderly or blind *married person* or *surviving spouse* adds $700 to the *basic standard deduction* ($1,400 on a *joint return*). The extra figure is $900 for *single taxpayers* who are elderly or blind ($1,800 for both combined). §63(f).

additional withholding allowances *exemption amounts* on *Form W-4 by employees* for purposes of their *employers'* computations of federal *employment taxes*. Employees with unusually large anticipated *deductions* characteristically claim additional withholding allowances in order to minimize current taxes.

addition to tax a term used as a synonym for *civil tax penalty*.

adequate accounting generally, the submission to an *employer* of an account book or comparable record with supporting documentary evidence which, in combination, satisfies the *adequate records* standards. Reg. §1.274-5(e)(4). *Employees* who incur *expenses* for the employer's benefit and charge them to the employer through advances or reimbursements are relieved of the §274(d) *substantiation* rules if an adequate accounting to the employer is made. Reg. §1.274-5(e). Also, if the employee *accounts* to his or her employer, he or she is entitled to simplified reporting of excess or inadequate reimbursements. Reg. §1.274-5(e)(2)(i). Regulation §1.162-17, covering employee reporting of reimbursements, is now largely or entirely displaced by Reg. §1.274-5(e)(2).

adequate and full consideration consideration measurable in monetary terms and equal to the value of the property transferred. If adequate and full consideration in money or money's worth is present and moves to the transferor from the transferee, the transfer is not a *gift* for federal *gift tax* purposes. Reg. §25.2512-8. Where some, but not full, consideration is paid by the transferee, the shortfall is deemed a gift. §2512(b). Consideration in money or money's worth excludes: (1) the release of marital rights such as *dower* or *curtesy*; or (2) promises of marriage or of gifts. In contrast, consideration in money or money's worth does include the release of duties to support and maintain an *individual*.

adequate disclosure rule in determining whether the *taxpayer* has omitted more than 25 percent of *gross income*, this rule prevents the *IRS* from including a questionable item of income that the taxpayer has omitted from gross income, thereby holding the *statute of limitations* to three, not six years. See Reg. §301.6501(e)-1(a)(1)(ii). For the questionable item of income to be excluded, the taxpayer must satisfactorily inform the IRS of the nature and amount of the omission by disclosing the omission on the tax return or on an addendum. *Id*. See Rev. Proc. 87-48, 1987 38 I.R.B. 45. See Rev. Proc. 91-19, 1991-10 I.R.B. 2 (adequacy of stated information). Such a disclosure benefits the taxpayer because it prevents the extension of the *assessment period. Id*. See *assessment period; statute of limitations*.

adequate disclosure, substantial understatement of income tax penalty a defense to a 20 percent penalty for substantial understatement of income tax, under which taxes attributable to non–*tax shelter* items that are adequately disclosed are not included in the year's understatement. (In the case of tax shelters, the *taxpayer's* position must more likely than not be correct.) *Proposed regulations* state that the disclosure statement must include a caption identifying the statement as a disclosure under §6662 (formerly §6661), the item for which disclosure is made, its amount, and either facts which, when evaluated by the *IRS*, suffice to identify the potential controversy about the item evaluated or a short description of the legal issue. Prior law Prop. Reg. §1.6661 et seq. See also Rev. Proc. 87-48, 1987-38 I.R.B. 45, relating to items as to which the forms alone are deemed to create adequate disclosure (e.g., medical expenses). See *penalty, substantial understatement of income tax*.

adequate records an account book, diary, statement of *expense*, or the like, used to record (at or near the time of expenditure) each element of an expenditure for *travel, entertainment*, or *business gifts*, as well as documentary evidence in the form of receipts, paid bills, and the like for lodging and other expenditures of not less than $25, showing the amount, date, place, and essential character of the expenditure. The record must usually include a written statement on the *business purpose* for the expenditure. If the *taxpayer* substantially complies with the adequate records requirement, a particular element of an expenditure may be substantiated with other adequate evidence. Reg. §1.274-5(c)(2). Despite the apparent finality of §274(d), the absence of adequate records is not always fatal since it may be possible instead to use corroborative evidence.

adequate stated interest, original issue discount rules a conclusion that arises where the stated principal amount of a *debt* is not greater than the testing amount (the sum of the *present values* of all payments due, using the *applicable federal rate* to discount the loan). §§1274(b)(2) and (3). For example, A owes B $50,000, payable at *x* percent interest. The payments sum to $100,000, and discounted at the applicable federal rate, $100,000 reduces to $60,000; therefore, there is adequate stated interest. Implicitly, the *x* percent rate exceeds the interest rate used for testing purposes. As a result, $50,000 is the issue price for *original issue discount* (OID) purposes. The OID is the excess of the redemption price at maturity less the *issue price*. If there is not adequate stated interest, an *imputed principal amount* must be determined.

adjustable life policy   see *flexible premium life insurance contract.*

adjusted basis   the *taxpayer's* original *basis of property,* typically its cost, increased for improvements and other *capitalized* items, and reduced by *depreciation allowed or allowable,* or *cost recovery, obsolescence, depletion, amortization,* and *bonus recovery* or *bonus depreciation.* §1016. Numerous other provisions can cause adjustments to basis; for example, §§108 and 1017 reduce basis by what would otherwise be *gross income* from the *discharge of indebtedness*; §§109 and 1019 combine to deny basis where a tenant's improvements are excluded from the landlord's *gross income*; and §266 increases basis for *capitalized carrying charges.* The adjusted basis of property determines the amount of *gain* or *loss* on its *sale* or *other disposition* (§1001), the base on which *depreciation* (§167) and *cost recovery* (§168) are allowed, and the basis of *gift* property (§1015) and of property taken in various tax-deferred exchanges (e.g., §§1031 and 1033).

adjusted current earnings (ACE)   a separate parallel system to both a corporation's alternative minimum tax (AMT) and taxable income for tax years beginning after 1989. §56(g). The purpose of the ACE adjustment is to ensure that the mismatching of financial statement income and taxable income will not produce inequitable results. The starting point for computing ACE is alternative minimum taxable income (AMTI). This is defined as regular taxable income after AMT adjustments (other than the net operating loss (NOL) and ACE adjustments) and tax preferences. Other adjustments comprising the ACE preference formula include the following: (1) income items which are included in earnings and profits but will never be included in taxable income or AMTI (§56(g)(4)(B)(i)); (2) *depreciation deductions* for post-1989 years computed under the *alternative depreciation system* (§56(g)(4)(A)(i)); (3) no *deduction* permitted for an expense disallowed for earnings and profits purposes, subject to certain exceptions for *dividends-received deductions,* (§56(g)(4)(C)); (4) other adjustments, including intangible drilling costs and organization expenditures §56(g)(4)(D)(i); and (5) special rules for items such as depletion and certain owner-

ship changes (§56(g)(4)(E)). The final ACE adjustment can be either a positive or negative amount. See *business untaxed reported profits.*

adjusted excess deductions account   the beginning balance in the *excess deductions account* less the current year's *farm net income.* Former §1251.

adjusted exploration expenditures   a construct designed to identify the portion of *mining exploration expenditures* that should, when *recapture* occurs, be treated as *ordinary income,* because it reflects the additional benefits of electing to *deduct* mining exploration expenditures under §617, as opposed to *capitalizing* and writing them off using more conservative *cost depletion.* See §617(f)(1). In general, the term is defined as the excess of the exploration expenditures previously allowed as *deductions* over the reduction in the *depletion* allowance which results from the deduction of exploration expenditures. When a property reaches the *production stage,* the *taxpayer* can elect full recapture of exploration costs or, by not electing, can forego an equal amount of depletion *deductions* (i.e., adjusted exploration expenditures) until the prior deductions are used up. Recapture also occurs on the *disposition* date. Exploration expenditure deductions taken into account in determining the adjusted exploration expenditures for any *property* or mine include those made by the taxpayer and his or her predecessors with respect to the property. See *production stage, resources; recapture, mining exploration expenditures.*

adjusted grossed-up basis   *grossed-up basis* of *recently purchased stock* of a *target corporation,* adjusted to include the basis of non–recently purchased stock, liabilities of the target, and other relevant items. Reg. §1.338(b)-1T(c). The details are elaborate. It may be more or less than the net value of the assets of the target company. Adjusted grossed-up basis is allocated to the assets of the target company in order to assign the basis using the *residual method.* It is assigned in sequence, first to *Class I assets,* then to *Class II assets,* etc., then to *goodwill* and *going concern value.* This has the effect of allocating basis to the assets most easily valued first. If there is a shortfall of purchase within a class, the shortfall is allocated to each asset in the class according to its relative *fair market value.* Reg. §1.338(b)-2T(c)(1). This system applies to corporate purchases under §338 as well as to business purchases controlled by §1060. See *Class I assets, Class II assets, Class III assets, Class IV assets.*

adjusted gross estate   the *gross estate* less expenses described in §§2053 and 2054. The principal expenses described in §§2053 and 2054 are for the administration of the *decedent's estate,* the decedent's debts (i.e., claims against the estate), and the *casualty* and *theft losses* allowed to the estate. The determination of the adjusted gross estate is necessary in testing for the extension of time for installment payment of estate taxes under §6166.

adjusted gross income   a tax computation unique to *individuals*, determined by subtracting a limited group of *expenses* from *gross income*. §62. These expenses include *business* expenses, expenses attributable to the *production of rent or royalty income*, a *capital loss deduction up to $3,000*, contributions to an individual retirement account (IRA), and certain personal expenses such as *alimony*. These deductions are said to be for adjusted gross income. See also *gross income*.

adjusted income from rents, personal holding company   see *rents, personal holding company income*.

adjusted income, low income housing rehabilitation anticipated total annual income of tenants occupying rehabilitated property as to which 60-month *amortization* of expenditures to improve such property is sought. To assure that the purpose of the law (i.e., providing housing for persons of low and modest incomes) is not subverted, former Reg. §1.167(k)-3(b) demanded that the tenant's adjusted income not exceed certain local limits set by HUD and computed under HUD procedures. Former Reg. §1.167(k)-3(b)(3) contains the principal requirements.

adjusted investment in the contract   the investment in an *annuity contract* or other contract to which §72 applies, less the value of a refund or period certain guarantee. The figure is used to determine the numerator of the *exclusion ratio* for an annuity contract where the above refunds or the period certain guaranteed features are present. §72; Reg. §1.72-7.

adjusted issue price   the *issue price* of a *debt instrument* plus daily additions of *original issue discount*, determined by compounding, minus *interest* actually payable for the same period. §1272(a)(4). On the issue date of an instrument issued at a discount, the adjusted issue price and the issue price are the same. Thereafter, adjusted issue price is increased as described by yearly adjustments. As a result, the *Code* defines adjusted issue price as the issue price plus adjustments. §1272(d).

adjusted life insurance reserves   the mean of the *life insurance reserves*, other than *pension plan reserves*, at the beginning and end of the *taxable year*. §816(b)(4).

adjusted net book income   an element of the calculation of the enormously complex *adjustment* for *business untaxed reported profits* in determining *alternative minimum taxable income* for 1987 through 1989. §56(f). It starts with net income shown on the *taxpayer's applicable financial statement*. §56(f)(2)(A). Such net income should reconcile with the *corporation's* balance sheet and be the same amount used in any computation of changes in owner's equity. See *alternative minimum taxable income*.

adjusted net income, private foundations   basically, a *private foundation's taxable income* computed as if it were a business *corporation*, excluding *net long-term capital gains*, but including otherwise *tax-free interest* income (after costs of earning such interest) and certain other adjustments. §4942(f). The concept was used in the past as part of an alternative base to determine the *excise tax* on the *undistributed income* of a private foundation imposed by §4942. See Reg. §53.4942(a)-(2)(d) for details. For the present standard, see *minimum investment return*.

adjusted net minimum tax   see *minimum tax credit*.

adjusted ordinary gross income (AOGI)   a term used in connection with the determination of *personal holding company* status of a *corporation* imposed by §541. In ascertaining whether a corporation is a personal holding company, personal holding company income divided by adjusted ordinary gross income must equal 60 percent or more. Adjusted ordinary gross income is the corporation's gross income less capital gains and §1231 gains, and certain expenses. §543(b)(2). See also *personal holding company income*.

adjusted prime rate charged by banks   the average predominant prime rate of interest quoted by commercial banks to large businesses, as determined by the Board of Governors of the Federal Reserve System. Former §6621(c). The term was formerly used to fix interest rates on *underpayments* and *overpayments of taxes*.

adjusted reserve rate   the lower of the *average earnings rate* or the *current earnings rate*. §805(b)(1). The term is peculiar to the taxation of *life insurance companies*.

adjusted sales price   for purposes of §1034, involving tax-deferred *rollovers of principal residences*, the term means the *amount realized* on the sale of the residence (i.e., sales price less costs of the sale such as an attorney's fees and a broker's commission) less *fixing-up expenses*. Fixing-up expenses are expenses for short-term improvements and repairs incurred in order to sell the home, done in the 90-day period ending on the day the sales contract is executed, and paid not later than 30 days after the sale. Reg. §1.1034-1(b)(6). Fixing-up expenses cannot be *itemized deductions*, and include wallpapering, installing new Venetian blinds, etc. If the cost of the new *principal residence* is at least as great as the adjusted sales price of the former principal residence, *gain* realized can be deferred under the mandatory rules of §1034.

adjusted taxable gifts   total *taxable gifts* made by the *decedent* after 1976, other than gifts which are *includible* in the *gross estate* of the decedent. §2001(b)(2) (applicable to the estate of decedents dying and *gifts* made after 1981).

adjusted taxable income a special term used for purposes of calculating *carryovers* of *capital losses*. It is defined as *taxable income* plus the applicable §1211(b)(1) or (2) limit and any *deductions* for *personal* or *dependency exemptions*. An excess of deductions over *gross income* produces negative taxable income. See §1212(b)(2).

adjusted taxable income, PSC a term used in connection with determining if a *personal service corporation* (PSC) satisfies a minimum distribution requirement in order to permit its payments to owner-employees to be fully deductible despite having made a *section 444 election*. Adjusted taxable income means *taxable income* determined without regard to *applicable amounts*. Adjusted taxable income for the *deferral period* of the *applicable election year* equals the adjusted taxable income that would result if the PSC filed an *income tax return* for the deferral period of the applicable election year under its normal method of accounting. A PSC may make a reasonable estimate of such an amount. Any net operating loss (NOL) carryover must be reduced by the amount of carryover attributable to the deduction of applicable amounts. The portion of the NOL carryover attributable to the deduction of applicable amounts is the difference between the NOL carryover computed with the deduction of such amounts and the NOL carryover computed without the deduction of such amounts.

Example: X-Corporation is a PSC with a taxable year ending January 31. For its taxable year beginning February 1, 1993, X-Corporation makes a §444 election to retain its taxable year ending January 31. X-Corporation does not satisfy the minimum distribution requirement for its first applicable election year, and the applicable amounts for that year exceed the maximum deductible amount by $54,000. The $ 54,000 excess carries over to X-Corporation's taxable year beginning February 1, 1994. If X-Corporation continues its §444 election for its taxable year beginning February 1, 1994, and wants to use the three-year average test for such year, the $54,000 will not reduce adjusted taxable income for that year.

adjusted tax attributes a *qualified person's* (i.e., a certain farmer's) *tax attributes,* allowing only one dollar per every three dollars of *general business credits* and *foreign tax credit carryovers.* §108(g)(3)(B). This amount plus tax farmer's aggregated *adjusted basis* of *qualified property* sets the limit on *qualified farm indebtedness* that can be excluded from gross income. §108(g)(3)(A). See *qualified farm indebtedness; qualified property, discharge of farm debt; tax attributes, Bankruptcy Tax Act.*

adjusted value the *gross estate* less debt attributable to the *estate* (defined in §2053(a)(4), or when speaking of particular property, the value of the property less debt described in §2053(a)(4)). §2032A(b)(1)(A), (B), and (3).

adjustment generally a change in a *taxpayer's tax return* asserted by the *IRS*.

adjustment, alternative minimum tax see *adjustments, alternative minimum tax.*

adjustment of purchase price see *purchase price adjustment.*

adjustments, alternative minimum tax part of the base on which the *alternative minimum tax* falls. It consists of an extensive series of modifications to the components of a *taxpayer's taxable income.* See §56. The alternative minimum tax (AMT) is aimed at recovering some of the tax savings generated by a variety of other deductions and methods for computing tax liability. Some adjustments have to be made solely by *corporate* taxpayers while others have to be made solely by *noncorporate* taxpayers. *All taxpayers, whether corporate or noncorporate,* must make certain adjustments for (1) depreciation (§56(a)(1)); (2) mining exploration and development deductions (§56(a)(2)); (3) long-term contracts (§56(a)(3)); (4) alternative net operating loss deductions (§56(a)(4) and (d)); (5) pollution control facilities (§56(a)(5)); (6) the installment method of accounting (§56(a)(6)); and (7) alternative tax energy preference deductions (§56(h)). *Corporate taxpayers* must make adjustments involving (1) a portion of the difference between the alternative minimum taxable income and the adjusted current earnings (ACE) (§56(c)(1) and (g)); (2) Merchant Marine Capital Construction Funds (§56(c)(2)); and (3) special adjustments relating to Blue Cross and Blue Shield organizations under §833(b) (§56(c)(3)). *Noncorporate taxpayers* must make adjustments involving (1) alternative tax itemized deductions (§56(b)); (2) personal exemptions and the standard deduction (§56(b)(1)(E)); (3) circulation and research expenditures (§56(b)(2)(A)(i)); (4) incentive stock options (§56(b)(3)); (5) passive farm tax shelter losses (§58(a)); and (6) other passive business activity losses (§58(b) and (c)). See *alternative minimum tax; items of tax preference.*

adjustment to gross income a term often used to describe the process of arriving at *adjusted gross income* under §62. The process involves subtracting amounts allowed as *above-the-line deductions* from *gross income.*

administration, estate the activity of an *executor, executrix, administrator,* or *administratrix* in supervising and winding up a *decedent's estate.* Its term begins at the date of death and ends with the complete distribution of the estate's assets and the discharge of its liabilities.

administration expenses expenses actually and necessarily incurred in the administration of the *decedent's estate,* including *executors'* or *administrators'* commissions, attorneys' fees, and miscellaneous expenses. Reg. §20.2053-3. Administration expenses will be allowed even if the expense has not been paid at the time of filing the *return* or has not been fixed in amount. Reg. §20.2053-1(b)(3). Such expenses are allowable for *estate taxes* or *income taxes,* but not both. §642(g); Reg. §1.642(g)-1.

administrative powers   powers held by a *grantor* of a *trust* (or a *nonadverse party,* or both) to deal with trust *income* or *corpus* for less-than-adequate consideration. §675. The existence of administrative powers causes taxation to the grantor. The principal powers are to borrow on inadequate terms (i.e., too low an interest rate, or with inadequate security) and to engage in unfair *sales* or *exchanges* with the trust. In addition, §675(4) taxes grantors who can acquire options over trust property or who can direct investments and voting power over *corporations* identified with the grantor. In addition, failure to repay loans from the trust by year-end causes the grantor (or *spouse*) to be taxed on unpaid balances.

administrative pronouncement   a pronouncement of the *IRS* that taxpayers can rely on, to the same extent as on a *revenue ruling* or *revenue procedure.* See Reg. §1.6661-3(b)(2) and, e.g., Notice 89-91, 1989-33 I.R.B. 18. Such a pronouncement constitutes *substantial authority* for purposes of the penalty under §6661, which creates the *substantial understatement penalty.* See *penalty, substantial understatement of income tax.*

adopted child   for purposes of determining whether a *child* is a *dependent,* the term refers to either a legally adopted child or a child who is a *member of the household,* provided the child was placed by an *authorized placement agency* pursuant to a formal application filed with the agency. Reg. §1.152-2(c) details the agency's authority and the *taxpayer's* filing requirements. Legal adoption is a matter of local law. See, e.g., Rev. Rul. 54-70, 1954-1 C.B. 69.

adoption agreement   an agreement under which an affiliated *employer* enlists under the plan (e.g., a *pension* or *profit-sharing plan*) of a related corporation, usually a parent company. See Reg. §1.410(a)-2(e), examples. It also refers to an agreement whereby an employer adopts a *master* or *prototype plan* (e.g., one sold by a life insurer). See, e.g., Reg. §601.201(a)-2(e)(ix).

ad valorem penalties   a synonym for *civil tax penalties.*

ad valorem taxes   taxes imposed on the basis of the value of property. Ad valorem taxes may be *deductible* under §164. Section 164(b) defines *personal property taxes* as ad valorem taxes imposed on an annual basis in respect of personal property. Likewise, state, local, and foreign *real property taxes* are almost invariably ad valorem taxes, and, as such, are deductible under §164(a), regardless of any *gain*-seeking intent on the part of the *taxpayer.* See *personal property taxes.*

advance pricing agreement   a *ruling* issued in advance of a transaction, which ruling approves related party pricing plans. See 50 Tax Notes 562 (1991). This can be used to resolve §482 issues before they emerge.

advance refunding bond   when speaking of potentially *tax-exempt* bonds, a bond issued to refund another bond, where the second bond is issued more than 90 days before the redemption of the refund bond. §149(d)(5). See §141(i)(4), applying the *volume cap* to such issues, if they are *private activity bonds.*

advance ruling   a *ruling* issued by the *IRS* to a *taxpayer* in anticipation of a proposed transaction.

advance royalties   same as *advanced royalties.*

advanced royalties   royalties advanced to an owner in anticipation of future royalties from actual exploitation. The practice is common in the oil and gas industry. Such royalties may be the subject of *cost depletion deductions.* Reg. §1.613-3(b) and (d); §§613(e)(4) and 613A(d)(5). They are recoupable out of future production and are avoidable for nonproduction. The payor (lessee) must generally *capitalize* and later deduct them when production occurs, unless they qualify as *minimum royalties.* Reg. §1.612-3(b)(3).

adverse interest   the interest of an *adverse party.*

adverse party   a party who has a substantial *beneficial interest* that could be negatively affected by the exercise (or presumably, nonexercise) of a power granted him or her by a *trust* instrument, with "substantiality" measured in comparison to the total trust property subject to the power. §672(a); Reg. §1.672(a)-1(a). The term is significant for questions of whether income earned by a trust should be taxed to the *grantor* or to the trust and its *beneficiaries.* For example, under §674(a), if the *grantor* can shift a right to trust income among adult beneficiaries only if each beneficiary agrees to the shift, then, because those parties who would be adversely affected by the shift can veto it, the power would be so limited as to not cause taxation of such income to the grantor. In this instance, the beneficiaries are clear adverse parties. Beneficiaries and persons with *general powers of appointment* are generally considered to be adverse parties, although a party is always only adverse to the extent of his or her share of the income or *corpus* of the trust. Reg. §1.672(a)-1(b).

adverse ruling   a *ruling* issued by the *IRS* to a *taxpayer,* taking a position adverse to the conclusion sought by the taxpayer with respect to a transaction.

affected item   any item on a *partners' income tax return* to the extent it is affected by a *partnership item.* §6231(a)(5). Affected items are significant to the procedures relating to *audits* of partnerships and a special *statutes of limitations.* See *unified proceedings.*

affected shareholder   a shareholder who receives a *distribution* from an *S corporation* which is electively treated as a *dividend* out of *earnings and profits.* §1368(e)(3)(B).

affected target   a *target affiliate* as to which there is a deemed election under §338. See Reg. §1.388-6T, which prevents multiple taxation where a *target corpo-*

ration in a *section 338 election* holds stock of an affected target. See *section 1.338-6T shareholder.*

affiliated corporation generally, a *corporation* connected to another corporation through a pattern of common ownership, either as a parent and a direct or indirect subsidiary or as a member of brother-sister corporations with common owners. The term is usually defined in terms of 50 percent or 80 percent levels of common ownership, the types of corporations (e.g., *life insurance companies* and *S corporations*) that may be included, and so forth. The details vary by the particular subject area. See, e.g., Reg. §§1.167(j)-7(a) (*section 1250 property* acquired from affiliates); 1.542-4(b) (*personal holding companies*).

affiliated corporation, redemption see *redemption by affiliated corporations.*

affiliated corporation, worthless stock or securities *securities* of a *corporation* in which the *taxpayer* owns at least 80 percent of the voting stock of all classes entitled to vote and at least 80 percent of each class of nonvoting stock (excluding nonvoting preferred stock), and more than 90 percent of the corporation's aggregate gross receipts throughout its existence is from sources other than *royalties, rents, dividends, interest, annuities,* or *gains* (ignoring *losses*) from *sales* and *exchanges* of stock and securities. §165(g)(3). If the taxpayer is a *domestic corporation,* then losses on the *worthlessness* of securities in such affiliates may be treated as *ordinary losses.* §165(g)(2).

affiliated group a group of *includible corporations* under sufficient common control to qualify for the privilege of filing a *consolidated income tax return.* A consolidated return is unavailable to *foreign* and *possession corporations* which make the *section 336 election, regulated investment companies, real estate investment trusts,* and *domestic international sales corporations (DISCs).* There must be one or more chains of includible corporations connected through stock ownership with a common parent corporation if 80 percent or more of the voting power of all stock *and* 80 percent or more of the value of all outstanding stock of each corporation (except the common parent) is directly owned by the other corporations. The common parent must own at least 80 percent of the voting power of all outstanding stock *and* at least 80 percent by value of all outstanding stock of at least one of the other corporations. Convertible preferred and preferred with a higher-than-market-rate yield are both considered stock for these purposes. One disregards preferred stock, meaning nonparticipatory, nonconvertible stock with a reasonable liquidating or redemption preference or premium. §1504. See *includible corporation; preferred stock, consolidated returns; stock, affiliated group.*

affiliated service group a *service organization* (basically an enterprise the principal function of which is to provide personal services) plus one or more organizations which meet one of the following tests: (1) where the related organization is a service organization, it must be a *partner* or shareholder in the first organization and perform services regularly for it, or be regularly associated with it in performing services for third persons; or (2) regardless of whether the related organization is a service organization, a significant portion of its business must consist of performing services for the first organization (or one of its affiliates), which services must be of a type historically performed by *employees,* and at least 10 percent of the interest in the related organization must be held by officers, highly compensated employees (§414(q)), or owners of the service organization. §414(m). This elaborate mechanism is designed to overcome the *Kiddie-Garland rule,* which permitted evasion of pension *coverage* requirements for *qualified plans* by formation of partnerships consisting of incorporated professionals. The new rules treat affiliated service groups as being trades or businesses under common control, thereby forcing coverage of employees of professional partnerships. In other words, the real significance is that for *plan years* starting in 1984, separate organizations must be aggregated for pension coverage purposes where one organization is set up by an executive or manager of a different organization that consists of rank-and-file employees. §414(m)(3). See *professional service corporation.*

affiliation privilege terminology for relief accorded corporate shareholders in foreign concerns from multiple taxation of dividends. The United States reflects the concern in the *dividend-received deduction.*

affirmative action carryover election terminology used in Reg. §1.338-4T(f)(6)(i)(A) to describe a deemed *section 338 election* that arises from an asset acquisition during the *consistency period.* The *IRS* can waive such deemed elections.

after-tax dollars a popular expression for money that has already been taxed. For example, a *corporation* paying taxes at a 34 percent rate receives only 66 cents in after-tax dollars.

agency corporations a nontechnical term used to describe *corporations* formed to act as *agents* of other persons, usually in order to hold property.

agency of a church an organization exempt from tax under §501 and either controlled by, or associated with, a *church.* For example, an organization, a majority of whose officers or directors are appointed by a church's governing board or by officials of a church, is considered controlled by a church. An organization is associated with a church if it shares common religious bonds and convictions with that church. Reg. §1.414-1(d)(2). See *church plan.*

agent   a person acting on behalf of another (the principal) by agreement. Income and expenses of agents are commonly taxed to their principals as they are *realized.*

agent driver or commission driver   a class of *statutory employees* for *FICA* and *FUTA* purposes. The term generally contemplates drivers engaged in distribution of meat, vegetable, fruit, and bakery products, beverages (other than milk), or laundry or dry cleaning services for a principal, provided such services are performed for remuneration. If the driver also distributes products other than those set forth above, he or she will still be a statutory employee if the delivery of such products is merely incidental to delivery of the other products. Certain further tests must also be met. Reg. §31.3121(d)-1.

age sixty-five   for purposes of determining whether the *taxpayer* qualifies for an extra *personal exemption* on account of age, the term refers to attaining age 65 on the last day of the *taxable year.* Regulation §1.151-1(c)(2) moves the taxpayer's birthday back one day; hence, birthdays falling on January 1, for tax purposes, fall on December 31 of the prior year.

aggregate deemed sales price   the deemed sales price of a *target corporation* that uses a *section 338 election* such that the target is deemed to go through a hypothetical *liquidation* and repurchase of its own assets. See §338(h)(11). The term "aggregate deemed sales price" appears in the *regulations.* See Reg. §1.338-4T(h).

aggregate theory   a basic notion of *partnership* taxation under which the partnership is viewed not as a separate entity but rather as a collection of participants. The antonym is the *entity theory.* Both theories are at work in the area.

aggregation group   see *top-heavy group.*

aggregation of mineral interests   an election available to a *taxpayer* who owns two or more separate *operating* mineral interests (other than oil and gas wells or geothermal deposits) that constitute part or all of the same *operating unit.* Under the election, those operating mineral interests may be aggregated and treated as one property for all federal *income tax* purposes. §614(c)(1); Reg. §1.614-3(a). A taxpayer may elect to form more than one aggregation within an operating unit, and each aggregation may include interests comprising one or more mines, but if an aggregation includes any separate operating mineral interest which is part of a mine it must include all such interests that comprise that mine. *Id.* Faulty aggregation may cause each separate operating mineral interest to be treated as a separate property. See *invalid addition; invalid basic aggregation.*

aggregation of plans   the process of combining different *plans* into an imaginary single plan, typically to test for *discrimination* against rank-and-file *employees.* See, e.g., §401(a)(5).

agreed case   a case (*taxpayer's tax return*) *audited* by the *IRS,* the *adjustments* to which the taxpayer agrees.

agreement vessel   see *qualified vessel, Merchant Marine Construction Fund Act.*

agricultural by-product steam, credit for producing fuels from nonconventional sources   steam produced from solid agricultural by-products other than timber. Such steam is a *qualified fuel* for purposes of the *credit for producing fuel from nonconventional sources* and is treated as having been sold by the *taxpayer* to an unrelated person on the date on which it is used. §29(c)(5).

agricultural cooperative   "a business organization usually incorporated, owned and controlled by its member agricultural producers, which operates for the mutual benefit of its members or shareholders, as producers or *patrons,* on a cost basis after allowing for the expenses of operation and maintenance and any other authorized *deductions....*" Farmer Cooperative Service, *United States Department of Agriculture Bulletin* 10 (1957). "Operates on a cost basis" signifies that profits are disbursed to the membership. Cooperatives are designed either to market farm products or to buy farm materials (e.g., seeds) at favorable prices. State laws often control their powers, and §521 grants special *deductions* to so-called *exempt farmer's cooperatives* if various conditions are met. Sections 1381–1388 generally tax the *entity* as a *corporation* to the extent its patrons do not report their share of the cooperative's *taxable income* as their own.

agricultural labor   a form of service partially exempt from *Social Security (FICA) taxes* imposed on *employers* and from federal *income tax withholding.* §§3121(a)(8)(B), (g), 3401(a)(2) (the FICA definition controls). The term includes all services performed for an owner, tenant, or farm operator on a farm, or in the employ of any person in connection with soil cultivation, raising or harvesting agricultural or horticultural commodities, including caring for, raising, training, shearing, feeding, and managing livestock, bees, poultry animals, and wildlife. §3121(g)(1). Timber operations and landscaping services are excluded. Reg. §31.3121(g)-1(a)(1).

agricultural organization   an organization formed to promote agricultural purposes. §501(c)(5). The term "agricultural" includes the art or science of cultivating land, harvesting crops, *harvesting aquatic resources,* or raising livestock. §501(g). Such organizations can qualify for *exempt organization* status.

aiding and abetting tax liability understatement, penalty   see *penalty, aiding and abetting.*

aircraft, luxury tax   any aircraft propelled by a motor and capable of carrying one or more *individuals.* §4003(b).

air transportation tax an 8 percent *excise tax* on air transportation of persons if the trip begins and ends in the *United States,* supplemented by a 5 percent tax on the air transportation of property from one point in the United States to another point in the United States (or, in certain cases, from a point outside the United States to a point in the United States), §4271 (or, in certain cases, if the trip begins or ends in, or passes through, the United States).

Alaska Native Corporation a *corporation* organized under the Alaska Native Claims Settlement Act. These corporations were entitled to exceptional tax benefits whereby they could in effect sell their *losses* via relaxed *consolidated return* rules. These benefits have been repealed, subject to exceptions for certain existing contracts and pre-existing *Title Eleven cases.* See *TAMRA* §5021 and §60(b)(5) of the *Tax Reform Act of 1984.*

alcohol fuel credit a two-part credit against *income tax* for alcohol that may be used in an internal combustion engine, but which is not produced from petroleum, coal, or natural gas. The credit does not apply if the tax exemption for alcohol fuels applies. Generally, the credit is only available to an *individual* who blends or uses such alcohol in a *trade or business,* and it must be used in the year in which the qualified sale or use occurs. The credit is 40 cents per gallon for alcohol that is not less than 190 proof, and 30 cents per gallon for alcohol that is between 150 and 190 proof. Integration of the alcohol fuel credit with the federal *excise tax* exemption creates an incentive to use fuels with an over-10-percent alcohol content. The credit has been extended through the year 2000. See §40.

alcoholic beverages tax an *excise tax* on alcoholic beverages imposed at varying rates. §5041.

alien an *individual* who is not a *citizen* or *national* of the United States. Aliens are classified as *residents* or *nonresidents* of the United States, as the facts may dictate. See *resident alien.*

alienation of income a reference to transferring away the right to a stream of income without disposing of the underlying property. The United States solution is the *assignment of income doctrine.*

alimony amounts paid to a former *spouse* in connection with a divorce, payable in different periods. The term is a state law characterization and does not control divorce-related *federal income tax* issues, although alimony payments are generally taxed to the payee and *deductible* by the payor. §§71, 215. See *alimony or separate maintenance payment; property settlements.*

alimony in gross *alimony* payments called for by certain states under which payments are made for a period of years, perhaps beyond the payee's death. Such alimony payments could lose their *deductibility* as a result of §71(b)(1)(D).

alimony or separate maintenance payments a class of payments which are taxed to a recipient (ex-*spouse* or separated spouse) and are deductible by the payor. Such payments must (1) be made in cash and (2) be received under a *divorce or separation instrument,* (3) which instrument does not designate the payment as a payment not includible as alimony under §71 and not allowable as a *deduction* under §215; (4) the payor and payee spouses must not be members of the same household; (5) there must be no liability to make any alimony payment (or substitute payment) after the death of the payee spouse, and the instrument so states; (6) the payment must not be disguised *child support;* and (7) the payments must be for a three-year or longer period (purportedly to prevent excess "frontloading" and resulting *recapture* of *excess alimony payments*). Life insurance payable to the recipient spouse does not affect the other payments, and payments for child support which decline on contingencies or at a time clearly associated with contingencies (e.g., graduation from private school) are treated as child support, not alimony or separate maintenance. Moreover, the payor spouse will be required to report the payee spouse's *taxpayer* number. §71. See *frontloading of alimony.*

alimony recapture a reference to the inclusion of excessively frontloaded alimony in the payor's *gross income* in the third year of such payments, with a corresponding *deduction* for the payee. See *frontloading of alimony.*

alimony trust trust established in contemplation of divorce to secure payments for the benefit of a former *spouse,* to divide property, or to support children. They are taxable as trusts, rather than under §71 (relating to alimony). See §682.

all earnings and profits amounts positive or negative *earnings and profits* for years attributable to *stock* in a *foreign corporation* which was liquidated into a *domestic* parent *corporation* or whose assets were acquired by a domestic corporation in a *Type C reorganization* under the principles of §1246 or §1248, and as the case may be, applying those sections without regard to distinctions between pre- and post-1963 accumulations. Temp. Reg. §7.367(b)2(f).

all events test one of the requirements that must be met in order for an *accrual method taxpayer* to report an item of *income* or *expense.* The gist of the requirement is that all the events which determine the fact of the right to *income* or the existence of liability must have occurred. Reg. §§1.451-1(a) (income), 1.461-1(b)(2) (expense). *Note:* The all events test looks to the existence of the facts needed to fix liability; the presence or absence of actual legal liability is irrelevant. In fact, taxpayers' consistent bookkeeping practices can also influence the moment of accrual (e.g., shipping and delivery). Once the particular test is met, the accrual is usually required, even if later in the same *taxable year* it becomes clear that the accrual should be reversed. If there are contingencies, an inability to ascertain the amount with reasonable accuracy, or doubts as to collectibility, then the obligation to report the income or to deduct the expense is eliminated. The all events test generally will not be satisfied until *economic performance* has occurred. §461(h).

allocable cash basis items   see *retroactive allocations.*

allocable costs, uniform capitalization rules   in general, the *costs* associated with the production or acquisition for resale of *property* subject to the *uniform capitalization rules.* Such costs include *direct labor costs, direct material costs, indirect resale costs,* and *indirect production costs,* but not marketing, selling, advertising, and distribution expenses, nor bidding expenses associated with contracts not obtained, nor administrative expenses not directly benefiting a production or resale activity, nor *losses* under §165, nor *depreciation, amortization,* and *cost recovery* allowances on idle facilities or equipment, nor *income taxes,* nor contributions that relate *past service costs* under a pension plan, nor cost attributable to strikes. Reg. §1.263A-1T(b)(2)(5). Past service costs are determined under the *minimum funding rules* or under the plan's benefit formula. Joint Comm. on Taxation, General Explanation of the Tax Reform Act of 1986 513 (1987). The only affected costs are those that would otherwise be considered in calculating *taxable income.* §263A(a)(2). Materials, services and labor provided by a related party at less than an *arm's length* charge must be *capitalized* at an arm's length rate, unless capitalized by the related party and not *deducted* sooner than they would have been deducted by the *taxpayer* if initially *capitalized.* See §482 for *reallocations of income and deductions by Commissioner.* Reg. §1.263A(b)(2)(vi). See *allocation methods, uniform capitalization rule; direct labor costs, uniform capitalization rules; direct material costs, uniform capitalization rules; indirect resale costs, uniform capitalization rules; indirect production costs, uniform capitalization rules.*

allocable installment indebtedness   the amount of income deemed received in the year of sale as a result of applying the former *proportionate disallowance rule.* It is derived by first cumulating the seller's *debt,* other then debt secured by personal use property or note received on the sale of such property. Former §453C(b)(3)(B). It is generally determined at year-end, but certain *dealers* must determine the amount quarterly. Former §453C(b)(1)(A). This figure is then multiplied by an "installment percentage" to yield allocable installment indebtedness. The installment percentage is the fraction:

face amount of all applicable installment obligations
———————————————————————
face amount of all installment obligations plus aggregate *adjusted bases* of all the *taxpayer's* other property

The resulting figure (the fraction times debt) is allocated to applicable installment obligations in the present and past years. Former §453C(b)(1)(B). The portion of the debt assigned to applicable installment obligations from sales in the current year is the allocable installment indebtedness. The proportionate disallowance rule was generally repealed by the *Revenue Act of 1987.*

allocable installment obligations   the type of *debt* taken back in an *installment sale* that attracts the *proportionate disallowance rule* which accelerated the reporting of *gains.* Former §453C(a). There are three types: (1) notes received for sales of *personal property* of a type the seller regularly sells on the *installment method*; (2) a note taken back on the *dealer* sale of *real property*; and (3) a sale of real property for over $150,000 which was used in the seller's *trade or business* or held for rental. Former §453(c)(e). Farm-related notes are generally exempt. The proportionate disallowance rule was generally repealed by the *Revenue Act of 1987.* Former §453C(e)(1).

allocable parental minimum tax   the *alternative minimum tax* (AMT) analog of the *allocable parental tax,* used if the child is subject to the AMT. §59(j)(2). In essence, it is the parent's hypothetical *alternative minimum taxable income* (AMTI) if one added the particular child's unearned AMTI plus all the children's *regular taxes* caused by their *net unearned income minus* their parents' independent AMT liability. §59(j)(2)(A). There are further modifications. Once the allocable parental tax is determined, the child is in essence taxed on the greater of (1) his or her AMT or (2) the child's share of the *allocable parental minimum tax* plus [the child's AMT minus his or her net unearned AMTI] and [the child's *regular tax* attributable to net unearned income]. The child's exemption amount is $1,000 plus earnings.

allocable parental tax   the amount of additional *federal income tax* that the parents would be required to pay if the child's *net unearned income* were included in the parent's *taxable income,* including *includible gains* attributed to a *grantor* parent. This amount is determined by subtracting the tax actually imposed on the parent's taxable income if that income included the *net unearned income* of each child under age 14. §1(g)(3)(A). If the child is subject to the *alternative minimum tax,* one uses the *allocable parental minimum tax instead.* §59(j)(2). See *kiddie tax.*

allocation   the practice of segregating items with tax significance (e.g., *basis, amount realized, interest expense*) to transactions or to activities or property with which they can be fairly associated (e.g., tracing investment advice expenses to particular stock market transactions). The primary allocation methods involve *tracing, stacking,* and *proration.* In a *partnership* context, items of *income, gain, expense, credit, deduction,* as well as overall *gains,* can be specially allocated or allocated in gross among the partners by agreement, provided the allocation itself has a *substantial economic effect*. §704(b)(2). See Reg. §1.704-1.

allocation methods, uniform capitalization rules methods to allocate costs to *property* subject to the *uniform capitalization rules*. See Reg. §§1.263A-1T(b)(3)–(5). Uniform capitalization rules generally require capitalization of direct costs and an allocable portion of indirect costs attributable to producing real and tangible personal property or acquiring real and personal property used in the taxpayers trade or business or in an activity engaged in for profit. If taxpayers are subject to the uniform capitalization rules, they may have to change their accounting method to properly value their inventories. Simplified methods of accounting for resale costs and for production costs may be elected by certain taxpayers. See *allocable costs, uniform capitalization rules; uniform capitalization rules*.

allocation of basis, partnerships the rules under which *basis* is allocated to property distributed by the *partnership* to a *partner* (§732(c)) or *adjustments* to basis are spread among partnership property (§755).

allocation of forfeitures the treatment of *accrued benefits* when an *employee* terminates employment or otherwise loses such benefits. Among other things, accrued benefits under *defined benefit plans* cannot be used to increase benefits for other employees if the plan is to be a *qualified plan*. §401(a)(8). Employee forfeitures cannot benefit employees who are shareholders of *S corporations*. §1379 for pre-1984 years. Forfeitures under *stock bonus* and *profit-sharing plans* may be applied on a nondiscriminatory basis to remaining employees. Reg. §1.404-4(a)(1)(iii). See Reg. §1.401-7 for estimated forfeitures in determining the costs of a qualified plan.

allocation of profits and losses, partnerships a loose term referring to the *allocation* of *partnership items*. See *distributive share; special allocations*.

allocation ratio, uniform capitalization rules the ratio of resale costs, subject to *capitalization* under the *uniform capitalization rules,* to the *taxpayer's* purchases for the *taxable year*. The amount of purchases remaining in *closing inventory* are multiplied by the ratio to determine what portion of resale costs must be capitalized in *inventory*. Reg. §1.263A-1T(d)(4)(ii). See *uniform capitalization rules; allocation methods, uniform capitalization rules*.

allowable depreciation the amount of *depreciation* a *taxpayer* is entitled to claim for property written off under §167. If the taxpayer has selected a method of depreciation, that method applies; otherwise, *straight-line depreciation* applies. Allowable depreciation can result in a reduction of *basis* which then leads to an increased taxable *gain*, even though there was no *tax*

benefit from the reductions in basis. §1016(a)(2). This seemingly harsh result is designed to prevent manipulation of depreciation *deductions*. In the case of *recovery property* under *ACRS,* it appears that the allowable cost recovery amount (i.e., allowable depreciation) is generated by applying the tabular rates found in §168(b). The slight uncertainty surrounding recovery property exists because Congress has not yet drawn the terminology of §1016 into line with ACRS. See *allowed or allowable*.

allowed depreciation the amount of *depreciation* actually claimed, whether or not legally excessive. Such amounts reduce the *adjusted basis of property* under §1016, and can create *gain* or reduce *loss* to the extent the *deduction* produced a *tax benefit*. See *allowed or allowable*.

allowed or allowable a reference to terminology of §1016, which limits *taxpayers'* latitude to select methods of *depreciation* under §167, and *cost recovery* under §168 or *depletion deductions* under §§611-613A. It requires that *basis* be reduced by depreciation allowed or allowable in order to bar taxpayers from manipulating depreciation (or cost recovery) by failing to claim it in low income years, or simply by failing to claim *depreciation* or cost recovery *deductions*. §1016(a); Reg. §1.1016. If depreciation actually allowed was more than the amount lawfully allowable, the balance reduces basis as if the taxpayer enjoyed a *tax benefit* from the excessive claim. §1016(a)(2). On the other hand, failure to claim allowable depreciation can result in unexpected *gains,* although not *recapture* of depreciation or of cost recovery, provided the taxpayer can adequately prove the depreciation allowed was less than that allowable. §§1245(a)(2), 1250(b)(3).

all substantial rights to a patent for purposes of §1235, rights that can turn what might otherwise be considered a *royalty* arrangement into a *sale* or *exchange* taxed as *long-term capital gains*. The term refers to rights, whether or not then held by the *grantor* of the rights, which have value at the time of transfer. All substantial rights to a patent do not include (1) geographically limited rights, (2) rights for a term shorter than the life of the patent, (3) rights for exploitation in less than all the trades or industries to which it applies, or (4) rights for less than all the claims or inventions covered by the patent. The foregoing cases, based on principles of federal taxation developed before passage of §1235, may be treated as creating a royalty. Reg. §1.1235-2(b)(1). Regulation §1.1235-2(b) lists some trivial rights which will not interfere with a transfer that falls under §1235. See *reduced to practice*.

almond or citrus grove one or more trees of the rue family (citrus) or one or more trees of the prunus amygdalus species (almonds). Reg. §1.278-1(a)(2). Section 278(a) is designed to limit *tax shelter* activities by generally requiring *capitalization* of the costs of planting, cultivating, maintaining, or developing almond or citrus groves for the first four years after planting.

alternate section 414(s) compensation *employers* can use a different definition of §414(s) compensation than one of the *safe harbor* definitions. An alternate §414(s) compensation definition must satisfy three conditions: (1) the definition must be reasonable; (2) the definition may not by design favor highly compensated *employees*; and (3) the plan must satisfy a nondiscriminatory compensation percentage test. The *regulations* do not provide specific guidelines regarding conditions (1) and (2). An alternate definition probably would satisfy conditions (1) and (2) if the definition excluded specified categories of compensation applicable to employees in general or to a nondiscriminatory classification of employees. For example, a definition of compensation which excludes bonuses or overtime should satisfy conditions (1) and (2) and the employer would be concerned only with condition (3). See §414(s)(3).

alternate substance, biomass property, energy investment credit any organic substance other than oil, natural gas, coal (including lignite), and any of their products. §48(1)(15)(B)(i). Alternate substances include waste, sewage, sludge, grain, wood, oceanic and crop residues. It also includes waste materials, such as municipal and industrial waste, which contain processed products of oil, natural gas or coal such as used plastic containers and asphalt shingles. Use of an alternate substance as the primary fuel is a prerequisite to qualifying certain equipment as *biomass property* for purposes of the *energy investment credit.* §48(1)(15). A $3-a-barrel credit (adjusted for post–79 inflation) is provided for fuel produced from nonconventional sources such as oil produced from shale or tar sands, gas from geopressured brine and biomass, and synthetic fuels produced from coal. Under the CNEPA of 1992 (Pub. L 102-486), the nonconventional fuels credit is extended but only with respect to gas from biomass and synthetic fuels from coal. §1918. The extension doesn't apply to oil produced from shale or tar sands.

alternate valuation date the date six months after the *decedent*'s death. See *alternate valuation date election.*

alternate valuation date election an election permitting the *executor* or *administrator* of a *decedent's estate* to value all the assets of the estate on the *alternate valuation date,* which is six months after decedent's death, rather than value all the assets at their *fair market value* at the time of the decedent's death. §2032. This rule is subject to various exceptions: (1) any assets sold, distributed, exchanged, or otherwise disposed of during the six-month period are valued as of the date of disposal (Reg. §20.2032-1(a)); and (2) the change in value of certain assets during the six months solely due to a mere lapse in time, such as the decrease or increase in the value of a *patent, annuity,* or *life estate* of another, is

disregarded in assessing the value of the assets six months later. The election to value the assets six months after death must be made on the estate tax return and is irrevocable. The executor cannot make the election on an item-by-item basis; all the assets are valued either immediately after death or six months later. The election can be made only if the value of the gross estate and the estate tax (after credits) decline as a result of its use; this is consistent with the statute's purpose of giving relief where values decline rapidly after the decedent's death.

alternative depreciation life a term sometimes used to describe the *recovery periods* for property written off under the *alternative depreciation system* of §168(g).

alternative depreciation system a variant of *cost recovery* using the *straight-line method of depreciation* over fairly long fixed lives and a zero *salvage value,* applicable after 1986. §168(g). It is sometimes elective and sometimes mandatory. It is mandatory as to *tangible property* used predominantly outside the United States, *tax-exempt use property, tax-exempt bond-financed property,* and property imported from some countries (*covered imported property*). It even covers tangible property (other than nonresidential housing) leased to a *foreign person* unless over 50 percent of the foreigner's *gross income* is subject to *federal income taxes.* For the election, see §168(g)(7). It is mandatory for purposes of computing *earnings and profits.* §312(k)(4).

alternative economic effect test part of the *economic effect test* for validating *allocations* in *partnerships.* It is a pro-*taxpayer* exception, applicable where there is not an absolute duty to restore deficits in *capital accounts.* It provides that as long as the capital account maintenance rules are otherwise adhered to, allocations to the *partner* have economic effect as long as they do not increase or create a capital account deficit. Reg. §1.704-1(b)(2)(ii)(d). If a partner must restore a deficit only up to a particular dollar amount, allocations to the partner are given effect as long as they do not produce a deficit that exceeds that amount. Reg. §1.704-1(b)(2)(ii)(f). In determining if allocations would create a deficit or an excessive deficit, certain capital amount adjustments for future years (e.g., certain future *distributions*) have to be anticipated. Also, allocations to a partner who does not have an unlimited obligation to restore a deficit lack economic effect and are invalid under the alternative economic effect test unless the *partnership agreement* provides a *qualified income offset* expressed in the partnership agreement. See *substantial economic effect test.*

alternative energy property, energy investment credit specific types of equipment that use an *alternate substance* as a fuel or feed stock or convert an alternate substance to a synthetic fuel. The equipment must fall within the following categories of property: (1) a boiler that uses an *alternate substance* as the primary fuel; (2) a burner for a combustor, other than a boiler if the burner uses an alternate substance as the primary fuel; (3) equipment for converting an alternate substance into a synthetic liquid, gaseous, or solid fuel; (4) equipment for modifying existing equipment so that an alternate source is at least 25 percent of the alternate fuel or feed stock; (5) equipment to convert coal (including lignite), or any nonmarketable substance derived from coal, into a substitute for a petroleum or natural gas; (6) pollution control equipment required by federal, state, or local regulations to be installed in connection with equipment in items (1)–(5); (7) equipment to unload, transfer, store, reclaim from storage, and prepare, at the point of use, an alternate substance to be used in any equipment in items (1)–(6); (8) equipment to produce, distribute, or use exclusively geothermal energy, but only, in the case of electrical generation, up to the electrical transmission stage; and (9) equipment that converts ocean thermal energy to usable energy and is placed in service at either of two locations designated by the *IRS.* §48(1)(3)(A); Reg. §1.48-9(c). *Public utility property* (defined in §46(f)(5)) is excluded from alternative energy property. §48(1)(17); Reg. §1.48-9(n)(2). Alternative energy property is *energy property* for purposes of the energy *investment credit.* §48(1)(2)(A); Reg. §1.48-9(a).

alternative IID   a mechanism described in Notice 88-131 which provides administrative guidelines for *accrual of benefits* under a *qualified deferred compensation plan* for post-1988 *plan years.* See PRD ERISA Newsletter No. 91-2 (1991).

alternative minimum funding standard account   a complex *minimum funding* account used to determine whether an *employer's* contributions to *qualified pension plans* are adequate. §412(g). The account is credited with (1) *employer contributions* and debited normal costs (calculated alternatively), (2) the shortfall of the value of plan assets over the present value of *accrued benefits,* and (3) the shortfall of past years' credits over past years' contributions. It operates as an alternative to the usual *full funding* standard and can be viewed as a relief provision vis-à-vis that of §412(c). See §412(h) for certain excluded plans. See *funding, qualified plans.*

alternative minimum tax   an extremely intricate tax designed to flush out income that has been concealed by clever tax planning. The tax base is the excess of the *tentative minimum tax* for the *taxable year* over the *regular tax* (as modified by §55(c) with respect to certain *tax credits*) for the *taxable year.* §55(a). The tentative minimum tax is basically 24 percent (21 percent for *corporations*) of the *taxpayer's alternative minimum taxable income* (AMTI) minus an *exemption amount* ranging from $20,000 to $40,000, depending on the *taxpayer.* §55(b). Those exemption amounts phase out (i.e., gradually disappear) for high income taxpayers. §55(d)(3).

There is also a special increase of at least $20,000 worth of AMTI for *married taxpayers* filing *separate returns. Id.* By far the most difficult aspect of the tax is determining its base, which consists of a series of *adjustments* to *taxable income* under §56 and the inclusion of *items of tax preference* under §57. Once the tax is established it becomes the tax for the year if it is higher than the regular tax. Finally, §53 contains an *alternative minimum tax credit* which can be carried forward to future years and used as a *credit* against future years to the extent that regular tax liability for that year exceeds minimum tax liability for that year; however, it is available only for application against so-called *deferral preferences* and not *exclusion preferences,* e.g., *depreciation* as opposed to *tax-exempt interest.* To make things more complex, for the year the minimum tax might apply, one subtracts all tax credits from regular tax credits but only reduces alternative minimum taxes by the *foreign tax credit* and *refundable* credits. To soften the blow, to the extent that any *nonrefundable credits* are unused as a result of this gyration, they too are carried forward for application against future regular taxes. The CNEPA of 1992 (Pub. L 102-486) repealed the alternative minimum tax energy deduction for tax years beginning after 1992. §1915.

alternative minimum taxable income   the base of *alternative minimum tax* (AMT), i.e., the *taxpayer's tentative minimum tax* for the *taxable year* minus the *regular tax* for the year. §55(a). The calculation is complex. Its elements are as follows: (1) *taxable income* (or the analogous base, such as *unrelated business taxable income*) less income that qualified for the *possessions tax credit,* (2) plus or minus *adjustments* in determining the AMT, (3) plus *items of the preference,* (4) less an *exemption amount* (ranging from $40,000 to $20,000, depending on the taxpayer). *Taxpayers* then (5) multiply the resulting number by the applicable tax rate (20 percent for *corporations* and 21 percent for other taxpayers), (6) subtract the *alternative minimum tax foreign tax credit* (items 1–6 yield tentative minimum tax), and (7) subtract the *regular tax.* See §55(a)-(b). A portion of the AMT is allowed as a *credit* against later years' regular income taxes. Only *deferral preferences* (not *exclusion preferences*) produce this benefit. §53(a), (b), and (d). One applies the *passive loss rules* in modified form (§58(b)) and denies *tax shelter farm losses* (§58(a)). See *adjusted net minimum tax; alternative minimum tax; regular tax, alternative minimum tax.*

alternative minimum tax bond   a bond whose *interest* is subject to the *alternative minimum tax*—generally, a *private activity bond* issued after August 7, 1986, other than a *qualified 501(c)(3) bonds.* The *arbitrage bond* rules do not apply to investments of proceeds of tax-exempt offerings in tax-exempt obligations other than AMT bonds. §148(d). See *arbitrage bond.*

alternative minimum tax credit   a *credit* against later years' tax liabilities caused by a carryforward of *alter-*

native minimum taxes imposed in earlier years. See §53. The credit applies against later years' *regular tax* to the extent that the regular tax liability for that year exceeds minimum tax liability for that year. Except for *corporations,* the credit can be used only against *deferral preferences* (e.g., *depreciation,* but not against *exemption preferences* (e.g., nontaxable interest). The credit is increased by the amount of *orphan drug credit* disallowed solely because of the tentative minimum tax credit. §53(d)(1).

alternative minimum tax foreign tax credit   a modified form of the *foreign tax credit,* applicable to the *alternative minimum tax* (AMT), the practical effect of which is that the foreign tax credit, including pre-1987 *carryforwards,* is available to offset the AMT. See §59(a). It is allowable only to the extent of the foreign tax on *alternative minimum taxable income* (AMTI) from foreign sources. The credit against *tentative minimum tax* is generally computed on the tax base against which the alternative minimum tax rate is applied, while the regular tax which reduces it is computed by using the regular foreign tax credit. §56(A). The *foreign tax credit limitation* (§904) is applied separately for AMTI and regular tax purposes, and by a percentage of the *book income adjustment* (§56(g)) is deemed from United States sources to the extent of the ratio of other domestic source AMTI to total AMTI. A key feature is that, for most corporations, not over 90 percent of tentative minimum tax liability, before foreign tax credits, is reduced by foreign tax credits, even though, under §904, over 90 percent of the liability could be offset by the foreign tax credit, with the balance carried forward or back. §59(a)(2). See §59(a)(2)(C) for the exception.

alternative minimum tax foreign tax credit carryover   a *relief provision* under which, in cases where the *alternative minimum tax foreign tax credit* exceeds the 90 percent limit, the excess can be carried forward or backward, like the *foreign tax credit.* §59(a)(2)(B). See *alternative minimum tax.*

alternative substance, alternative energy property   any substance other than oil and natural gas and any product of oil and natural gas. §48(1)(3)(B). For purposes of this provision, alternate substances include coal, wood, and agricultural, industrial, and municipal wastes or by-products. Alternate substances do not include synthetic fuels or other products produced from an alternate substance if the alternate substance underwent a significant change in chemical composition. Reg. §1.48-9(c)(5)(ii). Use of an alternate substance as the primary fuel is a prerequisite to qualifying certain equipment as *adjustments, alternative minimum tax; alternate energy property; items of tax preference* for purposes of the *energy investment credit.* §48(1)(3); Reg. §1.48-9(c).

alternative tax energy preference deduction   an amount that can be subtracted in computing the *adjust-*

ments to *taxable income* in determining the tax base of *taxpayers* other than an *integrated oil company.* §56(h)(1)(A). The CNEPA of 1992 (Pub. L 102-486) repealed the alternative minimum tax energy deduction for tax years beginning after 1992. §1915. See *integrated oil company, alternative tax energy preference deduction.*

alternative tax net operating loss deduction   a modified version of the *net operating loss deduction* (§172) used as an *adjustment* in determining *alternative minimum taxable income.* It is calculated in the first instance by applying *alternative minimum tax* concepts (e.g., adding back *items of tax preference*), denying losses from *tax shelter farm activities,* and applying the *positive loss rules,* and is further modified by: (1) limiting the *deduction* to 90 percent of alternative *minimum taxable income*; and (2) not adding back the *items of tax preference* to the extent they did not increase the loss for *regular tax* purposes. §56(d). There are also minor modifications which are primarily in the nature of *transition rules.*

amended refund claim   see *specific refund claim.*

amended return   a *tax return* filed as a corrective supplement to or a replacement of an original *tax return,* either to correct an error (i.e., a corrective return) or as the basis of a new *claim for refund or credit.* For this purpose, individuals must use Form 1040X and a corporation Form 1120X. Other taxpayers may use a regular return form. The words "Amended Return" should be written across the top of the regular amended return. An explanation of the error must also be attached. The IRS is not obligated to accept an amended return.

amortizable bond premium   the premium paid for a *bond* that can be *amortized.* See §171. See *amortizable bond premium of the taxable year.*

amortizable bond premium election   an election to *amortize* premiums over face amount paid for taxable bonds. The election permits an annual *deduction,* on a yield to maturity basis. §171. The amortized premium used to be treated as pure *interest,* but is now subject to being offset against interest income on the bond.

amortizable bond premium of the taxable year   the portion of *bond premium* that can be written off by the holder (other than a securities dealer) in the present year. §171(b)(1). Bond premium means *original issue premium* plus *market discount or premium* incurred by a holder of a *bond,* as well as miscellaneous *capital expenditures* such as commission costs to the extent that in combination these premiums result in a cost in excess of maturity value. §171(b); Reg. §1.171-2(a). For example, assume a bond with a face value of $1,000 is issued for $1,050 and rises in value to $1,075. The *taxpayer* purchases it for $1,095, which includes a $20 commission. The amortizable bond premium is $95. Premiums attributable to a conversion feature are not amortizable. §171(b)(1). For the elaborate details of amortizable bond premiums, see RIA Federal Tax Coordinator 2d paragraph K-8000 et seq. See *bond, amortization.*

amortization the systematic recovery of the cost or other *basis* of an *intangible asset* for *income tax* purposes over its *useful life* in the owner's hands. Amortization is claimed on the *straight-line* method only. Section 167(a) allows the *deduction* and §167(c) imposes the limitation to the straight-line method subject to specialized cases, such as subscription lists. Examples of amortizable *intangible property* include leasehold interests and *patents. Goodwill,* on the other hand, is not amortizable. Amortization of particular items may be regulated by particular *Code* sections (e.g., §171 *bond premium*). In fact, the Code often confuses the definition of amortization by using the term in connection with writing off the basis of *tangible property,* such as *low income housing rehabilitation* expenditures (former §167(k)) and *certified pollution control facilities* (§169). In such cases, the term is really used to mean what most accountants would understand as *accelerated depreciation.*

amortization of pollution control facilities, corporate income tax preference a reduction of 20 percent of the *basis* of any *certified pollution control facility* for which corporate *taxpayers* elect 60-month *amortization.* §291(a)(5).

amount at risk any amount considered *at risk* by §465. See *at-risk rules, generally.*

amount at risk, life insurance the face amount of a policy less accumulated reserves.

amount loaned, below-market loan see *below-market loan.*

amount realized for purposes of determining the amount *of gain* or *loss* on a *sale or other disposition* of property under §1001(a), the amount received in money, and the *fair market value* of property and services received. §1001(b). If the *fair market value* of the property received cannot be ascertained, the value of the surrendered property is used. Purchasers' obligations are generally accounted for at fair market value by *cash method taxpayers,* whereas *accrual method taxpayers* use the face amount of the obligations. Indebtedness assumed by or (in the case of *nonrecourse debt*) taken subject to the transferee is also included in amount realized. See *barter exchange method.*

amount received as an annuity the amount to which the *exclusion ratio* is applied to determine the nontaxable portion of a payment received after the *annuity starting date* under an *annuity* contract or a *life insurance* or *endowment* settlement option. Generally, such amounts qualify only if they are payable regularly and

in periodic installments, and if the total amount payable can be ascertained. Reg. §1.72-2(b)(2).

amount loaned see *below-market loan.*

amounts held by the insurer with respect to a beneficiary death benefits under a *life insurance contract* payable to a *beneficiary.* Former §101(d); Reg. §1.101-4(b). These amounts were prorated over the payment period, with amounts actually paid in excess of the prorated base treated as *interest* income. For example, if the contract had a $10,000 death benefit, but was payable at the rate of $1,100 per year for 10 years, then $100 per year was interest.

amounts not received as an annuity amounts taxable under §72 other than as *annuities* and *interest* payments. Examples include lump-sum surrenders of *life insurance policies,* dividends paid on annuity policies, most loans and guaranteed refunds paid under refund life annuity settlements. Prior to August 14, 1982, such amounts were taxed under *cost recovery method* principles, which generally continue to apply to life insurance and *endowment* contracts, but after August 13, 1982, most amounts paid out before the annuity starting date are treated first as a return of income. §72(e); Reg. §1.72-11. There is also a 10 percent *civil tax penalty* for various premature distributions from annuities. §72(q).

amounts properly paid or credited by estate all amounts properly paid, credited, or required to be distributed by an *estate* to a *beneficiary* during the *taxable year* other than *income for the taxable year required to be distributed currently.* Such amounts may be *deducted* in determining the *taxable income* of an estate. §661(a)(2); Reg. §1.661(a)-2.

amounts properly paid or credited by trust all amounts properly paid, credited, or required to be distributed by a *trust* to a *beneficiary* during the *taxable year* other than *income for the taxable year required to be distributed currently.* Such amounts may be *deducted* in determining the *taxable income* of a trust. §661(a)(2); Reg. §1.661(a)-2. Permissible *deductions* include discretionary distributions of income or *corpus,* the payment of an *annuity* to the extent it is not paid out of income for the taxable year, and a distribution of property in kind. Reg. §1.661(a)-2.

ancillary benefits additional benefits. See *incidental benefits, pension, annuity, and profit-sharing plans.*

ancillary refund jurisdiction the power of the *Tax Court* to determine that a *taxpayer* is entitled to a *refund or credit* by virtue of its finding that the taxpayer overpaid taxes in the disputed year. §6512.

announcement an *IRS* statement. There are several meanings. The formal variety is numbered and appears in *Internal Revenue Bulletins* and later in *Cumulative Bulletins,* advising *taxpayers* of matters other than interpretations of law (e.g., that the IRS is studying an area). The term is also used to refer to a *news release,* and to certain internal memoranda distributed to IRS personnel.

annual accounting concept a fundamental concept of *tax accounting,* the gist of which is that events with tax significance should be recorded in and by reference to the present *taxable year* alone even though other disparities may result or their eventual outcome is doubtful; correspondingly, future events are left for future years. The doctrine provides certainty as to how to account for events, and facilitates the closing of *taxable years.* The doctrine has a few exceptions. Most notably, §1341 allows *restorations* of previously taxed items (e.g., a bonus erroneously paid in a prior year and repaid this year) to be deducted or credited by reference to the tax burden in the prior year. Likewise, §111 provides a special *recovery exclusion* under which recoveries of previously deducted items are *excludable* from *gross income* by reference to the deductibility of the prior amount.

annual addition limitation, qualified plans the maximum allowable *annual addition* (discussed below) to a *participant*'s account under a *defined contribution plan.* §415. A plan will be disqualified if the addition in any year, as to any *participant,* exceeds this amount. §415(a). The general limit is the lesser of $30,000 or 25 percent of *compensation.* §415(c)(1). The annual addition for each participant is the sum for any year of (1) *employer* and *employee* contributions, and (2) *forfeitures.* Contributions by retired non-*key employees* are ignored if for medical coverage. §415(c)(2). See *annual benefit limitation* as to *defined benefit plans.* Section 415(e) provides intricate limitations when both types of plans cover the same employee. See *annual additions, qualified plans; combined plan fraction; qualified participant, qualified plans.*

annual additions, qualified plans aggregate *employer contributions* allocated to a *participant's* account, plus allocated *forfeitures* and the lesser of (1) a half of the participant's contributions, or (2) all of the participant's contributions that exceed 6 percent of compensation. §415(c)(2). Such additions to *defined contribution* and *defined benefit plans* are subject to limitations under §415. See *annual addition limitation, qualified plans.* The term includes contributions allocated to an *individual medical benefit account* of a retired 5 percent (or more) owner.

annual benefit limitation, qualified plans the maximum allowable *annual benefit* (discussed below) that a *defined benefit plan* may provide for its *participants.* §415. An otherwise *qualified plan* will be disqualified unless its provisions preclude the possibility that any annual benefit exceeding this amount will be payable at any time. Reg. §1.415-3(a). The limit generally is the lesser of $90,000 or 100 percent of the participant's average *compensation* for the high three years. The dol-

lar limit falls 10 percent per year to the extent of participation under 10 years. §415(b)(1) and (5). For a parallel rule regarding *defined contribution plans,* see *annual addition limitation, qualified plans; combined plan fraction.*

annual benefit, qualified plans a benefit under a *defined benefit plan,* payable annually as a straight *life annuity* with no ancillary benefits under a plan to which *employees* do not contribute, and which contains no *rollover contributions.* Reg. §1.415-3(d). This definition establishes a standard of comparison to determine whether annual benefits actually provided are excessive, so as to disqualify the plan. §415(b). See *annual benefit limitation, qualified plans.*

annual gift tax exclusion a *Code* provision under which a *donor* may exclude the first $10,000 of total *gifts* made during each *calendar year* to each *donee.* The exclusion is not allowed if the gift is of a *future interest* or if the value of a present interest is not ascertainable. In the case *of joint gifts* (often referred to as split gifts) by *married persons,* the annual exclusion is $20,000 per donee, regardless of who actually supplied the property. §2503(b).

annualization of income a process of accommodating certain *short periods* (e.g., short *taxable years*) by hypothesizing an *income tax* computed as if the *taxpayer's taxable income* for the short period reflected income for an entire year, and then reducing the tax to reflect the brevity of the period. §443(b)(1).

annual premium deferred life annuity an *annuity contract* calling for the payment of annual premiums beginning at once during the *accumulation phase,* in exchange for a *life annuity* beginning at a specified age during the application or annuitization period.

annual statement, life insurance companies the annual report made by an *insurance company* stating the company's receipts, disbursements, assets, and liabilities at the close of the calendar year. The statement is prepared in accordance with the statutory method of accounting prescribed by the National Association of Insurance Commissioners (NAIC) and is filed with the various State Departments of Insurance in those states where the company operates.

annuities, personal holding company income annuities to the extent includible in *gross income* under §72. Reg. §1.543-1(b)(4); Prop. Reg. §1.543-4(d). Annuities create *personal holding company income.* §543(a)(1).

annuity, generally a contractual arrangement between an obligor (*an insurance company* in the case of a *commercial annuity*) and a contract holder, in which a payee (*annuitant*) is entitled to periodic payments, which for federal *income tax* purposes are deemed to consist of a *return of capital* portion and an *ordinary income* portion. Rev. Rul. 55-639, 1955-2 C.B. 230 defines an annuity as a "contract which provides primarily for periodic installment payments to the annuitant named therein, and under which the death benefits at any time cannot exceed the larger of the reserve or the total premiums paid for the annuity benefits." The ratio that determines the proportion of taxable (ordinary income) to tax-free (return of capital) amounts is known as the *exclusion ratio.* Annuities may be fixed (i.e., the return is predictable) or variable (i.e., the payout depends upon the performance of a fund from which annuity payments are made). They may be payable during several lives, may contain refund features that provide a special return in the case of the early death of the annuitant, and in general are capable of almost limitless variations. See §72.

annuity or other payment   an *annuity,* lump-sum payment, or more than one payment, however timed, even if conditional and sporadic. Reg. §20.2039-1(b)(1). This is a transfer tax definition, not an *income tax* definition. Generally, the present value of annuities or other payments receivable by a *beneficiary* as a result of surviving the *decedent* are includible in a decedent's *gross estate* to the extent that the annuity or other payment's value is attributable to amounts paid by the decedent's *employer* or the decedent, but only if (1) the annuity or other payment was payable to the decedent (alone or with another) at least for the decedent's life, or (2) the decedent had the right to receive the annuity or other payment (alone or with another). §2039(a) and (b).

annuity payment   an amount payable at regular intervals over a period of more than one full year from the date on which the payments are deemed to begin, provided the total of the amount so payable or the period for which they are to be paid can be determined as of that date. Reg. §1.72-2(b)(2). Annuity payments are apportioned between *returns of capital* and *ordinary income* by §72. See *annuity, generally.*

annuity plan   see *qualified annuity plan.*

annuity starting date   the first day of the first period for which an *annuity* payment is received. §72(c)(4); Reg. §1.72-4(b). In the case of *qualified plans,* amounts paid prior to the annuity starting date are generally prorated between *returns of capital* and *gross income.* §72(e)(7)-(9). See *amounts not received as an annuity.*

annuity starting date, qualified plans   generally, the date that payments begin under a *qualified deferred compensation plan*. It is generally the first day the retirement annuity is supposed to begin. §417(f)(2). If the payment is not in the form of an annuity, the date is the first day that all the events fixing the payee's right to payment have taken place. §417(f)(2).

annuity valuation tables   tables issued by the *Treasury Department* that incorporate an *annuitant's* life expectancy for purposes of the taxation of *annuity* payments. Reg. §1.72-9.

annuity wrappers   see *wraparound annuities.*

annulment   invalidation of a marriage by virtue of its illegality, as opposed to divorce, which is the dissolution of a legal marriage. Courts strain to treat annulments under the same tax rules as a divorce.

anti-churning rules   see *churning.*

anticipation of income doctrine   acceleration of *gross income* through the *sale* of rights to income to be realized in the future. For example, a *cash method taxpayer* who sells the right to future dividends from stock must report the full amount of the income at the time of sale.

anticipatory assignment of income   see *assignment of income doctrine.*

anticipatory sales   a term sometimes applied to the *sale* of property in advance of a transaction that will create *ordinary income* (e.g., a large *stock dividend* from a closely held *corporation*). Such attempts to convert *ordinary income* into *capital gain* are subject to reclassification by the IRS.

anti-coupon stripping rules   Under *TEFRA,* applicable to coupon stripping after July 1, 1982, stripped bonds and stripped *coupons* in the hands of a purchaser are treated as bonds issued at a discount. §1286(a). The discount is the excess of the redemption price of the bond, or the amount payable on maturity of the coupon, over the purchase price allocable to the bond or coupon. The purchaser must include the discount in income under the *original issue discount rules.* The seller of a stripped bond or stripped coupon must, immediately before the *disposition,* allocate the *basis* of the bond (with coupons) between the bond and coupons in accordance with their values, thus preventing artificial *losses* from the sale of stripped bonds. §1286(b)(2). Accrued interest required by the new rules to be included in income upon the disposition of a stripped bond or stripped coupons does not include any interest theretofore included in income by the *taxpayer* (e.g., by an *accrual basis* taxpayer). §1286(b)(1). A person who retains a tax-exempt bond after disposition of the coupons is treated much like a purchaser of a stripped tax-exempt bond. The definition of "coupon" is essentially any right to receive interest on a bond whether or not evidenced by a coupon. See *coupon, coupon stripping.*

anti-discrimination rules   a general requirement, often imposed on an *entity* (usually an *employer*) as a prerequisite to qualification for a *tax benefit,* usually to the effect that the benefit will not be accorded unless the underlying activity provides rank-and-file *employees* with treatment as beneficial as that provided to more elite employees and owners (usually those who are officers or shareholders, or are highly compensated). The most familiar applications are found in the *pension plan* area. §§401(a)(4), 410(b), 411(d)(1). The requirement appears (among other places) in §§105(h) (self-insured *medical reimbursement plan*), 120(c) (*group legal service plans*), 124(c) (employer-provided transportation), 274(b)(3) (*qualified plan awards*), 501(c)(17).

Anti-Injunction Act   section 7421 of the *Code,* prohibiting *taxpayers* and others from suing to restrain the *assessment* or *collection of taxes.* In turn, §6212(a) allows injunctions against the *IRS* in cases of assessment where no *deficiency notice* was issued, and §6213(a) allows injunctions when, (1) despite notice to the taxpayer, the assessment took place before the 90-day period during which the taxpayer can file a *petition* in the *Tax Court* had elapsed, and (2) an assessment is made before the Tax Court has rendered a final decision. Section 7426 provides a further exception to the anti-injunction rule for improper seizures.

anti-pledge rule   a synonym for §453(d). See *secured indebtedness.*

anti-scalper rule   reference to §274(b), limiting most *deductions* for entertainment tickets to their face amount.

anti-stuffing rule   tax slang for either of three rules. First, it is a nickname for §382(l)(1)(A), which ignores *capital contributions* which are part of a plan whose principal purpose is to avoid the limits of §382, including all contributions made within two years before the *change date,* except as provided in *regulations.* This rule is needed to prevent *tax avoidance,* because the limit on *loss carryovers* found in §382(b) depends on the value of the loss *corporation* at the time of the *ownership change.* Second, it refers to §336(d)(2) under which corporations going through *liquidations* are denied losses on *sales, exchanges,* and *distributions* of certain contributed property with *basis* in excess of *fair market value.* Third, it refers to §341(e)(7), which backs out from the calculation of a pro-taxpayer fraction contributed assets designed to inflate the recipient corporation's asset base.

appeal bond   see *bond to stay assessment and collection.*

Appeals Conferee   the predecessor of the *Appeals Officer.*

Appeals Conference   a meeting between the *taxpayer* or *taxpayer representative* and the *Appeals Office* in connection with cases to which the *District Director* has issued a *thirty-day letter.* The conference is with an *Appeals Officer* of the *IRS* and is available at the taxpayer's request. Although the procedure is informal, it commonly requires the submission of a written *protest* and affidavits in support of some factual allegations. Following the conference, an offer of settlement is commonly made by the taxpayer or the taxpayer's representative. Settlement offers are considered by the IRS on an issue-by-issue basis and according to the probability of litigating outcomes (the *hazards of litigation* standard).

appeals coordinated issues   tax issues common to industry or occupational groups or to large groups of *partners* or *shareholders* which call for centralized, coordinated *IRS* treatment. See Rev. Proc. 79-4, 1979-2 C.B. 498, for details on how to handle such appeals. The *unified proceedings* for *partnerships* or *S corporations* partly displace the revenue procedure.

Appeals Division   a segment of the *National Office* of the *IRS* which reports to the *Assistant Commissioner, Compliance,* and which is responsible for national policy with respect to the administrative settlement of disputes and avoiding litigation by *taxpayers* and government.

Appeals Office   the Office of Regional Director of Appeals, the principal arm of the *IRS* for resolving tax controversies. It reports to the Regional Commissioner and is vested with broad settlement power on a *hazards of litigation* basis. *Taxpayers* generally find their way into the Appeals Office either as a result of a *protest* from a *proposed adjustment* (*thirty-day letter*), the so-called *nondocketed case,* or as a result of a *notice of deficiency* issued by the *District Director's* office, followed by the taxpayer's petition to the *Tax Court,* so-called *docketed cases.* After a docketed case has been filed, the Appeals Office has a limited period in which to settle. See Rev. Proc. 79-59, 1979-2 C.B. 573, Statement of [IRS] Procedural Rules §§601.105 to -106. See *Appeals Conference.*

applicable amounts   otherwise *deductible* payments from *personal service corporations* to their owner-employees. The deductibility of such amounts are limited by §280H if the payor chooses to use a fiscal year via a *section 444 election.* See Reg. §1.280H-1T(b)(4). Deductions that are disallowed because of failure to meet the minimum distribution requirements are allowed as deductions in the next taxable year. §280H(e). See *maximum deductible amount, section 444 election.*

applicable asset acquisition   any direct or indirect transfer of assets constituting a *trade or business* in the hands of either the seller or the buyer, if the transfer was either a fully taxable *sale* or a taxable *exchange* that was partially tax-*deferred* under §§1031 (*like-kind exchanges*), 1035 (exchanges of *life insurance policies*), or 1036 (*stock* for stock in the same *corporation*). §1060(c) and Temp. Reg. §1.1060-1T(b)(1) and (4). A group of assets constitutes a trade or business if its use would qualify as an *active trade or business* under §355 (*corporation divisions*) or if its character is such that *goodwill* or *going concern value* could attach to the assets under any circumstances. This latter determination is made on the basis of *all facts and circumstances,* including the fact that the price paid exceeds the book value of the assets other than goodwill and going concern value, and the existence of related contracts such as *leases, covenants not to compete,* and employment and management contracts. Temp. Reg. §1.1060-1T(b)(2). If the *taxpayer* engaged in an applicable asset acquisition, the *residual method* must be used for *allocating basis* among assets so acquired. Section 1060 can apply to the valuation of goodwill and going concern value of *partnerships* solely for purposes of §755, the operative rules for *partnership* basis allocations, and for reporting purposes on §1060(b). §1060(d) and (e). See *residual method; section 338 acquisition.*

applicable banking day the day after the day when there is $100,000 or more to be deposited in *withheld income taxes* and *Social Security taxes.* Employers with aggregate taxes due of $3,000 or more at the end of an eighth-monthly period must deposit the payment within three banking days after the end of that period. Employers on this "eighth-monthly" system must deposit withheld income and Social Security taxes by the close of the "applicable banking day" after any day when the amount to be deposited is $100,000 or more. §6302(g).

applicable CFC a class of *controlled foreign corporation* (CFC) which is treated as if it were a *nonresident alien individual,* hence not taxed on *portfolio interest.* See §904(g); §127(g)(3) of the *Tax Reform Act of 1984.*

applicable corporation, CERT a *C corporation* which acquires *stock,* or the stock of which is acquired, in a *major stock acquisition;* a C corporation making *distributions* with respect to, or redeeming, its stock in connection with an *excess distribution;* or any C corporation which is a successor corporation of such a corporation. §172(b)(1)(E)(iii). The term is used in connection with *corporate equity reduction transactions.*

applicable depreciation method the schedule according to which property is written off under §168 (the modified ACRS system in place after the *Tax Reform Act of 1986).* §168(b). In general, it calls for *declining-balance depreciation,* except that *straight-line depreciation* is used for *real estate* and property written off under the *alternative depreciation system.* Most property subject to *declining-balance depreciation* is written off at a 200 percent rate, switching to straight-line at the optimum moment. A 150 percent declining-balance method applies to *fifteen-year* and *twenty-year property* and to other property electively written off on the 150 percent schedule. In all cases zero *salvage value* is assumed. The period over which it is written off is called the *applicable recovery period.*

applicable dividends any *dividend* which, in accordance with the *ESOP* plan provisions: (1) is paid in cash

to participants in the *plan* or their *beneficiaries;* (2) is paid to the plan and is *distributed* in cash to participants in the plan or their beneficiaries not later than 90 days after the close of the *plan year* in which paid; or (3) is used to make payments on a loan, the proceeds of which were used to acquire the *employer securities* (whether or not allocated to participants) with respect to which the dividend is paid. §404(k). An *employer* can *deduct* applicable dividends used to repay a loan used to acquire securities, if the dividends are on securities acquired with the loan (known as *applicable employer securities).* See *ESOP loan.*

applicable election period a period during which *participants* can electively waive *qualified joint and survivor annuities* (90 days ending on annuity starting date) and *qualified pre-retirement survivor annuities* (period beginning on first day of *plan year* in which the participant attains age 35 and ends on his or her death). §417(a)(1) and (6).

applicable election year any *taxable year* in which a *personal service corporation* has a *section 444 election* in effect. If, for any applicable election year, the corporation does not satisfy the minimum distribution requirement of §280H(c), the deduction otherwise allowable for applicable amounts can not exceed the *maximum deductible amount.* Any amount not allowed as a deduction in an applicable election year is allowed as a deduction in the succeeding taxable year.

applicable employer cost (a) an *employer's* "qualified current retiree health liabilities" for the *taxable year,* divided by (b) the number of *individuals* to whom applicable health benefits coverage was provided during the taxable year. §420(c)(3)(B)(ii).

applicable employer securities with respect to any *dividend, employer securities* which are held on the record date for the dividend by an *ESOP* and are maintained by a *corporation* paying the dividend, or a related member of a *controlled group of corporations* under §409(l)(4) (viz., modified §1563 meaning). §404(k)(3). See *ESOP loan.*

applicable exclusion see *specified fringe benefit plan.*

applicable federal interest rate the rate used for discounting purposes by property and casualty insurance companies, based on the rates in effect, with adjustments for annual compounding, as of the beginning of each of the calendar months in the most recent 60-calendar month period ending before the beginning of the *calendar year* for which the determination is made. §§807(d)(4)(A)(i), 846(c), 1274(d). It is based on the *federal mid-term rate.*

applicable federal rate the rate of *interest* determined under §1274(d). The rate is used to impute interest on a *below-market loan* and to search for *original issue dis-*

count. The rate is determined by the *Treasury Department* and redetermined for each six-month period beginning January 1 and July 1. §1274(d)(1)(B) and (C). The federal rates are categorized based on the term of the instrument, taking any renewal or extension options into account. A short-term rate applies to obligations with a term of up to three years; a medium-term rate applies to obligations with a term of over three years, but not over nine years. Beyond that is the long-term rate. The rates are based on the average market yield for outstanding marketable federal obligations of comparable duration.

applicable financial statement the financial statement used as the starting point for calculating the *adjustment* for *business untaxed reported profits.* §57(f)(2)(A). Generally, it is the statement the *taxpayer* provides for regulatory or credit purposes, for the purpose of reporting to shareholders or other owners, or for other substantial nontax purposes. If it has more than one financial statement, rules of priority determine which statement is the applicable financial statement (AFS). §57(f)(3)(A) and (c). Highest priority is given financial statements that must be filed with the SEC. Second are audited financial statements certified by a professional accountant and used for credit purposes for reports to shareholders or other owners. Third are income statements that must be provided to the *federal* government or its agencies, a *state* government or its agencies, or a *political subdivision.* Fourth is any financial statement or report used for credit purposes, for reporting to shareholders or other owners, or for any other substantial nontax purpose. A *taxpayer* without an AFS or with only a fourth category AFS can irrevocably elect to use *current earnings and profits* to compute the book income preference, without reduction by *distributions.* Deadlocks between statements of the same priority are to be broken by *regulations.* §56(f)(3)(B).

applicable fraction the smaller of the *unit fraction* or the *floor-space fraction.* The unit fraction is a fraction, the numerator of which is the number of *low-income units* in the building, and the denominator of which is the number of residential units in the building. The floor-space fraction is a fraction whose numerator is the total floor space of the low-income units in the building, and whose denominator is the total floor space of the residential rental units in the building. §42(c)(1)(B)-(D).

applicable fraction, low-income housing credit see *qualified basis, low-income housing credit.*

applicable Government price index see *simplified dollar-value LIFO method.*

applicable health benefits health benefits or coverage provided to retired employees who, just before a *qualified transfer,* are entitled to receive both the health benefits or coverage and also pension benefits under the plan, as well as their *spouses* and *dependents.* §420(e)(1)(C)(i).

applicable high-yield discount obligation a debenture that has the following four characteristics: (1) it is issued by a *corporation*; (2) it has a maturity date more than five years from the date of issue; (3) its *yield to maturity* is at least 5 *percentage points* higher than the *applicable federal rate* in effect for the month in which it was issued; and, it is issued with significant *original issue discount.* §163(e)(5). *Interest* on a *payment in kind debenture* is treated the same way as original issue discount. §163(i). The concept of *significant OID* is defined elsewhere. The implications of being an applicable high-yield discount obligation are partial *deferral* and partial disallowance of *interest expense deductions* to the obligor. The disallowance falls on the *disqualified portion* of the yield; however, the recipient may claim a *dividends-received deduction* on such amounts. See *disqualified yield; payment assumption rule; significant OID.*

applicable housing price ratio either the *new housing price ratio* or the *existing housing price ratio,* whichever results in the housing cost/income ratio being closer to 1. §143(g)(5)(D)(ii).

applicable median family income the greater of median gross income in the area in which the residence is located, or the *state*wide median gross income. §143(f)(4). *Qualified mortgage bonds* and *mortgage credit certificate-assisted* loans generally cannot be to people with family incomes greater than 115 percent of median family income, except for *targeted area residences* or high-cost areas. §143(f). There are upward adjustments for larger families. See *area median gross income.*

applicable percentage, intangible drilling and development costs (IDCs) a series of percentages used to determine the portion of *intangible drilling and development costs (IDCs)* that *taxpayers* had to elect to *amortize* over five years. Former §58(i)(4). *Straight-line* recovery is now assumed. §57(a)(2).

applicable percentage, low-income housing credit see *low-income housing credit.*

applicable percentage, recapture of depreciation or cost recovery a percentage (ordinarily 100 percent) by which amounts potentially subject to *recapture* of *depreciation* or *cost recovery* are multiplied to reduce such recapture. The term is designed to afford relief to certain depreciated residential realty and *separate improvements.* Note, recapture under §1250 is based solely on the amount of *accelerated depreciation* or cost recovery in excess of depreciation (or cost recovery) that would have been claimed under the straight-line method.

applicable period the period during which a *participant* in a *qualified plan* must be given notice of the qualified preretirement *annuity* arrangements in anticipation of the participant's election to drop the annuity. The term is defined as the latest of: (1) the period beginning with the first day of the *plan year* in which the participant attains age 32 and ends with the close of the plan year preceding the plan year in which the participant attains age 35; (2) a reasonable period of time after the *individual* becomes a plan participant; (3) a reasonable period of time after the survivor benefit applicable to a participant is no longer subsidized as defined in §417(a)(5); or (4) a reasonable period of time after the survivor benefit provisions (§401(a)(11)) become applicable with respect to a participant. §417(a)(3)(B)(ii)(IV).

applicable preferred stock   *preferred stock,* as defined in §1504(a)(4), in a subsidiary *corporation,* which is a *member of an affiliated group* of corporations, provided the stock was issued after November 17, 1989, and is held by a *person* other than a member of the affiliated group. §1504(f)(3)(D). This is part of an ornate provision designed to put an end to special purpose subsidiaries which are used to pay preferred stock dividends to corporate investors while using the parent company group's *credit* (*group credit items*) or *losses* (*group loss items*) to shelter the sub's profits.

applicable rate, generation-skipping transfer tax the rate of *generation-skipping transfer tax* applied to the value of property transferred in *generation-skipping transfers.* See *direct skip, generation-skipping transfer tax; inclusion ratio, generation-skipping transfer tax.*

applicable recovery period   the period over which property is written off under §168 (the modified *ACRS* system in place after the *Tax Reform Act of 1986*). The periods range from 3 years to 31.5 years. §168(c). See *accelerated cost recovery system.*

applicable stock price, deep-in-the-money option see *deep-in-the-money option.*

applicable valuation date   the later of the beginning of the *taxable year* of the *passthrough entity* when the owner of an interest in the entity disposes of the interest or the date the *disposition* occurs. Temp. Reg. §1.469-2T(e)(3). In general, when an owner disposes of an interest in a *partnership* or an *S corporation,* a ratable part of the *gain* or *loss* is allocated to each *trade or business* in which the entity owned an interest on the applicable valuation date. Temp. Reg. §1.469-2T(e)(3)(ii)(A). The previous day is used if the entity engages in major dispositions of interests or property it holds or if the holder of the interest contributes substantially appreciated or depreciated property. Temp. Reg. §1.469-2T(e)(3)(ii)(D)(1). See *passive loss rules.*

applicable value, liquidations   see *qualified corporation, liquidations.*

application for quick refund   see *application for tentative carryback adjustment.*

application for tentative carryback adjustment   an application (Forms 1139 or 1045) used in lieu of an *amended return* to obtain a *refund or credit* for a *carryback* of a *net operating loss, capital loss,* or *unused general business credit* for a previous year. §6411. Prompt filing is demanded. See *tentative carryback adjustment.*

apportionment   allotment. For example, *depreciation deductions* to which a *trust* is entitled must be apportioned between the trust and its *beneficiaries* as directed by the trust instrument. §§167(h) and 611(b)(3). See *proration; stacking; tracing.*

apportionment, appointive property   an exception to the general rule that state law governs the determination of who will ultimately bear the burden of the *federal estate tax* in the absence of an expression of the *decedent's* intent. Under the *Code,* one who receives property over which the decedent had a power of appointment must contribute to the payment of the tax if such property is included in the decedent's *gross estate.* §2207.

apportionment plan   an agreement by *members of an affiliated group* of *corporations* that directs the *allocation* of the *surtax exemption* (superannuated—the real reference is now to *graduated income taxes* on corporate *taxable income*) and the *accumulated earnings credit* among each of the members of the group. If an apportionment plan is not elected, the surtax exemption and the accumulated earnings credit must be divided equally among the members of the affiliated group. §1561(g).

appraisal summary   a report that contains information to be prescribed by *regulations* and must (1) be signed by the *qualified appraiser* who prepared the *qualified appraisal* on which the summary is based; (2) bear the qualified appraiser's identifying number; and (3) be acknowledged by the signature of the donee. *Tax Reform Act of 1984* §155(a)(3).

appreciated inventory   see *substantially appreciated inventory items.*

appreciated property   in a general, nontechnical sense, property which has risen in value. For more technical tax purposes the term means property with a *fair market value* greater than *adjusted basis.* This latter format, for example, used in taxing *corporations* under §311(b) on *stock redemptions* performed with appreciated property, establishing *basis* under §1014(e) of appreciated property which was transferred by *gift* to a *decedent* within one year before death and which was reacquired by the *donor* from the decedent, taxing the transferors under §84 of appreciated property transferred to *political organizations,* and the impact of §170(e) on certain transfers of property to charities. Reg. §§1.311-2(a)(3); 1.170A-4.

appropriate exchange rate   for the purpose of translating *earnings and profits* of a *foreign corporation* into a *taxpayer's functional currency,* the spot rate of exchange between the taxpayer's functional currency and any *nonfunctional currency* at the time any nonfunctional currency distribution of *earnings, profits* or deemed *dividends* are included in the *gross income* of the *taxpayer.* §939(b). In case of amounts included in the income of *United States shareholders* in *controlled foreign corporations, foreign personal personal holding companies,* or *qualified electing funds,* the appropriate exchange rate is the *weighted average exchange rate* for the *taxable year.* §989(b)(3). See *functional currency.*

appurtenant   when speaking of *realty,* property which functions as an accessory to another piece of realty. See, e.g., Reg. §1.280A-1(c)(1).

arbitrage bond   an otherwise tax-exempt *state or local bond* obligation which is denied tax-exempt-bond status because some or all of the proceeds are reasonably expected to be used (1) to acquire obligations which may be reasonably expected to produce a yield during the term of the government obligation which is materially higher than the yield on the exempt issue of *higher yielding investments*; or (2) to replace funds used to acquire such investment property. §148(a)(1) and former Reg. §1.103-13(b). See *alternative minimum tax bond; six-month temporary investment exception; tax-exempt bond; TRAN; twenty-four-month construction issue exception.*

arbitrage exception, short sales   transactions of *stock, securities,* and *rights* to acquire stock or securities in which the *taxpayer* intends to profit from the current difference between the price of the asset purchased and the price of the asset sold, provided the asset purchased, if not identical to the asset sold, entitles or will entitle the taxpayer to acquire assets identical to those sold (e.g., convertible bonds). §1233(f)(4). Such transactions, if promptly and clearly identified, are exempt from the rule of §1233(e), which shortens the *holding period* of *substantially identical stock or securities* held by a short seller.

architectural and transportation barrier removal expense   expenditures incurred for the purpose of making any *facility* or *public transportation vehicle,* owned or leased by the *taxpayer* for use in connection with his *trade or business,* more accessible to, and usable by, *handicapped individuals* and *elderly persons.* §190(b)(1). See *qualified architectural and transportation barrier removal expense.*

architectural barriers deduction   a common shorthand reference to a *deduction* of up to $35,000 per year for easing the lives of *elderly* and *handicapped individuals.* §190. For the formal terminology, see *architectural and transportation barrier removal expense; qualified architectural and transportation barrier removal expense.*

area median gross income   low-income housing credit not yet defined. The *IRS* has announced that the definition will be based on *regulations* consistent with HUD's §8 housing definition, which uses a different income base from the one used for *federal income tax* purposes. Notice 88-80, 1988-30 I.R.B. 28. The low-income housing credit expired on June 30, 1992. See *low-income housing credit.*

area median gross income, low-income housing bonds   not specifically defined in the *Code*; rather it is determined according to the principles used to determine lower-income families and area median gross income under §8 of the Housing Act of 1937, and includes adjustments for family size. §142(d)(2)(B). One disregards the *interest* income exclusion under the *below-market loan* rules for certain loans to continuing-care facilities in determining an income. §142(d)(2)(B). The term is important in evaluating whether the projects being funded qualify for tax-exempt financing.

area of chronic economic distress   a poverty area that a *state* designates as meeting the standards of §163(j)(1), which designation HUD has approved. §163(j)(1)(B) provides criteria to guide HUD. Such areas can enjoy special benefits in connection with *qualified mortgage bonds* and *mortgage credit certificates.*

area of interest, natural resource exploration   generally, a noncontiguous subpart of a *project area* which a *taxpayer* selects to do further exploration. General *geological and geophysical costs* are apportioned to areas of interest retained after the project area has been studied. Detailed survey expenses are then apportioned by area of interest. See Rev. Rul. 83-105, 1983-2 C.B. 51 for a generous but confusing treatment. Where only detailed survey is done, then the area of interest and the project area are the same. Rev. Rul. 77-188, 1977-1 C.B. 76.

arm's length   a standard used to determine how a transaction would be carried out if the parties were independent of each other. The term is of special significance under §482, which authorizes the *Commissioner* to reallocate *income, deductions,* and other items between *trades, businesses,* and organizations under common control in order to eliminate *evasion* of taxes or *distortion of income.* See *abuse of discretion; reallocation of income and deductions by Commissioner.*

arm's length transaction   a transaction undertaken at *arm's length* that is with, or as if with, an independent party.

Arrowsmith doctrine   a judicial doctrine requiring that *restorations* of income associated with prior *closed transactions* take their tax character from the prior transactions. Specifically, corporate shareholders who had claimed *capital gain* on receipt of proceeds of a *corporate liquidation* were compelled to report repayments on a later judgment against the *corporation*. The repayments were found to be linked to the prior liquidation and were held as *capital losses* rather than simple *deductions*. The doctrine is complemented by similar rules involving recoveries. For example, if a company wrote off certain worthless notes as an ordinary deduction but later sold the notes for $18,000, the receipts would be taxable as *ordinary income*.

Art Advisory Council a panel of experts in the employ of the *IRS*, which meets periodically to assign values to particular works of art for *federal income, estate* and *gift tax* purposes.

ascertainable standard, power of appointment powers to consume, invade, or appropriate property for the benefit of the *donees* or *decedent* which are limited by an ascertainable standard relating to the health, education, support, or maintenance of the donee or decedent. Reg. §§25.2514-1(c)(2) (*gift taxes*), 20.2041-1(c)(2) (*estate taxes*).

ascertainable useful life a *useful life* of property in the *taxpayer's* hands that is reasonably capable of estimation. The term seems impossible to define. Examples include such diverse rules as: (1) *trademark* and *tradename* expenditures have useful lives that cannot be estimated and are instead in the nature of *goodwill,* and (2) renewable television licenses which have an indefinite duration also do not have ascertainable useful lives.

asserted liability an item that, absent a contest, could be *deducted* (e.g., a bill for services of a noncapital nature submitted to a business). §461(g); Reg. §1.461-2(b)(1). Thus, a proposed but *unassessed deficiency* is not enough. Section 461(g) authorizes a *deduction* for payments of certain contested liabilities by *accrual method taxpayers,* provided that, in addition to other conditions, there is an asserted liability. See *contest; contested liabilities.*

assessable penalty see *civil tax penalty.*

assessment establishment of a legal liability to pay a tax *deficiency*. The process of assessment of a deficiency involves formal entry of the alleged deficiency on ledgers maintained by the *IRS;* failure to assess means a tax deficiency cannot be collected administratively. Moreover, failure to assess a deficiency within periods fixed by *statutes of limitations* found in the *Code* precludes government action on the deficiency. On the other hand, failure by the *taxpayer* to enter a timely *petition* in the *Tax Court* after a *statutory notice of deficiency* results in exclusion from that court and a duty to pay the assessment. Interestingly, when taxes are paid in the ordinary course, accompanying *returns* are verified and the stated liability is assessed automatically, forming the justification for the government's retention of the funds. §6203; Reg. §301.6202-1.

assessment period the statutory period during which a *deficiency* can be *assessed* by the *IRS* (typically three years), unless extended by agreement of the parties. §6501. The period starts to run on the day after the *return* is filed or on the day after the last day the *taxpayer* can file the return (e.g., April 16), whichever is later. There is disagreement about when a return is filed. The IRS asserts that a return is filed when they receive it. See *filing, return; statute of limitations; waiver of restrictions on assessment and collection.*

asset depreciation period see *class life asset depreciation range system (ADR).*

asset depreciation range (ADR) a range of statutorily imposed *useful lives* applicable to property under the *class life asset depreciation range system*. The asset depreciation range for an asset consists of a statutory midpoint (e.g., 10 years) bounded by a 40 percent range (e.g., the ADR is 8–12 years). Within the ADR, *taxpayers* could choose a useful life with impunity. Reg. §1.167(a)-11(b)(4)(i)(B). The taxpayer's selection was the *asset guideline period*. See *class life asset depreciation range system (ADR).*

asset guideline class, class life asset depreciation range system a category of assets, including subsidiary assets, subject to the *class life asset depreciation range system* (ADR) for which a separate guideline period is in effect for the *taxable year*. Reg. §1.167(a)-11(b)(4)(i). For example, class 00.11 contained office furniture, fixtures, and equipment. The classification in turn determines the property's *useful life* expressed as both a midpoint and within a range and a *repair allowance*. Reg. §1.167(a)-11(b)(2); Rev. Proc. 72-10, 1972-1 C.B. 721, as amended. For example, water transportation equipment is ascribed a midpoint life of 20 years and an asset repair allowance of 8 percent. ADR never included buildings.

asset guideline period, class life asset depreciation range the *useful life* of property selected by a *taxpayer* under the *class life asset depreciation range system*. The period is a midpoint on a range called the *asset depreciation range*. See *class life asset depreciation range system (ADR).*

assets of a qualified business see *qualified business unit.*

assets test, domestic building and loan associations one of three tests used to determine if various savings and loan associations qualify as *domestic building and loan associations.* §7701(a)(19). To satisfy the assets test, at least 60 percent of the association's assets must consist of assets as defined in §7701(a)(19) and Reg. §301.7701-13A(d) and (e). Examples of such assets include cash, government obligations, and passbook loans. See *domestic building and loan association.*

assets test, operating foundation one of three alternative tests used by the *IRS* as part of the definition of an *operating foundation*. A *private foundation* satisfies the assets test if at least 65 percent of its assets are either: (1) devoted by the foundation directly to its *charitable exempt purposes* or to functionally related *businesses*, or both; or (2) are under the *control* (80 percent under §368(c)) of a *corporation* at least 85 percent of the assets of which are so used, or (3) some combination thereof. §4942(j)(3)(B)(i); Reg. §53.4942(b)-2(a). See also *endowment test; support test.*

asset use test one of two tests used to determine if *fixed or determinable periodical income* or *gains* and *losses* from *sales* or *exchanges* of property are *effectively connected* with the conduct of a *United States trade or business,* hence, treated as *income from* sources within the United States. If the income is derived from assets used in the conduct of a United States trade or business, it will be deemed United States source income and will be taxed as if earned by a *United States person.* This test is of primary significance with respect to *interest* and *dividends* earned by capital-intensive *foreign taxpayers* which maintain *branches* or *subsidiary* operations in the United States. §864(c)(2)(A); Reg. §1.864-4(c). See §864(c)(2)(B) for service-intensive businesses.

assigned property *recovery property* whose *class life, recovery period,* or classification is specifically placed into *three-year property, five-year property, seven-year property, fifteen-year property,* or *twenty-year property* classes by §168(e)(3) as well as a variety of assets assigned special *recovery periods* or *class lives* under former §168(g)(3)(B)-(D). §168(i)(1)(E). After 1982 the *Treasury Department* is authorized to change "assigned items" (the class lives, classifications, or recovery periods) of assigned property. Former §168(i)(1)(B).

assignment of income doctrine a judicial doctrine that treats attempts at gratuitous transfers of income interests as ineffective to shift income to another. If the doctrine applies, the transferor is taxed when the transferee receives the income that was the subject of the attempted transfer. Generally, if the transfer is of an underlying *property* interest (e.g., a copyright), the transfer will be effective to shift income from the property, except as to amounts earned prior to the transfer.

assignment or alienation, qualified plans a nonexclusive term including: (1) any arrangement which provides for payment of benefits under a *qualified plan* to the *employer* that would otherwise go to a *participant*; and (2) any arrangement whereby a party acquires a right to a plan benefit from a participant or *beneficiary* that is, or may become, payable to a participant or beneficiary. Reg. §1.401(a)-13(c)(1). For the key exception, see *qualified domestic relations order.*

Assistant Commissioner, Compliance the principal assistant to the Commissioner of the *IRS,* whose duty is to achieve maximum voluntary compliance with Internal Revenue laws. Numerous divisions report to this office: Appeals Division; *Examination Division; Collection Division; Criminal Investigation Division*; and *Foreign Operations Internal Revenue District.*

Assistant Commissioner for Taxpayer Services an *IRS* officer charged with providing telephone, walk-in, and educational services as well as designing and producing tax publications and tax forms. §7802.

associate company a company which is a member of a *holding company system* with another company. Public Utility Act of 1935, §2(a)(1), 15 U.S.C. §79b(a)(10) (1981), §1083(b) provides the precise meaning. *Gain* or *loss* may go *unrecognized* where securities in a registered holding company are transferred under a SEC order to an associate company (also a registered holding company) in exchange for securities. §1081(a); Rev. Rul. 54-192, 1954-1 C.B. 99.

associated entertainment and meal expenses *entertainment* and *meal expenses* which are not *directly related,* but are associated with the active conduct of the *taxpayer's trade or business* or investment activities. Such expenses are generally *deductible* only if the entertainment or meal occurs during or directly precedes or follows a *substantial and bona fide business discussion.* §274(a)(1)(A), Reg. §1.274-2(d). Expenses are generally associated with the active conduct of a trade or business if the taxpayer has a clear business purpose for incurring the expenditure (e.g., to develop new business or to encourage existing business relationships). Entertainment occurring on the same day as the business discussion is automatically considered as directly preceding or following the business discussion. However, if the entertainment does not occur on the day of the discussion, all facts and circumstances are considered. For example, if the customer is from out of town, entertainment on the day before or the day after the discussion generally will qualify. Reg. §1.274-2(d)(3)(ii). The cost of entertainment allocable to the *spouses* of the participants in the business discussion is deductible if there is a business, rather than a personal or social, purpose for including the spouses. Reg. §1.274-2(d)(2).

associates for purposes of classifying an *entity (partnership, trust,* etc.) as an *association taxable as a corporation,* Reg. §301.7701-2(a)(2) demands the presence of associates, meaning *persons* who, except in the case of *one-man corporations,* join together for profit. It has been held, in what may be an unreliable decision, that a trust established by will cannot have associates. The associates in a corporation are its *shareholders*; in a trust, the *beneficiaries*; and in a partnership, the *partners.* The latter two entities may be reclassified as associations taxable as corporations; the presence of associates is a necessary but inconclusive factor.

association "a body of persons united without a charter, but upon the methods and forms used by incorporated bodies for the prosecution of some common enterprise." The word is also used as an abbreviation of the term *association taxable as a corporation.*

association property all property held by the owners of a *condominium management association* or *residential real estate management association,* each of which is a *homeowners' association,* or commonly held by the members of a homeowners' association; property owned by a government unit and used for the benefit of the members; or property within the organization privately held by members of a homeowners' association. §528(c)(4). The term is significant because the *Code* grants a *federal income tax* exemption to two classes of homeowners' associations, provided they hold association property. The first class is an organization formed to acquire, construct, manage, maintain, and care for association property consisting primarily of a condominium project in which substantially all the units are used by *individuals* as residences (§528(c)(1) and (2))—so-called condominium management associations. The second class of organization is formed for the same purposes as the first, but with respect to the association property, consists of subdivisions on which substantially all the lots or buildings are used by individuals for residences (§528(c)(1)(f) and (3))—so-called *residential real estate management associations.*

association taxable as a corporation an *organization* (e.g., *corporation, trust,* or *partnership* under state or foreign law) which is classified as a *corporation* for *federal income tax* purposes pursuant to §7701(a)(3) and Reg. §301.7701-2. Six factors are applied to an *entity* to determine whether it is an association taxable as a corporation. Two mandatory factors for identifying an association are that the entity has (1) *associates,* and (2) a purpose to earn profits and to divide *gains.* The remaining four factors are used to establish whether the entity has more corporate than noncorporate attributes. Under current law, the presence of three of the factors (in addition to the mandatory two) results in finding an association: (1) *continuity of life;* (2) *centralized management;* (3) *free transferability of interests;* and (4) *limited liability.* Generally, the contests involve recharacterizing a *limited partnership* or a *trust.* §301.7701-4(b). See *limited liability company (LLC).*

"assumed or taken subject to" a term commonly used to describe how debt on encumbered property is treated. The concept is that debt is either assumed, meaning that the transferee entered into a new agreement with the lender promising to be personally liable for the debt, or that the encumbrance merely followed the property, as is always the case with *nonrecourse debt.* The confusing issue is how one treats *recourse*

debt that the transferee did not assume. The logical answer is that it was neither assumed (a fact) nor should it be deemed taken "subject to" because it is not nonrecourse debt and the transferor remains personally liable. The issue is unsettled. The issue is bound up with the treatment of *wraparound mortgages.*

assumption agreement an agreement under which a person agrees to undertake the liability of another. An assumption agreement makes *limited partners* liable for *partnership* borrowings, and is relatively common in *tax shelter* offerings because of its effect on *basis* under §752 and on amounts *at risk* under §465.

assumption of liabilities a transaction in which a transferee of property personally undertakes liabilities attached to the property, typically a mortgage obligation, and the transferor is released. Contrast the transaction in which property is merely transferred subject to a liability without accepting personal liability. Liabilities assumed or taken generally become part of an asset's *basis* in the transferee's hands, and part of the transferor's *amount realized.* See "*assumed or taken subject to.*"

athletic facilities, fringe benefits a type of *fringe benefit* which may be *deductible* by the *employer* and nontaxable to the *employee* under §132(h)(5). The benefit includes the use of gyms or other athletic facilities located on the premises of the *employer,* operated by the employer, and used almost exclusively by the employees, their *spouses,* and dependent children. Eligibility is not conditioned upon *nondiscrimination rules* as to *highly compensated employees* (§414(q)), but §274(e)(4) denies a *deduction* to the employer for costs attributable to a facility which is primarily for the benefit of highly compensated employees.

at-risk limitation see *at-risk rules, generally.*

at-risk rules, generally at-risk rules apply to all activities engaged in a trade or business or for the production of income. §465(c). Under at-risk rules, loss deductions are limited to the amount of the taxpayer's cash contribution and the adjusted basis of other property which he or she contributes to the activity, plus any amounts borrowed for use in the activity if the taxpayer has personal liability for the borrowed amounts or has pledged assets not used in the activity as security for the borrowed amount. The following amounts are considered at risk: (1) cash; (2) the *adjusted basis* of property contributed to the activity; (3) borrowings to be used in the activity, if subject to personal liability; and (4) borrowings secured by pledged property to the extent of its *fair market value,* other than (a) property contributed to the activity, and (b) pledged property outside the activity which is directly or indirectly financed by property contributed to the activity. §265(b)(1) and (2). The taxpayer will not be considered at risk with respect to nonrecourse financing, guarantees, stop-loss agreements, or similar arrangements. §465 (b). The two activities not subject to at-risk rules are: (1) the holding of real estate, other than mineral property, placed in service before January 1, 1987, and the leasing of equipment by *closely held corporations*. A closely held corporation is one where five or fewer individuals own more than 50 percent of the stock. §465(c)(4). See *recapture, at-risk rules*.

at-risk rules, investment tax credit   a system of proportionately reducing the *credit base* (*basis* for new property or cost for used property to the extent such *basis* qualifies for the *investment credit*) of an asset for purposes of calculating the former investment credit. The pattern is to reduce the credit base by *nonqualified nonrecourse financing,* that is, *nonrecourse* financing other than *qualified commercial financing* with respect to the property. §49(a)(1))A). Later increases or decreases in nonqualified nonrecourse financing cause *recapture* of the credit, or allow an increased credit, respectively. The credit is apportioned to *partners* and shareholders of *S corporations,* but the latter are deemed personally liable for their share of financing provided to the S corporation by a *qualified person* if the *debt* was *recourse* at the corporate level and is provided for *qualified business property.* §49(a)(1)(E).

attorney-client privilege   an evidentiary privilege that bars the forced disclosure of confidential communications by a client between attorney and client. It arises where professional legal advice is sought from an attorney, acting as such. It can be waived.

Attorney's Fees Award Act   obsolete federal statute that allowed discretionary attorney's fees to be a prevailing defendant in a civil action or proceeding initiated by the United States to enforce a provision of the 1954 Code. See *accountant's fees, recovery of; attorney's fees, recovery of; position of the United States; prevailing party; reasonable administrative costs; reasonable litigation costs; Taxpayer's Bill of Rights.*

attorney's fees, recovery of   reasonable fees for attorneys in a judicial or administrative proceeding and the fees of any *individual,* whether or not an attorney, who is authorized to practice before the *Tax Court* in a proceeding in the Tax Court. §7430(c)(3). The *prevailing party* in a civil tax proceeding brought by or against the United States may recover such fees, if reasonable, up to $75/hour unless the court states otherwise. §7430. Such fees are recoverable if the *position of the United States* was not "substantially justified." Because accountants can be admitted to *practice before the IRS* or be specially admitted to the Tax Court, they can recover either as "attorneys" or as other participants, such as expert witnesses or as preparers of reports and studies. See *position of the United States; prevailing party; reasonable administrative costs; reasonable litigation costs; Taxpayer's Bill of Rights.*

attribution   in tax parlance, the process of associating ownership of something from one *person* to another. See *attribution rules.*

attribution of ownership   see *attribution rules.*

attribution rules   a term used to describe any number of statutory schemes in which the ownership of *stock* is imputed to and from various related *persons.* While there is no universal set of stock attribution rules to find and shift ownership, §318 contains those most commonly used. Other major sources of attribution rules are §§544 (*personal holding companies*), 267(c) (*losses* between related *taxpayers*), 1239 (certain *sales* to related taxpayers), and 1563(e) (denial of certain *tax benefits* to related *corporations*). The rules of §318 are set forth as follows: First, §318(a)(1) and (2) attribute stock from others to the *taxpayer;* stock owned by a *spouse,* child, grandchild, or parent is attributed to the taxpayer; stock owned by *estates, partnerships,* and *trusts* (other than *exempt pension trusts*) is attributed proportionately to the taxpayer; and stock owned by corporations is attributed to the taxpayer only if the taxpayer has at least 50 percent of the corporation's stock by value. Second, §318(a)(3) attributes stock from the taxpayer to *entities;* the taxpayer's stock is attributed to partnerships, trusts (other than exempt pension trusts), and estates in proportion to the taxpayer's interest in such entities; and the taxpayer's stock is attributed to corporations only if the taxpayer has at least 50 percent of the stock of the corporation. Third, §318(a)(4) treats options as creating outright ownership of the optioned stock. See Rev. Rul. 68-601, 1968-2 C.B. 214 (warrants and convertible debt as options). For other major rules of attribution, see §§168(f)(5) (churning *recovery property*), 555 (*foreign personal holding companies*), and 1565 (*brother-sister controlled groups*) and *option attribution rules under §382.* The term "attribution rules" is synonymous with the term *constructive ownership.*

audit   the investigation of a *taxpayer's tax returns* in order to verify accuracy. Audits traditionally fall into the office variety, which occur at an *IRS* facility, or the field variety, which occur at the taxpayer's *business* or residence. The third type, correspondence audits, occur by mail. §7605.

Audit Division   the predecessor of the *IRS Examination Division,* not to be confused with the Internal Audit Division.

audit fee, private foundations   an *excise tax* characterized as a fee to cover the cost of *IRS* audits of *private foundations.* The fee equals two percent of the organization's *net investment income* and is levied on exempt foundations, those which have lost their §501(c)(3) exemption, and nonexempt private foundations, but in the latter case, subject to modifications for regular corporate or *trust* taxes. §4940. A private foundation that has been publicly supported for at least a decade or was an operating foundation as of its last pre-1984 *taxable year,* which is classified as an *exempt operating foundation,* is exempted from the audit fee, and a private foundation which makes certain *qualifying distributions* is subject only to a 1 percent tax. See *net investment income, private foundation excise tax.*

audit standard   a view of the tax laws applied by the *IRS* in auditing *taxpayers' tax returns.*

authority   see *substantial authority.*

authorized placement agency   any agency which is authorized by a state, the District of Columbia, a *possession* of the United States, a foreign country, or a political subdivision of any of the foregoing to place children for adoption. Reg. §1.152-2(c)(2). See *child, dependency exemptions; dependent, generally.*

automatic dividend rule   a description of either of two concepts: (1) treating part of any salary payment as inherently containing a *dividend* component; and (2) the unrelated notion that *boot* received in a *corporate reorganization* is a *distribution.* Both concepts have fallen into disrepute. Note that §356(b)(2) contains such a rule in cases of distributions of boot in otherwise tax-free *corporate divisions.*

automatic energy control system, energy investment credit   equipment that automatically reduces energy consumed in an industrial or commercial process for purposes such as environmental space conditioning (i.e., lighting, heating, cooling, or ventilating). Automatic energy control systems include, for example, automatic equipment setting controls and relay devices used as part of such system. Property such as computer hardware installed as a part of the energy control system also qualifies, but only to the extent of its *incremental cost.* Reg. §1.48-9(f)(10). A qualified automatic energy control system may qualify for *tax credits* as *specially defined energy property* for purposes of the *energy investment credit.* §48(1)(5). Reg. §1.48-9(f).

automatic extension   a statutorily based right to file an annual *income tax return* late. *Individuals* in the *United States* may file four months late if they file for an extension and pay in full by the due date. Reg. §1.6081-4. If they are outside the United States or Puerto Rico, no application is needed. Reg. §1.6081-2. Individuals use Form 4868. *Corporations* may file six months late, but full payment is due on the original due date, using Form 7004. No additional payment is made if a corporation has its records outside the United States or Puerto Rico and makes the proper application. Reg. §1.6081-2(a)(2). See also Reg. §1.6081-2(a)(1) (*partnership* outside the United States or Puerto Rico).

auxiliary benefit   see *annuity starting date, qualified plans.*

average acquisition cost method   a method of valuing increments of *inventory* under the *dollar-value method* by which current year's cost of *closing inventory* is determined on the basis of average acquisitions or production costs over the year. Reg. §1.472-8(e)(2)(ii)(C).

average acquisition indebtedness   see *unrelated debt-financed income.*

average adjusted basis   see *unrelated debt-financed income.*

average annual compensation   the *participant's* highest average annual *compensation* for any consecutive three-year period (or his or her period of service, if shorter). §401(1)(5)(C). The term is used for purposes of determining whether *integration* with Social Security is impermissible or by contradistinction merely creates a *permitted disparity,* as in the case of an *excess defined contribution plan.* See *compensation, generally; integration, Social Security; excess plan; participant, qualified plans.*

average area purchase price, qualified mortgage issue   the average purchase price of single-family residences (see below) in a *statistical area,* which were purchased during the most recent 12-month period for which sufficient statistical information is available. §143(e)(2); former §103A(f)(2). Bonds issued by an issuing authority to provide owner financing will not qualify as tax-exempt *qualified mortgage bonds* if the acquisition cost of any residence so financed exceeds 110 percent of the average area purchase price (120 percent for *targeted area residences*). The term "single-family residences" includes a two-, three- or four-family residence that was first occupied at least five years before the mortgage was executed, provided the owner occupies a part of the residence. §143(c)(7); former §103A(j)(9).

average basis method election   a convenient election under Reg. §1.1012-1(e) by which *taxpayers* who buy *stock* left in the hands of a *custodian* or *agent* can use an average cost method for determining the *basis* of stock purchased at different prices of a *regulated investment company* operating as a *mutual fund* or *unit investment trust.* The election covers all accounts in the same issuer, with a modification for stock received by *gift.* Taxpayers may choose either the *single category method* (all shares are placed in one account and divided by total cost, sales on first-in, first-out assumption) or the *double category method* (shares are broken into more-than-a-year and one-year-or-less holding period categories; the basis of shares in each account is determined by dividing total cost in each category by number of shares).

average benefit percentage   with respect to a group of *employees,* the average benefit percentages calculated separately for each employee in the group (whether or not a *participant* in the plan). The "benefit percentage" is the *employer contributions,* including forfeitures, or benefits attributable to an employee under the *employer's* qualified plans, stated as a percentage of that employee's *compensation.* Contributions have to be converted into benefits for this purpose. §410(b)(2)(B). See *minimum coverage rules.*

average benefits test an alternative test used to determine if the *coverage rules* for *qualified plans* are met. The test is met if the plan benefits *employees* set up under a nondiscriminatory classification (i.e., one not stacked in favor of *highly compensated employees,* likely applying the so-called *fair cross-section test* described under the heading *minimum coverage rules*) and the *average benefit percentage* for non–highly compensated employees is at least 70 percent of the average benefit percentage for the highly compensated group. One counts all the *employer's* benefits for this purpose, and one uses either a single *plan year* or a group of consecutive years. See *average benefit percentage; minimum coverage rules.*

average daily marginal production production calculated annually, determined by dividing the *taxpayer's* total marginal production of domestic crude oil or natural gas during the *taxable year* by the number of days in the taxable year. If the taxpayer holds a partial interest in production from a property (including in a *partnership*) production is an amount determined by multiplying total production from the property by the percentage participation in the property's revenues. Marginal production is deemed to some before regular production for purposes of the 1,000 barrel/day limit on *percentage depletion,* unless the taxpayer elects to the contrary. §613A(c)(6)(G). See *marginal production.*

average daily production the *taxpayer's* aggregate post-1974 production of oil and gas, and to which *gross income* is attributable during the *taxable year,* divided by the number of days in such year. Thus, the exemption amount and *percentage depletion* rate for production extracted in one year and sold in the next are determined in accordance with exemption amount and rate for the year of sale. See T.D. 8348, 1991-22 I.R.B. 5, 6.

average tax rate a *taxpayer's* tax liability divided by *taxable income.*

average unpaid balance the sum of the unpaid balances outstanding on the first day of each month beginning during the *taxable year,* divided by 12. The average unpaid balance times 6 percent is used to derive the interest expense component where interest is separately charged but unascertainable on an installment purchase of an education service or personal property payment. §163(b)(1); Reg. §1.163-2. See *installment method.*

averaging convention a method for arbitrarily solving the problem of when to consider *depreciable* assets *placed in service,* especially where there are multiple asset accounts with numerous annual additions and *retirements* during the *taxable year.* An illustrative minor convention involves an assumption of uniform additions and retirements. Reg. §1.167(a)-10(b). For major conventions, see *half-year convention; modified half-year convention.*

aviation fuel tax an *excise tax* on sales of aviation (nongasoline) fuel by producers and importers at varying rates. §§4081 and 4091. See also §4041 (noncommercial aviation).

avoided cost debt *debt* determined under the *avoided cost method.* See *eligible debt.*

avoided cost method a method referred to in §263A(f)(2)(A)(ii) under which indirect *interest expenses* are *capitalized* to the extent the *taxpayer's interest* expenses could have been reduced if production expenditures were confined to those paid out of borrowings directly attributable to such expenditures.

away from home overnight, travel expenses not in the general area of the *taxpayer's tax home* in circumstances where it is reasonable for the taxpayer to need *sleep or rest* during nonworking time in order to meet the requirements of the *trade or business* (or other *gain-*seeking activity). Being away from home can render *travel expenses* (e.g., fares, meals, lodgings, and telephone) *deductible.* Reg. §§1.162-2, 1.212-1(d).

B

B notice tax jargon for a notice given to payees who are subject to *backup withholding*. The notice is provided by payors of *interest* and *dividends* after the *IRS* notifies the payor of an incorrect *taxpayer identification number*. See Notice 89-88, 1989-33 I.R.B. 15.

BHC an abbreviation for *bank holding company* used in §304(b)(3).

BNA Bureau of National Affairs, a tax publisher.

BTA Board of Tax Appeals, the predecessor of the *Tax Court*.

BURPs an acronym for *business untaxed reported profits*.

background file document a communication relating to a *written determination (ruling, Technical Advice Memorandum* and *determination letter)* between the *IRS* and a *taxpayer* or a *taxpayer representative,* as well as a communication between the IRS and another party (except the Department of Justice in the case of civil or criminal suits), received before issuance of the determination. §6110(b)(2). Taxpayers may request and inspect such material, after names have been expunged, usually in order to fashion their own requests for determinations. See §6103 (confidentiality). Section 6110(j) permits the IRS to charge fees for providing such materials. Section 6110 permits administrative appeals and suits to restrain disclosure of such materials.

back-in farm out a *farm-out agreement* which provides that the *grantor's* retained *nonoperating interest* can later be changed into a specified undivided *working* or *operating interest.*

back loading generally, a slow rate of *accrual benefits* in a *defined benefit plan.* An excessive case of backloading would occur in a *defined benefit plan* when the plan provides that a *participant* in the plan will have no *accrued benefits* until the year prior to *normal retirement age.* Back loading is harmful to the *employee* with many *years of service,* as he will receive nothing upon retirement prior to the year in which benefits accrue. The *Code* has reduced the potential harm of back loading by requiring a *minimum* rate of accrual. §411(b). See *accrued benefits.*

back pay awards, sex discrimination Title VII of the Civil Rights Act awards recovery of back pay due to sex discrimination. *Such awards are includable in income* because Title VII did not provide tort-type remedies.

backup withholding tax a 31 percent tax is levied and withheld on an array of payments to payees. For tax years up to 1992, gambling winnings were subject to withholding at the rate of 20 percent, generally subject to a $1,000 threshold ($5,000 for state-run lotteries). Effective for payments received after 1992, the withholding rate on gambling winning is increased to 28 percent, while the threshold amount is increased to $5,000. Taxpayers who failed to furnish, or furnish obviously incorrect, *taxpayer identification numbers,* were subject to backup withholding at a rate of 20 percent. For amounts paid after 1992, the rate is increased from 20 percent to 31 percent. CNEPA of 1992 (Pub. L 102-486). §1935.

bad boy clauses clauses inserted in *deferred compensation* agreements to cause forfeitures in the event of actions such as working for competitors. They are used most commonly in *restricted property* cases to meet the requirements of §83, or to elude the rule of §411 requiring nonforfeitability of vested benefits under *qualified plans.* To avoid disqualifying an otherwise qualified plan, such clauses would have to create forfeitures which do not violate the vesting rules.

bad check penalty see *penalty, bad check.*

bad debt a *bona fide debt* that has become partially or entirely *worthless.* See *business bad debt; nonbusiness bad debt.*

bad debt loss a *loss* occasioned by a *bad debt.* §166.

bad debt, recovery exclusion see *recovery exclusion.*

bad debt reserve see *reserves for bad debts.*

badges of fraud indicia of knowingly misstating *gross income* or *deductions,* such as failure to report entire sources of income, claims of fictitious deductions, accounting irregularities, and other such conduct. Such behavior indicates a need for a thorough audit and perhaps serious penalties.

bailout an informal term for any technique used by owners of an *entity* to withdraw earnings of the enterprise at favorable tax rates. It is most commonly applied to withdrawing profits from a *corporation* at *capital gains* rates rather than distributing *dividends* at *ordinary income* rates to its shareholders. Section 306 is specifically designed to bar *preferred stock bailouts.*

balance sheet an accounting document showing a party's financial strength. It contains assets (usually on an historical cost basis), liabilities, and equity.

bank a bank or trust company incorporated and doing business under the laws of the United States (including laws relating to the District of Columbia) or any state, provided (1) a substantial part of the business consists of receiving deposits and making loans and discounts, or exercising fiduciary powers similar to those granted national banks under authority of the Comptroller of the

Currency, and (2) it is subject by law to supervision and examination by state or federal authority having supervision over banking institutions, including a *domestic building and loan association.* §581. Part I of subchapter H of the Code provides numerous tax benefits to banks, especially with respect to *reserves for bad debts.* The term includes industrial loan associations and Morris Plan banks.

bank deposit method an indirect method of determining income whereby all deposits to checking and savings accounts are totaled, and all deposits from nontaxable sources and transfers between the *taxpayer's* accounts are subtracted. The net figure of deposits minus nonincome items equals income, and if that income exceeds *exemptions* and *deductions,* the income is *taxable.*

bank deposits, international taxation investments that can be made by a *nonresident alien* or *foreign corporation* free of United States tax if they are not *effectively connected* with a United States *business.* §861(a)(1)(A) and (c); Rev. Rul. 72-104, 1972-1 C.B. 209; Rev. Rul. 75-449, 1975-2 C.B. 285. It includes *interest* on S&L accounts and amounts held by *insurance companies* as settlement options.

bank holding affiliate any organization: (1) that directly or indirectly owns or controls either a majority of the capital stock of a bank or more than half the shares voted to elect directors of any bank at the preceding election, or controls the election of a majority of the directors of any one bank; or (2) for the benefit of whose shareholders or members all or a substantial part of the stock of a member bank is held by trustees. Federal Reserve Act (1913), 12 U.S.C. §221(a) and (c) (1976). §§535(b)(8) and 601.

bank holding company a bank holding company as defined in §2 of the Bank Holding Company Act of 1956. §1103(a). The statute provides that: "Bank holding company means any company: (1) which directly or indirectly owns, controls, or holds with power to vote, 25 per centum or more of the voting shares of each of two or more banks or of a company which is or becomes a bank holding company by virtue of this Act; or (2) which controls in any manner the election of a majority of the directors of each of two or more banks, or (3) for the benefit of whose shareholders or members 25 per centum or more of the voting shares of each of two or more banks or a bank holding company is held by trustees; and for the purposes of this Act, *and* any successor...." Bank Holding Company Act of 1956, 12 U.S.C. §1841 et seq. (1976).

banking, financing, or similar business see *active conduct of a banking, financing, or similar business.*

Bankruptcy Tax Act of 1980 a major overhaul of the tax implications of *discharges of indebtedness* in bankruptcy and outside bankruptcy. Debtors in a *Title 11 case* need not recognize *gross income* from discharged debts, but at the price of reducing favorable tax *attributes* (e.g., *net operating losses, tax credits, basis* in *property,* in particular order) or electively reducing basis in *depreciable* property or *realty* held as *inventory* or *dealer property.* §§108 and 1017. *Solvent taxpayers* outside bankruptcy can generally avoid debt discharge income by electively reducing basis in *depreciable property* subject to later recapture. The act also adds the *Type G reorganization* and codifies prior law exempting cases involving purchase price adjustments from taxation.

Bardahl formula a test to determine whether a company's accumulations of *working capital* are excessive, for purposes of imposing the *accumulated earnings tax* of §532. In the *Bardahl Manufacturing Corp. v. Commissioner,* 24 T.C.M. (CCH) 1030 (1965), the Tax Court established a mathematical formula based on accounts receivable turnover and inventory that permitted the corporation to accumulate a sufficient amount of working capital to pay one operating cycle's expenses. An operating cycle means the period of time that it takes to turn cash into raw materials, then into an inventory of finished goods, then into sales, then back into cash. Once the operating cycle has been determined (e.g., six months), it is multiplied by the sum of the corporation's annual operating costs (ignoring expenses that do not require a cash reserve, such as *depreciation*) plus the annual *costs of goods sold.* If the resulting amount is less than net current assets (i.e., short-term assets less short-term liabilities), an accumulation of working capital is justifiable. The formula may be a good estimate of working capital needs of manufacturing businesses, but it has limited applicability to service companies where inventory is not a major balance sheet component. See *working capital.*

bare legal title the *legal title* to property without the beneficial right to property. For example, although a *nominee* has legal title to property, the realistic power to use, enjoy, encumber, and dispose of the property is held by another person. See *beneficial ownership.*

bargain purchase an acquisition of property for less than its *fair market value.* The acquisition may be in part a *gift,* a corporate *distribution,* disguised compensation, or some other method of transferring value. In a *bargain sale to charity,* a portion of the consideration paid potentially may be taxable *gain* if a portion of the transfer is treated as a taxable sale and the balance as a nontaxable charitable contribution. See Reg. §§1.170A-4(c)(2), 1.1011-2 (*basis* in charitable transactions), 1.1015-4 (basis of property received in noncharitable bargain sales). See §83 for treatment of bargain sales as compensation for services.

bargain sale to charity a transaction in which property is sold at a bargain price to charity. Such *sales* produce partially *taxable gain* by apportioning the *basis* of the property between the portion sold and the portion donated based on the *fair market value* of each portion. For example, if a *taxpayer* sells property with a basis of $100 and a fair market value of $1,000 to a charity for $500, the transaction is deemed as a half sale and a half gift. The sale portion results in a gain of $450, calculated as follows:

Amount realized	$ 500
Basis of property deemed sold	(50)
Taxable gain	$ 450

The remaining $500 is viewed as a contribution. Reg. §§1.170A-4(c)(2), 1.1011-2, 1.1015.4.

barred years years with respect to which the *IRS* can no longer assess or collect tax *deficiencies,* interest, and penalties because the year has been closed by the *statute of limitations.* Sections 6501, 6531, 6532, 6601, 6872, and 7405 contain various statutes of limitations that vary with the *taxpayer's* transaction (e.g., fraud versus negligence) or the proposed IRS action (e.g., imprisonment versus imposing interest charges). See *statute of limitations.*

barrel forty-two United States gallons. §§613A(e)(4) and 4996(b)(2). The term is important for *depletion.*

barter exchange any organization of members providing property or services who jointly contract to trade or barter such property or services. §6045(c)(3). A barter exchange is considered a *broker* for purposes of filing a *return* (§6045(a)), and a *third-party recordkeeper* for purposes of notice requirements for *third-party summonses* served after December 31, 1982. §7609(a)(3).

barter exchange method a method of determining *amount realized* in an *exchange.* It is used where the thing received (e.g., a franchise) cannot be valued, but the thing given up (e.g., land) can be by using the value of things given up as the amount realized.

base amount, credit for increasing research activities see *credit for increasing research activities.*

base amount, golden parachutes the payee's annualized includible compensation for a certain base period consisting of the most recent five years ending before the date on which the ownership or control of the corporation changed or the portion of this period during which the individual was an employee of the corporation. §280G(b)(3)(A). See *excess parachute payment, golden parachute agreement.*

base amount, Social Security a dollar-denominated floor below which Social Security benefits are untaxed. It is currently $25,000 for *single persons,* $32,000 if married filing *joint returns,* and zero if *married persons* filing separate returns unless the couple lived apart all year, in which case it is $25,000. §86(c). See *modified adjusted gross income Social Security benefits.*

base benefit percentage benefits provided on *average annual compensation* not in excess of the *integration level,* stated as a percentage of such compensation. §401(1)(3)(A)(ii). See *permitted disparity.*

base company informal terminology for a company (usually a *corporation*) established in a low-tax jurisdiction, through which income is channeled. The United States attacks this abuse via *subpart F* of the *Code* and §482. See *subpart F income.*

base contribution percentage the percentage of *compensation* that the *employer* contributed under the plan on compensation not over the *integration level.* §401(1)(2)(B)(ii). See *permitted disparity.*

base erosion rule an element of an anti-*treaty-shopping* provision in United States *tax treaties,* which applies if over half of the income of a recipient company is paid-out *royalties* or *interest* to residents of third countries. See *qualified resident, branch profits tax.*

base period, credit for increasing research activities see *base period research expenses.*

base period, debt-financed portfolio stock see *debt-financed portfolio stock.*

base period, golden parachutes see *base amount, golden parachutes.*

base period research expenses generally, average *qualified research expenses paid or incurred* for each *taxable year* in the three-year "base period" before the year for which the credit is determined (the "determination year"). §41(c)(1). Base period research expenses are always at least half of the qualified research expenses for the determination year. §41(c)(3). The growth of *qualified research expenses* over base period research expenses and the *basic research payments* generates the 20 percent *credit for increasing research activities.* §41(a). See *credit for increasing research activities.*

bases of valuation a term used to describe the cost, or *lower of cost or market* methods of valuing *inventory.* Reg. §1.471-2(c).

base stock method, inventory valuation a method of accounting, now discarded, under which the cost of *inventories* held by manufacturers was determined by including only additions to a base amount of inventory as the *cost of goods sold.*

base-year cost, LIFO the aggregate of the cost of all items in an *inventory pool,* determined as of the beginning of the taxable year for which the *last-in, first-out* (LIFO) inventory method is first adopted. Reg. §1.472-8(a).

basic benefit, Keogh plans a benefit in the form of a straight life *annuity,* commencing at the later of age 65 or the day five years after the day the participant's *current period of participation* began under a plan, which provides no *ancillary benefits* and to which *employees* do not contribute. §401(j)(5)(A); Reg. §1.401(j)-1(c)(2). The basic benefit concept is used to set the limit on permissible benefits to be paid out of defined benefit *Keogh plans.* The inquiry is whether the basic benefit provided by the plan exceeds amounts prescribed by Reg. §1.401-11(b)(3). Violation of these rules results in disqualification of the plan. See also §418E(a), (c)(3), (e)(1)(B), and (e)(3) relating to the insolvency of *multiemployer plans,* which evidently relies on ERISA §4001(a) and (b), referring to several guaranteed employee benefits. See *defined benefit plan.*

basic research   any original investigation for the advancement of scientific knowledge, not having a specific commercial objective, which research is conducted in the *United States,* and is not research in the social sciences, arts, or humanities. §41(e)(7)(A). See *credit for increasing research activities; university basic research credit.* The basic research credit expired on June 30, 1992. See *basic research payments.*

basic research payments   any amount paid in cash during the *taxable year* by a *corporation* (but not an *S corporation,* a *personal holding company,* or a *service organization*) to any *qualified organization* for *basic research* performed (in most cases) by the qualified organization. §41(e)(7)(E). The payment must be made under a written agreement between the *corporation* and the qualified organization. §41(e)(2)(A)(i)-(ii). Basic research payments that can qualify for the 20 percent credit for *increasing research activities* consist of such amounts *minus* the qualified organization base period amount; if there is no excess, then the payments are deemed *contract research expenses.* §41(a)(1). See *credit for increasing research activities; corporate grants for basic research by colleges, universities, or certain scientific research organizations.*

basic standard deduction   the usual *standard deduction* for *individuals.* §63(c)(2),(3). For 1993, the standard deductions are as follows:

Married filing joint and surviving spouse	$6,200
Heads of household	5,450
Unmarried individuals	3,700
Married filing separate	3,100
Additional standard deductions for age 65 and blind	
Individual who is married and surviving spouses	700
Individual who is unmarried and not a surviving spouse	900

basis   see *basis of property.*

basis in partnership interest   a *partner's basis* in his or her share of a *partnership,* a dynamic account that begins with the amount of money plus the *adjusted basis* of *property* contributed to a partnership. §722. The partner's share of the partnership's liabilities for which the partner is liable, and those that no partner is liable for are deemed to be a contribution of money and increase the partner's basis. §752. Liabilities of the partnership are generally allocated among the partners according to loss-sharing ratios, except for *nonrecourse liabilities* of *limited partnerships,* which allocate partnership debt according to profit-sharing ratios. Reg. §1.752-1(e). Direct assumption of the partnership's liabilities increases a partner's basis in the partnership interest. Basis is also increased by the partner's share of partnership income and the excess of *depletion deductions* over the basis of the depletable property; however, basis is reduced by partnership distributions and *losses, nondeductible, noncapitalized expenditures,* and limited oil and gas depletion. See §§705, 722, 742 and 752. Reductions in a partner's share of liabilities are treated as *distributions* of money to the partner, and correspondingly reduce basis. §752(b). The partner's basis in the partnership interest serves to limit loss deductions (§704(d)), and to determine *gain* or *loss* on sale or *liquidation* of the interest or on distributions of money in excess of basis. §§731 and 732.

basis, installment obligations   the face amount of an *installment obligation* less the income that would be reported if the obligation were paid in full. If, however, the obligation is disposed of other than by *sale* or *exchange,* the *fair market value,* rather than face amount of the obligation is used. §453B(b). Thus, in both cases the basis in the obligation approximates the *taxpayer's* unrecovered capital investment.

basis of property   a monetary figure designed to reflect the *taxpayer's* investment in property. Basis is used to determine *gains* and *losses* on *disposition* of the property, and the amount of *depreciation, obsolescence, depletion,* and *cost recovery* expense *deductions.* The basis of property depends on the nature of the transaction in which the property was acquired. In a taxable *exchange,* the basis of the property acquired is ordinarily its cost; the cost is purchase price for a *purchase* or the *fair market value* of the property received in an exchange. §1012. The basis of *inventory* is the last value assigned to inventory. §1013. Property acquired from a *decedent* has a basis equal to the property's value at the date of death or on the *alternate valuation date.* §1014. Property received by *gift* or transfer in *trust* takes a basis equal to the sum of the transferor's basis, plus an adjustment for *gift taxes* paid or, in the case of transfers in trust, *gain* or loss to the *grantor.* §1015. Basis is not reduced by encumbrances. After property has been acquired, §1016 and various other *Code* sections modify basis, at which time it becomes known as *adjusted basis.* Basis in property before adjustments is commonly referred to as original basis or unadjusted basis. See *adjusted basis; carryover basis; cost basis; substituted basis.*

basis reduction account an account established by Reg. §1.1501-327(a) to modify the *basis* of *stock* of a deconsolidated *subsidiary corporation* which is retained by the group. Basis declines by *distributions* of *dividends* to the extent of the account balance.

Bausch & Lomb doctrine a poorly clarified rule to the effect that a *Type C reorganization* result will be denied, and a taxable *liquidation* will be found, where an acquiring *corporation* first buys *stock* of a target corporation. The parent corporation then issues its own stock to the acquired corporation in exchange for the subsidiary's assets, and finally it liquidates the subsidiary. In such cases the subsidiary's assets are really acquired in part (as to the initial block of stock) for the subsidiary's stock in a *liquidation* rather than for the parent's stock in a *Type C reorganization* because the Type C reorganization was defective because there was too much boot in the form of the initial block of stock. In the actual decision, the transaction was suppose to be a *Type B reorganization,* but it failed because it was followed by a *liquidation,* hence had to be classified as a Type C (if anything). The doctrine is easily eluded. See *creeping acquisitions.*

bearer shares certificates of stock in a corporation that do not identify the owner. Rather, the holder of the certificate, whoever that might be, is the owner. Bearer stock assures anonymity and is often used to conceal concentrations of ownership in corporations which might otherwise attract tax problems (e.g., the *foreign personal holding company* rules). The antonym is registered stock. See *registered form bond; registration-required obligation.*

begins business, amortization of corporate organizational expenditures the time when the activities of the *entity* "have advanced to the extent necessary to establish the nature of the business operations." Reg. §1.248-1(a)(3). See *pre-opening expenses.*

below-market federal loan a term used in §429(i)(2)(D) relating to the *low-income housing credit.* It refers to any loan funded, even in part, with federal funds at a rate below the §1274(a)(1) (as of the date of lending) rate (§1274(a)(1) related to *original issue discount* and refers to *adequate stated interest*), except for loans under §§106-108 of the Housing & Community Act of 1974. Affordable housing loans under §721 of FIRREA are exempt. Reg. §9.42-3(a). Below-market federal loans disqualify a property for the credit. The low income housing credit expired on June 30, 1992.

below-market loan a *gift loan* or *demand loan* (see below) bearing an interest rate lower than the *applicable federal rate* (an objectively determined rate of interest) or a *term loan* (a loan other than a demand loan)

whose *amount loaned* exceeds the present value, discounted at the *applicable federal rate,* of all payments due under the loan. §7872(e). A demand loan for these purposes is either a loan fully payable at the lender's demand or a nontransferable loan whose interest benefits are contingent on the performance of substantial future services by an *individual* (e.g., a low-interest loan to a professional athlete whose low rate depends on playing a fixed number of games per season). §7872(f)(2)(B). The amount loaned means the amount received by the borrower (in contradistinction to the face amount of the loan). §7872(f)(4). Below-market loans are reorganized by §7872 as if the borrower actually paid (potentially *deductible*) interest at the applicable federal rate, which the lender reported (as a *gross income*), combined with a *gift* or a compensation payment to the borrower (referred to as *gift loans, compensation-related loans,* or *corporation-shareholder loans,* respectively). (*Tax avoidance loans* of some other nature may also be affected.) For example, if in the case of a gift loan, Parent lent $200,000 to Child at 5 percent at a time when the applicable federal rate was 15 percent, §7872 would treat Parent as receiving an extra $20,000 (the 10 percent of so-called *foregone interest*) and Child as being entitled to a further $20,000 potential interest expense *deduction.* In addition, Parent would be viewed as having made a $20,000 gift to Child. The below-market loan rules are designed to prevent a form of *income shifting* as a means of tax avoidance. See *loan, below-market loan.*

below the line a nontechnical term used to indicate that a *deduction* is an *itemized deduction* rather than an *adjustment to gross income* (i.e., a deduction claimed above the line). For the antonym, see *above the line.*

benchmark, deep-in-the-money option see *deep-in-the-money option.*

beneficial enjoyment, control over the power to direct the application of incidents of a *trust.* In particular, §674 taxes the *grantor* (or his or her *spouse*) of a trust if the grantor or a *nonadverse party,* or both, can dispose of trust income or *corpus* without the consent of an *adverse party.*

beneficial interest the property or contract right of a person as distinct from *legal title* which may be held by another person. For example, a *beneficiary* of a *trust* has the beneficial interest in property held by the *trustee.*

beneficial ownership an interest in property to which another may have *legal title,* and which can be enforced in *equity* against the legal owner. Typical beneficial owners are *beneficiaries* of *trusts* or *estates.*

beneficial ownership of stock, consolidated returns *beneficial* or *equitable* ownership of *stock,* used for the 80 percent stock ownership test. Such stock is included when determining whether a group of *corporations* is entitled to file a *consolidated return* as an *affiliated group* under §1504(a). For example, the parent may count such stock where the *nominee* is legally obligated to vote according to the parent's orders even though the nominee holds *legal title*. Rev. Rul. 70-469, 1970-2 C.B. 179. See *consolidated return; stock*.

beneficiary a *person* having an interest in property, but not *legal title*, for whose benefit the property is owned. Such parties include *beneficiaries* of *trusts* and *estates*, and payees of life insurance proceeds. Reg. §1.643(c)-1 states that a *beneficiary* is an *heir, legatee*, or *devisee* (including an estate or trust).

beneficiary limitations, small issue exemption see *small issue exemption, beneficiary limitations*.

benefit bank synonymous with a *flexible spending account*.

benefit percentage see *average benefit percentage*.

benefits and burdens of ownership a standard used to identify the true owner of property for *federal income tax purposes*. Using this standard, the courts inquire into which party bears the risk of loss or the chance for profit, and which party has the practical right to dispose of the property. Rev. Rul. 82-144, 1982-2 C.B. 34 Once true ownership has been established, the implications of ownership come into play. For example, the party properly entitled to claim *depreciation* or *cost recovery deductions* can do so.

benevolent life insurance associations one of a grouping of miscellaneous *exempt organizations*, including benevolent life insurance associations of a purely local character, *mutual ditch or irrigation companies*, and *mutual or cooperative telephone and electric companies*, and similar companies. There seems to be no formal definition of a benevolent life insurance association, although there is authority on whether or not it is of a purely local character. See, e.g., Rev. Rul. 64-183, 1964-2 C.B. 151. The exemption is granted on the primary condition that at least 85 percent of the organization's income is collected from members for the sole purpose of meeting losses and expenses. The *unrelated business taxable income* of such companies is taxed even if they satisfy the 85 percent test. §501(c)(12). No *charitable contribution deduction* is allowed for transfers to such organizations.

bequest a noncompensatory transfer of *personal property* by means of a will. Bequests are generally *excluded* from *gross income*. §102(a). See *inheritance*.

billing month the period for which the seller provides the customer with a periodic statement of charges and credits. Reg. §1.453-2(d)(6)(iii). The customer's agreement to pay part of the bill each billing month is a required element of a *revolving credit plan*.

binding commitment test see *step transaction doctrine*.

bingo games bingo games that, if carried on by an otherwise *exempt organization*, do not result in the activity being treated as an *unrelated trade or business* subject to income taxation. Such games must be legal under local law and operated openly (i.e., wagers laid, winners determined, and prizes awarded), and must not ordinarily be operated on a noncommercial basis nor compete with bingo games conducted on a commercial basis. §513(f).

biological a biological product (e.g., serum or vaccine); one form of *prescribed drug* for purposes of the *medical expense deduction*. §213(d)(2).

biomass, credit for fuels from nonconventional sources organic material that is an *alternate substance* as defined in §48(1)(15) (i.e., any substance other than oil, natural gas, or their products) other than coal, including lignite, or any product of such coal. §29. Biomass can qualify for the *credit for producing fuels from nonconventional sources* and the *energy investment credit*. See *alternate substance, biomass property, energy investment credit*.

biomass property, energy investment credit property that is one of the following: (1) a boiler that uses an *alternate substance (biomass)* as the primary fuel; (2) a burner for a combustor, other than a boiler, that uses an alternate substance (biomass) as the primary fuel; (3) equipment for converting an alternate substance (biomass) into a *qualified fuel*; (4) pollution control equipment required by federal, state, and local regulations to be installed on or in connection with equipment in items (1)–(3); and (5) equipment to unload, transfer, store, and prepare an alternate substance (biomass) at the point of use as a fuel or feedstock in any equipment in items (1)–(4). §48(l)(15)(A) and (B). *Public utility property*, defined under §46(f)(5), is excluded from biomass property. §48(l)(17). Biomass property is *alternative energy property* and may qualify as *energy property* for purposes of the *energy investment credit*. §48(l)(2). Under the CNEPA of 1992 (Pub. L 102-486), the nonconventional fuels credit is extended but only with respect to gas from biomass and synthetic fuels from coal. §1918. The CNEPA also provides a production credit of 1.5 cents per kilowatt-hour for electricity produced from wind energy and "closed-loop" biomass facilities, effective for biomass facilities placed in service after 1992. See *alternate substance, biomass property, energy investment credit*.

black lung benefit trusts *trusts* organized under United States law from contributions by anyone other than an insurer and which pay black lung death and disability benefits, premiums for black lung liabilities, as well as administrative costs. Their investments are closely confined, at the peril of loss of tax-exempt status. §501(c)(21). Section 192(a) provides a *deduction* for transfers to such trusts. See *black lung tax deduction*.

black lung tax deduction a *deduction* allowed for the *taxable year* equal to the sum contributed by the *taxpayer* during the taxable year to a *trust* or trusts established to satisfy liability for claims for compensation for death or disability due to pneumoconiosis under the Black Lung Acts. See *black lung benefit trusts.*

blanket withholding certificate see *withholding certificate.*

blind for a *taxpayer* to qualify for an additional *personal exemption* due to blindness, the condition must involve: (1) central visual acuity of not greater than 20/200 in the better eye with correcting lenses, or (2) visual acuity exceeding 20/200 but with a field of vision at the widest diameter subtending an angle of not greater than 20 degrees. §63(f)(4); Reg. §1.151-1(d)(3). Regulation §1.151-1(d)(3) and (4) describe the necessary certificate to be attached to the return in cases of partial blindness. Blind people get an extra *standard deduction.* §63(c)(3).

blocked currency, subpart F generally, a currency or other restriction or limitation imposed by the laws of a foreign country on the distribution of *earnings and profits* of a *controlled foreign corporation.* §964(c); Reg. §1.964-2(a). A restriction or limitation is determined on the basis of all the facts and circumstances in each case. Generally, such a restriction or limitation must prevent (1) ready conversion (directly or indirectly) of such currency into United States dollars or into property of a type normally owned by such *corporation* in the operation of its business or other money readily convertible into United States dollars, or (2) distribution of *dividends* by such a corporation to its *United States shareholders.* Reg. §1.964-2(b)(2). Blocked income is not deemed distributed, and earnings otherwise imputed to United States shareholders may be deferred until the blocking ceases. Reg. §1.964-2(c). Also, if the foreign currency can be paid to a United States shareholder overseas, the blocking exception falls. Reg. §1.964-2(c)(3).

block of timber an operational unit or a geographical area containing *timber* established to determine timber *depletion deductions* under §611. Operationally, the block may be a timber area which contains trees that are expected to grow to a single given point of manufacture, or all the timber which would likely be removed in a single logging development. *Taxpayers* are expected to maintain accounts that segregate immature growth, tree types, and other characteristics and which contain all the timber of one block, separating out timber held under cutting contracts of separate accounts. Reg. §1.611-3(d)(1).

"blue book" a nickname for a book often produced by the staff of the *Joint Committee on Taxation* after a major change in the tax laws. The book is designed to explain the content of the new law. The book is usually captioned General Explanation of [name of the Act and its year].

Board of Tax Appeals the predecessor of the *Tax Court.*

boiler, energy investment credit a device for producing vapor from a liquid. In general, boilers have a burner in which fuel is burned, a fire box, a containment shell, boiler tubes, pumps, pressure and operating controls and safety equipment, but not pollution control equipment. Reg. §1.48-9(c)(3)(ii). A boiler that uses an *alternate substance* as its *primary fuel* may qualify as alternative energy property. §48(1)(3); Reg. §1.48-9(c).

bona fide good faith. The standard is commonly applied in business transactions to distinguish a transaction motivated by tax avoidance purposes.

bona fide cost-sharing arrangement a written agreement, between two or more members of a group of controlled entities, providing for the sharing of the *costs* and risks of developing *intangible property* in return for a specified interest in the intangible property that may be produced. It must reflect a good-faith effort by the participating members to bear their respective shares of all the costs and risks of development on an *arm's length* basis. Reg. §1.482-2(d)(4). The *IRS* will not make *allocations,* except as may be necessary to reflect each participant's arm's length share of costs and risks, where a party acquires an interest in intangible property as a participant in a bona fide cost-sharing arrangement. *Id.* Such agreements also affect apportionment of research and development expenditures, within and without the United States, of controlled parties on the basis of relative sales. Reg. §1.861-8(e)(3)(ii)(D). See *cost-sharing election, possessions corporations.*

bona fide resident a *United States citizen* or *national* who, under standards applicable to determining whether an *alien* is a *resident alien* in the United States, is found to be a resident of a foreign country. §911(d)(1)(A). The *Code* demands bona fide residence for at least a year and denies the status to persons who represent to foreign tax authorities that they are not residents. One can enjoy partial exclusion for the year of arrival if one expects to meet the test. §911(d)(5). Bona fide residence abroad can authorize major exclusions of *foreign earned income* and a *foreign housing cost exclusion* and *deduction.* See *foreign earned income exclusion; foreign housing cost exclusion; resident aliens.*

bona fide resident of Puerto Rico an *individual* whose contracts with Puerto Rico are comparable to those of an *alien individual* who is classified as a *resident alien* in the United States. Reg. §1.933-1(a) (referring to the standards of §871). Such individuals and United States *citizens* who reside in Puerto Rico for more than two years are not taxed on Puerto Rican source income unless it is earned as a United States federal *employee*. §933. See *resident alien*.

bona fide selling price, inventory   generally, the actual price at which goods are offered during the 30-day period after the date of the inventory. The *bona fide* selling price less the cost of *disposition* is used to value *inventory* goods which are not salable at normal prices due to damage or other imperfections. Reg. §1.471-2(c).

bond   see specific type, e.g., *private activity bond; qualified mortgage bond; qualified student loan bond; qualified veteran's mortgage bond*. Sometimes the term refers to security made available to assure performance. For example, the *IRS* often requires the posting of a bond in exchange for relaxing a restriction of some sort. See, for example, §42(j)(6) (posting bond in case of transfer of property subject to *low-income housing credit*).

bond, amortization   a bond, debenture, note, or other evidence of an indebtedness, but not an obligation in the nature of *inventory, stock in trade,* or *dealer property*. §171(d). See *amortizable bond premium of the taxable year*.

bond discount   generally, the excess of the price to be paid by the issuer of the bond at maturity over the price paid for the bond. The issuer of the bond can generally *deduct* the discount as an *expense* over the term of the bond, while the holder of the bond generally reports the discount, to the extent it is *original issue discount*, as income over its term. See *accrual of bond discount; original issue discount*.

bonded warehouse   a place where goods can be stored on a tax or duty-free basis until withdrawal, at which time they attract a tax or duty. The warehouse owner posts a bond to cover irregularities.

bond for payment of tax   a performance bond often required of *taxpayers* when they seek an extension of time to pay tax.

bonding requirements, ERISA   a requirement that every *fiduciary* and every *person* who handles funds or other property of a *qualified retirement plan* must be bonded in an amount not less than 10 percent of the amount of the funds handled (i.e., ERISA bonds). *Employee Retirement Income Security Act of 1974*, §412, 29 USC §1112 (1976).

bond issuance premium   generally, the excess of the *issue price* of a *bond* over the amount payable at maturity. Reg. §1.61-12(c)(4). *Corporations* report bond issuance premium as *gross income* ratably over the life of the bond. Reg §1.61-12(c)(2).

bond, market discount, original issue discount, and coupon stripping   a bond, debenture, note, certificate,

or any other evidence of indebtedness. §1278(a)(3). The term is now defined in §1286(e)(1) for *coupon-stripping* purposes, but it is apparently dropped for *original issue discount* purposes and displaced by the term *debt instrument*.

bond premium   the excess of a *taxpayer's basis* in a *bond* over its redemption value. See *amortizable bond premium of the taxable year*.

bond purchase plan   see *qualified bond purchase plan*.

bond retirement premium   a premium that arises where a *debt instrument* is repurchased by the issuer at a price that exceeds the *issue price* of the old debt, plus *original issue discount* that was *deductible* before the repurchase, minus any premium included in *gross income*. The premium is treated as deductible *interest*. Reg. §1.163-4(c)(i).

bonds bought flat   bonds traded at prices that do not reflect unpaid interest due. If such prepurchase interest is later paid, it can be reported as a nontaxable *return of capital*. Reg. §1.61-7.

bond, state or local bond   any obligation. No formal note is required, and the obligation can, for example, arise from a *sale* of property. §150(a)(1).

bond to stay assessment and collection   a bond posted with the *IRS* to defer *assessment and collection* of taxes. See §7485 (premiums not recoverable against the United States). This bond arrangement arises after an appeal from the *Tax Court's* ruling, seeking a review of the decision. It is not required in order to take an appeal, but it is required to stay *assessment* and collection if the appeal is of an adverse ruling.

bonus exhaustion rule   a reference to a requirement that a *person* who claimed *depletion* of a *bonus* must exclude a proportionate part of the bonus in order to calculate *percentage depletion*. See Reg. §1.613-2(c)(5)(ii). To illustrate how it might operate, assume a lessee paid $20,000 as a bonus to a lessor. Assume that in the first year of operations 1/10th of the oil in the ground was removed. The bonus exhaustion rule would force the lessee to reduce *gross income from the property* by 1/10th of the bonus, i.e., by $2,000. This reduces the base on which the lessee's percentage depletion is calculated.

bonus expensing   see *bonus recovery*.

bonus insurance plan   a *welfare benefit plan* in which an *employer* pays for *life insurance* on the life of an *employee,* usually a well-paid executive. The premiums paid are taxable to the employee.

bonus, natural resources   ordinarily, the nonrefundable cash received by a lessor on the signing of a lease agreement payable either in a lump sum or in installments and due whether or not there is production. Such bonuses are common in the mineral, oil, and gas industries. Bonuses may take other forms, including extended *overriding royalty* interests. Bonuses relating to natural resources are subject to *cost depletion* by the lessor. §613A(d)(5).

bonus recovery an elective provision pursuant to which a *taxpayer* (other than an *estate* or a *trust*) may write off (i.e., *deduct*) up to $10,000 of new or used *personal property* to which §168 (*cost recovery*) applies, which property the taxpayer bought for use in a *trade or business* and which is *section 38 property*. §179. For this purpose, cost of property excludes *basis* that is determined by reference to other property the taxpayer held (e.g., property received in a *like-kind exchange*). The *deduction* cannot produce a current *business loss,* but it can be carried forward. §179(b)(3). The election and deduction under §179 are also referred to as bonus expensing. See *section 179 election to expense certain depreciable business assets.*

book entry registration see *registered form bond.*

book entry security a federal security recorded by an entry on a Federal Reserve Bank's records. They include transferable Treasury bonds, notes, bills, contracts of indebtedness, and so on, as well as Postal Service obligations. Reg. §1.1012-1(c)(7); Rev. Rul. 71-537, 1971-2 C.B. 262. The identification for *income tax* purposes of book entry securities which are sold depends on (1) a specification system in which the *taxpayer* assigns such securities sequential lot numbers, or (2) a confirmation by the bank or other agent of the date, amount, and description of the securities sold. Failing these steps, a *first-in, first-out rule* applies. Reg. §1.1012-1(c)(2) and (7). Such securities are deemed to be in *registered form* for purposes of the definition of *registration-required obligations.* §§163(f)(3) and 149(a)(3). The book entry method may be used to segregate securities of a *dealer* which the dealer holds for *investment.* Reg. §1.1236-1(d)(i) and (ii).

book income adjustment a term used to describe an element of the *alternative minimum tax* applicable to *C corporations,* increasing the tax base by a fraction of financial statement income (or *earnings and profits*) over *alternative minimum taxable income* as otherwise determined. §56(f)-(g). See *business untaxed reported profits.*

booking date the date of origination of a *section 988 transaction.* In transactions involving *debt* instruments, it is the date of acquisition or when the *taxpayer* becomes the obligor. §988(c)(2)(A). For transactions involving payments or receipts, it is the date of *accrual* or when taken into account. §988(c)(2)(B). The difference in the value of the object of a §988 transaction on the booking date and the *payment date* due to change in exchange rates equals the *foreign currency gain or loss.*

§988(b). *TAMARA* eliminated the date on which the financial instrument was entered into or acquired as a booking date.

book inventories see *perpetual inventories.*

books and records materials maintained by *taxpayers* that enable them to prepare their *federal income tax returns.* Regulation §1.6001-1(a) requires taxpayers to "keep permanent books of account or records, including inventories" sufficient to establish information required in any federal income tax return. However, for *individual taxpayers,* checkbooks, sales contracts, and receipts are generally sufficient. §§441, 446.

book up tax slang for increasing hypothetical *capital accounts* of *partners* under the *special allocation* provisions in the regulations. See Reg. §1.704-1(b)(2)(iv)(f)(5). The restatement of accounts can in fact be upwards or downwards.

book value the value ascribed to an asset after subtracting liabilities associated with it. Book values are ordinarily determined on the basis of historic cost valuation rather than on *fair market values.*

book value shares plan a *nonqualified deferred compensation* plan under which participants are entitled to buy newly issued *stock* at *book value,* which can be resold to the company or converted fully into publicly traded common stock. The scheme is to obtain *capital gains* treatment for the greater of the appreciation in book value or in *fair market value* from the date the stock is acquired.

boot property that is not like-kind property, including cash. Although the term "boot" does not appear in the Code, tax practitioners commonly use it rather than using "property that is not like-kind property." The receipt of boot will trigger recognition of gain if there is realized gain. The receipt of boot does not result in recognition if there is realized loss.

boot relaxation rules the contents of §368(a)(2)(B), the gist of which is that *boot* may be used in a *Type C reorganization,* provided at least 80 percent of the *fair market value* of the assets of the transferor (target) corporation are acquired in exchange for voting stock of the acquiring corporation. The rule is treacherous because if any boot is given, the *debt* assumed is also treated as boot, which may disqualify the reorganization. §368(a)(2)(B).

bootstrap acquisitions transactions in which the assets of the acquired *entity* are used to fund the acquisition. For example, a seller of corporate stock can sell a portion of his stock, followed by a *redemption* of the remaining stock.

bottom-hole contributions, mineral property an agreed-upon monetary contribution to an oil or gas operation made when a well reaches a specified depth, regardless of its production. The tax treatment of a bottom-hole contribution depends on whether (1) the well is productive, (2) the associated bottom-hole agreement is made pursuant to a purchase, and (3) the recipient of the contribution elected to *capitalize* or deduct *intangible drilling and development costs.*

bottom-line allocations a colloquialism for overall *allocations* of profits and losses of a *partnership*. The validity of such allocations are now clearly subject to the *substantial economic effect test* of §704(b)(2).

bottom-line consolidations, life insurance companies a post-1981 *consolidated return* reporting technique under which life *insurance companies'* results of operations may be combined with those of non–life insurance companies. *Taxable income* is determined first for each component member of the *affiliated group* (e.g., *taxable investment income* for some companies and *gain from operations* for others) and then consolidated by adding those separate company taxable income bases. See §1504(c).

boycotting country any country which is described in §999(a)(1)(A) and (B), which requires participation in an *international boycott activity*. Prop. Reg. §1.999-l(b)(l). See Notice 81-11, 1981-2 C.B. 543 for a current list of such countries.

boycott participation income, subpart F a term sometimes used to describe the mandatory increase in *subpart F income* arising from participation or cooperation in an international boycott. The amount of boycott participation income included in subpart F income is the *controlled foreign corporation's* total income that would otherwise be deferred, despite the other effects of *subpart F*, multiplied by the *international boycott factor*. §952(a)(3). This amount is imputed to the corporation's *United States shareholders*. §952(a)(2). See *international boycott activity, participation and cooperation.*

boycott reports reports required of *individuals* or *corporations* reporting on *international boycott activity*. They are filed on Form 5713 (International Boycott Report) with the Philadelphia Service Center with the other attached to the *taxpayer's tax return*. Treasury Release B-653 (Jan. 20, 1978).

bracket creep a shorthand term for rising tax burdens of a *taxpayer* who is pushed into higher *marginal brackets* as a mere result of inflation. *Indexing for inflation* is supposed to prevent this circumstance.

branch a geographically separate business location of an enterprise. The term is especially significant to foreign operations; a branch is considered an extension of the operations of an American enterprise into a foreign country, which causes immediate taxation of the United States *entity,* whereas a foreign subsidiary owned by the United States enterprise can frequently defer United States taxation until the earnings are repatriated. The

IRS asserts that incorporation of a loss branch compels *recapture* of *losses* and the *foreign tax credit*. §904(f). See *recapture, foreign losses.*

branch book/dollar pool method an elective method by which foreign banks apportion *interest expense deductions* to the United States *branch*. See Reg. §1.882-5(b)(3). The method determines the deduction on the basis of *interest expenses* to third parties according to the United States branch's books, with a system of adjusting such expenses where recorded liabilities vary from liabilities statutorily deemed attributed to the United States branch. For the alternate method, see *separate currency pools method.*

branch income, foreign income earned by a foreign branch of a *United States corporation*. Such income is taxed immediately to the United States corporation.

branch level interest tax a 30 percent *withholding tax* (or lower *tax treaty* rate) imposed on *interest* payments from United States *branches* to *foreign persons*. The base includes the actual amount by which the foreign corporation's *deduction* for interest allowed by Reg. §1.882-5 for interest paid by the United States *trade or business* exceeds the interest actually paid by a United States branch to third parties. This *excess interest* is deemed paid by a *domestic corporation* to its foreign parent company; this in turn makes it subject to *withholding*. To be deductible, the interest paid must be with respect to one of four classes of liabilities. The provision is complex. See *branch profits tax.*

branch profits tax a 30 percent tax, in addition to the corporate *income tax,* imposed on businesses operated in the *United States* by *foreign corporations* on income that is (or is deemed) *effectively connected* with the United States *trade or business*. §884(a). The amount subject to this tax is the *dividend equivalent amount,* which in turn is equal to the adjusted *effectively connected earnings and profits* for the *taxable year,* increased for declines in *United States net equity* and vice-versa. §884(b). The effectively connected earnings and profits are generally profits from conducting a trade or business within the United States. The purpose of the branch profits tax is to treat United States operations of foreign corporations in much the same manner as United States corporations owned by foreign persons. Various *international organizations* are exempt. See *branch level interest tax.*

branch rule a nickname for a provision embodied in §954(d)(2) which can have the effect of deeming an unrelated foreign manufacturing corporation to be the foreign manufacturing branch of a *controlled foreign corporation* (CFC). The gist of the rule is that where the CFC's activities are conducted through a branch outside the CFC's country of incorporation and where this has substantially the same effect as if the branch were a wholly owned sub, branch income is treated as if earned by a sub of the CFC and is treated as *foreign base company sales income.*

break in service   continuous period of separation from an *employer.* See *one-year break in service.*

bribes and kickbacks   see *illegal bribes, kickbacks, and other payments.*

broker   a term, for purposes of determining who must file a *broker's return* (§6045), which includes a *dealer,* a *barter exchange,* and any other *person* who, for a consideration, regularly acts as a middleman of property or services, but not a farm manager. §6045(c)(1). More generally, it means a person whose income is earned by commissions as opposed to *gains* from dealing in property he or she owns, the latter generally being a dealer in real estate transactions. See also *real estate reporting person.*

brokers or dealers in securities, inventories   *taxpayers* who may generally *deduct* from *gross income* market fluctuations in the value of securities held as *inventory.* A broker or dealer in securities is a merchant in securities—whether as an *individual, partnership,* or *corporation*—with an established place of business and who is engaged in the purchase of securities and their resale to customers for *gain* and profit. A dealer must regularly inventory these securities in order to qualify for the *deduction.* Reg. §1.471-5.

broker's return   a *return* required of every *person* doing business as a real estate *broker.* The return shows the name and address of each *customer* (any person for whom the broker has transacted any business) and any additional information regarding gross proceeds of or other information on the broker's business as required by *regulations.* §6045.

brother corporation   see *brother-sister corporations.*

brother-sister controlled group   two or more *corporations,* if five or fewer *persons* who are *estates, trusts,* or *individuals* own at least 80 percent of the *stock* (by voting power or by value) of all classes of each corporation, provided such persons own more than 50 percent of the stock of each corporation (by vote or by value of all classes) taking into account the stock of each such person only to the extent such stock ownership is identical with respect to each such corporation. §1563(a)(2). Sections 1563(d), (e), and (f) supply *attribution rules.* Corporations which are *component members* of such controlled groups are entitled to only one *accumulated earnings credit,* treated as one *taxpayer* for purposes of determining their claim to the payment of graduated income taxes, and get only one $25,000 *small business deduction* accorded to *life insurance companies.* §1561(a). See *controlled group of corporations, graduated taxes, and other benefits.*

brother-sister corporations   *corporations* under common control of a shareholder or group of shareholders. Section 304(a)(1) may treat sales of *stock* of one of the corporations to the other as a *distribution* rather than as a sale. In the simplest example of brother-sister corporations, 100 percent control of two corporations is held by the same shareholders and sales of the stock of one corporation to the other will generally yield a *dividend* to the shareholder. See *redemption by affiliated corporations.*

brother-sister groups under common control, qualified plans   a group of two or more *sole proprietorships, partnerships, trusts, estates,* or *corporations* in which the same five or fewer *individuals,* trusts, estates, or corporations own (directly and by *attribution*) a controlling interest (basically, 80 percent of the enterprise or *entity*) of each organization, and such persons are in *effective control* of each organization, taking into account the ownership of each such person only to the extent such ownership is identical with respect to each such organization. Such groups are aggregated to determine whether their plans satisfy the requirements necessary to be classified as *qualified plans,* as a species of "two or more trades or businesses under common control." Reg. §1.414(c)-2(a). See *effective control, brother-sister groups—qualified plans.*

building, FIRPTA   same as *building, investment tax credit* (below). In addition, Reg. §1.897-1(b)(3)(ii) states that the term generally means any structure or edifice enclosing a space within its walls, and usually covered by a roof, the purpose of which is, for example, to provide shelter or housing or to provide working, office, parking, display, or sales space.

building, investment tax credit   generally, a structure or edifice with enclosed walls and a roof. Former Reg. §1.48-1(e). While buildings do not qualify for the *investment tax credit,* there are major *rehabilitation tax credits* and *energy investment credits* for which they, or certain components and systems, do qualify. The term "building" also appears, among other places, in the definition of *section 1245 property* (generally *personal property*), but the above-cited investment tax credit regulations are specifically referred to for its definition. Reg. §1.1245-3(b)(2).

built-in deduction   a *deductible* item, such as a *theft loss, casualty loss, interest expense,* or *depreciation deduction,* which accrued in an economic sense in a *separate return limitation year* (basically, a year before a *corporation* was acquired by another corporation), but which is recognized in, or carried over to, a year in which the company becomes a member of an *affiliated group.* Reg. §1.1502-15(a). Generally, such items are deductible only by the acquired company, and not by the acquiring group in a *consolidated return.* Reg. §1.1502-15(a)(4) contains a *de minimis* exception.

built-in gain   a common term describing the excess of *fair market value* over *adjusted basis* of property. Built-in *gains* commonly arise in connection with gifts and tax-free *contributions* of property to *corporations* or *partnerships*, although the term is not confined to these transactions.

built-in gain on property contributed to partnerships a partner who contributes appreciated property to a partnership recognizes the gain if the partnership distributes that property to another partner within five years of the contribution. §704(c)(1)(B). Under a new rule imposed by the CNEPA of 1992 (Pub. L 102-486), which applies to partnership distributions *after June 24, 1992,* the gain recognized is the lesser of (1) the excess of the fair market value of the property, other than money, over the predistribution basis (reduced by any cash distribution), or (2) "*net precontribution gain.*" "Net precontribution gain" is the net amount of precontribution appreciation on all property the partner has contributed to the partnership during the preceding five years. The CNEPA of 1992, §1937. See *precontribution gain on partnership redemptions.*

built-in gain tax, S corporation a corporate level tax imposed primarily on *S corporations* that used to be *C corporations,* imposed on any *unrealized gain* at the time of a post-1986 conversion to S status. It applies secondarily to appreciated assets received with a *carryover basis* from C corporations. To the extent *gain* is *recognized* on the *disposition* of assets at any time in the 10-year *recognition period* (such gain is called *net recognized built-in gain*), it is taxed at maximum *corporate income tax* rates. §1374. Shareholders report the gain, but reduce the pass-through of income to themselves by the built-in gain tax paid; the tax can also be reduced by *alternative minimum tax credit carryovers* and *general business credit carryovers* from taxable years when the entity was a C corporation. §1374(b). *Business credit carryforwards, capital loss carryovers and net operating losses* can reduce the tax. §1374(b)(2) and (3). See *qualified corporation, liquidations; recognition period, S corporation.*

bulk sale a sale of substantially all the *inventory* and similar property of a *taxpayer's* line of *business* to one buyer in one transaction. Such sales used to qualify for tax-free treatment in the course of 12-month liquidations under former §337. See former §337(b)(2). A bulk sale also allows a *corporation* going through a *complete liquidation* to use the *installment method* for sales of *inventory* and similar property. §453(h)(1)(B). The bulk sale concept is sometimes used as an exception to treating property as *dealer property* under §1221(1), thereby qualifying the sale for *capital gain* or *loss* treatment.

bulk storage facility see *storage facility.*

bulky tool rule the rule that the additional commuting costs of carrying tools or other bulky business equipment needed for work are *deductible* (e.g., airline pilots' use of a cab because the use of public transportation was impracticable). Rev. Rul. 76-453, 1976-2 C.B. 86 states that only the incremental costs of using the same mode of transportation are deductible.

bulletproof statutes *limited liability company (LLC)* statutes containing mandatory provisions concerning limited liability, transferability of interests, centralized management, and continuity of life, which are designed to ensure that an LLC organized under the statutes will be classified as a partnership for federal tax purposes. The LLC statutes of Colorado, Virginia, and Wyoming are examples of bulletproof statutes. See *limited liability company (LLC).*

bump-and-strip a transaction that can be illustrated by the following example. Parent *corporation* owns a first-tier subsidiary, which in turn owns a second-tier subsidiary, the *stock* of which has a $10 basis, representing the *earnings and profits,* and a *fair market value* of $100. The first-tier subsidiary distributes the stock of the second-tier subsidiary to its parent, which takes a $100 *basis* according to Reg. §1.1502-31(a). The former second-tier subsidiary borrows $80 and distributes it to the parent. Of that $80, $10 is a *dividend* and $70 is a *return of capital.* The former second-tier subsidiary then sells $60 worth of newly issued stock to an unrelated buyer, and uses the $60 to pay down its debt. Thus, the unrelated buyer now owns 75 percent of the value of the second-tier subsidiary, and the parent owns the rest.

burden of proof the obligation to persuade a trier of fact of the validity of a factual assertion. In civil tax cases, the burden of proof is characteristically on the *taxpayer.* In *fraud* cases, the burden is on the *IRS.* The burden in civil cases shifts from the taxpayer to the IRS in cases such as where the government introduces new theories or where the taxpayer timely replies to an assertion of an *accumulated earnings tax* liability. The burdens also vary qualitatively, e.g., "preponderance of the evidence" (more than 50 percent, the typical civil standard), or "proof beyond a reasonable doubt" (the criminal standard).

burden rate method, uniform capitalization rules a method that *apportions indirect production costs* to various items of production and *closing inventory.* The allocation depends on some other factor(s) such as direct costs, hours, or similar items or similar formulae. The method requires that any net negative or net positive difference between total predetermined indirect production costs allocated to production and inventory and the total amount of such costs actually be allocated to such goods (that is, the under- or overapplied burden be treated as an adjustment to the ending inventory in the *taxable year* in which the difference arises, unless the adjustment is insignificant in amount and not allocated in the *taxpayer's* financial reports). Reg. §1.263A-1T(b)(3)(iii)(C). See *allocation methods, uniform capitalization rules.*

burial or funeral benefit insurance company a company which directly engages in the manufacture of funeral supplies or the performance of funeral services. Such companies are not *life insurance companies* for *federal income tax* purposes. §816(g). However, they may be tax-exempt.

burned-out tax shelter   a *tax shelter* that becomes financially burdensome. See *cross the line.*

business   an activity carried on by a *taxpayer* with a reasonable degree of regularity, continuity, and sincere profit motivation so as to qualify it for various tax benefits such as expense *deductions* under §162, *depreciation* deductions under §167, or *cost recovery* under §168.

business activities test   a test used to determine if *fixed or determinable periodical income* or income from capital transactions earned by *foreign persons* are considered from *United States* sources. Where the activities of a United States *trade or business* are a material factor in the realization of periodical income, the test is satisfied and the income will be considered from United States sources. §864(c)(2)(B); Reg. §1.864-4(c)(3). A good example would be royalties a foreign taxpayer earns from its business of licensing patents in the United States.

business associate   a *person* with whom the *taxpayer* could reasonably expect to engage or deal in the active conduct of the taxpayer's *trade or business,* such as the taxpayer's customer, client, supplier, *employee,* agent, partner, or professional adviser, whether established or prospective. Reg. §1.274-2(b)(iii). The term is used for purposes of §274's limitations on *travel, entertainment,* and *business gift deductions.* See *substantial and bona fide business discussion.*

business bad debt   a *business debt* that has become entirely or partially *worthless.* §166(a). Business bad debts qualify as *ordinary losses,* unlike *nonbusiness bad debts* that merely qualify for *short-term capital loss* treatment, and then only if they are entirely worthless.

business credit carryforward or carryback   a *carryforward* or *carryback* of the *general business credit* under §39. Such credits can generally be carried back 3 and forward 15 years. See §39(a)(1).

business day   the normal business hours of a day in which a traveler's primary activity is the pursuit of *trade or business.* See Reg. §1.274-4(d)(2) and (f)(4). Such days also include (1) days spent traveling to and from a foreign business destination by a reasonably direct route; (2) days that must be spent in a foreign country for a specific business purpose; (3) days that a traveler is in a foreign country and unable to conduct business due to conditions beyond his or her control; and (4) any weekend, holidays, or stand-by days abroad that fall between business days while the traveler is in a foreign country. The business day concept is used to *apportion transportation expenses* to and from a foreign country and to distinguish *deductible* from *nondeductible travel expenses* while overseas. See *foreign travel.*

business debts   *debts* created, acquired, or incurred in connection with the *taxpayer's trade or business.* §166(d). *Losses* on such debts are treated as *ordinary*

losses, whether entirely or partially *worthless.* §166(a). Because the *deduction* can only be claimed for the year of worthlessness, the area is highly contentious. The same rules that apply to lenders now apply to guarantors and indemnitors. See *worthless debt.*

business development company   a closed-end company described in 15 USC §80a-2(a)(48). Such a company is treated as a *regulated investment company* and is granted relief from some of the rigors of being such a company. §851(a)(1) and (e).

business discussion, entertainment expenses   see *substantial and bona fide business discussion.*

business energy credit   a term often used instead of the somewhat more precise term *energy investment credit.* This credit expired on June 30, 1992.

business exigencies rule   a rule applied to *travel expenses* that essentially requires the *transportation expenses* to be appropriate and helpful to the *taxpayer's,* or the taxpayer's *employer's, trade or business* in order for them to qualify for *deduction.* The cost of traveling from a taxpayer's home to his employer's headquarters is *nondeductible,* because the expenses do not serve any business purpose of his employer, but rather reflected a personal housing preference. On the other hand, where temporary employment elsewhere makes it impracticable to move a principal residence, and duplicative costs arise, the taxpayer may deduct meals and lodging at the temporary worksite, since the requirements of the business force the maintenance of two places of abode.

business expense   an *expense paid or incurred* during the *taxable year* in carrying on any existing *trade or business.* If appropriate, helpful, and current in nature, such expenses are *deductible* under §162(a) and, in most cases of an involved *individual,* are used as *adjustments to gross income.* §62. Salaries, travel and entertainment, and rental payments for leased business property are but some examples of business expenses. As with other expenses, they must be *capitalized* if they create, prolong, or improve a capital asset. §263. There is continuing authority that deductible expenses must be "ordinary" in the sense of not being bizarre.

business gifts   *gifts,* in the *income tax* sense (i.e., nontaxable gratuitous transfers), made in a *trade or business* setting for which the donor may seek a *deduction* under §§162 or 212. Deductions for business gifts, whether made directly or indirectly, are limited to $25 *per recipient* per year. Items that are clearly advertising in nature, such as pens embossed with the company's name, that cost $4 or less do not figure into the $25 limitation. §274(b)(1).

business leagues   *exempt organizations* described in §501(c)(6), including (and often loosely called) trade associations, chambers of commerce, boards of trade, and professional football leagues. Regulation §1.501(c)(6)-1 defines business leagues as associations of persons with common business interests and a purpose to promote those interests but who are not engaged in a regular *business* of a kind ordinarily carried on for profit. Business leagues are allowed secondary purposes to earn a profit, in which case the tax on *unrelated business taxable income* applies. §512. *Trade show* income can, however, be *exempt.* §513(d)(3).

business lease   see *debt-financed property.*

business losses   *losses* involving property incurred in the *taxable year* in the course of the *taxpayer's trade or business,* and not compensated for by insurance or otherwise, and which result in a *closed transaction.* §165(a) and (c)(1). *Individuals* can claim losses under §165(c) only if they are trade or business losses, losses from a *transaction entered into for a profit,* or certain *casualty* and *theft losses. Corporations* are not so constrained, since they are presumptively always engaged in a trade or business. The amount of a business loss is determined by the *adjusted basis* of the disposed property. The term "business losses" is often used in the vernacular instead of the more precise term *operating losses.* The courts seem to take a lenient attitude toward the "property" requirement for purposes of showing a loss.

business operations test, domestic building and loan associations   one of three tests used to determine if a *domestic building and loan association* qualifies for special tax treatment. §7701(a)(19). Such an association satisfies the business operations test if its assets are used in a business that consists of (1) acquiring the savings of the public, and (2) investing in loans. In general, the business of a savings association meets part 1 if more than 75 percent of the total deposits are held during the *taxable year* by the general public. Reg. §301.7701-13A(c). A domestic building and loan association meets part 2 if more than 75 percent of its *gross income* consists of interest or dividends on certain assets (cash, government obligations, "deposit insurance company securities," interest on loans, and other categories of income defined in Reg. §301.7701-13A(c)(3)). See *assets test, domestic building and loan associations; domestic building and loan association; supervisory test, domestic building and loan association.*

business premises   for purposes of the exclusion from *gross income* for *meals and lodging* supplied on the *employer's* business premises, the term means a place where activities of the employer are conducted such as a factory or an office. The *Tax Court* includes places such as a house provided for a hotel manager next door to the hotel, or a rented hotel suite used by officers for lunchtime conferences. Leased property can qualify if used to perform a business function of the employer. Reg. §1.119-1(c)(1).

business purpose   a requirement common to *corporate reorganizations* that demands a reason for the transaction germane to the business of the *corporation* undergoing the reorganization. Failing such a purpose, the benefits of a tax-free reorganization may be denied. The business purpose requirement also applies to *corporate divisions* (Reg. §1.355-2(b)), and has been said to be an implicit requirement in any commercial or industrial transaction.

business start-up expenses   see *start-up expenditures.*

business tax credit   see *general business credit.*

business transfer exception   a provision, embodied in Reg. §25.2512-8, the gist of which is that a transfer which might otherwise be subject to federal *gift taxes* will not be if it arises in a business context. The transfer must be at *arm's length* and the transferor must lack the intention to make a gift.

business trust   a *trust* whose objective is to carry on a joint business enterprise for a profit. Reg. §301.7701-2(a)(2) and -4(a). They are taxed as *corporations.*

business untaxed reported profits   an *adjustment* used in calculating *alternative minimum taxable income* designed to flush out additional taxes from *C corporations.* See §56(f). The excess of *adjusted net book income* over *alternative minimum taxable income* is added to the base. The preference is 75 percent of the excess of *adjusted current earnings* over income based on the use of adjusted net book income. §56(g). This adjustment does not apply to *S corporations, regulated investment companies, real estate investment trusts* or *REMICS.* §56(f)(4). Adjusted net book income (or loss) essentially is the corporation's income (or loss) reported on its *applicable financial statement.*

buy-sell agreement   an agreement, common in *closely held corporations* and *partnerships,* that upon the death or withdrawal of one owner the enterprise or the co-owner is obligated to buy out the interest of the *decedent* or the withdrawing party. Such agreements are commonly funded by *life insurance contracts.* Buy-sell agreements involving the enterprise's duty to buy out an owner are often called *entity buy-sell agreements.*

buy-sell basis   an arrangement in which the buyer of a product for resale is entitled to keep, as all or part payment for his services, all or part of the difference between the purchase price and the resale price. §6041A(b)(2)(A). The provision seems geared to cases in which *individuals* become intermediary buyers for wholesalers and take their own mark-up. Persons earning $5,000 or more annual income on the buy-sell basis are considered engaged in direct sales and must provide certain annual *returns* to the government. See *direct sales returns.*

C

C corporation a regular *corporation,* as opposed to an *S corporation,* subject to the taxation of *Subchapter C* for the year. §1361(a)(2).

C short year see *S termination year.*

CAF an acronym for *central authorization file.*

CAF number an identification number assigned to *taxpayer representatives* by the *IRS.*

CARVM an acronym for The Commissioner's Annuities Reserve Valuation Method prescribed by the National Association of Insurance Commissioners, which is in effect on the contract's date of issuance and is used in the computation of an *insurance company's life insurance reserves* for purposes of determining its *taxable income.* It is a so-called *tax reserve method.* §807(d).

CB Cumulative Bulletin. Official pronouncements of the *IRS* issued cumulatively, by year. For example, the term 1972-2 C.B. 7 indicates the second volume of the Cumulative Bulletin for 1972 at page 7.

CCH Commerce Clearing House, a major tax publisher. Its principal tax publications are the United States Tax Cases service (i.e., U.S.T.C.) and the Standard Federal Tax Reporter.

CDO an acronym for a collateralized debt obligation. The term is used in connection with reporting requirements for *REMICs* to issuers of such obligations. See Notice 89-136, 1989-44 I.R.B. 42.

CERT an acronym for a *corporate equity reduction transaction.*

cert. denied an abbreviation of the term *certiorari* denied, meaning that the United States Supreme Court has declined to hear an appeal of a case from a lower court. Such denials have no particular significance, since the Supreme Court hears only a handful of tax cases each year.

CFR the *Code of Federal Regulations.*

CID investigation an investigation conducted by the *Criminal Investigation Division.*

CIF an acronym for cost, insurance, and freight, also known as "landed price." The term is commonly used in connection with sales of goods across international borders.

Cl. Ct. an abbreviation for *Claims Court* (formerly the Court of Claims).

CMO an acronym for *collateralized mortgage obligation.*

CNEPA an acronym for the Comprehensive National Energy Policy Act of 1992 (Pub. L. No. 102-486). The law contains a range of energy tax incentives for both businesses and individuals, offset by revenue increase measures.

COBRA an acronym for Consolidated Omnibus Budget Reconciliation Act, passed in 1986. Pub. L. No. 99-172, 100 stat. 82.

CODA an acronym for a *cash or deferred arrangement.*

COLA an acronym for *cost of living adjustment.*

Conf. Rep. Conference Report, an official report of a House-Senate Conference.

CRCO an acronym for *consolidated return change of ownership.*

CRVM an acronym for the Commissioner's Reserve Valuation Method prescribed by the National Association of Insurance Commissioners. It is a so-called *tax reserve method.* §807(d).

CRY an acronym for consolidated return year.

Ct. Cl. an abbreviation for *Court of Claims,* or *Claims Court.* The Claims Court has been renamed the United States Court of Federal Claims.

Ct. D. an *IRS* abbreviation used to indicate a judicial decision.

cafeteria plan a plan for the benefit of *employees* (and communicated to them) in which all *participants* are employees and may choose among two or more benefits consisting of cash or *qualified benefits deferred compensation* plans, certain *cash or deferred plans,* or certain group retirement plans for employees of *educational organizations described in §170(1)(A)(ii).* §125(c)(1). Qualified benefits are generally a short list of otherwise nontaxable benefits, namely *accident and health plans, dependent care assistance programs, group-term life insurance,* and contributions to a *section 401(k) plan.*

calendar year a 12-month period beginning January 1 and ending on December 31. *Taxpayers* who keep no *books and records,* who have no other annual *accounting period,* or whose *taxable year* is not a *fiscal year* must use the calendar year as their *taxable year.* §441(d) and (g). A growing list of *entities,* such as *trusts,* are obligated to use the calendar year.

call a transferable contract that empowers the owner to buy securities at a specified price (in lots of 100) for a specific period of time (generally, one to nine months).

Revenue Rul. 78-182, 1978-1 C.B. 265, provides that the premium paid for an *option* is a *capital expenditure* and thus is not a *deductible expense* at the time it is purchased. If the option holder sells the option, §1234(a)(1) treats the sale as a *capital transaction* if the underlying property is a *capital asset*. A lapse is generally deemed a *sale* under §1234(a)(2).

call, partnerships a duty to make further contributions to a *partnership*. A *limited partner's* duty to make further contributions increases his or her *basis in the partnership interest* for purposes of §704(d) capping *losses* reportable by a partner. Reg. §1.752-1(e).

call premium generally, an amount in excess of the face amount of an obligation that an issuer must pay for the privilege of calling (redeeming) debt prior to maturity; it explicitly excludes the premium associated with conversion features. See §§171 (holder's *amortization* of *bond premium*), 249 (issuer's *deduction* for call premium at maturity).

camp *lodging* provided by or on behalf of the *employer* for the convenience of the employer in a remote area where satisfactory housing is not available to the *employee* in the open market. §119(c)(2). The camp is considered part of the employer's *business premises* and the value of camp lodging overseas is *excludible* from *gross income*. §119(c)(1).

cancellation of indebtedness income the discharge of a *taxpayer's* liability for less than the face amount of a genuine uncontested and enforceable obligation. Such discharges are considered to increase the taxpayer's *net worth,* thereby creating *gross income* unless intended as a *gift,* or an *inheritance* or unless *excluded* under some other *Code* provision. §61(a)(12). For example, a corporation's repurchase of its own bonds for less than face causes taxable *gain*. On the other hand, cancellation as a result of a gift or inheritance (§102) or as a *contribution to capital* by a shareholder-creditor (Reg. §1.61-12(a)) is a nontaxable transaction. See *stock for debt exception; workout.*

candidate for a degree one who is pursuing studies or conducting research to meet the requirements for an academic or professional degree conferred by colleges or universities. Reg. §1.117-3(e). In the case of *individuals* other than students attending a primary or secondary school or pursuing a degree at a college or university, the term "candidate for a degree" means a student (whether full-time or part-time) who receives a scholarship for study at an *educational institution* (described in §170(b)(1)(A)(ii)) that (1) provides an educational program that is acceptable for full credit toward a bachelor's or higher degree or offers training to prepare students for gainful employment in a recognized occupation, and (2) is authorized under federal or state law to provide such a program and is accredited by a nationally recognized accreditation agency. These candidates may be able to earn nontaxable scholarships. See also Reg. §1.117-3(e). See *scholarship.*

capital generally, a *taxpayer's adjusted basis* in *property.* See *return of capital.*

capital account, corporation for purposes of §312(c), charging a *corporation's* capital account when *stock* is redeemed, the term refers to the amount paid into the corporation for its common stock, which generally means the proprietorship account other than retained earnings. Rev. Rul. 82-72, 1982-17 C.B. 57; Rev. Rul. 79-376, 1979-2 C.B. 33.

capital account, partnership for purposes of *partnership* taxation, money and the agreed value of contributions to a partnership (but not liabilities) used to reflect each partner's equity in the enterprise. Once the partnership begins operations, each partner's account is increased by allocable *gains* and reduced by allocable *deductions, losses,* and *distributions.* It generally corresponds to the partner's *outside basis* disregarding debt. The capital account is of special importance in determining whether allocations can withstand scrutiny under the *substantial economic effect test* posed by §704(b).

capital asset *property,* as contemplated by §1221, not listed in the exceptions to §1221, nor otherwise excluded. Section 1221 specifically excludes (1) *stock in trade, inventory* and property primarily held for sale to customers in the ordinary course of a trade or business (*dealer property*); (2) *realty* and *depreciable property* used in a *trade or business*; (3) certain nonindustrial intellectual property; (4) accounts and notes payable acquired in the ordinary course of business for services or sales of property described in (1) above; (5) short-term (one year or less) government obligations issued at a discount (as to pre-June 24, 1981, periods); (6) United States government publications that were not purchased. See *ordinary gain and loss.*

capital contribution generally, a transfer of *property* by a *shareholder* or *partner,* acting in such capacity, to a *corporation* or *partnership.* Such transfers are generally nontaxable. See §§351, 721–724, and 1632. As long as such transfers are noncompensatory, they are not taxable to the transferee or the transferor. §§118 and 721. Corporations may generally *exclude* business subsidies and other transfers, provided they are not payments for goods or services or used to induce limited production. Capital contributions are generally added to the transferor's *adjusted basis* in the transferee, if any. See *contributions in aid of construction; debt-equity rules.*

capital expenditure an *expenditure* that, because it results in the creation, prolongation, or improvement of a *capital asset,* must be added to the *taxpayer's basis* in the asset rather than *deducted* from income. Section 263 is the principal authority. *Asbestos removal costs must* *be capitalized* based on the facts of increased health and safety, reduced risk of liability for owners and investors, and increased marketability, IRS Letter Ruling, Control No. TR-32-00038-91 (1992). See §1016 regarding adjustments to basis resulting, among others, from such expenditures.

capital gain *gain* from the actual or *constructive sale* or *exchange* of a *capital asset.* §1221. Such gains are generally subject to modestly favorable tax treatment in that they may be offset by *capital loss carryovers.* See *net capital gain.*

capital gain net income the excess of *gains* from *sales* or *exchanges* of *capital asset* or *section 1231 assets* from such sales or exchanges. §1222(9).

capital gain property property that is a *capital asset* or *section 1231 asset* in the hands of a *donor* if a *sale* of the asset at its *fair market value* at the date of the *charitable contribution* would have resulted in a *long-term capital gain.* §170(b)(1)(C)(iv). An *individual* is generally allowed a *deduction* of up to 30 percent of his or her *contribution base* for the contribution of capital gain property to *public charities,* with any contributions in excess of the 30 percent limit subject to a five-year carryover. §170(b)(1)(C)(i) and (ii). But see §170(e).

capital gains and losses *gains* and *losses* on *constructive* or actual *sales* or *exchanges* of *capital assets.* The term is often mistakenly used to refer to *long-term capital gains* and *losses.* See *capital gain; capital loss.*

capital gains dividend, regulated investment company any timely *dividend* or part thereof that is designated by a *regulated investment company* as a *capital gains* dividend and which represents a *distribution* of *gains* from *sales* or *exchanges* of *capital assets.* §852(b)(3)(C). A regulated investment company is allowed a *deduction* for capital gains dividends paid to its *shareholders.* Reg. §1.852-2(b)(1). Shareholders are required to treat capital gains dividends as gains from the sale or exchange of capital assets held for the *long-term holding period.* §852(b)(3)(B). However, if the declared amount of capital gains dividends is greater than the excess of the *net long-term capital gains* over *net short-term capital losses* of the *taxable year* (the excess), only the proportion that the excess bears to the total dividend is deemed to be a capital gains dividend. Reg.§§1.852-2(b) and 1.852-4(c). The distribution retains its *character* in the hands of the distributee shareholders.

capital interest in partnership generally, a *partner's* share in the *basis* of *partnership assets.* Such an interest in assets of a *partnership* is distributable upon withdrawal or *liquidation* at the *entity's adjusted basis* in its assets (*inside basis*). The right to participate in the profits of a partnership is not a capital interest. Reg. §1.704-1(e)(1)(v). Such interests are ordinarily created by con-

tributions to the enterprise, and are modified by later *gains, losses,* and *distributions* to partners. Where, however, a capital interest in a partnership is received in consideration for prior services, the service partner must include the value of the interest in income in the year of receipt. Reg. §§1.61-2(a)(1) and 1.721-(b)(1). For the antonym, see *profits interest in partnership.*

capitalization a reference to an *entity's* capital structure (loans, equity, etc.) or to the treatment of an *expenditure* that must be *capitalized.*

capitalize generally, to treat as an item of *capital* rather than as a current *expense.* For example, *taxpayers* are obligated to capitalize brokerage fees associated with acquiring *stock* held for investment by adding such costs to their *basis* in the stock. §§263 and 1016.

capitalized interest generally, any *interest* payment or *accrual* that has been *capitalized.* See *capitalized taxes, interest and other carrying charges.*

capitalized taxes, interest and other carrying charges a reference to the effects of §266, which allows *taxpayers* electively to *capitalize property taxes,* various sales taxes, *interest,* and other carrying charges in lieu of expensing them. The items that can be so treated are annual taxes, *mortgage interest,* and payroll taxes.

capital loss a *loss* from the actual or *constructive sale* or *exchange* of a *capital asset.* Losses that do not result from actual sales or exchanges may nonetheless result in capital losses as a result of statutorily or judicially deeming the transaction a sale or exchange. See, e.g., §§165(g) (worthless *securities*), 166(d) (*nonbusiness bad debts*), 301(c)(3) (corporate *distributions* in excess of *basis*), 331 (*corporate liquidations*). Capital losses are combined with *capital gains* to determine *taxable income* for the year. Generally, capital losses are treated less favorably than *ordinary losses.*

capital loss carryback the process of treating the excess of current year's net *losses* from *sale* or *exchanges* of *capital assets* as *short-term capital losses* in prior years. Under §1212(a)(1), such losses are carried back to the third year, and to the extent not absorbed, to the second, then to the preceding year, then forward. The practice applies to *corporations* only. Note that such carrybacks may not produce or increase *net operating losses* in the years to which they are carried. §1212(a)(1)(A)(i).

capital loss carryovers *long-term* and *short-term capital losses* that are not absorbed in the present *taxable year* but can be applied against income in other taxable years. Such losses preserve their *character* in the other years to which they are carried over. Noncorporate *taxpayers* can only carry forward capital losses, but they can do so indefinitely. §1212(b). Corporate taxpayers can generally carry their capital losses back three years, then forward five years, but only to offset *capital gains* in such other years. §1212(a).

capital receipts the aggregate dollar amounts received by a *small business corporation* for its stock, as *contributions to capital* and as paid-in surplus. §1244(c)(3)(A); Reg. §1.1244(c)-2(b)(1). Capital receipts are used as the measure to determine whether a corporation's capitalization is too large to qualify it as a small business corporation. For these purposes, money, other than property, is valued at its *basis* in the hands of a contributing *shareholder,* less any associated liabilities. §1244(c)(3)(B); Reg. §1.1244(c)-2(b)(1).

capital recovery concept the view that a *taxpayer* should not be taxed in a transaction where the result was the receipt of consideration short of the taxpayer's capital investment in property being disposed of. §453(j)(2); Reg. §15A.453-1(c).

capital structure expenditures a colloquial term used to describe *expenditures* in connection with issuing or selling stock or other securities, such as commissions, professional fees, and printing costs. Such expenditures are neither *deductible* nor *amortizable.* As a result, selling and issuing expenses associated with an original stock issue must be separated from *organizational expenses* occurring at approximately the same time. Reg. §1.248-1(b)(3). Comparable rules apply to forming *partnerships.* §709 (*syndication fees, partnership*).

capital transaction a term used to identify transactions that give rise to *long-term* or *short-term capital gains* or *losses.*

captive insurance company a *corporation* (generally foreign) that insures the risks of its shareholders. The establishment of a foreign captive insurance company is intended to (1) provide *deductions* for the shareholders who pay premiums to it, and (2) provide a tax-free base in which to accumulate the insurance company's profits offshore. Several court decisions have found the risk-shifting inadequate to support a section 162 trade or business deduction. See Rev. Proc. 82-41, 1982-30 I.R.B. 17; Rev. Proc. 82-22, 1982 C.B. 469; Rev. Rul. 89-61, 1989-19 I.R.B. 4; Rev. Rul. 77-316, 1977-2 C.B. 53; Rev. Rul. 78-338, 1978-2 C.B. 107. The *subpart F rules* may operate to tax *insurance income* of a captive to its corporate owners. §953(c). See *insurance income, subpart F.*

captive mine a mine operated by a *corporation* that holds bare *legal title* to a mineral property, operating it at cost for the benefit of its shareholders. The corporation and the shareholders are treated as separate taxable *entities* for federal *income tax* purposes. Rev. Rul. 77-12, 1977-1 C.B. 161.

career average unit benefit plans see *unit benefit plans.*

carried directly or indirectly by the employer a requirement for the *deduction* of *group-term life insurance* under §79. Regulation §1.79-0 considers group-term life insurance to be carried directly or indirectly by the *employer* if (1) the employer pays any part of the insurance directly or through another person; or (2) if the employer or two or more employers arrange for payment of the cost of the life insurance by their *employees* and charge at least one employee less than the cost of the insurance as determined by *IRS* premium tables, and at least one other employee is charged more than the cost of insurance under the IRS premium tables. If all the other requirements of §79 are met, then the employer is allowed a deduction for insurance costs, while an employee generally does not include the value of up to $50,000 in group-term insurance in *gross income.*

carried interest a fractional interest in oil, gas, or mineral *property,* typically via a *lease,* in connection with which the owner is not obligated to pay operating costs; instead, the owners of the remaining fraction (the *carrying party* or parties) pay such costs, reimbursing themselves out of production from the property. The person who holds a carried interest is the *carried party.* Such interests can take varied forms, depending on the terms of the agreement among the parties. §636(a); Reg. §1.613A-7(f)(3).

carried party someone who holds a *carried interest.* See *carried interest.*

carryback generally, to shift a net amount (e.g., a *capital loss*) to a prior *taxable year.*

carrybacks and carryovers of net operating losses see *absorption rules, net operating loss carryovers and carrybacks.*

carryforward synonymous with *carryover.*

carrying charges amounts charged consumers in transactions involving extension of credit (e.g., credit card sales); such charges often consist of both *interest* charges and service charges. For methods of sorting the two, hence creating the opportunity to claim a *deduction* for *interest expenses,* see §163(b); Reg. §1.163-2; Rev. Rul. 71-98, 1971-1 C.B. 57; Rev. Rul. 72-315, 1972-1 C.B. 498; Rev. Rul. 73-136, 1973-1 C.B. 68; Rev. Rul. 73-137, 1973-1 C.B. 68. An alternative meaning is costs to hold or improve property. Carrying charges are exempt from the *imputed interest* rules of §483. §483(d). As to the latter, see *capitalized taxes, interest and other carrying charges.*

carrying on a trade or business presently undertaking a *trade or business.* The term is found in §162(a), and its impact is to deny *deductions* for *expenditures* to enter a *new* business. See *begins business, amortization of corporate organizational expenditures; intramural expansion.*

carrying party   someone who pays operating costs for the benefit of the person holding the *carried interest*. See *carried interest*.

carryover   generally, to shift an amount to a future *taxable year*.

carryover basis   a *basis* in *property* in the hands of a transferee determined by reference to the transferor's (e.g., *donor's*) basis. See *transferred basis*.

carryover dividend   a component of the *dividends-paid deduction* of a *personal holding company* consisting of the excess of *dividends* paid in the prior two years over the *corporation's taxable income*, as modified. §564.

carve-out   a colloquialism for a lesser interest in a right that falls short of being classifiable as *property* for purposes of the *assignment of income doctrine*, as a result of which the transferor will continue to be taxed on income earned from the transferred interest. See *carved-out production payment; production payment*.

carved-out drill site transaction   a nickname for an oil and gas transaction which can be illustrated as follows. B, an oil drilling enterprise, acquires a permanent 50 percent (or some other percentage) interest in the entire oil and gas prospect and a temporary 50 percent *working interest* in a test well plus some surrounding acreage. B will hold the temporary working interest until the drilling costs are recouped out of production. As to the residual land, B has a 50 percent working interest and pays its pro rata share of expenses only.

carved-out oil payment   same as *carved-out production payment*.

carved-out production payment   a *production payment* transferred to another *person* out of a previously owned interest. For example, if A, who is entitled to the first 1,000 barrels of crude oil from Blackacre, transfers the right to the first 500 barrels to B, A is said to have transferred a 500-barrel carved-out production payment. Carved-out production payments are generally treated as *loans*, while retained interest transactions are generally viewed as *purchase money mortgages*. The seller is not taxed on the sales proceeds in the case of a carve-out, but is generally taxed on production and is allowed *depletion deductions*. Retentions can result in immediate taxation of the seller on the value of the retained interest as part of the *gain* from *sale*, but the buyer gets a claim to depletion deductions. §636. The term is virtually synonymous with the carved-out oil payment except that an oil payment is limited to one natural resource.

cash and carry commodities transaction   a tax-motivated commodities transaction that operates as follows: a *taxpayer* buys a quantity of a commodity (e.g., gold) and simultaneously enters into a *short sale* for a higher price, for delivery quite far in the future, setting the stage for a *long-term capital gain*. The taxpayer then treats the costs of carrying the commodity (e.g., *interest* and insurance) as *deductible expenses*. Note that §263(g) now forces *capitalization* of *carrying charges* and *interest* allocable to *personal property* which are part of a *straddle* (as defined in §1092(c)), less *compensatory* payments. It generally does not apply to *hedging transactions*.

cash basis   see *cash method*.

cash basis in a tax shelter   generally, one's direct investment in a *tax shelter*, a limit on current *deductions* for prepaid *IDC deductions* with respect to oil and gas *tax shelter* investments. More specifically, the term means a *partner's adjusted basis* of the *partnership interest*, ignoring (1) any partnership liability; and (2) any amount borrowed by the partner through a loan arranged by the partnership or certain other persons involved in the enterprise or secured by partnership assets. The "other persons" consist of anyone who participated in the organization, sale, or management of the partnership, or persons related to them, very broadly defined. Similar rules apply to tax shelters that are not partnerships. §461(i)(2)(B) and (C). Section 461(i) provides relief for oil and gas tax shelter deductions where economic drilling begins within 90 days of year-end. See *tax shelter, economic performance*.

cash discounts   reductions in amount otherwise payable if payment is made within a specified period of time. In valuing *inventory*, at the option of the *taxpayer*, the cost of the merchandise may be calculated using the invoice price less any cash discount. Reg. §1.471-3(b). Alternatively, the taxpayer may elect to treat the cash discount as financial income derived from business funds. Rev. Rul. 73-65, 1973-1 C.B. 216.

cash equivalents   items that are the equivalent of cash, considered *gross income* of a *cash method taxpayer*. Illustrations include checks and the *fair market value* of property. The impact of the doctrine on written promises to pay is unsettled, although freely transferable, readily marketable obligations have fairly regularly been held to be cash equivalents. For a closely related concept, see *economic benefit doctrine*.

cash expenditures method   see *cash flow method*.

cash flow   the amount of cash generated by an investment or activity, as opposed to *taxable income* or income reported for financial purposes. The major modification in deriving cash flow from traditionally determined income is to add back *depreciation, depletion,* and *amortization*, since these *expenses* are merely on paper, and to subtract principal payments on debts.

cash flow investment   temporarily invested of cash generated by underlying *qualified mortgage* of a

REMIC before distribution to investors. §860G(a)(b). It is a *permitted investment* of the REMIC.

cash flow method   an indirect method for showing understatements of income by contrasting annual expenditures, other than those from capital, with reported income. The fact that consumption exceeds *taxable income* can create an inference of concealment. It is also referred to as the cash expenditures method and the source and application of funds method.

cash, immediate jeopardy assessment   United States currency, foreign currency, bearer obligations, or any medium of exchange that has been used frequently in illegal activities and is specified as a cash equivalent by *regulations*. §6867(d). The term is defined in connection with specific rules and presumptions regarding *persons* in possession of a large amount of cash, allowing the *IRS* to *assess* an immediate 50 percent tax as if a *jeopardy assessment* were involved.

cash merger   a *merger* in which shareholders of the target company receive cash for their *stock*. For example, assume Mrs. A owns all the stock of T, and T is merged as a matter of state law into P, an unrelated corporation, and P pays A $1 million for her ownership interest; the result is a cash merger.

cash method   a *method of accounting* authorized by §446(c)(1) pursuant to which *gross income* (whether in the form of cash, property, services or *cash equivalents*) is reported when actually or *constructively* received, and *expenditures* are reported when actually paid. The method is subject to limitations. For example, some *deductions,* such as *depreciation,* are fixed by statute and operate independently of the *taxpayer's* accounting method. The term "cash basis" is used interchangeably. *C corporations, partnerships* with *partners* that are C corporations, and *tax shelters* generally cannot use the cash method. §448. There are exceptions as to the former two for *farming businesses, qualified personal service corporations,* and entities with gross receipts under $5 million. §448(b). See *constructive receipt doctrine; tax shelter, economic performance.*

cash method debt instrument   a *debt* instrument with a face amount of not over $2 million issued to a non-*dealer,* provided the property does not qualify for the *investment tax credit.* §1274A(c). The *imputed interest* rules of §483 apply to such obligations. The practical effect in the case of *cash method taxpayers* is *imputed interest* income being deferred until cash changes hands.

cash option, cash or deferred arrangement   another name for a *qualified cash or deferred arrangement* which is applied by reducing the *employee's* bonus. See *salary reduction plans.*

cash option mergers   *mergers* in which target company shareholders have an opportunity to take cash in lieu of *stock* of the acquiring company. Such mergers can be tax-free *Type A reorganizations* provided, among other things, the *continuity of proprietary interest doctrine* is satisfied by seeing that a sufficient percentage of the consideration received is stock of the acquiring company or its parent.

cash option plan   see *salary reduction plans.*

cash or deferred arrangement   a feature of a *qualified profit sharing* or *stock bonus plan* which offers *participants* a choice between receiving a specified amount of cash as extra taxable compensation or having the same amount directed to the plan. §401(k)(2). If the plan is structured properly, the *constructive receipt doctrine* is dispelled and the offer of cash is ignored for *federal income tax* purposes. In order for the system to work in the payee's favor, the plan must be a *qualified cash or deferred arrangement.* This calls for compliance with complicated nondiscrimination rules.

cash or deferred plans   plans which permit *employees* to take current cash compensation to defer such payments. See *qualified cash or deferred arrangement; qualified deferred compensation plan; salary reduction plans.*

cash out   a nickname for present *distribution* of the entire *vested accrued benefit* of a *participant* in a *defined benefit plan* or a *defined contribution plan.* The distribution may be voluntary on the part of the *employee* or involuntary (by the *employer* upon the termination of the employee's participation in the plan). §411(a)(7)(B); Reg. §1.411(a)-7(d)(4)(i) and (ii). If the distribution is involuntary, the amount distributed must not be in excess of $3,500. §411(a)(7)(B)(i); Reg. §1.411(a)-7(d)(4)(i). There is no like distribution limit on a voluntary cash out. §411(a)(7)(B)(ii); Reg. §1.411(a)-7(d)(4)(ii). In both types of cash outs, the distribution must be made on termination of the employee's *participation* in the plan. §411(a)(7)(B).

cash receipts and disbursements method   same as *cash method.*

cash, reporting   any monetary instrument, whether or not in bearer form, with a face amount not over $10,000, with minor exceptions for checks drawn on the writer for certain financial institutions. §6050. If it is over $10,000 in cash or foreign currency, in one or more related transactions, and is received by a person engaged in a *trade or business,* in the course of the trade or business, the recipient must report it to *IRS* and provide a statement to the payor. §60501. The term also includes cashier's checks, bank drafts, money orders, traveler's checks, or any combination thereof where the amount is $10,000 or more. §1.6050I-1(c)1,2.

cash settlement option   an *option* which can be settled in cash or property other than the underlying property (e.g., options on stock market indices). §1234(c)(2)(B).

cash surrender value the amount of cash a life insurer would pay to an owner of a *life insurance contract* if the contract were tendered to the company for cancellation. See section 7702(f)(2).

cash value accumulation test an alternative test used to determine whether a contract, which is otherwise a *life insurance contract,* can cause the *tax-free inside build-up* and death *proceeds* to be nontaxable to the insured. §7702. The test is met as long as the contract's *cash surrender value* (ignoring surrender charges, policy loan or reasonable termination dividends, and dividends on deposit at interest with the insurer) does not exceed the net single premium needed to fund the contract's future benefits. §7702(b)(1). Future benefits mean death and endowment benefits. See *cash value corridor test; guideline premium requirement; life insurance contract.*

cash value corridor test a test used in part to determine whether a contract which is otherwise a *life insurance contract* for federal tax purposes will so qualify. §7702(d). The gist of the test is that the contract's death benefit must be at least a specified percentage of its *cash surrender value.* §7702(d). The test is used in conjunction with the *guideline premium requirement.* See *life insurance contract.*

casual sale of personal property a *sale of personal property* that would not be includible in the *taxpayer's inventory* nor constitute *dealer property.* The general *installment method* may be used to report income from such sales unless the taxpayer is a *dealer* in such property. Reg. §§15A.453-1(a), -1(b)(1) and -1(b)(4).

casualty a sudden, unexpected, or unusual force that causes a complete or partial destruction of property. Fire, storm, and shipwreck are explicitly characterized as casualties. *Other casualties* include automobile collisions, sudden freezes, vandalism, quarry blasts, floods, sonic booms, and the like. Suddenness seems to be a principal earmark of other casualties. §165(c)(3). See *casualty loss.*

casualty loss physical damage to the *taxpayer's* property resulting from a *casualty.* §165(c)(3). Declines in value of property are not enough (e.g., where risk of mudslide causes the value of a residence to decline). The most contentious area involves casualty losses to personal use property of *individuals,* who can claim a tax benefit only under §165(c)(3), which allows a *deduction* for uncompensated *losses* resulting from fire, storm, shipwreck, or *other casualty,* or from *theft.* Note that the amount of the loss is in all cases allowed only to the extent *not compensated for by insurance or otherwise.* Such losses are treated as *itemized* deductions by individuals if they arise in a personal setting, but only to the extent they exceed $100 per casualty and 10 percent of the taxpayer's *adjusted gross income* and only if an

insurance claim (if available) is submitted. §165(h)(4)(i) and (c)(3); Reg. §1.165-1. If, however, the property loss relates to *trade or business* property or property acquired in a *transaction entered into for profit,* then the limitations of §165(c)(3) do not apply. Personal casualty losses involve losses of property not connected with a *transaction entered into for profit,* as well as property not connected with a *trade or business.* §165(c)(3). If the subject of the casualty is property held for more than one year, then the tax effects of the loss may be regulated by §1231. See *section 1231 assets.*

catch-all rule, annuities a method of treating miscellaneous payments under *annuity* contracts, including amounts paid before the *annuity starting date.* The approach is to treat only the amounts in excess of the *taxpayer's investment in the contract* as income. §72(e). That rule has been largely reversed by *TEFRA,* generally treating such payouts as income first. See *amounts not received as an annuity.*

catch-up election, tax-deferred annuities for exempt and educational organization employees a reference to one of several elections available to *employees* of hospitals, educational organizations, and *home health service agencies, churches,* and conventions or associations of churches, and certain church-related persons (defined in §414(e)(3)(B)(ii)) that allows them to direct their *employers* to make enlarged catch-up contributions to take account of past years' failure to make maximum contributions, without violating the limitations of §415(c).

catch-up provision, tax-deferred annuities for exempt and educational organization employees a term used to describe the operation of the §403(b)(2)(A) *exclusion allowance* when the *employer* contributes less than the maximum permissible amount to a tax-sheltered annuity. Thus, rising compensation permits the employer to contribute greater amounts to acquire annuities in such years without causing current taxation of the employee. For a distinct concept, see *catch-up election, tax-deferred annuities for exempt and educational organization employees.*

catch-up rule, eligible state deferred compensation plan the contents of §457(b)(3), allowing an individual participating in an *eligible state deferred compensation plan* electively to defer amounts which could have been, but were not, deferred within the $7,500/33$\frac{1}{3}$ percent limit of *includible compensation,* §457(b)(2), but never over an aggregate of $15,000 in the last three years. In computing the underused deferral limit, the participant must, however, use actual plan limitations if they are less than allowed by the law. See *eligible state deferred compensation plan.*

category A method of accounting jargon for a method of *tax accounting* not specifically authorized by *Code, regulations,* or case law. In Rev. Proc. 84-74,

1984-2 C.B. 736, the *IRS outlines special treatment of adjustments arising from a change of accounting method* as applied to category A methods.

category B method of accounting all *methods of accounting* other than those determined to be *category A methods of accounting*. See Rev. Proc. 84-74, 1984-2 C.B. 736. These are subject to the usual *§481 adjustments* where there has been a *change of accounting method*.

cattle breeding shelters a form of *tax shelter* in which the investor purchases an interest in a herd of cattle to be bred with a view to profitable sales of the progeny. The principal tax benefits are the availability of the *investment tax credit* (until 1987) and *cost recovery* with respect to the breeding herd, and the current *deductibility* of the costs of holding and breeding the herd. But see §263A. Finally, if the breeding herd is sold, it qualifies as *section 1231 property*; hence, it could attract a favorably taxed *long-term capital gain.*

cattle feeding shelters a *tax shelter* that can offer substantial deferral opportunities, designed to provide major (often year-end) *deductions* for the cost of feed, with a reversal of the deduction when the cattle are sold after fattening in commercial feedlots. Such shelters are now sharply confined by the *farming syndicate* rules, which allow the deduction only when the feed is consumed (§464), the *cash method* accounting isn't used, (§§448 and 461(i)), and the *passive loss rules* (§469) are ignored. See Rev. Rul. 79-229, 1979-21 C.B. 210, relating to the deductibility of prepaid feed expenses.

ceiling rule another name for Reg. §1.704-1(c)(2)(i) which limits *partnership allocations* of *depreciation* or *gain* or *loss* to *partners* under §704(c) to the depreciation allowable to the partnership or the amount of gain or loss *realized* on the *sale* of the property. For example, if A contributes $10,000 in cash and B contributes a building worth $10,000 but having a $4,000 *adjusted basis,* A can claim only $4,000 of depreciation over the life of the building even though A is deemed to have bought it for one-half its value ($5,000) for the purposes of §704(c). B can claim no depreciation on the building. Reg. §1.704-1(c)(2)(i) example 1.

cemetery companies *exempt organizations* owned and operated exclusively for the benefit of the members on a nonprofit basis, or chartered exclusively for the purpose of burying or cremating human bodies, provided that the organization is not permitted by its charter to engage in any business not incident to this purpose and that none of its net earnings *inure* to the benefit of any *private shareholder or individual.* §501(c)(13).

census tract a geographical tract based on federal census data. Such tracts may be *qualified census tracts,* in which case *interest* on certain indebtedness issued to subsidize home mortgages in the tract may be tax-

exempt as a *qualified mortgage issue* rather than as a taxable *private activity bond.* See §143(j)(2). See Rev. Proc. 83-51, 1983-2 C.B. 555 for a listing of the tracts.

central authorization file an automated system for maintaining *taxpayer representative* information. See Reg. §601.502(b)(2).

central withholding agreements agreements that enable *nonresident aliens* who are entertainers, athletes, and similarly situated *individuals* to enjoy an alternative method of *withholding* of income earned in the United States under reduced rates. See Rev. Proc. 89-47, 1989-29 I.R.B. 29.

centralized management a characteristic that helps distinguish an *association taxable as a corporation* from other *entities.* The term refers to concentrating the power to make managerial decisions in the hands of *individuals* appointed by the owners and without need for ratification, as opposed to dispersing such authority among all owners, as is the case in *general partnerships.* Reg. §301.7701-2(c)(4) provides that a *limited partnership* has centralized management if substantially all the interests in the partnership are owned by the *limited partners.* See Reg. §301.7701-2(c).

certain future obligations the sum of administrative and incidental expenses of a *black lung benefit trust,* plus an actuarially determined, level-funded amount needed to discharge the coal mine operator's outstanding liability for *black lung benefit claims* already filed, as well as anticipated claims. §192(b)(2). *Deductible* contributions to these trusts are limited to current year obligations or certain future obligations, whichever are greater. §192(b).

certificate credit rate the percentage of mortgage interest eligible for a *mortgage credit certificate (MCC).* In general, the amount of the tax *credit* is equal to the certificate credit rate multiplied by the *interest* paid on the mortgage. To qualify, it must be at least 10 percent but not more than 50 percent; the maximum available for assumptions is 25 percent. §25(d)(1). If the credit rate exceeds 20 percent, the maximum annual credit is $2,000. §25(a)(2). The credit may be carried over to any of the next three years, but unused credit is not refundable and cannot be carried back to a prior *taxable year.* The *taxpayer's deduction* for interest on the qualifying mortgage is reduced by the amount of the credit. §163(g).

certificate of beneficial interest, trusts a certificate, similar in nature to a share of common stock, evidencing ownership of a portion of a *Massachusetts trust* or *business trust.* Such shares are most commonly issued by *real estate investment trusts.*

certificate of loss of nationality of the United States a certificate issued by the Department of State certifying that a party is no longer a *citizen of the United States.* Consulates of the United States can issue such certificates to expatriate Americans on a showing of their having achieved foreign citizenship and renunciation of United States citizenship. See *expatriation to avoid tax.*

certificate of official record an *IRS*-generated internal form (Form 2866) that is apparently used to keep track of tax liabilities of particular taxpayers, with an emphasis on timing questions.

certificate of overassessment see *overassessment; overassessment notice.*

certificate of release of lien a certificate issued by an *IRS District Office* acknowledging the IRS's *release* of a *federal tax lien* because of unenforceability or satisfaction. See T.D. 7886 (Apr. 20, 1983). See *release of lien.*

certified historic structure a *building* and its *structural components* (1) individually listed in the National Register of Historic Places maintained by the Department of the Interior in Washington, D.C., or (2) located in a *registered historic district* and certified by the Secretary of the Interior as being of historical significance to the district. §48(g)(3)(A). 46 Fed. Reg. 56, 183 (1982). Rehabilitation expenses for a certified historic structure can qualify for a 20-percent *credit* against federal *income taxes.* The rehabilitation must be certified, however. See also §280B relating to demolition of historic structures using the same definition. See *rehabilitation credit.*

certified pollution control facility a new *pollution control facility,* identifiable as such, which qualifies for 60-month *amortization* if it was added to or used in connection with a plant in operation before January 1, 1976. §169(a). Where the property to be amortized is placed in service before 1981, the amortization deduction is available only for the portion of the property's basis attributable to the first 15 years of its useful life. §169.

certified rehabilitation, historic structure expenditures an expenditure for the rehabilitation of a structure, which has been certified by the Secretary of the Interior as consistent with the historic character of the property or the district in which it was located. §47(c)(2)(c). Particular expenditures that may qualify include plumbing, wiring, flooring, reconstruction (but not enlargement) of the structure, partitions, walls, and air conditioning. See *rehabilitation credit.*

certiorari a form of appeal from a federal appellate court to the United States Supreme Court.

cestui a *beneficiary* of a *trust,* an abbreviation of the quasi-Latin term cestui que trust.

chain acquisition an informal term for an acquisition involving §338, in which the purchase of a *parent corporation* is deemed to entail a *qualified stock purchase* of lower-tier chains of controlled *subsidiaries* on a single *acquisition date.* See §338(h)(3) and Reg. §1.338-4T(c)(3). A target *recognizes* no *gain* or *loss* on the deemed *sale* of *stock* of an affected target that is a Reg. §1.338-6T *shareholder* if a §338(g) election is made with respect to an *affected target.*

chain attribution see *reattribution.*

chain deficit rule reinstated relief provision for *controlled foreign corporations* ("CFCs"). Under prior law, if a *foreign corporation* had a deficit in its *earnings and profits,* a CFC in the same chain of ownership could reduce its earnings and profits for *subpart F* purposes to take account of the deficit. Under current law, §952(c) permits holders of CFC *stock* to reduce *subpart F income* by their ratable shares of *"qualified deficits."* Qualified deficits are pre-1986 deficits in earnings and profits of corporations that were CFCs when the deficits arose, which were attributable to a *qualified activity* and not previously used to reduce the CFC's subpart F income. §952(c)(1)(B). See *qualified chain member.*

chain liquidations a reference to *liquidations* of parent and controlled subsidiary *corporations* carried out in accordance with former §337(c)(3). The gist of the provision was that subsidiaries may sell their property tax-free as a part of a one-year *liquidation,* but only if the parent liquidates within 12 months of the subsidiary's adopting its plan of liquidation. If the subsidiary was controlled by one or more intervening subsidiaries, then they also had to liquidate in the 12-month period. Higher-tier corporations which received timely liquidating distributions were classified as distributee corporations if they were in the "chain of includible corporations," a term defined synonymously with the stock ownership (basically 80 percent control) standards under §1504 relating to *consolidated returns,* former §337(c)(3)(B).

chain of includible corporations undefined, but used for purposes of §1504(a), relating to *consolidated returns.* See *affiliated group; chain liquidations.*

chambers of commerce see *business leagues.*

change date, neutrality principle the date of the last component of an *owner shift involving a five-percent shareholder* or of an *equity structure shift.* §382(j). After the change date the *section 382 limitation* steps in to assure that the tax benefit of *net operating loss carryovers* and certain other *tax attributes* are limited to those hypothetically available to the *old loss corporation.* See *neutrality principle.*

change of accounting method a switch by the *taxpayer* from one overall *method of accounting* to a different method or the alteration in the treatment of a *material item* (basically, any regularly recurring incidence of *income* or *expense* which involves the time when it is reported). Reg. §1.446-1(e)(2)(i). The term includes the following: a switch from the *cash method* to the *accrual method* or vice versa; a switch from cash or accrual method to one of the *long-term contract* methods or vice versa; a switch to a *depreciation* method other than *straight-line depreciation*; a switch from one *inventory valuation* method to another; and a switch to or from a specialized *basis* method (e.g., *crop method* by farmers). Reg. §1.446-1(e)(2)(ii). The term can also encompass a change in accounting methods from an incorrect method to a correct method unless the erroneous method was not used consistently. The taxpayer is generally required to obtain permission from the *IRS* to compute income under a different method within 180 days after the beginning of the *taxable year* for which the change is sought. §446(e). The IRS grants permission to change an accounting method if the taxpayer agrees to certain conditions, one of which is spreading increased or decreased income over a specified period (usually the year of the change and the following nine tax years). In selected situations, the consent of the IRS is not required in order to change an accounting method (e.g., use of the *installment method* under §453). In addition, the IRS, using the powers granted by §446(b), may compel a change of accounting method. See *method of accounting; Silver Queen Motel doctrine.*

change of business   a change in continuity of the *business* enterprise, indicated by such factors as changes in *employees,* location, equipment, products, or other significant items. Former Reg. §1.382(a)-1(h)(5) defined a change of business and provided that an objective test was used to determine if such a change has occurred. Before 1987, the test was used in conjunction with §382(a) to determine whether *net operating loss carryovers* and other *tax attributes* of an acquired business survived the acquisition. The change of business provision also appears in §382(a), relating to *survival of tax attributes.*

change of ownership   changes in the ownership of corporate stock, which, if of sufficient magnitude, can result in the termination of various *tax attributes* of the *corporation* whose stock changed hands. See §382 (*neutrality principle*); Reg. §§1.1502-1(g) and -22(d) (*consolidated return change of ownership*). See *ownership change.*

change of use provisions   section 150(b)(1)–(4), the core idea of which is that if the proceeds of a *qualified bond* are misapplied in the sense that the funds are not used for the kind of activity that can be financed with *tax-exempt bonds,* then (in addition to the usual result of the bonds losing their exempt status), the user of the bond-financed property loses its *deductions* for *rent, interest,* or equivalent amounts. See *private activity bond; qualified bond; tax-exempt bond.*

character, gain or loss   the classification of an item of *gain* or *loss* as *ordinary* or *capital.* The issue concerns the quality of an item, as opposed to its quantity. For example, the sale of *inventory* results in ordinary gain or loss, whereas the sale of one's personal residence results in capital gain or loss. The exceptions to §1221 are primarily responsible for sorting ordinary from *capital assets,* but one must also ask questions such as whether the item is *property* (if not, then there can only be ordinary gain or loss) or whether the interest is a *substitute for ordinary income.*

character, income or deduction   the nature of an item of *income* or *deduction* in terms of whether it is *ordinary, capital, exempt,* and so forth. For example, the character of income and deductions flowed through from *partnerships* to *partners* are preserved by the *Code.*

charge-back provision, partnership   a provision that requires *allocations* of *income* or *gain* to a *partner* with reference to losses or *deductions* previously allocated to that partner. See *substantial economic effect test.*

charge-off method, bad debts   the *taxpayer's* recording of the uncollectible amount of a *debt* on his books and records in the year of partial or entire *worthlessness.* Reg. §1.166-3(a). The charge-off method is permissible for *business bad debts* and mandatory for *nonbusiness bad debts.* The alternative method, or *reserve method,* for recording bad debts may only be used by small banks and thrift institutions.

charges, revolving credit plans   *sales* of property and services, including finance and service charges in addition to *federal excise taxes* and state and local sales taxes. Reg. §1.453-2(d)(6)(ii); Rev. Rul. 68-163, 1968-1 C.B. 201. Charges under a *revolving credit plan* may be treated as an element of sales on the *installment method* to the extent provided by *regulations.* Reg. §1.453-2(d). After 1986, dealers generally cannot use the installment method. See *sale on the installment plan.*

charitable   as used in §501(c), defining entities organized and operated exclusively for "charitable" purposes, and §§170(c)(2)(B), 2055(a), and 2522, defining "charitable" organization to which *charitable contributions* can be made, the term contemplates virtually any activity that advances the public welfare. Examples include improving a lake used by the public (Rev. Rul. 70-186, 1970-1 C.B. 128), supporting a women's national honor society (Rev. Rul. 71-97, 1971-1 C.B. 150), and lessening the burden of government (Rev. Rul. 71-99, 1971-1 C.B. 151).

charitable annuity   see *charitable gift annuity.*

charitable bequest   a gift made to a *charitable organization* or religious organization under a will or before death which is *included in the gross* estate. Section 2055 allows a *deduction* in determining the *taxable estate* of a *decedent* for the value of charitable bequests, legacies, devises, or other transfers. See *charitable contribution.*

charitable contribution   generally, a gift to charities. Contributions are deductible, subject to various restrictions and ceiling limitations, if made to a qualified non-profit charitable organization. A cash basis taxpayer is entitled to a deduction solely in the year of payment. An accrual basis corporation may accrue contributions at year-end if the payment is properly authorized before the end of the year and payment is made within two and one-half months after the end of the year. §170.

charitable contribution deduction   a *deduction* claimed under §§170, 2055(a), and 2522 for a *charitable contribution.* It must be an *itemized deduction* if made during an *individual taxpayer's* lifetime. See *charitable contribution.*

charitable deduction property   property transfers (particularly real estate) subject to ceiling limitations on the amount of the deductions allowed in any one year (50 percent, 30 percent, or 20 percent of adjusted gross income, as the case may be) to a qualified charitable organization. §170(b)(1)(2). See *qualified appraisal.*

charitable gift annuity   an *annuity,* a portion of the purchase price of which is *deductible* for *income* and *estate tax* purposes as a *charitable contribution* and which meets the requirements of §514(m)(5).

charitable lead trust   a tax planning device under which a *taxpayer* transfers property *inter vivos* or by will, to a *trust* which transfers its earnings to a charity for a determinable period, after which the *corpus* of the trust reverts to the transferor or goes to another party. The donor is entitled to a *charitable contribution deduction* for the value of the stream of income over the period during which income is payable to the charity, providing the donor is taxable on such income under the *grantor trust rules* of §§671 et seq. Reg. §1.170A-6(c). A practical example is the transfer of $100,000 worth of 5 percent tax-free municipal bonds to a trust for a term of nine years, with a reversion to the transferor.

charitable organizations   organizations described in §501(c)(3), that is, tax-exempt entities "organized and operated exclusively for...charitable...purposes." While such organizations may engage in incidental business (which will be taxed as such), there must be no *inurement* of any part of the organization's *net income* to a *private shareholder or individual.* The donee organization must avoid participation or intervention in political campaigns on behalf of political candidates. Once such status is achieved, not only is the entity exempt from federal *income taxes* under §501(a), but contributions received are also *deductible* for *income, estate,* and *gift tax* purposes. See *action organizations; charitable; inurement of earnings to a private share-*

holder or individual; primary purpose standard, charitable organization.

charitable purpose or use   see *charitable.*

charitable trust   an *exempt organization* operated exclusively for *charitable* and other purposes described in §501(c)(3). The taxation of such trusts is controlled by §§501–528, relating to *exempt organizations,* rather than by *subchapter J,* relating to trusts.

chemical feedstocks tax   a tax imposed on the sale (by the manufacturer, producer, or importer) of over 40 organic and inorganic chemical feedstocks. §4662. If the manufacturer, producer, or importer of a taxable chemical feedstock uses the feedstock, then tax is imposed on the use of the feedstock in the same manner as if the feedstock has been sold. It is one of the three *Superfund taxes.*

Chief Counsel, IRS   the legal advisor of the *Commissioner* of Internal Revenue and an assistant general counsel to the *Treasury Department.* The Chief Counsel's duties include supervision of personnel responsible for general litigation, *refund* litigation, referral of criminal matters to the *Justice Department* interpretation, and legislation and *regulations.* In order to remain objective, the Chief Counsel reports to the Secretary of the Treasury rather than to the Commissioner of Internal Revenue. At the local level; delegates of the Chief Counsel litigate *Tax Court* disputes.

Chief Counsel orders and notices   statements of official policies and practices of the *Office of Chief Counsel* of the *IRS.* Such statements commonly concern the form and content of *requests for rulings.*

child and dependent care credit   a *nonrefundable credit* based on *employment-related expenses* for household services for the care of so-called *qualifying individuals* (basically, *dependents*), ranging from $720 to $1,440 per year. The amount of expense that qualifies for the credit is $2,400 for one individual and $4,800 for two or more individuals. If *adjusted gross income* is $10,000 or less, the credit is 30 percent. The credit declines by 1 percent for every $2,000 (or fraction) of *adjusted gross income* over $10,000, declining to 20 percent for *taxpayers* with adjusted gross income of more than $28,000. The credit is available to persons who maintain a household (i.e., provide more than one-half the cost of maintaining a household, considering such expenses as mortgage *interest,* utilities, property insurance, and food consumed in the home but not such general items as clothing, medical care, or the value of the claimant's services) for one or more qualifying individuals. The credit is limited to the *earned income* of the taxpayer or, if married, of the lower-earning *spouse.* §21. Section 21(d)(2) provides a presumptive level of earnings for incapacitated spouses and spouses who are students. See *qualifying individuals, child and dependent care credit.*

child, dependency exemptions a son, stepson, daughter, stepdaughter (§151(c)(3)), and children by adoption (§152(b)). Illegitimate children are also included. Rev. Rul. 54-498, 1954-2 C.B. 107. It is not clear whether an illegitimate grandchild could qualify. Stillborn children, but not those who have very brief lives, do not qualify. See generally Reg. §1.151-3(a). Note that an adult can be a "child" for these purposes.

child, earnings of evidently, refers to, but is not explicitly defined as a minor child, as determined under state law. §73(c); Reg. §1.73-1(c). Earnings from the services of a child are taxed to the child, notwithstanding state law that might make the property the parent's. §73(a).

child's share of allocable parental tax the amount of potential *income tax* allocable to each child that results from the taxation of the child's *net unearned income* at the parent's *marginal rate* of taxation. The amount is determined by multiplying the ratio of the child's *net unearned income* to the sum of the net unearned income of all the children of such parent under age 14 times the total *allocable parental tax*. See *kiddie tax*.

child support the common informal substitute for the term "payment to support children" used in §71(c). Section 71(c)(1) defines it as any part of the payment which the terms of the *divorce or separation instrument* fix (in terms of money or part of the payment) as a sum payable for the *support* of children of the payor. Section 71(c) is written so as to minimize the chances that payors will obscure their payments so as to turn them into *deductible alimony or separate maintenance payments* and to treat deferred payments as child support first. See *alimony or separate maintenance payments*.

chose in action a right to *personal property* or money not presently in possession, but which can be recovered in an action at law, or a note, bond, or other written obligation on which suit may be instituted. The term is used in §1031(a) (*like-kind exchanges*) to disqualify the property from §1031 tax-free exchange treatment.

Christmas tree oil and gas terminology for valves and fitting placed atop a casing head to regulate the flow of oil and gas to tanks and pipelines. The moment the Christmas tree is installed, the well and its equipment are generally considered *placed in service,* subject to *depreciation*. Rev. Rul. 70-414, 1970-2 C.B. 132.

church a church, or *convention or association of churches* (e.g. the Southern Baptist Convention), including religious orders and other organizations, which, as integral parts of the church, whether or not incorporated, are engaged in carrying out the functions of the church. §170(b)(1)(A)(i); Reg. §1.170A-9(a). See *church, unrelated trade or business*.

church employee income *gross income* from services. See §§3121(b)(8) and 1402(j)(4). Such income is exempt from *FICA* taxes. §1402(j)(1).

church, IRS investigations any organization claiming to be a church or any convention or association of churches. §7611(h)(1). See *church tax inquiry*.

church plan a *deferred compensation* plan established and maintained for *employees* (or their *beneficiaries*) of a *church,* or of an association or a convention of churches, exempt from taxation under §501, as well as (until 1983) *agencies of a church*. §414(e). Such plans may elect to be covered by *ERISA*. See §414(e)(2), excluding plans for employees engaged in *unrelated trades or businesses* and plans maintained by several *employers,* one of which is not a tax-exempt church, convention, or association of churches. The definition contains further refinements. See also Reg. §1.414(e)-1(e) and §89(i)(4) (exclusion from *statutory employee benefit plan* rules). See *life insurance contract*.

church records all corporate and financial records regularly kept by a *church,* including minutes and lists of names of members and contributors, but not records acquired under an *IRS summons* or from any governmental agency. §7611(h)(5). Such records are afforded certain protections under §7611. See *church, IRS investigations*; church tax examination.

church tax inquiry any inquiry to a *church* or *convention or association of churches* (other than an examination), however groundless the claim to church status, which serves as a basis for determining the church's right to exemption under §501(a) or determining whether it is carrying on an *unrelated trade or business* or is otherwise engaged in taxable activities. §7611(h)(2). Such inquiries are restricted to §7611 in that they can occur only if the Regional Commissioner (or higher official) reasonably believes, on the basis of written facts and circumstances, that the organization is taxable or is engaged in taxable activities. §7611(a)(2). The inquiry may be undertaken only after adequate notice to the *taxpayer*. §7611(a)(1)(B) and (b)(3). If the inquiry is ineffectual, further inquiries and examinations are barred for five years. §7611(f). See *church, IRS investigations; Regional Office*.

church, unrelated trade or business unclear. It includes a religious organization that carries out sacerdotal functions and conducts religious worship. That which constitutes religious worship or ministration of sacerdotal functions depends upon the tenets and practices of the particular religious organization. Reg. §1.511-2(a)(3)(ii) (*unrelated business taxable income*).

churning a nontechnical term for the practice of transferring property in order to qualify it for *cost recovery* under the *accelerated cost recovery system* (ACRS). Various transactions disqualify the property for ACRS treatment and cause §167 to apply for purposes of fixing *depreciation deductions.* §168(f). *Antichurning* rules may also require the use of pre-TRA of 1986 ACRS rules on property placed in service after December 31, 1986. **Circuit Court** one of 11 federal courts of appeal. They lie between the *District Courts* and *The Supreme Court of the United States.*

Circular 230 a *Treasury Department* publication that establishes standards for *practice before the IRS.* Reg. §10.1-3. The standards apply to attorneys, enrolled agents, enrolled actuaries, and certain other individuals eligible to represent clients before the IRS. Recent changes permit enrolled agents to use the term "certified" in connection with a professional attainment not relating to tax services per se, such as "certified financial planner." Final Amendments, Circular 230; *Fed. Register,* 9/9/92.

circulation expenditures costs incurred by publishers of newspapers, magazines, and other periodicals in connection with establishing, maintaining, or increasing circulation. §173. Such *expenditures* (other than for the purchase of land or *depreciable property* or for the acquisition of circulation through the purchase of any part of the business of another publisher of a newspaper, magazine, or other periodical) may be *deducted* under §173 at the *taxpayer's* election. The cost of a subscription list bought from another publisher is *nondeductible,* because it represents a purchase of part of another business. Rev. Rul. 74-103, 1974-1 C.B. 62. The cost of binders, tab guides, envelopes, boxes, looseleaf paper, and printing ink used in the publication and distribution of a periodical do not qualify as circulation expenditures. Rev. Rul. 67-201, 1967-1 C.B. 66. Taxpayers may irrevocably elect to *capitalize* circulation expenditures that are properly chargeable to *capital account.* §173.

citizen of the United States every *individual* born or naturalized in the *United States* and subject to its jurisdiction. In contrast, a foreigner who has filed his or her declaration of intention of becoming a citizen, but who has not yet been admitted to citizenship by a final order of a naturalization court, is an *alien.* Reg. §1.1-1(c). See also *national.*

civic achievement, prizes or awards exemplary, unusual behavior of general value to the community. It does not cover athletic achievement. Awards primarily for civic achievement are *excluded* from *gross income* provided they were granted without effort to enter a contest or proceeding, without a requirement to render substantial future services, and are given away to a governmental unit or certain charities. §74(b). See *prizes and awards.*

civic league or organization same as *social welfare organization.*

civil action a noncriminal lawsuit.

civil action against the IRS a civil lawsuit against the *IRS.* See, e.g., §§7432 (damages for failure to release a *lien*), 7433 (damages for unauthorized activity in *collection of taxes*), and 7430 (*reasonable litigation costs; reasonable administration costs*).

civil fraud a form of tax *fraud* that does not carry criminal liabilities. §6663(b). See *penalty, civil fraud.*

civil proceeding any civil action. §7430(c)(3). *Reasonable litigation costs* in civil tax proceedings may be recoverable by the *prevailing party* in such proceedings. §7430(a) and (c)(1)(A).

civil tax penalty a *nondeductible* monetary extraction from *taxpayers* who run afoul of any one of an extensive list of requirements imposed by the *Code* and which are not classified as being criminal in nature. The most significant ones are probably the so-called *negligence* penalty and the *civil fraud penalty.* The penalties are generally measured as a percentage of the taxpayer's tax liability and are *assessed* and collected administratively as part of the tax. See *penalty, fraud; penalty, negligence by tax return preparer.*

claim for abatement a procedure to appeal administratively a tax as to which an *assessment* has been made before making payment of the assessment, usually to correct an administrative error as to *employment taxes* or *excise taxes.* One uses Form 843. There is no right to file such a claim in *income, estate,* or, *gift tax* settings. §6404(b). See *abatement; ministerial act.*

claim for refund or credit a claim (which may be informal) submitted by a *taxpayer,* ordinarily on a form provided by the *IRS,* in which a taxpayer asserts a right to a repayment of cash (*refund*) or a *credit* against subsequent taxes, and provides the IRS with adequate information to process the request. §6402; Reg. §301.6402-2 and -3. The usual cause is the taxpayer's subsequent discovery of a legal or factual error (most often an overlooked *deduction*) on a prior *return.* While the claim may be made informally, excessive informality can be fatal. See Reg. §301.6402-2(b)(1) for the effect of the *statute of limitations* (generally three years from filing or two years from payment, whichever is longer). A timely filed claim for refund (or likely also a credit) must be made in order to prosecute a claim for refund in court. The matter is crucial in cases where a taxpayer pays a *deficiency* following an *audit* and sues for a refund after denial of the claim. Modest amendments to claims in the course of being processed after the statute has run are permissible.

claim of right doctrine a judicial doctrine that demands that *earnings* in the form of cash or property received by a *cash* or *accrual method taxpayer* be reported as *gross income* even though the earnings might have to be repaid, provided the recipient has an unrestricted right to the earnings. It confuses accrual method taxpayers. Although the doctrine requires a taxpayer to include the earnings (and perhaps prepayments) in income in the year of receipt, a *deduction* is generally allowed if a repayment is made. Examples of earnings that have been considered by the courts and subjected to the doctrine include contingent legal fees that were later repaid, taxes collected under a contested will, and dividends that were later repaid. Section 1341 provides somewhat intricate statutory relief from the doctrine by granting a *credit* or deduction (whichever is more advantageous to the taxpayer) if amounts previously included in income are later repaid, provided (among other things) the taxpayer had an apparently unrestricted right to the funds in the prior year (e.g., embezzled funds cannot qualify).

Claims Court   the new name for the *Court of Claims,* a court of limited jurisdiction headquartered in Washington, D.C. The Court of Claims was recently reorganized, but the successor performs the same tax-related functions as its predecessor, except that appeals of trial judges' decisions go to the *Federal Circuit.* The court hears tax *refund suits* and will travel to other cities.

clarified   an *IRS* term used to indicate an instance where the language of a prior *revenue ruling* or *revenue procedure* is being explained because it has caused, or may cause, some confusion. It is not used where a prior position is being changed.

Class I assets   assets of an acquired business consisting of cash and certain bank deposits. Reg. §1.338(b)-2T(b)(1). Purchase price of a business (*adjusted grossed-up basis* in the case of a *section 338 acquisition*) is assigned first to these assets, then to *Class II assets,* then to *Class III assets,* before basis is assigned to *Class IV assets,* which are *goodwill* and *going concern value* under the *residual method* for allocation of purchase prices.

Class II assets   liquid assets such as certificates of deposit, federal securities, and other readily marketable stock and securities. For the significance, see *Class I assets.*

Class III assets   all other *tangible* and *intangible* assets, excluding *goodwill* and *going concern value.* For the significance, see *Class I assets.*

Class IV assets   *goodwill* and *going concern value.* For the significance, see *Class I assets.*

class life   the *useful life* of property for *depreciation* purposes under prior law. §§168(i)(1) and 167(m). See *class life asset depreciation range system (ADR); class life period.*

class life asset depreciation range system (ADR)   an elective system designed to minimize disputes between *taxpayers* and the *IRS* over determination of the *useful life* of new or used *tangible property, salvage value,* and

repairs, as opposed to *capital expenditures.* §162(m); Reg. §1.167(a)-11. It is applicable to assets *placed in service* after December 31, 1970 (but not to property subject to the *accelerated cost recovery system* (ACRS)), and must be elected annually on Form 4832 (Class Life and Asset Depreciation Range (ADR) System). The system classifies assets by general character into *asset guideline classes,* which are listed in Rev. Proc. 77-10, 1977-1 C.B. 548 (as supplemented and amended). Each class of property listed in Rev. Proc. 77-10 is ascribed an *asset guideline period,* also known as the *midpoint life,* or *class life* (e.g., 10 years for dental equipment) and a range of years that is generally about 20 percent above and below the guideline period. Salvage value under ADR is much the same as under regular depreciation, except that *net salvage values* are not allowed for *vintage accounts.* If the taxpayer elects the ADR system, all eligible assets acquired during the year must be included. Eligible assets are generally all *section 1245 property* and such *section 1250 property* associated with commerce and industry. A taxpayer's election to use ADR cannot be revoked or modified after the last day prescribed for filing the election. *The Economic Recovery Tax Act of 1981* repealed ADR, but it still remains in the sense that it is used as a reference for classification purposes under the *accelerated cost recovery system* (ACRS), and may continue to control property placed in service before 1981.

class life period   a component of the *reserve ratio test* for *depreciation* of pre-1971 assets to determine if the retirement and replacement practices for assets are within the guidelines of the class life used. The procedure for applying the test is in Rev. Proc. 62-21, Part II, §5.02, 1962-2 C.B. 418. The system is now defunct.

class year plan   a *profit-sharing, stock bonus,* or *money purchase pension plan* which provides for the separate nonforfeitability of *employees'* rights to or derived from the contributions for each plan year. §411(d)(3).

classified account   assets segregated according to use without regard to *useful life,* for example, machinery and equipment, furniture and fixtures, or transportation equipment, grouped for *depreciation* purposes. Reg. §1.167(a)-7(a). See Reg. §§1.167(b)-1(b) (illustrations), 1.167(b)-2 (*declining-balance* method) and 1.167(b)-3.

clean-burning-fuel cars (electric vehicles)   the CNEPA of 1992 (Pub. L. 102-486) provides a *credit of 10 percent* of the cost of vehicles powered by electricity. The credit cannot exceed $4,000 (i.e., 10 percent of a $40,000 vehicle). The credit is available for vehicles placed in service after June 30, 1993. §1913.

clean-burning-fuel refueling property   the CNEPA of 1992 (Pub. L. 102-486) provides a *deduction of up to $100,000* for the cost of clean-burning-fuel refueling property effective for property placed in service after June 30, 1993. §1913.

clean slate doctrine a judicial doctrine to the effect that a *corporation* which goes through a bankruptcy reorganization cannot use its pre-reorganization *net operating losses* on the theory that the reorganized company is a new *taxpayer*.

clear reflection of income a standard embodied in §446(b), pursuant to which the *IRS* may force the *taxpayer* to change *accounting methods* for tax purposes if the one used does not clearly reflect income. The term is not defined, but it is clear that the concept contemplates not honesty, but rather accuracy. Realistically, because the taxpayer can overcome an IRS-imposed change of accounting method only by showing an *abuse of discretion,* and because the courts do not care for conceptual accounting disputes, the IRS tends to win these issues; hence, the term "clear reflection of income" has never been properly developed.

clerical errors see *mathematical or clerical errors.*

Clifford regulations *Treasury regulations* issued in 1946, designed to establish coherent standards for determining when to tax a *grantor* of a *trust.* The regulations have been displaced by the *Clifford rules* or *grantor trust rules,* found in §§671-679. In a Clifford trust, the income is taxable to the *grantor* (also referred to as a *grantor trust*).

cliff vesting a general term for a *vesting schedule* for pension benefits under which, in the extreme case, full vesting for a participant occurs after five *years of service,* with zero vesting theretofore. §411(a)(2)(A). A special parallel three-year cliff vesting rule applies as an alternate standard for *top-heavy plans.* §§411, 416(b) and (g).

clinical testing expense credit see *orphan drug credit.*

clone funds see *wraparound annuities.*

close corporation see *closely held corporation.*

closed case generally, an *audit* which the *IRS* has signed off on. A case agreed at the *District Office* level is closed when the *taxpayer* is notified in writing, after district conference (if any), of adjustments to tax liability or acceptance of the taxpayer's *return* without change. An unagreed *income, estate,* or *gift tax* case is closed when the period for filing a *petition* with the *Tax Court* specified in the statutory *notice of deficiency* issued by the *District Director* expires and no petition was filed. An unagreed excise or employment tax case is closed when the period specified in the preliminary letter for filing a protest and requesting consideration by the *Appeals Office* expires and no protest or request for Appeals consideration is filed. See Rev. Proc. 83-19, 1983-12 I.R.B. 18. *IRS* policy discourages reopening

closed cases except for especially good reason. See *second examination.*

closed-end account see *vintage account.*

closed-end multiple asset accounts see *vintage account.*

closed transactions transactions in which the *amount realized* on a *sale* or other *disposition* can be established, such that a *gain* or *loss* can properly be viewed as *realized.* For example, a *cash method taxpayer* who sells property and receives notes intended as payment and reasonably estimated to be worth $10,000 plus cash of $3,000 has engaged in a closed transaction and, unless the *installment method* applies, must report a $13,000 amount realized at the present time. The term modifies §1001(b) (amount realized). Other transactions that can result in closed transactions include unqualified abandonments, retirements, and demolitions. See *amount realized; open transactions.*

closed year a *taxable year* for which the *statute of limitations* has expired. Unless voluntarily extended in a timely manner, *deficiencies* must be *assessed* and collected, and *claims for refunds or credits* for overpayment of taxes must be made before the statute of limitation period expires. The purpose of the statute of limitations is to compel finality, something of benefit to both *taxpayers* and the government. See, however, §§1310-1314 for special mitigation provisions.

closely held business see *interest in a closely held business.*

closely held C corporation a *C corporation,* more than 50 percent of the value of whose *stock* is owned, directly or indirectly, by five or fewer *individuals.* §§465(a)(1)(B) and 542(a)(2). Ownership is determined by *attribution rules* of §544. Such corporations are unaffected by the *at-risk* rules as to their *qualifying businesses.* The same term is used for purposes of the *passive loss rules,* where it means the same thing. §469(j)(1). Such corporations cannot offset *portfolio income* with *passive activity losses* and *passive activity credits* if their owners do not participate adequately. §469(e)(2) and (h)(4). See *at-risk rules, generally; passive loss rules.*

closely held corporation another name for a *corporation,* the stock of which is owned by a relatively small group of shareholders, often family members. Such corporations are often subject to special scrutiny and statutory control because of their potential for tax abuse. See, for example, the *personal holding company tax* imposed by §541.

closely held corporation, valuation overstatement a *corporation* more than 50 percent owned (by value) by five or fewer *individuals.* §§465(a)(1)(B), 542(a)(2), and 6659(f)(2).

closely held pass-through entity   any *partnership, S corporation,* or *trust* where 50 percent or more of the value of the *beneficial interests* in the entity are owned directly or indirectly by five or fewer *persons* at any time during any *taxable year* for which there is income under the *long-term contract.* §§460(b)(5)(C)(iii) and 460(b)(5)(A)(iii). The *simplified look back rule* does not apply to a closely held pass-through entity. §460(b)(5)(B).

closing agreement   a written agreement between a *taxpayer* and authorized *IRS* official pursuant to which tax liabilities and facts, such as *basis* in property, can be finally and irrevocably settled, except for misrepresentation or as to future laws, whether previously disputed or not. Such agreements can cover any tax period (including future periods) and some or all of the issues. §7121. Reg. §301.7121-1; Rev. Proc. 68-16, 1968-1 C.B. 770. If the agreement settles a year or years only, then Form 866 is used. If it permanently settles one or more issues (e.g., property value), Form 906 is used.

closing inventory   *inventory* as of the end of the *taxable year.* There are various methods for valuing inventory, and the choice of method may significantly affect tax liability. See *cost, inventory valuation; first-in, first-out (FIFO); last-in, first-out (LIFO); lower of cost or market, inventory valuation.*

closing of partnership year   the division of a partnership's *taxable year* into two or more portions to reflect a *termination,* or with respect to a *partner* who sells his or her entire interest or whose entire interest is liquidated. §706(c). There is a general rule of nonclosing for other events such as admission of a new partner. §706(c)(1). See *retroactive allocations.*

closing transaction, puts and calls   a termination of an option writer's obligation to buy or to sell other than through a lapse or exercise of the option.

club   an *exempt organization* formed and operated to permit *individual* members to join in fellowship and cooperate in an attempt to achieve some common good, none of the *net income* of which *inures* to any *private shareholder or individual.* §501(c)(7). See *social club.*

coal tax   an *excise tax* on the extraction of coal (but not lignite), ranging from 50 cents to $1.10 per ton of coal extracted, paid by the producer. §4121(a) and (b). It helps defray costs under the Black Lung Benefits Act of 1977.

Code of Federal Regulations (CFR)   an authoritative federal publication containing regulations of the various federal agencies, including those of the *Treasury Department.*

cogeneration equipment, energy investment credit   property that is an integral part of a system for using the same fuel to produce both qualified energy and electricity at an industrial, agricultural, or commercial facility at which, as of January 1, 1980, electricity or qualified energy was produced. §48(1)(14)(A). For purposes of this provision, qualified energy means steam, heat, or other forms of useful energy (other than electric energy) to be used for industrial, agricultural, commercial, or space-heating purposes other than in the production of electricity. §48(1)(14)(D).

Cohan rule   a judicial doctrine which allows *taxpayers* to estimate certain *deductible expenses* when they do not have adequate records to document such expenses. The *Cohan* rule is applicable only if the taxpayers can prove that they are entitled to some *deduction,* and it does not apply to *travel, entertainment,* and *business gift* expenses. §274.

coinsurance   a form of *indemnity reinsurance* under which the reinsurer in effect becomes a full participant in its share of the ceded policy, roughly as if it had participated in the sale of the policy. The ceding (reinsured) company sells a portion of its *life insurance contracts* to the assuming (reinsuring) company, which assumes a proportionate part of all of the obligations arising out of the issuance of the reinsured policies. The reinsurer is obligated on and accounts for such contracts substantially in the same manner as if it were the original issuer. With respect to *participating contracts,* the *IRS* has ruled that the reinsurer is not permitted the *nonparticipating contract deduction* under former §809(d)(5) with respect to such policies pursuant to reinsurance under a coinsurance or *modified coinsurance* arrangement. Rev. Rul. 65-236, 1965-2 C.B. 229; see also Rev. Rul. 65-237, 1965-2 C.B. 230. The term is peculiar to the life insurance business.

collapsible asset   same as *hot asset.*

collapsible corporation   generally, a *corporation* which is made use of to give the appearance of a long-term investment to what is in reality a mere venture or project in manufacture, production, or construction of property with the view of converting inventory profits into capital gain. A shareholder will be required to treat gains as ordinary income if (1) he or she actually or *constructively* owns over 5 percent in value of the corporation's outstanding stock directly or indirectly; (2) 70 percent of the gain from the property transaction is attributable to the property manufactured, built, produced, or bought; or (3) gain from the tainted transaction is realized within three years after the completion of the manufacture, construction, production, or purchase of the property. §341(d). See *collapsible corporation, rebuttable presumption of collapsibility; section 341 assets; section 341(f) election; subsection (e) assets, collapsible corporation.*

collapsible corporation, rebuttable presumption of collapsibility   an objective formula that, if met, renders a *corporation* a *collapsible corporation,* absent evidence to the contrary. §341(c). Specifically, a *corporation* will be presumed collapsible if, at the time the corporation's assets are distributed or its shareholders engage in a *sale* or *exchange* of the corporation's *stock,* the *fair market value* of the corporation's *section 341 assets* (basically, certain *inventory, unrealized receivables* or fees, and *depreciable property* used in its *trade or business,* all of which have been held for less than three years) is (1) 50 percent or more of the fair market value of its total assets; and (2) 120 percent or more of the *adjusted basis* of the §341 assets. To determine the fair market value of the total assets, cash, obligations that are capital assets in the hands of the corporation, and stock in any other corporation are not included. Since the *IRS* can, on *audit,* declare a corporation a collapsible corporation, this presumption seems unimportant.

collapsible partnership rules   the rules of §751, which characterize a *partnership* interest as giving rise, in part, to *taxable ordinary income* based upon *both liquidating* and *nonliquidating disproportionate distributions of §751 assets.* These assets are often referred to as "tainted" or "hot" assets and are defined as unrealized receivables and substantially appreciated assets. Section 751 stands as an exception to §741, which generally treats an interest in a partnership as a *capital asset,* and to §732, which govern distributions of money and other property, respectively. See *inventory items; section 751 assets; substantially appreciated inventory items; unrealized receivables, partnerships; collapsible corporation.*

collapsing a transaction   disregarding a series of steps in order to ascertain the tax characterization of the overall arrangement; synonymous with applying the *step transaction doctrine.*

collateral   property used to secure a debt. The term is often used adjectivally to suggest remoteness (e.g., collateral relatives or matters).

collateral agreement   several meanings. One refers to secondary agreements entered into between *IRS* and the *taxpayer* under which the IRS forfeits collection of a delinquent account, but in exchange gets additional security interests in the taxpayer's property. See Reg. §301.7701-1. Another meaning is any secondary arrangement; for example, the IRS commonly exacts demands of taxpayers who successfully obtain compromises of liability by such means as abandoning future *tax benefits.* Forms 2261 and 2261-A are used for this particular set of circumstances.

collateral assignment   for purposes of *split-dollar life insurance,* a technique for splitting interests in a *life insurance policy,* such that the *employee* owns the policy but assigns the policy to the *employer* as collateral for the employer's loans. See *endorsement.*

collateral estoppel   a judicial doctrine that may be used in the interest of *equity* to prevent relitigating points or issues actually decided in a prior judicial proceeding involving the same parties against whom judgment was obtained, the same facts, and the same law. It does not apply if there has been an intervening change in the law or facts, or as to issues not raised in the prior determination.

collectibles   artwork, rugs, antiques, metals, gems, stamps, most coins, alcoholic beverages, or any other similar property the Secretary of the Treasury may specify. §408(m)(2) and (3). Individually directed plans described in §401(a) and *individual retirement accounts* may not invest in collectibles for *taxable years* ending after December 31, 1981. §408(m). 31 U.S.C. §5112(a) and (e) permit *qualified plans* to invest in certain United States gold and silver coins.

Collection Division   the segment of each *District Office* (and corresponding offices at higher organizational levels) of the *IRS* responsible for the *collection of taxes.*

collection gain   *gain realized* when a creditor is paid by the debtor in an amount greater than the *adjusted basis* of the obligation in the creditor's hands. The gain is viewed as *ordinary income,* on the theory that no property remains after the transaction (the *creditor release rule*); hence, the gain is ordinary in nature. The rule is equally applicable to *losses.* See §1271 for statutory *sale* or *exchange* treatment granted to terminations of a right or obligation with respect to actively traded property.

collection loss   see *collection gain.*

collection of taxes   the procedures and mechanisms by which the *IRS* collects taxes imposed by the Internal Revenue laws. Chapter 64 of the *Code* (§6301 et seq.) gives the IRS collection authority, including the power to enforce *liens* and to seize property. See *levy.*

collection period   the time during which the *IRS* can actually collect taxes due. It is normally six years, unless extended by *waiver,* after *assessment.* §6502(a)(1).

collectively bargained plan   a plan the Labor Department finds to be maintained under a collective bargaining agreement between *employee* representatives and *employers,* provided the plan constitutes a single plan of one or more employers. §413(a). The term "single plan" generally refers to one that, on an ongoing basis, makes all its assets available to pay all employee benefits. Collectively bargained plans are subject to most of the general requirements imposed on *qualified plans,* provided they are *bona fide.* See §7701(a)(46) (general standards for collective bargaining agreement).

combat pay   compensation (other than pensions and retirement pay) for combat service by members of the

Armed Forces of the United States. Section 112 prescribes eligibility, what area constitutes a *combat zone,* and for what period of time such zone qualifies. Importantly, commissioned officers are entitled to at most a $500-per-month exclusion. *Gross income* earned while a prisoner of war or while missing in action is similarly *excluded.* Members of the Armed Forces who served in Operation Desert Storm received favorable tax treatment for their military pay. Specified geographic areas were designated as a combat zone (Operation Desert Shield/Storm) effective January 17, 1991. For enlisted personnel, all military pay is nontaxable; for commissioned officers, $500 a month is nontaxable.

combat-related injury an injury or sickness that is incurred as a result of or caused by (1) armed conflict; (2) engagement in extra hazardous service, even if a person is not in combat; (3) conditions simulating war, including maneuvers or training; or (4) an instrumentality of war, such as military weapons. §104(b)(3). Amounts received for such injuries are excludable from *gross income* under §104(a)(4). Any *individual* who was a member of the armed forces of any country is eligible for the exclusion.

combat zone any area that the President of the United States by Executive Order designates, for purposes of §112 or corresponding sections relating to tax benefits for members of the *armed forces,* as an area in which armed forces of the United States are or have engaged in combat after June 24, 1950. §112(c)(2). Service in a combat zone is considered to be performed only on or after the date designated by the President's Executive Order as the date of the commencing of combatant activities in such zone and on or before the date designated by the President by Executive Order as the date of the termination of combatant activities in such zone.

combat zone exemption a provision that grants the *estate* of a American soldier who was killed or died as a result of wounds, disease, or injuries suffered while serving in a combat zone. §2201. See *combat zone.*

combination loan another name for a loan which is not entirely a *qualifying real property loan.* See §§593(d)(2) and 7701(a)(19) and Reg. §301.7721-13(k), which apportion the loan between the qualifying and nonqualifying portion. The definition relates to the right of certain financial institutions to claim favorable additions to *reserves for bad debts.* See *qualifying real property loans, mutual savings banks.*

combined deemed sale return a *return* filed by all *target corporations* acquired by a purchasing corporation on the same *acquisition date* in a *§338 acquisition,* if the targets were all members of the same *selling consolidated group.* §338(h)(15); Reg. §1.338-4T(l)(4). This is a simplifying rule, but it does not shift tax liability from the newly constituted target.

combined group three or more *corporations,* each of which is a member of a *brother-sister controlled group* or a *parent-subsidiary controlled group,* where one of the corporations is both a common parent and a member of a brother-sister controlled group. §1563(a)(3). A minimum pattern would be the case where Mrs. Smith owns 80 percent of B and C corporations, and B corporation owns 80 percent of S corporation. *Component members* of such groups are subject to §1561, which disallows *graduated tax* rates, multiple *accumulated earnings credits,* and multiples of the *exemption amounts* under the *alternative minimum tax* and the $2 million threshold for the *environmental tax.* §1561(a). Difficulties are exacerbated by §1563(c), which excludes Treasury stock, preferred stock, and a list of *excluded stock* from consideration as stock for purposes of finding a controlled group. See *controlled group of corporations, graduated taxes, and other benefits.*

combined plan a combination plan offered by an *employer* which consists of a *defined benefit plan* and a *defined contribution plan.* Despite the so-called *combined plan limitation,* this type of plan can be somewhat more lavish than either standing alone. See §415(e).

combined plan fraction a fraction found in 415(e), used to limit benefits and contributions to *combined plans.* It operates by altering the usual limits of §§415(b) and (c) and limiting the sum of the two to 1. See *combined plan limitation, benefits and contributions.*

combined plan limitation, benefits and contributions a reference to §415(e), which limits benefits and contributions under a combination consisting of a *defined benefit plan* and a *defined contribution plan* so as to assure that the combination offers pension benefits at most a fourth greater (for *participants* with high incomes) than either plan standing alone. In more formal terms, the limit is exceeded if the sum of the *defined benefit plan fraction* plus the defined contribution plan fraction exceed 1.0. §415(e)(2).

combined plan limitation, deductions a limit on *deductible employer contributions* to more than one qualfied plan (e.g., *defined benefit plan* and a profit-sharing plan), not to exceed 25 percent of the compensation paid or accrued to the beneficiaries under such plans. §404(a)(7). Amounts that exceed the limit on deductible amounts are carried over to later years. §404(a)(7)(B). See also *combined plan.*

combustible gas recovery system, energy investment credit an item of equipment used to recover unburned fuel from combustion exhaust gasses. Reg. §1.48-9(f)(13). Qualified combustible gas recovery systems may qualify as *specially defined energy property* for purposes of the *energy investment credit.* §48(1)(5); Reg. §1.48-9(f).

comfort ruling a *private letter ruling* provided with respect to a matter that does not call for a ruling because there is adequate, clear legal authority "in the statute, regulations or other authority published in Internal Revenue Bulletins." See Rev. Rul. 89-51, 1989-36 I.R.B. 19. The *IRS* is swamped with requests for comfort rulings and wants to cut back that burden. But see Rev. Proc. 90-42, 1990-31 I.R.B. 59 replacing Rev. Proc. 90-1, 190-1 I.R.B. 8.

commercial annuity an *annuity contract* written by a *life insurance company,* as opposed to a so-called *private annuity*. The two are taxed quite differently. The former is taxed as a true *annuity*; the latter is subject to complicated taxation, partly as a true annuity and partly like a sale.

commercial annuity, withholding an *annuity, endowment,* or *life insurance contract* issued by an *insurance company* licensed to do business under the laws of any state. Temp. Reg. §35.3405-1. Such annuities are subject to withholding under §3405.

commercial traveler exception see *trade or business within the United States.*

commercial type insurance generally, any insurance or annuity coverage of a type provided by commercial insurance companies, other than coverage provided substantially below cost to a class of charitable recipients; incidental health coverage provided by an HMO of a sort it typically provides; property or casualty insurance, or retirement or welfare benefits provided by *churches* or conventions or associations of churches solely for themselves; or *charitable gift annuities*. The term "insurance" includes *annuities* for this purpose. §501(m)(3) and (4).

commingled funds concept the notion that a *cash method taxpayer* can claim *interest expense deductions* through the use of borrowed money only if the funds borrowed to pay the interest are first commingled with the taxpayer's other funds, then paid out. The effect is to treat funds withheld as nondeductible, a highly formalistic rule that is becoming popular in the courts. See *leveraged loan.*

commission driver see *agent driver or commission driver.*

Commissioner when speaking of the *IRS,* the reference is to the Commissioner of Internal Revenue, an *individual* appointed by the President, serving under the Secretary of the Treasury, and charged with the administration of the IRS.

commitment fees amounts charged by lenders to make loan money available on demand. According to the *IRS,* such fees must be *capitalized* and *amortized* over the life of the loan if the loan closes. Rev. Rul. 81-160, 1981-23 I.R.B. 23. If the loan does not close, the fees may be currently *deductible business expenses.* Rev. Rul. 69-455, 1969-2 C.B. 9. See *points.*

commodities movable articles of value that can be bought or sold.

commodity credit corporation loans loans secured by agricultural commodities, granted to farmers by the federal Commodity Credit Corporation. Taxpayers may *electively include* such loans in *gross income* in the year the loan is received, provided they do so consistently. §77(a); Reg. §1.77-2. The effect is an increase in the *basis* of pledged farm property to the extent the loan is included in income. The basis is later reduced to the extent the farmer is discharged from liability. Reg. §1.1016-5(e).

commodity future synonymous with *commodity futures contract.*

commodity futures contract a contract to purchase a fixed amount of a commodity at a future date, either for speculation or hedging. Hedging results in *ordinary gains and losses* if it relates directly to the *taxpayer's business.* §1233(g); Reg. §1.1233-1(b). If the futures transaction is subject to the rules of a board of trade or commodity exchange, the gain or loss on a sale or exchange is long-term if the contract has been held for more than six months—even when the normal holding period is over one year. §1222.

commodity straddle see *loss deferral rule, straddles.*

common law employee an *individual* whose activities are subject to a right of control by the person paying for his or her services. The usual formulation follows: "generally the relationship of *employer* and *employee* exists when the person for whom services are performed has the right to control and direct the individual who performs the services, not only as to the result to be accomplished by the work but also as to the details and means by which this result is accomplished. That is, an employee is subject to the will and control of the employer not only as to what shall be done but how it shall be done. In this connection, it is not necessary that the employer actually direct or control the manner in which the services are performed; it is sufficient if he has the right to do so. The right to discharge is also an important factor indicating that the person possessing that right is an employer. Other factors characteristic of an employer, but not necessarily present in every case, are the furnishing of tools and the furnishing of a place to work to the individual who performs the services. In general, if an individual is subject to the control or direction of another merely as to the result to be accomplished by the work and not as to the means and methods of accomplishing the result, he is not an employee." Reg. §31.3401(c)-(1)(b) (federal *income tax withholding,* reflecting the common law standards). The same concept applies for *FICA* and *FUTA* purposes.

common law employee, Keogh plan any *employee* who is not a *self-employed individual*. See *self-employed individual, Keogh plans.*

common law state a *state* that relies on the common law system of England. Louisiana is the only civil law jurisdiction among the 50 states, although several other states, like Louisiana, have *community property* systems. Except for community property, these states too have common law.

commonly controlled organizations, trades or businesses see *reallocation of income and deductions by Commissioner.*

common parent exception a rule in the *consolidated return* area to the effect that *separate return years* of the common parent *corporation* for the *consolidated return year* to which a *credit* or *loss* is to be carried do not constitute *separate return limitation years* unless there has been a *reverse acquisition* or unless an election under §1562 (now repealed) was made. The corporation can, therefore, utilize losses against *members of an affiliated group* if it becomes the group's parent. The exception is also known as the lonely parent rule.

common paymaster a *corporation* that receives remuneration from several related corporations, disburses it to an *individual* who is employed by the related corporations, and keeps payroll records of such an *employee* or employees. §§3121(s) and 3306(p). If there is a common paymaster, the payee is treated as having only one *employer*; hence, *Social Security tax* payments and *withholdings* can be minimized. Compare Rev. Rul. 81-21, 1981-1 C.B. 482 (common treasurer was ruled not to qualify as a common paymaster for lack of an authorized corporation).

common stock not specifically defined. Generally it means *stock* (i.e., an equity interest in a *corporation*) which interest has no preference as to participation in earnings or in proceeds on the termination of the corporation. See *debt-equity rules.*

common stock, section 306 stock generally, nonredeemable *stock* that is not limited as to either *dividends* or *liquidation* rights. Revenue Rul. 79-163, 1979-1 C.B. 131, and Rev. Rul. 76-387, 1976-2 C.B. 96, treat nonvoting, nonredeemable stock that has no dividend or liquidating preference as common stock. The *IRS* has treated stock with a cash dividend preference as common stock. Rev. Rul. 75-222, 1975-1 C.B. 105. See *debt-equity rules; preferred stock; section 306 stock; stock.*

common trust fund a nontaxable *trust* in which the participants of the fund are taxed as income is earned, regardless of distribution. A common trust fund is defined in §584 as a trust established and maintained by a *bank* or an affiliated group of banks for the purpose of collective investment and reinvestment of money contributed to the fund by the bank in its capacity as an *executor, administrator, guardian,* or *trustee.* The *calendar year* is used. §584(h). See *common trust fund income.*

common trust fund income the *taxable income* of a *common trust fund,* meaning taxable income as computed for *individuals,* except that (1) *gains* and *losses* from *sales* or *exchanges* of *capital assets* are segregated; (2) computing ordinary taxable income, consisting of the excess of *gross income* over *deductions,* or an ordinary net loss, consisting of the excess of the deductions over the gross income, is disallowed; and (3) *charitable contributions* and the *standard deduction* are disallowed. Reg. §1.584-3(a)-(d). Each participant in a common trust fund reports his or her share of each of the above items whether or not distributed. Reg. §1.584-2.

communication satellite system income foreign corporate earnings derived from the ownership or operation of a communications satellite system by a foreign *entity* designated by a foreign government to participate in such ownership or operation. Such earnings are *exempt* from United States taxation if the United States, through its designated entity, participates in such a system pursuant to the Communications Satellite Act of 1962. §883(b).

communications services tax an *excise tax* based upon amounts paid for local telephone service, long-distance telephone service, and teletypewriter exchange service. §4251(b)(2).

community foundation see *community trust (or foundation).*

community income income from *community property* as well as salaries, wages, and other compensation of either *spouse* domiciled in a *community property state* or foreign country with a community property system. Half of such income is taxed to each *spouse,* unless the parties contractually agree to a separation of such income before it is earned. See *IRS* Pub. No. 555, Community Property and the Federal Income Tax 1-2 (1979). Note that if spouses file *separate returns* in such states, each reports half the total joint income. The Tax Reform Act of 1984 bars the use of foreign community property laws to split the United States earned income, trade or business income, partnership share of trade or business income, or community income from separate property, of one spouse. The spouse receiving such income is subject to United States tax at the rates applicable to *married persons* filing *separate returns.* §879(a), as amended. See *domicile.*

community property property held by a married couple domiciled in a *community property state* or foreign country with a *community property* system as the property of both. Generally, amounts earned by the labor of either *spouse,* and the income from such amounts, once invested, become community property as do improvements to *separate property* from community sources, while property brought to the marriage, and gifts and bequests during marriage remain separate property. See *separate property.*

community property states those states (Arizona, California, Idaho, Louisiana, New Mexico, Nevada, Texas, and Washington) whose property law systems follow those common in Continental Europe. The rights of *married persons* are the principal issue, particularly because in community property states one-half of the earnings of each *spouse* is deemed the property of the other spouse; whereas in other states the income is considered the distinct property of each spouse. *Community property* laws vary among the community property states. See generally *IRS* Pub. No. 555, Community Property and the Federal Income Tax 1 (1979).

community trust (or foundation) an *exempt organization* which is a *trust, corporation,* association, or some combination of these, established to receive contributions from the public and to apply them for charitable purposes primarily in the organization's areas. Regs. §1.170-9(e)(11)(i).

commuting costs the cost of commuting between home and work or job site in the area of the *taxpayer's tax home,* regardless of the mode of transportation. Such expenses are, in the opinion of the *IRS, nondeductible personal expenses.* Rev. Rul. 66-80, 1966-1 C.B. 57. The IRS asserts that the incremental expenses of carrying bulky tools by the same mode of transportation are, however, allowable as a *deduction.* Rev. Rul. 75-380, 1975-2 C.B. 59. Transportation between two different job locations, as well as the costs of going from a principal office located in the home to another job location, may be *deductible.* See Reg. §1.162-2(e), (f). See *bulky tool rule.*

comparable uncontrolled price method a standard used to determine whether sales between commonly controlled businesses are proper. Under this standard the proper price is the amount that an unrelated party paid in an *arm's length* transaction (*uncontrolled sales*) involving the same or immaterially different property and circumstances. Reg. §1.482-2(e)(2) and -2(e)(1)(ii) provides that if such sales can be found or derived, then those prices should be used. If such prices do not reflect the intercompany sales but can be corrected by a reasonable number of adjustments, then the *regulations* direct that such modifications be made. *Id.* Absent such sales, the regulations direct the use of the *resale price method* as the next best model. See *control, reallocations.*

compensable injury injury to business or property sustained as a result of the infringement of a United States *patent,* a breach of contract or fiduciary duty, or violations of §4 of the Clayton Act. §186(b). The lesser

of the *compensatory amount* or *unrecovered losses* resulting from such injuries is *deductible* under §186(a) upon receipt by the victim or when accrued. Section 186 is designed to allow an offset against taxable recoveries to the extent the payor's action created *operating losses* that generated no tax benefit (*unrecovered losses*).

compensating payments, cash and commodity straddles and short sales a shorthand term for payments and *distributions* in the nature of *ordinary income* arising from lending securities, but not *extraordinary dividends.* §263(h)(5). This rule applies to *short sales* as well as so-called *cash and carry commodities straddles.* §265(h)(6). See *extraordinary dividend, short sale.*

compensating use tax the *tax* on the use, storage, or consumption of goods bought in another jurisdiction (a use tax) that complements a state's sales tax. See *general sales tax.*

compensation, annual benefit and annual addition limitation currently taxable compensation for services rendered by an *employee,* paid by an *employer* maintaining the plan. Regulation §1.415-2(d)(1), which includes an extensive list of particular items, especially *wages* for *FICA* and *income tax withholding* purposes. Reg. §1.415-2(d)(2). The *regulations* also provide guidelines for the partial inclusion of such items as payments under accident and health plans and reimbursement of moving expenses. For the self-employed, the term "compensation" means *earned income* for pension plan purposes as defined in §401(c)(2), ignoring the *foreign earned income exclusion.* §415(b)(3) and (c)(3). See *annual addition limitation, qualified plans; annual benefit limitation, qualified plans; compensation, qualified plans.*

compensation for personal services, passive loss rules compensation paid to or on behalf of an *individual for services performed by the individual.* It only includes earned income, including compensatory payments from a *partnership* to a *partner;* property received for services (see §83); amounts received under *qualified plans;* other *deferred compensation;* taxable Social Security benefits; and, other income the *IRS* may identify. It excludes partners' and *S corporations'* shareholders' distributive shares of income from the *entity.* Such income is not *passive activity gross income.* See Reg. §1.469-2T(c)(4). See *passive activity gross income; passive loss rules.*

compensation, generally that which is given in return for something else, such as satisfaction for loss or injury, payment for property taken, or consideration for a privilege granted. Compensation for services, includible in *gross income* under §61(a)(1), includes (but is not limited to) wages, salaries, commissions, tips, bonuses, rewards, severance pay, jury fees, military pay, retirement pay, and pensions. Reg. §1.61-2(a). If compensation is given in a form other than cash, such as property or services, it is measured by its *fair market value.* Reg. §1.61-2(d).

compensation, highly compensated employee   *participant's compensation* as defined in §415(c)(3) relating to limits on *defined contribution plans,* disregarding: *cafeteria plans; employer contributions* under a *qualified cash or deferred arrangement*; employer contributions to a *SEP*; and *employer* contributions for *section 403(b) annuities* under a *salary reduction agreement.* §414(q)(7). A special set of rules is imposed upon so-called *top-heavy* plans to discourage retirement plans from conferring disproportionate benefits upon key employees. Top-heaviness is determined on an annual basis.

compensation, individual retirement arrangements *earned income,* as defined in §401(c)(2), the general pension plan definition (largely *net earnings from self-employment*). §219(f)(1). The term also includes taxable *alimony* or *separate maintenance payments.* §219(a). It excludes investment income earned by an investment *partnership.* §401(c)(2)(A) (referring to §1402(a)). Compensation does not include earnings and profits from property, such as rental income interest income, dividend income, pension and annuity income, deferred compensation, foreign earned income and housing cost amounts that are excluded from gross income, and any other amounts that are excluded from income. §219(f)(1). Individuals may annually deduct up to $2,000 or compensation (whichever is less) for contributions to individual retirement arrangements.

compensation otherwise paid or accrued   all compensation *paid or accrued* for the services of *employees,* excluding *deductible* contributions to a *qualified plan.* Reg. §1.404(a)-9(b) and (a)-13(a). This definition is used for limiting deductible contributions to qualified *stock bonus* and *profit-sharing plans,* alone or in combination with pension or annuity plans, and applies regardless of the plan's definition of compensation. Rev. Rul. 80-145, 1980-1 C.B. 89.

compensation, qualified plans   same definition (currently taxable compensation for services rendered by an *employee,* paid by an *employer* maintaining the plan) as *compensation, annual benefit and annual addition limitation* (§415(c)), disregarding certain deferrals unless the *employer* elects to the contrary. §414(s). The deferrals are those for *§401(k) plans, cafeteria plans, SEPs,* and *tax-deferred annuities for exempt and educational organization employees.* See *compensation, annual benefit and annual addition limitation.*

compensation-related loan   any *below-market loan* directly or indirectly between *employer* and *employee,* or *independent contractor* and recipient of the services. §7872(c)(1)(B). *Foregone interest* on such loans is treated as taxable compensation.

compensation, tax-deferred annuities for exempt and educational organization employees   see *includible compensation, tax-deferred annuities for exempt and educational organization employees.*

compensation, unemployment   see *unemployment compensation.*

compensatory amount   one measure of the amount of *deductions* allowable under §186(a) for violations of *patent* laws or anti-trust laws, or breaches of contract or fiduciary duty. §186(c). Such amounts are those received or accrued in the *taxable year* as damages as a result of an award or a settlement of a civil action for recovery of a *compensable injury,* reduced by amounts *paid or incurred* in the taxable year in securing the award or settlement. Compensatory amounts are limited to those amounts included in the *taxpayer's gross income.* §186(a). Thus, if a *business taxpayer* pays $10,000 of attorney's fees for a breach of contract, and receives a $50,000 settlement, the $40,000 is *includible* in the taxpayer's gross *income* as a compensatory amount. However, §186(a)(2) provides that if the taxpayer's *unrecovered losses* are less than the compensatory amount, then they are the measure of his or her deduction, consistent with the purpose of §186 to limit taxable recoveries by allowing a *deduction* to the extent that the losses that the recovery was based on were incapable of creating a *tax benefit.* See *compensable injury.*

compensatory damages   amounts awarded by a court to restore the recipient to a condition existing before the damage or injury took place. Such amounts are generally excluded from income, unless paid to restore lost income. §104.

compensatory royalty   an amount paid as a substitute for paying a *royalty.* The issue typically arises where a *lessee* contracts to drill on two tracts but wishes to pay an enlarged royalty for drilling on one tract only rather than being compelled to drill on both tracts.

competence   the ability to manage one's affairs in an adequate fashion. When speaking of minors who claim the status of genuine *partners,* the term refers to sufficient skill at managing their property to be able to undertake business affairs as equals of adults by the world. The issue is especially apt to arise in the context of a *family partnership.* Absent competence, a *trust* for the child is typically used as the partner. Absent competence or a trust, there may be no *partnership.* §704(e).

competent authority   an official designated under a *tax treaty* who has authority to regulate the application of the treaty to a particular transaction or *taxpayer,* notifying government officials of changes in the tax laws of the parties to the treaty, or of how the treaty was applied in litigation or administrative action. The provision is especially useful as a device to avoid the imposition of *double taxation.* The *Treasury Department* is typically the competent authority in this country.

competition, agreement against   see *covenant not to compete.*

complementary use tax   see *compensating use tax.*

completed contract method   a *method of accounting* authorized by Reg. §1.451-3(b)(2) in which profit or loss on a contract is not reported until the contract is fully performed. Upon its completion, income under the contract as well as associated *expenses (contract costs)* are reported, subject to an allowance for materials and supplies on hand. *Period costs* (those not allocable to the contract) are *deducted* when *paid or incurred.* The *IRS* has demanded a business need for the method as a condition to its use. Rev. Rul. 70-67, 1970-1 C.B. 117. See also *percentage of completion method of accounting.*

completed crop pool method of accounting   a *method of accounting* under which *gain* and *loss* is computed separately for each *crop year pool* in the year in which the last of the products in the pool are disposed of. §1382(g)(2). The method may not be used for *income tax* purposes, except by certain *cooperatives* under limited circumstances. §1382(g)(1); Rev. Rul. 69-71, 1969-1 C.B. 207.

completed film tax shelter   a *tax shelter* whereby investors purchase a completed film, claiming the *investment tax credit,* provided it was a new *qualified film.* §48(k)(1)(B). *Depreciation* (or possibly *cost recovery*) write-offs are often claimed for the film, through use of the *income forecast method* (depreciation only). Rev. Rul. 64-273, 1964-2 C.B. 62; Rev. Rul. 60-358, 1960-2 C.B. 68. The investors then turn the film over to distributors to market it. Because the *at-risk rules* and *passive loss rules* apply to these transactions, they have lost their appeal as tax shelters.

completed transfer   a direct or indirect transfer of a *present* or *future interest* in which the transferor (*donor*) relinquishes all dominion and control over the property (even if remote, such as the power to borrow without adequate interest or security), thereby attracting a potential federal *gift tax* liability. Reg. §25.2511-2(b). The term is not synonymous with the descriptive state law term *absolute gift.*

complete liquidation, corporate   a transfer by all shareholders of their *stock* to the *corporation* that issued the stock in exchange for the corporation's property. §331. A status of complete liquidation exists when the corporation ceases to be a going concern and its activities are merely for the purpose of winding up its affairs, paying its debts, and distributing any remaining balance to its shareholders. A complete liquidation may be completed prior to the actual dissolution of the liquidating

corporation, and in any event a legal dissolution of the corporation is not required. The mere retention of a nominal amount of assets for residual claims or to preserve the corporation's legal existence will not disqualify the transaction. Reg. §1.332-2(c). Generally, the shareholder treats amounts received in liquidation as *amounts realized* in a *sale* or *exchange* of a *capital asset.* §331. The amount of *gain* or *loss* depends on the shareholder's *adjusted basis* of his stock, the value of the property distributed by the liquidating corporation, or both. Whether such gain or loss is *long-* or *short-term* depends upon the length of time the shareholder held the stock. *Ordinary gains* or *losses* may also arise in certain circumstances, as, for example, where the stock is not a *capital asset* in the shareholder's hands, or where the shareholder elected under former §333 not to *recognize* the gain upon liquidation. The corporation is taxable on gains in liquidation, subject to anti-abuse rules to prevent injecting high-*basis,* low-value assets before the liquidation. A liquidation that is a step in continuation of the business is no liquidation. See *de facto liquidation; liquidation of a subsidiary; partial liquidation.*

complete payout period, natural resources   the portion of a *farmout* period during which the *carrying party* recovers its costs, including the costs of operating the mine(s) or well(s) to produce such income. Rev. Rul. 70-336, 1970-1 C.B. 145. If the carrying party can recover 100 percent of production before the carried party begins to share in production, then the carrying party can deduct all *intangible and drilling and development costs* and *depreciation* even though its final share is less than 100 percent of production. Reg. §1.612-4; Rev. Rul. 80-109, 1980-1 C.B. 129. See *fractional interest rule,* which this concept modifies.

complex trust   a *trust* other than a *simple trust*; in other words, a trust that may accumulate income, distribute *corpus,* or have a charitable *beneficiary.* The term includes a simple trust that engages in accumulations. §§661-663.

compliance period   the 15-year period during which there is ratable *recapture* of the *low-income housing credit.* §42(i)(1). It begins at the beginning of the *credit period,* meaning when the building is *placed in service* or the next year, if the *taxpayer* so elects. See §42(f). Failure to comply with the requirements of §42 during the compliance period generally causes recapture on the spot. §42(j)(1). The low-income housing credit expired on June 30, 1992. See *low-income housing credit.*

component depreciation   a *depreciation* method that fragments an item of property, often a building, into its elements (e.g., shell, plumbing, and wiring) and applies *individual useful* lives and *salvage values* to each such component. The result, if available, can be significant enhancement of depreciation *deductions.*

component member a *corporation* counted as a member of a *controlled group of corporations* for purposes of limitations on claims to *graduated taxes* on income, multiple *accumulated earnings credits,* and certain other *tax benefits.* §1563(b). Specifically, §1563(b) defines a component member, as of December 31 of any *taxable year,* if it (1) is a member of the controlled group as of December 31 and is not an *excluded member,* or (2) is not a member on December 31, but is treated as an *additional member.* An additional member is basically a corporation that is not an excluded member, but was a member of the controlled group at any time during the calendar year, but not on December 31. §1563(b)(3). Excluded members are primarily grouped by tax characteristic (e.g., *foreign* corporations and *exempt organizations*). In order to be a member of a controlled group of corporations, the corporation must be a component member. §1563(a). See *controlled group of corporations, graduated taxes, and other benefits.*

composite account a broad grouping of assets included in an account for *depreciation* purposes regardless of their character or *useful lives.* Reg. §1.167(a)-7(a). See Reg. §§1.167(b)-1(b) (illustrations), 1.167(b)-2 (*declining-balance* method) and 1.167(b)-3 (*sum-of-the-years'-digits method*).

composite depreciation a method of *depreciation* under which a major asset (e.g., an apartment building) is depreciated as a single asset, although it is in fact an aggregation of a great number of lesser items (e.g., wiring, shell, plumbing, and so forth). The method typically uses the weighted average of the separate *useful lives* of all the assets, changing the overall rate as major additions and retirements occur. Reg. §1.167(a)-7(d).

compromise undefined. It refers to an arrangement, which is preceded by an *offer in compromise,* under which the *taxpayer* and the *IRS* settle a delinquent taxpayer account for less than its face amount via mutual concessions. See *compromise agreements; offer in compromise.*

compromise agreements settlements arrived at by mutual concessions by the *IRS* or the *Justice Department* and *taxpayers,* finally settling tax liabilities for a taxable period. Such agreements need not cover all issues for the period and can relate to civil and criminal liabilities, provided they relate to regulatory provisions and not fraud penalties. Although such agreements can be based on uncertainties about liability, they usually relate to collectibility. Such agreements cannot be upset except for falsification, concealment of assets, or mutual mistake of a material fact, and in any case do not remit criminal liabilities other than the modest cases described above. §7122; Reg. §301.7122-1. See Rev. Proc. 80-6, 1980-1 C.B. 586. Such agreements are triggered by an *offer in compromise* (Form 656) tendered by the *taxpayer.* See *doubtful collectibility; offer in compromise.*

compulsory conversion see *involuntary conversion.*

computer see *qualified technological equipment.*

concentrates ores that remain after the initial processing, usually in advance of transportation for further processing. Concentration is generally considered *mining* for *income tax* purposes, particularly with respect to *percentage depletion.*

conclusive presumption see *presumption.*

condemnation the taking of property pursuant to government authority in exchange for a reasonable amount of compensation. For purposes of §1033 (*involuntary conversions*), the term refers to the time when the right to the *condemnation award* is fixed. See IRS Pub. No. 549 for examples.

condemnation award money or property received for property that is condemned, or conveyed under *threat or imminence of condemnation.* See *involuntary conversion.*

conditional sales agreement a transaction in which a seller reserves title to property until the buyer pays for the goods, at which time the condition is fulfilled and title passes to the buyer. Such arrangements may be recast as *leases,* or leases may be recast as conditional sales agreements. See also Rev. Rul. 55-540, 1955-2 C.B. 39 (concentration on intention of parties and factual context; factors listed) and I.R.M. 7299-4.

condition of employment generally, a feature of an employment relationship (e.g., a pleasant office or a parking lot), which might be considered *gross income* on the theory it is a *cash equivalent,* but which for reasons of convenient tax administration is excluded. The term is also used in §119, involving the exclusion from income of *employer*-provided *meals and lodging*; that particular language "required as a condition of employment" has been read to mean "required in order to perform properly the duties of the *taxpayer's* employment." Reg. §1.119-1(b). See *fringe benefits.*

condition precedent a condition that must be met if a contractual obligation is to arise. For example, if A promises to pay B $10 if the sun rises tomorrow, the sunrise is a condition precedent to the duty to pay. Conditions precedent are said to keep transactions open for purposes of reporting *gains* and *losses.* See, for example, Rev. Rul. 70-68, 1970-1 C.B. 122. See *accrual method; open transactions.*

condition subsequent a condition that, if met, eliminates a contractual obligation to perform. For example, if A promises to pay B $10 now for work, but if the sun rises tomorrow, then B must repay A, then tomorrow's sunrise is a condition subsequent to B's claim to the $10. Such conditions are said not to be sufficient to keep a transaction *open* for *income tax* purposes. See *accrual method; open transactions.*

condominium legal relationship involving *real estate* in which there are multiple owners of common areas and separate areas of privately owned property. Owners of condominium units who *itemize* their *federal income taxes* can claim *deductions* for their shares of such items as *taxes* and *interest expenses*. See *association property*.

condominium management association a type of *homeowners' association* that can elect to be *exempted* from federal *income taxes*. See *association property*.

conduct of a trade or business see *trade or business within the United States*. The term is used in §§864(c), 871(b), and 882(a).

conduit concept a tax law principle applied to *entities* that preserves the *character* of *gross income, losses, gains, expenses,* and *credits* in the hands of the *partners*. Partnerships are viewed as pure conduits in that they are mere reporting entities and not *taxpayers*. *Estates, trusts,* and *S corporations* and numerous intermediaries (e.g., *cooperatives*) are not true conduits, although they may achieve the same practical results. See *aggregate theory; entity theory*.

conduit IRA see *IRA rollovers*.

confiscation an expropriation, intervention, seizure, or similar taking by a foreign government in that foreign country. §172(h).

confiscation loss a confiscation, fixed by an *identifiable event*, that results in less compensation received than the *taxpayer's adjusted basis* in the confiscated property, even if there was a manifestation of intent of the taker to pay at some future time but no realistic effort to pay occurred. Rev. Rul. 62-197, 1962-2 C.B. 66. Confiscation losses are permissible *deductions* for *individuals* if they arise in the course of a *trade or business* or a *transaction entered into for a profit*. §165(c)(1). Such losses result in extended *net operating loss carryovers*. §172(b)(1).

conformity a shorthand word for the notion of conformity of the *tax accounting* with the *taxpayer's* financial records. The conformity requirement is found in §446(a), which demands the computation of *taxable income* under the *method of accounting* the taxpayer regularly uses in computing book income. The drive for greater conformity of the tax laws to accounting rules has generally failed.

Congressional Budget Office a segment of the United States Congress responsible for the details of federal budget matters.

Congressman's newsletter expenses the cost of newsletters, questionnaires, and reports sent to a representative's constituents. They are permissible *itemized deductions* for the legislator. Rev. Rul. 74-429, 1974-2 C.B. 83.

consent dividend a *dividend* deemed paid (hence *deductible*) by *personal holding companies* and *corporations* subject to the *accumulated earnings tax*. This imaginary dividend is made by election, and it is treated as a year-end dividend, followed by an imaginary contribution of such amounts back to the paying corporation. §565(c). The election calls for shareholder consents, filed with the tax return, and may be made up to the date for filing the corporation's *tax return*. §565(a); Reg. §1.565-1. Such dividends must not be *preferential*, and amounts that would not have qualified as a dividend if they actually had been paid are not considered part of the consent dividend. §565(b). See *preferential dividend*.

consenting corporation a *corporation* that elects to be controlled by §341(f). The practical effect is to free shareholders of what might otherwise be a *collapsible corporation* from *ordinary income* treatment on the sale of their *stock* in such a company. The corporation pays the price of having to submit to such treatment when it disposes of certain assets. See Reg. §1.341-7 for details. It must not be a *foreign corporation*. See *section 341(f) election*.

consent stock stock on which *consent dividends* can be paid, thereby allowing *corporations* to avoid the *accumulated earnings tax* or *personal holding company tax*. Consent stock is the class (or classes) of stock entitled to share in *current distributions* of *earnings and profits* after dividends on preferred stock are paid. In essence, it is the class or classes of stock entitled to residual earnings; it may, therefore, include participating preferred stock. §565; Reg. §1.565-6.

consent to extend statute of limitations the stricter terminology for the phrase *waiver of statute of limitations* when used in a federal tax setting.

conservation easement see *qualified conservation contribution*.

conservation purpose generally, the preservation of land areas, open space, and *certified historic structures,* or the protection of a relatively natural habitat. Section 170(h)(4)(A) for additional requirements. *Qualified conservation contributions* must be exclusively for conservation purposes in order for the *taxpayers* to claim a tax *deduction*. §170(h)(5).

consistency, duty of see *duty of consistency*.

consistency period, section 338 acquisitions the period beginning a year before a *twelve-month acquisition period,* plus the acquisition period up to and including the *acquisition date,* plus one year. §338(h)(4)(A). The period may be extended by the *IRS*. §338(h)(4)(B). See *consistency requirements, section 338 acquisitions*.

consistency requirement, partnership see *partnership item*.

consistency requirements, section 338 acquisitions rules found in §338(f), the gist of which is that during the *consistency period*: (1) an acquisition of *stock* or assets by any member of the *affiliated group* of the *purchasing corporation* is deemed an acquisition by the purchasing corporation; and (2) if the purchasing corporation makes *qualified stock* purchases with respect to a *target corporation* and one or more of its affiliates, an election under §338 with respect to the first target also applies to later purchases. See *section 338 acquisition.*

consolidated accumulated earnings tax the *accumulated earnings tax* (§531), applied to an *affiliated group* of *corporations.* See Reg. §1.1502-43, which also describes parallel concepts such as consolidated *accumulated taxable income,* consolidated *dividends-received deduction* and the consolidated *accumulated earnings credit,* all of which are multicorporation variants of the corresponding single *entity* concepts.

consolidated application an application by a *person* (often a *fiduciary*) representing more than 10 *trusts* or *estates* needing *employer identification numbers.* Rev. Proc. 70-22, 1970-2 C.B. 503 provides the procedures for acquiring multiple numbers.

consolidated charitable contribution carryovers excess *charitable contributions* of an *affiliated group* of *corporations* plus any excess charitable contributions of members of the group arising in *separate return years* of the members. Reg. §1.1502-24(b). The *separate return limitation year* rules do not apply to *charitable contributions,* and, therefore, charitable contributions of *individual* members of the affiliated group arising in separate return years are added to consolidated charitable contributions and used together. Reg. §1.1502-24.

consolidated charitable contributions deduction the lesser of the *charitable contributions* of each *member of an affiliated group,* plus any *consolidated charitable contribution carryovers,* or 10 percent of the adjusted *consolidated taxable income,* rather than *separate taxable income* of the individual members. Reg. §1.1502-24.

consolidated deemed sale election a mechanism that allows a group of *target companies* in *section 338* election to file a *consolidated return* if they were acquired on the same *acquisition date.* See *section 338 election.*

consolidated dividends received deduction see *consolidated accumulated earnings tax.*

consolidated group an informal term for an *affiliated group* of *corporations* that files a *consolidated return.*

consolidated income tax return synonymous with a *consolidated return.*

consolidated net operating loss a loss during a *consolidated return year* determined by taking into account the separate *taxable income* of each *member of the affil-*

iated group, any consolidated *net capital gain,* any consolidated *section 1231 net loss,* any *consolidated charitable contributions deduction,* and any consolidated *dividends-received deduction.* Reg. §1.1502-21(f). Computation of the consolidated net operating loss is necessary to determine the amount of any consolidated net operating loss *carryover* and *carryback.*

consolidated net operating loss deduction any consolidated *net operating losses* of the *affiliated group,* plus such net operating losses sustained by *members* of the group in *separate return years* as can be *carried over* or *carried back* to a different *taxable year.* Reg. §1.1502-21(b). The consolidated net operating loss *deduction* is computed on a consolidated, not a company-by-company basis and is deducted regardless of whether the affiliated group member or members sustaining the loss have income in the carryback or carryover year.

consolidated return a federal *income tax return* electively filed on Form 1120 by an *affiliated group* of *corporations* under the authority of §1501. The essence of such returns is to treat the group as one *taxpayer,* by combining their several *gross incomes, deductions, credits, losses,* etc., and eliminating *intercompany transactions.* The group is not only taxed as a single *entity* for purposes of §11, the *corporate income tax* levy, but it is also so treated for *personal holding company tax* (§541) and *accumulated earnings tax* (§531) purposes. Reg. §1.1502-43 to -47. The return creates *joint and several liability* for the tax.

consolidated return regulations an extensive set of *legislative regulations* issued under §1502.

consolidated return year a *taxable year* for which a *consolidated return* is filed, or is required to be filed, by the consolidated *affiliated group of corporations.* Reg. §1.1502-1(d).

consolidated section 1231 net gain or loss the aggregate of the *gains or losses* from dealing in *section 1231 assets* of each of the *members of an affiliated group* for the *consolidated return year.* Reg. §1.1502-23. The determination of whether there are *net section 1231 gains or losses* is made on a consolidated, not a separate company, basis. Reg. §1.1502-23.

consolidated taxable income *taxable income* of an *affiliated group of corporations.* In essence, it is the net income of the group after *intercompany transactions* are eliminated. See Reg. §1.1502-11. Consolidated taxable income is arrived at by aggregating the *separate taxable income* or loss of each member of the affiliated group, subject to intricate computational adjustments.

consolidated tax liability actual tax liability for the *taxable year* after *credits* of an *affiliated group* of *corporations* filing a *consolidated income tax return.* Reg.

§1.1502-2. Computation of consolidated tax liability is necessary in order to allocate the tax liability to members of the affiliated group under §1552 for purposes of computing each member's *earnings and profits*. Reg. §1.1502-33(d).

consolidation   the combining of two or more *corporations* into a single new corporation. Consolidations may qualify for tax-free *corporate reorganization* treatment under §§368(a)(1)(A), 354 and 361.

consolidation, partnerships   the *merger* or *consolidation* of two or more *partnerships,* treated as a continuation of any consolidated partnership whose members own 50 percent or more *capital* and profits *interest* in the resulting partnership. §708(b)(2)(A).

conspiracy   see *criminal conspiracy.*

constant interest rate method   an elective method of calculating discount on certain obligations on a constant daily basis by *yield to maturity* based on the cost of the obligation and daily compounding. §1283(b)(2). It is used to define the daily portion of *acquisition discount* under the *original issue discount* rules as they relate to *short-term obligations.* See *daily portion; ratable accrual method.*

constant rental amount   the amount which, if paid as of the close of each lease period (12-month period beginning on the first day the agreement applies), would have a *discounted present value,* using 120 percent of the *applicable federal rate* compounded semi-annually as the discount factor, equal to the discounted present value of the aggregate payments required. §467(e)(1). For example, in the case of a lease calling for a lump-sum payment at the end of the term, the constant rental amount is that amount which, if paid on the last day of each lease year into a bank account bearing interest at the indicated rate, would produce an account balance at the end of the lease equal to the present value of the deferred payment. See *rent-leveling rules.*

constant yield method   a method for treating *amortizable bond premium* under which the premium paid for the *bond* is computed on the basis of the *taxpayer's yield to maturity,* using the taxpayer's *basis* for the *bond,* and compounding at the close of each accrual period. §171(b). Accrual periods are generally the six-month periods ending on the date corresponding to the maturity date of the bond or the date that is six months prior to the maturity date. For this purpose, if the amount payable on an earlier call date is used to determine the amount of bond premium attributable to the period before the call date, the bond is treated as though it had matured on the call date for the redemption amount and was reissued on that date for the same amount. §171(b)(3)(B). See *amortizable bond premium; bond, amortization.*

construction of property, collapsible corporation   an unclear term that, whatever it may mean, goes so far as to include mere subdividing or rezoning of land or drilling of oil wells. See, e.g., Rev. Rul. 68-472, 1968-2 C.B. 138; Rev. Rul. 56-137, 1956-1 C.B. 178. The construction of property can trigger the *collapsible corporation* rules. §341(b)(1).

constructive   deemed or implied. A constructive receipt of property, for example, arises if the recipients can take possession of property if they cared to, even though there has been no actual receipt.

constructive disproportionate distribution   one of various transactions affecting shareholders' relative interests in a *corporation,* which have the effect of increasing *shareholders'* proportionate interests in the corporation's assets or *earnings and profits.* §305(c). Transactions that result in disproportionate distributions generally cause shareholders to be taxed under the general *stock dividend* rules of §305(b). Illustrations of such constructive distributions include various call premiums, escalating redemptions prices, recapitalizations, and anti-dilution clauses. §305(c). The term could also mean *partnership* distributions arising in odd cases such as changes in loss-sharing ratios that reduce allocable debt and produce an imaginary distribution. See *stock dividend.*

constructive dividend   a direct or indirect *dividend* by a *corporation* to a *shareholder,* in his or her capacity as such, which is treated for tax purposes as a *distribution* of property described in §301, even though a distribution to shareholders has not been formally declared by the corporation. Constructive dividends most commonly arise as a result of *IRS audits* of *closely held corporations* whose dealings with their shareholders are, more often than not, characterized by informality. Examples include a corporate loan to a shareholder where there is no intent to create a *bona fide* creditor-debtor relationship, a corporate expenditure incurred primarily for the personal benefit of the shareholder, a *sale* of property by a corporation to its shareholders for less than *fair market value,* excessive salaries paid to a shareholder, and excessive payments made by the corporation on purchasing or leasing a shareholder's property. The term is often used synonymously with the term "disguised dividend," although the latter term tends to suggest *tax avoidance* or *tax evasion.* See *triangular dividend.*

constructive ownership   ownership of stock and, in some instances, other property that is imputed to another related person. See *attribution rules.*

constructive receipt doctrine   a doctrine to the effect that a *cash method taxpayer* cannot postpone the reporting of *gross income* by failure to exercise his or her unrestricted power to collect it. Reg. §1.446-1(c)(1). However, income is not constructively received if a valuable right or privilege must be relinquished to receive payment, if the right to receive payment is disputed by the parties, or if there is a binding agreement that postpones payment to a year other than the completion date of the transaction.

constructive short-term capital gain   an elegant invention of §1212(b)(2) relating to *capital loss carryovers* of noncorporate *taxpayers,* the effect of which is to reduce the amount of *capital losses* carried out to the extent they were used up in a prior year. The purpose is to assure that the limitations of §1212(b) are not eliminated in the year to which the capital loss is carried.

consumer loan   any loan to an *individual* secured by an interest in *tangible personal property* which is not held for *investment* and which is not used in a trade or business. §6050J(b). Foreclosures and the like on such loans are subject to certain *IRS* reporting procedures.

consumption tax   a tax policy concept which would design the law to *defer* taxation of *income* until it is eventually applied for personal consumption. The concept already appears implicitly in such provisions as §1031 (*like-kind exchanges*) which defer taxation until *gains* are withdrawn from investment. The term also refers to any tax, typically a sales tax, that is imposed on consumption items, such as a sales tax on cigars.

contemplation of death   in the light of impending death.

contemporaneous records   not precisely defined, but apparently means records created simultaneously with or near in time to a given action or event. See Reg. §1.274-5(c)(1)–(3) (substantiation requirements for *business gifts, travel, entertainment,* and the like).

contest   a contest arises when there is a bona fide dispute as to the proper evaluation of the law or the facts necessary to determine the existence or correctness of the amount of asserted liability. It is not necessary to institute suit in a court of law in order to contest an asserted liability. Reg. §1.461-2(b)(2). A contest is needed in order for the *deduction* for *contested liabilities* under §461(a) to become available.

contested liabilities   a reference to §461(f), which allows a *deduction* for amounts paid in satisfaction of an asserted, but uncertain, liability which persists after the transfer, and which would have been *deductible* but for the contest. See *asserted liability, contested liabilities deduction.*

contested liabilities deduction   a *deduction* allowed to *taxpayers* for payments made (other than *foreign* or *possession* taxes), but which may be returned in later years because of a contest. §461(f). The deduction is rather narrowly confined, because it violates the usual rules of the *accrual method* of accounting. The deduction is allowed if (1) the taxpayer contests an asserted

liability but transfers money or other property to provide for the satisfaction of the asserted liability; (2) the contest with respect to the asserted liability exists after the transfer; and (3) but for the fact that the asserted liability is contested, a deduction would be allowed for the *taxable year* of the transfer (or, in the case of an accrual method taxpayer, for an earlier taxable year for which such amount would be accruable). See Reg. §1.461-2(a)(1)(i)–(v).

contiguous countries, generally   Canada and Mexico.

contiguous country life insurance branch   a Mexican or Canadian branch of a *domestic life insurance company.* Such a branch may qualify to elect to be separately accounted for, excluding its income from *life insurance company taxable income,* if three conditions are met. Specifically, the branch must (1) use insurance policies insuring risks in connection with the lives or health of residents of Canada or Mexico; (2) have its principal place of business in Canada or Mexico; and (3) be able to qualify as a *mutual life insurance company* if the branch were a *domestic insurance company.* §814(b).

contiguous foreign country corporation   a *corporation* organized under the laws of Canada or Mexico which is maintained solely for the purpose of complying with the laws of such country as to title and operation of property all of the stock of which is owned or controlled, directly or indirectly, by a *domestic corporation.* §1504(d). See, e.g., Rev. Rul. 70-379, 1970-2 C.B. 179. Generally, a *foreign corporation* is not allowed to join in filing a *consolidated return,* but the parent of a contiguous foreign country corporation may elect to include the contiguous foreign country corporation in its consolidated return. §1502(d).

contiguous, natural resources   resources having common boundaries, but not merely touching at the corner. Reg. §1.614-5(a). Contiguous *tracts or parcels of land* may be treated as a single *property* under §614, which is concerned with identification and aggregation of natural resource properties.

contiguous noncovered service   service not with an *employer* or employers maintaining an *employee* plan within a job classification or class of employees covered under the plan. Labor Reg. §2530.210(c)(3)(iii). Noncovered service is generally contiguous if (1) the noncovered service comes before or after *covered service;* and (2) the employee does not terminate employment between such covered service and noncovered service. Labor Reg. §2530.210(b)(3)(iv)(A).

continental shelf areas   the seabed and subsoil of those submarine areas adjacent to the territorial waters of the *United States,* a United States *possession,* or a foreign country, which, in accordance with international law, has exclusive rights with respect to exploration and exploitation of natural resources, provided the foreign country exercises, directly or indirectly, taxing jurisdiction with respect to such exploration or exploitation. Reg. §1.638-1(a). The rule applies to *income tax* provisions relating to mines, oil and gas wells, and other natural deposits for such purposes as determining sources of income and *withholding taxes.*

continental shelf income income from wells, mines, and employment arising from the exploration of the *United States'* continental shelf over which this country has exclusive rights as a matter of international law. Such income is treated as income from United States sources. Conversely, income from continental shelves of the United States *possessions* and foreign countries is *foreign source income* if those countries exercise taxing jurisdiction over such exploration. §638.

continental United States the District of Columbia and the 48 states other than Alaska and Hawaii. Reg. §§1.912-1(b) and 49.4262(c)-1(a). Certain presidentially approved cost-of-living allowances are excluded from *gross income* for civilian officers or *employees* of the *United States* government stationed outside the continental United States. §912(2). For purposes of the *excise* tax on air transportation (§4261), the term also expressly includes all inland waters or parts of inland waters lying within the boundary of the United States, and waters within three miles of the coastline. Reg. §49.4262(c)-1(a).

contingent compensation compensation, the amount of which depends on future events, especially profitability. See *free bargain concept.*

contingent income assets a term used in Reg. §1.1060-1T(f)(4) to include only those particular assets, such as patents, with respect to whose productivity contingent payments of purchase price are directly related. The benefits of such status are that later purchase price increases are *allocated* directly to those assets and they are not appraised according to their *fair market value* as of the acquisition date (hence subject to the limit on *Class III assets*).

contingent interest It is a general reference to the type of seller financing that would not be eligible for the exclusion from *acquisition indebtedness* under §514(c)(9) per §514(c)(9)(B)(ii).

contingent liabilities liabilities, the existence or amount of which depends on future events.

contingent payment sales a term used in the *regulations* under the *installment sales* rules to describe a *sales* contract, the price terms of which are not fixed by the end of the year of sale. Reg. §15A.453-1(c). See *sale for contingent payments.*

contingent retirement payments, partnership payments to a retired *partner* or deceased partner's *estate* that are dependent upon *partnership operations* and treated as *distributive shares* thereof. §736(a)(1).

contingent serial payments a term used in the heading of §1253(d)(1). It refers to payments for the transfer, sale, or other disposition of a *franchise, trademark,* or *trade name* that are contingent on the productivity, use, or disposition of the assets transferred, provided (1) the contingent amounts are part of a series of payments that are payable at least annually throughout the term of the transfer agreement; and (2) the payments are (a) substantially equal in amount or (b) payable under a fixed formula. §1253(d)(1).

continuing health coverage see *group health plan, deduction; health care continuation rules.*

continuing multiple asset accounts accounts used for *depreciation* purposes, kept open as long as accumulated depreciation is less than the cost of the assets. Additions to and retirements from the account are made as they take place. T.I.R. 503, August 21, 1963. Contrast the *vintage account,* which contains only assets *placed in service* in a particular year.

continuity of business enterprise doctrine a judicial requirement imposed on *corporate reorganizations,* the gist of which is that the acquiring company in a reorganization must continue a *business* enterprise after the reorganization, although not necessarily the one carried on by the target company. Continuity is also required if *net operating losses* and certain other *tax attributes* of target companies are to survive under the *neutrality principle.* Current *regulations* demand that the acquiring company must use a significant portion of the target company's *historic business assets* or continue at least one of the target company's historic businesses. Reg. §1.368-1(a). The continuity of business enterprise rules do not apply to *recapitalizations (Type E reorganizations).* Rev. Rul. 82-34, 1982-1 C.B. 59.

continuity of interest see *continuity of proprietary interest doctrine.*

continuity of life a characteristic of corporate status that arises when an *entity's* existence is not legally dissolved by death, bankruptcy, retirement, resignation, or expulsion of any member. Reg. §301.7701-2(b).

continuity of proprietary interest doctrine a judicial requirement imposed on *corporate reorganizations,* the gist of which is that the former owners of the target company in the reorganization must get a continuing proprietary stake in the acquiring corporation, represented by equity (generally common or preferred stock whether or not entitled to vote, but sometimes debt which gives the owners an intimate interest in the acquiring company). The continuity of proprietary interest requirement issue is most significant in *Type A reorganizations.* The term "continuity of interest" is often used instead.

contra a term used to indicate an authority that contradicts another authority.

contract costs a term often used to describe costs allocated to a long-term contract that are not reported until the contract is completed. See *completed contract method.*

contraction of business a voluntary or involuntary diminution in the operations of a *corporation* sufficient to be considered a *partial liquidation,* such that *individual shareholders* who *redeem* their *stock* in connection with the partial liquidation are entitled to treat their redemptions as *exchanges.* §302(b)(4). Illustrations of qualifying contractions include changing from a major department store to a small apparel store (Rev. Rul. 74-296, 1974-1 C.B. 80), and distribution of a major part of a business to shareholders to be operated by individuals. See §302(e) for a safe harbor provision.

contract research expenses 65 percent of amounts paid for *qualified research* to anyone other than an *employee* of the payor. §41(b)(3)(A). Prepayments are prorated. §41(b)(3)(B). Contract research expenses are a type of *qualified research expense* that forms part of the base on which the *credit for increasing research activities* is based. §41(b)(2) and (a)(1)(A). See *credit for increasing research activities.*

contractual right to cut timber the right to sell *timber* cut under a contract for the *taxpayer's* own account or for use in the taxpayer's *trade or business.* Reg. §1.631-1(b)(1). The concept applies both to the *hypothetical sale election* and to a *disposal with a retained economic interest* treated as a *section 1231 asset.*

contract with a retained economic interest see *disposal with a retained economic interest.*

contributed property, partnership allocations property that a *partner* contributed to the *partnership,* as opposed to property subject to claims of creditors of the partnership or property the partnership is merely entitled to use. Reg. §1.704-1(c)(1). The term is used for purposes of §704(c)(1) and (2), which generally treat contributed property as if purchased by the partnership, subject to the partners' duty to specially allocate *depreciation, depletion, gain,* or *loss* as to such property so as to compensate for differences between the cost and the value of the property.

contribution see *political contribution.*

contribution and benefit base a dollar amount (e.g., for 1993, $57,600 maximum earnings on which 6.2 percent Social Security tax will be imposed, and maximum earnings of $135,000 on which 1.45 percent Medicare tax will be imposed) determined pursuant to the Social Security laws. 42 U.S.C. §430. §§3101, 3121, 6413(c). Similarly, *self-employment taxes* are imposed on *net earnings from self-employment* up to this base amount,

reduced by wages earned. §1402(b). The net effect is that regardless of the number of *employers* an *individual* has (including himself), the *employee* will pay these taxes on no more than the base amount of earnings, although each employer must contribute a full share. As a result, Social Security contributions by employers can be duplicated.

contribution base an *individual's adjusted gross income,* computed by disregarding *net operating loss carrybacks.* §170(b)(1)(E). Generally, an individual's annual *charitable contribution deductions* cannot exceed 50 percent of the contribution base. §170(b)(1)(A). Section 170(b)(1)(B) and (C) contain further complex limitations, which are again geared to the individual's contribution base.

contribution not made under a salary reduction agreement *contributions* made: (1) under an *employee's* one-time irrevocable election at the time the employee first becomes eligible to participate; or (2) under a similar arrangement. If a contribution is not made under a salary reduction agreement, then it is not subject to the §402(g) annual limit on *elective deferrals* for *qualified employees* of *qualified organizations.* A similar arrangement has to involve a one-shot irrevocable election, in order that contributions be deemed not made under a salary reduction agreement. §403(b)(12)(A). The importance of the term is that *tax-deferred annuities for exempt and educational organization employees* and state and local governments are subject to nondiscrimination rules for contributions that are not made under a salary reduction agreement. See *tax-deferred annuities for exempt and educational organization employees.*

contribution percentage, matching contributions a fraction determined for each *employee* within a group of employees subject to testing for *nondiscrimination* in connection with *matching contributions* and *contributions by employees.* The fraction equals (1) aggregate matching contributions and contributions by the employees under the plan on behalf of each employee for the *plan year,* divided by (2) the employees's *compensation* (§414(s) definition) for the plan year. §401(m)(3). If the contribution percentage is within tolerances, the plan will not be disqualified. See *matching contribution.*

contribution to capital see *capital contribution.*

contributory plans *pension* or *profit-sharing plans* funded by contributions from both the *employer* and the *employee.*

control, acquisition to evade or avoid tax the ownership of *stock* having at least half of the total combined voting power of all classes of stock entitled to vote, or at least half of the total value of all classes of stock. §269(a).

control, applicable retained interest the holding of at least 50 percent by vote or value of the *stock* of a *corporation,* or at least 50 percent of the *capital* or *profits interests* in a *partnership,* or, in the case of a *limited partnership,* any interest as a *general partner.* §2701(b)(2).

control, corporate reorganizations, divisions, and transfers to controlled corporations the ownership of at least 80 percent of the total combined voting power of all classes of *stock* entitled to vote and at least 80 percent of the total number of shares of all other classes of stock. §368(c). The IRS asserts that 80 percent of the shares of all other classes of stock means 80 percent of each class of stock. Rev. Rul. 59-259, 1959-2 C.B. 115. Entitlement to vote refers to present voting rights. Rev. Rul. 66-339, 1966-2 C.B. 274. *Acquisitive D reorganizations* are subject to a 50 percent test. §368(a)(2)(H).

control, estate freezes at least 50 percent by vote or value of the *stock* of a *corporation,* at least 50 percent of the *capital* or *profits interest* in a *partnership,* or, in the case of a *limited partnership,* any interest held as a *general partner.* §§2701(b)(2) and 2704(c)(1). This term relates to the treatment of lapsing rights and restrictions on *liquidations* of corporations and partnerships.

control group test for purposes of determining whether attorney-client communications regarding tax matters are privileged, hence not subject to discovery, the term refers to limiting the privilege to those in control of corporate affairs.

controlled corporation, transfers see *transfers to controlled corporations.*

controlled entity see *related person, sales of depreciable property to.*

controlled foreign corporation (CFC) a *foreign corporation* in which more than 50 percent of the combined voting power of all classes of *stock* entitled to vote is owned by *United States shareholders* on any day of the *taxable year.* §957. A United States shareholder for these purposes is a *United States person* who owns a 10 percent or larger block of voting stock. Thus, if 11 unrelated United States shareholders each own equal shares, there can never be a CFC; but there can be a CFC if there are 9 equal shareholders. *Attribution rules* apply to determine *constructive ownership* of stock. §958.

controlled group, bonus recovery for purposes of the definition of the term *purchase* for *bonus recovery* purposes and the dollar limitations on bonus recovery, the term has the same meaning as under §1563(a), but using a 50 percent (rather than an 80 percent) level of *stock* ownership to find a controlled group. §179(b)(7). See *controlled group of corporations, graduated taxes, and other benefits.*

controlled group of corporations, graduated taxes and other benefits *corporations* falling into a *parent-subsidiary controlled group, a brother-sister controlled group,* or a *combined group.* Section 1563 defines these groups, and §1561(a) forces the aggregation of (1) graduated *corporate income taxes*; (2) the *accumulated earnings credit,* (3) the $40,000 *exemption amount* granted against the *alternative minimum tax,* and (4) the $2 million *environmental tax* threshold into one imaginary corporation and apportions the four benefits. Corporations caught in the net of §1561(a) include only *component members* (§1563(b)(1) and not so-called *excluded members.*

controlled partnerships a *partnership* in which a *partner* owns, directly or indirectly, more than half of the *capital interest* or *profits interest. Losses* on *sales* and *exchanges* of property between partners and controlled partnerships, or between two partnerships, each of which is a commonly controlled partnership (50 percent of profit or capital interests in both partnerships owned by one or more *persons*), are disallowed (subject to relief on later *dispositions*). §707(b)(1). Also, §707(b)(2) provides that if the sale or exchange is with or between 50 percent controlled partnerships and the transferred property is not a *capital asset* in the transferee's hands (e.g., a rental property sold at a *gain* to a 50 percent controlled partnership that is a real estate *dealer*), the *gain* on the sale or exchange is *ordinary income.* The *attribution rules* of §267(c) *impute* ownership from others to the controlling partner for purposes of §707(b)(1) and (2). §707(b)(3).

controlled sale a *sale of tangible property* between members of a commonly controlled group. The term is used for purposes of the *Commissioner's* power to reallocate income, *deductions, credits,* and so forth under §482. Reg. §1.482-2(e)(1)(i). See *control, reallocations; reallocation of income and deductions by Commissioner.*

controlling interest see *parent-subsidiary group under common control, qualified plans; two or more trades or businesses under common control.*

control, reallocations practical control, whether or not legally enforceable, with a presumption of control if the treatment of items of *gross income* or *deductions* is arbitrary. Reg. §1.482-1(a)(3). The presence of common ownership or control of two or more organizations, *trades,* or *businesses* is a prerequisite to the application of §482, which gives the IRS power to reallocate income, deductions, and the like between such *taxpayers.* The courts have been liberal in applying the IRS's view of the meaning of the term. See *reallocation of income and deductions by Commissioner.*

control, regulated investment companies for purposes of the diversification of investment rules of §854(b)(4)(B) so that the company can qualify as a *reg-*

ulated investment company, the term refers to ownership of 20 percent or more of the total combined voting power of all classes of voting *stock.* §851(c)(2).

convenience of the employer for purposes of §119, the value of meals and lodging provided to the employee and the employee's spouse and dependents is excluded from income if the meals and/or lodging are *furnished* by the employer, on the employer's *business premises* for the *convenience of the employer.*

convention and trade show activity see *qualified convention and trade show activity.*

convention of association of churches no clear definition. The only formal guidance seems to be in §414(e)(3)(D) which states that "an *organization,* whether a civil law *corporation* or otherwise is associated with a church or a convention or association of churches if it shares common religious bonds and convictions of that church or convention or association of churches." The term has the same definition for purposes of certain *annuities* (§403(b)(2)(C)) and the definition of *life insurance* (§7702(j)(3)(A)). It is not clear if a uniform meaning is intended for the entire *Code.*

conversion legally, a nonconsensual taking or destruction of another's property. For example, fatally shooting a neighbor's dog is a conversion. The term is commonly used in connection with government or quasi-governmental takings. See, e.g., §§1033 (*rollovers* of proceeds of *involuntary conversions*) and 1231 (*gains* from conversions of property held for more than six months). The word also refers to two similar tax planning concepts. One involves claiming *depreciation* (or *cost recovery*) *deductions* that are not subject to *recapture* of gain as *ordinary income* on *sale* (e.g., *straight-line depreciation* or *cost recovery* of real estate) but which instead generate *long-term capital gains.*

conversion of ordinary income into capital gain see *conversion.*

conversion return method a method of ascribing a *fair market value* to timber for purposes of the *hypothetical sales election* of §631(a), under which the *taxpayer* determines the price of the first marketable product at the mill (e.g., logs) and then subtracts costs and a risk and profit margin to determine value when cut.

converted wetland generally, land which has been drained or filled so that it can be used for agricultural purposes. The land must be held by the person who converted it or who now farms it. The *basis* of the land is determined by reference to the basis on the land of the person who converted it. Converted wetland is defined in 16 USC §3801(4). *Gains* on the *disposition* of the land are treated as *ordinary income,* and *losses* are treated as *long-term capital losses.* §1257. *Highly erodable croplands* are subject to similar treatment.

convertible bond, amortization or premium not clearly defined. Evidently, any conversion privilege, even if based on detachable warrants, gives rise to a convertible bond if the holder can exercise the privilege. Reg. §1.171-2(c)(3). The value of the conversion privilege must be extracted in determining the amount of the *bond premium.* §171(b)(1). See *amortizable bond premium of the taxable year.*

convertible debentures plan a *deferred compensation* plan under which participants purchase convertible debentures subject to restrictions on transferability.

convertible override oil and gas jargon for an arrangement under which an owner of an *overriding royalty* can convert that interest into a *working interest* at some future date.

convertible override farm-out a *farm-out* arrangement under which the *farmor* retains an *overriding royalty* which may, at the farmor's option, be converted into a share of the *working interest* on the *farmee's* payout. It is a form of subleasing arrangement used in the oil and gas industry.

cooperation and participation see *international boycott activity, participation and cooperation.*

cooperative bank an institution without capital stock, organized and operated for mutual purposes and without profit, that is either insured or subject to the supervision and examination of a state of federal authority, and meets the *assets test* and *business operations test* imposed on *domestic building and loan associations.* §7701(a)(32). Such organizations are entitled to claim a *deduction* for amounts paid or credited to their depositors. §591; Reg. §1.591.1. They are treated as *domestic building and loan associations.* Reg. §301.7701-14. For these purposes, the term excludes banks for cooperatives organized under the Farm Credit Act of 1933. Rev. Rul. 73-497, 1973-2 C.B. 314. It is basically a state-chartered savings and loan association peculiar to a fairly small number of states.

cooperative hospital service organization, exempt an organization that is organized and operated solely to provide certain centralized services for a *tax-exempt* hospital (or several exempt or government hospitals), which services would be exempt if performed by the hospital itself. The services are data processing, purchasing, warehousing, billing and collection, food, clinical, industrial engineering, laboratory, printing, communications, record center, and personnel (including selection, testing, training, and education of personnel) services. Such organizations are deemed tax-exempt hospitals, gifts to which qualify for the *charitable contribution deduction.* §501(e).

cooperative housing corporations *corporations* having one class of *stock,* each *shareholder* of which has a right to occupy an apartment in a building or development owned or leased by the corporation, none of whom has a right to *current distributions* that are not out of *earnings and profits,* which derive 80 percent or more of their gross income from *tenant-shareholders.* §216; Reg. §1.216-1(d). Such corporations (co-ops) generally cause their tenant shareholders to be treated as the true owners of the *real estate,* such that they can deduct their pro rata shares (based on stockholdings) of *depreciation,* mortgage *interest,* and *taxes* paid by the corporation, but in doing so, they deprive the corporation of its entitlement to *deductions* so claimed. The determination of exempt co-op status is made annually. (Co-ops must report the *proportional share of interest* paid by *tenant-shareholders* to the IRS annually.) Rev. Rul. 59-257, 1959-2 C.B. 101. See Private Letter Rul. 8338018, June 15, 1983 (offices as cooperative housing units).

cooperative member see *member, cooperatives.*

cooperatives *corporations operating on a cooperative basis* and allocating amounts to their *patrons* on the basis of business done with or for them. Reg. §1.1381-1(a). Nonfarm cooperatives are subject to a set of general rules, the gist of which is that the organization goes untaxed to the extent it distributes its earnings to its *patrons,* who are in turn generally taxed, while failure to make distributions results in taxation of the *entity* as a business *corporation.* Cooperatives appear to fall into several different functional classifications, namely those for consumers (often called purchasing cooperatives), those for producers, and those for workers. Rev. Rul. 61-47, 1961-1 C.B. 147 as to the latter. See *cooperative housing corporations; patronage dividend.*

cooperative service organizations of operating educational organizations, exempt basically, *exempt organizations* investing the funds of tax-exempt educational organizations. §501(f). The *Code* defines these entities as organizations that are organized and operated solely to hold and invest (including overseeing independent investment services), in *stocks* and securities, moneys contributed by their members, and to collect *income* thereon, turning it over, net of expenses, to their members. Such organizations must be organized and controlled by one or more of their members. If these conditions are met, the entity is granted exempt status, and *deductions* to them evidently qualify as *charitable contributions,* since §501(f) deems the organization a *charitable organization.*

cooperative telephone companies see *mutual or cooperative telephone companies.*

coordinated examination program team *audits* of large businesses using experienced *revenue agents, engineer agents, economists,* and so forth. See I.R.M. 42(11)l et seq. and M.T. 4200-381 (Jan. 29, 1980).

co-ownership of property fee ownership of property divided between or among two or more *persons.* Co-ownership may or may not constitute a *partnership.* Passive co-ownership, such as a joint undertaking merely to share expenses, is not a partnership. Reg. §1.761-1(a). However, co-owners who actively carry on *a trade* or *business* are considered partners. For example, where two or more *individuals* own an apartment building, lease space, and provide services to the occupants either directly or through an agent, they are considered partners. Reg. §1.761-1(a). Section 761 authorizes certain enterprises to elect out of partnership status. See *section 761 election.*

copycat ruling a request for *ruling* based on theories and facts all but identical to a prior ruling submitted by a different *taxpayer.* The pattern is facilitated by the IRS's obligation to provide *background file documents* on request.

copyright royalties *royalties* generated from the licensing or other use of copyrighted musical, literary, or other artistic works. See Reg. §1.543-1(b)(12)(iv) for an elaborate definition for the taxation of *personal holding companies.*

core benefits not defined in the *Code,* but it apparently refers to *accident or health plan* benefits other than coverage for dental, vision, psychological, orthodontia, or psychological help. The term is used for purposes of defining *excludable employees* for purposes of certain *welfare benefit plans.*

core testing a term used in the oil and gas industry to describe the geological practice of drilling below the topsoil in order to evaluate the structure and formation of subsurface samples.

Corn Products doctrine a judicial doctrine that narrows the definition of a *capital asset* (§1221) to exclude inventory-related property that is integrally tied to the day-to-day operations of a *business.* For example, if stock acquired by a shareholder was held for purposes connected with the taxpayer's trade or business, then, under the *Corn Products doctrine,* the gain or loss may be considered ordinary. For example, stock in a corporation may have been purchased to ensure the taxpayer an adequate supply of raw materials for his business.

corporate acquisition indebtedness *debt* obligations (as defined generally under the *debt-equity rules* of §385) issued after October 9, 1969, for the purpose of directly or indirectly acquiring either the *stock* or two-thirds of the noncash operating assets of another corporation, but only if (1) the debt is subordinated; (2) the debt is convertible into *stock* or is issued along with *warrants* to buy stock; and (3) the debtor corporation is either thinly capitalized (debt to net book worth is over 2:1), or its average earnings for the three-year period ending with the year the debt is issued are not more than twice its annual interest costs. For these purposes, interest includes *unstated interest* and *original issue discount* as well as disguised interest. §279(b). In order to limit debt-financed corporate takeovers, §279(a) provides that organizations may not *deduct* more than $5 million per year of *interest* on corporate acquisition indebtedness.

corporate contraction a standard used to test for a *partial liquidation*. See *contraction of business.*

corporate division the separation, often without recognition of *gain* or *loss* to the *shareholders* and security holders, of two or more existing *trades or businesses* (whether or not separately incorporated at the outset) formerly operated, directly or indirectly, by a single *corporation* (the distributing corporation). §355, Reg. §1.355-1(a). If a corporation has control (80 percent control as defined in §368(c)) of another corporation, stock in a subsidiary can be distributed to the shareholders of the parent corporation tax-free if certain requirements of §355 are met. When a subsidiary is newly formed to perfect a corporate division, §355 applies through §368(a)(1)(D) (a corporate divisive reorganization). However, if the subsidiary already exists, §355 alone applies. Three types of transactions are used to effect a corporation division: *spin-off, split-off,* and *split-up.* See also *Type D reorganization.*

corporate equity reduction transaction a transaction in which one *corporation* (an *applicable corporation*) acquires 50 percent or more by vote or by value of the *stock* of another corporation (a *major stock acquisition*) or when a corporation makes an extraordinarily large *distribution* (including a *major stock redemption*) to its *shareholders* (*an excess distribution*). §172(m)(3)(A). Section 172(m) limits the ability of a *C corporation* involved in a CERT to carry back a *net operating loss* incurred in the year of the CERT or in either of the two succeeding years to a pre-CERT *taxable year,* thereby preventing a corporation that engages in a leveraged buyout or leveraged recapitalization from using *losses* generated by *interest expense deductions* to get *tax refunds* paid in prior years.

corporate income tax an *income tax* imposed on *corporations* at rates varying from 15 percent to 34 percent of *taxable income.* §11.

corporate liquidation the winding up of a *corporation* and the *distribution* of its assets, regardless of whether it is legally dissolved. See *complete liquidation, corporate.*

corporate preference item items that may result in the imposition of the corporate *alternative minimum tax.* §§55–58. Because they produce tax savings, tax preference items must be added back to a corporation's taxable income to compute alternative *minimum taxable income (AMTI)* so that unreasonably high tax breaks can be recaptured. Tax preference items include depletion, excess intangible drilling costs, bad debt reserves, private activity bonds interest, appreciated property charitable deductions, and accelerated depreciation and

amortization on pre-1987 property. §57(a). See *alternative minimum tax.*

corporate reorganization for federal *income tax* purposes, one of an exclusive list of specific transactions defined in §368(a)(1), under which corporate structures may be rearranged on a potentially tax-free basis, varying from simple *recapitalizations* and changes on a potentially tax-free basis of state of incorporation to complex acquisitions, *mergers,* and *consolidations.* See *Type A reorganization; Type B reorganization; Type C reorganization; Type D reorganization; Type E reorganization; Type F reorganization; Type G reorganization.*

corporation generally, an organization formed under state, federal, or foreign corporation laws, having shareholders, directors, officers, and limited liability. For federal *income tax* purposes the term refers to an *association (trust, estate,* or *partnership)* with a requisite set of corporate characteristics, regardless of its label under local law. *See* Reg. §301.7701-2. See *association taxable as a corporation.*

corporation-shareholder loan any *below-market loan* directly or indirectly between a *corporation* and one of its *shareholders.* §7872(c)(1))(C).

corpus the principal (res) of a *trust* or an *estate* as opposed to its income.

correction of an error the correction of a deviation from a permissible *method of accounting* that does not require *IRS* approval. The *regulations* generally provide that any consistently applied accounting practice is a method of accounting, whether or not permissible, and that IRS consent to change such a method is required. Reg. §1.446-1(e). Nonetheless, an inconsistently used impermissible method should be a mere error (not a method of accounting) that can be corrected without IRS consent. Also, bookkeeping errors and miscategorizations are not methods of accounting. Reg. §1.446-1(e)(2)(ii)(b).

correction period generally, a statutorily fixed period during which some particular wrongdoing can be reversed, thereby avoiding penalties. See, e.g., §§4941 (*self-dealing* by a private foundation), 4943 (*excess business holdings*), 4944 (*speculative investments*), and 4975 (*prohibited transactions* by *qualified plans*).

correction period, private foundations a period beginning with the occurrence of an act of *self-dealing,* (or other proscribed acts) and ending on the earliest of (1) when the *IRS* issues the taxpayer a *deficiency notice* based on the act; or (2) when it assesses the deficiency; or (3) when the act is reversed ("corrected"). §4941(e)(1). The taxable period measure applies to the additional penalty taxes on *undistributed income* (§4942(j)(2)), *excess business holdings* (§4043(d)(3), and *speculative investments* (§4945(i)(2)).

correction period, qualified plan see *taxable period qualified plan.*

corrective return see *amended return.*

correct tax the tax determined by the *IRS for deficiencies.* The term includes liabilities for *self-employment taxes* and certain penalties. §§6211(a), 6659(a) and (b). The term is important because no *assessment* of deficiencies is permissible without a *statutory notice of deficiency (90-day letter),* and without knowledge of the correct tax, there can be no deficiency.

correlative adjustment generally, a term referring to adjustments to account for reallocations imposed on *taxpayers* under §482. Reg. §1.482-1(d)(2). For example, if a brother *corporation's* income is reduced by $1,000 as a result of correction of a bargain purchase of property from its sister corporation, the correlative adjustment is an increase of the sister corporation's income of $1,000. The purpose of the correlative adjustment is to place related business taxpayers on the footing they would have been on had they engaged in *arm's length* transactions with each other. See *reallocation of income and deductions by Commissioner.*

correlative deductions and credits, mitigation of the statute of limitation and other provisions a reference to the headings of §1312(5) and (6). These subsections effectively allow the elimination of inconsistencies in (1) *inclusions* and *deductions* for *trusts, estates,* and *beneficiaries*; or (2) *deductions* and *credits* of affiliated corporations, which might otherwise be impossible. See *mitigation of effect of statutes of limitations and other provisions.*

correspondence audit an *audit* undertaken by the *IRS* using the mail. Ordinarily, such audits relate to relatively minor issues. It is also called a correspondence examination.

corrupt interference with tax administration see *interference with tax administration.*

cost basis *basis of property* purchased or acquired in a purchase or taxable *exchange* on or after March 1, 1913. Cost refers to cash paid or the *fair market value* of property or services received in the exchange. §1012; Reg. §1.1012-1. If the value of the property received cannot be determined, the value of the property given up becomes the cost basis of property received. Thus, if property is taken in exchange for services or other property of uncertain value, the value of the property will become its basis under the *barter exchange method.* Liabilities assumed by and taken subject to the acquiror in connection with the acquisition or encumbering of the property at the time of the acquisition are included as part of basis, provided they arise out of *arm's length* transactions, and are not speculative.

cost, bonus expensing of recovery property the cost of *recovery property,* excluding the portion of the property's *basis* determined by reference to the basis of property held by the *taxpayer* at any time. §179(d)(3). Thus, if *recovery property* is received in a trade-in or in some other *like-kind exchange,* only the additional consideration (e.g., cash payment) is part of the cost of the property received.

cost completion method a method of determining the percentages of completion of a contract in the year, applied by comparing the costs incurred under the contract with total contract costs. Reg. §1.451-3(c)(2)(i). It is one application of the *percentage of completion method of accounting.*

cost, defined benefit plan for purposes of determining the limitation on allowable *deductions* for contributions to *defined benefit plans,* the term means the actuarially determined amount needed to adequately fund the plan over the coming years, taking into account intricate considerations such as anticipated plan earnings, mortality, turnover, including amounts needed to *amortize past service liabilities.* §404(a)(1).

cost depletion a method of *depletion* applied to exhaustible natural resources, including timber. The method depends on dividing the *adjusted basis* of the resources by the number of *recoverable units* (e.g., barrels or cubic feet) of the natural resource, and then *deducting* the cost of the portion of the recoverable units extracted and sold during the *taxable year.* The *deduction* can be claimed until the total investment is recovered. §§611 and 612. For example, if the adjusted basis of coal in the ground is $1,000 and there are 100 recoverable tons of coal in the ground, and the *taxpayer* extracts and sells 10 tons of coal this year, the cost depletion for the year is $100.

cost, inventory valuation a method of valuing year-end *inventories* by which goods on hand at the beginning of the year are valued at the inventory price, and goods purchased during the year are valued at cost, less discounts (unless consistently included in income), plus transportation and other costs of acquisition. The cost of manufactured goods includes the cost of raw materials and supplies and direct labor as well as certain indirect production costs (e.g., a share of management expenses) as demanded by *full absorption accounting.* Reg. §1.471-3 and -11. Section 263A (*uniform capitalization rules*) greatly expands the components of cost to include rather remote elements.

cost of goods sold opening *inventories* plus purchases of further inventory during the *taxable year* minus *closing inventory.* This amount is subtracted from annual sales to determine *gross income* (or *loss*) from *businesses* that use *inventory accounting.* Section 471 authorizes the *IRS* to compel the use of inventory accounting where appropriate. By its nature, inventory accounting includes, in cost of goods sold, the cost of such expenses as pilferage and casualties.

cost-of-living adjustments, qualified plans adjustments based on §215(i)(2)(A) of the Social Security Act, which increase maximum contributions and benefits payable to or for *participants* in *qualified plans.* §415(d) (increasing contribution or benefit bases during employment). For example, defined contribution plan contributions are limited to the smaller of $30,000 or 25 percent of the employee's compensation. The $30,000 limit is not increased until the defined contribution limit (which is adjusted for inflation) is in excess of $120,000. After the $120,000 amount is exceeded, the defined contribution amount is then 25 percent of the defined benefit limit. §415(c). See also *qualified cost-of-living arrangement.*

cost oil see *production payment.*

cost or market inventory see *lower of cost or market, inventory valuation.*

cost-plus method in business parlance, the provision of goods or services at a price reflecting the provider's cost plus a fixed mark-up. In connection with the *IRS's* power to adjust transactions between commonly controlled *taxpayers,* Reg. §1.482-2(e)(4) describes a cost-plus system applied for purposes of §482 to sales of property between such taxpayers. See *comparable uncontrolled price method.*

cost recovery *depreciation* claimed under §168, relating to the *accelerated cost recovery system.*

cost recovery method a synonym of the *open transaction* method of reporting *gains* or *losses.* See *open transactions.*

cost-sharing arrangement see *bona fide cost-sharing arrangement.*

cost-sharing election, possessions corporations an election by a *possessions corporation* in lieu of being subject to the provisions relating to *intangible property income.* The election applies where a United States parent corporation or another United States affiliated corporation (*mainland affiliate*) transfers certain manufacturing intangibles to its United States subsidiary or affiliate operating in a possession (*island affiliate*), but only if the island affiliate shares the annual *product area research expenditures* of the mainland affiliate and its affiliates (as defined under §482), and has a *significant business presence* in the possession (Puerto Rico or United States Virgin Islands). If these conditions are met, the possessions corporation is entitled, in computing its *taxable income,* to a *deduction* for its share of the collective cost of researching and developing the intangible. See Reg. §1.936-6(a)(4). The corporation must usually pay the costs to members of its affiliated group

that bore the costs not later than when its *tax return* is due. The payees treat the payments as cost reductions. Assuming the election is properly in place, the *intercompany pricing rules* of §482 are used to determine a full and fair return on manufacturing intangibles. §936(h)(5)(C)(i). An alternative to the cost-sharing plan is the *profit-split method.*

cost-sharing payments, conservation generally, payments made by a government to a landowner (commonly an owner of timber lands) to reimburse a share of improvements made to land in the interest of conservation. Section 126 provides that a limited amount (the so-called *excludable portion*) of specialized cost-sharing payments under certain government programs do not constitute *gross income,* to the extent the value of the *taxpayer's* property is not increased by the payment. §126(b)(1). *Recapture* is required for amounts excluded from *gross income* when property that qualifies for §126 treatment is disposed of. §1255. See *section 1255 recapture.*

coupon, coupon stripping generally, any right to receive *interest* on a bond (whether or not evidenced by a coupon). §128(e)(5). The definition is modified for certain pre–July 2, 1982 purchases. *Id.*; §1286(c). See *anti-coupon stripping rules.*

coupon stripping the tax avoidance practice of detaching interest coupons from a bond and promptly selling the bond as a *dealer* so as to recognize an immediate *ordinary loss.* For the legislative remedy under *TEFRA,* see *anti-coupon stripping rules.*

courtesy discounts discounts on purchases furnished or offered by the *employer* to *employees,* generally in order to boost health, goodwill, contentment, or efficiency of employees. Regulations §31.3401-1(b)(10) disregards such items as *wages,* and they are generally viewed as excludable from income. Free railroad passes are also so treated. O.D. 946, 4 C.B. 110 (1921). However, §132 now handles them as potential *qualified employee discounts.* See *qualified employee discounts* for a group of nontaxable courtesy discounts that appears to overlap with this entry.

Court Holding Company doctrine a tax law doctrine with continuing vitality, the effect of which is that if sales of corporate property really occur at the corporate level, the *corporation* will be taxed as the true seller.

Court of Appeals, Federal any of 13 federal courts (one per circuit plus the *Federal Circuit*) that, among other things, hears appeals of decisions of the *Tax Court,* the Federal *District Court,* and the *Claims Court.*

Court of Appeals for the Federal Circuit see *Federal Circuit.*

covenant not to compete a contract in which the seller of a business agrees not to compete with the buyer.

Generally, amounts paid pursuant to such covenants are treated *as deductible* to the buyer and *ordinary income* to the seller and will not be recharacterized absent *strong proof* to the contrary. It was generally agreed that specific allocations of purchase prices on the sale of a business cannot be attacked by the parties to the transaction in the absence of fraud, duress, or undue influence. See *residual method*.

coverage, qualified plans a *participation requirement for qualified plans*. The term refers to the group of *employees* required to be benefited under the retirement plan. Since a qualified plan must be primarily for the benefit of employees and must be nondiscriminatory, the plan has to cover a reasonable percentage of the company employees. There are three tests for determining reasonable coverage; meeting any one test will satisfy the coverage requirement. The first two tests are both numerical tests and a discrimination test. The numerical tests require that 70 percent or more of all employees must benefit, and that certain *minimum age and service requirements be met*. §410(a)(1). Under the discrimination test, the plan must not discriminate in favor of employees who are officers, shareholders, or *highly compensated*. §410(b)(1)(B); Reg. §1.410(b)-1(b)(2). §410(b)(3); Reg. §1.410(b)-1(b)(2) and -1(c). See *minimum age and service requirements*. See also *collectively bargained plan; qualified deferred compensation plan*.

covered compensation for an *employee,* the amount of compensation with respect to which old-age and survivors insurance benefits would be provided under the Social Security Act, if for each year until age 65 annual compensation is at least equal to the *taxable wage base* (the top amount on which Social Security taxes are imposed). Rev. Rul. 71-446, 1971-2 C.B. 187. The term is important for *integration* with Social Security. Section 401(1)(4)(C) and (5)(C) have a specific definition for purposes of future *regulations* relating to integration. See *permitted disparity*.

covered sale see *profit-split method*.

covered service employment with one or more *employers* who maintain a *qualified plan* covering specific job classifications or classes of *employees*. Labor Reg. §2530.210(c)(3)(ii) and (iii). The term is used to calculate *coverage* and *participation*. The definition could reasonably be applied elsewhere in the qualified plan area. Noncovered service is service with such an employer or employers that is not covered service. See *coverage, qualified plans; participation requirement, qualified plans*.

Crane doctrine a judicial doctrine stating that the *basis of property* (§1011 et seq.) includes *debt* assumed or attached to property at the time of acquisition; such *debt* is included in the *amount realized* for determining *gain* or *loss* under §1001.

credit an amount that directly offsets tax liabilities, as opposed to a *deduction* that only reduces the tax base. The credits are found in §§21–53. Credits may either reduce income taxes for the year (e.g., *energy investment credits* for certain machinery) or operate as prepayments of tax in determination of net taxes due for the year (e.g., *estimated tax* payments and *wage* withholdings). Certain credits are *refundable,* in that, if such credits exceed *taxable income* for the year, the excess is paid to the *taxpayer*. Others are *nonrefundable*.

credit for certain uses of gasoline and special fuels a *refundable credit* allowed to ultimate buyers of gasoline and other fuels. It is generated by the manufacturers' *excise tax* on such fuels in cases where the fuel is used for off-highway purposes, on farms, by local transit systems, operators of buses for nontaxable purposes, and for diesel fuel vehicles. The tax arises under §§6420, 6421, and 6427. The credit arises under §34(a).

creditable foreign taxes the term used to describe *foreign taxes* that qualify for the *foreign tax credit*.

credit for increasing research activities a twofold means of encouraging research and experimental activities: (1) Research and experimental expenditures may be either deducted or capitalized and amortized over a period of 60 months or more under §174; and (2) a 20 percent tax credit for increasing qualified research expenses as well as a 20 percent credit for basic research payments is available under the tax law. §41(a). The research credit expired on June 30, 1992. See *basic research payments; in-house research expenses; qualified research*.

credit for interest on certain home mortgages a *nonrefundable credit* of up to $2,000, designed to allow certain low-income *taxpayers* to obtain a *tax benefit* for home *mortgage interest expenses* related to their *principal residences,* available in states that have not fully used their authority to issue tax-exempt *mortgage subsidy bonds*. See §25.

credit for overpayment of tax a *refundable credit* for overpaid taxes. §6401. See *refund or credit*.

credit for producing fuels from nonconventional sources a *nonrefundable credit* allowed for the *domestic* production of *qualified fuels* (such as fuel from coal seams, tar sands, and geopressured brine) and sold to unrelated *persons,* generally at the rate of $3 per energy equivalent of one barrel of oil produced and sold from a well drilled, or a facility *placed in service,* before 1993 if the fuels are sold before 2003. (The credit is reduced by the excess of the aggregate *general business credit* claimed on a project that got the *enhanced oil recovery credit* over the aggregate amount of credit that was *recaptured*). See *gas from geopressured brine, Devonian shale, coal seams or a tight formation, credit for producing fuels from*.

credit for state death taxes the *credit* that a *decedent's estate* receives against its *federal estate tax* liability for payments of *state* inheritance, estate, legacy, or succession taxes. The credit allowed is limited to the lesser of the amount of the tax actually paid or the amount provided for in a table contained in §2011(b). The table amount is based on the adjusted taxable estate, which for this purpose is the taxable estate less $60,000. No credit is allowed if the adjusted taxable estate is $40,000 or less.

credit for tax withheld from foreign taxpayers a *refundable* credit against *federal income* taxes granted to *nonresident aliens* and *foreign corporations* that were subjected to United States withholding taxes. §33. See *withholding of tax at source.*

credit for the elderly and disabled a *nonrefundable* credit equal to 15 percent of a limited base, the amount of which depends on whether the taxpayers are over *age 65* or under 65 and retired due to permanent and total disability. The general credit is based on different initial amounts, depending on age and filing status: $5,000 for one 65-year-old *spouse,* or $7,500 if both are over 65 and filing a *joint return,* but $3,750 if filing separately. These initial amounts are reduced by amounts received as pension, annuity, or disability benefits that are excludable from gross income and by *adjusted gross income* over certain fixed amounts. In effect, the maximum credit is $1,125 (15 percent × $7,500) for a joint return, both age 65 or older, phasing out at the rate of 50 cents on the dollar to zero if their adjusted gross income is $17,500 or more.

credit for withholding of tax at source a *refundable* credit granted by §§1462 and 1464 for excessive *withholding of tax at source* on *nonresident aliens* and *foreign corporations.* Section 1462 lets the *foreign person* credit the withholding against taxes due, and §1464 generally directs that the *withholding agent* gets the credit.

credit life company a company that writes *life insurance policies* designed to ensure that creditors will be paid in the event of the death of the debtor-insured; the coverage is ordinarily the unpaid balance of the loan. Although they may merely act as reinsurers, such companies can qualify as *life insurance companies.*

creditor release rule a term that reflects the view that because no *property* remains after a debtor pays off an obligation, there can be no *sale or exchange* of property in such circumstances, and that the creditor has *ordinary income* if the *amount realized* by the creditor differs from the creditor's *basis* in the property. For example, X issues a note with a face amount of $1,000 to a seller. The seller transfers the note to Y for $800 in cash. Y later recovers $900 on the note from X. Y's *gain* of $100 is *ordinary income,* according to the creditor release rule, because no property survives the transaction (other than cash Y now holds). §1271.

credit period, low-income housing credit see *eligible basis, low-income housing credit.*

credit unions, exempt credit unions operating without capital stock, if organized and operated for mutual purposes and without profit, as well as nonstock organizations formed before September 1, 1957, to provide reserve funds and insurance to *domestic building and loan associations, cooperative banks,* and *mutual savings banks* without shares. §501(c)(14). Such organizations are entitled to operate on a tax-exempt basis, but no *charitable contribution deduction* is allowed for transfers to them.

creeping acquisitions a colloquial term for acquisitions of one *corporation* by another in a series of steps; the term has not been set in concrete. For example, in *Type A reorganizations* if cash purchases of major amounts of *stock* are followed by a *merger* of the target into the acquiring corporation, the result may be a failed reorganization, on the proper theory that target company shareholders sold out, such that there is insufficient *continuity of proprietary interest.* Type B reorganizations may safely creep in the sense that *control* of the target need not be obtained in a single transaction. §368(a)(1)(B). Multistep acquisitions create some of the most difficult classification problems in corporate tax law and call for scrupulous planning.

crew leader rules tax jargon for rules that specify who is the *employer* of certain agricultural workers, under which the crew leader is considered the employer if he or she furnishes *individuals* to perform *agricultural labor* for another *person* and pays those individuals without having a written contract (with that other person) designating the crew leader to be the employee of that other person. §3121(o). For purposes of *income tax withholding,* similar rules apply. §3401(h).

criminal conspiracy a conspiracy by two or more persons to defraud the United States government, or any of its agencies, in any fashion, provided at least one of the conspirators does an act to effect the object of the conspiracy. 18 U.S.C. §371. This general provision can apply to tax oriented conspiracies and can result in five years in prison, a $10,000 penalty, or both.

criminal fraud a nontechnical term for a series of *willful* deceptions practiced on the *IRS,* which result in the imposition of criminal penalties. §§7201–7207. See *civil fraud; fraud; willful attempt to evade tax.*

Criminal Investigation Division a division of each *District Office* of the *IRS,* responsible for the criminal statutes applicable to federal tax laws. The Division develops information about alleged criminal violations, evaluates indications of such violations to determine whether investigations should begin, and recommends prosecution, if warranted. Criminal Investigation Division personnel assist IRS and *Justice Department* attorneys in grand jury proceedings and trials of criminal tax cases.

criminal referral   referral of a case under civil *audit*, or in *collection*, etc., to the *Criminal Investigation Division* for consideration as a possible criminal case.

criminal tax evasion   see *tax evasion*.

criminal tax penalties   fines and/or imprisonment for violation of revenue laws, enforced only by prosecution. In general, unless imprisonment is possible, even the most extortionate monetary penalty retains its character as "civil" as long as the legislature does not slip and call it "criminal."

crop-financing organizations, exempt   a *corporation* organized by an *exempt farmers' cooperative* or its members for the purpose of financing the ordinary crop operations of the members or other producers, and operating in conjunction with the co-op. Such organizations are granted flexibility as to having stock and reserves. §501(c)(16); Reg. §1.501(c)(16)-1. They can operate on a tax-exempt basis, but no *charitable contribution deduction* is allowed for transfers to them.

crop method   a *method of accounting* authorized by Reg. §162-12(a) by which *farmers* raising a crop (e.g., sugar cane) that requires more than one year between the time of planting and disposal, may *defer expenses* until *realization* of the *income* from the crop. The *IRS*'s consent is required in order to use this method. Reg. §1.162-12(a).

crop year pool   annual harvests received by a tobacco growers' *cooperative* as collateral for farm price support loans and held for sale when a price approved by the Commodity Credit Corporation can be obtained. §1382(g). See *completed crop pool method of accounting*.

cross purchase agreement   an agreement between or among owners of a *business* under which the continuing owners purchase the ownership interest of the withdrawing or deceased owner. See also *buy-sell agreement; entity buy-sell agreement*.

cruise ship   *taxpayers* can deduct $2,000 ($4,000 on a joint return) for seminars, etc., on a United States registered cruise ship that sticks to United States and *possessions* ports, providing the meeting is sufficiently profit-oriented. §274(h)(2) and (5).

Crummey trust provisions   the language in a *trust*, giving the *beneficiary* (usually a minor) the right to demand a withdrawal of funds from the trust for some reasonable period of time, sometimes combined with provisions to the effect that all accumulated, unexpended income is to be paid to the minor upon his or her reaching majority. See PLR 8004172, (Nov. 5, 1979); Rev. Rul. 81-7, 1981-1 C.B. 474.

Cumulative Bulletins   official publications that contain compilations of *Internal Revenue Bulletins*, classified by year, volume number, and page. Thus, 1976-2 C.B. 211 indicates page 211 of the second volume of Cumulative Bulletins for 1976.

cumulative list of exempt organizations   a list of organizations that the *IRS* declares exempt from federal *income taxes*, referred to as IRS Publication No. 78, upon which *taxpayers* are generally entitled to rely in claiming *charitable contribution deductions*. Rev. Proc. 72-39, 1972-2 C.B. 818. An organization not on the list may still be exempt.

current earnings and profits   a tax account maintained by *corporations* to determine the extent that *distributions* are allocable to current *income*, hence, taxable as *dividends* to *shareholders* under §301. Current earnings and profits are not defined in the *Code*, but they are determined by beginning with current *taxable income* and making the following principal adjustments: (1) subtract items that reduce wealth but are not *deductible* (e.g., *fines and penalties* and *federal income taxes*); (2) add items that are not taxable but that increase wealth (e.g., tax-free interest income); and (3) add *deductions* that do not deplete wealth (e.g., *depreciation* in excess of *straight-line* and the *dividends-received deductions*). Accumulated earnings and profits consist of net accumulations of prior positive and negative current earnings and profits, as reduced by distributions from the account. To the extent of a positive balance in current earnings and profits at the end of the year, it is added to the accumulated earnings and profits account (which may be positive or negative), thereby increasing the account (or reducing the deficit) in the following year. Likewise, negative year-end current earnings and profits reduce the accumulated account or increase its deficit. §316; Reg. §1.316-1 and -2. The computational details are complex. If there are no earnings and profits, a distribution represents a tax-free return of capital rather than a taxable dividend.

current life insurance protection, qualified plans   generally, the excess of amounts payable at the death of the insured over the life insurance policy's *cash surrender value* at year-end. Reg. §1.72-16(b)(3). The *employee* is taxed on the imputed value of such coverage in amounts not less than the values generated under the so-called *PS-58 rates*, provided the *trust* is not entitled to retain the *death proceeds*. §72(m)(3)(B); Reg. §1.72-16 (b)(6).

currently distributable income of estate   income that the *fiduciary* has a duty to distribute to *beneficiaries* under the terms of the *decedent's* last will. Such distributions may be *deducted* from the *estate's taxable income* and may be payable from the *income* or *corpus*. §661(a)(1); Reg. §§1.661(a)(2), 1.651(a)-2(a). See *fiduciary accounting income*.

currently distributable income of trust income that the *fiduciary* has a duty to distribute to *beneficiaries* under the terms of the *trust* in a *taxable year*. Such distributions may be *deducted* from the trust's *taxable income* and may be payable from the *income* or the *corpus*. §661(a)(1); Reg. §§1.661(a)(2) and 1.651(a)-2. See *income, fiduciary accounting income*.

current period of participation any period of consecutive *plan years of participation* beginning with the first day of the first *plan year* of participation in the period and ending with the last day of the last consecutive plan year of participation in the period. The status of an *employee* at the time the employee's current period of participation began (i.e., as a *common law employee, self-employed individual,* or *shareholder-employee*) is not relevant. Reg. §1.401(j)-1(c)(4)(ii). It is used in calculating the *basic benefit* accruing under a *defined benefit plan* that covers self-employed individuals or shareholder-employees, to determine whether the benefits under the plan are excessive. Reg. §1.401(j)-1, -3 and -5.

current-year business credit a credit equal to the sum of the *investment tax credit, targeted jobs credit, alcohol fuels credit, research credit,* and *low-income housing credit* determined for the taxable year. §38(b). It is part of the *general business credit.* The targeted jobs credit and low-income housing credit expired on June 30, 1992.

current-year cost, LIFO the cost of *inventory* at current-year prices. Such values are used in various aspects of the *last-in, first-out* (LIFO) inventory method. See, e.g., *dollar-value method; double-extension method; index method.*

current-year loss deficit rule section 959(c), which limits a *controlled foreign corporation's subpart F income* to its *earnings and profits* for the year. This permits the corporation to offset subpart F income with other categories of income. This benefit reverses itself in later years. See §959(c)(2). A companion provision—the *accumulated deficit rule*—lets prior years' deficits reduce subpart F income.

current-year obligations, black lung benefit trust the total funding needed to increase the amount in a *black lung benefit trust* to the sum needed to disburse all amounts payable out of the trust for the *taxable year.* The coal mine operator (or other *taxpayer*) may *deduct* the amount *contributed* to pay such claims if the *trust* has insufficient funds to do so. §192(b)(2).

custodial account an account, typically established with a bank or securities firm pursuant to the *Uniform Gifts to Minor Act,* which has the practical effect of a *trust.* The custodian may pay *income* to or for the

minor, or simply accumulate the funds. The child for whom the account is established is taxed on and entitled to the account's income, and becomes entitled to the principal and undistributed income on attaining majority. In the interim, legal title to the property is held by the custodian, often a parent. See Rev. Rul. 56-484, 1956-2 C.B. 23.

custodial account, qualified plan an account established with banks (defined in §401(d)(1)) or other *IRS*-approved *custodians* and used as intermediaries for the investment of funds of various *deferred compensation* arrangements. §401(f). To be eligible for *qualified plan* status such accounts must meet the general requirements of §401(a) regarding *qualified trusts.* §401(f)(1). If they do, for practical purposes these accounts become trusts (e.g., such that the funds may be freed from current taxation).

custodial parent the parent who has custody of a child. Regulation §1.152-4(b) provides an order of priority for determining who has primary custody. One first evaluates the most recent decree (or if none, the *written separation agreement*). If there is no answer because the parents suggest split custody or are silent as to custody of the child during the year, then greater actual custody generally controls which person can claim the child as a *dependent.*

custodian someone who has been lawfully appointed to take custody of a thing or *person.* The *Uniform Gifts to Minors Act* calls for putting property for the benefit of minors into the hands of a custodian.

customer a person for whom a *broker* has transacted any business. §6045(c)(2). Under §6045(a), a broker may have to furnish the *IRS* with such persons' names and addresses in a *return.* §6045(a). A broker will be required to give all customers included in his return a written statement showing the name and address of the person making the return, and the information included about the customer in the return. §6045(b). The customer must receive this information from the broker by January 31 of the year following the year that the broker's return was made. §6045(b). See *broker's return.*

cut-off method, bad debts an elective method whereby *large banks* stop claiming *deductions* for additions to *reserves for bad debts* after 1986 and sort their loans between those made before a fixed cut-off date and those made thereafter. The old loans can continue to be handled under a bad debt reserve method, but the new loans cannot be so handled. If a bank affected by the change in bad debt rules does not elect this method, it must *recapture* bad debt reserves as *gross income* over a four-year spread period. §585(c). There is a relief provision for financially troubled institutions.

D

D reorganization see *divisive reorganization; Type D reorganization.*

DEFRA an acronym for the *Deficit Reduction Act of 1984.*

del. order an abbreviation for a *delegation order.*

DIF CORR program an *IRS* program used at *Service Centers* which corrects simple *itemized deductions* on small *returns.*

DIF score an acronym for *discriminant function system.*

DISC an acronym for *domestic international sales corporation.* The DISC provisions have been largely repealed and replaced by the *foreign sales corporation* (FSC) provisions. A DISC can elect to be an interest charge DISC, whose benefits are geared toward small businesses deferring a portion of qualified export receipts. §995(f). An existing DISC, regular corporation, or new domestic corporation must make an election to become an interest charge DISC. The election is made on Form *4876A* (Election to Be Treated as an Interest Charge DISC).

DLN an acronym for *document locator number.*

DNI an acronym for *distributable net income.* Distributable net income is an amount that sets the limit on the deduction of a domestic estate or trust for distributions to beneficiaries. It may also limit the amount of the distribution taxable to the beneficiary, and it is a factor in application of the *conduit* rule.

DPC an acronym for a *designated payor corporation.*

daily portion, acquisition discount a term of art used in the *acquisition discount* area to describe the hypothetical *interest* income a *taxpayer* must generally report with respect to *short-term obligations.* It is derived by one or two proration methods. See §1283(b). A simple daily method or *constant yield method* (which uses compounding).

daily portion, original issue discount the share of *original issue discount* allocable to each particular day on which the *taxpayer* held the *debt instrument.* One then determines *yield to maturity* by using semi-annual compounding of *interest* on a constant rate. The periods selected are based on half-year periods, one of which invariably ends on the obligations maturity date. §1272(a)(3)(A) and (5). See *original issue discount.*

damages recoveries for deliberate or accidental harm done the recipient or the recipient's property. Section 104(a)(2) excludes damages for *personal injury or sickness* from *gross income,* perhaps on the theory that they represent a recovery of "human capital." Section 104(a) extends the exclusion to amounts received in settlement and, according to recent *IRS* authority, to *punitive damages* in connection with personal injury claims and sickness. Rev. Rul. 75-45 1975-1 C.B. 47. Such items as interest on the award or settlement, amounts received as *medical expenses* that were previously *deducted,* and amounts received for lost profits are not excluded. The regulations demand that the damages received be based on tort or "tort type" rights. Reg. §1.104-1(c). Generally, damages for taking or injuring property are viewed as reducing the property loss or creating income to the extent the recovery exceeds the loss. See *personal injuries or sickness.*

dam rehabilitation property, energy investment credit any amount properly chargeable to a *capital account* for property (or additions or improvements to property) in connection with the rehabilitation of a hydroelectric dam. §48(1)(13)(D). For example, capital costs for repairing or restoring existing nonfunctional generating equipment would qualify. Dam rehabilitation property may qualify for the *energy investment credit* as *qualified hydroelectric generating property.* §48(1)(3).

dealer one who engages in regular transactions in property directly with customers. Such person's *gains* and *losses* generate *ordinary gains and losses* as a result of §1221(1), which treats *inventory, stock in trade,* and *property primarily held for sale to customers in the ordinary course of the trade or business* as noncapital assets. (The latter property is often referred to as *dealer property.*)

dealer disposition a dealer in real and personal property may not use the installment method to report the gain from "dealer dispositions." A "dealer disposition" includes any disposition of personal property by a person who regularly sells such property on the installment plan, or any disposition of real property that is held by the taxpayer for sale to customers in the ordinary course of business. §453(l)(1). See *installment method.*

dealer equity option as to an *options dealer,* a *listed option* which is an *equity option* bought or granted by such a dealer in the normal course of business and listed on the qualified board or exchange where the dealer is registered. §1256(g)(4). Such options are *section 1256 contracts.* See *listed option* for a definition of *qualified board or exchange.* See *mark-to-market system.* See *listed option.*

dealer property a shorthand term for the phrase "property held primarily for sale to customers in the ordinary course of the *taxpayer's* trade or business."

§1221(1). Such property is excluded from *capital asset* status, and therefore generates *ordinary gain and loss.* While it is clear that "primarily" means "of first importance," the precise meaning of the phrase remains confused. When leased property is available for sale, it is in effect characterized as dealer property under §1231(b)(1)(B), the definition of *section 1231 assets.* Securities dealers are, however, allowed to identify a security as an investment provided they do so by the close of the business day the security is acquired. Such transactions are subject to the rule that no security which is part of an offsetting position may be so treated unless all securities belonging to an offsetting position are timely and properly identified. *Floor specialists,* on the other hand, have seven days for identification. §1236(a) and (d).

dealer, securities   a *taxpayer* in the *business* of holding an *inventory* of securities that are sold directly to the public. Stocks and securities in the hands of dealers are not *capital assets* (§1221(1)), but §1236 allows dealers to promptly identify securities held for investment, which may then qualify as *capital assets.* See *dealer.*

death benefits, employer provided   amounts paid by reason of an *employee's* death, which are *excludable* from *gross income* of the deceased employee's *beneficiary* in amounts of up to $5,000 by §101(b).

death proceeds, life insurance contract   amounts received as a result of the death of the insured, paid pursuant to a *life insurance contract.* Section 10l(a) generally excludes such amounts from *gross income,* except to the extent there was a *transfer for value,* or the interest component on life insurance proceeds paid under a settlement option. §101(a)(2)and (d).

death tax   an estate, inheritance, legacy, or succession tax imposed by any state or the District of Columbia. Reg. §1.2011-(a). Section 2011 allows a *credit* for such taxes. See credit for state death taxes.

debt   a legally enforceable obligation to pay a fixed or determinable sum of money at a future date. The debt must be genuine in that, from the outset, the lender must intend to seek repayment rather than to engage in a transaction out of friendship, affection, or so forth. In short, the obligation must arise out of a debtor-creditor relationship. Reg. §1.166-1(c) *(bad debt deduction).* The term "debt," and synonyms, appear at various points throughout the Code, especially in connection with *bad debt deductions* (§166) and *interest expense deductions* (§163), but is believed to have a uniform meaning.

debt discharge amount   debt discharged in a bankruptcy, insolvency, or certain other cases which are excluded from *gross income* by §108. Generally, the debt discharge amount reduces certain *tax attributes* (then basis in *depreciable property*) unless the *taxpayer*

elects first to reduce basis in depreciable property. §108(b).

debt-equity ratio   the ratio of corporate liabilities to *shareholders'* equity. A high debt-equity ratio indicates that what parades as corporate debt may really be equity *(stock)* in the corporation. If debt is reclassified as equity, then all interest previously paid becomes taxable as dividends and favorable tax treatment is lost. §385. See *debt-equity rules.*

debt-equity rules   a series of factors set forth in §385 (and endless judicial decisions) which attempt to sort equity investments in a *corporation* from *debt* owed by the corporation (i.e., *stock*). The problem arises because *taxpayers* commonly attempt to substitute "debt" for equity in order to allow the paying corporation an *interest expense deduction* for disbursements to the holder of "debt." If the purported debt is recharacterized as equity, upon distribution the corporation will not be entitled to an *interest expense deduction,* and the "debt" holders will be taxed under rules governing *dividend* distributions rather than repayment of debt. Perhaps the single best test to determine if a transfer results in debt or equity is to ask whether the purported debt would have arisen in a transaction between the corporation and a disinterested third party.

debt-equity swap   retirement of old, low-value corporate *debt* in exchange for *stock* of the debtor, cast as a transaction falling within former judicial and statutory exceptions to the general rules requiring recognition of *gain* in *discharge of indebtedness.* To complete the ritualistic exchange, investment bankers may serve as intermediaries to buy debt and sell stock. The goal is that shareholders not be taxed even if they receive stock with a value greater than their *bases* in the debt (§354(a)), and that the *corporation* avoid tax on the *gain.* §§368(a)(1)(E) and 1032, §§354 and 356(a). See *Type E reorganization.*

debt-financed acquisition   see *corporate acquisition indebtedness.*

debt-financed income   see *debt-financed property; unrelated debt-financed income.*

debt-financed portfolio stock   the dividends-received deduction is reduced for dividends received from *debt-financed portfolio stock* by a percentage related to the amount of debt incurred to purchase such stock. The reduction is calculated by multiplying the difference between 100 percent and the average portfolio indebtedness by 70 percent (80 percent in the case of 20 percent-owned corporations). §246A.

debt-financed property   any property held by an *exempt organization* for the production of income, on which, at any time during the year, there is an *acquisition indebtedness.* Income for this purpose includes *gain* on *disposition* as well as current income. Reg.

§1.514(b)-l(a). If, however, property is disposed of during the present year, it is not debt-financed property unless there was acquisition indebtedness on the property at some time during the 12-month period before the disposition. Also excluded from debt-financed property are property related to an *exempt organization's exempt function*; property otherwise generating *unrelated trade or business* income; property producing income from research; and property used in certain exempt related trades or business. §514(b)(1)(A)-(D). See *acquisition indebtedness*.

debt-for-debt swap　　a transaction in which a *corporation* exchanges outstanding *debt* for new debt. The repeal of the *corporate reorganization* exception (§368(a)(1)(E)) that prevented the issuing corporation from being taxed on *cancellation of indebtedness income* in these transactions, except in bankruptcy or *insolvency*, has taken much of the attraction out of these deals. See §1274(a)(4) and (5), *Type E reorganization*.

debt instrument　　a bond, note, debenture, certificate, or other evidence of indebtedness. §1275(a). The term is used in connection with defining *original issue discount*.

debts owed by political parties　　a reference to the caption of §271, which denies *bad debt losses* or *worthless security* losses for debts owed by *political parties*. It is subject to an important exception that permits *deductions* for *accrual method taxpayers* who provide substantial goods or services to political parties and make substantial continuing efforts at collection (e.g., a phone company). Section 271 is designed to prevent evasion of the limitation on deductions for *lobbying expenses* by arranging sham loans. See also *indirect contributions to political parties*.

decedent　　a dead individual.

decedent's estate　　the *estate* of a *decedent*.

decedent's return　　a return on *Form 1040* or 1040A that must be filed for a *decedent* who would have been required to file a *tax return* had he lived. It covers that part of the year during which the decedent was alive and is filed by the *executor* or any other person responsible for the decedent's affairs. That person may file a *separate* or *joint return* with the surviving *spouse* and may claim the same filing benefits (e.g., extra *standard deduction* for being over age 65) as the decedent would have been entitled to while alive. Reg. §1.443-1(a)(2).

declaratory judgments　　judicial pronouncements of a legal conclusion, a specific equity power vested in most courts. A declaratory judgment is commonly used for such things as to declare a regulation invalid or to confirm the validity of a contract. Declaratory judgments are generally unavailable in federal tax litigation. 28 U.S.C. §2201.

decline in principal method, cost depletion　　a method for computing *cost depletion* of a *production payment* fixed in terms of dollars, under which the *taxpayer* multiplies the adjusted cost of the production payment at year-end, before *subtracting* depletion, by a fraction:

$$\frac{\text{Money received and used to reduce the balance of the production payment}}{\text{Balance of production payment at the beginning of the year}}$$

This method tends to result in level combined *deductions* of *interest* and cost depletion over the life of the production payment. See Rev. Rul. 65-10, 1965-1 C.B. 254. See also *sum-of-the-dollars method, cost depletion; unit of production method, cost depletion*.

declining-balance depreciation　　a method of *depreciation* under which a uniform rate of depreciation (e.g., 150 or 200 percent of straight-line) is applied to the *basis* of an asset, as reduced by prior depreciation *deductions*, stopping once a reasonable *salvage value* is reached. §167(b). Section 167(e)(1) permits an unchallenged switch from the declining-balance method to the *straight-line depreciation*. The effect is that depreciation (or *cost recovery* under §168) in early years exceeds amounts otherwise available under *straight-line depreciation*. For example, assume that an item of property costs $200, has a salvage value of $10, and a *useful life* of 10 years, and that the *taxpayer* is entitled to claim 200 percent declining-balance depreciation.

The first year's deduction would be $80:

$$\frac{\$200}{5} \times 200 \text{ percent}$$

The next year's depreciation would be $48:

$$\frac{\$120}{5} \times 200 \text{ percent}$$

The pattern would continue until *adjusted basis* equaled a *reasonable salvage value* ($10). The declining-balance method is generally used under the *accelerated cost recovery system*, except that the limitation to salvage value is eliminated (§168(f)(9)).

deconsolidation　　ceasing to file a *consolidated return*. For purposes of the *loss disallowance rules*, the term means any event that causes a share of *stock* of a subsidiary that remains outstanding to be no longer owned by a member of any *consolidated group* of which the subsidiary is also a member. Reg. §§1.337(d)-2 and 1.1502-20(b)(2).

deductible debt discharges　　a reference to §108(e)(2), in which the *discharge of indebtedness* of items which would have been *deductible* if paid (e.g., obligation to pay an *employee* his or her salary) does not generate *gross income*.

deductible interest an interest that *passes from the decedent* to his or her surviving *spouse,* which thereby permits a *marital deduction* in determination of the *taxable estate.* The value of the interest must have been included in the decedent's *gross estate.* Reg. §20.2053(a)-2(b). It may also refer to *interest expenses* that are *deductible.* See *marital deduction.*

deductible repair a *repair* cost that can be currently *deducted* under §§162 (*trade or business* expenses) or 212 (*investment expenses*). In contrast, a repair cost that cannot be currently deducted must generally be *capitalized* under §263 and deducted according to the rules for *depreciation* or *cost recovery.* See *repair.*

deduction equivalent under the *passive loss rules,* the amount of *passive activity credits,* which, if allowed as a *deduction,* would reduce *regular tax liability* by an amount equal to such credits. §469(j)(5). Passive activity credits are subject to the passive loss rules. See *passive loss rules.*

deduction for estate tax an *income tax deduction* allowed for federal *estates taxes* imposed on post-death income of a *decedent,* which *income* was included for federal estate tax purposes. §691(c). The deduction is allowable to the *person,* which may or may not be the estate, required to report *income in respect of a decedent.* §691(c)(1); Reg. §1.691(c)-1(a).

deductions, estate tax see *estate tax deductions.*

deductions in respect of a decedent *deductions* which have *accrued,* in an economic sense, prior to the *decedent's* death, but which are not allowable on the *decedent's* final *income tax return* because of the decedent's *accounting* method. Instead deductions in respect of a decedent are reported on the income tax return of the *estate* or on the *individual* income tax return of the heir liable for the debt. §691(b).

deduction year, foreign tax credit a year in which a *taxpayer* chose to *deduct* foreign taxes rather than claim the benefits of the *foreign tax credit.* Reg. §1.904-2(d). See §§164(a)(3) and 275(a)(4).

deem consider as done. Numerous hypothetical tax-related transactions begin with the word "deemed," e.g., a *deemed distribution* from *corporation* to *shareholder.*

deemed death benefit a figure derived from applying the formula in Reg. §1.79-1(d)(3) to a *whole life insurance* policy provided for an *employee* under a *group-term life insurance* plan. The so-called deemed death benefit must not be less than the total death benefits, less the group-term life insurance benefits designated as such by the *employer,* otherwise the policy does not qualify under §79; Reg. §1.79(1)(b).

deemed distribution, partnership a loose term for a number of hypothetical *distributions* from a *partnership* to a *partner.* Examples include: (1) imaginary distributions of property under §751 relating to *disproportionate distributions*; and (2) a reduction in a partner's share of partnership liabilities when another partner takes over such liabilities.

deemed dividend, consolidated return an elective provision that allows a member (or members) of an *affiliated group* to treat a wholly owned subsidiary as if it had disgorged its *accumulated earnings and profits* to its corporate owner(s) on the first day of the year, and the owner(s) in turn contributed the distribution to the subsidiary. The subsidiary must have been owned by members of the *affiliated group* on each day of the subsidiary's *taxable year.* Reg. §1.1502-32(f)(2). The election permits simplified accounting for *earnings and profits.*

deemed election, section 338 acquisitions the *constructive* making of a *section 338 election.* The asset acquisition consistency rule provides that if a purchasing corporation acquires an asset of the target or a target affiliate at any time during the (extensive) *consistency period,* the purchasing corporation is deemed to have made an election for the target. If the requirements of §338 are met (i.e., the purchase of at least 80 percent of the target corporation's stock in one or more purchases within a 12-month acquisition period), a purchasing corporation can elect to treat the target (1) as having sold all of its assets in a single transaction for their fair market value and (2) as if it were a new corporation purchasing the assets on the day after the acquisition. §338(e). It may also arise if a parent corporation purchases the stock of a subsidiary and *elects* to treat the stock purchase as a purchase of assets. §338(f). The deemed or election itself essentially enables the parent to obtain the same basis that it would have obtained had it purchased the assets directly (i.e., a basis equal to fair market value rather than a carryover basis).

deemed maturity date for purposes of defining a *life insurance contract* under §7702, the deemed maturity date is no earlier than age 95 and no later than age 100. §7702(e)(1)(B).

deemed paid foreign tax credit a *foreign tax credit* that a *domestic corporation* (other than an *S corporation*) and certain *individuals* may claim for its share of taxes, by a *foreign corporation's* share of taxes deemed to be paid or accrued, by a foreign affiliate. The credit is claimed in the year that a United States corporation receives a *dividend* from the *foreign corporation,* and is only available if the domestic corporation owns at least 10 percent of the *voting stock* of the foreign corporation when the dividend is paid. §902. The credit is also applicable to dividends from *second-* and *third-tier corporations,* provided the domestic corporation has at least a 5 percent indirect voting *stock* investment in the lower-tier corporations. The effect is to impute taxes paid by foreign affiliates to the domestic shareholder, which then combines the imputed taxes to determine its foreign tax credit. See *voting stock, foreign tax credit.*

deemed sale return a return filed by a *target corporation* in a *liquidation.* It may be a single "combined deemed sale return" if the targets are members of a *consolidated group.* §338(h)(15).

deemed unrelated income the income of a nonexempt *welfare benefit fund* that would be *unrelated business taxable income* of the fund if it were a tax-exempt *social club, VEBA, SUB,* or *GLSO.* In determining deemed unrelated income, the *employer* may elect to treat two or more nonexempt welfare benefit funds as a single fund. §419A(b)(1). The aggregation rules for *qualified pension plans* apply. Deemed unrelated income of a nonexempt welfare benefit fund is taxed to the employer maintaining the fund. §419A(g)(1).

deep-in-the-money option an option having a strike price (exercise price) lower than the lowest qualified benchmark. The "lowest qualified benchmark" means, in general, the highest available strike price that is below the applicable stock price (the closing price of the optioned stock on the most recent date on which it was traded before the date of option grant or the opening price of the stock on the option grant date if the opening price is more than 110 percent of the closing price on its last previous trading date). However, in the case of options for more than 90 days and a strike price of more than $50, the lowest qualified benchmark is the second highest available strike price that is less than the applicable stock price, and the lowest qualified benchmark cannot be lower than 85 percent of the applicable stock price where the stock price is $25 or less, and it cannot be lower than the applicable stock price minus $10 for stock priced at $150 or less. For example, exchange rules provide for option strike prices at $5 intervals (benchmarks) in the case of stock trading at under $100. Hence, for stock trading at $50, an exchange-traded call option with a strike price of $45 or more would qualify for the exception. §1092(c)(4)(C). Straddles involving options which are not deep in the money are not exempt from the *loss deferral rule* and the forced *capitalization* rule of §263(g). See *qualified covered call options.*

deep rent skewed project residential rental projects that are funded by *tax-exempt bonds* under income distribution rules that favor especially poor tenants. See §142(d)(4). If the projects meet certain requirements, bonds issued to fund the projects can be deemed *exempt facility bonds, interest* on which is nontaxable to the holder.

Deep Rock doctrine a bankruptcy law doctrine that treats as stock *debt* held by controlling shareholders which was received at the time of organizing the corporation. Section 510 of the Federal Bankruptcy Code

implements the doctrine, evidently limiting it to cases of wrongdoing. The doctrine also applies in tax cases. The doctrine may be significant in sorting debt from equity. See *hybrid instruments.*

de facto liquidation a *corporation's* attainment of such a state of dormancy that its existence can be considered at an end. The effect may be to bar *carrybacks* of *net operating losses* or other tax benefits to previous years. Because of the general similarity of *partnership* taxation, the doctrine presumably applied to them also.

defer report as an *income* or *deduction* in a later tax period.

deferral entity includes a *partnership, S corporation, personal service corporation,* or *grantor trust.* Reg. §1.444-2T(d). A partnership, S corporation, or personal service corporation is a member of a *tiered structure* for *section 444 election* purposes if it directly owns any part of, or is directly owned in whole or part by, a deferral entity on the applicable date, namely the end of its *required taxable year.* Id. See *section 444 election of fiscal tax year by partnership, S corporation, or personnel service corporation (PSC).*

deferral period, section 444 election the number of months that occur after the end of the *taxable year* desired under §444 and through the close of the *required taxable year.* §444(e). The term is central to the §444 election.

deferral preferences *items of tax preference* and *adjustments* that are not of a permanent character (e.g., *accelerated depreciation* as opposed to an exclusion for *interest* on *tax-exempt bonds*). Such items can count towards the *minimum tax credit* against *regular tax* under §53. See *alternative minimum tax.*

deferred annuity an *annuity* contract in which payouts begin at some future time.

deferred asset method a method for dealing with *interest expenses* of related parties under the *related party avoided cost rules.* Those rules are a subset of the *uniform capitalization rules.* The deferred asset method calls for the related party to *capitalize* interest incurred in the production period in an amount equal to the amount the producing *taxpayer* would have capitalized had the taxpayer incurred the expense on the *eligible debt* of the related party (known as the *related party avoided cost debt*). Notice 88-99, 1988-36 IRB 29, §IX.(A)(1). The related party treats the capitalized interest as an asset, taking into account the same way (and time) as the producing taxpayer would have accounted for it. Id., §IX(B)(2). It is an alternative to the *substitute cost method,* which is elective.

deferred benefit generally, a benefit which, if deemed to be compensation, would be *deferred compensation.* §404(b)(2). The determination of when an amount is included in *gross income* will be made without regard to whether it is excludable from gross income. Thus, for example, an *employer* can deduct such a benefit only when the benefit is enjoyed by the recipient. Certain vacation pay arrangements and benefits provided under *welfare benefit funds* are exempted from the deferred compensation *deduction* limits. §404(b)(2)(B).

deferred compensation compensation for services presently rendered, but to be paid for in the future. Such compensation may be nonqualified (i.e., the arrangements do not allow an immediate *deduction* by the payor nor deferred taxability of earnings on such funds) or qualified (i.e., permitting immediate deductions for contributions and tax-deferred growth in earnings, but subject to complex rules designed to protect *employees*). In general, unfunded *deferred benefit* plans (e.g., contractual promises to provide educational benefits for *employees'* children) also generate deductions only when funded (as if they were deferred compensation). §404(b). See *deferred benefit; qualified plan; welfare benefit fund.*

deferred intercompany transaction a *sale* or *exchange* of *property,* or the performance of services where the expenditure for services is *capitalized,* or any other expenditure where the amount is capitalized, if the sale, exchange, or expenditure takes place during a *consolidated return year* between *corporations* that are members of the same *affiliated group* immediately after the transaction. Reg. §1.1502-13(a)(2). The amount of *gain, loss, income,* or *deduction recognized* by affiliated group members on deferred intercompany transactions is determined under Reg. §1.1502-13(c)(1). Generally, the deferred intercompany transaction rules are considered one of the benefits of filing a consolidated return because any gains on intercompany sales of property are not recognized in the year of sale but instead are recognized over the life of the asset when the property is sold outside the group, or when the transferee ceases to be a member of the group.

deferred like-kind exchange a *like-kind exchange* under §1031 where the receipt of the exchanged property is deferred. There are now time limits on such exchanges and regulations as to their details. See *like-kind exchange; reverse Starker exchange.*

deferred payment sale a broad term describing a *sale* for which payment is not completed in one *taxable year.* Such sales may or may not be on the *installment method* of reporting. Generally, *cash method taxpayers* must report the full *fair market value* of the buyer's obligations received in the sale, reporting discount income as payments are made; whereas *accrual method* taxpayers include the full face amount of the buyer's obligations as an amount realized in the year of sale. Most deferred payment sales are now presumptively on the *installment method.* §453(d).

deferred statutory or tort liability loss the lesser of (1) the *net operating loss* for the year, reduced by any amount attributable to *foreign expropriation* or *product liability losses,* or (2) amounts allowable as *deductions* for federal or state statutory or tort claims, if the act of omission causing the statutory claim arose at least three years before the beginning of the *taxable year,* or, in the case of tort claims, if the liability arises out of acts or omissions over an extended period of time, a substantial portion of which occurred at least three years before the beginning of such taxable year. §172(k)(1)(B). The classic example is a slow chemical poisoning of an *employee.* The effect of finding such a loss (e.g., tort recovery by the employee) is to allow the *taxpayer* (e.g., chemical company) a 10-year *carryback* of the loss (hence, tax *refunds*). A potentially far longer carryback period applies to claims arising from nuclear decommissioning. §172(k)(2).

deferred tax liability the amount of *federal income tax* for any *taxable year* that a *taxpayer* will pay in later years on collecting obligations arising under the *installment method,* assuming the taxpayer is always taxed at top *marginal rates.* See §453A(c). The term is used for purposes of calculating an interest charge on tax deferrals resulting from big ticket sales of *real property* by *nondealers.*

deficiency underpaid tax. It is formally defined as the *correct tax* less the tax shown on the *return,* plus previous *assessments* less *rebates.* §6211(a). Reg. §301.6211-1(a). Section 6201 authorizes the *assessment* of *deficiency,* an internal operation of the *IRS,* for which notice is provided. Deficiency-related procedures are of extreme importance. For example, the existence of a proposed deficiency gives the *Tax Court* jurisdiction to hear the case without payment of taxes. Some *refundable taxes* are processed under deficiency procedures, even though the tax shortfall is negative (i.e., the tax is less than zero).

deficiency dividend, personal holding company a procedure designed to alleviate the *personal holding company tax* after liability for the tax has been established. §547. It permits the *corporation* to distribute an *actual cash dividend* which the corporation elects to treat as a distribution of personal holding company income for the year at issue, and it is taxable to shareholders. A deficiency dividend effectively reduces the amount of the penalty tax. See *determination, personal holding company tax.*

deficiency dividend, real estate investment trust (REIT) a current distribution by a *REIT* made within 90 days of determination of an *audit* adjustment, available to preserve the trust's status as a REIT against the charge of its having failed annually to distribute enough of its *real estate investment trust taxable income* to preserve its status. §860. See *determination, deficien-*

cy dividend by regulated investment companies and REITs.

deficiency dividend, regulated investment company a current distribution by a *regulated investment company* made within 90 days of determination of an *audit* adjustment, available to preserve the company's status as a regulated investment company against the charge of its having failed annually to distribute enough of its *investment company taxable income* to preserve its status. §860. See *determination, deficiency dividend by regulated investment companies and REITs.*

deficiency suit a suit that originates from the *IRS's assessment* of a *deficiency* against the *taxpayer*. The term is confusing because the jurisdiction of courts, other than the *Tax Court,* in such suits requires as an interim step that the taxpayer pay the tax and that the IRS reject the subsequent *claim for refund or credit.*

Deficit Reduction Act of 1984 the name of the act, Pub. L. No. 98-369, 98 Stat. 494, that incorporates the *Tax Reform Act of 1984* (Division A) and the *Spending Reduction Act of 1984* (Division B). Division B contains miscellaneous tax-related provisions involving such matters as Social Security taxation of church *employees* and technical corrections of prior law.

defined benefit plan under a defined benefit plan, the annual benefit payable is limited to the smaller of $112,221 (in 1992 and continually indexed for future years) or 100 percent of the employee's average compensation for the highest three years of employment. This benefit is subject to a $10,000 de minimis floor. §415(b).

defined benefit plan, ERISA a *pension plan* other than an *individual* account plan. *ERISA* §3(35).

defined contribution plan, Code a *deferred compensation* plan that provides an individual account for each *participant* and for retirement benefits based solely on the amount contributed to the participant's account or used to reduce future *employer contributions*. The participant's account is subject to any *income, expenses, gains,* and *losses,* and any *forfeitures* of accounts of other participants allocated to the participant's account. §414(i). Examples include *individual retirement arrangements, profit-sharing plans, stock bonus plans, money purchase pension plans,* and *target benefit plans.*

defined contribution plan, ERISA a *pension plan* that provides an *individual* account for each *participant* and for benefits based solely upon the amount contributed to the participant's account. The individual account is subject to any income, expenses, *gains* and losses, and any forfeitures of accounts of other participants allocated to such participant's account. ERISA §3(34). Defined contribution plans are covered by Pension Benefit Guaranty Corporation Insurance. ERISA draws numerous other practical distinctions

between defined benefit and defined contribution plans (e.g., reporting, disclosure, funding). See *employee pension benefit plan, ERISA.*

degree candidate see *candidate for a degree.*

delay rental an amount paid for the privilege of deferring development of mineral or oil and gas property and which could have been avoided by abandoning the mineral or oil and gas lease, by beginning development operations, or by obtaining production. Reg. §1.612-3(c)(1). Reg. §1.612-3(c)(2) declares that such rentals are taxable rental income to the payee and are not depletable, however the payor may *deduct* or elect under §266 to *capitalize* them.

delayed vesting a term used to describe *vesting* in installments, or all at once in the future, of benefits from *deferred compensation* plans.

delegate When used in reference to the *Secretary of the Treasury* (see *Secretary*), any officer, *employee,* or agency of the *Treasury Department* duly authorized by the Secretary of the Treasury directly, or indirectly by one or more redelegations of authority, to act in his behalf. §7701(a)(12).

delegation order an order of the Commissioner of the *Internal Revenue Service* granting lower-echelon officers authority formerly lodged at some higher level. Common examples include the delegation of authority to settle tax disputes.

deletions list a periodic list of charities that have lost their exempt status. It is an update of Publications 78 and appears in the *Internal Revenue Bulletin.*

delinquency amount amounts paid or accrued because of a failure to file a *tax return* or to pay a tax when due, and which were allowed as a *deduction* or *credit* (e.g., *interest* on delinquent taxes). These amounts, as well as numerous others, are subject to the *recovery exclusion* of §111. Reg. §1.111-1.

demand loan, below-market loan a loan payable on demand by the lender. The term also includes (other than for purposes of determining the *applicable federal rate*) any loan, if the benefits of the *interest* arrangements of the loan are nontransferable and are conditioned on the future performance of substantial services by an *individual.* §7872(f)(5). See *below-market loan; Crown loan.*

de minimis minimal or trivial.

de minimis fringe benefits a type of *fringe benefit* which may be *deductible* by the *employer* and nontaxable to the *employee* under §132(a)(4). They are defined as fringe benefits with a value so small that accounting for them is unreasonable or administratively impractical. §132(e)(1). This exclusion covers subsidized cafeterias on or near the employer's business, provided revenues from the facility are equal to or greater than direct operating costs. §132(e)(2). Eligibility for subsidized cafeterias (although not for *de minimis* fringe benefits in general) is conditioned upon *nondiscrimination rules* as to highly compensated employees.

de minimis loan a loan directly between *individuals* which in the aggregate never exceeds $10,000. §7872(c)(2). It excludes *gift loans* directly attributable to carrying income-producing assets. §7872(c)(2)(B). If the loan is compensation-related or between *corporation* and shareholder, there must be no tax avoidance intent if the lender is to avoid being taxed on hypothetical interest income under §7872. See *below-market loan.*

de minimis rule any rule that has the effect of relaxing another rule for relatively trivial cases. For example, §1272(a)(3) excludes from the definition of *original issue discount* (the redemption price less the issue price) any amount less than 0.25 percent of the redemption price times the number of years to maturity of an obligation.

demolition costs and losses any amount expended for or any *loss* sustained on account of the demolition of any structure (including a certified historic structure). These costs must be capitalized as part of the basis of the land on which the structure was located. §280B.

dependency exemption a $2,350-per-*dependent* (1993) "exemption" granted to *individual taxpayers,* which operates as a *deduction* from *adjusted gross income.* §151(c). The exemption is indexed for inflation and is phased out when adjusted gross income reaches certain levels. See *exemption.*

dependent agent an *agent,* especially a distributor, who is the exclusive representative of a *foreign* manufacturer, or an agent whose activities are otherwise so extensive as to have them imputed to the foreign manufacturer he represents, thereby causing the foreign manufacturer to be taxed as if a United States *taxpayer* on net United States source sales income. The concept is implicit in §§881 and 882. The concept is also found in *tax treaties* to determine whether a foreign person has a *permanent establishment* in a contracting state as well as in the *Code.* The power to fill contracts freely or from a stock of United States goods generally results in finding a dependent agent. See, e.g., Rev. Rul. 70-424, 1970-2 C.B. 150.

dependent care assistance programs nondiscriminatory, written plans for the exclusive benefit of *employees* established by *employers,* including *partnerships* and *sole proprietorships,* to provide dependent care assistance, meaning payments or provisions of services which, if paid by the employee, would qualify under the *child and dependent care credit* as necessary for gainful employment. §129. Such payments or services are *excludable* from the employee's *gross income* up to

$5,000 ($2,500 in the case of separate return by a married individual). The exclusion cannot exceed the earned income of an unmarried employee or the earned income of the lower-earning spouse of married employees. See *benefit bank; flexible spending account.*

dependent care center a facility that provides care for six or more *individuals* and is compensated through fees, payments, or grants. §21A(b)(2)(C). The *child and dependent care credit* may be claimed where the *expenses* are incurred for care outside the home at a dependent care center, provided the center complies with all applicable laws and regulations. The facility must provide care regularly to be classified as a dependent care center.

dependent care credit see *child and dependent care credit.*

dependent care expense see *child and dependent care credit.*

dependent, generally the term refers to: (1) any *individual* living with the *taxpayer* (providing the relationship is not illegal under local law) and for whom the taxpayer provides at least 50 percent of his or her *support*; and (2) certain relatives (parents, children, siblings, stepchildren, stepsiblings, stepparents, nephews, nieces, aunts, uncles, children-in-law, parents-in-law, grandparents, and grandchildren), regardless of where they live, for whom the *taxpayer* provides at least 50 percent of their support. *Adopted children* qualify as children and siblings, as do most foster children. §152(b)(2). Section 152(b)(3) excludes persons who are not United States *citizens* or *resident aliens* except where United States *taxpayers* adopt Canadian or Mexican citizens who make their homes with the taxpayer. For each dependent, the taxpayer is allowed a deduction of $2,350 for 1993. See *multiple support agreement.*

dependent, qualified group legal services plan the general definition provided by §152 applies to these plans, which can provide tax-free legal services for *employees, spouses,* and their *dependents.* §120(d)(4).

depletable gas quantity 6,000,000 cubic feet of *domestic* natural gas per day (larger in earlier years). §613A(C)(4). Such amounts are subject to *percentage depletion* under the *small producers' exemption.*

depletable interest see *economic interest, depletion allowance.*

depletable oil quantity 1,000 *barrels* of *domestic crude oil* per day (larger in earlier years). §613A(c)(3). Such amounts are subject to *percentage depletion* under the *small producers' exemption.*

depletion the decrease in natural resources, including timber, due to their extraction. Taxpayers with a so-called *economic interest* in the resources select annually whichever of two methods, *cost depletion* or *percentage depletion,* yields the larger *deduction,* although only cost depletion is allowed for timber. Section 612 authorizes cost depletion (i.e., depletion based on the cost of the resource) for virtually all exhaustible natural resources, while §§613 and 613A authorize percentage depletion (depletion based on a percentage of sales) for most hard minerals and, to a lesser extent, oil and gas. Percentage depletion is unique because the deduction can exceed the cost of the resource.

depletion, restoration a requirement, imposed by Reg. §1.612-3(a)(2) and (b)(2), that *depletion* claimed before extraction (e.g., *bonuses* and *advanced royalties*) of a resource that has been paid for, must be returned as *gross income* to the extent extraction or production never takes place.

depletion unit, timber a *taxpayer's basis* in timber, divided by the volume of timber subject to depletion for the year (e.g., $0.01 per standing board foot). See Reg. §1.611-3(b)(2). The depletion unit is multiplied by annual cutting to fix timber *depletion* for the year.

deposit a transfer of money or property that is intended as security rather than payment, such as a deposit paid to a landlord. Deposits are not taxable to the recipient. Alternatively, it may mean the payment of various required federal taxes at a Federal Reserve Bank or at an authorized local bank, accompanied by appropriate depositary receipt forms. Deposits of tax payments include those for *Social Security taxes, federal income tax* withholdings, *excise taxes, estimated taxes,* and *FUTA.* See *penalty, failure to make timely deposits.*

deposit administration contract basically, a group *annuity* contract that provides *deferred annuities* for *employees.* The *life insurance company* accumulates the *employer contributions* in a so-called *deposit administration* fund at a guaranteed interest rate under a contract that ordinarily allows for declarations of excess interest. When employees retire, retirement annuity contracts are bought for them at annuity rates guaranteed by the issuer. Deposit administration contracts must qualify under §816 to qualify as *life insurance reserves* or under §401(a) to qualify as *pension plan reserves.*

deposit administration plan a contractual arrangement with an *insurance company* by which funds are turned over to the company in order to fund anticipated retirement benefits under a pension plan, often with a guaranteed minimum return. Because monies held by regulated insurers qualify as de facto *trusts,* there is no actual need for a trust in order for the plan to be treated as a *qualified plan.* §401(f).

deposit-commission basis an arrangement in which the buyer of a product for resale is entitled to keep, as complete or partial payment for the buyer's services, all or part of a purchase deposit paid by the customer in connection with the transaction. §6041 A(b)(2)(B). Persons with an annual income of $5,000 or more from this type of business are considered engaged in direct sales and must provide certain return information. See *direct sales returns.*

deposit method an *inventory accounting* method under which returnable containers are considered fixed assets, income from which is deferred until they clearly will not be returned. See Rev. Rul. 60-243, 1960-2 C.B. 160.

deposit, natural resources each different quantity of oil, gas, or mineral in the ground. For example, three seams of coal in one tract are three deposits. Reg. §1.614-1(a)(5), ex. (1). It is said that even oil, gas, and distillates are separate property. The term is used for purposes of defining *natural resource property* for *depletion* and other purposes. See *property, depletion.*

depreciable interest an interest in *tangible property* that qualifies the holder to claim *depreciation, amortization,* or *cost recovery.* For example, a tenant who builds improvements on leased property generally has the depreciable interest and, therefore, is entitled to the *depreciation* or *amortization deduction* for the improvement. Reg. §1.167(a)-4. See *benefits and burdens of ownership; economic interest, depreciation.*

depreciable property generally, *tangible property* which by its nature loses its value through exhaustion, wear, tear, and obsolescence. The term appears in various places in the *Code,* sometimes with particularized meaning. See especially §§108(d)(5), 167(a), 453(f)(7), 1017(b)(3)(B), 1239, 1245(a)(3), 1250(c). Depreciated property refers to property that has been the subject of *depreciation* or *cost recovery deductions.* Such property is unlike property subject to *depletion* because depletion involves the extraction (or in the case of timber, harvesting) of natural resources. It is unlike *amortization* because amortization involves *intangible property.* See *contingent serial payments; listed property.*

depreciable property, debt discharge any property of a *character subject to depreciation* (provided basis reduction would reduce depreciation or *amortization* allowable for the period immediately before the reduction, e.g., not property used by a tenant which the tenant must restore), *real property* held as *inventory* (§1221(1)), *stock* in an affiliate which is a member of the same *affiliated group of corporations* filing a *consolidated return* in the year of debt discharge, or an interest of a *partner* in a *partnership* to the extent of the partner's interest in depreciable property. Certain debtors may elect under §108 to reduce the *basis* of depreciable property rather than *recognize cancellation of indebtedness income.* §108(b)(5) and (d)(4).

depreciation the systematic recovery of the *cost* or other *basis* of *tangible property,* other than natural resources, due to the exhaustion, wear, tear, and obsolescence of such assets over their *useful lives* in the *taxpayer's* hands. *Depreciable property* held for use in a *trade or business,* or *held for the production of income* (even if idle), may be written off over various periods that are based on the property's useful life in the taxpayer's hands. §167. However, the amount of depreciation may not exceed a reasonable *salvage value.* In 1981, a *cost recovery* system was introduced that parallels depreciation and performs a similar function for tangible property *placed in service* after 1980. §168. The cost recovery system does not pretend to reflect reality in an accounting sense.

depreciation agreement an agreement between the *IRS* and a *taxpayer* in which the *useful lives, salvage values,* and *methods of depreciation* are agreed upon for periods after the agreement is executed. §167(d); Reg. §1.167(d)-1. It does not apply to property which qualifies under §168 (*cost recovery*).

depreciation guidelines a standard formerly used to classify various assets according to *useful lives.* The *guideline lives* are still useful in cases where neither the *accelerated cost recovery system* nor the *class life asset depreciation range system* applies. In particular, of continuing importance, are *real estate* improvements, ascribing to these properties the following useful lives: apartment buildings, theaters, and hotels—40 years; factories, machine shops, garages, dwellings, and office buildings—45 years; banks and loft buildings—50 years; commercial buildings, warehouses, and grain elevators—60 years. Rev. Proc. 62-21, 1962-2 C.B. 418.

depreciation rate the percentage applied to the cost or other *basis of property* in order to calculate the amount of *depreciation deduction* for a particular year. The percentage depends upon the *useful life* and *method of depreciation* applied to the property. The term appears on Form 4562 (Depreciation and Amortization).

depreciation recapture the shorthand term commonly used in lieu of the cumbersome phrase *recapture of depreciation* as *ordinary income.* See *recapture, depreciation.*

designated blighted area an area which a local government unit so designates on the basis of the following factors: excessive vacant land where there used to be structures; empty buildings; substandard structures; vacancies; and delinquent property taxes. §143(c)(4)(C). Up to 25 percent by value of the realty in the local government's jurisdiction can qualify. Designated blighted areas can be financed with *qualified redevelopment bonds*; such bonds are *qualified bonds* and produce tax-exempt *interest* to the holder. See *tax-exempt bond.*

designated B method a *method of accounting* that the *IRS* considers to be erroneous, even though not unlawful under the *Internal Revenue Code, regulations,* or case law. If there is a *change of accounting method* as to a designated B method, it is subject to a short phase-in under §481 and is subject to other considerations set forth in Rev. Proc. 84-74, 1984-2 C.B. 736. See *category B method of accounting; section 481 adjustment.*

designated distribution any distribution or payment from or under an *employer's* plan of *deferred compensation,* an *individual retirement plan,* or a commercial *annuity,* but not an amount paid as *wages,* nor the portion of a distribution or payment not reasonably included in *gross income.* §3405(d)(1). For designated distribution purposes an employer's deferred compensation plan means any *pension, annuity, profit-sharing plan, stock bonus plan,* or other *deferred compensation* plan. §3405(d)(5).

designated hedge a hedging transaction that arises if (1) the *taxpayer's* risk of *loss* with respect to any position is reduced because the taxpayer has an option to sell, is under a contractual obligation to sell, or has made (and not closed) a *short sale* of substantially identical property; or (2) the taxpayer is the *grantor* of an option to buy; or (3) the taxpayer holds one or more positions as to be provided in *regulations.* The position must be identified. Increases and decreases in the value of positions in a designated hedge are netted for purposes of the 30 percent requirement relating to the definition of *regulated investment companies.* §851(g).

designated nondeductible IRA contributions for *taxable years* beginning after 1986, to the extent *individual taxpayers* are not eligible to make *deductible IRA* contributions, they may still make *nondeductible* contributions, under §408(o) to the extent of: (1) the excess of the lesser of $2,000 ($2,500 for a *spousal IRA*) or 100 percent of *compensation over*; (2) the IRA *deduction* limit for the taxpayer. The funds can grow tax-free until withdrawn.

designated payor corporation any *United States–owned foreign corporation* under §904(g)(6)), any *regulated investment company,* and any other *foreign corporation* in which the *taxpayer* is a United States shareholder at any time during the *taxable year* of the foreign corporation (whether or not a *controlled foreign corporation*). *Dividends* or *interest* paid by a designated payor corporation (DPC) to a *United States shareholder* (one owning over 10 percent of its voting power) is *separate limitation interest* income if the distribution is attributable to separate limitation interest that the DPC receives. This complexity was designed to prevent evasion of the separate calculation of the separate *foreign tax credit limitation* on interest.

designated settlement fund any fund established primarily for resolving and satisfying tort claims against the *taxpayer* (or a *related taxpayer* as defined in §267(b)) arising out of personal injury, death, or property damage. The fund must be established by court order to completely satisfy such liabilities and the taxpayer's selection must give the taxpayer (or related person) no *beneficial interest* in income or *corpus* and must be administered by parties independent of the taxpayer. No amounts may be transferred from the fund except in *qualified payments*. Payments to the fund are deemed *economic performance* under §461(h) and are *deductible* when paid to the fund. §468B(d)(2). Investment income of the fund should be taxable to the fund as if it were a *trust* or *estate*. See *qualified payment, designated settlement fund; related taxpayers, loss and deduction denial*.

designated summons an IRS *summons* issued in order to determine the amount of tax, issued at least 60 days before the statute of limitations (plus extensions) under §6501 (regarding the *assessment* of that tax) expires. It should clearly state that it is a designated summons under §6503(k)(2). §6503(k)(2)(A). If a designated summons is issued with respect to a *tax return* of a *corporation,* the *statute of limitations* regarding the *assessment* of tax on that return is suspended in a specified manner. §6503(k)(1).

designation agreement, broker's return an agreement that can be used to designate specifically who the *real estate reporting person* is in any particular transaction, provided the agreement is written and executed by the designated real estate reporting person at or before closing; designates a person who is eligible to be a real estate reporting person, that is, a person responsible for closing the transaction, the transferee's or transferor's attorney, the disbursing title or escrow company, or the *mortgage lender*; includes the name and address of the transferor and transferee, the address of (and any additional information necessary for identifying) the real estate being transferred, and the name and address of the designated real estate reporting person and all other parties, if any, to the agreement; is signed and dated by all parties to the agreement and retained for four years following the calendar year in which the closing occurs; and is made available for inspection on request by the *IRS* or any person involved in the transaction who was not a party to the agreement.

determination date, qualified plans the last day of the *plan year*; but if the plan is new, the last day of the prior plan year. §416(g)(4)(C). The term is used to evaluate whether a *qualified plan* or group of plans is *top-heavy*.

determination, deficiency dividend by regulated investment companies and REITs either a decision by the *Tax Court,* a final judgment or other final order by a court of competent jurisdiction, a *closing agreement* under §7121, or an agreement between the *IRS* and the qualified investment *entity* relating to that entity's tax liability. §860(e). If the determination results in any

adjustment, *deficiency dividends* by *real estate investment trusts* (REITs) and *regulated investment companies* (together called qualified investment entities) may be included in the special *deduction* for dividends paid to shareholders, absent fraud. §860(a) and (i).

determination letter an opinion issued by the *District Director* at the request of a *taxpayer,* or a *taxpayer representative,* based on facts stated in the taxpayer's inquiry that defines the legal implication of the stated facts. Such letters are available if the answer can be based on clear precedent, and they are commonly issued on the status of pension plans and nonprofit organizations. Reg. §601.201(c)(4) and (5).

determination, mitigation of statute of limitations and other provisions a decision by the *Tax Court*; a judgment, a decree, or other order by any court of competent jurisdiction which has become final; a *closing agreement* made under §7121; a final disposition by the *Treasury Department* of all or a part of a *claim for refund or credit*; or an agreement filed pursuant to the *regulations* under §1313 (Form 2259). §1313(a). A determination must exist before the relief of §§1311-1314 is available against the hardships caused by the *statute of limitations* and certain other circumstances. See *mitigation of effect of statutes of limitations and other provisions*.

determination, personal holding company tax the process by which a *deficiency dividend deduction* becomes available to *personal holding companies*. The determination may be made by a decision of the *Tax Court,* a judgment, decree, or other order by any court of competent jurisdiction which has become final; a *closing agreement* made pursuant to §7121; or a written agreement entered into between the *taxpayer* and the *Secretary* or his *delegate* pursuant to *regulations* controlling the amount of *personal holding company tax* due. §547(c)(1)-(3).

developer-assister rules a reference to Reg. §1.482-2(d)(1)(ii), which sets standards for evaluating who owns *intangible property*, hence, who is therefore entitled to be compensated. The regulations study all the facts, concentrating on relative costs and risks in the development process. Section 482 adjustments for developers (as opposed to "assisters") are somewhat deferred.

developer rule a nickname for a provision that allows real estate developers to reduce their *passive activity gross income* by reclassifying *net income* and *gains* earned from certain *real estate* as nonpassive, provided the property is not held for 12 months between its development and its disposition. Reg §1.419-2T(f)(5). The exception is available to *taxpayers* who materially or significantly participate in value-enhancing services with respect to the property during any taxable year.

The basic idea is to treat developers' services as active, including lease-up services, unless over half the property is leased. Under Reg. §1.469-2T(f)(5)(ii)(b), the 12-month rental period begins when the property is acquired, the rental portion is held out for rent, and no significant value-enhancing services (other than lease-up) remain to be done. See *passive loss rules; material participation, passive loss rules.*

development corporation a *corporation* principally engaged in the development or exploitation of inventions, technological improvements, and new processes that were not previously generally available to the world at large. §851(e)(1); Reg. §1.851-6(a)(1). If a *regulated investment company* provides capital to development corporations, it can become a *venture capital company,* and thus subject to more liberal diversification-of-investment rules. §851(e)(1).

development expenditures, minerals *expenditures* for the development of mineral property, *paid or incurred* after the disclosure of minerals (other than oil, gas, or geothermal) of commercially marketable quantities. §616(a); Reg. §1.616-1(a). See Rev. Rul. 77-308, 1977-2 C.B. 208, Rev. Rul. 70-288, 1970-1 C.B. 146. Section 611 offers an election to *deduct* such amounts annually. Unlike hard mineral exploration expenditures, hard mineral development expenditures are not subject to *recapture* except on *disposition.* Development expenditures may be *capitalized* and *amortized* at the *taxpayer's* election. §616(b).

development, oil, gas, and geothermal the drilling of wells that bring oil and gas into commercial production. Development follows exploration and discovery of oil and gas. Oil and gas exploration is, in large measure, done by drilling and precedes the production phase. Although oil and gas exploration costs must be *capitalized* and later written off as a *loss* if worthless (Rev. Rul. 77-188, 1977-1 C.B. 76), *intangible drilling and development costs* (IDCs) incurred by an *operator* are electively *deductible,* even if it is "wildcat" drilling. §263(c).

device limitation, corporate divisions a requirement for granting tax-free status to *corporate divisions* that the division not be used principally as a "device" for the *distribution* of the *earnings and profits* of the parent or the subsidiary. §355(a)(1)(B). The term underlines a general purpose to prohibit tax-free divisions in which the *shareholders* can promptly withdraw liquid or salable assets from either company at *capital gain* rates by a *liquidation* or sale of the *stock.* The focal point of the inquiry is whether the distribution is a mechanism whereby earnings and profits could be extracted from either *corporation,* or both, in lieu of payment of a *dividend.*

diagnostic procedures routine medical exams, blood tests, and X-rays. Not included are (1) treatments or cures of an illness; (2) testing for unknown illness or disability; or (3) treatment or testing for a physical energy, complaint, or specific symptom of a bodily malfunction. Reg. §1.105-11(g)(1). Health and medical reimbursement plans may discriminate with respect to diagnostic procedures.

diesel and aviation fuels excise tax an *excise tax* of 29.1 cents (15 cents + 14 cents + 0.1 cents ((§4091)(b)(1))) per gallon imposed on the importer or producer (including refiners and wholesalers) on sales of these products. There are broad exemptions for railroads, heating oil, commercial aviation, off-highway users, and state and local governments, among others. See §§4091-3 and 7232.

differential earnings amount, life insurance companies an amount which a *mutual life insurance company* must use in reducing its *general deduction* for *policyholder dividends.* §809. If the resulting number is n gative, the company reduces its *reserves* and may be forced to report some further *life insurance gross income.* §809(a)(2). See *life insurance deductions; differential earnings rate; policyholder dividend, life insurance companies.*

differential earnings rate the *imputed earnings rate* for the *taxable year.* The imputed earnings rate basically reflects the higher earnings of *stock life insurance companies,* and the average mutual earnings rate reflects the lower, post-dividend, earnings of the *mutual life insurance companies.* There are numerous further adjustments. See *life insurance deductions average equity base; differential earnings rate; policyholder dividend, life insurance companies.*

difficulty of care payments payments, beyond actual costs, made to *taxpayers* for caring at home for a *qualified foster individual* who is physically, mentally, or emotionally handicapped, which the state determines are needed and which are designated as compensation. §131(c). Such amounts are excludable from *gross income.* §131(a), (b). See *qualified foster care payments.*

digest ruling a *ruling* without an analytical rationale. For a reference to such a ruling, see G.C.M. 39043, Aug. 5, 1983.

dimension or ornamental stone blocks and slabs of natural stone, subsequently cut to definite shapes and sizes and used or sold for such uses as building and monumental stone. Dimension or ornamental stone can qualify for a 14 percent depletion rate. §613(b)(6)(A). See *percentage depletion.*

direct costing a financial accounting concept under which production costing is performed by including direct and variable indirect costs in *inventory* costs, and treating fixed indirect production costs as currently deductible period costs.

direct credit a shorthand term for *credit* for *taxes* allowed to *resident aliens, citizens, domestic trusts, estates,* and *corporations,* as well as to *foreign corporations* and *nonresident aliens* engaged in a *United States business* as to their *effectively connected income* from sources without the United States. §901. It is limited to taxes *paid or accrued* by the *taxpayer.* The credit directly offsets *federal income tax* liabilities.

direct five-percent shareholder an *individual* who owns, at any time during the *testing period* a direct ownership interest in the *stock* of the *loss corporation* of 5 percent or more. Reg. §1.382-2T(g)(1). The term is used in connection with determining if there has been an *ownership change* in the loss corporation such that the *section 382 limitation* might apply under the *neutrality principle.* See *option attribution rules under §382.*

direct labor costs wages paid for work performed on a specific unit of production or in a specific department, including vacation pay, overtime, and so forth. Reg. §1.471-11(b)(2). See *full absorption accounting.*

direct labor costs, uniform capitalization rules *wages* paid for work which can be identified or associated with a particular activity, including overtime pay, vacation and holiday pay, sick leave pay, shift differential, and *payroll taxes.* Reg. §1.263A-1T(b)(2)(i). These costs are a type of *allocable cost* which are subject to the *uniform capitalization rules.* They can be allocated by any reasonable method. See *allocable costs, uniform capitalization rules.*

directly related test, entertainment and meal expenses one standard for determining whether meal or *entertainment* expenses are *deductible gain*-seeking expenses or merely *nondeductible personal expenses.* To meet this test the *taxpayer* must show that (1) the principal aspect of the meeting was the transaction of *business*; (2) business was engaged in during the meal or entertainment period; and (3) the taxpayer had more than a general expectation of deriving income or some other specific benefit in the future. The business conversation must be more than incidental to the entertainment. In any event, entertainment on yachts, at lodges, or on hunting or fishing trips presumptively is not "directly related." Reg. §1.274-2(c)(3)(iii).

direct material costs cost of substances which can be identified with a specific unit of production or with a department or process. Reg. §1.471-11(b)(2). See *full absorption accounting.*

direct material costs, uniform capitalization rules the *cost* of substances and materials which become an integral part of *property,* and the costs of those materials consumed in the ordinary course of producing property. Reg. §1.263A-1T(b)(2)(i). These costs are a type of *allocable cost* which are subject to the *uniform capitalization rules.* See *allocable costs, uniform capitalization rules.*

directory rule an instruction, especially to *IRS* personnel, that does not create legal rights for the *taxpayer.* Most rules in the *Internal Revenue Manual* are directory. Failure to meet a directory *regulation* should not result in loss of tax benefits. For the antonym, see *mandatory rules.*

direct production costs the cost of materials and labor which can be directly tied to manufactured products under *full absorption accounting* for *inventory valuation.* Reg. §1.471-11(b)(2)(i), (ii), and (d) allows some latitude in treating direct production costs as indirect production costs. The direct cost method of valuing manufactured *inventory* is no longer acceptable. Instead, *full absorption* is required. Reg. §1.471-11. See *production costs.*

direct public group any 5 percent *public group* of a *loss corporation* and any public group of the loss corporation resulting from the application of the segregation rules. Reg. §1.382-2T(j)(2)(ii). See *neutrality principle.*

direct reallocation method an *allocation* method used in connection with the *uniform capitalization rules* in which total costs of a *service department* are allocated solely to departments or cost centers that are engaged in production or resale activities and then from those departments to particular activities. It ignores interservice department benefits and removes other service departments from the allocation base. Reg. §1.263-1T(b)(4)(iii)(A). See *step-allocation method.*

direct sales returns filings required of any person engaged in a *trade or business* who, in the course of the trade or business, sells consumer products to any buyer on a *buy-sell basis,* a *deposit-commission basis,* or any similar basis which the *Secretary* prescribes by *regulations.* The buyer or any other person must hold the products for resale in the home or otherwise, rather than in a permanent retail establishment. The information in such filings is compiled on a *calendar year* basis and must include the name and address of each buyer to whom the aggregate amount of such sales is $5,000 or more. §6041A(b)(1). The term "person" includes any governmental unit and any agency or instrumentality. §6041A(d)(1). A direct sales return is not required if a statement for the services is required under §§6051 (receipts for *employees*), 6052 (*returns* regarding payment of *wages* in the form of *group-term life insurance*), or 6053 (reporting of tips). §6041A(c).

direct seller a *person* engaged in the *business* of selling consumer products for consumption or resale, which sales take place in the home or in a location other than a permanent retail establishment. §3508(b)(2). Such persons are treated as *independent contractors* for federal *employment tax* purposes.

disabled access credit part of the *general business credit* under §38. It is 50 percent of the *eligible access* *expenditures* paid by an *eligible small business.* The base is expenditures during the *taxable year* that exceed $250, but are not over $10,250. §44.

disabled persons credit see *credit for the elderly and disabled.*

disappearing basis rule a remedial provision designed to rectify cases when an actual or *constructive stock redemption* is characterized, for federal *income tax* purposes, as a *distribution.* Specifically, when a shareholder's *stock* is redeemed and the proceeds are taxed as *distributions,* the shareholder is unable to recover, tax-free, his or her investment (basis) in the surrendered shares. To prevent the inequity of having a shareholder both lose his basis in the redeemed stock and suffer a distribution, the rule declares that the basis of the shareholder's remaining stock is increased by the basis of the redeemed stock. Reg. §1.302-2(c). See *stock redemption.*

disaster loss a *loss* attributable to a designated cause which occurs in an area declared by the President of the United States as a disaster area entitled to federal assistance. §165(h). *Taxpayers* may choose to claim such *losses* in the year the disaster took place, or in the preceding year. Note that a disaster can be more inclusive (e.g., drought) than a *casualty,* but in the case of *individuals* a disaster loss is *deductible* only if incurred in a *casualty,* in a *trade or business,* or in a *transaction entered into for a profit.* Reg. §1.165-11.

discharge of lien see *release of tax lien.*

disclaimer, estate and gift taxation a refusal to accept a *gift* or a *bequest, devise,* or *inheritance.* For an effective disclaimer, called a *qualified disclaimer,* to be made, thus preventing federal *estate, gift or generation-skipping transfer tax* liability, the (identical) conditions enumerated in §§2518(b) and 2045 must be met. Such a disclaimer has the effect of deeming there to have been no transfer to the disclaiming party. See *qualified disclaimer.*

Disclosure Office see *Disclosure Operations Division.*

Disclosure Officer the *individual,* housed in *District Offices,* responsible for administering the *Freedom of Information Act,* the *Privacy Act,* and other disclosure obligations.

Disclosure Operations Division the division of the *National Office* of the *IRS* responsible for supervising disclosures of information under the *Freedom of Information Act* and IRS *regulations.* Requests for information may be directed either to the National Office or to one of many *Regional Offices* and *districts.* Mailing and walk-in addresses are found in Reg. §601.701(g).

discount generally, the amount by which the amount paid for *debt* is less than its face amount. Financial dis-

counts may be either *original issue discount* or *market discount.* Original issue discount arises where the actual amount borrowed is less than the face amount of the debt. §1272. Market discount occurs where the *fair market value* of debt slips in price as a result of market forces. See *accrual of bond discount; cash discounts.*

discounted present value the value of a future dollar disbursed or received, expressed in current dollars. Discounting is widely used for valuation purposes.

discounted stock option an informal term for a plan under which executives or directors are granted the right to purchase *stock* of the *corporation* at a deep discount. They may be taxable at once if there is *constructive receipt of income,* however.

discretionary-contribution plan another term for a profit-sharing plan. See *profit-sharing plan, Code.*

discriminant function system a computer program which screens and scores federal *tax returns* for possible *audits.*

disguised dividend a transfer which in form is not a *dividend,* but which is intended or operates as a dividend. The distinction between disguised dividends and *constructive dividends* seems more semantic than practical. See *constructive dividend.*

disguised sales between partners and partnerships a situation where a partner transfers property to a partnership and there is a related transfer of money or other property from the partnership to the partner. Taken together, the transfers are viewed *as a sale or exchange and are treated as such for tax purposes.* Disguised sale treatment is applicable in the following circumstances: (1) the partnership's transfer of money or other property wouldn't have been made but for the partner's transfer of property to it; and (2) the partnership transfer isn't dependent on "entrepreneurial risks" of partnership operations. Reg. §§1.707-3 through 1.707-9.

disposal with a retained economic interest the *disposition* of timber, timber interests, coal (including lignite), or domestic iron ore held for more than a year, while retaining an *economic interest* in the subject matter of the sale. Under the mandatory rules of §631(b) (timber) or 631(c) (coal or domestic iron ore), what might otherwise have been royalties are converted into *long-term capital gains* or *ordinary losses* under the principles of §1231 such that overall *gains* produce capital gains and losses, but overall *losses* produce ordinary income and losses.

disposition virtually any transaction that terminates an interest in property. The term is never adequately defined, although it appears frequently throughout the *Code* in such critical portions as §§1001 (*gains* and *losses* from dealing in property) and 1245 et seq. (*recapture* of *gains* as *ordinary income*). See *benefits* *and burdens of ownership; beneficial interest; exchange; sale.*

disposition, installment obligation   a *sale, exchange, gift,* transfer from a *trust,* repossession of property sold, or other *transfer,* or cancellation of an *installment obligation.* Distributions of installment obligations to shareholders in certain *corporate liquidations* are neither dispositions of the installment obligation nor taxable to the corporation: instead the shareholders are treated as if they stepped into the corporation's shoes. §453(h)(1)(A). Generally, disposition of an installment obligation accelerates taxation by creating *gain* equal to the obligation's *fair market value* (disposition other than by *sale* or *exchange*) or *amount realized* (disposition by sale or exchange), less the *taxpayer's basis in the installment obligation.* §453B(a).

disposition of entire interest in a passive activity generally, an *arm's length sale* to an unrelated party. When a taxpayer disposes of a passive activity in a taxable transaction, the economic gain or loss generated by the activity can be computed, and the suspended losses of that activity may be deducted against the taxpayer's other income. However, the amount of the total net economic loss from the asset that is disposed of must first offset any passive income from other passive activities. §469(g). See *passive loss rules.*

disproportionate   not pro rata.

disproportionate distribution, partnerships   a *distribution* of property to a *partner* which has the effect of decreasing her or his proportionate share of *hot assets* and correspondingly decreasing her or his share of other assets, or vice versa. The *Code* provisions governing such distributions are very complex; their effect is to manufacture hypothetical taxable *exchanges* in order to limit tax abuse. §751.

disproportionate distribution, stock dividend   basically, a *distribution* of *stock* or stock rights to one group of shareholders and cash or other property to another group of shareholders. If the distribution (or series of distributions) results in an increase in the proportionate interest of the other shareholders in the corporation's assets or earnings and profits, then the stock or stock rights distributed to the shareholder on the common stock of the corporation must be treated as a taxable distribution. §305(b)(2). The disproportionality can also arise from various *constructive disproportionate distributions* under §305(c). See *constructive disproportionate distributions.*

disproportionate redemption of stock   see *substantially disproportionate redemption.*

disproportionate sharing arrangement   an arrangement common in the oil and gas industry under which the sponsor/operator bears a certain percentage of all costs while sharing in a higher proportion of the program revenues. Commonly, the sponsor pays 25 percent of the costs and receives 50 percent of the revenues.

disputed liabilities deduction   see *contested liabilities deduction.*

disqualified benefits   (1) post-retirement or life insurance benefits for a *key employee* not paid out of a separate account where one is required; (2) discriminatory benefits of the type described above; or (3) any of the welfare benefit fund reverting to the *employer's* benefit. §4976(b)(3). An *excise tax* falls on employers who provide disqualified benefits provided by a fund under a welfare benefit plan. The tax is 100 percent of the disqualified benefits provided during a *taxable year.* See *excise tax, disqualified welfare plan benefits.*

disqualified individual   a *substantial contributor* to a *private foundation*; an owner of over 20 percent of the votes of a *corporation*, the *profits interest* in a *partnership,* or the *beneficial interest* of a *trust* or unincorporated enterprise, which, during such ownership, is a substantial contributor; or the family (per §4946(d)) of any of the above. See §4946(a)(3) and (4) for further *attribution rules.* See *exempt operating foundation.*

disqualified individual, golden parachutes   includes any *officer, shareholder, or highly compensated individual (including a personal service corporation or similar entity).* §280G. A corporation that enters into a contract to pay an employee in excess of his or her usual compensation is barred from taking a deduction for an "*excess parachute payment*" to a "disqualified individual." The disqualified individual is subject to an excise tax of 20 percent of the excess parachute payment in addition to the income tax due. §4999.

disqualified interest   any *interest paid or accrued* directly or indirectly to a related *person* if no *United States income tax* is imposed on such interest, but it excludes: (1) interest on any *demand loan* or other loan without a fixed term which was outstanding on July 10, 1989, to the extent attributable to periods before September 1, 1989; (2) interest paid or accrued under indebtedness with a fixed term which was (a) issued before July 11, 1989, or (b) was issued after July 10, 1989, under a written binding contract in effect on July 10, 1989, and at all times between that date and the date on which the debt was issued. §163(j)(3)(B). A corporation will be disallowed a deduction for excessive interest paid to a tax-exempt related person. The provision is designed to put an end to bleeding off corporate earnings via interest payments to related charities or foreign owners. See *earnings stripping provisions.*

disqualified lease   any *lease* of property to a *tax-exempt entity,* but only if (1) part of all of the property was financed (directly or indirectly) by an obligation, the interest on which is exempt from tax under §103(a) (i.e., a *tax-exempt bond*), and the entity (or related entity) participated in such financing; (2) under such lease there is a fixed or determinable price purchase or sale option which involves such entity (or related entity) or there is the equivalent of such an option; (3) the lease has a term in excess of 20 years or such lease occurs after a *sale* (or other transfer of the property by, or lease of the property from, such entity (or related entity) before such sale (or other transfer) or lease. §168(h)(1)(B)(ii). Such leases can give rise to *tax-exempt use property* which is subject to relatively slow cost recovery. See *tax-exempt bond–financed property*.

disqualified leaseback or long-term agreement   any *§467 rental agreement* if it is part of a *leaseback transaction* or *long-term agreement,* meaning one for a term longer than 75 percent of the property's statutory *recovery period* (generally, the *ACRS* recovery period, whether or not the property qualifies for ACRS treatment)—but in any case only if a principal purpose for increasing rents is *tax avoidance.* §467(b)(4). Such leasebacks and agreements are subject to remedial provisions forcing level rental accruals by lessors and lessees. See *rent-leveling rules.*

disqualified person, black lung benefit trusts   a person who is one of the following: (1) a contributor to the *black lung benefit trust*; (2) a *trustee* of the *trust*; (3) an owner of more than 10 percent of (a) the total combined voting power of a *corporation,* (b) the *profits interest* of a *partnership,* or (c) the *beneficial interest* of a *trust* or unincorporated enterprise, which is a contributor to the trust; (4) an officer, director, or *employee* of a person who is a contributor to the trust; (5) the *spouse,* ancestor, lineal descendant, or spouse of a lineal descendant of an *individual* described above; (6) a corporation of which the persons described above own more than 35 percent of the total combined voting power; (7) a partnership in which persons described above (except corporations not described) own more than 35 percent of the profits interest; or (8) a trust or *estate* in which persons described above (except the corporations and partnerships described in (6) and (7) above) hold more than 35 percent of the beneficial interest. §4951(e)(4). Special *attribution rules* apply in determining stock ownership. §4951(e)(5). Disqualified persons are subject to various penalties for improper dealings with black lung benefit trusts. See *self-dealing tax, black lung benefits trust.*

disqualified person, private foundations   for transactions with *private foundations,* a series of people who are subject to various *excise taxes* (which can rise to 200 percent) designed to penalize various prohibited acts. The list of persons includes: (1) a substantial contributor to the foundation; (2) a *foundation manager*; (3) someone who owns more than 20 percent of a *business* or *trust* which is itself a substantial contributor; (4) a mem-

ber of the family of the *individuals* described in (1)–(3) above; (5) a *partnership,* trust, *estate,* or *corporation* more than 35 percent owned by anyone described in (1)–(4) above; or (6) a *government official.* §4946. Another private foundation controlled by, or receiving substantially all its contributions from, the same persons described above is also included for purposes of the excise taxes on *excess business holdings.* Section 4946(a)(3) provides *attribution rules* for determining ownership levels of entities and thus greatly extends the reach of the excise taxes. See *government official, private foundations; self-dealing tax, private foundations.*

disqualified person, qualified plans   a term used in the *qualified deferred compensation plan* area to describe *persons* who are potentially subject to *excise taxes* imposed on *prohibited transactions* (basically, transactions that might be disadvantageous to plan participants). Such persons can include fiduciaries, which can include an administrator, officer, *trustee,* or *custodian,* among others), a lawyer for or *employee* of a plan, or a relative of these people. A disqualified person may also include someone who provides services to the plan, or a person who owns a 50-percent-or-more interest, directly or indirectly, in an employer, any of whose employees are covered by the plan. §4975(e)(2).

disqualified portion   see *disqualified yield.*

disqualified preferred stock   certain *preferred stock,* *dividends* on which are per se deemed to be *extraordinary dividends* so as to reduce the *basis* of such stock in the hands of a *corporation* holding such stock. The stock so affected is preferred stock if (1) when issued, such stock has a dividend rate which declines (or can be reasonably expected to decline) in the future; (2) the stock's issue price exceeds its liquidation rights or its stated redemption price; or (3) such stock is otherwise structured to reduce tax through a combination of *dividends-received deductions* and *loss* on the *disposition* of such stock. §1059(f). See *extraordinary dividend, basis reduction.*

disqualified property   property which is acquired by a liquidating *corporation* during the five-year period preceding the liquidation if the *property* was acquired through a *section 351 transaction* or a *contribution to capital.* §336(d)(1)(B). A liquidating corporation cannot recognize a *loss* on a *distribution* to a *related taxpayer* if the distributed property is disqualified property or is not made *pro rata* among *shareholders.* §336(d)(1). A related taxpayer is defined in §267. Thus, a distribution of depreciated property to a shareholder who directly or indirectly owns more than 50 percent of the liquidating corporation's *stock* cannot generate a tax loss for the corporation. Even post-contribution losses are affected. Section 361(d)(2) buttresses these rules. See *related taxpayers, loss and deduction denial.*

disqualified stock includes *stock* in the distributing *corporation* if it was acquired by purchase (as defined) on the date of the *distribution* or at any time in the five-year period immediately before that date but after October 9, 1990. Stock in a controlled corporation is disqualified stock if it was (1) acquired by purchase on the date of the distribution or at any time during the five-year period immediately before that date, but after October 9, 1990; or (2) received in the distribution and attributable to distributions on disqualified distributing corporation stock or *securities* in the distributing corporation acquired by purchase on the date of the distribution or at any time during the five-year period immediately before that date (but after October 9, 1990). §355(d)(3).

disqualified stock, debt cancellation any *stock* with a *stated redemption price at maturity* that (1) has a fixed redemption date; (2) is callable by the issuer; or (3) is puttable by the holder. §108(e)(10)(B). Disqualified stock is not treated as stock for purposes of the *de minimis* and proportionality disqualification of the *stock-for-debt exception* to the cancellation of indebtedness rules as to stock issued after October 9, 1990. §108(e)(8), (10)(a)-(c), and (11). The concept is geared to removing preferred stock from the mix of consideration received by creditors. This means bankrupt or insolvent taxpayers must reduce their *tax attributes* to the extent the discharged debt exceeds the value of the disqualified preferred stock.

disqualified yield the portion of the yield on an obligation that exceeds the *applicable federal rate* when it was issued plus 6 percentage points. §163(e)(5)(C)(ii). The portion of the yield on an *applicable high-yield discount obligation* that is not treated as *interest* (and is, therefore, not *deductible* by the obligor) is known as the *disqualified portion* of the OID. It is the portion of the total return on the obligation that bears the same ratio to the total return as the disqualified yield bears to the total yield to maturity on the instrument.

disqualifying disposition see *incentive stock option.*

disregard of corporate entity the practice of treating a *corporation* as if it were nonexistent for tax purposes, thereby causing the *shareholders* to be taxed directly on their share of all corporate *gains, losses,* and other tax incidents.

dissolution, corporation the legal termination of a *corporation.* Such terminations ordinarily accompany *liquidation* of the corporation and relieve the corporation of the duty to file *federal income tax returns.* If a calendar-year corporation dissolves on June 30, it must file a short-period return covering the period January 1 to June 30. In addition to filing its regular income tax return, a corporation that has adopted a resolution to dissolve itself or liquidate all or part of its stock must file

Form 966 (Corporate Dissolution or Liquidation) to notify the IRS of its plans. §6043 and reg. §1.6043-1. See *de facto liquidation.*

dissolution, partnership the legal termination of a *partnership* as a matter of local law. It typically arises on a change in the identity of members, death, bankruptcy, or insanity of a *general partner.* Reg. §301.7701-(2)(b)(2). The possibility of a dissolution in such cases generally results in the absence of the corporate feature of *continuity of life,* even though the partnership agreement provides for continuation of business by the remaining members and even though no *termination* for tax purposes takes place. *Id.*

distortion of income the opposite of a *clear reflection of income.* For example, current *deductions* are exaggerated for expenditures that properly relate to future periods or by transactions engaged in with related parties that result in *gains* or *losses* that would not have occurred if the transactions had been with strangers.

distraint see *levy.*

distributable amount, private foundation the *minimum investment return,* reduced by the sum of taxes imposed on the *private foundation* for the taxable year. §4942(d). A 15 percent *excise tax* on a private foundation's undistributed income is levied on the distributable amount less *qualifying distributions.* §§4942(a) and (c), 4942(d)(1). See *undistributed income excise tax, private foundation.*

distributable net income an amount used: (1) to limit the *deductions* allowed to *estates* and *complex trusts* under §§651 and 661 for amounts paid, credited, or required to be distributed to *beneficiaries*; and (2) as the measure of *taxable income* reportable by *beneficiaries.* The *character* of such income is preserved in the hands of the beneficiaries. §§652(b), 662(b).

distributed amount, real estate investment trust see *excise tax, undistributed income of a REIT.*

distributed amount, regulated investment company see *excise tax, undistributed income of a RIC.*

distributed, sold, exchanged, or otherwise disposed of, alternate valuation date with respect to the rules relating to the *alternate valuation date,* the ways of transferring property that will accelerate the date of valuing property in the *gross estate.* If the alternate valuation date has been elected, property in the gross estate is valued six months after death rather than on the date of death. However, property distributed, sold, or otherwise disposed of within the six-month period is valued on the date transferred rather than six months after death. §2032(a)(1).

distribution, corporation an actual or *constructive* transfer of *property* (including money, *securities,* and *debt* of the *corporation*), other than *stock* or *rights* to acquire stock in the corporation, by a corporation to a *shareholder* in his or her capacity as a shareholder. §§301(a), 317(a). Distributions may be current (i.e., not in liquidation) or as an aspect of a *corporate liquidation*. The following material sketches the taxation of *current distributions*. The amount of the distribution equals the cash plus the *fair market value* of noncash property conveyed. §301(b). Distributions may be treated or taxed in three ways: (1) the portion of the distribution that constitutes a *dividend* (as defined in §316) out of *earnings and profits* is included in the shareholder's *gross income* as *ordinary income* (modified for *twenty-percent corporate shareholders*); (2) the portion of the distribution that does not constitute a *dividend* is tax-free and is applied against and reduces the *adjusted basis* of the recipient's stock; and (3) the portion of the distribution that does not constitute a *dividend*, but does exceed the adjusted basis of the stock (i.e., exceeds the amount determined in (2) above), is included in *gross income* as *gain* from the *sale* or *exchange* of property. §301(c). The corporation can *recognize gains* but not *losses* on nonliquidating distributions of property. Distributions of stock may be taxable to recipients under §305 relating to *stock dividends*. See *complete liquidation, corporate*.

distribution, generally a transfer of money or other property from an *entity* (e.g., *trust, estate, partnership,* or *corporation*) to a *beneficiary, partner,* or *shareholder*.

distribution in kind a *distribution* from a *partnership, trust,* or *corporation* of property other than money.

distribution in redemption of stock see *stock redemption*.

distribution in reorganization a *distribution* by an acquired *corporation* in connection with a *corporate reorganization*. Section 361(c) does not recognize *losses* on distribution of depreciated assets, but it does recognize *gains* on the distribution of appreciated assets to *shareholders*, subject to an exception for distributions of *qualified property*. See *qualified property, corporate reorganizations*.

distribution, partnership a transfer of money or other property from a *partnership* to a *partner,* in the partner's capacity as a partner rather than in the capacity of a third party. Distributions from partnerships are generally tax-free and, by virtue of §705(a)(2), merely reduce the partner's *basis in the partnership interest*. However, distributions of money in excess of basis are treated as a sale or *exchange* of the *partnership interest* and, therefore, generally result in *capital gains* to the partner. §731. See §735 for the *character* of *gain*. See *collapsible partnership rules*.

distribution, qualified plan generally, any direct or indirect payment to a *beneficiary* from a *qualified plan*. It includes loans other than those described in §72(p)(2),

as well as pledges and assignments other than loans and amounts the *plan administrator* approves for distribution even if a smaller amount is withdrawn. Rev. Rul. 71-332, 1971-2 C.B. 210. See *uniform minimum distribution rules*.

distribution right a right to *distributions* from a *corporation* with respect to its *stock* and a right to distributions from a *partnership* with respect to a *partner's* interest in the partnership. §2701(c)(1)(A). It excludes a right to distributions with respect to any *junior equity* interest, any *liquidation, put, call, or conversion right,* or any right to receive any *guaranteed payment* (§707(c) meaning). §2701(c)(1)(B).

distribution, trusts and estates generally, transfers to *beneficiaries* that are not *gifts, bequests,* or *devises*. §663(a)(1).

distributive share a *partner's* agreed-upon participation in a *partnership's income, gain, loss, deduction,* or *credit*. Such shares preserve their tax *character* in the hands of partners and must be reported for *federal income tax* purposes, whether or not distributed. They are recorded on *Schedules K-1* which are transmitted to each partner after the close of the partnership's *taxable year*. Reg. §1.702-1(a). See *allocation: special allocations; substantial economic effect test*.

distributive share, piggyback taxation the income of a *trust* or *estate* that is taxable to the *taxpayer* as a *beneficiary* under applicable *federal income tax* rules, and the *undistributed taxable income* of an *S corporation* taxable to the taxpayer. Reg. §301.6362-5(c)(3).

distributor's agreement cancellation a cancellation of an agreement for the distribution of goods. If the distributor has a substantial capital investment in the distributorship, amounts paid to the distributor can be deemed received in *exchange* for the agreement and may result in a *capital gain or loss*. §1241.

District a geographical area of *IRS* jurisdiction, a subpart of an IRS region, administered by a *District Office*. See *Regional Office*.

District Counsel the chief attorney for the particular *District Office* of the *IRS*. This *individual* controls a sizeable staff of lawyers whose primary function is to litigate cases in the *Tax Court*. The office is ultimately controlled by the *Chief Counsel* of the IRS, but it is under the immediate supervision of a *Regional Counsel* in the *Regional Office*.

District Court a federal court of general jurisdiction. District courts are subdivisions of circuit courts to which appeals are taken. District courts are the forums most often used for possible recovery of denied *claims for refunds* (following the payment of assessed *deficiencies*), proceedings for enforcement of *IRS summonses,* and criminal tax matters.

District Director the District Director of Internal Revenue for an *Internal Revenue District,* and the Director of International Operations. Reg. 301.7701-10. District Directors are charged with administering the internal revenue laws in their Internal Revenue District.

District Office an administrative office of the *IRS,* which is most notable to *taxpayers* because it houses *revenue agents* and is the standard point of origin of *audit* controversies. The District Offices contain five subgroups: Examination, Collection, Taxpayer Service, Criminal Investigation, and Resource Management. Some districts contain an Employee Plans and Exempt Organization Division. District Offices are run by a *District Director* who reports to the *Regional Director.*

diversification in general, the practice of distributing risk by broadening investments or activities. For purposes of §351(e), two or more unrelated persons who transfer separately owned property to a controlled corporation in exchange for its stock or securities are permitted to achieve a degree of diversification without recognizing gain. The nonrecognition principle of §351 is *inapplicable* to transfers of property "to an investment company." The general nonrecognition rules also do not apply to gain realized upon a contribution of property to a partnership "investment company." §§721(a), 721(b). See *partnership swap fund; swap fund.*

dividend a *distribution* of money or *property* (as defined in §317 to include anything other than *stock* and rights to acquire stock) in the ordinary course of *business* to *shareholders* of the distributing *corporation,* in their capacities as such, by a *domestic* or *foreign corporation* out of either post–February 13, 1913, *accumulated earnings and profits* or *current earnings and profits* of the year in which the dividend is paid, computed without regard to the amount of the current earnings and profits at the time the distribution is made. §316; Reg. §1.316-1(a)(1). A dividend is defined differently for purposes of federal *income taxes* and state corporate law. Therefore, a corporate distribution may be a dividend for tax purposes under §§316(a) and 301, even though unlawful under state law (e.g., impairs capital). Distributions that are dividends are taxed as *ordinary income.* §§61 and 301. See *earnings and profits*; *property, corporate distributions.*

dividend announcement date for purposes of reducing *basis* in stock for *extraordinary dividends,* the earliest of the dates when the payor *corporation* declares, announces, or agrees to either the amount or payment of the dividend. §1059(d)(1)(A). See *extraordinary dividend, basis reduction.*

dividend carryover a reference to §564(a) which allows *deductions* for *dividends* paid in the two preceding years to the extent dividends exceed *taxable income* (as adjusted) in those prior years. The provision reduces

the base on which the *personal holding company tax* falls. See *dividends-paid deduction, corporate.*

dividend equivalent amount, branch profits tax the base on which the *branch profits tax* falls. It is the amount of a *foreign corporation's* United States branch's earnings that are subject to the *branch profits tax.* §884(a). The amount equals its *effectively connected earnings and profits* for the *taxable year,* reduced for any rise and increased for any decline in *United States net equity* from a previous year. §884(b). Increases in the dividend equivalent amount due to equity decline may not exceed *accumulated effectively connected earnings and profits* as of the close of the prior year. §884(b)(2)(B). The general tax rate is 30 percent. See *effectively connected earnings and profits, branch profits tax.*

dividend in kind *dividends* paid by *corporations* in property, as opposed to cash. See *noncash dividends.*

dividend, life insurance See *policyholder dividend, life insurance companies.*

dividend, personal holding company income A dividend received by a corporation which is part of its *personal holding company income* for purposes of determining whether the *entity* is a *personal holding company.* §543(a)(1).

dividends-paid deduction, corporate generally a *deduction* that permits diminution of the base on which the *accumulated earnings tax* or the *personal holding company tax* is imposed, or that permits a *REIT* or *RIC* to preserve its status as a *conduit.* §§535(a), 545(a), 860. The taxable base of the accumulated earnings tax is a company's accumulated taxable income (ATI). The taxable income of the corporation is modified as follows: ATI = Taxable income ± certain adjustments − dividends-paid deduction − the accumulated earnings credit. See *deficiency dividend, personal holding company; deficiency dividend, real estate investment trust; deficiency dividend, regulated investment company; preferential dividend.*

dividends-paid deduction, public utilities a *deduction* allowed to public utility corporations on certain *preferred stock* issued before October 1, 1942. §247.

dividends-received deduction a deduction available to corporations on dividends received from a domestic corporation. The dividends-received deduction is generally 70 percent of the dividends received. If the recipient corporation owns 20 percent or more of the stock of the paying corporation, an 80 percent deduction is allowed. The dividends-received deduction is 100 percent of the dividends received from another member of an affiliated group, if an election is made, §§243–246.

dividends to policyholders Dividends on life insurance and endowment policies are normally not taxable because they are considered to be a partial return of premiums paid. §301. The dividends are taxable to the extent that the total dividends received exceed the total premiums paid. If the dividends are left with the insurance company and earn interest, the interest is taxable. See *policyholder dividend, life insurance companies,* for the current definition.

dividend stripping a nickname for the practice of *corporations* by which they bought *stock* that was about to pay a *dividend,* received the dividends subject to the *dividends-received deduction,* and then sold the stock at a *short-term capital loss* or diminished gain. The practice has been curtailed by §§301(f), 312(n), 246(c) and 1059. The Code limitations tend to increase the chance that a distribution will be treated as a *return of capital* rather than a tax-deductible dividend. This basis reduction makes it more likely that the sale of the distributee corporation will be at a taxable *gain.* Section 1059 is discussed under the heading *extraordinary dividend, basis reduction.*

dividend within gain principle the notion that *boot* distributed in a *corporate reorganization* should give rise to *dividend* treatment only to the extent the shareholder has *recognized gain* on the transaction. §356(a)(1). Whether there is a dividend at all, however, depends upon the boot's being qualitatively similar to a dividend from the transferor corporation. §356(a)(2). Thus, if a shareholder exchanges one share of A Corp stock, which cost $10,000, for one share of Z Corp stock worth $10,000 plus $10 of cash in a tax-free merger, there is $10 of recognized gain. Whether the $10 is taxable as a *capital gain* or as a dividend depends on whether the $10 has the *effect of a dividend. Corporate divisions* are not subject to the dividend within gain limitation. §356(b).

divisible tax a federal tax which can be broken into smaller units (e.g., *excise taxes*), such that the *taxpayer* can pay one of the smaller units, seek a *refund,* and eventually go to a court other than the *Tax Court* to seek a judicial determination of the tax.

division of partnership the division of *partnership* property or business into two or more partnerships, provided the members of the original partnership had a more-than-50-percent combined *capital* and *profits interest* in the prior partnership. The new partnership is deemed a continuation of the predecessor without *termination.* §708(b)(2)(B).

divisive reorganization a *Type D reorganization* that meets the requirements of §355. They may involve a transfer of assets to a new or pre-existing *corporation,* or a break-up of a single corporation or other formats, but they are always followed by a distribution of the controlled *corporation's stock* in a §355 *spin-off, split-off,* or *split-up.* See *corporate division.*

divisive Type D reorganization a reorganization that must take place as part of a plan of reorganization and satisfy the requirements of both §§368(a)(1)(D) and 355. There are three forms of *divisive Type D reorganizations:* spin-offs, split-offs, and split-ups. See *spin-off; split-off; split-up.*

divorce or separation instrument a decree of divorce or *separate maintenance* or a written instrument issued incident to that decree, a *written separation agreement,* or a decree of any type of court order requiring a spouse to make payments for the support or maintenance of the other spouse, including a temporary decree, an interlocutory (not final) decree, and a decree of alimony *pendente lite* (while awaiting action on the final decree or agreement). §71(b)(2). Payments pursuant to such instruments may be treated as *deductible alimony or separate maintenance payments.* §71(b).

docketed case a federal tax dispute in which a *petition* has been filed in the *Tax Court* following the issuance of a *notice of deficiency* (the so-called 90-day letter). Reg. §601.106(d)(2). Depending on the circumstances under which the case was docketed, settlement authority may vest in the *Appeals Office,* the Office of the *Chief Counsel of the IRS,* or both. Reg. §601.106(d)(3). See also Reg. §601.106(a)(1)-(3) and Rev. Proc. 78-9, 1978-1 C.B. 563, for further details regarding settlement of such cases.

documentary evidence, substantiation of travel, entertainment, and gift expenses a receipt, paid bill, or similar evidence to support an expenditure. Documentary evidence is required for any expenditure for lodging and any other expenditure of $25 or more in *travel away from home,* except if the evidence for a transportation charge is not readily available. Reg. §1.274-5(c)(2)(iii). Adequate documentary evidence ordinarily discloses the amount, date, place, and the essential character of the expenditure. A canceled check payable to a named payee is not adequate unless other evidence, such as a bill or invoice from the payee, is also presented.

document locator number a number the *Service Center* assigns to each incoming *return* and associated check. The number is used to track the return in the National Computer Center.

dollar approximate separate transactions method the normal way of calculating *gross income, taxable income,* and *earnings and profits* of a *qualified business unit* (QBU) whose *functional currency* is the United States dollar. §985(b)(3) and Reg. §1.985-2, 3. To oversimplify: the method works by taking an income statement in local currency, modifying it to conform to United States *tax accounting* principles, and applying the average United States/local currency exchange rate for the month to which the item on the statements relate.

Finally, the dollar amount of income or loss is adjusted to reflect currency gain or loss. It is generally done by determining the change in the QBU's *net worth* from the beginning to the end of the *taxable year*. The change in net worth less the dollar income (or plus the dollar loss) is the amount of currency gain or loss. This method applies for purposes of *subpart F income* and the separate limitations on the *foreign tax credit*. See Prop. Reg. INTL 29-91, 1991-31 I.R.B. 38 for a discussion.

dollar-value method the more popular of the two basic methods of computing *inventory* cost in a *last-in, first-out* (LIFO) inventory system. The dollar-value method determines cost by using a *base-year cost* expressed in total dollars rather than cost based on the quantity and price of specific goods. Any increment in base-year cost of *closing inventory* over that of opening inventory is treated as a separate "layer" of inventory for the current and future years. Reg. §1.472-8(a). An advantage of the dollar-value method is that inventory pools (groupings of goods) may be larger (and thus fewer), each generally encompassing a *natural business unit*. Reg. §1.472-8(b). The larger pools are less subject to fluctuations and thus better serve the goals of the LIFO method. Various methods of determining costs of inventory by the LIFO method include the *double-extension method, index method, link-chain method,* and *retail inventory method*. For the other LIFO method, see *specific goods method*.

dollar-value pool, LIFO see *dollar-value method*.

domestic when applied to a *corporation* or *partnership,* the term means created or organized in the *United States* or under the laws of the United States or of any *state*. §7701(a)(4) (implicitly rendering *possessions* not domestic).

domestically controlled REIT a *real estate investment trust* (REIT) in which, throughout the "testing period," less than 50 percent in value of its *stock* was held directly or indirectly by *foreign persons*. §897(h)(4)(B). The testing period is the shortest of (1) the period beginning on June 19, 1980, and ending on the date of *disposition* of the stock; (2) the five-year period ending on the date of the disposition; or (3) the period during which the *REIT* was in existence. An interest in a domestically controlled REIT is not a *United States real property interest*; therefore, sales of the stock of such REITs are not subject to the provisions applicable to dispositions of United States real property interests. §897(h)(2).

domestic building and loan association a domestic building and loan association, a domestic savings and loan association, a federal savings and loan association, or any other like savings institution under federal or state charter and supervision which meets the *supervisory test*, the *business operations test*, and the *assets test*.

§7701(a)(19); Reg. 301.7701-13A(a). While the general rules of corporate taxation apply, such institutions qualify for particularized methods of computing *reserves for bad debts* (§593) and *deductions* for *dividends* or *interest* on demand accounts (§591) §7701(a)(19); Reg. §1.591-2.

domestic corporation a *corporation* created or organized in the *United States* or under the laws of the United States or of any *state*. §7701(a)(3) and (4).

domestic crude oil or natural gas, percentage depletion *crude oil* and natural gas extracted in the *United States* and its *possessions,* including the *continental shelf areas*. §613A(e)(3).

domestic fraternal societies see *fraternal benefit societies*.

domestic international sales corporation a *domestic corporation,* often a shell, that exports goods produced in the *United States,* meets various statutory tests, and makes a revocable election to be treated as a *domestic international sales corporation* (DISC). The DISC provisions have been largely repealed and replaced by the *foreign sales corporation* (FSC) provisions. See *DISC*.

domestic investment income gross investment income from *United States* sources less the *expenses* allocable to such income. §842(b)(5). Gross investment income includes *interest* (including *tax-exempt interest*), *rents, royalties,* total *dividends* received (not reduced by the *dividends-received deduction*), and the net *gain* (or *loss*) from the *sale* of investment assets. §832(b). The expenses taken into account include interest (including interest that is incurred or continued to purchase or carry tax-exempt obligations), taxes (other than *federal income taxes*), salaries and other similar items, and *depreciation* and *depletion,* to the extent allocable to gross investment income. §842(c). Domestic investment yield for the year is multiplied by *required U.S. assets* to determine a net investment income that is *effectively connected income* associated with the operations of *foreign insurance companies*. §834(b)(1). Such companies can elect to substitute *current worldwide investment yield* for domestic investment yield. §842(b)(4). This provision was added in 1987.

domestic iron ore any ore used as a source of iron that is mined in the *United States*. Reg. §1.631-3(e). Such ore may be the subject of a *disposal with a retained economic interest,* taxed as a *capital gain* or as an *ordinary loss* as a *section 1231 asset*.

domestic partnership a *partnership* created or organized in the *United States* or under the laws of the United States or of any state. §7701(a)(2) and (4).

domestic production see *domestic crude oil or natural gas, percentage depletion*.

domestic savings association see *domestic building and loan association.*

domestic service services of a household nature, meaning work, ordinarily performed as an integral part of household duties including work done by cooks, waiters, butlers, and housekeepers. §3401(a). If both the employer and employee agree, withholding is permitted for such services. Withholding is specifically excluded for amounts of casual employment (less than $50 paid and less than 24 days worked in that quarter, tips amounting to less than $20, etc.). §3121(a). Remuneration paid for services performed in or about the private home of the person is exempt from federal *income tax withholding* if the services are of a household nature. Payments for domestic services in a private home of household nature are not subject to *FICA taxes* unless and until they exceed $50 or more cash wages in a calendar quarter, regardless of the number of days they work. §3121(a). Such services are exempt from *FUTA taxes* unless one pays $1,000 or more in cash in any quarter of the current or prior year for such services. §3306(c)(2).

domestic trust a trust other than a *foreign trust.* §7701(a)(30)(D).

domicile generally, where an *individual* resides and intends to stay indefinitely or permanently. For determining whether a person is domiciled in a *community property state,* it has been held that federal standards control.

donative intent a legal standard used to determine whether there is a *gift* as a matter of state law. The intent called for is simply the intent to make a gift. While transfers regarded as gifts for state law purposes are sufficient to find them as gifts subject to federal *gift taxes,* such gifts are excludable from *gross income* only if they arise out of "detached or disinterested generosity" and are made "out of affection, respect, admiration, charity or like impulses." See *gift, income taxation; gift tax.*

donee the recipient of a *gift* or a *power of appointment.*

donor the person who makes a *gift* or a transfer of a *power of appointment.*

double attribution see *reattribution.*

double category method, securities identification see *average basis method election.*

double declining-balance depreciation a method of *depreciation* authorized under §167(b) for new property acquired after 1953 and before 1981, with a *useful life* of more than three years. The method applies a constant rate, equal to twice the *straight-line* rate, to a declining base without regard to *salvage values.* For example, if

an asset has a five-year useful life and costs $10,000, the straight-line rate would be $2,000. The double declining balance would yield a $4,000 *deduction.* In the following year the remaining $6,000 basis would result in a $1,200 deduction (i.e., $6,000 times 20 percent). The pattern automatically prohibits actual depreciation deduction claims from exceeding a *reasonable salvage value.* Variations of the above system include 175 percent, 150 percent, and 125 percent declining-balance methods. They all use the same computational system described above by merely substituting the alternate figures (e.g., 175 percent) for 200 percent. See *declining-balance depreciation.*

double dummy technique a corporate acquisition practice in which two tiers of subsidiaries are used; the second-tier (lower) subsidiary exists temporarily only for the purpose of the acquisition and afterwards is promptly liquidated into the first-tier (higher) subsidiary. The second-tier subsidiary could be used as a transitory acquiring company in a taxable *cash merger,* followed by its *liquidation* into the higher-tier subsidiary under former §334(b)(2).

double-extension method one of the approved methods for computing the *base year cost and current-year cost* of a *dollar-value method* pool in a *last-in, first-out* (LIFO) *inventory* system. Reg. §1.472-8(e). An *index method* may be used without prior approval in certain instances, but otherwise an index method or a *link-chain method* may be used only where the double-extension method is impractical or unsuitable. *Id.* Double extension means the quantity of each item in the pool is extended at both base-year unit cost and current-year unit cost. These costs are then separately totaled for all items in the pool, thus yielding the base-year and current-year cost of the inventory in the pool. Reg. §1.472-8(e)(2). Comparing the base-year costs computed for the *closing inventory* with those computed for the *opening inventory* shows whether an increment in, or liquidation of, inventory has occurred. The ratio of the current-year cost to the base-year cost is then used to find the value of the increment. This increment is then treated as a separate layer of inventory in future years. Sample computations are provided at Reg. §1.472-8(e)(2)(v). See *dollar-value method.*

double jeopardy the practice of repeated prosecutions for the same offense, prohibited by the Fifth Amendment to the Constitution. While the rule generally applies in the tax area, it does not prevent imposition of a civil penalty against a person already tried for criminal fraud.

double taxation, corporate the characteristic of imposing two taxes on one corporate profit. A typical *corporation* pays the first tax on corporate *income,* while the *shareholders* pay the second tax when corporate earnings are distributed to them. Dividends represent distribution of corporate profits and are therefore not deductible by the corporation.

doubtful collectibility a consideration that eliminates the duty to *accrue* an item of *gross income,* the gist of which is that if there is a "reasonable doubt" as to collectibility, then an item should not be accrued. The prospect of total default must be "quite substantial." For example, the fact that the debtor is in bankruptcy is not in itself conclusive, since the creditor may be paid.

downstream de minimis rule a provision, which is met, for the testing period, if the "5 percent adjusted taxable income test" or the "2 percent gross income test" is met. Reg. §1.444-2T(c)(2)(i). The 5 percent test is met if all *deferral entities* accounted for not over 5 percent of the *partnership's, S corporation*'s, or *qualified personal service corporation*'s (PSC) adjusted taxable income. In the case of a partnership or an S corporation, adjusted *taxable income,* the sum of pass-through items reportable by the partners or shareholders (other than credits and tax-exempt income) plus applicable payments to partners or *shareholders* that the entity *deducted,* and *deductible guaranteed payments* as defined in §707(c). For a PSC, adjusted taxable income is taxable income of the PSC, with deductible payments to shareholders added back. The 2 percent test is met if all deferral entities accounted for not over 2 percent of the partnership's, S corporation's, or PSC's gross income for the testing period. See *section 444 election by partnership, S corporaton, or personal service corporation (PSC); tiered structures.*

downstream exchange a term used to describe a *corporation's* exchange of outstanding bonds for new common or preferred *stock.* Such transactions can apparently qualify as tax-free *Type E reorganizations* such that accrued *interest* on the bonds can remain untaxed.

downward ratchet rule a rule built into §4943(c)(4)(A)(ii) and Reg. §53.4943-4(a) to the effect that if a *private foundation* and its associated *disqualified persons* held more than 20 percent (or 35 percent) of a business enterprise on May 26, 1969, the special relief for such coverages will be reduced whenever their interests decline. The image is of a ratchet not moving back once a diminution occurs. Decreases in the holdings of the private foundation are disregarded if: (1) the decreases are due solely to the issuance of *stock* (or to the issuance of stock coupled with later stock redemptions) of the business enterprise; (2) the net percentage decrease does not exceed 2 percent; and (3) the number of shares the private foundation holds is not affected by the stock issuance or any stock redemption that was coupled to the stock issuance. §4943(c)(4)(A).

draws advances by a *partnership* to a *partner* in anticipation of future earnings. Such amounts are treated at year-end as *distributions* made on the last day of the part-

nership's *taxable year,* unless there is a duty to repay, in which event they are considered debts. Reg. §1.731-1(c)(2). Such amounts are usually *deductible* under §162(a) if treated as *guaranteed payments* under §707(c).

dribble out IRA an *IRA* scheduled to make small distributions before age $70\frac{1}{2}$ and thereafter major distributions over a fixed term not longer than the owner's (or owner's and *spouse's* joint) life expectancy. See *IRA dribble out; excise tax, failure to make minimum distributions.*

drop down the transfer of the assets or *stock* of a target company into one or more subsidiaries following a *corporate reorganization.* See, e.g., §368(a)(2)(C); Rev. Rul. 68-261, 1968-1 C.B. 145.

drugs and medical expenses prescribed medicines and insulin, and a wide range of medical, dental, and other diagnostic and healing services that are deductible *from adjusted gross income.* §1.213-1(e)(1)(ii). Expenditures for toiletries, cosmetics, toothpaste, shaving cream, hand lotions or vitamins are not deductible. Amounts qualifying as medicines and drugs are deductible to the extent they *exceed $7\frac{1}{2}$ percent of adjusted gross income.* §213(b); Reg. §1.213(e)(2). *Cosmetic surgery does not qualify* as a deductible medical expense unless it is necessary to correct a deformity arising from a congenital abnormality. §213(d)(9)(A).

dual capacity taxpayer a *taxpayer* who pays a foreign taxing authority amounts which are both for specific benefits (hence not usable for purposes of calculating the *foreign tax credit*) and foreign charges which do qualify as creditable taxes. Taxpayers are entitled to show their dual status, and corresponding entitlements to foreign tax credits, by various methods. Regs. §§1.901-2(a)(2)(ii)(B) and 1.901-2A.

dual consolidated loss any *net operating loss* of a *domestic corporation* which is subject to an *income tax* of a *foreign* country on its income without regard to whether that income is from sources within or without that country, or is subject to that tax on the basis of *residence* as opposed to source. §1503(d)(2)(A). Such losses cannot offset income of United States affiliates filing a *consolidated return.* §1503(d)(1). See Reg. §1.1503-2T. This prevents the double use of worldwide *losses.* A relief provision lets *domestic corporations* with *qualified excess loss accounts* reorganize by transferring their assets to foreign corporations and have the foreign corporation deemed a United States corporation. See §1503(d)(3)-(4). The corporations affected by these rules are referred to as *dual resident* corporations. See Ann. 90-17, 1990-6 IRB 26.

dual filing a term sometimes used to describe the system of filing a *federal income tax return* with the United States and the United States Virgin Islands under §932(a)(2). It applies to people who are not full-time residents but who, nevertheless, have income from the United States Virgin Islands.

dual purpose summons   a *summons* issued on a *taxpayer* for both civil and criminal purposes.

dual resident   a *taxpayer* that is a *United States resident* and a resident of another country. See *dual consolidated loss.*

dummy corporation   a *corporation* whose existence is so meaningless that it is disregarded and its owners are taxed on its income. Generally, a corporation will not be disregarded if its purpose is the equivalent of business activity or if its formation is followed by the carrying on of business by the corporation.

dummy, limited partnerships   a *general partner* who exercises no independent action, who instead functions as a representative of the *limited partners*. Reg. §301.7701-2(d)(2). A *partnership* with a sole general partner that is a dummy and has no substantial assets possesses the corporate characteristic of *limited liability*. Moreover, if no general partner has unlimited liability, the limited partnership may be treated as a general partnership for income tax purposes. See *limited liability company (LLC).*

duplicated loss, loss disallowance rules   an amount (which is fixed immediately after a *disposition* or *deconsolidation*) of a subsidiary. The computation, which is complex, essentially involves the excess, if any, of the sum of the aggregate *adjusted basis* of the assets of the *subsidiary* other than any *stock* and *securities* that the subsidiary owns in another subsidiary over the sum of the value of the subsidiary's stock and any liabilities of the subsidiary. Reg. §1.1502-20(c)(2)(vi). See *loss disallowance rules.*

Dutch auction rate preferred stock   *preferred stock* sold via a process in which orders to purchase to sell the stock are submitted through a designated auction agent.

In each auction, existing holders that wish to increase their holdings along with new holders bid to buy shares offered for sale. See Rev. Rul. 90-27, 1990-14 I.R.B. 7, describing one issuer's form of Dutch auction. The ruling holds that the payee of a *distribution* on such stock is entitled to the *dividends-received deduction,* even though the security has the flavor of short-term commercial paper.

Dutch sandwich   a term used to describe a chain of *corporations* with a Netherlands corporation in the middle of the chain. One common example involves the foreign investor who forms a Netherlands Antilles *corporation,* which in turn owns a Netherlands corporation, which owns a Netherlands Antilles creditor corporation. This structure enables the Netherlands Antilles corporate grandchild to receive *interest* income from a *United States* payor free of United States withholding tax.

duty of consistency   a judicially imposed requirement that a *taxpayer* take consistent positions with respect to the facts asserted in a prior *taxable year.* For example, the duty would prevent a *shareholder* from treating the receipt of cash from the company as a loan while the *statute of limitations* was open and to declare it a *dividend* once the statute had expired.

dwelling unit, low or moderate income rental housing rehabilitation   a house or apartment used to provide living accommodations in a building or structure, but not a unit in a hotel, motel, inn, or other establishment in which more than half the units can be *used on a transient basis.* §167(k)(3)(C).

dwelling unit, vacation home rule   quarters that a human can inhabit as residential space, and *appurtenant* structures (e.g., a mobile home and an adjacent freestanding garage used to house the family car). The term does not include that portion of a unit exclusively used as a hotel, motel, or the like. §280A(f)(1); Reg. §1.280A1(c).

E

e & p   an abbreviation for *earnings and profits.*

E Bonds   see *series E Bonds.*

EDA   an acronym for *excess deductions account.*

EE Bonds   see *series EE Bonds.*

EIN   an acronym for *employer identification number.*

EO   an acronym for executive order.

EP/EO agent   an *IRS* agent in a *key district* who specializes in *audits* of plans for *employees,* related *trusts,* and *exempt organizations.*

ERISA   an acronym for *Employee Retirement Income Security Act of 1974,* Pub. L. No. 93-406, 88 Stat. 829 (Sept. 2, 1974).

ERISA bonds   see *bonding requirements, ERISA.*

ERTA   an acronym for Economic Recovery Tax Act of 1981, Pub. L. No. 97-34, 95 Stat. 172 (1981).

ESOP   an acronym for *employee stock ownership plan.*

ESOP credit   the now-defunct *tax credit employee stock ownership plan (TRASOP).*

ESOP loan   a nontechnical term for a loan by a commercial lender to an *employee stock ownership plan* (ESOP) or to a *corporation* where the ESOP uses the money to buy *employer securities.* The formal term is a *securities acquisition loan.* The lender must be a *bank, insurance company, regulated investment company,* or active money-lending corporation. Such a loan allows the lender to report only one-half of the *interest* for a seven-year excludable period if certain conditions are met. §133. The employer can *deduct applicable dividends* used to repay securities acquisition loans, provided the dividends are on securities acquired with the loan (known as "*applicable employer securities*"). §404(k). See *securities acquisition loan.*

ESOT   an acronym for *employee stock ownership trust,* which is a *trust* that holds assets of an *employee stock ownership plan* (ESOP), an investment *tax credit employee stock ownership plan* (TRASOP), or a *payroll credit employee stock ownership plan* (PAYSOP). The terms ESOP and ESOT are used more or less interchangeably. See *employee stock ownership plan.*

ETC   an acronym for an *export trade corporation.*

EWOC   an acronym for an *eligible worker-owned cooperative.*

earlier call date   any ascertainable call date before maturity (the date a security is redeemed on the issuer's demand), but not necessarily the earliest call date, selected by the *taxpayer.* §171(b)(1)(B)(i); Reg. §1.171-2(b)(1). See *amortizable bond premium of the taxable year.*

earliest acquisitions cost method   a method of valuing *inventories* under the *dollar-value method* whereby current-year costs of items in *closing inventory* are determined on the basis of the earliest costs of products purchased or produced during the year. Reg. §1.472-8(e)(2)(ii)(b).

earliest retirement age   the earliest date on which, under a *qualified retirement plan,* the *participant* can elect to receive retirement benefits. §401(a)(11)(G)(ii).

earliest retirement age, qualified domestic relations order   see *qualified domestic relations order.*

early retirement benefit   actuarially reduced retirement benefits payable upon the *participant's* attainment of a certain age, provided a minimum term of service has been completed. Reg. §1.401(a)-14(c).

early retirement date   a retirement date (e.g., the day the *participant* attains age 55) which is earlier than the *normal retirement date* (e.g., age 65), at which point retirement benefit payments begin. Early retirement date provisions are permissive, but if included, must comply with the *early retirement rule.*

early retirement rule   a rule expressed in Reg. §1.401(a)-14(c) to the effect that any *participant* who has met the plan's minimum service requirements for *early retirement benefits,* but who terminates service before the *early retirement date* fixed by the plan, must be entitled to at least the full *early retirement benefit* upon reaching the early retirement date fixed by the plan. However, no benefits need accrue for the interim period between actual retirement and the early retirement date prescribed by the plan. The absence of an early retirement rule disqualifies the plan. §401(a)(14).

early survivor annuity   an *annuity* for the life of the *participant's spouse,* the payments under which must not be less than the payments which would have been made to the spouse under the *joint and survivor annuity* if the participant had so elected immediately prior to retirement and if his retirement had occurred on the day before his death and within the period during which an election can be made.

early termination limitations   restrictions on maximum benefits that can be paid to the 25 highest-paid *employees* (the "restricted group" or "restricted class") if a *pension plan* is terminated within 10 years of its establishment, or if benefits become payable to a member of the restricted class, before certain *funding* requirements have been satisfied. Reg. §1.401-4(c).

earned income generally, income earned from services as opposed to capital. The term is defined variously throughout the *Code*, §911 being the most common source (earned income, foreign earned income).

earned income, child and dependent care credit *wages,* salaries, tips, and other *employee* compensation, and *net earnings from self-employment* (or such net *losses*), as defined in §1402(a) (roughly, *gross income* from a *trade or business* less *attributable deductions* plus the *distributive share of partnership taxable income* or loss), computed without regard to *community property* laws. The term excludes: (1) amounts received as a pension or *annuity*; or (2) amounts to which §871(a) (relating to a *nonresident alien's* non*effectively connected income*) applies. Reg. §1.44A-2(b)(2).

earned income credit a *refundable credit* that is available to a low-income individual who has a qualifying child, has earned income, and meets adjusted gross income thresholds. §32. For 1992, the maximum basic earned income credit for a qualifying taxpayer with one child is $1,324 ($7,520 × 17.6 percent) and $1,384 for a taxpayer with two or more qualifying children ($7,520 × 18.4 percent). For 1992, the credit is zero when adjusted gross income or earned income is $22,373 or more. See *earned income, earned income credit; eligible individuals, earned income credit.*

earned income, credit for increasing research activities see *earned income, pension plans.* §41(b)(2).

earned income, dependent care assistance programs exclusion see *earned income, earned income credit.* §129(e)(2).

earned income, earned income credit *wages,* salaries, tips, and other *employee* compensation, plus *net earnings from self-employment* (or such net *losses*), excluding amounts received as a pension or an *annuity* or not *effectively connected* with a United States *trade or business* received by *nonresident aliens*. Earned income is determined without regard to community property laws. A modified form of this definition is used for purposes of *dependent care assistance programs.*

earned income eligibility certificate Form W-5, filed by *employees* with their *employers,* certifying to eligibility for the *earned income credit.* Filing such a certificate is a precondition to advance receipt of the earned income credit, paid as part of the employee's paycheck. §3507(a).

earned income, foreign earned income *wages,* salaries or professional fees, and other amounts received for personal services rendered, but not compensation derived for personal services rendered to a *corporation* that represents a *distribution* of *earnings and profits* rather than a reasonable allowance for personal services. §911(d)(2)(A); Reg. §1.911-(2)(b)(1). In the case of a noncorporate *taxpayer* engaged in a *trade or business* in which both personal services and capital are *material income-producing factors,* earned income may not exceed 30 percent of the share of net profits of the trade or business. §911(d)(2)(B). When the taxpayer is a professional and employs assistants, earned income includes all professional fees received, provided the taxpayer's patients or clients look to the taxpayer as the person responsible for the services rendered. Reg. §1.911-2(b)(3). See *foreign earned income.*

earned income, treatment of community income where spouses live apart see *earned income, foreign earned income.* §66(b).

earnings and profits a measurement of the capacity of a corporation to make distributions to shareholders which are not a return of capital. The basic rule is to tax distributions to shareholders as *ordinary income* to the extent of the corporation's *current* and *accumulated earnings and profits,* applying year-end *current earnings and profits* first. §316. See *accumulated earnings and profits; current earnings and profits.*

earnings and profits of the current taxable year synonymous with *current earnings and profits.*

earnings credit see *earned income credit.*

earnings stripping provisions a reference to §163(j), which *defers interest expense deductions* for interest *paid or accrued* by a *corporation* to a nontaxable related person, if the corporation has a high *ratio of debt to equity.* The deferral applies only to *disqualified interest* for any *taxable year* in which the corporation has *excess interest expense* and a ratio of debt to equity greater than 1.5 to 1. The provision is designed to put an end to bleeding off corporate earnings via interest payments to related charities or *foreign* owners.

economic accrual concept the notion of reporting *interest income* (and perhaps other income) realistically on a current basis regardless of when it is actually paid or how it is paid. See Rev. Rul. 83-84, 1983-1 C.B. 9.

economically disadvantaged ex-convict any *individual* who is certified by the *designated local agency*: (1) as having been convicted of a felony under state or federal laws; (2) as being a *member of [an] economically disadvantaged family*; and (3) as having a hiring date that is not more than five years after the last date on which such individual was so convicted or was released from prison. §51(d)(7). The term relates to the *targeted jobs credit.* The targeted jobs credit expired on June 30, 1992.

economically disadvantaged family a family that the *designated local agency* determines had an income that on an annual basis would be 70 percent or less of the Bureau of Labor Statistics' lower living standard. §51(d)(11). The determination is based on the family's income during the six-month period immediately preceding the determination date. The term relates to the *targeted jobs credit*. The targeted jobs credit expired on June 30, 1992.

economically disadvantaged youth   any *individual* who is certified by the *designated local agency* as meeting certain age requirements and is a member of an *economically disadvantaged family*. An individual meets the age requirements of this subparagraph if he or she has attained age 18 but not age 23 on the hiring date. §51(d)(3). The term relates to the *targeted jobs credit*. The targeted jobs credit expired on June 30, 1992.

economic effect   a partnership allocation generally has economic effect if it increases or decreases the partner's *capital account,* if *liquidation* proceeds are distributed in accordance with capital accounts, and if there is a duty to restore deficits. Reg. §1.704-1(b)(2)(ii)(b). This really means that allocations result in genuine effects to the partners—usually felt in cash. This is the primary test for "economic effect." This is also an *alternative economic effect test* and an *economic effect equivalence test.* For a slight relaxation of the economic effect test for potential losses attributable to *nonrecourse debt,* see *qualified income offset.* See *substantial economic effect test.*

economic effect equivalence test   a standard found in Reg. §1.704-1(b)(2)(ii)(I), which validates *allocations* of *partner's distributive shares* if the practical effect is the same as if the basic requirements for *economic effect* (i.e., *capital account* maintenance, *liquidation* in accordance with *capital accounts,* and a duty to make up deficits) existed. It can be used as a substitute for the rigid three-part test. See *substantial economic effect test.*

economic effect, partnership allocations   one element of the *substantial economic effect test* which is used to determine whether *partnership allocations* will be validated for federal *income tax* purposes. See Reg. §1.704-(b). Section 704(b)(2) is the central provision. Generally speaking, the test will be met if the allocations reflect cash transactions over the life of the partnership; those transactions are measured by *capital accounts* of the partnership, there is an unconditional duty to make up deficits in the capital accounts, and properties are assigned *fair market value* in this analysis. See *substantial economic effect test.*

economic family concept   a notion in the self-insurance area that when an affiliated *corporation* is used to insure risks of a related company there is no real insurance arrangement because when the captive receives a dollar, its net worth and its affiliate's rise by a dollar, and when the captive pays out a dollar, the converse occurs. See Rev. Rul. 77-316, 1977-2 C.B. 53. See *captive insurance company.*

economic interest, depletion allowance   an interest in natural resource property sufficient to justify a claim

for a *depletion deduction* for the exhaustion of the resource. The term is vaguely defined in Reg. §1.611-1(b)(1) and (2).

economic interest, depreciation   an interest in property that justifies claims for *depreciation* (or *cost recovery*) of the property. Depreciable property is often acquired through involved transactions that leave the property subject to the control or claims of several parties. In such cases, the general rule is that the person entitled to claim depreciation *deductions* for the property is the person who assumes or retains the burden of ownership, that is, the person whose capital investment suffers the economic loss which depreciation represents. See *depreciation; economic interest, depletion allowance.*

economic performance   a requirement of the *all events test* which must be met before *deductions* can be reported under the *accrual method* of taxation. Economic performance with respect to a particular liability generally occurs when all activities have been performed that are required to satisfy that liability. §461(h). See *tax shelter, economic performance; tax shelter, penalty for substantial understatement of income tax.*

Economic Recovery Tax Act of 1981   Pub. L. No. 97-34 (1981), commonly known by its acronym ERTA.

economic substance   a term used to indicate the presence of significant nontax economic possibilities associated with undertaking an activity or transaction, so as to permit *deductions* and *losses* with respect to the activity or transaction. The absence of economic substance renders the activity or transaction vulnerable to being classified as a *sham.* See *purposive economic activity doctrine; sham transactions.*

educational assistance plan   payments of up to $5,250 per year received by an employee for tuition, fees, books, supplies, etc., under an employer's educational assistance plan may be excluded from gross income. §127. Any excess is includible in the employee's gross income and is subject to employment and withholding taxes. This exclusion is limited to amounts paid for educational assistance provided before June 30, 1992. See *scholarship.*

educational expense deduction   a *deduction* allowed to an *individual* for costs undertaken to maintain or improve a skill needed by the individual in his or her employment or other *trade or business,* or to meet the express requirements of the individual's *employer,* or the requirements of law or regulations, imposed as a condition to the individual's retention of an established employment relationship, status, or rate of compensation. Such costs include books, tuition, fees, and like expenditures. Reg. §1.162-5. No *deduction* is allowed for expenditures required of the *taxpayer* to meet the minimum educational requirements for qualification in his or her present employment, trade, or business, or to qualify the taxpayer for a new trade or business. *Travel expenses* for education are also deductible to the extent attributable to a period of travel directly related to allowable educational activities. Travel as education is *nondeductible.* §274(m)(2).

educational gift see *medical and tuition expenses, gift tax exclusion.* §170(b)(1)(A).

educational institution a school maintaining a regular faculty and established curriculum, and having an organized body of students in attendance. The term includes primary and secondary schools, colleges, universities, normal schools, technical schools, mechanical schools, and similar institutions, but it does not include noneducational institutions, on-the-job training, correspondence schools, night schools, and so forth. Reg. §1.151-3(c). See *educational organization described in §170(b)(1)(A)(ii).*

educational organization, catch-up election an *educational organization described in §170(b)(1)(A)(ii)* that qualifies as a *fifty-percent charity.* §415(c)(4)(D)(ii). *Employees* of such an organization qualify for the special catch-up election under §415(c)(4). See *catch-up election, tax-deferred annuities for exempt and educational organization employees.*

educational organization described in §170(b)(1)(A)(ii) an educational organization that normally maintains a regular faculty and curriculum and that normally has a regularly enrolled body of pupils or students in attendance at the place where its educational activities are regularly carried on. The term includes institutions such as primary, secondary, preparatory, or high schools, colleges and universities, as well as federal, state, and other publicly supported schools that otherwise come within the definition. Reg. §1.170A-9(b). The term appears in numerous *Code* provisions.

educational services any services, including lodging, purchased from an *educational institution* and provided for a student of the *educational organization* described in §170(b)(a)(A)(ii). §163(b)(1). Section 163(b) provides a method for determining the portion of such payments for such services attributable to *interest.*

education, gift for see *medical and tuition expenses, gift tax exclusion.*

effective control, brother-sister groups—qualified plans ownership of more than 50 percent of all classes of *stock,* by vote or value. Prop. Reg. §1.414(c)-2(c)(2). Related *employers* are aggregated for qualification purposes (e.g., §§401, 408(k), 410, 411, 415, and 416) if they are sufficiently aligned. A brother-sister group of *trades or businesses* under common control occurs and compels aggregation of employers (hence, also of their

employees) where there are two or more trades or businesses which meet certain tests. See Reg. §1.414(c)-4 for *attribution rules.*

effective control, private foundation's excess business holdings the direct or indirect possession of the power to direct or cause the direction of the management and policies of a business enterprise, whether through the ownership of voting *stock* or the use of *voting trusts,* contractual arrangements, or otherwise, looking at its legal substance, not its form. §4943(c)(2)(B).

effective control, private foundation's minimum investment return same definition as for purposes of *effective control, private foundation's excess business holdings.* Reg. §53.4942-2(c), relates to the valuation of certain securities for purposes of the *excise tax* on a private foundation's undistributed income. See *undistributed income, private foundation.*

effectively connected earnings and profits, branch profits tax the earnings of a *foreign corporation* that are attributable to income that is connected with conducting a *trade or business* in the United States. §884(d)(1). Such *earnings and profits* are not diminished by any distributions made during the *taxable year.* See *dividend equivalent amount, branch profits tax.*

effectively connected income *income from sources within the United States,* and to some extent from *foreign* sources, that is so bound up with the present *conduct of a trade or business* within the United States that it is taxed at graduated *federal income tax* rates. §§864(c) *(definition),* 871(b) *(individuals),* 882(a)(1) *(corporations).* See *asset use test; business activities test; permanent establishment; trade or business within the United States.*

effective tax rate the actual tax rate based on *taxable income.* For example, a tax of $61,250 based on corporate taxable income of $200,000 would result in an effective tax rate of 30.625 percent.

effect of a dividend a standard used to determine whether *boot* distributed in a *corporate reorganization* should be treated as a *capital gain* or as a *dividend.* §356(a)(2). Generally, the same standards apply in this area as in the analysis of *stock redemptions,* to determine whether a redemption is more like an *exchange* or a *distribution.*

eighteen-year real property (prior law) for purposes of the *accelerated cost recovery system (ACRS),* the term refers to *section 1250 class property* with a present *class life* under the *class life asset depreciation range system* of more than 12.5 years; it does not include *low-income housing.* Former §168(c)(2)(D). Real property has since been moved up to 27.5 or 31.5 years by the 1986 Act.

eighty-percent distributee a parent *corporation* holding 80 percent of the outstanding *stock* of a subsidiary, by vote and by value. §§337(c) and 332(b)(1). Unless the parent is an *exempt organization* of a certain type, or a *foreign corporation, liquidating distributions* of *property* to the parent are generally nontaxable to parent or subsidiary. The *consolidated return regulations* are disregarded for this purpose. The term "*corporate distributee*" seems synonymous. The term "corporate distributee" is used in §334, relating to *basis,* whereas "eighty-percent distributee" is used in §337, relating to *nonrecognition* of *gain* or *loss.*

eighty-percent owned entity   a *corporation* of which at least 80 percent of the *stock* (by value) is owned directly or indirectly by or for the *taxpayer,* or a *partnership* in which at least 80 percent of the *capital interest* or *profits interest* is owned by the taxpayer. §1239(c). The *attribution rules* of §318 apply, except that the family includes only: (1) *spouses* (the 50 percent limitations of §318(a)(2)(C) and (a)(3)(C) do not apply); and (2) *trusts* of which the taxpayer is a *beneficiary,* but not a *remote contingent interest in trust.* See *related person, sales of depreciable property.*

elapsed time method, qualified plans   a method of determining an *employee's period of service* for purposes of *accrual of benefits* by reference to the employee's total period of service, rather than actual or equivalent *hours of service.* A "period of service" is the time between the employment commencement date (the day *participation* begins) until the severance from service date (basically termination of employment or a one-year absence). Reg. §1.410(a)-7(a)(2). See *accrued benefits.*

elderly person   an *individual* who is age 65 before the end of his or her *taxable year.* Such a person gets an *additional standard deduction.* §63(f). An *individual* attains age 65 on the first moment of the day preceding his or her 65th birthday. Reg. §1.151-1(c)(2). See *age sixty-five; standard deduction.*

elderly person, architectural and transportation barrier removal expense   pertains to an *individual* age 65 or over. Reg. §1.190-2(a)(4). See *qualified architectural and transportation removal expense.*

election not to carry back a net operating loss   an irrevocable election to forgo the entire *carryback* period with respect to a *net operating loss* for any *taxable year* ending after December 31, 1975. §172(b)(3)(C). Generally, a net operating loss may be carried back three years, but in certain situations where the *carryback* of a loss provides little benefit, it may be beneficial to elect not to carry back the net operating loss and instead use the *carryforward* period only.

election out of subchapter K   see *section 761 election.*

election to be treated as resident   an election under §7701(b)(1)(A)(iii) and (4) under which someone who is otherwise a *nonresident alien* can elect to be treated as a *resident alien.* The alien must not have qualified as a resident for the prior *calendar year,* must meet the *substantial presence test* in the post-election year, must be physically present in the *United States* for at least 31 consecutive days in the election year, and must be present in the United States for at least three-fourths of the number of days in the period starting with the first day of the 31-day period and ending with the last day of the election year. Section 6013(g) offers a parallel provision for *married persons* pursuant to which the nonresident alien spouse is treated as if he or she were a resident alien.

elective corporation   an *S corporation.*

elective deferrals   as to any *taxable year,* the sum of: (1) *employer contributions* under a *qualified cash or deferred arrangement,* to the extent they are not *includible* in *gross income*; (2) the same as to amounts deferred under a *simplified employee pension plan* pursuant to a salary reduction agreement; and (3) the same under a *tax-deferred annuity for exempt and educational organization employees.* §402(g)(3). In the first two cases the cap on such amounts is presently $7,000 per year, and $9,500 per year as to the third item. This does not prevent the employer from contributing on its own. Excess (taxable) employee deferrals are subject to allocation and permissive distribution early in the following year (although referred to as "required distributions" in the *Code*), in which case income earned on the excess is taxable. See §72(t). They are subject to *FICA* and *FUTA taxes.*

electronic filing (ELF)   a method of filing tax returns with the IRS. Practitioners must first register with the IRS by filing Form 8633, which identifies what role the practitioner plans to play—originator or transmitter—and is a basis for assignment of an identification number or EFIN. A practitioner may not participate until officially notified of acceptance. See publication 1345 and IRS Rev. Proc. 91-69. Problems with electronic filing include administrative delays by the IRS, learning and training delays, rejected returns, delayed refunds, and security problems in the form of an outsider tapping into the practitioner's computer system through a modem. To safeguard the integrity of the ELF program, the IRS will alter the procedure regarding the receipt of a tax return and a possible refund. Effective for the 1994 filing season (i.e., for the filing of 1993 returns), the IRS acknowledgment sent to an electronic transmitter will specify only that a taxpayer's return has been received and filed. It will not indicate whether a refund is going to be issued.

elevators and escalators   "elevator" means a cage or platform and its hoisting machinery for conveying persons or freight to or from different levels and functionally related equipment which is essential to its operation. "Escalator" means a moving staircase and functionally related equipment which is essential to its operation. The definitions of 27.5-year residential real property (real estate used for human habitation) and 31.5-year nonresidential real property (offices, warehouses, factories, stores) include elevators and escalators for purposes of *recapture* of *depreciation* or cost recovery. §§1245, 1250, 168(e)(2)(A), 168(e)(2)(B).

eleven-percent qualified energy property   See *energy property, energy investment credit.*

eligibility   synonymous with coverage. See *coverage, qualified plans.*

eligible access expenditures   amounts *paid or accrued* by an *eligible small business* to let it comply with the Americans with Disabilities Act of 1990. §44(c)(1)(A). The expenditures must be for the purpose of removing architectural, communication, physical, or transportation barriers which prevent a business from being accessible to, or usable by, individuals with disabilities; providing qualified interpreters or other methods of making aurally delivered materials available to individuals with hearing impairments; providing qualified readers, taped texts, and other effective methods of making visually delivered materials available to individuals with visual impairments; acquiring or modifying equipment or devices for individuals with disabilities; or providing other similar services, modifications, materials, or equipment. The term also includes reasonable amounts *paid or incurred,* but it excludes amounts paid or incurred in connection with any facility first placed in service after November 5, 1990. Such expenditures can qualify for the *disabled access credit.* The amount of the credit is 50 percent of the amount of eligible access expenditures for a year that exceed $250 but that do not exceed $10,250.

eligible basis, low-income housing credit   *adjusted basis* in the case of a new building, or in the case of an existing building, its acquisition costs plus *depreciable* improvements added in the first *taxable year* of the building's *credit period.* §42(d). In order to have any *basis* for this purpose, the *building* must have been acquired by purchase from an unrelated person and (unless the condition is waived by the *Treasury Department*) at least a decade must have elapsed since it was last *placed in service* or (if longer) was the subject of a *nonqualified substantial improvement.* A nonqualified substantial improvement means a *capital expenditure* of 25 percent or more of the *adjusted basis* of the building to which five-year §167(k) *amortization* was allowed or to which *ACRS* applied. §42(d)(2)(D)(i)(I). In *high-cost areas,* eligible basis is boosted by 30 percent. §42(d)(5). The low-income housing credit expired on June 30, 1992.

eligible debt   a class of *debt* that is subject to *allocation* under the *uniform capitalization rules* of §269A. It refers to all the *taxpayer's* debt other than debt whose *interest* is permanently *nondeductible,* debt that is *personal interest,* debt whose interest is *qualified residence interest,* debt incurred by an *exempt organization* (unless directly related to a taxable business), and debt between the taxpayer and a related person (as defined in §§707(b) and 267(b)) if the rate is inadequate. Such debt is traced under the rules of Reg. §1.163-8T. The part of the eligible debt that is traced directly to production expenses for produced property is considered *traced debt* and interest thereon must be *capitalized.* Other debt is evaluated to determine whether it is *avoided cost debt.* That determination is made by assuming that all expenditures made for producing property were instead made to repay debt. The amount of interest that that taxpayer would therefore have avoided has to be capitalized. See Notice 88-99, 1988-36 I.R.B. See *uniform capitalization rules.*

eligible deferred compensation plan   an unfunded *deferred compensation* plan established by a state, a *political subdivision* of a state, the District of Columbia, or any agency or instrumentality of either of them, (see §457(d)(9) for definition) and *tax-exempt organizations* under which income of their *employees* and *independent contractors* can defer current compensation. §457. These entitities are called *eligible employers.* Noncompliance with §457 results in current taxation of such employees. The plan must meet certain principal requirements. §457(c)(2); Reg. §1.457-1 through -4. The *uniform minimum distribution rules* apply. §457(d)(2).

eligible dividends   *dividends* paid out of a *foreign corporation's earnings and profits* for a *taxable year* during which all of the foreign corporation's *stock* is owned by a *domestic corporation* to which the dividends are paid, and all of the foreign corporation's *gross income* is *effectively connected income.* A 100 percent *deduction* is permitted for such eligible dividends received by the *domestic* corporation. §245(b)(1) and (2).

eligible employee, cash or deferred arrangement   an *employee* who is directly or indirectly eligible to make an employee *contribution* or to receive an *allocation* of *matching contributions* (including from forfeitures) under the plan for a *plan year.* An employee is an eligible employee even if he or she cannot make an employee contribution or receive an allocation of matching contributions merely because compensation is less than a stated dollar amount. §401.

eligible employer   a state or local government, but not a church or an organization controlled by a church (see §3121(w)(3) for church-related definitions for this purpose). §453(e)(13). Eligible employers can adopt *eligible deferred compensation plans.* See *eligible deferred compensation plan; eligible state deferred compensation plan.*

eligible individuals, earned income credit generally, all *married* persons entitled to a *dependency exemption* for a *child, surviving spouses,* and *heads of households* who maintain a household for a child. In each case, the child must reside with the taxpayer in the *United States.* §43(c). People who claim the benefits of §911 (*foreign earned income exclusion*) and §931 (relating to *possessions*-source income) are excluded. §43(c).

eligible loan a type of loan with respect to which certain lenders, other than *large banks,* can claim the *percentage method* of calculating additions to *reserves for bad debts.* Understanding the term calls for defining the term "loan," then determining which loans are eligible. For these purposes, a loan is generally a *debt* for purposes of §166 (*bad debts*), but it includes overdrafts in one or more deposit accounts by a customer in good faith, a bankers' acceptance purchased or discounted by a bank, and a loan participation to the extent that the *taxpayer* bears a risk.

eligible physicians and surgeons' mutual protection and interindemnity arrangement or association any mutual protection and interindemnity arrangement or *association* that provides only medical malpractice liability protection for its members or medical malpractice liability protection in conjunction with protection against other liability claims incurred in the course of, or related to, the professional practice of a physician or surgeon. Contributions to such associations are generally *deductible,* and refunds are deductible by the association to the extent taxed to the recipient.

eligible property, asset depreciation range system *tangible depreciable property,* which is subject to *recapture* of *gains* as *ordinary income* (i.e., *section 1245 property* and *section 1250 property*), which is first *placed in service* by the *taxpayer* after 1970 and before 1981, provided an *asset guideline class* and an *asset guideline period* are in effect in the year of election. The property may be new or used, and may be a property improvement or *excluded addition.* Reg. §1.167-11(b)(2).

eligible retirement plan a term used to limit the kinds of plans to which *rollovers* of *distributions* from *qualified plans* can be made. See §402(a)(5)(E)(iv). It covers *IRAs, IRA annuities, qualified trusts,* or retirement *annuities* under §403(a) (*qualified annuity plans*). Numerous results flow from this structure. For example, *partial distributions* can only go to *IRAs.* §402(a)(5)(D)(ii).

eligible small business *Eligible small businesses* can elect a *disabled access credit* for expenditures to acquire or modify facilities to accommodate the disabled.

eligible small business, LIFO generally, a *taxpayer* with average annual gross receipts of not more than $5 million for the three *taxable year* periods ending with the taxable year. §474(b). If the taxpayer is a member of a *controlled group,* all *corporations* that were *component members* of the group at any time during the calendar year are treated as one taxpayer for the year for purposes of determining the *gross receipts* of the taxpayer. *Regulations* under §52(b) are used to define a controlled group for these purposes. *Id.* Eligible small businesses that use the *simplified dollar-value method* of pricing *inventory* under the *last-in, first-out* method may elect to use one *inventory pool* per *trade or business.* §474(a). See *simplified dollar-value LIFO method.*

eligible small ethanol producer see *small ethanol producer credit.*

eligible state deferred compensation plan a type of *deferred compensation* plan set forth in §457(d), as in effect before 1989. This type of plan is much the same as its successor, the *eligible deferred compensation plan* (for post-1988 years), except that the latter allows more *employers* to qualify.

eligible worker-owned cooperative an *exempt farmers' cooperative,* or a taxable *corporation operating on a cooperative basis,* where a majority of the members are *employees,* a majority of the voting *stock* is owned by members, a majority of the directors are elected by members, at one vote each, and a majority of the allocated earnings and losses are *allocated* to members on the basis of patronage, *capital contributions,* or both combined. §1042(c)(2). Among other benefits, sales of securities by such organizations can be free of current taxes as in the case of *ESOPs.* See *employee stock ownership plan.*

eligible work incentive employees *individuals* who have been certified by the *designated local agency* as being eligible for financial assistance under part A of title IV of the Social Security Act and as having continually received such financial assistance during the 90-day period before their hiring date, or having been placed in employment under a work incentive program established under §432(b)(1) of the Social Security Act (42 U.S.C. §632(b)(1) (1976)). Wages paid to these individuals qualify for the *targeted jobs credit.* The targeted jobs credit expired on June 30, 1992.

eminent domain the power of government or its delegate to take a private property for public purposes. Section 1033 provides relief from taxation when property is taken under an actual or imminent exercise of this power and when the *taxpayer* realizes a *gain* on the transaction and reinvests in comparable property. See *involuntary conversion.*

employee achievement award an item of tangible *personal property* transferred from *employer* to *employ-*

ee for length of service or safety achievement, as part of a meaningful presentation, under circumstances that do not suggest disguised compensation. §274(j)(3). Such awards cannot be *deducted* beyond $400 per employee per year. §274(j)(2)(A). If they are *qualified plan awards,* a higher limit applies. §274(j)(2)(B). Such awards may be *excludable* from the transferee's *gross income* by §74(c). If and to the extent they are lavish (meaning *nondeductible* because of §274(j)), they are *excess deduction awards* which are taxable to the transferee. §74(c)(2). See *length-of-service award.*

employee association an organization composed of two or more *employees,* including (but not limited to) an exempt *social welfare organization. Self-employed individuals* may also be included. In any event, to qualify as an employee association, some nexus between the employees (such as having a common *employer* or identity) must exist. Reg. §1.408-2(c)(4)(ii). Such associations may be the subject of collective *individual retirement arrangements.* §408(c); Reg. §1.408-2(c)(4)(ii). See *voluntary employees' beneficiary associations.*

employee award see *employee achievement award.*

employee benefit organizations, exempt see *voluntary employees' beneficiary associations.*

employee benefit plan an *employee welfare benefit plan* or an *employee pension benefit plan* or a combination of both. Reg. §1.401(d)(1)-1(f)(8)(iv). ERISA §3(3). Labor Reg. §2510.3-3.

employee benefit trust a *trust* holding the assets of an *employee benefit plan.* See also *supplemental unemployment benefit trusts.*

employee business expenses *trade or business expenditures* of an *employee* for the benefit of his or her *employer.* Such expenses are *deductible* from *gross income* (to the extent reimbursed) or from *adjusted gross income.* The unreimbursed element is an *itemized deduction* (if deductible at all). §63(a)(2). The unreimbursed element may be subject to the *two percent of adjusted gross income floor for miscellaneous itemized deductions* (§67).

employee death benefits amounts received by the *beneficiaries* or the *estate* of an *employee,* paid by or on behalf of an *employer,* by reason of the employee's death. The first $5,000 of such death benefit is tax-exempt and is not included in the *gross income* of the *beneficiaries* or the employee's *estate.* §101(b)(1).

employee, Federal Insurance Contribution Act an *individual* performing services for another, whose relationship with the other *person* falls into one of three following classifications: (1) an officer of a *corporation* is an *employee* unless he performs only minor services for the corporation and receives no compensation (Reg. §31.3121(d)-1(b)); (2) an individual is an employee if he

or she qualifies as one under the common law rules used for *income tax withholding* purposes (Reg. §31.3121(d)-1(c)); or (3) an individual, in certain occupations whose contract of service contemplates that the individual will personally perform substantially all of the services, has no substantial investment in the facilities to be used and performs services as part of a continuing relationship and not a single transaction (Reg. §31.3121(d)-1(d)). The following are the specific occupations: (1) *agent drivers or commission drivers* engaged in distributing certain food products, laundry, or dry-cleaning services for their principals; (2) *full-time life insurance salesmen;* (3) *homeworkers* (workers performing work in their homes on materials furnished by their principals); and (4) *full-time traveling or city salesmen engaged* in the solicitation of orders on behalf of their principals. See *common law employee; Social Security tax.*

employee, Federal Unemployment Tax Act an *individual* performing services for another whose relationship with the other *person* meets any of the tests for *employee* status for purposes of the Federal Insurance Contribution Act (*FICA*), except that *full-time life insurance salesmen* and *home workers* are excluded. §3306(i). See *employee, Federal Insurance Contribution Act.*

employee, income tax withholding every *individual* performing services if the relationship between him or herself and the *person* for whom he or she is performing such services is the legal relationship of *employer* and *employee,* determined by common law rules. Reg. §31.3401(c)-1(a). Generally, the relationship exists when the person for whom the services are performed has the right to control or direct the individual who performs the services. Reg. §31.3401(c)-1(b). Usually, physicians, lawyers, and others who follow an independent *trade, business,* or profession in which they offer their services to the public, are not employees. Reg. §31.3401(c)-1(c). See *common law employee.*

employee, Keogh plans generally, an individual with *self-employment income,* even if the *trade or business* shows no net profits. §401(c)(1); Reg. §1.401-10(b). Such persons may also be employed by other persons in separate capacities. Reg. §1.401-10(b)(2). In effect, the term refers to anyone (other than a *full-time life insurance salesman*) who has or had earned income from a profession or other business enterprise which he or she independently owns or conducts, or is a general partner in. The employee is not entirely dependent on the technicality of having earnings from self-employment, because certain *employees* (e.g., ministers) who are deemed to have such earnings for *self-employment tax* purposes are expressly excluded. Reg. §1.401-10(b)(3)(i).

employee organization, ERISA any labor union, or any organization of any kind, or any agency or *employ-*

ee representation committee, association, group, or plan in which employees participate and which exists for the purpose, in whole or in part, of dealing with *employers* concerning an *employee benefit plan,* or other matters incidental to employment relations, or any employees' *beneficiary* association organized for the purpose, in whole or in part, of establishing such a plan. ERISA §3(4).

employee-owner an *employee* who owns, directly or through very slightly modified *attribution rules* of §318, more than 10 percent of the outstanding *stock* of a *personal service corporation.* §269A(b)(2). The modification is that a 5 percent threshold is used to attribute stock held by a corporation to its shareholders. In certain cases the income of a personal service corporation may be *allocated* to its employee-owner. The existence of employee-owner helps to detect the existence of a personal service corporation for purposes of §269A, allowing reallocations from the company to its employee-owners. Under the *passive loss rules,* the term is defined the same way except that they are people who own any stock, and stock is attributed from corporate portfolios to shareholders *pro rata* (i.e., not even a 5 percent threshold).

employee pension benefit plan, ERISA any plan, fund, or program established or maintained by an *employer* or by an *employee* organization, or by both, to the extent that, by its express terms or as a result of surrounding circumstances, the plan, fund, or program: (1) provides retirement income to employees; or (2) results in a *deferral* of income by employees for periods extending to the termination of covered employment or beyond, regardless of the method of calculating the benefits under the plan or the method of distributing benefits from the plan. *ERISA* §3(2). Both *defined benefit plans* and *defined contribution plans* fall under this rubric. ERISA §3(3). Certain severance pay arrangements, bonus programs, *individual retirement accounts,* gratuitous payments to pre-ERISA retirees, and *tax sheltered annuities,* are not, however, deemed *employee pension benefit plans.* ERISA §3(2)(B). Labor Reg. §2510.3-2.

employee, pension plan see *employee, qualified plan.*

employee plan benefit and contribution ceilings various employee plan benefit and contribution limitations are subject to annual cost-of-living adjustments. For 1993, the maximum deferral under a 401(k) plan is $8,994. Elective contributions in excess of the maximum limitation are taxable in the year of deferral. §4981A.

employee, qualified plan a *common law employee,* a *full-time life insurance salesman* (as defined for *Social Security tax* purposes), or a *self-employed person* (someone who has *net earnings from self-employment*) in a *trade or business* in which the personal services of the *individual* are a material income-pro-

ducing factor, but only for *Keogh plan* purposes. §§401(c)(1) and (2); 7701(a)(20). Individuals may occupy multiple statuses (e.g., a moonlighting professional who is also an employee of a large corporation). Generally, employee status is required in order to enjoy the benefits of a *qualified plan,* and coverage of a nonemployee can disqualify a plan. Certain *leased employees* are also included for purposes of testing the plan's status as a qualified plan. See *recipient leasing employees.*

employee relocation loan a mortgage loan on an *employee's* new residence. It is exempted from the *below-market loan* rules if it is nontransferable and is conditioned on future employment; the employee certifies that he or she expects to claim *itemized deductions* every year; and the loan agreement requires that the loan proceeds will only be used to acquire a new residence. See *below-market loan; compensation-related loan.*

Employee Retirement Income Security Act of 1974 a statute designed to assure equitable treatment of *employee* benefits. It is enforced both by the United States Department of Labor and the Treasury Department.

employees' beneficiary association see *voluntary employees' beneficiary association.*

employees' beneficiary association, ERISA an organization which the Department of Labor finds that (1) membership in the association is conditioned on employment status—for example, membership is limited to employees of a certain employer or union; (2) the association has a formal organization, with officers, by-laws, or other indications of formality; (3) the association is organized for the purpose, in whole or in part, of establishing a welfare or pension plan; and (4) the association generally does not deal with employers. ERISA §3(4).

employee, self-employment tax the same as for FICA purposes. §1402(c)(2). *Individuals* who are *employees* are by nature not subject to *self-employment taxes.* See *employee, Federal Insurance Contribution Act.*

employee stock ownership plan either a *qualified stock bonus plan* (QSB) or a combination QSB and *qualified money purchase plan.* An ESOP is funded by a contribution of the employer's stock. This stock is held for the benefit of the employees. ESOPs are attractive because the employer is allowed to reduce taxable income by deducting any dividends that are paid to the participants or their beneficiaries in the year such amounts are paid. §§409(a), 4975(e)(7). See *employer securities, ESOPs, EWOCs, PAYSOPs, and TRASOPs; excise tax, prohibited allocation of ESOP and EWOC stock; leveraged ESOP; qualified participant, ESOP.*

employee stock ownership trust a *trust* used as the funding vehicle for an *employee stock ownership plan.*

employee trust, qualified a *trust* set up for the benefit *of employees,* as described in and meeting the requirements of §401(a), and which is exempt from tax under §501(a). Reg. §1.401-0(b)(2). See *qualified deferred compensation plan.*

employee welfare benefit plans, ERISA any plans, funds, or programs established or maintained by an *employer* or by an *employee* organization, or both, to provide participants or their beneficiaries with medical, surgical, or hospital care or benefits; benefits in the event of sickness, accident, disability, death, or unemployment; vacation benefits; apprenticeship or other training programs; day care centers; scholarship funds; prepaid legal services; or any benefit described in §302(c) of the Labor Management Relations Act, 1947 (other than pensions on retirement or death, and insurance to provide such pension). ERISA §3(1)(A) and (B). Labor Reg. §2510.3-1. Certain payroll practices, maintenance of on-premise facilities, holiday gifts, sales to employees, maintenance of hiring halls, remembrance funds, strike funds, industry advancement programs, group or group-type insurance programs, or unfunded scholarship programs are not deemed employee welfare benefit plans. Labor Reg. §2510.3-1(b)-(k).

employee who performs services for an educational institution see *public school employee.*

employee withholding exemption certificate See *Form W-4.*

employer contribution not explicitly defined. It appears to mean anything of value, whether in cash or *property,* contributed by an *employer* to a *deferred compensation plan.* Such contributions are *deductible* when paid under the provisions of §404 if in connection with *qualified plans.* The *deduction* is not available under any other *Code* section in the case of *annuity plans* and *stock bonus* and *profit-sharing plans,* and no deduction is allowed in excess of §415's limits. §404(j). Promissory notes of the employer are not contributions. See *matching contribution; qualified deferred compensation plan.*

employer deferred compensation plan, withholding see *designated distribution.*

employer, employment taxes generally any *individual* or *entity* that employs and compensates others to perform services as *employees* and has control over the *wages* paid, including persons paying wages on behalf of *foreign persons,* is considered an *employer.* §3401(d) (income taxes). For *Federal Unemployment Tax Act* purposes, the term refers to a person who paid $1,500 or more of wages in the present quarter or prior calendar year, disregarding certain agricultural labor and domestic service payments. §3306(a). Employers can, therefore, include *individuals; corporations; partnerships;*

trusts; estates; joint stock companies; associations; syndicates; pools; *joint ventures;* religious and charitable organizations; educational and social institutions; the United States government; state governments and local subdivisions as well as governmental agencies. Reg. §31.3401(d)-1(c) and (d). There is no general definition of the term for *Social Security tax* (FICA) purposes. See *common law employee.*

employer, generally one who hires another to perform services on his behalf and who has a right to control the payee's manner of performance and tasks. The *Code* does not seem to focus on the existence of *employers,* but rather concentrates on the presence of *employees* in the important areas, especially *employment taxes* and *qualified plans.* See *common law employee; employer, employment taxes generally.*

employer identification number an identifying number issued under the authority of §6011(b) or §6109, or corresponding provisions of prior law. The nine-digit number is separated by a hyphen, as follows: 00-0000000. Reg. §301.7701-12. See Reg. §31.0-2(a)(11) with respect to *employment taxes.* Various *IRS* filings demand the inclusion of an *employer* identification number. See §6109 and *regulations* thereunder. A number is obtained by application to the IRS using *Form SS-4.*

employer, income tax withholding any *person* or *entity* (including governments and their agencies and instrumentalities) for whom an *individual* performs or performed services as an *employee.* §3401; Reg. §301.3401(d)-1(a). Because the term contemplates past services, withholding taxes on *wages* may be due on *deferred compensation.* See *income tax withholding.*

employer reversion the cash plus the value of other property directly or indirectly received by an *employer* from its *qualified plan.* §4980(c)(2)(A). §4980(c)(1). Reversions exclude distributions from *multiple employer plans* based on mistake of fact, or plans that were not qualified or that produced nondeductible contributions. §4980(c)(2)(B). There are also certain exceptions for reversions from *ESOPs* and *TRASOPs.* §4980(c)(3).

employer securities, ESOPs, EWOCs, PAYSOPs, and TRASOPs for purposes of *deductions* and *credits* with respect to contributions of qualified securities to *ESOPs, EWOCs,* (formerly) *PAYSOPs,* and *TRASOPs,* the term means common *stock* issued by the *employer* which is either readily tradable on an established securities market, certain convertible preferred stock, or nontradable common stock that have voting power and dividend rights and that are not inferior to any other class of common stock issued by the employer. §§409(1)(ESOP), former 44G(c)(6) (PAYSOP), 1042(c) (EWOC). A mix of employer securities which reasonably reflects the outstanding securities of the employer can also qualify.

employer securities, qualified plan distributions *stocks* and bonds or debentures with interest coupons or in *registered form* issued by an *employer,* its *parent,* or *subsidiary.* §402(a)(3)(A) and (B). See §425(e) and (f) (definition of parent, or subsidiary). *Distributions* of employer securities from a *qualified plan* may, unlike other property, be reported at their cost or other *basis* to the *qualified trust* when paid out as part of a *lump-sum distribution;* if the distribution is not a lump-sum distribution then the employer need not report the *unrealized appreciation* attributable to his or her contributions. In either event, the unrealized appreciation is *recognized* later when the securities are *sold* or otherwise *disposed of* unless this privilege is waived. §402(e)(4) and (a)(1).

employer withdrawal liability an *employer's* liability under Title IV of *ERISA* to pay its share of a *defined benefit plan's* unfunded *vested benefits* at the time of the employer's complete or partial withdrawal from the plan. ERISA §4210 et seq. Unfunded vested benefits are the excess of nonforfeitable benefits over plan assets. ERISA §4211.

employer withdrawal liability trust a *trust* set up for *multiemployer plans* by *plan sponsors* to pay *employer withdrawal liabilities* and similar payments to such plans. §501(c)(22). Section 194 allows *deductions* for *contributions* to such trusts.

employment commencement, qualified plans the first day for which the *employee* is entitled to be credited with an *hour of service.* Labor Reg. §2530.202-2(a). The initial eligibility computation period used to determine whether an employee has computed his or her first *year of service* begins on the employment commencement date. §410(a)(3)(i); Labor Reg. §2530.200b-2(a). The date is used for measuring years of service thereafter as well. §410(a)(3)(A).

employment, FICA taxes services of any type by an *employee* for the person employing him or her, regardless of the payee's citizenship, in the *United States* and on United States vessels and aircraft under most circumstances, as well as outside the United States by a *citizen of the United States* or a *resident alien* when working for a United States *employer.* §3121(b). There are innumerable exceptions such as those for for servants, children in their parents' employ, and prison inmates. *Social Security taxes* fall on *wages,* which §3121(a) defines as remuneration for "employment" and then goes on to exclude a variety of payments from being remuneration.

employment-related expenses, child and dependent care credit expenses for household services or for the care of *qualifying individuals* that enable a *taxpayer* to search actively for employment or to remain *gainfully employed* (e.g., not to do volunteer work). §21(b)(2). Household services means services in and about the taxpayer's home.

employment taxes a general term used to describe the *Social Security tax, federal unemployment tax, income tax withholding,* and various state and local payroll taxes. Generally, any *wages* paid to an *employee* are subject to such taxes.

endowment policy a form of *life insurance contract* which provides for termination of coverage at a predetermined age, at which time the policyowner receives a fixed sum. Death proceeds of such contracts are generally treated as *life insurance proceeds* and are *excludable* from *gross income* under §101. At maturity, such proceeds (if in excess of net *policyholder dividends*) are taxable as *ordinary income.* §72(e); Reg. §1.72-11(d). Government life insurance proceeds are largely excludable. See 38 U.S.C. §3101(a) (1976); Rev. Rul. 71-306, 1971-2 C.B. 76.

endowment test one of three alternative tests used as part of the definition of an *operating foundation.* A *private foundation* satisfies the endowment test if it normally distributes an amount equal to at least two-thirds of its *minimum investment return* directly for its *charitable purposes.* §4942(j)(3)(B)(ii); Reg. §53.4942(b)-2(b). See also *assets test.*

end use test, natural resources a standard for classifying hard minerals for *percentage depletion* purposes under §613 of the *Code.* The standard demands that a mineral (e.g., limestone) be classified according to its ultimate use (e.g., ornamental use versus road building).

energy credit a component of the *investment credit,* which, in turn, is an element of the *general business credit.* The energy credit applies at a 10 percent rate (the *energy percentage*) to *energy property,* except to the extent of the proportion of such property subject to *subsidized energy financing* or to proceeds of a *private activity bond* which pays *tax-exempt interest.* §48(a). This credit expired on June 30, 1992.

energy property, energy investment credit energy property on which the 10 percent energy investment credit may be taken. Energy property includes the following: (1) solar or geothermal property; (2) property constructed or reconstructed by the taxpayer; (3) property that is *depreciable* or *amortizable*; and (4) property that meets certain quality and performance standards. §48. Qualified investments in energy property made during the specified credit periods (before 1992) are eligible for the *energy investment credit.* §§46, 48.

engaged in a trade or business within the United States see *trade or business within the United States.*

engaged in the business of farming actively engaged in agriculture for profit, including as a nurseryman or as a landlord operating on the sharecropping method, or as a landlord who materially participates in the operation of a rented farm, but not as a hobby farmer or as a person engaged in forestry. Reg. §§1.175-3, 1.182-2 and-1(b).

engineer agent an *IRS* agent who has specialized skills at engineering or valuation issues. This person is commonly called in by audit personnel in order to render a specialized finding (e.g., *salvage value*), which is embodied in an *engineer's report*. See Statement of [IRS] Procedural Rules, Reg. §601.105(b)(3).

enhanced oil recovery credit a 15 percent *credit* is provided for costs incurred in connection with oil recovery projects that involve tertiary recovery methods such as cyclic steam injection or in situ combustion. §43. The base is *qualified enhanced recovery costs* for the *taxable year*. The credit is part of the *general business credit*. §38(b). The credit phases out proportionately over a $6 phase-out range as the average per barrel wellhead price of domestic crude oil (the *reference price*) for the last *calendar year* that ended before the tax year in question exceeds $28 (as adjusted for inflation). *Deductions* otherwise allowed for any cost taken into account in computing this credit are reduced by the amount the credit is attributable to such cost. §43(d)(1). The credit is subject to the *passive activity loss* and *credit* rules and the *at-risk rules*. §43(c)(3).

enlargement of building an expansion of a building's overall volume. Reg. §1.48-11(b) (before amendment of §48, but likely controls *rehabilitation tax credits* for lack of contrary Congressional direction). Reg. §1.167(k)-3(a)(3) uses similar language but exempts related facilities (e.g., building a garage). Tax benefits for rehabilitation of buildings do not extend to enlargements. §48(g)(2)(B)(3); Reg. §1.167(k)-3(a)(3). See *external walls requirement*.

enrolled actuary a *person* enrolled by the Joint Board for the Enrollment of Actuaries established under Subtitle C, title III of the Employee Retirement Income Security Act of 1974. §7701(a)(35). Such *individuals* are authorized to perform numerous actuarial activities in connection with *qualified plan* calculations.

enrolled agents *individuals* authorized to practice before the *IRS* based on their competence. Former IRS personnel with sufficient experience may be enrolled without an examination. IRS Circular 230, §10.4(b)(3)(i)-(iv). Form 23 is used to apply for this status.

enrollment card form 294, a permanent document authorizing someone other than an attorney or CPA to *practice before the IRS*. 5 U.S.C. §10.6(b) (1976).

entertainment any activity generally considered to constitute not entertainment, amusement, or recreation, using an objective standard in the context of the *taxpayer's trade or business* or, presumably, investment activities. Reg. §1.274-2(b)(1)(1). *Entertainment expense deductions* are sharply limited by §274.

entertainment expense deduction a *deduction* granted by the general language of §162 *(trade or business)* or §212 (investor's) for *ordinary and necessary* expenses for entertainment. While there is nothing special about the availability of the deduction under those sections, §274 places rather elaborate restrictions on otherwise *deductible* expenditures, largely because of their inherently personal nature. Meal and entertainment expenses are generally *deductible* only to the extent of 80 percent of cost. §274(n)(1). See *associated entertainment and meal expenses; qualified meeting; directly related test, entertainment and meal expenses.*

entertainment facilities property owned, rented, or used by the *taxpayer* for or in connection with *entertainment*. Reg. §1.274-2(e)(2)(i). Examples include yachts, hunting lodges, bowling alleys, fishing camps, and the like. Reg. §1.274-2(c)(2)(ii) exempts facilities used only unsubstantially for entertainment, or activities inherently not entertainment to the taxpayer (e.g., a trade show attended by a dress manufacturer). Section 274(a)(2)(C) exempts social, athletic, and sporting clubs, if used primarily for business, as to items directly related to the conduct of the taxpayer's trade or business, and eating clubs are even more liberally treated. Generally, however, §274(a)(1) denies *deductions* in connection with entertainment facilities.

entity buy-sell agreement an arrangement under which the *entity* purchases the interest of a deceased or withdrawing owner. When the entity is a corporation, the agreement generally involves a stock redemption on the part of the withdrawing shareholder. §302(b). §303.

entity five-percent public group a *public group* of either a *first-tier entity* (or a *higher-tier entity*) that is treated as a *five-percent shareholder*. Reg. §1.382-2T(g)(1). The term is used in connection with determining if there has been an *ownership change* under the *neutrality principle* such that the §382 *limitation* might apply.

entity segregation rules rules applicable to certain *dispositions* by *first-tier entities* (or higher-tier entities) of *stock* of a *loss corporation* and to certain other transactions. The term is used in connection with determining if there has been an *ownership change* under the *neutrality principle* such that the *§382 limitation* might apply.

entity theory a basic notion of *partnership* taxation under which a partnership is viewed as an organization separate from its participants. For example, the partnership has its own *taxable year* and *accounting method*. The antonym is the *aggregate theory*. In fact, both theories are at work in the federal *income tax* treatment of partnerships.

environmental tax a tax imposed at a very low rate as a *surcharge* on a modified form of the *alternative minimum taxable income* over $2 million. *Tax Reform Act of 1984*. See *Alaska Native Corporation*.

Equal Access to Justice Act   an act that allows a discretionary right to a *prevailing party* (not limited to a prevailing defendant) to recover attorney's fees in civil litigation against the federal government that commence before March 1, 1983, unless the government action was substantially justified or special circumstances make an award unjust. 28 U.S.C. 2412 (1976). The fees are generally limited to $75/hour. §504(a)(2). Section 7430, however, supersedes the act effective for *Tax Court* proceedings commenced after February 28, 1983. See *accountant's fees, recovery of; attorney's fees, recovery of; position of the United States; prevailing party; reasonable administrative costs; reasonable litigation costs; Taxpayer's Bill of Rights.*

equitable recoupment   a judicial doctrine, not available in the *Tax Court,* that allows *taxpayers* and the government to offset obligations to each other with amounts arising out of the same transaction, which are otherwise time-barred. See Rev. Rul. 81-287, 1981-2 C.B. 83 for an illustration of the doctrine's application. See *mitigation of effect of statutes of limitations and other provisions.*

equity capital, qualified stock options   in the case of a single *corporation,* the sum of its money and the *adjusted basis* of its other property, less its indebtedness (other than indebtedness to shareholders); and in the case of a group of corporations consisting of a parent and its subsidiaries, the sum of the equity capital of each such corporation, adjusted to eliminate the effect of intercorporate ownership and transactions. §422(c)(3); Reg. §1.422-2(h)(3). See §425(e) through (g) for definitions of parent and subsidiary corporations. The term is important in determining whether a shareholder owns *qualified stock options.* §422(b)(7).

equity-financed lending activity   any *activity* which, for the *taxable year,* involves a *trade or business* of lending money in which the average outstanding balance of the liabilities for the year is not over 80 percent of the average outstanding balance of the interest-bearing assets held in the activity for the year. Temp. Reg. §1.469-2T(f)(4). Net *interest* income from equity-financed lending is treated as *nonpassive income.* Temp. Reg. §1.469-2T(f)(3). See *passive loss rules.*

equity interest   *stock* or any *partnership* interest. §2701(a)(4)(B)(ii).

equity option   any *option* to buy or sell *stock,* and any other option whose value is determined by reference to any stock (or group of stocks) or stock index. §1256(g)(6). Equity options held by dealers are subject to taxation under the rules of the *mark-to-market system.* §1256(g)(4). See *dealer equity option; mark-to-market system.*

equity structure shift   any tax-free *corporate reorganization* under §368(a)(1) (other than a *divisive reorganiza-*

tion, a *Type F reorganization,* or a Type G reorganization) as well as other transactions to be specified by *regulations.* §382(g)(3). An equity structure shift is one of the events that triggers the limitations on *net operating losses* and other limits on *tax attributes* under the *neutrality principle,* but only if there is also an ownership increase of 50 *percentage points* by *five-percent shareholders.* See *neutrality principle; section 382 limitation.*

equivalent exemption   a provision of a *foreign* air or sea transport law that exempts *United States* registered aircraft or ships from taxation on revenues earned from aircraft or shipping activities in such countries. Aircraft and ships registered in such countries are exempt from United States taxation on aircraft and shipping income allocable to United States ports and airports. For purposes of the equivalent exemption rule the failure of a foreign country to grant an exemption to a domestic *corporation* is not taken into account if the corporation is subject to tax by the foreign country on a residence basis, under standards to be prescribed by the *IRS.* §883(a)(5). *Possessions* using a *mirror tax* system qualify under this system. §§872, 883. See §893(b) for a comparable rule regarding the taxation of *employees* of foreign governments and *international organizations.* See *foreign shipping income.*

erroneous refund or credit   any *refund or credit* paid in error. §7405. Payment after the *statute of limitations* for filing a *claim for refund or credit* is an example. §6514(a)(1). The government is authorized to recover such amounts through a civil action. §7405.

escheat   a reversion or forfeiture of real or personal property to the state due to the absence of anyone competent to inherit or as a result of default.

escrow   the placing of money or other property in the hands of a third party to provide security for an obligation. Escrow arrangements are technically viewed as creating *trust* relationships as a legal matter. The money or property remains in escrow until conditions fixed by the escrow arrangement (e.g., the buyer's raising money to buy escrowed property) are met. Escrow funds are generally taxable as *trusts.* §483B(g).

eskimo pie   a slang name for a transaction in which *losses* of *Alaska Native Corporation* could in effect to be sold to outsiders. §60(b) of the *Tax Reform Act of 1984.* See *Alaska Native Corporation.*

essentially equivalent to a dividend, redemptions   see *redemption not essentially equivalent to a dividend.*

established securities market   includes a national securities exchange registered under §6 of the Securities Exchange Act of 1934 and an exchange which is exempted from registration under §5 of the Securities Exchange Act of 1934 because of its limited volume of transactions and any over-the-counter market. Reg. §1.453-3(d)(4); 15A.453-1(e)(4). An over-the-counter market is reflected by the existence of an interdealer quotation system, meaning any system of general circulation to brokers and dealers which regularly disseminates quotations of obligations by identified brokers or dealers, other than a quotation sheet prepared and distributed by a broker or dealer in the regular course of business and containing only quotations of such broker or dealer. The National Daily Quotation Sheet ("yellow sheets") is an interdealer quotation system and, therefore, reflects an over-the-counter market which constitutes an established securities market within the meaning of the regulations. Reg. §15A.453-1(e)(4)(v), example 2. The term is used for purposes of the *installment method* and the *OID rules*. Prop. Reg. §1.1273-2(c)(1).

estate an artificial *entity* that comes into being as a result of death (a *decedent's* estate) or bankruptcy. Decedent's estates are taxed in much the same way as *complex trusts,* and terminate for *federal income tax* purposes after a reasonable period, a limitation designed to control *tax avoidance*. Reg. §1.641(b)-3(a). Estates of *individuals* are viewed as separate *taxpayers,* not *conduits*. §§6012(a)(9) and 1398(c)(1). In legal parlance, the term refers to *present* or *future interests* in property. For an example, see *estate for years*. An estate may also arise for the benefit of a minor or incompetent. See Rev. Rul. 74-9, 1974-1 C.B. 241 (such estates are not permissible *S corporation shareholders*).

estate freeze any method by which future appreciation in value of assets is controlled, thereby reducing prospective *estate taxes*. The most common device is to recapitalize a *corporation* so as to give older members preferred stock, leaving younger members the sole opportunity to garner future appreciation in the value of the enterprise. Section 2036(c) represented an extreme attempt to limit the practice. See *control, applicable retained interest; control, estate freezes; distribution right; equity interest; liquidation, put, call, or conversion right*.

estate tax the federal tax, enacted in 1916, that is imposed on the privilege of a *decedent* to transfer his or her property. It is not a tax levied on an heir receiving property, but rather falls on property owned at death. The stated purpose of the estate tax is to limit the accumulation of great wealth in America. The federal estate tax is now bound into the federal *gift tax* through a *unified transfer tax* system which is designed to achieve tax parity between *inter vivos* and *testamentary* transfers. A unified credit of *$192,800* is available to an estate. The main reason is to eliminate the estate tax liability on small estates. Based on current estate tax rates, the credit covers a tax base of $600,000. The estate tax is determined by (1) combining the *taxable estate* and *adjusted taxable gifts* (basically, inter vivos gifts) and multiplying them by the uniform transfer tax rate; (2) subtracting gift

taxes actually or constructively paid during the decedent's life; and (3) subtracting the *unified credit* and various other minor *credits*. §§2001, 2011-2016.

estate tax charitable contribution a *deduction* used to reduce a *gross estate* of a *decedent* to compute the *taxable estate*. The amount of the allowable *charitable contribution deduction* cannot be greater than the value of the transferred property, which must be included in the decedent's gross estate. §2055(d).

estate tax credits an exclusive list of *nonrefundable credits* that may be applied against *federal estate tax* liabilities: the *unified credit*; the *gift tax credit* (§2012); the *credit for state death taxes* (§2011); *foreign death tax credits* (§2014); and the *credit for tax on prior transfers* (§2013). The unified credit is applied first and the foreign death tax credit is credited last if it arises under *tax treaty*. Reg. §20.2014-1(a)(1). See *estate tax*.

estate tax deductions an exclusive list of *deductions* from *the gross estate* of a *decedent* for certain items which actually reduce the amount of wealth which a decedent can transmit to his or her *beneficiaries*; it is used to determine the *taxable estate*. The list consists of funeral and administrative expenses, legally enforceable predeath claims against the estate, and unpaid mortgages on (or indebtedness in respect of) property that is included in the value of the decedent's gross estate. These deductions are allowed for such expenses only if they are properly allowable under local law. §2053.

estate tax marital deduction see *marital deduction*.

estate trust a *trust,* the income of which is either distributed to the *surviving spouse* or accumulated during his or her lifetime, the principal and accumulated income of which is payable to his or her *estate*. A transfer to such a trust will qualify for the *marital deduction* despite the *terminable interest rule*. See §2056.

estimated tax, corporations *federal income tax* paid in advance of year-end on the basis of anticipated tax liabilities not covered by withholdings. Such taxes are now an integral part of the federal tax scene. Failure to pay on time can produce substantial additional liabilities. The term was defined as the amount of *federal income tax* expected to be owed by a *corporation,* including the *alternative capital gains tax,* less any expected *credits* against tax. If a corporation owes such taxes, but does not make adequate quarterly estimated tax payments, then it may be liable for the *penalty [for] underpayment of estimated tax* imposed by §6655. The tax includes the *alternative minimum tax*. See *exceptions to estimated tax, corporate; large corporation, estimated taxes*.

estimated tax due dates dates on which *estimated tax* payments must be made in order to avoid the *penalty [for] underpayment of estimated tax*. The usual estimated tax due dates for *calendar-year individuals* are April

15, June 15, September 15, and January 15 of the succeeding year. §6153(a)(1). Calendar-year *corporations* are generally subject to the same due dates, except that the final payment is expected on December 15. §6154(b). If estimated payments are timely filed and paid in the proper amounts, then a *taxpayer* will not owe any penalty for underpayment of estimated tax. §§6654(a), 6655(a).

estimated tax, individuals If an individual expects to owe estimated tax in excess of $500, then the *taxpayer* must make quarterly estimated tax payments or run the risk of being subject to a penalty for *underpayment of estimated income taxes* under §§6654, 6015(a), and Reg. §1.6015(c)-(1)(a). Most *trusts* and *estates* must pay estimated taxes in much the same manner as individuals. The tax includes the *alternative minimum tax*.

estimated wages the aggregate amount the *employee* reasonably expects will constitute *wages* for his or her *taxable year*. §3042(m)(2)(B). The term is used for purposes of setting *withholding allowances* in connection with withholding of *federal income taxes* on wages. §3402(m)(1). See *income tax withholding*.

estimation days days on which *estimated taxes* are due, generally the 15th of April, June, and September, and January of the following year for *calendar-year individual taxpayers*. §6073. Special rules apply to farmers, fishermen, and *nonresident aliens*.

estimation year the computation period for *estimated taxes*. A calendar-year individual should determine, on or before March 31 of the current tax year, whether or not he or she will have an underpayment of estimated tax for the year. In making this determination, the individual should estimate the income tax, taking into account any alternative minimum and self-employment tax that will be due for the year, and deduct any tax credits. If an underwithholding of $500 or more is expected, the taxpayer should make quarterly estimated tax payments. The term is used to form the period with respect to which employees determine their *estimated wages* and *estimated itemized deductions* for purposes of claiming their *withholding allowances*. See Reg. §31.3402(m)-1(a).

estoppel a doctrine developed in the courts of *equity*—those courts authorized to do justice with special remedies such as injunctions and declaratory judgments as opposed to merely applying the law to grant monetary awards—to the effect that one cannot profit from a misrepresentation. Representations by agents of the *IRS* may occasion application of the doctrine. Although the majority view appears to be that the doctrine is inapplicable against the IRS, in a number of cases the doctrine has in fact been applied to the benefit of *taxpayers*.

evergreen trees, hypothetical sales election applies

to pine, spruce, fir, hemlock, cedar, and other conifers. Reg. §1.631-1(b)(2). If the trees are more than six years old when severed from the roots and are for ornamental purposes, they qualify for the *hypothetical sales election*. §631(a).

evidence of indebtedness *debt* that is manifested in some documented form such as bonds, debentures, notes, or certificates; a term referred to in various sections of the *Code*. See, e.g., §§1232, 1083(e)(1), 453(f)(3).

Examination Division (1) a division within the *Service Center* that examines tax returns, communicating with *taxpayers* by letter; (2) a division of a *District Office* that selects and examines returns and conducts office and field examinations; and (3) a division of the *National Office* headed by the Assistant Commissioner, comparable to the office of the Assistant Regional Commissioner. See Statement of [IRS] Procedural Rules, Reg. §601.105(a) and (b) as to the first two items. See *audit*.

examination report generally, a report prepared by a *revenue agent* following an *audit*, designed to inform *taxpayers* and the *IRS* of the details of the examination. Such reports follow fairly rigid formats, designed for different types of cases (e.g., *income tax* or *estate tax*). See, e.g., I.R.M. Pt. IV—Audit §4237, *Report Writing Guide for Income Tax Examining Officers* 7301 et seq. See *Revenue Agent's Report*.

examination review a procedural and quality check of *examination reports*. This is normally an internal function within each *District Office*, but it is performed by certain large *prime districts* for small *streamlined districts* which do not have the staff for it. I.R.M. 1118.3(2).

excepted agreed case a tax dispute with the *IRS* which is agreed but which involves one of several classes of special situations, such an audit of a *personal holding company*. IRS Procedures: Audits and Appeals A-24-25.

excepted exchange a *foreign corporation's* exchange of its *stock* of one (old) foreign corporation for stock of another (new) foreign corporation, provided (1) the exchange is to effect a mere change in form of a single corporation; (2) the old and new corporations differ only in form; (3) ownership of the entities is the same; and (4) the first transfer begins during or after 1968. In these cases, a *section 367 ruling* to avoid immediate taxation can be granted before or after the transfer. Temp. Reg. §7.367(a)-1(b)(5) and -1(d)(4)(ii).

exceptions to estimated tax, corporate statutory provisions (also known as safety zones) that allow a corporate *taxpayer* to avoid the *penalties [for] underpayment of estimated tax*. §6654(d). Current law requires a *corporation* to make its *required annual payments* of its estimated tax in four equal installments, regardless of when income is actually earned. The payments are based on the lesser of 90 percent of the tax due on the *return* or 100 percent for *large corporations* of the tax reported on the original return for the prior *taxable year*. §6654(d)(1)(B). There are exceptions to the penalty when the corporation has based its payments on annualized income earned in the immediately preceding quarter (§6655(e)(2)), a seasonal income exception that allows the use of payments that track the income pattern of the prior year (§6655(e)(3)) and corporations with less than $500 of tax for the prior year (§6655(f)). §6655(d)(2)(A). If none of these exceptions apply and there is a sufficient underpayment, then the taxpayer will be subject to a penalty for the period of underpayment. §6655(a). For years beginning in 1992, the required annual payment, which includes a corporation's alternative minimum tax liability, is the lesser of 93 percent (94 percent for 1993 and 1994, and 95 percent for 1995 and 1996) of the corporation's final tax, or (2) 100 percent of the tax for the preceding year if that was a 12-month tax year. The minimum tax is slated to return to 90 percent for 1997. §§6655(d) and (e) as amended by the Tax Extension Act of 1991.

exceptions to estimated tax, individual   two statutory provisions (also known as safety zones) that allow an *individual taxpayer* to avoid the *penalty for underpayment of estimated tax*. §6654(d). The exceptions are generally referred to as "*last year's tax*" (meaning 100 percent of the tax shown on the prior year's initial *return*) and the "tax on annualized current year's income," which can protect *taxpayers* whose incomes balloon late in the year. §6654(d)(1). If neither of these exceptions apply and there is an underpayment, then the taxpayer will be subject to a penalty for the period of underpayment. §6654(a). There is also no penalty if (1) there was no tax in the prior year; (2) net tax liability after *wage* withholding *credits* is under $500; or (3) the *IRS* determines it would be unfair because the underpayment was caused by a casualty or disaster, recent retirement at age 62 or older, or recent disability. §6654(e)(1) and (3). To avoid an underpayment penalty, taxpayers whose adjusted gross income increases by more than $40,000 from a prior year and whose adjusted gross income is more than $75,000 must make estimated tax payments at least equal to 90 percent of the current year's tax liability rather than 100 percent of the prior year's tax liability. The Internal Revenue Service is also authorized to abate any underpayment in 1992 caused by the underwithholding due to the issuance of revised withholding tables (effective March 1992). §6654(d).

excess accumulations, IRA   a shortfall in distributions from an *individual retirement account* or *annuity*. §4974(a). *IRAs* are supposed to begin paying out before the *individual* reaches age 70½. Section 4974 imposes a 50 percent *excise tax* on failure to make minimum dis-

tributions demanded by §408(a)(6), (7) or (b)(3), (4) during the payee's *taxable year*.

excess aggregate contributions   as to any *plan year*, the excess of aggregate *employee matching contributions* and *contributions* by *employees* (plus any *qualified nonelective contributions* and elective contributions included in computing the *contribution percentage*) paid on behalf of *highly compensated employees* over the maximum permissible amounts under the contribution percentage limitation of §401(m)(3). §401(m)(6)(B). Such amounts can be purgatively distributed so as to avoid disqualification of the plan. See *matching contribution*.

excess alimony payments   see *frontloading of alimony*.

excess benefit percentage   benefits provided on *average annual compensation* above the *integration level*, stated as a percentage of such compensation. §401(1)(3)(A)(i)(I). See *permitted disparity*.

excess benefit plan, ERISA   a *nonqualified deferred compensation* plan maintained by an *employer* solely for the purpose of providing benefits for certain *employees* in excess of the limitations on contributions and benefits imposed by §415 on plans to which that section applies, without regard to whether the plan is *funded*. To the extent that the Secretary of Labor determines that a separable part of a plan is being maintained by an employer for such a purpose, that part is treated as an *excess benefit plan. ERISA* §3(36). These plans are a popular post-ERISA mechanism for maximizing tax-favored retirement planning.

excess benefit plan, integrating Social Security and pension plans   plans that pay a benefit based exclusively on amounts over a base, referred to as the plan's *integration level,* the effect of which is generally to permit proportionately enhanced benefits to highly paid *employees*. The maximum integration level is determined by the *Social Security wage base*. See *integration, Social Security*.

excess business holdings excise tax, private foundations   a tax imposed on a *private foundation* at the rate of 5 percent of the value of its *excess business holdings*, with an additional 200 percent tax if such holdings are not disposed of by the time a *notice of deficiency* is mailed. The purpose of these elaborate rules is to disentangle private foundations from business enterprises and to minimize unfair competition with taxable enterprises arising out of the tax benefits available to private foundations. §4943.

excess business holdings, private foundations   for purposes of the five-percent *excess business holdings excise tax* imposed on *private foundations* by §4943(a)(1), the term refers to stock or other interests in business enterprises that the foundation would have to dispose of to someone other than a *disqualified person* in order for its remaining holdings to be permitted holdings. §4943(c)(1). See *effective control, private foundation's excess business holdings.*

excess business holdings redemption needs   the amount needed (or reasonably anticipated to be needed) to redeem stock from a *private foundation* pursuant to the 20 percent *excess business holdings* rule of §4943. §537(b)(2). Amounts accumulated for this purpose are considered reasonable accumulations for purposes of the *accumulated earnings tax.* §537(a)(3). See *reasonable needs of the business, accumulated earnings tax.*

excess contribution, black lung benefit tax   the excess of amounts contributed to a *black lung benefit trust* over the amount permitted to be *deducted,* adjusted by excess contributions from the preceding *taxable year.* This excess amount is taxed at a rate of 5 percent to the person making the excess contribution. §4953(a) and (b).

excess contribution, CODA   see *qualified cash or deferred arrangement; excise tax, excess contributions to cash or deferred plans, SEPs, and tax-sheltered annuities for exempt and educational organization employees.*

excess contribution percentage   the percentage of *compensation* that the *employer* contributed under the plan on compensation over the *integration level.* §401(1)(2)(B)(i). See *permitted disparity.*

excess contributions, excise tax   excess contributions to cash or deferred plans, SEPs, and tax-sheltered annuities for exempt and educational organizational *employees.* See *excise tax, excess contributions to cash or deferred plans, SEPs, and tax-sheltered annuities for exempt and educational organization employees.*

excess contributions excise tax, individual retirement arrangements and section 403(b) annuities   an *excise tax* imposed on an *individual* for making contributions to an *individual retirement arrangement* or *section 403(b) annuity* in excess of the *deductible* limits, and on cumulative excesses from previous years, reduced by certain distributions. See §408(d)(5). The tax is imposed each year at a rate of 6 percent of the accumulated excess as determined at the end of the year, but it may not exceed 6 percent of the value of the *IRA.* §4973.

excess contributions, qualified deferred compensation plans   generally, any contribution to a *qualified pension plan* larger than the amount the contributor can *deduct* for *federal income tax* purposes. Such an amount may be subject to penalties, but it can generally be carried forward for *deduction* in later years. See especially §404(a)(1)(D).

excess credits   any unused *general business credit* (§39) and any unused *minimum tax credit* (§53).

§383(a)(2). Limitations similar to those applicable to *net operating loss carryforwards* are also applied to excess credit carryforwards after an *ownership change,* under *regulations* to be issued. §383(a)(1). See *neutrality principle.*

excess deduction award   an *employee achievement award* that is partially taxable because of its magnitude. §74(c). See *employee achievement award.*

excess deferral, CODA   an elective deferral of an *employee's* earnings in excess of the indexed $7,000 cap on deferrals under a *qualified cash or deferred arrangement.* §408(g)(2)(C). Such excess amounts must be returned to the employee, who is taxable on the income earned on the excess deferral when the distribution is made. The excess deferral itself is taxed in the year in which it occurs. §402(g)(1), (2)(C) and 401(a)(30) (disqualification of plan in absence of indexed $7,000 cap on elective deferrals). See *qualified cash or deferred arrangement.*

excess defined benefit plan   see *excess plan.*

excess defined contribution plan   see *excess plan.*

excess depletion   an informal term for *item of tax preference* consisting of the excess of *percentage depletion* deducted for the year over the *adjusted basis* of the *property* at the end of the year (computed property by property without regard to the depletion allowance for the *taxable year*). §57(a)(1). This excess can attract *alternative minimum tax.* The CNEPA of 1992 (Pub. L 102-486) repeals the alternative minimum tax for tax preferences for excess intangible drilling costs and excess depletion for tax years beginning after 1992. §1915.

excess distribution   a transaction that occurs if a *corporation's distributions* (including *redemptions*) with respect to its *stock* (aside from §1504(a)(4) *preferred stock*) in a single *taxable year* exceed the greater of (1) 150 percent of the average of such distributions made by the corporation during the preceding three taxable years or (2) 10 percent of the *fair market value* of the stock of the corporation (excluding §1504(a)(4) *preferred stock*) at the beginning of the taxable year. §172(m)(3)(C), (E). Excess distributions are a kind of *corporate equity reduction transaction* (CERT) in the interest of limiting tax abuses in the context of a leveraged recapitalization of a single corporation or group of corporations. See *corporate equity reduction transaction.*

excess distribution, CERT   the excess of the aggregate *distributions* (including redemptions) made in a *taxable year* by a *corporation* with respect to its *stock* over the greater of 150 percent of the average of such distributions in the three taxable years immediately before that year or 10 percent of the *fair market value* of its stock as of the beginning of the year. Certain preferred stock and certain stock issuances are ignored.

§172(m)(3). This term is an element of the definition of an *applicable corporation, CERT*. See *corporate equity reduction transaction* for the significance.

excess distribution, passive foreign investment company a *distribution* to a *shareholder* of a *passive foreign investment company* that is subjected to current taxation plus an interest charge for the *tax deferral* caused by the fact that the income was generated in an untaxed foreign investment company. §1291(b). The details are elaborate.

excess distribution, trusts an *accumulation distribution* by a *complex trust*. Such amounts are subject to the complicated *throwback rules* of §§665–668.

excess FICA taxes *Social Security taxes* collected by two or more *employers* in a *taxable year,* with the result that the *employee* paid more than the *FICA* ceiling for the taxable year as did the employers. Employees are entitled to a return of the excess. Reg. §31.6413(c)-1.

excess intangible drilling and development costs (excess IDCs) *intangible drilling and development costs* (IDCs) that relate to productive oil, gas, and geothermal wells in excess of amortization of IDCs that would have arisen had the *taxpayer capitalized* them, then written them off over 10 years or using *cost depletion,* whichever resulted in a lower excess. §57(a)(2)(B). The CNEPA of 1992 (Pub. L 102-486) repeals the alternative minimum tax for tax preferences for excess intangible drilling costs and excess depletion for tax years beginning after 1992. §1915.

excess interest allocation to the extent Reg. §1.882-5 allocates a *branch* of a *foreign corporation* an *interest deduction* in excess of interest actually paid, that excess is treated as interest paid by a United States subsidiary to the foreign corporation on a hypothetical loan from the foreign corporation. §884(f)(1)(B). See *branch level interest tax; branch profits tax.*

excess interest deduction *interest* credited to holders of *deferred annuities* issued by *life insurance companies* that represent amounts in excess of rates required by applicable state insurance laws to support annuity contracts. *TEFRA* interceded by generally declaring *qualified guaranteed interest* (i.e., guaranteed interest relating to future periods) alone *deductible*. See §§805(g), 818(c) and (h). The term is also used in reference to interest on so-called *flexible premium life insurance policies'* cash values where the insurer claims *interest paid*. See *policyholder dividend, life insurance companies.*

excess interest expense a *corporation's* excess interest expense for a *taxable year* is the excess, if any, of the corporation's *net interest expense* over the sum of half of its *adjusted taxable income* for the year plus any *excess limitation carryforward* from the three prior taxable years. §163(j)(2)(B). The limitation on the interest

deduction is designed to put an end to bleeding off corporate earnings via interest payments to related charities or foreign owners. See *earnings stripping provisions.*

excess investment interest see *interest on investment indebtedness limitation.*

excessive compensation see *unreasonable compensation.*

excessive profits any amount which constitutes excessive profits within the meaning of the Renegotiation Act of 1951, as amended, any part of the contract price of a contract with the United States or any agency thereof, any part of the subcontract price of a subcontract under such a contract, and any profits derived from one or more such contracts or subcontracts. §1481(a)(1)(B). See *renegotiation of government contracts.*

excessive salaries see *unreasonable compensation.*

excess limitation carryforward the excess limitation, if any, arising in any of the *corporation's* three prior *taxable years* and not taken into account in any of those three prior taxable years. An excess limitation arising in any taxable year carries over to the corporation's first, second, and third succeeding taxable years to the extent it is not taken into account in any of those three succeeding years. §163(j)(2)(B)(ii). The limitation on the interest deduction is designed to put an end to bleeding off corporate earnings via interest payments to related charities or foreign owners. See *excess interest expense; earnings stripping provisions.*

excess lobbying expenditures see *tax on lobbying expenditures.*

excess loss account a negative account in common *stock* of a *subsidiary* held by a *parent corporation* where the companies file *consolidated returns*. Reg. §1.1502-32 compels parent corporations to reduce their *basis* in the stock of a consolidated subsidiary by the subsidiary's deficit in *earnings and profits,* as well as certain other items. When the parent's basis in such stock turns negative, an excess loss account arises. Reg. §1.1502-19(b) in turn triggers *gain* to the parent on various *dispositions* (principally *sales, exchanges, worthlessness* of the sub stock; certain discharges of subsidiary indebtedness; and cessation of filing of a consolidated return). See Reg. §1.1502-19(e). If the subsidiary is insolvent at the time, the gain will commonly be *ordinary,* not *capital gain.* Parent corporations can no longer minimize taxation on dispositions of such stock by electing to reduce the basis in sub debt, but it is possible to reduce the basis in stock subsidiary. See Reg. §1.1502-19.

excess net passive income the base on which the corporate rate tax imposed by §1375(a)(1) falls. §1375(b)(1). If an *S corporation,* which was formerly a

C corporation (i.e., a regular corporation), had *earnings and profits* in prior years and has *passive investment income* in excess of 25 percent of its *gross receipts,* then a tax falls on the excess, as defined. The calculation involves determining net passive income by subtracting directly connected allocable *expenses* (undefined but excluding *net operating loss deductions* under §172 and deductions under §§241–250) from *passive investment income,* determining the extent to which it exceeds 25 percent of gross receipts ("the excess"), and then multiplying net passive income by:

$$\frac{\text{The excess}}{\text{Total passive investment income}}$$

Section 1375(a) imposes the top corporate tax on excess net passive income, but only to the extent it is not greater than the corporation's *taxable income.* §1375(b)(1)(B).

excess parachute payment   the amount by which a *parachute payment* exceeds the *base amount* allocated to it. §280G(b)(1). For example, if an executive's base amount is $100,000 and she gets a $400,000 parachute payment, one multiplies the $100,000 by three to get the base amount and determines that there is a $100,000 excess parachute payment. Section 4999 imposes a 20 percent tax on such payments in addition to the income tax due. See *base amount, golden parachutes, parachute payment.*

excess pension assets   assets the amount of which can be transferred in a *qualified transfer.* Assets transferred to a *section 401(h) account* in a *qualified transfer* can be used only to pay *qualified current retiree health liabilities* for the taxable year of the transfer. See *qualified transfer, health benefit account.*

excess plan   a plan that provides benefits or contributions with respect to *employee compensation* in excess of compensation that is covered by Social Security, or a plan that provides greater benefits or contributions on such excess compensation. Such a plan may be a *defined benefit plan* ("*excess defined benefit plan*") or a *defined contribution plan* ("*excess defined contribution plan*"). For post-1988 years, §401(l)(2) provides further restrictions. See *integration, Social Security; permitted disparity.*

excess prepaid farm supplies   prepaid farm supplies for the *taxable year* to the extent the amount of such supplies exceeds 50 percent of *deductible* farming expenses for the *taxable year* other than prepaid farm supplies. §464(f)(4)(A). Deductible farming expenses include *depreciation* or *amortization* which is properly allocable to the *trade or business* of farming. §464(F)(4)(C). See *farming, farming syndicate.*

excess reimbursements, medical plans   benefits actually provided to *highly compensated individuals*

under *self-insured medical reimbursement plans* but not to other *employees,* or a formula amount derived by multiplying other reimbursements to highly compensated employees under a discriminatory plan times the following fraction:

$$\frac{\text{Total reimbursements to highly compensated employees}}{\text{Total reimbursements}}$$

§105(h)(7). Such amounts are *includible* in the *gross income* of highly compensated individuals. §105(h)(1). See *highly compensated individual, medical reimbursement plans.*

excess reserves for losses on bad debts of financial institutions   In the case of *banks, mutual savings banks, domestic building and loan associations,* and certain *cooperative banks,* the *deduction* for additions to *reserves for bad debts* computed on the basis of actual experience. §291(e)(1)(A). Such excess reserves are treated as a *corporate preference item,* 15 percent of which must be eliminated as a tax deduction. §291(a)(3).

exchange   a transfer of property in exchange for other property (not money). Section 1001(a) is the principal authority defining *gains* and *losses* from exchanges. An exchange is considered an appropriate occasion for finding a *realization* of gain or loss, such that it must be reported for *federal income tax* purposes, absent an applicable *nonrecognition provision.* Exchanges may be *constructive* as well as actual; see, e.g., §165(g) relating to *worthless securities.* Generally, a sale or exchange is required for purposes of finding a *capital transaction.* §1222. The term is not defined for purposes of §267(c), relating to denial of losses on transactions, including exchanges, between *related taxpayers,* but there seems to be no reason to develop a different definition.

exchanged basis   a synonym of *substituted basis.*

exchanged basis property   *property* received by a transferee in a *nonrecognition transaction* in which the *basis* of the property is determined at least in part by the *taxpayer's* basis in other property. §7701(a)(44). The term is used in connection with the taxation of *market discount bonds.* See §1272(c)(2).

exchanged employee, highly paid employee   see *top paid group.*

exchange funds   see *swap fund.*

exchange group   properties transferred and received in a *like-kind exchange* to the extent they are all of a like-kind or *like class.* Money; *stock in trade;* other property held primarily for sale; *stocks;* bonds; notes; other securities, or indebtedness, or interest; interests in a *partnership; certificates of beneficial interest;* or *choses in action* do not qualify. Each exchange must consist of at least one property transferred and one received in the exchange. Reg. §1031(f)-1(b)(2)(i). In multiproperty *like-handed exchanges,* properties transferred and properties received by the taxpayer in the exchange are separated into *exchange groups* and a *residual group.* Reg. §1.1031(f)-1(b)(2).

exchange group deficiency the excess of the aggregate *fair market value* of the properties transferred in an *exchange group* over the aggregate value of the properties received (less the amount of any excess liabilities the *taxpayer* assumes and which are *allocated* to that exchange group) in the exchange group. Reg. §1.1031(f)-1(b)(2)(iv). The term is used in connection with multiproperty *like-kind exchanges* where there are excess liabilities.

exchange group surplus the excess of the aggregate value of the properties received (less excess liabilities the taxpayer assumes and which are *allocated* to the *exchange group*) in an exchange group over the aggregate value of the properties transferred in the exchange group. Reg. §1.1031(f)-1(b)(2)(iv). The term is used in connection with multiproperty *like-kind exchanges* where there are excess liabilities.

exchange offer a financing device (also known as a "roll up") in the oil and gas industry and, to a lesser extent, the real estate business, which provides an opportunity for *limited partners* to exchange their interests for freely tradable stock or publicly traded limited partnership interests on a potentially tax-free basis. Under the scheme, the new *entity,* whether a *corporation* or a *limited partnership,* would acquire and consolidate the assets of several ventures in these tax-free exchanges, and the shareholders would acquire liquidity and the possibility for *capital gains.* The availability of such tax-free treatment is a *no ruling area.* Rev. Proc. 83-22, 1983-13 I.R.B. 14; Rev. Proc. 83-16, 1983-11 I.R.B. 10; Rev. Proc. 82-56, 1982-41 I.R.B. 17. See *publicly traded partnerships.*

excise tax a tax imposed on the manufacturing, selling, or using of goods or on an occupation or activity. A license tax is an excise tax on the privilege of engaging in a certain business, occupation, or profession. Under §1491, a United States person who transfers appreciated property to a foreign corporation as paid-in surplus or as a contribution to capital to a foreign partnership must pay an excise tax on the transfer. Federal excise taxes are also imposed on fuels (gasoline, diesel fuel, etc.), luxury items, gas-guzzling cars, heavy trucks and trailers, firearms, tobacco, and alcohol.

excise tax, dispositions of §133 securities an *excise tax* of 10 percent of the *amount realized* (or *fair market value* in certain cases) on various *dispositions* of *section 133 securities.* §4978B. This is designed to stop the practice of borrowing money to buy such securities and then disposing of them, under circumstances in which the party that advanced the money to buy the section 133 securities *excludes* half the *interest* from *gross income.*

excise tax, disqualified welfare plan benefits an *annual excise tax* on *employers* whose *welfare benefit funds* provide *disqualified benefits.* The tax equals 100 percent of the disqualified benefit. §4976. Section 4976(c) imposes a further tax on funded welfare benefit plans which include a discriminatory employee benefit plan.

excise tax, early dispositions by ESOPs and EWOCs an *excise tax* of 10 percent of the *amount realized* on the disposition of *qualified securities* by an *ESOP* or *EWOC* that did not hold the stock for at least three years. There are various exceptions. §4978. It only applies if the *employer*–original seller of the securities bought *qualified replacement property* pursuant to §1042.

excise tax, early withdrawals a 10 percent *excise tax* imposed on the recipient of early distributions from any *qualified retirement plan, qualified annuity, IRA,* or *tax-deferred annuity for exempt and educational organization employees* before age 59½.

excise taxes, private foundations a set of miscellaneous taxes, generally imposed on a *private foundation* and sometimes its insiders for acts or omissions not in accordance with proper foundation operations. Taxes are imposed on investment income (the *audit fee,* which is not based on bad acts) (§4940), on *self-dealing* (§4941), on *undistributed income* (§4942), on *excess business holdings* (§4943), on *speculative investments* (§4944), and on *taxable expenditures* (§4945). See *audit fee, private foundations; excess business holdings excise tax, private foundations; self-dealing tax, private foundations; speculative investments excise tax, private foundations; undistributed income excise tax, private foundations.*

excise taxes, qualified plans a set of miscellaneous taxes imposed for certain misdeeds associated with *qualified plans, IRAs,* and so forth. Imposition of one or more of these taxes does not affect eligibility for tax-privileged status under §401 et seq. Rather, these taxes are imposed on an *employer* who fails to meet the §412 *minimum funding standards* (§4971), on an employer who makes *excess contributions* (§4972), on an individual who makes *excess contributions* to an *individual retirement arrangement* (§4973), on an individual who receives insufficient distributions from an *individual retirement account* or *annuity* (§4974), and on certain *persons* who participate in a *prohibited transaction* with an IRA or a qualified plan (§4975). The amount of the taxes and the base on which they are imposed are treated under separate headings. See *accumulated funding deficiency; excess accumulations, IRA; excess contributions, excise tax; minimum funding excise tax; prohibited transactions, penalties.*

excise tax, excess contributions to cash or deferred plans, SEPs, and tax-sheltered annuities for exempt and educational organization employees a 15 percent *excise tax* on *employers* who make undue contributions consisting of *excess contributions* in connection with *salary reduction plans* and so forth and *excess aggregate contributions* in connection with *matching contributions*. §4979. No tax is imposed on any excess contribution or excess aggregate contribution if it is *distributed* (with any income allocable to that contribution) or forfeited before the close of the first two and one-half months of the *plan year*. §4979(f).

excise tax, excess distribution from qualified plans a 15 percent *nondeductible excise tax* on so-called excess distributions from *qualified plans* and *IRAs*. §4980A (formerly 4981A). The base of the tax is the excess of *actual distributions* over $112,500 for the year (indexed for inflation) or $150,000, if greater. The payee bears the tax.

excise tax, failure to make minimum distributions an *excise tax* equal to 50 percent on the shortfall of any minimum required distribution under an *IRA*, a *qualified deferred compensation plan*, a *section 403(b) annuity*, or a *qualified annuity plan*. §4974. See also *minimum distribution rules*.

excise tax, failure to provide health care continuation a $100 per person (e.g., *employee*, spouse, and *dependents*) per day *excise tax* on the *employer's* failure to provide the employee with an option to buy continuing health care coverage on terms at least as favorable as that provided to continuing employees. The excise tax is aimed at stopping abuses of *deductions* for health care coverage. See *group health plan, deduction; health care continuation rules*.

excise tax, funded welfare benefit plans see *disqualified benefits*.

excise tax, greenmail see *greenmail payments*.

excise tax, minimum funding see *minimum funding excise tax*.

excise tax, nondeductible contributions to qualified plans a 10 percent *excise tax* imposed on *employers* who make *nondeductible* contributions to *qualified plans*, determined as of the close of the payors' *taxable year*. §4972. This prevents overfunding as a technique to generate tax-free income on interim overpayments. The plans affected include *qualified pension, profit-sharing or stock bonus plans, SEPs*, or *annuity plans*.

excise tax, political expenditures an *excise tax*, initially of 5 percent, imposed on *private foundations* and their management with respect to amounts *paid or incurred* to carry on propaganda, influence legislation, influence the outcome of a public election, or carry on a voter registration drive. §4945(d). Such expenditures are one form of *taxable expenditures*.

excise tax, premature disposition by ESOP of employer securities acquired with securities acquisition loan an *excise tax* imposed by §4978B imposed on the employer if there is voluntary disposition by ESOP of employer securities acquired with securities acquisition loan within three years after the acquisition. The tax is 10 percent of the *amount realized*. The tax technically falls on dipositions of *section 133 securities*, defined in §4978B to mean employer securities acquired by the ESOP with a *securities acquisition loan*.

excise tax, premiums to foreign insurers an *excise tax* on insurance policies, annuities, indemnity bonds, and reinsurance policies issued by *foreign* insurers and reinsurers either (1) to, for, or in the name of a *United States person* as to whole or partial United States risks or (2) to, for, or in the name of a foreign person enagaged in a United States *trade or business* as to United States risks. §4371.

excise tax, prohibited allocation of ESOP and EWOC stock a 50 percent *excise tax* on the amount involved when an *ESOP* or *EWOC* allocates *employer securities* acquired in a transaction under §1042 or (now repealed) §2057, where the *allocation* violates §409(n) or any benefit accruing to a person in violation of §409(n). It is imposed on the *employer*. See §§4979A(b)(1) and (c) and 409(n)(2)(B). See *nonallocation period*.

excise tax, reversion of excess pension funds an *excise tax* imposed on the amount of pension plan assets which are transferred to a plan's *sponsor* after the plan terminates and satisfies its obligations. The rate is 20 percent if any of three specified circumstances apply and 50 percent for all other plan terminations. The specified circumstances arise if the plan sponsor: (1) is in Chapter 7 bankruptcy liquidation (or similar state court proceedings) on the plan termination date; (2) provides certain pro rata benefit increases under the terminating plan; or (3) establishes or maintains a *qualified replacement plan*. §4980.

excise tax, taxable substances an *excise tax* imposed on importers of a long list of chemicals (*taxable substances*) which is subject to being lengthened by the *Treasury Department*. See *chemical feedstocks tax*.

excise tax, transfers to foreign corporations, trusts, estates, and partnerships a 35 percent *excise tax* generally imposed on the appreciation, that is, the excess of *fair market value* over the *basis* plus the amount of *recognized gain* on the transfer, when a *United States person* moves property to a *foreign corporation, estate, trust*, or *partnership*. §1491. Since foreign entities are generally not subject to United States income tax, they can offer a means of tax-free accumulations of income. See *outbound transfers.*

excise tax, undistributed income of an REIT   an *excise tax* on certain undistributed income of a *real estate investment trust* (REIT). See §§857 and 4981.

excise tax, undistributed income of an RIC   a *nondeductible excise tax* equal to 4 percent of the *excess,* if any, of the *required distribution* for the calendar year, *over the distributed amount* for the calendar year. The excise tax is to be paid not later than March 15 of the succeeding calendar year. To determine the amount to be distributed, a RIC may reduce its capital gain net income by its net ordinary loss— the company's net operating loss for the calendar year determined in the same manner as ordinary income. See §§852(b) and 4982.

excise tax, undistributed income of a private foundation   see *undistributed income excise tax, private foundation.*

excludable employee, cafeteria plan   see *excluded employee.*

excludable employee, minimum coverage rules   any *employee* who needs not be counted for purposes of determining if the *minimum coverage rules* involving *qualified plans* are satisfied. See §410(b)(2)-(4). One can generally disregard an *employee* who does not meet the plan's *minimum age and service requirements.* §410(b)(4)(A).

excludable period   a period (generally seven years) during which certain parties that lend money in the form of a *securities acquisition loan* to an *ESOP* can exclude half the *interest* thereon. §133(e)(2).

excludable portion, section 126 payment   see *cost-sharing payments, conservation.*

excluded addition, class life asset depreciation range system   an *expenditure* of more than $100 for *property* which is for an additional identifiable unit of property (including certain replacements) which substantially increases the productivity or capacity of an existing identifiable unit of property by at least 25 percent or adapts it for a substantially different use. Excluded additions had to be *capitalized* and treated as new assets or be placed in a *vintage account* for the year that they were first *placed in service,* or for the year that their costs were paid or incurred. Reg. §1.167(a)-11(d)(5) and (6).

excluded employee   generally, an *employee* who is not counted for purposes of testing for a *discriminatory employee benefit plan.* §89(h). They are employees: (1) who have not completed one year of service; plan; (2) who normally work less than $17\frac{1}{2}$ hours per week; (3) who normally work no more than six months during any year (or any shorter period specified in the plan);

(4) who are included in a unit of employees covered by an agreement found by the *IRS* to be a *collective bargaining agreement;* (5) who have not reached age 21 (or an earlier age specified in the plan); or, (6) who are *nonresident aliens* and who receive from the *employer* no earned income from United States sources. See §125(b)(3).

excluded employee, highly paid employee   see *top paid group.*

excluded member   a *corporation* that was a member of a *controlled group of corporations* on December 31, but (1) was a member of the group for less than half the days of the *taxable year* before December 31; (2) is an *exempt organization* (under §501), unless it is subject to the tax on *unrelated trade or business* income; (3) is a *foreign corporation* subject to *federal income taxes* under §881 (the 30 percent flat rate, or as reduced by treaty) on *gross income from sources within the United States*; (4) is one of several types of *insurance companies* (except for a group of life insurance companies); or (5) is a *franchised corporation.* §1563(b)(2). An excluded member is, by virtue of §1563(b), not a *component member* of a controlled group of corporations and can, therefore, claim a separate right to graduated income taxes, the *accumulated earnings credit,* and the $25,000 *small business deduction* granted *life insurance companies.* §1561(a). See *brother-sister controlled group; combined group; controlled group of corporations, graduated taxes, and other benefits; excluded stock, controlled group of corporations; parent-subsidiary controlled groups.*

excluded property, alternate valuation   *property* not included in valuation of the *gross estate* because the increase in value was not property owned by the *decedent.* Examples include *interest* accrued after the date of death on interest-bearing notes, rental payments, and cash dividends declared to shareholders as of a record date after the decedent's death. Such property is excluded despite the selection of the *alternate valuation date.* Reg. §20.2032-(1)(d).

excluded stock, controlled group of corporations   *stock* that is not counted in determination of whether a *corporation, individual, estate,* or *trust* owns 50 percent or more of the total combined voting power or total value of all classes of a corporation's *stock* for purposes of finding either a *parent-subsidiary* or a *brother-sister controlled group.* §1563(c)(2)(A) and (B). Excluded stock for purposes of the parent-subsidiary test is stock in the subsidiary held by a *trust* that is a part of a *deferred compensation* plan, stock owned by a principal officer or *shareholder* of the parent, stock owned by an *employee* of the subsidiary where the right to dispose of the stock is substantially restricted by the parent, and stock owned by an *exempt organization* that is controlled by the parent or one of its subsidiaries, or an individual, estate, or trust that is a principal shareholder. §1563(c)(2)(i) through (iv). Excluded stock for purposes of the brother-sister requirements is stock held by a *qualified trust* for the benefit of the corporation's employees; stock held by an employee of the corporation, the *disposition* of which is substantially restricted: and stock of an exempt organization that is controlled by the corporation or an individual, estate, or trust that is a principal shareholder (someone with 5 percent or more interest by vote or value). §1563(c)(2)(B)(i) and (iii). See §1563(c)(2) for details. See *controlled group of corporations, graduated taxes and other benefits.*

exclusion allowance a limitation on the extent to which an *employer's* payments to purchase *tax-deferred annuities* for teachers and *employees* of charitable organizations can be excluded from the *employee's gross income.* The exclusion allowance is 20 percent of *includible compensation,* basically meaning all employer-paid taxable compensation as well as excluded *accident and health plan* pay and *foreign earned income.* §§403(b)(2)(A), 415(c)(4); Reg. §1.403(b)-1. If the exclusion allowance is exceeded, the balance is currently taxable. To the extent of such prior inclusions in income, later payouts under the annuity go untaxed on the theory that they are part of the *investment in the contract.* §403(c). See *tax-deferred annuities for exempt and educational organization employees.*

exclusion for gift of education and medical care costs an unlimited *gift tax exclusion* provided in §2503(e) for direct payments by a *donor* to an institution or *person* furnishing *educational services* and *medical care* to a *donee.* An example would be a grandparent's payment of her grandchild's college tuition. The medical care must qualify under §213(e); the *educational institution* must be an *educational organization described in §170(b)(1)(A)(ii).* See *medical and tuition expenses, gift tax exclusion.*

exclusion from gross income a receipt or accrual that would, but for a specific *exclusion* provided by the *Code* or administrative action, be included in a *taxpayer's gross income.* Particularly common exclusions are those for *gifts* and *inheritances* (§102) and *death proceeds* paid under a *life insurance contract* (§101).

exclusion preference a type of *items of tax preference* and *adjustments* that cannot be used as a *credit* in later years against *regular taxes.* It grows out of a tax benefit of a permanent nature as opposed to one that merely defers income; the latter are referred to as *deferral preferences.* See §53(a), (b), and (d). See *minimum tax credit.*

exclusion ratio a ratio applied to *annuity, endowment, or life insurance contracts* to determine the nontaxable portion of each payment, defined as the proportion that the *investment in the contract* bears to the *expected return* under the contract (figured as of the *annuity*

starting date). An equivalent proportion of any *amount received as an annuity* (under an *annuity,* or under an *endowment* or *life insurance contract* under an installment payment option) is not included in *gross income.* §72(b). For example, if one invests $100 in the contract (e.g., in net premiums) and has an expected return of $400, then 25 percent of each payment is excluded from gross income.

Executive Order instruction issued by the President of the United States. Such order may be addressed to the *Treasury Department* among others.

executor a *person* appointed by a will to manage and wind up a *decedent's estate.* For liability of executors, see Reg. §20.2203-1.

executor's commissions amounts paid, or reasonably expected to be paid, by a *decedent's estate* for services of an *executor* or *administrator.* Reg. §20.2053-3(b)(1). Such commissions are *deductible* for purposes of determining the *taxable estate.*

exempt cooperatives see *exempt farmers' cooperative.*

exempt corporation a *corporation* that is exempt from *federal income taxes.* See *exempt organizations; federal corporation.*

exempt facility bond a *state or local bond,* at least 95 percent of the *net proceeds* of which are used to provide for a number of specified public facilities such as government-owned airports, docks, and wharves; *mass commuting facilities; solid waste disposal facilities;* etc. §142(a). Such bonds may be tax-exempt even though they are otherwise classified as *private activity bonds* by virtue of being *qualified bonds,* provided a major network of requirements is satisfied. §§103(b)(1) and 141. See *private activity bond; tax-exempt bond.*

exempt farmers' cooperative farmers', fruit-growers', or like *persons'* associations organized and *operating on a cooperative basis* (and not for its own profit): (1) for the purpose of marketing the *members'* products or other products and turning back to members the proceeds of sales, less necessary marketing expenses, on the basis of either the quantity or the value of the products furnished by them; or (2) for the purpose of purchasing supplies and equipment for the use of members or other persons and turning over such supplies and equipment to them at actual cost, plus necessary expenses; or for both purposes (1) and (2). §521(b)(1). Reg. §1.521-1(c). These cooperatives can have capital stock, but the *IRS* insists that 85 percent of the ownership be in the hands of the producers. §521(b)(2). Exempt farmers' cooperatives are taxed like run-of-the-mill *cooperatives,* but they are permitted special *deductions* pursuant to §1382(c) for dividends on stock and functional equivalents (e.g., revolving fund certificates) and for patronage distributions for business done for the

United States or from earnings from other nonpatronage sources (e.g., rental income). §1382(c)(1) and (2). See *member, cooperatives.*

exempt foreign trade income, FSC   that portion of the *foreign trade income* generated by a *foreign sales corporation* or *DISC* which is tax-exempt. §921. The amount of the exemption varies. §§482, 923(a), 925.

exempt function income, homeowner associations membership dues, fees, and assessments received from owners of residential units and lots in their capacities as owner-members, but not amounts charged for special services. Payments for special use of facilities such as swimming pools are exempt function income if not paid more frequently than annually (e.g., not hourly use). §528(d)(3). Such income is not part of *homeowner's, association taxable income* and is tax-exempt to the *homeowner's association.* §528(d)(1)(B).

exempt function income, political organization amounts received in the form of *political contributions* of money or other property; membership dues; membership fees or assessments from members of the political organization; proceeds from a political fund-raising or an entertainment event; amounts received to make certain reimbursements; proceeds from sales of political campaign materials, provided they are not received in the ordinary course of any *trade or business*; and bingo game proceeds. §527(c)(3). Provided such amounts are properly segregated for use by the organization in its *exempt function,* they are not subject to *federal income taxes.* §527(c)(1)(B). See *debts owed by political parties; political organization taxable income.*

exempt function income, social clubs and voluntary employee beneficiary associations   generally, *gross income* from dues, fees, or similar amounts paid by members of the organization to provide such members or their dependents or guests with goods, facilities, or services in furtherance of the same purposes for which the tax exemption was granted. It can also mean income set aside for a religious, charitable, scientific, literary, educational, or anti-cruelty purpose, or, in the case of *voluntary employees' beneficiary associations,* income to provide for payment of life, sickness, accident, or other benefits. §512(a)(3)(B). Exempt function income of *exempt organizations* is, by definition, not *unrelated trade or business income,* and eludes the tax on such income imposed by §511. §512(a)(3)(A). See also §§512(a)(3)(C) (comparable to rule for *title-holding corporations*) and 512(a)(3)(D) (limitations on taxation of *gains* on *sales* or property used in performance of an *exempt function*).

exempt function, political organization   influencing or attempting to influence the selection, nomination, election, or appointment of any *individual* to any federal, state, or local public office or office in a political organization, or presidential or vice-presidential elec-

tion, whether or not such individual or elector is selected, nominated, elected, or appointed. §527(e)(2). See *exempt function income, political organization.*

exempt income   amounts which would otherwise be considered *gross income* but which are *excluded* therefrom. See *exclusion from gross income.*

exempt income expenses   *expenses* properly allocable to earning *tax-exempt income.* Such expenses are generally rendered *nondeductible* by §265.

exempt individual   see *resident alien.*

exempt information, Freedom of Information Act disclosure requirements   see *Freedom of Information Act.*

exempt interest dividends, regulated investment companies   *dividends* paid by *regulated investment companies* that are entirely or partially exempt from taxation. Section 852(b)(5) allows a regulated investment company to pay exempt-interest dividends if more than 50 percent of the value of its assets consists of obligations described in §103(a) (*tax-exempt bonds*). In turn, shareholders treat the nontaxable portion of such dividends as exempt. As a practical matter, §852(b)(5) enables mutual funds to offer tax-exempt-bond funds to the public.

exemption   a *deduction* (after 1989, subject to *indexing for inflation*) granted to *individuals* under various circumstances. One class is the so-called *personal exemption* ($2,350 for 1993) available to individual *taxpayers.* §151(b), (d). The second type is the *dependency exemption,* which generally entitles individual taxpayers to a like *deduction* for each *dependent.* §151(e). The term also refers in a general sense to relieving certain classes of income or taxpayers from taxation. For example, various *charitable organizations* can claim a general exemption from *federal income taxes* under §501(a). See *exemption amount.*

exemption amount   the dollar amount allowed for each permissible *personal exemption* and *dependency deduction*—$2,350 in 1993 and inflation-adjusted amounts thereafter. Such amounts, together with either the standard deduction, or itemized deductions, are deducted from *adjusted gross income* when an *individual's taxable income is determined.* §63(b)(2).

exemption amount, alternative minimum tax   an offset in determining the AMT. For *corporations,* it is $40,000 less 25 percent of the amount by which *alternative minimum taxable income* exceeds $150,000, but not less than zero. §55(d)(1)(A), (d)(8), and (d)(3)(A). Component members of a *controlled group of corporations* have one $40,000 exemption which, unless the members consent to an unequal allocation, is shared equally. The *alternative minimum taxable income* of all members is taken into account, and any resulting reduction of the $40,000 exemption is shared equally among them unless all consent to an unequal allocation. For *married persons* filing jointly and *surviving spouses,* the amount is $40,000 less 25 percent of the amount by which alternative minimum taxable income exceeds $150,000, but not less than zero. For *single persons* who are not surviving spouses, the amount is $30,000, less 25 percent of the amount by which alternative minimum taxable income exceeds $112,500, but not less than zero. For married persons filing separately, *estates* and *trusts,* the amount is $20,000, less 25 percent of the amount by which alternative minimum taxable income exceeds $75,000, but not less than zero. §55(c). See *alternative minimum tax.*

exemption certificate, estimated taxes   Form W-4, filed by *individuals* on which they claim one withholding allowance for each exemption they report on their return. In addition, they can also claim a withholding allowance for the standard deduction and other additional withholding allowances.

exemption certificate, exempt private schools   an information certificate that the *IRS* required private schools to submit annually on Form 990 if the school had not yet obtained a *ruling* or a *determination letter* establishing its status as an *exempt organization* under §§501(a) and 401(a). The IRS's position is that the tax-exempt status of private nonprofit schools will be denied and *charitable contributions* to these schools will be *nondeductible* if the IRS deems the school's operation to be discriminatory and in violation of the United States government's civil rights policies.

exemption equivalent trust   a *trust* established to take property worth $600,000 so as to take advantage of the $600,000 exemption from *federal estate taxes.* These trusts are also known as *by-pass trusts, family trusts, B trusts, and shelter trusts.* The idea is to assure that the trust will have $600,000 which will be subject to estate taxes; the rest commonly goes to the *surviving spouse* on a tax-free basis.

exemption letter   a letter issued by the *IRS* approving the tax-exempt status of an organization under §501 or §521. Such letters are submitted to the local *District Office,* which will refer them to the *National Office* in uncertain cases. See Rev. Proc. 72-4, 1972-1 C.B. 706. Such exemptions may be requested on a group basis for multiple organizations. Rev. Proc. 73-8, 1973-1 C.B. 820; Reg. §601.201(n)(7). See *group exemption letter; exempt organizations.*

exempt operating foundation   an *operating foundation* which has been a *publicly supported organization* as defined in §170(b)(1)(A)(vi) or §509(a)(2) for over 10 years. Such foundations are generally exempt from the so-called 2 percent *audit fee* and the *taxable expenditures excise tax* of §4945. See §§4940(d) and

4945(d)(4). Operating foundations in existence on January 1, 1983, automatically meet the 10-year test. See *audit fee, private foundations; publicly supported organizations; taxable expenditures, private foundations.*

exempt organization master file   an information system kept by the *IRS* containing records on all acknowledged *exempt organizations.* Ann. 68-55, 1968-34 I.R.B. 54.

exempt organizations   organizations described in Subchapter F (*exempt organizations*) of the *Code* that are generally exempt from *federal income taxes* to the extent they earn income other than from an *unrelated trade or business.* §§501–528. They are, however, taxable on their unrelated trade or business income and on their *debt-financed income* and are potentially subject to a number of *excise taxes,* including a modest annual *audit fee* designed to cover the federal cost of their administration. The types of organizations range from *charitable organizations* and *exempt private foundations* to such diverse entities as *trade associations, labor unions, social clubs, and certain nonprofit day care facilities.* §501(k). Exempt organizations file *Form 990* (Return of Organization Exempt from Income Tax). See *primary purpose standard, charitable organization.*

exempt pension trust   see *qualified trust.*

exempt person   a governmental unit (a state or local governmental unit and in certain instances the United States and its agencies and instrumentalities) described in §501(c)(3), or a type of organization (a school, charity, etc.) that is exempt from taxation under §501(a) but only with respect to a *trade or business* which is not a taxable *unrelated trade or business.* Reg. §1.103-7(b)(2).

exempt property, broker's returns   see *real estate transaction.*

exempt purpose   the objective of an *exempt organization,* such as carrying on educational or scientific activities in the public interest. Income that relates to the exempt purpose is generally tax-free, rather than *unrelated trade or business* income.

exempt purpose expenditures   see *tax on lobbying expenditures.*

exempt sales, luxury tax   certain sales exempt from the luxury excise taxes: passenger vehicles to be used exclusively in the active conduct of a *trade or business* of transporting persons or property for compensation; boats to be used for commercial fishing, transporting persons or property for compensation; etc. §4221(c) and (d)(1).

exempt transfer, broker's returns   see *real estate transaction.*

exempt transferors, broker's returns *corporations*; governmental units; or *exempt volume transferors* (basically dealers). In the case of an exempt transferor, unless the *real estate reporting person* has actual knowledge to the contrary, the real estate reporting person is entitled to treat a transferor as a corporation if (1) the name of transferor unambiguously expresses corporate status; (2) the name of transferor contains the words "insurance company"; or (3) documents used in the transaction clearly indicate the corporate status of transferor. A governmental unit of the transferor means the *United States,* any *state,* a *political subdivision* of the United States or any state, or a *foreign* government. §7701(a)(18). Reg. §1.6045-4.

exempt volume transferor, broker's return a status that requires the *real estate reporting person* to receive a *certification of exempt status.* Such a certification must contain the taxpayer's name, address, and *taxpayer identification number*; enough information to identify otherwise *reportable real estate* which has not been reported by virtue of the transferor's exempt status; and a declaration stating that the transferor has sold or exchanged during either of the prior two *calendar years,* has *sold* or *exchanged* during the current calendar year, or, as of the closing date, reasonably expects to sell or exchange at least 25 separate items of reportable real estate to at least 25 separate transferees. The certification itself must be signed under penalties of perjury. Reg. §1.6045-4.

existing housing price ratio the ratio which the *average area purchase price* for existing homes in that area bears to the average purchase price for existing homes in the United States. §143(f)(5)(D)(iv).

expatriation to avoid tax a *citizen of the United States'* departure from the United States and renunciation of citizenship in order to avoid paying *federal income, estate,* or *gift taxes.* United States tax law limits the advantage of expatriation for tax purposes by retaining jurisdiction to tax the expatriate in cases of tax avoidance. §877. This provision applies only to United States source income earned within 10 years of the date of expatriation. No tax is imposed on foreign-source income, including income from the *disposition* of appreciated foreign assets, however.

expected return the amount that the *annuitant* expects to receive under an *annuity contract.* If a life contingency is involved, the *IRS* annuity tables must be consulted. §72(c)(3); Reg. §1.72-5. The expected return is the denominator of the fraction *(exclusion ratio)* which is applied to each annuity payment to determine the taxable and nontaxable components. See *exclusion ratio.*

expedited rulings requests for *rulings* that are given accelerated treatment for good cause. See Rev. Proc. 80-20, 1980-1, C.B. 633, §10.

expenditure, political a nonexclusive list of transactions, including a payment, distribution, loan, advance, deposit, or gift of money or anything of value, including a contract, promise, or agreement to make an expenditure, whether or not legally enforceable. The term is used to help define exempt *political organizations,* and it is used with respect to the worthlessness of any debt owed by a political party. §271(b)(3). See *debts owed by political parties.*

expenditure responsibility a reference to requirements imposed on *private foundations* if they are to avoid the *taxable expenditures excise tax* of §4945. It calls upon private foundations to vigorously police their grants to other organizations (other than to exempt *charitable organizations* other than private foundations), including obtaining reports from grantees and submitting relevant information to the *IRS.* See §4945(b). See *taxable expenditures, private foundations.*

expenditure responsibility rules a subpart of the *taxable expenditure* rules of §4945. See *taxable expenditures, private foundations.*

expenses for the management, conservation, or maintenance of property held for the production of income a class of *expenses* that are not *trade or business expenses* that *individuals, trusts, estates, partners,* and evidently (in practice despite contradictory statutory language) *corporations* may *deduct* under the authority of §212(2), provided they are not *capital expenditures* (§263) or related to earning nontaxable income (§265). The subsection contemplates expenses proximately related to property held for the production of *capital gains,* or even the minimization of *losses* (Reg. §1.212-1(b)), provided it is held primarily for economic, not personal, reasons or for the production of tax losses. Typical management, conservation, or maintenance expenses include rental of a safe deposit box to hold investment assets, the cost of cleaning artwork held for appreciation, expenses incurred to maintain a vacation home which has clearly been placed on the market for sale at a gain, and the costs of litigation to recover embezzled securities. See *proximate relationship standard.*

expenses for the production or collection of income a class of non–*trade or business expenses* which *individuals, trusts, estates, partners,* and evidently (in practice despite contradictory statutory language) *corporations* may *deduct* for *gain*-seeking activities under the authority of §212(1), provided they are not *capital expenditures* (§263) or related to earning nontaxable income (§265(1)). Examples include proximately related expenditures for collecting or generating taxable alimony, taxable prizes and awards, claims for wrongful firing, expenses of asserting claims to an income interest in a will contest, and expenses relating to investment income such as an investment adviser's fees and clerical help. See Reg. §1.212-1(b)(7) and -1(g). See *proximate relationship standard.*

expenses in connection with the determination, collection, or refund of any tax a class of expenses that may be *deducted* by *individuals, estates, trusts,* and *partners* even though they do not arise in a *trade, business,* or other *gain-seeking activity.* §212(3); Reg. §1.212-1(1). The scope of the provision is broad, extending to foreign, state, local, or federal taxes, regardless of whether the tax is *deductible* for *federal income tax* purposes. The tax involved, however, must be the liability, even if indirect, of the person claiming the *deduction.* Common examples of deductions include tax return preparation charges, the cost of having a *claim for refund or credit* prepared, the cost of having donated property valued, and the cost of advice about the tax aspects of estate planning and tax aspects of a divorce.

expense test, net lease see *interest on investment indebtedness limitation.*

experience-based refund see *policyholder dividend, life insurance companies.*

experience method a method of determining *practical capacity* on the basis of the *taxpayer's* actual manufacturing output experience while it is operating at practical capacity. An alternative method is the *theoretical capacity method.* See *full absorption accounting; practical capacity determination.*

experience method, reserves for bad debt a method for additions to *reserves for bad debts* of *banks, mutual savings banks, cooperative banks,* and *domestic building and loan associations, small business investment companies,* and *business development corporations* under which the addition is calculated on the basis of actual bad debt experience over a six-year period. §§585(b)(3), 593(b)(3). "*Large banks*" (generally those with over $5 billion in average *adjusted basis,* separately or as a parent-sub group, cannot *deduct* additions to such reserves. §585(c)(2).

exploration expenditures, minerals amounts paid or incurred before the mine reaches the development stage, to ascertain the existence, location, extent, or quality of an ore or other mineral deposit, which amounts are not otherwise *deductible* and which do not represent amounts paid to acquire operating or working interests. Exploration ends (and development begins) when the facts reasonably justify commercial exploitation by the *taxpayer.* Examples of mining exploration expenditures include initial core drilling and expenditures for exploratory drilling from within a producing mine to ascertain the existence of what appears to be a different ore. Reg. §1.617-1(a) and (b)(3). See *development expenditures, minerals; recapture, mining exploration expenditures.*

exploration, oil, gas, and geothermal activities undertaken in the search for oil and gas before the *taxpayer* has decided to drill at a particular site for the purpose of extraction in commercial quantities. Operators of a domestic oil, gas, or geothermal well may elect to currently deduct intangible drilling and development costs rather than charge such costs to capital, recoverable through depletion or depreciation. §263(c) Reg. §1.612-4. See *exploration expenditures, minerals.*

exploration or development expenditure an *expenditure* which is necessary for ascertaining the existence, location, extent, or quality of a deposit or which is incident to and necessary for the preparation of a deposit for production. Reg. §1.636-1(b)(1).

export financing interest *interest* received from financing the *disposition* of *property* originating in the *United States* for use outside the United States. §904(d)(2)(G). The goods must be manufactured, produced, grown, or extracted by the *taxpayer* or a *related person,* and no more than half of their value may be attributable to imported goods. This interest is *excluded* from *passive income, high withholding tax interest,* and financial services income, but it is included in §904(D)(1)(I) residual category. Also, income that is formally export-financing interest paid to a United States shareholder of a *controlled foreign corporation (CFC)* out of its passive income goes into the shareholder's passive basket and not its overall basket. See *section 904(d)(1) "basket"; related person, controlled foreign corporation; passive income, foreign tax credit.*

export trade corporation largely supplanted by *domestic international sales corporations* (DISC). The DISC provisions were largely repealed by the 1984 Tax Reform Act.

export trade income see *export trade corporation.*

expropriation loss a *loss* from a taking by a foreign government or instrumentality. See *foreign expropriation loss.*

extended long-term contracts generally, building, installation, construction, and manufacturing contracts that are not expected to be completed within the two-year period beginning on the contract commencement date. *TEFRA* §229(b)(1). Real estate construction contracts to be completed within three years can be entered into by *taxpayers* whose annual average gross receipts for the three pre-contract years are not more than $25 million. TEFRA §229(b)(2)(A). See *long-term contract; seventy-percent PCM.*

extended low-income housing commitment a requirement for claiming the *low-income housing credit* for buildings with low-income tenants. It generally requires the owner to maintain the percentage of low-income tenants for at least 15 years, which commitment the low-income tenants can enforce and which is binding on the owner's successors. §42(h)(6). The low-income housing credit expired on June 30, 1992.

extension of assessment period   see *waiver of statute of limitations.*

extension of time to pay tax   an extension of the due date of *federal income taxes,* granted in the discretion of the *IRS* for periods of up to six months—or longer for *taxpayers* abroad or on a showing of *undue hardship.* §6161(a)(1). Such extensions do not limit obligations to pay interest in such cases. Reg. §1.6161-1(d).

external walls requirement   a requirement that must be met in order for a property to qualify for the *rehabilitation credit.* The idea is that at least 75 percent of the original walls must be left in place (which must consist of at least 50 percent remaining external walls) and at least 75 percent of internal structural framework must also be left intact. §47(c)(1)(A)(iii)(II). The rule does not apply to *historic properties.*

extraction, natural resources   not defined, but applied in its common sense meaning of being dug up or otherwise separated from the earth by mechanical or presumably chemical means for later sale. Extraction is a precondition to claims for *depletion* of natural resources other than timber. (Timber is "cut" or "harvested.")

extraordinary dividend, basis reduction   an unusually large *dividend* in comparison to the recipient's *basis* in the *stock* of the *distributing* corporation, determined by objective factors set forth below. The term generally applies to dividends that have not been held for more than two years as of the dividend announcement date (i.e., the earliest of the date the dividend is declared, announced, or agreed on). The definition is used in connection with a loophole-closing provision designed to prevent corporate shareholders from buying stock in anticipation of an unusually large *dividend* and then selling the stock at a *short-term capital loss.* The provision sting is that it reduces *basis* in the stock (but not below zero) by the "nontaxed portion" (basically, the amount of the applicable *dividends-received deduction*) of the dividend. §1059(a). A dividend is extraordinary if it exceeds 5 percent of the *stock's basis* in the case of dividends on preferred stock and 10 percent as to dividends on common stock. §1059(c)(1)-(2). All dividends received by the shareholder with respect to a share of stock which have *ex-dividend* dates within the same period of 85 consecutive days are combined and deemed one dividend. §1059(c)(3)(A). Extraordinary dividends automatically include *stock redemptions* in *partial liquidation* or non–pro rata redemptions of stock to the extent of any amount treated as a dividend, regardless of the *holding period* of the stock or the relative magnitude of the distribution. §1059(e)(1).

Alternatively, the *taxpayer* can elect to test the status of the dividend as extraordinary by reference to the *fair market value* (not adjusted basis) of the stock as of the day before the ex-dividend date, a wise decision if the stock has appreciated in value. §1059(c)(4). Dividends on *disqualified preferred stock* are deemed to be extraordinary. §1959(f). See *dividend announcement date; qualified corporation, extraordinary dividends; qualifying dividends, dividends-received deduction.*

extraordinary dividend, short sale   same as *extraordinary dividend, basis reduction* except that the *taxpayer* uses the *amount realized* in a *short sale* as his or her *adjusted basis* in *stock* in order to determine if the *dividend* is large enough to be considered "extraordinary." §263(h)(3). This is part of a provision that prevents taxpayers who make payments in lieu of *dividends* on stock held to close a short sale soon (generally 45 days) after the date of the short sale from claiming a *deduction* for such payments. §263(h)(1).

extraordinary gain disposition   an actual or deemed *disposition* of (1) a *capital asset;* (2) *section 1231 assets* (regardless of *holding period*); (3) an asset described in §1221 (1), (3), (4), or (5), if substantially all the assets in such category from the same *trade or business* are disposed of in one transaction (or series of related transactions); (4) assets disposed of in an *applicable asset acquisition;* (5) a *change of accounting method* resulting in a *positive section 481 adjustment;* (6) a *discharge of indebtedness;* (7) any other event (or item) identified by the IRS in *revenue rulings* and *revenue procedures.* Reg. §1.1502-20(c)(2)(i). This is limited to post–November 19, 1990 *income* or *gain* for purposes of computing *earnings and profits* (net of directly related *expenses*). The term is important in determining the effect of the *loss disallowance rules.* See *loss disallowance rules.*

extraordinary gain factor   *earnings and profits* from *extraordinary gain dispositions.* Reg. §1.1502-20(c) allows *losses* to the extent in excess of the extraordinary gain factor, the *positive investment adjustment factor,* and the *loss duplication factor.* See *loss disallowance rules.*

extraordinary personal services   personal services provided by an *individual* in connection with the use of property in circumstances in which the customer's use of the property is merely incidental to receiving the service, such as the provision of sleeping facilities at a hospital or boarding school. Temp. Reg. §1.469-1T(e)(3)(v). By contrast, providing extensive services in connection with leasing out photocopying equipment does not involve extraordinary personal services. *Id.* If a *taxpayer* provides extraordinary services in connection with providing property, then the income from the activity is not income from a *rental activity.* That means that if the taxpayer is otherwise active enough, the income may be classified as not income from a *passive activity*. See *passive loss rules*.

extraordinary retirement, ADR depreciation the retirement of one of the following types of assets from a *vintage account*: (1) *§1245 property* retired due to a *casualty*; (2) §1245 property retired in the *taxable year* due to the curtailment of a business or facility, or production operation, if the *unadjusted basis* of all the assets retired as a result of such an event is greater than 20 percent of the unadjusted basis of the account just before the event; or (3) any *section 1250 property*. Reg. §1.167(a)-11(d)(3). *Gains* and *losses* are generally *recognized* on extraordinary retirements. See *ordinary retirement, ADR depreciation*.

extravagant expenditures, meals, lodging, and entertainment see *lavish or extravagant, meals, lodging, and entertainment*.

F

FICA an acronym for *Federal Insurance Contributions Act*. See *Social Security tax*.

FICA taxes see *Social Security tax*.

FIFO an acronym for *first-in, first-out*.

FIRPTA an acronym for the *Foreign Investment in Real Property Tax Act* of 1980.

FIRPTA withholding a term used to describe requirements of the *Foreign Investment in Real Property Tax Act* (FIRPTA), under which *foreign persons* who dispose of *United States real property interests* generally must pay tax on any *gain* realized on the *disposition* of such interests at top tax rates. Enforcement occurs through *withholding* of tax on the purchase price paid by the transferee unless the transferee gets a sworn statement *(nonforeign affidavit)* that the transferor is a *United States person* or some other exception applies. §1445. The withholding tax can be as high as 34 percent (certain distributions of *gains* to *partners* and *beneficiaries* or distributions of appreciated real property interests by *corporations*), but it is generally set at 10 percent of the sale price. §1445(e)(2),(3),(4). See *withholding certificate*.

FISC an acronym for *foreign international sales company*.

FNMA an acronym for Federal National Mortgage Association.

FNMA purchase price the gross amount of consideration agreed upon between the *Federal National Mortgage Association* and the initial holder for the purchase of mortgage paper, without regard to any *deduction* therefrom (such as capital contribution or a purchase or marketing fee). The initial holder is the original purchaser who is issued stock of the Federal National Mortgage Association pursuant to §303(c) of the Federal National Mortgage Association Act, and who appears on the books of the Association as the initial holder. The initial holder is considered to have acquired the stock as of the date of issuance. §162(d).

FOGEI an acronym for *foreign oil and gas extraction income*.

FOGEI taxes *foreign taxes* on *foreign oil and gas extraction income*. Reg. §1.907(a)-0(b)(3).

FOIA an acronym for the *Freedom of Information Act*.

FORI an acronym for *foreign oil-related income*.

FORI taxes *foreign taxes* on *foreign oil-related income*. Reg. §1.907(a)-0(b)(4).

FPAA an acronym for *final partnership administrative adjustment*.

FPHC an acronym for *foreign personal holding company*.

F.R. an abbreviation for *Federal Register*.

FSC an acronym for a *foreign sales corporation*.

F.2d an abbreviation for Federal Reporter, second series, an official compilation of decisions of the *Claims Court* and Federal *Circuit Courts*. See *Court of Appeals; Federal Circuit*.

F. Supp. an abbreviation for Federal Supplement, the official compilation in which the decisions of the United States Federal *District Courts,* the United States Court of International Trade, and rulings of the Judicial Panel on Multidistrict Litigation are reported.

FUTA an acronym for *Federal Unemployment Tax Act*.

FUTA taxes an acronym for taxes imposed by the *Federal Unemployment Tax Act*.

face-amount certificate any certificate, investment contract, or other security that represents an obligation on the part of its issuer to pay a stated or determinable sum or sums at a fixed or determinable date or dates more than 24 months after the date of issuance. Investment Company Act of 1940, §2(a)(15) 15 U.S.C. §80a-2(a)(15). Face-amount certificates are treated as *endowment contracts* for *annuity* taxation purposes (§72(1)) and are on occasion referred to as permissible pension investments.

face amount, life insurance the amount stated on the face of the policy that will be paid in case of death or at the maturity of the policy. It does not include additional amounts payable under accidental death or other special provisions or amounts acquired through the application of policy dividends.

facilities for the furnishing of water facilities for the provision of water for any purpose, if the facilities are operated by a governmental unit which makes or will make available water to the general public (including commercial users). §142(a)(4), (e) and prior law 103(b)(4)(G). It must not be a production facility. If the facility is not owned by a government unit, it is sufficient if the rates are established or approved by a *state* (or *political subdivision* of a state), by an agency or instrumentality of the *United States,* or by a public service or public utility commission or similar body. §142(e). If *private activity bonds* issued after August 15, 1986, are used for facilities that furnish water, and if

95 percent or more of the bond issue *net proceeds* are to be used for such purposes, then such bonds are "exempt facility bonds" that pay *interest* that is exempt from *federal income tax.*

facility, architectural and transportation barrier expense   all or any portion of buildings, structures, equipment, roads, walks, parking lots, or similar real or personal property. Reg. §1.190-2(a)(1).

faculty member   typically, an *individual* who meets one of the following tests: (1) his or her service counts towards tenure or he or she has tenure; (2) the institution is providing retirement plan contributions; or (3) he or she can vote in faculty affairs. Reg. §1.162-5(b)(2). Faculty members are deemed to have met minimum levels of education if there are no normal institutional requirements as to education for a position. *Id.* Accordingly, *expense deductions* claimed by a faculty member in such circumstances cannot be rejected on the grounds that they were paid or incurred to meet a minimum level of qualification for the job. See *educational expense deduction.*

fair market value   the price at which property would change hands between a willing buyer and a willing seller, neither being under any compulsion to buy or to sell, and both having reasonable knowledge of the relevant facts. Reg. §20.2031-1(b). One looks at the "most active marketplace" if there is a market. Rev. Rul. 8069, 1980-1 C.B. 55. The term is used throughout the *Code.*

false or fraudulent return   a shorthand term used to describe a *return* filed in violation of §6501(c)(1) and (2) relating to a "false or fraudulent return" filed with the intent to evade taxes, or in a "*willful* attempt in any manner to defraud or evade" taxes other than *estate* or *gift taxes.* In effect, such returns create an open-ended *statute of limitations. Id.* For standards to determine the requisite intent, see *penalty, fraud.*

family   defined variously throughout the *Code,* depending on the particular subject matter. Leading definitions are found in the general *attribution rules* relating to *stock* ownership of §318 (*spouses* who are not *legally separated,* children, grandchildren, and parents) and §267 relating to expenses and losses on transactions between related persons (brothers and sisters by the whole or half-blood, spouses, ancestors, and *lineal descendants*).

family attribution rules   provisions of the *Code* that attribute the ownership of *stock* or other property from one member of a family (as variously defined) to another member (e.g., §§318(a)(1)(A) and 267(c)(2)). See *attribution rules.*

family corporation   a term used in the heading of §447(c) to describe a class of *corporations* exempt from §447(a)'s requirement that large corporate farmers use the *accrual method of accounting* for years beginning after 1986. Corporations engaged in the farming business are exempt from this requirement. Large corporate farmers include one-family corporations and those composed of two- or three-family corporations. A one-family corporation is exempt from the capitalization requirement if at least 50 percent of the combined voting power of all classes of *stock* entitled to vote and at least 50 percent of the total number of shares of all other classes are owned by members of the same family. §447(d)(3)(C)(ii). A two-family corporation exists if members of two families have directly or indirectly owned at least 65 percent of the voting stock and at least 65 percent of all other classes of stock, in which case the corporation qualifies. §447(d)(2)(C)(ii) and (h)(1)(A). Finally, if members of three families have directly or indirectly owned at least 50 percent of the voting stock as well as at least 50 percent of all other classes of stock, and if substantially all the other stock is owned by the corporation's *employees* or by members of their families or by an exempt employee *trust,* then the corporation qualifies as a family corporation. §447(h)(1)(3). Members of an employee's family are defined under §267. §447(h)(2)(A). See *family, losses and expenses; preproductive period.*

family, farming syndicates   siblings, ancestors, descendants, *spouses* of grandparents, and the *spouses* of the foregoing *individuals.* §464(c)(2). Members of the family of four classes of individuals are excepted from being classified as *limited partners* or *limited entrepreneurs* for purposes of determining whether there is a *farming syndicate.* §464(c).

family foundation   a colloquial term for a *private foundation* under the control of a single family. Such foundations give the founder flexibility to achieve his or her own charitable goals and to perpetuate his or her name.

family income splitting   a tax planning area that focuses on shifting *taxable income* from family members in high federal income tax brackets to those in lower brackets through such devices as short-term *trusts* with a view to minimizing the aggregate tax burden imposed on the family as a whole. See *kiddie tax.*

family, losses and expenses   brothers and sisters, by the whole- or half-blood, *spouses,* ancestors, and lineal descendants. §267(c)(4). Losses and certain unpaid expenses between family members are disallowed or deferred by §267(a). See *related taxpayers, loss and deduction denial.*

family partnership   a *Code* heading to §704(e) that affects a *partnership* in which the *partner* received an interest by *gift* (§704(e)(1)) or is a family member who purchased his or her interest from a relative. §704(e) attempts to regulate artificial family partnerships and improper allocations designed to shift income to lower-bracket partners. The Code recognizes partnership interests acquired by gift if that person owns a *capital interest in a partnership* in which capital is a *material income-producing factor.* Otherwise, a *bona fide* intent to form a partnership is required. Section 704(e)(2) limits *allocations* of partnership income reportable by such buyers and *donees* by demanding a reasonable allocation of income to the donor (typically a parent) for services and that there not be an overallocation (as a percentage of the parties' *capital accounts*) to the *donee.* In interlocking fashion, §704(e)(3) treats sales of partnership interests among family members as gifts of money, followed by contributions to capital. For this purpose, family members include only *spouses,* ancestors, lineal descendants, and any *trusts* for the primary benefit of such persons. *Id.* Most family partnerships in which minors are partners are likely to be *limited partnerships.*

family, percentage depletion of oil and gas   one's *spouse* and *minor children.* §613A(c)(8)(D)(iii) and (10)(G)(ii). The family must share a single 1,000 barrel/day of oil (6,000,000 cf/day of gas) exemption that qualifies for *percentage depletion.* The term is also used for purposes of certain incorporations of *proven properties* under §613A(c)(10).

Fannie Mae   see *Federal National Mortgage Association.*

farm   defined as in the dictionary, including fish, poultry, dairy, stock, plant, and truck farming, as well as ranches, orchards, hatcheries, plantations, and all land used for farming. Reg. §§1.61-4(d), 1.175-3, 1.182-2; Rev. Rul. 59-12, 1959-1 C.B. 59. The term is defined throughout the *Code* with minor but sometimes important variations, and it should be evaluated in its particular setting. See, e.g. §6420(c)(2) See *farmer; fish farm.*

farm cooperatives   see *exempt farmers' cooperatives.*

farm corporation   see *family corporation.*

farmer   a *person* who cultivates, operates, or manages a *farm* or farms for *gain* or profit, as owner or tenant. Reg. §1.61-4(d). The concept of the farm or farmer is sprinkled somewhat inconsistently throughout the *Code.* See, e.g., §§175, 180, 464, 1251, 6073, 6420. The term is generally read to generously include investors and ranchers, including persons who raise fur-bearing animals (Rev. Rul. 57-588, 1957-2 C.B. 305). A major tax advantage of being a farmer is the general right to use the *cash method* of accounting, without using *inventories.* See *farm.*

farmer, self-employment tax   an *individual* engaged in a *trade or business,* which, if it were carried on exclusively by *employees,* would constitute *agricultural labor* for Social Security *self-employment tax* pur-

poses. §3121(g). Farmers are entitled to use the *farm optional method* for determining *net earnings from self-employment.*

farmers' cooperatives   see *exempt farmers' cooperatives.*

farming business, uniform capitalization rules   a *trade or business* involving the cultivation of land or the raising or harvesting of any agricultural or horticultural commodity. Reg. §1.263A-1T(c)(4)(i)(A). It includes nurseries, sod farms, and trees other than fruit, nut, or ornamental trees that are raised and harvested. See *uniform capitalization rules.*

farming business, use of the cash method   A farm business which is a *partnership* with a *C corporation* partner, or simply a C corporation, neither of which is a *tax shelter,* can use the *cash method* of accounting. §447. See *tax shelter, cash method disallowance rules.*

farming, farming syndicate   any farming partnership or enterprise, other than a corporation that is not an S corporation, if at any time (1) interests in the enterprise or partnership have been offered for sale in an offering required to be registered with any federal or state agency having authority to regulate such offering, or (2) more than 35 percent of the losses during any period are allocable to limited partners or entrepreneurs. §464(c). See *farming syndicate.* See *syndicate; limited entrepreneur; limited partner.*

farming preproductive period   see *preproductive period.*

farmland recapture   see *farm recapture on land sale.*

farm optional method, self-employment tax   a simplified method for determining Social Security *self-employment taxes* for *farmers.* A self-employed farmer has to pay self-employment tax if his net earnings from self-employment are $400 or more. §1402(b). However, an optional method for reporting income from farming is available to the farmer. If his gross income is not more than $2,400, he can report two-thirds of his gross income as net earnings from self-employment §1402(a). If a farmer has more than $2,400 of gross income from farm operations, he may report his actual earnings. If his net earnings are less than $1,600, the $1,600 may be reported as net earnings. See *farmer, self-employment tax.*

farm or closely held business real property, special use valuation   see *farm, special use valuation; interest in a closely held business.*

farm-out   a synonym for *farm-out agreement.*

farm-out agreement   one of any number of agreements common in the oil and gas industry under which the risks and costs of drilling and *development* are moved between contracting parties. A typical case involves an agreement between an oil and gas *operator* who owns a lease and does not want to *undertake* drilling operations and another operator. The transferor-operator transfers the lease, or a share of the lease, to the other party who agrees to exploit the tract on the condition that the transferee actually drill one or more wells. The transferor commonly retains a *production payment* or an *overriding royalty*. The transferor is often referred to as the *farmor* and the transferee as the *farmee*.

farm price method a method of valuing *inventories* of livestock and other farm products, using their market values minus the direct costs of disposing of the items. Reg. §1.471-6(d).

farm recapture on land sale if farm land held for *nine years or less* is disposed of, a percentage of the total post-1969 deductions for soil and water conservation expenditures and land clearance expenditures will be recaptured as ordinary income. §1252. If the land is held for five years or less, the recapture percentage is 100 percent. The recapture percentage is 80 percent within the sixth year after acquisition. For the seventh, eight, and ninth years, the recapture percentages are 60 percent, 40 percent, and 20 percent, respectively. There is no recapture after the ninth year.

farm-related taxpayer a *taxpayer* whose principal occupation is farming, whose *principal residence* (§1034) is on a farm, or who is a member of the family (as defined) of such a person. §464(f)(3)(B). See *qualified farm-related taxpayer,* of which definition this is an element.

farm, special use valuation a term that includes stock, dairy, poultry, fruit, and furbearing animals; truck farms, plantations, ranches, nurseries, ranges, greenhouses, or other similar structures used primarily for the raising of agricultural or horticultural commodities; and orchards and woodlands. §2032A(e)(4). Such land may qualify for favorable *special use valuation* for federal *estate tax* purposes.

farm syndicate rules see *farming, farming syndicate.*

federal certifying authority, pollution control facilities the administrator of the Environmental Protection Agency. Reg. §1. 169-2(c)(3).

Federal Circuit an Article III federal court located in Washington, D.C., that, among other things, takes appeals from the Claims Court. Appeals from the Federal Circuit go to the United States Supreme Court.

federal corporation a *corporation* formed pursuant to an act of Congress. Such organizations are exempt if the Congress provides for exempting them from federal *income taxes*. Illustrations of such corporations include the Farmers Home Corporation, the Federal National Savings Association, and the federal reserve banks.

federal estate taxes *estate taxes* imposed by the *Code*. See *estate tax.*

Federal Home Loan Bank one of the regional member Federal Home Loan Banks. They are suspect to special treatment as to *dividends* on *Freddie Mac* stock.

Federal Home Loan Mortgage Corporation a federal corporation engaged in the mortgages market. It lost its federal tax exemption as of 1985. Tax Reform Act of 1984, §178.

federal income tax a tax authorized by the *Sixteenth Amendment,* which authorizes the taxation of income "from whatever source derived." The tax is principally manifested in §§1 *(individuals, estates,* and *trusts)* and 11 *(corporations),* but it also pops up throughout the *Code* (e.g., §§871 and 888—taxes on *nonresident aliens* and *foreign corporations).*

Federal Insurance Contributions Act (FICA) see *Social Security tax.*

Federal Lien Tax Act of 1966 an act that establishes priorities among creditors, including the *IRS,* with respect to claims against debtors, and which affects various *collection* procedures.

federal long-term contract a contract with the United States or any of its agencies and instrumentalities as well as related subcontracts. §460(d). Such contracts are subject to special cost *allocations* under §460(c)(2).

federal long-term rate the rate of *interest* on taxable *federal* debt with a term of over nine years. §1274(d)(1)(A). The rate is determined monthly by the *Secretary.* §1274(d)(1)(B). It is used for a variety of purposes, especially the determination of *original issue discount.*

federally assisted building, low-income housing credit see *eligible basis, low-income housing credit.*

federally registered partnership any *partnership,* interests in which have been offered for *sale* at any time during the *taxable year* or a prior taxable year in any offering required to be registered with the *SEC,* or which, at any time during such *taxable year* or a prior taxable year, was subject to the annual reporting requirements of the SEC which relate to the protection of investors in the partnership. §6501(q)(4). Section 6501(o) provides a four-year (from filing date) *statute of limitations* that governs the *assessment* period for a *deficiency* attributable to any partnership item of a federally registered partnership. §6501(o)(1).

federally subsidized, low-income housing credit financed (as to construction or acquisition) to any extent (at any time) by an obligation whose *interest* is *tax-exempt* under former §103 of the *Code,* or a direct or indirect federal loan if the rate is less than the *applica-*

ble federal rate. §42(i)(2). The percentage of *qualified basis* that can be claimed as *low-income housing credit* declines if the project got a federal subsidy. If the subsidy was in the form of an exemption on *interest* paid on a loan, the owner can claim a higher credit if *basis* is reduced by the principal amount of the loan.

federal mid-term rate   the rate of interest on taxable *federal* debt with a term of over three but under nine years. §1274(d)(1)(A). The rate is determined monthly by the *Secretary*. §1274(d)(1)(B). It is used for a variety of purposes, especially the determination of *original issue discount.*

Federal National Mortgage Association   a federally sponsored private *corporation* that operates under the Federal National Mortgage Association Charter Act (12 U.S.C. §1716b (1976) et seq.), which acts as a mortgage banker with power to purchase, service, or sell certain insured or guaranteed home mortgages, established for the purpose of boosting mortgage lending and home building activities. 12 U.S.C. §1716b (1976) et seq. Sales of mortgage paper to the Association tax in exchange for its stock allow the seller to deduct the excess of the issue price (the *FNMA purchase price*) of the stock over its market price on its date of issuance. §162(d). See §1054 for *basis* adjustment.

Federal Register   the official publication in which federal agencies' *regulations* first appear.

federal savings and loan association   see *domestic building and loan association.*

federal short-term rate   the rate of interest on taxable *federal* debt with a term of not over three years. §1274(d)(1)(A). The rate is determined monthly by the *Secretary*. §1274(d)(1)(B). It is used for a variety of purposes, especially the determination of *original issue discount.*

federal tax lien   a legal claim in favor of the United States on the property of a delinquent *taxpayer*. Once a federal tax has been *assessed* it becomes a *lien,* until paid, on *real* and *personal property* of the *taxpayer*. §§6321, 6322. The priority of the claim, however, depends on its having been properly filed, the time of its filing, and the competing liens. See *levy.*

federal thrift savings fund   a fund for federal *employees,* including members of Congress, to which such persons can make elective deferrals of up to 10 percent of basic pay. See 5 U.S.C. §§8347 and 8437. They are treated much like plans under §401(k) (i.e., *salary reduction plans*).

Federal Unemployment Tax Act (FUTA)   a tax imposed on *employers* to provide unemployment benefits for *employees*. The maximum amount of *wages* subject to FUTA tax is $7,000 of wages paid, during the *calendar year* to each employee at a rate of 6.2 percent

of taxable wages paid in covered employment. §§3301, 3306(b)(1). The tax applies only to employers who employed at least one *individual* in covered employment on at least one day in each of 20 weeks in the current or prior *calendar year* or who paid wages in covered employment of $1,500 or more in a calendar quarter in the current or prior calendar year. Employers are allowed a *credit* against the federal unemployment tax for contributions paid into state unemployment funds. The maximum credit allowable is 5.4 percent of taxable wages. To obtain the full amount of the credit, the employer must pay the state unemployment tax liability before the due date for filing the federal unemployment tax *return,* which is January 31 of the following year. A credit is allowable for late payments, but the amount of credit is limited to 90 percent of the credit which would be allowable if the state tax had been timely paid. §3302.

federated farmers' cooperatives   associations of *farmers' cooperatives* that combine to improve their marketing and purchasing activities for the benefit and protection of the *individual* cooperatives. Such federations can be *tax-exempt,* if appropriate evidence is provided to the *IRS* on Form 1028. Rev. Proc. 72-16, 1972-1 C.B. 738.

feeder organizations   a nontechnical term used to describe organizations that turn over their operating proceeds to affiliated charities. Section 502 provides that organizations carrying on *business* will not be exempt merely because they turn their profits over to charities. The purpose of the feeder organization rules of §502 is to force feeders to run the same tax gauntlets as regular charities, and if they are found nonexempt, then to tax them on all their income.

feeder trust, employee benefits   an arrangement under which an actuarial excess of funds from a *group annuity contract* that covers one group of *employees* can be transferred to a similar contract that covers a different group of employees. To avoid disqualification of the plan, both contracts must be part of a single *qualified plan.* Rev. Rul. 68-242, 1968-1 C.B. 156. A qualified plan must contain specific provisions regarding the transfer of plan assets or liabilities. Reg. §1.401-2(a).

feedstock taxes   a commonly used term for the *excise taxes* imposed by §§4661-2 on a substantial list of chemicals made in entering the *United States*. The rates range from $4.87 to $0.24 per ton. They are a component of the "Superfund taxes."

fee royalty   a synonym for *landowner's royalty.*

fellowship grant   an amount paid to or for an *individual* to aid in the pursuit of study or research. It includes the value of services or accommodations, tuition, matriculation, and other fees, as well as family allowances, but it excludes amounts paid by individuals to help a friend, relative, or other person where the *grantor* is motivated by family or philanthropic motivations. Reg. §1.117-3(c). Fellowships may be excludable from *gross income* under §117, within closely confined limits, described under the heading *qualified scholarships.* Fellowships and *scholarships* are generally treated as exceptions to the general rule of §74, taxing *prizes and awards.*

fertilizer expenditures a loose term for expenditures by persons *engaged in the business of farming* for fertilizer, lime, and the like to improve the productivity of land used in farming, including the cost of applying the materials. §180. Such expenditures may be *deducted* currently despite their long-term value.

fiduciary a *person* who occupies a position of special confidence, especially a *trustee, guardian,* receiver, conservator, *executor,* or *administrator.* Such a person has *legal title* to property, which she or he holds for the benefit of others, subject to strict state law duties. §§6012(b)(4), 7701(a)(6); Reg. §301.7701-6. Many, but not all fiduciaries are compelled to file *returns* on behalf of the *entity* (e.g., *trust* or *estate*) for which they are responsible.

fiduciary accounting income income of a *trust* or *estate* as determined by the *fiduciary.* Fiduciaries are bound by the trust instrument and local law as well as the *Code* in determining income. In addition, they have latitude to determine whether *expenses* are properly allocable to *corpus* or income. See §643(b); Reg. §1.643(b)-1.

fiduciary liability the liability of a *fiduciary* for the federal taxes of another during the period of occupying that status. §6903(a). The liability, however, is not personal to the fiduciary, but rather to the property held by the fiduciary. The practical effect is that the *IRS* can proceed against the fiduciary as if moving against the *beneficiary-taxpayer.*

fiduciary, qualified plans anyone who exercises any discretionary authority or control with respect to management of a *qualified plan* or management or disposition of its assets; anyone who provides investment advice, for compensation, with respect to plan assets or who has any authority or responsibility to do so; or anyone who has discretionary authority or responsibility in the administration of the plan. This includes *trustees, plan administrators, employers* and investment advisors, as well as advisors with de facto authority or control. §4975(e); ERISA §3(21)(A). Such fiduciaries have extensive duties and liabilities.

field attorney an attorney from a *Regional Office* of the *IRS* who is assigned to a *criminal fraud* case. After such an attorney has studied the case, she will typically offer to meet with the *taxpayer,* the taxpayer's representative, or both. *Id.* If the taxpayer elects to meet with the

field attorney, the field attorney will advise the taxpayer of constitutional rights and proceed to gather information to fill in the legal elements of the case.

field audit an *audit* of the *taxpayer's* books and records, undertaken outside the offices of the *IRS,* typically at the taxpayer's principal place of business.

field examination same as *field audit.*

field prototype plans *IRS*-approved plans used by *plan sponsors* for the purpose of submitting requests for determination of the qualification of plans for clients. See Rev. Rul. 77-23, 1977-2 C.B. 530.

fifteen-year property includes *taxable personal property* with a *class life* of 20 years or more but less than 25 years, as well as municipal wastewater treatment plants, telephone distribution plants, and other comparable equipment used for the two-way exchange of voice and data communications, i.e., equipment used by nontelephone companies for two-way exchange of voice and data communications other than cable television equipment used primarily for one-way communication. §168(e)(3)(E). This class of *recovery property* is the product of the *Tax Reform Act of 1986.*

Fifth Amendment see *self-incrimination, privilege against.*

fifty-fifty split, possessions corporations an elective procedure whereby a *possessions corporation* can avoid imputation of *intangible property income* to its *shareholders.* The election entitles the *island affiliate* to 50 percent of the combined *taxable income* from the sale of products produced or services rendered in a *possession* by the island affiliate and sold to third parties or foreign affiliates by it or a *mainland affiliate,* with the remainder of the combined taxable income allocated to mainland affiliates. §936(h)(5)(C)(ii)(III). In order to qualify, an island affiliate must meet one of the *significant business presence* tests under the *cost-sharing election* for the product or service. §936(h)(5)(C)(ii)((II).

fifty-percent charities a term often used to describe *exempt organizations* listed in §170(b)(1)(A), that is, those to which a *taxpayer* can make *charitable contributions* and in general *deduct* an amount up to 50 percent of his or her *adjusted gross income* in the year of the contribution. The term includes typical charities, governments and several types of *private foundations.* See *section 170(b)(1)(A) organizations.*

fifty-two, fifty-three week taxable year an elective *accounting period* that varies from 52 to 53 weeks but ends on the same day of the week (e.g., the second Thursday of March) or the day closest to the last day of the month (e.g., the Tuesday closest to the last day of March). §441(f). This unusual year is designed to accommodate taking *inventories.*

filing date, statute of limitations see *statute of limitations.*

filing, return filling out and submitting a *return* to the appropriate place, as defined in the *regulations.* Reg. §301.6091-1. In most instances the regulations specify that the return must be filed with a particular *Service Center*; however, a return can be filed by hand-carrying it to a local *District Office.* Generally, timely mailing of the return or other document is deemed timely filing. See *timely mailing rule.*

filing status the *taxpayer's* marital and family status and filing selection (e.g., *single, married* filing jointly, *surviving spouse, head of household,* or married filing separately). Filing status has a significant impact on *federal income tax* rates.

final decision, Tax Court a nonappealable decision of the *Tax Court.* This occurs after the 90-day appeal period expires. §7481.

final determination generally, some administrative or judicial act, or both, used as a measure of finality. The term is defined in disparate ways throughout the *Code,* depending on the particular subject matter. See, e.g., Reg. §§1.46-6 (public utilities—an incontestible ratemaking determination) and 1.401-13(d) (excess contributions to *qualified plans*—a final judicial decision or order or a *closing agreement*). The word "determination" is often used with the same import. See *final decision, Tax Court; final determination, regulated public utilities investment tax credits.*

final determination, regulated public utilities investment tax credits a determination regarding public utility property that determines the effect of the former *investment tax credit* allowed to a *taxpayer* on its cost of service or rate base for rate-making purposes with respect to which all rights to appeal and review have been exhausted or have lapsed. Reg. §1.46-6(8)(iii); §46(f)(4)(C)(i), (f)(1), and (f)(2). If such a determination was inconsistent with a taxpayer's claimed credit, the taxpayer's credit was disallowed. §46(f)(4)(A).

final partnership administrative adjustment a notice sent to all *notice partners,* which the *IRS* must issue prior to *assessment* of a *deficiency.* It is comparable to a *statutory notice of deficiency.* The notice gives the *tax matters partner* 90 days to file a *petition* for readjustment in the *Tax Court, Claims Court,* or the *District Court.* §6223. See *unified proceedings.*

final regulations *regulations* in their final, effective form, as opposed to *proposed* or *temporary regulations.*

finance charges generally, amounts charged on installment *debt,* treated as *interest* to the extent for the use of money. See especially Rev. Rul. 72-315, 1972-1 C.B. 49 (amounts designated as finance charges under Truth in Lending Act on accounts deemed interest). Consumer finance charges are not *deductible* as interest.

financial accounting accounting for nontax purposes. For federal tax purposes, *tax accounting* dictated by the *Code* preempts financial reporting when they conflict.

financial asset any asset reflecting a fixed amount of foreign currency (e.g., cash on hand and loans receivable) and securities unless they have been or are reasonably expected to be held for at least six months. Advances on open account to any *corporation* in which the *taxpayer,* certain related persons, or both hold at least 10 percent of voting power are not financial assets if they have remained open for more than one year. Reg. §1.964-1(e)(5)(i). The term is used for purposes of determining *earnings and profits* of *foreign corporations* for *subpart F* purposes. Specifically, exchange *gains* are reflected in United States dollars, showing financial assets at the year-end exchange rate.

financial institution, disallowance of interest expenses any *person* who accepts deposits from the public in the ordinary course of the *trade or business* and is federally or state regulated as a financial institution, and most *banks,* including United States *branches* of *foreign* banks. §265(b)(5). Financial institutions can not *deduct interest expense* allocable to *tax-exempt interest.* §265(b)(1). There is an exception for tax-exempt obligations acquired before August 8, 1986, and for *qualified tax-exempt obligations* acquired after August 7, 1986.

financial institution, insolvent see *qualified financial institution.*

financial institution preference item *excess reserves for losses on bad debts of financial institutions,* and *interest* on debt to carry *tax-exempt obligations* acquired after December 31, 1982. §291(e)(1). The amount allowable as a *deduction* for such items must be reduced by 20 percent. §291(a)(3). See *corporate preference items.*

financial institutions' deduction for interest on tax-exempt obligations *interest* paid by *banks* and certain financial institutions on customers' deposits, where the deposits are used to acquire obligations that generate *tax-exempt income.* Twenty percent of such interest expenses are disallowed under §291 as a *corporate preference item.* §291(a)(3) and (e). §291(e) (calculations to determine interest allocable to such obligations).

financial lease a nickname for a lease commonly used in *tax shelter* operations under which the manufacturer of property sells the property to a *partnership* which finances the *lease* with debt from a third party and then net leases the property to a third party. The tax issue is whether the lease is really a lease or a *sale.* See Rev. Rul. 55-540, 1955 2 C.B. 39.

financially troubled thrift institutions building and loan associations, cooperative banks, and mutual savings banks involved in a case under the jurisdiction of the Federal Home Loan Bank Board, the Federal Savings and Loan Insurance Corporation (FSLIC), or, if neither has supervisory authority, the equivalent state authority. Tax-free *corporate reorganizations* undertaken in connection with such a case are allowed without regard to the *continuity of proprietary interest* requirement. *Stock* or *securities* in the transferee corporation do not need to be received or distributed in the transaction. Additionally, the recapture rule for distributions out of excess *bad debt reserves* (§593(e)) does not apply to distributions in redemption to the FSLIC with respect to an interest in a thrift institution received in exchange for financial assistance. *Id.*, §368(a)(3)(D). Their *loss carryovers* are also more freely preserved in *title 11 or similar cases.* §382(l)(5)(F). The special tax benefits for financially troubled thrift institutions are generally set to expire in 1990.

financial services income a category of *foreign service income* to which *foreign tax credit limitation* applies separately. It consists primarily of income which is received or *accrued* by a *person* predominately engaged in the active conduct of a banking, insurance, financing, or similar *business,* including income from the investment by an insurance company of its unearned premiums or reserves that are ordinary and necessary for the proper conduct of its business, and insurance income as defined by §953(a), with a minor exception. §904(d)(2)(C)(i)(I) and (ii). If an *entity* is predominantly involved in a banking, insurance, financing, or similar business for the *taxable year,* any income that is *passive income* will be financial services income as will *export financing interest* which would otherwise be *high withholding tax interest.* §904(d)(2)(C)(i)(II)-(III). The term excludes *export financing interest, high withholding tax interest,* and *dividends* from *noncontrolled §902 corporations.* Due to the mobile nature of financial services income, businesses had been given incentive to locate such income in low-tax jurisdictions using unrelated excess credits to avoid United States taxation of the financial services income. The creation of this separate category destroys that incentive. See *export financing interest; high withholding tax interest; section 904(d)(1) "basket."*

financing lease a euphemism for a long-term *lease* with characteristics of a *mortgage* or other financing device.

findings of fact generally, the conclusions regarding the facts of a case, determined by a trial court.

fines or penalties fines or similar penalties paid to a government unit for violation of any law. Such expenses are *nondeductible* under §162 or implicitly under §212, in the view of the *IRS,* even (according to some judicial authority) if they are in the nature of *interest* or merely to encourage prompt payment or other action. §162(g). Examples of nondeductible fines and penalties are (1) those paid as a result of a nolo contendere or guilty plea in a criminal proceeding; (2) amounts paid as a fine or penalty to settle an actual or potential liability, whether the liability is civil or criminal; and (3) forfeited collateral posted in a proceeding that could result in a fine or penalty. Reg. §1.162-21(a).

fire department bonds see *qualified volunteer fire department.*

first-in, first out (FIFO) a method for determining *closing inventories,* which uses the assumption that goods on hand are those most recently acquired and which ascribes costs on that basis. For example, if a store has 1,000 towels on hand, the most recently acquired 500-towel batch costs $120, and the prior 500-towel batch cost $90, then the FIFO method dictates a *closing inventory* cost of $210, regardless of when the towels were in fact acquired. Closing inventory is vital to determining *cost of goods sold* for *taxpayers* using *inventory accounting.* The first-in, first-out assumption is commonly used for other purposes as well (e.g., absorption of *investment credit carrybacks* under Reg. §1.46-1(1) and (m)). See *inventory accounting; last-in, first-out (LIFO).*

first-in, first-out rule, securities identification a rule of convenience, the gist of which is that when securities are sold from lots acquired at different times or at different prices, and the identity of the lots cannot be determined, the securities sold are deemed to be the earliest purchases of such securities. Reg. §1.1012-1(c).

first marketable product or group of products, natural resources the product, or group of essentially the same products, produced by the *taxpayer* as a result of the application of a nonmining process, in the form or condition in which such product or products are first marketed in significant quantities by the taxpayer or by others in the taxpayer's marketing area. Reg. §1.613-4(d)(4)(iv), which also provides examples. The term is used under the *proportionate profits method* to determine *depletion deductions* that can be claimed by taxpayers who are engaged in integrated mining and manufacturing. See *proportionate profits method, minerals; sudden death rule.*

first post-separation year see *frontloading of alimony.*

first retail sale the first sale, for a purpose other than resale, after manufacture, production, or importation. §4011(a). The term is used for purposes of the *luxury taxes* to limit the tax to new items.

first-tier beneficiary a *beneficiary* who receives mandatory distributions *(income for the taxable year* *required to be distributed currently*) from an *estate* or *complex trust*. §662(a)(1).

first-tier corporation, foreign tax credit   a term used to describe a *foreign corporation* in which a *domestic corporation* owns at least 10 percent of the voting *stock*. §902. The term is important in determining the availability of the *deemed paid foreign tax credit*.

first-tier entity   an *entity* (defined in the usual way in Reg.§1.382-2T(f)(7)) that at any time during the *testing period* owns a 5 percent or more direct ownership interest in the *loss corporation*. Reg. §1.382-2T(f)(9). The term is used in connection with determining if there has been an *ownership change* of the *loss corporation* for purposes of the *neutrality principle* so as to cause the *section 382 limitation* to apply.

first-tier excise tax   an informal term for any of the *excise taxes* imposed on *private foundations*. §§4941, 4951-2, 4955, 4971, or 4975. §4963(a). If the first-tier tax is left uncorrected, much higher *second-tier* taxes are imposed. See *excise taxes, private foundations*.

first-tier partnership   a *partnership* which holds interests in another *(second-tier)* partnership. The tiers can be infinite.

first-year election   see *election to be treated as resident*.

first-year expensing   a synonym for *bonus depreciation*. §179.

fiscal year   a 12-month *accounting period,* other than a *calendar year,* ending on the last day of a particular month, for example, July 1 to June 30 of the following year. Numerous *taxpayers* are free to select a fiscal year in which to report *taxable income*.

fish farm   a place where fish are grown and raised. Reg. §1.175-3. A major benefit of being a farmer (even a fish farmer) is the right to use the *cash method* of accounting. Reg. §§1.61-4(a), 1.476-6(a). The *estimated tax* definition is confused, treating fish farming as fishing but oyster raising as farming. See Reg. §1.6073-1(b).

fishing boat services   employment on a boat engaged in catching fish or other forms of aquatic animal life. Under an arrangement with the owner or operator, the *taxpayer* receives no cash remuneration other than his or her share of the catch, with the share dependent solely on the amount of the catch, if the operating crew of the boat (captain included) normally numbers less than 10. §3121(b)(20). Such compensation is generally exempt from *FICA, FUTA,* and *income tax withholding*. §§3401(a)(17), 3306(c)(18), and 3121(b)(20).

fishing crew member   an *individual* on a boat, with an operating crew normally of fewer than 10, engaged in catching fish or other aquatic animal life, is to be treated as an *independent contractor* for federal tax purposes if the following conditions are met: (1) the individual does not receive any cash remuneration other than a share of the proceeds from the sale of the catch; (2) the individual receives a share of the boat's catch or a share of the proceeds from the sale of the catch; and (3) the amount of the individual's share depends on the amount of the boat's catch. §§1402(c)(2)(F); 3121(b)(20). Section 6050A requires the boat operators to report information regarding the portions of any catches and any shares of the proceeds from the sale of any catches which are distributed to each crew member.

five-percent notice group   a group of *partners* who for the *partnership's taxable year* had *profits interests* that aggregated 5 percent or more. §6231(a)(11). A five-percent group can designate one of its members as the person who must receive notice of the beginning and completion of any proceedings by the *IRS*. §6223(b)(2). See *unified proceedings*.

five-percent owner, employee plans   an *employee* who, at any time during the *plan year* or any of the four preceding plan years, is or was a five-percent owner. A five-percent owner is the owner of more than 5 percent of the *stock* or voting power of the *employer corporation* (directly and via the *attributes* rules of §318—as modified) or of more than 5 percent of the capital or profit interest in an unincorporated employer. §416(i)(1)(B). A five-percent owner is a *key employee*.

five-percent owner, neutrality principle   any *individual* who owns, at any time during the *testing period,* a 5 percent or greater direct ownership interest in a *first-tier entity* or *higher-tier entity*. Reg. §1.382-2T(f)(10). The term is used in connection with determining if there has been an *ownership change* for purposes of the *neutrality principle* so as to cause the *section 382 limitation* to apply to the *loss corporation*.

five-percent shareholder   any *person* holding 5 percent or more in value of the *corporation's stock* at any time during the (generally three-year) *testing period,* both before and after each shift. §382(k)(7). Nonvoting, nonconvertible preferred stock, which does not participate in corporate growth to any significant extent and which has redemption and liquidation rights which do not exceed the issue price of such stock (except for a reasonable redemption or liquidation premium) is excluded. §382(k)(6)(A). Five-percent shareholders are scrutinized to determine whether an *ownership change* of an *old loss corporation* has occurred, so as to attract the *section 382 limitation* and related provisions. Complex *attribution rules* expand the likelihood of finding five-percent shareholders. §382(b)(3). Also all persons holding under 5 percent are deemed a single five-percent shareholder. §382(g)(1). Reg. §1.382-2T(g)(1). See *direct five-percent shareholder; indirect five-percent shareholder; neutrality principle*.

five-to-fifteen-year vesting a *vesting* alternative authorized under §411(a)(2)(B) pursuant to which *employees* in *qualified plans* develop vested interests in their *employer contributions* according to the following schedule:

Years of Service	Vested Percentage
1	0
2	0
3	0
4	0
5	20
6	30
7	35
8	40
9	45
10	50
11	60
12	70
13	80
14	90
15	100

This is one permissible form (to be eliminated) of vesting that satisfies the minimum vesting requirements for qualified plans. It is being phased out in favor of more rapid vesting. See *vesting schedules.*

five-year forward averaging an elective method whereby *participants* (or their alternate payees) in *qualified deferred compensation plans* can elect to treat *lump-sum distributions* as if they were received in equal amounts over the current and next four years. It is available once in a lifetime and is available only to persons at least $59\frac{1}{2}$ years of age. §402(e)(4)(B). It replaces *ten-year forward averaging* and applies to post-1986 distributions. Some computational details are discussed under the heading *ten-year forward averaging.* See *lump-sum distribution, qualified plans.*

five-year property generally property with a *class life* of more than 4 years and less than 10 years, including (1) cars; (2) light general-purpose trucks; (3) *qualified technological equipment*; (4) switching equipment; (5) biomass properties that are small power production facilities within the meaning of §(3)(17)(C) of the 16 U.S.C. §796(17)(C), as in effect on September 1, 1986; (6) any property used for *research and experimentation*; (7) semi-conductor manufacturing equipment; and (8) *geothermal, ocean thermal, solar,* and *wind energy properties.* §168(e)(3)(B). This class of *recovery property* is the product of the *Tax Reform Act of 1986.*

five-year recovery property certain property subject to the *accelerated cost recovery system,* specifically *section 1245 class property* (basically, *tangible personal property*) not included in any other class (e.g., heavy-duty trucks, most office equipment, lathes, ships, aircraft), *single-purpose agricultural and horticultural structures,* petroleum storage facilities which are classed as §1245 (i.e., *personal*) property, and public utility property not granted a 10-year or longer *ACRS* life.

five-year vesting an alternative minimum *vesting schedule* under which *employer contributions* are fully vested after five *years of service.* §411(a)(2)(A). Such a vesting schedule can satisfy the requirements relating to vesting of benefits under *qualified plans* or *trusts.* The alternative is *three-seven vesting.* See *vesting schedules.*

fixed base percentage see *credit for increasing research activities.*

fixed benefit plans a form of *defined benefit plan* under which benefits are fixed in terms of a specified percentage of a *participant's compensation,* commonly for some specific number of highest-paid consecutive years of service out of the participant's last years of service. Benefits are often scaled down for late entry. A typical benefit formula might be 20 percent of a participant's average monthly compensation for the highest three consecutive years of service out of the last eight years of service.

fixed investment trust see *unit investment trust.*

fixed or determinable annual or periodical gains, profits, and income a residual class of *income* taxable to *foreign corporations* and *nonresident aliens* from sources within the *United States* other than *business* activities, which is generally taxed at a flat 30 percent rate unless reduced by a *tax treaty.* "Fixed" income paid means income in predetermined amounts. Income is "determinable" if there is a basis of calculation by which the amount to be paid can be ascertained. "Periodical" means from time to time, though not necessarily at regular intervals. Thus, alimony, prizes, and gambling income, for example, are included. *Gains* from *sales* or property are excluded. Whether the payment itself is in a lump sum or in installments is irrelevant to the conclusion. Reg. §1.1441-2(a). Unless the income is fixed or determinable annual or periodical income, it is not taxed when earned by nonresident aliens and foreign corporations in a nonbusiness context. It is, however, taxable to foreigners as if earned by a United States person if it is *effectively connected* with the *active conduct of a trade or business* in the United States. §§871(a)(1)(A) (*individuals*), 881 (*corporations*).

fixing-up expenses see *adjusted sales price.*

flat benefit excess plan a *defined benefit plan* that provides a retirement benefit equal to a flat percentage of compensation in excess of some *integration level.* Such plans are subject to *integration* rules set forth in Rev. Rul. 71-446, 1971-2 C.B. 187, §5. See *integrated plan; integration, Social Security.*

flat benefit plan   a form of *defined benefit plan,* common to collective bargaining agreements, the benefits of which are independent of the *participant's compensation*. In the undiluted form, the participant is entitled to a flat monthly pension at the *normal retirement date* (e.g., $500 per month regardless of the period of service or level of compensation). In a less diluted form: the pension may be defined as a specified dollar figure (e.g., $50 per month times years of service).

flexible benefit plan   a synonym for a *cafeteria plan.*

flat bonds   see *bonds bought flat.*

flexible premium life insurance contract   a *life insurance* arrangement (generally *universal life* or *adjustable life*) that provides for the payment of one or more premiums, which are not fixed by the insurer as to both timing and amount. In order for *death proceeds* to be *excludable* from *gross income,* a flexible premium life insurance policy must satisfy one of two alternative requirements: (1) the sum of premiums paid under the contract at any time cannot exceed a specifically computed *guideline premium limitation,* and any amount payable on the death of the insured cannot be less than the "applicable percentage" of the contract's cash surrender value as of the date of death; or (2) the *cash surrender value* must never exceed the net single premium for the death benefit. §101(f).

flexible spending account   a type of *cafeteria plan* which includes one or more reimbursement accounts under which cash that is forgone by an *employee,* by means of salary reductions or otherwise, is credited to a bookkeeping account of the *employer* and drawn down by the employer to reimburse the employee for uninsured medical or dental expenses (e.g., deductibles), to which §105(b) applies, or for *dependent care expenses,* to which §129(a) applies. Cafeteria plans often provide both insurance coverage options and reimbursement accounts. See *dependent care assistance programs; medical care; use it or lose it rule.*

flexible statutes   statutes which allow a *limited liability company's (LLC) organizers* broad flexibility in structuring the LLC and which allow the provisions concerning transferability of interest, centralized management, and continuity of life to be varied by the agreement of the owners of the LLC, with "default" provisions that otherwise govern. The danger is that by not following the default provisions in the flexible statutes, there is the risk that the LLC will not be structured properly from a federal tax standpoint (i.e., the ability for practicing professionals to limit their exposure to vicarious liability without the costs of a professional corporation). Delaware, Texas, and Illinois have flexible statutes. See *bulletproof statutes.*

floating rate convertible notes   corporate securities, the interest rates of which are tied to the issuer's divi-

dend yield on its common *stock* and which are convertible into the issuer's common stock. In Rev. Rul. 83-98, 1983-2 C.B. 40, the *IRS* ruled such issues to be *stock,* not *debt,* and disallowed *deductions* for alleged interest payments, principally because of the likelihood that the obligations would be converted into stock. See *debt-equity rules.*

floor offset plan   an arrangement whereby benefits payable under a *defined benefit plan* are offset by the benefits of a separate *defined contribution plan.*

floor plan   a *defined benefit (pension) plan,* which provides for the reduction of pension benefits by an amount receivable from another plan maintained by the same *employer,* usually a *profit-sharing plan.* Rev. Rul. 76-259, 1976-2 C.B. 111. See §414(k).

flower bond   a certain low-interest bond issued at a discount by the United States Treasury prior to March 3, 1971, that the *decedent's* representative can use at face value to pay federal *estate tax* liability, provided the decedent actually owned the bonds at the time of death. See Rev. Rul. 69-489, 1969-2 C.B. 172.

flow-through accounting   a technique used by public utility companies to pass tax savings on to customers in the form of reduced rates. This is accomplished by applying tax benefits to reduce the company's cost of service for ratemaking purposes or to reduce the base to which the company's rate of return for ratemaking purposes is applied. Flow-through treatment of the *investment tax credit* was and is prohibited, except under certain transitional provisions, for *public utility property placed in service* after 1980. §46(f); *ERTA* §209(d).

flow-through private foundation   a *private nonoperating foundation* that, not later than the fifteenth day of the third month following the close of its *taxable year* in which contributions are received, makes qualifying distributions to *public charities* or to *private operating foundations* that are treated as distributions out of *corpus* in an amount equal to all such contributions. Gifts to such foundations qualify for the 50 percent contribution ceiling (i.e., are so-called *fifty-percent charities*). §170(b)(1)(A)(vii) and (E).

focal point analysis   an analysis under which *home office deductions* are denied if an *employee's* principal place of business (§28(c)(1)(A)) is not at home, which evaluates the place where business is done (e.g., a symphony hall), not where most time is spent (e.g., at home practicing).

forced type B reorganization   situation in which there is a *reverse triangular reorganization* involving a transitory *subsidiary* established for the transaction. It arises if the reorganization fails a condition of §368(a)(2)(E). In such cases the transaction can be nontaxable if it satisfies the standards of a *Type B reorgani-*

zation, but no *boot* is allowed. (The presence of boot would render the transaction fully taxable.)

foreclosure gain as to the owner, *gain* on *foreclosure* of property subject to *recourse debt* is *realized* to the extent that the value of property exceeds the owner's *basis* in the property. Further debt is *cancellation of indebtedness income.* Reg. §1.1001-2(c), Example 8.

foreclosure loss as to the owner of property subject to *recourse debt, loss* on *foreclosure* arises to the extent that the owner's *basis* exceeds the property's *fair market value.* Further debt is *cancellation of indebtedness income.* Reg. §1.1001-2(c), Example 8. In the case of *nonrecourse debt,* there is a *loss* to the extent the *basis* of the property exceeds the debt. As to the *mortgagee* (lender), loss arises to the extent that the mortgagee's basis in the discharged debt (including legal and other expenses, and accrued *interest* reported as *gross income*) exceeds the fair market value of the property received (or the proceeds from the sale). The mortgagee's loss is generally treated as a *bad debt.*

foreclosure property, real estate investment trust any interest in *realty* and incidental *personal property* acquired after 1973 as a result of *foreclosure* by a *real estate investment trust* (REIT), or as a result of default or the imminence of default on a lease of the property or on a debt secured by the property. It does not apply to property acquired as a result of debt arising from the REIT's purchase of *dealer property* if it was not originally acquired as foreclosure property. §856(e)(1).

foreclosure property, REMIC foreclosure property under *real estate investment trust* provisions which is acquired as a result of default or imminent default of a *qualified mortgage.* §860G(a)(8). It retains that status for a year, during which time it is a *permitted investment* of the *REMIC.* Net income from such properties are taxed to the *REMIC* at top corporate *income tax* rates. §860G(c). See *foreclosure property, real estate investment trust.*

foregone interest *interest* not charged on a loan. The term is used in connection with *below-market loans,* and is formally defined as the excess of (1) interest that would have been payable on the loan for the period of interest accrued at the *applicable federal rate* and payable annually at the end of the calendar year over (2) interest payable on the loan, properly allocable to such period. §7872(e)(2). Foregone interest is generally treated as paid from borrower to lender, then generally retransferred as a *gift, dividend,* or *compensation* to the borrower. §7372(a)(1).

foreign when applied to a *corporation* or *partnership,* the term means a corporation or partnership which is not *domestic.* §7701(a)(5) (implicitly rendering *possessions* foreign). *Trusts, estates,* and other *taxpayers* are classified under more difficult standards.

foreign affiliate, FICA taxes any *foreign entity* in which a *United States employer* has a direct or indirect interest of 10 percent or more. If it is a *corporation,* then the United States employer must hold at least 10 percent of the foreign corporation's voting *stock;* otherwise, it must hold at least a 10 percent interest in the foreign entity's profits. §3121(1)(8). An American employer can agree with the *IRS* to extend Social Security coverage to *United States citizens* and *resident aliens* who are employed by any or all of the United States employer's foreign affiliates. §3121(1). Form 2032 is used.

foreign affiliate tax credit see *deemed paid foreign tax credit.*

foreign areas allowances an extensive series of *nontaxable* benefits for federal *employees* posted abroad: (1) allowances under Title IX of the Foreign Service Act, §4 of the Central Intelligence Agency Act of 1949, Title II of the Overseas Differentials and Allowances Act, or §§1(e) and (f) or 22 of the Administrative Expenses Act of 1946; (2) cost-of-living allowances (other than amounts received under Title II of the Overseas Differentials and Allowances Act), treating officers or employees serving in Alaska or Hawaii as serving abroad for this purpose; and (3) amounts received as allowances by Peace Corps volunteers and volunteer leaders, except for termination payments, leave allowances, family allowances received by a volunteer leader training in the *United States,* and such parts of living allowances as the President may determine to be basic compensation allowances, and other items which, in the case of military personnel, must be purchased out of basic compensation. §912.

foreign base company an undefined element of the *subpart F* rules. The underlying *subpart F* concept is to prevent corporate *taxpayers* from selectively operating out of low-tax jurisdictions or running their transactions through low-tax jurisdictions via foreign subsidiaries (*controlled foreign corporations*). See *foreign base company income.*

foreign base company income a category of *subpart F income* that consists of (1) *foreign personal holding company income,* (2) *foreign base company sales income,* (3) *foreign base company services income,* (4) *foreign base company oil-related income,* and (5) *foreign base company shipping income.* §954(a)(1)-(5). Such income is imputed to *United States shareholders* of *controlled foreign corporations* (CFCs).

foreign base company oil-related income a form of *subpart F income* consisting of income from processing, transporting, distributing, and selling oil and gas, and oil and gas products, income from dispositions of assets used in such activities, and certain passive income, but not income from the extraction of oil and gas. §954(h).

foreign base company sales income   a component of *foreign base company income* of a *controlled foreign corporation* (CFC), which may be imputed to its *United States shareholders* as a component of *subpart F income*. §§954(a)(2), 952(a)(2). The thrust of the provision is to limit the use of foreign subsidiaries in low-tax countries to act as receptacles for sales income ultimately generated in third countries. See *related person, controlled foreign corporation; substantial transformation test.*

foreign base company services income   a form of *foreign base company income,* specifically income from rendering services (comprehensively defined) outside the *controlled foreign corporation's* (CFC's) country of incorporation for a related party, disregarding certain services related to the sale of property made, grown, or extracted by the CFC. §954(e).

foreign base company shipping income   a form of *foreign base company income* (hence, *subpart F income*), principally, income earned from vessels and aircraft in foreign commerce from sources other than the *controlled foreign corporation's* (CFC's) country of incorporation. §954(f) and (g).

foreign-based documentation   a United States document (including books and records) outside the *United States* that may be relevant or material to the tax treatment of an examined item. §982(d)(1). The term includes documents held by a *foreign entity,* even if the entity is not controlled by the *taxpayer.* Items are foreign-based if they are directly or indirectly from a source outside the *United States* or if they arise outside the United States or are otherwise dependent on transactions outside the United States. §982(d)(3). If a taxpayer does not substantially comply with a request for a foreign-based document in 90 days, it cannot be used as evidence in a court proceeding, subject to a *reasonable cause* exception.

foreign branch   when speaking of a *United States taxpayer,* an overseas office or any other center of activity of a *United States* enterprise. Branches are not separable for tax purposes from the United States enterprise even if separately managed; accordingly all income from a foreign branch automatically flows through to the United States enterprise and is taxed as earned. See Rev. Rul. 78-201, 1978-1 C.B. 91.

foreign central bank of issue   a bank that is the principal authority for issuing instruments intended to circulate as currency, operating by authority of law or government sanction. §861(a)(1)(E); Reg. §1.861-2(b)(4). Its investment income is generally *exempt* from United States taxation if the bank is owned by its government and is not engaged in commerce here. §892. Income

from bankers' acceptances issued by such banks is considered *gross income from sources without the United States.* §861(a)(1)(E).

foreign citizen   see *alien.*

foreign collapsible corporation   an informal term meaning a *foreign corporation* which is subject to the *collapsible corporation* rules. Such corporations generally cannot make a *section 341(f) election.* §341(f)(8).

foreign convention   any convention, seminar, or similar meeting held outside the *North American area* (i.e., United States, Mexico, Canada, Puerto Rico, United States possessions, and the trust territory of the Pacific and other jurisdictions), including a growing list of other countries included under treaties. §274(h)(6). The *deductibility* of *expenses* for such conventions are subject to sharp restrictions. §274(h). See *North American area.*

foreign corporation   a *corporation* organized under any law other than that of the United States, a state, or the District of Columbia. A foreign corporation does not include a corporation created or organized on Guam. Foreign corporations engaged in a United States *trade or business* are taxed at regular United States corporate tax rates on income from United States sources that is *effectively connected* with that business and at 30 percent on United States source income not effectively connected with that business. §§7701(a)(3), (4), and (9); 881(a), 882(a). Guamanian corporations are treated as not foreign for purposes of the 30 percent flat tax imposed by §881. §881(b). See also *foreign; branch profits tax.*

foreign corporation's post-1986 foreign income taxes   generally, the sum of a *foreign corporation's foreign income taxes* for the year a *dividend* is paid plus all prior years after 1986, reduced by the portions of the *foreign income taxes* allocable to dividends paid in such prior years (including distributions to shareholders that are not eligible for the *deemed paid foreign tax credit.* §902(c)(2). See *deemed paid foreign tax credit; foreign income taxes; foreign income, war profits and excess profits taxes; foreign tax credit; foreign tax credit limitation; functional currency.*

foreign country equity adjustment   an adjustment for *mutual life insurance companies* to cover the risks of foreign strife. §809(g)(5).

foreign country, foreign earned income   a *foreign* country or territory under the sovereignty of a foreign government, but not a United States *possession* or territory. Temp. Reg. §§5b.913-3(d), 5b.911-7. Trust territories administered by the United States on behalf of the United Nations are territories under the sovereignty of a foreign government. The Panama Canal Zone, the Antarctic region, the Northern Marianas Islands, and territorial waters the United States recognizes as part of a foreign country are also foreign. Rev. Rul. 80-167, 1980-2 C.B. 176; Rev. Rul. 68-608, 1968-2 C.B. 309; Rev. Rul. 67-52, 1967-2 C.B. 166; Rev. Rul. 63-50, 1963-1 C.B. 129. Personal service income earned in a foreign country is entirely or partially excluded from *gross income*. See *continental United States; foreign earned income exclusion*.

foreign currency contract a contract that requires delivery (or the settlement of which depends on the value) of a foreign currency in which positions are also traded through a regulated futures market, traded in the interbank market, and entered into at arm's length at a price determined by the interbank market. §1256(g)(2). Such contracts are treated like *regulated futures contracts* and other *section 1256 contracts*.

foreign currency gain or loss the difference in the value of the object of a *section 988 transaction* between the *booking date* and the *payment date* (or delivery date if the *taxpayer* takes delivery) due to fluctuations in exchange rates. §988(b). Generally foreign currency *gain* or *loss* is treated as *ordinary income*, but in special circumstances it can be *capital gain* or *interest* income. §988(a)(1). See *qualified fund, foreign currency gain or loss; section 988 transaction*.

foreign death tax credit a *credit* against *federal estate tax* for the amount of *foreign estate, inheritance, legacy,* or succession taxes actually paid on *property* located in foreign countries or *possessions* that is included in a *decedent's gross estate*. §2014. The credit is subject to limitation.

foreign development costs any *expenditures paid or incurred* with respect to the *development* of a mine or other natural deposit (other than oil, gas, or geothermal well) located outside the *United States*. Such expenditures are, at the election of the *taxpayer*, (1) included in *adjusted basis* for purposes of computing the amount of *depletion deductions,* or (2) allowed as *deduction* ratably over the 10-*taxable year* period beginning with the *taxable year* in which such expenditures were *paid or incurred*. §616(d). See *development expenditures, minerals*.

foreign distributee for purposes of §367, this term is defined as a *foreign person* who receives a *distribution* of *stock* or *securities* of a *domestic* or *foreign corporation*. Reg. §1.367(e)1T. If the transaction qualifies under §355 (nontaxable corporate fissions), the distributing corporation generally reports only *gains* but not *losses* on such transactions. Otherwise, the term is undefined, but presumably it means any foreign person who receives a distribution from any source.

foreign earned income an *individual's earned income* from foreign sources attributable to services performed while a resident of a *foreign country* or

countries. §911(b)(1)(A). Residence is determined by either being a *bona fide resident* abroad or under a *physical presence test*. See *earned income, foreign earned income; foreign earned income exclusion; housing cost amount*.

foreign earned income exclusion a relief provision pursuant to which a *qualified individual taxpayer* may elect to exclude $70,000 of *foreign earned income*. §911(a) and (b). The taxpayer must elect between this exclusion and the *foreign tax credit*. Note that this exclusion and the *foreign housing cost exclusion* or deduction cannot exceed foreign earned income for the *taxable year*. §911(d)(7). See *earned income, foreign earned income; housing cost amount; qualified individual, foreign earned income*.

foreign economic process, FSC requirements that certain sales and direct cost activities of a *foreign sales corporation* (FSC) be performed outside of the *United States* in order for receipts from such activities to be qualified as *foreign trading gross receipts*. To qualify, the FSC (or person under contract with the FSC) must participate outside the United States in either the solicitation (other than advertising), negotiation, or making of the contract relating to the transaction giving rise to the receipts, and the FSC's *foreign direct costs* attributable to the transaction must equal or exceed 50 percent of the FSC's total direct costs incurred with respect to the transaction. §924(d).

foreign estate an *estate* of a *decedent* who had his *domicile* in a *foreign* country at the time of his death. §7701(a)(31). Foreign domicile is the criterion for determining whether an estate is a foreign estate. Rev. Rul. 62-154, 1962-1 C.B. 148.

foreign estate tax credit see *foreign death tax credit*.

foreign exploration costs any *expenditures paid or incurred* before the *development stage* for the purpose of ascertaining the existence, location, extent, or quality of any deposit of ore or mineral (other than an oil, gas, or geothermal well) located outside the *United States*. Such expenditures are, at the election of the *taxpayer*, (1) included in *adjusted basis* for computation of the amount of any *depletion deductions,* or (2) allowed as a *deduction* ratably over the 10-*taxable year* period beginning with the taxable year in which such expenditures were paid or incurred. See §617(h). See *exploration expenditures, minerals*.

foreign expropriation capital loss a *loss* sustained by appropriation, intervention, seizure, or similar taking of property by the government of a *foreign* country and any political subdivision thereof, or any agency or instrumentality of the foregoing, or losses from *securities* that become worthless for one of the reasons given by the statute (appropriation by the government of a foreign country, etc.). §1212(a)(2). Such *capital losses* qualify for a special 10-year *carryforward* period when sustained by *corporations*. §1212(a)(1)(C)(ii).

foreign expropriation loss aggregate *losses* sustained by reason of expropriations, interventions, seizures, or similar takings of property by the government of any country, any political subdivision thereof, or any agency or instrumentality of the foregoing, including *business-related debts* that are rendered *worthless* as result of such acts. §172(h). They exclude loss transactions in *capital assets, section 1231 assets, worthless securities* and *Cuban expropriation losses* (which are specially treated). Reg. §1.172-11(b)(1).

foreign gift tax credit a *credit* for foreign *gift taxes* paid. It is awarded to *United States residents* and *citizens* for transfer subject to *foreign gift taxes,* and arises solely as a result of *tax treaty* provisions.

foreign government-related individual a class of *individuals* who do not become *resident aliens* by virtue of time spent (the *substantial presence test*) in the *United States.* The term refers to any individual temporarily present in the United States because of (1) diplomatic status, or a visa which the *Treasury Department,* after consultation with the State Department, determines represents full-time diplomatic or consular status for purposes of defining resident alien and *nonresident alien*; (2) being a full-time *employee* of an *international organization*; or (3) being a member of the immediate family of an individual described in (1) or (2). §7701(b)(4)(B).

foreign housing cost deduction a *deduction* available to *citizens of the United States* or *resident aliens* of the United States, pursuant to which a *qualified individual* is entitled to deduct a limited amount of housing costs arising from foreign employment. The deduction is limited to the individual's *foreign earned income* for that year minus the amount of such income subject to the *exclusion* for foreign earned income. §911(c)(3)(A). See *foreign earned income exclusion.*

foreign housing cost exclusion an *exclusion* available to *citizens of the United States* or *resident aliens* of the United States overseas pursuant to which a *qualified individual* may elect to exclude from *gross income* a limited amount of *employer*-provided overseas housing costs as a result of foreign employment. §911(c). The *taxpayer* must elect this exclusion. Election of the exclusion results in a partial diminution of *foreign tax credits.* See *resident alien.*

foreign housing costs see *housing cost amount.*

foreign income see *gross income from sources without the United States; taxable income from sources without the United States.*

foreign income tax, subchapter S corporations foreign taxes paid by an S corporation that pass through as

such to the shareholders, who can elect to treat them as deductions or credits on their individual tax returns. §1373(a).

foreign income, war profits and excess profits taxes *taxes* (as opposed to *deposits, fees,* penalties, *royalties,* and so on) paid to a foreign country, including a local government or a *possession of the United States,* that are imposed on *income, war profits,* or *excess profits,* or are imposed in lieu of such taxes. §901(b). The search is for substantial resemblance to the United States *federal income tax.* If a foreign tax meets these tests, it can be used as a *credit* against United States tax liabilities. §901(a).

foreign insurance company a *foreign corporation* that carries on an insurance business. Such companies may be taxed as *domestic insurance companies* on their insurance business carried on in this country. Reg. §1.881-1(d)(1) and (2).

foreign insurer premium excise tax a tax imposed on insurance, indemnity bond, annuity contract, or reinsurance policies issued by any foreign insurer or reinsurer. §§4371–4374.

foreign international sales corporation (FISC) a foreign selling corporation whose assets and activities must be export-concentrated. §993(a), (b), and (e)(1). Reg. §1.993-5(b). A FISC is one of three types of *related foreign export corporations.*

foreign investment company a *foreign corporation* registered under the Investment Company Act of 1940, or engaged (or holding itself out as being engaged) mainly in the business of investing, reinvesting, or trading in securities (using the Investment Company Act definition), commodities, or any interests in securities or commodities (including futures or forward contracts or options) when at least 50 percent of the voting power of all classes of voting *stock* or value of all classes of its stock is held by *United States persons.* Any *long-term capital gain* realized on the *sale* or *exchange* of stock in a foreign investment company is generally treated as *ordinary income* to the extent of the *taxpayer's* share of the company's *earnings and profits* generated while the shareholder held the stock (other than *subpart F income* previously reported.) §1246. Additional rules cause a *carryover* of ordinary income potential to *donees* and *heirs.* Its stock is considered held by *persons* with *beneficial ownership* therein. See §1247 for a relief provision in cases where certain foreign investment companies elect to make current *distributions.*

foreign investment company stock *stock* in a *foreign corporation* that was a *foreign investment company* at any time in the period during which the *taxpayer* owned the stock. If the *holding period* of the stock was more than six months as of the date of the *sale* or *exchange* of the stock, then any *gain* on the sale or exchange is treated as *ordinary income* to the extent of the *taxpayer's* ratable share of the corporation's *earnings and profits* accumulated for *taxable years* beginning after 1962. §1246(a).

Foreign Investment in Real Property Tax Act a complex statute passed in 1980 in order to subject *foreign* investors to *United States income taxes* on direct and indirect investments in United States *real estate*. For example, the act taxes *dispositions* of direct interests in United States real property by *nonresident aliens* and *foreign corporations* as *effectively connected income,* and it also taxes *sales* or *exchanges* of stock in *United States corporations* that are *United States real property holding corporations.*

foreign items any items of *interest* upon the bonds of a *foreign* country or of a nonresident *foreign corporation* not having a fiscal or paying agent in the *United States* (including Puerto Rico as part of the United States), or any items of *dividends* upon the stock of such a corporation. Reg. §1.6041-4(b). If the total of such items paid to a *citizen* or *resident of the United States,* or to a *partnership* with such a member, in a *taxable year* is $600 or more, then a bank or collecting agent accepting such items for collection must file a *Form 1099.* §6041.

foreign living expenses the election by an individual to exclude part of her or his income attributable to housing expenses. Expenses include utilities and insurance, but not taxes and interest. §911(c)(1).

foreign management, FSC a requirement that the management of an *FSC* take place outside the *United States* in order for the FSC's income to be classified as *foreign trading gross receipts,* and thus partially tax-exempt. The requirement is met if (1) all meetings of shareholders and directors occur outside the United States; (2) the FSC's principal bank account is maintained outside the United States at all times during the *taxable year*; and (3) all the FSC's dividends, legal and accounting fees, and salaries of officers and members of its board of directors are reimbursed out of bank accounts maintained outside the United States. §924(c). The requirement does not apply to a *small FSC.*

foreign mineral income income from the extraction of minerals, the processing of them into primary products, and the transportation, distribution, or sale of such raw minerals or their primary products, as well as *dividends* received that are attributable to such income and with respect to which taxes are "deemed paid" under §902 and *partnership distribute shares* attributable to such income. Reg. §1.903-3(b); §901(e)(2). Section 901(e) forces a diminution of *foreign tax credits* attributable to such income if the *taxpayer* used *percentage depletion* with respect to any part of such income for

the *taxable year.* Reg. §1.901-3(a)(3). The diminution is applied by reducing *creditable foreign taxes* by tax savings arising from *percentage depletion,* calculated on a country-by-country basis. §901(e)(1). See *deemed paid foreign tax credit.*

foreign oil and gas extraction income *taxable income* derived from sources without the *United States* and its *possessions* from the extraction (by the *taxpayer* or any other person) of minerals from oil or gas wells, or the *sale* or *exchange* of assets used by the *taxpayer* in such a business. It also includes actual and *constructive dividends* with respect to which *deemed paid foreign tax credits* are available, *domestic corporations'* foreign source dividends, and *partnership* shares related to such income. §907(a)(2) and (c)(5). Extraction *losses* incurred in one country offset extraction gains in another, thereby reducing creditable oil and gas extraction taxes (eliminating the *per country extraction loss rule*) subject to a limited *carryover* under §907(f).

foreign oil and gas extraction taxes see *oil and gas extraction taxes.*

foreign oil and gas tax credit shorthand term for the effects of §907(b), which force a separate calculation of *foreign tax credits* with respect to *foreign oil-related income.*

foreign oil extraction loss the amount by which the *taxpayer's foreign oil and gas extraction income* is exceeded by the sum of the *deductions* properly *apportioned or allocated* to such income, ignoring *net operating loss deductions, foreign expropriation loss* deductions, and *casualty* or *theft* losses. §907(c)(4)(B). See *recapture, foreign extraction losses.*

foreign oil-related income *taxable income* derived from sources outside the *United States* and its *possessions* from the processing of oil and gas into their primary products; the transportation, distribution, or *sale* of *oil* and gas as primary products; or the sale or *exchange* of assets used by the taxpayer in the foregoing *trades* or *businesses* and the performance of related services (after 1982). §907(c)(2). There are various other complex inclusions. See Reg.§1.907(c)-1(d). The term foreign oil-related income is broader than *foreign oil and gas extraction income,* since it includes, for example, transport and processing and even sale of its primary products.

Foreign Operations Internal Revenue District The District is responsible for administering the tax laws with respect to *United States persons* residing or doing business overseas, *foreign persons* with United States source income, and persons obligated to withhold taxes on United States source income.

foreign partnership a *partnership* created or organized under *foreign* law. §7701(a)(2) and (a)(5).

foreign partner, withholding any *partner* who is not a *United States person.* §1446(e). Such partners are subjected to top *corporate* or *individual income tax* tax rates on their *distributive shares* of *effectively connected income,* subject to an eventual *credit* against the year's tax bill. More specifically, if the partnership has *effectively connected [taxable] income* which is allocable to a foreign partner, it must pay a withholding tax. The foreign partner gets a credit for its share of the tax withheld. An amount equal to the credit is deemed distributed by the partnership to the partner, which reduces the partner's *outside basis.* The partner is treated as receiving a *distribution* on the earlier of (1) the last day of the partnership's *taxable year,* or (2) the date on which the partnership pays the tax. §1446(a).

foreign pension and profit-sharing plans see *qualified foreign plan.*

foreign person a *nonresident alien,* or a *foreign corporation, partnership, trust,* or *estate.* Reg. §301.7701-5. See *United States person.*

foreign personal holding company any *foreign corporation* that meets the following tests: generally, (1) at least 60 percent of its *gross income* in its first year is *foreign personal holding company income* (50 percent after the first tax year); and (2) at any time during the *taxable year* more than 50 percent in value of its outstanding voting and nonvoting *stock* is owned directly or indirectly by not more than five *resident aliens* or *citizens of the United States.* §§552,553. See *related person dividend or interest; subpart F income; foreign personal holding company income; foreign personal holding company income, subpart F.*

foreign personal holding company income in general, passive or investment income from *domestic* or *foreign* sources earned by a *foreign personal holding company.* §553(a). The principal items of such income include *dividends; interest; royalties* other than *active business computer software royalties;* net *gains* from *sales* or *exchanges* of stock, securities, and commodity futures contracts; income from certain *personal service contracts;* compensation for the use of corporate property by a 25-percent-or-more *shareholder; rents,* if they constitute less than half of *gross income;* and certain *related person factoring income.* See *foreign personal holding company; foreign personal holding company tax; related person, controlled foreign corporation.*

foreign personal holding company income, subpart F a modified form of *foreign personal holding company income* used for *subpart F purposes.* It consists of dividends; interest, including certain *related person factoring* income and "income equivalent to interest"; *rents; royalties;* and net *gains* from the sales of property, especially stocks, bonds, and other property that produced dividends, interest, rents, and royalties that were FPHC income. Foreign personal holding company income, as

defined for *subpart F* purposes, is a component of *foreign base company income* (§954(a)), which is in turn a form of *subpart F income,* which is taxed to *United States shareholders* as it is earned, regardless of whether it is actually distributed. §952(a)(2). Note that the regular foreign personal holding company rules control if they overlap. §951(d). See *controlled foreign corporation; related person, controlled foreign corporation; subpart F income.*

foreign personal holding company tax a federal tax imposed on the American *shareholders* of a *foreign personal holding company* by §551. The base on which the tax falls is *undistributed foreign personal holding company income.* See Reg. §1.551-2. The tax is calculated by adding such income to the shareholders' *gross income.*

foreign person, foreign corporate reporting a *person* who is not a *United States person,* i.e., not a *citizen* or *resident,* a *United States partnership* or *corporation,* or an *estate* or *trust* whose foreign income is subject to United States tax. §§6038A(c); 6038C(e).

foreign person, UNICAP any *qualified business unit* of a *foreign person,* as defined in Reg. §1.989(a)-1T, or any *foreign branch* of a *United States person,* provided the branch constitutes a separate qualified business unit. Notice 88-104, 1988-38 I.R.B. 20. The term is used for purposes of identifying people who can use the simplified *uniform capitalization rules* applicable to foreigners.

foreign plan, qualified see *qualified foreign plan.*

foreign presence test an objective standard used to determine if a *taxpayer* is a *qualified individual* under §911. To satisfy the test, the *citizen of the United States,* in a period of 12 consecutive months, must be present in one or more foreign countries during at least 330 days. §911(d)(1)(B). United States citizens who satisfy the test may elect to exclude a limited amount of *foreign earned income* and to *exclude* or *deduct* a limited amount of *foreign housing costs.* §911(a) and (b). Compare the *foreign residence test,* which is subjective in nature.

foreign property see *property predominately used outside the United States.*

foreign regulated investment company a *regulated investment company* organized outside the *United States* and registered under the Investment Company Act of 1940. Such a company can elect the benefits of §1247 under which, if major current *distributions* are made, then *gains* on *sales* of *stock* are not reclassified as *ordinary income.* Reg. §1.1247-1(b).

foreign residence test a subjective standard used to determine if a *citizen of the United States* is a *qualified individual* under §911. To establish foreign residence, a citizen of the United States must show that he or she has been a *bona fide resident* of one or more foreign countries for a uninterrupted period, which includes an entire *taxable year*. §911(d)(1)(A). Factors used to determine foreign residency include the existence of a foreign bank account, local contracts, type of foreign visa held, and so on. Qualified individuals living abroad may exclude a limited amount of *foreign earned income* and partially *exclude* or deduct *foreign housing costs*. §911(a) and (b). Contrast this to the *foreign presence test*, which is objective in nature. The standards used to determine residence are the same as those used to determine residence on an alien individual in the United States. Reg. §1.911-2(c). See *resident alien*.

foreign sales corporation a type of *foreign corporation* designed for export promotion purposes. It is the successor of the *DISC*. If eight requirements of §922 are met and an election is made in timely fashion under §927(f), then a portion of the FSC's *foreign trade income* will be tax-exempt at the corporate level provided it is derived from the *foreign presence and economic activity* of the FSC. To be eligible, the FSC must (1) be (a) created under the laws of either a *foreign* country which is either a party to a bilateral or multilateral agreement or an income *tax treaty* partner of the United States for the exchange of information, or (b) a *possession of the United States*; (2) have not over 25 *shareholders* at any time in the *taxable year*; (3) have no outstanding preferred stock during the tax year; (4) maintain an office with permanent books and records outside the *United States* or in a *possession*; (5) have at least one *nonresident alien* director; (6) at no time during the taxable year be a member of a *controlled group* of which an interest charge DISC is a member at any time during the tax year (§922(a)(1)); (7) have a tax year that conforms to the tax year of the shareholders or group of shareholders who have the highest percentage of voting power (§441(h)); and (8) have shareholders who each must consent to the election to be an FSC or a small FSC (§927(f)(91)(B), Reg. 927(f)-1). For the meaning of the term "controlled group," see *controlled group of corporations, graduated taxes, and other benefits*.

foreign separate limitation loss recapture see *recapture, foreign losses*.

foreign service allowances see *foreign areas allowances*.

foreign shipping income foreign source income from the operation of ships or aircraft documented or registered under the laws of a foreign country. This income may be *excluded* from *gross income* of a *nonresident alien* or *foreign corporation* if the laws of the foreign country where the ship or aircraft is documented or registered provides an *equivalent exemption* for the benefit of *United States persons*. §§872(b), 883(a); Reg. §§1.872-2, 1.883-1(a)(2).

foreign source capital gain net income *capital gain net income* from sources without the *United States,* or *capital gain net income,* whichever is less. §904(b)(3)(A). One effect is to assume that *gains,* perhaps manipulatively *realized* overseas, are held to overall *net capital gains*. Section 904(b)(3)(C) also limits *taxpayers'* abilities to realize gains from certain *sales of personal property* in foreign jurisdictions with especially low taxes (so as to drive up the numerator of the limitation of the *foreign tax credit*) by treating certain gains as United States source gains. Corporate taxpayers' capital gains are limited to foreign source capital gain net income, diminished by a fraction of *foreign source net capital gains* known as the *rate differential portion*. §904(b)(2)(B)(i). See *foreign tax credit limitation*.

foreign source earned income see *earned income, foreign earned income*.

foreign source income a term commonly used instead of the more cumbersome term *gross income from sources without the United States*. The reason for the *Code's* verbosity is to encompass, for example, shipping income from beyond the three-mile limit—income not attributable to any foreign source, but still outside the United States. The principles for sorting United States source from foreign source income are extensive and often confusing. See §§861–865. *Tax treaties* sometimes prescribe special source rules. See *source rules*.

foreign source net capital gain *net capital gain* from sources without the *United States,* or net capital gain, whichever is smaller. §904(b)(3)(B). The term is significant in calculating limitations of *foreign tax credits*. §904(b).

foreign subsidiary a *foreign corporation* controlled by a *corporation* formed in a different country (e.g., a United States subsidiary of a United Kingdom company).

foreign tax credit a *credit* allowed for *foreign income, war profits,* and *excess profits* and "*in lieu of*" taxes imposed by *possessions of the United States* and foreign countries, which can be applied against *United States income taxes* subject to the limitations of §904. The credit is designed to ease the burden of double taxation that occurs when both the United States and foreign countries tax income from foreign sources. §901. However, it cannot offset United States tax on United States source income. §904. See *deemed paid foreign tax credit; foreign corporation's post-1986 foreign income taxes; foreign income tax, subchapter S corporations; foreign income, war profits and excess profits taxes; foreign tax credit limitation; functional currency; section 904(d)(1) "basket"; separate foreign levy*.

foreign tax credit carryover and carryback provisions granting *taxpayers* the right to carry the *foreign tax credit limitation* back two years and forward five years. See §904; Reg. §1.904-2. The purpose is to reduce the hardships of the limitation of such credits, since they represent actual costs of doing business. See §907(f) for a special limitation relating to *oil and gas extraction taxes.*

foreign tax credit limitation   a limitation, often referred to as the overall limitation, to the effect that the amount of credit for *foreign income, war profits, and excess profits and "in lieu of" taxes* may neither exceed the amount of foreign taxes paid or accrued, nor, in effect, what the *federal income tax* would be on that income (the *tentative tax*) if earned in the United States. This limitation may be expressed by the following formula:

$$\text{United States tax before credit} \times \frac{\text{taxable income from all foreign sources}}{\text{total taxable income}}$$

Any foreign tax so disallowed may be carried back two years and carried forward five years. §904. Reg. §1.904-2 describes the *carryover* and *carryback* rules. See *section 904(d)(1) "basket."*

foreign tax deduction   a *deduction* allowed for foreign taxes *paid or accrued,* available in lieu of the *foreign tax credit.* §164(a).

foreign tax haven   see *tax haven.*

foreign trade income, FSC   the *gross income* of a *foreign sales corporation* attributable to *foreign trading gross receipts.* §923(b). It includes both the profits earned by the FSC itself from exports, and commissions earned by the FSC from products or services exported by others. A portion of foreign trade income is treated as *exempt foreign trade income* and is tax-exempt. The remainder is nonexempt income treated as *taxable foreign source income.*

foreign trade zones   areas exempted from customs duties, such as the New York Foreign Trade Zone. Such exemptions are granted by the federal government.

foreign trading gross receipts, FSC   the gross receipts of an FSC attributable to transactions involving certain goods and services, analogous to the *qualified gross receipts* of the now-superseded *DISC.* These receipts include those from (1) sale or lease of export property for use outside the *United States*; (2) services related or subsidiary to the sale or lease of export property; (3) certain engineering or architectural services; and (4) export management services. §924(a). For these items to be classified as foreign trading gross receipts, the FSC must also meet *foreign management* and *foreign economic process* requirements. If all these requirements are met, then a portion of such receipts is considered *exempt foreign trade income* and is exempt from *federal income taxes.*

foreign travel   for purposes of §274's limitations on *travel expenses,* the term refers to costs allocable to periods after leaving the last point in the *United States.* For example, if Mrs. X leaves New York on a business trip to Tokyo, the entire New York–Tokyo flight is foreign travel. If, however, the plane stopped over in San Francisco, then only the San Francisco–Tokyo leg is foreign travel. The *regulations* view that last point in the United States in the case of public transportation as the last point of embarkation; the last point in the United States for an automobile is the United States border; the last point for a private aircraft appears to be the last airport actually used. §274(c); Reg. §1.274-4(e).

forfeiture   the loss of *unvested benefits* under *pension* and *profit-sharing plans.* When unvested benefits are lost through forfeiture (e.g., because the *participant* is terminated), depending on the kind of plan involved, the forfeitures may be allocated to other *participants'* accounts, refunded to the *employer,* or used to reduce later employer contributions. §401(a)(8); Reg. §§1.401-2(b)(1), -4(a)(1)(iii), and -7.

forfeiture case   a tax case involving commercial or financial transactions subject to reporting requirements, noncompliance with which results in forfeiture of the property. See §§6050 and 7302 and Title 18 §§981, and 1956-1967 and Title 31 §§5313 and 5324. These cases are directed at money laundering and drug trafficking.

Form 706   the *estate tax* form.

Form 709   the *federal gift* form.

Form 851   the common parent corporation, when filing a consolidated return, must attach Form 851, Affiliations Schedule. See *Form 1122.*

Form 866   see *closing agreement.*

Form 870   a form (Waiver of Restriction on Assessment and Collection of Deficiency in Tax and Acceptance of Overassessments) that, when signed by the *taxpayer,* allows the *IRS* to assess a proposed *deficiency* without the necessity of issuing a statutory *notice of deficiency* (90-day letter), as a result of which the taxpayer must pay the deficiency and may not file a *petition* in the *Tax Court.* See §6213(d).

Form 870AD   see *offer of waiver of restrictions on assessments and collections.*

Form 872   a form that, when signed by the *taxpayer,* extends the period of time during which the *IRS* can make an *assessment* or *collection of taxes*; that is, it extends the applicable *statute of limitations.* See §6501(c)(4). The variant Form 872-A is used in the *Appeals Division.* See *waiver of statute of limitations.*

Form 906   see *closing agreement.*

Form 966 part of the general liquidation process. Section 6043(a) requires a corporation to file Form 966 (Information Return under Section 6043) *within 30 days after the adoption of any resolution or plan* calling for the liquidation or dissolution of the corporation. Form 966 must be filed by the liquidating corporation whether the shareholders realized gain or not. See *section 331 liquidation; section 332 liquidation; section 338 acquisition.*

Form 990 the annual report for *exempt organizations* (other than *churches*). See §6033.

Form 990-PF an annual information return applicable to *private foundations* required to be filed with the *IRS* and a relevant state official, and available in the foundation's principal office for public inspection. The form requires information pertaining to *private nonoperating* and *operating foundations* both by categories of expense and types of administrative expenses (including *grant administrative expenses*). §6033(a). The foundation must also publish a notice of availability of this form (with the telephone number of the foundation's principal office) in a general-circulation newspaper in the county of the office.

Form 1040 the general *individual income tax return.*

Form 1040A all individuals use Form 1040, unless they are eligible and choose to use short form (1040A or 1040EZ). Individuals may use Form 1040A if all of their income is from wages, tips, unemployment insurance, interest, and dividends, and if they do not itemize. Taxable income must be under $50,000. Because Form 1040A (and 1040EZ) cannot be filed by taxpayers with taxable income of $50,000 or more, tax tables for use with these forms end at taxable income of $50,000.

Form 1040ES the form prescribed for *individuals* who must make estimated tax payments. Each payment voucher has a date when the voucher is due for the calendar year.

Form 1040EZ a simplified *federal income tax return* for *single persons* with no *dependents*. Because Form 1040EZ (and Form 1040A) cannot be filed by taxpayers with taxable income of $50,000 or more, tax tables for use with these forms end at taxable income of $50,000.

Form 1040X amended returns can be used to correct errors on filed returns. For this purpose, *individuals must use Form 1040X.* Other taxpayers may use a regular return. Reg. §301.6402-3(a).

Form 1041 the general *fiduciary income tax return.*

Form 1065 the *partnership tax return.*

Form 1099 the form used by the payor of income items such as *rents, royalties, dividends,* and other *non-wage* amounts. The form has various suffices (e.g., Form 1099-Div for dividends).

Form 1120 the general corporate *income tax return.*

Form 1120A the short form corporate tax return that may be filed if (1) gross receipts or sales do not exceed $500,000; (2) total assets do not exceed $500,000; (3) the corporation is not involved in a dissolution or liquidation; (4) the corporation is not a member of a controlled group under §§1561 and 1563; (5) the corporation does not file a consolidated return; (6) the corporation does not have ownership in a foreign corporation; and (7) the corporation does not have foreign owners who directly or indirectly own 50 percent or more of its stock.

Form 1120S the *S corporation income tax return.*

Form 1120X amended returns can be used to correct errors on filed returns. For this purpose, *corporations must use Form 1120X.* Other taxpayers may use a regular return. Reg. §301.6402-3(a).

Form 1122 a form signed by an officer of a subsidiary *corporation* that states that the subsidiary consents to be included in the filing of a *consolidated return.* Reg. §1.1502-75(h)(2). Form 1122 must be filed for each subsidiary and included in the initial *consolidated return* for the return to be valid. Reg. §1.1502-75(h)(2).

Form 2210 the form prescribed for *individual taxpayers* to report penalties for *underpayment of estimated taxes.* Reg. §1.6654-1(b). If an exception to estimated tax applies, then the taxpayer can use Form 2210 to compute any diminution in the penalty.

Form 2220 the form prescribed for corporate *taxpayers* to report penalties for *underpayment of estimated taxes.* Reg. §1.6655-1(b). If an exception to estimated tax does apply, then the taxpayer can use Form 2220 to compute any diminution in the penalty.

Form 2553 the form required in order for a small business to make a valid S corporation election. The election must be filed in a timely manner and all of the corporation's shareholders must consent to the election. §1362(a)(2).

Form W-2 The form used by the payor of *wages* and salaries to report wage and *withholding* information to both the *IRS* and the *employee.* Form W-2P is used to report pension for *annuity* income.

Form W-4 the *employee withholding exemption* certificate.

Form W-5 see *earned income eligibility certificate.*

formal document request any request to produce any *foreign-based documentation.* Such a request is made by registered or certified mail to the *taxpayer* after the normal request procedures fail. It must set forth: (1) the time and place to produce the documentation; (2) a statement of the reason why any documentation already produced is insufficient; (3) a description of the documentation that is sought; and (4) the consequences of taxpayer's failure to satisfy the request. §982(c)(1). Such a request is supposed to follow the normal request procedures.

former DISC a *domestic international sales corporation* (DISC) that has lost its status as such. §992(a)(3); Reg. §1.992-1(h). Upon the *corporation's* losing DISC status, its accumulated tax-deferred income is gradually deemed *distributed* to its *shareholders* in equal annual installments, numbering twice the number of immediately preceding qualifying years but not exceeding 10. For purposes of subsequent distributions, both the former DISC and its shareholders continue to be subject to the DISC rules. §§995(a), 996(a) and (b). A former DISC can reelect DISC status. §992(b); Reg. §1.992-1(e)(4). The *Domestic International Sales Corporation* (DISC) generally has been replaced by a system of foreign sales corporations (FSCs).

former passive activity an *activity* that was a *passive activity* in some former *taxable year* but not in the current taxable year. §469(f)(3). Previously suspended *losses* and *credits* from such activities remain suspended and continue to be deemed *passive activity losses* or *passive activity credits,* but they can continue to be used against net income (other than *portfolio income*) from the former passive activity. This avoids discouraging *taxpayers* from *material participation* in activities. §469(f)(1)(A). See *passive loss rules.*

form versus substance see *substance over form doctrine.*

forward triangular merger a three-party *Type A reorganization* cast as a *merger,* whereby the transferee *corporation* (acquiring subsidiary) receives *substantially all of the properties* of the transferor corporation (target) in exchange for the *stock* of its controlling corporation (parent), and the target merges into the subsidiary. Provided the merger would have qualified as a Type A reorganization had it been a merger into the parent corporation, i.e., there is *continuity of proprietary interest* and no subsidiary stock is used in the transaction, the merger can qualify as a tax-free reorganization. §368(a)(2)(D); Reg. §1.368-2(a)(2) and -2(b). The forward triangular merger rules are extended to *Type G reorganizations.* §368(a)(2)(D).

foster care payments see *qualified foster care payments.*

foster child a child in the care of a person or persons, other than the parents or adoptive parents of the child, who care for the child as if their own. The circumstances under which a foster child becomes a *member of*

the household are irrelevant. §152(b)(2); Reg. §1.152-2(c)(4). A foster child who is a member of the household for the entire *taxable year* can qualify as a *dependent* and can also qualify a *taxpayer* for *head of household* rates. §§151, 2(b). See also Reg. §1.43-1(c)(ii) *(earned income credit* uses the same definition).

foundation manager an officer, director, or *trustee* of a *private foundation,* or any other *individual* with similar powers or responsibilities, and any *employee* of a foundation with authority or responsibility with respect to any act or failure to act. §4946(b). Foundation managers are subject to *excise taxes* for improper conduct, such as *self-dealing, speculative investments,* or making *taxable expenditures.* §4940.

foundation, private see *private foundation.*

fourth-quarter exception a nickname for §6654(h), which provides that if an *individual* files his *tax returns* on or by January 31 and pays in full, there can be no penalty for underpayment of the fourth *required installment.* See *penalty, underpayment of estimated tax by individuals.*

fractional interest rule, natural resources a rule to the effect that a *carrying party* in a *farm-out* can deduct *intangible drilling and development costs* (IDCs). §1.612-4. For example, if L, a land-owner, farms out a property for O, an operator, to exploit by drilling a well on the property and if the parties agree that O will get an undivided 40 percent interest in the property, then O has a 40 percent fractional share and can generally deduct only 40 percent of the IDCs. This rule is modified by the *payout concept,* which allows 100 percent of the IDCs to O under certain circumstances. See *complete payout period, natural resources.*

fractional rule, accrued benefits a rule relating to *defined benefit plans,* the generality of which is that other *accrued benefits* to which a *participant* is entitled upon separation from service must be at least the benefit available at *normal retirement age,* times the participant's years of participation before such separation, divided by the years of participation if the participant had worked until *normal retirement age.* §411(b)(1)(C). This rule is one of three alternate minimums, only one of which need be satisfied in order for a plan to be deemed a *qualified plan* with respect to this issue. §411(a).

franchise for purposes of the §1253 10-year *amortization,* all public or business franchises, except those specifically excluded, that satisfy the three elements of §1253(b)(1): (1) an agreement (2) which gives one of the parties the right to distribute, sell, or provide goods, services, or facilities (3) within a specified area. Franchise terminations enjoy favored tax treatment in the form of *capital gains.*

franchised corporation a *corporation* that is otherwise a member of either a *brother-sister* or *parent-subsidiary controlled group* in which for more than one-half of the days of the *taxable year* preceding December 31, the *stock* of the corporation was under an agreement to be sold to one of its *employees* under a plan to eliminate the stock ownership of the parent or common owner. The selling price must have been reasonable and paid out of a portion of the employee's share of profits, and the employee must have owned more than 10 percent of the total value of all classes of stock. More than 50 percent of the *inventory* of the corporation must have been acquired from other members of the *controlled group of corporations*. §1563(f)(4). A franchised corporation is excluded from the controlled group for purposes of applying the limitations applicable to a controlled group on *graduated taxes* and *other benefits*. §§1563(f)(4), 1561(a).

franchise taxes taxes imposed on the privilege of carrying on a business in corporate form. Numerous states impose franchise taxes which are measured by the corporation's income (i.e., disguised income taxes).

fraternal benefit societies societies, orders, or associations that (1) *operate under the lodge system,* or for the exclusive benefit of members of a society, which itself operates under the lodge system, and provides life, sick, accident, or other benefits to members or their dependents; or (2) operate under the lodge system, devoting their *net earnings* exclusively to religious, charitable, scientific, literary, educational, and fraternal purposes without providing life, sick, accident, or other benefits. §501(c)(8) and (c)(10). The Elks Club could be an example. Such organizations qualify for tax-exempt status, but contributions to them are *deductible* only to the extent used for certain *charitable* and other purposes. §170(c)(4).

fraud *taxpayer* behavior that may attract civil or criminal liabilities. *Civil fraud* may result in a penalty of 75 percent of the part of the underpayment attributable to fraud. §6663(b). *Criminal fraud* may result in fines, imprisonment, or both. §§7201–7207. Civil and criminal fraud both require an intent to evade tax, not mere negligence, and criminal fraud requires the further showing of *willfulness*. The burden is on the government to prove such fraud. See *penalty, civil fraud.*

fraud penalty see *penalty, civil fraud.*

fraudulent conveyances an improper transfer of property undertaken by debtors in order to place their property beyond the reach of creditors. State law defines whether a transfer is fraudulent. If so, creditors, including the *IRS* in the course of collecting taxes, may enforce liens against such property in the hands of the transferee (the fraudulent transferee). Fraudulent conveyances are said to create a trust fund for the creditors. See *transferee liability.*

fraudulent return see *false or fraudulent return.*

Freddie Mac a nickname for the Federal National Mortgage Association.

free bargain concept a limited relief provision relating to disputes over the extent to which compensation paid is unreasonable in amount and therefore nondeductible. The notion is that if the recipient and the payor freely entered into an *arm's length* agreement to provide compensation based on future economic contingencies (e.g., a fixed percentage of gross revenues), then the resulting compensation will generally be allowed to stand. Reg. §1.162-7(b). Dominance of the payor by the payee will negate a finding of a free bargain. See *unreasonable compensation.*

Freedom of Information Act a disclosure statute applicable to federal agencies, the purpose of which is to ensure reasonable public access to information in government hands. 5 U.S.C. §552 (1976). Generally, the statute divides agency information into three categories and outlines the means for making each available: (1) material of a general, informative nature must be published in the *Federal Register*; (2) opinions, orders, and other materials of specific nature and public importance must be made available at regional locations for public inspection and copying, unless they are promptly published and offered for sale, with identifying information deleted to avoid invasions of the personal privacy of *individuals* involved, and a written justification for the deletion must accompany the edited document; and (3) any other materials not exempt from disclosure that are in the possession or control of the agency must be made available to any individual who makes a reasonably descriptive *Freedom of Information Act request*. See Reg. §601.701. The act specifically exempts certain information from disclosure, including certain privileged or confidential information, certain inter- or intraagency correspondence, certain *investigatory records* compiled for law enforcement purposes, and information exempted by other statutes (e.g., §6103).

Freedom of Information Act request a request for disclosure of specific information pursuant to the *Freedom of Information Act,* 5 U.S.C. §552 (1976). In the case of requests on the *IRS,* a request must be in writing, signed by the party making the request, and addressed and mailed or hand-delivered to the office of the appropriate IRS officer (as listed in Reg. §601.702(g)) and must contain the following: (1) a statement that the request is made pursuant to the Freedom of Information Act; (2) a description of the records in reasonably sufficient detail to enable IRS *employees* familiar with the subject area of the request to locate the records without undue difficulty; (3) sufficient identification and statement of the requester's right to the disclosure; (4) the address where the requesting party may be contacted; (5) a statement as to whether the requester wishes to inspect the records or wants a copy made and furnished without first inspecting them; and (6) a firm agreement to pay the appropriate fees, as determined under Reg. §607.702(f), or justification for reduction and waiver of fees, or a request for an estimate of the fees involved. The requirements are further explained in Reg. §601.702(c). In practice most requests are easily made, through use of a preprinted IRS form.

free transferability of interests   the corporate characteristic of freely being able to transfer ownership interests in an *entity* without dissolving the entity. Reg. §301.7701-2(e)(1) provides that an *organization* has the characteristic of free transferability of interests if each of its members or those members owning substantially all of the interests in the organization have the power, without the consent of other members, to substitute for themselves in the same organization a person who is not a member of the organization. In order for this power of substitution to exist in the corporate sense, the member must be able, without the consent of other members, to confer upon the substitute all the attributes of her or his interest in the organization. Thus, the characteristic of free transferability of interests does not exist in a case in which each member can, without the consent of other members, assign only the right to share in profits but not in the management of the organization. Rights of first refusal, however, modify, but do not eliminate, the characteristic. Reg. §301.7701-2(e)(2) (relating to *limited partnership/association* distinctions).

free well farm-out   a *farm-out agreement* under which the *farmee* agrees to pay a disproportionate share of the costs of one or more wells, but production revenues are shared in accordance with their respective shares of the *working interests*. The tax benefits to the farmee are limited by the *fractional interest rule*. See *fractional interest rule, natural resources*.

freight-in   transportation and other charges incurred in acquiring goods. Such charges are included in *inventory* cost. Reg. §1.471-3.

fresh start rule, life insurance companies   a special relief provision granted by §211(b) of the *Tax Reform Act of 1984,* pursuant to which charges in calculating *reserves* forced by the new law are not treated as a change in method of computing reserves, and which result in no *gain* or *loss.* The 1986 Act contains changes which clarify the 1984 provisions concerning reserves previously denied a fresh start. See §216(b)(1), (b)(3)(A), and (b)(3)(C) of the Tax Reform Act of 1984.

fringe benefits   a term used to describe noncash benefits conferred on *employees,* many of which are either statutorily excluded (e.g., *group-term life insurance*) or disregarded as a *condition of employment.* §132. The Act set forth six categories of benefits which, if granted to an employee, are *deductible* by the *employer* and nontaxable to the employee: (1) *no additional cost services;* (2) *qualified employee discounts;* (3) *working condition fringe benefits;* (4) *de minimis fringe benefits;* (5) *athletic facilities;* and (6) *qualified tuition reduction.* The value of *outplacement services* is generally excluded from gross income unless the services are offered in lieu of severance pay. Fringe benefits are often confined by the *anti-discrimination* rules and the need for an *employer.* Effective for years after 1992, the CNEPA of 1992 (Pub. L 102-486) limits the exclusion for employer-provided parking to $60 a month. Any excess payment above this amount must be included in income. §1911.

frivolous return   see *penalty, frivolous return.*

frivolous return controversy   a reference to a courtroom controversy under §6703(c) in which the *taxpayer* seeks to prevent the imposition of penalties under §§6700 (promoting *abusive tax shelters*), 6701 (aiding and abetting an understatement of tax), or filing a *frivolous return.* See *penalty, frivolous return.*

frontloading   a term used to describe a *defined benefit plan* that provides the *employee* with an *accrued benefit* equal to the full retirement benefit after only one year of *participation* in the plan, or some other fast rate of accrual of benefits. Such an excessive rate of accrual is freely allowed; however, it is costly to the *employer.* It is also used in connection with *alimony* or *separate maintenance payments.*

frontloading of alimony   a reference to major *alimony* or *separate maintenance* payments in the early years following divorce or separation. As a safeguard against a property settlement being disguised as alimony, special rules apply to post-1986 agreements if payments in the first and second year exceed $15,000. If the change in the amount of the payments exceeds statutory limits, *alimony recapture* results to the extent of excess alimony payments. In the *third year,* the payor must include the excess alimony payments for the first and second years in gross income, and the payee is allowed a deduction for these excess alimony payments. § 71(f). The recapture formula for the first post-separation year is as follows:

$$\text{Excess payment} = \text{alimony paid in year 1} - \left[\$15,000 + \frac{\left(\begin{array}{ccc}\text{alimony} & \text{excess} & \text{alimony}\\ \text{paid in} & - \text{ payments} & + \text{ paid in}\\ \text{2nd year} & \text{in 2nd year} & \text{3rd year}\end{array}\right)}{2}\right]$$

To determine the excess payments in the first year, one has to determine the excess payments in the second year. The excess payments in the second year are the excess (if any) of the amount of alimony paid during the second year over the sum of the amount of alimony paid in the third year plus $15,000.

$$
\begin{array}{c}
\text{Excess} \\
\text{payments} \\
\text{in year 2}
\end{array}
=
\begin{array}{c}
\text{alimony} \\
\text{paid in} \\
\text{2nd year}
\end{array}
-
\left(
\begin{array}{c}
\text{alimony} \\
\text{paid in} \\
\text{3rd year}
\end{array}
- \$15,000
\right)
$$

After the excess payments for both the first and second post-separation years have been determined, the results are summed to determine the amount that must be recaptured in the third post-separation year. The recapture rules do not apply to decrees for support or maintenance. §71(f)(5)(B).

fuels, energy investment credit   materials that produce usable heat from combustion. Reg. §1.48-9(c)(5)(ii). Electricity and waste heat are not fuels. Reg. §1.48-9(c)(3)(iii).

fuels from nonconventional sources   a 10 percent business energy credit is allowed for qualified solar and geothermal property placed in service before July 1, 1992. §48. The CNEPA of 1992 (Pub. L. 102-486) permanently extends these credits retroactive to property placed in service after June 30, 1992. §1916. See *credit for producing fuels from nonconventional sources.*

full absorption accounting   a *method of accounting* used by manufacturers in valuing *inventories,* under which *direct* and *indirect production costs* are included in inventory by some appropriate method (e.g., the *manufacturing burden rate* or the *standard cost method*). The practice is mandatory for *federal income tax* purposes. Reg. §1.471-11. See §263A. See also Rev. Rul. 81-272, 1981-2 C.B. 116, for a description of the types of supply, labor, and incidental expenses that must be reported as direct production costs. See *manufacturing burden rate method.*

full and adequate consideration in money or money's worth   consideration that is the full equivalent of the monetary value of property received. If property is transferred for less than an adequate and full consideration in money or money's worth, there is ordinarily a *gift* to the extent that the value of the property is greater than the value of the consideration received. The result is the possible imposition of a *federal gift tax.* Reg. §25.2512-8.

full day   twenty-four consecutive hours, beginning at midnight. Full days are counted to determine whether a *citizen of the United States* is physically present overseas long enough to qualify for the exclusion of *foreign earned income* granted by §911. See Reg. §1.913-2 (510-day test; elliptical explanation.) See *physical presence test.*

full funding limitation, qualified pension plans   an alternate funding standard that, if satisfied, assures that

the *minimum funding standards* of §412, applicable to *qualified pension plans,* will be satisfied. §412(c)(6) and (7).

full payment rule, refund suit   the requirement that *assessed deficiencies* be paid in full in order for a *taxpayer* to be allowed to bring a *refund suit.* Note that *divisible taxes* (those where *assessments* can be divided into separate portions or transactions) can be the basis for selective refund suits.

full-time life insurance salesman   a class of *statutory employee* for *FICA* purposes. The term contemplates an insurance salesman whose exclusive business activity (aside from occasionally or incidentally placing other insurance) is soliciting life insurance, annuities, or both, for one insurance company. §3121 (d)(3)(B). Reg. §31.3121(d)-1. Rev. Rul. 59-103, 1959-1 C.B. 259.

full-time salesman   an *employee* devoting full time in his or her employment to selling as opposed to providing service and delivery. Reimbursements of employment-related expenses by an employer or by a third party are generally included in the employee's gross income. Therefore, the law provides that the employee may deduct the related expenses in determining adjusted gross income up to the amount of the reimbursement, provided that the employee has made an *adequate accounting to the employer* and the employee does not have the right to retain any amount in excess of the substantiated expenses. §62(c).

full-time student   see *student, dependency deduction, and child and dependent care credit.*

full-time traveling or city salesman   a class of *statutory employees* for *FICA* purposes. The term contemplates a salesman who works exclusively for one principal, regardless of how many hours; hence a salesman who deals with many product lines from different companies is not an employee under this standard. Reg. §31.3121(d)-1.

functional allocation   a sharing arrangement common in the oil and gas industry in which investment *partners* are typically allocated *current expenses,* while the sponsor/operator is allocated *nondeductible* costs. The principal, currently *deductible expenses* are *intangible drilling and development costs.*

functional currency   The currency by which all *federal income tax* determinations must be made for certain foreign business operations. It is usually the currency in which most of the businesses' activities are conducted. §985(b)(1)(C)(ii). For most *taxpayers* the dollar will be their functional currency, the only exceptions being for *qualified business units* which may use the currency of the economic environment in which they conduct a significant part of their activities. All foreign currency dealings must be translated into the taxpayer's functional currency on a transaction-by-transaction basis. It must be used in determining a *foreign corporation's post-1986 undistributed earnings* and the numerator for the §902 fraction for purposes of calculating the *deemed paid foreign tax credit*. §986(a)(1) and Notice 87-54, 1987-31 I.R.B. 21. See *deemed paid foreign tax credit; foreign corporation's post-1986 foreign income taxes; foreign income, war profits and excess profits taxes; foreign tax credit; foreign tax credit limitation; functional currency; section 988 transaction.*

functionally related business, operating foundations a *trade or business* that (1) is not an *unrelated trade or business,* or (2) is an activity that is part of a larger overall group of activities related to an organization's *exempt purpose.* §4942(j)(5). See *operating foundation.*

functionally unrelated distribution a characterization applied to transfers of property to *shareholders* that purport to be made in the context of a *corporate reorganization,* which are instead classified as mere current *distributions* on the theory that they are not genuinely bound up with the reorganization. It is possible to characterize a purported *recapitalization (Type E reorganization)* involving a swap of *stock* for bonds as a mere *dividend* from a continuing corporation.

functional use test, involuntary conversions an *IRS* test requiring that replacement property be applied in a manner closely similar to that of the replaced property, such as a slide rule replaced with a computer, in order for the owner-user to qualify for deferral of *gains* from an *involuntary conversion* (i.e., the excess of compensation over the *adjusted basis* of the converted property) under §1033. Owner-lessors of *real property* only need to satisfy the *like-kind property* standard of §1031. §1033(g).

fundamentally inconsistent event an event that, had it occurred in the same *taxable year,* would have precluded a *deduction* (e.g., a distribution in *liquidation* of towels that were previously written off by a laundry corporation). Such events can cause taxation under the *tax benefit rule* (e.g., because the towels have remaining value) even though there is no actual recovery of value. Presumably other tax benefits, such as *credits,* are subject to the fundamentally inconsistent event rule.

funded deferred compensation *nonqualified deferred compensation* arrangements that have the feature of providing some secured benefit for the payee, such as placements in escrow or funding with an *annuity contract* in the name of the payee. Such arrangements result in current taxation unless they are nontransferable, and they are subject to a *substantial risk of forfeiture.* Rev. Rul. 60-31, 1960-1 C.B. 174.

funded insurance trust a *trust* used to hold an insurance policy, usually on the life of the *grantor* to which money has been transferred to pay future premiums.

funded nonqualified plan see *funded deferred compensation.*

funded welfare benefit plan see *welfare benefit plan.*

funding period, black lung benefit trusts see *certain future obligations.*

funding, qualified plans generally, the method by which obligations of a *qualified plan* are met. Section 412 establishes ornate *minimum funding standards* for *qualified pension plans* and a backstop in the form of the *Pension Benefit Guaranty Corporation* to assure adequacy of funding, the violation of which is penalized by *excise taxes* on *accumulated funding deficiencies.* The result is a strong impetus to make contributions adequate to meet plan liabilities.

funeral expenses for purposes of filing the estate tax return (Form 706), amounts properly allowable as funeral costs out of property subject to claims as determined under local law. Reg. §20.2053-2. Reg. §20.2053-1(c).

futures contract a contract that calls for the *sale* and delivery of property at a fixed price at some future date. See *commodity futures contract.*

G

G.C.M. an abbreviation for *General Counsel's Memorandum.*

GLSO an acronym for a *group legal care services organization.*

GMbH a German organization comparable to a *limited partnership,* ruled a *corporation.* P.L.R. 8114095 (Apr. 15, 1981).

GNP implicit price deflator the first revision of the implicit price deflator for the gross national product as computed and published by the Secretary of Commerce. Not later than April 1 of any *calendar year* the *IRS* must publish the inflation adjustment factor for the preceding calendar year. §43(b)(3)(B).

gain chargeback a provision in a *partnership agreement* pursuant to which inter*partner* disparities between final *distributions* from the partnership in its *liquidation* and their *capital account* balances are eliminated by retroactive adjustments to partnership *gains* or *losses.* Making such adjustments may validate the *allocation* provisions of the partnership by assuring that they have *substantial economic effect.* The most common case involves adjusting *gains* on *sales* of *real estate* held by partnerships.

gain corporation any *corporation* with *net unrealized built-in gain.* §384(c)(8). Section 384 makes it unattractive to combine gain corporations with corporations having preacquisition losses. See *preacquisition loss limits.*

gain or loss generally, the difference between a *taxpayer's amount realized* on the *disposition* of property less the taxpayer's *adjusted basis* in the property. A positive result is a *gain,* and a negative result is a *loss.* §1001(a).

gain recognition agreement an agreement between the *IRS* and a *taxpayer* pursuant to which the taxpayer consents to *recognize gain* on the later *disposition* of *stock* transferred out of the *United States* on a nontaxable basis. See Notice 87-85, 1987-2 C.B. 395. No such agreement is generally required as to assets used in an *active business* as described in §355(b). See *outbound transfers.*

gambling losses see *wagering.*

gas from geopressured brine, Devonian shale, coal seams, or a tight formation, credit for fuels from

nonconventional sources gas produced from geopressured brine, Devonian shale, coal seams, or a tight formation, as determined by §503 of the National Gas Policy Act of 1978. Gas produced from a tight formation includes only gas the price of which is regulated by the United States, and gas for which the maximum lawful price applicable under the Natural Gas Policy Act of 1978 is not less than 150 percent of the then-applicable price under former §103 of that act. §29(c)(2). Such gas may qualify for the *credit for producing fuels from nonconventional sources.*

"gas guzzler" tax an *excise tax* on the manufacturer of inefficient automobiles. See §4064. Section 1016(d) forces a reduction in *basis* of such autos.

gasohol later-blending rule a retailer's blending of gasohol with gasoline in a tank after production of gasohol which does not attract a tax under §4081(b) if the percentage of alcohol is not under 10 percent. The CNEPA of 1992 (Pub. L. 102-486) has modified the partial excise tax exemption for gasoline that is mixed with ethanol or other alcohol. §1920.

gasoline and special fuels credit see *credit for certain uses of gasoline and special fuels.*

gasoline, special fuels and lubricating oil credit a *refundable credit* for *federal excise taxes* imposed on gasoline, special fuels, and lubricating oil used for farming, taxicabs, and certain nontaxable purposes. Section 34 grants the credit, which is claimed on Forms 4136 or 4136T.

gasoline tax an *excise tax* imposed on manufacturers of gasoline. The rate is 14.1 cents per gallon, which is the sum of the Highway Trust Fund financing rate of 11.5 cents a gallon, the Leaking Underground Storage Tank Trust Fund financing rate of 0.1 cent a gallon, and the deficit reduction rate of 2.5 cents per gallon. §§4081(a)(2), 4081(c)(4).

gas payment see *production payment.*

general asset accounts a synonym for *mass asset accounts.*

general assistance recipient generally, any *individual* who is certified by the *designated local agency* as receiving assistance under a qualified general assistance program for any period of not less than 30 days ending within the preemployment period. For these purposes, *"qualified general assistance program"* means any program of a state or a *political subdivision* of a state which provides general assistance or similar assistance which is based on need, and consists of money payments, and which is approved by the *IRS,* after consultation with the Secretary of Health, Education, and Welfare. §51(d)(6). *Wages* paid such persons can qualify for the *targeted jobs credit.* The targeted jobs credit expired on June 30, 1992.

general business asset classes *depreciable tangible personal property* described in one of asset classes 00.11 through 00.28 and 00.4 of Rev. Proc. 87-56, 1987-2 C.B. 674. Reg. §1.1031(a)-2(b)(2). It can qualify as *like-kind property*. See *like class*.

general business credit a reference to the heading for §38 which combines certain *nonrefundable credits,* namely, the *investment credit* (i.e., reforestation, *energy* and *rehabilitation credits*), *targeted jobs credit, credit for increasing research activities, low-income housing credit,* the enhanced *oil recovery recovery credit,* the *disabled access credit,* and the *alcohol fuels credit* into a single *general business credit.* Section 38(c)(1) generally limits the general business credit to the taxpayer's *net income tax* reduced by the greater of (1) the tentative minimum tax, or (2) 25 percent of the *net regular tax liability* that exceeds $25,000. §38(c). The targeted jobs credit and low-income housing credit expired on June 30, 1992.

General Counsel's Memorandum a memorandum prepared by the Office of the *Chief Counsel* of the *IRS* explaining adoption of positions in public and private *revenue rulings* and *Technical Advice Memoranda.*

general deductions a series of *deductions* granted by §805 to *life insurance companies.* They are a subset of so-called *life insurance deductions.* The latter are used in determining the *income tax* base of life insurance companies. §805.

generally enforced state law a state law, unless it is never enforced or the only persons normally charged with violations thereof in the state (or the District of Columbia) enacting the law are infamous or those whose violations are extraordinarily flagrant. A criminal statute of a state is generally enforced unless violations of the statute brought to the attention of appropriate enforcement authorities do not result in any enforcement action in the absence of unusual circumstances. Reg. §1.162-18(b)(2). See *illegal bribes, kickbacks, and other payments.*

general matching provisions a term used to describe §467(a), which forces *lessors* and *lessees* under *§467 rental agreements* to *accrue* annually the *rent* and *interest* allocable to the *taxable year* where actual payment of the rent and interest is deferred to some future period.

general post fund a trust established by Congress to be administered by the Veterans Administration for the benefit of ex-service people dependent on the government for care. 31 U.S.C. §725s(a)(45) (1976); 38 U.S.C. §§5101–5228 (1976). The value of a deceased veteran's property that passes to the United States as *trustee* for this fund is *deductible* from the *gross estate* as a *charitable bequest,* charitable pledge, or liability imposed by law, depending upon the circumstances.

See generally RIA Federal Tax Coordinator 2d, paragraph R-6118.

general refund claim a *claim for refund or credit* filed by a *taxpayer* that states general grounds for believing that an overpayment was made. RIA Federal Tax Coordinator 2d, paragraph T-6901. The courts may allow amendment, but the *IRS* asserts the power to reject a general refund claim as too indefinite without considering its merits. See also *specific refund claim.*

General Utilities doctrine the basic doctrine that a corporation's *distribution* of *appreciated* property to *shareholders* is not taxable to the *corporation,* a concept embodied in §311(a) but profoundly eroded in the balance of that section as well as by various judicial doctrines and §336.

general welfare fund payments a catchall phrase for a wide variety of governmental payments to persons in need. Such payments, which to some extent include *Social Security benefits,* are generally not taxed unless they are in exchange for services of the recipient. See, e.g., Rev. Rul. 76-230, 1976-1 C.B. 19; Rev. Rul. 70-217, 1970-1 C.B. 12. Government subsidies, however, are generally taxable. See, e.g., Rev. Rul. 60-32, 1960-1 C.B. 23.

general written determination any *written determination* that is a *ruling, determination letter,* or *Technical Advice Memorandum* other than a *reference written determination.* §6110(b)(3)(B). The majority of post–July 4, 1967, general written determinations and *background file documents* are the subject of mandatory disclosure under §6110(a) and (h), although general written determinations relating to certain trivial accounting issues do not need to be disclosed at all. Such documents may be disposed of not sooner than three years after being made available for public inspection. §6110(j)(2); Reg. §301.6110-2. The term is an aspect of the *Freedom of Information Act* as embodied in the *Code.*

generic tax shelter a nickname for a *tax shelter* that is devoid of economic substance, as opposed to one having a real profit motive.

geological and geophysical costs a vague, nontechnical term for costs incurred in the search for minerals, oil, and gas. Geological and geophysical costs must generally be capitalized until the *taxpayer* abandons the area under investigation. See Rev. Rul. 78-188, 1978-1 C.B. 76.

geothermal deposit, depletion a geothermal reservoir consisting of natural heat that is stored in rocks or in an aqueous liquid or vapor (whether or not under pressure) in the *United States* or a *possession of the United States.* §613(e). The depletion allowance is 15 percent.

gift and loanback a *tax avoidance* transaction in which a heavily taxed *individual* gives money to a modestly taxed individual (usually a child), who in turn lends the money back to the *donor*. The result is an opportunity to shift income to the child and *deductions* to the parent. Revenue Ruling 82-94, 1982-1 C.B. 31 treats such arrangements as shams where they are part of a preconceived plan.

gift, gift taxes a direct or indirect lifetime transfer of property by a competent *donor*, in *trust* or otherwise, for less than *full and adequate consideration in money or money's worth*. See Reg. §25.2511. If property is transferred for less than full and adequate consideration in money or money's worth, then the amount by which the value of the property exceeds the value of the consideration is a *gift*, although a *sale* or *exchange* made in the ordinary course of *business* in an *arm's length* transaction is made for full consideration in money or money's worth. §2512(b); Reg. §25.2512-8. Donative intent is not mandatory. The transfer must be of a *beneficial interest* in property, not a transfer of *bare legal title* to a *trustee* in order for the *gift tax* to apply. Reg. §25.2511-1(g)(1).

gift, income taxation a transfer excluded from *gross income* if the dominant motive for the transfer is "detached and disinterested generosity" arising "out of affection, respect, admiration, charity, or like impulses." §102.

gift loans loans at below-market rates (using the *applicable federal rate*) where the *forgone interest* is in the nature of a gift to the borrower. §7872(f)(3). See *below-market loan.*

gift splitting a device whereby a *spouse* makes a *gift* to a third party and, in order to obtain two *annual gift tax exclusions* (of $10,000 each) with respect to the one gift, the other *spouse* consents to treat the gift as being made one-half by each spouse. §2513. Both spouses must be *citizens of the United States* or *resident aliens*; both must be married at the time of the gift; and the donor spouse cannot remarry during the year of the gift. See *annual gift tax exclusion.*

gift tax a cumulative, progressive *excise tax* imposed on the *donor* of a *gift* of *property,* measured by its *fair market value,* applicable only to *individuals*. Its practical purpose is to prevent the avoidance of *estate taxes* by giving property away before death. See §§2501–2524. The gift tax is now incorporated in the *unified transfer tax*; hence, while *inter vivos* gifts may be made with minor or no gift tax burdens, to the extent such gifts are not taxed because of the unified credit, the credit against estate taxes will be correspondingly reduced.

gift tax credit a *credit* against the federal *estate tax* liability based on federal *gift taxes* previously paid. The credit arises when property is first subject to a gift tax, then to an estate tax because it was the subject of an *inter vivos* transfer which was ineffective in removing it from the decedent's *estate*. §§2012 (inapplicable to gifts made after December 31, 1976), 2012(e). In a much looser sense, it refers to the use of gift taxes actually or constructively paid as an offset against the *unified transfer tax*. §2001(b)(2).

gift tax exclusion see *annual gift tax exclusion.*

gift tax exclusion, medical and tuition expenses see *medical and tuition expenses, gift tax exclusion.*

gift tax marital deduction a reference to §2523, the gist of which is that interspousal transfers are free of federal *gift taxes*. See *gift tax.*

gift tax return an annual *tax return* (Form 709) reporting *taxable gifts,* to accompany *federal gift tax* payments. They are generally due on April 15 (for the prior year) or on the due date of a *decedent's estate tax* return, including extensions. §§2501(a), 2502(a), 6019, 6075(b).

going concern value an accounting concept that is supposed to reflect the value inherent in the fact that a business can continue despite being taken over. It is sometimes calculated by subtracting the value of the *tangible* and *intangible* assets from the total purchase price; the residue consists of going concern value and *goodwill*. Such allocations are required in connection with purchases of businesses. §1060. *Taxpayers* are expected to use Temporary Reg. §1.338(b)-2T which *allocates* the price to cash and similar items, then marketable securities, etc., then other assets, then residually to *goodwill* and going concern value. See *residual method.*

golden parachute agreement basically, an employment agreement that provides a lavish payment to an *employee* of a company if the company becomes a takeover candidate. The *Code* defines it as an agreement that calls for payments or property transfers that are contingent on a change in a *corporation's* ownership or control, or change of a significant part of its assets, under which payments are made to a *disqualified individual* (basically owners and top executives), where the discounted present value of the contingent payments (determined under §1274) equals or exceeds 300 percent of the individual's annualized includible compensation from the corporation for any *taxable year* during the five-year period before the change of ownership (the base amount), where at least some part of the payments is not *reasonable compensation* for services actually rendered. The rules are structured to prevent *deductions* for *excess parachute payments,* meaning *parachute payments* in excess of a base amount, and to impose an excise tax on that excess. See *disqualified individual, golden parachutes; parachute payment.*

good-faith agreement, tip income   a written agreement that is consented to by the *employer* and at least two-thirds of the members of each occupational category of tipped *employees* which provides for an allocation of the "*excess amount*" (the amount by which 8 percent of gross receipts exceeds total reported tips) based on good-faith approximation of the actual distribution of tip income among the employees. Such agreements are effective prospectively beginning with any payroll period that begins within 30 days of its adoption and terminates not later than the last day of the *calendar year* in which it is first effective. Temp. Reg. §35.6053-1(e). A good-faith agreement is one mechanism with which employers can allocate the excess amount among tipped employees.

goodwill   no single definition. Generally, it refers to an *intangible* asset that reflects an expectation of earnings greater than a fair return on property invested in the business or other means of production or any other positive attribute a firm acquires in the progress of its business. Rev. Rul. 59-60, 1959-1 C.B. 237. It is usually said to depend on an expectation of continued patronage. According to the *Tax Court,* goodwill will be found only if it is transferable. Goodwill is generally viewed as a *capital asset* that cannot be *amortized,* since it generally lacks an *ascertainable useful life. See applicable asset acquisition; going concern value; mass asset theory; residual method.*

goodwill entertainment   *entertainment* designed to promote commercial goodwill toward the person providing the entertainment. The term has evidently not been defined, perhaps because its meaning is so intuitively clear. According to the *regulations,* goodwill entertainment expenditures are *deductible* if they are "*associated*" *entertainment expenses.* Reg. §1.274-2(f)(2)(i)(a); Rev. Rul. 63-144, 1963-2 C.B. 129. Code amendments also demand a business connection. See *associated entertainment and meal expenses.*

governing instrument test, private foundations   a nickname for §508(e), which refuses to exempt *private foundations* from taxation unless the governing instrument (e.g., declaration of *trust*) (1) compels the *distribution* of investment income so as to avoid the *excise tax* on undistributed income imposed by §4942, and (2) prohibits self-dealing, retaining *excess business holdings,* making *speculative investments,* or making *taxable expenditures.*

governmental plan   a term often used to describe *pension plans* established and maintained for the benefit of the *employees* of the federal government or of a state or its *political subdivisions,* or by an agency or instrumentality of one of the foregoing; Railroad Retirement Act plans; and plans of international organizations which are *tax-exempt* under the International Immunities Act. §§414(d), 503(a)(1)(B), 4975(g)(2).

See P.L.R. 9040065 (plan forming integral part of state governmental plan qualifies). Governmental plans in existence before *ERISA* are exempt from present law requirements concerning the *participation, vesting,* and *funding* standards of §§410–412. Such plans (or their *trusts*) can lose their tax-exempt status if participants have engaged in *prohibited transactions* after March 1, 1954. §503(a)(1)(B). See also *eligible state deferred compensation plan.*

governmental plan, ERISA   a plan established or maintained for its employees by the government of the United States, by the government of any state or political subdivision thereof, or by any agency or instrumentality of any of the foregoing. ERISA §3(32). Section 4(b)(1) of ERISA excludes governmental plans from coverage by title I of ERISA.

government official, private foundations   generally, someone holding elective office in the federal government, a federal judge, presidential appointee, or highly paid federal civil servant. Elected or appointed state and local government officials are also so classified if they are paid at an annual rate of $15,000 or more. §4946(c). Financial dealings between a *private foundation* and a government official are prohibited by §4941 and taxed by §4941(d). See *disqualified person, private foundations.*

graduated taxes   taxes whose rates rise with the amount transferred or earned; synonymous with *progressive taxes.*

grandfathered fiscal years   *fiscal years* of *S corporations* and *partnerships* that are allowed as to initial *taxable years* beginning on or after January 1, 1987, despite general rules requiring the use of the *calendar year.* The year must be one as to which *IRS* permission was obtained on or after July 1, 1974, granting over three months of *deferral.* See Rev. Proc. 87-32, 1987-2 C.B. 396. These years do not call for *required payments* to the IRS.

grant administrative expenses, private foundation   a type of administrative expense of *private foundations* incurred in donors' making qualified grants (any contribution, gift, or grant which is a *qualifying distribution*), as distinct from administrative expenses incurred in the active conduct of the foundation's exempt activities. Grant administrative expenses paid during a *taxable year* that can be partiallly taken into account in calculating the foundation's qualifying distributions. §4942 (g)(4). See *qualifying distributions, private foundations.*

grass roots expenditures   expenditures by *public charities,* to influence the general public or any segment thereof. §4911(c)(3). A communication is generally not grass roots lobbying unless it refers to specific legislation, reflects a view on that legislation, and encourages the recipient of the communication to take action with respect to that legislation. In general, an electing charity's grass roots expenditure limit is 25 percent of its total lobbying limit. See *tax on lobbying expenditures.*

grass roots lobbying   any attempt to influence the general public, or a segment of the public, with respect to legislative matters, elections, or referendums. §162(e)(2)(B). Amounts *paid or incurred* (whether by way of contribution, gift or otherwise) are *nondeductible* as *business expenses.*

gravesite   any type of interment sold by a cemetery, including, but not limited to, a burial lot, mausoleum, lawn crypt, niche, or scattering ground, where the fund or cemetery has an obligation of care and maintenance. Reg. §1.642(i)(2)(c). A limited *deduction* may be taken by perpetual-care fund trusts for distributions used for the care and maintenance of gravesites. §642(i).

Great Lakes Fishery Commission   an organization exempt from United States *income taxes* as a public international organization in which the United States participates under a treaty with Canada. §892; Reg. §1.892-1(b)(1); 6 U.S.C. 2836. The Commission is entitled to the privileges, exemptions, and immunities provided by the International Organizations Immunities Act. Exec. Order 11059. Reg. §1.893-1(b)(3).

green-card test   a nickname for a standard under which *foreign individuals* are tested to determine whether they are *resident aliens.* The inquiry is whether the person is lawfully present in the *United States,* i.e., carries a so-called "green card" evidencing permanent resident alien status for immigration law purposes. §7701(b)(5). See *resident alien.*

greenmail payments   any consideration transferred by a *corporation* (or anyone acting in concert with the corporation) to directly or indirectly acquire its *stock* from any *shareholder* if the shareholder's *holding period* was under two years, if the shareholder, someone acting in concert with the shareholder, or a person related to either of them (using §§267 and 707(b) definitions), threatened to make or made a public tender offer for its stock pursuant to an offer not made on the same terms to all shareholders. §5881(b). Section 5881(a) imposes a 50 percent *excise tax* on the *gain* or other *income* of the payee of the greenmail. Such payments are *nondeductible.* See *stock redemption payments.*

grossed-up basis   a term used as shorthand for the effects of §338(b)(2) in cases where the acquiring corporation (A) purchases less than all of the *target company's* (T) *stock,* and T goes through a hypothetical *liquidation. Basis* of T's assets is increased (i.e., grossed up) by multiplying A's basis in T's assets by the fraction:

$$\frac{100 \text{ percent}}{\text{Percent (by value) of T stock held by A on } \textit{acquisition date}}$$

The effect is to create an increased hypothetical purchase price and a full step-up (or step-down) in basis of T's assets. Only T stock purchased during the 12-month acquisition period is counted. If the purchaser also held *nonrecently purchased stock,* it is also added (sometimes subject to its own step-up under an election provided by §338(b)(3)). Liabilities are added as well, and there may be further adjustments. Reg. §1.338-1T(f)(1). See *adjusted grossed-up basis.*

grossed-up dividends   *dividends* distributed from a *foreign corporation* to certain corporate shareholders, increased by the proper hypothetical allocable share of certain *foreign taxes* attributable to the dividend. See *gross-up, foreign tax credit.*

grossed-up required distribution, real estate investment trust   see *excise tax, undistributed income of an RIC.*

grossed-up required distribution, regulated investment company   See *deemed paid foreign tax credit.*

gross estate   the total value of all interests held by a *decedent* who was a *citizen of the United States* or *resident alien* described in §§2033–2044. Specifically, §2033 includes in the *gross estate* any interest in property that a decedent had at the time of death.

gross income   income subject to *federal income taxes.* The term contemplates accretions to wealth after *deducting costs of goods sold* and *basis of property* transferred away but before any reduction by expenses associated with acquiring such wealth, unless the accretion is excluded by a specific *Code* section or a judicial or administrative rule. §61. The form of the receipt is immaterial and may include such items as the value of services received, windfall *gains, cancellations of indebtedness,* and capital receipts in excess of the *taxpayer's* investment in the property or savings of *expenses* and other *economic benefits.* The courts demand *realization* in order to find income, a term that generally means a sufficient change in the taxpayer's position to justify the imposition of a tax (e.g., trivial changes in the terms of a debt obligation received compared to those of the debt obligation tendered will be disregarded). See *capital; return of capital.*

gross income, adjusted   see *adjusted gross income.*

gross income, adjusted ordinary gross income test   *gross income* as defined under §61. To determine whether a closely held *corporation* is to be taxed as a *personal holding company, personal holding company income* must exceed 60 percent of *adjusted ordinary gross income.* This gross income includes all income as defined by §61 and the corresponding *regulations.* The adjustments to gross income are made pursuant to §543(b)(2).

gross income from sources without the United States same as *foreign source income.*

gross income from the property the base on which *percentage depletion* is calculated. See *gross income from the property, mining.*

gross income from the property, mining the *taxpayer's* share of sales of production attributable to the taxpayer's interest in the *deposit.* Consists of the sales price of minerals after *mining* (a defined term which can include the cost of up to 50 miles of *mining transportation* — sometimes more — and levels of processing specified in §613(c)(4)), or a *constructive* sales price when mining ends if minerals are sold after further processing, in both cases less *rents* and *royalties.* §613(c); Reg. §1.613-4. *Percentage depletion* is based on gross income from the property. §613(a).

gross income from the property, oil and gas the *taxpayer's* share of sales of production attributable to the taxpayer's interest in the deposit. Consists of the sales price of oil and gas in the *immediate vicinity of the well,* or the *representative market or field price* if the product is transported or refined (without subtracting transport or refining costs), less *rents* or *royalties* in which the royalty owner has an *economic interest.* §613(c); Reg. §1.613-3(a). Gross income from the property is the base on which *percentage depletion* for oil and gas is computed. §613(a).

gross income, insurance companies in general, the sum of investment income, underwriting income, *gain* from the *sale* or *other disposition* of property, and all other items constituting *gross income* for a *corporation.* §832(b)(1). The term relates to the taxation of stock nonlife insurers, mutual marine insurers, and certain mutual fire or flood insurance companies, as well as mutual casualty insurance companies. §832(a)(2).

gross income method an optional method of allocating and apportioning *interest expense* provided in Regs. §1.861-8. Allocations and apportionment of interest expense are to be made under an asset method, using either the *tax book method* or relative *fair market values.*

gross income, tax return filing requirements *gross income* in the usual tax sense, modified by disregarding *capital losses* and the *net capital gains deduction,* excluded *foreign earned income,* and the $125,000 *exclusion* allowed for persons over 55 on the sale of their *principal residences.* §6012. Special rules apply to residents of Puerto Rico.

gross investment income, charities *gross income* from *interest, dividends, rents,* and *royalties,* except to the extent that they are considered *unrelated business taxable income.* §509(e). Gross investment income can determine whether a *tax-exempt organization* is a *private foundation.* Specifically, one exception from pri-

vate foundation status is for a type of *public charity,* namely those receiving more than one-third of their annual *support* from the *general public* and less than one-third from gross investment income and income from *unrelated trades or businesses.* §509(a)(2)(B)(i).

gross investment income, life insurance companies the sum of *interest; dividends; rents; royalties;* certain income arising from entering into, altering, or terminating certain agreements; *short-term capital gains* in excess of *net long-term capital loss; and noninsurance trade or business* income.

grossly erroneous items see *innocent spouse rule.*

gross profit, installment sales the *selling price* of property, less its *adjusted basis.* §453(c); Temp. Reg. §15a. 453-1(b)(2)(v). For this purpose, the selling price is the consideration the seller receives, unreduced by interest, selling expenses, and encumbrances. However, gross profit is reduced by amounts not *recognized* by reason of the *like-kind exchange* rules of §1031.

gross profit percentage, employee discounts see *qualified employee discounts.*

gross profit percentage method see *percentage mark-up method.*

gross profit ratio, installment sales the proportion of *gross profit* realized or to be realized to the *total contract price.* The ratio is used in calculating the part of payment to be taxed on the *installment method.* Reg. §15a.453-1(b)(2). See *total contract price.*

gross receipts, DISC total receipts from the sale, lease, or rental of property held primarily for sale, lease, or rental in the ordinary course of the *trade or business* of a *corporation* seeking to be a *domestic international sales corporation* (DISC) and *gross income* from all other sources, reported in accordance with its *method of accounting.* §993(f). Unless certain minimum gross receipts tests are met, a corporation cannot qualify as a DISC. *The Domestic International Sales Corporation* (DISC) generally has been replaced by a system of foreign sales corporations (FSCs).

gross receipts, filing requirements the gross amount received from all sources by an *exempt organization,* unreduced for any costs or expenses, cost of operations, or expenses of earning, raising, or collecting such amounts, including contributions, gifts, grants, dues assessments, or receipts from business activities, including *unrelated trades or businesses* activities, all sales proceeds, and investment income. Reg. §1.6033-2(g)(4). *Exempt organizations* other than *private foundations* do not need to file tax *returns* if their gross receipts generally do not exceed $10,000. Reg. §1.6033-2(g)(1). See Ann. 77-62, 1977-17 I.R.B. 22 for details.

gross receipts, S corporation election amounts received or *accrued,* applying the *corporation's tax accounting* method, from *sales,* services, and investment, without reduction for cost, returns, and allowances or other permissible *deductions.* Amounts received from nontaxable *sales* or *exchanges,* borrowings, loan repayments, and *contributions to capital* are excluded. Reg. §1.1372-4(b)(5)(iv). Assumptions of the corporation's liabilities are also gross receipts. Rev. Rul. 68-364, 1968-2 C.B. 371. Only *joint venture* gross receipts are counted. Rev. Rul. 71-455, 1971-2 C.B. 318. The term excludes *returns of capital* on the sales of *capital assets.* §1362(d)(3)(C). If more than 25 percent of a corporation's gross receipts (20 percent under prior law) are consistently from *passive investment income,* then the corporation may face termination of the election. §1362(d)(3).

gross receipts test see *foreign income.*

gross receipts test, section 1244 stock see *largely an operating company.*

gross rent, low-income housing credit rental payments made to the landlord, the cost of any utilities (other than telephone); also, the *IRS* may include in gross rent any utility allowance under §8 of the United States Housing Act of 1937. The term is vital in defining whether a unit is a *rent-restricted unit* such that the *low-income housing credit* might apply. §42. See *rent-restricted unit, low-income housing credit; qualified low-income housing project, low-income housing credit.*

gross sales (actual or constructive), natural resources the total of the *taxpayer's* actual competitive *sales* to others of the *first marketable product or group of products,* plus the taxpayer's *constructive* sales of the first marketable product or group of products used or retained for use in his own subsequent operations, subject to certain adjustments. Reg. §1.613-4(d)(4)(v)(A). The term is used in the *proportionate profits method* of calculating *gross income* from *mining* for purposes of *percentage depletion.* Reg. §1.613-4(d).

gross sales, foreign or domestic source income the *sales* of *personal property* produced, in whole or in part, by the *taxpayer* within the *United States* and sold within a *foreign* country or produced, in whole or in part, by the *taxpayer* within a foreign country and sold within the United States. Reg. §1.863-3(c)(3), example 2. This form of the term is used for *allocation* or *apportionment* when income from the sale of *personal property* is derived partly from sources within and partly from sources without the United States. §863(a); Reg. §1.863-3.

gross salvage value the estimated *amount realized* on a *sale* or other *disposition* of property when it is no longer useful in the *taxpayer's trade or business* or in the production of income and is to be retired from ser-

vice, without reduction for the cost or removal, dismantling, demolition, or similar operations. Reg. §1.167(a)-11(d)(1)(i). Gross salvage is mandatory for *class life asset depreciation range system* purposes; dismantling, etc., costs are treated as *current expenses.*

gross transportation tax a tax of 4 percent imposed on *United States* source "gross transportation income" of *nonresident aliens* and *foreign corporations.* §887(a). Income subject to this tax is not subject to the 30 percent *withholding tax* or the tax on *effectively connected income.* The transportation income is gross income derived from, or in connection with, the hiring, use, or leasing of a vessel or aircraft, or the performance of directly related services.

gross-up, estate tax a colloquialism for a rule embodied in §2035 that the *decedent's gross estate* must be increased by *gift taxes* paid by the *decedent* or the *decedent's estate* on *gifts* made by the decedent or the decedent's *spouse* after 1976 and during the three-year period which ends with the decedent's death. §2035(c).

gross-up, foreign tax credit the practice of treating a *distribution* from a *foreign corporation,* in which a *United States corporation* has a major share (at least 10 percent) of the voting *stock,* as also having distributed a proportionate share of its *creditable foreign taxes* when it makes a *distribution* to such a United States corporation. §78. The effect is to increase the distributee's *gross income* and *foreign tax credits.* §902. There is no gross-up for foreign taxes as to which the recipient of the dividend cannot claim a *foreign tax credit.* §901(j)(3). The gross-up applies as far down as the third tier of foreign corporations.

gross valuation overstatement any statement as to the value of any property or services if the value so stated exceeds 200 percent of the correct amount and the value is directly related to a *deduction* or *credit.* §6700(b). See *abusive tax shelters, penalties, injunctions, and crimes; penalty, promoting abusive tax shelters.*

group account assets similar in kind with approximately the same *useful lives,* grouped for *depreciation* purposes. Reg. §1.167(a)-7(a). Such accounts may be further segregated by location, acquisition date, cost, character, use, and so forth. See Reg. §1.167(b)-1(b) (illustrations), -2 (*declining-balance method*), and -3 (*sum-of-the-years-digits method*).

group annuity plans an arrangement designed to fund a *pension plan* under which the *employer* purchases, directly or through a *trust,* a group *annuity* from an insurance company to provide promised benefits under the plan. Because regulated insurers are considered de facto *trustees,* there is no actual need for a *trust* in order for the plan to be treated as a *qualified plan.* §401(f).

group exemption letter a letter from the *IRS* recognizing the exempt status of a group of affiliated organizations controlled by a parent organization. See Rev. Proc. 72-4, 1972-1 C.B. 706, §3. The exemption, if granted, can apply to both the parent and all the affiliates (e.g., the National Chamber of Commerce and all its affiliates). See *exemption letter*.

group health plan, deduction any plan of, or contributed to by, an *employer* to provide *medical care* (as defined in §213(d)) to his *employees,* former employees, or the families of such employees or former employees, directly or through insurance, reimbursement, or otherwise. §162(i). See *excise tax, failure to provide health care continuation*; *qualifying event*.

group insurance any *insurance* plan by which a number of *employees* (and their *dependents*) or members of some other homogeneous group are insured under a single policy, issued to their *employer* or lender with *individual* certificates provided to each insured individual or family unit. Commonly written lines are life, accidental death and dismemberment, weekly benefits, and hospital, surgical, and medical expense.

group legal care services organizations *exempt organizations* whose sole function is to form part of a *qualified group legal services plan* as defined in §120. §501(c)(20). They are not disqualified by virtue of providing legal service or indemnification against the cost of services unassociated with a qualified group legal care service plan. Although such organizations are tax-exempt, transfers to them are not *deductible* as *charitable contributions*. See *qualified group legal service plans*.

group legal services plans see *qualified group legal services plans*.

group life insurance *life insurance* purchased for the benefit of a group of insureds. See *group-term life insurance*.

group of employees, group-term life insurance all *employees* of an *employer*, or less than all employees if membership in the group is determined solely on the basis of age, marital status, or factors related to employment such as union membership, compensation, duties performed, length of service, etc. Reg. §1.79-0. That *regulation* provides additional examples of factors which do and do not relate to employment. Life insurance is not *group-term life insurance* for purposes of §79 unless it is provided to a "group of employees" and meets certain other requirements. Reg. §1.79-1(a). The phrase appears throughout the *Code*, especially in the *deferred compensation* area, but without a specific definition.

group of financially related corporations any *affiliated group* of *corporations* as defined in §1504 (with-out regard to the exceptions by type of industry in §1504(b)), using a 50 percent ownership test in place of the 80 percent ownership test. The term also covers any other group of corporations which issue consolidated financial statements or reports to shareholders or others. §472(g)(2). Such groups are subject to the *LIFO conformity rule*.

group-term life insurance a common *fringe benefit* which permits *employees* pure life insurance coverage (i.e., no *permanent benefits* such as a cash value) of up to $50,000 tax-free, the premium cost of which the *employer* may *deduct*. §§79, 162. Retirees are entitled to greater tax-free coverage. §79(b). The imputed cost of amounts of coverage over $50,000 is determined by Reg. §1.79-3(d)(2), Table 1.

group trusts, qualified plans see *pooled fund, qualified plans*.

guaranteed interest contract a group *pension plan* contract issued before 1984 that specified that the renewal or maturity rate and the funds deposited by the contract holder plus interest at the guaranteed rate are paid as directed by the contract holder. *Tax Reform Act of 1984*, §217(1)(3).

guaranteed payment any payment or *accrual* from a *partnership* to a *partner* in his or her capacity as a partner, for services or for the use of capital, which is made without regard to income of the partnership. §707(c). Such amounts are treated as if paid to an outsider for purposes of §§61 (*gross income*) and 162 (*trade or business deductions*). The timing of these deductions and *gross income* is controlled at the partnership level. Reg. §1.707-1(c).

guaranteed payment option a feature of an *annuity* that assures the *annuitant* a minimum return, measured either by a guaranteed period minimum amount or a guarantee of a refund of premiums. The method for handling this feature is to subtract the value of the guarantee from the *investment in the contract*. See Reg. §1.72-11(c)(2).

guarantee fund certificates certificates issued by a *mutual insurance company* to provide a fund required by many states to allow the company to issue policies without contingent liability on the part of the holders. The certificates generally have attributes that indicate both debt and equity interests, but they are deemed to be debt for tax purposes, thus enabling the company to *deduct* as *interest* periodic payments made to holders.

guarantor one who guarantees a debt of another. Guarantors forced to honor their obligations are generally treated as if they were the primary obligor, hence, entitled to *bad debt loss deductions*. The same rules apply to indemnitors, endorsers, and comparable persons with secondary liability. Reg. §1.166-9(e)(1).

guardianship   an arrangement subject to judicial supervision whereby one person, a guardian, has the duty to care for another, the *ward,* and his or her property. Guardianships are established because of the ward's inability to legally act on his or her own behalf because of minority or incapacity. The ward is taxed on income from the property subject to the guardian's control, unless it discharges another's duty of *support.* Rev. Rul. 56-484, 1956-2 C.B. 23.

guideline class   see *asset guideline class, class life asset depreciation range system.*

guideline life   the anticipated *useful life* of certain properties under Rev. Proc. 62-21, 1962-2 C.B. 418. See *asset guideline period, class life asset depreciation range system.*

guideline premium limitation   the greater of the *guideline single premium* or the sum of level annual amounts payable over the longest period permitted under the contract, but ending no sooner than 20 years from the date of issue or no later than age 95, if earlier. The term is important in evaluating whether a *flexible premium life insurance* contract qualifies as *life insurance* under §101 for purposes of excluding the death proceeds from *gross income.* It applies to flexible premium contracts issued before 1985, payable by reason of death.

guideline premium requirement   a test used in part to determine generally whether a contract is a *life insurance contract.* §7702(a)(2). Failure to meet the test as to post-1984 contract can result in taxation of the *tax-free inside build-up* and taxability of *death proceeds,* among other things.

H

H.R.   abbreviation for *House Report.*

H.R. 10 plan   see *Keogh plan.*

H. REP. No.   abbreviation for House Report Number.

HSOP   an *ESOP* with a §401(h) health plan for *employees.* The advantage of such a plan is that the *employer* can *deduct contributions* to the plan (including to the health component), and employees may be able to exclude the contribution from *gross incomes.*

half-year convention   an accounting convention used for *depreciation* purposes under which a property *placed in service* during the *taxable year* is deemed placed in service on the first day of the last half of the year. For example, if a *calendar year taxpayer* placed one truck in service on January 12 and a second truck in service on September 3, then each is deemed placed in service on July 1 and depreciated accordingly. Reg. §1.167(a)-11(c)(2)(iii) (ADR system) and -10(b) (non-ADR). A half-year convention is also generally assumed with respect to *recovery property* under §168(d)(1) (*accelerated cost recovery system*). See *modified half-year convention.*

handicapped individual   someone with a physical or mental disability (including blindness or deafness) which for the *individual* constitutes or results in a functional limitation to employment, or someone who has any functional or mental impairment (including sight or hearing) which substantially limits one or more major life activities of the individual. §190(b)(3). The term is used in connection with the *deduction* for the *removal of architectural barriers* and the deduction for *impairment-related work expenses.*

handicapped, schools for   see *special school.*

harbor maintenance tax   an *excise tax* of .04 percent of the value of commercial cargo that is loaded or unloaded at any United States port. A Unites States port includes any port that is open to public navigation and is not an inland waterway. Commercial cargo includes the value of the actual charge paid for the transfer of passengers for hire. See §4461.

hardship, tax extensions for   see *undue hardship, extension of time for paying tax or deficiency.*

harvesting of aquatic resources   both fresh- and salt-water fishing and related activities, but not including reaping mineral resources. Harvesting of aquatic resources is considered agricultural as the term is used in §501(c)(5) and (g) in defining certain *agricultural organizations* exempt from federal *income taxes.*

hazardous duty pay, armed forces   see *combat pay.*

hazards of litigation   the uncertainties associated with a lawsuit. Officers at the appeals level of the *IRS* are directed to consider such hazards when entering into settlements with *taxpayers* over *audit* liabilities and to make settlements on the basis of probable litigating outcomes when the odds are not over four-to-one for or against the IRS. See *Appeals Conference.*

head of household   an *individual,* other than a *nonresident alien,* who meets the three following tests. First, the *taxpayer* must have been unmarried or have lived apart from his or her *spouse* for the last half of the year. Second, the taxpayer must have maintained as his or her home a household in which one or more of the following individuals lived as the *principal place of* abode: (1) a child, stepchild, grandchild; or (2) any other individuals for whom the taxpayer could claim a *dependency exemption,* except a cousin or unrelated person living in the household. However, as long as the taxpayer maintained his or her parent's household, it need not have been the taxpayer's home. Third, the taxpayer must have contributed more than half the cost of maintaining the home. §§2(b) and 7703(b). Head of household status qualifies the taxpayer for favored *head of household* tax rates under §1(b), which offer about half the tax advantage afforded in a *joint return.*

health and accident plan   see *accident and health plan.*

health benefits account   same as a *section 401(h) account.*

health care continuation payments   see *group health plan, deduction.*

health care continuation rules   the requirements of §4980B, which, if met, prevent the imposition of an *excise tax* on failure to provide continuing health care coverage for *covered employees* or *qualified beneficiaries.* Current law generally requires the party who provided health care coverage to provide an opportunity to continue to participate for a specified period in the payor's health plan despite the occurrence of an event that would otherwise eliminate the person's right to participate. The obligation generally expires if the payee is admitted to another person's plan as long as the new plan does not contain exclusions or limitations for pre-existing conditions. Other requirements must also be met. See *excise tax, failure to provide health care continuation.*

health insurance credit   a component of the earned income credit. §32. The earned income credit is the sum of three components: the basic earned income credit §32(b)(1)(D); a supplemental young child credit; and a supplemental health insurance credit. §32(b)(2).

health insurance deduction for the self-employed a *deduction* allowed under §162(l) to *self-employed persons* in an amount up to 25 percent of the cost of health insurance coverage for that person, as well as his or her *spouse* or *dependents*. However, no deduction is allowed if the self-employed person is also eligible to participate in any subsidized health plan of an employer or of a spouse's employer. The deduction is limited to the taxpayer's earned income derived from the trade or business for which the insurance plan was established.

heat exchanger, energy investment credit equipment consisting in part of fixed heat transfer surfaces separating two media. It recovers energy, usually in the form of waste heat. Reg. §1.48-9(f)(7). A qualified heat exchanger may qualify as *specially defined energy property* for purposes of the *energy investment credit*. §48(1)(5); Reg. §1.48-9(f). See also Rev. Rul. 83-21, 1983-5 I.R.B. 5.

heat pipe, energy investment credit heat pipes recover energy, usually in the form of waste heat, from high-temperature fluids to heat low-temperature fluids. Reg. §1.48-9(f)(9). A heat pipe may qualify as *specially defined energy property*. §48(1)(5); Reg. §1.48-9(f).

heat wheel, energy investment credit an item of equipment used to recover energy, usually in the form of waste heat, from exhaust gases to preheat incoming gases. Reg. §1.48-9(f)(5). A heat wheel may qualify as *specially defined energy property*. §48(1)(5); Reg. §1.48-9(f).

heavy oil oil with a weighted gravity of 20 degrees API or less (corrected to 60 degrees Fahrenheit). §613A(c)(6)(F). The term is used for purposes of enhanced *percentage depletion* from difficult properties. See *marginal production*.

hedge agreement an agreement commonly embodied in corporate resolutions or by-laws, or in contracts with *employees,* to the effect that the payee will reimburse the *employer* for salaries or expenses charged to the company to the extent they are disallowed to the payor for tax purposes because they are unreasonable or lavish. The *IRS* takes the view that such repayments may be *deductible* by the repaying *individuals* as §162 (*trade or business*) *expenses,* but that they do not qualify for special relief under §1341 on the theory that the *taxpayer* had an unrestricted right to the receipt in the prior year, a limitation imposed by §1341(a)(2). See *reasonable compensation; restoration*.

hedge bond basically, an otherwise *tax-exempt obligation interest* which is rendered taxable because it was issued early to hedge against *interest* rate increases. *Interest* on hedge bonds is taxable unless two requirements are satisfied: (1) the *reasonable expectations test*;

and (2) the *issuance costs test*. §149(g)(1). Under the reasonable expectations test the issuer must reasonably expect that 10 percent of the *spendable proceeds* of the issue will be spent for the governmental purposes. Under the issuance costs test, payment of legal and underwriting costs associated with the issue must be definitely payable and not contingent. §149(g).

hedging exception, mark-to-market rule, loss deferral, and capitalization rules see *identified hedging transactions*.

hedging exception, short sales an exception to the general rules of §1233 governing *short sales,* which exempt hedging transactions in *commodity futures*. §1233(g). The practical importance is that *gains and losses* on such transactions are not *capital gains* or *losses,* regardless of the *character* of the property used to close the transaction. The exception applies only to *bona fide* hedging transactions used for some good *business purpose*. Reg. §1.1231-1(b).

hedging loss deduction limit a reference to §1256(e)(5), which limits the hedging *loss deduction* available to *limited partners* and *limited entrepreneurs* to the *taxpayer's* nonhedging income from the underlying *trade or business*. Losses in excess of the limit are carried over to the succeeding year as hedging transaction deductions. If there is an economic loss (e.g., hedging losses in excess of aggregate unrecognized *gains* as of year-end), the limit generally does not apply, however.

hedging transactions, mark-to-market rule, loss deferral and capitalization rules see *identified hedging transactions*.

held for sale the status of being held with a view to *sale*. The term appears at various points with varied meanings. For example, *depreciation, amortization,* and *cost recovery* are denied to property held for sale, referring to property described in §1221(1), (i.e. *inventory, stock in trade,* and *dealer property*).

held for the production of income held in order to realize income from current operations or, in the case of *investment* assets, a later *sale*. The term is used in a number of contexts. Section 212(2) allows *investment expense deductions* with respect to such property, even if currently unproductive (e.g., a vacant residence held for post-departure appreciation) or held solely to minimize a loss. Reg. §1.212-1(b). For purposes of *depreciation* and *cost recovery* under §§167 and 168, the term is primarily designed to encompass *rental property* held by investors. The term also appears in §871(d)(4)(A) (United States realty income), §4940(c)(3) (*private foundation audit fee*), and §4942(f)(3) (retention of earnings by private foundations), but without clarification.

held for the production of rents or royalties   held for the purpose of producing *royalties* and *rents*. *Expenses* for such properties generate *deductions* from *gross income* (not *itemized* deductions) under §62(4) and allow *depreciation* and *cost recovery deductions* under §§167 and 168, respectively, if the property is of a *character subject to depreciation*.

higher-tier entity   any *entity* (defined as usual in Reg. §1.382-2T(f)(7)) that, at any time during the *testing period*, owns a 5 percent or greater interest in a *first-tier entity* or in any higher-tier entity. Reg. §1.382-2T(F)(14). The term is important for purposes of determining if there has been an *ownership change* in the *loss corporation* so as to cause the *section 382 limitation* to apply under the *neutrality principle*.

higher-tier limitation member   a higher-tier *corporation* (referring to level of ownership within a recently acquired *affiliated group* of corporations filing a *consolidated return*) that was not a member of the group before its acquisition and that was not the acquiring corporation in a *Type A, Type C,* or *Type D reorganization*. Reg. §1.1502-19(g)(2)(ii). If any *stock* of a member of the affiliated group (as it exists after the acquisition) is *disposed of,* then a higher-tier limitation member owning stock of the disposing member may be required to make certain adjustments in the *basis* of its *stock* to reflect an increase in *earnings and profits* attributable to a portion of the *excess loss account*. Reg. §1.1502-19(g)(2)(i) and -32.

higher-yielding investments   any *investment property* that yields a return over the life of the *tax-exempt bond* issue which is materially higher than the yield on the tax-exempt issue. §148(b)(1). Investment property is (1) any *security*; (2) any *obligation*; (3) any *annuity contract*; (4) any investment-type property and; (5) as to non–*private activity bonds,* any residential property for family units outside the issuer's jurisdiction and not to meet desegregation mandates. §148(b)(2). Investments generally exclude tax-exempt obligations but not *specified private activity bonds* (unless the source of the arbitrage funds is a specified activity bond). See *arbitrage bond; security, worthlessness; specified private activity bond.*

highest permitted benefit   see *excess benefit.*

highest tier entity   a *first-tier entity* or a *higher-tier entity* that is not owned, even in part, at any time during the *testing period* by a higher-tier entity. Reg. §1.382-2T(f)(16). The term is used for purposes of determining if there has been an *ownership change* in the *loss corporation* so as to cause the *section 382 limitation* to apply under the *neutrality principle.*

highly compensated employee   an *employee* who during this current or preceding year was at any time a *five-percent owner,* received *compensation* from the employer in excess of $75,000 (indexed), received *compensation* from the employer in excess of $50,000 (indexed), and was in the *top paid group* of employees (top fifth in compensation), or was at any time an officer and received compensation greater than 50 percent of the annual benefit limitation for a *defined benefit plan* (i.e., $45,000 with deferred indexing for inflation). Family members of highly compensated people are generally aggregated and treated as one person under §414(q)(6). Also, employees who are excluded from consideration under the top paid group test are also excluded from officer status. §414(q)(6)(C)(1). The term "employee" for this purpose excludes *nonresident aliens* with no United States source *earned income* from the employer. §414(q)(11). This uniform definition is used for purposes of various *nondiscrimination rules,* including those relating to *qualified salary reduction plans* and *fringe benefits.* See *five-percent owner, employee plans,* as applied to *top-heavy plans.*

highly compensated employee, cash or deferred plans   for purposes of §401(k) (*cash or deferred plans*), any *employee* who is more highly compensated than two-thirds of all eligible employees. §401(k)(4). After 1988, the uniform (§414(q)) meaning applies. §401(k)(5).

highly compensated individual, medical reimbursement plans   for purposes of §105(h), an *individual* who is (1) one of the five highest paid officers; (2) a *shareholder* who owns, applying the *attribution rules* of §318, more than 10 percent in value of the *stock* of the *employer;* or (3) among the highest paid 25 percent of all *employees.* §105(h)(5). It excludes nonparticipating employees who (1) have not completed three *years of service;* (2) have not attained age 25; (3) are part-time or seasonal employees; (4) are covered under a good-faith bargaining agreement, if accident and health benefits were part of such agreement; or (5) are *nonresident aliens* who receive no *earned income* (within the meaning of §911(b)) from the employer, which constitutes *gross income from sources within the United States* within the meaning of §861(a)(3). §105(h)(3)(B). Self-insured medical reimbursement plans that discriminate in favor of highly compensated individuals as to eligibility or benefits cause *excess reimbursements* of medical expenses to be currently taxed to them. §105(h)(1).

highly erodable cropland   any highly erodable cropland as defined in 16 U.S.C. 3801(6) if at any time the *taxpayer* used the land for farming purposes other than grazing animals. *Gains* from *dispositions* of this *property* produce *ordinary income,* whereas *losses* are *long-term capital losses.* §1257. *Converted wetlands* are subject to similar treatment.

high-taxed income, foreign tax credit   for purposes of the limitation on *passive income* in connection with the *foreign tax credit,* any income otherwise qualifying as passive income, but having been taxed by *foreign income, war profits and excess profits tax* systems at rates in excess of the highest *federal income tax* rates under §1 or §11 (whichever is applicable). §902(d)(4)(F). *Foreign taxes* include both taxes actually *paid or accrued* and those *deemed paid*. High-taxed income is included in the §904(d)(1)(I) catchall category. By excluding high-taxed items from the passive income category, the *credits* which result from the high-taxed income cannot be applied to the low-taxed passive income. It can include passive income from *foreign personal holding companies* or *qualified electing funds*. See *passive income, foreign tax credit; deemed paid foreign tax credit; section 904(d)(1) "basket"; qualified electing fund, passive foreign investment company.*

high three years the three consecutive years in which a *participant* in a *defined benefit plan* earned his or her top levels of compensation. §415(b)(3). The term is used for purposes of calculating permissible maximum retirement benefits. See *annual benefit, qualified plans.*

high withholding tax interest a category of *foreign source income* which is treated as not *passive income* and to which the *foreign tax credit limitation* applies separately. This category consists of any *interest* subject to a *withholding tax* (or a tax determined on a gross basis) of a *foreign country* or *possession of the United States* equal or greater than 5 percent. §904(d)(2)(B)(i). See *section 904(d)(1) "basket."*

historical cost the cost of property based on actual prices paid, as opposed to making any adjustments for *fair market value,* inflation, and so on. *Basis of property* is typically based on historical cost.

historic business generally, the business a *corporation* most recently conducted, provided it was not entered into as part of a *plan of reorganization.* Reg. §1.368-1(d)(3)(iii). See *continuity of business enterprise.* The historic business of the acquired corporation is used as a measure of *continuity of business enterprise* in a *corporate reorganization* and in applying the *neutrality principle.* There can be more than one historic business.

historic business assets the assets used in a *corporation's historic business,* including such operating assets as *goodwill, patents,* and *trademarks,* whether or not they have a tax *basis.* Reg. §1.368-1(d)(4). Continuation of the use of historic business assets by a successor corporation is a measure of *continuity of business enterprise* in a *corporate reorganization* and in applying the *neutrality principle.*

historic district, registered see *registered historic district.*

historic structure see *certified historic structure.*

historic structure rehabilitation expenditures see *qualified rehabilitation expenditures.*

hobby an activity that the *taxpayer* does not engage in for a profit. See *hobby loss rules.*

hobby loss rules rules embodied in §183 to the effect that *current losses* that may be *deducted* from an investment or *activity not engaged in for profit* cannot exceed associated *gross income,* after *deducting casualty losses* and *taxes.* For example, if a *taxpayer* raises dogs for pleasure rather than for profit, incurring $100 of *interest expenses* and $800 in miscellaneous costs, and generates $200 of income, then §183 allows only $100 of miscellaneous costs, since the first $100 is absorbed by the interest expense *deduction.* The rule applies to *individuals, S corporations,* and, according to the *IRS, estates* and *trusts.* Reg. §1.183-1(a). Section 183(d) creates a *rebuttable presumption* of *gain*-seeking intent if a profit is shown in three out of any five (seven in the case of horses) consecutive years, and §183(e) creates an opportunity to extend the statute of limitations with respect to this issue for an extra two years in order to allow taxpayers to take advantage of these presumptions. The rule has been applied to publicly distributed *tax shelters.* See *activity not engaged in for profit.*

holder, patents the *individual* who created the property or another individual who acquired an interest in the *patent* for money, or money's worth, before the patent was reduced to practice. As to acquirors, the person is not a holder if at the time of acquisition she or he is the inventor's *employer* or a *related taxpayer* (as defined in §267(b) and modified by §1235(d)). §1235(b). Section 1235 treats various patent transfers by holders, even if they bear some of the earmarks of licenses or *royalties,* as *sales* or *exchanges* of *long-term capital assets,* provided the transfer is of *all substantial rights to the patent* or an undivided interest in such rights. Reg. §1.1235-2(d).

holding companies generally, *corporations* of a relatively or completely passive nature that in turn control other corporations, often in order to limit liabilities incurred by the subsidiaries.

holding company affiliate see *bank holding affiliate.*

holding company bailouts a practice largely banished by *TEFRA* under which stock of *corporations* with substantial *earnings and profits* was transferred tax-free under §351 to newly formed passive corporations, with the principal results that current *distributions* from the new (holding) company could not be *dividends,* for lack of earnings and profits, and preferred stock of the holding company would not be *section 306 stock.*

holding company system a holding company, its subsidiaries, and all mutual service companies of which such a holding company or any subsidiary thereof is a member company. See Public Utility Holding Company Act of 1935, 15 U.S.C. 79 et seq., §1083(b). An *associate company* that is a registered holding company within such a system may transfer securities with another registered holding company under an order of the SEC for other securities (other than nonexempt property) on a tax-deferred basis. §1081(a); Rev. Rul. 54-192, 1954-1 C.B. 99.

holding or investment company   see *mere holding or investment companies, accumulated earnings tax.*

holding period   the length of time an asset is held before it is disposed of. This period is used to determine whether a gain or loss is long- or short-term. To be classified as a long-term capital gain or loss, the capital asset must be held more than one year. §1222. To determine the holding period, the day of acquisition is excluded and the disposal date is included. Rev. Rul. 70-598, 1970-2 C.B. 168. Section 1223 provides a series of specialized holding period rules for particular cases relating to specified properties and transactions. Section 1223 controls holding periods, imposes a series of important rules relating to such matters as *tacking* in the case of *exchanges* and *distributions,* and grants most property received from a *decedent* an automatic *long-term holding period.*

holding periods, tacking rules   see *tacking of holding periods.*

holding real estate, at-risk   includes holding of *personal property* and providing of services incidental to making *real property* available as living accommodations. §465(b)(6)(E)(i). (By contrast, borrowing to finance personal property and working capital are not so covered.) Mineral property never qualifies. §465(b)(6)(E)(ii). The activity of holding real property is exempt from the *at-risk rules* of §465. Thus, *nonrecourse debt* can be used and forms the basis of *deductions,* as long as the lender is suitably unrelated. §456(b)(6). There is uncertainty as to how long the owner must plan to hold the property.

holiday   see *legal holiday.*

home construction contract   a contract as to which at least 80 percent of the estimated costs are for building, constructing, reconstructing, or rehabilitating improvements to *real property* directly related to and located at the site of *dwelling units* (§167(k) definition) in a building with four or fewer dwelling units. It includes the cost of installing any integral component to, or improvement of, real property. §460(e)(6)(A). A townhouse or rowhouse counts as one separate building for this purpose, regardless of how many other such rowhouses or townhouses may be attached. The *percentage of completion— capitalized cost method* does not (and the *completed contract method* can) apply to such contracts, and they enjoy

favorable treatment under the *alternative minimum tax.* §§56(a)(3) and 460(e)(1)(A). All home construction contracts, regardless of duration or amount, are exempt from the general rule requiring use of the percentage of completion method for alternative minimum tax purposes. §56(a)(3). See *dwelling unit, low- or moderate-income housing rehabilitation; residential construction contract.*

home equity indebtedness   a form of *debt* that can support a *deduction* for *qualified residence interest paid or accrued.* It must be secured by a *qualified residence,* meaning a *principal residence,* or a property *used as a residence* under the *vacation home rules* or not at all during the *taxable year.* §163(h)(3)(C). It cannot exceed the excess of the *fair market value* of the residence over the *acquisition indebtedness* encumbering the property, and total home equity indebtedness is limited to $100,000 ($50,000 on a separate return). Nothing stops the use of such debt for nonresidential purposes, hence the use of credit card arrangements secured by homes. See *qualified residence interest.*

home health service agencies, catch-up election   an organization *exempt from federal income taxes* under §501(c)(3) that HEW (presumably HHS nowadays) determines to be a home health agency as that term is defined by of the Social Security Act, i.e., a public or private agency providing medical items and services at home. §415(c)(4)(D)(iii). *Employees* of such agencies qualify for the special *catch-up election* of §415(c)(4). See *tax-deferred annuities for exempt and educational organization employees.*

home leave, foreign service officer   home leave as described in the Foreign Service Act of 1980, §903, 22 U.S.C.A. §4083 (1981 Supp.), from a foreign country. Such leave is mandatory after three years of continuous foreign service by *citizens of the United States* who are members of the foreign service and must be taken in the United States, its *possessions,* territories, or Puerto Rico. Amounts expended for such home leave are *deductible travel expenses* under §162. Rev. Rul. 82-2, 1982-1 C.B. 12. P. Postlewaite & M. Collins, *International Individual Taxation,* §4.08 (1982).

home mortgage credit   see *credit for interest on certain home mortgages.*

home office   see *home office deductions.*

home office deductions   *deductions* arising from having a place of *business* in the home. Section 280A generally denies any deductions (other than for *interest, taxes,* and *casualties*) in connection with a personal residence. However, §280A(c)(1) relaxes that prohibition with respect to deductions allocable to a portion of the residence used exclusively and regularly (1) as a principal place of business for some particular *trade or business*; (2) as a place of business used regularly by patients, clients, or customers in meeting and dealing with the *taxpayer* in the normal course of his or her *trade or business*; or (3) merely in connection with the taxpayer's trade or business, in the case of separate structures. *Employees* must also show such expenses are for the *convenience of the employer* if claimed as a result of employee status. See *vacation home rules.*

homeowners' association an organization that can elect to be· *exempt* from *federal income taxes* by virtue of being a *condominium management association* or real estate management association. §528(c). Alternatively, it can elect to be taxed on its *homeowners' association taxable income* (basically, income earned from *businesses* or *investments*) at top corporate rates. See also *association property.*

homeowners' association taxable income *gross income* of a *homeowners' association* other than *exempt function income,* less otherwise allowable *deductions* for the production of such *gross income,* subject to certain modifications, principally a $100 deduction, no *net operating loss deductions,* and no intercorporate *dividends-received* deductions. §528(d). A *homeowners' association* can elect to be taxed on such income as if it were a *corporation* in the top corporate income tax brackets. The effect is basically to tax it on net investment income and net *trade or business* income.

home rent allowance for clergyman see *parsonage allowance.*

homestead exemption provisions of state laws that exempt the home from creditors' claims. No provision of a state law may exempt property or rights to property from *levy* for the *collection* of any federal tax. Thus, property exempt from execution under state personal or homestead exemption laws may, nevertheless, be subject to levy by the United States for collection of its taxes, although the personal residence is generally exempt under the *Taxpayer's Bill of Rights.* See §7403 and Reg. §301.6334-1(c).

home, travel expenses see *tax home.*

homeworker basically, a cottage industry worker. Such *individuals* if not *common law employees,* are *statutory employees* for *FICA* purposes if they have over $100 in wages per year, and meet a series of tests: (1) the arrangement between *employer* and the employee contemplates that all material aspects of the services to be performed are to be performed by the homeworker personally; (2) the homeworker has no substantial investment in any of the facilities used in connection with the services to be performed (facilities include the premises and equipment not commonly provided for by the employees, but not any vehicle that the homeworker uses for transportation in the performance of services); and (3) the services to be performed by the homeworker are of a continuing nature, although the homeworker

need not work an eight-hour day, five days a week, nor need the services be performed on consecutive workdays. Reg. §31.3121(d)-1.

horizontal cut oil payment an assignment of part of an *oil payment* under which the payee receives a fixed aggregate amount before the assignor is paid.

horizontal double dummy technique a corporate acquisition technique. It posits two publicly held *corporations* used to combine enterprises (T1 and T2) which will be kept separate with minimum taxes due on the combination. The notion is to form a new corporation (Newco) which owns two subsidiaries, S1 and S2, with S1 merging into T1 and S2 merging into T2 and thereafter having T1 and T2 file *consolidated returns.*

horticultural organization an *exempt organization* not defined in the *Code* or *regulations,* evidently the same as an *agricultural organization,* except that its objective presumably relates to improving fruit, vegetables, flowers, or ornamental plants. §501(c)(5). See *agricultural organization.*

hospital, charitable contributions a private or governmental organization, the principal purpose of which is to provide medical or hospital care, education, or research, including rehabilitation institutions, extended-care facilities, drug treatment centers, outpatient clinics, but not convalescent or visiting home health care organizations. See Reg. §1.170A-9(c)(1). Hospitals can qualify as publicly supported charities for purposes of *charitable contribution deductions.* §170(b)(1)(A).

hospital insurance tax (1) a part of an *independent contract's self-employment tax.* The rate is 2.90 percent of *net earnings from self-employment.* §1401(b). Every *individual* who has self-employment income for a tax year must pay, in addition to other taxes, a self-employment tax comprised of an *old-age, survivors, and disability insurance tax* and the companion hospital insurance tax. §1401(b). The tax applies until net earnings from self-employment reach the level specified in §3121(x), which is $135,000 for 1993. §1402(k). (2) *Employers* and *employees* together also contribute the same 2.90 percent hospital tax. §3101(b).

hospitalization insurance see *accident and health plan.*

hospital service organization see *cooperative hospital service organization, exempt.*

hostility, family attribution rules see *redemption not essentially equivalent to a dividend.*

hot assets a term sometimes used for assets that trigger the *collapsible partnership rules* upon the *sale* or *exchange* of a *partnership interest* or a disproportionate distribution of partnership property. See *collapsible partnership rules.*

hour of service, qualified plans each hour for which an *employee* is paid or entitled to be paid for the performance of duties for the *employer* during the applicable computation period, including hours for which an employee is paid or entitled to be paid by the employer, during which no duties are performed due to vacation, holiday, illness, incapacity (including disability), layoff, jury duty, military duty, or leave of absence. The latter hours are creditable up to 501 hours in any continuous period of not working. Hours of service also include each hour for which back pay, irrespective of mitigation of damages, is either awarded or agreed to by the employer. Labor Reg. §2530.200(b)-2(a)(1), (2) and (3).

House Committee on Ways and Means the committee of the United States House of Representatives responsible for revenue laws. The Constitution requires tax bills to originate in the House.

household and dependent care expenses see *child and dependent care credit.*

Housing and Community Development Act of 1974 an act primarily to establish a program of community development block grants and to amend and extend laws relating to housing and urban development. Pub. L. No. 93-383, 88 Stat. 633 (1974).

housing cost amount an amount *excludable* from *gross income* of a *citizen of the United States* resident overseas, if paid for by the *employer,* or *deducted above the line* if paid by the *taxpayer* rather than by the employer. §911(a) and (c). The exclusion or *deduction* is equal to the excess of the taxpayer's actual *housing expenses* over a base housing amount. The base housing amount is 16 percent of the salary of an *employee* of the United States whose salary grade is step 1 of grade GS-14. The amount of the deduction is limited, subject to a special carryover rule, to the *individual's foreign earned income,* which is not otherwise excluded from gross income under this provision.

housing cost exclusion see *foreign housing cost exclusion.*

housing credit dollar amount a figure used to limit the cumulative installments of the *low-income housing credit.* See §42(h). The limit is determined by the action of state agencies allocating a $1.25 per person per state amount among owners of low-income housing, such that each property is subjected to a particular dollar cap.

housing development bonds bonds, the proceeds of which are used to finance residential rental property described in §103(b)(4)(A). The *interest* on such bonds may be *exempt* from *federal income taxes.* See *targeted area projects.*

housing expenses reasonable *expenses* paid or incurred during the *taxable year* by or on behalf of an *individual* for housing of the individual, his or her spouse, and any *dependents* in a *foreign* country. Such expenses include expenses attributable to housing, such as insurance, but not *deductible interest* or taxes. The costs of maintaining a second overseas household for the *taxpayer's* spouse and dependents are also included if the second household is needed because of the adverse living conditions at the first household. §911(c)(2). To the extent overseas housing expenses exceed a base level, they can be *deducted,* or if paid by the *employer, excluded* from *gross income.* §911(a) and (c)(3). See *foreign housing cost deduction; foreign housing cost exclusion; housing cost amount.*

husband and wife, exclusion of gain on sale of residence for purposes of §121 (i.e., granting a $125,000 exclusion of *gain* on the *sale* of a *principal residence*), the term refers to persons who are married on the date of the *sale* or *exchange.* §121(d)(6)(A). It excludes persons who are separated under decrees of separate maintenance or divorce. T.I.R. 573 (Apr. 20, 1964). See *married person.*

hybrid accounting method any combination of an acceptable *methods of accounting* permitted by the *regulations.* §446(c)(4). An example of a hybrid method occurs when a retailer uses the *accrual method* of accounting for purchases and sales and the *cash method* for all other items of income and expense. This is authorized by the *regulations,* because although the accrual method must be used in connection with *inventories,* mandatory accrual accounting does not extend beyond the treatment of inventories. Reg. §1.446-1(c)(1)(iv) and -1(c)(2)(i).

hybrid instruments financial instruments that are neither entirely *stock* nor entirely *debt,* such as convertible debentures and income bonds or participating bonds that call for contingent payments to the holder (other than a *call premium*). An example would be income debenture bonds, paying noncumulative contingent interest, subordinated to other debt, without management powers). Such instruments create difficulties in determining whether they are debt or equity. See *debt-equity rules.*

hybrid plan a *defined benefit plan* under which benefits are based partially on a separate account for the *participant* (e.g., a *money purchase pension plan* that provides a minimum defined benefit).

hybrid Type A reorganization see *forward triangular merger; reverse triangular merger.*

hydroelectric generating facilities, qualified see *qualified hydroelectric generating facility, industrial development bond.*

hyperinflationary currency one that has inflated at a rate of at least 100 percent in the last 36 months immediately preceding the *taxable year.* Reg §1.985-2(b). See *United States dollar approximate separate transactions method.*

hypothetical sales election an election applicable to *timber* held for more than a year that allows an owner of standing timber or of a *contractual right to cut timber* to have the cutting of timber deemed a *sale* when the timber is cut. §631(a); Reg. §1.631-1(a). The timber so cut is considered *section 1231 assets.* Timber is deemed cut at the beginning of the year in which, in the ordinary course of *business,* the amount of timber felled can first be defi- nitely ascertained (usually at scaling). The election can convert a great deal of what would otherwise be *ordinary income* into *long-term capital gains.* Reg. §1.631-1(a)(4).

hypothetical transactions a transaction that will only theoretically take place. The *IRS* will not issue rulings in such cases, although it will rule on transactions sub- ject to contingencies.

I

IDB an acronym for *industrial development bond.*

IDC an acronym for *intangible drilling and development cost.*

IDR an acronym for *information document request.*

IMPACT an acronym for the *Improved Penalty Administration and Compliance Act of 1989.*

IR an Internal Revenue news release. See *news release.*

IRA an acronym for *individual retirement arrangement* or *individual retirement account.*

IRA annuities nonforfeitable, nontransferable *annuities* purchased as the funding medium for *individual retirement arrangements.* §408(b).

IRA dribble out the practice of electing to receive modest distributions from an *individual retirement arrangement* before the year in which the retired *individual* attains age $70\frac{1}{2}$ and thereafter receiving larger, substantially identical distributions, computed under *regulations* for the rest of the applicable life expectancy. The practice may avoid the imposition of substantial taxes that results from having distributions deferred until $70\frac{1}{2}$. But see *uniform minimum distribution rules.*

IRA endowment contracts nontransferable, nonforfeitable *endowment contracts* purchased as the funding medium for an *individual retirement arrangement.* §408(b). Such contracts are subject to numerous limitations, set forth in Reg. §1.408-3(e).

IRA rollovers generally, a transfer from one *individual retirement arrangement* (IRA) to another (directly, or indirectly through the *taxpayer),* or a *qualifying rollover distribution* from a *qualified pension, profit-sharing,* or *stock bonus plan* to an IRA. Each type is tax-free, if completed within 60 days. §§402(a)(5), 408(d)(3)(A)(i). See §403(a)(4) for parallel rules regarding rollover of the *employee's* credit balance under *qualified annuity plans.*

IRB an acronym for industrial revenue bond, another name for *industrial development bonds.*

IRD an acronym for *income in respect of a decedent.*

IRM an acronym for *Internal Revenue Manual.*

IRS an acronym for *Internal Revenue Service.*

IRS valuation guide for income, estate and gift taxes a publication issued by the *IRS* under the title "IRS Appeals Office Valuation Training Program" for use in the negotiation of settlements relating to the valuation of *realty* and *personal property.* The publication is made available through Commerce Clearing House.

ISO an acronym for an *incentive stock option.*

I.T. Income Tax Unit Ruling, an early form of *ruling.*

ITC an acronym for an *investment tax credit.*

identical securities a term used in §1058 that exempts securities lending transactions from taxation, provided, among other things, the lender receives back certificates identical to those lent out.

identifiable event a term often used in connection with determining when a *loss* (e.g., *worthless securities*) has taken place. See Reg. §1.165-1(b). It is frequently most difficult to find such an event where the loss occurs gradually and the property is not abandoned or otherwise *disposed of.*

identifiable event, worthless debt or security an event such as bankruptcy, the occurrence of which causes or evidences *worthlessness* for purposes of §§165(g) *(worthless securities)* and 166 *(bad debts* other than where the *taxpayer* uses *reserves for bad debts).* No particular event is uniformly conclusive of worthlessness, since other facts or circumstances may indicate the existence of value. See Reg. §1.166-2(a)-(c). The term also has significance in establishing the *closed transaction* needed to establish property-related *losses* of all varieties. Reg. §1.165-1(b).

identified hedging transactions transactions entered into by a *taxpayer* in the normal course of the *trade or business,* primarily in order to reduce the risks of price or currency fluctuations with respect to property held or to be held, fluctuations in interest rate or price changes, currency fluctuations with respect to borrowings made or to be made, or obligations incurred or to be incurred by the taxpayer. Furthermore, the transaction must create *ordinary gains or losses* and, by the end of the day, must be identified as a hedging transaction on the taxpayer's records. §1256(e)(2). The *loss deferral* (§1092), *mark-to-market* (§1256), and *capitalization* rules (§263(g)) do not apply to identified hedging transactions. §§263(g)(3), 1092(e), 1256(e)(1). The *Code* uses the term "hedging transaction," but it seems the term "identified hedging transaction" is the more common usage. See *syndicate, hedging exception.*

identified straddle a *straddle* that is clearly identified on the *taxpayer's* books as such on the day the straddle was acquired, that is either *disposed of* on the same day or held by the taxpayer at year-end, and that is not part of a larger straddle (e.g., a "butterfly"). §1092(a)(2)(B). *Losses* on such straddles (and related *gains*) are *recognized* when the taxpayer disposes of all the positions accompanying the straddle on the same day. §1092(e)(2)(A)(ii). The advantage of these straddles is that *unrealized gains* in such straddles do not need to be reported.

illegal bribe, kickback, or other payment to a foreign government official   direct and indirect payment to a foreign official, *employee,* or agent-in-fact of a foreign government if the payment is unlawful under the Foreign Corrupt Practices Act of 1977, which exempts traditional "grease" payments. §§162(c)(1), 964(a), 995(b)(1)(F)(iii). Such amounts may not be *deducted* as *trade or business expenses* under §162 or as other *gain*-seeking or tax-saving expenses under §212, are treated as *deemed distributions* of a *DISC* under §995(b)(1)(F)(iii), and do not reduce *earnings and profits* of a *controlled foreign corporation* under §964(a).

illegal bribes, kickbacks, and other payments   various illegal payments. For purposes of the claim for *deductions* under §162 (*trade or business expenses*) or §212 (various *gain*-seeking or tax-saving expenses), the term refers to three classes of payments. The first class consists of direct or indirect payments to any official or *employee* of any government or agency or instrumentality of any government if the payment is an illegal bribe or kickback, or in the case of foreign governmental officials and employees, if the payment is illegal under the Foreign Corrupt Practices Act. §162(c)(1). The latter rule became effective with the passage of *TEFRA* and narrows the prior law definition. Second, §162(c)(2) supplements the first class of payments by rendering direct or indirect payments to nongovernmental persons *nondeductible* if they are illegal bribes, kickbacks, or other payments under federal law, or under state law, provided it is a *generally enforced state law* that subjects the payor to criminal penalty or loss of authority to engage in a *trade or business.* Third are Medicaid and Medicare rebates, bribes, and kickbacks in connection with payments for goods or services, including referrals, which are rendered nondeductible by §162(c)(3). As to payments potentially *nondeductible* under Code sections other than §§162 and 212, see *public policy limitation.* Illegal payments to foreign officials under §162(c)(2) are treated as *deemed distributions* of a *DISC,* (§995(b)(1)(f)(iii)) and have the adverse feature of not reducing *earnings and profits* of a *controlled foreign corporation* under §964(a). See *illegal bribe, kickback, or other payment to a foreign government official; illegal rebates; public policy limitation.*

illegal drug trafficking   see *narcotics trafficking.*

illegal rebates   reductions in selling prices that violate local law. The courts have allowed such rebates to reduce *taxable income* of the seller.

immediate annuity   an *annuity contract* under which payments begin promptly after purchase. For the antonym, see *deferred annuity.* There is a limited definition for purposes of §72(u) (immediate taxation of *taxpayers* other than *individuals* owning annuities), which defines an excepted immediate annuity as one bought with a single payment, beginning not later than a year from purchase with substantially equal payouts occurring at least annually. §72(u)(4).

immediate assessments   *deficiencies* that are promptly *assessed* without the usual formalities. See *jeopardy assessment; termination assessment.*

immediate distribution rules   see *cash out.*

immediately after the exchange, transfers to controlled corporations   the time at which 80 percent *control* of a transferee *corporation* is measured to determine whether the transfer can qualify for tax-free treatment under §351. §351(a). A corporate transferor only needs to have momentary control if it distributes *stock* or *securities* to its *shareholders.* §351(c). See *section 351 transactions.*

immediately after the transfer   an element of §368(a)(1)(D) that relates to *Type D reorganizations,* conditioning the benefits of that paragraph on the transferor's, its *shareholders',* or both, holding 50 percent *control* of the transferee *corporation.* The term is read to have the same meaning as *immediately after the exchange* under §351.

impairment of capital   violation of state corporate law rules designed to preserve the solvency of a corporation.

impairment-related work expenses   *ordinary and necessary expenses* (claimed as *itemized deductions*) of a *handicapped individual* in order for the *individual* to be able to work. It includes attendant care services at the place of employment and other *expenses* in connection with the place of employment which are necessary for the individual to be able to work. §67(d). "Handicapped individual" is defined the same as for purposes of the *business expense deduction* for the cost of removing architectural barriers to the handicapped. §67(d)(1). See *architectural barriers deduction.*

imported property   property completed outside the *United States,* Puerto Rico, or *possessions of the United States,* or less than 50 percent of the *basis* of which is attributable to value added within the United States. §168(g)(6)(B). Such property is subject to the relatively slow *alternative depreciation system.*

Improved Penalty Administration and Compliance Act of 1989   a major overhaul of the penalty and compliance provisions of the *Internal Revenue Code,* passed in 1989. It has significantly streamlined the system.

improvement, recapture of depreciation   see *separate improvement.*

improvements generally, structures, buildings, and other man-made additions to land.

improvements by lessee see *lessee improvements.*

impute to attribute. The term is used in a number of situations, the most common of which involve finding *interest* in transactions for deferred payments where no interest or inadequate interest is provided for in the parties' agreement. See, e.g., *imputed interest.*

imputed earnings rate a supposedly realistic figure drawn from *life insurance* industry data that reflects the profitability of the 50 largest *domestic stock life insurance companies.* It is used to determine the *differential earnings amount* that reduces *(deductible) policyholder dividends* of *mutual life insurance companies* under §809(a)(2).

imputed income the value of the consumption of self-produced goods, crops, and services or the use of personally or family-owned property. At the judicial level, the Supreme Court has made an unauthoritative statement that the value of occupying one's own home is not taxable.

imputed income limitation a figure used to determine if a unit in a building is a *rent-restricted unit.* The imputed income limit applicable to a unit is the income limit under the set-aside requirement applicable to people occupying the unit if the number of occupants has been as follows: in the case of a unit without a separate bedroom, there has been one occupant, and if there has been at least one separate bedroom, 1.5 *individuals* per bedroom. §42(g)(2)(C)(i)-(ii).

Illustration: Assume the relevant §8 Housing Program makes the very low income figure for a family of four $19,000 and $21,000 for a family of five. Assume a three-bedroom unit is the subject of the inquiry; it presumably contains 4.5 people. The very low income figure for this unit is the average of the four- and five-member family incomes, that is, $20,000. Therefore, the gross rent limitation for a three-bedroom rent-restricted unit is 30 percent of $20,000, that is $6,000, or $500/month.

imputed interest imaginary *interest income,* created by §483 of the *Code.* (The Code uses the term *unstated interest,* but imputed interest seems to be the more common usage). Section 483 is designed to thwart the practice of setting unrealistically low interest charges with respect to *sales* of property payable in installments. The effect of §483 is to turn part of the sales price into interest, creating a *deduction* for the buyer and interest *income* for the seller, since §483 creates interest for all tax purposes.

imputed principal amount, original issue discount rules the sum of the *present values* of all payments due under an obligation, computed as of the *sale* or *exchange* date, using the *applicable federal rate* (com-

pounded semi-annually). §1274(b)(1) and (2). Unless there is *adequate stated interest,* this is used as the issue price in connection with an obligation issued for property to determine *original issue discount* absent a *potentially abusive situation.* See *potentially abusive situations, original issue discount.*

inactive participant a person not in *covered service* under a qualified plan, who is in pay status under the plan or who has a nonforfeitable benefit under the plan. §418D(e). The term as defined here is applicable only in regard to §418D, regarding reorganizations of *multiemployer plans.*

inactive subsidiary an 80-percent-or-more controlled subsidiary *corporation* that is inactive. For this purpose, inactivity exists if the subsidiary neither began business after formation before the close of its parent's *taxable year* nor had *taxable income* during the period included within such a taxable year. §1361(c)(6). An *S corporation* may own an inactive (but not an active) subsidiary without losing its status.

inadvertent termination rule, S corporations a statutory provision designed to prevent loss of *S corporation* status in the event of inadvertent disqualification. Any S corporation that was terminated because it ceased to be a *small business corporation* or because it had too much *passive investment income* continues to be an S corporation for a period to be specified by *regulations,* provided that the *IRS* determines that the termination was inadvertent and that the corporation and its shareholders act promptly to restore the corporation to compliance. §1362(f).

inbound toll charge a so-called *toll charge* on *transfers* into the *United States* by *foreign corporations,* or on the disposition of *stock* in *foreign corporations,* generally converting overseas accumulations of *earnings and profits* into *dividends.* See §§367, (prior law) 1248.

incentive stock option a compensation device through which *employees* are issued *stock options,* the term of which may not exceed 10 years, at an option price at least equal to the *fair market value* of the stock at the time of the grant. The options do not attract *federal income taxes* until stock purchased under the incentive stock option (ISO) is sold. The special appeal of such stock options is that the full spread between the exercise price and the sale price can be a *long-term capital gain.* §422. The exercise of ISOs creates an *adjustment* under the *alternative minimum tax.* §57(a)(3).

inception-of-title rule a concept used in *community property states* to determine the ownership of property, under which the character of the interest before marriage controls its later character. It is used to determine the character of *ordinary life insurance.*

incidence of tax the party on whom the burden of a

tax falls. For example, it is often said (whether or not correctly) that in the long run the incidence of the *federal income tax* on *corporations* actually falls on the consuming public.

incidental benefits, pension, annuity, and profit-sharing plans   permissible benefits, aside from retirement benefits (e.g., life insurance), provided under *qualified pension, annuity, profit-sharing,* or *stock bonus plans.* Such plans may generally provide life, accident, and health insurance benefits to a modest extent, even though they are unrelated to the primary purpose of §401, namely to provide retirement benefits. Reg. §§1.401-1(b)(1)(i) and (ii), 1.401-14. Rev. Rul. 74-307, 1974-2 C.B. 126; Rev. Rul. 61-164, 1961-2 C.B. 99; Rev. Rul. 60-84, 1960-1 C.B. 159; and Rev. Rul. 60-83, 1960-1 C.B. 157 provide objective tests with respect to *life insurance contracts.*

incidental life insurance   in the case of a *benefit plan,* life insurance coverage not greater than 100 times the projected monthly benefit; in the case of a *defined contribution plan,* coverage is incidental if under 50 percent of contributions are used to acquire *whole life insurance* coverage or under 25 percent of contributions are used to buy *term insurance* coverage. See Rev. Ruls. 60-83, 1960-1 C.B. 157; 66-143, 1966-1 C.B. 79; and 76-353, 1976-2 C.B. 112. Incidental life insurance is a permissible feature of many *qualified plans.* See, e.g., *profit-sharing plan, Code.* See *individual medical benefit account; subordinate benefit rule.*

incidental or subordinate   see *individual medical benefit account.*

incidents of ownership   for *federal estate tax* purposes, the right of the insured or his or her *estate* to one or more of the economic benefits of a *life insurance policy.* Section 2024 requires *inclusion* in the *gross estate* of proceeds of insurance on the *decedent's* life, even though the proceeds are not receivable by or for the benefit of the decedent's *estate,* if at the date of death the decedent possessed incidents of ownership in the policy.

incident to a qualified scholarship to which section 117(a) applies   a term used to described payments made to students who are *nonresident aliens,* which are subject to 14 percent withholding at source under §1441. This is a favorable rule. See §§141(b), 871(c), 3121(b)(1), 3231(e)(1), 3306(c)(19), and 7701(b)(5)(D)-(i)(I). This lowers the tax rate for people on F, J, or M visas. The lower rate applies only to payments of *qualified scholarships.*

incident to divorce   no gain or loss shall be recognized on a transfer of property from an individual to a spouse incident to a divorce. §1041(a). A transfer between former spouses is incident to divorce if it occurs within one year after the marriage ceases or is related to the cessation of the marriage. §1041(c).

Transfers incident to divorce are generally treated like *gifts.* §1041(b).

included property, alternate valuation   all property which is included in the *gross estate* at the time of the *decedent's* death under §§2033–2044, although valued at the former *alternate valuation date.* Reg. §20.2032-1(d) and (e). See *excluded property, alternate valuation.*

includible compensation, eligible state deferred compensation plans   compensation for services performed for a state or other government unit that is currently *includible* in *gross income,* ignoring *community property* laws. §457(d)(5) and (7). See *tax-deferred annuities for exempt and educational organization employees.*

includible compensation, tax-deferred annuities for exempt and educational organization employees   wages and salaries and other taxable compensation for the most recent year of service (when earned, as opposed to when paid) (ending not later than the close of the *taxable year)* as well as excludable payments from *accident and health plans,* and otherwise excludable *foreign earned income,* but not amounts paid by the *employer* to buy annuities under the plan or other employer contributions to *qualified plans. Foreign* income is excluded, even if untaxed under §911, but one excludes taxable *annuity* premiums, taxable *P.S. rate* cost of life insurance, state deferred compensation plan deferrals, as well as compensation from other employers. §403(b)(3). Includible compensation is the base on which to determine the *exclusion allowance,* which in turn decides the extent to which *employees* of educational institutions and certain other exempt organizations can exclude their employers' purchases of *deferred annuities* from current income. See *eligible state deferred compensation plan.*

includible corporations   *corporations* eligible to join in filing a *consolidated return.* Section 1504 defines the term to mean any corporations other than (1) corporations exempt from tax under §501 (*exempt organizations* subject to an exception relating to *title holding corporations* under §1504(e)); (2) *insurance companies* (but see §1504(c)(1); (3) *foreign corporations* (except for electing *contiguous foreign country corporations*); (4) *possessions corporations*; (5) *regulated investment companies* and *real estate investment trusts*; (6) *domestic international sales corporations* (other than former DISCs, for limited purposes) and corporations with post–1984 DISC accumulations of income; (7) *China Trade Act corporations*; (8) unincorporated businesses that are taxed as corporations (an inference arising from the repeal of former §1361); (9) *S corporations* (see §1361); and (10) *terminal railroad corporations* (unless filing as a common parent under §281(d)). Some complexities remain, however, especially as to *S corporations.*

includible insurance companies *insurance companies* that can be members of an *affiliated group* for purposes of filing a *consolidated return.* §1504(c). Generally, insurance companies are not *includible corporations* for purposes of filing a consolidated return, but §1504(c) makes two exceptions. First, two or more affiliated *domestic life insurance companies* taxable under §812 may file a consolidated return together. §1504(c)(1). Second, a parent corporation may elect to include a domestic life insurance company taxable under §801 in its consolidated return if the insurance company has been a member of the affiliated group for the five *taxable years* immediately preceding the *taxable year* for which the consolidated return is filed. §1504(c)(2)(A). See *bottom-line consolidations, life insurance companies.*

includible tax-exempt organization an *organization* exempt from tax under §501 which joins together with other such organizations and files a *consolidated return.* §1504(e). Generally, an *exempt organization* is not allowed to join in filing a consolidated return, but two or more tax-exempt organizations, one or more of which are exempt under §501(c)(2) as corporations organized for holding title to property, collecting income, and then turning over the entire amount to an organization that is also exempt from tax, and other corporations that derive income from a tax-exempt title-holding organization may join together and file a consolidated return. §1502(e).

income assignment see *assignment of income doctrine.*

income certification statement, low- or moderate-income housing a statement of anticipated income for the household for the certification year, that is, the 12 months during which the tenant(s) will occupy a *low- or moderate-income rental unit* for which the owner seeks 60-month *amortization* under former §167(k). The content of the certification statement is designed to show annual economic resources of all the occupants, using H.U.D. standards. Reg. §1.167(k)-3(b)(3) and (4).

income earned abroad see *foreign earned income exclusion.*

income effectively connected to a United States trade or business see *effectively connected income.*

income forecast method of depreciation a method of *depreciation* under which the *basis* of *depreciable* property is written off in proportion to total anticipated future *gross income* from the property, taking *salvage values* into account. Rev. Rul. 64-273, 1964-2 C.B. 62; Rev. Rul. 60-358, 1960-2 C.B. 68. Thus, if a film cost $120, has a salvage value of $20, and is expected to yield total income of $200, of which there is $80 of income in year one, $60 in year two, $60 in year three, and nothing thereafter, then of the $100 that can be depreciated, $40 is written off on the first year (i.e., $80 × $200/$100).

income for the taxable year required to be distributed currently, estate or trust amounts the *fiduciary* is required to *distribute* currently, even if made after the close of the *taxable year,* often called *first-tier distributions.* Such amounts are generally *deductible* under §651(a) for *simple trusts* and under §661(a) (but, when combined with certain discretionary payments, not in excess of *distributable net income*) for *complex trusts* and *estates,* and are taxable to *beneficiaries* to the extent of distributable net income. §§651(b), 661(a). In the case of complex trusts and estates, the *deduction* is the lesser of *first-* and *second-tier distributions* or distributable net income. §661(a). Income required to be distributed currently (*currently distributable income*) is income reported in compliance with the terms of the trust or will and local law that must be distributed promptly or periodically, even if the distribution is subject to minor discretion on the part of the fiduciary. See *other amounts properly paid or credited or required to be distributed, estate or trust; tier system.*

income from sources within the United States *United States* source *gross income.* Section 861(a) provides a long series of mechanical rules for attributing gross income to a particular jurisdiction. For example, §861(a) generally classifies the following as being from United States sources: *interest* on obligations of *persons* resident in the United States; income from *sales* of *real estate* located in the United States; and underwriting income from insuring *United States risks.*

income from sources without the United States *foreign* source *gross income.* §862. Specific mechanical rules provide, for example, that income from sales of *real estate* and *royalty* income turns on the location of the particular property. §862(a)(4) and (5). Section 862 is largely redundant, since it is merely the counterpoint of §861 which defines *income from sources within the United States.*

income in respect of a decedent amounts of *gross income* to which a *decedent* was entitled prior to death but which were not reported because of his or her *method of accounting.* Such amounts can relate to the year of death or a *prior taxable year,* and they are taxed to the recipient of the income when received. Reg. §1.691(a)-2.

income not reduced to undisputed possession windfall *gains* held by someone who does not yet have good title against persons other than the true owner. See *treasure trove.*

income of a foreign government income earned by foreign governments and their subdivisions from investments in the *United States* in *stocks,* bonds, other domestic securities, and *interest* on United States bank deposits. Such income is exempt from *federal income tax,* provided the government does not engage in more than minimal commercial activities in the United States. The exclusion also applies to income earned by any organization created by a foreign government. §892.

income of international organization income earned by an *international organization* from investments in the United States in *stocks,* bonds, other domestic securities, and *interest* on United States bank deposits. Such income is exempt from *federal income tax, provided the organization does not engage in more than minimum commercial activities in the United States. §892.*

income splitting the practice of fragmenting income among numerous *taxpayers* in order to minimize overall *income taxes* on a group by taking advantage of lower tax rates imposed on the transferees. It is most commonly practiced within the family in an effort to shift income from higher-bracket members, typically parents, to lower-bracket members, typically children, by such devices as *gifts* of income-producing property.

income tax a tax based on the *taxpayer's* income. The primary tax in the United States is the *federal income tax,* which is imposed by §1 of the *Code.*

income tax return preparer see *tax return preparer.*

income tax withholding the mandatory practice of having *employers* act as collectors of current *federal income taxes,* based on the *employee's wages, filing status,* and *exemptions.* §3402. Employers are personally liable for such amounts. §3403. Such withholding creates *credits* against the employee's income tax liability. §31. See *responsible person.*

income, trusts and estates generally, income of a *trust* or *estate* as determined under the terms of the governing instrument (trust document or will) and local law, subject to the fiduciary's limited power to allocate receipts to either corpus or to income. §643(b). See *fiduciary accounting income.*

incoming Treasury letter an informal term for a letter sent by or for a *taxpayer* to the *National Office* of the *IRS* seeking legal advice on how to deal with some particular tax matter. The response is called an *outgoing Treasury letter.*

incomplete transfer any transfer that would not be treated as a *gift* whether or not consideration was received for the transfer. §2702(a)(3)(B). Under *proposed regulations,* an incomplete transfer would be a transfer for which no portion would be treated as a completed gift without regard to any considerations received by the transferor. Prop. Reg. §25.2702-1(c)(1).

inconsistent position see *maintenance of an inconsistent position, mitigation of effect of statutes of limitations and other provisions.*

incorporated municipality see *municipal corporations.*

incorporated pocketbook a colloquialism for a *tax avoidance* device to avoid the graduated *income tax* imposed on *individuals,* whereby an individual would organize a *corporation* to hold *investment* securities so that the *dividends* and *interest* received would be taxed at the relatively lower corporate income tax rate. The *personal holding company tax* (§§541–547) is designed to deal with this device, among others.

incorporated talents a term used for a *tax avoidance* device to avoid the graduated *income tax* imposed on *individuals,* whereby a highly paid individual providing personal service skills (e.g., an actor) would organize a *corporation* and contract to work for it at a relatively small salary. The corporation would then contract out her services at *fair market value.* The difference between the amount received by the corporation for her services and the salary paid to the individual would be taxed at the relatively lower corporate rates. A corporate tax deduction also becames possible for expenses that are essentially personal costs of the *shareholder.* The *personal holding company tax* (§§541–547) is designed to deal with this device, among others.

incorporation the formation of a *corporation* under federal, state, or foreign laws. See *section 351 transactions* for tax-free incorporation.

increase in earnings invested in United States property, subpart F a form of *constructive distribution* to *United States shareholders* of a *controlled foreign corporation* (CFC), calculated by subtracting the *entity's* year-end *basis* in its *United States property* from its beginning-of-year investments in such property; in both cases liabilities encumbering the property are considered to reduce *basis.* §951(a)(1)(B). The underlying notion is that investments in such property are a de facto repatriation of earnings, hence, an appropriate moment to levy an *income tax.* §956.

incremental cost, energy investment credit the excess of the total cost of equipment over the amount that would have been expended for the equipment if the equipment were not used for a qualifying purpose. Reg. §1.48-9(k). The incremental cost of property (e.g., a computer associated with *automatic energy control systems*) can qualify for the *energy investment credit.* Reg. §1.49-9(e)(10).

incremental research credit see *credit for increasing research activities.*

incurred in a trade or business undertaken or sustained in connection with and in furtherance of a *trade or business.* Determining whether a *taxpayer's* activities constitute a trade or business is the usual difficulty. Once this is established, however, a *taxpayer* must still show, in order to be entitled to a *deduction,* that an *expense* (§162(a)), a *loss* (§165(c)(1)), or *business bad debt* (§166(d)) was incurred in that trade or business. In cases in which an expense or loss cannot be *apportioned* between business and nonbusiness motivations, the courts require that the taxpayer's business motives be dominant. See *carrying on a trade or business; trade or business.*

indebtedness see *debt.* For distinguishing debt of a *corporation* from equity, see *debt-equity rules.*

indebtedness of the taxpayer, income from discharge of indebtedness debt, for which *taxpayer* is personally liable or subject to which the taxpayer holds property. §108(d)(1). Section 108 offers numerous relief provisions when indebtedness of the taxpayer is discharged in a fashion that would otherwise generate *gross income.*

indefinite job, travel expenses see *travel expenses.*

indemnitor one who undertakes to indemnify (make good) another's losses. See also *guarantor.*

indemnity an undertaking to make good another's losses.

indemnity reinsurance a mechanism by which one *insurance company* (the direct writer or ceding company) transfers all or a portion of the risk under its insurance contracts to another company (the assuming company or reinsurer). In indemnity reinsurance, the ceding company remains solely liable to the policyholder, whether all or a portion of the risk is transferred to the assuming company. Therefore, the liability of the reinsurer in an indemnity reinsurance transaction is to the ceding company, and not to the policyholder of the reinsured policy.

independent contractor an *individual* subject to the control and direction of another only as to the result of his or her work, and not as to the means. Reg. §31.3401(c)-1(b). The term "independent contractor" is complementary to the term *"employee"* in that they each pertain to different employment relationships but together they include all employment relationships. However, since the term "employee" is broader in scope for purposes of *Social Security tax* (FICA) and *federal unemployment tax* (FUTA) than it is for purposes of *income tax withholding,* the term "independent contractor" is correspondingly narrower in scope for purposes of FICA and FUTA than it is for purposes of income tax withholding. Thus, *agent-drivers, full-time salesmen,* and other so-called *statutory employees* may be treated as employees for Social Security tax purposes but as independent contractors for income tax withholding purposes. There are many anomalies. For example, individuals who render *fishing boat services* are deemed independent contractors for employment tax and *quali-*

fied deferred compensation plan purposes. See §§401(c) and 3121(b)(20).

independent producer, percentage depletion Section 613A generally disallows *percentage depletion* for oil and gas, but it provides a 1,000 *barrel*/day of oil or 6 million barrel/day of gas (or some combination thereof) exemption for *taxpayers* other than major *retailers* and major *refiners* of petroleum products. See *percentage depletion.*

independent producers and royalty owners exemption a synonym for *small producers' exemption.*

indexing for inflation adjusting dollar amounts for the destructive effects of inflation. In particular, *individual, estate* and *trust* income tax rates and *exemptions* are indexed to reflect the amount of inflation. §151(d).

index method a method for computing the *base-year cost* and the *current-year cost* of a *dollar-value pool* in a *last-in, first-out* (LIFO) *inventory* system. An index is a representative measure of change, which is then applied to the pool as a whole, and may be computed either by extending a representative portion of the inventory by both current-year unit cost and base-year unit cost and comparing the two, or by using other appropriate statistical methods. Reg. §1.472-8(e)(1). Taxpayers may use specified published government indices without prior approval, if certain requirements are met. Reg. §1.472-8(e)(3)(v).

Indian tribal government the governing body of any tribe, band, community, village, or group of Indians determined by the Secretary of the Treasury on consulting with the Secretary of the Interior to exercise substantial government functions. It includes subdivisions that have been found to have been delegated one or more essential government functions of the tribal government. §§7701(a)(4), 7871. Such governments are generally treated as *states,* or *political subdivisions* as the case may be, for various purposes. Furthermore, interest on their bonds may be *exempt* from *federal income taxes.*

indirect contributions to political parties a reference to §276, which denies *deductions* for advertising in a *political party's* convention program, admission expenses for political dinners and programs, and admission expenses to inaugural balls and other political bashes, and to a lesser extent to §271, relating to *debts owed by political parties.*

indirect costs, uniform capitalization rules any costs that are not direct costs. These costs are capitalized into property that they directly benefit, or if they are incurred because of the performance of a production or resale activity. Reg. §1.263-1T(b)(2)(ii).

indirect five-percent shareholder an *individual* who owns, at any time during the *testing period,* an indirect ownership interest in the *stock* of the *loss corporation* of five percent or more by virtue of an ownership interest in any one *first-tier entity* or *higher-tier entity*. Reg. §1.382-2T(g)(1). The term is important for purposes of determining if there has been an *ownership change* such that the *section 382 limitation* might apply under the *neutrality principle*.

indirect foreign tax credit   same as the *deemed paid foreign tax credit*.

indirect partner   a *person* having an interest in a *partnership* through one or more *pass-through partners*. §6231(a)(10). See *unified proceedings*.

indirect production costs   the cost of labor and materials that can be indirectly tied to manufactured products under *full absorption accounting* for *inventory valuation*. Such costs fall into three groupings. One grouping (repairs, maintenance, utilities, rent, indirect labor and production supervisory wages, indirect materials and supplies, tools and equipment not *capitalized,* and costs of quality control and inspection) is subject to mandatory inclusion in the cost of *inventories*. Reg. §1.471-11(c)(2)(i). The second grouping (marketing, advertising, selling, and other distribution expenses, interest, research and experimentation costs, *percentage depletion* in excess of *cost depletion, depreciation* and *amortization* claimed for *federal income tax* purposes in excess of amounts claimed for financial reporting purposes, income taxes related to income received on the sale of inventory, certain pension contributions, general and administrative expenses, and officers' salaries related to nonmanufacturing activities) consists of expenses that cannot be classified as production costs, and it is subject to permissive inclusion in inventory costs. Reg. §1.471-11(c)(2)(ii). The third grouping (certain taxes, *depreciation* and *depletion,* some *employee* benefits, strike and spoilage costs, factory administrative expenses, officers' salaries, and insurance costs) is included in inventory costs if properly so recorded for financial reporting purposes. Reg. §1.471-11(c)(2)(iii). See *full absorption accounting*.

indirect production costs, uniform capitalization rules   the *costs* of labor and material that can be indirectly tied to produced property under the *uniform capitalization rules*. They include repair of equipment or facilities; maintenance of equipment or facilities; utilities relating to equipment or facilities; *rent* of equipment; facilities, or land; indirect labor and contract supervisory *wages*; indirect materials and supplies; tools and equipment not otherwise *capitalized*; quality control and inspection; taxes, other than state, local, and foreign taxes, that relate to labor, materials, supplies, equipment, land, or facilities; *depreciation, amortization,* and *cost recovery* allowances on equipment and facilities; *depletion,* whether or not in excess of cost; direct and indirect *service costs* or *mixed service costs*;

insurance on plant, machinery, or equipment, or the property produced; contributions paid under a stock bonus, pension, profit-sharing, or annuity plan; bidding expenses incurred in the solicitation of contracts; engineering and design expenses; storage, purchasing, and handling expenses. Reg. §1.263A-1T(b)(2)(iii). These costs are a type of *allocable cost* which are subject to the *uniform capitalization rules*. See *allocable costs, uniform capitalization rules*.

indirect resale costs, uniform capitalization rules generally, *costs* associated with the purchasing, handling, off-site storage, and administration of *realty* and *personal property,* of an *inventory* or *dealer property* nature, which the *taxpayer* acquires for resale. §263A(b)(2)(A). Purchasing costs include labor costs, office machines, supplies, telephone, travel, and general and administrative expenses. Reg. §1.263A-1T(d)(3)(ii)(B)(5). Handling costs include processing, assembly, repackaging, transportation from place of purchase to the taxpayer's storage facility and from the storage facility to the outlet where the sale of the delivered property occurs, as well as direct and indirect labor, tools, vehicles and equipment, maintenance of vehicles and equipment, *rent* and *depreciation* and insurance on vehicles and equipment, materials, supplies, and general and administrative expenses. Reg. §1.263A-1T(d)(3)(ii)(C). Off-site storage costs include direct and indirect labor costs, rent, *depreciation,* insurance, security, taxes, utilities, maintenance, materials, supplies, and general and administrative expenses. Reg. §1.263A-1T(d)(3)(ii)(A)(5). Administration costs include service or support functions or departments that directly benefit or are incurred by reason of purchasing, handling and off-site storage activities. Reg. §1.263-1T(d)(3)(ii)(D). These costs are a type of *allocable cost* which are subject to mandatory *capitalization* under the *uniform capitalization rules*. See *allocable costs, uniform capitalization rules*.

individual   in general, a human being. The term is used to identify this particular class of *taxpayers*. The *individual* may be contrived; an *S corporation* in its capacity as a *shareholder* of another *corporation* is defined as an individual for corporate tax law provisions. §1371(a)(2).

individual account plan, ERISA   a pension plan which provides for an individual account for each participant and for benefits based solely upon the amount contributed to the participant's account, and any income, expenses, gains and losses, and any forfeitures of accounts of other participants which may be allocated to such participant's account. ERISA §3(34).

individual account plans   see *defined contribution plan, Code*.

individually designed plan   a term used to describe a *qualified deferred compensation plan* that was drawn up to meet the particular needs of the *employer,* as contrasted with a *model, master,* or *prototype plan* that already has been approved for bulk use by the *IRS.*

individually directed account   an account in a *qualified defined contribution plan* or *IRA* which permits the plan *participant* to exercise control over assets in the participant's account.

individual medical benefit account   any separate account which is established for a retired *participant* under a *pension* or *annuity plan* and from which sickness, hospitalization, and other medical benefits described in §401(h) are payable solely to the retired participant, the participant's *spouse,* or *dependents* for whom the account was established. §415(1)(2). *Contributions* that are *allocated* to such accounts are treated as *annual additions* to *defined contribution plans* for purposes of §415(c), which limits such contributions. See *five-percent owner, employee plans.* See *subordinate benefit rule.*

individual retirement account (IRA)   a type of *individual retirement arrangement,* using as its funding medium either a *trust* or *custodial account.* §408(a) and (h). Such accounts commonly allow the *taxpayer* great flexibility in the selection of investments. They are defined in §408, which demands numerous features, including: (1) maximum contributions of $2,000 (based on the taxpayer's *compensation*); (2) a prohibition on purchasing life insurance; (3) nonforfeitability; and (4) limitations on commingling assets. Such a trust or custodial account can be maintained only by a limited class of financial institutions. §408 (a)(2) and (h). See *compensation, individual retirement arrangements.*

individual retirement annuity   a fairly closely confined form of commercial *annuity* or *endowment contract,* which can be used as the funding vehicle for *individual retirement arrangements.* The principal features of such contracts are (1) nontransferability, (2) nonforfeitability, (3) flexible premiums, (4) a $2,000 limit on annual premiums, and (5) upper limits on distribution dates. §408(b). There are further limitations in the case of endowment contracts.

individual retirement arrangement (IRA)   a form of *domestic qualified deferred compensation plan,* the principal features of which are (1) an annual maximum *deduction* of *compensation* or $2,000, whichever is less, as an *adjustment to gross income* (§62(a)(7)); (2) accumulations free of current *federal income taxes* (§408(e)(1)); (3) fully taxable distributions (§61(11)); (4) *distributions* that begin at age 70½; but (5) no *five-year forward averaging* of *lump-sum distributions.* IRAs generally cannot be used by *employees* if they are *active participants* in various *qualified plans* of their *employers.* The permissible funding media are *trusts, custodial accounts, annuities, endowment contracts,*

and, in the past, certain *retirement bonds,* but not most *collectibles.* See *conduit IRA.*

industrial and commercial profits   a *tax treaty* term generally meaning a *foreign person's* net income from the conduct of a *business,* as opposed to investment or personal service income. Tax treaties generally provide that foreign persons who have a *permanent establishment* in a host country will be taxed by the host country on their industrial and commercial profits.

industrial show   see *trade show.*

ineligible corporation, S corporations   a *corporation* which, by virtue of its character, is disqualified from being treated as an *S corporation.* §1361(b). There are five such cases: (1) a member of an *affiliated group*; (2) a financial institution to which §585 or §593 applies (various banking organizations); (3) an *insurance company* taxed under *subchapter L*; (4) certain corporations that are entitled to the *section 936 credit* for doing business in *possessions*; and (5) a *domestic international sales corporation* (DISC) or former DISC. See *section 936 election.*

influencing legislation   see *lobbying expenses* and *lobbying taxable amount.*

information at source   a reference to information provisions of the *Code* under which payors of various sorts (e.g., *employers* paying *wages* and *corporations* making *distributions* to *shareholders*) report their disbursements to payees and to the government. *Form W-2* is used for *wages* and other compensation while variants of *Form 1099* are used for other payments.

information document request   a standard request by a *revenue agent* for information from a *taxpayer* in the course of a routine *audit.*

information letter   a writing issued by the *National Office* or *District Director* to a *taxpayer* that refers to established rules or principles of tax law, but without applying the rules to a particular fact pattern. Reg. §601.201(a)(4).

information release   see *news release.*

information returns   annual 1099 series returns transmitted together with Form 1096 for paper filings (or Form 4804 for magnetic media filings) provided by payors to the *IRS* designed to report certain payments. The most common examples include the following: corporate distributions of $600 or more pertaining to partial or complete liquidations (Form 1099-DIV); interest (Form 1099-INT); certain governments payments, including tax refunds of $10 or more (Form 1099-G); rent and bonus payments of more than $600 and prizes and awards of $5,000 or more (Form 1099-MISC). §§6041–6049. See *information at source.*

information returns program an *IRS* program used at *Service Centers* which picks up items not included as *gross income* by matching them against the taxpayer's *return.*

informers' rewards rewards to tax informers, provided in the discretion of the *IRS*, not always conditioned on a criminal conviction, based on the value of the information, and not to exceed 10 percent of the additional taxes, penalties, and fines collected as a result of the information. §7623; Reg. §301.7623-1(c). Anonymity is assured. Reg. §301.7623-1(e) and (f).

inherently permanent structure any *property* (other than a *building*) that is affixed to *real property* and that will ordinarily remain affixed for an indefinite period of time. Property that is not classified as a building for purposes of *investment tax credit* (ITC) may be an inherently permanent structure. For purposes of *FIRPTA*, affixation to real property may be accomplished by weight alone. Reg. §1.897-1(b)(3)(iii). See *building, investment tax credit.*

inherently personal a catchphrase for *nondeductible expenditures* that fall into the family, personal, or living expenses classification of §262. Examples include personal grooming and business suits. The term seems to have little analytical value, because even some of these items are *deductible* if needed for *gain*-seeking purposes (e.g., certain high-fashion clothing purchased by a model).

inheritance *noncompensatory* amounts devolved from a *decedent's estate* under local law as the result of death in the absence of a will. In some states inheritances, like *bequests* and *devises,* are tax-free to the recipient. §102(a).

inheritance tax a tax imposed on the recipient of an *inheritance, bequest,* or *devise* from a *decedent,* as distinguished from an *estate tax.* Many states impose an inheritance tax as well as an estate tax. Section 2011 allows a limited *credit* for such taxes in determining the *federal estate tax.*

inherited individual retirement account or annuity an *individual retirement account* or *annuity* acquired by the *beneficiary* as a result of the death of another *individual,* provided the beneficiary is not the decedent's surviving *spouse.* §408(d)(3)(C). Such amounts may not be rolled-over tax-free, nor may *deductible* contributions be made to them. §219(d)(4). A parallel system applies to *individual retirement bonds.* §409(b)(3)(C).

in-house research expenses *wages paid or accrued* by an *employer* for *qualified services* by an *employee,* as well as amounts paid or incurred for supplies used in the conduct of *qualified research,* and amounts paid or incurred to another person for the right to use computers in the conduct of qualified research. §41(b)(2)(A).

General overhead and marketing services do not qualify. §41(b)(2)(b)(ii). Supplies are defined as tangible property other than land or improvements to land and depreciable property. In-house research expenses are a subset of *qualified research expenses,* and may enjoy the *credit for increasing research activities.* See *credit for increasing research activities; qualified research expenses; qualified service, credit for increasing research activities; research and experimental expenditures.*

initial holder, FNMA see *FNMA purchase price.*

initial inventory amount the *intercompany profit amount* of a *member of [an] affiliated group* for the *separate return year* that precedes the filing of a *consolidated return.* Reg. §1.1502-18(b). The initial inventory amount must be added to the income of the *corporation* for the *consolidated return year* in which the goods to which the initial inventory amount is attributable are *disposed of* outside the group or in which the corporation becomes a nonmember. Reg. §1.1502-18(b). See *unrecovered inventory amount.*

injunctions see *Anti-Injunction Act.*

injunctions, promoters of abusive tax shelters a reference to §7408, which permits the United States government to seek injunctive relief against any person engaging in conduct subject to the penalty for organizing or selling *abusive tax shelters.* §6700. *Venue* is generally the federal judicial district in which the promoter resides, has his or her principal place of business, or has engaged in the conduct subject to penalty under §6700. See *penalty, promoting abusive tax shelters.*

injured spouse a *spouse* not responsible for support obligations. The term is used in connection with procedures under which certain *taxpayers* who are delinquent in their support payments may lose their *refunds* to state governments that provided aid to the family. See I.R.M. 6810, §(16) 25.3, for filing procedures by an injured spouse to avoid mistaken loss of refund. See *past-due support.*

injuries, compensation for see *personal injuries or sickness.*

injury period the period used to determine *unrecovered losses*; only losses that arose in the injury period can give rise to recoveries *deductible* under §186(d)(1). Specifically, the injury period means any one of three periods, depending on the *compensable injury* sustained: (1) in the case of patent infringement, the period in which the infringement occurred; (2) in the case of breach of contract, *fiduciary* duty, or relationship, the period during which amounts would have been received if there had been no breach; and (3) in the case of violations of antitrust laws, the period in which such injuries were sustained. §186(d)(2). See *unrecovered losses.*

in kind a term loosely referring to payments, distributions, or other transfers of property other than money. Such transfers are often treated with substantially different and generally more lenient tax effects than similar transfers made in money. See, e.g., §731(a).

in-kind distributions see *distribution in kind.*

inland waterways fuel tax an *excise tax* on liquid fuels for vessels in commercial waterway transportation. It rises from 10 cents per gallon in 1990 to 20 cents per gallon after 1994, and includes a 0.01 cent per gallon surcharge for the *Leaking Underground Storage Tank Trust Fund.* §4042.

"in lieu of" taxes taxes imposed in the place of overseas *taxes* that would otherwise qualify for the *foreign tax credit.* §903. In order to qualify as such, the foreign country or *possession of the United States* must have a general income tax law in force to which the *taxpayer* would otherwise be subject, but for the "in lieu of" tax.

in-lieu payments see *substitute payments.*

innocent spouse rule an exception to the general rule of *joint and several liability* on a *joint return,* which exempts a *married person* if (1) there is unjustifiable understatement of tax attributable to *grossly erroneous items* of one *spouse* (e.g., omitted *gross income,* inflated *deductions, basis,* or *credits*) of over $500; (2) the other spouse establishes that in signing the return he or she did not know of, and had no reason to know of, the omission; and, (3) after consideration as to whether the innocent spouse significantly benefited from the omission and in light of all the other facts and circumstances, it is inequitable to hold the innocent spouse liable for the deficiency in tax. If these conditions are met, then the innocent spouse is relieved of the liability attributable to the omission. In order for an understatement to be substantial, it must exceed specified percentages of the innocent spouse's *adjusted gross income,* except for omissions of *gross income.* Also, community property law rules are ignored for this purpose. §6013(d)(3) and (e); Reg. §1.6013-5. There is somewhat analogous provision under §66 for *community property states'* residents. See also *TAMRA* §6004 (transitional relief).

in oil payment see *production payment.*

inside basis a general term for the *basis of property* in the hands of a *partnership* and correspondingly for each *partner's* share of that basis, as contrasted with *outside basis,* which is the partner's or partners' *basis in the partnership interest.* Although generally the same, outside and *inside basis* may differ because of transactions affecting partnership interests. For applications of the term, see especially §§723, 734, and 754. See *partnership's basis in assets.*

insolvency exception a rule to the effect that to the extent debtor is *insolvent* (liabilities in excess of *fair market value* of assets) after a *discharge of indebtedness,* the debtor does not realize *gross income.* §108(a)(1)(B) See *insolvent debtor.*

insolvency reorganizations a *Type G reorganization* whereby all or part of the assets of a debtor corporation are transferred to an acquiring corporation in a bankruptcy or similar proceeding in a federal or state court. The debtor corporation's creditors must receive voting stock of the acquiring corporation for debt representing 80 percent or more of the total fair market value of the debt of the debtor corporation. §368(a)(1)(G).

insolvent the opposite of *solvent.* See *solvency.*

insolvent debtor a person, the *fair market value* of whose assets is less than that person's debts (i.e., a person who has a negative net worth). §108(d)(3). Insolvent debtors who are not in a *title eleven case* (federal bankruptcy), and whose liabilities are reduced, exclude such discharges from *gross income* to the extent the debtor thereafter has no net worth. §108(a)(1)(B) and (a)(2)(B). Negative net worth is determined immediately before the discharge. See *solvency.*

installed capacity, energy investment credit with respect to any *qualified hydroelectric site,* the installed capacity of all electrical generating equipment placed in service at the site, including the capacity of equipment installed during the three *taxable years* following the taxable year in which the equipment was placed in service. §48(1)(13)(E). To qualify as *energy property* for purposes of the *energy investment credit,* hydroelectric generating property must meet the rules with respect to its installed capacity under §48(1)(13).

installed capacity fraction a fraction derived from the *installed capacity* of a hydroelectric generating facility. The numerator is 25, reduced (but not below zero) by the number of megawatts by which the installed capacity exceeds 100, and the denominator is the number of megawatts of installed capacity, not exceeding 100. §103(b)(8)(D). The fraction is used to limit and phase out federal tax subsidies for financing more powerful hydroelectric facilities. The same fraction is used in §48(1)(13)(C) to reduce or eliminate the *energy investment credit* for such facilities. See *installed capacity, energy investment credit; qualified hydroelectric generating property, energy investment credit.*

installment gifts an *estate planning* term for *gifts* of property made in annual installments in order for the donee to enjoy the benefits of the *annual gift tax exclusion.* The practice of making such gifts by sale of property to the intended *donee,* followed by systematic forgiveness of parts of the debt, generated considerable controversy, but the practice is now sharply confined by §453B(f).

installment method generally, a *method of accounting* for reporting *gains* on *sales* of property. The method applies to sales of property (other than most *dealer property* and *inventory*), with at least one payment to be made in a year after the *taxable year* the sale is made; as a result, *gains* (not *losses*) are reported ratably as *payments* are made. §453. The *character* of the gain is preserved in later years and is determined as of the date of the sale. The gain with respect to each payment is determined by a *profit ratio*, which is basically the ratio of the *gross profit* on the sale to *total contract price.* The result is to treat a constant fraction of each payment as gain. To take a simple case, assume a sale of a car that cost the *taxpayer* $500 and which he or she now sells for $1,000; $600 is payable this year, and $400 next year. The profit ratio is $500 over $1,000, or 50 percent. Thus, $300 of gain is reported this year, and $200 next year. See *nondealer real property installment obligations; related person, sales of depreciable property; related person, sales of depreciable property.*

installment obligation generally, an obligation taken back from a buyer by a seller of property who reports the *sale* on the *installment method.*

installment obligation, one-year liquidations If a corporation makes an installment sale of its assets in the course of a 12-month liquidation, and if it distributes the installment obligations that it received from the sale during the 12-month period beginning when the plan of liquidation is adopted, the shareholders are not taxed when they receive the obligations. It is the subsequent payments received by the shareholders on the installment obligations, rather than the obligations distributed to the shareholders, that are treated by the shareholders as *liquidation payments* received by them for their stock. The liquidation exchange is reported by the shareholder on the installment method. §453(h). See *section 331 liquidation.*

installment payment any payment made under the *installment method,* including encumbrances in excess of *basis,* which are treated as payments in the year of sale.

installment payment annuity rule a colloquial term for a method of determining *taxable income* derived by an *annuity.* The approach is to divide the *investment in the contract* by the period during which it will be paid, and to treat that portion of each payment as a tax-free *return of capital.*

installment payment arrangement a plan whereby a taxpayer, who has agreed to a definite tax liability, attempts to negotiate an installment payment arrangement. This is done with a revenue officer but may also be done through the automated collected system (ACS). §6159. The IRS will not agree to an installment payment arrangement without the taxpayer submitting a detailed financial statement on *Form 433.* See *offer in compromise.*

installment payment of estate tax a permissive tax payment method available to *estates* that allows an estate to pay a portion of its estate tax liability in installments if a substantial portion of the estate consists of the decedent's interest in a closely held business. §6166(b). An estate is eligible if more than 35 percent of the *adjusted gross estate* consists of the value of such an interest. The percentage of the estate tax liability that can be deferred is based on the ratio of the value of the closely held business to the value of the adjusted gross estate. The tax deferred under §6166 is payable in *10 equal installments.* The rate of interest is 4 percent interest on the portion of the estate tax, after *credits,* attributable to the proportionate value of the closely held business. In a sense, the estate can borrow a certain amount of dollars from the government at 4 percent, and the rest at a higher, but still favorable, rate. See §§6166(a),(b).

installment percentage, proportionate disallowance rule see *allocable installment indebtedness.*

installment plan see *revolving credit plan; sale on the installment plan.*

installment sale a *sale* of property where at least one *payment* will be received in a *taxable year* following the year of sale. Reg. §15a.453-1(b). *Gains* from installment sales are generally reported on the *installment method,* unless the seller elects out under §453(d). *Dealer dispositions* of *personal property* and *inventory*-type property are not installment sales. §453(b)(2).

installment sale method another term for *installment method.* The *Code* uses the term installment method in the key place. §453(a).

institutional advertising advertising that keeps the *taxpayer's* name in the public eye. Such expenditures are generally *deductible* as *trade or business expenses* if they relate to patronage the taxpayer might reasonably expect in the future. Likewise, costs of advertising that present views on economic, financial, social, or other subjects of a general nature (not involving political lobbying for the promotion or defeat of legislation, the election or defeat of political candidates, or the influencing of the public to approve or reject a measure in a referendum or similar procedure) are deductible if they otherwise meet the requirements of §162. Reg. §1.162-15(c)(1) and -20(a)(2). Such advertising is often referred to as goodwill advertising.

institution of higher education an educational institution in any state that (1) admits as regular students only *individuals* that have a certificate of graduation from a high school, or the recognized equivalent of such a certificate; (2) is legally authorized within such a state to provide a program of education beyond high school; (3) provides an educational program that awards a bachelor's or higher degree, provides a program that is acceptable for full credit toward such a degree, or offers a program of training to prepare students for gainful employment in a recognized occupation; and (4) is a public or other nonprofit institution. §3304(f) (state compliance with federal unemployment tax). The term is used in §41 for purposes of the *credit for increasing research activities* and in §170(e)(4)(B) regarding *charitable contributions* of property used for research purposes.

insubstantial authority list   a list the *IRS* is required to publish annually which shows positions believed to lack *substantial authority.* §6662(d)(2)(i). See *substantial authority.*

insubstantial rights, retention   minor rights, the retention of which by a charitable *donor* does not cause the transfer to be classified as a *partial interest* so as to bar a *charitable contribution deduction.* The focus is on whether the charitable *donee* is still a full owner, despite the retention. Examples of transfers with insubstantial retained rights include the right to train hunting dogs on donated land (Rev. Rul. 75-66, 1975-1 C.B. 85), the right to hunt on donated property (Letter Rul. 8140002, May 27, 1981), and the right to store personal property in a vacation home (Rev. Rul. 75-420, 1975-2 C.B. 78).

insurance   undefined in the *Code,* but generally it is an agreement whereby for a consideration one promises to pay money or its equivalent to another for the destruction, death, loss, or injury of someone or something from specified perils. See *captive insurance company; life insurance proceeds.*

insurance company   a company, more than half of whose annual business is issuing *insurance* or *annuity contracts* or reinsuring risks underwritten by insurance companies. §816(a).

insurance company deductions   all *ordinary and necessary trade or business expenses, interest expenses, deductible taxes,* various allowable *losses* on the *disposition* of assets to meet business needs. See §832(b)(5); *capital losses; tax-exempt interest; depletion deductions; charitable contributions* and *deductions* and allowances for items like contributions to *pension, profit-sharing,* and *stock bonus plans; dividends* and similar *distributions* paid or declared to policyholders; certain *dividends-received deductions*; and the *mortgage guaranty company deduction.* §832(c). *Insurance company taxable income,* the tax base of *insurance companies* other than *life insurance companies,* consists of its *gross income* less *insurance company deductions.* §832(a). See *gross income, insurance companies.*

insurance company group, limitations on graduated taxes, and other benefits   two or more *life insurance companies* taxable under §801 that are considered members of either a *brother-sister controlled group,* a *parent-subsidiary controlled group,* or a *combined group.* §1563(a)(4). Insurance company groups are subject to the controlled group provisions. See also *includible corporations.*

insurance company taxable income   the heading of §832, referring to, in general, *gross income* of an *insurance company* as defined in §832(b)(1), less the *deductions* permitted in §832(c). §832; Reg. §1.832-1. The term relates to the taxation of stock nonlife insurers, mutual marine insurers, and certain fire or flood insurance companies.

insurance contract plans, qualified plans   certain *qualified plans,* funded with *individual* or *group insurance* or *annuity contracts,* which are exempt from the Code's *minimum funding standards.* The principal requirements are that the insurer be state-regulated. See §412(i); Reg. §1.412(i).

insurance income, subpart F   net premiums or other consideration received by a *controlled foreign corporation* (CFC) for its *insurance,* reinsurance, or issuance of an *annuity* contract in connection with property in or a liability arising from health or mortality risks located in a *foreign country* where the CFC is not incorporated. §953(a)(1)(A). See *United States risks.*

insurance reserves required by law, deductibility   The amount of the deduction for dividends or similar distributions to policyholders for any tax year is the amount of policyholder dividends paid or accrued during the year rather than the amount of the increase in the reserves for policyholder dividends. Thus, no income or loss is recognized with respect to amounts in existing policyholder dividend reserves. §808(c).

insured medical reimbursement plans   *employer-*paid medical care plans provided under an *individual* or group accident or health insurance policy issued by a licensed insurance company under, or under an arrangement in the nature of, a prepaid health care plan. *Employer* contributions are *deductible,* and the benefits of the plan can be *excluded* by employees. §§105(b) and (h)(6), 106, 162.

intangible drilling and development costs   *expenditures* incurred by an *operator* that have no *salvage value* and are incident to and necessary for the drilling of wells and the preparation of wells for the production of oil and gas and geothermal energy. These costs including wages, fuel, repairs, hauling, supplies used in the drilling, clearing of ground, draining, road making, surveying, and geological works necessary in preparation for the drilling of wells and in the construction of physical structures necessary for the drilling and preparation of wells for the production of oil or gas. Operators may elect to currently deduct intangible drilling and development costs rather than charge such costs to capital, recoverable through depletion or depreciation. §§263(c), 612; Reg. §1.612-4(a). See *develop-*

ment, oil, gas, and geothermal; exploration, oil, gas and geothermal.

intangible drilling cost preference the amount by which *alternative minimum taxable income* would be reduced if it were calculated without the *intangible drilling cost* preference or the *adjusted current earnings* IDC preference, adjustment from wells not drilled for any geothermal deposits. §56(h)(7)(A). The part of the intangible drilling cost preference attributable to *qualified exploratory costs* is prorated in accordance with how much of the *taxpayer's* IDCs (including those *capitalized*) in the search for oil and gas are qualified exploratory costs. §57(h)(7)(B). The CNEPA of 1992 (Pub. L. 102-486) repeals the *alternative tax energy preferences* for excess drilling costs effective for tax years beginning after 1992. The repeal of the excess intangible drilling costs can't result in a reduction of more than 40 percent (30 percent for tax years beginning in 1993) in the taxpayer's alternative minimum taxable income. §1915.

intangible property income income, attributed to certain *intangible personal property*, earned by *possessions corporations* claiming the *possessions tax credit* and taxed to the corporation's *shareholders* whether or not distributed. The construct imposes United States taxes on intangibles that add value to products produced by a possessions corporation whose intangibles are received from related domestic *taxpayers*. This reverses excessive allocations of income to such intangibles by possessions corporations, which shield the income with the possessions tax credit. Intangible property income is defined as the *gross income* of a possessions corporation attributable to any intangible property other than that which has been licensed to it since before 1948 and used by it on the date of enactment of *TEFRA*. §936(h)(3)(A).

intangible property of possessions corporations see *intangible property income.*

intangible property or rights goodwill, *stock* in a *corporation,* or a *patent* right. If such property can be written off at all, it is done by means of *amortization,* not *depreciation* or cost recovery.

intangibles see *intangible property or rights.*

integrated auxiliary of a church an *exempt organization* whose principal activity is exclusively religious, and which is affiliated with a *church,* meaning controlled by or associated with a church, *convention, or association of churches.* The entities share common religious bonds and convictions; examples include seminaries, youth groups, and religious schools. Reg. §1.6033-2(g)(5)(iii). Such auxiliaries are not required to file *federal income tax returns.* §6033(a)(2)(A)(i).

integrated benefit a benefit under an *integrated plan.*

integrated financial transactions multipart transactions such as debt-financed acquisitions of foreign currency debt obligations or other comparable arbitrage transactions. Section 864(e)(7)(8) authorizes *regulations* to provide for the direct *allocation* of *interest expense* incurred to income generated from the assets acquired with borrowed funds. The *IRS* may also allocate interest expense directly to interest or other passive income if doing so is needed.

integrated oil company, alternative tax energy preference deduction any producer of crude oil which does not qualify for *percentage depletion* because of its status as a *retailer* or *refiner* under §614A(d)(2) or (4). §56(h)(6)(D).

integrated plan a *deferred compensation* plan in which *Social Security benefits* are considered in fixing benefits under what is intended to be a *qualified plan.* Such plans can remain qualified (and not illegally discriminatory) despite differences in proportionate benefits that favor more highly paid *employees,* if such differences are appropriately offset by old age, survivors, and disability insurance benefits attributable to *employer contributions* under the *Federal Insurance Contributions Act* (Social Security tax). Rev. Rul. 71-446, 1971-2 C.B. 188. See *integration, Social Security.*

integrated transaction doctrine a synonym for *step transaction doctrine.*

integration level the level of compensation at or below which, under a *qualified plan's* benefit formula, *compensation* is partly or entirely disregarded in the calculation of contributions to or benefits from the plan. §401(l)(5)(A)(i). For example, a plan might provide for greater contributions for participants whose wages exceed $15,000; the plan would have an integration level of $15,000. See *permitted disparity.*

integration rate the retirement benefit provided by a *qualified plan,* stated as a percentage of *compensation* which exceeds the *integration level.* Integration rates are limited by the *Code.* §401(a)(5).

integration, Social Security a practice, authorized by §401(a)(5), Rev. Rul. 71-446, 1971-2 C.B. 188, and Reg. §1.401-3(e), under which contributions to a *qualified plan* may be diminished to take account of the *employer's* contributions to the Social Security system. This relaxation makes it easier for the plan to meet *nondiscrimination* tests relating to *employer-provided contributions and benefits.* For plan years beginning after 1983, contributions to defined contribution plans must be integrated at a uniform rate. Thus, if the rate of employer contribution exceeds the FICA rate, then corrective contributions must also be made for *employees* whose *wages* fall below the *Social Security wage base.* §401(1). See *integrated plan.*

intellectual property a loose term for *patents, copyrights,* secret processes, trade names, *trademarks,* and similar property. Such properties generally *qualify* as *capital assets* under §1221 unless held by the creator or his or her *donee*(s). §1221(3).

Intelligence Division the predecessor of the *Criminal Investigation Division.*

intentional disregard of rules and regulations a knowing failure to pay tax, but without intent to defraud. See *penalty, negligence by tax return preparer.*

intercept program see *past-due support.*

intercompany dividends dividends received by a *member of [an] affiliated group* of *corporations* from another member during a *consolidated return year.* Reg. §1.1502-26(b). Intercompany dividends are eliminated from *consolidated taxable income* for purposes of computing the group's *consolidated tax liability.* Reg. §1.1502-14(a).

intercompany pricing prices charged for *sales* of goods between commonly controlled business organizations. Section 482 authorizes the *IRS* to establish different prices, if the prices charged do not reflect an *arm's length* standard, and a series of standards to determine how to set intercompany prices. See *advance pricing agreement; comparable uncontrolled price method; cost-plus method; resale price method.*

intercompany profit amount profits of a *corporation* arising in transactions with other members of the *affiliated group* with respect to goods that are, at the close of the *corporation's taxable year,* included in the *inventories* of any other member of the group. Reg. §1.1502-18(a). If a corporation files a *consolidated return* with members of an *affiliated group* and filed a *separate return* for the preceding year, then the intercompany inventory profit amount of the corporation for the *separate return year* is added to the income of the corporation for the *consolidated return year* in which the goods containing the intercompany profit are *disposed of* outside the group or in which the corporation becomes a nonmember. Reg. §1.1502-18(b).

intercompany transaction a transaction during a *consolidated return year* between *corporations* that are *members of an affiliated group* immediately after the transaction. Reg. §1.1502-13(a)(1). An intercompany transaction may, for example, include a *sale* of property, performance of services, or the payment of *interest* by one affiliated group member to another group member. Reg. §1.1502-13(a)(1)(i). However, the term excludes *dividend* distributions or the sale or *other disposition* of stock or debt instruments between affiliated group members. Reg. §1.1502-13(g)(1)(ii). Intercompany transactions that are considered *deferred intercompany transactions* are *recognized* only to the

extent required under Reg. §1.1502-13(c)(2), consistent with the basic view that an affiliated group is a single *taxpayer.* All intercompany transactions besides deferred intercompany transactions are treated as if the transactions were between the corporation and a nonaffiliated group member. §1.1502-13(b). It is consistent with the basic view that an affiliated group is a single taxpayer.

interest for purposes of §163, allowing a *deduction* for *interest expenses* on *debt,* the term traditionally refers to a charge for the use, forebearance, or detention of money. Interest is commonly imputed under the *Code,* for example, by §§453A(d) (interest on certain *tax deferrals*), 483 (*imputed interest*), and 1232 (*original issue discount*). An indebtedness for these purposes is an unconditional, reasonably ascertainable, and legally enforceable obligation for the payment of money. See *debt; imputed interest; indebtedness; original issue discount; rule of seventy-eights.*

interest and carrying charges, straddle the excess of (1) the sum of *interest* on *debt* incurred, or continued, to purchase or carry *personal property* that is part of a *straddle,* and amounts *paid or incurred* to insure, store, or transport that personal property; over (2) the sum of the amount of *interest income,* including *original issue discount,* from the property *includible* in *gross income* for the *taxable year,* and any amount treated as *ordinary income* under §§1271, 1278, and 1281 (relating to certain *acquisition discounts.* §263(g)(2). Such amounts (less *compensating payments* paid to a securities lender) must be *capitalized.* §263(g)(1). The rule is designed to thwart *cash and carry commodities transactions.*

interest charge DISC a *domestic international sales corporation* (DISC) which has $10 million or less of *qualified export receipts.* Under the interest charge DISC system, a nondeductible interest charge tied to the Treasury bill rate is imposed on the *shareholders* of a DISC, based on the shareholder's DISC-related tax-deferred liability. §995(f). As in the case of a *small FSC,* small exporters can elect to use the interest charge DISC operates as a relief provision for smaller companies, following the general elimination of the DISC by the *Tax Reform Act of 1984.*

interest coupons coupons attached to bonds that can be removed and tendered to the obligor for payment of interest. Corporate and government debt obligations with interest coupons are *securities* for purposes of special treatment as *statutory sales* when they become worthless, provided they are *capital assets* in the *taxpayer's* hands. §165(g); Reg. §1.165-5(a)(3). When older bonds with interest coupons attached are redeemed, *gain* can result in *capital gain* treatment. §1232(c).

interest deduction see *interest expense deduction.*

interested parties, qualified plans persons entitled to notification of a *determination letter* request relating to the status of a *deferred compensation* plan. The term includes *employees* who are eligible to participate and other employees whose principal place of employment is the same as that of any eligible *employer*. Reg. §1.7476-1(b)(l)(ii).

interest expense generally, the implicit or express price charged per unit of time for the use of a creditor's money, or for the creditor's forebearance in demanding repayment. Rev. Rul. 72-458, 1972-2 C.B. 514. See *interest; interest expense deduction.*

interest expense deduction a *deduction* allowed for *interest paid or accrued* on *debt* in the *taxable year.* §163. The interest expense may take the form of *bond discount,* and it does not depend on a *business purpose* for *deductibility.* However, if incurred in a business setting or in connection with property *held for the production of rents or royalties,* then it can be deducted as an *adjustment to gross income.* §62(5). The deduction may be contingent on the obligation being registered. There are severe restrictions on deductions for *investment interest,* and *personal interest* is entirely *nondeductible.* §163(d) and (h). See *registration-required obligation.*

interest-free loans loans that bear no *interest.* Interest-free loans impose imputed interest income to the lender. At the same time, the borrower is deemed to have incurred interest expense equal to the imputed income. §7872(a)(1). Imputed interest is calculated with the rate the federal government pays on new borrowings and is compounded semiannually. Since such loans (and *below-market loans*) have been rendered taxable to the lender, they may be subject to *gift taxes.* See *below-market loan; compensation-related loan; gift loans.*

interest in a closely held business a major proprietary interest in a *business,* entitled to favorable *estate tax* treatment. The term refers to (1) an interest as a proprietor in a *trade or business* carried on as a *proprietorship*; (2) an interest as a *partner* in a business *partnership* if (a) 20 percent or more of the total *capital interest in the partnership* is included in determination of the *gross estate* of the *decedent,* or (b) it has 15 or fewer partners; or (3) *stock* in a business *corporation* if (a) at least 20 percent of the voting stock by value is included in determination of the gross estate of the decedent, or (b) it has 15 or fewer shareholders. §6166(b). *Estates* that consist in large measure of such interests are granted a substantial *deferral* of time to pay estate taxes and a reduced rate of interest on the estate tax on the first $1 million in value of the business interest. §6166.

interest income generally, the implicit or express price due per period of time for the use of a creditor's money, or for the creditor's forebearance in demanding repayment. Rev. Rul. 72-458, 1972-2 C.B. 514. It is explicitly an item of *gross income.* §61.

interest in the dwelling unit, vacation home rules unclear, but of sufficient interest to attract the limits of §280A. See Priv. Let. Rul. 8247039 (Aug. 23, 1982) (partnership which leased residential realty to lessees with options to purchase at formula prices resulted in use by person without an interest in the property, hence vacation home rules were inapplicable). See *shared equity financing agreement; vacation home rules.*

interest on investment indebtedness limitation a limitation imposed by §163(d) which prevents noncorporate *taxpayers* from *deducting investment interest expenses* to the extent they exceed *net investment income* for the *taxable year.* The excess is not permanently disallowed but instead is carried forward to future years and subject to similar limits. §163(d)(2). Net investment income consists of *investment income* less *investment expenses.* Section 163(d)(6) provides a fairly generous phase-in rule. See *interest expense; investment income, interest on investment indebtedness limitation; investment expense, interest on investment indebtedness limitation; investment interest expense; net investment income.*

interest, personal holding company income any amounts, includible in *gross income,* received for the use of money loaned. Reg. §1.543-1(b)(2). *Interest* income may also include *redeemable ground rents* and *imputed interest* under §483(c). Carrying charges and loan origination fees (points) can also constitute interest. See, e.g., Rev. Rul. 70-540, 1970-2 C.B. 101. Interest income is *personal holding company income.* §543(a)(1).

interest, real estate investment trust for purposes of the 95 percent test, all *interest* except interest based on the net income of any person; for purposes of the 75 percent test, only *interest* on obligations secured by *mortgages* on *realty* or *interests in real property.* §856(c)(2)(B), (c)(3)(B) and (f). In both cases interest is used to determine whether the composition of the *entity's* income disqualifies it as a *real estate investment trust.* See *contingent interest; real estate investment trust.*

interests in real property, real estate investment trust (REIT) fee ownership and co-ownership of land cr improvements, leaseholds of land or improvements, or options to acquire land or improvements; mineral, oil, or gas royalty interests are excluded. §856(c)(6); Reg. §1.856-3(c). One of the tests to qualify as a REIT is that a substantial part of the enterprise's *gross income* must come from real property or interests in real property. §856(c). See *real estate investment trust.*

interest wholly exempt from tax *interest* that, by its character, is entirely free of *federal income taxes,* and subject to relaxation in the case of interest from certain *face-amount certificates,* but which includes current *tax-*

exempt interest dividends distributed by *regulated investment companies* (both as to the company and the shareholder). The term wholly is now antique; the qualification was used to exclude certain extinct federal obligations that created partially exempt interest. Interest on debt incurred or continued to purchase or carry obligations generating income wholly exempt from tax is rendered *nondeductible* by §265(2). In parallel fashion, §212 *deductions* (e.g., rental charged to an *individual* investor for a safe deposit box holding such securities) are disallowed by §265(1). *Gains* deferred by *nonrecognition provisions* or gains excludable if previously they generated no *tax benefit* are not considered income wholly exempt from tax.

interest, withholding Backup withholding tax is imposed on interest, dividends, and certain other payments if the payee fails to provide his or her taxpayer identification number. For amounts paid to December 31, 1992, the backup withholding rate was 20 percent. For amounts paid after 1992, the CNEPA of 1992 (Pub. L. 102-486) increases the backup rate to 31 percent. §1935. See *backup withholding tax.*

interference with tax administration actual or attempted intimidation of any officer or *employee* of the United States acting in an official capacity under the *Code,* or any other active or actual or intended obstruction or interference with the administration of the tax laws. §7212(a). The interference may be by force, by threats of bodily harm to an officer or employee or a member of his or her family, or by any means deemed to be corrupt (undefined), and it is punishable by fines, imprisonment, or both.

interim closing of books the calculation of income based on hypothesizing that the computation period should end as of some particular date, e.g., as of the day when a *partner* sells his entire interest in a *partnership* under §706(c)(1).

interlocutory during the course of a suit, pending a final decree. The issue often arises in the divorce area; in particular, interlocutory decrees of divorce or decrees of alimony pendente lite can qualify the payments as *periodic payments* that are *deductible* by the payor under §215 and includible in the income of the payee under §71. §71(a)(3); Reg. §1.71-1(b)(3).

interlocutory order an order made before final judgment, i.e., during the pendency of a proceeding but not the disposing of the proceeding. See, e.g., §7482(a).

Internal Revenue Bulletin an office bulletin containing compilations of *revenue rulings,* notices of *acquiescence* and *nonacquiescence,* legislative history of revenue laws, and the like, compiled by year, issue number, and page number. They are later incorporated into *Cumulative Bulletins.*

Internal Revenue Code the primary source of United States taxes. It is found in 26 U.S.C. §1 et seq.

Internal Revenue District see *District.*

Internal Revenue Manual a compilation of internal *IRS* practices and procedures, now made public under the *Freedom of Information Act* and reproduced by Commerce Clearing House. Among other things, the manual advises revenue agents on how to audit particular industries and *tax shelter* issues, and it commonly sets forth the government position on the applicable law.

Internal Revenue Service (IRS) the largest component of the *Treasury Department,* comprised of a *National Office* in Washington, D.C., and an extensive field organization. The field organization consists of seven Internal Revenue Regions, each of which is commanded by a Regional Commissioner; *Internal Revenue Districts,* each of which is commanded by a *District Director*; and ten Internal Revenue *Service Centers.* Some districts have further suboffices.

international air passenger departure tax a $6 tax per passenger on international fights departing from the *United States.* §4261.

international boycott activity, participation and cooperation generally, consenting with an unsanctioned boycott based on race, nationality, or religion. A *taxpayer* who, in order to do *business* in a certain country (or with its nationals or companies) agrees, expressly or impliedly, not to do business with another specified country or with a *United States person* who conducts business in such a blacklisted country, is considered to participate in an international boycott. §99(b)(3)(A)(i) and (ii). Likewise, if a *corporation* agrees to refrain from doing business with any company whose management is composed of persons of a particular nationality, race, or religion, or if it removes or refrains from selecting directors or *employees* of such origins, then there is cooperation. §999(b)(3)(A)(iii) and (iv). Finally, if a corporation, as a condition of the sale of its products, agrees to refrain from shipping on a carrier owned or operated by a person who is not cooperating with an international boycott, then there is boycott participation. §999(b)(3)(B). Compliance with official United States boycotts and with import or export laws of any country is, however, outside the definition. §999(b). The burdens of participation are forced inclusion of income from boycott operations under *subpart F* (§952(a)(3)), a reduction of the *foreign tax credit* (§908(a)), and a *deemed distribution* under the DISC rules (§995(b)(l)(F)(ii)), determined in part by reference to an *international boycott factor.* See Notice 82-16, 1982-36 I.R.B. 10 (list of boycotting countries). See *separate and identifiable operations exemption.*

international boycott factor a fraction, the numerator of which reflects the overseas operations for the *taxable year* of a *person* (or controlled group as defined in §993(a)(3)) related to a country or countries associated in carrying out an international boycott, and the denominator of which reflects total overseas operations of that *person* or group. §999(c)(1).

international boycott income an informal term used for the increase in *subpart F income* caused by participation in certain international boycotts. Specifically, a *United States shareholder* of a *controlled foreign corporation* (*CFC*) must report as income a pro rata share of the corporation's income from boycott operations which would otherwise not be currently taxed to it. §§952(a)(3), 999(c). See also §927(e)(2). See *subpart F income*.

international boycott income, DISC income deemed distributed to *shareholders* of a *domestic international sales corporation* (DISC) as a result of participation or cooperation in an international boycott. §995(b)(1)(F)(ii). See *international boycott activity, participation and cooperation*.

international communications income all income derived from the transmission of communications or data from the *United States* to any *possession of the United States* or *foreign country,* or from any foreign country or United States possession to the United States. §863(e). *United States persons* report half of such income as United States source income. See *source rules*.

international departure tax an *excise tax* used to fund the Airport and Airway Trust Fund (AATF) of $6 per person on international flights beginning in the *United States.* §4261(c).

international finance subsidiary a *corporation* established in a convenient *tax-haven* country (e.g., Netherlands Antilles) by a United States parent corporation. The subsidiary borrows money abroad, with the guarantee of the United States parent, and lends the money to the United States parent. If the subsidiary were located in a country with an attractive *tax treaty* with the United States, then the United States tax on *interest* remittances to the subsidiary could be trivial or zero.

international organization a public international organization entitled to the privileges, exemptions, and immunities granted by the International Organizations Immunities Act (22 U.S.C. 288-288f (1976)). §7701(a)(18). See Reg. §§1.892-1(b), 1.893-1 for details. Such organizations are generally *tax-exempt.* §892. Examples include the United Nations and World Bank.

interpretative regulations *regulations* issued pursuant to §7805(a), authorizing the *Treasury Department* to issue "needful rules and regulations." They are designed to interpret preexisting but incompletely expressed law found in the *Internal Revenue Code.* The validity of such regulations is complex and uncertain. Generally, such regulations will stand unless found inconsistent with the Code or legislative history, or

unreasonable. See *regulations, Treasury Administrative and Procedural.*

interstate cooperation laws, piggyback taxation state laws that may be in effect simultaneously with a *state agreement* and that provide for cooperation or reciprocal agreement between the electing state and another state with respect to *income taxes* applicable to *individuals.* Reg. §301.6363-1(a)(2)(iv). Certified copies of these laws must be filed with the Secretary of the Treasury prior to adoption of the *piggyback taxation* system.

interview audit generally, an *IRS audit* of a *taxpayer* of a face-to-face variety, as opposed to a *correspondence audit.* Such an audit may be held at the offices of the IRS (*office audit*) or elsewhere (*field audit*). The term is also used in reference demands for oral information in connection with summonses issued by the IRS. See *Q and A.*

inter vivos "during life" as opposed to "by will." For example, *trusts* may be established during the life of the *grantor* (*inter vivos trust*) or by will (*testamentary trust*).

inter vivos trust a revocable or irrevocable *trust,* formed during the life of the *grantor,* often called a living trust.

intestate without a will.

in the money put and calls put and calls that at a particular moment contain a guaranteed *gain* element. For example, if a call allows the *taxpayer* to purchase the stock of X Corp. for $40, and if the stock trades at $45, then the put is in the money to the extent of $5.

intragroup stock *stock* in one member of an *affiliated group* of *corporations* filing a *consolidated return* which is held by another member of the group. It can include a former member of the group that disposes of stock of another former member. §1503(e)(2). The *basis* of such stock is subject to complicated adjustments and its *disposition* can generate *gains* based on *excess loss accounts.*

intramural expansion a colloquial term describing the expansion of an existing *business* into a related field through acquisition or internally generated growth. Expenses for intramural expansion may be currently *deductible* under §162(a).

inure redound to the benefit of. See *inurement of earnings to a private shareholder or individual.*

inurement of earnings to a private shareholder or individual the derivation of improper benefits by insiders of various otherwise *exempt organizations,* the result of which is loss of the tax exemption. See, e.g., §501(c)(3), (4), (6), (7), and (9). The term contemplates improper diversion of a portion of such organizations' *net earnings* by a person in control of the disposition of the organizations' funds or related to such a person.

invalid addition   the improper combination of an *operating mineral interest* to an existing mineral aggregation, such as adding part of a *mine* to an aggregation that does not include other interests which are part of the same mine, or adding part of a mine in one *operating unit* to an aggregation that is in another operating unit. Invalid additions are generally treated as a separate *property,* unless the *IRS* consents to a change. Reg. §1.614-3(f)(8)(iii). Such additions may not be aggregated for *depletion* purposes. Reg. §1.614-3(f)(8)(i). See *aggregation of mineral interests.*

invalid basic aggregation   an aggregation that is initially invalid because, for example, it includes *operating interests* that are not part of the same *operating unit.* Separate *operating mineral interests* included in an invalid basic aggregation are treated as a separate *property* for the first year for which the election is made and thereafter unless the *IRS* permits a change. Reg. §1.614-3(f)(8)(ii). Such additions may not be aggregated for *depletion* purposes. Reg. §1.614-3(f)(8)(i). See *aggregation of mineral interests.*

invasion of corpus   usually, a trustee's taking of the principal of a *trust* for a *beneficiary.*

inventory   generally, all finished or partly finished goods, raw materials, and supplies that will become merchandise intended for sale, and containers as to which the buyer will receive title. Merchandise held for sale remains in a *taxpayer's inventory* even though it is subject to a contract for sale if it has not yet been segregated and applied to the contract, and goods shipped on consignment remain in the consignor's inventory. Likewise, merchandise to which the taxpayer has title but not possession is included. Reg. §§1.471-1 and -2(f)(5), 1.472-1(b). This definition results in the identification of items that must be included in opening and closing inventories and is critical to determining *cost of goods sold.* See *first-in, first-out (FIFO); last-in, first-out (LIFO); inventory methods.*

inventory accounting   a *method of accounting* under which income (or loss) is reported by determining sales revenues for the year and subtracting the *taxpayer's cost of goods sold.* Generally, inventory purchases and sales must be reported on the *accrual method.* Reg. §1.446-1(c)(2)(i). *Expenses* incurred in acquiring or producing manufactured inventory must be accrued and absorbed into the cost of the items and cannot, therefore, be *deducted* until they are sold. Reg. §1.471-2. Section 471 and Reg. §1.61-3(a) commonly combine to require the use of the method for manufacturers, merchandisers, and mining enterprises. Farmers and ranchers may elect out of the inventory accounting requirements. Reg. §1.471-6. See *full absorption accounting; uniform capitalization rules.*

inventory items   for purposes of the *collapsible partnership rules* of §751, the term refers to a class of *section 751 assets,* specifically: (1) *stock in trade* and *inventory,* in the usual sense; (2) property other than *capital assets* or *section 1231 assets* (e.g., *accounts receivable* for services); (3) property that would fall into any of these categories if held by the *partner,* unless they are in fact distributed to the partner; and (4) property subject to *ordinary income* treatment under §1246(a) (e.g., *foreign investment company* stock). §751(d)(2). Such items are *substantially appreciated* if their value exceeds 120 percent of their *adjusted bases* in the hands of the *partnership* and more than 10 percent of the *fair market value* of all partnership property other than money, in which case they can cause conversion of *capital gains* into ordinary income at the partner level. §751(d)(2). *Unrealized receivables* are added for purposes of the 10–120 percent tests. Reg. §1.751-1(d)(2)(ii). The term is also used in §735(a)(2) involving *dispositions* by *partners* of distributed property. See *collapsible partnership rules; section 751 assets; unrealized receivables, partnerships.*

inventory methods   the methods of identifying goods and of valuing them, for example the *LIFO* and *FIFO* methods. The choice of methods influences *cost of goods sold,* hence annual business profitability. Reg. §1.381(c)(5)-1 contains elaborate provisions on the subject of the survival of such methods in the case of *corporate reorganizations,* but the major rule is that the successor uses the predecessor corporation's inventory methods. §381(c)(5).

inventory pool election, small business   a term describing a relief provision under which *eligible small businesses* can elect to combine *inventories* of a single *trade or business* (even though they relate to multiple products) into a single *dollar-value LIFO pool.* See *simplified dollar-value LIFO method.*

inventory pools   groupings or classifications of *inventory* items for purposes of determining cost as part of a *last-in, first-out* (LIFO) inventory method. Once established, pools may not be changed unless required or approved by the *IRS.* Reg. §1.472-8(d). See *dollar-value method; simplified dollar-value LIFO method.*

inventory price computation method   an accounting method used in connection with *dollar-value method,* under which the consumer price index or the producer price index prepared by the Bureau of Labor Statistics is used for the purpose of determining inventory cost. See Reg. §1.472-8(e). See *dollar-value method; index method.*

investigation expenses   see *start-up expenditures.*

investigatory records   one class of information exempt from disclosure under the *Freedom of Information Act.* It includes records prepared for law enforcement purposes, whether civil, criminal, or administrative in nature, but only to the extent that disclosure would interfere with enforcement, violate rights, disclose confidential information, or endanger law enforcement personnel. 5 U.S.C. §552(b)(7) (1976); Reg. §601.701(b)(vii).

investment a general term used to describe an interest in *property* held for appreciation or the production of income, but not entailing more than minor personal efforts, as contrasted with a *trade or business*. For guidance in connection with the limits on *investment interest expenses* (§163(d)), see §163(d)(4)(B).

investment base see *tax shelter, registration*.

investment basis adjustment an annual adjustment used by *affiliated corporations* filing a *consolidated return*, requiring *parent corporations* to adjust the *basis* in common and preferred *stock* of *subsidiaries* in order to account for the subsidiary's operations. Undistributed *earnings and profits* and unused *losses* of the subsidiary increase the parent's basis in the account, while utilized losses of the subsidiary (not only current deficits, but also prior years' losses that are carried over from prior years and used in the present year) reduce the account. *Distributions* that are treated as *returns of capital* and those out of *earnings and profits* generated in post-1965 *consolidated return years* reduce basis in subsidiary stock. Reg. §1.1502-32. The investment basis adjustment system is one of the linchpins of the *consolidated return regulations*. See *intragroup stock*.

investment company for purposes of determining whether otherwise nontaxable contributions to *corporations* or *partnerships* are currently taxable, the term means a *regulated investment company*; a *real estate investment trust* (REIT); or an enterprise, more than 80 percent of the value of whose assets are held for investment and are readily marketable stocks, securities, or interests in regulated investment companies (e.g., mutual funds) or in REITs.

investment company, investment company reorganizations a *regulated investment company*, a *real estate investment trust*, or a corporation, at least half the value of whose total assets are *stock* and *securities*, and 80 percent or more of the value of whose total assets are held for investment. Stock and securities in any subsidiary are disregarded and the parent corporation is deemed to own its ratable share of the subsidiary's assets; a corporation is considered to own a subsidiary if it owns at least half of the combined voting power of all classes of stock entitled to vote, or at least half of the total value of shares of all classes of outstanding stock. §368(a)(2)(F)(iii). The term is significant for purposes of determining whether certain limits on tax-free *corporate reorganizations* apply. See *investment company reorganizations*.

investment company reorganizations *corporate reorganizations* involving *investment companies,* a practice curtailed by §368(a)(2)(F). Section 368(a)(2)(F) provides that if two or more investment companies merge, then tax-free corporate reorganization status will be denied as to the acquired company if its investments are inadequately diversified at the time of the reorganization. Also, §368(a)(2)(F)(iv) *denies losses* on mergers of commonly owned mutual funds that do not meet the requirements of §368(a)(2)(F) and imposes a *reverse acquisition* rule, which can penalize an undiversified acquiring investment company by making such transactions taxable. See *investment company, investment company reorganizations*.

investment company taxable income the taxable income of a *regulated investment company,* with the following adjustments: (1) *net capital gain* is excluded; (2) the *net operating loss deduction* (§172) is not allowed; (3) the special corporate *deductions* (§§241–250, *dividends received,* etc.), except for *organizational expenditure amortization* election (§248), are disallowed; (4) the *dividends-paid deduction* (§561) is computed without regard to *capital gain dividends* and *exempt interest dividends*; and (5) the provisions relating to computation of tax on a change of *accounting period* (§443(b)) is disregarded. §852(b)(2). Investment company taxable income, less deductions for dividends to shareholders, forms part of the base on which such corporations are taxed. See *preferential dividend; regulated investment company*.

investment credit a three-part system of *nonrefundable credits* granted as part of *general business credit* by §38 and defined by §§47 and 48 relating to a broad range of *tangible personal property* and some *real estate,* most of which credits can be cumulated. The components are the *rehabilitation credit,* the *energy credit,* and the *reforestation credit*. The credit rates vary from 20 percent (*certified rehabilitations* of *certified historic structures*) to 10 percent (most cases). Unused credits are subject to extensive carrybacks and carryforwards. §39. Fairly elaborate *at-risk rules* apply, in different degrees depending on the nature of the property. §49. *Basis* must generally be reduced by the half credit claimed. §50(c)(1). The full rehabit credit reduces basis. *Dispositions* and cessation of use of such property can cause partial or complete *recapture* of the credit. §50(a).

investment credit, at-risk limitation see *at-risk rules, investment tax credit*.

investment expense, interest on investment indebtedness limitation otherwise *deductible expenses paid or accrued* to purchase or carry property held for investment. Any interest held by the *taxpayer* in an activity involving a *trade* or *business* which is not a *passive activity* under the *passive loss rules* and in which he or she does not *materially participate* is deemed held for investment. An example would be an investment in a *working interest* in oil or gas. It also includes *interest expense* allocable to *portfolio income* under the passive loss rules, as well as the portion of interest paid or accrued to purchase or carry an interest in a passive activity to the extent allocable to portfolio income. It excludes *interest* used to determine income or loss from a passive activity, interest allocable to a rental real estate activity in which the taxpayer *actively participates,* and *qualified residence interest.* §163(d)(4)-(5). Such expenses reduce *investment income* for purposes of calculating the limit on *deductions* for *interest expenses* in connection with carrying investment property. See *interest on investment indebtedness limitation.*

investment expenses, generally a general term for (1) *expenses for the production or collection of income*; (2) *expenses for* the *management, conservation, or maintenance of property held for the production of income*; or (3) expenses paid or incurred in the determination or collection of any tax, even though they were not incurred in the course of a *trade or business.* Noncorporate *taxpayers* are entitled to *deduct* such expenses under §212.

investment income, interest on investment indebtedness limitation *gross income* from *property held for investment,* including net *gain* from the *disposition* of such property. §163(d)(4)(B). Property is considered held for investment if it generates income in the form of *dividends, interest, annuities,* or *royalties* or is an interest in a trade or business which is not a *passive activity* and in which the *taxpayer* does not materially participate. §§163(d)(5)(A) and 469(e). See *interest on investment indebtedness limitation; material participation, passive loss rules.*

investment income, insurance companies the *gross income* earned during the *taxable year* by an *insurance company* from *interest, dividends,* and *rent.* This amount is adjusted by adding *interest, dividends,* and *rents* due and *accrued* at the end of the taxable year and deducting all interest, dividends, and rents due and accrued at the end of the preceding taxable year. Investment income is considered part of *insurance company taxable income.* §832(b)(2).

investment interest *interest* allowable as a *deduction* (ignoring the limit on investment interest) *paid or accrued* properly allocable to property held for *investment,* but not *qualified residence interest* or interest used for computing income or *loss* from a *passive activity.* §163(d)(3)(A)-(B). It also includes amounts allowable as *deductions* in connection with *personal property* used to close a *short sale.* §163(d)(3)(C). Such interest expenses, if generated by noncorporate *taxpayers,* are subject to limitations on current *deductibility* but are subject to an indefinite *carryforward* of amounts so limited. See *interest on investment indebtedness limitation.*

investment interest limitations see *interest on investment indebtedness limitation.*

investment in the contract cumulative premiums or other considerations paid to acquire *annuities* or permanent life insurance coverage, including *endowment policies,* less cumulative dividends and other amounts paid before the *annuity starting date.* §72(c)(1). The figure is determined on the later of the starting date or the date of actual payment. Reg. §1.72-6(a). This figure determines the taxable portion of each payment to the insured or *annuitant* after payments begin under the contract. In principle, the investment in the contract is returned tax-free. See *exclusion ratio.*

investment in United States property, CFC the term includes (1) *tangible property* located in the *United States,* other than tangible *personal property* acquired for use abroad or for export; (2) *obligations* of one year or longer owned by a United States *individual* or *United States corporation* that is either a *United States shareholder* of the *controlled foreign corporation* (CFC), or at least 25 percent owned, directly or indirectly, by the CFC's United States shareholder; and (3) stock of a United States corporation that is either a United States shareholder of the CFC or at least 25 percent owned, directly or indirectly, by the CFC's United States shareholder, and obligations of United States persons, which a CFC guarantees or pledges. It excludes United States government obligations and United States bank deposits. §956(b)(2) and (c). The CFC's increased earnings invested in United States property are treated as *constructively* received pro rata by its United States shareholders, since they are so much like an outright repatriation of earnings. §§951(a)(1)(B), 956(a). See *increase in earnings invested in United States property, subpart F.*

investment partnership a term often used to describe arrangements whereby participants in a venture own property as co-owners, reserve the right to separately take or dispose of their shares of any property acquired, do not vest a representative with discretion to dispose of the property, and do not actively conduct a *trade or business.* Reg. §1.761-2(a)(2). An investment *partnership* may elect to be excluded from the partnership provisions of the *Code.* See *section 761 election.*

investment property when speaking of *tax-exempt bonds,* any *security,* any obligation, any *annuity contract,* or any investment-type property other than any *tax-exempt bond.* §148(b)(2). The use of proceeds of a tax-exempt bond to acquire investment property with a materially higher yield than the yield on the bond can convert the bond into an *arbitrage bond,* the *interest* on which is taxable. §103(b)(2) and 148(a). See *arbitrage bond; securities, worthlessness.*

investment tax credit enacted in 1962 to stimulate the economy. The Tax Reform Act of 1986 repealed the ITC for property placed in service after December 31,

1985. For property placed in service after 1990, the investment tax credit has been reconstituted as the sum of the following three components: (1) the rehabilitation credit; (2) the business energy credit; and (3) the reforestation credit. §§46, 47, and 48.

investment trust a *trust* established to invest in a portfolio of stocks, securities, or both, operated for the benefit of certificate holders. If the trust lacks power to vary its investments (except to accept more assets for investors or to dispose of assets), it will be taxed as a trust. Otherwise, it will be taxed as an *association* (i.e., business *corporation*). The latter type of trust is sometimes referred to as a management trust. Reg. §301.7701-4(c).

investment unit a bond or other security obligation (now called a *debt instrument*) sold in tandem with other property such as an option or warrant. Reg. §1.1232-3(b)(2)(i) (prior law but presumably valid). The *regulations* generally call for an allocation of *basis* between the elements of the unit in accordance with *relative fair market values*. The result is a method by which to infer *original issue discount*.

investor a nontechnical term often used to identify a *taxpayer* who is not a *trader* or *dealer*. Investors are viewed as not being engaged in a *trade or business* and must, therefore, claim many of their expenses under §212 rather than §162. On the other hand, property held by investors commonly qualifies as a *capital asset*.

involuntarily terminated CETA employee an *individual* certified by the *designated local agency* as having been involuntarily terminated after 1980 from employment financed in whole or in part under a program under part D of Title II or Title VI of the Comprehensive Employment and Training Act. §57(d)(10). Such an individual may qualify for the *targeted jobs credit* as a *member of a targeted group*. The targeted jobs credit expired on June 30, 1992.

involuntary cash out see *cash out*.

involuntary conversion partial or entire loss or destruction of property as a result of *theft, casualty, seizure, requisition, or condemnation*. The *recognition* of *gains realized* on an involuntary conversion can be *deferred* for *income tax* purposes if the owner reinvests the condemnation proceeds (e.g., government compensation or insurance) within a fixed period of time in property that is *similar or related in service or use* under the elective provisions of §1033. *Losses* are unaffected by §1033. *Tangible* and *intangible personal* and *real property* rights have been held to qualify, but substitutes for *ordinary income* (e.g., recoveries for business losses or lost opportunities) should not, as the origin of the doctrine involves requisitions and war losses. Involuntary conversions may be actual, threatened, or imminent appropriations, or they may be *casualties* or

thefts by an external force. Suddenness is not required, provided the destruction is unexpected and involuntary, if it is otherwise a *casualty* under Rev. Rul. 59-102, 1959-1 C.B. 200. See *reinvestment period, involuntary conversion; rollover, proceeds of involuntary conversion; threat or imminence of condemnation, involuntary conversions*.

irrevocable beneficiary designation the irreversible selection of another *person* to be the *beneficiary* of a *life insurance policy*. Such a designation is often made in the context of a divorce to assure the payor's right to claim a *deduction* under §215 for premium payments, or to avoid inclusion of the death proceeds in the transferor's *gross estate*. See *incidents of ownership; periodic payments*.

island affiliate a *corporation* that operates in Puerto Rico or the United States Virgin Islands and is affiliated with a *United States corporation* or has a United States parent. The rules of affiliation are supplied by §936(h)(3)(D). See *possession corporation; intangible property income*.

isolated redemption not defined. Reg. §1.305-3(e), examples 10 and 11, suggest that such *stock redemptions* must not be part of an overall plan periodically to redeem a *corporation's stock,* and they hint that a redemption in anticipation of an officer's retirement may improve the standing of redemption as isolated. Isolated redemptions are disregarded in determination of whether there are *constructive distributions* of stock under §305(c) to the remaining shareholders. See Rev. Rul. 77-19, 1977-1 C.B. 83. The provision for isolated redemptions mitigates the excesses of §305(b) (disproportionate redemptions) and (c). See *stock dividend*.

issuance costs test see *hedge bond*.

issue price generally, the cash received by an issuer for a *debt instrument* when it was issued. If the obligation was issued to *shareholders,* its issue price is generally its *fair market value*. See §1275(a)(5). If it was part of a public offering, it is the price the public buyers paid, not the amount the issuer receives on sale to the underwriter or broker. §1273(b)(1)-(2). In the case of an *investment unit,* it is the amount received that is allocable to the debt instrument, by relative *fair market value*. §1273(c). There are further complex details. The term is used for purposes of defining *original issue discount*. See *original issue discount*.

issuer a securities law term commonly used in the *Code* to indicate a *corporation* that has issued stock or securities.

issuing corporation the *corporation* whose *stock* is transferred to another corporation in a *redemption by [an] affiliated corporation*. The recipient is called the acquiring corporation. See *redemption by affiliated corporations*.

itemize   to claim *itemized deductions* rather than to use the *standard deduction.*

itemized deductions   a term commonly used to describe a limited group of *expenditures* by *individuals* electively allowed as *deductions* from *adjusted gross income* (e.g., *interest* paid on home mortgages, *medical expenses,* state *general sales taxes,* and itemized *charitable contributions*). §63(e). Section 63, which defines *taxable income,* authorizes their deduction from *adjusted gross income* and defines the term as meaning deductions other than (1) those used to determine adjusted gross income, and (2) *personal exemptions.* Such deductions are reported on Schedule A of *Form 1040.*

itemized deductions, two-percent floor on miscellaneous itemized deductions   *deductions* available for *individuals* in reduction of *adjusted gross income,* other than those for certain preferred deductions. The term is used for purposes of the *two-percent floor on miscellaneous itemized deductions.* For the particular items, see *two-percent floor on itemized deductions.*

items of tax preference   a series of *deductions* or preferentially treated income, found in §57(a), and forming part of the base on which the alternative minimum tax (AMT) falls. They consist of charitable *contributions of appreciated property, tax-exempt interest on certain private activity bonds, excess depreciation on property placed in service before 1987,* and the *bargain element* from the *exercise of an incentive stock option* (ISO) before 1988. For one to arrive at alternative minimum taxable income (AMTI), taxable income is increased by the tax preference items. For tax years beginning after 1992, the CNEPA of 1992 (Pub. L. 102-486) repeals the alternative minimum tax preferences for excess intangible drilling costs and excess percentage depletion. §1915. See also *adjustments, alternative minimum tax.*

J

jeopardy assessment　an immediate *assessment,* permitted in cases where the assessment or *collection* of an *income, estate, or gift* (or some *excise*) *tax deficiency,* including penalties and *interest,* may be jeopardized by delay. After assessment, the *IRS* must provide *notice and demand* for payment within 60 days thereof (assuming the assessment is made first). §6961. Jeopardy assessments must be considered in light of §7429, which generally calls for the IRS to provide written notice of the information on which the assessment is based and which states the *taxpayers'* rights to demand an IRS review of the determination and to sue the United States to determine the propriety of the assessment and its amount.

jeopardy levy　the seizure by the *IRS* of a *taxpayer's* property pursuant to §6331(d)(3), permitting seizure (*levy*) of earnings or other property on a finding that collection of the tax is in jeopardy. See §§6331(a)(3) and 7429. These actions are subject to judicial review.

jobs credit　see *targeted jobs credit.*

John Doe summons　another name for a *summons* issued on a *taxpayer* under §7602 that does not specifically identify the taxpayer under investigation. The power is limited by §7609(f), which allows such summonses only after judicial determinations that the subjects of the summonses are at least an ascertainable group of persons, that they may have failed to comply with the tax law, and that their identities and the information sought cannot be readily obtained from other sources.

joinder of parties, Tax Court　the addition of a party to a *petition* filed on behalf of another party or parties, done only with the court's permission and the consent of all petitioners. Joinder is permissible only where there is a common question of law or fact relating to all parties, and where each party's tax liability arises entirely or in part out of the same transaction, occurrence, or series of transactions or occurrences. *Tax Court* Rule 61.

joint and several liability　a legal relationship, the effect of which is to make each obligor individually and collectively liable for the entire amount of an obligation. In the tax area, §6013(d)(3) allows the *IRS* to collect the entire amount of tax from one or more of several *taxpayers.* Most especially, a husband and wife who file *joint returns* are collectively or individually liable for the entire balance of their income tax liability. See *innocent spouse rule.*

joint and survivor annuity　an *annuity* payable for two lives that does not expire with the death of the first *annuitant,* although the amount may vary after the first death. §72. Regulation §1.72-5 provides computational guidance. See *qualified joint and survivor annuity.*

joint and survivor annuity, qualified　see *qualified joint and survivor annuity.*

Joint Committee on Internal Revenue Taxation　a House–Senate committee of ten members, five from the *House Committee on Ways and Means* and five from the *Senate Finance Committee.* The committee has an army of experts that is lent to the process of formulating tax policy. §§8001–8023. It has extensive powers to generate data and to summon witnesses, and its review is required for *tax refunds* to be obtained on more than $1 million.

joint gifts　*gifts* to third persons by one *spouse,* other than gifts to the other spouse, which may be considered made half by each spouse, even though the entire *corpus* of the gift comes from one spouse's property. §2513. To qualify for such treatment, the following tests must be met: (1) at the time of the gift each spouse must be a *citizen* or a *resident alien* and the *donor* spouse must be *married* to the consenting spouse, and (2) both spouses must consent to split the gift. *Id.* Gift splitting is not permitted when the donor spouse creates in the donee spouse a *general power of appointment* over the transferred property. §2514(c). Such gifts are often referred to as split gifts. See *annual gift tax exclusion; gift, gift taxes; married person.*

joint hospital facilities exemption　see *cooperative hospital service organization, exempt.*

joint interests　generally, a loose reference to property held in *joint tenancy,* by the *decedent,* and therefore generally included in the decedent's *gross estate,* unless and to the extent the survivor can show his or her contributions to the cost of the property, in which case relative contributions determine the portion of the property to be included in the decedent's estate. §2040. See *marital deduction.*

joint operating agreements　agreements, common in the extractive industries, that provide for joint exploitation of mineral properties for the separate profit of each member. See I.T. 3930, 1948-2 C.B. 126, which treats these arrangements as co-ownership arrangements. See *section 761 election.*

joint return　generally, a *federal income tax return* filed together by husband and wife reporting their aggregate income, signed by both *spouses.* Reg. §1.6013-4(b) and -1(a)(2). §7701(a)(38). It includes a widow or widower with a *dependent child* for two years after the *taxable year* in which the spouse died. §6013. See §6013(a)(1) for *nonresident alien spouses.*

joint stock company a business organization created by Articles of Association that contractually renders the members personally liable for the enterprise's obligations, absent agreement to the contrary, with ownership evidenced by certificates. The board of directors is elected by shareholders to manage the company, and shareholders cannot bind the company by their acts. They are classified as *corporations* by §7701(a)(3).

joint tenancy undivided ownership of property by two or more persons with the right of *survivorship* (i.e., a right giving the surviving owner full ownership of the decedents' interest in the property). The interest is usually freely alienable. For *gift tax* consequences upon the creation of a joint tenancy in real estate between *spouses,* see §2515. For *estate tax* consequences upon the death of a *joint tenant,* see §2041.

joint tenants persons who hold *joint tenancies.*

joint venture a term used to describe a *partnership* for a limited purpose, such as constructing and later selling an apartment building. The tax rules concerning partnerships apply to joint ventures, providing the enterprise is indeed a partnership as that term is defined by Reg. §301.7701-2. See *partnership.*

judicial notice the cognizance of certain facts that a judge may act upon without hearing any proof establishing the veracity of the facts. A judicially noticed fact must be one not subject to reasonable dispute and must either be generally known in the jurisdiction or capable of accurate determination by resort to sources whose accuracy cannot be reasonably questioned. Matters of which judicial notice has been taken are considered fact, except in criminal trials. Fed. R. Evid. 201.

junior common stock plans *deferred compensation* plans under which a *corporation* issues and sells common stock that is subordinate to its presently outstanding common stock to its executives; the shares are significantly restricted and automatically become common *stock* on the occurrence of future events (e.g., high earnings). The *employee* would have *ordinary income* when the restrictions lapse, but by making the *section 83(b) election* when the junior stock is issued, the future appreciation may result in *capital gains.*

junk bonds high-yield, high-risk bonds often used in connection with corporate buyouts. They present the tax issue of potentially being *stock.* See §385.

jurat an oath or affirmation attached to a document, such as the oath found at the bottom of the facing page of a *Form 1040.*

Justice conference a conference between the *taxpayer* (or representative) with the *Department of Justice's Tax Division* to consider the prosecution of a criminal tax case. If prosecution is recommended, the case goes to the United States Attorney's office for handling.

Justice Department from a tax perspective, the federal department responsible for conducting all civil and criminal tax litigation other than litigation in the *Tax Court.* 28 U.S.C. §507(a) (1976). The Tax Division of the Justice Department litigates or supervises litigation of all such tax matters by United States Attorneys, with the exception of violations of liquor, wagering, narcotics, and firearms tax laws, the latter being handled by the Criminal Division.

K

KSOP an acronym for an *ESOP* operated in combination with a *section 401(k) plan.* This hybrid is gaining currency as of this writing.

Keogh plan a form of *qualified pension or profit-sharing plan* (also known as an H.R. 10 plan) for *self-employed individuals* (even if only part-time) and their *employees.* A self-employed individual may contribute the smaller of $30,000 or 25 percent of earned income from self-employment activity. §415(c)(1). A 15 percent deduction limit applies if the defined contribution plan is a profit-sharing plan. For purposes of the 25 percent calculation, earned income is reduced by the contribution made in behalf of the self-employed individual. §401(c)(2)(A)(v).

key district one of 19 *IRS Districts* containing an Employee Plans and Exempt Organizations Division, and/or designated for the management of Computer Assisted Audit, Engineering, and International Enforcement programs. A district that is a key district for one program may or may not also be a key district for other programs. I.R.M. 1118.4(2), (3), and (4).

key employee, anti-discrimination for *top-heavy plan* purposes, a special set of rules exists to discourage retirement plans from conferring disproportionate benefits upon key employees. Top-heaviness is determined on an annual basis. In general, a top-heavy plan allocates more than 60 percent of the cumulative benefits to key employees, or the plan is part of a top-heavy plan. Key employees, generally mean (1) officers; (2) the 10 employees owning the largest interest in the employer; (3) a greater-than-five-percent owner of the employer; or (4) a greater-than-one-percent owner of the employer with annual compensation in excess of $150,000. §416(i)(1). See *top-heavy plan; five-percent owner, employee plans.*

key-man insurance *life insurance* on the life of one or more vital *employees,* pursuant to which the *business employer* is a *beneficiary,* usually arranged to assure the company's survival or to fund a buy-out arrangement. Although premiums are *nondeductible,* the death benefits are *excludable* under §101. The proceeds will indirectly increase *federal estate taxes* to the extent the decedent owns corporate stock, the value of which is increased by the death proceeds.

kickbacks see *illegal bribes, kickbacks, and other payments.*

kiddie tax another name for §1(i) of the *Code,* the practical effect of which is to minimize the attraction of shifting income to children under the age of 14 (at year-end) by taxing such children's *unearned income* at their parent's *marginal rates* (if higher than their own marginal *regulate tax* or *alternative minimum tax* rates). One considers only the *custodial parent* if the parents are *divorced* or *separated.* In the typical case, the first $600 (for 1992 and for 1993) of a child's *taxable income* is exempt from tax and the next $600 is taxed at the child's rates, with the remaining *unearned income* of the child taxed at his or her parent's top marginal rates. Unearned income includes taxable interest, dividends, capital gains, rents, royalties, pension and annuity income (other than earned income). §1(i). See §59(j) for modifications of the kiddie tax if the child is subject to the *alternative minimum tax.* See *allocable parental minimum tax.*

Kintner regulations *regulation* §301.7701-1 through -3, issued after the decision in *United States v. Kintner,* 216 F.2d 418 (1954). The regulations sort *partnerships* from *associations taxable as a corporation.* They generally favor finding a partnership, whereas *Kintner* found a corporation in the case of an unincorporated clinic.

L

L and R an acronym for Legislation and Regulations, a section of the *Chief Counsel's* office. Its primary function is drafting *regulations.*

LIFO an acronym for *last-in, first-out (LIFO).*

LIFO conformity rule the requirement that a *taxpayer* who uses the *last-in, first-out inventory* valuation method for tax purposes also uses it for financial reporting purposes. §472. The *regulations* in fact grant taxpayers substantial flexibility in such reporting. See Reg. §1.472-2(e).

LIFO pool see *dollar-value method; inventory pools.*

LIFO recapture see *recapture, LIFO inventories.*

LIFO recapture amount the excess of the *inventory's* value, determined by using a *"FIFO"* flow assumption over its *LIFO* value. §312(n)(4)(B). *Earnings and profits* are increased or decreased by rises and falls in this amount. §312(n)(4)(A). See *recapture, LIFO inventories.*

LIFO reserves the excess of *LIFO* over *FIFO* costs. See *LIFO recapture amount.*

LUST an acronym for the *Leaking Underground Storage Tank Trust Fund.*

labor, agricultural, and horticultural organizations class of *exempt organizations* formed to better the conditions of people engaged in labor, agricultural, or horticultural pursuits, to improve the grade of their products, or to develop greater efficiency in their occupations. §501(c)(5). Reg. §1.501(c)(5)-1a(2). For these purposes, the term "agriculture" extends to harvesting live aquatic resources, cultivating crops, and raising livestock. §501(g). In the case of labor organizations, typical labor benefits such as strike and lockout benefits as well as accident, health, and death benefits are acceptable. Rev. Rul. 62-17, 1962-1 C.B. 87. As usual, if any part of the *net income* from these organizations *inures* to the benefit of any *private shareholder or individual,* then the organization's tax benefits will be lost. Gifts to these organizations cannot be claimed as *charitable contribution deductions.* See *agricultural organization; horticultural organization; labor organization.*

labor-based simplified service cost method a method of *allocating mixed service costs* under the *uniform capitalization rules.* It involves multiplying total mixed service costs by a ratio, the numerator of which is labor costs allocable to the taxpayer's production activi-

ties under §263A (other than labor costs included in mixed service costs) for the *taxable year,* and the denominator of which is total labor costs included in the taxpayer's operation of the *trade or business* (aside from labor costs included in mixed service costs) for the taxable year. See 1988-34 I.R.B. 10 §II.(B)(1).

labor organization an *exempt organization* (principally a union), provided it meets certain tests. First, no member may benefit from any income earned by the organization, and second, the organization must be formed and operated to improve the working conditions of the members. §501(c)(5) and (g); Reg. §1.501(c)(5)-1(a). For example, an association of public school teachers formed to improve the teachers' professional abilities with seminars, courses, etc., and to act as a bargaining unit qualifies. Rev. Rul. 76-31, 1976-1 C.B. 157.

labor union see *labor organization.*

lapse restriction a restriction on the transferability of *property* other than a restriction which by its terms will never lapse. Reg. §1.83-3(h).

large corporate underpayment an underpayment of taxes (including *interest* and penalties) that is subject to an interest rate of 5 percent plus the *applicable federal rate.* §6621(c)(1). The rate generally has to exceed $100,000, known as a *threshold underpayment.* See Reg. §301.6221(c)-3T. This rate applies only to the period after the thirtieth day following the earlier of *IRS's* sending a *thirty-day letter* or a *ninety-day letter.* §6621(c)(2)(A).

large corporation, estimated taxes a *corporation* if it or any predecessor corporation had *taxable income* of $1 million (disregarding *net operating loss carryovers* and *carrybacks*) or more during the testing period. The testing period is generally the three immediately preceding *taxable years.* In the case of *controlled groups,* the $1 million is divided equally among the members, unless they all consent to a plan calling for unequal allocation. §6655(i). Large corporations are subjected to more restrictive rules regarding underpayment penalties. §6655. See *penalty, underpayment of estimated tax by corporations.*

large deposit a nickname for a federal tax deposit in excess of $20,000. It must in fact be made by the deposit's due date in order for late payment penalties to be avoided. §7502(e). See *timely mailing rule.*

large farm corporation another name for a *corporation* engaged in the *trade or business* of farming if it or a predecessor corporation had gross receipts in excess of $1 million for any *taxable year* beginning in or after 1976. §447(e). All members of a controlled group of corporations are treated as one corporation. Large farm corporations that are not *S corporations* or *family corpo-*

rations (i.e., those in which at least 50 percent of the total voting power and of the total number of shares of other *stock* are owned by members of one family) are required to use the *accrual method* of accounting. §447 (lists additional restrictions and exceptions).

large food or beverage establishment   any *trade or business,* or portion thereof, that provides food or beverages, that normally employs more than 10 *employees* on a typical business day during the preceding *calendar year,* and in which the tipping by customers of employees serving food or beverages is customary. §6053(c)(4). Such establishments are required to report information with respect to tips for calendar years beginning after December 31, 1982. The 10-employee test is applied by combining affiliated businesses. §6053(c)(4). Persons owning 50 percent or more of the *employer* are not employees for purposes of defining this term. §6053(c)(4), as amended.

largely an operating company   a requirement that, in order to qualify its stock as *section 1244 stock,* during the previous five years the issuing company must have derived more than 50 percent of its gross receipts from sources other than *rents, royalties, dividends, interest, annuities,* and *sales* or *exchanges* of stocks or securities. This requirement is also known as the gross receipts test. §1244(c)(1)(C). However, a company that is economically unsuccessful, and therefore exempted from the gross receipts test by §1244(c)(2)(C), must still be largely an operating company and show that if gross receipts had been received, it is probable that they would have met the 50 percent gross receipts test. Reg. §1.1244(c)-1(e)(2).

large oil producer   a *foreign corporation* that has average daily oil and gas production, within the related group to which the corporation belongs, of at least 1,000 barrels (or its equivalent in gas). A related group means a group that consists of the foreign corporation and any other *person,* whether or not *domestic* or a United States *resident,* in control of the foreign corporation, or a corporation that controls or is controlled by the foreign corporation, or a sibling corporation controlled by the same person that controls the foreign corporation. For these purposes, control means ownership of more than 50 percent of the total combined voting power of all classes of *stock* entitled to vote (direct or indirect), using *attribution rules,* and average daily production is determined comparably to the *independent producers'* and *royalty owners'* 1,000-barrel-a-day *percentage depletion* ceiling amount. §954(h). Only large oil producers are reached by the rules relating to *foreign base company oil-related income.*

last acquisition cost method   a method of valuing *inventories* under the *dollar-value method,* whereby current year costs of items in *closing inventory* are determined on the basis of latest costs incurred during

the year. Reg. §1.472-8(e)(2)(a). It is also referred to as the natural acquisition cost method.

last-in, first-out (LIFO)   a *method of accounting* used to determine *inventory* costs, which presumes that inventory on hand consists of the earliest acquired units. §472(b)(1). It tends to minimize reportable income in times of inflation by increasing *costs of goods sold* as a result of having only low-cost items on hand at year-end. If *closing inventory* quantities exceed *opening inventory* quantities (an increment), then the excess is considered acquired during the *taxable year,* and the closing inventory LIFO value is determined by adding the current-year cost of the increment to opening inventory LIFO value. If closing inventory quantities are less than opening inventory quantities (a liquidation), then no items are treated as acquired during the taxable year, and the most recent opening inventory quantities (and their applicable LIFO values) are subtracted to the extent of the liquidation. To take a simplified example using a *specific goods* (rather than a *dollar-value) method,* if a retail store buys and sells numerous towels over the course of the year and has 1,000 towels on hand at year-end, and if the historic first batch of 500 towels it bought cost $50 and the second historic batch of 500 towels it bought cost $65, then the closing inventory cost would be $115, regardless of when the towels on hand were in fact acquired. For a contrasting convention, see *first-in, first-out (FIFO).* See *dollar-value method; specific goods method.*

last known address   generally, the address the *IRS* reasonably believes the *taxpayer* wants his or her mail to be sent to. Section 6212(b)(1) requires the IRS (absent a fiduciary relationship) to send *deficiency notices* to the taxpayer's last known address. See Reg. §310.6212-1(b). The IRS must exercise due diligence. Thus, if the IRS has notice of the new address in their computer files but mails a notice of deficiency to an old address, the requirement of due diligence has not been met and the taxpayers have *not* received proper notice. (*IRS v. Powell,* No. 92-452, November 1992).

last year's tax, exception   an exception to the *civil tax penalties* for underpayment of *estimated tax* provided to those *individuals* who paid at least an amount equal to their tax liabilities shown on their *tax returns* for the preceding *taxable year.* §6654(d)(1). This exception is the most generally used basis for making reduced estimated tax payments. To avoid an underpayment penalty, taxpayers whose adjusted gross income increases by more than $40,000 from the prior year and whose adjusted gross income is more than $75,000 must make estimated tax payments at least equal to 90 percent of the current-year's tax liability rather than 100 percent of the prior year's tax liability. The IRS is also authorized to abate any underpayment in 1992 caused by under-withholding due to the issuance of revised withholding tables effective March 1992). §6654(d). See *penalty, underpayment of estimated taxes by individuals.*

latest acquisition cost method   same as *last acquisition cost method.*

lavish or extravagant, meals, lodging, and entertainment expenses   expenses that are excessive under the circumstances of the case. It certainly does not per se preclude deluxe accommodations and services. §162(a)(2); Rev. Rul. 63-144, 1963-2 C.B. 129 (extravagance limit extended to *entertainment*; extravagance standard opaquely discussed). Apparently, §274 would not disallow exceptionally large meals and lodging expenses, provided they are not lavish or extravagant. On the other hand, §§162(a) and 212 would allow only *deductions* that are both reasonable and not lavish or extravagant.

Leaking Underground Storage Tank Trust Fund   a fund to pay cleanup and related costs for petroleum tanks, to be used where there is no other solvent taxpayer. It is funded by a 1 cent-per-gallon tax on gasoline, diesel fuel, nongasoline aviation fuels, and special motor fuels. The details are fairly complex. See §§4041–4093. Section 9508 establishes a fund to which revenues from various sources are transferred, viz:

1. Motor vehicles fuels tax under §4041(d)
2. A share of the federal gasoline tax exacted under §4081
3. A share of the proceeds of the tax on diesel fuel and aviation *fuel excise* tax received from §4091
4. A share of the inland waterways fuel tax under §4042
5. Amounts received under §9003(h)(6) of the Solid Waste Disposal Act

leapfrog withholding   a method used by *employers* to reduce the costs of preparing payrolls by curtailing the number of payroll periods, thereby enabling the employer to reduce the number of *withholding* computations and associated paperwork. See RIA Fed. Tax Coordinator, 2d paragraph S-7133. Under such a method, *employees* receive their paychecks as frequently as before; the difference is that the first check in the pay period is treated as advance salary. However, the *Treasury Department* has determined that the advance payment is a payment of *wages,* requiring the employer to withhold taxes. See §3402(a). The leapfrog method cannot be used to avoid the required *deposits* employers make when paying wages to employees. See Rev. Rul. 66-376, 1966-2 C.B. 495.

lease   a contract to rent *realty* or *personalty.* The tax law will look at the substance of the transaction, disregarding labels attached by the parties to determine whether an arrangement is indeed a lease for federal tax purposes. *The Tax Reform Act of 1984* provides objective criteria consisting of the following unranked factors: (1) the recipient of the services physically possesses controls or has a significant possessory or economic interest in the property; (2) the party providing the services does not bear any economic risk if there is non-performance under the contract; (3) the party providing the services does not concurrently use the property to provide significant services to entities unrelated to the recipient of the services; and (4) the total contract price does not substantially exceed the rental value of the property for the contract period. §7701(e)(1). See also *financing lease; royalties, generally; sale and leaseback.*

lease at-risk payment   any rental payment against which the lessee is not protected against loss by *nonrecourse financing,* guarantees, stop-loss arrangements, etc. §48(d)(6)(C)(v). See *at-risk rules, investment tax credit.*

leaseback   a transaction in which a transferee leases property to the transferor. The original transfer may be a *gift* or a taxable *disposition.* See *sale and leaseback.*

leaseback transaction   a term used in §467, referring to a transaction which involves a leaseback to any *person* who had an interest in the property at any time within two years before the transaction (or a related person). §467(e). Certain leaseback transactions are classed as a subset of *disqualified leasebacks or long-term agreements* and are singled out for special attack by §467.

lease bonuses   another name for an additional amount paid to a lessor at the time of entering into a lease. Such amounts must generally be reported as *gross income* when *paid* or *accrued* by the lessor but must be *amortized* by the lessee. Such bonuses may be depletable by the lessor when paid with respect to an oil, gas, or other mineral property. *Percentage depletion* cannot be claimed as to bonuses and other advance payments. §§613(e)(4) and 613A(d)(5). See *bonus, natural resources.*

lease cancellation payment   an amount paid to a tenant in cancellation of a lease. Such an amount is treated as a *sale* or *exchange* of the leasehold by the tenant. §1241. If the landlord is paid by the tenant, however, the result is *ordinary income* to the landlord.

leased employee   any *person* who provides services to another (the *recipient*) if (1) the *person* has performed such services for the recipient, or for the recipient and related persons (per §103(b)(6)(C)), on a substantially full-time basis for at least a year; (2) the services are provided pursuant to an agreement between the recipient and any other person (the leasing organization); and (3) the services are of a type historically performed, in the recipient's business field, by *employees.* §414(n)(2). A leased employee will be treated as an employee of the recipient for purposes of certain *qualified plan* requirements, such as *minimum participation* and *vesting* standards, *nondiscrimination,* and others as listed. §414(n)(1). See *employee, qualified plan; recipient, employee leasing.*

leasehold a tenant's interest in a *lease.*

lease, natural resources a transaction in which the holder of a *working interest* transfers his or her interest, retaining only a continuing *nonoperating interest* (e.g., royalty) in production from the property. The concept of the lease is especially significant in distinguishing such transactions from *sales* for *federal income tax* purposes; the two transactions yield radically different results.

legacy a transfer of cash or other *personal property* from a *decedent's estate* to another person under the terms of a will.

legal age the age of majority, 21 years of age as a federal matter. See *minor.*

legal holiday a legal holiday in the District of Columbia, and in the case of acts called for elsewhere within a *Revenue District,* a statewide holiday in the state in which the *District Office* is located. §7503. See Reg. §301.7503-1(b)(1) for legal holiday in the District of Columbia.

legal interest either an interest protected by law or a rate of *interest* that is not usurious.

legal life estate an outright *life estate* in property as opposed to one held beneficially (i.e., in *trust*). Such *estates* have the advantage of generally not being includible in the holder's *gross estate,* because they expire at death. The legal life estate can be a powerful *estate planning* tool if §2036 can be avoided.

legally separated authorized to live apart from one's *spouse* pursuant to a judicial order (more than entitled to separate maintenance—the latter merely entitles one to continuing support payments), often called a decree of separation from bed and board. The term appears in §21A(f)(3) (*child and dependent care credit*), Reg. §1.71-1T(a)A-2, 71(a)(1) (divorce, etc.), and §7703 (determination of marital status).

legal representative a *person* who is legally responsible for overseeing the affairs of another *person* or that person's *estate,* such as a *guardian, executor,* or *administrator.*

legal separation see *legally separated.*

legal title an enforceable formal right of ownership and possession in property. The holder of such title may or may not have any *beneficial interest* as opposed to one who retains an *equitable title* in the property. An example of someone with no beneficial interest would be a *trustee* holding legal title to property. Absent some adverse equitable interest, however, the legal owner has full possessory rights.

legatee someone who receives *personal property* under a will.

legi-care plans see *qualified group legal services plans.*

legislation or proposed legislation, business expenses bills and resolutions introduced in the United States Congress or other legislative body for consideration, as well as oral or written proposals for legislative action submitted to the body, a committee, or members. Reg. §1.162-20(c)(2)(ii)(a). Section 162(e)(1) permits certain *trade or business deductions* in connection with legislation or proposed legislation, despite the limitations or *lobbying expenses.*

legislative day for purposes of §162(c), allowing state legislators to treat their residences in their legislative districts as their *tax homes,* the term refers to any day during the *taxable year* that the legislature is in session (including any day the legislature is not in session for a period of four consecutive days or less), or any day the legislature is not in session but the physical presence of the legislator is formally recorded at a meeting of a committee of the legislature. §162(i)(2). The legislator must reside more than 50 miles from the state capitol in order to qualify for the election. The number of legislative days is multiplied by certain per diem amounts to arrive at a (*deductible*) *travel expense* figure. See Rev. Rul. 82-33, 1982-1 C.B. 28.

legislative history historical materials and facts surrounding the enactment of legislation. In the case of federal tax laws, the reports of the *House Ways and Means Committee,* the *Senate Finance Committee,* and the *House-Senate Conference* reports (reconciling the preferences of the two bodies) are the vital sources. Legislative history plays a vital role in interpreting the *Code.*

legislative regulations *Treasury Administration and Procedural Regulations* that represent a delegation of legislative authority from the Congress. They are virtually impossible to overturn. The *consolidated return regulations* are the leading example. See *regulations, Treasury Administrative and Procedural.*

leg, straddles one position that forms part of a *straddle.* For example, if the *taxpayer* bought a put to sell 100 I.B.M. shares at $60 and a call to buy 120 shares of I.B.M. at $60, each position is a leg. The term is used commonly in tax and financial parlance.

lending or finance business, corporate acquisition indebtedness a *business* of making loans or purchasing or discounting *accounts receivable,* notes, or installment obligations. §279(c)(5). See *corporate acquisition indebtedness.*

lending or finance company, personal holding companies a *business* that primarily (1) makes loans; (2) purchases or discounts accounts receivable, notes, or installment obligations; or (3) renders services or provides the facilities connected with the above activities. Such companies are exempt from the *personal holding company tax* if various tests are met. See §542(c)(6) and (d)(1). Companies that make long-term (more than five years) loans are generally not considered engaged in the lending or finance business.

length-of-service award a special award given to *employees* for a long period of employment. Generally, *deductions* for *business gifts* are limited to $25 per *individual* for each *taxable year*. See §274(b). The length-of-service award is an exception to this limitation. To qualify for the exception, the award must be *tangible personal property* awarded as part of a meaningful presentation under circumstances not likely to involve disguised compensation. It cannot include an award made in the first five years of employment or received by the recipient (unless the award was *excludable* as in *de minimis fringe benefit*) during the current or any of the prior four years. §274(j)(4)(B). Such awards are *employee achievement awards* over which may be deducted up to $400 per employee per year if not *qualified plan awards* and up to $1,600 if they are. §274(j)(2),(3)(B). The employee can exclude the value of the award from his or her *gross income* to the extent it is *deductible* as an *employee achievement award*. See *employee achievement award; excess deduction award; qualified plan award*.

less-developed country corporations certain *foreign corporations* that benefited from special relief provisions under *subpart F*. The definition is still of some significance with respect to *withdrawals of previously excluded subpart F income* under present §955. Also, §1248(g)(3) provides certain exclusions from *earnings and profits* accumulated before 1976 in the determination of the effects of *sale, exchanges,* and *distributions* of *stock* in certain foreign corporations.

lessee improvements the value of improvements made by a *lessee* to the *lessor's* property. Such improvements are not included in the lessor's *gross income* unless the improvements were made in lieu of rent. Reg. §1.109-1. Factors indicating an intention to provide a rent substitute are a lease term shorter than the life of the improvement, or a lease terminable by the lessor.

letter, determination see *determination letter.*

letter ruling see *ruling.*

level funding a common actuarial method applied to *defined benefit plans* by which the *employer's* annual contribution to the plan for each *employee* is calculated. The method is used to determine a constant assumed annual *contribution* needed to fund the anticipated retirement benefits, in which expected earnings of the fund, mortality, expected withdrawals, changes in compensation, and retirements at various ages are taken into account. Other factors may also be considered. Reg. §1.404(a)-3(b).

level payment loan a loan in which each installment is substantially equal, a portion of each installment being attributable to repayment of the principal, which increases as the portion of each installment attributable to *interest* correspondingly declines. §49(a)(1)(F) incorporating former §46(c)(8)(F)(iv).

leveraged ESOP a *defined contribution plan* that (1) is a qualified *stock bonus plan* or a combination qualified stock bonus plan and qualified *money purchase pension plan*; (2) is designed to invest primarily in *qualifying employer securities*; (3) is otherwise defined in the *regulations*; and (4) meets certain other requirements of §409A(b)-(h). The advantage of these plans is that they are free of certain *prohibited transactions* rules; accordingly, the *employer* or a shareholder can sell stock to the *ESOP,* which can use the stock as collateral, often guaranteed by the *employer corporation,* to finance the stock purchase. §4975(e)(7). The employer in turn makes *deductible* contributions to the ESOP, the proceeds of which are used to *amortize* the loan. The use of this pattern permits corporations the flexibility to "go private," to buy out an owner, or to sell the company to *employees.* See §§404 (a)(10) and 415(c)(6)(C) for limitations. See *prohibited transactions, penalties; qualified plan.*

leveraged lease a transaction especially common in the equipment leasing field, in which an outside lender provides loan funds for the acquisition of property to be purchased and held by a *lessor* (usually a *limited partnership* or specialized leasing company), typically with a view to having the lessor garner *investment tax credits* and substantial *depreciation* or *cost recovery deductions,* in exchange for which the lessee's rental terms are improved. The vital tax question is whether the transaction is really a *sale* to the putative lessee as opposed to a financing arrangement such as a *mortgage.* The standards are unclear. See *leveraged lease guidelines; safe harbor leasing.*

leveraged lease guidelines a term used for a set of guidelines relating to *leveraged leases* issued in 1975 by the *IRS* in Rev. Procs. 75-21, 1975-1 C.B. 175 and 75-28, 1975-1 C.B. 752. These guidelines apply for *advance ruling* purposes only. The guidelines' principal demands are that (1) the *lessor* have throughout the lease term at least a 20 percent equity investment in the property; (2) the *lessee* not have an equity or security interest in, or lending position with respect to, the property; (3) the expected residual value of the property be at least 20 percent of original cost (ignoring inflation) and have a remaining *useful life* of at least 20 percent of its originally estimated useful life; (4) the lessor's rent plus residual value exceed the lessor's equity investment plus debt service, ignoring tax benefits; (5) rents exceed debt service payments; and (6) the lessee not have a bargain-rate call option and the lessor not have a put option. These are not an *audit standard*. The term applies to leveraged leases of equipment.

leveraged loan   a loan, a portion of which is used to pay interest on the loan. For example, if Mr. M. borrows $100 in January, of which $10 is for *interest* to pay interest due in the year of the borrowing, the result is a leveraged loan.

leveraged preferred stock   a *corporation's* use of debt to purchase preferred stock. The practice typically involves a group of corporations that organizes a *trust* that borrows money to buy the preferred stock of the ultimate borrower; the tax leverage to the beneficiaries of the 70 percent *dividends-received deduction* and the *interest expense deduction* means the ultimate borrower (likely a corporation without a tax burden) can pay a low *dividend* rate on its preferred stock.

levy   an *IRS* enforcement power to seize or sell "by any means" nonexempt property of the *taxpayer* to satisfy tax obligations. §7701(a)(21). The power arises under §§6331–6344 and applies to property held by the *taxpayer* or others. The rules, which are available without the need for court action, are complex. Section 6334 exempts many classes of property and modestly limits garnishment of income. Section 6331(a) generally requires *notice and demand,* a 10-day wait (21 days for bank accounts), and a notice of *levy* to the person who holds the property or who is obligated to the taxpayer. Section 6332(c)(2) also grants the power to impose a 50 percent penalty. Section 6332(e) provides immunity to all concerned for the party honoring the levy. Section 6337 provides limited (180-day) redemption rights and §6334(a) grants various exemptions (e.g., the *principal residence,* $1,100 worth of books and tools of the trade). The *Code* does not appear to draw the distinction with any care; instead, the term is evidently used synonymously with distraint. See *jeopardy levy; lien; notice of levy; property exempt from levy; release of levy.*

liability   no formal definition in the *Code.* The term is used to refer to the obligation to pay a *debt* and also to include a *lien* representing a debt to which property is subject. See *at-risk rules; deemed distribution; like-kind exchange; nonrecourse liabilities.*

liability, contested   see *contested liabilities.*

liability, joint and several   see *joint and several liability.*

liability, limited   see *limited liability.*

liability, partnership taxation   an obligation that creates increased *basis* in *partnership* property, that produces a *deduction* for the partnership, or that is neither *deductible* nor *capitalized.* Reg. §1.752-1T(g). *Accounts payable* and *accrued liability* of a *cash method taxpayer* are ignored, as they do not create basis in a partnership asset and are not yet deductible. This is now a general definition for purposes of §752 and in turn is subdivided into *recourse liabilities* and *nonrecourse liabilities.* See *nonrecourse liabilities; recourse liabilities, partnership taxation.*

lien   generally, a claim that attaches to or encumbers property owned by the debtor and used to secure a *debt,* which may arise voluntarily or involuntarily. If *taxpayers* fail to pay *assessed* taxes for which they are liable, the *Code* makes the amount due a lien against the taxpayer's property (including after-acquired property) until the debt is discharged or, in most cases, until the six-year *statute of limitations,* during which the *IRS* can enforce its lien, expires. §§6321, 6322, 6502. The lien attaches 10 days after demand for payment and is unaffected by judgments. §6331. There can be immediate demand in *jeopardy assessment* cases. The *IRS* is empowered to enforce liens in federal *District Courts* under §7403, the most significant effects of which are ordering the rights of creditors and decreeing that property subject to the lien be sold in *foreclosure.* See §6326 (appeal to release publicly filed tax lien). See also §§6324–6324B, involving liens for federal *estate* and *gift taxes;* the principal feature is that they apply to property included in the *decedent's gross estate,* whether or not probated, and to *gift* property, subject to a special *shifting lien* provision. See *certificate of release of lien; levy.*

lien date, accrual of real estate taxes   the date a *real property tax* causes a *lien* for its payment to attach to the property. The date is determined under local law. Reg. §1.164-1(a) provides that the real estate taxes are *deductible* in the year *paid or accrued,* depending on the *taxpayer's accounting method,* but does not set forth any special accrual rule. The case law provides that real property taxes accrue when the obligation to pay them becomes fixed and the amount of liability certain, and that real property taxes cannot accrue against taxpayers until both the tax base and rate of taxation are determined, the tax becomes due and payable, and a lien on assessed property or *personal property* attaches, as the case may be.

life annuity   an *annuity* that provides retirement payments and requires the survival of the *participant* or his or her *spouse* as one of the conditions for any payment or possible payment under the annuity. For example, annuities that make payments for 10 years or until death, whichever occurs first or whichever occurs last, are life annuities. It excludes an annuity, or portion of an annuity, which provides those benefits that would not be taken into account in the determination of the *normal retirement benefit* or *early retirement benefit* (referring to §411(a)(9), e.g., Social Security supplements). Reg. §1.401(a)-11(b)(1).

life beneficiaries generally, *persons* entitled to the use of or income from property during their lives.

life expectancy rule another term for a method of calculating the taxable component of an *annuity*. The approach is to divide the *investment in the contract* by the *annuitant's life expectancy,* and to treat that portion of each payment under the contract as a nontaxable *return of capital.*

life income funds arrangements under which a *donor* gives property to a *pooled income fund* of a charity, reserving a right to income from his share of the fund during his life. Done properly, the result is an immediate *charitable contributions deduction* for the value of the *remainder interest,* and a stream of income during the donor's life.

life insurance risk-shifting arrangements under which an insurer contracts to pay *death proceeds* to the *estate* of an insured or his or her *beneficiary(ies).* For certain regulatory purposes, no risk-shifting arises if the insured purchases an offsetting *annuity contract.* For the recent statutory definition, see *life insurance contract*. See *insurance.*

life insurance company a company whose primary and predominant purpose and activity (more than 50 percent of the activity) during the year is issuing insurance or annuity contracts or reinsuring risks underwritten by insurance companies. §816(a).

life insurance company taxable income the major tax base for *life insurance companies.* §801(a)(1). It consists of *life insurance gross income,* minus *life insurance deductions.* §801(b). In addition, there is a separate alternative tax on *net capital gains.* §801(a)(2). Life insurance company taxable income is taxed at general corporate *income tax* rates under §11.

life insurance contract a contract that qualifies as a life insurance contract under applicable law (and certain *church* death benefit plans) and meets one of two alternative tests. §7702(a). Note that this definition is used for all *Code* purposes, not just for purposes of §101 which excludes the death benefits paid under such a contract from *gross income. Endowment policies* can qualify also. §7702(h).

life insurance contract, qualified plans a retirement income, *endowment,* or other contract that provides *life insurance* protection. Reg. §1.72-16(a). It includes an *individual* or group *annuity* contract that provides *incidental life insurance* protection. Rev. Rul. 74-76, 1974-1 C.B. 30. The imputed cost of current life insurance protection under a life insurance contract is generally

includible in the *gross income* of insured *participants* in *qualified plans* who are provided such coverage if the *death proceeds* are payable to the participant or the participant's *beneficiary.* §72(m)(3); Reg. §1.72-16(b)(1) and (2).

life insurance deductions two *deductions* allowed by §804 and used as the subtraction from *life insurance gross income* in determining *life insurance company taxable income (LICTI),* the base on which *life insurance companies* are taxed. The two deductions are (1) the *general deductions* (§805), and (2) the *small life insurance company deduction* (if any) of §806(a). §804.

life insurance gross income includes policy premiums, life insurance reserve decreases, and other amounts generally included in gross income, such as investment income. §806.

life insurance proceeds amounts received from an insurer under a *life insurance contract* as a result of the death of the insured. Section 101(a) generally *excludes* such amounts from *gross income* unless there was a *transfer for value.* Such proceeds are, however, included in a *decedent's gross estate* to the extent receivable under policies on his or her life or from proceeds payable to others where the decedent had *incidents of ownership* in such policies. §2042.

life insurance reserve amounts set aside to mature or liquidate, either by payment or reinsurance, future unaccrued claims arising from life insurance, annuity, and noncancellable accident and health insurance contracts (including life insurance or annuity contracts combined with noncancellable accident and health insurance). §816(b).

lifetime gift a *gift* given during the *donor's* life.

lifetime marital trust a type of *trust* designed to take maximum advantage of the *unified credit.* The idea is for a wealthy and a nonwealthy *spouse* to maximize the credit by having the wealthy spouse transfer the credit equivalent (say $600,000) to a *trust* for the other spouse. That means each spouse is positioned to have a full credit equivalent at death.

lifetime transfer a transfer during the transferor's lifetime, synonymous with *inter vivos* transfer.

like class *depreciable tangible personal property* held by the *taxpayer* for productive use in its *trade or business.* It is considered to be of a like class to other depreciable tangible personal property to be held by the taxpayer for productive use in its business, provided the exchanged properties fall either within the same *general business asset class* or within the same *product class.* Reg. §1.1031(a)-2(b)(1).

like-kind and grade mining terms used to determine whether representative minerals and ores used by the *taxpayer* in assessing *depletion deductions* are sufficiently similar to the ores and minerals owned by the taxpayer. See Reg. §1.613-4(c) and (d). Ores and minerals are of a like-kind and grade if, in customary commercial practice, they are sufficiently similar in chemical, mineralogical, or physical characteristics to the ores and minerals used by the taxpayer. See Reg. §1.613-4(c)(2).

like-kind exchange an *exchange* of *business* or *investment* property pursuant to §1031. *Recognition* of *gains* and *losses* on such exchanges is tax-deferred, except to the extent of nonqualifying property (*boot*) received or paid over (to the extent of any built-in gain or loss). For example, if a taxpayer exchanges investment land with an adjusted basis of $10,000 and worth $100,000 for an apartment (business) worth $100,000, the transaction will result in no immediate taxation. However, the apartment will have a *basis* of $10,000. Such exchanges may be simultaneous or deferred, but if the exchange was with a *related taxpayer,* it generally does not qualify for *nonrecognition of gain or loss* if either party *disposes of* the property within two years, or longer if and to the extent there is a diminution of risk of *loss* with respect to the property. §1031(f). The extent of delay permissible in deferred exchanges is generally limited to 180 days. §1031(a)(3). Section 1031 is mandatory, and the price exacted is a basis in the acquired property which is reduced to the extent of any deferred gain. The exchange is evaluated property by property; for example, an exchange of assets of a business for the assets of a similar business does not qualify. Rev. Rul. 89-121, 1989-47 I.R.B. 8. See *like-kind property; related taxpayers, loss and deduction denial; three-cornered exchange.*

like-kind property qualitatively similar *business* or *investment* property. For purposes of §1031, which authorizes tax-deferred *exchanges* of *business* or *investment* properties, the term "like-kind" limits the types of properties that can be so exchanged. Generally speaking, the term is broadly defined with respect to *real estate*. Stocks, bonds, *partnership* interests, and *choses in action* are expressly excluded from §1031, as are livestock of different sexes and *foreign real property* as opposed to real property located outside the *United States*. Note that business property can be swapped for investment property and vice versa, and that it is the property's use in the hands of the *taxpayer* seeking the benefits of §1031 that counts.

limitation periods see *statute of limitations.*

limitation year, qualified plans the *calendar year,* unless the *employer* selects a *fiscal year* or a 52- or 53-week year, with a requirement that affiliated employers select a consistent year. Reg. §1.415-2(b); Rev. Rul. 75-481, 1975-2 C.B. 188. The limitation year is used in the determination of whether otherwise *qualified plans* pro-

vide for excessive benefits or contributions, thereby jeopardizing their qualification.

limited entrepreneur a *person* who has an interest in a farming enterprise, other than as a *limited partner,* and does not actively participate in the management of the enterprise. §464(e)(2). §464(c). Section 464(a) limits *deductions* for seed, feed, etc., until they are consumed, but the limit applies if an undue share of the losses is claimed by limited entrepreneurs. See *family, farming syndicate; farming syndicates.*

limited liability a term used in the context of characterizing an organization as an *association taxable as a corporation,* as opposed to another *entity* such as a *partnership.* Generally, limited liability exists as to an owner if the owner's legal exposure to debts or other liabilities of the organization is limited to contributed capital. However, the entity will not have the characteristic if any owner is individually liable without limit for the organization's debts or claims, unless in the case of *limited partnerships* that party is a *dummy* with no substantial assets acting as the *agent* of the other *partners.* Reg. §301.7701-2(d).

limited liability company (LLC) a relatively new form of entity that combines the S corporation characteristic of limited liability for all investors with the income flow-through attributes of a partnership. The *IRS* has ruled that a limited liability company created pursuant to the laws of Wyoming would be treated as a partnership for tax purposes. Rev. Rul. 88-76, 1988-2 C.B. 360. A limited liability company which meets certain requirements for classification as a partnership can provide the following benefits: (1) pass-through of tax attributes; (2) limited liability for all members; (3) control over the business by the members without their being subjected to unlimited liability; and (4) freedom from S corporation eligibility requirements. Only certain states permit businesses to form limited liability companies.

limited membership VEBA an *IRS* term for a *voluntary employees' beneficiary association* with a high ratio of officers, shareholders, and highly compensated members to rank-and-file members. The IRS considers that such VEBAs result in *inurement.*

limited overriding royalty, natural resources an *overriding royalty,* the term of which is shorter than the term of the *lease,* hence treated as *carved-out production payment.*

limited partner a member of a *limited partnership* other than a *general partner.* Limited partners are exposed to the liabilities of the limited partnership only to the extent of their capital contributions, agreed future contributions, and certain *distributions* from the partnership. An improperly formed limited partnership may be attacked and reclassified as an *association taxable as* *a corporation.* See Reg. §301.7701-2 and -3. A vital state law characteristic is that, in order to maintain *limited liability,* limited partners must not participate in the management of the partnership's affairs.

limited partnership, passive loss rules an interest designated as a *limited partnership* interest in the *partnership agreement* or certificate, whether or not the *partner's* liability is limited at state law, or an interest as to which the liability of the partner for partnership obligations is limited under the law of the state in which it is formed to a determinable fixed amount. Temp. Reg. §1.469-5T(e)(3). In general, a limited partner's *distributive share* of a limited partnership's income of loss is automatically passive in nature. Passive losses may be used to offset income from other passive activities, but may not be used to offset either active or portfolio income. See *passive loss rules.*

limited use property property not expected to be useful to or usable by a *lessor* at the end of the *lease* term, except for continued leasing to the lessee. Rev. Proc. 76-30, 1976-2 C.B. 647. The *IRS* will not issue *private letter rulings* regarding the question of whether a lease relating to such property is a true lease.

linear algebra method a method of *allocation* of the costs of a mixed *service department* pursuant to the *uniform capitalization rules.* It uses a series of linear algebra equations that recognize all services provided by service departments to other service departments. Matrix algebra must be used. The method provides a more accurate allocation of service-cost than the direct or step allocation methods.

line of business exception a provision found in §414(r) under which, if an *employer* for genuine *business* reasons maintains more than one line of business, *employees* in different lines of business may be tested separately when determination is made as to whether a *qualified pension plan* meets the *coverage requirements.* §410(b)(5). See *coverage, qualified plans; line of business limitation.*

line of business limitation another name for a provision pursuant to which the favorable tax treatment of certain *fringe benefits* in the form of goods and services is limited to those which are offered for sale by the *employer* to the public in the ordinary course or *business.* In general, the recipient of the benefit must be employed in the line of business to which the benefit relates. Reg. §1.132-4. See *qualified employee discounts.*

line of business, passive loss rules one of 79 types of *business* activity, based on *SIC* standards in OMB's *Standard Industrial Classification Manual.* See Rev. Proc. 89-38, 1989-1 C.B. 920. Similar or commonly controlled lines of business are combined under the *regulations* under the *passive loss rules.*

link-chain method generally an impermissible method for computing the *base-year cost* and *current-year cost* of a *dollar-value pool* in a *last-in, first-out* (LIFO) *inventory* system. A link-chain method may be approved only if the *taxpayer* demonstrates to the satisfaction of the *District Director* that the *double-extension method* and the *index method* would be impractical and unsuitable and that the particular link-chain method used is appropriate, accurate, and reliable. Reg. §1.472-8(e). Generally, the procedure involves double-extending a representative portion of the inventory and using the two totals to compute a yearly index, which is then multiplied by the cumulative index from the beginning of the year, yielding the percentage relationship of current-year costs to base-year costs.

link companies another name for *corporations* which are subject to mixed rules for determining whether they are *domestic* or *foreign* for *federal income tax* purposes. Under the general rules, the determination of whether corporations are foreign is made by reference to the laws of their place of incorporation. See *dual consolidated loss.*

liquidated damages amounts established as due to a contracting party in anticipation of a possible default by the other party. Liquidated damages are treated as *gross income* to the recipient.

liquidating distribution a *distribution* from an *entity* to its owner(s) in the course of *liquidation.* In the case of a *corporation,* the distribution may also be made in the course of a so-called *partial liquidation,* although the concept is highly confined after *TEFRA.* Such distributions are generally taxable to the *shareholder* (§331) and the corporation (§336(a)). But see *section 332 liquidation.* For transitional relief, see *qualified corporation, liquidations.* As to *partnerships,* see *distribution, partnership; liquidation of a partner's interest.*

liquidating gains or losses a nontechnical term for *gains* and *losses recognized* by *corporations* on the *distribution* of *appreciated* or *depreciated property.* Such distributions are commonly called *liquidating distributions.* After 1986, that is the general rule, subject to §§332, 337, and 336(d)(2)(A), involving *losses* on property contributed to corporations with a view to *recognizing* a loss. §336.

liquidating partnership a *partnership* established to complete the *liquidation* of a *corporation.* Such partnerships enable corporations to undertake tax-free liquidations or to meet *IRS* demands for promptness in completing liquidations. The transfer to the partnership is viewed as an indirect taxable *distribution* to *shareholders* under §331, followed by a nontaxable transfer to the partnership under §721.

liquidating trust a *trust* for the benefit of corporate *shareholders,* to which assets of a *corporation* undergoing *liquidation* or bankruptcy are transferred. Reg. §301.7701-4(d). Such trusts enable corporations to undertake tax-free liquidations pursuant to former §337 or to meet *IRS* demands for promptness in completing liquidations where the property is not susceptible to prompt sale or distribution to shareholders. Such trusts were structured as *grantor trusts*. Thus, the transfer to the trust was a *taxable event* to shareholders and trust *income* and *loss* was thereafter attributable directly to the shareholder-*beneficiaries*. Provided the trust's primary purpose and activity is to complete the liquidation of assets in an orderly fashion, it will not lose its status as a trust. Because of IRS hostility to these trusts, *partnerships* were commonly used instead.

liquidation   generally, the actual winding up of an *entity* and the *distribution* of its assets, or proceeds from the sale of its assets, to its proprietors or *beneficiaries*. The concept is distinct from *dissolution,* which refers to legal termination of the entity.

liquidation, corporate   see *complete liquidation, corporate.*

liquidation of a partner's interest   the termination of a *partner's* entire interest in a *partnership* by means of a *distribution* or series of distributions to the partner by the partnership. §761(d) (used as the general definition under *subchapter K*—relating to the *income taxation* of partners and partnerships).

liquidation of a subsidiary   generally, the *liquidation* of a subsidiary into its parent. The *Tax Reform Act of 1986* repealed the *twelve-month liquidation* provisions of §337 and replaced them with a new §337 that provides an exception to the general rule requiring *recognition* of *gain* on the *distribution* of *appreciated property* by a *corporation* going through a liquidation. Under new §337, no *gain* or *loss* is *recognized* by a liquidating subsidiary on the distribution to an *eighty-percent distributee* (parent corporation) of any property in a complete liquidation under §332; companion §336(d) also denies corporate level losses on distributions of property to minority shareholders in such liquidations. Property distributed to an eighty-percent distributee in satisfaction of a debt owned by the subsidiary is deemed a distribution in liquidation, and no gain or loss is recognized to the distributing corporation. The price of these liquidations is that the distributee correspondingly takes the distributing corporation's basis. §334(b). Nonrecognition treatment is not available for distributions to eighty-percent distributees that are *foreign corporations*. §367(a).

liquidation, partial   see *partial liquidation.*

liquidation, partnership   see *partnership liquidation.*

liquidation, partnership interest   the *redemption* of a *partner's interest in the partnership* by the *partner-*

ship. It can occur at once or in stages. See Reg. §1.761-1(d). It is sometimes difficult to distinguish a liquidation from a *sale* of a partnership interest; the key issue is who is primarily responsible for paying the retiring partner or his or her *estate*. Section 736 controls the taxation of *liquidating distributions*. See *section 736 payments.*

liquidation, put, call, or conversion right   any *liquidation, put, call,* or conversion (e.g., from *debt* into *equity*) right, or any similar right, the exercise or nonexercise of which affects the value of the transferred interest. §2701(c)(2)(A). See *distribution right.*

liquidation, reincorporation   see *reincorporation.*

liquidation trust   see *liquidating trust.*

liquidation year   the *taxable year* in which a *qualified liquidation* occurs. §473(d)(1).

listed option   any option (other than a right to acquire stock from the issuer) that is traded on (or subject to the rules of) an SEC-registered national securities exchange, a domestic board of trade designated as a contract market by the Commodity Futures Trading Commission, or *IRS*-designated security exchanges, markets, or boards of trade. §1256(g)(5). The various markets are known as *qualified boards or exchanges*. §1256(g)(7). See *dealer equity option; nonequity option.*

listed property   a *passenger automobile*; other property which is used as a means of transportation; property of a type generally used for entertainment, recreation, or amusement; home computers and peripheral equipment; cellular telephones and similar telecommunication equipment; and other property the *Treasury Department* identifies by *regulation*. §280F(d)(4). Such property is subject to special *substantiation* requirements and limitations as *cost recovery deductions, expensing* and to specialized *recapture* rules. §280F(b). See *mixed use property.*

livestock, section 1231 assets   the usual farm animals and all other mammals, but not fish, frogs, reptiles, poultry, or other birds. Reg. §1.1231-2(a)(3). Livestock held for draft, breeding, dairy, or sporting purposes can qualify as *section 1231 assets* if held for more than 24 months.

living expenses   actual, reasonable, and necessary expenses, incurred as a result of the loss of the use or occupancy of the *principal residence,* to maintain the *taxpayer* and members of his household in accordance with their customary standard of living. Such items generally include the cost of temporary housing, utilities, meals at restaurants that would otherwise have been prepared at home, and other comparable expenses (e.g., groceries). Reg. §1.123-1(b)(2). Section 123 grants an *exclusion* from *gross income* of insurance recoveries that reflect reimbursement of additional living expenses caused by *casualty* or government action relating to an actual or threatened casualty (e.g., forced evacuation in advance of hurricane).

living trust   see *inter vivos trust.*

loan, below-market loan   any extension of credit and any transaction under which the owner of money lets another person use the money for a period of time, after which the money is to be transferred to the owner or applied according to an express or implied agreement with the owner. For example, a father could transfer money to his daughter interest-free for her to invest. The daughter would receive income and pay a tax, presumably at a lower rate. Under the Code, the father is required to recognize imputed interest income equal to what the federal government pays on new borrowings. §7872(a)(1).

loaned employee   see *leased employee.*

loan origination period requirements, pooled financing bonds   see *pooled financing bond.*

loan, percentage method   see *eligible loan.*

lobbying activities   see *lobbying expenses.*

lobbying expenditures, charities   *expenditures* by a *charitable organization* to influence legislation. For an exempt organization to maintain its exempt status, no substantial part of its activities can consist of propaganda or activities that attempt to influence legislation or attempt to participate or intervene in any political campaign. §501(c)(3). However, a public charity may elect, on Form 5768, instead of meeting a "substantial part of activities test," to meet a sliding scale limitation on expenditures made to influence legislation. §501(h); Reg. §1.501(h)-2, 4911(b),(c).

lobbying expenses   amounts *paid or incurred* (in any form) for participation or intervention in any political campaign on behalf of any candidate for public office, or in connection with any attempt to influence the general public, or segments thereof, with respect to legislative matters, referenda, or elections. §§162(e)(2) and 4911(d)(1) *excise tax.* Such *expenditures* are generally not *deductible* as *trade or business expenses.* Id. However, expenses (including *travel* and costs of preparing testimony) associated with legislative appearances regarding *legislation or proposed legislation* of direct financial interest and associated statements are generally deductible. §162(e)(1)(A). Likewise, *taxpayers* are permitted to *deduct* expenses (including travel and costs of preparing testimony) of communicating with organizations to which they belong with respect to legislation or proposed legislation which is of direct interest to the organizations and the *taxpayers.* §162(e)(1)(B). Dues allocable to payments falling into §162(e)(1)(A) or (B) are also generally *deductible.* §162(e)(1).

lobbying nontaxable amount   The lesser of $1 million or a certain defined percentage of the *exempt purpose expenditures* of a *public charity.* §4911(c)(2). See *tax on lobbying expenditures.*

lobbying taxable amount   see *tax on lobbying expenditures; lobbying expenditures, charities.*

local benefit assessments   taxes for benefits that benefit only the property on which the tax is assessed, even if the tax results in an incidental public benefit. §164(c)(1). Such taxes are *nondeductible* under §164, although they may be *deductible* as *trade or business expenses.* Examples of such assessments include taxes for sewer, water, and waste-removal services that benefit only the assessed properties. Rev. Rul. 76-45, 1976-1 C.B. 51.

local benevolent life and mutual associations   apparently not defined. See *benevolent life insurance associations.*

local district heating or cooling facility   property used as an integral part of a *local district heating or cooling system.*

local district heating or cooling system, exempt facility bond   any local system consisting of a pipeline or network that may be connected to a heating or cooling source, providing both water, chilled water, or steam to at least two users for residential, commercial, or industrial heating or cooling, or for process steam. §142(g). A local system includes facilities that furnish heating and cooling to an area that consists of a city and one contiguous county. Bonds to finance these facilities are *exempt-facility bonds, interest* on which is *tax-exempt interest.*

local furnishing of electrical energy or gas   the provision of electrical energy or gas in an area comprising no more than two contiguous counties, or one city and a contiguous county. §142(f). *Private activity bonds* issued after August 15, 1986, that are part of an issue, 95 percent or more of whose net proceeds are to be used for such purposes, qualify as *exempt facility bonds,* interest on which is exempt from *federal income tax.*

local teachers' retirement funds, exempt   teachers' retirement funds of a "purely local character," whose income comes only from assessments on teachers, local taxes, and investment income, provided there can be no *inurement of earnings to any private shareholder or individual.* §501(c)(11). These organizations can operate on a tax-exempt basis.

location, passive loss rules   see *undertaking, passive loss rules.*

lockout benefits   see *strike and lockout benefits.*

lodge system   a form of organization, comprised of local branches chartered by a parent organization and primarily self-governing, called lodges, chapters, or the like. Reg. §1.501(c)(8)-1. *Fraternal benefit* societies are *exempt* from tax under §501(c)(8) if *operating under the lodge system.* There is a recent trend away from a strict interpretation of this last requirement. Rev. Rul. 73-192, 1973-1 C.B. 224; Rev. Rul. 73-370, 1973-2 C.B. 184.

lodging   for purposes of the *exclusion* under §119 for certain *meals* and the use of lodging, the term implicitly means facilities usable for human housing on the *business premises* of the *employer,* and it explicitly includes certain *qualified campus lodging.* See Reg. §1.119-1(c) and §119(d).

lodging plus meals and incidental expenses per diem under this per diem method, the amount of the employee's expenses deemed substantiated is equal to the lesser of the per diem allowance or the amount computed at the federal per diem rate for the locality of travel in which the employee was away from home. The federal per diem rate may be based travel in CONUS (the 48 contiguous states the District of Columbia) or OCONUS (outside the conterminous United States). Rates for CONUS and OCONUS are published under the Federal Travel regulations for government travel.

longevity benefit payment   see *length-of-service award.*

long-term agreement   see *disqualified leaseback or long-term agreement.*

long-term capital gains   *gains* from the *sale* or *exchange* of a *capital asset* held for more than one year. §1222. Such sales or exchanges may be actual or *constructive,* for example, the retirement of government securities, under §1272(a), that are not in fact either sold or exchanged. See *holding period.*

long-term capital losses   *losses* from *sales or exchanges* of *capital assets* held for more than one year. §1222(4). Such sales or exchanges may be actual or *constructive*; for example, losses on *worthless securities* are deemed to arise from sales or exchanges by §165(g). See *holding period.*

long-term contract   generally, a building, installation, construction, or manufacturing contract that is not completed within the *taxable year* in which it was entered into. §460(f)(1). A manufacturing contract is deemed a long-term contract only if it involves the manufacture of unique items not usually carried as finished goods by the *taxpayer* or items that will normally require more than 12 months to complete. §460(f)(2). The taxpayer is generally limited to the *percentage of completion method of accounting.* §460(a). All *costs* which directly benefit or are incurred by reason of a long-term contract are allocated in the same way as costs associated with *extended period long-term contracts* under Reg. §1.451-

3(b)(5). §460(c)(1). In general, *interest expense* is allocable to contracts such as under the *uniform capitalization rules* of §263A(f). Percentage of completion (or even *percentage of completion—capitalized cost methods*) are not required as to *home construction contracts* and certain small construction contracts (the *"small contractor exception"*) if the contract is expected to be completed within a two-year period, and if the contract is performed by a taxpayer whose average annual gross receipts for the three taxable years preceding the year the contract is entered into do not exceed $10 million. §460(e)(1)(A), (B). See *extended long-term contracts; percentage of completion method of accounting; percentage of completion—capitalized cost method; residential construction contract; uniform capitalization rules.*

long-term holding period   generally a *holding period of* property of more than one year. §1222. Holding periods may be "tacked" by virtue of §1223. Property so held may qualify for favorable *long-term capital gains* treatment. If a futures transaction is in a commodity subject to the rules of a board of trade or commodity exchange, the gain or loss on a sale or exchange is long-term if the contract has been held for more than 6 months—even when the normal long-term holding period is over one year. See *tacking of holding periods.*

long-term tax-exempt rate   for the purposes of the *section 382 limitation,* the *federal long-term rate* under §1274(d), downwardly adjusted so as to reflect rates on tax-exempt bonds. §382(b)(1)(B) and (f). Section 1274 applies to determination of *issue price* when certain *debt instruments* are issued for property. See §1274(d). The long-term rate turns on the average market value yield on outstanding marketable federal obligations with remaining periods to maturity of over nine years. See *applicable federal rate; neutrality principle; section 382 limitation.*

long useful life   see *uniform capitalization rules.*

look-back method, long-term contracts   a special provision under the *percentage of completion method* of accounting for *long-term contracts.* §460(b)(3). It provides that when the contract is completed, the contractor calculates the income which would have been reported in all of the years of the contract if one had used actual total contract costs instead of estimated total contract costs. If and to the extent the contractor overestimated total contract costs, he or she owes the government interest on the tax deferral, and if and to the extent the contractor underestimated total costs of completing the contract, a refund of *interest* is due. Section 460(b)(4)(B) exempts contracts completed within two years of the contract commencement date (the first date on which cost allocable to a contract, other than a binding or negotiating cost, is incurred, §460(g)) if the gross contract price does not exceed $1 million or 1 percent of the taxpayer's average gross receipts for the three taxable years prior to the year the contract was entered into. Section 460(b)(4)(A) authorizes the *IRS* to prescribe a *simplified method* of allocating costs of a long-term contract for purposes of applying the percentage of completion method. The simplified method cannot be used by contractors using the *percentage of completion—capitalized cost method* for accounting for long-term contracts. This simplified method is mandatory for * *AMT* purposes under §56(a)(3). §1007(b) of *TAMRA*.

look-back method, percentage of completion method of accounting   a *tax accounting* rule under which, in the *taxable year* that a *long-term contract* is completed, the *taxpayer* must determine whether *federal income taxes* paid in the prior years of the contract were more or less than what would have been paid if actual rather than expected costs and contract price had been used to compute *gross income*. If there is an underpayment of tax (computed on the basis of actual contract price and cost) the taxpayer must pay *interest* on the *deferral* of tax; a taxpayer is entitled to receive interest if there is an overpayment of tax. Interest on the overpayment or underpayment is computed by use of the overpayment rate under §6621, compounded daily. §460(b)(3). There are further details. See *percentage of completion—capitalized cost method; simplified look-back method.*

look-through entity   a term used in Reg §1.904-5(h)-(i) to denote *partnerships* and other unspecified entities that are taxed as *conduits.*

loss   generally, the *amount realized* on a *disposition* of *property* in a *closed transaction* to the extent it falls short of the property's *adjusted basis.* §1001(a). See §165. In another sense, the word refers to negative operating revenues. See *net operating loss (NOL).*

loss carryovers and carrybacks   see *capital loss carryback; capital loss carryovers; loss carrybacks, regulated futures contracts; net operating loss carrybacks; net operating loss carryovers.*

loss corporate freeze recapitalization   a method of recapitalizing a *corporation* with a history of *net operating losses* without violating the *neutrality principle.* The trick is to assure that the former *shareholders* retain at least half the recapitalized corporation's equity. As a result, there is no *ownership change* and therefore the *section 382 limitation* does not come into play.

loss corporation   generally, a *corporation* that has unexpired *net operating losses* or *capital losses.* The term includes any corporation that is entitled to a *prechange loss* for the *taxable year* in which an *ownership change* took place (including an *NOL* or NOL *carryover*). For purposes of the *neutrality principle,* it is defined as a corporation that is entitled to use a net operating loss carryover. §382(k)(1).

loss deferral rule, straddles   a rule to prevent *deferral* of income and to prevent conversion of *ordinary income* and *short-term capital gain* into *long-term capital gain* on *straddle* transactions. Generally, the *deduction* of *losses* on straddle *positions* involving property not on the *mark-to-market system* is limited to the amount by which such *losses* exceed *recognized gain* on any *offsetting positions.* §§1092, 1256. As a result, if a *taxpayer* recognizes a loss on the *disposition* of one or more positions in a straddle, the amount of loss that may be *deducted* is the excess of the loss over the *unrecognized gain* (if any) in positions that offset the loss positions and that were acquired before the taxpayer disposed of the loss position. See *position, unregulated commodities contracts.*

loss disallowance rules   a loose reference to the rule embodied in Temp. Reg. §1.1502-20T. The rule disallows a parent *corporation's loss* on the *sale* of the *stock* of a subsidiary (or a deconsolidation) which was a *member* of an *affiliated group.* Reg. §1.1502-20(c) allows loss to the extent it exceeds an amount determined by a formula: (1) *E&P* from *extraordinary gain dispositions* (extraordinary gain factor); (2) positive investment adjustments in excess of the amount described in (1) (positive adjustment factor); and (3) *duplicated loss* (loss duplication factor). The formula is designed to protect against the elimination of corporate level tax while permitting *economic loss* to the extent feasible without tracing.

losses   either operating deficits incurred in a *trade or business* or *investment*-related transactions involving property (e.g., *sales*) in which the *taxpayer* fails to recover his capital. Operating losses are described in §172 (*net operating losses*), basically as a failure by a *person* engaged in a *trade or business* to earn *gross income* at least equal to gross *expenses,* but with numerous qualifications. Transactional losses are described in §165 as transactions implicitly involving property (§165(b)), which are not compensated for by insurance or otherwise. §156(a). If incurred by *individuals,* they are *deductible* only if incurred in a trade or business, in a *transaction entered into for a profit,* or as a result of *theft* or *casualty.* Further limitations are imposed by §165(d) (*wagering losses*), (f) (*capital losses*), and (g) (*worthless securities*).

losses incurred, insurance companies   an amount computed by adding the salvage and reinsurance recoverable left outstanding at the end of the preceding *taxable year* to the *losses* paid during the *taxable year,* then *deducting* the salvage and reinsurance recoverable at the end of the taxable year. To this result, one adds all unpaid losses and all *discounted unpaid losses* outstanding at the end of the *taxable* year and deducts those outstanding at the end of the preceding taxable year to arrive at the figure for total losses incurred for the taxable year. §832(b). The resulting number, losses incurred, is a *deduction* used in calculating *insurance company taxable income*. §832(c).

loss of member or function of body   generally, the substantial or complete loss, or loss of use, of an eye, ear, or extremity. Reg. §1.105-3. Acute, completely debilitating cancer also qualifies. Rev. Rul. 63-181, 1963-2 C.B. 74. If the loss is permanent, then compensatory payments for the loss may be excluded from the payee's *gross income*. §105(c).

loss payment pattern   an *insurance company's* historical *loss* payment pattern, determined every five years with respect to each line of business in accordance with a loss payment pattern schedule provided by the *Treasury Department*.

loss reserves   accounts established to reflect, by means of a present *deduction*, anticipated future *losses*. While such accounts are allowed for financial reporting, the *IRS* and the *Code* virtually never allow them. See §461(h).

low-cost articles   unsolicited gifts from *exempt organizations* which the *donee* can keep in all events as part of solicitation of *charitable contributions*. The aggregate of these gifts must cost the organization less than five dollars in 1986. The five-dollar amount will be adjusted by the cost of living. §573(h)(2)-(3). Income from distributing such articles and from renting or exchanging associated donor lists is not treated as being from an *unrelated trade or business*. §573(h)(1).

lower of cost or market, inventory valuation   a method for determining *closing inventory* under which goods are valued at the lesser of their *fair market value* or their *cost* at the end of the *taxable year*. Reg. §1.471-2(c) authorizes the use of cost alone (mandatory for *LIFO* accounting) or a lower of cost or market. A major practical effect is to allow *taxpayers* to treat declines in inventory value to below cost as *current expenses*. However, *Thor Power Tool doctrine* demands that excess stocks of merchandise whose value has been written off must actually have been offered for sale for prices below replacement cost in order for such write-offs to be valid. See *cost, inventory valuation; market, inventory valuation; subnormal goods*.

low-income housing   for purposes of the *accelerated cost recovery system* and *construction period interest and taxes,* the reference is to residential realty described in §1250(a)(1)(B)(i) through (iv), including (1) property whose *mortgage* is insured under §§221(d)(3) or 236 of the National Housing Act, or under comparable state or local law subject to rental limits described in §1039(b)(1)(B); (2) property qualifying under §8 of the United States Housing Act of 1937 or comparable state or local law.

low-income housing credit   A nonrefundable income tax credit is available on a per unit basis for low-income units in qualified low-income buildings in qualified low-income housing projects placed in service generally before 1992. §42. The owner of a qualified low-income housing project may claim a credit over a 10-year period. The *tax credit* was to encourage rehabilitation or construction of housing for people with low incomes, based on *area median gross income*. The low-income housing credit expired on June 30, 1992. See *low-income unit, low-income housing credit*.

low-income rental housing   see *low- or moderate-income rental housing*.

low-income unit, low-income housing credit   any unit in a *qualified low-income building* if it is a *rent-restricted unit* whose occupants meet an income limitation elected for the project; the unit must be habitable on a nontransient basis, and if it is a building with four or fewer units, it must not have the owner or a related person as one of its occupants. §42(i)(3). See *eligible basis, low-income housing credit; qualified basis, low-income housing credit*.

low- or moderate-income rental housing   a building, the *dwelling units* of which are held for rental occupancy by families and *individuals* of low or moderate income as determined by the *IRS,* consistent with the §8 subsidy program under the Housing Act of 1937. Specifically, a household is not low or moderate income if its adjusted annual income exceeds 80 percent of the median income for the geographical area as determined by HUD. Reg. §1.167(k)-3(b)(2).

lump-sum distribution, qualified plans   a payment or distribution of an *employee's* entire credit balance (including an *annuity* in certain cases) under all the *employer's qualified pension* or *profit-sharing plans* in a single *taxable year,* paid because of the payee's death, reaching of age $59\frac{1}{2}$, *separation from service,* or *disability* as defined in §72(m)(7). §402(e)(4)(A). Under current law, a *five-year forward averaging convention* is available if an individual is a participant in a qualified pension or profit-sharing plan for at least five years and receives a lump-sum distribution from the plan. §402(e). The forward averaging provisions are generally available for lump-sum distributions received on or after age $59\frac{1}{2}$. §402(e)(4)(B). A distribution from an IRA does not qualify for five-year forward averaging.

lump-sum rollover, annuities   a reference to §72(h), which permits lump-sum payments under *annuity contracts* to be reinvested within 60 days thereof, free of *federal income taxes*.

luxuries   items that are not *necessities*. The provision of luxuries is not counted in determining who, if anyone, can claim another *individual* as a *dependent*. §151(c). See *necessities*.

luxury automobiles, limitation on depreciation
additional *MACRS* depreciation restrictions apply to so-called luxury automobiles. The limitations apply even if such automobiles are used *100 percent* of the time for business. The *MACRS* depreciation for automobiles placed in service in 1991 is subject to a $2,660 ceiling limitation for the first year, $4,300 for the second year, $2,550 for the third year, and $1,575 for each succeeding year in the recovery period. §280F(a)(2).

luxury tax *excise taxes* imposed on the acquisition or holding of luxury articles such as boats (10 percent of the excess, if the price exceeds $100,000), aircraft (10 percent of the excess, if the price exceeds $250,000), jewelry and furs (10 percent of the excess, if the price exceeds $10,000), and passenger vehicles (10 percent of the excess, if the price exceeds $30,000). Taxicabs are exempt.

M

MACRS   an acronym for *modified ACRS.*

MCC   an acronym for a *mortgage credit certificate.*

machine readable form   see *magnetic media reporting.*

magnetic media reporting   procedures whereby *taxpayers* submit electronic data processing tapes in lieu of written papers for various tax reporting purposes. See, e.g., Rev. Proc. 83-8, 1983-27 I.R.B. 7. See §6011(e) for mandatory reporting in machine readable form for taxpayers obligated to file numerous *information returns.*

mail order ministries   *tax evasion* schemes by which *taxpayers* are typically solicited to acquire materials showing them how to purchase credentials to become affiliates of central church organizations, or simply to form their own totally unaffiliated churches. The usual scheme is to organize a church to which the *taxpayer* transfers all his or her property and future income and for the benefit of which he or she takes a vow of poverty, while characterizing personal living expenses disbursed by the church as *excludable* from the recipient's *gross income.* Such schemes have met hostile judicial and administrative reactions, largely because of the *inurement* of benefits to founders, in violation of §503(c). Also, *assignments of income* to such churches invariably fail.

mainland affiliate   a *United States* parent or affiliate of a subsidiary or affiliate operating in Puerto Rico or the United States Virgin Islands. The rules of affiliation are supplied by §936(h)(3)(D).

maintaining a household, child and dependent care credit   providing more than half the maintenance costs of a household for the *taxable year.* §21(f)(1); Reg. §1.44A-1(d)(1).

maintenance of an inconsistent position, mitigation of effect of limitations and other provisions   a requirement that the party (*taxpayer* or *IRS*) against whom a mitigating correction is sought generally take a position with respect to an *open year* that conflicts with an erroneous prior treatment in order to use the mitigation provisions to correct an error. §1311(b)(1). For example, if there is a *determination* that a taxpayer erroneously claimed a *deduction* in a prior *closed year* and now claims it for an open year, the taxpayer has taken an inconsistent position, and the IRS may bring §§1311–1314 to bear against the taxpayer. In other words, the existence of an inconsistent position ordinar-

ily means one party is trying to get a double benefit (e.g., two taxes on one transaction by the IRS) by changing a prior interpretation of how the item should be treated. See *duty of consistency; mitigation of effect of statutes of limitations and other provisions.*

maintenance of income-producing property   see *expenses for the management, conservation, or maintenance of property held for the production of income.*

maintenance repair allowance deduction   see *repair allowance.*

major category   see *simplified dollar-value LIFO method.*

majority interest taxable year   the *taxable year,* if any, which on each testing day (generally, the first day of the *partnership's* putative taxable year) constituted the taxable year of one or more *partners* (on such day) then having over one-half the aggregate *capital interest* and *profits interest* in the partnership. §706(b)(4)(A). This year is the *Code's* mandatory first choice for the selection of a taxable year. §706(b)(1)(B). Once selected, the choice generally sticks for two years. §706(b)(4)(B). The majority interest taxable year is the first preference. If it does not exist, one uses the year of the *principal partners.* Failing that, one generally uses a *calendar year.* §706(b)(1)(B).

majority-owned subsidiary company, registered holding company   a *corporation* in which a registered holding company, its other subsidiaries, or both, own more than half of the total combined voting power of all classes of *stock* entitled to vote, not including stock that votes only on default or nonpayment. §1083; Reg. §1. 1083-1(c). Under certain circumstances, interests in such companies may be transferred tax-free pursuant to SEC orders.

majority United States shareholder   see *specified foreign corporation*

majority United States shareholder year   see *specified foreign corporation.*

major stock acquisition   a transaction in which an *acquiring corporation* , or it and any group of *persons* acting in concert with it, acquires 50 percent or more by vote or by value of the target's *stock* (§1504(a)(4) *preferred stock*). For this purpose, all stock purchases during any 24-month period are aggregated, and stock purchases separated over 24 months are aggregated if made pursuant to a plan. If this type of *corporate equity reduction transaction* (CERT) occurs, both corporations are considered to have undergone a CERT. §172(b), (m). There are exceptions for purchases followed by *section 338 elections* and for cases where immediately before the acquisition, the target was a member (but not the common parent) of an *affiliated group.* See *corporate equity reduction transaction.*

major stock acquisition, CERT   a planned acquisition by a *corporation* (alone or in concert) of *stock* of another corporation that represents 50 percent or more by vote or value of the stock in such other corporation; it excludes a *qualified stock purchase* under §338, or an acquisition of the stock of another corporation which, immediately before the acquisition, was a *member* of an *affiliated group* of corporations. All plans are combined and all acquisitions occurring in a 24-month period are combined. §172(m)(3). This is an aspect of an *applicable corporation* for purposes of the *corporate equity reduction transaction* restrictions. See *applicable corporation, CERT.*

make-up provision, partnerships   an agreement that any *partner* with a *deficit* in his or her *capital account* following *distribution* of *liquidation* proceeds must restore the amount of the deficit to the *partnership*. See Reg. §1.704-1(b)(2)(ii)(c). Absent such a provision, partnership allocations can lack *substantial economic effect*. See *charge-back provision, partnership.*

management, conservation, or maintenance of property held for the production of income   see *expenses for the management, conservation, or maintenance of property held for the production of income.*

management contract   in a *tax shelter* setting, an agreement between an investor in an equipment leasing venture and an equipment management enterprise. In the typical case an investor buys a railroad boxcar and contracts out the management of the boxcar and claims the *investment tax credit*, asserting that the arrangement is not a *lease* which could attract problems under §46(e)(3) relating to limits on availability of the credit to noncorporate lessors. A management contract will evidently be found if the investors retain control over, and risk of loss in, the venture.

management contract retirement plan   a *nonqualified deferred compensation* plan collectively designed for *employees'* (usually only executives') retirement, used in lieu of *qualified deferred compensation plans.*

management corporations   *corporations* providing managerial services, frequently to related entities. Such corporations are sometimes formed to bleed off earnings of affiliates in order to limit *accumulated earnings tax* and *unreasonable compensation* problems, or to provide favorable *fringe benefits* to parties associated with the management corporation. Such corporations may be *personal service corporations.*

managing executive   an *employee* who, by reason of her authority and responsibility, is authorized, without effective veto procedure, to decide upon the necessity of her foreign business trip. Reg. §1.274-4(f)(5)(i)(a). Such an *individual* is not automatically exempted from the limits on foreign *travel expense deductions* imposed by Reg. §1.274-4. Reg. §1.274-4(f)(5) (first sentence).

mandatory contributions   amounts contributed to a *retirement plan* as a condition of employment, plan *participation*, or obtaining the benefit of *employer contributions*. §411(c)(2)(C) (*vesting* purposes under *defined contribution plans*, used to define *accumulated contributions*). Mandatory contributions (possibly having the same meaning) may be found discriminatory if unduly burdensome and can, therefore, disqualify a plan. Reg. §1.401-3(d). See Rev. Rul. 80-307, 1980-2 C.B. 136. See also Rev. Rul. 74-56, 1974-1 C.B. 90, and Rev. Rul. 74-55, 1974-1 C.B. 89, as to withdrawals.

mandatory retirement age   for purposes of §105 relating to *accident and health plans*, the term refers to the age set by an *employer* for the mandatory retirement of *employees* in the class to which the *taxpayer* last belonged, unless that age has been set higher than that at which it has been the practice of the employer to terminate, due to age, the services of his or her employees, or for purposes of *tax avoidance*. If no age is set for mandatory retirement, the term means the greater of age 65 or the age at which it has been the practice of the employer to terminate, due to age, the services of the class of employees to which the taxpayer belongs. Reg. §1.105-4(a)(3)(i)(B). *Employer contributions* to the plan made after mandatory retirement age are not *excludable* from the employee's *gross income*. Reg. §1.105-4(a)(3)(i)(A).

mandatory rules   instructions, especially those to *IRS* personnel, that create legal rights for *taxpayers*. Some procedural rules set forth in the *Internal Revenue Manual* are mandatory. Generally, a procedural rule will be found mandatory only if it preserves a substantial interest of a taxpayer, especially a Constitutional right. For the antonym, see *directory rule.*

manufacturing burden rate method   a method that apportions *indirect production costs* to various items of *closing inventory*. The method requires that any net negative or net positive difference between total predetermined indirect production costs allocated to the goods in *closing inventory* and the total amount of such costs actually required to be allocated to such goods (that is, the under- or overapplied burden) be treated as an adjustment to the closing inventory in the *taxable year* in which the difference arises, unless the adjustment is insignificant in amount and not allocated in the *taxpayer's* financial reports. The *regulations* provide that periodic adjustments of the burden rate to adapt to current conditions are not *changes in accounting method*. See Reg. §1.471-11(d)(2).

manufacturing intangibles   see *cost-sharing election, possessions corporations.*

manufacturing overhead costs   sometimes known as manufacturing expenses, these are the variety of *indirect production costs* that cannot be identified and allocated, or that are inexpedient to attempt to allocate, to specific units of production. Reg. §1.471-11.

marginal production *domestic* crude oil or domestic natural gas produced during any *taxable year* from a *property* that is a *stripper well property* for the *calendar year* in which that *taxable year* begins, or a *property* substantially from which all the production during the calendar year in which that tax year begins is *heavy oil.* §613A(c)(6)(D)(ii). The term is used for purposes of enhanced *percentage depletion* from difficult properties. The benefit is that the usual 15 percent rate rises by one percentage point for each whole dollar by which the average wellhead price per *barrel* of domestic crude oil (the *reference price*) falls below $20 (not adjusted for inflation) for *calendar year.* §613A(c)(6). The benefit applies only to so much of a *taxpayer's average daily marginal production* that does not exceed 1,000 barrels/day of oil or 6 million cubic feet of gas. §613A(c)(6)(A). See *property, depletion.*

marginal rate the rate of tax applied to the last dollar of the *tax base.* For example if between $16,000 and $20,000 of *taxable income* were taxed at 20 percent and the *taxpayer* had $16,500 of taxable income, the marginal rate would be 20 percent.

marital deduction an unlimited *deduction* used in determining *taxable gifts* or the *taxable estate* for interspousal transfers. §§2056, 2523. By making the marital deduction unlimited in amount (a 100 percent marital deduction), neither the gift tax nor the estate tax is imposed on outright interspousal transfers of property. The unlimited marital deduction even includes one spouse's share of the community property transferred to the other spouse. See *estate tax; gift tax; passes from the decedent to his surviving spouse, estate tax marital deduction; qualified domestic trust.*

marital deduction trust a *testamentary trust* for the benefit of a *surviving spouse.* Presently, §2056(a) grants an *unlimited marital deduction,* but much *estate planning* apparently now revolves around transferring to other people the maximum creditable amount ($600,000 after 1986) under §2505 and placing the balance in a marital deduction trust. Examples of such trusts include *marital estate trusts, QTIP trusts,* and any other *present interests* transferred in trust.

marital gifts interspousal gifts. They are generally free of federal *gift taxes.* §2522(a). See §1042 for *income effects* (*gift* treatment applied).

marketable securities, second disposition rule for installment sale any security for which there was market on an established securities exchange or otherwise, on the date of resale by the related buyer. §453(f)(2). The term includes securities listed on the New York Stock Exchange, the American Stock Exchange, or any city or regional exchange in which quotations appear on a daily basis, including foreign securities listed on a recognized foreign national or regional exchange; securities regularly traded in the national or regional over-the-counter market, for which published quotations are available; securities locally traded, for which quotations can readily be obtained from established brokerage firms; and units in a *common trust fund.* Mutual fund shares, for which redemption prices are published, also would be considered marketable securities. S. Rep. No 1000, 96th Cong., 2d sess. 15 (1980) 1980-2 C.B. 494, note 20. A second disposition of marketable securities by a related person may accelerate *recognition* of *gain* from the first *installment* sale between such related person and the related party from whom he acquired the property, even if the second disposition occurs more than two years after the installment sale. See *second disposition rule, installment sales.*

market discount bond a bond (meaning a bond, debenture, note, certificate, or other evidence of indebtedness) purchased after its initial issuance (subject to certain exceptions) having *market discount,* other than a short-term obligation (not more than a year from issue date to maturity date), *tax-exempt obligation, United States savings bond,* or *installment obligation* (§453B sense, but not demand debt when issued). §1278(a)(1). Section 1278 defines market discount immediately after its acquisition by the buyer, subject to a *de minimis rule. Gain* on *disposition* of a market discount bond in the hands of a *cash method taxpayer* is *ordinary income* to the extent of *accrued market discount.* §1276(a). See *market discount, income.*

market discount, income the excess of a bond's *stated redemption price at maturity* (e.g., $100) over the *taxpayer's basis* for the bond immediately after its acquisition (e.g., $90). §1278(a)(2). The market discount ($10) is now generally treated as generating eventual *ordinary income* on disposition or, at the *taxpayer's* election, ratably over the life of the bond. See *market discount bond; stated redemption price at maturity, market discount.*

market discount or premium a discount below the issue price, or a premium above the issue price of a debt obligation, respectively, arising because of changes in an obligation's value after its issuance. Reasons for such fluctuations might be changes in overall levels of interest rates or the issuer's credit rating. As to post–July 18, 1984 bonds, market discount can be *accrued* ratably, on a daily basis or under *OID* principles, at the holder's election, for purposes of converting the gain on sale to *ordinary income* under §1276(a). The holder may also elect to include market discount in *gross* income ratably.

market discount rules Sections 1276–1278, the core ideas of which are that purchasers of bonds trading at a market discount and issued after July 18, 1984, at a discount (below stated redemption price), subject to a *de minimis* exception under §1278(a)(2) must identify the market discount. *Interest expense deductions* on loans to purchase such bonds are generally deferred until the bond is disposed of. §1277. *Taxpayers* can elect to report market discount annually over the life of the bond and add the imaginary income to the *basis* of the bond, thereby reducing *gain* on the disposition. §1278(b). See *market discount or premium; market discount bond; market discount, income.*

marketing cooperative   a *cooperative* whose purpose is to market the output of its members (e.g., a truck farmer's selling co-op). See *cooperatives; exempt farmers' cooperatives.*

market, inventory valuation   generally, the current bid price (open-market replacement cost) prevailing at the *inventory* valuation date for a particular item of merchandise in the volume most commonly acquired by the *taxpayer*; it is applied to goods that have been purchased as well as to those on hand, and to the basic elements of cost (i.e., materials, labor, and overhead) of goods in the process of being manufactured and to finished goods on hand produced by the taxpayer. Reg. §1.471-4(a). Inventory valuation at the *lower of cost or market* is a common pricing practice. Reg. §1.471-2(c).

market or cost, inventory valuation   see *lower of cost or market, inventory valuation.*

mark-to-market system   a method of accounting used by commodities exchanges under which people who trade on such exchanges are credited with *unrealized gains* and *losses* on a daily basis. Losses require immediate cash deposits and *unrealized* gains permit cash withdrawals. As a result of this accounting, the position of each member of the exchange is determined daily, and their customers' accounts are immediately credited or charged. The term's importance relates to the definition of *regulated futures contracts* and other so-called *section 1256 contracts. Unrealized capital gains* on such contracts are deemed *recognized* at year-end, and they are treated as if 60 percent were *long-term capital* and 40 percent were *short-term capital gains* (or *losses*). The system is also applicable to *nonequity listed options* and *dealer's equity options.* The mark-to-market provisions do not apply to *hedging transactions,* unless they were undertaken by *syndicates.* §1256(e).

married person   someone who maintains a legal relationship with a *spouse* recognized as a marriage by state law. For tax purposes, one's marital status is determined on the last day of one's *taxable year,* but in the event one spouse should die during the *taxable year,* marital status is determined as of the date of death, such that a *joint return* can be filed that year. §7703(a). Generally, one is regarded as a married person even if the spouses

live separately, unless they have been *legally separated* or divorced. The *IRS* will recognize a common law marriage if it is recognized by state law. Rev. Rul. 68-277, 1968-1 C.B. 60. Section 7703(a)(2) treats people who are legally separated under a decree of separate maintenance or divorce as not married, and the *runaway spouse rule* of §7703(b) deems certain *heads of household* to be unmarried so as to qualify for married head of household *income tax* rates.

Massachusetts trust   a form of *trust,* organized under Massachusetts law, that is designed to engage in *business* enterprises, managed by its *trustees,* the ownership of which is evidenced by transferable *certificates of beneficial interest.* Such trusts are taxable in the same manner as *corporations.* Reg. §301.7701-4(b). *Real estate investment trusts* are commonly organized as Massachusetts trusts, but are granted special tax relief that entitles them to *deduct dividends* to *shareholders,* making them effectively nontaxable.

mass asset retirement   the retirement of *mass assets* from service. The subject is simple in the case of a normal retirement (retirement proceeds are added to the *depreciation* reserve). In the case of *extraordinary retirements,* however, the problems of identifying the vintage of the asset has led to Reg. §1.167(a)-11(d)(3)(v)(d), which allows the use of a mortality dispersion table generated by the *taxpayer* to solve the problem.

mass asset rule   synonymous with the *mass asset theory.*

mass assets   a mass or group of *individual* items of property not necessarily homogeneous, each of which is minor in value relative to the total value of such mass or group, numerous in quantity, usually accounted for only on a total dollar or quantity basis, and with respect to which separate identification is impracticable. The term includes portable air and electric tools, jigs, dies, railroad ties, overhead conductors, hardware, textile spindles, and minor items of office, plant, and store furniture and fixtures, as well as returnable containers and other items that are considered subsidiary assets for purposes of computing the allowance for *depreciation.* Reg. §1.47-1(e)(4). Mass asset retirements affecting the *investment tax credit* could be done on the basis of careful estimates. Reg. §1.47-1(e)(2). The term is synonymous with unitary assets.

mass asset theory   a judicial concept that elements of *goodwill* cannot be broken down into distinct items, such as customer lists, which have identifiable *useful lives* so as to be separately *amortized,* on the theory that the particular *intangibles* are submerged in the larger enterprise. However, *taxpayers* who support their claims with string evidence have prevailed. See Rev. Rul. 74-456, 1974-2 C.B. 65. But see *residual method.*

mass commuting facilities, exempt facility bond includes *real property* together with improvements and *personal property* used therein, such as machinery, equipment, and furniture, serving the general public commuting on a day-to-day basis by bus, subway, rail, ferry, or other conveyance which moves over prescribed routes. It also includes terminals and facilities which are functionally related and subordinate to the mass commuting facility, such as parking garages, car barns, and repair shops. Bonds issued to finance such facilities are generally *private activity bonds, interest* on which may be exempt to their holders. See *state or local bond; tax-exempt bond.*

mass submitter   generally, a *person* which can establish that if it gets a favorable notification letter from the *IRS* with respect to a *regional prototype plan,* there are at least 50 sponsors who will adopt the plan verbatim. Rev. Proc. 89-13, 1989-7 I.R.B. 25, at 27. Such plans qualify for favorable processing by the IRS by virtue of being *mass submitter regional prototype plans.* See *mass submitter program.*

mass submitter program   an *IRS* program authorized by Rev. Proc. 89-9, 1989-6 I.R.B. 59.04 as a permanent program to provide expedited review of *qualified plans* submitted in accordance with the requirements of §18 of the same revenue procedure. See Form 4461-B, to be used to request applications on behalf of sponsoring organizations which are adopting plans that are identical to or minor modifications of mass submitter plans.

mass submitter regional prototype plan   a *defined benefit plan* or *defined contribution plan* made available to plan sponsors by a *mass submitter,* provided the plan otherwise qualifies as a *regional prototype plan.* Rev. Proc. 89-13, 1989-7 I.R.B. 25, at 27. Such plans are subject to cookie-cutter processing by the IRS. One key advantage is that the *National Office* of the *IRS* considers such plans for approval, and if approved, they can be approved nationwide. See *mass submitter program.*

master limited partnership   a term used to describe a *partnership* which is used as a vehicle for an *exchange offer.* The idea is to contribute "burned out" *partnership interests* that have lost their values as *tax shelters* on a tax-free basis to larger partnerships, interests in which may be publicly marketed. Such partnerships may be *publicly traded partnerships.* See *publicly traded partnership.*

master plan   a model form of an *IRS*-approved *qualified plan* in which the funding medium's (e.g., an insurance company separate account) identity is specified. Rev. Proc. 80-29, 1980-1 C.B. 681, §3.02. Adopting such plans results in administrative savings.

matching concept, accounting   a basic accounting concept under which items of *income* and *expenses* are associated in a manner designed to clearly reflect income or loss over time. The concept is only occasionally adopted for purposes of *tax accounting.*

matching contribution   an *employer contribution* to a *qualified plan* on behalf of an *employee's* contribution, or an employer's contribution on behalf of an employee on account of the employee's *elective deferral* of compensation. According to the *legislative history* of *TAMRA,* it may be made to the same or a different plan and it includes an employer contribution to a *tax-sheltered annuity* on account of employee contributions or elective deferrals. See generally §401(m)(4)(A).

matching taxable year of election   the *taxable year* of each *member of an affiliated group,* which includes the last day of the *taxable year* of the common parent *corporation,* for which an election by the affiliated group is made pursuant to §243(b)(2) to deduct 100 percent of the *qualifying dividends* received by the recipient corporation. Reg. §1.243-4(c)(1)(iii). All the subsidiaries must consent to elect the 100 percent *deduction* if they were members of the affiliated group at any time during the matching year, which included the parent's year-end; absent such consent, the 100 percent *dividends-received deduction* is prohibited. §243(b)(2). For example, if P were on a *fiscal year* ending June 30, and the only subsidiary were on a *calendar year,* and the parent made the election for the fiscal year ending June 30, 1992, then the subsidiary would have to consent for its calendar year 1992.

material costs, direct   see *direct material costs.*

material income-producing factor, capital   several *Code* sections attempt to sort *income* from *capital* as opposed to income from services on the basis of whether capital is a material income-producing factor or merely incidental to the performance of personal services, especially §§704(e)(1) *(family partnerships)* and 911(d)(2)(B) *(foreign earned income).* Capital is a material income-producing factor if a substantial portion of the *gross income* of the *trade* or *business* is attributable to the employment of capital as reflected, for example, by a substantial investment in *inventories,* plant, machinery, or other equipment, such as a laundering and dry cleaning business. Capital is generally not a material income-producing factor where the *gross income* of the business consists principally of fees, commissions, or other compensation for personal services performed by an *individual.* Accordingly, capital is usually regarded as incidental to the professional practice of a doctor, dentist, radiologist, architect, lawyer, or accountant, even though the practitioner may have a substantial investment in professional equipment or in the physical plant constituting his or her office. Reg. §1.1348-3(a)(3)(ii). Examples are set forth in Reg. §1.1348-3(a)(6). See also Reg. §§1.704-1(e)(l)(iv) and 1.911-2(b).

material income-producing factor, services not clearly defined. See Reg. §§1.37-3, 1.401-13, and 1.1402(a)(1); G.C.M. 34160 (July 9, 1969) which do not clarify the issue.

material item a recurring incidence of *gross income* or *expense* (e.g., vacation pay), which calls for determining the proper time for *inclusion* of the item in *gross income* or for taking a *deduction*. Reg. §1.446-1(e)(2)(ii)(A). Generally, the treatment of any material item constitutes a *method of accounting*. Reg. §1.446-1(e)(2)(ii)(A). Accordingly, a change in the manner of recording such items for *federal income tax* purposes generally constitutes a *change of accounting method*, which calls for *IRS* approval.

material modification of debt a change in the terms of a *debt* that is so great as to constitute an *exchange* under Reg. §1.1001-1(a). See, e.g., Rev. Rul.89-122, 1989-47 I.R.B. 6. The standards as to when such a modification have taken place are definitely not clear. Instead a mass of unranked factors must be considered.

material participation, passive loss rules a regular, continuous and substantial activity with respect to an *undertaking*. §469(h)(1). *Limited partners* are generally incapable of material participation. §469(b)(2). Certain retired farmers and their *spouses,* however, are deemed to materially participate, and the activity of one spouse is often attributed to the other spouse. §469(h)(3) and (5). *Closely held C corporations* and *personal service corporations* are considered to materially participate via their shareholders. §469(h)(4). The issue is contextual and depends in each case on the particular *trade or business* under scrutiny. *Partners* and *shareholders* of *S corporations* are active directly or not at all. In general, material participation by a *taxpayer* suffices to avoid the *passive loss rules*. In the case of certain real estate activities, *active participation* suffices.

mathematical or clerical errors various computational or clerical errors shown on *tax returns*. Section 6213(f) defines such errors to include (1) arithmetic errors; (2) incorrect use of tax tables; (3) inconsistent entries on a tax return where it is apparent which entry is correct; (4) omission of supporting schedules, which are required to support an entry on a return; and (5) a *deduction* or *credit* that exceeds a statutory limit. When such an error occurs, the *IRS* is allowed to make a summary *assessment* by sending a notice to the *taxpayer*. The taxpayer is then given 60 days to file an *abatement* request; the *IRS* is precluded from collecting the assessment until 60 days have passed or the taxpayer agrees to the assessment. After the 60-day abatement period, the IRS must follow the regular *deficiency* procedures. §6213(b)(1); Reg. §301.6213-1. See *notice of deficiency*.

maximum deductible amount, section 444 election the sum of (1) the *applicable amount* paid during the *deferral period* of the *applicable election year,* plus (2) the product of (a) the amount determined under (1) above, divided by the number of months in the deferral period of the applicable election year, multiplied by (b) the number of months in the nondeferral period (i.e., the portion of the applicable election year after the portion of such year constituting the deferral period) of the applicable election year. Reg. §1.280H-1T(d).

Illustration: PSC, Inc., is an accrual method PSC with a taxable year ending January 31. It makes a section 444 election to retain a year ending January 31 for its taxable year beginning February 1, 1992. For its applicable election year beginning February 1, 1992, PSC, Inc., does not satisfy the minimum distribution requirement. Furthermore, PSC, Inc., has three employee-owners, G, H, and I. Both G and H have been employee-owners of PSC, Inc., for 10 years. Although I has been an employee of PSC, Inc., for 4 years, I did not become an employee-owner until December 1, 1992, when I acquired 5 of the 20 outstanding shares of PSC, Inc., stock. For PSC, Inc.'s applicable election year beginning February 1, 1992, G earns $5,000 a month plus a $40,000 bonus on January 15, 1990, and H and I each earn $4,000 a month plus a $32,000 bonus on January 15, 1993. Thus, the total of the applicable amounts during the deferral period of the applicable election year beginning February 1, 1992, is $143,000. Based on these facts, PSC, Inc.'s deduction for applicable amounts is limited to $156,000, determined as follows: $143,000 (applicable amounts during the deferral period) plus $13,000 (applicable amounts during the deferral period, divided by the number of months in the deferral period, multiplied by the number of months in the nondeferral period).

maximum tax, FIRPTA withholding the maximum amount of tax on *ordinary income* or *capital gains* associated with the *disposition* of a *United States real property interest*. The term is used in connection with obtaining a certificate permitting exemption from *FIRPTA withholding*. See §1445(c) and Rev. Proc. 88-23, 1988-19 I.R.B. 32 at §4.01.

meals for purposes of §119, allowing an *exclusion* for *employer*-provided meals (or meal subsidies), the term clearly includes meals in kind and excludes cash allowances. Whether groceries are included as meals is unclear.

meals and lodging see *lodging; meals.*

meaningful barriers to collection doctrine a minority view that a *cash method taxpayer* who can only collect available property (e.g., a check) at year-end with almost superhuman effort will not be taxed on such *gross income* under the *constructive receipt doctrine*. See *cash method; method of accounting.*

meaningful reduction of a shareholder's proportionate interest see *redemption not essentially equivalent to a dividend.*

medical and tuition expenses, gift tax exclusion medical and tuition payments (so-called *qualified transfers*) made directly to the service provider. §2503(e). Gifts of such expenses are free of *federal gift taxes*. Qualifying medical expenses are those defined in §213 as *medical care* (i.e., those incurred for the diagnosis, cure, mitigation, treatment, or prevention of disease, etc., including drugs and medical insurance, in short, medical care expenses) paid directly by the *donor* to the *individual* or organization providing medical services (i.e., not reimbursement to the *donee*, as intermediary).

medical care generally, care received for the "diagnosis, cure, mitigation, treatment, or prevention of disease, or for the purpose of affecting any structure or function of the body, for transportation primarily for and essential to medical care or for insurance covering medical care." See §213(d); Reg. §1.213-1(e)(1)(ii). Medical expenses include the entire *medical insurance premium*. Deductions for medical care must be for costs incurred primarily for the prevention or alleviation of physical or mental illness or defects. Costs expended for general beneficial care to the *individual* do not qualify. Also excluded from the deduction are costs incurred for needless cosmetic surgery, illegal operations and treatments. The term includes transportation expenses essential to medical care (§213(d)(1)(B), including certain lodging up to $50 per night), so-called *special schools* (often in full—Reg. §1.213-1(e)(1)(v)(a)), domestic nursing services (including board), care dispensed by dentists, *prescribed drugs* and insulin, chiropractors, Christian Science practitioners, acupuncturists, and various others (see, e.g., Rev. Rul. 72-593, 1972-2 C.B. 180), and *capital expenditures* to the extent they do not add value to the property (Reg. §1.213-1(e)(1)(iii)). See *medical expense deduction*.

medical expense deduction an *itemized deduction* allowable *to individuals* for unreimbursed payments on their own behalves, and on behalf of their *dependents* for *medical care* and for certain drugs. The "floor" on medical expense deductions is 7.5 percent of *adjusted gross income*. See *medical care*.

medical expenses, exclusion see *medical and tuition expenses, gift tax exclusion*.

medical insurance premiums premiums paid for insurance policies, or membership in associations providing cooperative or "free choice" group medical care, that provide hospitalization, surgical fees, or other *medical care* expenses or for drugs, either in cash or in-kind. Amounts paid other than for medical care (e.g., for loss of a limb) do not qualify. Reg. §1.213-1(e)(4).

medical reimbursement plans *fringe benefit* plans for *employees* under which the *employer* directly or indirectly reimburses the *medical care* expenses of *employees* and their *spouses* and *dependents*; such reimbursements are generally *excluded* from *gross income* under §105 but *deducted* by the employer under §162(a).

medical research the conduct of investigations, experiments, and studies to discover, develop, or verify knowledge relating to the causes, diagnosis, treatment, prevention, or control of physical or mental diseases and impairments of human beings. In order to qualify as a *medical research organization,* the *entity* must have or must have continuously available for its regular use the appropriate equipment and professional personnel necessary to carry out its principal function of engaging in medical research. Medical research encompasses the associated disciplines spanning the biological, social, and behavioral sciences, (e.g., physical chemistry, medical electronics, and epidemiology). Reg. §1.170A-9(c)(2)(iii). See *medical research organization*.

medical research organization generally, an organization that qualifies for the 50 percent *deduction* ceiling by virtue of its principal purpose or function *of medical research* and its being directly engaged in the continuous active conduct of medical research in conjunction with an exempt, nonprofit, or governmental hospital. See Reg. §1.170A-9(c)(2).

medical supplies includes drugs, medicines, and medical devices. Reg. §1.164-3(g)(3).

medicines see *biological; prescribed drug*.

member, cooperatives in the case of *exempt farmers' cooperatives,* anyone who shares in the profits of the cooperative and is entitled to participate in its management. Reg. §1.521-1(a)(3). For purposes of the general rules of taxation of cooperatives, the *regulations* define "member" more broadly as any *person* entitled to participate in the management of a cooperative. Reg. §1.1388-1(c)(3)(ii)(cc).

member of an affiliated group any *corporation,* including the common *parent,* that is included within an *affiliated group*. Reg. §1.1502-1(b). See *affiliated group; consolidated return*.

member of an economically disadvantaged family someone who the *designated local agency* determines to be a member of a family that had an income during the six months immediately preceding the month in which such determination occurs, that, on an annual basis, is 70 percent or less of the Bureau of Labor Statistics lower living standard. The definition applies to persons beginning work after August 31, 1981, for purposes of the *targeted jobs credit*. The targeted jobs credit expired on June 30, 1992.

member of a targeted group any one of the following: (1) a *vocational rehabilitation referral*; (2) an *economically disadvantaged youth*; (3) an *economically disadvantaged Vietnam-era veteran*; (4) an *SSI recipi-*

ent; (5) a *general assistance recipient*; (6) a *youth participating in a cooperative education program*; (7) an *economically disadvantaged ex-convict*; (8) an *eligible work incentive employee*; (9) an *involuntarily terminated CETA employee*; or (10) a *qualified summer youth employee*. §51(d)(1). *Qualified wages* for these *individuals* can qualify for the *targeted jobs credit*. The targeted jobs credit expired on June 30, 1992.

member of a uniformed service, federal insurance contribution act (FICA) any person appointed, enlisted, or inducted into the Army, Navy, Air Force, Marine Corps, or Coast Guard (including a reserve component), or as a commissioned officer of the Coast and Geodetic Survey, or the Regular or Reserve Corps of the Public Health Service (including retired members of any of those services), and any person serving in the Army or Air Force under call or conscription. §3121(n). Section 3121(i) imposes *FICA taxes* with respect to basic pay only and §3121(m) provides special FICA rules in cases of active service and activities while on leave without pay.

member of the faculty see *faculty member*.

member of the household an *individual* for whom the household is the principal place of abode. Reg. §§1.2-2(c)(1), 1.85-1(b)(4). The term is used periodically throughout the *Code* and *regulations* without specific definition, but the context of its usage coupled with the application of the *plain meaning rule* supports this interpretation. See also §§21 (*child and dependent care credit*), 123 (certain *living expenses*), 143(b) (marital status), 152 (*dependent* defined), 170(g) (certain students), and 217(b)(3)(C) (*moving expenses*). Note that in most cases the duration of the status is important. For example, a *married person* may qualify under §21 for the *child and dependent care credit,* but the individual's *spouse* must not have been a member of the household at any time during the last six months of the year. §21(e)(3). On the other hand, to qualify under §152 as a dependent, an unrelated individual must be a member of the household for the entire year, except for certain temporary absences due to such cases as illness, education, vacation, business, or military service. Reg. §1.152-1(b).

members of targeted groups *individuals* who are *vocational rehabilitation referrals, economically disadvantaged youths, economically disadvantaged Vietnam-era veterans, SSI recipients, general assistance recipients, youths participating in a cooperative education program, economically disadvantaged ex-convicts, eligible work incentive employees, or qualified summer youth employees.* §51(d)(10). Members of targeted groups can generate *targeted job credits*.

membership organization for purposes of §456, which allows these entities to defer prepaid dues

income, the term means a *corporation, association,* federation, or other organization without capital stock and no part of the *net earnings* of which is distributed to any member. §456(e)(3). See also §277, which allows *social clubs* and other "membership organizations" *deductions* for furnishing goods and services to members. It does not define the term.

memorandum decision a decision of the *Tax Court* that is considered not to contain novel issues. Such cases are cited by a volume number, followed by T.C. Memo or T.C.M.

merchandise return period unless the *taxpayer* selects a shorter period with respect to any *taxable year,* in the case of magazines, the period of two months and 15 days first occurring after the close of the *taxable year,* or in the case of paperback books and records, the first four months and 15 days after the close of the taxable year. §458(b)(7). Section 458 allows *accrual method* taxpayers to elect to *exclude* returns of merchandise from *qualified sales* if the return occurs within the merchandise return period.

merchant marine construction fund a fund to which United States shippers can make *deductible* contributions.

mere holding or investment companies, accumulated earnings tax two types of *corporations* automatically exposed to the *accumulated earnings tax* because they were presumptively formed to avoid taxes on their *shareholders.* §533(b). First, Reg. §1.533-1(c) provides that a company is a mere holding company if it has practically no activities other than holding property and collecting income. Second, if instead it engages substantially in the buying and selling of securities and other investments, the same regulation classifies it as a mere investment company. Managing leased property lifts the corporation out of this status, even if the corporation is primarily a holding or investment company. Mere holding and investment companies are entitled to no more than $250,000 in *accumulated earnings credit.* §535(c)(3).

merger the fusion of two companies under state or federal corporate law, which causes one *corporation's* existence to cease. Characteristically, shares of the disappearing corporation are converted into shares of the surviving company by operation of law. Mergers are among the transactions defined as *corporate reorganizations* and are potentially tax-free to the corporate participants as well as shareholders and security holders of the disappearing company. *Partnerships* are also capable of mergers. §708(b)(2).

method of accounting a system by which a *taxpayer* may report terms of *gross income, gain, loss,* and *deductions* either on an overall basis (an *overall method*) or with respect to any *material item*. The methods themselves are conventions (e.g., *cash method, accrual method,* or *installment sales method*), applied consistently to produce a meaningful picture of profitability and solvency. §446. The *Code* dictates accounting methods that may depart from financial accounting; where they diverge, the *Code*'s methods control for *federal income tax* purposes. See *tax accounting.*

methods of depreciation various mutually exclusive schedules or formulas that can be used to write off the *basis* of *tangible property,* provided the result is a reasonable allowance. Use of the *straight-line method,* for example, results in an equal annual *depreciation deduction.* The *sum-of-the-years'-digits* and *declining-balance methods,* by contrast, result in enlarged early years' deductions. The *Code* authorizes the use of potentially unlimited alternatives, provided they are consistently applied and do not result in undue deductions in early years. §167(b)(4).

middleman for purposes of *backup withholding,* the term means the person collecting or receiving the payment, irrespective of whether he is acting as the agent of the payee or as agent for the issuer of the instrument. Section 1.6049-4(f)(4) of the regulations defines a "middleman" as any person who makes payment of interest for or collects interest on behalf of another person, or who acts as an intermediary between a payor and a payee. This definition includes all *brokers* as defined in §6045(c).

midmonth convention an accounting convention allowing *depreciation* beginning in the middle of the month for the month that the property is first *placed in service.* §168(d)(2) and (4)(b). It applies to *real property* under *ACRS.*

midpoint life an element of the *class life asset depreciation range system,* which assigns each class of listed assets an assumed useful life, subject to a range from 80 percent to 120 percent of the assumed *useful life.* The midpoint is the center of that range. See Rev. Proc. 77-10, 1977-1 C.B. 548, as revised. It is synonymous with the term *asset guideline period.*

midquarter convention an assumption for *depreciation* purposes that all *tangible personal recovery property* is *placed in service* midway during the calendar quarter in which it is actually placed in service. §168(d)(4)(C). It is an alternative to the *midyear convention,* and is used in §168(d)(3) to prevent excessive *deductions* for property placed in service in the last quarter of the *taxable year.* See *accelerated cost recovery system.*

mileage allowance an amount, classified in pennies per mile, granted by the *IRS* to *taxpayers* who use their cars for *gain*-seeking, medical, educational, and charitable purposes in order for them to *deduct* costs incurred for such *expenses.* See, e.g., Rev. Proc. 80-7, 1980-1

C.B. 590, modified by Rev. Proc. 82-61, 1982-2 C.B. 849. This allowance, or standard optional rate, may be used by the taxpayer rather than his or her attempting to calculate the exact costs of operating the car, and it displaces expenses other than those for fees and tolls. Once the taxpayer has fully depreciated the car, the taxpayer is limited to a lower fixed rate per mile. See I.R.S. Pub. No. 463. The current allowance for medical, charitable, moving, and educational travel is typically still lower per mile. Electing this method displaces the *accelerated cost recovery system* or *depreciation deductions.* Rev. Proc. 82-61, 1982-2 C.B. 849.

military housing allowance not formally defined, but evidently referring to nontaxable housing allowances granted to United States military personnel and certain others. *Mortgage interest* and *taxes* paid by such personnel are *deductible* despite the *exclusion* from *gross income* of the housing allowance. §265(a)(6). For purposes of this rule, the term "military personnel" includes members of the National Oceanic and Atmospheric Administration, the Public Health Services, the Army, Navy, Air Force, Marine Corps, and Coast Guard. See also *qualified military benefit.*

Mimeograph an early form of *ruling* by the *IRS.*

mine, election to deduct mineral exploration expenditures any quarry, pit, shaft, well, or any other excavation or working for the purpose of extracting any known mineral deposit. Reg. §1.617-3(b)(1). *Deductible mining exploration expenditures* are limited to those incurred with respect to mines. See §617(a)(1).

mineral interest a property right in minerals, oil, and gas pursuant to which the holder can enter the land and extract the resource. Such interests may be created by deed or lease and can be of varying durations.

mineral payment a *production payment* with respect to minerals. See *production payment.*

minerals, depletion in effect, all minerals (including metal ores, coal, oil, gas, geothermal, and all other metallic and nonmetallic deposits) other than those from inexhaustible sources such as air or sea water. Reg. §1.611-1(d)(5) (*cost depletion*); §613(b), Reg. §1.613-1 (*percentage depletion*). Curiously, the *cost depletion* definition includes the percentage depletion definition and vice-versa. Reg. §§1.611-1(d)(5), 1.613-1. Oil, gas, sod, dirt, water, or mosses are expressly excluded by §613(b)(7)(A) and (C). Oil and gas are separately treated by §613A, which allows restricted percentage depletion only.

minimum accumulated earnings tax credit generally $250,000, but $150,000 in the case of *corporations* whose principal *business* consists of rendering services in the fields of health, law, engineering, architecture, accounting, actuarial science, performing arts, or consulting. §532(c)(2) and (3) (effective for years after 1981). The effect is that corporations can always accumulate these minimums with no fear of imposition of the *accumulated earnings tax.* See *mere holding or investment companies, accumulated earnings tax.*

minimum age and service requirements   one of several *participation* requirements necessary for a plan to be deemed a *qualified retirement plan.* Under the general rule, an *employee* must be able to participate in the plan at age 21, provided he or she completes one *year of service.* §410(a)(1)(A). If the plan allows for 100 percent *vesting* of the *accrued benefits* after not more than two years of service, then the one-year-of-service requirement may be extended to not more than two years of service. §410(a)(1)(B)(i).

minimum coverage rules   a body of tax law rules that must be met in order for a *deferred compensation plan* or related *trust* to be a *qualified plan* or *qualified trust.* §410(b). In general, before 1989, a plan must benefit at least 70 percent of all *employees* or, if it benefits at least 80 percent of employees eligible to benefit, at least 70 percent of all employees must be eligible (the "percentage test"). If this test is not met, one can still demonstrate satisfaction of the minimum coverage rules by showing it benefits a classification of employees that is not discriminatory in favor of *highly compensated employees* (the so-called *fair cross-section test*). After 1988, a plan must meet one of the following tests: (1) the plan benefits at least 70 percent of all non–highly compensated employees (another version of the percentage test); (2) the plan benefits a percentage of non–highly compensated employees which is not less than 70 percent of the percentage of highly compensated employees covered under the plan (the so-called ratio test); or (3) the plan meets the so-called *average benefits test,* which basically requires that run-of-the-mill employees get benefits not less than 70 percent of the benefits available to the highly compensated. Certain *excludable employees* can be disregarded. See *accrued benefits; excludable employee, minimum coverage rules.*

minimum distribution rules   rules found in §401(a)(9) that disqualify otherwise *qualified deferred compensation plans* if they fail to contain provisions limiting deferred payouts to retired persons. See *uniform minimum distribution rules.*

minimum funding excise tax   an *excise tax* on an *employer* who maintains a *qualified plan* subject to the *minimum funding standards* imposed for each *taxable year* in which there is an *accumulated funding deficiency* as of the close of the *plan year* ending with or within that taxable year. §4971. The tax is imposed at the initial rate of 5 percent of the accumulated funding deficiency, with an additional 100 percent tax if the deficiency is not corrected by the earlier of the mailing of a *notice of deficiency* or the *assessment* of the tax.

minimum funding standard account   a mandatory account maintained by *qualified pension plans* to evaluate compliance with the *minimum funding standards.* §412(b). See *minimum funding standards.*

minimum funding standards   a concept applicable to *qualified pension plans* that assures that the *employer* will provide sufficient contributions to maintain the integrity of the benefits promised under the plan. §412. In the case of *defined benefit plans,* the analysis of adequate funding calls for a complete actuarial study and includes assumptions respecting such matters as *employee* turnover, mortality, morbidity, and employee behavior with respect to the reelection of benefits, as well as expected investment returns and administrative expenses. §4971(a) and (b) impose *excise taxes* on employers who violate the minimum funding requirements. The *minimum funding standard account* is the benchmark of compliance. *Profit-sharing* and *stock bonus plans,* certain *government* and *church plans,* certain *employee-pay-all plans,* and certain *insurance contract plans* are largely or entirely exempt from the minimum funding requirement. §412(h).

minimum gain chargeback   a provision in a *partnership agreement* under which an *allocation* of *deductions* based on *nonrecourse debt* may trigger an obligation to specially *allocate* any *gain* (referred to as *partnership minimum gain*) resulting therefrom to whoever enjoyed the deduction. See Reg. §1.704-1(b)(4)(iv)(d)(3), (e). Such a provision (or a *deficit make-up* provision) can validate a *deduction* allocable to nonrecourse debt, provided various other requirements summarized in Reg. §1.704-1(b)(4)(v)(d) are met. See *substantial economic effect test.*

minimum investment return   five percent times the *fair market value* of a *private foundation's* assets, other than those directly used in carrying out its *exempt purpose,* less its *acquisition indebtedness.* §4942(e)(1). Generally, fair market values are used, subject to a *blockage rule.* §4942(e)(2). Failure to make minimum payouts attracts a 15 percent *excise tax.* §4942(a) and (b). See *undistributed income excise tax, private foundation.*

minimum marital deduction   a *prior provision* under which a minimum *marital deduction* of $250,000 was allowed for *federal estate tax* purposes if such an amount of qualifying property passed to the *surviving spouse.*

minimum net earnings from self-employment   *net earnings from self-employment* of under $400. Such amounts are *excluded* from the Social Security *self-employment tax.* §1402(b)(2).

minimum participation standards   standards imposed on *qualified deferred compensation plans* by §401(a) and 410 which fix the minimum number of *employees* who can be included in the plan if the plan is to qualify for the vital tax benefits that make such arrangements attractive. See *participation, qualified retirement plans.*

minimum required distribution   see *excise tax, failure to make minimum distributions.*

minimum royalties, natural resources   a *royalty* expressed in dollars paid at least annually to a mineral owner, payable regardless of production. Such amounts may or may not be chargeable against future production. If such royalties are chargeable against future production (i.e., are *advanced royalties*) and are payable in a substantially uniform amount over at least the lesser of the life of the *lease* or 20 years, they are classified as paid pursuant to a "*minimum royalty provision,*" and they may, at the payor's election, be currently *deducted,* despite the general proscription against deducting *advanced royalties.* Reg. §1.612-3(b).

minimum royalty provision   See *minimum royalties, natural resources.*

minimum set aside   see *qualified low-income housing project, low-income housing credit.*

minimum tax credit   a *nonrefundable credit* against *regular income tax* liabilities attributable to the portion of the *taxpayer's alternative minimum tax* liability attributable to timing differences. The alternative credit for the tax year is the amount by which the alternative minimum tax exceeds the regular tax for the year due to timing differences. Many taxpayers may pay an alternative minimum tax with respect to some transactions long before they would be required to pay a regular tax on those transactions. The credit can be carried forward indefinitely. §53.

minimum term rules   a reference to former §71(f)(1) which rendered *alimony or separate maintenance payments* in excess of $10,000 per *calendar year* nondeductible unless such payments were to be made to the payee *spouse* in each of the six *post-separation* years. Some separations and divorces remain subject to these rules. For current law, see *frontloading of alimony.*

minimum vesting rules   rules setting minimum rates at which benefits under *qualified plans* vest (i.e., become irrevocably fixed in favor of the *participant*). §411. See *vesting schedules.*

mining   extraction of minerals, including certain statutorily prescribed degrees of processing and transportation set forth in §613(c)(4). The *Treasury Department* has authority to define further treatment processes. §613(c)(4)(I). The term is significant in determining *gross income from the property* for purposes of calculating *percentage depletion.*

mining development expenditures   see *development expenditures, minerals.*

mining exploration expenditures   see *exploration expenditures, minerals.*

mining transportation   transportation of extracted minerals for the first 50 miles from the point of extraction, unless lengthened with the permission of the *IRS.* It excludes transportation for marketing, distribution, storage, or delivery for the application of non*mining* processes. Reg. §1.613-4(g)(3). See also Rev. Rul. 73-474, 1973-2 C.B. 200. Mining transportation is considered a part of *mining* and as such the value added in effect becomes part of the base on which *percentage depletion* is calculated under §613. See *mining.*

ministerial act   act which involves obedience to instructions without special discretion, skill, or judgment. If such an act causes error or delay by the *IRS,* then §6404(e) authorizes *abatement* of *interest* by the IRS on associated *assessments.* See *abatement.*

minister of the gospel   a clergyman of any faith, but only if duly ordained, commissioned, or licensed. §1402(e)(1); Reg. §1.107-1(a) (which bows to Reg. §1.1402(c)(5)); Rev. Rul. 59-270, 1959-2 C.B. 44. See *parsonage allowance.*

minor   someone who is not an adult. The federal tax standard is under age 21. State standards will be applied only where compelled by express language or necessary implication.

mirror tax   the *Code,* as adopted by the United States Virgin Islands and Guam. The United States Virgin Islands and Guam have adopted the Code, substituting the words "Virgin Islands" or "Guam" where "United States" appears in the Code and vice versa.

miscellaneous expense deductions   a term used on Schedule A to *individuals' Form 1040* to describe *deductions* not specifically set forth on the Schedule. The Schedule expressly refers to *medical, interest, state* or *local taxes, charitable,* and union dues expenses. Typical miscellaneous expenses include safe deposit charges connected with safeguarding securities and tax return preparation costs. It should be distinguished from the concept of *miscellaneous itemized deductions,* which involves the *two-percent floor on itemized deductions* (§67).

miscellaneous itemized deductions   *itemized deductions* of *individuals, estates,* and *trusts* other than a fairly extensive list of deductions that are listed under the heading *two-percent floor on itemized deductions.* §67(b). Thus, they are a disfavored class. See *two-percent floor on itemized deductions.*

miscellaneous payroll period   a payroll period other than daily, weekly, biweekly, semimonthly, monthly, quarterly, semi-annually, or annually. §3401(b). See *payroll period, withholding.*

missing status   the status of an *employee* in or under an executive agency or a military department who is in active federal service, or of a member of a *uniformed service* who is officially carried or determined to be absent in a status of (1) missing; (2) missing in action; (3) interned in a foreign country; (4) captured, beleaguered, or besieged by a hostile force; or (5) detained in a foreign country against his or her will. §6013(f)(3); 5 U.S.C. §5561(5) (1976); 37 U.S.C. §551(2) (1976). The *spouse* of an individual in a missing status as a result of service in a *combat zone* may elect in certain instances to file a *joint return*. §6013(f)(3). The period during which the *individual* is in a missing status is disregarded in determination of whether acts such as *filing* a *return,* paying a tax or installment, filing a claim or a suit upon a claim, and others, are performed within the time prescribed. §7508(c). See also §§2(a)(3) (surviving spouse), 112(d) (tax-free compensation, Vietnam conflict), and 692(b) (member of the armed forces exempt from *income tax* for year of death determination).

mitigation of effect of statutes of limitations and other provisions   a reference to §§1311–1314, which in specified circumstances have the effect of preempting *statutes of limitations* or other causes for closing a *taxable year,* in the interest of fairness to the *taxpayer* or the government, generally to correct inconsistencies such as double *inclusions* or *exclusions* of *income* or double *deductions* or *credits* or their double denials, which affect the taxpayer alone or the taxpayer and a *related taxpayer*. These rules are inapplicable to *estate taxes*. See *determination, mitigation of statutes of limitations and other provisions; maintenance of an inconsistent position, mitigation of effect of statutes of limitations and other provisions; related taxpayer, mitigation of effect of statutes of limitations and other provisions.*

mixed service costs, uniform capitalization rules   *service costs* that benefit a production or resale activity as well as other functions or activities of the *taxpayer*. These kinds of costs must be allocated to the function or activity they serve based on some basis reasonably calculated to relate the cost to the activity it serves. Those costs relating to or incurred by resale or production activities must be *capitalized* under the *uniform capitalization rules*. Reg. §1.263A-1T(b)(4)(ii). See *service costs, uniform capitalization rules; allocable costs, uniform capitalization rules; allocation methods, uniform capitalization rules.*

mixed straddle   a *straddle* of which at least one, but not all, of the positions are *regulated futures contracts* (RFCs) (for example, a regulated futures contract in silver offsetting an actual holding of silver) and each position of which is clearly identified as constituting part of the straddle in the *taxpayer's* records of the day of acquisition of the first RFC. §1256(d)(4). Regulated futures contracts are normally treated under the *mark-to-market system* requirements, but the taxpayer may elect (1) to exempt all the positions in mixed straddles, including regulated futures contracts and other property, in which case they are subject to the *loss deferral rules* of §1092 applicable to straddles, or (2) to treat all such positions under the mark-to-market rules. §1256(d).

mixed use property   an informal term for automobiles or other *"listed property"* generally used in part for business purposes and in part for personal purposes or *investment* activity. Depending on the relative proportion of use for *trade or business* purposes, the *property* may be eligible for *accelerated cost recovery system (ACRS) deductions*. §280F. Listed property includes any *passenger automobile* or other property used as a means of transportation, entertainment, recreation, or amusement; computers or peripheral equipment; or any other property specified in the regulations. §280F(d)(4). Subject to a 50 percent business use threshold requirement, the *taxpayer* was entitled to claim the portion of the maximum *investment tax credit* and can claim *depreciation deductions* which correspond to the business use percentage. Special rules govern the depreciation of *luxury automobiles*. §280F(a). If business use falls below 50 percent, then the tax benefits conferred are subject to *recapture* or prior deductions and subsequent depreciation under the alternative depreciation *system*. §280F(b)(3). Deductions and credits for mixed use property must be well-substantiated. §274(d)(4).

model pension and profit-sharing plans   *pension* and *profit-sharing plan* documents prepared by the *IRS* for use in easy cases by corporate *employers*. Such plans meet the drafting requirements for *qualified plan* status under §401(a). See Rev. Proc. 77-15, 1977-1 C.B. 572.

moderate income, low-income housing rehabilitation amortization   see *low- or moderate-income rental housing.*

modification equipment, energy investment credit   equipment designed to modify existing equipment. Modification equipment qualifies as *alternative energy property* if (1) as a result of the modification, the existing equipment, which used oil or natural gas as a fuel or as feedstock, can now use either a substance other than oil and natural gas or oil mixed with an *alternate substance,* and (2) after the modification, the alternate substance is at least 25 percent of the total fuel or feedstock. §48(l)(3)(A)(iv); Reg. §1.48-9(c)(6)(i). Such property can qualify for the *energy investment credit*.

modified ACRS   the *ACRS* system as rewritten by the *Tax Reform Act of 1986*. In comparison to prior law, it generally slows the rate at which *cost recovery deductions* are available and introduces the *alternative depreciation system (ADS)* of §168(g). It generally classifies *recovery* property into eight classes based on its *class* *life asset depreciation range* category and assigns specific *applicable recovery periods* to them. §168(e). Section 168(a) further compels the use of particular *applicable depreciation methods* and *applicable conventions.*

modified adjusted deemed sales price a hypothetical price determined formula found in Reg. §1.338(h)(10)-1T(f) in connection with *section 338(h)(10) elections* to impose tax liability on the deemed *liquidation* to the seller. It calls for determining the aggregate deemed sales price of assets by reference to the actual purchase price of the *stock* of the *target corporation,* adjusted for liabilities of the target and certain other items. See *section 338(h)(10) election.* The method is elective. It is useful when target stock is sold at a bargain price because it uses a modified stock sales price (the *grossed-up basis* of *recently purchased stock* of the target company, determined under Reg. §1.338-4T(h)(3)) which has the effect of reducing *gain* to the selling *corporation.*

modified adjusted gross income, passive loss rules *adjusted gross income* computed without regard to any *passive activity loss,* taxable Social Security or Railroad Retirement benefits, or *deductions* for contributions to an *IRA.* §469(i)(3)(D). The $25,000 *de minimis* exception to the *passive loss rules* for rental real estate losses by people who engage in *active participation* in the operation diminishes as the *taxpayer's* modified adjusted gross income exceeds a certain amount (e.g., $100,000 for married couples.) See *passive loss rules.*

modified adjusted gross income, Social Security benefits *adjusted gross income* (ignoring Social Security benefits) plus *exempt income.* §86. The lesser of half the *taxpayer's* annual Social Security benefits, or the excess of modified adjusted gross income plus half the benefits received in excess of a *base amount,* ($25,000 for all other individuals, $32,000 for married filing jointly, $0 for married persons filing separately but not living apart) are included in *gross income.* See *base amount, Social Security.*

modified alternative minimum taxable income the base on which the *environmental tax* falls. §59A. It is basically *alternative minimum taxable income,* determined without regard to the *alternative tax net operating loss deduction, alternative tax energy preference deduction,* or the deduction for the environmental tax. §59A(b).

modified half-year convention an accounting practice used for *depreciation* purposes under the *class life asset depreciation range system* (ADR). Under this convention, property *placed in service* during the first half of the year is presumed placed in service at the beginning of the year, with post-mid-year property deemed placed in service at the beginning of the following year.

Reg.§1.167(a)-11(c)(2)(ii) (ADR system) and -10(b) (non-ADR).

money-laundering penalty a penalty found in 18 U.S.C. §1956 which imposes enormous monetary sanctions as well as long prison terms on money laundering or transporting of money and other instruments to or from the *United States* in violation of law. The statute is extremely broad and can sweep in any activity that indirectly involves violations of a long array of violations of other statutes. It buttresses the Currency and Foreign Transactions Reporting Act, and is known under the short title of the Money Laundering Control Act of 1986.

money or money's worth, gift tax consideration that can be measured in monetary terms, not just consideration sufficient to render a contract enforceable. The following items have no monetary value: moral obligations; promises of marriage; or love and affection. If property is transferred for less than an adequate and full consideration in money or money's worth, then the excess of the value of the property over the consideration is generally a *taxable gift.* §2512(b). See *gift, gift taxes.*

money purchase pension plan a form of *defined contribution plan* that provides retirement benefits determined on the basis of formula contributions by *employers* and accumulated income on such contributions. Such plans can be *qualified plans* if, among other things, *employer contributions* are controlled by a fixed formula. Reg. §1.401-1(b)(1)(i). *Employer contributions,* earnings, and *losses* are actuarially allocated to *individual* accounts for *participants,* with actual pensions based on the amounts in those individual accounts, with *forfeitures* reallocated to reduce employer contributions. Thus, no actual promise as to the actual benefits is made to *employees.* Rather, the participant's account at retirement is controlling. No withdrawals before retirement or separation from service are allowed.

mortality gain or loss the difference between the cost of *life insurance* coverage and the *death proceeds* received. For example, if someone buys a policy with a face amount of $10,000 for $100 and dies next month, the insured has a $9,900 mortality gain. Section 101(a) generally renders such gains nontaxable.

mortgage credit certificate a type of mortgage financing device issued by state and local governments authorized to issue *mortgage subsidy bonds.* The *Tax Reform Act of 1984* authorized these governmental entities to convert a portion of their mortgage bond issuing authority to MCCs. These in turn grant *tax credits* to eligible persons who obtain mortgages to purchase first-time residences. §25(c)(1). See *applicable median family income; private activity bond; tax-exempt bond.*

mortgage lender, broker's return   see *real estate reporting person.*

motor carrier operating authority   a certificate or permit held by a common or contract motor carrier of property and issued pursuant to subchapter II of chapter 109 of Title 49 of the United States Code. ERTA §266 (Pub. L. No. 94-37, 95 Stat. 172). The *adjusted basis* of such certificates can be written off over 60 months, if held (or subject to purchase contract) on or before July 1, 1980. This provision does not appear in the *Code.*

movie shelters   see *completed film tax shelter; production company film tax shelters*

moving expense deduction   an *itemized deduction* allowed to *employees* and *self-employed individuals* for the reasonable expenses of moving from one location to another, but only if the move is incidental to commencement of work in a new location. §217. The following describes the high points of the deduction in capsule form. The deduction (for items other than for *qualified residence sale, purchase or lease expenses* and of post-employment house-hunting expenses) is limited to $3,000, and the expenses for house-hunting trips and temporary living expenses at the new job location are limited to $1,500 of that $3,000. These dollar limitations apply for each new employment or self-employment position. *Spouses* are subject to the same overall ceiling, even if each begins a new job, unless both spouses commence work at new *principal places of work* at least 35 miles apart and do not reside at the same residence during the year, or if they plan to share the same residence within a determinable time. To qualify for the deduction, the distance between the *taxpayer's* new principal place of employment and his previous residence must be 35 or more miles greater than the distance from the former primary place of work to the previous residence, and minimum permanency of employment tests must be met, except in specified cases of hardship. See *moving expenses.*

moving expenses   the reasonable expenses of (1) moving household goods and personal effects from the former residence to the new residence; (2) *travel* (including meals and lodging) from the former residence to the new place of residence; (3) traveling (including meals and lodging), after obtaining employment, from the former residence to the general location of the new *principal place of work* and return, for the principal purpose of searching for a new place of residence; (4) meals and lodging while occupying temporary quarters in the general location of the new principal place of work during any period of 30 days after obtaining employment; and (5) items that constitute *qualified residence sale, purchase, or lease expenses.* §217(b). See *moving expense deduction.*

multiemployer pension plan liability   see *employer withdrawal liability.*

multiemployer plan   a collectively bargained *qualified plan* between *employee* representatives and several *employers* under one or more collective bargaining agreements to which more than one employer must contribute, and which satisfies other Labor Department requirements. §414(f)(1). Such plans are subject to somewhat relaxed standards. §§411–414. The multiemployer plan is a subset of *multiple employer plans.* See *collectively bargained plan.*

multiemployer plan, ERISA   a *defined benefit plan* to which more than one employer must make contributions and that is maintained under a collective bargaining agreement between an employee organization and more than one employer. ERISA §4001(a)(3). Such plans are somewhat more loosely regulated; employers who withdraw from such plans are subject to liability.

multiform partnerships   a term sometimes used to describe *partnerships* that consist of several types of participants (e.g., *corporations* and *individuals*).

multiple asset accounts   accounts that contain more than one asset, established for purposes of *depreciation* or cost recovery *deductions.* See *closed-end multiple asset accounts; open-end multiple asset accounts; vintage account.*

multiple employer plans   generally, *qualified deferred compensation plans* maintained by more than one *employer.* If such plans are maintained by related employers, they are aggregated to test for such items as overall *qualified plan* status, adequate *participation, vesting,* and *accrual of benefits.* §414(b) and (c). The term also refers to plans maintained under a good-faith collective bargaining agreement between one or more employers and *employee* representatives. §414(a). See *collectively bargained plan.*

multiple levies rule   a rule of Reg. §1.901-2(e)(4) to the effect that if under *foreign* law a *taxpayer's* tentative liability for one levy (the first levy) is or can be reduced by its liability for a different levy (the second levy), then the amount deemed paid under the second levy is the entire amount of that levy, and the rest of the amount paid is considered paid pursuant to the first levy.

multiple pooling, LIFO   an elective method of applying the *last-in, first-out* (LIFO) method of accounting, under which several *LIFO pools* are maintained for *inventory* items that are not within a *natural business unit* pool. This election is in lieu of *natural business unit pooling.* In the case of a business enterprise with more than one natural business unit, a *taxpayer* may elect to use a natural business unit pool for one of the natural business units, and multiple pooling with respect to another. Reg. §1.472-8(b)(3)(i)(a). Even in the case of a business with a single natural business unit, multiple pooling may be elected. Reg. §1.472-8(b)(1). Each of the multiple pools normally contains a group of inventory items that are substantially similar, although a miscellaneous pool may also be used. Selection of pools requires factual determinations for which detailed comments are not feasible. Reg. §1.472-8(b)(3)(i). See *dollar-value method; inventory accounting.*

multiple support agreement a collective agreement to support an *individual,* the effect of which may be to create a *dependency deduction* where none might otherwise be available. Reg. §1.152-1. If more than one-half of the recipient's *support* during the *calendar year* was furnished by two or more *individuals,* each of whom would have been entitled to the *deduction* but for his or her failure to furnish more than one-half of the individual's support, then one of them is entitled to the *exemption* for the *dependent* if he or she furnished more than 10 percent of the support and if all the others who contributed more than 10 percent of the support file a declaration (Form 2120) that they will not claim the individual as a dependent for any *taxable year* beginning in that calendar year. §152(c); Reg. §1.152-3.

multiple surtax exemption currently, a reference to graduated corporate *income taxes,* used in reference to multiple *corporations* that can potentially profit from filing *separate returns* so as to exploit such graduated rates, compared to filing a *consolidated return.* Sections 269, 1551, and 1561 through 1563 are designed to limit the availability of graduated corporate taxation of related corporations, in effect forcing them to specifically *apportion* the so-called *graduated bracket amount* (i.e., the part of the corporation's *tax base* that is under the 34 percent rate). See *controlled group of corporations, graduated taxes, and other benefits; graduated taxes.*

municipal bonds a loose term to describe securities issued by municipalities, which generate *tax-exempt interest,* or even more inaccurately any other debt security, the income of which is *excludable* from the holder's *gross income.* §§103, 141–150.

municipal corporations undefined. In general terms, it is a status conferred upon a local governmental unit (e.g., city, mass transportation authority, board of education) by state law, giving the unit certain autonomous operating authority such as the power of taxation, power of eminent domain, police power, and regulatory power. The *IRS* apparently will recognize a unit as a municipal corporation if it is recognized as such by the state. Rev. Rul. 80-136, 1980-1 C.B. 25. Municipal corporations are permitted to issue *tax-exempt bonds* under §103(a). See *political subdivision.*

mustering-out pay payments to members of the *armed services* of the United States as departure pay. Such amounts are *excluded* from *gross income.* §113.

mutual and stock companies insurance companies that are eligible for exemption from tax if their written net premiums or direct written premiums (whichever is greater) do not exceed $350,000. §501(c)(15). The law allows mutual and stock companies with written net premiums or direct written premiums (whichever is greater) in excess of $350,000 but less than $1,200,000 to elect to be taxed only on taxable investment income. §831(b).

mutual fund a nontax term for a *regulated investment company,* the shares of which are either freely redeemable at net asset value (open end) or merely publicly traded (closed end). Such funds are taxed as *corporations* but can qualify for special *dividends-paid deductions* and related relief so as to be rendered *conduits* for all practical purposes. §§851–855.

mutual fund custodial accounts certain *custodial accounts* that invest in the stock of domestic *regulated investment companies.* §403(b)(7). Such accounts can be used in place of *annuity contracts* in connection with *tax-deferred annuity* programs. Such accounts must satisfy the general qualification requirements of §401(f). See *custodial account, qualified plan.*

mutual interdependence test see *step transaction doctrine.*

mutual or cooperative electric companies the electrical power analog of *mutual or cooperative telephone companies,* except that *qualified pole rentals* are not excluded. §501(c)(12). See *benevolent life insurance associations; mutual or cooperative telephone companies.*

mutual or cooperative telephone companies telephone companies of a purely local character, granted *exempt organization* status if at least 85 percent of their income is from members and for the sole purpose of meeting losses and expenses. For purposes of the 85 percent test, such organizations exclude income from (1) nonmember telephone companies for services involving members; (2) *qualified pole rentals;* and (3) the sale of directory displays (i.e., yellow pages advertising) in directories furnished to members. §501(c)(12). Cancellation of debt under the Rural Electrification Act of 1936 is not income for purposes of the 85 percent test. §501(c)(12)(B)-(C). See *benevolent life insurance associations.*

mutual savings bank undefined in the *Code* or *regulations.* For *taxable years* ending after August 13, 1981, the term expressly includes any bank that has capital stock that may be represented by shares, and which is subject to and operates under federal or state laws relating to mutual savings banks. §591(b) (*deduction* for dividends paid on mutual savings bank, etc., deposits). These newly included banks are occasionally referred to as *mutual stock associations.* Under current banking law relating to the Federal Deposit Insurance Corporation, a mutual savings bank is a bank without capital stock and that transacts a savings bank business, the net earnings of which inure wholly to the benefit of its depositors after payment of obligations for any advances by its organizers. 12 U.S.C. §1813(f) (1976).

mutual savings bank life insurance life insurance offered by *mutual savings banks* without capital stock. Such banks may conduct an insurance business through a separate department if their books are separately maintained, provided the department would itself quali-fy as a *life insurance company* under §801. §594; Reg. §1.594-1.

mutual stock association any bank that has capital stock represented by shares and is subject to and operates under federal or state laws relating to mutual savings banks. The term is not found in the Code or *regulations,* but it is sometimes used to describe those banks that, after *ERTA,* become subject to the rules governing *mutual savings banks.* §591(b). See *mutual savings banks.*

mutual thrift institutions see *troubled thrift institutions.*

N

NOL an acronym for *net operating loss.*

NOL carryback the shifting of an *NOL* to a prior taxable year. It may produce a *tax refund.*

NOL carryover the shifting of an *NOL* to a later taxable year.

NOLD an acronym for a *net operating* loss *deduction.* See *net operating loss.*

naked title see *bare legal title.*

narcotics trafficking undefined, but apparently a reference to the illegal dealing of substances described in Schedules I and II of the Controlled Substances Act (21 U.S.C. §812 (1976), as amended). §280E. *Deductions* (other than for *cost of goods sold*) and *credits* are disallowed for any amounts *paid or incurred* in carrying on a *trade or business* that consists of narcotics trafficking.

national a *citizen,* or a *person* who, although not a *citizen* of the *United States,* owes permanent allegiance to the United States. 8 U.S.C. §1101(a)(22) (1976). A person is a national, but not a citizen, of the United States at birth, if that person is (1) born in an outlying *possession* of the United States (American Samoa or Swain's Island, 8 U.S.C. §1101(a)(29)) on or after the date of its formal acquisition; (2) born outside the United States and its outlying possessions of parents both of whom are nationals but not citizens of the United States and have had a residence in the United States or one of its outlying possessions prior to the person's birth; or (3) of unknown parents and who, while under the age of 5, is found in an outlying possession of the United States, until shown, prior to his or her attaining the age of 21 years, not to have been born in such outlying possession. 8 U.S.C. §1408 (1976). Reg. §1.1-1(c).

National Office a shorthand term for the National Office of the *IRS,* headquartered in Washington, D.C. The *Commissioner* of the IRS is its highest official. Beneath the Commissioner, there are seven Assistant Commissioners: Inspection, Administration, Compliance, Accounting, Collection and Taxpayer Service, Planning and Research, and Technical. The IRS is provided formal legal advice by the Office of the *Chief Counsel,* a separate subdivision of the *Treasury Department.*

natural acquisition cost method a method of valuing *inventories* under the *dollar-value method,* whereby current-year costs of items in *closing inventory* are determined on the basis of latest costs it incurred during the year. Reg. §1.472-8(e)(2)(a). It is also called the *last-acquisition cost method.*

natural business unit not explicitly defined. Generally, a whole range of activities from production through sales; it may encompass one or several product lines. Whether a business consists of one or several product lines can turn on such nebulous factors as managerial division, accounting segregation, and, most importantly, separation of production processes and facilities. See Reg. §1.472-8(b)(2)(i). All items within the natural business unit go into a single *inventory pool.* See *dollar-value method; natural business unit pooling.*

natural business unit pooling an elective method of *last-in, first-out* (LIFO) accounting under which *inventory pools* are maintained for each *natural business unit,* which can be claimed in lieu of *multiple pooling.* Reg. §1.472-8(b)(3)(i)(a). The method is used in order to isolate a *taxpayer's inventory* investment for separate accounts under the *dollar-value method.* See *dollar-value method; inventory accounting.*

natural business year for enterprises with peak and slow periods, the *fiscal year* ending shortly after the close of the peak period. Rev. Proc. 74-33, 1974-2 C.B. 489. A need to change from some other *taxable year* to a natural business year can be used to justify the change as a matter of business purpose. See *change of accounting method.*

natural person an individual, not a corporation. A corporation is deemed an *artificial* entity.

necessary appropriate and helpful in advancing the *taxpayer's trade business* or income-producing activity. §§162, 212. *Welch v. Helvering,* 290 U.S. 111 (1933). See *ordinary and necessary expense.*

necessary working capital, operating cycle formula see *Bardahl formula.*

necessities generally, the minimal expenditures a court can require a parent to make for his or her children, usually for food, shelter, clothing, education, medical and dental care, recreation, and transportation. This is significant in meeting the *support test* for determining who qualifies as a *dependent* under §151(e). However, it has been held that support also includes expenditures other than for traditional necessities, such as cars. For the antonym, see *luxuries.*

negative net salvage value a case in which the cost of removal is expected to be greater than the salvage realized, or in which demolition costs will be incurred without realization of any *salvage value.* Negative salvage value has been allowed where the *taxpayer's* past experience substantiated the reasonableness of the alleged removal cost. The *IRS* rejects the concept. Rev. Rul. 75-150, 1975-1 C.B. 73.

negative section 481 adjustment a *section 481 adjustment* that results in a ratable *deduction* for the current year under the *passive loss rules*. It is treated as a *passive activity deduction*. §1.469-2T(e)(1).

negligence a breach of the civil duty of care owed by *individuals* in favor of the property and persons of others in the light of their particular factual circumstances, arising through unreasonable behavior that actually and proximately causes harm to another person or persons. The term finds its way into various penalty provisions of the *Code*.

negligence, negligence penalty includes any failure to make a reasonable effort to comply with the requirements of the *Code*. §6662(c).

negligent tax return preparation see *penalty, negligence by tax return preparer; penalty, unrealistic position by tax return preparer; return preparer penalties*.

negotiable certificates see *stock*.

neighborhood land rule an exemption of certain land from consideration as *debt-financed property* for purposes of the tax on *unrelated business taxable income* of an *exempt organization*. The exemption applies to *real property* which is acquired by an exempt organization for the principal purpose of using the land in the exercise or performance of the organization's *exempt purpose*, and which, at the time of the acquisition, is "in the neighborhood of" other property owned by the organization and used in such a manner. §514(b)(3)(A). See *acquisition indebtedness; debt-financed property; unrelated business taxable income*.

net adjustment the aggregate of duplicated or omitted items that arise as a result of a *change of accounting method*. For example, if a *taxpayer* changed from the *accrual method* to the *cash method* of accounting, accounts receivable could be reported twice. These amounts are combined and create a net figure which is then spread forward, typically over six years under the authority of Rev. Proc. 84-74, 1984-2 C.B. 736. See *section 481 adjustment*.

net amount realized the *amount realized* from the *approved disposition* of a *qualified housing project* less expenses paid or incurred by the *taxpayer*, which are directly connected with the approved disposition, and the amount of *taxes* (other than *income taxes*) paid or incurred by the taxpayer, which are attributable to the approved disposition. Reg. §1.1039-1(c)(5). If a taxpayer reinvests the net amount realized from an approved disposition of certain low-income housing projects in a timely manner, then the *gain* on the disposition may be deferred. §1039.

net capital gain the excess of *net long-term capital gain* for the year over *net short-term capital losses* for the year. §1222(11). *Individual taxpayers* enjoy a maximum tax rate of 28 percent on net long-term capital gain for the year after 1990. §1(h).

net capital loss *capital losses* in excess of the *deduction* allowable under §1211. §1222(10). The term is used in §1212(a) and (b) for calculating *capital loss carryovers* and *carrybacks*. That is, to the extent losses are unabsorbed in the present year, there is a net capital loss that may be absorbed in prior years (*corporations* only) or subsequent years (all *taxpayers*).

net casualty loss the excess of *personal casualty gains* over *personal casualty losses*. This net figure is subject to a floor of 10 percent of *adjusted gross income* on personal casualty loss *deductions*. §165(h)(2). An excess of *gains* over *losses* is deemed a *sale* of *capital assets*. §165(h)(2)(B).

net earnings, exempt organizations earnings after expenses. The net earnings concept seems to be generally ignored. See *inurement of earnings to a private shareholder or individual*.

net earnings from self-employment generally, an *individual's gross income* from a *trade or business* carried on as a *sole proprietorship* less *expenses* attributable to the proprietorship, plus *guaranteed payments* from a *partnership,* and his or her *distributive share* of the income or *loss* from the partnership's trade or business. §1.1402(a)-1. *Interest, dividends*, real estate *rent*, and *capital gains* are not included unless received in the *taxpayer's* capacity as a *dealer*, nor are wages and salaries. The distributive share of income from an *S corporation* is not self-employment income, since it is considered a *distribution* of corporate profits. §1402(a). Net earnings from self-employment is the base on which Social Security *self-employment taxes* (*SECA or Self-Employment Contributions Act of 1954*) fall. The self-employment tax is 15.3 percent and consists of two taxes—an OASDI (i.e. Social Security) tax of 12.4 percent and a Medicare tax of 2.9 percent. See *self-employment tax; trade or business, self-employment tax*.

net earnings, patronage dividends net earnings from *business* done with or for the *patrons* of a *cooperative,* as reported by the cooperative for *federal income tax* purposes. §1388(a); Rev. Rul. 74-274, 1974-1 C.B. 247. *Patronage dividends* only qualify as such if determined by reference to net earnings of the organization. §1388(a)(3).

net gift a *gift* in connection with which the *donee* pays the *gift tax*. If the *donee* pays the gift tax as a condition of receiving the gift, then the *donor* has a taxable *gain* equal to the gift tax paid by the donee minus the *taxpayer's basis* in the property. The *IRS* asserts that a voluntary payment also creates income. Rev. Rul. 75-72, 1975-1 C.B. 310. The gift tax falls on the net gift (i.e., the value of the transferred property, less gift tax) only.

net income   generally, *gross income* less appropriate *deductions*, provided there is still a profit. The term is used broadly in the *Code*, but with many nuances.

net income basis election   a reference to §367(a)(3)(C), which codifies the *IRS* view that when a *foreign branch* of a *domestic corporation* is incorporated, *gain realized* on the incorporation must be *recognized* to the extent of prior foreign *losses*, reduced by any later branch income and amounts subject to *recapture* under §904(f)(3).

net interest income   the excess of total interest income (including *original issue discount*) includible in the year over interest *paid or accrued* during the year on debt incurred or continued to purchase or carry a *market discount bond*. §1277(b)(1)(c). *Taxpayers* may electively *deduct* interest on market discount bonds to the extent of net interest income. §1277(b)(1)(A) and (b)(3).

net investment income   for purposes of §163(d), which limits current *investment interest expense deductions* of noncorporate *taxpayers*, the term means *investment income* minus *investment expenses*. §163(d)(3). Net investment income set the current limit on such interest expense deductions, although disallowances may be *carried forward* to future years. §163(d). The term is also used in connection with limitations on the rules surrounding *below-market loans*. See §7872(d)(1). See *interest on investment indebtedness limitation; investment expenses, interest on investment indebtedness limitation; investment income, interest on investment indebtedness limitation.*

net investment income, interest on investment indebtedness limitation   the figure which imposes the limit on *deductions* for *investment interest expenses*. It consists of *investment income* less *investment expenses* (other than *interest*) which are directly connected to the production of investment income. §163(d)(4)(C). If *depreciation* or *depletion deductions* are allowed with respect to investment property, then one uses the actual deductions allowable for such expenses. Also, the *percent floor on miscellaneous itemized deductions* applies before the §163(d) limit. *Passive activity income* and expenses are not included in the calculation. There are important transition rules. See *interest on investment indebtedness limitation.*

net investment income, private foundation excise tax   gross investment income from *dividends, interest, rents,* and *royalties* (except to the extent they were subjected to the tax on *unrelated business taxable income*), plus *capital gains* from properties held for investment or used in the production of *unrelated business taxable income* (again, except to the extent included in computing the tax on unrelated business taxable income), subject to special rules regarding *basis* of such assets. Appropriate *ordinary and necessary deductions* incurred to produce or collect such income, or in the management of assets, are *deductible* from such income. §4940(c). The term is used to calculate the 2 percent *excise tax* imposed on the foundation's net investment income. §4940(a). See *audit fee, private foundations.*

net invoice method   a method of accounting for cash discounts under which such discounts are *excluded* from *gross income* until the discounted goods are *sold*. Reg. §1.471-3(b).

net liquidation value   the amount, after *expenses* and *taxes*, that can be *realized* for listed and readily marketable securities held by a *corporation* subject to the *accumulated earnings tax*. Liquid assets are studied to determine whether there has been an unreasonable accumulation of earnings such that a corporation can be presumed to have the requisite intention to avoid taxes required to attract the accumulated earnings tax. §§532 and 533. See *accumulated earnings tax.*

net long-term capital gains   the excess of *long-term capital gains* for the *taxable year* over *long-term capital losses* for the *taxable year*. §1222(7).

net long-term capital loss   the excess of *long-term capital losses* for the *taxable year* over *long-term capital gains* for the year. §1222(8).

net loss   generally, *gross income* in excess of appropriate *deductions*. The term is used broadly in the *Code*, but with many nuances.

net negative overhead variance   see *standard cost method.*

net operating loss (NOL)   generally, the excess of allowable *deductions* over *gross income* from a *trade or business*, with adjustments. §172(c). The principal adjustments are (1) no *NOL* deductions may be carried from other years to the present year; (2) in the case of noncorporate *taxpayers, capital losses* are *deductible* only to the extent of *capital gains*, and in computing the net operating loss, the former deduction for 60 percent of *net capital gain* for noncorporate taxpayers is disallowed; (3) in the case of noncorporate taxpayers, no deduction is allowed for *personal exemptions*, and *estates* and *trusts* may not claim the deduction in lieu of the deduction for *personal exemptions*; (4) in the case of noncorporate taxpayers, nonbusiness deductions are allowed only to the extent of nonbusiness income; and (5) *dividends-received deductions* for *dividends* from a *domestic corporation, dividends-paid deductions* on preferred stock of public utilities, and deductible dividends from certain *foreign corporations* are generally allowed without regard to the limitations based on *taxable income*. Reg. §1.172-2 and -3. Net operating losses from one source offset current year's income from all other sources, and, if they result in negative income after being so combined, the overage is *carried back* or *carried over* to other *taxable years*. See *net operating loss carrybacks; net operating loss carryovers.*

net operating loss carrybacks *net operating losses* applied to a *taxable year* earlier than the *taxable year* in which the loss arose. Generally, net operating losses are first carried back to the third year preceding the year of loss, and then to the second year preceding the year of loss, etc., until the loss is fully absorbed and paid as refunds. §172(b)(1)(A). If a net operating loss has not been fully used up during the carryback period, then the loss can generally be *carried forward* 15 years. §172(b)(1)(B). Recent legislation allows *taxpayers* to forego the carryback and instead to carry their NOLs forward 15 years. §172(b)(3)(C). See *net operating loss carryovers.*

net operating loss carryovers *net operating losses* utilized in a *taxable year* after the year in which the loss was incurred. Generally, a net operating loss must be carried back three years before it is *carried forward.* §172(b)(1)(A). But see §172(b)(3)(C). For losses that are carried forward, the carryover period for most *taxpayers* is 5 taxable years for pre-1976 losses and 15 taxable years for post-1975 losses. §172(b)(1)(B). Certain industries and transactions qualify for sharply different carryover periods (e.g., 20 years for *Cuban expropriation losses*).

net operating loss carryovers, corporate reorganizations and acquisitions see *neutrality principle.*

net operating loss deduction an amount equal to the aggregate of the *net operating loss carryovers* to such *taxable year,* plus the net operating loss carryovers or *carrybacks* to that year. §172(a). The net operating loss *deduction* is treated as a deduction from *gross income* and may generate a *refund* of previously paid taxes.

net passive income, subchapter S corporations see *excess net passive income.*

net positive overhead variance see *standard cost method.*

net premiums premium paid minus dividends received on a *life insurance policy.*

net proceeds, state or local bonds proceeds of an issue of *bonds,* reduced by amounts in a reasonably required reserve or replacement fund. §150(a)(3).

net profits interest a share of gross production of oil, gas, or minerals from a property, determined on the basis of net profits from the operation of the property. It is a *nonoperating interest.* Rev. Rul. 75-182, 1975-1 C.B. 176. It is generally an *economic interest,* entitling the holder to *depletion deductions.*

net recognized built-in gain, S corporation the amount that would be an *S corporation's taxable income* if (except as provided under *net operating loss carryover* rule) only *recognized built-in gains* and *recognized built-in losses* were taken into account. If it elected subchapter

S status before April 1988, net recognized built-in gain for any *taxable year* would not exceed its taxable income for that year. This definition applies during the 10-year *recognition period* following adoption of S corporation status by a former *C corporation.* §1374(d)(1). *Gains* on the *disposition* of such assets are generally taxed at top corporate rates. See *built-in gain tax, S corporation; recognition period, S corporation.*

net rental election a generally advantageous election available to *nonresident aliens* and *foreign corporations* to treat rents as being from the conduct of a United States *trade or business,* such that United States taxes will fall on rents after appropriate *deductions* at graduated rates, rather than on gross rents. §§871(d) (*individuals*) and 882(d) (*corporations*). The election is also found in certain *tax treaties.*

net salvage value the excess of gross salvage over the estimated cost of removal, permissible except under the *asset depreciation range system.*

net section 1231 gain the excess of *section 1231 gains* over *section 1231 losses.* §1231(c)(4). See *unrecaptured net section 1231 losses.*

net section 1231 loss the excess of *section 1231 losses* over *section 1231 gains.* §1231(c)(4). See *unrecaptured net section 1231 losses.*

net short-term capital gain the excess of *short-term capital gains* for the *taxable year* over the *short-term capital losses* for that year. §1222(5).

net short-term capital loss the excess of *short-term capital losses* for the *taxable year* over *short-term capital gains* for the year. §1222(6).

net unearned income, kiddie tax a child's *adjusted gross income* which is not attributable to *earned income* (using the §911(d)(2) meaning relating to expatriate Americans) minus: (1) the greater of $600 (as adjusted for inflation) or the child's earned income, plus (2) the greater of (1) or the child's *itemized deductions* in connection with generating unearned income. §1(g)(4). This figure may in effect be taxed to the child at the parent's top *marginal rate* if the so-called *kiddie tax* applies. See *kiddie tax.*

net United States real property gain for purposes of the special taxes imposed on foreigners' sales of interests in *realty* located in the *United States,* the term means the excess of the aggregate of the *gains* for the *taxable year* from *dispositions* of *United States real property interests* over the aggregate of the *losses* for the taxable year from dispositions of such interests. §897(a)(2)(B). See *Foreign Investment in Real Property Tax Act.*

net unrealized appreciation, collapsible corporations the overall appreciation in a *corporation's* assets, in which *unrealized appreciation* is viewed as values in excess of *adjusted bases* and *unrealized depreciation* is viewed as values less than adjusted bases. §341(e)(6). Net unrealized appreciation in certain assets of a corporation is included in the definition of *subsection (e) assets*. §341(e)(5). See *collapsible corporation*.

net unrealized built-in gain, neutrality principle the reverse of a *net unrealized built-in loss*. If the value of the *loss corporation's* nonliquid assets exceeds the value of its aggregate *bases* by over 15 percent on the *change date*, the *section 382 limitation* increases by any built-in gain (up to total *net unrealized built-in gain*) that is *recognized* during the five-year period following the change date. §382(h)(1). This is pro-*taxpayer* adjustment. See *net unrealized built-in loss, neutrality principle*.

net unrealized built-in gain, preacquisition loss limits same as *net unrealized built-in gain, neutrality principle* (§382(h)(3)), but the *acquisition date* is substituted for the *change date*. §384(c)(4). The amount of *recognized built-in gain* for any *taxable year* is limited to net unrealized built-in gain minus recognized built-in gains from prior years in the *recognition period* which, but for §384, would have been offset by preacquisition losses. §384(c)(1)(C). A *de minimis rule* treats the net unrealized built-in gain as zero unless it exceeds the lesser of $10 million or 15 percent of the *fair market value* of the *corporation's* assets. One disregards liquid assets in calculating the 15 percent. See *preacquisition loss limits*.

net unrealized built-in gains, S corporation see *built-in gain tax, S corporations*.

net unrealized built-in loss, neutrality principle corporate assets whose aggregate value just before an *ownership change* is less than their aggregate *adjusted bases*. §382(h)(3)(A)(i). This figure is adjusted by amounts that would have been built-in gain or loss if recognized during the *recognition period* (e.g., *installment sales* whose first payments begin in a decade); *carryovers* of *net operating losses* and *capital losses* simply offset recognized built-in gain to the extent otherwise permitted under the applicable section. §382(h)(6)(B),(C). If a *loss corporation* has a net unrealized built-in loss, any *recognized* built-in loss during the five-year *recognition period* is treated as a *prechange loss* and is capped by the *section 382 limitation*. §338(h)(3)(B). The same definition is used for purposes of the *preacquisition loss limits* under §384, in which the *acquisition date* is substituted for the *change date* and a *de minimis rule* is added which treats the net unrealized built-in loss as zero unless it exceeds the lesser of $10 million or 15 percent of the *fair market value* of the *corporation's* assets. §384(c)(8). See *neutrality principle*.

net unrealized depreciation, collapsible corporations the excess of a *corporation's unrealized depreciation* (*adjusted bases* of property in excess of value) over its unrealized appreciation (values in excess of adjusted bases) in its assets. §341(e)(6). Net unrealized depreciation in certain assets of a corporation is included in the definition of *subsection (e) assets*. §341(e)(5).

net worth, collapsible corporations the *fair market value* of a *corporation's* assets at day's end plus amounts *distributed* in *complete liquidation* on or before day's end minus its liabilities at day's end. Assets infused during the year ending at day's end are disregarded if they were received without good business reason in exchange for *stock*, as a *contribution to capital*, or as paid-in surplus. §341(e)(7). The latter rule is designed to avoid padding net worth. Net worth is used as a base to determine whether a corporation can elude *collapsible corporation* status under §341(e). See *subsection (e) assets, collapsible corporation*.

net worth method a method of determining omissions from *gross income*, pursuant to which understatement of tax can be shown. The analysis runs as follows: if a *taxpayer* realizes an increase in net worth during the course of a year and in addition pays out funds for *nondeductible* items and services, the resulting total, reduced by nontaxable receipts, represents income to the taxpayer.

net worth method, currency translation a method of reflecting effects of foreign currency values, under which profits are determined by calculating fixed assets at historical costs and net worth of current assets and liabilities at the beginning of the year at currency rates then prevailing, and adding remittances during the year and subtracting year-end current net worth at year-end rates. The net figure is viewed as reflecting profits or losses (if negative) for the year.

neutrality principle the concept underlying §§382 and 383, limiting the survival of *net operating losses, net unrealized built-in losses, excess credits, foreign tax credits,* and certain other *tax attributes* in a corporate acquisition context. The idea is that the tax laws should give the acquirer of a loss business an annual tax saving no greater than the taxes that would have been saved by the loss corporation if it had invested its funds conservatively and offset such income with its historic losses. The event that triggers the limitation is an *ownership change*, meaning *an owner shift involving a five-percent shareholder* or an *equity structure shift*, both combined with a 50 *percentage point* shift in *stock* ownership. The target company's hypothetical income stream is called the *section 382 limitation*. It is derived by multiplying the value of the *old loss corporation stock* immediately before the ownership change by the *long-term tax-exempt rate* posted by §1274. The product of the two items is the annual cap on usable net operating losses, known as the *section 382 limitation*. Section 382 can also limit *deductions* for losses from sales of assets of corporations with *net unrealized built-in loss* before the ownership change, which includes certain *depletion depreciation* and *amortization*. §382(h). §382(l)(5). Section 383 applies parallel provisions for various other tax attributes, especially credits, and §384, discussed under the primary heading *preacquisition loss limits* controls trafficking in profitable corporations to counteract the rules of §382 via stock and asset acquisitions.

new construction, rehabilitation generally, construction in circumstances in which the foundation or outer walls of a building are not retained, including enlargement of the total area of a building. Reg. §1.167(k)-3(a)(2) and (3).

new-housing price ratio the ratio which the *average area purchase price* for new homes in that area bears to the average purchase price for new homes in the United States. §143(f)(5)(D)(iii).

new loss corporation a *corporation* which has a *net operating loss carryforward* after an *ownership change*. §382(k). Such a change attracts the limits of §382 as to annual losses available to the *new loss corporation*. The new loss corporation and the *old loss corporation* are often the same, (e.g., a recapitalization), but in the case of a loss corporation's merger into a profitable corporation, the target is the old loss corporation and the survivor becomes the *new loss corporation*. See *neutrality principle; ownership change; section 382 limitation*.

news gathering service an organization (e.g., AP) that is primarily engaged in the *business* of gathering news and distributing it to its members. Such organizations are exempt from §277 which limits, for a *membership organization*, the *deduction* attributable to furnishing services to its members to the income derived from such services. §277(b).

news release an irregularly issued *IRS* publication concerning matters on which the public needs to be informed and that generally have nationwide applicability or interest. The Public Affairs Division of the IRS is responsible for determination of need, development in final form, and issuance of news releases. I.R.M. 1(17)12.13. Such releases sometimes relate to matters of tax policy.

new theory a clarification or development of an original *IRS* determination, which does not shift the *burden of proof* to the IRS in the *Tax Court*.

next-day transactions one of four principal types of transactions taking place on the New York Stock Exchange under which the *settlement date* in the sale of stock or securities is the next business day following the date of sale. The settlement date is determined by the New York Stock Exchange and depends on the type of transaction involved. Next-day transactions are mostly used by *cash method taxpayers* at year-end to accelerate the year in which *gains* are *recognized* by having payment made before year-end. Settlement dates control when a cash method taxpayer reports *capital gains*. Rev. Rul. 72-381, 1972-2 C.B. 233.

next-lower-tier entity with respect to a *first-tier entity*, it is the *loss corporation*. The next-lower-tier entity with respect to a *higher-tier entity* is any first-tier entity or other higher-tier entity in which the higher-tier entity owns, at any time during the *testing period*, a 5 percent or more direct ownership interest. Reg. §1.382-2T(f)(17). The term is important for purposes of determining if an *ownership change* has taken place, such that the *section 382 limitation* might apply to the *loss corporation* under the *neutrality principle*.

nimble dividend rule a state corporate law rule that allows corporations to pay dividends out of current profits, despite cumulative losses. The concept is reflected in §316(a)(2), which treats *distributions* from *current earnings and profits* as creation of *dividends*, even though the corporation has an accumulated deficit.

1984 Act an abbreviation for the *Deficit Reduction Act of 1984* or the *Tax Reform Act of 1984*.

1986 Code the *Internal Revenue Code of 1986*, as amended, supplanting and largely re-enacting the *Internal Revenue Code of 1954*, as amended.

1990 Act the Revenue Reconciliation Act of 1990, Pub. L. No. 101-508. It contains a variety of technical changes in the tax law, including a reinstatement of a preference for *capital gains*.

1992 Energy Act the Comprehensive National Energy Policy Act of 1992. H.R. 776. Pub. L. 102486.

ninety-day letter see *notice of deficiency*.

no additional cost services a type of *fringe benefit* which is typically *deductible* by the *employer* and non-taxable to the *employee* under §132(a)(1). This benefit is available only if the services are normally offered to customers (the so-called *line of business limitation*) and the employer incurs no substantial additional cost in providing the service. §132(b). Eligibility is conditioned upon *nondiscrimination rules* as to *highly compensated employees*. §132(h). Employers may also enter into agreements to provide exempt services to each other's employees on a reciprocal basis. §132(g). See *nondiscrimination rules, fringe benefits*.

no-change letter a letter issued in a *correspondence audit* indicating that the return is accepted as filed (Form 590 (DO)). Reg. §601.105(c)(1)(i). It does not prevent further audits.

"no-comfort" policy an *IRS* policy to not issue *comfort rulings*.

nominal or taken shares an amount of *stock* issued to creditors that is so small it prevents application of the favorable *stock-for-debt exception*. The *IRS* specifies that the transfer must be worth at least 10 percent of the value of the existing stock and securities. §108(e)(8).

nominee a party who holds *bare legal title* to property for the benefit of others, or who receives and disburses funds for the benefit of others, sometimes to avoid usury laws applicable to *individual,* but not to corporate, borrowers. Nominees are now capable of being treated as conduits. See *agency corporations.*

nominee trust a *nominee* arrangement in which a *trust* is used, usually without disclosure of record of the *beneficial* owners. The form is frequently used in Massachusetts but is not to be confused with a *Massachusetts trust.* In Illinois, where they are popular with slumlords, such trusts are often called Illinois trusts and have a bank *trustee.*

nonaccountable plan an expense reimbursement plan under which an *employee* is not required to substantiate expenses nor return all amounts which are not substantiated. Reg. §§31.3121(a)-2T(b), 31.3306-2T(b), and 31.4301(a)(-2T(b). Such plans force reporting to the *IRS* and employee all advances and reimbursements. See *accountable plan.*

nonaccountable plans an informal term for arrangements under which the *employee* is not required to substantiate the *expenses* covered by the arrangement to the party providing the reimbursement, or the employee has the right to retain amounts in excess of the substantiated expenses covered under the arrangement. After 1988, unreimbursed employee business expenses *paid or incurred* under such plans are *deductible* only as an *itemized deduction,* subject to the *two-percent floor on itemized deductions.* §62(c).

nonaccrual experience method a provision for service providers found in §448(d)(5). It states that *accrual method taxpayers* need not report amounts due for services rendered that, based on past experience, is likely not to be collected. To qualify, there must be no charge (e.g., interest) for delayed payment.

nonacq. see *nonacquiescence.*

nonacquiescence formal disagreement by the *Commissioner* of the *Internal Revenue Service* regarding a decision on an issue decided adversely to the government by the *Tax Court.* Nonacquiescence may be as to one or more issues. Such announcements appear first in the *Internal Revenue Bulletin* and later in final form in the *Cumulative Bulletins.* They are frequently cited in the form "nonacq." or "NA." The Commissioner is not obligated to issue an acquiescence or nonacquiescence for any Tax Court decision. For the antonym, see *acquiescence.*

nonallocable receipts receipts from carryout sales or services to which a service charge of at least 10 percent is added. §6053(c). Such amounts need not be reported as *gross income* under the rules covering tip income.

nonallocation period the period beginning with the later of the date on the *sale* of *qualified securities* or of the plan allocation attributable to final payment of the *securities acquisition loan.* §409(n)(3). No part of such securities, or assets attributable to them, can be allocated by the *ESOP* or *EWOC* in the nonallocation period to (1) a *decedent* whose *estate* makes the sale to a *related taxpayer* (§267(b) meaning), or (2) anyone who owns, using §318 *attribution rules,* over 25 percent of any class of *stock* of the issuer or of any related *corporations.* §409(n)(1). There are some exceptions. §409(n)(3)(A). Violations of the rule attract an *excise tax* under §4979A. See *excise tax, prohibited allocation of ESOP and EWOC stock.*

nonbusiness asset see *substantial nonbusiness assets.*

nonbusiness asset, neutrality principle any asset held for *investment.* §382(l)(4)(C). See *substantial nonbusiness assets.*

nonbusiness assets share of indebtedness see *substantial nonbusiness assets.*

nonbusiness bad debt a *nonbusiness debt* that becomes entirely *worthless* in the *taxable year.* If such debts are held by noncorporate *taxpayers,* they are deemed *sales or exchanges* of *capital assets* held for one year or less and result in *short-term capital losses.* Such debts do not qualify for *deductions* for *partial worthlessness,* nor may *reserves for bad debts* be established. §166(a)(2), (c) and (d). *Worthless securities* are excluded. §166(e). See *worthless debt.*

nonbusiness day, foreign travel days other than *business days.* Reg. §1.274-4(d). See *business day.*

nonbusiness debt a *debt* that is neither created nor acquired in connection with the *taxpayer's trade or business* nor which becomes *worthless* in connection with the taxpayer's trade or business. §166(d)(2). See *nonbusiness bad debt; worthlessness.*

nonbusiness expense not defined. The *Treasury* uses the term nontrade or nonbusiness *expenses* in the captions to *regulations* under §212, relating to various *deductible expenses* of an *investment* nature or relating to tax determinations. See *nonbusiness expense deduction.*

nonbusiness expense deduction a confusing colloquial term for *expenses* that are not incurred in the course of a *trade or business* but which are nevertheless *deductible* under §212, relating to *investment* and tax-related expenditures.

noncancellable accident and health policies accident and health (A&H) policies that obligate the issuer to renew or continue coverage at a specified premium, and with respect to which a *reserve* in addition to the unearned premiums must be carried to cover the obligation. Stipulated age termination, if age 60 or more, does not vitiate the noncancellable character of the policy until that age is reached. Reg. §1.807-3(c) (defining prior law terminology). The term is important for purposes of determining whether a company is a *life insurance company* under §816.

noncapital asset an asset other than a *capital asset*. Noncapital assets include inventory, trade receivables, certain properties created by the effects of the taxpayer (such as works of art), depreciable business property and business land, and certain government publications. §1221.

noncash dividends any *dividends* in a form other than cash or the distributing *corporation's* own *stock* and rights to acquire such stock. §317 (defining *property* for corporate *distribution* purposes). The distributing corporation generally *recognizes gain* or *loss* on the distribution of a noncash dividend. §311. Also, an individual who receives a noncash dividend is taxed on the *fair market value* of the property received, while corporate recipients are taxed on the lower of the property's *adjusted basis* (plus gain recognized by the transferor) or *fair market value*. §301.

noncommunity property separate, as distinguished from *community property*. The term is used in the context of community property matrimonial regimes (e.g., California) and refers to property owned by a *spouse* before the marriage or received by *gift, inheritance, devise,* or *bequest* during the marriage.

noncompete agreements agreements by which a seller of a business agrees not to compete with the buyer of the business, not to compete for a certain length of time, or not to compete within a certain geographic area. Provided the agreement is a *bona fide* arm's length transaction, amounts paid pursuant to such agreements are generally *deductible* to the payor and *ordinary income* to the payee. Rev. Rul. 69-643, 1969-2 C.B. 54. See *covenant not to compete*.

noncompliance rule the nickname for an *IRS* power to determine the correct treatment of any transaction with a *foreign related party*. This power arises when (1) a foreign related party fails to authorize a *twenty-five percent reporting corporation* to act as its agent in limited circumstances; (2) the twenty-five percent reporting corporation fails to substantially comply with a *summons* for information regarding transactions with a foreign related party; or (3) the summons is quashed because the *records* were not maintained or the reporting corporation cannot provide the records requested in the summons. §6038C(d). This rule applies to any *related party transaction* if the foreign related party does not

agree to authorize the reporting corporation to act as its limited agent for purposes of §7602 (examination of books and witnesses), §7603 (service of summons), and §7604 (enforcement of summons) for any request to examine records or produce testimony and requests for information with respect to foreign corporations engaged in United States business. §6038C(d)(1). The rule also applies to a transaction or item to which the summons relates to determining a reporting corporation's proper *federal income tax* liability, the IRS issuing a summons to the reporting corporation to produce (directly or as agent) records or testimony, §6038C(d)(2)(A). The IRS need not first begin an action to enforce the summons. §6038C(d)(2). See *penalty, foreign corporation's failure to furnish information or retain records; records, foreign corporate reporting; related party, foreign corporate reporting.*

noncontributory pension or profit-sharing plan a *pension* or *profit-sharing plan* funded entirely by the *employer* (i.e., no contributions made by the covered *employees*).

noncontrolled section 902 corporation a *foreign corporation* (as defined for *controlled foreign corporation* purposes) in which a *domestic corporation* owns at least 10 percent of the voting *stock*. §904(d)(2)(E). *Dividends* and *qualified electing fund* inclusions taxed to the domestic corporation are generally segregated for separate application of the *foreign tax credit limitation*. §904(d)(i)(E). The use of the word "each" in §904(d)(1)(E) creates an additional segregation which allows the tax credit to be applied only to *distributions* from each *noncontrolled section 902 corporation* individually. *High withholding tax interest* (to the extent over 5 percent) received by a noncontrolled §902 corporation is deemed paid by the distributee but is included in the *high withholding tax interest* category, thus avoiding cross-crediting against the lesser taxed dividends. See *financial services income; section 904(d)(1) "basket."*

nonconventional source fuels see *credit for producing fuels from nonconventional sources.*

nonconvertible currency, tax payments foreign currency that is not convertible (nor in fact converted) into United States dollars or into any other currency that is convertible into United States dollars, because of monetary, exchange, or other restrictions imposed by the foreign country, agreements entered into with the United States, or the terms and conditions of the United States government grant to which the currency relates. Reg. §301.6316-2(b). In certain cases, United States taxes may be paid in such currency. Reg. §301.6316-7 and 17 U.S.C. §1704(h)-(p) (1976).

noncustodial parent the parent not having custody of the child. Normally, the custodial parent is entitled to the dependency exemption. This right is inapplicable when the custodial parent releases his or her right to the child's dependency exemption to the noncustodial parent. This release must be executed in writing (*Form 8332* or similar release) and attached to the noncustodial parent's tax return for each year the exemption is released. §152(e)(2). The *execution of a multiple support agreement* will also allow the child to be claimed as a dependent by a taxpayer other than the custodial parent. §152(c).

nondealer real property installment obligations   an informal term for *installment obligations* that arise out of the *disposition* of any property whose sales price exceeds $150,000, to the extent that deferred payments from all such dispositions exceed $5 million in any year. It excludes any installment obligation that arises out of the disposition of *personal use property* as defined in §1275(b)(3) (e.g., a home), or the disposition of any property that is used or produced on the *farm* as defined for *special use valuation* purposes. The term also excludes any installment obligation that arises out of a disposition of the residential lot (as to which the seller or a related person will not make improvements) or *time-share* if the *taxpayer* elects to pay *interest* on the amount of the deferred tax attributable to the use of the installment method. §453A(a)-(c). The term no longer appears in the *Code,* but it is useful shorthand. It is the kind of property affected by §453A(d), which taxes pledges of *secured indebtedness.* See *installment method.*

nondeductible expenditures   expenditures that cannot be *deducted.* Some such expenditures (e.g., a personal swimming pool) may have to be *capitalized,* depending on the facts.

nondeductible IRA contributions   see *designated nondeductible IRA contributions.*

nondepreciable property   property for which *depreciation deductions* cannot be claimed. Examples include raw land, artwork with an enduring value, and goodwill. The term also refers to property not used in the *trade or business* or *held for the production of income.* See §167(a).

nondevice factor   see *device limitation, corporate divisions.*

nondiscrimination certificate, private schools   an *information return* required of private schools, certifying that they do not practice racial discrimination. See T.I.R. 1449 (Mar. 19, 1976). The *IRS* recently has been denied funding to act to disqualify otherwise exempt schools. Treasury, Postal Service, and General Government Appropriation Act of 1980, Pub. L. No. 96-74, 93 Stat. 559 (1980), and §§614–615.

nondiscrimination clause   a *tax treaty* term assuring that a country that is a party to a treaty will not impose

tax burdens on treaty *citizens* and enterprises more burdensome than those imposed on their own citizens and enterprises.

nondiscrimination, qualified pension, profit-sharing, and stock bonus plans   a requirement demanded of *qualified pension, profit-sharing,* and *stock bonus plans,* at the risk of their losing qualified status, that contributions to the plans and benefits under them not discriminate in favor of *highly compensated employees.* §401(a)(4). In testing for discrimination, certain union employees whose pension plans are subject to good-faith collective bargaining are excluded from discrimination calculations, as are *nonresident aliens.* Id. While a plan can generally cover salaried employees only, be directly tied to base compensation, and be based solely on compensation in excess of the *Social Security wage base,* provided the plan is *integrated,* the determination of whether a plan is discriminatory remains difficult because it is made case by case and looks for internal disparities, not absolute numbers. These rules are distinct from the provisions of §401(a)(3), concerning *minimum participation standards* which demand fairly broad participation, but says nothing about who gets what.

nondiscrimination rules, fringe benefits   a limitation whereby the favorable tax treatment of certain *fringe benefits* is dependent upon the *employer's* making the benefits available on substantially the same terms to each member of a group of *employees* which is defined under a reasonable classification set up by the employer that does not discriminate in favor of *highly compensated employees.* §132(h)(1). If the availability of the fringe benefit does not satisfy this nondiscrimination test, the exclusions for *no-additional cost services* and *qualified employee discounts* apply only to those recipient employees who are not members of the highly compensated group.

nondividend distributions   current *distributions* by a *corporation* to a *shareholder,* in his or her (or its) capacity as such which are not treated as a *dividend,* but rather as a *return of capital* or, if the amount distributed exceeds the *taxpayer's basis* in his stock, a *gain.* §301(c). Such distributions arise if and to the extent the distributing corporation lacks *earnings and profits.*

nondivisive Type D reorganization   see *Type D reorganization.*

nondocketed case   see *Appeals Office.*

nonequity option   *listed options* other than *equity options.* §1256(g)(3). The term would, for example, include stock index options. See *section 1256 contract.*

nonexempt charitable trust   a *trust* organized for charitable purposes, but that does not qualify as *tax-*

exempt under §501(c)(3). By giving away its current incomes to charitable donees, the trust can get practical effects of tax *exemption*. There is no limit on a trust's ability to claim *charitable contribution deductions*; hence, the trust can give away all its income and avoid taxation, although the *alternative minimum tax* may apply.

nonexempt cooperative any organization not exempt under §521, *operating on a cooperative basis* and determining its allocations to *patrons* on the basis of business done with or for its patrons. §1381(a)(2). Such a cooperative can *deduct* from its *gross incomes* the amounts of certain *patronage dividends* and distributions but it does not get the full complement of benefits available to an *exempt farmers' cooperative*. It can transact any amount of business with nonmembers, but such business is taxable. But see Rev. Rul. 72-602, 1972-2 C.B. 511.

nonexempt income any income that must be *included* in *gross income*. Reg. §1.265-1(b).

nonexempt person a *person* other than an *exempt person*. The term is used in connection with *industrial development bonds*.

nonexempt private foundation a *private foundation* that has lost its *exemption* from *federal income taxes*.

nonfarm optional method an elective method of determining Social Security *self-employment taxes* for *individuals* who are regularly self-employed but with modest amounts ($1,600 or less) of income (or even losses) from nonfarm self-employment. Such earnings must be less than two-thirds of the *taxpayer's gross income* from such self-employment. The benefit of the method is that if the *taxpayer's gross income* from all nonfarm *trades or businesses* is not more than $2,400, then he or she may report two-thirds of the gross income from nonfarm business as *net earnings from self-employment*. If, instead, gross income from all non-farm trades or businesses exceeds $2,400, then the taxpayer may report $1,600 as his or her net earnings from nonfarm self-employment. §1402(a). See *IRS* Pub. No. 533, Self-Employment Taxes 4. See *farmer, self-employment taxpayer*.

nonforeign affidavit an affidavit provided by a transferor of a *United States real property interest* stating that the transferor is not a *foreign person* and giving the transferor's *taxpayer identification number,* and other information the *IRS* calls for by *regulation*. §1445(b)(2). Transferees who receive such affidavits in good faith are relieved from *FIRPTA withholding*. §1445(b)(1).

nonforeign statement same as *nonforeign affidavit*.

nonforfeitable, qualified deferred compensation plans for purposes of the *vesting* requirements of

§411, the term generally means an unconditional right to an *accrued benefit*. Thus, rights that are conditioned upon a sufficiency of plan assets in the event of a termination or partial termination are considered to be forfeitable because of the condition. On the other hand, a plan does not violate the nonforfeitability requirements merely because in the event of a termination an *employee* does not have any recourse for satisfaction of his nonforfeitable benefits from other than the plan assets or the *Pension Benefit Guaranty Corporation,* or because of *integration* with Social Security. Rights that must be prospectively nonforfeitable under the vesting standards are nonforfeitable and may not be forfeited until it is determined that such rights are, in fact, in excess of the vesting standards. Paraphrased from portions of Reg. §1.411(a)-4(a). See Reg. §1.411(a)-4(b) and (c) for limitations and exceptions. See *integration, Social Security; qualified plan*.

nonforfeiture options the choices available if the policyholder discontinues premium payments on an *insurance* policy with a *cash surrender value*. This, if any, may be taken in cash, as extended *term insurance,* or as reduced paid-up insurance.

nonfunctional currency generally, any currency other than the *functional currency* of a *taxpayer,* but for purposes of §988, it also includes demand notes, time deposits, or similar instruments issued by a bank that are denominated in a currency other than the taxpayer's functional currency. §988(c)(1)(C)(ii). See *functional currency; section 988 transaction*.

nongovernmental output property *tangible or intangible property* that before its acquisition has been used (or held for use) by any *person* other than a state or a local governmental unit (e.g., by an investor-owned utility, a *cooperative,* or the federal government) in connection with an *output facility*. Output property includes electric and gas generation, transmission, distribution, and other related facilities. §143(d). Bonds issued to acquire such property are generally treated as taxable *private activity bonds* unless they are issued to acquire such property for the furnishing of electric energy or gas and are issued as *exempt facility bonds* or issued in connection with the furnishing of water, with several modifications. There are major exceptions under which what would otherwise be nongovernmental activity bonds are declassified if they are used to finance existing service areas and incursions into annexed areas. See *output facility; private activity bond*.

nonhighway fuels credit see *gasoline, special fuels, and lubricating oil credit*.

nonintegrated pension benefit a benefit under a *pension plan* which is calculated without reference to *Social Security benefits*. The term is particularly important in determining whether a *deferred compensation* *plan* can retain its status as a *qualified plan* under the strictures of §416. *See integrated plan.*

nonmanufacturing intangibles see *cost-sharing election, possessions corporations.*

nonnotice partner a *partner* other than a *notice partner.* Such partners are generally bound by settlements entered into by the *tax matters partner* in a *TEFRA audit.* §6224(c)(3). See *unified proceedings.*

nonoperating foundation see *private nonoperating foundation.*

nonoperating interest an interest in an oil, gas, or mineral property other than an *operating interest.* The term is especially significant for purposes of the *depletion* of natural resources. Examples include *landowners' royalties* and *net profits interests.* For the antonym, see *working interest.* See *operating interest.*

nonoperating mineral interest a *mineral interest* other than an *operating mineral interest.* Reg §1.614-5(g). Section 614(e) allows limited permission to aggregate such interests for *depletion* purposes if *IRS* consent is granted.

nonparticipating royalty an interest in oil, gas, or other mineral that entitles the holder to be paid if and when production occurs, but which requires no payment of expenses by the holder. It does not entitle the holder to share in bonuses, rentals, lease execution rights, exploration, or development.

nonpartnership items items that are not, or are not treated as, *partnership items.* §6231(a)(4). See §6231(b)(1) for numerous special cases in which partnership items can evolve into nonpartnership items. The concept is central to the *TEFRA audit* procedures. One important feature is that if a *partnership item* becomes a nonpartnership item, the *IRS* has an extra year to assess a *deficiency.* §6229(f). See *unified proceedings.*

nonpassive gain *gain* other than gain from a *passive activity.*

nonpassive income income other than *passive income.* The term appears in various places in the *regulations.* The usual significance is that such income cannot offset *passive activity deductions.* See *passive loss rules.*

nonperiodic distribution a *designated distribution* that is not a *periodic payment.* §3405(d)(3). Nonperiodic distributions that are not *qualified total distributions* are subject to *withholding* at a rate of 10 percent unless the payee elects against withholding. §3405(b)(2).

nonpreferential dividend a *dividend* other than a *preferential dividend.* See *preferential dividend.*

nonprofit corporations *corporations* exempt from *federal income taxes.* The term is used descriptively.

See, e.g., §6044; Reg. §§1.103-1 (interest on obligations of a state, territory, etc.), 1.277-1 (allowable deductions for expenses incurred by certain *membership organizations*), 1.501(c)(13)-1 (*cemetery companies*), 1.522-1 (farmers' cooperative marketing and purchasing associations exempt under §521), and 1.6033-2 (returns by *exempt organizations*).

nonprofit day care center an informal term for a day care center whose enrollment is based on the financial need of the family, or where the center offers preschool-age children of working parents an educational program provided by a professional staff of qualified teachers. For purposes of *exempt organization* status under §501(c)(3) and eligibility for *deductible charitable contributions* under §§170, 2055, and 2522, the term "educational purposes" includes the providing of care of children away from their homes if (1) substantially all of the child care provided by the organization is for the purpose of enabling *individuals* to be gainfully employed, and (2) the services provided by the organization are available to the general public. Such day care centers may qualify as nonprofit organizations, and *charitable contributions* to them can be *deductible.* See *exempt organizations.*

nonprofit organizations an alternative term for the imprecise phrases *exempt organizations* and not-for-profit organizations. Note that not all not-for-profit corporations are entitled to tax exemption.

nonpurpose investment any *investment property* which is acquired with the gross proceeds (including income from the proceeds and amounts to be used to pay debt services) of a *tax-exempt bond issue* and which is not required to carry out the governmental purpose of the issue. §148(f)(6). See *private loan financing test.*

nonpurpose obligation a term used generally for a security or any obligation that is *not tax-exempt,* which is acquired with the gross proceeds of an issue, and which is not acquired in order to carry out the governmental purpose of the issue. §103(c)(6)(H)(i). The term is generally used in the context of *industrial development bonds (IDBs).* See *arbitrage bond.*

nonqualified amount see *output facility.*

nonqualified annuity generally, an *annuity* other than one acquired by a *participant* in a *qualified annuity* or by an *employee* of an *exempt organization* used for pension purposes. Section 403(a)(1) provides that participants receiving payments pursuant to such arrangements are taxed under the general rules taxing annuities (§72) rather than on the full value of the annuity made available.

nonqualified deferred compensation *deferred compensation* for services other than *qualified deferred compensation.* While the gross income is generally not reportable until paid, nonqualified deferred compensation arrangements *do not benefit* from being able to grow without current taxation or allowing a *deduction* to the payor before it is reported by the payee.

nonqualified guaranteed contract an *insurance contract* (as well as a reasonable premium stabilization reserve) that provides only current insurance protection. The *Code* defines it as one as to which there is no guaranteed renewal and, aside from insurance protection, there is no promise of refunds or dividends, except to the extent they are experience rated and depend on factors other than *welfare benefits* paid to or on behalf of participants. §419(e)(4)(B). Such amounts are not viewed as funds held in connection with *welfare benefit* plans, as the insurer carries risk of loss. See *welfare benefit fund.*

nonqualified nonrecourse financing, at-risk rules for investment credit commercial financing which is not qualified. In order for commercial financing for any property to be qualified, it must not be convertible debt, and (1) the property must not have been acquired from a *related taxpayer* (per §267(b)); (2) nonrecourse financing cannot exceed 80 percent of the credit base; and (3) the financing must either be from a *qualified person,* or represent a loan from any federal, state, or local government or instrumentality, or be guaranteed by any federal, state, or local government. §49(a)(1)(D)(i) and (ii). See *at-risk rules, investment tax credit; related taxpayers, loss and deduction denial.*

nonqualified per-unit retain certificate any *per-unit retain certificate* that has not met the requirements to be a *qualified per-unit retain certificate.* §1388(c). *Cooperatives* can in effect *deduct* such certificates only when redeemed, at which point the *patron* reports the income. §§1382(b), 1383, and 1385. See Reg. §1.1388-1(c)(3) (tax benefit adjustment).

nonqualified plan generally, a *deferred compensation* plan that is not a *qualified plan.* Such plans offer only limited tax benefits. See *qualified deferred compensation plan.*

nonqualified stock option a *stock option* whose grant is nontaxable, but as to which the transfer of the underlying stock is subject to the *restricted property rules* (§83), such that when the option is exercised, one subtracts the amount paid for the option from the *fair market value* of the *stock* (ignoring nonlapse restrictions) and treats that excess as *ordinary income.* The inclusion in *gross income* occurs when the recipient's rights to the transferred property become transferable or free of any *substantial risk of forfeiture.* See Reg. §1.83-4(b).

nonqualified substantial improvement see *eligible basis, low-income housing credit.*

nonqualified tax-exempt organization, safe harbor leasing generally, any organization (or predecessor organization that was engaged in substantially similar activities) that was *exempt* from *federal income taxes* at any time during the five-year period ending on the date the *safe harbor lease* was entered into, but not any *farmers' cooperative* described in §521 (*exempt farmers' cooperative*) whether or not exempt from taxation under that section. An organization is not considered a nonqualified tax-exempt organization with respect to any property used in an *unrelated trade or business* taxable under §511 (tax on *unrelated business taxable income*). §168(f)(8)(H)(ii). Property leased to nonqualified tax-exempt organizations did not qualify for *safe harbor leasing* under the rules imposed by *TEFRA.*

nonqualified written notice of allocation a *written notice of allocation* to *patrons* of a *cooperative* that is not a *qualified written notice of allocation* or is a *qualified check* that is not cashed on or before the ninetieth day after the close of the payment period for the *taxable year* for which the *distribution* of which it is a part is made. §1388(d). *Patronage dividends* paid with such notices are not *deductible* by the cooperative under §1382(b)(1), but they are deductible under §1382(b)(2) when redeemed in money or other property, subject to a *tax benefit* computation, at which time they are reported as *gross income* by the *patron* under §1385. See Reg. §1.1383-1.

nonrecently purchased stock *stock* bought before the *twelve-month acquisition period* began. See *recently purchased stock.*

nonrecognition of gain or loss the failure to *recognize* a *realized gain* or *loss.* Numerous *Code* sections provide for such nonrecognition. See, e.g., *like-kind exchanges.* See *nonrecognition provisions.*

nonrecognition property property, the receipt of which does not cause *recognition* of income (e.g., *like-kind property* received in a *like-kind exchange*). The term is used explicitly in §358 regarding the basis of property received in *corporate reorganizations* and *divisions,* and in the *regulations* relating to *installment* sales, and is common tax parlance.

nonrecognition provisions provisions of the *Code* that bar immediate *recognition* of otherwise taxable (*realized*) *gains* and often *losses.* Examples include *like-kind exchanges* under §1031 and *rollovers of principal residences* under §1034. The effect of these provisions is generally reflected in the *basis of property* received in such transactions to the extent of the unrecognized gains. Thus, nonrecognition typically results in deferred gains that are reflected in the form of a reduced basis in property held by the *taxpayer,* whereas Code provisions excluding amounts from *gross income* result in permanent freedom from taxation.

nonrecognition transaction   a transaction (e.g., a *sale*) in which the *taxpayer* does not *recognize gain* or *loss* (in whole or in part), even though gain or loss is *realized*. An example would be a *like-kind exchange* under §1031. §7701(a)(45). See *nonrecognition provisions*.

nonrecourse deduction   a *deduction* that is based on *nonrecourse debt* of *partnership*. See Reg. §1.704-1(c) and (d)(3). The deduction equals the increase in the *partnership minimum gain* for the *taxable year*.

nonrecourse financing, at-risk rules for investment credit   includes amounts for which the *taxpayer* is protected against loss through guarantees, stop-loss agreements, or similar arrangements, and amounts borrowed from a *person* who has an interest, other than as a creditor, in the activity in which the property is used, or borrowed from a person related to the person (other than the taxpayer) having an interest in the activity. Future regulations will exempt certain persons from being treated as having an interest in the activity. Where the borrowing is by a *corporation* from a *shareholder*, the *shareholder* will not be treated as a person with an interest in the activity. §49(a)(1)(D)(iii). See *at-risk rules, investment tax credit; nonqualified nonrecourse financing, at-risk rules for investment credit*.

nonrecourse liabilities   secured liabilities for which the borrower is not personally liable. Rather, the creditor's rights on default are limited to using the property to satisfy unpaid liabilities. Liability in excess of the *adjusted basis* of the property can give rise to *gain* on foreclosure even when liability exceeds value. In fact, the determination as to whether a debt is really nonrecourse can be extremely uncertain. What, for example, is a debt that is guaranteed by an insolvent corporation where the borrowing was undertaken by a corporate general partner which is also insolvent? See also *nonrecourse liabilities, partnership taxation*.

nonrecourse liabilities, partnership taxation   in general, *liabilities* for which no *partner* is personally liable. They are a residual category, left over after determination of which liabilities are *recourse liabilities*. See *liability, partnership taxation; recourse liabilities, partnership taxation*.

nonrefundable credits   *tax credits* that cannot do more than reduce a *taxpayer's* tax liabilities to zero. Examples include the *foreign tax credit, general business credit*, and the *nonconventional source fuel credit*.

nonresident alien   an *individual* whose residence is not within the *United States* and who is not a *citizen* of the United States, including a nonresident *fiduciary*. Reg. §§1.871-2 and 301.7701-5. Such persons are generally taxed only on *dividends, rents, royalties, interest,* and other *fixed or determinable annual or periodical income* from sources within the *United States*, as

are citizens of *possessions* other than Puerto Rico, Guam, and the United States Virgin Islands. For *federal gift* and *estate tax* purposes, the term includes an individual who is neither a citizen nor a *domiciliary* of the United States at the date of transfer or death, respectively. Reg. §§20.0-1(b)(2) and 25.2501-1(b). An alien may, therefore, be a resident of the United States for income tax purposes but not for estate and gift tax purposes. The term is now formally defined as a person who is neither a United States citizen nor a *resident alien* of the United States. §7701(b)(1)(B). See *resident alien*.

nonresidential real property   all *section 1250 property* with no *ADR midpoint life* or a midpoint life of 27.5 or more years. §168(e)(2)(B). Such property may generally be written off over not less than 31.5 years, if it was *placed in service* after 1986. §168(c). See *accelerated cost recovery system (ACRS)*.

nonseparately computed income or loss, S corporations   *gross income* minus allowable *deductions*, determined by excluding all items of income (including *tax-exempt income*), *loss, deduction,* or *credit*, the separate treatment of which could affect any *shareholder's* tax liability. §§1366(a)(1)(B) and (a)(2). Such items need not be broken down but rather can be computed in the aggregate. Items, the separate treatment of which could affect the liability of any shareholder (e.g., *investment interest expense*), are reported separately. §1366(a)(1)(A). See *separately computed items*.

nonsimultaneous exchange   an exchange which is *deferred*. See *like-kind exchange*.

nonstatutory options   *stock options* that are not issued pursuant to *employee stock purchase plans, qualified stock options, restricted stock options,* or *incentive stock options*. Such options generally create *ordinary income* when exercised, to the extent of the spread between the value of the stock and the option price. If the option has an ascertainable value and is granted as compensation, then the spread is treated as ordinary income when granted. Absent such a value, the spread is taxable as ordinary income at the date of exercise, unless there are significant restrictions on the stock, in which case compensation is realized when the stock is sold or the restrictions lapse. §83. For a special election, see *restricted stock plans*.

nontaxable exchange   see *like-kind exchange; nonrecognition provisions*.

nontaxed portion   the amount of *basis* in *stock* that must be reduced by an *extraordinary dividend*. It is the excess of the total amount of the dividend over the taxable portion, namely, the part of the dividend includible in *gross income* after the *dividends-received deduction* has been applied. §1059(b). If the nontaxed portion exceeds the recipient's *basis* in the stock, the excess is treated as a *gain* from the *sale* or *exchange* of property if and when the owner sells or disposes of the stock. §1059(a)(2). See *extraordinary dividend, basis reduction.*

nontrade expenses not defined. The *Treasury Department* uses the term "nontrade or nonbusiness expenses" in the captions to *regulations* under §212 in relation to various *deductible expenses* of an *investment* nature or in relation to *tax determinations.* Reg. §1.212-1.

nontrusteed plan, qualified plans a term used to describe *qualified plans* for *employees,* the assets of which are not held in *trust* but rather are funded through such media as group *annuity* contracts, the purchase of certain *retirement bonds,* or bank *custodial accounts* that are considered as secure as a trust arrangement.

non-USRPHC certificate an affidavit of a *domestic corporation* issued to the transferee of an interest in the corporation, stating under penalty of perjury that the corporation is not and has not been a *United States real property holding corporation* during the five-year period ending on the date of the transfer. See §1445(b)(3). This prevents *FIRPTA withholding.*

non-USRPI statement a statement given to the buyer, certifying that the interest transferred is not a *United States real property interest.* Reg. §1.1445-2(c)(3). The transferor can avoid *FIRPTA withholding* on the acquisition of an interest in a *domestic corporation* (or a *foreign corporation* that made a *section 897(1) election*) whose *stock* is not publicly traded, or if the transferee receives a non-USRPI statement from the corporation. *Id.* See Reg. §1.897-2(h)(1)(v) for compliance and §1.1445-2(c)(3)(ii) for right to rely on the statement. See *FIRPTA withholding.*

no prosecution letter a communication from the Justice Department stating that it declines to prosecute a potential criminal tax case.

normal call premium generally, a *call premium* on a convertible obligation in an amount equal to a call premium, specified in dollars, on a nonconvertible obligation which is comparable to the convertible obligation (e.g., if a $1,000 twenty-year convertible bond has a call premium of $60, but a comparable nonconvertible bond has a call premium of $40, the normal call premium is $40). The Code limits *deductible* call premiums on repurchase to normal call premiums on nonconvertible debt, with the balance treated as a part of the corporation's capital structure. §249(a).

normal cost, qualified deferred compensation plan an alternate calculation used to determine the amount an *employer* can *deduct* for *contributions* to *pension plans.* In the case of *defined benefit plans,* the calculation determines the contribution that would be needed to keep the plan in force if it had existed since the beginning of service of all covered *employees,* and assuming

all prior costs had been paid, and that the various assumptions as to interest, mortality, and the like were correct.

normalization accounting, public utilities accounting methods under which tax liabilities that would have been incurred had the utility not claimed a *tax benefit* (e.g., *investment tax credit* or *accelerated cost recovery*) are added to *reserves* for future taxes, thereby causing higher utility rates. Absent such treatment, the lower utility rates would result in lower *taxable income* to the utility and lower federal tax revenues. In contrast, the *flow-through* method of ratemaking lowers rates by reflecting tax benefits in current customer charges. The normalization system is controversial because the *Code* grants certain *federal income tax* benefits on the condition that the utility use normalization accounting, thereby depriving ratepayers of the current tax benefits enjoyed by the utility. See *flow-through accounting; public utility property, accelerated cost recovery system.*

normal rehabilitation period the period reasonably expected to be required for the rehabilitation of the building, beginning when rehabilitation starts (or at the end of the first year of the election to claim *investment credits* ratably as the building is improved, if later) and ending when it is expected the building will be available to be *placed in service.* §47(d)(3). See *progress expenditure.*

normal retirement age for *vesting* purposes, the earlier of (1) the time that a plan specifies as normal retirement age, or (2) the latest of (a) the time a *participant* attains age 65 or (b) the fifth anniversary of the time a participant began *participation* in the plan. §411(a)(8) (formerly one also considered the tenth anniversary); ERISA §3(24)(B). Plans customarily provide for normal retirement at age 65 with a full pension benefit. Normal retirement age is a vital factor in determination of the commencement of *normal retirement benefits.* §411(a)(9). The date is important in determination of both costs and benefits for structuring retirement arrangements. The *Code* demands full *vesting* of normal retirement benefits at normal retirement age. See *vesting schedules.*

normal retirement benefit the periodic benefit that begins at early retirement, if available, or at *normal retirement age,* whichever is greater. §411(a)(9); Reg. §1.411(a)-7(c)(1). *Qualified plans* covered by *ERISA* must provide for nonforfeitable normal retirement benefits when the *participant* reaches *normal retirement age.* §411(a).

normal retirement date see *normal retirement age.*

North American area the *United States,* its *possessions,* the Trust Territory of the Pacific Islands, Canada, and Mexico. §274(h)(3)(A). It includes the United

States Virgin Islands, Guam, and American Samoa (Rev. Rul. 82-151, 1982-34 I.R.B. 5) as well as Puerto Rico (Rev. Rul. 78-23, 1978-1 C.B. 79). See §274(h) for limits on convention expense *deductions* under §§162 and 212 for conventions outside the North American Area. Other treaties include Bermuda, Grenada, Palau, Barbados, Manihall Islands, and Micronesia. The United States–Jamaica Tax Treaty, Article 25, includes Jamaica in the North American Area. Also, the Caribbean Basin Economic Recovery Act, Pub. L. No. 98-67, expanded this definition to include Caribbean and Central American countries if designated "beneficiary countries" by the President of the United States. Bermuda automatically qualified. See §274(h)(3)(B). See *foreign convention.*

no ruling area a subject on which *private letter rulings* and *determination letters* will not be issued, either because the area is inherently factual, hypothetical, expressed alternatively, or *tax-avoidance motivated,* or because the *IRS* perhaps feels disadvantaged by ruling on the subject, as well as in numerous detailed circumstances. These areas are periodically announced in *revenue procedures.*

not compensated for by insurance or otherwise a term limiting the extent to which a *loss* is *deductible.* §165(a). The meaning of the term is controversial in that there is a split in authority as to whether a *taxpayer's* waiver of an insurance claim for good business reasons nonetheless reduces the loss. The *regulations* take the view that as long as there is a reasonable prospect of a recovery, the claimed loss must be correspondingly reduced. Reg. §1.165-1(d)(2)(i). Filing an insurance claim is precondition to some *casualty loss* deductions under the *Code.* §165(a)(4)(i).

not-for-profit activities see *activity not engaged in for profit; hobby loss rules.*

notice and demand an *IRS* communication which insists on payment of an unpaid tax. Such communications are called for within 60 days after an *assessment* and a *deficiency's* determination in the *Tax Court,* and where installment payments of taxes are accelerated. §§6303, 6215, and 6152. Notice and demand is a condition to the enforcement of a federal *tax lien, distraint,* and in certain other cases.

notice of deficiency a communication (also called a *ninety-day letter*) issued by the *IRS* which notifies the *taxpayer* that a *deficiency* has been *assessed* and that the *assessment* will become final within 90 days from the date of the letter (Form 531 (DO)). Without such a notice, the IRS may not assess and *collect* the deficiency, absent: (1) a taxpayer's waiver; (2) a *jeopardy assessment;* or (3) the IRS's closing of the *taxable year.* Only during the 90-day period may taxpayers file a *petition* in the *Tax Court* (which permits adjudication

without prior payment of the assessment). After the 90-day period expires, the IRS will demand payment and enforce collection, and the taxpayer may only pay the tax and submit a *claim for refund or credit,* followed by a *refund suit* to recover the alleged overpayment in the federal courts if the IRS denies the claim. §§6211–6213. The notice is issued under circumstances in which the *statute of limitations* is about to run against the IRS, no settlement is reached at an *Appeals Conference,* or the issue cannot be resolved administratively. It may even be issued at the taxpayer's request. See *rescission, statutory notice of deficiency.*

notice of disallowance of claim for refund or credit an official rejection of a *taxpayer's claim for refund or credit.* The only statutory requirement is that the notice be sent by certified or registered mail, but it may be expected that the notice will identify the claim by month and year and will state that notice of disallowance is being sent as provided by law. §6532. Mailing of the notice begins the running of the two-year period, after which a *refund suit* may not be brought, unless the taxpayer files a waiver of statutory notice, in which case the two-year period begins on the date of the filing of the waiver. §6532(a)(1) and (3). The two-year period may be extended by agreement. §6532(a)(2). See *full payment rule, refund suit; suit for refund.*

notice of levy a notice mailed to delinquent *taxpayers* and used to attach property, such as bank accounts, held by third parties. I.R.S. News Release 83-57 (Mar. 31, 1983). The date and time the notice is delivered to the person to be served is the date and time the *levy* is made. A person with more than one office may designate one office to which notices of levy are to be sent, by writing to the *District Director.* Reg. §301.6631-1(c). Prelevy notice is mandatory, absent jeopardy to the government.

notice partner a *partner* in a *partnership* who is entitled to notice from the *IRS* of the start and completion of a TEFRA *audit* of the partnership. §6231(a)(8). It excludes less-than-one-percent partners in partnerships having more than 100 partners, unless they form a *five-percent notice group.* §§6223(b)(2) and 6231(a)(3). See *unified proceedings.*

notification test, private foundations a standard applicable in determination of the *deductibility of transfers* to *private foundations,* disallowing *deductions* unless (as to organizations organized after October 9, 1969) the foundation notifies the *IRS* of its application for recognition of tax-exempt status. §508(d)(2)(B).

notified payee underreporting an event that triggers *back-up withholding.* See Temp. Reg. §35a.3406-2. It occurs when the *IRS* finds underreporting of *interest* or *dividend* income and mails at least four notices over

120 days, and (as to filers) the IRS *assesses* a *deficiency* of tax attributable interests. This triggers notice to payors and brokers to begin withholding.

notional principal contracts sophisticated financial contracts such as interest rate swaps and interest cap or floor agreements. They are generally used to manage *interest* rate risks, which usually affects the overall cost of interest-bearing liabilities or the return on interest-bearing assets. See Notice 89-89, 1989-33 I.R.B. 18. *The regulations* on currency transactions define the term as a financial instrument that calls for the payments of amounts by one party to another at specified intervals measured by *interest* rates and notional principal amounts in exchange for specified consideration or a promise to pay similar amounts. Reg. §1.98-1T(a)(2)(iii)(B)(2).

O

OASDI an acronym for *Old-Age, Survivors, and Disability Insurance*. See *OSADI*.

OBRA an acronym for the Omnibus Budget Reconciliation Act of 1987.

OD an acronym for the early term Office Decision (i.e., an early *revenue ruling* of the *IRS*).

OID an acronym for *original issue discount*.

OID obligation any bond or other evidence of indebtedness having *original issue discount* as defined under §1273. §871(g)(1)(A). It excludes obligations payable within 183 days of the date of issuance and *tax-exempt bonds*. §871(g)(1)(B). OID obligations are generally subject to 30 percent *withholding of tax at source*, unless they produce *portfolio interest*. §§871(a)(1)(C) and 881(a)(3)(B). The 30 percent rate may be reduced by *tax treaties*.

OSADI an acronym for Old-Age, Survivors, and Disability Insurance, the major component of the *self-employment tax* and *FICA* taxes shared by *employers* and *employees*. See *self-employment tax*.

obligation generally, an indebtedness. Distinctions are drawn between *securities* and other *obligations* in corporate transactions. Other obligations (generally short-term notes) are treated as the equivalent of cash. See *security, corporate taxation*.

obligation, interest reporting for purposes of reporting interest payments, the term includes bonds, debentures, notes, certificates, and other evidences of indebtedness. §6049(d)(2).

obligation, original issue discount any bond, note, certificate, or other evidence of indebtedness issued by a corporation. Reg. §1.163-4(a)(1) (deductions). The term *debt instrument* has since replaced "obligation." See *debt instrument*.

obligation, tax-exempt bonds and securities defined as including certificates issued by a political subdivision for public improvements which evidence special assessments against specific property, which become liens, which the issuer must enforce. Reg. §1.103-1(b). Thus, there need not be the backing of the issuer's full faith and credit, and indeed, the debt may be privately insured. Rev. Rul. 72-134, 1972-1 C.B. 29. Because current law §103(c)(1) uses the term "obligation" in connection with defining the key term *state or local bond,* this definition seems to remain important.

obligation well doctrine a judicial and administrative doctrine to the effect that a *taxpayer lessee* who is required to drill wells as a condition of obtaining a capital interest in the wells must *capitalize* the otherwise *deductible intangible drilling and development costs (IDCs)* attributable to such wells. See Reg. §1.612-4(a), which allows IDCs only as to operating rights in which the taxpayer acquires an interest. See *operating mineral interest*.

obsolescence the process that renders an asset economically useless to the *taxpayer* regardless of its physical condition, thereby diminishing its *useful life* to the taxpayer. Obsolescence may be attributed to technological improvements and reasonably foreseeable economic changes. The process of normal obsolescence is one basis for claiming *depreciation* or *cost recovery expenses* for tax purposes. Reg. §1.167(a)-7, -8 and -9 (*depreciable property*); see also Reg. §1.165-1(b). In addition, deductions for *extraordinary obsolescence* may be claimed on an adequate showing of some objective external cause (e.g., an armistice that renders a munitions plant of diminished utility).

obsoleted an *IRS* term used to describe a *revenue ruling* or *revenue procedure* that the government does not consider determinative of future transactions, sometimes because it has been included in later *regulations*.

occupancy test, residence sold by persons age fifty-five or over a condition imposed on the *taxpayer* to *exclude* from *gross income* the *gain* from the *sale* or *exchange* of property if the taxpayer has attained age 55 before the date of the sale or exchange. The gist of the requirement is that during the five-year period ending on the date of the sale or exchange, the property must have been owned and used by the taxpayer as his or her *principal residence* for periods aggregating three years or more (the occupancy test). The property does not need to be the taxpayer's principal residence at the time of sale. Reg. §1.121-l(b), example 1. The amount of the gain excluded from gross income may not exceed $125,000. §121.

ocean thermal equipment, energy investment credit equipment placed in service at either of two locations to be designated by the *IRS,* which converts ocean thermal energy to usable energy. §48(l)(3)(A)(ix). Ocean thermal equipment qualifies as *section 38* property under §48(a)(2)(B)(xi) even though used outside the United States. Such equipment includes turbines, generators, and related equipment. Qualified ocean thermal equipment is *alternative energy property* and can qualify for the *energy investment credit*. §48(l)(3).

offer in compromise an offer by a *taxpayer* submitted on Form 656 under the authority of §7122, under which the taxpayer proposes to pay less than the delinquent account, on the theory that the account is either not collectible in full or because the alleged liability for taxes is defective. See Reg. §302.7122-1(a). The compromise may be acceptable only if the taxpayer enters into *collateral agreements* with the *IRS*. In 1992, the IRS issued new guidelines (IRM 57(10)) to encourage the making of offers. The guidelines state that the objectives of compromise are as follows: (1) to resolve accounts receivable that cannot be collected in full; (2) to effect collection of what can reasonably be collected; (3) to give the taxpayer a fresh start to voluntarily enable him or her to comply with the new law; and (4) to collect any funds that may not be collectible through any other means. See *installment payment arrangement.*

offer of waiver of restrictions on assessments and collections an offer that is submitted by *taxpayers* using Form 870-AD to settle a *nondocketed case* and that is filed in the *Appeals Office* of the *IRS*. The offer must be accepted by the IRS in order to be effective, but once accepted it signals practical termination of the dispute on the IRS's part. See Statement of [IRS] Procedural Rules §601.106(d)(3)(i). The authority for the procedure flows from §7122. Compare with the *waiver of restrictions on assessment and collection* (Form 870), which is used at the *District Office* level as a traditional element of the settlement of a tax dispute.

office audit an *audit* of a *taxpayer's* return(s) by correspondence or interview at the offices of the *IRS*. See *correspondence audit; interview audits.*

office auditor an auditor with the *IRS* whose job it is to examine *individual tax returns.* Such an examination may be conducted by correspondence with the *taxpayer* or at the local IRS Office. §601.105(b)(2). Office auditors may examine the return from the year being examined, not returns of subsequent or prior years. The latter are generally conducted by more experienced auditors. Office auditors generally examine medium-income, nonbusiness returns or smaller *sole proprietorship* returns as well as *estate* and *gift tax returns.*

Office of Chief Counsel a formal description of the legal bureaucracy run by the *Chief Counsel* of the *IRS*. It is a unit of the *Treasury Department*. See *Chief Counsel, IRS.*

Office of International Operations the predecessor of the *Foreign Operations Internal Revenue District.*

Office of Regional Director of Appeals see *Appeals Office.*

Office of Regional Inspector the office of the *IRS* responsible for verifying financial transactions, analyzing operating practices, and conducting the Internal Security Program. There are seven Regional Inspectors, one in each Regional Office. Reg. §1115, [IRS] Statement of Organization and Functions.

Office of Tax Analysis a *Treasury Department* office responsible for revenue estimates and economic studies on current legislation, as well as fundamental questions of tax policy.

Office of Tax Legislative Counsel see *Tax Legislative Counsel.*

office or other fixed place of business within the United States generally, an office or other fixed facility, including such places, sites, and structures as factories, stores, workshops, or mines, through which *foreign persons* engage in *trade or business* in the *United States*. Reg. §7.864-7(a) and (b). The presence of such a place can convert certain foreign source income (*rents, royalties, gains* from intangibles, *interest dividends* on *stock* or securities gains, and income from the sale of *inventory*) earned by a *foreign person* into constructive *effectively connected income* from the conduct of a United States trade or business. §864(c)(4).

officer, qualified plans an *individual* who, on the basis of all *facts and circumstances,* is an administrative executive in regular and continuous service by virtue of his or her authority, duties, term of election, or appointment. Rev. Rul. 80-314, 1980-2 C.B. 152; Rev. Rul. 68-300, 1968-1 C.B. 159. The usual question is whether the person is one who in his or her regular and continuous duties has a voice in the management or administration of the *corporation.* Discrimination in contributions or benefits in favor of such persons can disqualify an otherwise *qualified pension, profit-sharing,* or *stock bonus plan.* §§401(a)(4) and 410(b)(1)(B).

off-return information, Privacy Act information not shown on a *taxpayer's tax return* but protected under the Privacy Act component of *return information.* See *return information.*

offset defined benefit plan a *defined benefit plan* that is structured so that Social Security benefits offset benefits provided under the plan. See §401(1)(4)(D). See *integration, Social Security; permitted disparity.*

offset plan, Social Security integration a plan containing a *defined benefit* below which no *participant* or compensation is excluded because of minimum compensation, but with a provision that offsets the benefit by a fraction of the participant's Social Security old-age retirement benefit. See Rev. Rul. 71-446, 1971-2 C.B. 188, and §401(l)(3)(B) (offset limit for post-1988 years). See *integration, Social Security; permitted disparity.*

offsets see *set-offs.*

offsetting allocation a type of *allocation* of *partner's distributive share* which fails the requirement that allocations be "substantial." This occurs if there is a strong likelihood that, as of the date the allocation is agreed on, the pretax detriment any particular partner may incur as a result of the allocation will be offset by the tax consequences of the allocation. Reg. §1.704-1(b)(iii)(a). See *substantial economic effect test*.

offsetting position, stock various interests in corporate *stock* which, because of their risk-neutralizing features as a result of being part of a *straddle,* are subjected to the special tax rules applicable to straddles. Such stock includes any stock which is part of a straddle, at least one of the offsetting positions of which is (1) an option with respect to that stock or substantially identical stock or securities, or (2) a position with respect to *substantially similar or related property* other than stock. §1092(d)(3)(B)(i). It also includes stock of a corporation *formed or availed of* to take positions in *personal property* which offset positions taken by any shareholder. §1092(d)(3)(b)(ii). See *substantially similar or related property, offsetting position, straddles, straddles in stocks.*

offsetting position, straddles a circumstance that arises if there is a substantial diminution of the *taxpayer's* risk of *loss* from holding any *position* with respect to *personal property* by reason of his or her holding one or more other positions with respect to personal property. §1092. A mere diversification of positions usually would not substantially diminish risk, but positions in personal property may be treated as offsetting whether or not the property is the same kind. §1092(c)(3)(A). *Identified straddles* are subject to separate treatment. The presence of an offsetting position is one element in the definition of a *straddle.* See *straddle, unregulated futures contracts.*

offshore trust a synonym for *foreign trust.*

oil and gas extraction taxes any *income,* war profits, and *excess profits* tax *paid or accrued* (or deemed to have been paid under §§902 and 960) during the *taxable year* with respect to *foreign oil and gas extraction income* or loss (ignoring a special loss-denial rule) that would be taken into account for purposes of the general *foreign tax credit* provisions. §907(c)(5). Such taxes are subject to special limits in determination of the foreign tax credits they generate. §§904 and 907(a).

oil import fee a fee (tariff) on foreign oil. The concept is that such a fee, which would reduce United States demand, would save the domestic oil and gas industry by stabilizing demand while weakening OPEC's grasp.

oil or gas substance, energy investment credit oil or gas and any primary product of oil or gas. Reg. §1.48-9(c)(2)(ii). An oil or gas substance is not an *alternate substance* for purposes of the *energy investment credit.* §48(1)(3)(B); Reg. §1.48-9(c)(2)(i).

oil payment an *oil production payment* that depends on the extraction of oil from the ground.

Oil Spill Liability Trust Fund tax an *excise tax* imposed on domestic crude oil and imported petroleum products to fund the Oil Spill Liability Trust Fund. The tax is to be paid by an operator of a United States refinery when oil is received at the refinery or by an importer of petroleum products when petroleum products enter the *United States.* The tax is imposed at the financing or oil spill rate of 5 cents a *barrel.* §4611(c)(2)(B). The tax is subject to complex limits. §4611(c)(2)(B)(3).

old-age exemption an additional exemption was permitted if the taxpayer was age 65 or over. Former §151(d); Reg. §1.151. It has been replaced by an *additional standard deduction.* See *age sixty-five.*

omission from income a *taxpayer's* failure to properly include and report an amount of *gross income.* See §6013 and Reg. §1.6013-5 (*innocent spouse rule*); §6501 (limitations on *assessment* and *collection*; six-year assessment period in case of 25 percent omission of gross income); §§1312–1317, and §1.1312-7 (*basis* of property after erroneous treatment of a prior transaction).

one-examination rule a shorthand term for the rather meek rule that a *taxpayer's* books of account may be inspected only once for each *taxable year,* unless the taxpayer requests otherwise, or unless the *IRS,* after investigation, notifies the taxpayer in writing that an additional inspection is necessary. This restriction pretends to prohibit unnecessary examinations or investigations of a taxpayer. §7605(b). See *closed year; second examination.*

one-family corporation see *family corporation.*

one hundred percent penalty See *penalty, failure to collect and pay overtax, or attempt to evade or defeat tax.*

one hundred twenty-five thousand dollar exclusion, gain on sale of residence a reference to the provisions of §121, the gist of which is that *individuals* who are 55 years of age or older may irrevocably elect to exclude from *gross income* the first $125,000 of *gain recognized* on the *sale* of their homes provided the home was a *principal residence* for at least three of the preceding five years. At least one spousal owner must be 55 years old on the date of sale and must meet certain ownership and use tests in order to qualify. §121(d). See *husband and wife, exclusion of gain on sale of residence.*

one-in-twenty test a test under which a *person* is an *employer* for *FUTA* purposes if at least one *individual* in covered employment is employed for some part of each of 20 days in the current or prior *calendar year,* each day being in a different calendar week. §3306(a)(1)(B).

one-man corporation   a *corporation* owned by one *individual*. Although the *regulations* generally demand several participants (*associates*) to find any business organization (other than a *sole proprietorship*), the regulations also parenthetically acknowledge the possibility of the one-man corporation. Reg. §301.7701-2(a)(1) and (2).

one-month liquidation   see *section 333 liquidation*.

one-year break in service   the failure of a *participant* in a *qualified retirement plan* to complete more than 500 *hours of service* during the *calendar year, plan year,* or other 12-month period designated by the plan. §411(a)(6)(A); Labor Dept. Reg. §2530.200b-4(a). Such breaks in service can result in loss of credits or suspension of *participation*. See §410(a)(5)(D). See *participation, qualified retirement plans*.

one-year lookback rule, qualified plans   a provision that may be inserted in *qualified plans* to the effect that an *employee* with a *one-year break in service* may be required to perform a year of service based on the eligibility computation period before being readmitted to the plan; once the employee is readmitted, all pre- and post-break service must generally be combined for benefit purposes, with readmission retroactive to the reemployment date. §411(a)(5) and (6).

one-year rule, temporary work away from home   a reference to the general view of the *IRS* that work-related absences of a year or more are not temporary and that *travel* and *temporary living expenses* are, therefore, not *deductible*. See Rev. Rul. 60-189, 1960-1 C.B. 60. The IRS considers two years a possibility also if certain further criteria are satisfied. See Rev. Rul. 83-82, 1983-22 I.R.B. 5.

one-year's interest rule, convertible bonds   see *normal call premium*.

on-premise athletic facility   an athletic facility located on the *employer's* premises (although it need not be its business premises; it may not be a facility for residential use), substantially all use of which must be limited to current, retired, or disabled *employees,* their *spouses,* and *dependent children*. The value of the use of such facilities can be a tax-free *fringe benefit*. §132(h)(5).

open-ended waiver   a waiver of the period during which the *IRS* can *assess* a *deficiency,* with no time limit. See §6501(c)(4). See *waiver of statute of limitations*.

open-end multiple asset accounts   accounts used to group similar or related assets in connection with *multiple asset account depreciation* not under the *class life asset depreciation range system (ADR)*. This grouping minimizes bookkeeping, since similar or related assets are thereby depreciated as a unit. Reg. §1.167(a)-7. The ADR system is far more restrictive, requiring among other things that only assets of the same *guideline class* be placed in a particular account. See *continuing multiple asset accounts*.

open-end mutual fund   a mutual fund (*registered investment company* for tax purposes) that has the feature of continuously allowing its *shareholders* to demand *redemption* of their *stocks* at their then-prevailing *fair market values,* in contrast to shares in closed-end funds, which can only be sold to other members of the public. Such funds are the most common type of registered investment company.

open-end selling price, installment sales   an *installment sale* without a fixed or limited selling price.

open transactions   *sales* or other *dispositions* in which the *cash* or *accrual method taxpayer's amount realized* is so uncertain that the only just result is to delay reporting *gains* or *losses* until the taxpayer has enjoyed a *recovery of capital*. The government position is that such transactions are extremely rare.

open year   a *taxable year* as to which the *statute of limitations* remains open. The statute varies by subject, so a year may be open for one purpose and closed for another.

operating agreement   a contractual arrangement for the joint production, extraction, or use of a natural resource property, the participants in which can elect to be excluded from taxation under the *federal income tax* laws relating to *partnerships*. §761(a). For the participants to qualify, Reg. §1.761-2(a)(3) requires that they (1) be co-owners or co-lessors of the property and have exclusive operating rights over the property; (2) reserve the right to separately take in-kind or dispose of their shares of any property produced, extracted, or used; and (3) not jointly sell services or the property produced or extracted. These rules do not apply to persons whose principal purpose is selling, manufacturing, or processing for nonmembers. It is also common in the oil and gas industry for co-owners or parties to a *unitization* or *pooling* agreement to test and develop property. Usually, one party is made an active *operator*. See *section 761 election*.

operating agreement partnership   see *operating agreement*.

operating corporation   a *corporation,* over 50 percent of the assets of which were used in the active conduct of a *trade or business* when the relevant securities were bought or before the close of the replacement period. It includes a broad range of financial institutions. §1042(c)(4)(B). Such corporations can be the issuers of *qualified replacement property* which can be used to roll over and defer *gains* on *sales* of *employer securities* to *ESOPs* and *EWOCs*. See *qualified replacement property*.

operating cycle formula see *Bardahl formula.*

operating day method, depreciation a *depreciation* method used if the major factor in depreciation of equipment, such as rotary oil-drilling rigs, is wear and tear arising from use, and obsolescence is not a material factor in causing its retirement. Rev. Rul. 56-562, 1956-2 C.B. 125. Depreciation in these cases may be computed by estimating the *useful life* of the equipment in terms of the total number of days it can be operated and the depreciable *basis* is prorated on the actual number of days used. A reasonable *salvage value* must be established, as well as an estimated total operating day life, both of which may be revised based on actual experience. The taxpayer must also establish that the method results in a reasonable annual allowance for depreciation. Prior to electing a change from some other method of depreciation to this method, *taxpayers* must apply for permission for a *change of accounting method.* See §167(e); Reg. §1.167(e)-1(a). Section 168(f)(1)(B) should permit the use of this method as to *ACRS* property.

operating expenses, Bardahl formula *cost of goods* sold plus other expenses incurred in production, excluding *depreciation.* This figure is multiplied by a derived percentage to obtain necessary *working capital* under the *Bardahl formula,* for purposes of the *accumulated earnings tax.* Profit-sharing contributions and *charitable contributions* are not operating expenses when the Bardahl formula is used. However, costs may be adjusted for inflation. *Id.* In addition, estimated taxes are also included.

operating foundation an *exempt organization* that makes direct *qualifying distributions,* excluding contributions to other exempt organizations, of substantially all its income (at least 85 percent of the lesser of *adjusted net income* or its *minimum investment return*) directly for its *charitable purposes* and that, in addition, satisfies the *assets test,* the *endowment test,* or the *support test* set forth in Reg. §53.4942(b)-1 and -2. §4942(j)(3). Private operating foundations are exempt from the *undistributed income* requirements of §4942(a)(1). Contributions to such organizations qualify for the 50 percent *charitable contributions* ceiling. §170(b)(1)(A)(vii).

operating interest see *operating mineral interest.*

operating lease, sale, and leaseback a colloquial term for a *sale* followed by a true *lease,* perceived as such by the parties, as compared to a *sale* followed by a *lease* with the earmarks of a financing arrangement (e.g., a *mortgage*). The concept is reflected in §46(e)(3), which denies the *investment tax credit* to noncorporate lessors if the lease is for one-half or more of the *useful life* of the asset, or if *trade or business deductions* are not at least 15 percent of the first 12 months' rents.

operating loss deduction a *deduction* for current *net operating losses* (NOLs), or a deduction for NOL *carryovers* or *carrybacks.*

operating mineral interest basically, the interest in a mineral, oil, or gas property held by the *persons* financially responsible for its operation. Typically, it is the mineral interest minus the royalty interest. Such interests can be created by *lease* (e.g., where the owner of real estate leases the property in exchange for a royalty) or by a grant in which the seller transfers the fee interest but retains a royalty interest. For tax purposes, the term is defined as an interest in respect of which the costs of production of the mineral are required to be taken into account by the *taxpayer* for purposes of computing the 100-percent-of-taxable-income limitation on *percentage depletion* provided for in §613. The term is synonymous with *operating interest* and *working interest.*

operating on a cooperative basis a mandatory feature of a *cooperative,* whether "exempt" under §521 or nonexempt, hence, subject to the rules of *subchapter T* alone. The term is nowhere precisely defined, but the basic notion is that the enterprise must turn its profits, if any, over to its owner-*patrons.*

operating under the lodge system carrying out activities on the basis of an organizational structure that consists of largely self-governing local branches chartered by a parent organization which are called lodges, chapters, and the like (e.g., the Moose). See Reg. §1.501(c)(8)-1(a). Generally, §501(c)(8) provides an exemption for various organizations that operate under the lodge system, and provides their members life, sick, accident, and other benefits. See *fraternal benefit societies.*

operating unit, aggregation of oil, gas, geothermal, or mineral interests in general, an aggregation of mineral, oil, gas, or geothermal interests that results in the treatment of several natural resource *properties* as one. Interests that are geographically widespread may not be considered parts of the same operating unit merely because one set of accounting records is maintained by the *taxpayer,* or merely because the products of such interest are processed at the same treatment plant. See Reg. §1.614-2(b)(c). Since aggregations can result in the creation of a single depletable property, a major tax-saving potential arises. See *property, depletion.*

operational test, exempt organizations a standard required of *§501(c)(3) organizations* (exempt charities, etc.) to the extent that they can be operated exclusively for *exempt purposes.* The gist of the test is that if more than an insubstantial part of the organization's activities are not in furtherance of an exempt purpose, then the exemption is lost. Reg. §1.501(c)(3)-1(c)(1). Examples of violating the test include undertaking major lobbying activities (Reg. §1.501(c)(3)-1(c)(2)) and conducting winter cruises for church members and ministers that involve substantial recreational and social time (Rev. Rul. 77-366, 1977-2 C.B. 192), but not mere weekend retreats for religious purposes with modest recreational interludes (Rev. Rul. 77-430, 1977-2 C.B. 194).

operations, international boycotts all forms of *business* or commercial activity, whether or not income-producing, including, but not limited to sales, purchases, banking, financing, extracting, processing, manufacturing, production, construction, transportation, and ancillary activities such as contract negotiating, advertising, and site selection. Performance of services is an operation, but an *individual* performing personal services as an *employee* does not have an operation. Treas. Dept. News Rel. B-653 (Jan. 20, 1978).

operator, intangible drilling and development costs and depletion a *person* who owns a *working* or *operating interest* in a tract or parcel of land, as an owner or under a *lease* or other contract, that grants working or operating rights. Reg. §1.612-4(a). Such operators who *undertake* drilling are entitled to claim *deductions* for *intangible drilling and development costs* and *depletion* deductions to the extent of their fractional interests. Reg. §1.611-1(b).

opinion letters writings issued by the *National Office* of the IRS regarding the acceptability under §§401 and 501 of *prototype* or *master plans* and related *custodial accounts*. Statement of [IRS] Procedural Rules, §601.201(a)(4).

opting out a reference to provisions found in *qualified retirement plans* permitting *employees* to opt out of the plan. Extensive opting out may create *coverage* problems, and if only highly paid *individuals* are allowed to opt out and their compensation is correspondingly increased, then the plan may be deemed a *cash or deferred plan*; and if only low-paid employees opt out, the plan may be discriminatory against them. Rev. Rul. 80-351, 1980-2 C.B. 152; Rev. Rul. 73-340, 1973-2 C.B. 134.

option generally, a contractual right to buy or sell a predetermined property at a fixed price in the future. §1234 (taxation of option holders and *grantors*).

option attribution rules under section 382 Section 382 limits net operating loss carryovers where there is an ownership change with respect to the loss corporation. An ownership change occurs with respect to a loss corporation if (1) the percentage of the stock of the loss corporation owned by *five-percent shareholders* has increased by more than 50 percentage points over the lowest percentage of stock owned by these shareholders at any time during the testing year. For this purpose, an option is treated as exercised if its deemed exercise would result in an ownership change. Under proposed regulations, an option would *not* be treated as exercised

unless it was issued for an *"abusive principal purpose."* An abusive principal purpose is manipulation of the timing of an owner shift to avoid or ease the impact of an ownership change. Prop. Reg. §1.382-4(d). See *direct five-percent shareholder.*

optional adjustment to basis see *optional basis election.*

optional basis election a *partnership* election whereby the *basis* of partnership assets are either increased or decreased due to a transfer of a partnership interest (the *section 734 adjustment*) or a *distribution* of partnership property (the *section 743 adjustment*). See §754 and Reg. §1.754-1 and the *regulations* under §755 for procedures. See *section 734 adjustment; section 743 adjustment.*

optional gross income method a method for apportioning *interest expenses* to sources within and without the *United States* on the basis of the ratio of foreign source gross income to total *gross income.* Reg. §1.861-8(e)(2)(vi).

optional mileage deduction see *mileage allowance* (synonym).

option privilege the right to benefit from increases in value of *stock* subject to an *option* without risking one's own capital. Reg. §1.421-1(a). The *IRS* asserts that a *nonstatutory stock option* that is not traded cannot have a readily ascertainable value unless the option privilege itself has a readily ascertainable value.

options dealer someone registered with a securities exchange as a market maker or specialist in *listed options* or *person* whom the *IRS* determines to be comparable. §1256(g)(8). The term is a component of the concept of a *dealer equity option.*

option stock generally, *stock* acquired through the exercise of an *option.*

ordinary commonplace or non*capital.* Current *trade or business deductions* under §162(a) and income-producing expenses under §212 are limited to those that are ordinary. The principal meaning of the term is that the expenses not be *capital expenditures* but rather be true current costs. A less common tax meaning of ordinary is more literal, namely, that the expenditure not be extraordinary.

ordinary and necessary expense an *expense* that is both *ordinary* (i.e., *current*) and *necessary* (i.e., appropriate and helpful). If the expense is *incurred* in a *trade or business* or is proximately related to an investment and does not violate some particular rule (e.g., §162(f) denying *deductions* for *fines or penalties*), it will generally be *deductible* and, thus, will affect current income (or perhaps create a *net operating loss*). §§162 and 212. Note that ordinary is occasionally applied in the sense of meaning not extraordinary. See *incurred in a trade or business; ordinary; proximate relationship standard.*

ordinary course of his trade or business an element of the definition of so-called *dealer property*. The phrase focuses on whether *property* was *disposed* of in connection with the *taxpayer's* regular *trade or business* or in an exceptional transaction. §1221(1). This element of the definition of dealer property does not seem to have attracted much attention. The term also appears in §1231(b)(1), where it has been read broadly to include rented property also available for sale. See *held for sale; section 1231 assets.*

ordinary expense generally, an expense that need not be *capitalized.* See *ordinary and necessary expense.*

ordinary gain and loss *gains* and *losses* that are not classified as arising from *sales* or *exchanges* of *capital assets.* The *ordinary income* result may occur because (1) there was no sale or exchange (e.g., an abandonment); (2) the property was not a capital asset (e.g., lots held by a real estate dealer); (3) the thing sold or exchanged was not *property*; (4) it represents the acceleration of a right to receive *ordinary income* (e.g., a mineral lease carve-out); or (5) a transaction otherwise properly treated as resulting in a capital gain or loss is so intertwined with a prior ordinary transaction that it is recharacterized so as to result in an ordinary gain or loss (e.g., *capital gain* on *liquidation* of a *corporation,* followed by later repayment of some proceeds in a later year; repayment of proceeds treated as a *capital loss*). Finally, some statutory provisions may alter the character of a transaction to or from ordinary gain or loss status (e.g., §165(g), which treats *worthless securities losses* as generally capital in nature, and §1231, which treats overall losses on certain business property as ordinary). See *substitute for ordinary income.*

ordinary gross income generally, *current ordinary income* of a *corporation.* More specifically, *gross income* as defined under §61 less (1) *gains* from the *sale or other disposition* of *capital assets*; (2) *section 1231 gains*; and (3) in the case of a *foreign corporation* wholly owned by *nonresident aliens* during the last half of the *taxable year,* all *personal holding company income* except income from *personal service contracts.* §543(b)(1). *Capital losses* and losses from the sale of *section 1231 assets* are not taken into account in determining ordinary gross income. The amount of gain from *section 1231 assets* that is treated as ordinary income by virtue of *recapture* provisions (e.g., §§1245 and 1250) is included in the computation of ordinary gross income. Ordinary gross income is used in connection with the *personal holding company tax,* serving as a preliminary figure in the calculation of *adjusted ordinary gross income* which, in turn, is essential in the 60 percent tainted income test of §542(a)(1) in the determination of the *personal holding company* status of a cor-

poration. The concept is also important in the decision whether certain income items constitute *personal holding company income.* See, for example, the "10 percent of ordinary gross income" *de minimis* standards under §543(a)(2)(B) and (a)(4)(B) in the declassification of *rents* and *copyright royalties* from personal holding company income status.

ordinary income *gain* from the *sale* or *exchange* of property that is neither a *capital asset* nor a *section 1231 asset.* In addition, income other than from actual or *constructive* sales or exchanges (e.g., *rents* or *wages*) is also commonly referred to as ordinary income. See §64.

ordinary income portion, lump-sum distribution see *lump-sum distributions, qualified plans.*

ordinary income property *property* which would produce *ordinary income* if *sold.* The concept appears in various locations in the *Code.*

ordinary income property, charitable contributions a nontechnical term used to describe property that would not have resulted in a *long-term capital gain* if sold by the *taxpayer* for its *fair market value* when contributed (e.g., *inventory,* self-produced artworks, memoranda, letters, *capital assets* held not longer than one year, and *section 306 stock*). §170(e)(1)(A). Only the *adjusted basis* of such property is *deductible* as a *charitable contribution.*

ordinary loss a *loss* resulting from the *sale* or *exchange* of property that is neither a *capital asset* nor a *section 1231 asset,* in addition to losses from *dispositions* that are not actual or *constructive* sales or exchanges. See §65. Ordinary losses are generally entirely *deductible,* unlike *capital losses.* See also §165.

ordinary retirement, ADR depreciation the retirement of property from a *class life asset depreciation range vintage account* that is not an *extraordinary retirement.* *Gains* and *losses* are generally not recognized in such cases, and proceeds are ordinarily added to the *depreciation reserve* for the *vintage account.* Reg. §1.167(a)-11(d)(3). See *extraordinary retirement, ADR depreciation.*

ordinary trust a *trust* designed to hold property for its *beneficiaries* under typical rules of probate and chancery courts. The term is commonly used to distinguish trusts engaged in business activities and therefore treated as *associations taxable as corporations.* See *business trust.*

organizational expenditures, corporate *expenditures incurred* before the end of the first *taxable year* incident to the creation of the *corporation,* chargeable to a *capital account,* and of a character that, if expended incident to the creation of a corporation having a limited life, could be *amortized* over its life. Examples include state filing fees and attorneys' fees for preparing documents such as the charter and by-laws, temporary directors' fees, costs of early organizational meetings, and the cost of designing an accounting system. These costs are generally *capitalized*, but a corporate *taxpayer* may elect to defer these expenses and *deduct* them over a period of at least 60 months after the corporation *begins business*. §248(a) and (b). The cost of raising equity capital (*capital structure expenditures*), however, is not *amortizable* or currently *deductible*. Reg. §1.248-1(b)(3)(i). Reorganization expenses can qualify if they directly result in the creation of a new corporation. Reg. §1.248-1(b)(4). See *capital structure expenditures.*

organizational expenses, partnerships   expenses of organizing *partnerships*. Under general tax principles, such expenditures should be *capitalized* but not *amortized* for lack of an ascertainable *useful life*. Section 709(b) permits *taxpayers* to elect to amortize such expenditures for *federal income tax* purposes over not less than 60 months. Such expenses are defined as expenditures incident to the formation of a partnership and chargeable to capital account which would be amortizable if the *entity* had an ascertainable life. Examples include state filing fees for recording the entity's existence and attorneys' fees for preparing the partnership agreement, but not the costs of selling interests in the entity (*syndication fees*). See Reg. §1.709-2(a)(4).

organizational test, exempt organizations   a condition to being granted *exempt organization* status under §501(c)(3), the gist of which is that the *entity's* articles of organization must limit its purposes to one or several *exempt purposes* and must have no explicit authority to engage in *business,* propagandizing, lobbying, political, or other activities that are not in furtherance of its exempt purpose, except as an insubstantial part of its activity. Reg. §1.501(c)(3)-1(b)(1). The standard applies both to the operating life of the organization and to the use of its assets on dissolution. That is, on dissolution, the assets must pass to another charity, a government unit, or the like. Reg. §1.501(c)(3)-1(b)(4).

organization expenses   see *organizational expenditures, corporate.*

organization, trade or business   a term found in §482, a provision that empowers the *IRS* to restructure transactions between commonly controlled *taxpayers* so as to place suspect transactions on *arm's length* footings. The term "organization, trade or business" is broadly defined in Reg. §1.482-1(a)(1) and (2) to encompass virtually any *foreign* or *domestic entity* or taxpayer (including a *sole proprietor*), and virtually any *trade or business*. See *reallocation of income and deductions by Commissioner.*

original basis   a term sometimes in reference to the *basis of property* in the hands of the *taxpayer* when first acquired by the taxpayer.

original issue discount   generally, the shortfall between the *issue price* of a *debt instrument* and its *stated redemption price at maturity*. §§1272(a)(1) and 1273(a)(1). In the case of a public cash offering, the issue price is the initial offering price to the public at which a substantial amount of the obligations are sold. §1273(b)(1). In the case of a private placement for cash, the issue price is the price paid by the first buyer of one of the obligations. §1272(b)(2). The stated redemption price of an obligation at maturity generally means the amount payable at maturity. §1273(a)(2). Holders must generally report as income the ratable *daily portion* of the original issue discount multiplied by the number of days that the *taxpayer* held the obligation. §1272(a)(1). Consistently, the issuer *amortizes (deducts)* the discount, on a level amortization basis. Reg. §1.163-4. See *adjusted issue price; stated redemption price at maturity, original issue discount.*

original issue discount obligation   a bond or other evidence of indebtedness having *original issue discount,* but not short-term (183 days or less) obligations or *tax-exempt* obligations. §871(g)(1). *Foreign persons* who engage in a *sale* or *exchange* or who retire such obligations at a *gain* are subject to tax on the gain (less *OID* taxed to them while they held the obligation), as well as tax on certain *interest* payments. See §§871(a)(1)(C), 881(a)(93), and 881(c).

original issue discount rules   a far-reaching body of *tax accounting* provisions found in §§1272–1288, the core concepts of which are (1) to tax holders of financial obligations issued at a discount (i.e., bearing inadequate *interest*) to accrue such interest ratably; (2) to apply a similar model for deferred payment sales of high-priced properties; (3) to tax discount on certain *short-term obligations*; and (4) to eliminate the tax benefits of *coupon stripping*. The *imputed interest* rules of §483 (relating to sales for deferred payments) can apply where the original issue discount rules do not. See *original issue discount.*

original issue premium   the excess (e.g. $3) of the actual issue price of a security (e.g., $103) over its face amount (e.g., $100). The term is the converse of the term *original issue discount* and is computed by reference to §1272-3 with the borrower ratably reporting income over the life of the debt. Reg. §1.61-12(a)(4). See *amortizable bond premium of the taxable year.*

original proceeds   net amounts, after payment of all expenses of issuing the obligations, received by a state or local governmental unit as a result of the sale of an issue. Illustrative expenses include advertising and printing costs, financial advisors' and counsel fees, initial fees of trustees, disbursement agents' costs, and costs for certification or authentication of agents. Prior Reg. §1.103-13(b)(2)(i). The term was used in connection with *arbitrage bonds.*

original purchaser, original issue discount   the first purchaser of an obligation, other than an underwriter or dealer, who purchases an obligation for resale. Reg. §1.1232-3(b)(4). The issuer and the original purchaser can connive to have an obligation called before maturity, thereby reducing the *capital gains* when the debt is *sold* or *exchanged*. §1271(a)(2)(A).

original use, depreciation   the first use to which property is put, regardless by whom. Regs. §§1.167(a)-11(c)(3)(v), 1.167(c)-1. Demonstration models may be considered first used by the buyer. Rev. Rul. 78-433, 1978-2 C.B. 121. A change of use does not result in an original use. Reg. §1.167(c)(2). Original use beginning with the *taxpayer* generally results in more generous *depreciation deductions* for property depreciated under §167, but it is not relevant for the *accelerated cost recovery system* of §168.

origin of the claim test   a retrospective standard used to determine the income tax treatment of attorneys' fees and other costs of litigation. The notion is that if the origin and nature of the litigation is personal (e.g., arises out of a divorce, even though it involves a husband's defense of his business property from an aggrieved wife), then its *deduction* will be disallowed as a *personal expense*. §262. Likewise, an admittedly *gain*-seeking legal expenditure (e.g., enforcement of a business contract) may have to be *capitalized* (§§263, 1016) if the legal action ultimately concerns a *capital expenditure* (e.g., an inventor's sale of a *patent,* even though the promise to transfer the patent arose in an employment context). The test is often criticized because of the practical difficulty of determining ultimate first causes. Multiple origins are possible.

orphan drug credit   a *credit* equal to 50 percent of *qualified clinical testing expenses* for the *taxable year*. §28(a). The credit is designed to stimulate research in human clinical testing of drugs to cure *rare diseases or conditions*. §28. The credit expired on June 30, 1992.

other amounts properly paid or credited or required to be distributed, estate or trust   for purposes of §661(a), which allowed *fiduciaries* of *estates* or *complex trusts* to report a *deduction* of these amounts, the term refers to noncurrent *distributions* that are actually made or unqualifiedly subject to the *beneficiary's* demand, aside from income that is required to be distributed currently. Amounts are proper if called for by the terms of the trust or estate, in light of local law. The amounts described in this paragraph are the so-called *second-tier distributions. Complex trusts* and estates can generally claim a deduction for the lesser of DNI or the two tiers of distributions. §661. See *tier system.*

other disposition   a term commonly used in connection with the term *sale* or *exchange* or simply sale to refer to a *disposition* other than by the named types, such as an abandonment, destruction, or comparable transaction. The most common use is in §1001(a).

other earnings and profits, DISC   the *accumulated earnings and profits* of a *DISC,* excluding *accumulated DISC income* and *previously taxed income*. §996(f)(3). The *Domestic International Sales Corporation* (DISC) generally has been replaced by a system of foreign sales corporations (FSCs). See §§921–927 and *domestic international sales corporation.*

other property   a term sometimes used to describe *property* that may not be received on a tax-free basis in what may be an otherwise nontaxable *exchange*. The term is synonymous with the colloquial term *boot.*

outbound toll charge   *IRS*-compelled imposition of tax on certain transfers to *foreign entities* by *United States persons* as a condition of granting *rulings* under §367, which treats otherwise tax-free *outbound transfers* as taxable *exchanges*. The term is also used in reference to §1491, under which the *unrealized gains* on a more extensive list of transfers are taxed at a flat 35 percent rate unless the transferor elects to treat the transfer as taxable. See *excise tax, transfers to foreign corporations, trusts, estates, and partnerships; section 367 rulings; outbound transfers; tainted assets, outbound transfers.*

outbound transfers   certain transfers of *property* by one or more *United States persons* to a *foreign corporation*. Such transfers are subject to §367, which, absent an exception, immediately taxes *unrealized gains* on outbound transfers that might otherwise be tax-free through the curious mechanism of treating the corporate transferee as not a *corporation,* such that the *nonrecognition provisions* relating to transfers to corporations are eliminated. §367(a)(1). The particular transfers are *liquidations* of *domestic* subsidiaries, *section 351 transactions, corporate divisions,* and *corporate reorganizations,* including incorporations of foreign *branches*; there may be a mandatory *recapture* of *overall foreign losses* under §904(f)(3). See *recapture, foreign losses; section 367 rulings; tainted assets, outbound transfers.*

outdoor advertising display   a rigidly assembled sign, display, or device permanently affixed to the ground or permanently attached to a *building* or other *inherently permanent structure* constituting, or used for the display of, a commercial or other advertisement to the public, including billboards planted with poles, pipes, or beams, whether or not with concrete footings. A *taxpayer* may elect to characterize outdoor advertising displays as *real property*. Thus, if there is an *involuntary conversion* of an outdoor advertising display and the taxpayer so elects, he or she may then purchase an interest in real property as replacement property for the converted property, with the replacement property treated as being of like-kind as the converted property. §1033(g)(3). See *involuntary conversion*.

outgoing Treasury letter   a letter the *IRS* sends to a *taxpayer* in response to a request for legal advice as to clarify the application of the law to some particular fact pattern.

out-of-pocket expenses   *expenditures* by a *taxpayer* of his or her own funds for *business* or personal use. Whether such expenses are for business use is one of the factors used to determine if an *entertainment facility* is primarily used for business. T.I.R. 628, August 27, 1963.

output bond   see *output facility*.

output facility   a facility for furnishing power (but not water), such as one for electric or gas generator, transmission, or related facilities. §141(b)(4). There is a special limit on financings of such facilities by *persons* other than government units and the general public. A *state or local bond*, at least 5 percent of whose proceeds are to be used with respect to any output facility (called an "*output bond*"), is deemed to satisfy the *private business use test* as well as the *private security or payment test* if, in general, the issue's so-called *nonqualified amount* is more than the excess of $15 million over aggregate nonqualified amounts as to all prior tax-exempt output bonds used to finance the same facility or a related one within a project. §141(b)(4). See *private activity bond; private business use test; private security or payment test; tax-exempt bond*.

outside basis   a *partner's basis in the partnership interest* as distinct from her or his share of the partnership's *basis* in its *property*. They may differ due to such factors as transfers of partnership interests, retirements, or death-related *distributions*. The term should be distinguished from *inside basis*, meaning the basis of property in the hands of a *partnership*. See *section 734 adjustment; section 743 adjustment*.

outside salesman   an *employee* who, through the performance of services, principally solicits business for an *employer* away from the employer's place of business. An outside salesman who incurs *unreimbursed* business expenses, including travel and transportation, can deduct these expenses as miscellaneous deductions. See Form 2106 (Employee Business Expenses).

outstanding stock, personal holding companies   all *stock* subscribed and paid for, even if certificates have not been issued, as well as securities convertible into stock, but not *Treasury stock*. Reg. §1.542-3(b). Generally, what constitutes outstanding stock is determined by local law. The term is used to determine whether stock of a *corporation* is closely held for purposes of determining whether it is a *personal holding company*.

overall foreign loss   the excess of (1) *expenses* and *deductions* allocable to *gross income from sources without the United States* plus a ratable part of general expenses and deductions, over (2) gross income from sources without the United States. For these purposes, *net operating loss deductions, capital loss carryovers* and *carrybacks* to the loss year, *foreign expropriation losses*, and *casualty* and *theft losses* are disregarded. §904(f)(2). The term sets an alternate limit to *recapture* of *foreign losses*. See *recapture, foreign losses*.

overall foreign loss, recapture   see *recapture, foreign losses*.

overall limitation, certain itemized deductions   the Revenue Reconciliation Act of 1990 established a cutback to certain itemized deductions for high-income taxpayers. The threshold amount for 1993 is $108,450 ($54,225 for married persons filing separately). The threshold will be adjusted annually for inflation. The itemized deductions that are otherwise deductible for the tax year are reduced by the *lesser* of (1) 3 percent of the excess of AGI over the annual threshold amount, or (2) 80 percent of the amount of itemized deductions otherwise deductible (e.g., state and city withholding taxes, mortgage interest, charitable contributions) for the year, excluding investment interest expenses, medical expenses, casualty losses, and wagering losses to the extent of wagering gains. §68.

overall limitation, foreign tax credit   a rule to the effect that the *foreign tax credit* cannot exceed the portion of United States taxes that would have been paid on the *taxpayer's* foreign source income had it all been earned in the *United States*. §904. Thus, if, for example, a taxpayer derives 25 percent of her *taxable income* from foreign sources, she can take a foreign tax credit equal to, at most, 25 percent of his United States tax liability (computed before application of the credit). The effect is to deny an immediate foreign income tax credit for overall foreign taxes imposed at a rate greater than that imposed by the federal government. The method by which the limitation is computed is called the overall method. §904(a). The limitation is computed with the following formula:

$$\frac{\text{Taxable income from foreign sources}}{\text{Worldwide taxable income}} \times \begin{array}{l}\text{United States}\\\text{tax liability}\end{array}$$

Unused tax credits may be carried back to the two preceding tax years and then forward to the next five succeeding tax years. §904(c). There are also separate limitations computations for certain categories of income. §904(d). See *per country limitation; section 904 (d)(1) "basket."*

overall method of accounting   a *method of accounting* used for general purposes, such as the *cash* or *accrual method*, as compared with some special method relating to a particular item, such as use of the *installment method* to report *gains* from a single large land sale. Taxpayers may use different methods of accounting for different *trades or businesses* as long as they maintain adequate records. §446(d).

overassessment the administrative determination of *overpayment* of taxes, often resulting from the *audit* process. The concept is needed in order to correct *IRS* records. (Its antonym is the *deficiency.*) A statement in the *taxpayer's* favor normally results from the partial or entire allowance of a *claim for refund or credit,* but it can also result from an audit without claim. See also *account stated.*

overassessment notice a communication from the *IRS* that it has received payments from the *taxpayer* in excess of the *taxpayer's* actual liabilities. *Overassessments* frequently result in suits based on *account stated.*

overlapping groups two or more *controlled groups* of *corporations* that have at least one common *component member.* §1563(b)(4). Despite the overlap, a corporation can be considered to be a *component member* of only one controlled group during a *taxable year.* §1563(b)(4). Where there are overlapping groups of controlled corporations, the common member may elect the group in which to be included. Reg. §1.1563-1(c)(2)(i). If no election is made, then the *IRS* determines in which group the common member is to be included. Reg. §1.1563-1(c)(2)(iii). See *controlled group of corporations, graduated taxes, and other benefits.*

overnight rule, travel expenses see *sleep or rest rule.*

overpayment of tax generally, the excess of the amount of taxes, if any, paid over the *correct tax.* The term does not appear to have been explicitly defined, although §6401 provides that it includes amounts *assessed* or *collected* after the *statute of limitations* has run and various excessive *credits.* An overpayment authorizes the IRS to grant a *refund* or *credit* of such overpayments. §6402.

overriding royalty an interest in oil and gas (or other minerals), free of the expense of production, and in addition to the usual *landowner's royalty* reserved to the lessor or assignor in an oil and gas (or other mineral) lease. It is an interest carved out of the lessor's or a sublessor's share, as distinguished from the owner's reserved royalty interest (hence, it cannot outlast the lease) and is commonly viewed as an interest in *real property* as a matter of state law. Such royalties should be subject to *depletion.*

overriding royalty owner the owner of an *operating interest* in a mineral property who retains an interest in the minerals in place when he assigns his operating or working interest to another who is subject to the

landowner's royalty and the overriding royalty. See *overriding royalty.*

overseas cost-of-living allowances see *foreign areas allowances.*

overwithholding of income tax an *employer's* withholding of *income taxes* in excess of the amount called for to meet the *employee's* actual liabilities. The practice of voluntarily requesting overwithholding is commonplace because such overpayments are spread back over prior quarters. §6654(e). The result is a diminution of *civil tax penalties* imposed on the employee for underpayment *of estimated taxes.* See *income tax withholding; penalty, underpayment of estimated tax by individuals.*

owner, coal or iron ore any *person* who owns an *economic interest* in coal or iron ore in place, including a sublessor. These owners can benefit from rules regarding the *disposal with a retained economic interest* of coal or domestic iron ore (§631(c)) and are entitled to *depletion deductions* (§§611–613).

owner-employee a self-employed *proprietor* of a *trade* or *business* or *a partner* with more than 10 percent *capital* or *profits interest.* §401(c)(3). The presence of an owner-employee subjects *Keogh plans* to special restrictions. §401(d). The same term is used in §408, which denies loans to such persons from *qualified plans* and *annuities* described in §403(b).

owner shift involving a five-percent shareholder basically, any change in common *stock* ownership that affects the percentage ownership of a *five-percent shareholder.* §382(g)(2)(A). It might, for example, occur via *purchases* of stock from other shareholders, stock issuances, foreclosures, or *redemptions,* or via the issuance of stock by a *corporation* in exchange for cash. Conversions of a *debt* to stock may also cause an owner shift. It cannot occur via *gifts, bequests,* divorce or separation, or certain transfers to *employee stock ownership plans.* §382(1)(3). If *owner shifts involving a five-percent shareholder* are significant enough, they can cause an *ownership change* which can attract the *section 382 limitation.* See *neutrality principle.*

ownership change a change in the control of a *corporation* which can result in limits on *carryovers* of *net operating losses* and other *tax attributes* under the *neutrality principle.* §§382 and 383. There are two elements. The first is either an *owner shift involving a five-percent shareholder* or an *equity structure shift.* §382(g)(1). The second is an increase in the *stock* ownership of one or more *five-percent shareholders* by over 50 percentage points over the lowest percentage of stock owned by such shareholders during the *testing period* (generally three years preceding the *change date*). Under a special exception, a purchase of *employer securities* by *TRASOPs* or plan *participants* does not constitute an ownership change as long as the buyer owns over 50 percent of the stock of the loss corporation by value and there are not mass defections from the TRASOP. §382(l)(3)(C). See *neutrality principle; new loss corporation; section 382 limitation.*

ownership change stock *stock* that is not described in §1504(a)(4) and is therefore not considered when determination is made as to whether an *ownership change* has taken place. See *stock, neutrality principle.*

ownership, exemption or reduced rate certificate a certificate used by nonresident persons in connection with their being paid income from *United States sources.*

owners or ownership in common owners of undivided interests in property without rights of *survivorship*. There may or may not be a *partnership* for tax purposes.

owner, timber any *person* who owns an interest in *timber*, including a sublessor and a holder of a *contractual right to cut timber*. Such a person must have a right to cut timber for *sale* for his or her own account. Reg. §1.631-2(e)(2). An owner of timber is subject to specific rules regarding the *disposal with a retained economic interest* of the timber (§631(b)) and is entitled to *depletion deductions* (§§611–613).

ozone-depleting chemical any substance which, at the time of sale or use by the manufacturer, producer, or importer, is listed as an ozone-depleting chemical, and which is manufactured or produced in the *United States* or entered into the United States for consumption, use, or warehousing. §4682(a). These chemicals are identified by the common names CFC-11 (trichloroflouromethane), CFC-12 (dichlorodiflouromethane), Halon-1211 (bromochloroflouromethane), Halon-2402 (dibromotetraflouroethane), etc. §4682(a)(2). The list can be changed by legislation, but changes in the Protocol (if any) will not necessarily change this list. This is part of the formula for determining the *ozone-depleting chemicals tax.*

ozone-depleting chemicals tax an *excise tax* on ozone-depleting chemicals designed to implement the Montreal Protocol. The base is the sale or use by a producer, manufacturer, or importer of certain *ozone-depleting chemicals*. The rate is $1.37 per pound in 1990 or 1991, $1.67 for 1992, and $2.65 for 1993 or 1994. These rates can be modified for the destructive capacity of the chemical ("*ozone depletion factor*"), subject to major exceptions for halons and rigid-foam insulation. §§4681, 4682. The tax is imposed for the calendar year the sale or use occurs. For calendar year 1995 and thereafter the rate rises 45 cents each year. §4861(b)(1)(C).

ozone-depletion factor the factor for a particular ozone-depleting chemical, determined by a comparison of the ozone depletion caused by a kilo of the chemical with the ozone depletion caused by a kilo of trichlorofluoromethane (CFC-11).

P

PAYSOP an acronym for a form of *employee stock ownership plan* (*ESOP*) permissible in 1983 through 1986. Former §44G.

PBGC an acronym for *Pension Benefit Guaranty Corporation.*

PBGC premium the annual flat rate per *participant* premium the *Pension Benefit Guaranty Corporation* charges *employers* for protecting certain *pension plans* from shortfalls in the event of termination. *ERISA* §4006(a). See *termination insurance, ERISA.*

PHC an acronym for *personal holding company.*

PL an acronym for public law (a federal statute).

PLR an acronym for a *private letter ruling.* See *ruling.*

Prop. Reg. an abbreviation for *proposed regulation.*

PS-58 rates tables used to determine the cost of the pure death benefit coverage attributable to an *employee* granted *life insurance* coverage under a *qualified plan.* Rev. Rul. 55-757, 1955-2 C.B. 228. For *split-dollar* plans and *tax-deferred annuities for exempt and educational organization employees,* see Rev. Rul. 66-110, 1966-1 C.B. 12, and Rev. Rul. 68-304, 1968-1 C.B. 179.

PTI an acronym for *previously taxed income.*

Pub. L. No. an abbreviation for public law (a federal statute).

paid-in surplus the excess of the amount paid by investors over the par or stated value of the *stock in exchange* for stock of a *corporation.* It is an accounting and state corporate law concept.

paid or accrued same as paid or incurred.

paid or incurred *paid* or *accrued* in accordance with the *taxpayer's method of accounting,* (i.e., *cash* or *accrual method,* respectively). §7701(a)(25). The term is also used in §162(a), with the difference that, in the case of *cash method taxpayers,* incurred colorably also means to undertake at a time when the taxpayer was engaged in a *trade or business,* or before being so engaged if the later duty to pay is contingent on successfully entering a trade or business.

paired plans a *defined benefit plan* plus a *defined contribution plan,* operated in tandem by the same *employer.* Such combinations offer maximum tax savings. See Ann. 88-116, 1988-37 I.R.B. 27.

paired stock see *stapled entities.*

parachute payment any payment in cash or property as compensation to or for the benefit of a *disqualified individual* (mainly top management) if (1) the payment is contingent on a 50 percent or more change in the ownership or effective control (which includes a imposed change in the majority of the board by a 20 percent or more *shareholder*) of the *corporation,* or in the ownership of a substantial portion (at least one-third by value) of the assets of the corporation; and (2) the aggregate present value of all such contingent compensation payments equals or exceeds three times a *base amount* (essentially, the payee's recent compensation). §280G(b)(2). The term also includes any compensation to or for a disqualified individual if the payment violates securities laws or regulations. §280G(b)(2)(B). The *excess parachute payment* is nondeductible and attracts a 20 percent *excise tax* on the recipient. §§280G and 4999. There are exemptions for *small business corporations* (those with not over 35 shareholders, all of whom are *resident aliens* or *citizens of the United States*), corporations without readily tradable common stock whose *shareholders* approve the payment, transfers to and from certain *qualified plans,* and payments of *reasonable compensation.* Fairly elaborate *proposed regulations* have been issued. See Reg. §1.280G-1. See *disqualified individual, golden parachutes; excess parachute payment; golden parachute agreement.*

parent corporation a nontechnical term for a corporation in control of another (subsidiary) corporation.

parent-subsidiary controlled group one or more chains of *corporations (component members)* in which a common parent directly or indirectly holds 80 percent or more of the *stock,* by voting power or value. §1563(a). Stock of a controlled corporation owned directly by other members is disregarded; thus, if P owns 70 percent of S1 and S2, and S1 owns 30 percent of S2, then P is deemed to own 100 percent of S2. Section 1563(d)(2) and (e) imports complex *attribution rules* to determine stock ownership, and §1563(b) arbitrarily includes and excludes certain corporations from consideration from the status of being a component member by classifying them as *excluded members.* Corporations that are component members of a *controlled group* are subject to §1561, disallowing graduated *income tax* rates and other benefits of free-standing corporations. See *controlled group of corporations, graduated taxes, and other benefits.*

parent-subsidiary group under common control, qualified plans a group that consists of one or more chains of organizations (*sole proprietorships, partnerships, trusts, estates,* or *corporations*) in which one or more of the organizations other than the common parent organization owns a controlling (basically 80 percent) interest in the other organizations and the common parent owns a controlling interest in at least one of the other organizations, aside from any direct ownership in the other organizations. Reg. §1.414(c)-(2)(a) and -2(b)(1). Such groups are aggregated to determine whether their plans satisfy the requirements necessary for them to be classified as *qualified plans,* as a species of *two or more trades or businesses under common control.* Reg. §1.414(c)-2(a). The *parent-subsidiary* group is also aggregated for computation of *minimum funding standards* and allowable contribution *deductions,* each of which is then apportioned among the members. For attribution rules, see Reg. §1.414(c)-(4).

parent's unused parental minimum tax exemption the excess, if any, of the parent's *exemption amount* under §55(d) over the parent's *alternative minimum taxable income.* §59(j)(3). See *exemption amount, alternative minimum tax; kiddie tax.*

parity provisions a reference to the numerous provisions of *TEFRA,* the overall effect of which is largely to eliminate the distinction between *Keogh plans* for the self-employed and *qualified plans* of corporate *employers.* See especially *top-heavy plan.*

parity rule see *rule of parity, qualified plans.*

parking benefits employer-provided parking benefits remain excludable under the CNEPA of 1992 (Pub. L. 102-486) but are capped at $155 a month for benefits provided after 1992. The $155 amount will be indexed for inflation. §1911.

parole evidence rule a rule against introducing extrinsic evidence regarding a written contract that is inconsistent with a clear written contract. The rule binds parties to a contract; therefore, the *IRS* is rarely hampered by the rule.

parsonage allowance an *exclusion* from *gross income* allowed for a residence (including utilities and furnishings) furnished to a *minister of the gospel* by the religious institution that employs him or her. §107; Reg. §1.107-1. Where no home is made available to a member of the clergy, that person may exclude from gross income the rental allowance given as part of compensation, to the extent it is used to provide a home. To benefit from the exclusion, the residence or rental allowance must be provided as compensation for the functions commonly performed by a member of the clergy. See also §265(6).

partial bad debt deduction a *deduction* for a partially *worthless debt,* allowed if (1) the debt is a *business debt*; (2) the *IRS* is satisfied that the particular debt is only partially recoverable; (3) the deducted amount was charged off within the *taxable year*; and (4) the debt is one not evidenced by a *worthless security* (basically, worthless corporate *stock* or corporate or government debt in *registered form* or with coupons attached). §166(a)(2), (d), and (e).

partial disallowance generally, the *IRS's* disallowance of a *taxpayer's deduction* or *credit* only in part.

partial distribution any *distribution* to an *employee* of any portion of the balance to his or her credit that is not a total distribution; in other words, any part of his or her credit balance in a *qualified trust* or *qualified annuity plan* that does not qualify as a *lump-sum distribution.* §§402(a)(5)(D)(2), (E)(v), and 403(b)(8)(B). See *lump-sum distribution, qualified plans.*

partial interests less than a complete share of each and every substantial interest or right in property owned by the *taxpayer.* §170(f)(3). Section 170(f)(3)(A) generally disallows *charitable contribution deductions* for gifts of such interests. Section 170(f)(3)(B) in turn provides various exceptions to the general rule.

partial liquidation *under prior law,* a *distribution* that either (1) was one of a series of *distributions* in *redemption* of all the *stock* of the *corporation* pursuant to a plan of complete *liquidation,* or (2) was a *redemption not essentially equivalent to a dividend,* was in redemption of a part of the stock of the corporation pursuant to a plan, and occurred within the *taxable year* in which the plan was adopted or in the succeeding *taxable year.* Former §346(a). See *active conduct of a trade or business; stock redemption.*

partially worthless bad debt a *debt* that has demonstrably become *worthless* in part during the *taxable year.* §166(a)(2). Only *business bad debts* give rise to a permissible *deduction* for partial worthlessness. *Id.*; §166(b)(2). The partial worthlessness must be established by some *identifiable event,* along the same lines as applied to *worthlessness* generally. See *worthless debt.*

partial redemption a *corporation's* acquisition of its own *stock* from a *shareholder,* without its entirely redeeming the shareholder's interest, in exchange for money or property, whether or not the stock so acquired is cancelled, retired, or held as *Treasury stock.* §317(b). Partial redemptions raise difficult questions as to whether the redemption is more like a *sale* of the stock, perhaps entitled to *capital gains* treatment, or a *distribution.* Sections 302 and 304 attempt to resolve most of these questions. See *redemption not essentially equivalent to a dividend; redemption by affiliated corporations; substantially disproportionate redemption.*

partial rollover a term used to refer to a transaction in which a *participant* in a *qualified plan* of some sort received a complete *distribution* of his or her account balance and rolled over part of that distribution into another qualified plan or an *IRA.* See §402(a)(6)(D)(iii). A lump-sum distribution from a qualified pension plan may be transferred to an IRA within 60 days so that tax on the lump-sum distribution can be avoided. §402(a)(5).

partial termination, qualified plans a major diminution in *employer contributions,* a major amendment to the plan that operates to exclude previously covered *employees* or to reduce their *vesting* rights, certain plan mergers and consolidations, and various other events that have significant adverse effects on covered employees. See Reg. §1.411(d)-2(b)(1) and (2); Rev. Rul. 73-284, 1973-2 C.B. 1939; Rev. Rul. 72-439, 1972-2 C.B. 223. Section 411 demands that *qualified plans* provide that affected employees be entitled to nonforfeiture of funded *accrued benefits* in the case of complete or partial terminations. §411(d)(3).

partial worthlessness of debt see *partial bad debt deduction; partially worthless bad debt.*

participant, common trust fund undefined, but includes any *estate* or *trust* for which monies have been distributed to the *common trust fund.* Reg. §1.584-1(a). Participants are taxed much like *partners.*

participant loan see *qualified plan loan.*

participant, qualified plans the status of being an *employee,* or former employee, whose service gives or has given rise to *accrual of benefits,* whether or not they vest, under a *qualified plan.* It is distinct from, and generally follows, *eligibility,* which is the status of being eligible to participate only after some predetermined period. While an employee is eligible but not participating, benefits do not accrue, but once admitted to the plan, the participant's preparticipation service may or may not be counted for accrual of benefit or *vesting* purposes, or both. Rarely will a person who is eligible to participate not participate, but examples of such cases include employees who do not make mandatory contributions, fail to take required physical exams for insured plans, or fail to meet other preconditions for participation.

participant's compensation the *compensation* the *employer* paid an *employee,* or *earned income* (defined in §401(c)) of a *self-employed person,* for the year. §415(c)(3)(A) and (B). In the case of disabled people who are not *highly compensated employees* who so elect, the term means compensation that would have been received for the year if he or she were not disabled. §415(c)(3)(C). This term is used for purposes of setting annual limits on benefits and contributions under *qualified plans,* but it is now the base of the generic definition of compensation for qualified plan purposes generally, found in §414. For the generic definition of compensation, see *compensation, qualified plans.*

participation and cooperation, boycott see *international boycott activity, participation and cooperation.*

participation certificate a certificate issued by *cooperatives* that evidences membership. See *member, cooperatives.*

participation, qualified retirement plans a catchall term encompassing the many requirements of §410(a) involving minimum participation standards in a *qualified plan.* Some of the principal features are: (1) the *minimum age and service requirements* as to the length of service an *employee* must complete as a condition of participation in the plan, generally age 21 or one *year of service;* (2) the prohibition against excluding employees who have attained a specified age from participation in the plan, unless the plan is a *defined* or *target benefit plan;* (3) requirements that the plan must benefit the lesser of 50 employees or 40 percent or more of all employees, except for collectively bargained *multiemployer plans* (§401(a)(26)); and (4) specification of the date when an employee who has satisfied the minimum age and service requirements must begin participating in the plan, generally the earlier of six months after she or he has satisfied the age and service requirements, or the plan's anniversary date. See *minimum age and service requirements; time of participation, qualified retirement plans.*

parties in interest, prohibited transactions a *fiduciary* (including the *plan administrator, trustee,* or *custodian* of plan assets), someone who provides services to a plan, an *employer* whose *employees* are covered by the plan, a relative (*spouse,* ancestor, lineal descendant, or spouse of a lineal descendant) of any of the foregoing *individuals,* as well as any employee, officer, director, or 10 percent shareholder (direct or indirect) of the employer maintaining the plan. ERISA §3(14). Such parties are within the scope of ERISA's rules against *prohibited transactions.* See *prohibited transactions, ERISA.*

partner a member of a *partnership,* whether a *general partner* with unlimited liability or a *limited partner.* §761(c). Distinguishing members from creditors and *employers* or *employees* can be difficult, and local law conclusions are not controlling. The essential question is whether the member intended to join with one or more other persons for joint profit. See *family partnership; partnership.*

partner nonrecourse synonymous with *partner nonrecourse debt.*

partner nonrecourse debt any *partnership liability* for which no *partner* is liable. See Reg. §1.704-2(b)(4). Regulation §1.704-2 provides complex rules for attributing such liabilities among partners.

partner, partnership audits actual *partners* as well as any other person whose tax liability is partially or entirely, directly or indirectly determined with reference to the partnership's *partnership items.* §6231(a)(2). It includes *passthrough partners* (i.e., conduits such as *subchapter S corporations*) and *indirect partners* (i.e., persons who hold interests in passthrough partners). §6231(a)(9) and (10). The term is specially defined for the purpose of assuring that the unified partnership *audit* procedures will be widely felt. See *unified proceedings.*

partner's distributive share   see *distributive share.*

partnership   an unincorporated *association,* but not a *corporation, trust,* or *estate,* by which any *business,* venture, or financial enterprise is carried on for the joint profit of its owners. It includes a *syndicate,* pool, group, or *joint venture.* §§761(a) and 7701(a)(2). The partners may be *individuals,* estates, trusts, or corporations. Mere passive *co-ownership of property* does not rise to the level of partnership status. The characterization of the organization turns on federal tax law rules, although state law determines the legal relations among the owners. Section 761(a) allows an election by investment organizations, raw material extractors, and co-owners of property to be excluded from the application of some or all of the partnership tax rules of *subchapter K.*

partnership agreement   a contract that regulates the operation of a *partnership.* Such agreements are frequently oral and informal. Generally, partnership agreements control *income* or *losses* reportable by the partners. §704(a). Amendments to agreements made on or before the partnership's *federal income tax* filing date (excluding extensions) are effective for the prior *taxable year,* subject to the rules of §704. §761(c). Where the agreement is silent, local law controls. Reg. §1.761-1(c).

partnership allocations   the allocation to each *partner* of the partner's *distributive share* of each *partnership item.* See *special allocations.*

partnership associations   a state law term for entities that may or may not be treated as *partnerships* for federal tax purposes. Reg. §301.7701-3(c).

partnership distribution   a transfer of cash or property from a *partnership* to a *partner* in his or her capacity as a partner. Distributions are generally tax-free, with stated exceptions. §731.

partnership flip   shift in interests of *partners* in profits and *losses,* or *partnership distributions,* at some time during partnership operations. The partnership flip provides needed flexibility in planning for partnerships where one or more partners contribute capital and the remaining partners contribute services. The flip is commonly used to increase *allocations* to service partners after passive partners have been allocated profits sufficient to recoup previous losses or achieve an agreed cumulative return on their investments. The *IRS* has asserted that a flip may be a *nonrecourse liability.* Tech. Adv. Mem. 7707260880A (July 26, 1977).

partnership information return   the *return* (Form 1065) required by §6031 which specifies *income* and *deductions* of a *partnership* and other items. *Form 1065, Schedule K-1* shows the individual partners' shares of the items shown on the partnership's return. Failure to file is governed by §6698.

partnership item   any item required to be taken into account for the partnership's taxable year to the extent the regulations provide that such item is more appropriately determined at the partnership level rather than at the partner level. §§6231(a)(3), 301.6231(a)(3)-1. Partnership items include (1) all items of partnership income, gain, loss, deduction or credit; (2) all other items that affect a partner's basis, tax preferences, credit recapture, at-risk amount, or §613A depletion with respect to oil and gas wells; (3) guaranteed payments; (4) optional adjustments to the basis of partnership property pursuant to a §754 election; (5) partnership contributions and distributions, payments to a partner under §707(a); and the application of §751(a) and (751(b) (unrealized receivables and inventory). See *unified proceedings.*

partnership liabilities   liabilities assumed by a *partnership* or to which its property is merely subject. §752. Such liabilities may create *basis* for *partners.* See Reg. §1.752-1. It excludes accrued by unpaid *expenses* and *accounts payable* of a partnership on the *cash method.* Rev. Rul. 88-77, 1988-38 I.R.B. 8.

partnership liquidation   in general, an event which occurs when no part of any *business,* financial operation, or venture of a *partnership* continues to be carried on by any of the *partners.* §708(b)(1)(A). It also occurs for technical tax purposes if 50 percent of the interests in *capital* and *profits* of the partnership are transferred by *sale or exchange* in any 12 month period, such that there is a termination. Reg. §1.708-1(b)(1)(iv). For purposes of validating *special allocations* or *bottom-line allocations* under §704(b)(2) Reg. §1.704-1(b)(2)(ii)(g). See *termination, partnership.*

partnership minimum gain   as to each *nonrecourse debt liability* of *partnership,* the excess of such debt over the *adjusted basis* of related encumbered property. Reg. §1.704-1(b)(4)(iv)(c). This sort of potential *gain* must be covered by an adequate *allocation* under §704(b)(2) *regulations.* See Reg. §1.704-1(b)(4)(iv)(d) for the requirements, including a *minimum gain chargeback* or a *deficit make-up* provision. See *substantial economic effect test.*

partnership nonrecourse liability   a *nonrecourse liability* of a *partnership.* See Reg. §1.704-1(i).

partnership's basis in assets   See *inside basis.*

partnership swap fund   a device that involves the tax-free formation of *partnerships* funded with *investment* securities in order to diversify investment risks. The *device is now sharply limited* by §721(b), which makes such formations taxable (as to *gains,* not *losses*) if the transfers are to a partnership *investment company*. The terminology of §721(b) is defined by reference to the standards of Reg. §1.351-1(c)(1). Section 721(b) applies only if contributions result in *diversification*.

partnership withholding tax a withholding tax is imposed on a partnership's "effectively connected taxable income" allocable to foreign partners at a rate of 31 percent (34 percent for foreign partners that are corporations). §1446.

partner's interest in the partnership the *partner's* practical economic position in a *partnership*. See Reg. §1.704-1(b)(3). The partnership interest, for example, has its own *basis* and is subject to complex adjustments, e.g., §722 (contributions), §733 (*distributions*), and §742 (transfers). It is used as the guide for the correction of defective *allocations* of *distributive shares* of partnership *income, gains, losses, deductions,* and *credits*. The concept is easy to express but extremely difficult to apply. An alternate meaning is the manner in which a *partner* has agreed to share the economic benefit of an item or items to be allocated. Reg. §1.704-1(b)(3)(i)-(iii). The *regulation* adds a presumption that all partners' interests are equal, on a per capita basis, in cases of doubt. This standard is applied to *special allocations* or *bottom-line allocations* of *partnerships' distributive shares* where the allocation provided for in the partnership agreement fails to have a *substantial economic effect,* or where the agreement does not provide for an allocation.

party-in-interest, ERISA anyone falling into one or more of the following general classes of *persons*: (1) *fiduciaries,* (including *plan administrators,* officers, *trustees* and *custodians,* counsel, and *employees*); (2) persons providing services to a plan; (3) the *employer* and the employees, officers, or directors and persons having similar powers or responsibilities or 10 percent shareholders, a level which may be lowered administratively; (4) controlling or controlled parties or parties under common control (generally defined as 50 percent ownership; (5) unions with members covered by the plan and their employees, officers and directors, and affiliates; and (6) certain relatives and partners of parties-in-interest. *ERISA* §3(14). See *prohibited transactions, ERISA.*

party to a reorganization a *corporation* that results from a *corporate reorganization,* or both corporations in the case of a reorganization consisting of the transfer of *stock* or properties from one corporation to another. §368(b). In addition, under either a *Type B* or *Type C reorganization,* if the acquiring corporation uses the stock of its parent as consideration, then the parent corporation is also a party to the reorganization. §368(a)(1)(B) and (C). In the case of a *Type A, Type B; Type C,* or *Type G reorganization,* if the acquiring corporation transfers all or part of the acquired assets or

stock to its subsidiary, the acquiring corporation and its subsidiaries are parties to the reorganization. In a *forward triangular merger* qualifying under §368(a)(2)(D), the parent is a party to the reorganization. In a *reverse triangular merger* qualifying under §368(a)(2)(E), the parent corporation is again a party to the reorganization. §368(b); Reg. §1.368-2(f). The term "party to a reorganization" is significant because, under §§354(a)(1) and 361(a), *nonrecognition* of *gain or loss* resulting from a reorganization is available only if exchanges of stock, securities, or properties of a party to a reorganization are involved.

passage of title test a standard used to determine the place where income from *personal property* is derived when such property is sold in international commerce. The inquiry is when and where the rights, title, and interest of the seller pass to the buyer, and it concentrates on *beneficial ownership* as opposed to mere *legal title* under local law. Reg. §1.861-7(c); Rev. Rul. 75-263, 1975-2 C.B. 28.

passenger automobile any four-wheeled vehicle made primarily for use on public streets, roads, and highways and rated at a gross vehicle weight of 6,000 pounds or less (unloaded), but not hearses, ambulances (or a hybrid) used in a *trade or business,* taxis, and other vehicles directly used to transport people and things for pay, or trucks or vans specified in regulations. §280F(d)(5)(B). See *listed property.*

passenger vehicle any four-wheeled vehicle manufactured primarily for use on public roads, which is rated at 6,000 pounds unloaded gross vehicle weight or less. §4001(b)(1). The weight limitation does not apply to limousines. A limousine is a passenger vehicle regardless of its weight. §4001(b)(2)(B). A truck or van is rated at 6,000 pounds gross vehicle weight rather than unloaded gross vehicle weight. §4001(b)(2)(A).

passes from the decedent to his surviving spouse, estate tax marital deduction is transferred from the *decedent* so as to vest the *surviving spouse* with *beneficial ownership* of the property only under one of seven categories. §2056(a) and (c). The statute provides that property that "passes or has passed" from the decedent to his (and implicitly, her) surviving spouse can qualify for the *marital deduction* for *federal estate tax* purposes.

passive activity generally a *trade or business activity* within the meaning of §162 with respect to which the *taxpayer* does not *materially participate,* on a regular, continuous, and substantial basis for the entire year or for the part of the year during which the activity was in existence. An interest as a *limited partner* and *rental activities* are inherently passive, unless rent involves a high level of turnover such as busy car rental operations and hotels or other specialized cases. The *Treasury Department* has broad authority to extend the definition to limit *tax avoidance*. §469(h)(2) and (c)(2). For this purpose, one considers services of the taxpayer's *spouse* as well, regardless of whether the parties filed a *joint return*. §469(h). See *activity, passive loss rules; material participation, passive loss rules; passive loss rules; rental activity*.

passive activity credit   the aggregate of most *tax credits* from all *passive activities* for the *taxable year* to the extent in excess of the *taxpayer's regular tax* liability for the taxable year allocable to all passive activities. §469(d)(2). The particular credits are the *general business credits, possession tax credit, orphan drug credit, credit for producing fuels from nonconventional sources* (not the *foreign tax credit*) from all *passive activities*. §469(d)(2); Temp. Reg §1.469-3T(b)(1)(i). Suspended credits are carried forward indefinitely for later application against income from passive activities. §469(d)(2). See *passive loss rules*.

passive activity deduction   generally, any *deduction* which arises in connection with the conduct of a *passive activity* for the *taxable year*, or a *carryover* of such a deduction from a previous year. Reg. §1.469-2T(d). It is calculated under the *taxpayer's method of accounting* as if *taxable income* for all years were determined without consideration of the passive loss rules or capital loss carryforwards. In general, a *taxpayer's passive activity loss* for the taxable year is the amount by which *passive activity deductions* exceed passive activity gross income for the taxable year. Reg. §1.469-1T(f)(2)(i)(B). Any unused suspended losses are allowed in full when the taxpayer disposes of his or her entire interest in the activity in a fully taxable transaction. §469(g). See *passive activity gross income; passive loss rules*.

passive activity gross income   *gross income* generated by a *passive activity*. See Reg. §1.469-2T. It excludes *portfolio income* (including income of a dealer if the property was held for investment at any time by the dealer); *gain* from disposition of an interest in the *activity* or property used in the activity if the activity was not passive when disposed of; *compensation for personal services* of an *individual*; gross income from *working interests* in oil and gas *properties* (subject to modifications); gross income from licensing *intangible property* the *taxpayer* produced; gross income from certain low-income housing projects; *tax refunds*; income from *covenants not to compete*; and, other nonpassive income determined under *regulations*. See *activity, passive loss rules; compensation for personal services, passive loss rules; operating mineral interest; passive loss rules*.

passive activity losses   aggregate *losses* from all *passive activities* for the *taxable year* to the extent in excess of aggregate income from such sources for the year. §469(d). Such losses are generally incapable of reducing income generated from sources other than *pas-*

sive activities. Special rules apply to losses from publicly traded partnerships (PTPs). See *publicly traded partnership*.

passive foreign investment company (PFIC)   a class of *foreign corporation*, based upon its characteristic of being predominantly organized for, or actually producing, *passive income*. A foreign corporation is a *PFIC* if either (1) 75 percent or more of its annual gross income is passive; or (2) 50 percent or more of its assets (by value) produce passive income. A foreign corporation may elect to make this determination based on the adjusted basis of its assets. A *PFIC* does not include a foreign investment company that has elected under §1247 to distribute income currently. §1296(a). See *excess distribution, passive foreign investment company; passive income, foreign tax credit; qualified electing fund, passive foreign investment company; related person, controlled foreign corporation*.

passive income   rarely defined but often referred to; the reference is presumably to such items as *rents, royalties, dividends, interest, annuities,* and the like. See *passive investment income, S corporations*.

passive income, foreign tax credit   a category of *foreign source income* to which the *foreign tax credit limitation* applies separately. This category primarily includes *foreign personal holding company income*, under *subpart F*, but also consists of amounts includible in *gross income* under §§551 and 1293 relating to shareholders of *foreign personal holding companies* and *qualified electing funds*. §904(d)(2)(A). The category is limited by four exceptions which are other *section 904(d)(1) "baskets," export financing interest, high-taxed income,* and *foreign oil and gas extraction income*. §904(d)(2)(iii). See *section 904(d)(1) "basket."*

passive investment income, S corporations   passive investment income means gross receipts derived from royalties, rents, dividends, interest (excluding interest on installment sales of inventory to customers), annuities, and sales or exchanges of stock or securities to the extent of any gains therefrom. §1362(d)(3)(D). See *excess net passive income*.

passive loss rules   a complex provision (§469) designed to prevent most *taxpayers* from *deducting losses* and *credits* from *trades or businesses* in which they are only passively involved from income from other sources, especially so-called *portfolio income* and income from personal services. The affected losses are referred to as *passive activity losses* and the affected credits are referred to as *passive activity credits*. The general concept is to defer such losses until the taxpayer's death (or there is a taxable *disposition* of the taxpayer's entire interest in the *activity*) or until (and to the extent) it turns a profit. §469(b) and (g). There is a *de minimis* rule for real estate activities; the general rule is that while all *rental activities* (narrowly defined) produce passive activity losses and credits, taxpayers who *actively participate* in real estate rental can deduct up to $25,000 per year. The $25,000, however, is reduced by 50 percent of the taxpayer's AGI in excess of $100,000. For this purpose, AGI is determined without regard to any passive loss. §469(i)(3)(A). See *activity, passive loss rules; former passive activity; material participation, passive loss rules.*

passive solar system, energy investment credit a system that is based on the use of conductive, convective, or radiant energy transfer. Passive solar property includes greenhouses, solariums, and mass or water drum walls. Reg. §1.48-9(d)(2)(iii). Materials and components of passive solar systems do not qualify as *solar energy property* for purposes of the *energy investment credit.* §48(1)(4); Reg. §1.48-9(d)(2).

passthrough entity a *partnership* or *S corporation.* The term is used in various places in the *Code* and *regulations.*

passthrough partner a *partnership, estate, trust, S corporation,* or *nominee* through which other *persons (indirect partners)* hold an interest in a partnership. §6231(a)(9). Any notices received by passthrough partners with respect to the beginning and completion of an *IRS audit* are required to be forwarded by the passthrough partner to the partners, *beneficiaries,* and *shareholders* of the passthrough partner within 30 days of receipt of the notice. §6223(h). See *unified proceedings.*

past-due support the amount of a delinquency determined by a court order or by a state administrative order for the support of a child or the parent with whom the child lives. Reg. §304.6402-1(b)(1). In certain cases the *IRS* must use overpayments of tax to offset past-due support, the practical effect of which is, in limited circumstances, to turn the IRS into an agency of the family courts in an effort to reimburse state governments that have provided help to the family under the so-called intercept program. If notified, the IRS will attempt to collect amounts exceeding $150 due for more than three months, provided the state has made a reasonable effort at collection as an assignee of the support obligation. See *I.R.M.* 6810, §(16) 25.2.

past service costs, minimum funding standard actuarially determined costs associated with the provision of pension benefits to *participants* on the basis of service performed for the *employer* in a prior year or years. They may arise for such reasons as retroactive increases in pension benefits. See, e.g., Reg. §1.412(b)-5. See *minimum funding standard account; minimum funding standards.*

past service credits credit for time put in by an *employee* under a *pension plan.* Credits may be given for work done for other *employers,* but the result may be unacceptable discrimination.

past service liability pension plan liabilities arising from services rendered by *employees* in the past, which have not yet been met by *employer contributions* and growth of the fund. *ERISA* imposes significant limitations on the ability to postpone indefinitely the funding of past service liabilities. Generally, employer funding must be sufficient to *amortize* such liabilities over a 30- or, in some cases, 40-year period, or the employer will be subject to significant excise taxes under §4971. §412(b)(2). See *accumulated funding deficiency; underfunding excise tax.*

patent for purposes of §1235, which grants certain transfers status as a *sale* or *exchange* of a *capital asset,* the term "patent" includes a patent granted or applied for under Title 35 of the United States Code or any foreign patent granting rights generally similar to those under a United States patent. §1235(a). Patents issued by the United States Patent Office have a term of 17 years, during which the inventor has a legal monopoly to exploit the patent. Section 1235 provides liberal *capital gains* treatment for production-based patent transfers. See *all substantial rights to a patent.*

patient includes a person (1) admitted to a hospital or clinic as an inpatient or outpatient; (2) refilling at the hospital a prescription written during treatment at the hospital; (3) participating in a hospital-administered home care treatment program; or (4) receiving treatment in a hospital-affiliated extended care facility qualified to participate in Medicare and other governmental programs. All income received from the sale of pharmaceutical supplies to such patients is not *unrelated trade or business income* of exempt medical organizations. Rev. Rul. 68-376, 1968-2 C.B. 246.

patron a person for whom or with whom a *cooperative* does business on a cooperative basis, but not necessarily a *member* of the cooperative. Reg. §1.1388-1(e). See Rev. Rul. 76-388, 1976-2 C.B. 180. Profits distributed from a cooperative are generally taxed to the *patron* when received. §1385(a)(1). See *operating on a cooperative basis.*

patronage dividend an amount paid to a *patron* by an exempt cooperative and a corporation operating on a cooperative basis. The patron is taxed on such distributed amounts. In addition, the exempt cooperative and a corporation operating as a cooperative are allowed deductions for patronage payments paid in money, qualified written notices of allocation, and property. §§1381–1388; Reg. 1.1381-1.1388-1. The patron generally includes such dividends in *gross income* under §1385(a)(1), unless §1385(b) excludes the dividends directly attributable to the purchase of capital items or personal use items. See *cooperatives; exempt farmers' cooperative.*

patronage dividend, withholding   the amount of a *patronage dividend* as defined in §1388(a), or any amount of certain nonpatronage *distributions* described in §1382(c)(2)(A) paid in money, *qualified written notice of allocation,* or other property other than a *nonqualified written notice of allocation.* See §3454(c)(2)-(4) (exceptions and special rules).

pattern plan   a plan submitted to the *District Director* by a law firm, or other authorized practitioners, that contemplates use of the form of such plan in the submitting of its *determination letter* applications on behalf of several adopting *employers.* See Rev. Proc. 76-15, 1976-1 C.B. 553.

pay-as-you-go profit sharing   *profit-sharing plans* with current payouts according to company profits. These are not *qualified plans,* because they involve no deferral.

payee statement   any one of a long list of statements that must be filed with the *IRS* and submitted to the payee of money or property and as to which such a statement is required. §6724(d)(2). See *penalty, failure to file correct payee statement.*

payment assumption rule   a rule to the effect that any payment to be made in the form of another obligation of the issuer (or related person) is not considered a payment at that time; rather it is assumed to be made later, when a payment under the obligation or *stock* must be made in cash or property other than such an obligation. The payment assumption rule applies to an aspect of an *applicable high-yield debt instrument* (AHYDO) as well.

payment date, foreign currency transactions   the date of completion of a *section 988 transaction.* It is the date payment is made or received. §988(c)(3). The difference in the value of the object of a section 988 transaction between the *booking date* and the payment date due to change in exchange rate, equals the *foreign currency gain or loss.*

payment, installment method   cash, property, foreign currency, marketable securities, evidence of indebtedness that is *readily tradable* or payable on demand (whether issued by the purchaser or someone else) under local law, evidence of indebtedness secured by cash or a cash equivalent (e.g., a *Treasury* note), evidence of indebtedness issued by *persons* other than the purchaser, the purchaser's cancellation of the seller's preexisting obligation, or *mortgages* of the seller to the extent in excess of the seller's *basis* (whether or not assumed). Certain installment obligations arising from a *corporate liquidation* are not payments. §453(h). Instead, amounts disbursed pursuant to the obligation

are "payments." The *installment sale method* causes a portion of each payment to be taxed in the year it is made. See §§453(a) and 453A(a).

payments for partnership goodwill   payments in *liquidation* of a retiring or deceased *partner's* interest made for *goodwill,* treated as *distributive shares* or *guaranteed payments* unless the agreement provides for payment for goodwill. §736. See *section 736 payments.*

payments in exchange for a partner's interest in partnership property   payments treated as *distributions* rather than as *distributive shares* of partnership income or as *guaranteed payments.* §736(b).

payment in kind debenture   a debenture, usually issued in leveraged buyouts, that permits or requires the issuer to issue more debt. Under §163(e) and (i), it also includes an obligation that requires or permits the issuer to issue *stock. Interest expense deductions* on such debt is subject to limitations. See *applicable high-yield discount obligation.*

payments in lieu of dividends   a concept used in connection with *short sales* under which payments made to the lender of *stock* used in a short sale reflect dividends that would otherwise have been received by the lender. Such payments are generally *deductible,* unless the short sale spans a 45-day (or shorter) period (a one-year or shorter period in the case of *extraordinary dividends*). §263(h). See *extraordinary dividend, short sale.*

payments to a partner for services or the use of capital   see *guaranteed payment.*

payments to a partner not acting in capacity as a partner   payments made to a *partner* from a *partnership* in which the partner does not act in the capacity of a partner, such as the *sale* of property or formal lending of money. §707(a). Such transactions are generally taxed as if undertaken with strangers. By contrast, *guaranteed* payments are received as a partner.

payment to support children   see *child support.*

payroll period, withholding   the period of service for which a payment of *wages* is ordinarily made to an *employee* by the *employer.* A miscellaneous payroll period is one other than daily, weekly, biweekly, semimonthly, monthly, quarterly, semiannually, or annually. If payroll periods occasionally vary, the period for which payment is ordinarily made is controlling even if it does not coincide with an actual particular period for which payment of wages is made. §3401(b); Reg. §31.3401(b)-1.

penalty, aiding and abetting   a $1,000 ($10,000 for a corporation) *civil tax penalty* imposed on *persons* who aid or abet in the understatement of the tax liability of another. §6701. The term "aiding and abetting" means (1) aiding, assisting, or giving advice in the preparation or presentation (e.g., during an *IRS audit*) of any portion of a *tax return* or other document in connection with any matter arising under the Internal Revenue laws; (2) knowing (or having reason to believe) that a portion of the return or document will be used in connection with any material matter arising under the Internal Revenue laws; and (3) knowing that, if the portion of the tax return or other document is used, an understatement of the tax liability of another person would result. §6701(a)(1)-(3). The penalty is mutually exclusive with the *tax return preparer* penalties and the §6700 penalty for promoting *abusive tax shelters*. Those aiding and abetting may also be subject to criminal penalties. §7206(2); 18 U.S.C. §1 (1976). See also §7408.

Penalty Appeal Office an office located in *Service Centers* and *District Offices* designed to allow *taxpayers* subjected to *civil tax penalties* to obtain a discretionary review following the *IRS*'s rejection of *abatement* of a penalty. Rev. Proc. 78-1, 1978-1 C.B. 500. The procedure has been established on a trial basis only.

penalty, bad check a penalty for a dishonored check tendered to the *IRS* in bad faith. The rate is 2 percent of the check, but $15 if the check is for under $750. It can be excused for *reasonable cause*. §6657.

penalty, civil fraud a *civil tax penalty* equal to 75 percent of the portion of an *underpayment of tax* due to fraud for each *taxable year*. §6663. Once fraud is shown, the burden shifts to the *taxpayer* to show by a *preponderance of the evidence* the portion not tainted by fraud. With respect to a *joint return,* the penalty does not apply to a *spouse* unless some part of the underpayment is caused by fraud by that spouse. For a comparison, see §7201 (*criminal fraud*). See §6664(c).

penalty, damages for proceedings before Tax Court for delay sanctions against *taxpayers,* lawyers, or other parties entitled to practice before the *Tax Court,* of up to $25,000, awardable by that court where it appears the proceedings begun or maintained by the *taxpayer* are frivolous or groundless. Section 6673 is designed to put an end to one form of tax protest in the form of obstreperous litigation in the Tax Court. See also §7482, which allows other courts to award like costs and sanctions and to collect them as if they were awarded by the Tax Court.

penalty, employer's failure to furnish Form W-2 to employee a $50-per-case *civil tax penalty* imposed on any *employer* who willfully furnishes a false or fraudulent statement or who willfully fails to furnish a statement on *Form W-2* describing the amount of taxes withheld from *gross compensation,* or on any employer who willfully fails to furnish such a statement in a timely fashion. §6624. Section 7204 imposes a criminal penalty of $1,000 or one year imprisonment, or both. See *willful.*

penalty, failure of employers of tax return preparers to file correct information report a *civil tax penalty* of $50 (not to exceed $25,000 for any return period) for each report by an *employer* of a *tax return preparer* not filed. §6695(e). The duty extends to self-employed preparers. See §6060. Such reports must include records of *employees'* names, tax return preparers' identification numbers, and principal places of employment. It can be waived for *reasonable cause.*

penalty, failure of income tax preparer to sign return a *civil tax penalty* of $50 for each failure of the *tax return preparer* to sign the return. §6695(b). It is not to exceed $25,000 per reporting period and it can be waived for *reasonable cause.*

penalty, failure of tax return preparer to furnish copy of return to taxpayer a *civil tax penalty* of $50 for each failure by a *tax return preparer* to return a copy of the *income tax return* to the *taxpayer,* not to exceed $25,000 per reporting period. §6695(a). It can be waived for *reasonable cause.*

penalty, failure of tax return preparer to furnish identification number a *civil tax penalty* of $50 imposed on any *tax return preparer* for each failure to furnish the proper identifying numbers on the return. §6695(c). It is not to exceed $25,000 per reporting period and it can be waived for *reasonable cause.*

penalty, failure of tax return preparer to retain copies of tax returns a *civil tax penalty* of $50 for each failure by a *tax return preparer* to keep copies of all *income tax* returns prepared. The maximum penalty for any one return period is $25,000 as to any one preparer. Copies must be retained for a minimum of three years. §6695(d). The penalty is not to exceed $25,000 per reporting period and it can be waived for *reasonable cause.*

penalty, failure to collect and pay overtax, or attempt to evade or defeat tax a *civil tax penalty* equal to the total sum of the tax evaded, not collected, or not accounted for and paid over, imposed on any *person* required to collect, truthfully account for, and pay over such tax under §6672(a), for *willful* failure to collect such tax, or truthfully account for and pay over such tax, or willful attempt to evade or defeat any such tax or the payment thereof. §6672(a). The tax falls on the so-called *responsible person* and is the iron fist of the *employment tax* system. The party may also be subject to criminal penalties under §7201.

penalty, failure to comply with specified information reporting requirements a *civil tax penalty* of $50, capped at $100,000 per *calendar year,* for each failure to file timely information reports, referred to in the statute as *specified information reporting requirements.* §6723. It can be waived for *reasonable cause.* §6724(a). See *specified information reporting requirements.*

penalty, failure to file a *civil tax penalty* imposed on all *taxpayers* who fail to file any *return* on time (taking into account automatic and discretionary extensions). §6651(a)(1). The penalty consists of an addition to the amount required to be shown as tax on the return, of an amount equal to 5 percent of the tax for failure to file of a month or less, plus 5 percent for each complete or partial month during which the failure continues, limited to 25 percent. The penalty can be excused for *reasonable cause*. Note, the *timely mailing rule* applies. Rev. Rul. 73-133, 1973-1 C.B. 605. Intentional failure to file may subject the taxpayer to criminal penalties under §7203. For a heavier penalty, see *penalty, fraudulent failure to file*.

penalty, failure to file correct information returns a *civil tax penalty* of $50 (often $100 or more, if deliberate) for each failure more than *de minimis* to file timely, complete, or accurate *information returns*. There is a three-tier penalty structure ranging from $15 to $50 per return and from $100,000 to $250,000 per *calendar year* as the ceiling, depending on how promptly the errors were corrected. §6721(d). The ceiling figures are reduced for smaller *taxpayers* (i.e., those with gross receipts of not over $5 million).

penalty, failure to file correct payee statement a *civil tax penalty* of $50 (often $100 or more, if deliberate) for each failure to file timely, complete, or accurate *payee statements*, limited to $100,000 per *taxpayer* per *calendar year* as the ceiling in innocent cases. The penalty is excused if the failure is based on *reasonable cause*. §6724(a). See *filing, return*.

penalty, failure to file partnership return a $50-per-month, summary per *partner civil tax penalty* for failure to file a sufficiently complete *partnership return*, assessed against the partnership, excusable for *reasonable cause*. §6698.

penalty, failure to furnish information regarding tax shelters a *civil tax penalty* of 1 percent of the aggregate amount invested, with a minimum penalty of $500 (and a ceiling of $10,000, if the failure was unintentional) imposed on the failure to comply with the *tax shelter* registration requirements of §6111(a). §6707(a). Failure to furnish an investor with the tax shelter registration number results in a $100 penalty per failure. §6707(b)(1). Investors who, without *reasonable cause*, fail to include the registration number in their returns are subject to a $50 penalty. §6707(b)(2). See *tax shelter, registration*.

penalty, failure to furnish payee statement a *civil tax penalty* for failure to furnish a *payee statement*, failure to include all the information required on the statement, or inclusion of incorrect information on or before the prescribed date, of $50 for each statement, with a maximum of $100,000 per *calendar* year. §6722(a) and

(b). If the *taxpayer* shows that the failure was based on *reasonable cause*, no penalty is imposed. In the event of intentional disregard, the penalty is the greater of $100 or 10 percent (5 percent for certain types of statements) of the amount required to be shown on the statement, with no limitation on the maximum penalty. §6722(c).

penalty, failure to maintain lists of investors in potentially abusive tax shelters a *civil tax penalty* imposed on a *tax shelter organizer's* failure, without *reasonable cause*, to maintain a list of participants in any *potentially abusive tax shelter* in accordance with *regulations* to be issued. The penalty is $50 per omission of an investor, up to $50,000 per calendar year. The penalty is imposed by §6708; the positive duty arises under §6112.

penalty, failure to make timely deposits a four-tier *civil tax penalty* of 2 to 15 percent of the amount of underpayment of any required *deposit* of federal taxes, which rises as the delay continues. §6656. Each rate is referred to as the "applicable percentage." §6656(b)(1). The depositor is subject to a penalty equal to 2 percent of the amount of the underpayment if the failure is corrected on or before five days after the due date. The penalty is 5 percent of the underpayment if the failure is corrected after 5 days but on or before 15 days after the due date. The penalty is 10 percent if the failure is for more than 15 days but on or before the date that is 10 days after the date of the first delinquency notice to the taxpayer per §6303. The penalty is 15 percent of the amount of underpayment if the failure is not corrected on or before the date that is 10 days after the date of the first delinquency notice. No penalty is imposed if the failure to make a timely deposit is due to *reasonable cause*. For purposes of the penalty, "underpayment" means the shortfall in required tax payments on the due date for payment. §6656(b)(2). The penalty may be avoided if the failure was shown to be due to reasonable cause and not willful neglect.

penalty, failure to meet information requirements a *civil tax penalty* for failure to set forth the information required on a *debt instrument* with *original issue discount* under §1275(c)(1), consisting of $50 for each instrument on which the information is omitted, unless the failure is due to *reasonable cause* and not willful neglect. §6706(a). A penalty of 1 percent of the aggregate issue price of the issue, with a maximum of $50,000, is also imposed for failure to furnish the information required under §1275(c)(2) to the *IRS*, unless the failure is due to *reasonable cause* and not willful neglect. §6706(c).

penalty, failure to pay tax a *civil tax penalty* for failure to pay the amount of tax shown on virtually any *return*, aside from *estimated tax*, when due (subject to automatic and discretionary extensions) and for failure to pay a *deficiency* within 10 days of the date of *notice* *and demand,* excusable for *reasonable cause.* §6651(a)(2). The penalty is assessed at the rate of one-half of one percent for each month or fraction of a month for which the tax or deficiency is unpaid, and is based on the net amount of tax shown on the return as filed, less tax paid on or by the beginning of the month for which the penalty is computed. The maximum penalty is 25 percent.

penalty, failure to report cash a formerly separate *civil tax penalty* of $50 per failure, up to $50,000 per year ($100 per failure, if deliberate, with no dollar limit), for failure to report cash transactions, including cashier's checks, bank drafts, money orders, traveler's checks, in a *trade or business* of over $10,000, excusable for *reasonable cause.* It is now part of the general penalty provision for *failure to file correct information returns.* §6721(a). See §6050I for the reporting requirements. See *tips, allocation of employee; cash, reporting.*

penalty, failure to report receipts of more than $10,000 the penalty for intentional disregard of these reporting requirements to the greater of $25,000 or the amount of cash, including cash equivalent monetary instrument, received in the transaction, to the extent the cash (or cash equivalent monetary instrument(s)) does not exceed $100,000. §6721(e)(2).

penalty, failure to supply identifying numbers a five-dollar-per-case *civil tax penalty* for failure to provide an identifying number when required to do so. §6676.

penalty, false or fraudulent exemption certificate information nonexclusive criminal penalty of up to $1,500, a year's imprisonment, or both, for the acts described in the heading, if the act is *willful* and has the effect of reducing taxes. §7205.

penalty, foreign corporation's failure to furnish information or maintain records a *civil tax penalty* of $10,000 for each *taxable year* to which a failure occurs. §6038A(d). The penalty falls on *foreign corporations* engaged in a *trade or business* in the *United States* at any time during the *taxable year* which fail to furnish information and maintain (or cause another *person* to maintain) records to determine the reporting corporation's tax liability. Once *IRS* mails notice of the failure to the reporting corporation and the failure continues for more than 90 days after the date the notice was mailed, an additional $10,000 penalty is incurred for each 30-day period (or fraction thereof) during which the failure continues after the end of the 90-day period following IRS notice, subject to a reasonable cause exception. See also §6038C(c) (same for foreign corporation engaged in *United States trade or business*).

penalty, fraud see *penalty, civil fraud.*

penalty, fraudulent failure to file a *civil tax penalty* consisting of a 15 percent surcharge on the net amount of tax due for each month that the *return* is not *filed,* up to a maximum of five months or 75 percent. §6651(f). The *IRS* has the burden of proof.

penalty, frivolous litigation see *penalty, damages for proceedings before Tax Court for delay.*

penalty, frivolous return a $500 *civil tax penalty* for filing a frivolous return, namely a return that on its face (1) does not contain information from which the correctness of the return can be determined; or (2) is substantially incorrect as to the tax liability shown. Even then, the penalty applies only if the conduct is due to a frivolous position or an intent to delay or impede the administration of the tax laws. §6702. See *frivolous return controversy.*

penalty, improper use of information a civil tax penalty of $250 to $10,000 imposed on a paid tax preparer who voluntarily discloses information given to prepare a *return* or who uses the information for any other purpose other than certain peer or quality review uses. §7216. There are associated *criminal tax penalties.*

penalty, negligence by tax return preparer a tax return preparer may, in good faith, rely upon the information furnished by the taxpayer and is not required to examine and review documents to verify the taxpayer's information. Reg. §1.6694-1(b)(2)(ii). However, the tax preparer may not ignore the implications of the information furnished and must make the appropriate inquiries required under the circumstances. See *penalty, unrealistic position by tax return preparer.*

penalty, negotiation of refund check by preparer a *civil tax penalty* of $500 for any *tax return preparer* who endorses or otherwise negotiates a refund check issued to a *taxpayer.* Certain limited exceptions apply to a bank that was the preparer. §6695(f).

penalty, payment of federal tax with bad check see *penalty, bad check.*

penalty, promoting abusive tax shelters a *civil tax penalty* imposed on *persons* who organize or sell any interest in a *partnership* or other *entity* or investment (e.g., even a *tax-exempt bond*), when, in connection with such organization or sale, the person makes or furnishes either (1) a statement, which the person knows or has reason to know is false or fraudulent as to any material matter with respect to the availability of any *tax benefit* said to be available by reason of participation in the investment; or (2) a *gross valuation overstatement* as to a matter material to the entity that is more than 200 percent of the correct value. §6700(a). This standard does not carry with it a duty of inquiry concerning the transaction. The penalty for promoting an abusive tax shelter is equal to the greater of $1,000 or 100 percent of the *gross income* derived, or to be derived, from the activity. Id. Participation in each sale of an interest is a separate punishable activity. §6700(a)(2)(B). The *IRS* is given authority to waive all or part of any penalty resulting from a gross valuation overstatement upon a showing that there was a reasonable basis for the valuation and that the valuation was made in good faith. Also, all activities subject to the penalty are enjoinable under §7408. See *abusive tax shelter, penalties, injunctions, and crimes.*

penalty, substantial understatement of income tax *civil tax penalty* of 20 percent of the portion of an *underpayment* attributable to an aggressive filing position that is not explained on the *taxpayer's return,* or as a result of a tax shelter, meaning a *partnership,* other *entity,* plan, or arrangement whose principal purpose is to avoid or evade *federal income tax.* Understatements are substantial if greater than both $5,000 ($10,000 for most *corporations* other than *S corporations* and *personal holding companies*) and 10 percent of the correct tax as redetermined by the *IRS.* Under prior law, and apparently also under current law, amounts refunded to taxpayers could be underpayments for purposes of §6661(a). There are various relief provisions (e.g., *taxable income* thresholds, *adequate disclosure,* and reliance on *substantial authority* for the position). §6662(d)(2)(B)(i) and (ii). The taxpayer must show that the treatment was more likely than not correct in cases involving *tax shelters.* §6662(d)(2)(C). See *accuracy-related penalty; secretarial list; underpayment of tax, accuracy-related penalty.*

penalty, unauthorized use of tax information   see *unauthorized use of tax information.*

penalty, underpayment of deposits   see *penalty, failure to make timely deposits.*

penalty, underpayment of estimated tax by corporations   a *civil tax penalty* imposed at variable rates for failure to pay timely any *required installment* of estimated taxes by a *corporation,* computed for the period of underpayment as to each required installment. It cannot be waived for *reasonable cause.* §6655. So-called *large corporations* are subjected to more onerous installment payment obligations and correspondingly increased likelihood of attracting these penalties. §6655(h). See §6655(d) (*safe harbor* exceptions to the estimated tax penalty). See *exceptions to estimated tax, corporate.*

penalty, underpayment of estimated tax by individuals   a *civil tax penalty* imposed at variable rates for failure to pay timely any *required installment* of estimated tax by an *individual taxpayer* obligated to pay such taxes, computed for the period of underpayment as to each *required installment.* It cannot be waived for

reasonable cause. §6654(a). For computations, see §6654(b). The underpayment is defined as the excess of the "required installment" over the amount paid as of the installment date. §6654(a). The amount of the required installment is generally defined as one-fourth of the "required annual payment," meaning the lesser of 90 percent of the tax for the year or 100 percent of last year's tax. §6654(d)(1). To avoid an underpayment penalty, taxpayers whose AGI increases by more than $40,000 from the prior year and whose AGI is more than $75,000 must make estimated tax payments equal to 90 percent of the current year's tax liability rather than 100 percent of the prior year's tax liability. §6654(d). See *exceptions to estimated tax, individual.*

penalty, unrealistic position by tax return preparer a *civil tax penalty* of $250 imposed on a *tax return preparer* if any part of an understatement of tax on a *return* or *claim for refund or credit* is attributable to an *unrealistic or hopeless position* and if the preparer knew or should have known of the position and did not make an *adequate disclosure* under §6662(d), or if the position was frivolous. §6694(a). It does not apply if there was *reasonable cause,* exercised in *good faith.* A $1,000 penalty applies to understatements caused by willful attempts to understate tax liability or reckless or intentional disregard of the rules. §6694(b). See *return preparer penalties.*

Pension Benefit Guaranty Corporation   a federal *corporation* designed to protect benefits under *defined benefit plans* by providing plan termination insurance. Premium charges, reporting, and disclosure are demanded by PBGC from defined benefit plans. Moreover, PBGC has the power to involuntarily terminate a plan under *ERISA* §4042, leaving the *employer* liable to pay PBGC potentially significant amounts. The PBGC rules do not apply to *individual* or *governmental plans, church plans* that have made the election under §410(d), or professional service plans with fewer than 25 participants.

pension plan contracts   that portion of *life insurance reserves* allocable to contracts (1) purchased by or for *stock bonus, pension,* or *profit-sharing plans* or *trusts,* which at the time of such purchase were qualified under §401(a); (2) purchased under *qualified annuity plans* for public school *employees*; (3) provided by a *life insurance company* for its own employees under stock bonus, pension, or profit-sharing plans, which for the *taxable year* satisfy the requirements of §401(a); (4) purchased to provide retirement annuities for its employees by an organization, which at the time of purchase was an exempt *section 501(c)(3) organization,* or purchased to provide retirement annuities for employees performing services for educational institutions of a state or local government; or (5) purchased by or for trusts, which at the time of purchase were *individual* *retirement accounts,* or purchased by or for *individual retirement annuities*; (6) or bought by certain *governmental plans* under §414(d) or *eligible deferred compensation* plans, or by certain governments to provide benefits under those two types of plans. §818(a).

pension plan, ERISA　see *employee pension benefit plan, ERISA.* The terms are synonymous.

pension plan, Internal Revenue Code　a *plan* established and maintained primarily to provide for the payment of definitely determinable benefits to *employees* after retirement. Reg. §1.401-1(b)(1)(c). Retirement benefits generally are measured by, and based on, such factors as *years of service* and *compensation* received by the employees. The determination of the amount of retirement benefits and the contributions to provide such benefits are not dependent on profits.

pension plan year　see *plan year.*

pension trusts, exempt　*trusts* organized and operated exclusively to fund *qualified pension, profit-sharing,* and *stock bonus plans.* §§401(a), 501(a). The key to qualifying such trusts for tax exemption in the vast majority of cases is meeting the comprehensive requirements of §401(a). See *qualified pension, profit-sharing, and stock bonus plan.*

percentage depletion　a method of *depletion* applied to most minerals, *geothermal deposits,* and, to a more limited extent, oil and gas, under which an arbitrary percentage of *gross income from the property* is allowed as a *deduction.* §§613. The rates range from 22 percent to 5 percent. The percentage depletion method has not been available to large oil and gas producers since 1974. However, it is still available to small oil and gas producers and royalty owners under specific exemption in the law, and for several types of mineral properties such as coal, iron, and gravel. §§613, 613A. Percentage depletion may not exceed 100 percent of taxable income before the deduction for depletion. The percentage limitation was 50 percent for years prior to 1991. See *small producers' exemption.*

percentage mark-up method　a method of showing concealment of income by merchants. The method assumes that sales are some percentage in excess of cost of sales. The result is an inferred figure for actual gross profit.

percentage of completion—capitalized cost method　a method by which 90 percent in most cases of the items (contract price and estimated cost) with respect to a *long-term contract* are taken into account, and income reported, under the *percentage of completion method,* and 10 percent are taken into account under the *taxpayer's* normal *method of accounting* (e.g., *completed contract* or *accrual method*) used for long-term contracts entered into and after June 20, 1988 until July 11, 1989,

when the method was *repealed,* subject to certain exceptions. §460(1)(A)-(B). There are significant exceptions to repeal in the case of smaller contractors, *qualified ship contracts, home construction contracts,* and *residential construction contracts.* §460(a)(2). See *percentage of completion method of accounting; completed contract method; small contractor exception.*

percentage of completion method of accounting　a *method of accounting* under which the taxpayer reports a percentage of the gross income from a long-term contract based on the portion of the work that has been completed. The portion of the total contract price reported in a given year is determined by multiplying the total contract price by the percentage of work completed in the year. The percentage is determined by dividing the current-year costs by the expected total costs. Reg §1.451-3(c(2). For alternative methods, see *completed contract method; extended long-term contracts; percentage of completion—capitalized cost method; small contractor exception.*

percentage of taxable income method, reserves for bad debts　a method of reporting additions to *reserves for bad debts* of *mutual savings banks, cooperative banks,* and *domestic building and loan associations* under which the lender can increase its *reserves* and, therefore, *deduct* an amount sufficient to inflate the reserve up to 8 percent of *taxable income.* §593(b).

percentage points　a change in position measured as a percentage of a total. For example, if Mrs. A owned 60 percent of a corporation in July and 90 percent that September, her ownership increased by 50 percent, but by only 30 percentage points. The standard is used under §382 to determine survival of *tax attributes.*

percentage test for coverage under qualified plan　see *coverage, qualified plans.*

percentage test, minimum coverage rules　see *minimum coverage rules.*

per country limitation　a method of computing the *foreign tax credit limitation* which is performed separately for each country in which it earns income. The method has been repealed in favor of an *overall limitation.*

per diem allowances　fixed amounts paid to an *individual* on a daily basis to cover living costs while he or she is in some particular status. See Reg. §§301.7601-1(d) (witnesses), 1.274-5(f) (authority of *IRS* to fix per diem allowances in connection with *travel expenses*), and 1.61-2(b) (inclusion of per diem expenses of persons in military and *uniformed services* of the United States).

period costs　generally, *expenses* that are excluded from *inventory* costs and instead can be *deducted* when *paid* or *incurred.* Reg. §1.471-11(c)(3)(ii). Also,

TEFRA §229 affects the treatment of period costs in the context of *long-term contracts.*

period costs, completed contract method under existing *regulations,* all *expenses* that are not incident and necessary to the performance of a *long-term contract,* as well as the following, whether or not incident to such a contract: (1) marketing and selling expenses, including bidding expenses; (2) advertising expenses; (3) other distribution expenses; (4) general and administrative expenses that benefit the *taxpayer's* business as a whole; (5) interest; (6) *research* and *experimentation expenses;* (7) *losses* under §165 and the *regulations* thereunder; (8) *percentage depletion* in excess of *cost depletion;* (9) *depreciation* on idle equipment and, for other equipment, tax depreciation in excess of book depreciation; (10) income taxes; (11) pension and profit-sharing contributions and other *employee* benefits; (12) costs attributable to strikes, rework, scrap, and spoilage; and (13) officer compensation that benefits the taxpayer's activities as a whole. Reg. §1.451-3(d)(5)(iii). Period costs are attractive to *taxpayers* since they may be currently *deductible.* See *uniform capitalization rules.*

periodic income see *fixed or determinable annual or periodical gains, profits, and income.*

periodic payment plan see *unit investment trust.*

periodic payments for purposes of the *federal income tax* on divorce payments under prior law (still in effect as to some prior divorces), the term refers to amounts includible in the recipient–ex-spouse's (or separated spouse's) *gross income* under former §71 and *deductible* by the payor-spouse (unless paid from an *alimony trust* or other *corpus*) under §215. To qualify, such amounts must be paid in light of a duty of support arising out of the marital relationship, pursuant to a decree of divorce, *separate maintenance,* or support, or pursuant to a *written separation* agreement.

periodic redemption plan not clearly defined, but apparently an arrangement whereby a *corporation* systematically repurchases small portions (e.g., 5 percent) of its own *stock.* Reg. §1.305-7(a); Rev. Rul. 78-115, 1978-1 C.B. 85. Such *stock redemptions* can result in increased proportionate interests in the corporation such that §305(b) may apply to tax both redeeming and nonredeeming shareholders. See *stock dividend.*

periodic report of actuary see *actuarial statement of valuation.*

period of service see *elapsed time method, qualified plans.*

permanent establishment a *tax treaty* term referring to a regular fixed place of *business* in one of the contracting countries.

permanent multiple asset accounts see *continuing multiple asset accounts.*

permanent preferences such *items of tax preference* or *AMT adjustments* as tax-exempt interest and *percentage depletion* in excess of *basis* that are permanent as opposed to transitory *timing preferences.* See §57(a)(5) and (a)(1). In the case of the noncorporate *taxpayer,* these items are excluded from the *minimum tax credit.* §53(d). See *alternative minimum tax.*

permitted disparity a disparity in contributions or benefits that does not disqualify a *defined benefit plan* or a *defined contribution plan* on the basis of discrimination against lower-paid *employees* whose benefits or *employer* contributions are diminished by *Social Security benefits.* §401. See *integration, Social Security.*

permitted investment a type of asset held by a *REMIC,* consisting of any *cash flow investment,* any *qualified reserve asset,* or any foreclosure property. §860G(a)(5). A REMIC's asset base must be primarily *qualified mortgages* and *permitted investments.* §860D(a)(4).

permitted property a term used in Prop. Reg. §1.453-1(f)(1)(iii) to refer to property that can be received on a *tax-deferred* basis, to which *basis* in the transferred property is first allocated where the *taxpayer* engages in an *installment sale* in connection with a *section 351 transaction,* taking back an obligation that is not a *security.*

permitted year a *calendar year* or a *fiscal year* of an *S corporation* approved by the *IRS.* §1378(a)(2). Approval requires a *business purpose.* §1378(b)(2). See *section 444 election of fiscal tax year by partnership, S corporation, or personal service corporation (PSC).*

perpetual-care fund a *trust* established pursuant to local law by a taxable cemetery for the care and maintenance of the cemetery. It is funded out of a percentage of the gross receipts from the sale of burial lots and crypts. The income of such a trust is applied to the perpetual care and maintenance of the cemetery, burial lots, and mausoleum crypts. §642(i). Section 642 provides a *deduction* for amounts *distributed* by perpetual-care fund trusts for the care and maintenance of gravesites. The deduction allowed is to be the amount actually distributed during the year for such care and maintenance (but not more than $5 per gravesite).

perpetual inventories book *inventories,* that is, inventories determined on the basis of recorded costs of purchases (or manufacture) and sales, rather than physical inventories. The *regulations* acknowledge the system but demand occasional physical inventories. Reg. §1.471-2(d).

person generally, an *individual, trust, estate,* or *corporation.*

personal casualty gain the *recognized gain* from any *involuntary conversion* of *property,* which is described in §165(c)(3), arising from fire, storm, shipwreck, or *other casualty,* or from *theft.* §165(h)(3)(A). See *net casualty loss.*

personal casualty loss any *loss* described in §165(c)(3), e.g., one from fire, storm, or shipwreck, which does not arise in a *business* or *transaction* entered into for a *profit*-seeking context, determined after the application of the $100 per casualty floor. §165(h)(3)(B). Section 1231 no longer applies to these losses. §1231(a)(3). See *net casualty loss.*

personal exemption $2,350 for 1993, to be deducted from adjusted gross income, together with either itemized deductions or the standard deduction, whichever is larger, in arriving at *taxable income.* §151. *Married* taxpayers filing *joint returns* may claim a total of two personal exemptions. §151(b). In addition, exemptions may be claimed for *spouses* who file *separate returns* and have no *gross income.* §151(b). The exemption on the basis of having dependents under §153(c) is usually referred to as a *dependency exemption.* The personal exemption is phased out (and *marginal tax rates* rise) at high levels of *adjusted gross income.* §151(d). See *dependency exemption.*

personal exemption, trusts and estates annual amounts, ranging from $600 for an *estate* to $100 for a *complex trust,* allowed as a *deduction* by the trust. §642(b). Such deductions are allowed in order to avoid the need to prepare *returns* with such trivial income.

personal expenses *expenses* disallowed (entirely, or if appropriate, allocably) by §262, on the underlying theory that only *gain-seeking* or legislatively preferred expenditures (e.g., *business* costs or *interest* charges) should be fiscally subsidized. "Personal expenses" is shorthand for the *Code's* term "personal, living, and family expenses." Illustrations, listed in Reg. §1.262-1(b), include insurance for one's personal residence, personal life insurance, and *losses* on transactions not entered into for a profit. *Corporations* are generally thought of as not subject to this rule, but, in fact, they are occasionally subject to it in the sense that in some cases the expenditure (e.g., swimming pool maintenance for a shareholder) may serve no business purpose as required by §162. A corporate expenditure may also be characterized as a *nondeductible disguised dividend* if its benefit flows to a *shareholder.*

personal holding company generally, a closely held *corporation* earning excessive amounts of certain types of income. The *Code* defines it as any corporation (1) at least 60 percent of whose *adjusted ordinary gross income* (AOGI) for the *taxable year* is *personal holding company income*; and (2) more than 50 percent in value of whose outstanding *stock* is owned directly or indi-

rectly, actually or *constructively,* by no more than five *individuals* at any time during the last half of the *taxable year.* §542(a); Reg. §1.542-1. Corporations excluded from the definition of personal holding company include *tax-exempt* corporations, *banks, building and loan associations,* certain lending or finance companies, surety companies, *life insurance companies, foreign personal holding companies,* most corporate bankrupts, certain other *foreign corporations,* and certain *small business investment companies* that are licensed by the Small Business Administration. §542(c). If the personal holding company tax applies, the tax is 28 percent of undistributed personal holding company income. §541. See *personal holding company income.*

personal holding company income *gross income* of certain passive investment and personal service varieties that may taint a corporation as a *personal holding company* if other tests under §542(a) are met. Section 543(a) defines the term as that portion of the *adjusted ordinary gross income* (AOGI) that consists of (1) *dividends*; (2) actual and *imputed interest*; (3) *royalties* (other than those described in items (6), (7), and (8) below); (4) *annuities*; (5) *rents* (excluding, inter alia, *active business software royalties*); (6) mineral, oil, and gas royalties; (7) *copyright royalties*; (8) *produced film rents*; (9) *compensation for use of corporate property by shareholders*; (10) income from *personal service contracts*; and (11) income from *estates* and *trusts.* §543; Reg. §1.543-1. This concept is essential in determining the personal holding company status of the corporation. If at least 60 percent of the corporation's AOGI is personal holding company income and if the *stock* ownership test (more than 50 percent owned by five or fewer *individuals*) is also satisfied, the corporation is a personal holding company. §542(a). Distributions in *partial liquidation* to a corporate shareholder are also personal holding company income if such distributions would otherwise be *dividends.* §543(a)(1). See *annuities, personal holding company income; copyright royalties, personal holding company income; dividend, personal holding company income; interest, personal holding company income; produced film rents; rents, personal holding company income; royalties, personal holding company income.*

personal holding company tax an additional surtax of 28 percent imposed on the *undistributed personal holding company income* of a *corporation* that meets the statutory definition of a *personal holding company* under §542. §541. This tax, if applicable, is in addition to the corporate *income taxes* of §§11 or 1201. It applies to *domestic* and *foreign* corporations (only as to United States source income as to the latter, unless they meet the definition of the term *foreign personal holding company* defined in §552) and, to the extent provided by §542(b), to an *affiliated group* of corporations filing a *consolidated return.* Reg. §1.541-1. The personal holding company tax was enacted to deal with *tax avoidance* devices such as *incorporated pocketbooks, incorporated talents,* and *incorporated yachts.*

personal injuries or sickness injuries to the *person,* or ill-health. Section 104(a)(2) and Reg. §1.104-1(c) create an *exclusion* from *gross income* for recoveries, even if by settlement, for unintentional and intentional torts that result in bodily injury or sickness but not as to the portion of the payment allocable to previously *deducted medical expenses.* Section 104(a)(3) provides a comparable exclusion for payments under policies purchased by the payee. Associated *punitive damages* are excluded, provided there is sickness or personal injury. §104(a). See §§104(a)(4) and 105, which provide comparable exclusions for *employee*-paid and *employer*-paid insurance covering personal injuries or sickness.

personal interest any *interest* otherwise *deductible* except for interest *paid or accrued* on debt occurred or continued in a *trade or business* of the *taxpayer* (other than performing services as an *employee*); *investment interest*; interest taken into account in computing of *income* or *loss* from a *passive activity; qualified residence interest*; or, interest on the deferred payment of *estate tax* under §6163 or §6166. §163(h)(2). It, therefore, includes such items as interest on credit cards, car loans, unsecured credit lines, and underpayments of income tax. It also includes interest on home mortgage loans unless the interest constitutes *qualified residence interest.* The status of interest paid to purchase or carry *life insurance* is unclear, but it seems to be *investment interest.* Personal interest is *nondeductible* by *taxpayers* other than *corporations.* §163(h)(1). There are grandfathering provisions for qualified residence interest, including refinanced debt.

personal living and family expenses see *personal expenses.*

personal losses *losses* that neither arise in a *trade or business* setting nor are a result of a *transaction entered into for a profit.* Section 165, the central loss provision of the *Code,* allows *deductions* for such losses for *individuals* only if they are *thefts* or *casualties.* Otherwise, as in the case of a home acquired as a residence and sold at a loss, there is in effect no federal tax subsidy.

personal property property other than *real property.* Personal property may be *tangible* (e.g., an automobile) or *intangible* (e.g., a patent). Personal property can also refer to property not used in a taxpayer's trade or business or held for the production or collection of income.

personal property, straddles any *personal property,* other than stock, that is regularly traded (e.g., gold, Treasury bills, grains, meats, foreign currency). §1092(d)(1). The term forms part of the definition of a *straddle.* §§1092(c)(1) and 1256(c)(2)(A). The straddle

rules extend to *stock options* and *offsetting position stock.* The latter term includes any *stock* which forms part of a straddle, at least one of the offsetting positions of which is an option on that stock or substantially identical stock or securities, or a position in substantially similar or related property other than stock. §1092(d)(3)(B)(i). It also includes stock of a *corporation* used to take positions in personal property that offset positions taken by any shareholder. §1092(d)(3)(B)(ii).

personal property taxes annual *taxes* imposed by a state or local government primarily on the value (i.e., ad valorem) of *personal property.* §164(b)(1). The tax is still a personal property tax even though it is associated with a privilege, such as operating a boat, provided it is based on value. Reg. §1.164-3(c)(3). Only the excess over a minimum fee can be *deductible,* since only the excess can be levied as a percentage of the property's value. See, e.g., Rev. Rul. 71-472, 1971-2 C.B. 123. State and local personal property taxes are deductible under §164(a)(2). See *ad valorem taxes.*

personal representatives generally, *executors* and *administrators* of *decedents' estates.*

personal service activity, passive loss rules the performance of personal services in the fields of health, law, engineering, architecture, accounting, actuarial science, performing arts, consulting, or any other *trade or business* in which capital is not a *material income-producing factor.* See Reg. §1.469-5T(d). If an *activity* is a personal service activity and the *individual materially participated* in the activity for any three years in the past, the individual is deemed to have materially participated. Reg. §1.469-5T(a). See *material participation, passive loss rules.*

personal service contract a contract under which a *corporation* furnishes personal services (e.g., dental services), if someone other than the corporation has the right to designate the *individual* to provide the services, or if the individual who will perform the services is designated in the contract, but in all cases only if during some part of the year the service provider owns at least 25 percent of the value of the *stock* of the corporation. §543(a)(7); Reg. §1.543-10(a). *Adjusted ordinary gross income* from such contracts is *personal holding company income.*

personal service corporation a *corporation,* the principal activity of which is performing personal services (e.g., medical services, law, accounting), which services are substantially performed by *employee-owners* (basically, more-than-ten-percent shareholders, applying modified *attribution rules* that include *stock* held by a five-percent-or-more-owned corporation). §§448(d)(2)(A), §269A(b). Section 269A grants the *IRS* broad authority to reallocate *gross income, deductions,* and other allowances between such corporations and their employee-owners where such entities are formed or used for the principal purpose of *avoiding* or evading *taxes* by securing otherwise unavailable *tax benefits,* and substantially all their business is done for one other *entity.* The principal activity is personal services if over 50 percent of annual compensation cost (salaries, *wages,* etc.) is for personal services or supporting the provision of such services. Personal services are "substantially performed" by employee-owners if they generate over 20 percent of the corporation's compensation cost. For purposes of the *section 444 election,* the term "personal service corporation" has the same meaning as under §269A(b)(1) except that any stock held by an owner-employee is counted and that ownership of a corporation's stock portfolio is attributed pro rata (i.e., not limited by a 50 percent threshold). Also, at least 10 percent of the stock (by value) must be held by employee-owners (as modified) and if the corporation is a member of a *consolidated group,* all members are considered in the decision as to whether it is a personal service corporation. §§444(f) and 441(i)(2).

personal service corporation, passive loss rules basically, a *corporation* whose principal *activity* is offering personal services of its *employee-owners.* §§469(j)(1) and 269A(b)(1). The definition is the same as for a *personal service corporation* under the reallocation rules of §269A, but with broader *attribution rules* for *stock* ownership. For this purpose, employee-owners are persons who owned any of the corporation's outstanding stock on any day of the *taxable year,* subject to a *de minimis* exception for corporations as to which only 10 percent or less of the value of the corporation's stock is held by employee-owners. §469(j)(2) and Reg. §§1.469-1T(g)(2) and 1.441-4T(d) (inclusion of §44 definition). The *attribution rules* of §318 are used, except attribution of stock ownership from corporations to shareholders is simply pro rata, with no 50 percent threshold under §318(a)(2)(C). §469(j)(2)(B). These corporations are subject to the *passive loss rules,* provided over 10 percent of the stock (by value) is owned by employee-owners. See *passive loss rules.*

personal service corporation, taxable year a personal service corporation may elect on *Form 8716* to use other than a required tax year. §444. Electing personal service corporations must make minimum distributions to their employee-owners by the end of a calendar year that falls within a tax year to avoid certain deduction deferrals for amounts paid to employee-owners. A personal service corporation may not deduct payments made to owner-employees before the tax year in which such persons must include the payment in gross income. For this purpose, a personal service corporation and any employee-owner are considered *related taxpayers.* §267(a)(2).

personal service corporation, tax rates same as *qualified personal service corporation.* Such corporations are taxed at the top *corporate income tax* rate. §§11(b)(2) and 448(d)(2).

personal use for purposes of the *vacation home rules* of §280A, relating to rentals of *dwelling units,* the term refers to use of a residence (which is broadly defined) for nonbusiness purposes by (1) a party having an interest in the property; (2) someone with a reciprocal right to use the property; or (3) someone who rents the property at a rate below *fair market value.* §280A(d)(2). See *use as a residence.*

personal use property property held for personal use as opposed to property held for *business* or profit. The concept appears sporadically in the *Code.* One multiple use definition appears under the heading *"personal use property, imputed interest."* See *casualty loss.*

personal use property, imputed interest *property,* substantially all of the use of which is by the *taxpayer* and is not in connection with a *trade or business* of the taxpayer or an *investment* activity under §212. §1275(b)(3). In the case of the *original issue discount rules,* this determination is made as of the time the *debt* is issued. §1275(c)(5).

per-unit retain allocation any *allocation,* by a *marketing cooperative* to its *patron* with respect to products marketed for the patron, the amount of which is fixed without reference to the net earnings of the organization, pursuant to an agreement between the organization and the patron (e.g., per dozen eggs). §1388(f). The cooperative can deduct such allocations to the extent paid in money, *qualified per-unit retain certificates,* or other property. §1388(b)(3). The patrons must take such certificates into *income* at their face amounts. §1388(h).

per-unit retain certificates a written notice of amounts allocated to and retained by a *cooperative* from *patrons* without regard to the earnings of the association, usually determined on the basis of the quantity and quality of patrons' products delivered to the cooperative. They are not *patronage dividends* because they are determined without regard to the cooperative's earnings. §1388(g); Reg. §1.1388-1(a)(2)(iv). On redemption, patrons receive extra money (or property) representing proceeds from sales on their behalf. The proceeds are taxed to patrons immediately if the certificates are *qualified per-unit retain certificates,* or when redeemed if they are nonqualified certificates. See *qualified per-unit retain certificate.*

petition for readjustment a *petition* that may be filed in the *Tax Court,* the *Claims Court,* or a Federal *District Court* in response to a notice of *final partnership administrative adjustment.* §6226(a). The petition is an important element of the TEFRA *audit* procedures for *S corporations* and *partnerships.* It is generally filed by the *tax matters partner*, but it may be filed by other partners if that partner fails to make a timely filing. §6226(b) through (d). See *unified proceedings*.

petition, Tax Court   a document used by *taxpayers* to gain the jurisdiction of the *Tax Court*. See Tax Court Rule 30-34. Generally, defects in form are disregarded, although the rules do offer a prescribed form.

petroleum tax   an informal term for an element of the collective *"Superfund taxes"* taxes. The base on which the tax is imposed is *crude oil* received at a *United States* refinery and petroleum products entering the United States for consumption, use, or warehousing. §4611. The details of the tax are complex, and it is subject to sunset provisions.

phantom gain   a reference to a *gain* which is not *realized* in cash. The most common example occurs when property which is encumbered by *nonrecourse debt* is transferred to the lender by means of a deed in lieu of foreclosure. The excess of the debt over the property's *adjusted basis* is taxable (phantom) gain under §1001(a).

phantom stock   stock of a designated *corporation*, used as a measuring device for *deferred compensation* plans. Such stock is not actually acquired and held but is simply used as an index of the payor's eventual obligations. See §404(a)(5).

phase-by-phase consolidations   a position taken in certain *rulings* that if a *life insurance company* filed a *consolidated return* with a nonlife company, then it had to aggregate *taxable investment income* and *gains from operations* before determining consolidated group accounts. Consolidated amounts would be determined by aggregating separate amounts for each member in a life subgroup, and a consolidated limitation would apply whenever a *deduction* was limited by an amount or percentage of an amount (including the 50 percent deferral for gain from operations in excess of taxable investment income and the limitation on policyholder dividends and special deductions). See *bottom-line consolidations, life insurance companies*.

physical asset   any asset other than a *financial asset,* including *goodwill, patents,* and other *intangibles.* Reg. §1.964-1(e)(5)(ii). The term is used for purposes of determining *earnings and profits* of *foreign corporations* under *subpart F*. Specifically, foreign exchange *gains* are reflected in United States dollars by showing physical assets (other than *inventory*) at the exchange rate for the translation period in which the historical cost of the asset was incurred. See *financial asset*.

physical completion method   a method of determining the *percentage of completion* of a contract in the year, applied by comparing the work performed under the contract with the estimated total work to be per-

formed. Reg. §1.451-3(c). It is an application of the *percentage of completion method of accounting* permissible for pre–March 1986 *long-term contract*.

physically handicapped person   not clearly defined. See *handicapped individual*.

physical presence test   an alternate standard to determine whether a citizen of the *United States* or *national* qualifies for the benefits of §911, allowing an *exclusion* of foreign source *earned income*. §911(d)(1)(B). The inquiry focuses on whether the *individual* was physically present abroad for 330 days during any 12-month period. For the other test, see *bona fide resident*.

physician   a doctor of medicine or osteopathy who is legally authorized to practice medicine and surgery by the state in which he or she practices; a doctor of dentistry or oral surgery who is legally authorized to practice dentistry by the state in which he or she practices, but only for surgery related to the jaw; a doctor of podiatry or surgical chiropody, but only for functions he or she is legally authorized to perform in the state in which he or she practices; a doctor of optometry who is legally authorized to practice optometry by the state in which he or she practices, but only with respect to determining whether a patient needs prosthetic lenses; or a chiropractor who is legally authorized to perform the services of a chiropractor in the state in which he or she practices. 42 U.S.C. §1395x(r). For a *prescribed drug* to be *deductible* as a *medical expense* under §213(b), it must be one that legally requires a prescription from a physician as defined above. See §213(b). The term is also used in connection with the $50 per night *deduction* for lodging for persons accompanying the ill person. §213(d)(2) (part of the definition of *medical care*).

physicians and surgeons mutual protection association   an *association providing only medical malpractice protection for its members (or provisional members) or medical malpractice coverage against claims relating to a doctor's professional practice. The association can generally exclude* from its *gross income* initial receipts from a new participant. *Current distributions* to members are deemed paid from surplus in excess of amounts not previously taxed. Its members can *deduct* initial payments (made in up to six installments) to the association as a *trade or business expense,* up to the amount payable to an independent insurer. §1031.

piecemeal cancellation of debt   cancellation of *debt* in serial fashion. It is a common *estate planning* device to transfer property by sale, in order to gain a *stepped-up basis* for the buyer, followed by *gifts* subject to the *annual gift tax exclusion*.

piggyback agreement   a nickname for the procedure under which *tax shelter* investors who have been audited agree to be bound by the judicial results of a test case.

placed in service, date the date *depreciable property* is first placed in a condition or state of readiness and availability for a specifically assigned function, a status that can arise long before the property is actually used (e.g., a farmer's purchase of a tractor in the fall for use next spring). Only at that time can *depreciation* (or *cost recovery*) *deductions* be claimed. Reg. §1.167(a)-11(e).

placed in service, qualified film the date a film is first exhibited to, or otherwise used by, the primary audience for which it was created. Reg. §1.48-8(a)(5).

plain-meaning rule a doctrine of statutory construction to the effect that as the first step in interpreting a statute, the courts should study and follow the plain meaning of the words and not engage in interpretative gymnastics when the meaning of the language is clear.

plan synonymous with *employee benefit plan* or *qualified plan*. Also, for purposes of *prohibited transactions penalties,* a *trust* described in §401(a) that forms a part of a plan, or a plan described in §403(a) or §405(a), which trust or plan is exempt from tax under §501(a); an *individual retirement account, individual retirement annuity,* or *retirement bond*; or a trust, plan, account, annuity, or bond that, at any time, has been determined by the *Secretary* to be such a trust, plan, account, or bond is a "plan." §4975(3). Note, the term implies a permanent, as distinguished from a temporary, program. Reg. §1.401-1(b)(2). See *qualified plan.*

plan administrator the *person* or persons specifically designated to act as the *administrator* by the terms of the instrument under which a *plan* is operated. Should no person or persons be specifically designated as the plan administrator, then the plan administrator is, (1) in the case of a plan maintained by a single *employer,* the employer (a *corporation* may be a plan administrator); (2) or in the case of a plan maintained by an *employee organization,* the employee organization; (3) in the case of a plan maintained by two or more employers, then the association, committee, or joint board of trustees who maintain the plan; and (4) in any case where (1), (2), or (3) above do not apply, then the person(s) actually responsible, directly or indirectly, for the control, disposition, or management of the cash or property received by or contributed to the plan. §414(g). Reg. §1.414(g)-1(a) and (b). A virtually identical definition to the foregoing is provided by *ERISA,* Pub. L. No. 83-406, §3(16)(A), 88 Stat. 829. See *plan sponsor* for administration in cases of default.

plan description materials, which may be *summary plan descriptions* and amendments, that the *plan administrator* of a *qualified retirement plan* must file with the Secretary of Labor within 120 days after the plan's adoption and every five years thereafter, with descriptions of material modifications to the plan filed within 210 days after the close of any year in which changes occur. *ERISA,* Pub. L. No. 83-406, §104, 88 Stat. 829.

plan loan see *qualified plan loan.*

plan of reorganization a statutory requirement imposed by §§354 and 361, which allows a tax-free *exchange* in a *corporate reorganization.* The term refers to a consummated transaction specifically defined as a reorganization under §368(a). Reg. §1.368-2(g). Reg. §1.368-3(a) demands officially recorded adoption of the plan by authorized corporate officials. A plan may, however, be found through an application of the *step transaction doctrine.* Informality is in fact tolerated, but the plan requirement remains an important limit on the definition of the term "*reorganization.*" The absence of a plan of reorganization may result in the finding of no reorganization, and the concept has been used to defeat *continuity of interest* and *continuity of business enterprise* claims, even though the term appears only in §§354, 356, and 361, and not in the definitional provisions of §368.

plan spin-off the division of a single *qualified plan* into two or more plans. Section 414(b) contains elaborate provisions to assure that each *participant's* post-spin-off minimum benefit is preserved.

plan sponsor (1) the *employer,* in the case of an *employee benefit plan* established or maintained by a single employer; (2) the *employee organization,* in the case of a plan established or maintained by an employee organization; or (3) the association, committee, joint board of trustees, or other similar group of representatives of the parties who establish or maintain the plan, in the case of a plan established or maintained by two or more employers or jointly by one or more employees and one or more employee organizations, *ERISA,* Pub. L. No. 83-406, §3(16)(B), 88 Stat. 829. A plan sponsor is the *plan administrator* if no person is specifically so designated by the terms of the instrument under which the plan is operated. *ERISA,* Pub. L. No. 83-406, §3(16)(A), 88 Stat. 829.

plan valuation a process, to be performed at least annually, of valuing the assets in a *qualified deferred compensation plan* using actuarial methods in order to determine if the plan satisfies the *minimum funding standards.* §411(c). See *accumulated funding deficiency.*

plan year a *calendar,* policy, or *fiscal year* on which the records of the plan are kept. *ERISA,* Pub. L. No. 83-406, §3(39), 88 Stat. 829; Labor Dept. Reg. §2602.2.

plan year of participation a *plan year* for which a *participant accrues* a benefit under the terms of the plan (determined only with respect to benefits provided by the plan and without regard to any plan provision not in effect that plan year). As a result, for example, benefits provided under the Social Security Act or past service benefits for prior years are not included in the determination of the plan year of participation. Reg. §1.401(j)-1(c)(4)(iii).

point in the United States see *foreign travel.*

points a fee charged for finding, placing, or processing a mortgage loan. To qualify as deductible interest, the points must be considered compensation to a lender solely for the use or forbearance of money. The points cannot be a form of service charge if they are to qualify as deductible interest. Rev. Rul. 67-297, 1967-2 C.B. 87. Points are required to be *capitalized* and *amortized* ratably over the life of the loan. A special exception permits the purchaser of a personal residence to deduct qualifying points in the year of payment. §461(g)(2). See §6050H(b)(2)(C) (lender's obligation to report points).

policy acquisition expenses *expenses* incurred in the generation of *life insurance* and other premiums. *Insurance companies,* whether life or nonlife, must *capitalize* and *amortize* policy acquisition expenses (and make certain reserve adjustments). §848. Reinsurance transactions are also subject to the amortization provisions. Amortization applies to each *specified insurance contract.*

policyholder dividend, life insurance companies any dividend or similar *distribution* to *policyholders* (as such), including (1) amounts paid or credited (including increases in benefits) where the amount depends on the *life insurance company's* experience or its management's discretion; (2) *excess interest*; (3) premium adjustment (premium reductions not demanded by the contract); and (4) experience-rated refunds (those based on the contract or the group's experience). §808(a) and (b). Excess interest means an amount paid or credited to a policyholder (as such) which exceeds the prevailing state assumed rate of interest. §808(d)(i). Dividends which increase *cash surrender values* or other benefits or which reduce premiums are not policyholder dividends, but returns of premiums. §806(e). Dividends on life insurance policies are normally not taxable because they are considered to be a partial return of premiums paid. The dividends are taxable to the extent that the total dividends received exceed the premiums paid. See *differential earnings amount, life insurance companies; excess interest deduction.*

policyholder, life insurance the person who owns a *life insurance policy.* This is often the insured, but it may also be a relative of the insured, a *partnership,* or a *corporation.*

policyholders' deduction the exclusion of the *policyholders' share* of *investment income* of a *life insurance company.*

political candidate for purposes of the denial of

deductions for indirect contributions to political parties, the term includes anyone who is generally believed, by the persons making the expenditures, to be one who is or in the reasonably foreseeable future will be seeking selection, nomination, or election to any public office. Reg. §1.276-1(f)(2). See *indirect contributions to political parties.*

political contribution a nonexclusive list of transactions, including a gift, subscription, loan, advance, or deposit of money or anything of value, including a contract, promise, or agreement to make a contribution, whether or not legally enforceable. §271(b)(2). The term is used for purposes of defining an exempt *political organization* (§527) and in relation to *bad debts* and *worthless securities* of *political organizations* (§271). §527(e)(3). Note that the *Code* uses the term "contributions" not "political contributions." See *debts owed by political parties; indirect contributions to political parties.*

political expenditure see *expenditure, political.*

political expenditures excise tax see *excise* tax, political expenditures.

political organization a party, committee, association, fund, or other organization (whether or not incorporated) organized and operated primarily to accept contributions, to make expenditures for an *exempt function* (basically, getting people elected or appointed to public office), or both. However, the organization does not need to engage exclusively in such exempt functions. §527(e)(1); Reg. §1.527-2(a)(1) through (3). Political organizations, although generally tax-exempt, are taxed on their *political organization taxable income,* which basically means net income from nonexempt sources (e.g., *capital gains, investment interest,* and the like) at top corporate rates, except for principal campaign committees of Congressional candidates, which enjoy graduated corporate rates. §527(b)(1) and (h)(1). The concept is a broad one; it explicitly includes *newsletter fund contributions* (§527(g)) and can, for example, include a bank account used to accept contributions and disburse campaign expenses. Rev. Rul. 79-11, 1979-1 C.B. 207. Gifts to political organizations are exempt from the federal *gift tax* (§2501(a)(5)), but gifts of appreciated property to political organizations result in taxable *gains* to the transferor. See *expenditure, political.*

political organization taxable income an amount equal to the excess (if any) of the *gross income* for the *taxable year* (excluding *exempt function income*), over *deductions* directly connected with the production of the gross income (excluding exempt function income), subject to some minor modifications, principally: (1) a specific deduction of $100; (2) no *net operating loss deductions*; and (3) no *dividends-received deduction.*

§527(b). This definition combines with other *Code* provisions to mean the organization is taxed at top corporate rates under §11 on its *ordinary income* from nonpolitical sources, regardless of the actual legal form the organization takes. See *political organization.*

political party, indirect contributions a political party; a national, state, or local committee of a political party; or a committee, association, or organization that accepts *political contributions* or makes expenditures for the purpose of influencing or attempting to influence the election of presidential or vice-presidential electors or of any *individual* whose name is presented for election to any federal, state, or local elective public office, whether or not such individual is selected, nominated, or elected. §276(b)(1). The significance of the term appears under the headings "*indirect contributions to political parties*" and "*political contributions.*"

political subdivision counties, townships, cities, or other authorities that have been delegated power by a state, *possession,* territory, or the District of Columbia. It can include authorities created by interstate compacts, such as the Port of New York Authority. The term is important in the determination of whether *interest* or certain obligations is *exempt* from *federal income taxation* under §103 by virtue of being a *state or local bond.*

pollution control equipment, energy investment credit Pollution control equipment, qualifying as energy property, which is financed by *industrial development bonds* or by other government means, is eligible for a reduced *energy investment credit.* §48(1)(11).

pollution control facility *state or local bonds* property to be used, in whole or in part, to abate or control water or air pollution by removing, altering, disposing, or storing pollutants, contaminants, wastes, or heat. For *amortization* of certain pollution control facilities, see *certified pollution control facility.*

Pomona plan a plan devised by Pomona College to attract contributions. The plan involves contributing appreciated securities under a life income plan; the college then invests the proceeds in *tax-exempt bonds,* distributing the income to *beneficiaries.* The result is a *charitable contribution* at full value without recognition of *gains* and a flow of *tax-exempt income.* Revenue Rul. 60-370, 1960-2 C.B. 203, would tax the gain on the transfer to the college or other charitable recipient.

pooled financing bond in general, any *bond* that is issued as part of an *issue,* more than $5 million of whose proceeds are, at the time of issuance of the bonds, reasonably expected to be used, or are intentionally used, directly or indirectly, to make or finance loans to two or more ultimate borrowers. §149(f)(4)(A). Unless there is an exception, pooled financing bonds are *tax-exempt bonds* only if (1) the issuer reasonably expects at least 95 percent of the *net proceeds* (modi-

fied definition) to be used within three years to make or finance loans to ultimate borrowers; (2) there are no contingent legal or underwriting fees; and (3) at least 95 percent of anticipated legal or underwriting costs of the offering will occur within 180 days of issuance. §149(f). See *required rebate.*

pooled fund, qualified plans arrangements under which separate *qualified trusts* of multiple *employers* combine their funds in a group trust to diversify their investments. Such group trusts can qualify as qualified trusts. Rev. Rul. 66-297, 1966-2 C.B. 234.

pooled income fund a *trust* for the benefit of a *public charity* to which several *donors* have transferred property, which is commingled and invested in assets other than *tax-exempt obligations,* with the income interest shared in proportion to the donor's contribution, payable to each donor or donor's *beneficiary* for life and the *remainder* irrevocably payable to charity. §642(c)(5) (containing further restrictions). The gift of the *remainder interest* is paid to the charity and qualifies as a currently *deductible charitable contribution.* §170(f)(3). Such funds are operated by numerous charitable organizations and are efficient alternatives to separately established *charitable remainder trusts.* The funds are taxed as *trusts.*

pooling agreement an agreement among owners of small tracts of land who join in order to meet state standards for spacing wells so that they can collectively exploit their oil and gas properties. Pooling avoids economic waste in the extraction of resources. R. Williams & C. Meyers, *Oil and Gas Law, Manual of Oil and Gas Terms* 555 (MB 1981). See *unitization, oil and gas properties.*

pooling method see *pooling-of-interest method.*

pooling method, foreign tax credit a method of determining the source out of which *foreign taxes* are considered paid for purposes of determining the *deemed paid foreign tax credit* for years after 1986, when dealing with a *foreign corporation's post-1986 undistributed profits.* See *deemed paid foreign tax credit; foreign corporation's post-1986 foreign income taxes; foreign income, war profits and excess profits taxes; foreign tax credit; foreign tax credit limitation; functional currency.*

pooling-of-interest method a *method of accounting* for corporate fusions, which is based on the theory that the *corporations* have blended together, with little or no distribution of assets. The balance sheets are simply combined. Since no *goodwill* is purchased, it will not be listed as a new-found asset after the acquisition. The pooling method may be used only if the stringent requirements set by the Accounting Principles Board Opinion No. 16 are met, including limits on intercompany ownership, type of stock involved, time for completion of the acquisition, and others. These are independent of the requirements for treatment as a tax-free *reorganization.* For the antonym, see *purchase method.*

pooling, oil and gas   see *pooling agreement.*

pool-of-capital doctrine a *federal income tax* doctrine of great importance to the oil, gas, and mineral industries, the gist of which is that the receipt of an *economic interest* in a mineral property in exchange for equipment, capital, or services directly used in the exploitation of the property does not result in the *realization* of *gross income,* on the theory that the parties are merely pooling their capital. The doctrine was most fully explored in G.C.M. 22730, 1941-1 C.B. 214, and has recently been confined so as to exclude from its protection the provision of services by promoters, attorneys, and certain corporate *employees* who receive royalties in connection with the acquisition and development of the properties out of which the royalties were created. Rev. Rul. 83-46, 1983-1 C.B. 16.

pool-of-capital investment, oil and gas   see *pool-of-capital doctrine.*

portability a reference to the power of a *participant* in a *qualified deferred compensation plan* to shift rights from one plan to another upon his or her changing employment. The most powerful form of portability arises when the new *employer* counts service for the previous employer in determining benefits under its plan. Section 402(a)(5) provides limited portability in that it permits some distributions from qualified deferred compensation plans to be reinvested in *individual retirement arrangements* or another qualified plan.

portfolio income another name for *interest, dividends, royalties, gains,* and *losses* on property held for *investment,* gains and losses on *dispositions* of property that normally produces interest, dividend or royalty income, and portfolio income passed through to the *taxpayer* from a *passive trade or business* activity, as well as interest on *installment sales* not in the ordinary course of *business.* §469(e)(1). It also includes licensing royalties, dividends from *C corporations, real estate investment trusts* and *regulated investment companies,* and *annuity* income. It excludes income earned in connection with current *trade or business* operations (including *sales* in the ordinary course of business, for example, interest earned by a bank). However, portfolio income earned from working capital reserves remains portfolio income. Such income cannot offset *passive activity losses.* See *passive loss rules.*

portfolio indebtedness any *debt* directly attributable to an investment in portfolio (investment) *stock* held by a *corporation.* §246A(d)(3)(A). The term refers to debt directly attributable to the carrying of portfolio stock as well as to debt directly attributable to the acquisition of portfolio stock. Debt that is clearly incurred for the purpose of acquiring *dividend*-paying stock or that is other-

wise directly traceable to such an acquisition is also portfolio indebtedness; therefore, margin borrowing for stock held in a margin account with a securities broker would constitute portfolio indebtedness, as would a nonrecourse loan secured in whole or in part by dividend-paying stock. Debt used to acquire all or substantially all of a corporation's stock is not directly attributable to any portfolio stock that the acquired corporation holds in the active conduct of a trade or business, but this rule applies only if the practice of making portfolio stock investments is an integral part of the target corporation's trade or business. Purchase money indebtedness is considered portfolio indebtedness. Hence, if a corporation buys stock in exchange for its own debt obligation to the seller, that obligation is portfolio indebtedness. Subject to numerous exceptions, §246A limits *dividends-received deductions* that corporations that carry such stock can claim. See *debt-financed portfolio stock.*

portfolio interest *interest* (including *original issue discount*) paid to *foreign persons* which is *exempt* from the 30 percent (or lower *tax treaty* rate) *withholding tax at source* under §§1441 and 1442. See §§871(h) and 881(c). It refers to *debt* issued after the enactment of the *Tax Reform Act of 1984,* generating (1) interest paid on obligations not in registered form as defined for purposes of *registration-required obligations,* provided there are arrangements reasonably designed to ensure that the obligation will be sold, or resold in connection with the original issue, only to non–*United States persons*; and (2) interest paid on an obligation in registered form (registered debt) for which a statement is filed that the *beneficial* owner is not a United States person. In any case, *interest on otherwise eligible obligations will be taxable if the IRS determines that the exchange of information between the United States and the foreign country is inadequate to prevent tax evasion* by United States persons. §§871(h) and 881(c)(5).

portfolio stock see *debt-financed portfolio stock.*

position of the United States the litigating position of the representative of the United States government in a judicial proceeding to which §7430(a)—allowing recoveries of *reasonable litigation costs* and *reasonable administrative costs*—applies, and a position taken by a representative of the United States in an administrative proceeding covered by §7430(a). In the latter case, the position is measured as of the earlier of the receipt of the final decision of the *Appeals Office* or the date of the *notice of deficiency.* §7430(c)(7). If the position is not substantially justified, the *taxpayer* may be awarded attorney's fees, (§7430(a)) if various tests are met. See *accountant's fees, recovery of; attorney's fees, recovery of; prevailing party; reasonable administrative costs; reasonable litigation costs; Taxpayer's Bill of Rights.*

position, unregulated commodities contracts an interest, including a futures or forward contract or option, in *personal property*. §1092(d)(2)(A). It generally includes an *option* to buy or sell actively traded *stock*, which is part of a *straddle*, unless the stock is traded on a United States exchange or designated foreign exchange and is of a type that normally expires in less than the *long-term holding period* (presently, six months and a day). §1092(d)(2)(B). A position does include stock if it involves an offsetting position that is (1) an option on such stock or substantially identical stock or securities or (under *regulations*) a position in substantially similar or related other property; or (2) any stock of a corporation *formed or availed of* to take positions in personal property that offset positions taken by any shareholder. §1092(d)(3).

positive adjustment factor   *earnings and profits* that result in adjustments with respects to the share under §1.1502-32(b)(1)(i) and (c)(1), but only to the extent the amount of these earnings and profits for a *taxable year* exceeds the amount described in Reg. §1.1502-2-(c)(1)(i) for the same taxable year. This factor is added to various others when determination is made as to the extent to which a *loss* is allowed on the *disposition* of a *subsidiary* that is a member of an *affiliated group* of *corporations*. Regulation §1.1502-20(c)(1) allows losses to the extent in excess of the *extraordinary gain factor*, the *positive investment adjustment factor*, plus the loss duplication factor described in this entry. See *loss disallowance rules*.

positive income sources   a term used in connection with the *passive loss rules* to refer to *gross income* from wages and investments which is typically offset by *tax shelters*. The purpose of the passive activity rules is to bar such effects. See *passive loss rules*.

positive section 481 adjustment   a *section 481 adjustment* that results in ratable *passive activity gross income* for the *taxable year* under the *passive loss rules*. Reg. §1.469-2T(c)(5).

possession   see *possession of the United States*.

possession bank   an informal term for a bank organized in a *possession of the United States*. Such banks are taxed on their *taxable incomes* and are subject to the *branch profits tax* as to their income from United States obligations other than *portfolio interest*. §882(e).

possession exemption   a reference to §931, the gist of which is that if a *citizen of the United States* derives at least 80 percent of his or her gross income (as defined) from sources within a *possession of the United States* and at least 50 percent of his or her gross income (as defined) from all sources from the active conduct of a *trade or business* within a possession, then the *taxpayer* may elect to be taxed on income from United States sources only. §931. Compensation paid by the United States government or its agencies is not *excludable*. §931(i). The Virgin Islands and Puerto Rico do not qualify as possessions for these purposes. §931(c).

possession of the United States   American Samoa, Guam, the Canal Zone (phasing out), Midway Islands, Johnson Island, Wake Island, Puerto Rico (generally), but not the Virgin Islands. §7701(d) and Reg. §1.931-1(a)(1). Note that Puerto Rico is a possession only for tax purposes, and that the *federal tax laws* (e.g., §901) often treat possessions as *foreign* countries.

possessions corporation   a term used to describe a domestic *corporation* that irrevocably (for a decade) elects, using Form 5712, the benefits of the *possession tax credit* under §936, the practical effect of which is that the corporation is taxed (if at all) on possession source income only. Such a corporation is not eligible to join in filing *consolidated returns*. To qualify, the corporation must derive at least 80 percent of its *gross income* from possessions sources (including Puerto Rico, but excluding the United States Virgin Islands) during the three-year period (or part thereof during which it was in existence) ending with the election, and at least 50 percent of the corporation's *gross income* (gradually rising to 65 percent) for the same period must be from the active conduct of a possession *trade or business*. §936(a)(1)(A) and (B). Such a corporation can qualify for an elective *credit* against United States taxes for taxes attributable to income from a possession, whether or not such possession taxes were actually paid or accrued. §936(a). However, such a corporation cannot be an *S corporation*. §1361(b). See *fifty-fifty split, possessions corporations; intangible property income*.

possession source investment income   see *qualified possession source investment income*. §936(d)(2).

possession tax credit   elective *tax credit* designed to stimulate economic activity in United States *possessions* and in Puerto Rico but not the United States Virgin Islands, which is in lieu of the regular *foreign tax credit* (§901) or a *deduction* for foreign taxes (§936). It is available to certain electing *domestic corporations* (*possessions corporations*) and is equal to the portion of federal income tax on the enterprise (whether or not actually paid) attributable to their business transacted in a possession or Puerto Rico and from *qualified possession source investment income*. For *taxable years* beginning after 1982, this freedom from United States taxation (and often from possessions taxes, since possessions tend to offer generous tax relief) is constricted by rules to the effect that income generated by *intangible* assets owned or leased by a possessions corporation is ratably taxable to its shareholders, unless the corporation elects to make sufficient current distributions to its shareholders. §936(h). The definition of the term "possessions corporation" is narrowed after 1982. The credit is actually granted by §27. See *cost-sharing election; fifty-fifty split, possessions corporations; intangible property income; possessions corporation; section 936 election*.

post-audit review the *IRS* process of randomly selecting and reviewing settlements by its examining agents, in the interest of evaluating the agent's actions and uniformity, usually performed by the *Regional Office* of the IRS. See Rev. Proc. 63-9, 1963-1 C.B. 488.

post-change year any *taxable year* ending after the *change date*. §382(d)(2). See *change date, neutrality principle*.

post-mortem estate planning planning after the death of the *decedent*. The typical tax issues involve *special use valuation, disclaimers, installment payment of estate taxes*, and use of the *alternative valuation date* so as to minimize *federal estate taxes*.

post-1986 accumulated earnings *earnings and profits* accumulated during all years after 1986, inclusive of the current year, reduced by all post-1986 *dividends*, exclusive of current dividends. §902(c)(1). *Domestic corporations* that receive dividends from a *foreign corporation*'s post-1986 accumulated earnings are considered to have paid a ratable share of the foreign corporation's foreign taxes for purposes of the *foreign tax credit*, provided the United States corporation is at least a 10 percent shareholder. §902(a). The term is also used for purposes of currency transaction implications of remittances from *qualified business units* overseas. See *deemed paid foreign tax credit*.

post or organization of war veterans see *veterans' organization*.

post-separation year any *calendar year* in the three-calendar-year period beginning with the first calendar year in which the payor *spouse* paid to the payee spouse (or former spouse) *alimony or separate maintenance payments* to which §71 applies (i.e., the first post-*separate return* year). §71(f)(6). The term is important for purposes of *alimony recapture*. For example, if a couple were *legally separated* but lived together in the year of divorce, and the husband moved out next year, the next year would be the first post-separation year. See *front-loading of alimony*.

post-termination transition period one or both of two periods, the first of which is the period that begins on the day after the last day of an *S corporation's taxable year* and ends on the later of (1) one year after that last day; or (2) the due date of the *return* for the last subchapter S year, including extensions. The alternate period is a 120-day span beginning on the date of a determination that S corporation status ended. §1371(e). Former S corporations are, accordingly, given substantial time to make *distributions* of money to their *shareholders* on a tax-free basis to the extent of the corporation's *accumulated adjustments account* and to the extent of the shareholder's *basis* in stock.

potentially abusive situations, original issue discount a transaction involving a *tax shelter* (§6662(d)(2(C)(ii) definition), or a potentially abusive situation or other situations where recent sales, *nonrecourse debt* financing, financing with a term beyond the economic life of the property, or other circumstances are determined under *regulations* to have a potential for *tax avoidance*. §1274(b)(3)(B). In the case of a potentially abusive situation, the *imputed principal amount* of the *debt* is the *fair market value* of the property adjusted to reflect other consideration used in the transaction. See *tax shelter, penalty for substantial understatement of income tax*.

potentially abusive tax shelter a *tax shelter* (as defined under §6111), which must be registered under that section and any other plan or arrangement having a potential for *tax avoidance* or the *tax evasion*, to be defined under *regulations*. §6112(b). Promoters who organize or sell interests in such shelters must keep lists of customers. §6112(a). See *tax shelter, registration*.

power of appointment a power that one *person* confers on another (a *donee*) to select the person who is to enjoy a property interest (which often includes being the *beneficiary* of a *trust*) upon the death of the *donor* of the power, or on the death of the donee. The distinction between a *general power of appointment* and a *nongeneral power of appointment* has tax significance because §2041 includes in the *gross estate* of one who possesses a general power of appointment the value of the property subject to that power. *Nongeneral powers of appointment* are outside the scope of §2041. The exercise or release of a power of appointment may result in a taxable *gift*. §2514.

power of attorney an authorization granted by a *taxpayer* to a person acting as a *taxpayer representative*. Powers of attorney are commonly prepared on Form 2848, and are principally required for extensions of the *statute of limitations*, receiving of *tax refund* checks, execution of *waivers of restrictions on assessment and collection* of a *tax deficiency*, waiving of *notice of disallowance of a claim for a refund or credit*, performance as substitute representatives, delegation of representation authority, and signing of *closing agreements*. See Statement of [IRS] Procedural Rules, §§601.502(c)(1) to .504(a). Outside the tax area, power of attorney can refer to virtually any enforceable delegation of authority. See *taxpayer representative; tax information authorization*.

power of invasion a power held by a *trustee* to extract *corpus* from a *trust*. The power exists to the extent granted by the trust instruments or local law. Powers of invasion create complicated *gift tax* results, but can be a useful *estate planning* device.

practical capacity concept a method of allocating a portion of fixed indirect production costs to a manufactured product under full absorption accounting for inventory. The percentage of practical capacity represented by actual production is used to determine the allocable portion. Reg. §1.471-11(d)(4). It lies between prime costing and direct costing. The concept may be used in conjunction with the manufacturing burden rate method or the standard cost method. The remaining portion is generally deductible as a current operating expense. See also Reg. §1.1263A-1T and T.D. 8148 (rejection of method in connection with uniform capitalization rules).

practical capacity determination a realistic appraisal of a manufacturer's output capacity, based on experience or theoretical capacity (maximum output less breakdowns, etc.). Reg. §1.471-11(d)(4). *Practical capacity* is used in *full absorption accounting* to determine fixed *indirect production costs* that must be allocated to *closing inventory*. To the extent the *taxpayer* operates below practical capacity, part of the indirect fixed production costs are excluded from *inventory* and currently *deductible,* a clear tax advantage. See *experience method.*

practical merger a term often used to refer to a *liquidation* of a subsidiary into its corporate parent. The term is also used in reference to a *Type C reorganization.*

practice before the IRS making an advocate's presentation to the *IRS* of a client's rights, privileges, or liabilities under the law and regulations. It includes correspondence, preparation of documents, and representation at meetings, conferences, and hearings. T.D. Circular No. 230, §10.2(a). It excludes *return* preparation and appearances as a witness. Being entitled to practice before the IRS does not automatically entitle people to practice law. See *Circular 230.*

preacquisition loss, preacquisition loss limits a *net operating loss* (NOL) *carryforward* into the year in which the *acquisition date* fell, any NOL for that year to the extent the loss arose before the acquisition, and any *recognized built-in loss.* §384(c)(3) and (d). The limits of §384 also extend to *excess credits* and *capital losses.* For the significance of the term, see *preacquisition loss limits.*

preacquisition loss limits a loose reference to §384 which prevents *corporations* with existing *losses* or *excess credits* that acquire the *stock* or assets of a *gain corporation* with *net unrealized built-in gains* from offsetting their own otherwise unavailable *preacquisition losses* with the target's *recognized built-in gains*; there is a parallel limit on acquisitions where either corporation is a gain corporation. The restriction applies for five years after the *acquisition date,* subject to an exception for cases where the loss corporation and the gain corporation were members of the same

controlled group of corporations (modified definition) for five years before the acquisition. §384(b) and (c)(2). The acquisition date means the date the acquiror gets control (using the *affiliated group* definition) or, in the case of asset acquisitions, the date of the transfer in a *Type A, C, or D reorganization.* §384(c)(2). For example, assume Mr. G owns all the stock of G, Inc., which operates at a profit. It owns a building with a *basis* of $10 and a value of $20. It contracts to sell the building to a stranger. Sensing the tax would be too high, G instead sells the stock of G, Inc. to Loss, Inc., a corporation with a record of losses of every variety, in exchange for $19 with a view to having G, Inc., and Loss, Inc., file a *consolidated return* and to have Loss's *NOLs* offset the *gain* on sale of the building. That is no longer possible, in the sense that G, Inc.'s built-in gain that is *realized* within five years of the acquisition of Loss cannot be sheltered by Loss's NOLs. See *preacquisition loss limits; recognized built-in gain, preacquisition loss limits.*

preaffiliation year any *taxable year* of a subsidiary which includes at least one day in which the subsidiary was not a *member of an affiliated group of corporations* filing a *consolidated return,* and each taxable year preceding such a year. Reg. §1.1502-32(d)(9). *Distributions* made by a subsidiary out of *earnings and profits* accumulated in preaffiliation years require the parent to reduce its *adjusted basis* in the subsidiary's *stock,* if the distribution occurred on or before August 9, 1979. Reg. §1.1502-32(b)(2)(iii)(b).

preceding-year test a test used to determine if a *personal service corporation* satisfies a minimum distribution requirement in order to permit its payments to owner-employees to be fully deductible despite its having made a *section 444 election.* The amount determined under the preceding-year test is the product of (A) the *applicable amounts* during the *taxable year* preceding the *applicable election year* (the "preceding taxable year"), divided by the number of months (but at least one) in the prior taxable year, multiplied by (B) the number of months in the deferral period of the applicable election year

Illustration: A PSC has historically used a taxable year ending January 31. For its taxable year beginning February 1, 1992, R makes a section 444 election to retain its January 31 taxable year. It is an accrual basis taxpayer and has one employee-owner, F. For its taxable year ending January 31, 1992, F earns $5,000 a month plus a $40,000 bonus on January 15, 1992. The amount determined under the preceding-year test for its applicable election year beginning February 1, 1992, is $91,667 ($100,000, the applicable amounts during R's taxable year ending January 31, 1992, divided by 12, the number of months in its taxable year ending January 31, 1992, multiplied by 11, the number of months in the PSC's deferral period for such year).

prechange loss a term that includes, (1) as to the *taxable year* in which an *ownership change* occurs, the portion of the *loss corporation's net operating loss* that is allocable (determined on a daily pro rata basis, without regard to *recognized built-in gains* or *losses*) to the period in such year before the *change date*; (2) *net operating loss carryforwards* that arose in a taxable year before the taxable year of the ownership change; and (3) certain *recognized built-in losses* and *deductions*. §382(d). This complex definition assures a way to handle changes of ownership in a loss year. This loss is subject to the *section 382 limitation* under the *neutrality principle*.

precontribution gain on partnership redemptions a partner who contributed appreciated property to a partnership will include the precontribution gain in income to the extent that the value of other property distributed by the partnership to that partner exceeds his or her adjusted basis in his or her partnership interest. The CNEPA of 1992 §1937. See *built-in gain on property contributed to partnerships*.

predecessor corporation, neutrality principle a distributor or transferor *corporation* that distributes its assets to an acquiring corporation in a transaction described in §381(a) (various *corporate reorganizations*). Reg. §1.382-2T(f)(5).

predecessor plan a *qualified plan* that provided retirement benefits and was previously terminated, in circumstances in which the *employer* established another such plan within the five-year period immediately preceding or following the date of the termination, and the termination occurred during a *plan year* to which the *vesting* rules of §411 applied. Reg. §1.411(a)-5(b)(3)(v)(B). One need not count time served for *vesting* purposes prior to the installation of a plan, in the absence of a predecessor plan. See §7476(c) for a description of the types of qualified plans treated as retirement plans for this purpose.

predominantly used outside the United States generally, property that is physically located outside the *United States* for more than half the time during the *taxable year,* or for more than half the time from when it is *placed in service* until the end of the taxable year. Rev. Rul. 71-178, 1971-1 C.B. 6.

pre-enactment activity see *pre-enactment interest.*

pre-enactment interest generally, an interest in a *passive activity* acquired before October 22, 1986, and held at all times thereafter by the *taxpayer*. §469(m)(3)(B)(i). The term is defined as a *qualified interest* in a *pre-enactment activity*. A qualified interest in an *activity* is any interest in an activity which was held by the taxpayer on October 29, 1986, and all times thereafter, or acquired by the taxpayer after that date, directly or indirectly, pursuant to one or more binding written contracts (as defined in §1.469-11T(c)(7)) to which the taxpayer was a party on that date, and held at all times thereafter. For this purpose, *stock* in a *C corporation* is not an interest in the corporation. §1.469-11T(c)(2). A pre-enactment activity is one conducted on October 22, 1986, or at least 50 percent of the value of the property used in the activity during the year was either in existence or under construction on August 16, 1986, or acquired or constructed by anyone (including the taxpayer or a related party) under a binding written contract in effect on August 16, 1986. For this purpose, it is immaterial whether the activity would have been a passive activity of the taxpayer for any *taxable year* beginning before 1987 had the *passive loss rules* been in effect for that year. §1.469-11T(c)(3).

pre-ERISA money purchase plan a *pension plan* which is a *defined contribution plan,* and which was in existence on June 27, 1974, and which, on that date, included a salary reduction arrangement, and under which neither *employee* contributions nor *employer* contributions can exceed the contribution formula in effect under the plan on June 27, 1974. §401(k)(5). Such plans, if they contain a *cash or deferred plan* feature, are subject, after 1984, to rules applicable to *qualified profit-sharing* and *stock bonus plans* containing cash or deferred features. §401(k)(1). See also §401(k)(2)(B) (earliest payout limits).

pre-examination procedures *IRS* activities that may precede an *examination* (i.e., audit) of a *taxpayer*. The IRS claims broad authority to ask questions that may or may not lead to an examination. See, e.g., G.C.M. 38875 (July 7, 1982) (pre-examination of Form 990-T filed by churches).

preferential distribution, partnerships see *priority distributions.*

preferential dividend any *distribution* that does not treat each *shareholder* the same as every other shareholder of the same class of *stock,* or that treats any class of stock other than in accordance with its dividend rights as a class. §562(c). If a preference exists, the distributing *corporation* will be denied the *dividends-paid deduction* and any *dividend carryover* (§564) for the entire distribution, not merely the preferential portion. §562(c); Reg. §1.562-1(a). The effect may be to attract or increase the *personal holding company tax* or the *accumulated earnings tax*. The concept is also used to disallow certain non–pro rata distributions from a *regulated investment company* except to the extent they reflect administrative savings passed on to $10-million-or-larger shareholders. See *dividends-paid deduction, corporate.*

preferred stock generally, *stock* that has a preference on *liquidation* which gives its holders limited priority over holders of common *stock* and limitations on *divi-*

dend rights. It is said to include redeemable common stock (Rev. Rul. 57-132, 1957-1 C.B. 115) and common stock convertible into stock other than common stock (Reg. §1.306-3(f)), but not stock merely subject to a right of first refusal by the corporation (Rev. Rul. 76-386, 1976-2 C.B. 95). Note, while §306 is referred to as an anti-*preferred stock bailout* provision, its approach is to attack stock that is "not common stock." §306(c). The *Code, regulations,* and *revenue rulings* are inconsistent in their definitions. For example, section 1504(a)(4) implicitly defines preferred stock as largely nonparticipating nonvoting stock, limited and preferred as to *dividends,* redeemable and liquidatable at no more than a reasonable premium, and not convertible into anther class of stock. See *common stock, section 306 stock; debt-equity rules; section 306 stock.*

preferred stock bailout a pattern of issuing *preferred stock* to *shareholders* tax-free, followed by *sales* of such *stock* to outsiders who *redeem* the stock. This abuse (elimination of some *earnings and profits* at *capital gains* rates) is controlled by §306. See *section 306 stock.*

preferred stock recapitalization a term sometimes used to describe a transaction in which a *corporation* is recapitalized by issuing *preferred stock,* typically to senior members alone, in order to achieve an *estate freeze.* It is an especially common *estate planning* device aimed at keeping future appreciation out of a *decedent's gross estate.* But see Rev. Rul. 83-120, 1983-2 C.B. 170 (valuation of preferred and common, tending to maximize the value of common stock, thereby attracting federal *gift taxes*).

prefiling notification letters from the *IRS* sent to investors, advising them that the *tax shelter* they have purchased is abusive, that the *deductions* the shelter will generate are not allowable, and that if they are claimed on the *taxpayer's* return, the return will be *audited* and the claimed deductions will be disallowed.

preheater a type of *energy property*; preheaters recover energy, usually in the form of waste heat from either combustion exhaust gases or steam, to preheat incoming combustion air or boiler feedwater. Preheaters are *specially defined energy property* and qualify for the *energy investment credit.* Reg. §1.48-9(f)(12).

preheater, energy investment credit equipment consisting, in part, of fixed heat transfer surfaces separating two fluids. Preheaters recover energy, usually in the form of waste heat, from either combustion exhaust gases or steam, to preheat incoming combustion air or boiler feedwater. Reg. §1.48-9(f)(12). A qualified preheater may qualify as *specially defined energy property* for purposes of the *energy investment credit.* §48(1)(5); Reg. §1.48-9(f).

premature distribution, retirement funds actual or *constructive distributions* to *taxpayers* before they

attain $59\frac{1}{2}$ years of age or are *disabled.* See, e.g., §401(d)(4)(B) (*Keogh plans*). Unless rolled over, such distributions are subject to penalty taxes. An example of a constructive distribution is the use of an *individual retirement annuity* as security for a loan. §408(e)(3). Also, §72(m)(5)(A) imposes a 10 percent penalty on a premature distribution from a *qualified plan* to a *five-percent owner.*

premium generally, the excess of the purchase price of a *debt* over its face amount. Such premiums are ratably included in the holder's *gross income* over the term of the obligation. §§1272 and 1273; Reg. §1.61-12(c)(2). See *amortizable bond premium of the taxable year.*

premium conversion plan this is a form of benefit for *employees* under which they can elect to use their paychecks as sources of payments for such benefits as *group term life insurance* or family coverage under a medical insurance plan. The advantage to the employee is that the benefit can be paid with money that has not been subject to *employment taxes.* The *employer* may save money as well because it may enjoy reduced obligations to make *FICA* and *FUTA* contributions on the employee's behalf. This is a common feature of a *cafeteria plan.*

pre-opening expenses start-up costs, or costs of investigating *businesses* before the decision to acquire or enter a new line of business. Such expenses must be *capitalized* and *amortized* over the *useful life* of identifiable assets under §167 or §168 (to the extent they can be allocated to such assets), or they may be electively *amortized* over 60 months under §195. The question of when a taxpayer *begins business* remains unclear. The majority view is that a business begins only when it performs the ultimate activities for which it was organized. See Reg. §1.248-1(a)(3). See *start-up expenditures.*

pre-operation expenditures, credit for increasing research activities any *contract research expense* attributable to *qualified research* to be conducted after the close of the *taxable year* in which the expense was actually *paid or incurred.* Former §44F(b)(3)(B). Such amounts are *deductible* only when the research is conducted. *Prepaid contract research amounts* that were treated as paid or incurred in a later year for this purpose were considered made in the later year for purposes of determining average yearly *base period research expenses* for credit computations in later years. See *credit for increasing research activities.*

prepaid contract research amount any *contract research expense* attributable to *qualified research* to be conducted after the close of the *taxable year* in which the expense was actually *paid or incurred.* Prior law §44F(b)(3)(B). Such amounts were *deductible* only when the research was conducted. Prepaid contract research amounts that were treated as paid or incurred in a later year for this purpose were considered disbursed in the later year for purposes of determining average yearly *base period research expenses* for credit computations in later years. *Section 41(b)(3)(B) now causes the same result.* See *credit for increasing research activities.*

prepaid expenses current payment of *expenses* that relate to future *taxable years.* Such expenses must generally be *capitalized* and *amortized* in the future period to which the expense relates. See Reg. §1.461-1(a)(1). Farmers, but not *farming syndicates,* may deduct such items as prepaid feed and seed if there is no material *distortion of income,* a *business purpose,* and if the payment is not a *deposit*; otherwise, they must be capitalized and matched to the year to which they relate. Rev. Rul. 79-299, 1979-2 C.B. 210. The tax treatment of these expenditures remains contentious. Prepaid expenses of *tax shelters* on the *cash method* are *deductible* only upon economic performance. §461(i). See *prepaid interest.*

prepaid farm supplies see *excess prepaid farm supplies.*

prepaid feed expenses a loose term used to describe payments for feed by *cash method* farmers made in one year, for consumption of the feed in a later year, often in a deliberate attempt to accelerate *deductions.* Farmers, but not *farming syndicates,* may deduct such items if (1) there is no material *distortion of income*; (2) there is a *business purpose*; and (3) the payment is not a *deposit.* Rev. Rul. 79-299, 1979-2 C.B. 210. The area remains litigious. See also *preproductive period expenses, farmers; farming, farming syndicate.*

prepaid income *gross income* received before it is earned. Such income has been included in *accrual method taxpayers'* income by virtue of the *IRS's* application of its powers under §446(b). See also *claim of right doctrine; prepaid services income.*

prepaid interest *interest* paid with respect to future periods. Such amounts are *nondeductible* to *cash method taxpayers* (except as to certain *points*) and to *accrual method* taxpayers, since the obligation to pay has in theory not yet arisen.

prepaid services income payments for services not yet rendered. Revenue Proc. 70-21, 1970-2 C.B. 501, allows *accrual method taxpayers* to defer the portion of prepayments of services (not *rents* and *interest*) allocable to the present and following *taxable year* (with no limit for bus tokens and photographic services). Such payments are, however, taxable to *cash method* taxpayers. See Reg. §1.451-5 (comparable rule for sales of goods).

prepaid subscription income amounts *includible* in *gross income* in connection with and directly attributable to a liability that extends beyond the close of the *taxable year* in which it was received and is income from a subscription to a newspaper, magazine, or other periodical. §455(d)(1). Section 455(a) permits *taxpayers* to elect to defer reporting such income until the liability to which it relates (e.g., to provide a magazine) arises. Rev. Rul. 82-68, 1982-1 C.B. 81, takes the view that the term includes prepaid postage and handling charges paid by the subscriber to the taxpayer.

preparer of tax return see *tax return preparer.*

prepayment credits a colloquial term for *credits* allowed to *individual taxpayers* for *employers' withholdings* of *federal income taxes* withheld from *wages* over the course of the year. *Social Security* (FICA) taxes withheld from wages may also be treated as a form of prepayment credit, applicable against federal income taxes. §31.

preproductive period in the case of *property* that has a *useful life* of more than one year, and more than one crop or yield, the period before the *disposition* of the first such marketable crop or yield, or in the case of any other property, the period before such property is disposed of. §447(b)(2). For purposes of determining the preproductive period, a disposition is considered to have occurred when the farmer uses any supply produced in such *trade or business.* Numerous *preproductive period expenses* are subject to mandatory *capitalization.* See *farming syndicate; prepaid feed expenses.*

preproductive period expenses, farmers any amount (except taxes, interest, and amounts incurred on account of fire, storm, flood, or other casualty, or on account of disease or drought) that is attributable to crops, animals, or any other property having a crop or yield during the *preproductive period* of such property. §447(b). Examples include such items as upkeep costs, carrying charges, water for irrigation, fertilizer, etc., before the farm or other agricultural property becomes commercially productive. The significance of the term is that while Reg. §1.162-12(a) generally grants *farmers,* orchard men, and ranchers the right to *deduct* or *capitalize* such disbursements until the productive period begins, §477 generally compelled most corporate farmers or farmers operating in *partnership* form with one or more corporate partners to capitalize such expenditures before 1987. Thereafter, the *uniform capitalization rules* applied.

prepublication expense an *expense paid or incurred* by the *taxpayer,* in connection with the *trade or business* of publishing, for writing, editing, compiling, illustrating, designing, or other development or improvement of a book, teaching aid, or similar product. The proper treatment of such expenditures is not settled. For example, Rev. Rul. 73-395, 1973-2 C.B. 87 requires capitalization of development and publication costs of texts and visual aids. Reg §1.263A-1T(a)(5)(iii)(A); §263A(h).

presale registration see *registration of tax shelters*.

prescribed drug a drug or biological material (e.g., serum) that legally requires a prescription from a *physician* (defined in 42 U.S.C. §1395x(R)) for its use by an *individual*. After December 31, 1983, only such drugs will be *deductible* as an *itemized medical expense*. See §213(b). See *medical expense deduction*.

present interest an unrestricted right to the immediate use, possession, or enjoyment of property, or to the income from property, such as a *life estate* or a *term for years* (but not *remainders* or *reversions*), is a present interest in property. Reg. §25.2503-3(b). Transfers of present interests in property qualify for the $10,000-per-*donee*, per-year *annual gift tax exclusion*, provided they have present ascertainable values.

present value synonymous with *discounted present value*.

present value method of valuation a method of evaluating the worth of property that creates a flow of income or is to be received outright in the future. The technique is to discount the income or property by some interest rate to reflect the impact of futurity. The method is used for general financial planning and for numerous valuation requirements of the *Code*, especially with respect to *estate* and *gift taxes*. See *discounted present value*.

present value method, valuation of mineral properties a technique for determining the *fair market value* of a mineral deposit on the basis of its anticipated production, net of cost, discounted for the time required for extraction and for risk. Reg. §1.611-2(d).

preservation clause, treaties a *treaty* term allowing *taxpayers* to use either a treaty provision or domestic law in order to prevent unintended tax increases from being caused by the treaty. See also §7852(d) for a domestic analog, preserving treaty terms when the 1954 *Code* was adopted.

presidential election fund an arrangement whereby *taxpayers* may elect to have one dollar of their tax payments contributed to a fund to be used in presidential election years, for use by major political parties which submit to certain limitations and restrictions as a condition to participating in the fund.

presumption an assumption, which is either rebuttable, meaning it can be overcome by a sufficient contrary showing, or conclusive, or "irrebuttable," meaning it cannot be overcome. The most common rebuttable presumption in the tax laws is that the *IRS*'s assertions of most facts are correct.

prevailing party a *taxpayer* that may be able to recover costs—either *reasonable litigation costs* or *reasonable administrative costs*—against the *IRS* following victory in a tax dispute. A number of tests must be met. The taxpayer must establish (1) that the *position of the United States* in the proceeding was not substantially justified; (2) that the taxpayer has substantially prevailed with respect to the amount in controversy or has substantially prevailed with respect to the most significant issue or set of issues presented; and (3) that a timely claim for reimbursement has been submitted. The term excludes the United States or any creditor of the taxpayer, along with taxpayers with substantial net worths who are excluded from benefiting under the *Equal Access to Justice Act*. The determination as to whether a party is a prevailing party is made by the court or by agreement of the parties in the case of litigation, but it is made by the IRS (in its wisdom) if the proceeding is administrative. §7430(c)(4)(A)(i)-(iii). See *attorney's fees, recovery of; position of the United States; reasonable administrative costs; reasonable litigation costs; Taxpayer's Bill of Rights*.

previously taxed earnings and profits an informal term for *earnings and profits* of a *controlled foreign corporation* that have already been taxed to the *United States shareholder*. When they are later paid out, they are not taxed. §959(a).

previously taxed income, DISC income of a *domestic international sales corporation* (DISC) deemed *distributed* and therefore actually taxed to *shareholders*. §995(b)(1). Any DISC income that is not deemed distributed remains in the DISC as tax-deferred income. §996(f)(1). The *domestic international sales corporation* (DISC) generally has been replaced by a system of foreign sales corporations (FSCs). See §§921–927 and *domestic international sales corporation*.

price level adjusted mortgage a mortgage, the *interest* charges on which vary with the market rate of interest.

primarily of first importance. See *dealer property*.

primarily for sale to customers see *dealer property*.

primarily used for business, entertainment expenses see *primary use test, clubs*.

primary adjustment an *IRS* adjustment made to a member or group of *taxpayers* under the authority of §482 (power to reallocate *income, deductions,* and the like). Reg. §1.482-1(d)(2). The existence of a primary adjustment by the IRS in turn triggers the *correlative adjustment* mechanism under which the related taxpayer's income is conversely affected. See *reallocation of income and deductions by Commissioner*.

primary product from coal coal and all products recovered from the carbonization of coal, including coke, crude light oil, and coal tar. Reg. §1.993-3(g)(3)(iii). These processes and their products may change with new technologies. Reg. §1.993-3(g)(3)(v). Such property generally does not qualify as *export property* for *domestic international sales corporation* (DISC) purposes. §993(c)(2).

primary product from gas   all gas and associated hydrocarbon components from gas wells or oil wells, whether recovered at the lease [sic] or on further processing, including (1) natural gas; (2) condensates; (3) liquefied petroleum gases such as propane and butane; and (4) liquid products such as natural gasoline, but not petrochemicals. Reg. §1.993-3(g)(3)(ii) and (vi). These processes and primary products may change with new technologies. Reg. §1.993-3(g)(3)(v). Such property generally does not qualify as *export property* for *domestic international sales corporation* (DISC) purposes. §993(c)(2).

primary product from oil   crude oil and all products derived from the destructive distillation of crude oil, including (1) volatile products; (2) light oils such as motor fuel and kerosene; (3) distillates such as naphtha; (4) lubricating oils; and (5) greases and waxes, and residues such as fuel oil. Reg. §1.993-3(g)(3)(i) and (vi). The primary products and the processes may change with new technologies. Reg. §1.993(g)(3)(v). Such property generally does not qualify as *export property* for *domestic international sales corporation* (DISC) purposes. §993(c)(2).

primary production   oil production that is recovered through the use of the natural energy source in the reservoir.

primary purpose standard, charitable organization   an *IRS* position that a *section 501(c)(3) organization* must not be organized or operated for the primary purpose of carrying on an *unrelated trade or business*. Furthermore, in the IRS's view at least, any unrelated trade or business must further the organization's *exempt purpose* and must not be for private benefit, meaning that excessive unrelated trade or business income can defeat the exemption. Whether the required primary purpose exists is determined on the basis of all the facts and circumstances. Reg. §1.507(c)(3)-1(e)(1).

primary use test, clubs   a test applied to determine whether a *deduction* for certain club expenditures will be allowed, as an exception to the general treatment of amounts paid or incurred in connection with an *entertainment facility*. §274(a)(1)(B) and (a)(2)(C). This test is satisfied if the *taxpayer* establishes that the facility was used primarily (more than one-half the time it was used) for the furtherance of his or her *trade or business* or that the expense items in question were directly related to the active conduct of such trade or business (or

presumably investment or tax-related activities). §274(a)(1)(A); Reg. §1.274-2(c)(6).

prime costing   a *financial accounting* concept under which the costing of production is performed by including direct production costs in *inventory* cost and deducting *period costs*.

prime district   one of seven relatively large *Internal Revenue Districts* which performs administrative support services and certain other functions (such as the *examination review* function) for one or more of the 12 small *streamlined districts*. I.R.M. 1118.4(5).

prime issue   an issue of major importance that has not been judicially resolved, typically, purely legal issues which may set important precedents, test important *regulations* or *rulings*, or have other serious implications to the government. Prime issues will not be conceded or settled by the *Audit Division*, although the examiner and the *taxpayer* may proceed to resolve any other issues involved in the case. Cases containing prime issues are reviewed by the *Appeals Office*, which, if it determines that the issue is clearly a prime issue and warrants trial, will ordinarily force the taxpayer into court. I.R.M. 8247.1 (Oct. 3, 1973) and I.R.M. 8247.5 (Sept. 3, 1974).

principal   (as a noun) property, rather than income, a term commonly used to describe the *corpus* of a *trust*, or the *person* who controls an *agent* and is responsible for the agent's acts and income. See *agent*.

principal owner   a *person* who owns, directly and by application of Reg. §1.414(c)-4, the following: (1) in the case of a *corporation*, 5 percent or more of the total combined voting power of all classes of *stock* entitled to vote in such *corporation* or of the total value of shares of all classes of stock of such corporation; (2) in the case of a *trust* or *estate*, an actuarial interest of 5 percent or more of such trust or estate; or (3) in the case of a *partnership*, 5 percent or more of the *profits interest* or *capital interest* of such partnership. Reg. §1.414(c)-3(d)(2). Principal owners' stock or other interests in a 50-percent-owned subsidiary organization is considered not outstanding for the purpose of determining whether the parent or subsidiary organization is a member of a commonly controlled *parent-subsidiary group* for purposes of aggregating *qualified plans*. Reg. §1.414(c)-3(b)(4).

principal partner   a *partner* with at least a 5 percent *profits interest* or *capital interest*. §705(b)(3). Unless §706(b)(1)(B)(i)—calling for use of the *taxable year* of majority *partners*—applies, a partnership must adopt as its *taxable year* the same year as that of all its principal partners, or (failing that) a *calendar year*, or some other *IRS*-approved year. §706(b). See *majority interest taxable year*.

principal place of abode roughly stated, a household that is the realistic home of a *dependent*, on the basis of which the *taxpayer* claims *head of household* status or the *earned income credit*. The taxpayer's mother and father do not have to live with the taxpayer in order to claim head of household status (i.e., taxpayers whose parents are in nursing homes can qualify as heads of households). Reg. §§1.2-2(c) and 1.43-2(c)(1). The *regulations* include reasonable flexibility to allow taxpayers to change homes, temporarily depart on account of illness or business travel, and to allow minors under joint custody to depart for periods just short of six months. The regulations assert that both the taxpayer and the person qualifying the taxpayer must occupy the household for the entire taxable year.

principal place of business as to the disallowance of *deductions* for use of a portion of a *dwelling unit* as a place of *business*, the term refers to the primary place of business of any particular *trade or business* the *taxpayer* conducts. §280A(c)(1)(A). Thus, if business is conducted only at the taxpayer's dwelling unit, then it is clearly the principal place of business. Where there are several places of business, home office deductions may be permissible by virtue of the exception provided by §280A(c)(1)(A). There appears as yet to be no method for determining which is the principal place, although the standards generated in connection with *travel expenses* are at least relevant, given the identical terminology. In the *IRS*'s view, factors to be considered in determination of the taxpayer's principal place of business with respect to *travel expenses* are (1) the total time spent in performing duties in each area; (2) the degree of business activity in each area; and (3) the relative amount of income from each area. The principal determining factors are where the taxpayer's most important business interests are and where the most time is spent. Rev. Rul. 54-147, 1954-1 C.B. 51.

principal place of work, moving expenses the place where the *taxpayer* spends all or most of his or her working hours. It must be a place where the taxpayer is permanently, rather than temporarily, employed. In instances where no single place of work exists, the center of the taxpayer's business activities is considered his or her principal place of work; for example, the place he or she reports for work. See Reg. §1.217-2(c)(3). The term is used for numerous purposes to determine whether particular expenditures are *deductible* as *moving expenses*. §217(b)(1)(C)-(D) and (b)(2)(B)-(C).

principal residence, deferral of gain see *rollover of principal residence*.

principal residence, rollover of principal residence and one hundred and twenty-five thousand dollar exclusion on sale of principal residence by person age 55 or older the place where the person genuinely does or did reside, based on *all facts and circumstances,* including the *taxpayer's good faith*. It does not need to be the principal residence at the time of sale, and temporary rentals of the property do not automatically disqualify it as a principal residence. Reg. §§1.1034-1(c)(3)(i) and 1.121-3(a). It excludes items other than realty and fixtures, but it can include nontraditional homes such as cooperatives, trailers, and so forth.

principal shareholder an *individual* who owns 5 percent or more of the combined voting power or of the total value of all the *stock* in the parent *corporation*. §1563(c)(2)(A)(ii). Stock of a *subsidiary* in a *parent-subsidiary controlled group* held by a principal shareholder is treated as *excluded stock* for purposes of finding a controlled group of corporations. See *controlled group of corporations, graduated taxes, and other benefits.*

priority distributions another term for preferential *distributions* of cash or property to *partners,* measured by the amount of the partner's *capital account* and the time preceding the distribution, generally as a form of compensation for the use of money, but subject to alternate characterizations.

priority of lien the rank granted to a lien, including a *federal tax lien.* Generally speaking, liens for federal taxes are accorded a particularly high priority in bankruptcy proceedings, but they must comply with state law regarding the filing and execution of liens in order to be perfected and made the basis of a *levy.* See *federal tax lien.*

prior unstated inclusion see *recapture, leaseback or long-term agreement.*

prior year's tax see *last-year's tax, exception.*

Privacy Act the Privacy Act of 1974, 5 U.S.C.A. §552(a) (1976), granting *individuals* access to agency records about themselves as well as restrictions on the collection and dissemination of personal information by federal agencies and to a lesser extent by other government personnel. The protection is against the unauthorized disclosure of personal information in the form of *returns, return information,* and *taxpayer return information,* unless the agency obtains prior consent from the subject of the records. There are exceptions for federal, state, and local law enforcement authorities, court orders, and routine agency uses if they are disclosed in the Federal Register. Agency records that are subject to compulsory disclosure under the Freedom of Information Act are exempt as well. Privacy Act rights can be enforced in *District Courts* after exhaustion of administrative remedies. The Privacy Act manifests itself in §§6103, 7213, and 7216. See *unauthorized use of tax information.*

private activity bond generally, a state or local *bond,* the proceeds of which are used to finance nongovernmental activities. They are generally the successor of the *industrial development bond*. More precisely, it means a bond issued as part of a *state or local bond* issue that meets both the *private business use test* and *private security or payment test* or that meets the *private loan financing test*. §141(a). Issuers of such bonds must notify the *IRS* with specified information soon after their issuance if the obligations are to be tax-exempt. §103(1). *The Tax Reform Act of 1984* enacted maximum aggregate amounts of *industrial development bonds (IDBs)* and *student loan* bonds that a state or locality can issue per calendar year, as well as restrictions on *cost recovery deductions* for property financed with IDBs. See *exempt facility bond; qualified bond; tax-exempt bond.*

private activity bond, limitations generally, volume limitations enacted by the *Tax Reform Act of 1984* affecting the tax-exempt status of several types of *private activity bonds*. This is a pre-1986 Act concept, and is now dated. In general, bonds issued in excess of certain limitations lose their tax-exempt status. §103(1).

private business use for the purpose of determining a *state or local bond* issue's status as a *private activity bond,* a use of funds or facilities which directly or indirectly supports a *trade or business* carried on by any *entity* or person other than governmental unit. §141(b)(6). State or local bonds which devote too great a percentage of their proceeds to support private interests are private activity bonds. See *private activity bond.*

private business use test one element of a two-part test used in determination of whether a *state or local bond* is a *private activity bond.* This test is met if more than 10 percent of the proceeds of a bond issue are used for *private business use.* §141(b)(1). In the case of bonds, 5 percent or more of their proceeds which are used for *output facilities* other than water facilities, the test is met when the aggregate of proceeds from all such issues that are used for private business use, or the private amounts securing the issues, exceed $15 million. §141(b)(4). A bond which meets both the private business use test and the *private security or payment test* is designated a *private activity bond.* §141(a)(1). The test is applied to bonds issued on or after September 1, 1986, with certain exceptions. See *private activity bond; private security or payment test.*

private foundation any *exempt organization* which got its status under §501(c)(3) (e.g., charitable and other types of organizations, but not a *church*), unless (1) it is a *publicly supported organization,* meaning more than one-third of its support normally comes from members of the public (excluding *disqualified persons*) and less than one-third of its income normally comes from investments and *unrelated business taxable income*; (2) it qualifies for the 50 percent *charitable contribution*

deduction described in §170(b)(1)(A)(i)-(vii) (basically, churches, schools, and hospitals); (3) it is a public safety testing organization; or (4) it is a *supporting organization,* formed to assist the functions or purposes of (1) and (2) above, that is not controlled by a *disqualified person* (other than a *foundation manager*). §509(a). Private foundation status triggers, among other things, a 2 percent excise tax on *net investment income* (the so-called *audit fee* of §4940), a 15 percent tax on failure to distribute income (§4942), taxes on *self-dealing* (§4941), taxes on *speculative investments* (§4944), taxes on lobbying expenditures (§4945 *taxable expenditures*), and a potentially crushing *termination tax* (§507). *Charitable contributions* to private foundations are subject to a somewhat greater limitation. §170(b)(1)(B). *The Tax Reform Act of 1984* added the *exempt operating foundation* to the list of private foundations. §4940(d)(2). See *section 501(c)(3) organizations.*

private foundation excise taxes see *excise taxes, private foundations.*

private institution, medical expense deduction an institution regularly engaged in providing *medical care* and services. For these purposes "regularly engaged" means that the persons providing the medical care devote a substantial portion of their time to its provision, and that the care is provided in exchange for an *arm's length* consideration, whether or not it is done for a profit. Thus, even a low-charge charity case can help qualify the institution as long as the charge is determined at arm's length. Rev. Rul. 69-499, 1969-2 C.B. 39. Hospital care in a private institution is *deductible.* Reg. §1.213-1(e)(1)(v).

private letter ruling see *ruling.*

private loan financing test one element of a two-part test applied to *state or local bond* issues to determine whether a bond is a *private activity bond.* §141(a)(2). This test is met (and *interest* on the loan is taxable) in the case of an issue as to which 5 percent or more of the proceeds or $5 million of the proceeds, whichever is less, are used to make or finance loans to private interests. §141(c). This rule does apply to bonds whose proceeds are used to make or finance loans that (1) let the borrower finance any governmental tax or assessment of general application for a specific essential governmental function; or (2) constitute a *nonpurpose investment.* §141(c)(2). See §141(b)(9) for a special election. See *private activity bond.*

private nonoperating foundation a *private foundation* that is not an *operating foundation.* Gifts to private nonoperating foundations qualify for the medium ceiling on *charitable contributions* if they distribute 100 percent of their contributions received in accordance with §170(b)(1)(D)(ii) and Reg. §1.170A-9(g). §170(b)(1)(A)(vii). The 20 percent ceiling on cash and *ordinary income property* is now a 30 percent ceiling. §170(b)(l)(B), as amended. The 20 percent ceiling on gifts of *capital gain property* is retained. See *private foundation; qualified appreciated stock.*

private operating foundation see *operating foundation.*

private papers doctrine a Supreme Court doctrine to the effect that compulsory production of a citizen's private books and records violates the *Fifth Amendment* privilege against self-incrimination.

private placement the issuance of securities without public registration with the SEC under the Securities Act of 1933. Section 4(2) of that Act provides an exemption, clarified in the form of safe harbor rules under SEC Regulation D, for distributions to a limited number of accredited investors (or those well represented) able to absorb significant losses. The private placement exemption is commonly availed of in *tax shelter* offerings.

private security or payment test an alternative test used in determining whether a *state or local bond* is a *private activity bond.* The test is met by a bond issue as to which the payment of more than 10 percent of the principal or *interest* is secured or satisfied, directly or indirectly, by interest in property used for a private business use or payments in respect of such property. §141(b)(2). The 10 percent limit is reduced to 5 percent in situations where the property or payments, securing or satisfying the issue, are used for or derived from a private business use unrelated or disproportionate to the governmental use for which the issue was undertaken. §141(b)(3). A bond meeting both the *private business use test* and the private security or payment test is designated a private activity bond, and is at first blush incapable of generating *tax-exempt interest.* §141(a)(1). The test is to be applied to bonds issued on or after August 15, 1986. See *private activity bond; private business use test; private loan financing test; unrelated or disproportionate use proceeds.*

private shareholder or individual a *person* having a personal and private interest in the activities of the *exempt organization.* Reg. §1.501(a)-1(c). The term includes members, *shareholders,* the creator, persons under the control of the foregoing, as well as major contributors, *trustees,* officers, or directors, and their families. Reg. §1.501(c)(3)-1(b)(4) and -1(d)(1)(ii); Rev. Rul. 77-367, 1977-2 C.B. 149; Rev. Rul. 76-441, 1976-2 C.B. 147. Evidently, anyone who is not a member of the charitable class may be a private interest. G.C.M. 38905 (June 11, 1982) (investment advisor with contingent compensation contract). *Inurement* of benefits to such persons may defeat the organization's tax exemption.

privileged communications communications between doctor and patient, attorney and client, and priest and penitent which are protected by traditional privileges against forced disclosure. They are generally beyond *IRS* investigation. §7602.

privilege tax a *tax* imposed on engagement in a particular activity, e.g., overseas oil extraction. Privilege taxes do not qualify for the *foreign tax credit,* but instead must be *deducted.* §901(a). See also *franchise taxes.*

prizes and awards contest awards, door prizes, and television giveaways that are taxable. Reg. §1.74-1(a). Awards for religious, charitable, scientific, educational, artistic, literary, or civil achievement, without action to enter by the recipient, are excluded from the recipient's income only if they are transferred *unused* by the taxpayer to a governmental unit or tax-exempt charitable, religious, or educational organization. §74. Employee achievement awards are excluded from gross income only to the extent that the cost of the award is allowable as a deduction by the employer. The excludable amount can be no more than $400 for nonqualified awards and $1,600 for qualified awards. §74(c). See *qualified plan award.*

probate estate a nontax term describing property of a *decedent* that is subject to *administration.* It is not the same as the *gross estate* for *federal estate tax* purposes.

Problem Resolution Officer a person charged with implementing the *Problem Resolution Program.* There people work at *IRS Service Centers* and *District Offices* and can be extremely helpful. See *taxpayer assistance order; Taxpayer Ombudsman.*

Problem Resolution Program a nationwide *IRS* program designed to assist *taxpayers* who feel that their tax problems are not receiving proper attention through normal IRS channels. Each IRS *District Office,* and apparently each *Service Center,* has a Problem Resolution Officer whose function is to attempt to quickly resolve problems. By monitoring the use of the program, the IRS hopes to be able to identify and alleviate common taxpayer difficulties. Despite the *news release,* the Problem Resolution Program apparently functions both as a complaint department and as a substitute for normal tax dispute resolution procedures. I.R. News Release 1838 (June 16, 1977).

procedural regulations a class of *regulations* whose purpose is to establish tax administration procedures, as opposed to *legislative* or *interpretative regulations,* which are concerned with the substantive rules of taxation.

proceeds of sale or exchange money or property received upon the *sale* or *exchange* of *property.* See *amount realized.*

process of experimentation see *qualified research.*

produced by the taxpayer see *uniform capitalization rules.*

produced film rents payments received in connection with an interest in a film or videotape for the use of, or right to use, such film or tape, but only to the extent that the interest was obtained prior to substantial completion of the film. Produced film rents will be treated as *personal holding company income* unless such rents are 50 percent or more of the company's *ordinary gross income*. §543(a)(5). In the case of a producer who actively participates in production of the film or tape, it also (and to that extent) includes a mere interest in the proceeds or profits from the film or tape. See *producer*.

producer a production company engaged in production activities such as the photography or taping of film or tape. Payments to a producer constitute *produced film rents* if such payments represent an interest in the proceeds or profits from the film and if the producer's interest can be attributed to production activities. §543(a)(5). A production company is considered a producer if it engages in production activities and is involved in principal photography or taping of the production.

producer's loan, DISC a loan with a term not more than five years made by a *domestic international sales corporation* (DISC) out of its tax-deferred profits to an affiliated *domestic* parent corporation which produced the *export property* or to any other United States exporter, whether or not affiliated, subject to various restrictions. Such loans do not cause taxation of the DISC or its parent. The *domestic international sales corporation* (DISC) generally has been replaced by a system of foreign sales corporations (FSCs). See §§921–927 and *domestic international sales corporation*.

producing stage the time when the major portion of mineral production is obtained from workings other than those opened for the purpose of development, or when the principal activity of the *mine* is the production of developed ores or minerals rather than development of additional ores or minerals for mining. Reg. §§1.616-2(b) and 1.617-3(c)(2). The term is used to delineate the development stage from the producing state, an important distinction for purposes of the specialized rules of §§616 and 617 (relating to mineral *exploration* and *development expenditures*). The definition is confused by some uncertainties as to the meaning of "development stage." See *development expenditures, minerals*.

product area, possessions corporations the output of a *possessions corporation* that makes the *cost-sharing election*. See §936(h)(5). The product area is determined by the three-digit classification of the Standard Industrial Classification Code, or another classification specified by the *Treasury Department*. See *possession tax credit*.

product area research expenditures direct and indirect *expenses* for *research and experimental expenditures* for the acquisition or use of manufacturing *intangibles,* costs of developing and purchasing research and development-related computer software, and the like, incurred by the *taxpayer* and all its affiliates. §936(h)(5)(C)(i)(1). Such research expenditures are determined on the basis of the *product area* for each activity in which an *island affiliate* operates. See *possession tax credit*.

product class *depreciable tangible personal property* that is listed in a product code. A property's product code is its five-digit product class under the product coding system of the United States Department of Commerce, Bureau of the Census, 1987 Census of Manufacturers and Census of Mineral Indutries, 1989 Reference Series: Numerical List of Manufactured and Mineral Products. Reg. §1.1031(a)-2(b)(3). It can qualify as *like-kind property*. See *like class*.

production company film tax shelters a form of *tax shelter* in which investors contribute funds to a company that will produce a film suitable for public distribution. Provided the film is a *qualified film,* production costs could be claimed as a basis for the *investment tax credit*. §48(k)(1)(B). The *income forecast method* could be used to claim *depreciation* or, conceivably, cost recovery for the film. §§167 and 168; Rev. Rul. 64-273, 1964-2 C.B. 62.

production costs for purposes of *full absorption accounting* for *inventory valuation,* costs are considered to be production costs to the extent that they are incident to and necessary for production or manufacturing operations or processes. Production costs include *direct production costs* and fixed and variable *indirect production costs*. Reg. §1.471-11(b)(1). Whereas production costs are not currently *deductible,* so-called *period costs* are.

production expenditures for purposes of the *uniform capitalization rules,* this term means the costs required to be *capitalized* under §263A with respect to the property (e.g., bricks and mortar). §263A(f)(4)(C). *Interest expenses* must be capitalized if traced to production expenditures that relate to property that is subject to the *interest* capitalization provisions. See *traced debt*.

production of income see *expenses for the management, conservation, or maintenance of property held for the production of income*.

production or collection of income see *expenses for the production or collection of income*.

production payment a share of oil, gas, or minerals (in cash or in kind) from a specific tract, generally free of costs of production, at the surface, which ends (1) when the holder has received a specific aggregate sum of money from production; (2) at a fixed date; or (3) when a fixed amount of the resource has been extracted. Such interests may be carved out by the owner of a working interest, transferred by an assignor of a lease, or reserved by a lessor, but in either case must be shorter than the economic life of at least one of the underlying burdened properties and must be an *economic interest* in the natural resource. Reg. §1.636-3(a)(1).

production royalties, natural resources   a synonym for *royalties* from the production of natural resources.

production sharing contract   an agreement common in the oil and gas industry pursuant to which a contractor is paid its costs out of production, up to a maximum percentage (e.g., 25 percent) of production. The oil taken by the contractor is often called "cost oil." The balance (profit oil) is shared in accordance with the profit-sharing ratio.

production stage, resources   see *producing stage.*

productive use or investment   the purposes for which property must be held to qualify for deferral of *gain* in a *like-kind exchange*. Property must be held for productive use in a *trade or business,* or must be held for *investment*. Neither the *Code* nor the *regulations* define either phrase. *Dealer property* does not qualify. §1031(a); Reg. §1.1031. Property that has been acquired for business use may qualify even if it has not yet been used, or even if it has been used but is now inactive. See *like-kind exchange.*

product liability   liability of a *taxpayer* for damages on account of physical injury or emotional harm to *individuals,* or damage to or loss of the use of property on account of any defect in any product which is manufactured, leased, or sold, but only if the injury, harm, or damage arises after the taxpayer has completed or terminated operations with respect to, and has relinquished possession of, the product. §172(f)(4). Generally, a business enterprise may carry back a *net operating loss* 3 years, but taxpayers with *product liability losses* for *taxable years* after September 30, 1979, may carry back their losses 10 years. §172(b)(1)(C). See *specified liability loss.*

product liability loss   the lesser of (1) the *net operating loss* of a *taxpayer* for the year, or (2) the *trade or business* and *loss deductions* attributable to *product liability* or expenses incurred in the investigation or settlement of, or opposition to, claims against the taxpayer on account of product liability. §172(f)(4). Generally, a corporation may carry back a net operating loss 3 years, but taxpayers with product liability losses may carry back their losses 10 years. §172(b)(1)(H). See *specified liability loss.*

product liability loss reserves   reasonable amounts of *reserves* (appropriations of retained earnings) accumu-

lated for the payment of reasonably anticipated *product liability losses*. §537(b)(4). Such loss reserves can be used defensively by *taxpayers* to ward off imposition of the *accumulated earnings tax*. That is, they are considered *reasonable needs of the business.*

professional corporation   a *corporation* carrying on a profession (e.g., medicine) through its owner-employees. §448(d)(2)(A). The *Treasury Department* now acknowledges that professional corporations or associations organized under state law can qualify as corporations for tax purposes, unless it is illegal at local law for corporations to engage in the particular profession. Reg. §301.7701-1 and -2; Rev. Rul. 70-101, 1970-1 C.B. 278; Rev. Rul. 70-455, 1970-2 C.B. 297. Professional corporations, which are also known as *personal service corporations (PSCs),* are denied the benefits of graduated corporate tax rates. §11(b)(2). Professionals covered include accountants, lawyers, actuaries, architects, chiropodists, chiropractors, MDs, dentists, engineers, optometrists, osteopaths, podiatrists, psychologists, and veterinarians. Generally, the states have specialized statutes authorizing professionals to incorporate. See *affiliated service group.*

professional football leagues   see *business leagues.*

professional partnerships   *partnerships* organized by professionals (i.e., doctors, lawyers, accountants). While partnerships have been the traditional form of organization used by professionals, a recent development has been the use of *professional corporations* as partners of professional partnerships (so-called multiform partnerships) in order to increase a professional's *pension* and *profit-sharing plan* benefits, the advantages of which have been largely reduced or eliminated by *TEFRA*. See §269A.

professional service corporation   see *professional corporation.*

profit-and-loss method, currency transactions   a method of reporting currency *gains* and *losses* under which net gains or losses are first determined on the basis of a foreign currency, with the results determined when the currency is converted into dollars and repatriated to the United States, with the unrepatriated balance determined at year-end. Rev. Rul. 75-107, 1975-1 C.B. 32.

profit motive   not defined in the *Code* or the *regulations*. The term is used in Reg. §1.183-2(b) relating to *hobby losses,* and refers to the subjective intention of a *taxpayer* to earn a profit. The Internal Revenue Code (§183) provides that if the taxpayer's activities are sufficient to support *deductions* under §162 (*trade or business expenses*) or §212 (certain *investment expenses*), then there is a profit motive. §183(c). See *hobby loss rules.*

profit ratio a fraction, used for reporting *gains* from *installment sales,* consisting of *gross profit* divided by *total contract price.* The ratio is applied to each *payment* made pursuant to the installment sales contract to determine the taxable component of each payment. §453. See *installment method; total contract price.*

profit-sharing plan, Code a *defined contribution plan* established and maintained by an *employer* to provide deferred benefits to *employees* or their *beneficiaries.* Reg. §1.401-1(b)(1)(ii). Such a plan is designed to permit all benefits to be paid in a lump-sum, even before retirement or separation from service. No current or accumulated profit is required. §401(a)(27). A profit-sharing plan must have a definite written formula for allocating profits among individual accounts maintained for the participants. Reg §1.402-1(b)(1)(ii). Today, the term "profit-sharing plan" is considered a misnomer since such a plan may qualify as profit sharing even if contributions exceed current and accumulated profits. A more accurate name would be "discretionary-contribution plan." Regulation §1.401-1(b)(2) demands that employer contributions be regular and substantial.

profit-sharing trust a *trust* used as the funding vehicle for a *profit-sharing plan.*

profits interest in partnership the interest of a *partner* in a *partnership's* future profits, as opposed to its capital. A partner's share of profits may diverge from his or her share of capital. For the antonym, see *capital interest in partnership.*

profit-split method a method of setting hypothetical *arm's length* charges for *sales* of goods between related parties when §482 (*Commissioner's power to reallocate income and deduction between related taxpayers*) is applied. The technique involves dividing profits between the parties so that each takes a realistic profit. It is an alternative to the *cost-sharing election. See intercompany pricing; reallocation of income and deductions by Commissioner.*

progress expenditure an expenditure with respect to property which it is reasonable to believe will qualify for the former *investment tax credit* when *placed in service* by the *taxpayer.* The property must have a *normal rehabilitation period* of at least two years. The *useful life* and the normal rehabilitation period are determined on the basis of the facts known at the close of the *taxable year* in which the construction begins or, if later, at the close of the first taxable year to which a progress expenditure election applies. §47(d) (relating to *rehabilitation credit*) and former §46(d)(2)(A) (using term "*normal construction period*"). If the property under construction by or for the *taxpayer* has a construction period of at least two years, the taxpayer can elect to treat progress expenditures made with respect to such property as part of the taxpayer's investment for the

taxable year. §47(d)(5). Progress expenditures qualify for the credit ratably as the property is improved.

progressive taxes *taxes* whose rates rise as the amount transferred or earned increases (e.g. *federal income taxes*). See *proportional tax.*

prohibited assets a class of assets which generally could not be the subject of a nontaxable *outbound transfer.* See §367(a) as administered under Rev. Proc. 68-23, 1968-1 C.B. 821. The assets included, with certain exceptions, *inventory* and *accounts receivable, stock* and securities, assets transferred in contemplation of *sale, lease* or *license* and leased or licensed assets, and United States *intangibles* used in connection with goods manufactured within the United States. Rev. Proc. 68-23, §3.302(1)(2) and (b). As to whether *partnership interests* are included as securities, compare Letter Rul. 8145034, Aug. 11, 1981, with Letter Rul. 8040070, July 11, 1980. There is an exception for certain stock or securities. See *same-country exception; section 367 rulings.*

prohibited group for purposes of testing whether a *retirement plan* is disqualified because of discrimination in its contributions and benefits, this nontechnical shorthand is used to refer to *highly compensated employees.* §401(a)(4). (It formerly included *officers* and *shareholders.*) *Employees* whose pensions have been the subject of good-faith collective bargaining agreements (as defined in §410(b)(3)(A)) and *nonresident aliens* with no United States source income from the *employer* (§410(b)(3)(B)) are not considered for these purposes.

prohibited interest a term sometimes used to describe an interest in a *corporation* which prevents a *shareholder* who claims *waivers of family attribution rules* from asserting a complete *redemption in termination of shareholder's interest.* See §302(b)(2)-(3). The interest is tested from the moment following the redemption and forward for a decade. Examples of prohibited interests include directorships; officer status; employee status; reacquisition of *stock* other than by *bequest* or *inheritance*; employment by a subsidiary of the redeeming corporation; custodianships under the *Uniform Gifts to Minors Act*; voting trusteeships; rights to payment that fluctuate with corporate income; acting as a legal advisor to the corporation; having a lawyer act as a limited director of the redeeming corporation until the stock is paid in full (as opposed to a nondirector-lawyer who attends meetings purely as advisor to the redeeming shareholder); excessively great or minor powers as a creditor. See, e.g., Rev. Rul. 59-119, 1959-1 C.B. 68. See *waiver of family attribution rules.*

prohibited transaction exemptions administrative exemptions from the *prohibited transactions* rules of *ERISA* and the *Code,* either as to an *individual* transaction (individual exemptions) or as to a class of transactions (class exemptions). Requests for such exemptions are filed with the Department of Labor. §4975(c); ERISA, Pub. L. No. 83-406, §408(a), 88 Stat. 829.

prohibited transactions, ERISA a series of transactions between *plans* and *parties in interest* that involves *retirement plans* or *welfare benefit plans* to which §406 of *ERISA* applies, thereby creating potential personal liability for any resulting losses to the plan. ERISA, Pub. L. No. 83-406, §409, 88 Stat. 829 (subject to defenses of *good faith*). Prohibited transactions arise in the case of (1) a direct or indirect *sale, exchange,* or leasing of any property between a plan and a party in interest; (2) the direct or indirect lending of money or other extension of credit between a plan and a party in interest; (3) the direct or indirect furnishing of any goods, services, or facilities between a plan and a party in interest; (4) the direct or indirect transfer of any plan assets to, or use of any plan assets by or for, the benefit of a party in interest; (5) the direct or indirect acquisition of securities of the *employer* under certain circumstances or in excess of certain maximum amounts; (6) a *fiduciary's* dealing with assets of the plan for personal *gain*; (7) a fiduciary's representation of any person in a transaction involving the plan if that party has interests adverse to the plan; and (8) a fiduciary's receipt of kickback from any person in connection with a transaction involving plan assets. *ERISA,* Pub. L. No. 83-406, §408(b), 88 Stat. 829.

prohibited transactions, loss of exemption a series of transactions between a limited class of *exempt organizations* and their creators, *persons* who have made substantial contributions to the organization, family members (as defined in §267(c)(4) which defines *related taxpayers*) of the foregoing persons, or certain *corporations* 50 percent or more controlled by such persons. The transactions subject to the proscription are (1) loans of any part of the *income* or *corpus* from the organization, without the receipt of adequate security and a reasonable rate of interest; (2) payment of excessive compensation; (3) provision of services by the organization on a preferential basis; (4) substantial purchases at inflated prices of securities or any other property by the organization from one of the foregoing persons; (5) bargain sales of any substantial part of the organization's securities or other property by the organization; or (6) any other transaction that results in a substantial diversion of the organization's income or *corpus*. §503(b). Such transactions, unless otherwise excepted, result in loss of the organization's tax exemption. §503(a). These rules are limited to *church plans, governmental plans, supplemental unemployment benefit trusts,* and certain pension trusts established before June 25, 1959. *Id.*

prohibited transactions, penalties transactions between *qualified plans* and *disqualified persons* that

are considered against public policy, on which the *Code* imposes a 5 percent penalty tax, based on the amount involved, for each year until the transaction is reversed (and a one-time, 100 percent tax if it is not promptly corrected after the *IRS* notification). In summary form, the transactions are (1) *sales, exchanges,* and *leases* of property (transfers of property that are subject to a security interest which the plan assumes, or that the transferor incurred within 10 years before the transfer, are also considered sales or exchanges); (2) extending credit to or from the plan; (3) furnishing goods, services, or facilities; (4) transferring plan income or assets to or for the use or benefit of a disqualified person or persons; (5) dealings by fiduciaries of the plan in plan assets or income for the fiduciaries' own account; or (6) a fiduciary's receiving consideration from a party dealing with the plan in connection with a transfer involving income or assets of the plan. §4975(c)(1). These limitations are modestly relaxed in order to allow fiduciaries to be paid, to benefit from plans in which they participate, and so forth. §4975(d). See *disqualified person, qualified plans; prohibited transactions, ERISA; prohibited transactions, loss of exemption.*

project area, natural resources a geographical territory that the *taxpayer* determines can be explored advantageously in a single integrated operation. Reg. §1.617-3(d)(3) and Rev. Ruls. 77-188, 1977-1 C.B. 76 (oil and gas) and 83-105, 1983-2 C.B. 51 (oil and gas). The term is important in determining how to apportion capitalized *geological and geophysical costs,* and to grant *deductions* for write-offs for surveys which do not yield natural resources.

projected income investment an investment which is not expected to reduce the cumulative tax liability of any investor for any year during any of the first five years ending after the date on which the investment is offered for sale. An investment reduces cumulative tax liability of an investor if projected cumulated *deductions* for the investor exceed cumulative projected income. Investors must be provided with a written financial projection or other writing that supports the conclusion. Temp. Reg. §301.6111, A-57. Projected income investments need not register as *tax shelters.* See *tax shelter, registration.*

proof of claim a submission in bankruptcy and insolvency proceedings by which creditors formalize their asserted rights. The *IRS* uses Form 4491 ("Proof of Claim for Internal Revenue Taxes—Bankruptcy Proceedings") and Form 4991 ("Proof of Claim for Internal Revenue Taxes") outside bankruptcy.

property generally undefined. While state law is frequently respected in the determination of whether an item (e.g., an *easement*) is property, the issue is a federal one. The most conservative guidance is perhaps found under §351, relating to tax-free incorporations and expansions, and to its companion §721, relating to contributions to *partnerships* in exchange for interests in partnerships. Those provisions treat such items as *goodwill, leaseholds,* certain *know-how,* trade secrets, *accounts receivable, patents, letters of intent, copyrights,* and loan agreements generated by the transferor's efforts, as property. Prudence dictates that the meaning of the term must be researched for the purpose of each relevant Code section.

property acquired by bequest, devise, or inheritance a series of transfers of property that are not *gross income* by the recipient. §102. See *bequest; devise; inheritance.*

property acquired from a decedent generally, any *property* received by *bequest, devise,* or *inheritance.* Property is deemed to have been acquired from a *decedent* if it is includible in the decedent's *gross estate* because of the acquisition, regardless of whether an *estate tax return* is required or an estate tax is payable. Such property takes a *basis* equal to its *fair market value* on the decedent's death or on the *alternate valuation date,* or a *special use valuation* basis. §1014(a).

property and liability insurance company generally, any *insurance company* other than a *life insurance company.* Such a company is taxed under §§831–846.

property, corporate distributions money, securities, and any other *property,* aside from *stock* in the *corporation* making the *distribution* (or rights to acquire such stock). §317(a). It includes any *debt* to the corporation making the distribution, as well as securities, whether issued by the distributing corporation or by another corporation. Reg. §1.317-1. Property distributions are taxed under §301(c). This definition applies for purposes of Part I of *subchapter C* relating to *distributions* by corporations. Distributions of property are subject to specialized tax rules. See *distribution, corporation.*

property, depletion each separate legal interest owned by the *taxpayer* in each mineral *deposit* in each separate *tract or parcel of land.* §614(a). Interest for these purposes means *economic interests* (e.g., *working interests, overriding royalties,* and *production payments*). Reg. §1.614-1(a)(2). Dissimilar economic interests in the same tract or parcel are treated as separate properties. Reg. §1.614-1(a)(3). Taxpayers who have several interests in a single tract or parcel of oil, gas, or geothermal resources must aggregate such interest unless they elect to separate them. §614(b). Section 614(c) allows taxpayers who have separate operating mineral interests that constitute some or all of a single operating unit to elect to aggregate the interests that make up one or more mines, and to treat amounts not so aggregated as separate properties. *Cost* and *percentage depletion* must generally be calculated separately for each property. §§612, 613. This definition of the property unit is ubiquitous in the *Code,* even though §614 states it only applies to depletion. The effect of the state law doctrine of merger of estates is unsettled.

property exempt from levy an exclusive list of property that the *IRS* cannot seize to satisfy its claims. Principal items are the *principal residence* (absent jeopardy to the government or high-level IRS approval); clothes; schoolbooks; tools of the trade; fuel; furniture; personal effects; unemployment benefits; worker's compensation; supplemental Social Security benefits for aged, blind and disabled people; state and local welfare and public assistance; Job Training Act payments; property whose estimated *fair market value* is more than the estimated costs of levy and sale; pensions and annuities; and a modest amount of weekly earnings. §6334(a). See *homestead exemption.*

property held for investment see *investment income, interest on investment indebtedness limitation.*

property held for sale see *held for sale.*

property held for the production of income see *held for the production of income.*

property held primarily for sale, capital transactions see *dealer property.*

property held primarily for sale, like-kind exchanges similar to the definition of *dealer property,* but materially broader; the scope of the term is unclear, but it definitely includes leased property that may predictably be sold to the *lessee.*

property, original issue discount rules includes services and the right to use property, but not money. §1273(b)(5). The *original issue discount* rules cover obligations issued for publicly traded and nontraded property.

property passing to spouse see *passes from the decedent to his surviving spouse, estate tax marital deduction.*

property predominantly used outside the United States see *predominately used outside the United States.*

property, restricted property rules any *real* and *personal property* other than an *unfunded, unsecured* promise to pay money in the future. In the case of a transfer of a life insurance, retirement income, or other contract providing life insurance protection, only the *cash surrender value* of the contract is property. Escrowed or trusted amounts are also property. Reg. §1.83-3(e). See *restricted property rules.*

property settlements a term used to describe transfers of property, not mere divisions, between *spouses* or former spouses in connection with a separation or divorce. No gain or loss is recognized to the transferor on a transfer of property (outright or in trust) between spouses or between former spouses incident to the divorce, nor is the value of the property included in the gross income of the transferee. §§1041(a), 1041(b)(1).

property tax   see *ad valorem taxes.*

property used in trade or business   see *section 1231 assets; used in the trade or business.*

proportional tax   a tax which takes the same proportion of each *taxpayer's* income, often called a "flat tax." See *progressive taxes.*

proportionate acquisition rules   the content of §382(g)(4)(B)(ii), to the effect that in determining whether an *equity structure shift* or later transaction is an *ownership change,* the acquisition of *stock* after an equity structure shift is treated as having been made proportionately from all *shareholders* immediately before the acquisition, unless a different proportion is established. See *neutrality principle.*

proportionate profits method, minerals   a method for determining *gross income* from mining for *depletion* purposes where *representative market or field prices* cannot be determined. The method assumes that each dollar spent to produce, transport, and sell the *first marketable product* earns an equal proportionate profit. The formula determines gross income on which depletion can be calculated by the following formula:

$$\text{Gross sales of the first marketable product of group of products} \times \frac{\text{mining costs}}{\text{all mining and nonmining costs}}$$

See Reg. §1.613-4(d)(4)(ii).

proportionate share of interest   the portion of *interest* bearing the same ratio to a *cooperative housing corporation's* total interest *expense* as the portion *tenant-shareholders* hold of the cooperative *stock* bears to the total outstanding corporate stock. Persons in *business or trade* receiving at least a $600 mortgage interest from an *individual* must file with the *IRS* an *information return* and provide a statement to the payor. §6050H(g).

proposed adjustment   an adjustment to a *taxpayer's return,* which the *IRS* proposes to make, following an *audit* of the taxpayer's return. Such proposals ordinarily trigger the taxpayer's appeal rights. §601.103(b).

proposed legislation   see *legislation or proposed legislation.*

proposed regulations   *regulations* that have been issued in a tentative form. Technically, they have no legal weight, but the *IRS* typically attempts to abide by them, and they do reflect the views of the government.

pro rata   proportionately. For example, if a *corporation* has four *shareholders,* each of whom owns 25 per-

cent of the *stock,* and if each *shareholder* received a $100 distribution, then the distribution would be pro rata.

pro rata redemptions of stock   *stock redemptions* from shareholders in proportion to their *stockholdings.* Such redemptions are generally treated as *distributions.* See §302.

pro rata stock distributions   *distributions* of *stock* to *shareholders* in proportion to their predistribution stockholdings. Such distributions are generally tax-free. §305(a).

proration   a method of *allocation* under which items are allocated proportionately.

proprietorship   see *sole proprietorship.*

pro se   on one's behalf, often used in reference to lawsuits undertaken without an attorney.

protective carryover basis election   an election by a purchasing *corporation* with respect to a *qualified stock purchase* of a *target corporation,* which election prevents certain asset purchases from the target or a *target affiliate* during the *consistency period* from causing a deemed *section 338 election* under §338(e). The election assures that the acquiror group's acquisition of an asset from the *target corporation* or from a *target affiliate* does not cause a deemed election under §338, even though an acquiror might have engaged in a *qualified stock purchase* during the *consistency period.* The price exacted for the election is that the purchased assets take a *transferred basis.* Reg. §1.338-4 T(f)(6). Not making the election is a major trap for tax planners and likely constitutes negligence. See also §338(i)(1). See *affected target; section 338 election treating certain stock purchases as asset purchases.*

protective claim for refund   a *claim for refund or credit* that is prepared and filed like any other such claim, except it is filed merely to keep a *taxpayer's* claim alive. See Rev. Rul. 83-79, 1983-20 I.R.B. 7. Such a claim is commonly used where the *IRS* has taken a view adverse to that of the taxpayer in pending litigation. See *claim for refund or credit.*

protective claim for refund or credit   See *protective claim for refund.*

protective ninety-day letters   *statutory notices of deficiency* sent to several related *taxpayers* when only one taxpayer is actually liable, in cases where the taxpayer with the actual liability is unclear.

protective refund or credit claim   see *protective claim for refund.*

protest return   a civil penalty of $500 imposed upon an individual who files a purported income tax return if (1) the purported return fails to contain sufficient information from which the substantial correctness of the tax liability can be determined, and (2) such conduct arises from either a frivolous position or from a desire to impede the administration of the tax laws. This penalty is imposed in addition to all other penalties. §6702.

protocol   either a preliminary treaty or a clarifying addendum to a treaty.

prototype plan   a model form of an *IRS*-approved *qualified plan* in which the identity of the funding medium (e.g., an *insurance company's separate account*) is left blank. Rev. Proc. 80-29, 1980-1 C.B. 681; Rev. Proc. 72-8, 1972-1 C.B. 716. Adopting such plans generally results in administrative savings.

proven oil or gas property   see *proven property.*

proven property   an oil or gas *property,* the principal value of which, when transferred, is demonstrated by prospecting, exploration, or discovery work. The principal value has been demonstrated if (1) any oil or gas has been produced from a deposit; (2) exploration indicates enough oil and gas to justify development; and (3) the property's current *fair market value* is at least half its value minus actual expenses for equipment and *development* costs of the transferee when production begins. Prop. Reg. §1.613-9.

proximate relationship standard   a standard reflected in *regulations* pursuant to §§166 (*business bad debt* losses) and 212 (*investment expenses*). Its purpose is to limit *deductions* under the foregoing sections to those which bear a reasonable and proximate relationship to the conduct of the *trade or business* the *taxpayer* was engaged in when the *debt* was incurred or when it became partially or entirely *worthless* (the §166 case); or to the production and collection of taxable income; or to the management, conservation, or maintenance of property held for the production of income (the §212 case). Reg. §§1.166-5(b), 1.212-1(d). In the case of investment expenses, it is a particularized subject of the more general *ordinary and necessary* standard.

prudent fiduciary rule   a requirement that a *fiduciary* must discharge his or her duties with respect to a *qualified plan* solely in the interest of the *participants* and *beneficiaries,* with the care, skill, prudence, and diligence, under the circumstances then prevailing, that a prudent person acting in a like capacity and familiar with such matters would use in the conduct of an enterprise of a like character and with like aims. It is a properly demanding standard. *ERISA,* §404(a)(1)(B).

pseudo corporation   see *S corporation.*

publication date, regulations   the date that *Treasury regulations* appear in the *Federal Register.*

public charities   a nontechnical term for *exempt organizations* that are described in §501(c)(3) but

which are not *private foundations.* §509(a). Briefly, the list of such organizations includes (1) a *church, convention, or association of churches*; (2) an educational organization that normally has a regular faculty, curriculum, and enrolled student body at the place where instruction is given (an *educational organization described in section 170(b)(1)(A)*); (3) a *hospital* or hospital-affiliated research organization; (4) a public or government-supported development organization that holds and invests property for a state or local college or university; (5) a federal, state, or local governmental unit; (6) an organization that normally receives a substantial part of its support from the public or from a governmental unit; (7) a *supporting organization* affiliated with a public charity described in §509(a)(1) or (a)(2); and (8) an organization that normally receives more than one-third of its support in each *taxable year* from the public, in the form of contributions, membership fees, and so forth, and not more than one-third of its support from gross investment income or unrelated business income (a *section 509(a)(2) organization*). §509(a)(1)-(4). The significance of being a public charity includes (1) qualification for the maximum 50 percent *charitable contribution* limit; (2) favorable treatment of donated *long-term capital gain property*; (3) qualification as *donees* of certain *split-interest* gifts; (4) avoidance of various punitive excise taxes (e.g., §§4941–4945); and (5) qualification as donees for *research and experimentation credits.*

public entertainment activity   any entertainment or recreational activity usually conducted at fairs or expositions for agricultural or educational purposes. Income from such an activity may be *exempt* if conducted by a qualifying organization and structured to meet the requirements set forth in §513(d)(2)(B). §513(d)(1) and (d)(2)(A).

public group   a group of *individuals, entities* or other *persons,* each of whom owns, directly or constructively, less than 5 percent of the *stock* of the *loss corporation.* Reg. §1.382-2T(f)(13). The term is important in the determination as to whether an *ownership change* has occurred for purposes of the *neutrality principle* such that the *section 382 limitation* might apply.

publicly offered registered investment company basically, a broadly offered mutual fund that for years beginning in 1988–1989 can generate expenses that are not subject to the *two-percent floor on itemized deductions* at the investor level. See §67(c). The term is ornate, but it is essentially defined as a *registered investment company* whose shares are publicly offered under §4 of the Securities Act of 1933, regularly traded on an established securities market, or held by or for at least 500 people at any time during the *taxable year.* The *IRS* has regulatory power to provide relief where there are sharp redemptions that violate the 500-shareholder rule. The 1989 cutoff for the regulatory power looks like a drafting error.

publicly supported organizations   an informal term for one of two kinds of *public charities.* The first type, described in §170(b)(1)(A)(vi), generally draw the bulk of their support from the general public or from a governmental unit. They consist primarily of museums of history, art, or science, etc. The second type is described in §509(a)(2) as a type of *section 501(c)(3) organization* which is expressly rendered not a *private foundation.* These organizations have no particular qualitative features, but they instead must satisfy two rigid mathematical tests relating to the minimum normal sources of support (generally, one-third must be public, and from permitted sources) and maximum level of income from *investment* and unrelated *business* sources. Organizations that fall into either of these categories are exempted from *private foundation* status and can qualify for the maximum level of *deductible charitable contributions.* §§509(a)(2), 170(b)(vi) and (viii).

publicly traded partnership   a *partnership* as to which interests are either traded in an established securities market or readily tradable on a secondary market or substantial equivalent thereof. §§469(k)(2) and 7704(b). They are deemed *corporations* by §7704(a) unless they meet the requirements of §7704(c) which relates to hefty minimum proportions of passive income (called *qualifying income*). The particular requirement is that at least 90 percent of its *gross income* be qualifying income, each year; unexcused failure results in a deemed liquidation of the partnership and a deemed formation of a corporation in a *section 351 transaction.* §7704(c)(2) and (f). Publicly traded partnerships (PTPs) can never escape corporate status if they would be *registered investment companies* (if *domestic* and registered), unless commodities, options, futures, or toward commodities contracts trading is one of their principal activities. §7704(c)(3). *The passive loss* rules are applied separately to each PTP, and the $25,000 relief provision for real estate does not apply to any PTP item, except for the *low-income housing credit* and the *rehabilitation tax credit* where such credits exceed *regular tax* liability attributable to nonpartnership income. Finally, on *exempt organization's distributive share* of the net income of a PTP that escapes corporate status is deemed to be from an *unrelated trade or business.* §512(c). See *qualifying income, publicly traded partnerships.*

publicly traded security, charitable contributions   a *security* (including a mutual fund) for which market quotations are readily available on an established securities market. Reg. §1.170A-13(c)(7)(xi). The *regulation* also provides that a security qualifies if it is regularly traded on an interdealer quotation system, if the issuer keeps records of trading prices and volumes, and

if trading prices and volumes are published in a newspaper of general circulation. Such securities enjoy favored status as *charitable contributions.* §170(e)(5). See *security, worthlessness.*

publicly traded security, ESOPs   a security that is listed on a national securities exchange or that is quoted on a system sponsored by a [registered] national securities association. Reg. §54.4975-7(b)(i)(iv). The term arises in connection with loans to *ESOPs.* The "pink sheets" do not qualify, according to the *IRS.* PLR 9036039 (June 13, 1990).

public owner   an *individual, entity* or other *person* that at all times during the *testing period,* owns less than a 5 percent interest in a *first-tier entity* or any *higher-tier entity.* Reg. §1.382-2T(f)(12). The term is important for purposes of determining if an *ownership change* has occurred in a *loss corporation* so as to cause the *section 382 limitation* to apply under the *neutrality principle.*

public policy limitation   a judicial rule that can result in the disallowance of *deductibility* of *expenses* or *losses,* if permitting the *deduction* would frustrate a sharply defined state or local policy. Rev. Rul. 77-126, 1977-1 C.B. 47. The doctrine does not apply to deductions claimed under §162 or §212, rather §162(c), (f), and (g) and Reg. §1.212-l(p) preempt the field, along with §280E (which denies deductions, other than *cost of goods sold,* for illegal drug trafficking).

public retirement system   a pension, annuity, retirement, or similar fund or system established by the United States, a *state,* a *possession,* any *political subdivision* of the foregoing, or the District of Columbia. §37(e)(9). Amounts received from a public retirement system specially affect claims to the *credit for the elderly.*

public school employee   someone who performs services as an *employee,* directly or indirectly, for an *educational organization described in section 170(b)(1)(A)(ii).* The principal, clerical employees, custodial employees, and teachers at a public elementary school are certainly employees performing services directly for such an educational institution, and an employee who performs services involving the operation or direction of a *state's* or *political subdivision's* education program as carried on through such educational organizations is an employee performing services indirectly for such institutions. Such persons can qualify for special tax-deferred annuities. See *tax-deferred annuities for exempt and educational organization employees.*

public transportation vehicle   a vehicle, such as a bus, a railroad car, or other conveyance, that provides transportation service to the public whether or not the owner/taxpayer is in the *business* of rendering transportation services. Reg. §1.190-2(a)(2). See *architectural and transportation barrier removal expenses.*

public utility dividend reinvestment plans   plans under which shareholders of *qualified public utilities* may elect to receive *distributions* in the form of common *stock* (*qualified common stock*) in lieu of money, and exclude up to $750 ($1,500 on a *joint return*) of such distributions from income, but must give the distributions a zero *basis*. §305(e).

public utility property, accelerated cost recovery system   same as *public utility property* for *depreciation* purposes, but only if the *taxpayer* uses *normalization accounting*. §168(f)(2).

public utility property, depreciation   property used predominantly in the *trade or business* of furnishing or selling (1) electricity, water, or sewage disposal services; (2) gas or steam through a local distribution system; (3) telephone services or certain COMSAT services; or (4) steam or gas transported by pipeline, provided in all cases the foregoing are subject to federal, state, or local rate regulation. §167(1)(3)(A). Such property is singled out for specialized *depreciation* under §167(1). See also §168(f)(2) and (i)(10).

public utility property, energy investment credit   *property* used predominantly in the *trade or business* of furnishing or selling (1) electrical energy, water, or sewage disposal services; (2) gas through a local distribution system; (3) telephone or telegraph service; (4) communications property of unregulated persons of the type used by persons engaged in providing regulated telephone or microwave communications services, if the property is used predominantly for communication purposes; or (5) steam through a local distribution system. Public utility property is excluded from qualifying as *alternative energy property, biomass property, solar* or *wind energy property, recycling equipment,* and *cogeneration equipment.* §48(e)(17); Reg. §1.48-9(n). See *normalization accounting.*

public utility stock dividends   see *qualified common stock, public utility stock dividends.*

Puerto Rican resident   a *resident* of Puerto Rico. One must apply the standards relevant to *alien individuals* to determine whether such a person is a *resident alien* in the *United States.* Reg. §1.933-1(a). Although subject to United States taxes, such a resident may exclude Puerto Rican source income, except to the extent paid for United States government services. §933(1).

punitive damages   damages awarded in civil litigation by a court in order to discourage the doing of especially bad acts. According to §104(a), such damages can be *excluded* from *gross income* only if they involve physical injury or sickness. Punitive damages, such as treble damages under antitrust laws, constitute taxable ordinary income. Reg. §1.61-14(a).

purchase accounting   see *purchase method.*

purchase, bonus expensing   acquisition of *property* other than from a related person (as defined) or from a *component member* of the acquirer's *controlled group,* but only if the *basis* of the acquired property is not determined in whole or in part by the *basis* of the property in the transferor's hands (e.g., a *gift*) or under §1014 (relating to property acquired from a *decedent*). §179(d)(3). In order to qualify for *bonus expensing,* property must be purchased. §179(d)(1).

purchased nonmining transportation   transportation beyond the mine by a third party, delivering the product to the customer, provided (1) the conveyances are not owned or leased by the *taxpayer*; (2) there is no further processing or packaging; and (3) the taxpayer ordinarily does not profit from the transportation. The transportation must be via a warehouse, terminal, or distribution facility the taxpayer owns, and it may be performed by an affiliate of the taxpayer as long as an *arm's length* rate is charged for the service. Reg. §1.613-4(e)(2). The term is used to fix *gross income* in the case of *percentage depletion* for mining.

purchase method   a *method of accounting* for corporate acquisitions, based on the theory that the acquiring corporation has purchased the assets and liabilities from the acquired corporation. Hence, the assets are accounted for on the balance sheet of the acquiring corporation at their cost to the acquiring corporation (usually *fair market value*) and not as they had been accounted for by the acquired corporation. This (ordinarily) higher cost will yield higher *depreciation* and *amortization expenses,* but any excess of the total consideration paid over the value of the identifiable assets acquired is treated as a purchase of *goodwill,* and it will be *amortized* for financial reporting purposes over its useful life, not exceeding 40 years.

purchase price adjustment   a reduction in the purchase price of specific property negotiated directly between the buyer of the property and the seller who financed the sale. Such renegotiations are treated as not giving rise to income from the *discharge of indebtedness,* provided the buyer is *solvent,* not in bankruptcy, and still holds the financed property; likewise, the seller must still hold the obligation. See §108(e)(5). Other post-sale adjustments are not excluded from *gross income,* unless perhaps as *gifts* or *inheritances.* See *insolvent debtor.*

purchase, section 338 acquisition   acquisitions of *stock* other than (1) stock with a *carryover basis* or from a *decedent*; (2) acquisitions to which §351 (tax-free *transfers to controlled corporations*) applies; and (3) acquisitions of stock from a person whose stock is deemed owned by the buyer under the *attribution rules* of §318(a), disregarding the attribution rule for *options* (§318(a)(4)). §338(h)(3). Stock is also not "purchased" if it is acquired as a result of an *exchange* to which §354 (relating to exchanges of *stock* and *securities* in certain corporate reorganizations), §355 (relating to corporate fissions), or §356 (relating to the receipt of *boot* in certain *corporate reorganizations* and divisions) applies. Also, an acquisition is not deemed a purchase if the stock is acquired in any other transaction described in *regulations* in which the transferor does not *recognize* the entire amount of the *gain* or *loss realized* on the transaction. §338(h)(3)(A)(ii), as amended.

purchasing corporation, section 338 acquisitions any *corporation* that makes a *qualified stock purchase* with respect to another corporation. §338(d)(1).

purpose obligations   see *acquired obligations.*

purposive economic activity doctrine   a tax law doctrine of uncertain scope to the effect that tax benefits, especially *deductions,* will be denied unless there is a realistic expectation of an economic profit, aside from tax savings, that is not minimal in amount. The doctrine is also referred to as the economic purpose doctrine and relates to the *economic substance* concept.

pursuit of trade or business   the course of an existing *trade or business,* as opposed to the search for one. By the terms of §162(a), business *travel expenses* are *deductible* only if incurred in pursuit of a trade or business. However, the rule permits travel *deductions* in connection with so-called *intramural expansions.*

push-up   a term used to describe a *corporate reorganization* in which the acquiring company transfers acquired assets to its parent company. See, for example, §368(a)(2)(E), which bars a push-up in a *reverse triangular merger.*

put   a transferable contract that entitles the holder to sell to the party who wrote the contract a fixed number of securities (usually in lots of 100) at a specified price for a specified period, generally ranging between one to nine months. Rev. Rul. 78-182, 1978-1 C.B. 265, treats the cost of a put as a *capital expenditure.* The *sale* is generally treated as the *sale* of a *capital asset;* lapse is deemed a sale.

Putnam doctrine   the generality that when a *taxpayer* lends money to his or her *corporation* and is not repaid, the result is a *capital loss* under §165(g)(1), if evidenced by a *security,* or under §166(d)(1), absent a security. See *security, worthlessness.*

pyramiding of income tax   another name for arrangements under which a payor agrees to pay the payee's taxes, which leads to potentially endless rounds of taxes. See Rev. Procs. 83-43, 1983-24 I.R.B. 60 and 81-48, 1981-2 C.B. 263, for the *IRS's* solution. Corporate *lessors* are granted comparable relief by §110.

Q

Q and A a colloquial term for a formal interview of a *taxpayer*, based on an *IRS summons*. It is in essence a deposition.

QTIP an acronym for *qualified terminable interest property*.

QTIP election an election by an *executor* of a *decedent's estate*, or by a *donor* in the case of a lifetime *gift*, to treat certain property passing to the decedent's *spouse* for the transferee's lifetime as not part of the decedent's *gross estate*, or as not subject to federal *gift taxes*, respectively. In the typical case, the executor will make an election to transfer property to a trust for the benefit of the survivor so as to maximize the marital deduction, and thereby he or she can defer the day that estate taxes fall on the property transferred into the trust until the survivor's death, at which point the survivor's estate will report the property.

QTIP trust a *trust* established by one *spouse* to which to transfer *qualified terminable interest property*.

qualified activity, controlled foreign corporations any activity producing *foreign base company shipping income, foreign base company oil-related income, foreign base company sales income, foreign base company services income, foreign base company insurance income* (if predominantly engaged in an active insurance business), or *foreign personal holding company income* (if predominantly engaged in an active banking, finance, or like business). §952(c)(1)(B)(iii). Deficits from qualified activities can give rise to *qualified deficits* which can reduce *subpart F income*. See *accumulated deficit rule; chain deficit rule.*

qualified alcohol-producing facility, industrial development bonds a facility that primarily produces alcohol, for which more than half of the feedstock is, or is derived from, *solid waste.* Former §103(g)(3). Substantially all of the feedstock derived from solid waste must be produced at a facility located at or adjacent to the site of the alcohol-producing facility, and both facilities must be owned and operated by the same person. *Interest* from obligations issued to furnish qualified alcohol-producing facilities is exempted from *federal income taxation.* §103(b)(4)(E). It appears to have disappeared from the scene, but it may still be a viable subset of a qualified *solid waste disposal facility* under §142(a)(6).

qualified allocation an *allocation* of a *partner's distributive share* that results in each partner that is a *qualified organization* having the same percentage interest in each item of partnership *income, gain, loss, deduction,* and *credit* at all times through the life of the partnership *and* has *substantial economic effect* under §704(b)(2). In general, a partnership's allocations satisfy the *fractions rule* if (1) such allocations cannot result in a partner that is a *qualified organization* having a share of overall partnership income for any *taxable year* that is greater than its share of overall partnership loss for the taxable year during which such partner's loss share is the smallest, and (2) such allocations have substantial economic effect.

qualified allocation plan a plan adhered to by a state housing agency that allocates the *state low-income housing credit limitation* in a way that ensures that the best interest of low-income tenants and the public is served. The definition appears in §42(m)(1)(B) and consists of an extensive list of criteria. See *low-income housing credit.*

qualified amateur sports organization an organization organized and operated exclusively to foster national or international amateur sports competition, if such organization is also organized and operated primarily to conduct national or international competition in sports or to support and develop athletes for national or international competition in sports, even if its membership is local or regional and even though it provides athletic facilities or equipment. §501(c)(3), (j)(1) and (2). If the *entity* is otherwise exempt, contributions can qualify as *charitable contributions.* §170(c).

qualified annuity plan a nontechnical term for an otherwise *qualified pension plan* that provides retirement benefits from individual or *group annuity* contracts bought by the *employer*, typically with no *trust* used to hold such contracts. §§403(a), 404(a)(2), 401(f) and (h) (medical and other benefits for retirees). Such annuities may have *incidental life insurance* features; or the plan may be funded with life insurance contracts with only incidental life insurance benefits. Reg. §§1.401(f); 1.404(a)-3(a).

qualified appraisal an appraisal prepared by a *qualified appraiser* and containing (1) a description of property; (2) its *fair market value* on the date of its *charitable contribution* and specific basis for valuation; (3) a statement that the appraisal was prepared for *income tax* purposes; (4) the appraiser's qualifications; (5) the appraiser's signature and identifying number; and (6) such additional information as the *regulations* may require. *Tax Reform Act of 1984,* §155(a)(4). The qualified appraisal is required for *charitable contributions* of over $5,000. The fee for the appraisal cannot be a percentage of the gift's value. §155(d)(1).

qualified appraiser an appraiser who is qualified to make an appraisal of the type of *property* donated. Such appraiser is not the *taxpayer*; a party to the transaction in which the taxpayer acquired the property; the *donee*; any person employed by any of the above-listed *persons,* or bearing a relation to any of the above-listed persons, who would bear the *deduction* of a *loss* on the *sale* of property to such a person under §267 (a *related taxpayer*); or any person whose relationship to the taxpayer would cause a reasonable person to question the appraiser's independence. In appropriate circumstances, an appraiser who is regularly retained by someone could be considered as an *employee* of that party where a longstanding relationship with the appraiser would cause a reasonable person to question the independence of the appraiser. Only a qualified appraiser can provide a *qualified appraisal.* See also §6659(f)(3)(B).

qualified appreciated stock   any *stock* of a *corporation* for which (as of the date contributed) market quotations are readily available on an established securities market and which is *capital gain property,* provided contributions of such stock to *private foundations* do not exceed 10 percent of the value of all of the corporation's stock. §170(e)(5)(B) and (C). Until 1995, contributions of such stock to or for the use of *private nonoperating foundations* can (for a 10-year period) be made without reduction by built-in *long-term capital gains.* §170(e)(5)(A).

qualified architectural and transportation barrier removal expense   an *architectural and transportation barrier removal expense* incurred in connection with bringing any facility or *public transportation vehicle* into conformity with standards set forth in *regulations.* §190(b)(2). The maximum deduction for a taxpayer (including an affiliated group of corporations filing a consolidated return) for any taxable year is $25,000. Reg. §1.190-1(b).

qualified asset account   an account maintained by a *funded welfare benefit plan* containing funds set aside to provide for payment of disability, medical, unemployment, severance pay, or *life insurance* benefits. *Deductions* for annual additions to such accounts are subject to complex limits designed to prevent their abuse. §419A.

qualified assignment   any assignment of a duty to make periodic payments as *damages* for *personal injuries or sickness* if an assignee (e.g., *life insurance company*) agrees to make the payments for the assignor, provided the payments are fixed and determinable as to amount and time of payment, and not subject to acceleration, deferral, increase, or decrease by the recipient (tort victim). The assignee's obligations cannot be greater than that of the person whose liability is assumed, and the periodic payments must be *excludable* from the recipient's *gross income* as damages for *personal injuries or sickness* under §104(a)(2). §130(c). See *qualified funding asset.*

qualified bank holding corporation   a *corporation* that controlled a bank within the meaning of the Bank Holding Company Act on July 7, 1970, or that is later considered a qualified bank holding company by virtue of (1) property it has acquired not later than July 7, 1970; (2) property it has received thereafter in a *distribution* from another qualified bank holding company; or (3) stock of a subsidiary it has required thereafter, provided the subsidiary was created in order to recover the property. §1103(a). Divestitures by such a corporation to a corporation or *individual* qualify for special tax relief. §§1101–1103.

qualified basis, low-income housing credit   the dollar value of the portion of each *qualified low-income building* on which the *low-income housing credit* is based. §42(c)(1). It equals the building's *eligible basis* times a so-called *applicable fraction* (i.e., the smaller of the fraction based on proportionate floor space or portion of residential units that are *low-income units,* including unoccupied units). It is reduced by provisions analogous to the general *at-risk rules,* with exceptions for *qualified commercial financing.* See *low-income housing credit.*

qualified beneficiary   someone who is related to a *covered employee* under the *health care continuation rules.* §4980B. Such beneficiaries consist of *spouses* and *children* who are *dependents.* §4980B(g)-(1)(A). Certain *nonresident aliens* are excluded. §4980B(g)(1)(C). In bankruptcy cases, the term expands to include retirees and widows. §4980B(g)(1)(C). See *group health plan, deduction; health care continuation rules.*

qualified beneficiary, excise tax, failure to provide health care coverage   see *excise tax, failure to provide continuation coverage.*

qualified benefits   when *cafeteria plans* are spoken of, the reference is generally to a benefit in employment which is *excludable* from *gross income* under some particular *Code* section, other than (1) *scholarships* and *fellowships*; (2) *educational assistance plans*; and (3) the six types of nontaxable *fringe benefits* described in §132. §125(f). In addition, *group-term life insurance* coverage in excess of $50,000 and other benefits to be prescribed in *regulations* are qualified benefits. Qualified benefits are crucial to the definition of *cafeteria plans.*

qualified board or exchange   includes a national securities exchange which is registered with the Securities and Exchange Commission. §1256(g)(7). See *listed option.*

qualified bond   a *state or local bond* that is classified as a *private activity bond* but is granted *tax-exempt bond* status due to the designated purpose for which the proceeds from the issue will be used. The types of such bonds are *exempt facility bonds, qualified mortgage bonds, qualified veteran's mortgage bonds, qualified small issue bonds, qualified student loan bonds, qualified redevelopment bonds* and *qualified section 501(c)(3) bonds.* §141(d)(1). See also §§148 (*arbitrage bonds*) and 149-150 (further restrictions). See *state or local bond; tax-exempt bond.*

qualified bond purchase plan a *qualified pension* or *profit-sharing plan* under which *employer contributions* are invested exclusively in specialized nontransferable federal bonds issued under the Second Liberty Bond Act in compliance with §405(b)(1). Such plans must satisfy most of the rules that apply to qualified plans (e.g., vesting, coverage, and so on), but no *trust* or *custodial* arrangement is required. The bonds are nonforfeitable, pay interest at redemption only, and must be bought in the name of the participant. They are redeemable at death or after age $59\frac{1}{2}$. Not more than $5,000 of such bonds may be bought for any person in a *calendar year.* To the extent redemption proceeds exceed *basis* in the bond on redemption, the result is fully taxable *ordinary income* to the participant. While such plans are not automatically *qualified deferred compensation plans,* the character of the bonds intrinsically causes such plans to meet many of the conditions of §401. Sales of such bonds have terminated. These plans were eliminated by the *Tax Reform Act of 1984.* §491.

qualified business indebtedness *debt* of the *taxpayer* if both (1) the indebtedness was incurred or assumed by a *corporation* or by an *individual* in connection with property used in the taxpayer's *trade or business,* and (2) the taxpayer makes an election to reduce the *basis* of depreciable assets or realty held as *inventory.* Discharges of such debt were tax-free under §108(a)(1)(C) prior to 1986. For the surviving concept, see *qualified farm indebtedness.*

qualified business property, at-risk rules for investment credit any property, aside from master *sound recordings* or other *tangible* or *intangible* assets associated with literary, artistic, or musical properties, if (1) the property is used by the *S corporation* in the active conduct of a *trade or business*; and (2) during the entire 12-month period ending on the last day of the corporation's *taxable year,* the corporation (a) had at least three full-time *employees* who were not owner-employees (i.e., did not own over 5 percent of the outstanding common *stock*) and substantially all of whose services were directly related to the *trade or business,* and (b) had at least one full-time employee substantially all of whose services were devoted to the active management of the trade or business. §49(a)(1)(E)(iii). See *at-risk rules, investment tax credit.*

qualified business unit a separate and clearly identified unit of a *trade or business* of a *taxpayer* which maintains separate books and records. §989(a). Designation as a qualified business unit is for the purpose of determining a *functional currency* and does not constitute a separate trade or business for portions of the *Code* other than *subpart J.* A taxpayer may have more than one qualified business unit. Reg. §1.989(a)-1T. Realistically, the term refers to *foreign branches* of United States *businesses* which used a net worth method of accounting before enactment of the *Tax Reform Act of 1986.* The term is significant for purposes of interim rules involving reporting profits and losses on foreign currency transactions. See TD 8207, 1988-28 I.R.B. 18. It is also used to define the term *foreign person* for purposes of allocations under the *uniform capitalization rules,* described under the heading "*United States ratio method.*"

qualified business use the kind of use that allows *listed property* (e.g., cars) for *business* and nonbusiness use to qualify for former *investment tax credits* and *accelerated cost recovery.* Basically, it means any use in a *trade or business* of the *taxpayer.* §280F(d)(6)(B). Use for the production of income (§212) does not qualify for purposes of the 50 percent threshold. The term excludes (1) leasing property to any *five-percent owner* of the taxpayer or to any *related* taxpayer (§267) (A *five-percent owner* is one who owns 5 percent or more of the voting power or outstanding *stock* of a *corporation* or who owns 5 percent or more of the *capital* or *profits interest* of a noncorporate *entity* as provided in §§416(i)(l)(B)(i) and 280F(d)(6) (D)(i)); (2) the use of listed property provided as compensation for services by a *five-percent owner* or a related person (§280F(d)(6)(C)(ii)); (3) the use of listed property as compensation for services by any person (other than a *five-percent owner* or related person), in connection with the business of the taxpayer, provided such use gives rise to *gross income* to the user (which, in the case of an *employee,* must also be treated as *wages* subject to *withholding*).

qualified buy-sell agreement an agreement, which has existed continuously since September 28, 1982, that calls for the surviving contracting owners of an *S corporation* (who were parties to the agreement on that date) to buy the *stock* of the *decedent.* §1378(c)(3)(D). The acquisition of stock of an S corporation pursuant to such an agreement cannot force the imposition of a *calendar year* on the corporation. §1378(c)(3)(A).

qualified campus lodging lodging furnished to an *employee* (including a *spouse* and any *dependents*) by or on behalf of an *educational institution* for use as a residence. It may be to nonfaculty personnel or to faculty, but it must in all cases be on or in the proximity of the campus. The value of such lodging is taxable to the extent the annual rent paid is less than the lesser of (1) 5 percent of the property's independently appraised value, or (2) average rentals paid to the landlord/employer for comparable housing by outsiders. §119(d). It may be entirely *excludable* from *gross income* under §119(a).

qualified cash or deferred arrangement an arrangement forming part of a *qualified profit-sharing* or *stock bonus plan, a pre-ERISA money purchase plan, or a rural electric cooperative's plan* under which, among other things, (1) *employees* may elect to have the *employer* make payments of up to $7,000 (indexed for inflation; the ceiling amount is $8,728 for 1992) as contributions to a *trust* under the plan on behalf of the employees or may make contributions directly in cash (the monetary ceiling applies to all trusts, not each trust); (2) amounts held by the trust and attributable to *employer contributions* made at the employee's election may not be distributable to *participants* or their *beneficiaries* earlier than retirement, death, *disability,* separation from service, hardship, or age 59½, and will not be distributable merely by reason of the completion of a stated period of participation or the lapse of a fixed number of years; and (3) each employee's right to his or her *accrued benefit* derived from employer contributions pursuant to his or her election is nonforfeitable. §§401(k)(2) and 401(a)(30). The benefit of a qualified cash or deferred arrangement is that employees can defer substantial amounts of their wages and salaries, which deferrals can grow tax-free until paid out. See *actual deferral percentage; salary reduction plans; salary reduction SEP.*

qualified C corporation a *closely held C corporation* other than a *personal holding company, foreign personal holding company,* or a *personal service corporation* (applying a 5 percent rather than a 10 percent measure). §465(c)(7)(B). Such corporations can elude the *at-risk rules* as to their *qualifying businesses.* See *at-risk rules, generally.*

qualified census tract a census tract in which at least 70 percent of the families have income which is not over 80 percent of statewide median income, based on the most recent decennial census data. §143(j). See *targeted area residences.*

qualified chain member a 100-percent-owned lower-tier *corporation* organized in the same country as the top-tier *controlled foreign corporation* (CFC), and which was 100 percent owned when the deficit arose. §952(c)(1)(C). Deficits in the *earnings and profits* of such corporations can reduce the CFC's *subpart F income* which is attributable to qualified activities (*foreign base company shipping income, foreign base company oil-related income, foreign base company sales income,* and certain income of an insurance company or *foreign personal holding company*). §952(c)(1)(B)(ii) and (c)(1)(C)(i).

qualified check, written notice of patronage allocations a check or other instrument redeemable for money, paid as part of a *patronage dividend* or a dividend for nonpatronage business to a distributee who did not consent to include an *allocation* of patronage earnings in income; such a check states that its endorsement or presentation constitutes consent to include the amount in *gross income.* §1388(c)(4). Failure to cash the check, or cashing it more than 90 days after the payment period to which it relates, renders the check a mere *nonqualified written notice of allocation,* which cannot be *deducted* by the *cooperative* until redeemed. §1388(d). See *cooperatives; written notice of allocation.*

qualified child care facility, amortization a facility that is particularly suited to provide child care services and specifically used by an *employer* to provide such services primarily for his or her *employees'* children, operated as a licensed or approved facility under applicable local law, if any, relating to the day care of children, and if directly or indirectly funded to any extent by the United States, established and operated in compliance with the requirements contained in part 71 of Title 45 of the C.F.R., relating to Federal Interagency Day Care Requirements. Reg. §1.188-1(d)(4). Expenditures made before 1983 to acquire or improve such property (if located in the United States and not of a *character subject to depreciation*—also known as §188 property) may be *amortized* over 60 months after the property is *placed in service.* §188(a).

qualified clinical testing expenses amounts paid or incurred by the *taxpayer* during the *taxable year* for human clinical drug testing, which would otherwise qualify for the *tax credit for increasing research activities,* but which (1) include all *contract research expenses*; and (2) exclude research funded through grants, contracts, and the like by another person or government unit, and foreign testing unless there is no adequate United States testing population. (Even then the overseas testing must be by unrelated parties.) §28(b). See *orphan drug credit.*

qualified commercial financing see *nonqualified nonrecourse financing, at-risk rules for investment credit.*

qualified common stock, public utility stock dividends authorized but unissued common *stock* designated by the directors as issued as a *qualified reinvested dividend* in connection with a dividend reinvestment plan. A qualified reinvested dividend refers to a *distribution* of qualified common stock (including fractional shares) to an individual on his or her common or preferred stock, pursuant to a plan whereby he or she can elect to take stock in lieu of cash or other property, treating the stock dividend as tax-free (but having a zero *basis*). §305(e)(2). In order for stock to be qualified common stock, the number of shares a shareholder receives must be based on the *fair market value* of the shareholder's stock immediately before the distribution, with a potential for error of 5 percent above or below the then–fair market value. §305(e)(4)(A). See *public utility dividend reinvestment plans.*

qualified conservation contribution   a type of partial interest in *property* that can qualify for a *deduction for charitable contributions,* provided it is of a *qualified real property interest* made to a *qualified organization* exclusively for *conservation purposes* (defined in §170(h)(1)). Irrevocable transfers of *easements* in real property made after 1986 to qualified organizations (defined in §170(h)(3)) are *deductible* as qualified conservation contributions for *estate* and *gift tax* purposes even though they do not satisfy the conservation purpose requirement of §170(h)(4)(A). See *qualified organization, qualified conservation contribution.*

qualified contract, low-income housing credit   a *bona fide* contract to acquire (within a reasonable period after the contract is entered into) the non-low-income portion of a building for *fair market value,* plus the low-income portion for the amount as determined under pre-1990 Act law. §42(h)(6)(F). The qualified contract for a mixed use building must specify a price for the non-low-income portion equal to *fair market value.* After the housing credit agency is notified of the *taxpayer's* intent to dispose of the property, it can only provide for continuation of the low-income status of the building if there is a qualified contract by a *person* who will continue that status. The term is used in connection with the *low-income housing credit.*

qualified contribution, corporate gifts   *charitable contributions* by *corporations,* other than *S corporations,* if all the following tests are met: (1) the recipient of the gift is a *section 501(c)(3) organization,* which uses the *property* to care for the ill, needy, or infants in a fashion related to its *exempt purpose;* (2) the recipient of the gift does not transfer the property for money, property, or other services; (3) the recipient of the gift furnishes a written statement to the *donor* that the foregoing requirements were satisfied; and (4) the property meets applicable FDA requirements. Section 170(e)(3)(A) provides an exception for such gifts from the general rule preventing any *deduction* for the *gain* built into such gifts, and the *IRS* can simplify related appraisal requirements.

qualified contribution, works of art   a transfer of property to a *qualified organization,* if the *property's* use is related to the transferee's *exempt purpose* (e.g., a gift of a copyrighted painting to a publicly supported art museum). Sections 2055(e)(4) and 2522(c) permit gifts of copyrighted *tangible personal property* ("works of art") to be severed into the copyright and the *tangible property* itself for *estate* and *gift tax charitable deduction* purposes. See *qualified organization, contributions of works of art.*

qualified convention and trade show activity   activity undertaken by qualifying organizations (meaning *exempt labor, agricultural* or *horticultural organizations, business leagues,* etc., described in §501(c)(5) or (6)) that regularly conduct as one of their substantial *exempt purposes* a qualified convention or trade show. A qualified convention or trade show in turn means a show that (1) is conducted by a qualifying organization; (2) the sponsor intends at least partly, to promote and stimulate interest in and demand for the products and services of the industry or industry segment of the members of the organization; and (3) is designed to achieve that purpose through the character of a significant portion of the exhibits or the character of conferences and seminars held at the convention or meeting. For these purposes, "show" includes an international, national, state, regional, or local convention, annual meeting, or show. Such activities can be carried on without creating *unrelated trade or business taxable income.* §513(d)(3).

qualified corporation, extraordinary dividends   any *corporation* (including a predecessor corporation) (1) as to which the *taxpayer* holds directly or indirectly for the corporation's entire existence at least the same ownership interest as the taxpayer holds in the corporation distributing what is otherwise an *extraordinary dividend,* and (2) which has no *earnings and profits* (e&p) which were earned by or which are attributable to *gain* on property which *accrued* during a period when it was not held by a corporation meeting the requirement of (1), above. §1059(d)(6)(B). In general, the rules forcing *basis* reduction of *stock* which is the subject of an extraordinary dividend do not apply with respect to any share of stock of the corporation to an original, continuous shareholder as long as the e&p of the distributing corporation was its own and not earned by the efforts or capital of another (nonqualified) corporation. §1059(d)(6)(A). See *extraordinary dividend, basis reduction.*

qualified corporation, liquidations   a *corporation* having an *applicable value* not over $10 million and having more than 50 percent of its *stock* (by value) owned by 10 or fewer *qualified persons.* The applicable value of a corporation is the value of its *stock* on the date of adoption of the plan of liquidation, or August 1, 1986, if the value was greater at that time. Generally, qualified persons are *individuals, estates,* and *trusts* that can hold *S corporation* stock. Stock held by a corporation, trust, or *partnership* is deemed owned proportionately by its *shareholders, beneficiaries,* or *partners.* Stock owned by members of the family (as defined in §318) is deemed owned by one person. Members of a *controlled group of corporations* are treated as one corporation. *Gain* or *loss* is *recognized* on the *liquidating distribution* of property that would produce *ordinary income* if sold, *short-term capital gain property,* and gain or loss on the disposition of *installment obligations,* and is phased out for qualified corporations valued at over $5 million. *Tax Reform Act of 1986,* §663(d). This relief provision limits or prevents taxation of the liquidating corporation in regular *corporate liquidations* or in hypothetical liquidations under §338. Similar rules apply to S corporations. See §633(d)(8). This is the primary *transition rule* under the corporate tax system following the quasi-repeal of the *General Utilities doctrine* in 1986.

qualified cost *qualified direct costs* for the *taxable year* plus certain additions (*reserve* increases) to the *qualified asset account.* (§419(c)(1)), reduced by after-tax income of the plan. (§419(c)(2)). The term is used in connection with the limits (subject to *carryovers* to later years) on *deductions* to *welfare benefit funds.*

qualified cost-of-living arrangement an arrangement under a *defined benefit plan* containing a cost-of-living adjustment (COLA) to a benefit provided under the plan or a separate plan subject to the *minimum funding standard.* The arrangement must meet the following requirements: (1) to the extent the increase exceeds 3 percent of the original retirement benefit, the COLA must be based on increases in the cost-of-living after the *annuity starting date,* using *IRS* standards; (2) electivity by the *participant* and availability to all participants under the same terms at specified times; (3) no pattern of discrimination with respect to *participation* in favor of *highly compensated employees. Key employees* (§416(i)(1) meaning, as modified) are generally excluded from participating. §415(k)(2)(B). Qualified cost-of-living arrangements offer security against post-retirement inflation.

qualified covered call as to *positions* established after 1987, this exception is limited to cases of *stock* disposed of at a *loss* in one *taxable year,* where *gain* is reportable in the following year. In such cases, the *taxpayer* must hold the call for at least 30 days after the related stock is *sold* at a loss. §1092(c)(4)(E), as amended.

qualified covered call options an *option* written by a *dealer* in the course of his option business and any option granted by the *taxpayer* to buy *stock* held by him, or acquired by the taxpayer in connection with such a grant. The option (1) must be traded on a national securities exchange registered with the SEC or similar *IRS*-designated market; (2) cannot be granted by an option dealer in connection with his option-writing activity, and *gain* or *loss* produced by it cannot be *ordinary income* or *loss*; (3) must have a term of more than 30 days; and (4) must not be a *deep-in-the-money option.* §1092(c)(4)(B). See also §1092(f) (special rule as to *capital losses*). What would otherwise be a *straddle* subject to the *loss deferral rule* can be declassified if it is a *qualified covered call option,* such that neither

the loss deferral rule nor the mandatory *capitalization* provisions for straddles apply. §1092(c)(4)(A).

qualified creative expense any one of various expenditures that self-employed photographers, artists, and authors can *deduct,* directly or as *qualified employee-owners* of *personal service corporations* (§269A(b) definition), currently in spite of the *uniform capitalization rules.* §263A(h). These are otherwise *deductible expenditures* which are *paid or incurred* by an *individual* engaged in the *business* of being a photographer, artist, or author. Creativity and uniqueness of the item as well as its aesthetic value is taken into consideration when determination is made as to whether a qualified creative expense is paid or incurred by an artist. Certain expenditures are explicitly not treated as qualified creative expenses, namely those related to printing, photographic plates, motion picture films, videotapes, and "similar items."

qualified current retiree health liabilities the aggregate amounts, including administrative expenses, related to *applicable health benefits* in the *taxable year,* which amounts would have been *deductible* by the *employer* for that year if the benefits were provided directly by the employer and the employer used the *cash method* of accounting. §420(e)(1)(A). *Key employees* (§416(i)) for any *plan year* ending in a taxable year are disregarded (§420(e)(1)(D)), and qualified current retiree health liabilities otherwise calculated are reduced by previous contributions to a *section 401(h) account* or a *welfare benefit fund* to pay for the qualified current retiree health liabilities (§420(e)(1)(B)). See *qualified transfer, health benefit account.*

qualified debt instrument, foreign currency see *qualified hedging transaction.*

qualified debt instrument, imputed interest any *debt instrument* that is issued by a buyer in connection with purchases of property (other than *section 38 property*) in a sale for *deferred* payments where the principal amount of the debt instrument does not exceed $2.8 million. §1274A(b). Section 1274 limits the interest imputed under §§1274 and 482 on such debt to 9 percent. See *imputed interest; original issue discount.*

qualified deferred compensation plan a *pension, profit-sharing,* or *stock bonus plan* that meets the requirements of §§401, 410, and 411 of the *Code.* Reg. §1.401-0(b)(1). The tax advantages of qualified plans include the following: (1) *employer contributions* are *deductible* within certain limits as *ordinary and necessary trade or business expenses*; (2) employer contributions to a *qualified trust* (or certain permissible substitutes for a trust) used to fund the plan are not *includible* in the *gross income* of *participants* until actually received; (3) investment earnings on plan assets held by a qualified trust—including *realized gains* and *losses*—

are not taxable until disbursed to *participants* in the form of plan benefits; and (4) *lump-sum distributions* to plan participants qualify for favorable long-term *capital gains* treatment (to a limited extent) and special *five-year forward averaging* for income tax purposes.

qualified deficit a deficit in a *controlled foreign corporation's earnings and profits* from a post–December 31, 1986 *taxable year,* to the extent attributable to the same activity as the current year's income activity under the *accumulated deficit rule,* and further to the extent not previously used to reduce *subpart F income.* §952(c)(1)(B)(ii). See *accumulated deficit rule.*

qualified depository institution a *bank* as defined in §581; a *mutual savings bank, cooperative bank, domestic building and loan association*; or bank, credit union, or any other savings or thrift institution chartered and supervised under federal or state law; or a credit union.

qualified designated distribution a *dividend* paid by a *regulated investment company* (RIC), formally designated as such with respect to a non-RIC year and made after a determination that RIC status is lost. §852(e)(2)(B). Absent fraud, such a distribution can salvage the RIC's status in the future. In some cases it will be a superior alternative to a *deficiency dividend.*

qualified direct cost the aggregate amount, including administrative expenses and premiums, which would have been allowable as a *deduction* to a *cash method taxpayer* with respect to benefits provided under a *welfare benefit fund* in the *taxable year* if the *taxpayer* had provided the benefits directly on a current basis. §419(c)(3)(A), (g).

qualified disability benefit, qualified plans a disability benefit that is not greater than the amount of benefit payable to a *participant* if the participant separated from service at *normal retirement age,* making the *normal retirement benefit* calculation for purposes of determining qualification of the plan without regard to ancillary benefits, such as medical benefits or disability benefits that are not in excess of the qualified disability benefit. §411(a)(9); Reg. §1.411(a)-7(c)(4). *Qualified plans* subject to *ERISA* must provide for nonforfeitable *normal retirement benefits* at normal retirement age. §411(a).

qualified disclaimer an irrevocable and unqualified refusal to accept all or an undivided portion of a *property* interest under a will, *intestacy* statute, or a *gift.* To make an effective qualified disclaimer, the conditions enumerated in §2518(b) must be met: (1) a written refusal must be sent by the transferor of the interest (the disclaimant), the transferor's legal representative, or the legal title holder of the property interest not more than nine months after the later of the transfer or the disclaimant's attaining age 21; (2) the disclaimant must not theretofore have accepted the interest or any of its benefits; and (3) the interest must pass without direction by the disclaimant, and pass to either the *decedent's spouse* or to a person other than the disclaimant. The effect of a qualified disclaimer is that the property interest disclaimed is treated as though it never had been transferred to the disclaimant for *estate, gift,* and *generation-skipping transfer tax* purposes. §2518(a).

qualified distributions, private foundations amounts paid by *private foundations* that have the effect of reducing the base on which the 15 percent/100 percent *excise tax* on failures to make minimum distributions falls. §4942(a). The term refers to amounts (including administrative expenses) paid in order to accomplish specific charitable purposes, as well as amounts paid for assets held, or held for use, in directly carrying out these purposes (but not *depreciation* on such assets). §4942(g); Rev. Rul. 74-450, 1974-2 C.B. 388. In general, contributions to controlled organizations or to *disqualified persons* (and contributions to *nonoperating foundations*) are not counted for this purpose. Certain *charitable set-asides* (reserves) for private foundations also qualify, if appropriate, in some cases without prior *IRS* approval. §4942(g)(2). See *excise taxes, private foundations; undistributed income excise tax; undistributed income, private foundation.*

qualified dividend reinvestment plan a plan adopted (or, in the case of an existing plan that required amendment, one amended) after August 12, 1981, and before the date of the particular distribution intended to be a *qualified reinvested dividend.* Such a plan must meet various specified requirements in order for the special benefits of *public utility dividend reinvestment plans* to be available to shareholders. See Temp. Reg. §5c.305-1 for details.

qualified domestic relations order a court judgment, order, or decree relating to provision for child support, alimony, marital property rights to a *spouse* (or former spouse, child, or other *dependent* of the *participant*) in a *deferred compensation plan,* including an *IRA,* pursuant to state law, that recognizes an alternate payee right, or assigns the alternate payee that right, to receive some or all of the benefits from a *qualified plan* or *trust.* §414(p). Benefits which are paid to an alternate payee such as a divorced spouse under a so-called *qualified domestic relations order* can be rolled over on a tax-free basis from a qualified plan into an *IRA,* and do not disqualify the plan or trust on grounds of permitting assignment or alienation of benefits. §401(a)(13)(B). See *qualified deferred compensation plan.*

qualified domestic trust a kind of *trust,* transfers to which qualify for the *marital deduction* for *federal estate tax* purposes despite the fact that the transferee *spouse* is not a *citizen of the United States.*

qualified dwelling any house, apartment, condominium, or mobile home not used on a *transient basis* (as defined in §7701(a)(19)(C)(v)), including all structures or other property belonging to or annexed to such a qualified dwelling. §56(e)(2). *Interest paid or accrued* during the *taxable year* on *debt* incurred in acquiring, constructing, or substantially rehabilitating such a qualified dwelling is a component of *qualified housing interest*. §56(e)(1)(B). *Individuals* can *deduct* qualified housing interest for *alternative minimum tax purposes*. §56(b).

qualified early retirement age the latest of (1) the earliest date under the *qualified retirement plan* on which the *participant* could elect, without prior approval, to receive retirement benefits (other than disability benefits); (2) the first day of the 120th month before the participant reaches *normal retirement age*; or (3) the date on which the participant begins participation. Reg. §1.401(a)-11(b)(4). Final *regulations* call for an automatic *joint and survivor annuity* for *employees* who retire at or after *normal retirement age* or qualified early retirement age. See *normal retirement age; participation, qualified retirement plans*.

qualified educational expenses see *qualified residence interest*.

qualified electing fund, passive foreign investment company a *passive foreign investment company* that provides the *IRS* with information concerning ownership of *stock*, earnings, and other facts, enabling the *shareholders* to elect to pay tax on the income of the company currently or *defer* payment until a specified future event occurs. §§1294–1295. Extension-terminating events are *distributions* of income, *disposition* of stock in the passive foreign investment company, or the passive foreign investment company's ceasing to be a *qualified fund*. §1294(c). Deferral is not available for amounts *includible* in the *gross income* of the *taxpayer* under §§551 and 951 (relating to *foreign personal holding companies*). If deferral is elected, then *interest* is due when the tax is paid on the deferral. See *passive foreign investment company; qualified fund, foreign currency gain or loss*.

qualified electing shareholder a *shareholder*, other than an *excluded corporation* (basically, a *corporation* that had at least 50 percent control of the corporation since 1954), who held any class of *stock* at the time of adoption of the plan of *liquidation* and duly elected the benefits of former §333 (*one-month liquidation*). See *section 333 liquidations*.

qualified employee, catch-up election an *employee* who has completed 15 years of service with a *qualified organization*. §402(g)(8)(C). See *catch-up election, tax-deferred annuities for exempt and educational organization employees*.

qualified employee discounts if the employer sells goods or services to the employee for a price that is less than the price charged regular customers, the employee

realizes income equal to the extent of the discount. For example, assume that a department store sells a washing machine to an employee for $200 when the regular price is $400. If the gross profit is 40 percent, then the employee must recognize income of $40, calculated as follows:

Customer price for washing machine	$400
Less: Gross profit (40%)	160
	$240
Employee price	200
Recognized income	$ 40

There is no exclusion for discounts on any personal *investment* or *real property*. In the case of services, the exclusion is limited to 20 percent of the customer price. Reg. §1.132-1(b). See *fringe benefits; line of business limitation*.

qualified employee-owner an *individual* who is an artist, author, or photographer who owns substantially all of the *stock* of a *personal service corporation* (§269A definition), directly and with members of his or her family (§267 definition). §263A(h)(3)(D)(ii). A personal service corporation can deduct *qualified creative expenses* which relate directly to the activities of a qualified employee-owner as if the expense were borne by the qualified employee-owner, in spite of the *uniform capitalization rules*. §263A(h)(c)(D)(i). See *qualified creative expense; related taxpayers, loss and deduction denial*.

qualified employee, section 403(b) annuities see *catch-up election, tax-deferred annuities for exempt and educational organization employees*.

qualified employer plan a *qualified plan* or *trust* for *employees* that satisfies the requirements of §401, a *governmental plan*, a *qualified annuity plan*, a *qualified bond purchase plan*, or a plan under which amounts are contributed by an *individual's employer* for a *section 403(b) annuity* contract. §219(e)(3) and (4). The term has the same meaning for purposes of §72(o) relating to distributions from *qualified plans* and *governmental plans*. §72(o)(5)(A).

qualified energy property, at-risk rules property that qualifies for the former *investment tax credit* (ITC), even though subject to extensive nonrecourse debt. The property consists of (1) *solar* or *wind energy property* (former §48(1)(2)(iii)); (2) *recycling equipment* (former §48(1)(2)(iv)); (3) *qualified hydroelectric generating property* (former §48(1)(2)(vii)); (4) *biomass property* (former §48(1)(5)); (5) equipment for converting an *alternate substance* into alcohol (former §48(1)(3)(A)(iii)); (6) *alternate energy property* (former §48(1)(2)(A)(i)), which is other property used to exploit *geothermal deposits* (former §48(1)(3)(A)(viii)) or *ocean thermal energy* (former §48(1)(3)(A) (ix)); and (7) property comprising a system to use the same energy sources for sequential generation of electrical or mechanical shaft power, or both, in combination with steam, heat, or other useful energy.

qualified enhanced oil recovery project   any project that uses one or more *tertiary recovery methods* in accordance with sound engineering principles, which is expected to result in more than an insignificant increase in the amount of crude oil that will ultimately be recovered, and which is located in the *United States* (including the seabed and subsoil of areas adjacent to such territorial waters over which the United States has exclusive rights under international law as to natural resources), and with respect to which the first injection of liquids, gases, or other matter begins after 1990, and with respect to which the operator provides the *IRS* with a petroleum engineer's certification that the project meets, and continues to meet, such requirements. §43(c)(2). See *tertiary recovery method, deduction of injectants.*

qualified enhanced recovery costs   *tangible property* which is an integral part of a *qualified enhanced oil recovery project* and is *depreciable* or *amortizable*; tertiary injectant costs *paid or incurred* in connection with a qualified EOR project, which costs are *deductible* as *qualified tertiary injectant expenses* (§193); currently deductible *intangible drilling and development costs* paid or incurred in connection with a qualified EOR project; and amounts a large refiner or retailer must *capitalize* under §291(b)(1). These costs can qualify for the 15 percent *enhanced oil recovery credit.*

qualified ethanol fuel production   ethanol which is produced by an eligible *small ethanol producer* and which is either (1) sold by the producer to another *person* for use by that other person in the production of a qualified mixture in that person's *trade or business* (except casual nonfarm production), or for use by the other person as a fuel in a trade or business, or for sale at retail to another person in which the ethanol is placed in the other person's fuel tank; or (2) used by the eligible small ethanol producer for any purpose in (1). §40(b)(4)(B). See *alcohol fuel credit.* If the fuel is not so used, the credit is *recaptured* by means of an *excise tax* imposed under §4081. §40(d)(3)(C).

qualified excess loss account   an *excess loss account* to the extent it is attributable to pre-1988 periods during which a *domestic corporation's* income was subject to a foreign income tax on a residence basis or without regard to its source. *TAMRA section 6126* allows dual-resident corporations with a qualified excess loss account to transfer their assets and liabilities to a *foreign corporation* in exchange for *stock* and then liquidate into the common parent, and it has the foreign corporation deemed a domestic corporation for *consolidated return* purposes, thereby minimizing the tax cost of the transaction. See *dual consolidated loss; dual resident.*

qualified expenditures   currently *deductible expenditures* for publishers *circulation expenditures, research and experimental expenditures, excess intangible drilling and development costs* and *mine development expenditures* and *exploration expenditures* for mines. §59(c)(2). *Taxpayers* can elect to write off these expenditures over longer periods (three years for the first and 10 years for all the others) for regular *income tax* purposes, thereby reducing their *alternative minimum taxable incomes.*

qualified export assets, DISC   *export property* within the meaning of §993(c)(1), basically: (1) *inventory* or rental property grown or produced here, other than by the *domestic international sales corporation* (DISC), (2) held primarily for sale, lease, or rental in the ordinary course of trade or business by or to a DISC, for direct use, consumption, or disposition outside the United States, and which has (3) not more than 50 percent of the fair market value of the property attributable to articles imported into the United States. The *domestic international sales corporation* (DISC) generally has been replaced by a system of foreign sales corporations (FSCs). See §§921–927 and *domestic international sales corporation.* See *affiliated group.*

qualified farm indebtedness   farm-related *debt* with respect to which the *taxpayer* can use the *exclusion* from *gross income* that arises when debt is discharged outside of bankruptcy or insolvency. §108(g). It means debt incurred directly in connection with the *trade or business* of farming (not specifically defined), but only as to farmers who got at least 50 percent of their annual gross receipts for the prior three years from farming. §108(g)(2). Only a *qualified person* as defined in §46(c)(8)(D)(iv) (including a *federal, state,* or local government agency or instrumentality thereof) can benefit. The exception from discharge of indebtedness income is limited to such a person's *adjusted tax attributes* and the *adjusted basis* of *qualified property.* See *qualified person, at-risk rules.*

qualified farming trade or business   the *trade or business* of farming: (1) sugar cane; (2) any plant with a preproductive period of two years or less, or (3) any other plant (other than any citrus or almond tree) if an election by the *corporation* is in effect, provided the plant has a preproductive period of more than two years. The *alternative depreciation system* must be used for all farm assets, and expense costs must be recaptured as *ordinary income* upon the *disposition* of the plants. §447(g)(4)(3)(i). The term is used in connection with the exemption of sugar cane farmers on the *accrual method* from the *uniform capitalization rules.*

qualified farm-related taxpayer a *farm-related tax-payer* who meets one of the following tests: (1) his or her aggregate prepaid farm supplies for the three preceding *taxable years* are less than half of his or her aggregate *deductible* farming *expenses* (other than prepaid supplies) for the same period; or (2) he or she has excess prepaid farm supplies for the taxable year by reason of a change in business operation directly attributable to extraordinary circumstances. §464(f)(3)(A). See *farming, farming syndicate.*

qualified financial institution a commercial *bank* (§581), *domestic building and loan association* (§591), insured credit union, or similar state or federally chartered institution. §165(1)(3). *Losses* on deposits usually create *short-term casualty losses. Qualified individuals* can elect to *deduct* up to $20,000 of *losses* that are not federally insured on deposits (including withdrawable accounts or shares) in such organizations as *personal casualty losses.* §165(1)(1). See *qualified individual, losses of insolvent financial institutions.*

qualified first-tier taxes *civil penalty* taxes for a violation of *private foundation* rules assessed in addition to the so-called *audit fee.* They include a 15 percent *excise tax* on *undistributed income* (§4942), taxes on *speculative investments* (§4944), taxes on *excess business holdings* (§4943), and taxes on *taxable expenditures* (e.g., lobbying, §4945). §4962(b). It does not include the initial tax on *self-dealing* (§4941(a)). All first-tier penalty taxes are, at the discretion of the *IRS,* subject to *abatement* if the IRS determines that the violation of foundation rules was (1) due to *reasonable cause* and not to willful neglect; and (2) corrected within the appropriate *correction period.* §4962(a).

qualified first-year wages see *targeted jobs credit.*

qualified foreign contract any contract issued on the life or health of a resident of a *foreign* country (not contiguous with the *United States*) by a foreign *branch* of a *domestic life insurance company* required by the foreign country to operate through a branch at the time it began its operations in that country. §807(e).

qualified foreign plan a *qualified deferred compensation plan* established by an *employer* for *nonresident aliens* who are *employees* and whose *compensation* is not subject to United States taxation. §404A. Employers may *deduct* contributions to such plans. §404A(a). Such plans can be either *qualified funded plans* or *qualified reserve funds.*

qualified foster care payments generally, amounts paid by a *state, political subdivision,* or *tax exempt* agency to the *taxpayer* for the costs of caring for a *qualified foster individual* at home, or a *difficulty of care payment.* §131(b)(1). Such amounts are *excludable* from *gross income.* §131(a).

qualified foster individual generally, an *individual* who lives in a foster home in which he or she was placed by a state, a *political subdivision,* or an exempt agency. §131(b)(2). See *qualified foster care payments.*

qualified fuel, biomass property, energy investment credit any synthetic solid fuel or alcohol for fuel purposes, if the primary source (more than 50 percent) of energy for the facility producing the alcohol is not oil or natural gas or a product of oil or natural gas. §48(1)(15)(C). Equipment that produces qualified fuel from an *alternate substance* (biomass) may qualify for the *energy investment credit.* §§48(1)(3) and (15)(B). See *biomass property, energy investment credit.*

qualified fuel, credit for producing fuels from non-conventional sources oil from shale or tar sands; liquid, gaseous, or solid synthetic fuel from coal or lignite (even as a feedstock); gas from geopressured brine, Devonian shale, coal seams, or a tight formation; *biomass; qualifying processed wood fuel*; and *agricultural by-product steam.* §29(c). *Taxpayers* are entitled to a credit of $3 times the barrel-of-oil equivalent of qualified fuels they produce and sell to unrelated persons. §29(a).

qualified fund a fund that takes money or property pursuant to a government order (federal, state, or local, and including a court order), which fund is independent of the transferor, but only if the transfer completely extinguishes the transferor's liability. There are further safeguards. The core idea is that under Prop. Reg. §1.461-6(c) a payment to a qualified fund constitutes *economic performance.* The provision is patterned along the lines of §468B. Other payment liabilities subject to this rule consist of those arising out of a workers' compensation act, breach of contract, or law violation.

qualified funded plan a *qualified foreign plan* other than a *qualified reserve fund.* §404A(f)(1). Such plans are subject to the usual *funding* requirements applicable to *qualified plans.*

qualified fund, foreign currency gain or loss a *partnership* with special characteristics that prevents it from being able to elect to benefit from an election to treat contracts not on the *mark-to-market system* as §988 transactions. *Taxpayers* can elect to treat such contracts as §988 transactions, except for partnerships that have elected *qualified fund* status. The term "qualified fund" means a partnership that (1) has at least 20 partners with none owning over 20 percent of its *capital interests* or *profits interests* at all times during the *taxable year* and each prior year to which an election applies (there is a look-through rule, and a 20 percent limit does not apply to a *general partner*); (2) has a regular principal activity of buying and selling *options,* futures, or forwards as to commodities; (3) has at least 90 percent of its *gross income* for the current and all prior years coming from *interest* and *dividends, gain* from the *sale* or *disposition* of *capital assets* held to produce interest or dividends, and income and gains from commodities, futures, forwards, and options as commodities; (4) derives not more than a *de minimis* amount of income for the current and all prior years from buying and selling commodities; and (5) has made a proper election. §988(c)(2)(E)(iii).

qualified funding asset   an *annuity* issued by a licensed *insurance company* or a United States government obligation bought within 60 days before or 60 days after a qualified assignee assumes an obligation to pay a defendant's periodic liabilities for damages for *personal injuries or sickness.* §130(d). The *Code* contains further modest limitations. The assignee who undertakes to pay the liability is not taxed except to the extent the annuity or United States obligation costs less than the claim. §130(a) and (b). The concept is designed to assure that tort victims who are paid off in periodic installments will not be taxed on such payments if a lump-sum payment would not have been taxable. See *qualified assignment.*

qualified general assistance program   a program certified by HUD and run by a state or its *political subdivision* that provides general assistance (or similar assistance) based on need. Such assistance consists of money, vouchers, or scrip. §51(d)(6)(B). The term is important in defining *general assistance recipients* for purposes of the *targeted jobs credit.* The targeted jobs credit expired on June 30, 1992.

qualified GIC   a group pension plan contract issued before 1984 that specified the renewal or maturity rate. Funds deposited by the contract holder plus interest at the guaranteed rate are paid as directed by the contract holder. §217(1)(3), Pub. L. No. 98-369 (July 18, 1984).

qualified grant   see *grant administrative expenses, private foundation.*

qualified group legal services organization   a nontaxable organization established to fund a *qualified group legal services plan.* These plans are subject to a sunset provision, but have proven durable. See §501(c)(20).

qualified group legal services plans   written, enforceable, permanent plans that provide prepaid legal services for the exclusive benefit of *self-employed persons, partners, employees,* and their *spouses* or *dependents* (modified definition), the benefits of which are adequately communicated. Such amounts are *excludable* from *gross income* by employees and are presumably *deductible* by business *employers.* §§89(k), 120, 162. The principal limit on such plans is that they may not discriminate in favor of *highly compensated employees,* and not more than 25 percent of the annual contributions may be for *shareholder*-owners with a 5

percent or more interest in *stock,* capital, or profits, and *spouses* and *dependents* of such persons. The funding may be through direct payments, insurance, a *qualified group legal services organization,* or a feeder organization. These plans are electively treated as *statutory employee benefit plans* and as such are subject to special *nondiscrimination* rules. They are subject to a sunset provision.

qualified group self-insurers' fund   any group of two or more *employers* that has been in existence for at least two years and who agree to pool their liabilities under a state's workers' compensation laws.

qualified hazardous waste facility   any facility for the disposal of nonradioactive hazardous waste by incineration or entombment, but only if (1) the facility is subject to final permit requirements under subtitle C of title II of the Solid Waste Disposal Act as in effect in October 22, 1986; and (2) the part of such facility which is to be provided by the issue does not exceed the portion of the facility which is to be used by persons other than the owner or operator of such facility, and any related person to such owner or operator, which requirement is satisfied if at least 95 percent of the net proceeds of the bond issue are to be used with respect to that portion of the facility used by persons other than the owner or operator or his relatives. §142(a)(10). *Private activity bonds* issued after August 15, 1986, that are part of an issue, 95 percent or more of whose net proceeds are to be used for such purposes, qualify as *exempt facility bonds, interest* on which is exempt from *federal income tax.*

qualified hedging transaction   a *qualifying debt instrument* in a *nonfunctional currency* plus a hedge that wipes out all foreign currency risk. These are combined and referred to as a *synthetic debt instrument.* Reg §1.988-5T(a)(9). The synthetic debt instrument is usually denominated in *taxpayer's functional currency.* Income and costs under the synthetic debt are treated as *interest income* and *expense.* Reg §1.988-5T(a)(1). *OID* principles may also apply. A debt instrument is a "qualified debt instrument" only if at least some of the payments are denominated in a nonfunctional currency and the instrument itself is not an *account receivable* or an *accounts payable* . Reg §1.988-5T(a)(3).

qualified higher education expenses   tuition and fees paid for the *taxpayer,* the taxpayer's *spouse,* or a *dependent* as to whom the taxpayer can claim a *dependency deduction,* to attend an eligible educational institution (basically a college, university, nursing school, or vocational school). §135(c)(2)(A) and (3). Tuition and fees must be reduced by nontaxable *scholarships* and *fellowships,* assistance provided by an *employer,* and other such amounts. If the payments are for sports, games, or hobbies, they do not count unless they lead to a degree. Taxpayers who redeem *qualified United States savings* *bonds* can do so tax-free if and to the extent the proceeds are used to pay qualified higher education expenses. §135(a). See *qualified United States savings bond.*

qualified home improvement loan   the financing, whether or not secured by a *mortgage,* of alterations, repairs, and improvements that substantially protect or improve the basic livability or energy efficiency of an existing residence. Such loans may not exceed $15,000 for any residence. §143(k)(4). Permissible items include renovation of plumbing or electrical systems, installation of improved heating or air conditioning systems, addition of living space, and kitchen renovation, but not recreational or entertainment facilities such as swimming pools, tennis courts, or saunas. Reg. §6a.103A-2(b)(9). Qualified home improvement loans were a permissible use of the proceeds of a *qualified mortgage issue* under former §103A, paying tax-exempt interest. Although §103A has been repealed, §§141–150 provide similar exempt bond issue rules.

qualified hospital bond   any bond issued as part of an issue, at least 95 percent of the *net proceeds* of which are to be used with respect to a hospital. §145(c). Hospitals include places for the mentally ill. Such bonds may be a type of *qualified 501(c)(3) bond* which enjoys more generous limits on the total volume of which can be issued on a *tax-exempt* basis.

qualified housing interest   *interest* that *individuals pay* or *accrue* during a *taxable year* which is *qualified housing interest* incurred in the acquisition, construction, or substantial improvement of any property that is either (1) the *principal residence,* as defined under §1034, of a *taxpayer* when such interest *accrues*; or (2) a *qualified dwelling* (house, apartment, condo, or mobile home not used on a transient basis, plus appurtenant structures and property) which is a *qualified residence.* §56(b)(1)(C)(i) and (e). It includes refinanced debt not greater than the original debt. §56(e)(1). It also includes pre–July 1, 1982 qualified residence interest on a principal residence or a qualified dwelling used by the taxpayer or his *family.* §56(e)(3). Such interest is added to other allowable *interest expense deductions* for the purposes of the *alternative minimum tax* on *items of tax preference.* §56(b)(1)(C). It is limited to debt equal to the lesser of the home's *fair market value* or purchase price plus improvements. See *family, losses and expenses.*

qualified housing project   a rental or cooperative housing project for lower-income families that has been constructed, reconstructed, or rehabilitated pursuant to a mortgage insured under §221(d)(3) or §236 (National Housing Act) provided that, with respect to the housing project disposed of and the replacement project, the owner of the project at the time of the *approved disposition* and before the close of the *reinvestment period* is limited as to rate of return on his or her investment in the project, and limited as to rentals or occupancy charges for units in the project, or is a nonprofit owner. Reg. §1.1039-1(c)(2). Generally, former §1039 allowed tax-free *rollovers* of the *net amount realized* from the sale of qualified housing projects.

qualified hydroelectric generating facility, industrial development bond   any *qualified hydroelectric generating property* that is owned, directly or through an agency or instrumentality, by a state or a *political subdivision* of a state. Former §103(b)(8)(A). Interest on *industrial development bonds* issued to provide qualified hydroelectric generating facilities is subject to the *installed capacity fraction* limitation, tax-exempt. Former §103(b)(4)(H). This exemption disappeared in 1986, subject to some territorial relief.

qualified hydroelectric generating property, energy investment credit   property installed at a *qualified hydroelectric site* that is (1) equipment for increasing capacity to generate electricity by water up to but not including the electrical transmission stage; and (2) structures for housing generating equipment, fish passageways, and *dam rehabilitation property,* required by reason of the installation of generating equipment. Former §48(1)(13)(A). The *energy investment credit* is allowed in full for a qualified hydroelectric site with less than 25 megawatts of *installed capacity.* Qualified hydroelectric generating property may qualify as energy property for purposes of the *energy investment credit.* Former §48(l)(2).

qualified hydroelectric generating property, industrial development bond   same as *qualified hydroelectric generating property, energy investment credit,* but excluding any property installed at the site of any dam described in former §48(1)(13)(B)(i)(I)) unless the dam was owned by one or more states, *political subdivisions* of states, or agencies or instrumentalities thereof, on October 18, 1979, and at all times thereafter until the obligations are no longer outstanding. Former §103(b)(8)(B). See also *qualified hydroelectric generating facility, industrial development bond.*

qualified hydroelectric site, energy investment credit   a site where there is a dam that was completed before October 18, 1979, and that has not been significantly enlarged since then, or where electricity is to be generated without any dam or other impoundment of water. The *installed capacity* at the site must be less than 125 megawatts. Former §48(l)(13)(B). To qualify as *energy property* under former §48(l)(2), *hydroelectric generating facilities* must be installed at a qualified hydroelectric site. Former §48(1)(13).

qualified income offset   a provision called for under *regulations* pursuant to §704(b)(2) relating to the validity of *partnership allocations.* The concept calls for having the *partnership agreement* provide that any and all future income will be allocated to *partners* with unexpected negative *capital accounts* as fast as possible. It applies in cases where a partner does not have an absolute duty to restore such deficits on *liquidation* of the partnership. If this alternative requirement is met, it helps show *economic effect*. It is only useful with respect to deficits in excess of make-up obligations to the extent the excess is caused by certain specified, unexpected events (namely, oil and gas *depletion* allowances, adjustments relating to donated interests in *family partnerships* under §704(e)(2) and changes in partnership interests under §706(d), taxable net distributions of *unrealized receivables* and *substantially appreciated inventory items* and other unanticipated net distributions). Regs. §1.704-1(b)(2)(ii)(d)(1)-(3). See *substantial economic effect test*.

qualified individual, child and dependent care credit a child under age 15 whom the *taxpayer* can claim as a *dependent* under §151(e), or a *spouse* or *dependent* who is physically or mentally incapable of caring for him- or herself. §21(c)(1). If the taxpayer maintains a household for such a person or persons, the taxpayer is entitled to a limited credit for *employment related expenses*. The credit is $720 for one spouse or dependent and $1,440 (maximum) for two or more spouses or dependents.

qualified individual, foreign earned income a *citizen of the United States* living overseas who is a *bona fide resident,* or a United States citizen or *resident alien* who meets the *physical presence test* of §911. Such a person may elect to exclude up to $70,000 of foreign earned income attributable to the period of his or her residing in a foreign country. §911(a)(1) and (b)(2). A taxpayer may also elect to exclude excess foreign housing costs. See *foreign earned income exclusion; foreign housing cost exclusion.*

qualified individual, losses of insolvent financial institutions any *individual* who is neither a one-percent (or more) owner, officer, nor party related to such a person, of an insolvent *qualified financial institution.* §165(1)(2). Such an individual can choose to treat a *loss* on a deposit for a nonbusiness account in an insolvent or bankrupt financial institution as a *personal casualty loss* in the year in which the loss can be reasonably estimated, in lieu of treating the loss under the existing *bad debt* provisions which consider such loss as a *short-term capital loss* that is *deductible* only in the year in which there is no prospect of recovery. §165 (1)(1).

qualified intercity bus, energy investment credit an automobile bus that is used predominantly on a full-time basis in the *trade or business* of furnishing intercity passenger transportation or intercity charter service by a common carrier regulated by the Interstate Commerce Commission or an appropriate state agency, as determined by the *IRS*. Qualified intercity buses may qualify as *energy property* for purposes of the *energy investment credit*. Former §48(l)(2).

qualified interest, passive loss rules see *pre-enactment interest.*

qualified intermediary a *person* who is not the *taxpayer* or a related party and who acts to facilitate a *deferred like-kind exchange* by entering into an agreement with the taxpayer for the exchange of properties (the *exchange agreement*), acquires the relinquished property from the taxpayer, transfers it, and acquires the replacement property and transfers it to the taxpayer. The transfer need only be of legal title. There are further minor details. Reg. §1.1031-2(g)(4)(iii). The term is used in connection with a *safe harbor rule* for financial go-betweens in deferred like-kind exchanges. See T.D. 8345, 1991-21 I.R.B. 5.

qualified inventory interruption generally, a regulation or request from the Department of Energy or an interruption resulting from any embargo, international boycott, or other foreign trade interruption that the *Secretary* determines has made the replacement of goods during the *liquidation year* difficult or impossible. §473(c)(2). It is the *taxpayer's* burden to establish that a *qualified liquidation* has resulted directly and primarily from a qualified inventory interruption in order to elect to have *gross income* adjusted pursuant to §473(b) and (c).

qualified investment entity see *determination, deficiency dividend by regulated investment companies and REITs.*

qualified investment, investment tax credit the aggregate of the *applicable percentage* of the *basis* of each new item of *property placed in service* by the *taxpayer* during the *taxable year*. §46(c). The applicable percentage, which is applied to the *basis* or cost of property, is determined by either the *useful life* or *recovery period* of the property, as the case may be. The applicable percentage depends on the estimated useful life of the property or recovery period.

qualified investments in foreign base company shipping operations certain overseas shipping and aircraft investments that could formerly protect a *controlled foreign corporation's* earnings in the form of *foreign base company shipping income* from being currently taxed to its *United States shareholders*. Former §954(g).

qualified joint and survivor annuity generally, a retirement *annuity* for the life of the *participant,* with an annuity to the *surviving spouse* which is at least half of the initial annuity, and which is the actuarial equivalent of a single annuity for the life of the participant. §417(b). In order to have a *qualified deferred compensation plan,* the spouse of the participant must either get a *qualified preretirement survivor annuity* or a qualified joint and survivor annuity, unless he or she waives the payout option during the *applicable election period.* §401(a)(11) and 417.

qualified low-income building, low-income housing credit   any building that is part of a *qualified low-income housing project* throughout the 15-year *compliance period* and to which §201 of the *Tax Reform Act of 1986* applies, beginning when the building is part of the project. §42(c)(2). Such buildings can qualify for the *low-income housing credit,* provided it does not get §8(e)(2) Housing Act of 1937 assistance. See *qualified basis, low-income housing credit.*

qualified low-income housing project, low-income housing credit   a residential rental project as to which (1) 20 percent or more of the residential units are rent-restricted units used by occupants whose incomes are 50 percent or less of *area median gross income*; or (2) 40 percent or more of the residential units are *rent-restricted units* used by occupants whose incomes are 60 percent or less of area median gross income. Such units must be suitable for occupancy, used on a nontransient basis (subject to certain exceptions for homeless people), and subject to a limit on *gross rent.* The restriction renders them *rent-restricted units.* §42(g)(1). This is known as the *minimum set-aside requirement,* one of the critical requirements for generating a *low-income housing credit.* To prevent recapture of the credit, the building must be part of such project from the first day of the *compliance period* and ending on the last of its compliance period. See *gross rent, low-income housing credit.*

qualified mass commuting vehicle   any bus, subway car, railcar ferry, or the like that is *recovery property* and is leased to a mass transit system wholly owned by one or more governmental bodies, and used by them in providing mass commuting service (or mass transportation service, if the vehicle is a ferry). Former §103(b)(9)(A). A variant of the term now appears in §142(a)(3) as a kind of *exempt facility bond.*

qualified matching contributions   *matching contributions* by an *employer* that satisfy certain additional requirements as though such contributions were elective contributions of the *employee,* without regard to whether such contributions are actually taken into account as elective contributions. Reg. §1.401(k)-1(g)(7)(i) and (iii). Except in limited cases, all or part of the *qualified nonelective contributions* and qualified matching contributions made with respect to *eligible employees* under a *cash or deferred arrangement* being tested for nondiscrimination can be treated as elective contributions under the arrangement, provided various tests are met. Reg. §1.401(k)-1(b)(3).

qualified medical expenses   see *qualified residence interest.*

qualified meeting   any convention, seminar, annual meeting, or similar *business* program with respect to which an expense for food or beverages is not separately stated, over half the participants are *away from home,* there is at least 40 percent attendance, and the food and beverages are part of a program that includes a speaker. §274(n)(3). The 80 percent cap on meal and entertainment expenses of §274(n) does not apply when such expenses are integral to qualified meetings. §274(n)(2)(D).

qualified military benefit   an allowance of in-kind benefits received by current or former members of the *uniformed services* (or their *dependents*) by reasons of military status or service and legally or administratively authorized and excludable on September 9, 1986. The use of vehicles is not a qualified military benefit. §134(b)(2). Such amounts are generally *excluded* from *gross income.*

qualified mineral interest   certain subsurface oil, gas, or other minerals and the right to access to such minerals. §170(h)(6). Section 170(h)(5) provides that where such an interest is the subject of a *charitable contribution,* the general requirement that a *qualified conservation contribution* be exclusively for *conservation purposes* will not be met if there may be extraction or removal of minerals by any surface mining method. Section 170(h)(5)(B)(ii) provides an exception for interests in mineral and surface rights that were severed before June 13, 1976, where mining is only a negligible possibility (i.e., qualified mineral interest).

qualified minority shareholder   a shareholder who owns less than 10 percent by value of a *bank holding company's* (BHC's) stock. §304(b)(3)(D)(i). Such persons may *exchange stock* for BHC securities (bonds, debentures, etc.) without risk of having the exchange run the gauntlet of §304(b)(3) *(redemptions by affiliated corporations).* The mechanism is to treat the securities as not *property* (taxable consideration) for purposes of §304, but only if various conditions are met. For example, assume Mrs. M owns 15 percent of Regional Bank, Inc., all of the stock of which is transferred to a BHC. The BHC issues her 11 percent of its stock and $1,000 worth of its securities. Because she owns more than 10 percent of the BHC, the $1,000 worth of securities may be taxable as property received in the redemption of the stock of an affiliated corporation. Had she received 9 percent of the stock of the BHC, she would have been a qualified minority shareholder and §304 could not apply, if the other conditions of §304(b)(3)(C) were met. See *redemption by affiliated corporations.*

qualified mixture   a mixture of alcohol and gasoline or alcohol and a special fuel that (1) is sold by the *taxpayer* producing such mixture to anyone for use as a fuel; or (2) is used as a fuel by the producer. §40(b)(1)(B). Such mixtures can qualify for a *credit* for production of alcohol fuels. For clarification as to who is the producer of such fuels, see Rev. Rul. 88-64, 1988-32 I.R.B. 5. See *alcohol fuel credit.*

qualified money purchase pension plan   a *money purchase pension plan* that is a *qualified plan.*

qualified mortgage bond   a bond issued as part of a *qualified mortgage issue* marketed before October 1, 1990.

qualified mortgage issue   an issue consisting of one or more bonds a *state or local bond* issued before October 1, 1990, by a state or *political subdivision,* all the proceeds of which are used to finance single-family owner-occupied residences to be occupied by families with relatively modest incomes. §143. Ninety-five percent of the *net proceeds* must be used to finance residence of first-time homebuyers with exceptions for homes in low-income areas and proceeds used for *qualified home improvement loans* and *qualified rehabilitation loans.* §143(d). Any bond issue meeting the *private business use test* or *private security or payment test* cannot be a qualified mortgage issue. §143(a)(2)(A)(iii). However, a *private activity bond* satisfying the *private loan financing test* may be a qualified mortgage bond. As such, the issue will be a *qualified bond* and the *interest* therefrom will be *tax-exempt.* See *applicable median family income; private activity bond; tax-exempt bond.*

qualified mortgage, REMIC   any obligation, including any participation or *certificate of beneficial interest* therein, that is principally secured directly or indirectly by an interest in *real property,* and that either (1) is transferred to the REMIC on or before the *start-up day;* or (2) is bought by the REMIC within the three-month period beginning on the start-up day. It can include a bond which has been stripped of its coupons. A *regular interest* in a REMIC that was transferred to the REMIC before the start-up day also qualifies. §860G(a)(3). They include *qualified replacement mortgages.* Substantially all of the REMIC's assets must consist of qualified mortgages and *permitted investments,* if it is to retain its special status.

qualified nonelective contribution   any contribution by an *employer,* except a *matching contribution,* as to which the *employee* cannot take cash in lieu of the contribution, provided the contribution is nonforfeitable when made, ineligible for withdrawal before age $59\frac{1}{2}$ death, *disability,* separation from service, sale of a subsidiary, or termination of the plan. §401(m)(4)(C). The employer can count such contributions in determining the *contribution percentage* for *matching contributions.* See *contribution percentage, matching contributions.*

qualified non-personal use vehicle   generally, any vehicle that is not subject to the *listed property rules* because of its nature. Example include marked police cars and fire vehicles, forklilfts, various farm and con-

struction equipment, ambulances, dump trucks, and garbage trucks. Reg §1.280F-6T(b)(2).

qualified nonprofit organization   a kind of organization that can lend money under special relaxations for low-income housing projects for purposes of the *low-income housing credit.* §42(h)(5). Technically, such an organization is exempt from *federal income taxes* under §501(a), which has as one of its *exempt purposes* the fostering of low-income housing and which is either a *civic league* or a *§501(c)(3) organization,* including a *corporation* whose *stock* is held by such organizations. The participation of such an organization can produce a *qualified low-income housing project.* §42(h)(5). Loans from such organizations enjoy relaxation of the special *at-risk rules* for low-income housing projects. §42(k)(2). See also §42(k)(3) for impact of low-interest rate.

qualified nonrecourse financing   generally, *nonrecourse* financing that is secured by the *real property* used in the activity of holding nonmineral *real estate,* including amounts loaned or guaranteed by *federal, state,* or local government or borrowed by the *taxpayer* from a *qualified person* and not convertible into an equity interest in the property. §465(b)(6)(B). The *at-risk rules* limit the *losses deductible* by *individuals* and certain *corporations* with respect to *business* and income-producing activities, including real estate activities, to the *taxpayer's* economic investment. However, in the case of *holding real estate* there is an exception for qualified nonrecourse financing from so-called *qualified persons* (as defined in §46(c)(8)(D)(i)), but with an exception for certain commercially reasonable loans from related persons. §465(b)(6)(A). Qualified persons from whom a taxpayer may borrow such money include persons actively and regularly engaged in the *business* of lending money, e.g., a bank, but not (1) the seller of the property (or related party); (2) any person who receives a fee with respect to the taxpayer's investment in the property (or related party); or (3) any person related to the taxpayer, unless that person is dealt with on the same commercial terms as with unrelated persons. §465(b)(6)(D). See *at-risk rules, generally; nonrecourse liabilities; qualified person, at-risk rules for investment tax credit.*

qualified oil corporation   an *S corporation* whose average daily production of *domestic crude oil* or natural gas in combination with any 40 percent *shareholder's* production exceeds 1,000 barrels. Such a corporation can elect to have the law that was in force prior to the *Subchapter S Revision Act of 1982* apply to it. See Pub. L. No. 97-354, §6(c)(3), 96 Stat. 1669, 1698. For a closer definition of the 40 percent shareholder, see *substantial shareholder.*

qualified organization   a *qualified pension fund,* an *educational organization described in section 170(b)(1)(A)(ii)* (see also §509(a)(3)), or a *title holding* *company* per §501(c)(25). Section 514(c)(9) provides that acquisition indebtedness does not include debt incurred to finance a real estate investment by any *qualified organization*, provided the investment satisfies certain requirements.

qualified organization base period amount an amount equal to the sum of the *minimum basic research amount* plus the *maintenance-of-effort amount*. §41(e)(3).

qualified organization, catch-up election any *educational organization, hospital, home health service organization*, health and welfare service agency, *church, convention or association of churches*, or §414(e)(3)(B)(ii) organization. §408(g)(8)(B). See *catch-up election, tax-deferred annuities for exempt and educational organization employees; educational organization, catch-up election.*

qualified organization, contributions of works of art a *charitable organization*, other than a *private foundation*, described in §501(c)(3). §2055(e)(4)(D). Such organizations can receive partial interests in *works of art*, with a resulting *charitable contribution deduction* for the donor.

qualified organization, credit for increasing research activities (1) an *educational organization described in section 170(b)(1)(A)(ii)* (i.e., one which normally maintains a regular faculty and curriculum and has regularly enrolled students), which is an *institution of higher education* defined in §3304(f), such as a college or university; (2) a tax-exempt *scientific research organization* qualified under §501(c)(3), other than a *private foundation*; (3) an *exempt organization* (other than a *private foundation*) that is primarily operated to promote scientific research by "educational institutions" under written agreements and that expends substantially all funds or basic research payments to accomplish that end (§41(e)(6)(C)); and (4) a certain grant organization which operates the same as under (2) or (3) above, and is exempt from tax (other than private foundations), organized and operated exclusively for the purposes of making grants to "educational institutions" under written research agreements for basic research, and which elects to be treated as a private foundation. §41(e)(6). Payments to qualified organizations can qualify for the 20 percent *university basic research credit*, which forms part of the *credit for increasing research activities*. The basic research credit expired on June 30, 1992. See *basic research; credit for increasing research activities.*

qualified organization, qualified conservation contribution a governmental unit, a *publicly supported organization*, or an *entity* controlled by one of the foregoing. §170(h)(3). *Taxpayers* can deduct *charitable contributions* of partial interests in property for *conser-*

vation purposes if they are made to one or more of the entities on this short list. See *qualified conservation contribution.*

qualified ownership interest an undivided interest for more than 50 years in the entire dwelling and any *appurtenant* land to which the *shared equity financing agreement* relates. §280A(d)(3)(D). The presence of such an interest may allow rentals of property to co-owners as *principal residences* to be freed of the *vacation home rules*, if rented at a fair rental price, since in such cases there is by fiat no *personal use* by the *lessor*. §280A(d)(3).

qualified participant, ESOP a *participant* in an *ESOP* who is at least 55 years old with at least 10 years of service. §401(a)(28)(B)(iii). Such a person can diversify his or her ESOP account. See *employee stock ownership plan; participant, qualified plans.*

qualified participant, qualified plans an *individual* who is a participant in a *defined benefit plan* of a *state* or *subdivision*, provided the period of service taken into account for determination of benefits under the plan has at least 15 years of service as a full-time fireman or policeman (male or female), or as a member of the *armed forces* of the *United States*. §415(b)(2)(H)(ii). For such a person, the reduction of benefits before age 62 does not reduce the annual benefit dollar limitation to under $50,000 at any age. See *annual benefit limitation, qualified plans.*

qualified partnership, farming trade or business (sugarcane) a *partnership*, consisting of *corporations* other than *personal holding companies* and *S corporations*, that is engaged in sugarcane growing. Such an entity may use the *accrual method* of accounting and currently can deduct *pre-productive period expenses*. §447(g).

qualified payment any *dividend* payable on a periodic basis under any cumulative *preferred stock* (or a comparable payment as to *partnership* interest) to the extent the dividend or comparable payment is determined at a fixed rate or is tied to a particular market interest rate. §2701(c)(3).

qualified payment, designated settlement fund any money or property which is transferred to any *designated settlement fund* other than amounts paid from the fund to the *taxpayer* (or any *related taxpayer* under §267(b)) or the transfer of the taxpayer's *stock* or liabilities to the fund. §468A(d)(1). See *designated settlement fund; related taxpayers, loss and deduction denial.*

qualified payment election an irrevocable election of *qualified payment* treatment or an election to waive qualified payment treatment. §2701(c)(3)(C)(iii). This is an aspect of the *estate freeze* provisions. See *qualified payment.*

qualified pension, profit-sharing, and stock bonus plan a *pension plan, profit-sharing plan,* and *stock bonus plan* that meets the requirements of §401(a). For the principal requirements of §401(a), see *qualified deferred compensation plan.*

qualified performing artist an *individual* who (1) performs services in the performing arts during the *taxable year* for at least two *employers*; (2) has total *trade or business deductions* attributable to the performance of such services that exceed 10 percent of the income received from such services; and (3) has an *adjusted gross income* of $16,000 (*single* or a *married person* filing a *joint return*) or less (determined prior to application of this provision). Employers from which an individual receives less than $200 for his services are not taken into account for purposes of meeting qualification (1). The *deductible business expenses* of a qualified performing artist are deductible against *gross income* to arrive at *adjusted gross income.* §62(b).

qualified periodic interest payment any one of a series of payments equal to the product of the outstanding principal balance of the *debt instrument* and a single fixed rate of interest, or a variable rate tied to a fixed index governed by Reg §1.1275-5 that is payable unconditionally (or will be constructively received under §451) at fixed periodic intervals of a year or less during the entire term of the *debt instrument,* including short periods. Interest payments that are not qualified periodic interest payments are included in the *stated redemption price at maturity.* See §1273(a)(2) and Prop. Reg §1.1273-1(b).

qualified person, at-risk rules Same as *qualified person, at-risk rules for investment tax credit* §465(b)(6)(D)(i). *Nonrecourse debt* on real estate held by the *taxpayer* which is borrowed from qualified persons is treated as an *amount at risk.* Certain commercially reasonable financing from related persons also counts. §465(b)(6)(d)(ii). See *qualified nonrecourse financing.*

qualified person, at-risk rules for investment tax credit any *person* actively and regularly engaged in the *business* of lending money, provided the person is not (1) related to the *taxpayer* (per §267(b)); (2) the person (or related to the person) from whom the taxpayer acquired the property; or (3) the person (or related person) who receives a fee with respect to the taxpayer's investment in the property. §49(a)(1). A qualified person can or could provide *nonrecourse financing* that would not jeopardize the *investment credit.* See *at-risk rules, investment tax credit; nonqualified nonrecourse financing, at-risk rules for investment tax credit; related taxpayers, loss and deduction denial.*

qualified person, liquidations see *qualified corporation, liquidations.*

qualified per-unit retain certificate any *per-unit retain certificate* that the distributee of a *cooperative* has agreed to report, at the certificate's stated dollar amount, as *gross income.* §1388(b). Such amounts can qualify as *patronage dividends* under §1382(b), are *deductible* by the cooperative when distributed, and are taxable to the *patron.* See *nonqualified per-unit retain certificate; patronage dividend.*

qualified plan generally, a term used instead of the more cumbersome term *qualified deferred compensation plan.*

qualified plan award an item of *tangible personal property* awarded to an *employee* as part of a permanent, written, nondiscriminatory plan for length of service, or safety achievement, accompanied by a meaningful presentation, which is unlikely to be disguised compensation. Such awards are classed as *employee achievement awards* and are *deductible* up to $1,600, provided the average annual award does not cost over $400 (awards of nominal value are ignored). §§74(c) and 274(j). See *length-of-service award; safety acheivement award.*

qualified plan loan a nontechnical term for any loan to a *participant* in a *qualified plan.* Such a loan may or may not be taxable as a *distribution,* depending on the circumstances. §72(p). In addition, the *Tax Reform Act of 1986* made *interest* payments under such a loan *nondeductible* to the borrower/*key employee* if the loan is secured by *elective deferrals* in a *CODA* or in a plan of *tax-deferred annuities for exempt and educational organization employees.*

qualified pole rental payments received by a *mutual cooperative telephone company* from rental of a pole used by the telephone or electric company to provide services to its members and to transmit other communications. These payments are disregarded when one determines whether the payee will be exempt from taxation. §501(b)(12)(A), (B), and (D). See *benevolent life insurance associations.*

qualified possession source investment income income from sources within a United States *possession* in which the *possessions corporation* actively conducts a *trade or business,* whether or not profitably, and *interest* paid by one possessions corporation to a second unrelated possessions corporation operating in the same possession, provided the funds invested were derived from the active conduct of a *trade or business* within that same possession and were actually invested in assets in that possession. The term also includes income from sources within the possession attributable to reinvestments of qualified possessions source investment income. Funds placed with an intermediary (such as a bank located in the possession) are treated as invested in that possession only if it can be shown that the intermediary did not reinvest the funds outside the possession. All such income is determined net of appropriate *deductions*. Certain net income from Puerto Rico is also included if it is exempt from Puerto Rican tax, is from Puerto Rican sources, and is received by possession corporations doing business in Puerto Rico. Temp. Reg. §7.936-1.

qualified preferred dividends   certain *dividends* that are generally deemed not *extraordinary dividends* for purposes of the *dividends-received deduction*. They are fixed dividends payable on any share of *stock* that provides for fixed preferred dividends payable at least annually and acquired without dividends in arrears. §1059(e)(3)(C)(i). Such dividends are deemed not extraordinary if the dividends received by the corporate *shareholder* during the period it held the stock do not exceed an annualized rate of 15 percent of the lesser of (1) the holder's *adjusted basis* in the stock; or (2) the liquidation preference of the stock where the *taxpayer* held the stock for over five years. §1059(e)(3)(A). (Shorter than five-year holding periods qualify for limited relief.) The reason for provision is that *dividend stripping* is not easily performed with preferred stock that was not bought with dividends in arrears. See *extraordinary dividend, basis reduction.*

qualified pre-1985 instrument   a decree of divorce, or separate maintenance, or written agreement executed before 1985, granting the *noncustodial parent* the *dependency exemption* for a *child,* which instrument is not modified to reverse the grant. §152(e)(3)(B). Such an instrument can form the basis for a continuing claim to the *dependency exemption* if the *noncustodial parent* provides at least $600 of *support* for the child. See *child, dependency exemptions; support, dependency exemptions.*

qualified preretirement survivor annuity   generally, a retirement *annuity* for the life of the *surviving spouse.* §417(c). In order to have a *qualified deferred compensation plan,* the spouse of the *participant* must either get a qualified preretirement survivor annuity or a *qualified joint and survivor annuity,* unless he or she waives the payout option during the *applicable election period.* The plan must provide an explanation of the annuity during the *applicable period.* §§401(a)(11) and 417; ERISA §205(c)(3)(B).

qualified property, corporate divisions   any *stock* or *securities* in the controlled corporation received in a *corporate division.* §§355(c)(2) and 361(c)(2)(B). Such stock or securities can be distributed free of *gain* to the distributing corporation in a §355 *corporate division.* By contrast, *distributions* of other appreciated property are taxable to the distributing corporation. See *corporate division.*

qualified property, corporate reorganizations   *stock, rights* or obligations of a distributing *corpora-*

tion, or of another corporation which is a *party to a reorganization* if received by the distributing corporation in the *exchange.* §361(c)(2)(B). *Gain* (but not *loss*) on *distributions* of appreciated property, other than qualified property, to its own *shareholders* are generally *recognized* by the distributing corporation even though distributions made in its capacity as a party to a reorganization. §361(c)(2). Transfers of qualified property to creditors to satisfy a *debt* are treated as *distributions* pursuant to a *plan of reorganization* and are nontaxable to the corporation. This helpful rule makes it possible for the target company to pay its debts on a tax-free basis with a limited class of consideration furnished by the acquiror. However, distributions of appreciated retained assets (i.e., assets not acquired in the reorganization) or *boot* (other than notes of the acquiror) that appreciated between the time of receipt and the date of distribution to shareholders result in taxation of gains. This will arise primarily in *type C reorganizations* to assure that the target company will go largely untaxed on its distributions to its shareholders as it disappears.

qualified property, discharge of farm debt   a farmer's property used or held for use in a *trade or business* or *held for the production* of income. §108(g)(3)(c). The aggregate *adjusted basis* of such property or of the beginning of the *taxable year* following the discharge of *qualified farm indebtedness* plus the farmer's *adjusted tax attributes* as of that date limit the amount of such *cancellation of indebtedness income* the farmer (*qualified person*) can *exclude* from *gross income* with respect to *qualified farm indebtedness.* §108(g)(3). See *qualified farm indebtedness; qualified person, at-risk rules for investment tax credit.*

qualified property or services   see *qualified employee discounts.*

qualified public entertainment activities   entertainment or recreational activities of a kind traditionally conducted at fairs or expositions for agricultural and educational purposes. They include, but are not limited to, any activities of which one of the purposes is to attract the public to fairs or expositions or to promote the breeding of animals or the development of products or equipment, and they are *qualified* in the sense that they are carried on by so-called qualified organizations (i.e., a *labor, agricultural,* or *horticultural organization,* or a *business league,* etc., described in §501(c)(5) or (6)). Such activities are not treated as taxable *unrelated trade or business* activities. §513(d)(1).

qualified public utility   a *domestic corporation* that, during the 10-year period ending the day before the beginning of the *tax year, placed in service qualified long-life public utility property* which in the aggregate cost at least 60 percent of all the *section 1245 property* acquired during that decade. §305(e)(3)(A). Such a utility can set up plans under which limited amounts of distributions of *qualified common stock* can be issued tax-free in lieu of cash or other property. See *public utility dividend reinvestment plans.*

qualified real estate agent a licensed real estate agent whose remuneration is substantially all directly related to sales or other output rather than to hours worked, and whose services are performed pursuant to a written contract between the agent and the person for whom the services are performed. The contract must provide that the agent will not be treated as an *employee* for *federal* tax purposes. §3508(b)(1). Such a person is treated as an *independent contractor* for *federal income* and *employment tax* purposes.

qualified real property interest the entire interest of the *donor* (other than a *qualified mineral interest,* which can be fragmented), a *remainder interest,* or a perpetual restriction on the property's use. §170(h)(2). It is an element of the term of art "*qualified conservation contribution.*"

qualified reclamation or closing costs two classes of mine reclamation and closing costs as well as solid waste disposal and closing costs which can be deducted under a uniform method before they actually occur, thereby creating an exception to the general rule that accrual method taxpayers can deduct expenses for a future year's activities only when economic performance (reclamation and closing) occurs. §468(d)(2)(A). The term also includes expenses incurred for land reclamation or closing activities in connection with a solid waste disposal site which is conducted in accordance with any permit issued pursuant to any provision of the Solid Waste Disposal Act (or in effect on January 1, 1984) which requires such activity, or any other federal, state, or local law imposing requirements substantially similar to that Act. §468(d)(2)(B). "Superfund" sites do not qualify. Acrual method taxpayers electing to deduct such future expenses can establish reserves for them on a sinking fund method, increasing the fund for current reclamation or closing costs (those which would be incurred if the reclamation or closing occurred currently), crediting it with interest, and reducing it by amounts actually paid for reclamation or closing. Excess amounts (deductions or reserves) returned to the taxpayer are taxable. §468(a)-(d).

qualified redevelopment bond a bond issued under state law authorizing their issuance for *designated blighted areas,* at least 95 percent of the *net proceeds* of which are used for *redevelopment purposes.* §144(c)(1) and (2)(A). Principal and *interest* on such *debt* have to be secured by general tax revenues or by a pledge of property tax increases reserved to pay debt service. §144(c)(2)(B). Even though such a bond may otherwise be a *private activity bond* (such that *interest* thereon would be taxable), it may be a *qualified bond* (whose interest is nontaxable) if it satisfies the requirements

imposed on qualified redevelopment bonds. See *tax-exempt bond.*

qualified rehabilitated building for purposes of the *rehabilitation credit,* the term refers to a building first *placed in service* before 1936 (unless a *certified historic structure*) and *placed in service* prior to the beginning of the rehabilitation or reconstruction, 50 percent or more of the existing external walls of which retained and at least 75 percent of the external walls and internal structural framework of which are retained, and that has been substantially rehabilitated, meaning that an amount in excess of the greater of the *adjusted basis* of the building or $5,000 was spent for *qualified rehabilitation expenditures* on the property within a 24-month period (in certain cases, 60 months, pursuant to a well-drawn plan). §47(c)(1). The walls and structural framework tests do not apply to a *certified historic structure.*

qualified rehabilitation expenditures depreciable *capital expenditures* made for *real property* (with a *class life* of at least 12.5 years) in connection with a (residential rental or nonresidential real estate or real estate with a *class life* of at least 12.5 years) *qualified rehabilitated building.* §47(c)(2). Both interior and exterior renovations can qualify. Expenditures for new plumbing, wiring, flooring, roofing, and heating and air conditioning systems should qualify for the credit, as should demolition costs incurred as a part of a qualified rehabilitation. It is unclear whether costs such as architectural and engineering fees, real estate commissions, developer's fees, and legal fees qualify for the investment credit. Costs incurred for reconstruction and increased floor space as a part of interior remodeling should qualify for the credit, provided the building's volume or overall size is not increased. See generally Reg. §§1.48-11(b)(4)(ii), 1.191-2(e) (under former §191). There are further limits. *Straight-line cost recovery* must be used; acquisition or enlargement expenditures do not qualify; it must not be *tax-exempt use property.* See *rehabilitation credit.*

qualified rehabilitation loan any owner financing from the proceeds of a *qualified mortgage issue* provided in connection with a *qualified rehabilitation,* or the acquisition of a residence with respect to which there has been a qualified rehabilitation, but only if the mortgagor to whom the financing is provided is the first resident of the dwelling after the completion of the rehabilitation. §143(k)(5)(A). See *qualified mortgage issue; qualified rehabilitation, qualified mortgage issue.*

qualified rehabilitation, qualified mortgage issue any rehabilitation of a building if (1) physical rehabilitation is begun at least 20 years after the building was first used; (2) at least 75 percent of the existing external walls are retained and at least 75 percent of the external walls and internal structural framework of the building are retained as such; and (3) the expenditures for the rehabilitation are at least 25 percent of the mortgagor's *adjusted basis* in the residence, determined as of the later of the acquisition of the residence, or the completion of the rehabilitation. §143(k)(5)(B). *Qualified rehabilitation loans* may be made with the proceeds of a *qualified mortgage issue*, which produces *tax-exempt interest* to the holder of the bond.

qualified reinvested dividends   see *qualified common stock, public utility stock dividends.*

qualified rental period   a consecutive period of 12 months or more, beginning or ending during the *taxable year*, during which a *taxpayer's principal residence* (as defined in §1034) is rented (other than to a brother, sister, *spouse*, ancestor, or *lineal descendant* of the taxpayer) or held for rental at its *fair market*, or a period of less than 12 months if the residence is *sold* or *exchanged* before it has been rented or held for rental for the full 12 months. If there is a qualified rental period, then, for purposes of the *loss* limitations of the *vacation home rules*, the taxpayer is not considered to have made *personal use* of the residence for any day in the taxable year before or after the 12-month consecutive period or before the shorter period preceding disposition. §280A(d)(3). The provision was added to prevent the disallowance of *deductions* based on previous use as a principal residence for the period after a residence was converted to rental property.

qualified rents   amounts that would be treated as rents from *real property* if they were received by a *real estate investment company*. §856(d)(6)(B). If a tenant gets most of its rents from subleasing most of the property, and if the tenant's rents are qualified rents, the payments to the REIT-landlord are also rents from real property for purposes of qualifying as a REIT even though the rents are tied to the profitability of the property. There is a similar rule for *interest* income. §856(f). See *real estate investment trust.*

qualified replacement mortgage, REMIC   a *qualified mortgage* which is transferred or purchased by the *REMIC* which is received for another obligation or for a defective obligation. §860G(a)(4). These acquisitions and dispositions are subject to strict time limitations. A REMIC's asset base must consist primarily of qualified mortgages and *permitted investments*. 860D(a)(4). A qualified replacement mortgage is a type of qualified mortgage. §860G (a)(3)(B).

qualified replacement property   securities issued by a *domestic corporation* that does not, for the *taxable year* prior to the year such stock is issued, have passive investment income—*royalties, rents, dividends, interest, capital gains*—that exceeds 25 percent of gross receipts for that year. §1042(c)(4). Banks and thrifts are exempt. Gains on certain *stock sales* to *ESOPs* and *EWOCs* can be rolled over into qualified replacement

property free of current taxes. See *eligible worker-owned cooperative; qualified securities; employee stock ownership plan.*

qualified research   a *research and experiment activity*, as defined in §174, that is conducted within the *United States*, fundamentally of a technological nature and intended to be useful in the development of a new or improved *trade or business* already being carried on by the *taxpayer*. §41(d)(1). Only costs of research in the laboratory or for experimental purposes, whether carried on by the taxpayer or on behalf of the taxpayer by a third party, are deductible. Computer software developed primarily for internal use qualifies if it is used in qualified research undertaken by the taxpayer or in a production process. §41(d)(4)(E). *Regulations* may also require all software to be innovative, to involve significant economic risk, and not to be commercially available for use by the taxpayer. No credit is allowed to the taxpayer when research is funded by another *entity*, including the government. §41(d)(4)(H). See §41(a)(1)(A). The following are not qualified research: (1) research after commercial production; adaptation of existing business components; (2) duplication of an existing business component; (3) or surveys, etc. §41(d)(A)-(D). See *research and experimental expenditures; in-house research expenses; credit for increasing research activities.*

qualified research contributions   *contributions* of *property* of an *inventory* nature by a *corporation* (other than an *S corporation*, a *personal holding company*, or a *service organization* defined in §414(m)(3)) to an *institution of higher education* for that college or university to use for research purposes or to a *section 501(c)(3) organization* dedicated to scientific research which is not a *private foundation*. To qualify: (1) the property must have been constructed by the *taxpayer*; (2) the contribution must be made within two years of substantial completion of construction of the property; (3) the original use of the property must be by the *donee*; (4) substantially all the use of the property by the donee must be for *research or experimentation* within the meaning of §174, including research training purposes; (5) the property must not be transferred by the donee in exchange for money, other property, or services; and (6) the taxpayer must receive the donee's written statement representing that the use and disposition of the property contributed will be in accordance with the preceding two requirements. §170(e)(4)(B). If these conditions are satisfied, the donor's *charitable contribution deduction* is generally for the sum of the taxpayer's *basis* in the property plus half of the *unrealized appreciation*. However, in no event is a deduction allowed for an amount that exceeds twice the basis of the property. §170(e)(4)(A).

qualified reserve asset, REMIC   a *permitted investment* for a *real estate mortgage investment conduit*

(REMIC). It is any *intangible property* held for investment and as part of a *qualified reserve fund.* §860G(a)(7). It is a *permitted investment* of the REMIC.

qualified reserve fund, REMIC a fund from which the *expenses* of a *REMIC* may be paid or amounts due on *regular interests* in case of default. §860G(a)(7)(B). The fund is disqualified if 30 percent of the *gross income* from the assets of the fund is derived from the sale or disposition of *property* held less than three months. §860G(a)(7)(C). It is a type of *qualified reserve asset,* which in turn is a *permitted investment* of a REMIC.

qualified residence a residence that can support a *deduction* for *qualified residence interest paid or accrued.* It is either a *principal residence* (§1034) or a second *dwelling unit* that is either *used as a residence* during the *taxable year* within the meaning of the *vacation home rules,* or not at all. Qualification is tested as of the time the interest accrues. §163(h)(4). See *qualified residence interest.*

qualified residence interest *interest paid or accrued* on *debt* secured by a so-called *qualified residence* (a status determined when the interest *accrues*). A qualified residence is the *taxpayer's principal residence* plus one other property chosen by the taxpayer, either of which is *used as a residence* during the *taxable year* under the *vacation home rules* of §280A (i.e., is used for *personal use* the greater of 14 days or 10 percent of the days for which the property is rented at fair value); the "used as a residence" requirement is waived if the property was not rented during the year. §163(h)(3)-(4). Effective for post-1987 *taxable years,* post-October 13, 1987, debt is limited to debt incurred to acquire or substantially improve a principal or second residence (up to a total cost of $1 million) plus other debt (not over $100,000) secured by a principal or second residence. In *Code* parlance, only *acquisition indebtedness* with respect to a qualified residence (§163(h)(3)(A)-(B)) and $100,000 of *home equity indebtedness* (§163(h)(3)(C)) generates qualified residence interest on post–October 13, 1987, debt (even if refinanced up to the original amount of the debt). For interest on debt incurred on or before October 13, 1987, the amount of qualified residence interest is limited to the interest on debt secured by a qualified residence to the extent the debt does not exceed the lesser of the *fair market value* of the qualified residence or the sum of the taxpayer's *basis* in the qualified residence (including improvements, but not including any adjustments to basis for *gains* deferred on the *sale* of previous personal residences under §1034) and the amount of *qualified medical expenses* and *qualified educational expenses* incurred after August 16, 1986, and within a reasonable amount of time before or after the debt is incurred. *Qualified medical expenses* are amounts paid for *medical care* of the taxpayer, his or her *spouse,* or his or her *dependents* (other than medical insurance), which are *deductible* as *medical expenses* under §213. §163(h)(3)(B). *Qualified educational expenses* are *qualified tuition and related expenses* of the taxpayer, his or her spouse, or his or her dependents for attendance at an educational institution, including tuition and room and board for college or high school. §163(h)(3)(C). See *acquisition indebtedness, qualified residence interest; home equity indebtedness.*

qualified residence sale, purchase, or lease expenses reasonable *expenses* other than *rent* incident to (1) the *sale* or *exchange* of the *taxpayer's* former residence, excluding expenses for work performed on the residence in order to assist in its sale, which would otherwise be taken into account in the determination of the *amount realized* on the sale or exchange; (2) the purchase of a new residence in the general location of the new *principal place of business,* which would otherwise be taken into account in determination of (a) the *adjusted basis* of the new residence, or (b) the cost of a loan other than payments or prepayments of *interest*; (3) the settlement of an unexpired *lease* on property used by the taxpayer as his or her former residence; or (4) the acquisition of a lease on property used as the taxpayer's new residence in the general location of the new principal place of work. §217(b)(2). Such expenses are considered *moving expenses.* See *moving expense deduction.*

qualified resident, branch profits tax a classification which determines the residency of a *foreign corporation* for the purpose of applying the *branch profits tax.* A foreign corporation is a qualified resident of the treaty country if it is a resident of the treaty country (under its concepts of residence) and either (1) 50 percent or more (by value) of its *stock* is owned, directly or indirectly, by *individuals* resident in the treaty country or by *citizens of the United States* or *resident aliens,* and more than 50 percent of its income is used to satisfy liabilities of persons resident in the treaty country or the United States (the *base erosion* rule); or (2) the stock in such corporation, or in a parent corporation organized in the treaty country, is primarily and regularly traded on an established stock exchange in such country. §884(e)(4). The primary need for determining the residency of a foreign corporation is to determine whether that corporation may claim exemption from the branch profits tax under a *tax treaty* the United States has with the country of residency, or whether that corporation is merely engaged in invalid *treaty shopping.* See Notice 87-5, 1987-35 I.R.B. 9. See *branch profits tax.*

qualified residential rental project, exempt facility bond a multifamily residential real estate project (which may include a single detached home) that at the issuer's election meets one of two primary tests, thereby making it possible for the bonds issued to finance the project to be classified as *exempt facility bonds*. The primary tests call for having either (1) at least 20 percent of the units occupied by people whose income is less than half the *area median gross income*; or (2) 40 percent of the units occupied by people whose income is 60 percent or less of area median gross income. §142(d). There are further alternative tests under which a small percentage of the units can be occupied by persons with still lower incomes, so as to have "deep rent skewing." §142(d)(4). All of these income-related tests must be made annually during the *qualified project period*, beginning the first day that at least 10 percent of the units are occupied and ending when the bonds are retired, when §8 subsidies end, or 15 years after 50 percent occupancy. §142(d)(2). See also §150(b)(2) (denials of *interest expense deduction* if bond does not qualify). See *deep rent skewed project; exempt facility bond; qualified bond; tax-exempt bond.*

qualified retiree moving expenses any *moving expenses* that are incurred by an *individual* whose former *principal place of work* and former residence were outside the *United States,* and that are incurred for a move to a new residence in the United States in connection with the *bona fide* retirement of the individual. Such expenses are *deductible* under relaxed limitations. §217(i)(1).

qualified retirement plan a *qualified plan* that is a *retirement plan.* Retirement plans fall into a number of subcategories. See *retirement plans.*

qualified sale, ESOPs and EWOCs pre-1992 *sale* of *employer securities* by the *executor* of the *estate* of a *decedent* to an *ESOP* or *EWOC*. §2057(b). *Qualified proceeds* of such sales are 50 percent *deductible* (up to $75,000) for *estate tax* purposes. The *qualified proceeds* from a *qualified sale* qualify for an *estate tax deduction.* For details, see *qualified proceeds.*

qualified sale, merchandise returns a *sale* of a magazine, paperback, or record if (1) at the time of sale, the *taxpayer* has a legal obligation to adjust the sales price of such magazine, paperback, or record if it is not resold; and (2) the sales price of such magazine, paperback, or record is adjusted by the taxpayer because of a failure to resell it. §458(b)(5). Section 458 allows *accrual method* taxpayers to exclude refunds for goods returned within statutorily fixed merchandise return periods or shorter taxpayer-selected return periods.

qualified sale, unstated interest a *sale* or *exchange* of land between an *individual* and a member of the individual's family, as broadly defined under §267(c)(4). If the sale provides for simple interest at a rate of at least 6 percent, it is exempted from the *unstated interest* rules of §483 as to the first $500,000 of such sales, provided no party to the *sale* is a *nonresident alien.* §463(e). See *related taxpayers, loss and deduction denial.*

qualified section 501(c)(3) bond a *private activity bond* issued as part of an issue if (1) all *property* which is to be provided by the *net proceeds* of the issued will be owned by a *section 501(c)(3) organization* or a governmental unit; and (2) the bond would not be a private activity bond if the organization were a government unit when its exempt activities were being conducted. §145(a). During the testing for a qualified section 501(c)(3) bond, the *private business use test* and the *private security or payment test* are applied by substituting "5 percent of the proceeds" for the usual "10 percent of the proceeds." §145(a)(2)(B). Because section 501 (c)(3) bonds are one type of *qualified bond,* they can be *tax-exempt bonds* despite the fact that they are private activity bonds. As a result, *interest* they pay can be nontaxable to their holders. See *tax-exempt bond; private activity bond; qualified bond.*

qualified securities *employer securities* issued by a *domestic corporation* or a member of its *controlled group of corporations* that has no *stock* outstanding that is readily tradable on an established securities market. The securities must be assets that would produce *long-term capital gains* if sold; they must not have been received by the seller from a *qualified plan* or pursuant to a right to acquire stock in connection with the performance of services or through a *qualified stock option,* an *incentive stock option,* an *employee stock purchase plan,* or a *restricted stock option.* §1042(c)(1). Such securities may be sold free of current tax if the proceeds are timely rolled over into *qualified replacement property.* Such securities are free of *market* discount. §1042(d). See *eligible worker-owned cooperative; employee stock ownership plan.*

qualified service, credit for increasing research activities an in-house research activity which can qualify for the *credit for increasing research activities.* §41(b)(2). "Research activities" include engaging in the actual conduct of research (e.g., a lab scientist engaging in experimentation), engaging in the immediate supervision of such persons (e.g., a research scientist who supervises lab scientists engaged in experimentation), or providing direct support for either or both of the foregoing activities (e.g., a lab assistant or secretary typing reports). §41(b)(2)(B). *Wages* paid to *employees* for such services are part of *in-house research expenses* and can qualify for the 20 percent *credit for increasing research activities.*

qualified ship contract any contract for the construction of not more than five ships within the *United States,* provided such ships are not constructed either directly or indirectly for the United States government and the taxpayer reasonably expects to complete the contract within five years of the contract commencement date. Revenue Act of 1987, §10203(b)(2). *Taxable income* from these contracts can be determined by using the *percentage of completion—capitalized cost method,* as modified by treating 40 percent of the long-term contract items under the *percentage of completion method* and 60 percent under the *taxpayer's* normal *method of accounting.*

qualified shipping investments, controlled foreign corporations   see *foreign base company shipping income.*

qualified small issue bond   a *state or local bond* as to which the aggregate amount of proceeds for all issues to be used by the same person (or various related persons) in the same municipality or county is $1 million or less and at least 95 percent of the *net proceeds* of which are used for the acquisition or improvement of land or *depreciable property.* §144(a). The $1 million figure rises to $10 million to the extent the issuer elects to take related *capital expenditures* into account. Despite being *private activity bonds,* qualified small issue bonds may nonetheless be *qualified bonds,* the *interest* on which is *exempt* from *federal income taxes.* §144(a)(12)(A)-(B). Post-1987 (pre-1992 for manufacturing facilities and certain farming) bonds or *refund bonds* with average maturities longer than those of the retired bonds generally cannot qualify. §144(a)(12).

qualified small issuer   an issuer (including its subordinate entities) which is not reasonably anticipated to issue over $10 million of tax-exempt obligations. §265(b)(3)(C). Such issuers can generate *qualified tax-exempt obligations* as to which *financial institutions* can deduct allocable *interest* expenses. §265(b)(3)(A). In applying the $10 million, one disregards most *private activity bonds* and certain other obligations. See §265(b)(3)(C)(ii). See *qualified tax-exempt obligation.*

qualified state judicial plan   a retirement plan for the exclusive benefit of state judges (1) that has been continuously in existence since December 31, 1978; (2) in which all judges eligible to benefit under the plan must participate and contribute the same fixed percentage of their basic or regular rate of compensation; (3) that does not provide an option to participants as to contributions or benefits, the exercise of which would affect the amount of the participant's currently includible compensation; (4) in which the retirement benefit under the plan is a percentage of the compensation of judges of the state holding similar positions; and (5) that does not pay benefits for a participant in excess of the limitation on benefits permitted under qualified *defined benefit plans. Participants* in such plans are not subject to the rule requiring participants in an ineligible *deferred compensation* plan to include plan benefits in *gross income* merely because there is no substantial risk of forfeiture. *TEFRA,* Pub. L. No. 97-248, §252, 96 Stat. 324, 532, amending §131 of the Revenue Act of 1978, Pub. L. No. 95-600, 92 Stat. 2763, 2779.

qualified steam-generating facility, industrial revenue bonds   a steam-generating facility for which more than half of the fuel is, or is derived from, *solid waste.* Former §103(g)(2). *Interest* on obligations issued to provide qualified steam-generating facilities is *tax-exempt.* Former §103(b)(4)(E). The exemption for such bonds may still be available under §142(a)(6) or (7), most likely as *solid waste disposal facilities.* They cannot now be used for further processing (e.g., to generate electricity). See Reg. §1.103-8.

qualified stock purchase, section 338 acquisitions   a transaction or series of transactions in which a *corporation purchases,* during a 12-month *acquisition period,* at least 80 percent of the combined voting power of all classes of voting *stock* and at least 80 percent of stock (aside from certain nonvoting stock limited and preferred as to dividends) by value. §338(d)(3). Such a purchase lies at the heart of an effective *section 338 acquisition,* the result of which can be to give the acquired corporation a *basis* in *target company* (its own) assets equal to their *fair market value.* One aggregates purchases made by members of an *affiliated group* of corporations to determine whether a qualified stock purchase was made and counts those purchases for other purposes as well. See §338(h)(8). The purchase may also arise through a combination of actual purchases plus *stock redemptions.* See *consistency period, section 338 acquisitions; purchase, section 338 acquisition; section 338 acquisition.*

qualified student loan bond   a bond issued to fund student loans issued pursuant to the Higher Education Act of 1965 Department of Education's Guaranteed Student Loan program or Parent's Loans for Undergraduate Students program, provided that 90 percent or more of the *net proceeds* of the issue are used to finance student loans. §144(b)(1)(A) and (2)(A). The issue includes a student loan bond issued under certain state supplemental student loan programs, and it requires that at least 95 percent of the net proceeds of such an issue be used to finance student loans. §144(b)(1)(B) and (2)(B). The bond is not qualified unless all loans made under it are to students who are either residents of the *state* issuing the bond or enrolled at an educational institution located in that state. §144(b)(3). Such a bond can be a type of *qualified bond,* with the result that *interest* thereon is *exempt* from federal *income taxes* under §103(a), despite being a type of *private activity bond.*

qualified subchapter S trusts   *trusts* (or independent separate shares thereof) defined in §1361(d)(3). Such trusts are permissible legal shareholders of *S corporations,* although their *beneficiaries* are derivatively considered *shareholders.* These trusts have the following characteristics: (1) they own *stock* in one or more S corporations; (2) their terms provide for only one *income* *beneficiary* at a time; (3) the income beneficiary is a *resident alien or citizen of the United States*; (4) all the income of the trust is or must be distributed currently to that beneficiary, and if *corpus* is distributed during the term of the trust, it too must be distributed to that beneficiary; (5) each income interest ends on the earlier of the death of the income beneficiary or on the trust's termination; and (6) if the trust terminates during an income beneficiary's life, it must distribute all its assets to that beneficiary. §1361(d)(3). Such trusts are popular devices for family *income shifting*.

qualified subsidiary a *corporation* that throughout its existence is wholly owned by a *title-holding corporation*. If a qualified subsidiary later stops satisfying the 100 percent ownership test, it is treated as a new corporation acquiring all its assets and assuming all its liabilities in *exchange* for its *stock* immediately before it ceases to qualify. Qualified subsidiaries of title-holding corporations are not treated as separate corporations for purposes of determining whether their ownership pattern is permissible. §501(c)(25)(E). See *title-holding companies*.

qualified summer youth employee a *member of an economically disadvantaged family*, hired at age 16 or 17, who performs services between May 1 and September 16 and was an *employee* any time during the 90 days before the period for which the *employer* claims the *targeted jobs credit*. §51(d)(12). The credit applies in 1983 and later. Hiring such *individuals* can qualify the *employer* for the targeted jobs credit, subject to certain limitations. The targeted jobs credit expired on June 30, 1992.

qualified survivor, moving expenses *moving expenses* that are paid or incurred by the *spouse* or any *dependent* of any *decedent* who, at the time of death, had a *principal place of work* outside the *United States*; such expenses are incurred for a move that begins within six months after the decedent's death and is to a residence in the United States from a former residence outside the United States, which (at the time of the decedent's death) was the residence of the decedent and the *individual* paying or incurring the expenses. Such expenses are *deductible* under relaxed limitations. §217(i)(1). See *moving expense deduction*.

qualified tax-exempt obligation a tax-exempt obligation issued after August 7, 1986, by a *qualified small issuer*, which obligation is not a *private activity bond* and which the issuer designates as an obligation that a *financial institution* can generate *deductible interest expenses* for holding. §265(b)(3)(B)(i). This provision allows people who acquired such a bond after August 7, 1986, to treat it as if it was acquired on that date such that generally only 20 percent (as opposed all) of the *interest expenses* are rendered *nondeductible*. *Qualified 501(c)(3) bonds* and certain refunding issues are

deemed not private activity bonds for this purpose. §265(b)(3)(B)(ii). In general, any particular issuer can designate not over $10 million worth of *qualified tax-exempt obligations* in any *calendar year*. §265(b)(3)(D)(i). Refundings of qualified tax-exempt obligations are not subject to the ceiling. §265(b)(3)(D)(ii).

qualified technological equipment a class of property which is not subject to the special limits on *cost recovery deductions* despite being leased to *tax-exempt entities*. The term contemplates tangible high-technology equipment used by a tax-exempt *entity* under a *lease* with a term of five years or less. (If the term is over five years, the equipment's cost is recovered over a five-year period with the straight-line method and no *salvage value*.) The term primarily refers to computers and related peripheral equipment, high-technology telephone station equipment installed on a customer's premises, and high-technology medical equipment. The terms "computer" and "related peripheral equipment" do not include any word processing equipment or video games or other devices used primarily for amusement or entertainment purposes. §168(i)(2). See also §168(g)(d)(C) (five-year *alternative depreciation system* life).

qualified temporary investment income *income* attributable to temporary *investments* in new *stock* or *debt instruments* during a one-year period after a *REIT* receives such capital. §856(c)(6)(D). Such investments qualify under the 75 percent test for determining REIT status. See *regulated investment company*.

qualified tender bond a bond that meets certain maturity limits, pays *interest* annually, and has an interest rate that is periodically reset to enable the bond to trade at par. The tender aspect means bondholders can liquidate their investments at designated tender intervals. Such bonds are generally viewed as not reissued when rates are adjusted, hence are generally not *arbitrage bonds*. See Notice 88-130, 1988-2 C.B. 543).

qualified ten-percent owned foreign corporation a *foreign corporation* (other than a *foreign personnel holding company* or *passive foreign investment company*), at least 10 percent of whose *stock* (by vote and value) is owned by the *taxpayer*. §245(a)(2). Distributees of *dividends* from such a corporation can claim a *dividends-received deduction* with respect to the United States source portion of such dividends. §245(a)(1). *Gains* on *sales* or *exchanges* of *stock* in *controlled foreign corporations* which are treated as dividends under §1248 do not qualify, however. §245(a)(11).

qualified terminable interest property (QTIP) a closely confined form of *property* in the form of a *terminable interest* that can qualify for the unlimited *mari-*

tal deduction, provided the *executor,* or, in the case of a *gift,* the *donor,* elects and various other conditions are met. §§2056(b)(7), 2523(f). In the case of QTIP gifts, the donor must make a *QTIP election* in order to qualify for the unlimited marital deduction.

qualified tertiary injectant expenses   any *cost paid or incurred* during the *taxable year* (whether or not chargeable to capital account) for any tertiary injectant (other than a hydrocarbon injectant, which is recoverable) used as a part of a tertiary recovery method. §193(b)(1). *Expenses* for such injectants used during the taxable year are *deductible.* §193(a). See *tertiary recovery method, deduction of injectants.*

qualified timber property   a woodlot or other site located in the *United States* that contains trees in significant commercial quantities and which is held by the *taxpayer* for the planting, cultivating, care, and cutting of trees for sale or use in the commercial production of timber products. §194(c)(1). Rapid *amortization* is allowed over a seven-year period of up to $10,000 per year of *capitalized reforestation expenditures* after 1979. The concept excludes ornamental trees (including Christmas trees) and *deductible* (§175) shelter belts, and the woodlot must be at least an acre in size, but the taxpayer claiming the benefits of §194 need not be the landowner. Reg. §1.194-3(a). In addition, a special *reforestation credit* is allowed for *reforestation expenditures.*

qualified total distribution   one or more *distributions* in a single *taxable year* of an *employee* in which he or she receives the balance in his or her account in a *qualified plan* on account of plan termination (or cessation of *contributions* to a *profit-sharing* or *stock bonus plan*), or as a *distribution* of the recipient's *accumulated deductible employee contributions* to the plan. §402(a)(5)(E). Such distributions can be rolled over tax-free into an *eligible retirement plan,* meaning an *IRA, qualified trust,* or *qualified annuity plan.* §402(a)(5). Such distributions are subject to §3405(d)(4) *withholding* on the *ordinary income* component at rates designed to reflect *five-year forward averaging.* The plan is not disqualified by such distributions. §401(a)(20). Qualified total distributions which are dumped into an *IRA* tax-free can be rolled over again tax-free. §408(d)(3). See *conduit IRA.*

qualified transfer, health benefit account   (1) a transfer of plan assets to fund a *section 401(h) account,* which transfer is of *excess pension assets* of a *defined benefit pension plan* to a health account which is part of the plan. It enables employers with pension plans with assets that exceed the *full funding limitation* to transfer plan assets to fund retiree health benefits.

qualified transfer, medical and tuition expenses   see *medical and tuition expenses, gift tax exclusion.*

qualified transferor   someone who held *stock* in an *S corporation* or predecessor *corporation* on December 31, 1982, or who acquired the stock from a family member (as defined in §267(c)(4)) by *gift,* by reason of the transferor's death, or by reason of a *qualified buy-sell agreement* from a qualified transferor (or his estate) who was a family member. §1378(c)(3)(B). Major post-1982 changes in stock ownership can result in forcing a *fiscal year* S corporation onto *a calendar year,* subject to exceptions for transfers involving qualified transferors. The *Tax Reform Act of 1984* provides that a qualified transferor also includes a person whose *estate* held the transferred stock on December 31, 1982. §1378(c)(3)(B)(i), as amended. See *related taxpayers, loss and deduction denial.*

qualified transportation   transportation in a *commuter highway vehicle,* regardless of when it was acquired or whether it was subject to an election under §46(e)(6)(B)(iv). §124(b). Such transportation, used for commuting purposes by *employees,* could be *excluded* from the employees' *gross income* under §124 (until 1987), subject to controls on discrimination and various other modest constraints, yet could create *deductible expenses* for the *employer* and provided for a 10 percent *investment tax credit.*

qualified trust   a *trust* used to fund a *stock bonus, pension,* or *profit-sharing plan* that meets the elaborate qualification requirements of §401(a). While a trust is generally required, plans that are funded with *custodial accounts, annuities,* and certain other contracts provided by state-regulated *insurance companies,* are characterized as trusts for this purpose. §401(f). If a trust is used as the funding vehicle, then the requirements for meeting §401(a)'s definition of a *qualified plan* must be met; in addition, the trust must be a *domestic trust* (§401(a)), and the trust document must assure that its funds cannot be diverted for purposes other than the exclusive benefit of *employees* and their *beneficiaries* until all liabilities to such persons are satisfied (§401(a)(2)). In order for the trust to be tax-exempt, it also must meet the standards of §501, something virtually assured by its satisfying §401. For a more complete list of required features, see *qualified deferred compensation plan.*

qualified tuition and related expenses   tuition, enrollment fees, as well as books, supplies, and equipment needed for courses of instruction. §117(b)(2)(B). Such *expenses* may form the basis for a nontaxable *qualified scholarship.*

qualified tuition reduction   the amount of any reduction in tuition provided to an *employee* of an *educational organization described in section 170(b)(1)(A)(ii)* for the education (below the graduate level) at such organization (or another such *employee,* or any person treated as an employee or whose use is treated as by an employee) under the rules of §132(f). §117(d)(2). If the reduction is available on substantially the same terms to a group of employees under a reasonable classification set up by the *employer* and if it does not discriminate in favor of *highly compensated employees* (within the meaning of §414(q)), then the highly compensated (along with all other) employees can *exclude* such reductions from *gross income*. §117(d)(1). *Excluded employees* under §89(h) are disregarded in the testing for discrimination. §117(d)(4). The denial of the exclusions for graduate study does not apply to graduate research teaching assistants. §117(d).

qualified United States savings bond   a United States savings bond issued after 1989 to an *individual* who has reached age 24, at a discount under 31 U.S.C. 3105 (Series EE). §135(c)(1). Such a bond can be *redeemed* and the *interest* therefrom can be excluded from *gross income* of the holder (the exclusion is available only to the buyer). The exclusion is available only if and to the extent the *taxpayer* pays *qualified higher education expenses*. The exclusion is limited by a phase-out that depends on the taxpayer's *modified adjusted gross income,* which for this purpose is defined as *adjusted gross income* in which the *foreign earned income exclusion* is ignored (special treatment accorded income of Puerto Ricans and *possessions* persons) is ignored but taxable *Social Security* benefits, *Railroad Retirement Act* benefits, the impact of the *passive loss rules,* and *IRA deductions* are included. §135(c)(4).

qualified vessel, Merchant Marine Construction Fund Act   any vessel built in the *United States* (and if reconstructed, also reconstructed in the United States) and documented under United States law, which by agreement with the Secretary of Commerce, will be operated in United States, foreign, Great Lakes, or noncontiguous domestic trade or in the fisheries of the United States. The term is not defined in the *Code*; moreover, the *Code* also uses the term "agreement vessel" in §7518. Reg. §3.11(a)(2); Merchant Marine Act of 1936, 46 U.S.C. §1101 et seq. (1976). See §7518(i) (definitions).

qualified veterans' mortgage bonds   *state or local bond* issues, 95 percent or more of the *net proceeds* of which are used to provide residence for veterans. §143(b). Only *states* issuing such bonds prior to June 22, 1984, may continue to do so. The amount permitted to be issued annually is based upon the average yearly issuance for such issuing state for the years between 1979 and 1984. *Refunding issues* are not included in the total. Only veterans serving before January 1, 1977, are eligible to be recipients of the proceeds from such issue. §143(1). Any bond meeting the *private business use test* or *private security or payment test* cannot be a qualified veterans' mortgage bond. §143(b)(4). However, a *private activity bond* satisfying the *private loan financing*

test may be a qualified veterans' mortgage bond. As such, the issue will be a *qualified bond* and the *interest* therefrom will be *tax-exempt.* See *tax-exempt bond; private activity bond.*

qualified voluntary employee contribution   a voluntary contribution made by an *individual* as an *employee* under a *qualified plan* (including a *governmental plan*), which the employee has not designated as *nondeductible.* This provision was repealed in 1986. In order to qualify, the plan had to permit an employee to make contributions that may be treated as qualified voluntary employee contributions. §219(e)(2)(A). The contribution was voluntary if not mandatory, meaning not required as a condition of employment or participation in a plan, or as a condition of obtaining *employer*-paid benefits. §219(e)(2)(B). See *qualified employer plan.*

qualified volunteer fire department   an organization that provides fire-fighting and emergency medical services, pursuant to a written agreement, to residents of an area not otherwise receiving fire-fighting services. §150(e)(2). If substantially all the proceeds of a debt issue are used to acquire, construct, reconstruct, or improve a firehouse or truck for such a department, the obligation is considered to have been issued by a *political subdivision* such that the *interest* on the debt can be tax-exempt. §150(e)(1).

qualified wages, targeted jobs credit   see *targeted jobs credit.*

qualified withdrawal, Merchant Marine Construction Fund Act   generally, amounts withdrawn from *capital construction funds,* which do not attract current *income taxes,* made with the agreement of the Secretary of Commerce for the purpose of acquiring, constructing, reconstructing, or converting a *qualified vessel* associated container or barge, or of paying down principal on *debt* for such a purpose. §7518(e).

qualified works of art   any archaeological, historic, or creative *tangible personal property.* §2503(f)(2)(A). Loans of such property may be exempt from *federal gift taxes.* §2503(f).

qualified written notice of allocation   a written notice used by a *cooperative* to inform *patrons* of earnings *allocated* to them, including the portion that consists of an allocation of a *patronage dividend.* At least 20 percent of such allocations must be paid in money or by *qualified check* and the patron who receives the notice must either have the chance to convert the allocation into cash within a period of not less than 90 days or must consent to include the stated dollar amount of the allocation in his or her *gross income.* §1388(c)(1). Valid consent may be given by various means discussed in §1388(c)(2)(A) through (C). The issuance of a qualified written notice of allocation permits the cooperative to *deduct* patronage dividends. §1382(b)(1).

qualifying alimony amounts reported as taxable *alimony or separate maintenance* payments under §71 relating to amounts received pursuant to a decree of divorce or separate maintenance or an associated written instrument. Former §219(b)(4)(B).

qualifying business, at-risk rules an actively conducted *business,* provided (1) for the *taxable year,* the *corporation* had at least one full-time *employee,* substantially all of whose services were in the active management of the business; (2) it had at least three full-time nonowner employees (employees with not over a five-percent ownership interest), substantially all of whose services were directly related to that activity; (3) the *deductions* for *trade or business* expenses, other than salary to more than five-percent owners and their families, under §162 and §404 benefit plan *contributions* exceed 15 percent of *gross income* from the business; and (4) the business does not involve equipment leasing or the use (except in the case of FCC licensee), exploration, sale, lease, or other disposition of master *sound recordings,* motion picture films, videotapes, or tangible or intangible assets associated with literary, artistic, or musical property, unless the *taxpayer* is entirely at risk for any amounts spent. §465(c)(7)(C). Such a business can elude the *at-risk rules* if run by a *qualified C corporation.* There are further definitional complexities. See *at-risk rules, generally; qualified C corporation.*

qualifying distributions, private foundations amounts paid out (including administrative expenses) to accomplish a *private foundation's exempt purpose* and to acquire assets used or held for use directly in carrying out an exempt purpose, and certain *set-asides* (i.e., reserves) for specific charitable projects to be used within five years, provided the *IRS* either approves the set-aside, or certain restrictive conditions are met. §4942(g); Reg. §53.4942(a)-3. Qualifying distributions reduce the base on which are imposed the 15 percent/100 percent *excise taxes* on private foundations' failures to make minimum distributions of income. See *undistributed income excise tax, private foundations; grant administrative expenses, private foundation.*

qualifying distribution, tax-deferred annuities for educational and exempt organization employees one or more *distributions* from a *tax-deferred annuity for educational and exempt organization employees,* which would be a *lump-sum distribution* (§402(e)(4)), disregarding the election requirements of §402(e)(4)(B) or the five-year minimum period of service requirement of §402(h)(4)(H)), if the annuity were bought under a *qualified annuity plan* or were a distribution of *accumulated deductible employee contributions.* §403(b)(8)(B). An *employee* who is paid the balance of the account in such annuities in a qualifying distribution is not taxed if he or she rolls over the distribution into another tax-

deferred annuity or an *individual* retirement plan. §403(b)(8)(A). The term disappears from post-1988 years.

qualifying dividends, dividends-received deduction the amount of the dividends-received deduction depends upon the percentage of ownership the recipient corporate shareholder holds in the corporation making the dividend distribution. §243(a). For dividends received or accrued, the deduction percentage is as follows:

Percentage of Ownership by the Corporate Shareholder	Deduction Percentage
Less than 20%	70%
20% or more (but less than 80%)	80%
80% or more	100%

The dividends received deduction may be limited by a percentage of the taxable income of the corporation computed without regard to the net operating loss deduction *(NOL),* the dividends received deduction, or any capital loss carryback to the current year. See *affiliated group; dividends-received deduction.*

qualifying employer securities, ESOP securities of an *employer corporation* in which a *leveraged ESOP* may invest. §4975(e)(8) defines the term to mean the same thing as *employer securities* within the meaning of §409(1). See *employer securities, ESOPs, EWOs, PAYSOPs, and TRASOPs.*

qualifying employment-related expenses see *child and dependent care credit.*

qualifying event one of various circumstances under which an *employer* must provide continuing coverage for current and even some retired *employees*—called *covered employees*—(and, in general *spouses* and *dependents,* collectively referred to as "*qualified beneficiaries*") under a *group health plan* or face a large *excise tax.* §4980B(f)(3) (formerly §§162(k)(3) and 106(b)). The events are (1) death of the covered *employee*; (2) termination (other than by reason of gross misconduct), or reduction of hours, of employment; (3) divorce or legal separation; (4) entitlement to benefits under title XVIII of the Social Security Act; (5) a dependent child's ceasing to be such under the plan; or (6) a bankruptcy of the payor-employer. See *excise tax, failure to provide health care continuation coverage; group health plan, deduction.*

qualifying income, publicly traded partnerships includes *interest, dividends, realty, rents, gains* from the *disposition of* realty, and income and gains from various activities involving depletable mineral or other natural resource deposits. It includes gain from disposition of a *capital asset* or *section 1231 asset* held for the production of income that is of a passive character. In addition, passive-type income includes income and gains from commodities (but *not inventory, stock in* *trade,* or *dealer property*) or futures, *options,* or forward contracts with respect to such commodities (including foreign currency transactions of a commodity pool) in the case of *partnerships,* a principal activity of which is the buying and selling of such commodities, futures, options, or forward contracts (i.e., typical commodity pools). In the determination of whether 90 percent of a partnership's *gross income* is passive-type income, gross income is not reduced by inventory costs when dealing with the disposition of real property. If at least 90 percent of a *publicly traded partnership's* gross income is qualifying income, the *entity* retains its character as a *partnership* rather than a *corporation.* §7704(a)-(c). There are further difficult details to this definition. See *publicly traded partnership.*

qualifying indebtedness, installment sales   *mortgages* and other *debts* encumbering *property* sold plus unsecured debt, which the buyer incurs or assumes incident to the purchase, holding, or operation of the property in the ordinary course of the buyer's *business* or *investment.* Reg. §15a.453-1(b). It excludes obligations the seller incurred incident in the disposition (e.g., legal fees) and obligations functionally unrelated to the acquisition, holding, or operation of the property (e.g., payment of the seller's medical bills). Any obligation that is incurred or assumed in contemplation of the disposition of the property is disqualified if recovery of the seller's *basis* in the *installment sale* is accelerated. Qualifying indebtedness is treated as reducing the *selling price* so as to arrive at *total contract price* for purposes of the *installment sales* provisions. Reg. §15a.453-1(b)(2)(iii).

qualifying individual, child and dependent care credit   an *individual* who is either (1) a *dependent* of the *taxpayer* who has not attained the age of 15 years, for whom the taxpayer is entitled to a *dependency exemption*; or (2) a dependent or *spouse* of the taxpayer who is physically or mentally incapable of caring for him- or herself. §21(c)(1). The *Code* applies a more liberal test for treating a child of divorced or separated parents as a qualifying individual. Basically, as long as more than half the *support* comes from the parents, the child (under age 15, or mentally or physically handicapped) is a qualifying individual as to the parent who had custody for the greater period during the *calendar year.* §21(f)(5). See *child and dependent care credit.*

qualifying processed wood fuel, credit for fuels from nonconventional sources   any processed solid wood fuel that has a BTU content per unit of volume or weight at the *taxpayer's* irrevocable election, determined without regard to any nonwood elements, which is at least 40 percent greater per unit of volume or weight than the BTU content of the wood from which it is produced (determined immediately before processing). Charcoal, fireplace products, or products used for ornamental or recreational purposes are excluded. §44D(c)(4). Such wood can qualify for the *credit for producing fuels from nonconventional sources.* §29(f)(2).

qualifying real property loans, mutual savings banks   generally, loans secured by *real estate* which will be used to improve upon the property, but not (1) loans evidenced with government or corporate *debt* coupons attached or in *registered form*; (2) loans, the primary obligor of which is a government or a subdivision or instrumentality of a government, a *bank* (§581 definition), or another member of the same *affiliated group* (as defined in §1504(a), but expanded); (3) any loans to the extent secured by a deposit in or a share of the *taxpayer*-lender; or (4) loans which, within a 60-day period beginning in one *taxable year* of the creditor and ending in its next taxable year, were made or obtained and then repaid and disposed of, unless they are *bona fide* transactions. §593(e)(1). *Mutual savings banks, domestic building and loan associations,* and *cooperative banks* without stock, which are organized and operated for mutual profit, are entitled to favorable treatment with respect to *deductions* for additions to *reserves for bad debts* for such loans. §593(b)(1)(B).

qualifying retirement plans   see *qualified plan.*

qualifying rollover distributions   *lump-sum distributions* (the five-year *participation* rule is ignored) and distributions of *accumulated deductible employee contributions* within one *taxable year* of a plan termination, or, as to *stock bonus* and *profit-sharing plans,* complete discontinuance of *employer contributions* of the entire balance of the *participant's* account. §402(a)(5)(E)(i). Such amounts can generally be rolled over tax-free into an *eligible retirement plan,* that is, a form of *individual retirement plan,* another *qualified deferred compensation plan,* or an *annuity plan* of §403(a) variety. Section 402(a)(5)(B) caps nontaxable rollover by reference to qualified total distributions. The term is also used in §402(a)(6)(D) (deferral of *gains* on sales of distributed property) and §402(a)(7) (surviving *spouse's* rollover).

qualifying statement   see *FIRPTA withholding; withholding certificate.*

quality review staff   a staff in the *IRS District Office* which checks the results of *audits* for such questions as computational accuracy of compliance with audit standards.

quasi-capital assets   a term sometimes used to refer to property held for the requisite *long-term holding period* and subject to *hotchpot* treatment under §1231. See *section 1231 assets.*

quasi-community property   a hybrid class of *property* developed in some *community property states* basically in order to adjust for the rights of a wife moving from a non–community property *state* into a *community property state*. The wife in a separate-property state would have *dower* or similar rights in her husband's separate property, but she would lose them upon moving to a community property state and would have no rights in community property. In fairness to such *spouses,* the quasi-community property concept treats property brought to a community property state as community property if it would have been community property had it been acquired while the individual domiciled in the community property state. See Ariz. Rev. Stat. Ann. §25-318 (1977); Cal. Civ. Code §4803 (West 1983); Idaho Code §15-2-201(b) (1979).

quasi-domestic corporation a *foreign corporation* that, pursuant to an applicable *tax treaty,* makes an election to be treated as a *domestic corporation* for purposes of §§897 and 6039C of the *Code.*

questionable payments an informal reference to payments that the *slush fund questionnaire* is designed to uncover. Essentially, it refers to bribes, loans, kickbacks, and political expenditures, whether lawful or otherwise, which have questionable deductibility under §162 as *trade or business expenses.* See I.R.M. 4200 (the five questions).

quick assets highly liquid assets such as cash, short-term investments, and notes receivable and accounts receivable. A high rate of quick assets to sales can indicate an unreasonable retention of earnings, which can in turn provoke the *accumulated earnings tax.* See *working capital.*

quick carryback refunds see *tentative carryback adjustment.*

quickie refund, application for see *tentative carryback adjustment.*

R

R and D   see *research and experimental expenditures.*

R and D credit   see *credit for increasing research activities.*

RAA   an acronym for *request for administrative adjustment.*

RAR   an acronym for *Revenue Agent's Report.*

REA   an acronym for the *Retirement Equity Act of 1984.*

Reg(s).   in the case of *federal* taxation, an abbreviation for *Treasury Administrative and Procedural Regulations.*

REIT   an acronym for *real estate investment trust.*

REIT year   any *taxable year* for which the provisions of part II of *subchapter M,* the *real estate investment trust* (REIT) provisions, apply to the *taxpayer.* §172(b)(1)(E)(iii). Generally, *net operating losses* of a *taxpayer* can be carried back three years, but a *net operating loss* from a REIT year cannot be carried back. §172(b)(1)(E)(i)(I). Also, a net operating loss from a non-REIT year cannot be carried back and deducted in any REIT year. §172(b)(1)(E)(iii).

REMIC   an acronym for a *real estate mortgage investment conduit.*

Rev. Proc.   an abbreviation for the term *revenue procedure.*

Rev. Rul.   an abbreviation for the term *revenue ruling.*

RIC   an acronym for *regulated investment company.*

Rabbi trust   tax slang for a *trust* established by an *employer* or other payor to fund *nonqualified deferred compensation* payments for *employees* and *independent contractors.* They are used to hold such assets as *annuities* owned by the obligor. The *beneficiary* must still be a *general creditor* of the trust. PLR 8113107 (Dec 30, 1980). Model provisions for a rabbi trust are found in Rev. Proc. 92-64, 1992-33 IRB. This model grantor trust is intended to serve as a safe harbor for taxpayers that adopt and maintain grantor trusts in connection with unfunded deferred compensation arrangements.

racially nondiscriminatory policy as to students   a policy of admitting students of any race to all the rights, privileges, programs, and activities of the school, and nondiscrimination by race as to educational policies, admissions policies, loans, scholarships, athletic, and other programs. Rev. Rul. 71-447, 1971-2 C.B. 230. Absence of such a policy imperils the tax exemption granted private schools. I.R.S. Ann. 79-38 (current *IRS* standards).

Railroad Retirement Tax Act (RRTA)   a statute that imposes a tax on both *employers* and *employees* to provide funds for retirement benefits of railroad employees. *Social Security taxes* do not apply to those employees subject to the RRTA tax. The benefit provisions of the RRTA are administered by the Railroad Retirement Board. The tax is covered in §§3201–3233. See §401(a)(5) and Reg. §1.401-3(e)(4) for integration of the RRTA with *qualified plans.* Rev. Rul. 70-149, 1970-1 C.B. 95.

rare disease or condition   any disease or condition that affects less than 200,000 people in the *United States* or affects more than 200,000 people in the United States if there is no reasonable expectation that the cost of developing and making available in the *United States* a drug to treat the disease or condition will be recovered from sales in the United States of the drug. A 50 percent *nonrefundable credit* is approved for *qualified clinical testing expenses* necessary in obtaining approval from the FDA for the sale of a drug for a rare disease or condition. §28(d). See *orphan drug credit.*

ratable accrual method   a general method of calculating currently taxable discount on certain *debt* obligations under which the discount is divided by the number of days from the date the *taxpayer* acquired the obligation, until the day of maturity. This amount is then added to daily *gross income.* See §§1276(b)(1) and 1283(b)(1). It is used to define the *daily portion* of *acquisition discount* under the *original issue discount rules* as they relate to *short-term obligations.* See *constant interest rate method.*

ratable share of acquisition discount   the *acquisition discount* of a short-term government obligation multiplied by the period the *taxpayer* held the obligation divided by the number of days between the time the taxpayer acquired the obligation and its maturity date. For example, if the acquisition discount is $1,000 on a one-year T-note and the taxpayer held the obligation for 10 days, then the *taxpayer's* ratable share of the *acquisition discount* is $1,000 × 10/365, or $27.40. To the extent the taxpayer recognizes a *gain* on the *sale* or *exchange* of such an obligation, the first $27.40 is *ordinary income,* and the balance will ordinarily be *capital gain.* See, e.g., §1271(a)(3).

rate differential portion   see *foreign source capital gain net income.*

rate of accrual   see *accrued benefits.*

ratio for exclusion, annuities   see *exclusion ratio.*

ratio of debt to equity a *corporation's* ratio of debt to equity is determined by dividing (1) its total indebtedness by (2) the sum of its money and all other assets less its total indebtedness (but not less than zero). §163(j)(2)(C). In the case of a debt having *original issue discount,* the amount included in total indebtedness is its *issue price* plus the portion of the original issue discount previously *accrued* without reduction for any acquisition premium paid by a holder of the debt instrument. §163(j)(2)(C)(ii). Other assets are included at their *adjusted basis* for purposes of determining *gain.* §163(j)(2)(C)(i). The provision is designed to put an end to bleeding off corporate earnings via interest payments to related charities or foreign owners. See *earnings stripping provisions.*

reacquired property see *repossession of property.*

readily ascertainable fair market value, nonstatutory options generally, an *option* that is actively traded on an established market, or, if not so traded, is otherwise readily ascertainable with reasonable accuracy. The *IRS* asserts that "with reasonable accuracy" calls for the *taxpayer* to be able to show that the following conditions exist when the option is granted: (1) it is freely transferable by the optionee; (2) it is immediately exercisable in full by the optionee; (3) the option or property is not subject to any restriction or condition, other than a lien or condition to secure payment of the purchase price, which has a significant effect on the value of the option or property; and (4) the *fair market value* of the *option privilege* is readily ascertainable. Reg. §1.83-7(b). The *regulations* make it hard to show that a nontraded option has a readily ascertainable value. As a result, the *section 83(b) election* to report *ordinary income* at the time of grant and *capital gain* treatment for appreciation in value of the property thereafter is made difficult. See *nonstatutory options.*

readily tradable, installment sales issued with interest coupons attached, in *registered form,* regularly quoted by brokers or dealers making a market in the obligation, or otherwise designed to in fact be traded in an established securities market. §453(f)(5); Reg. §15a.453-1(e)(4)(iii). A readily tradable governmental or corporate obligation (e.g., Treasury bill) is treated as *payment* in the year received rather than as an installment obligation embodying rights to payment in future years. §453(f)(4); Reg. §15a.453-1(e)(1)(i)(C). Registered debt may be shown to be not readily tradable. §453(f)(5)(A). See *payment, installment method.*

readily tradable security, golden parachutes a security that is regularly quoted by brokers or dealers making a market. Reg. §1.280G-1, Q&A 6. The term is used in connection with *golden parachute agreements* in §280G(b)(5)(ii)(II) involving certain *small business corporation* exemptions. See *small business corporation, S corporations.*

real and depreciable business property *real estate* and *depreciable property,* whether or not *real estate,* used in a *taxpayer's trade or business.* Such property, if held for more than one year (subject to some modest variations), qualifies as so-called *section 1231 property.* See *section 1231 assets; used in the trade or business.*

real estate see *realty.*

real estate assets *real estate* (e.g., land and improvements and interests in *real estate* other than minerals, oil, and gas); interests in *mortgages* on *real estate* (and their legal equivalents, including mortgage pool certificates and *debt* securing mobile homes); interests in mortgages on leaseholds of land and improvements; *regular* or *residual interests* in *REMICs*; and shares of other *REITs* on temporarily invested new capital placed in debt and equities for up to a year. §856(c)(6)(B); Reg. §1.856-3. The term is important in determination of whether the REIT qualifies as such by virtue of its having at least 75 percent of its total assets invested in *real estate* assets or certain other assets, or both combined. §856(c)(5)(A).

real estate holding company a *corporation* used to hold *real estate.* Rental property is often so held for various reasons, for instance, to avoid usury law ceilings, to conceal ownership, or to limit liabilities. Such an organization may encounter *personal holding company tax* problems, although §583(a)(2)'s definition of *rents* makes avoidance of the tax easy. The *S corporation* is a more popular format for this purpose.

real estate investment trust a *corporation, trust,* or *association* (usually a trust organized in Massachusetts, but not a *bank* or similar financial institution or an *insurance company*) taxable as if a *corporation,* unless it elects a special status under §§856–858, which allows it to be taxed much like a *regulated investment company.* To qualify as a REIT, the *entity* must be managed by one or several *trustees* or directors, and its *beneficial* ownership must be held by 100 or more *persons* for at least 335 days of the tax year, and five or fewer individuals may not own more than 50 percent of the stock. The REIT must also satisfy three income-related tests: (1) at least 95 percent of its *gross income* must be from *dividends, interest,* real property rents, *gains* from *sales* of certain securities (including gains or receipts from certain cap or swap agreements), and certain realty or *real estate* tax refunds and disbursements; (2) at least 75 percent of its gross income must be from *real estate rentals, mortgage interest, sales of certain realty and mortgages, real estate tax refunds and abatements, qualified temporary investment income, dividends from other REITs,* and similar items; and (3) not more than 30 percent of its gross income may be from dispositions of *stock* or securities. §856. At least 75 percent of the value of its assets must be *real estate,* cash receivables, or government securities, subject to limitations on holdings of a single issuer. §§856, 857. REITs are in effect taxed only on retained income, and they can pass *capital gains* through to their *shareholders,* provided they distribute at least 95 percent of their *real estate investment trust taxable income* (less excess noncash income), other than *net capital gains,* to their shareholders. §§857, 858. The rationale for the REIT is to allow the small investor to participate in the real estate industry. *See excise tax, undistributed income of an REIT.*

real estate investment trust taxable income   *taxable income* generally computed as if for a *corporation,* with the following primary adjustments: (1) the *dividends-received deduction* is not allowed; (2) the *dividends-paid deduction* is allowed and is computed without regard to the portion of such deduction attributable to net income from foreclosure property; (3) §443(b) does not apply, so that *taxable income* for a period of less than 12 months is not *annualized*; (4) net income from *foreclosure property* is excluded; and (5) taxes imposed for failure to satisfy the income tests required to qualify as a REIT may be deducted. Net income derived from prohibited transactions is excluded. There are further intricate details. §857(b)(2); Reg. §1.857-2(a).

real estate mortgage investment conduit   an *entity,* known as a REMIC, generally not subject to *federal income tax,* which issues multiple classes of interests to investors in a fixed pool of mortgages. The income of a *REMIC* passes through to the holders of interests, thus avoiding double taxation. §860A. However, the REMIC is taxed on any income resulting from certain prohibited transactions. §860F. There must be an affirmative election to be a REMIC. §860D(b). To qualify, its *taxable year* must be a *calendar year,* substantially all its assets must consist of *qualified mortgages* and *permitted investments* as of the end of the third month following the *start-up day* and each subsequent quarter, and all interests must be *regular interests* or *residual interests* (being limited to one class, distributions being pro rata with respect to such interests). §860D(a). Section 860 contains other complex provisions. Distributions on residual interests are not included in gross income to the extent they do not exceed the *adjusted basis* of the interest (basis being increased by the amount taken into account as taxable income and decreased by the amount of any *distribution* or loss). §860C.

real estate reporting person   every person doing business as a broker is required to furnish the government with information pertaining to each customer, including gross proceeds due to any sales or exchanges. §6045(a). This requirement includes real estate brokers. A real estate broker means any person involved in the real estate transaction, including the person responsible for the transaction, the mortgage lender, the seller's broker, or the buyer's broker. §6045(b). The information provided by the broker to the government must be

reported to each customer on Form 1099-B. §6045(b).

real estate taxes   see *real property taxes.*

real estate tax shelter   a *tax shelter* involving investments in improved *real estate.* Although this type of tax shelter takes various forms (e.g., existing properties, *sale* and *leasebacks,* or new construction), the common trend has been for investors to engage in *deferral* of income through *depreciation* (or *cost recovery*) *deductions* with respect to improvements (buildings or structures) followed by a *sale,* some or all of which is reported as *capital gain.* The basic aims of most tax shelters are as follows: (1) the maximization of tax incentives for investors; (2) the reduction of current income tax liability and the deferral of taxation to future tax years; and (3) the ability of investors to use borrowed money to finance their original investments (leveraging). Tax shelters attempt to satisfy all three aims, if possible. Section 42(g) adds an incentive to rehabilitate real estate in exchange for major *tax credits.* Accordingly, some *real estate* tax shelters can combine tax credits with significant conversion and deferral features. The *passive loss rules* are the big obstacle nowadays. Note that the *at-risk* rules of §465 do not apply to holding *real estate*; hence, leverage can be maximized. See *tax deferral.*

real estate transaction   a transaction which consists in whole or in part of the *sale* or *exchange* (whether or not currently taxable) of *reportable real estate* for money, *debt,* property, or services. §6045 and Reg. §1.6045-4. Such transactions produce a duty to issue a *broker's return.* Exempt transactions fall into two categories, namely, *exempt transfers* and *exempt property.* An "exempt transfer" is (1) a transfer which is not a sale or exchange, e.g., gift, bequeath, financing, refinancing; or, (2) a transfer in full or partial satisfaction of debt, e.g., foreclosure, transfer in lieu of foreclosure, or abandonment. There is an exception for a *de minimis* transfer, meaning a transfer as to which total consideration (without regard to allocation of proceeds) is under $600.

real property   see *realty.*

real property holding company, DISC   a *foreign corporation* formed solely to hold title to *foreign* realty for use by the *DISC.* §993(e)(2). *Stock* in such *corporations* are *export assets* if the *DISC* cannot hold title to property at local law and has more than 50 percent of the *corporation's* stock. See also §993(b)(6). Such *corporations* are classified as *related foreign export corporations.* The *domestic international sales corporation* (DISC) generally has been replaced by a system of foreign sales corporations (FSCs). See §§921–927 and *domestic international sales corporation.*

real property taxes   *taxes* imposed on the value of interests in *real estate* (but not excises on occupancy or transfers) that are levied for the general public welfare and are imposed at a like rate against all property in the taxing jurisdiction. Reg. §§1.164-3(b) and -4(a). *Local benefit assessments* do not qualify, but assessments allocable to maintenance, repair, or interest charges incurred in connection with maintenance, repair, or interest on improvements are deductible as real property taxes. Reg. §1.164-4(b)(1). Real property taxes are rendered *deductible* by §164(a). See *local benefit assessments; tax.*

real property tax year the period that, under the law imposing a *real property tax,* is regarded as the year to which the tax relates. Reg. §1.164-6(c). Beyond that, the *regulations* provide no guidance and refuse to identify some other time (lien date, fiscal year, assessment date, and so on) that determines the real property tax year. The local *District Director* can typically supply the real tax year applicable to the *taxpayer's* jurisdiction.

realization a difficult tax law concept that limits the finding of *income, gain,* or *loss* by demanding a change in the *taxpayer's* economic position sufficient to justify the imposition of a tax or to grant a tax allowance. For example, borrowing against appreciated property is not considered a realization, whereas a *sale* for cash clearly is. In order for an *exchange* to result in realization of *gain* or *loss,* there must be a *material difference* between the two things.

realize see *realization.*

realized gains and losses *gains* and *losses* arising from *sales* or *other dispositions* of property. Gains are the excess of the *amount realized* (usually, the sales price) over the *adjusted basis* of the property. Losses are the reverse. §1001(a). A gain or loss is realized when there has been a sufficient change in the *taxpayer's* economic position to justify recognizing the effect of the transaction for tax purposes. Gains or losses that are realized may still not result in any immediate tax consequence because some other *Code* section bars them from *recognition.* Examples of nonrecognition of realized gains or losses include the following *tax-free exchanges*: (1) exchanges of *like-kind property* under §1031; (2) *exchanges* of *stock* in *corporate reorganizations*; and (3) transactions in which *partnerships* or *corporations* are formed. Section 1001(c) requires that all realized gains or losses be *recognized,* unless some other Code section precludes their recognition. See *realization; recognition.*

reallocation of income and deductions by Commissioner a power granted the *IRS* by §482 to reallocate "*income, deductions, credits* or allowances" between commonly controlled *organizations or trades or businesses* to prevent *tax evasion* (under the *regulations, avoidance*) or to clearly reflect income. Control for these purposes means practical control, however maintained. Reg. §1.482-1(a)(3). Such reallocations cannot be upset unless they represent an *abuse of dis-*

cretion, a difficult showing for *taxpayers* to make. If the IRS reallocation stands, then the adjustment made by the IRS should be symmetrically applied among or between the commonly controlled taxpayers so as to avoid double-counting. The purpose of the §482 power is to place commonly controlled taxpayers in the same tax position as if they were doing business with each other at *arm's length.* See *clear reflection of income; correlative adjustment.*

reallocation, personal service corporations see *personal service corporation.*

realty an ownership interest related to land, improvements, and fixtures. Some interests insufficiently touch or concern land to qualify (e.g., temporary licenses that fall short of being leases). Fixtures are defined somewhat differently from state to state, although the differences merely revolve around the degree of permanence required to characterize something (e.g., a boiler or heat duct) as a fixture, hence, realty. The general rule against granting fixtures status as *tangible personal property* is modified by the *Code,* which generally takes the view that items that can be removed without significant damage or alteration to the rest of the property could qualify for the former *investment tax credit* (former §§38–48) and are, therefore, subject to depreciation *recapture* under §1245. See Reg. §§1.1250-1(e), 1.1245-3(c). See *inherently permanent structure; personal property.*

reasonable administrative costs a class of costs allocable to the United States government (and no other party) that are recoverable against the *IRS* under §7430(a)(2) as the result of a judicial award or a settlement where the *taxpayer* is a *prevailing party.* The dispute can relate to the determination, collection, or refund of any tax, interest, or penalty. Such costs include any administrative fees or other charges imposed by the IRS, and the reasonable expenses of compensating expert witnesses, paying for necessary studies and reports, and paying attorney's fees, based on prevailing market rates for the kind or quality of services provided. §7430(c)(2). No expert can be paid more than the top rate paid for government witnesses, and attorney's fees are generally capped at $75/hour. The IRS determines the reasonableness of attorney's fees and the costs of studies and reports in an administrative proceeding before the IRS. No award will be made to the extent the taxpayer unreasonably protracted the proceedings. §7430(c)(2)(B). Anyone who is admitted to practice before the *Tax Court* is deemed an attorney for purposes of recovering reasonable administrative and attorney's fees. The clock begins ticking on recoverable administrative expenses only after the earlier of the date of a *notice of deficiency* or a final decision of the *Appeals Office.* This is a major restriction. See *accountant's fees, recovery of; attorney's fees, recovery of; prevailing party; reasonable litigation costs; Taxpayer's Bill of Rights.*

reasonable allowance for exhaustion, wear and tear the *deduction* for *depreciations* allowed by §167 under a method described or allowed in that section or required or allowed by §168 (*cost recovery*).

reasonable and proximate relationship see *proximate relationship standard.*

reasonable cause, generally a basis for avoiding a raft of *civil tax penalties* or other burdens imposed on *taxpayers* for such acts as underpayment, tardiness, and failure to file various *returns*. The standard appears to be uniform, but only the *regulations* relating to late filing penalties define the term. The excuse is typically phrased "reasonable cause and not willful neglect"; the willful neglect language seems redundant. Sometimes reasonable cause is explicit. For example, under §§4912 and 4915 (pertaining to certain political activities by *exempt organizations*), a manager is liable for the excise tax only if the IRS shows that, in agreeing to the making of the lobbying expenditures, the manager knew that such expenditures constituted lobbying expenditures and (under §4912) knew that as a result of such expenditures the organization was likely to lose its tax-exempt status under §501(c)(3), and only if the manager failed to obtain an opinion of counsel concerning the expenditures that would protect the manager under the reasonable cause exception. Reg. §53.4945-1. In the case of *charitable deduction property*, when the *accuracy-related penalty* is involved for a valuation overstatement, this calls for a *qualified appraisal* by a *qualified appraiser* and independent investigation by the taxpayer. §6654(c)(2). For illustrations of the standard, see *reasonable cause, late filing penalties.*

reasonable cause, late filing penalties a basis for avoiding late tax payment penalties, on showing *reasonable justification* for delay. Regulation §301.6651-1(c) states: "If the taxpayer exercised ordinary business care and prudence and was nevertheless unable to file the return within the prescribed time, then the delay is due to a reasonable cause." The reasonable cause issue has been a litigious subject. Reasonable cause for delay was found in the following situations: the taxpayer relied on the advice of a competent adviser; the return was prepared on time, but late filing was due to an oversight by an *employee* or by the preparer of the return; and, the taxpayer was ill. Reasonable cause for delay was not found in the following situations: the taxpayer relied on the advice of an attorney inexperienced in *federal income tax* matters; the taxpayer's accountant failed to obtain an extension; the taxpayer erroneously believed that no tax was due; the taxpayer's accountant was too busy; the taxpayer had an erroneous belief as to due date of the return.

reasonable compensation compensation for services actually rendered which does not constitute *unreasonable compensation*. Reasonable compensation *paid or*

incurred in connection with a *trade or business* is *deductible* under §162(a), provided it is *ordinary and necessary*. See *unreasonable compensation.*

reasonable expectation test, hedge bond see *hedge bond.*

reasonable litigation costs reasonable court costs, reasonable *expenses* for expert witnesses in civil proceedings, reasonable costs of preparing any study or report that the court deems necessary for the preparation of a party's case, and reasonable *attorney's fees* in a civil proceeding other than a *declaratory judgment* (except as to loss of *tax-exempt* status), but only after exhausting administrative remedies. 7430(a)-(c). The dispute can relate to the determination, collection, or refund of any tax, interest, or penalty. Nonlawyers admitted to the *Tax Court* or to *practice before the IRS* count as lawyers in Tax Court cases. Only costs allocable to the United States (and not to any other party) count, and they are unavailable to the extent the *taxpayer* unreasonably protracted the litigation. The *prevailing party,* in a court proceeding brought by or against the United States, may generally recover such costs in a court of the United States as long as the *position of the United States* was not "substantially justified." §7430(a). A party generally may not, however, recover such costs in excess of $75/hour. §7430(c)(1). If the dispute never went to court, and sometimes if it did, it may still be possible to recover *reasonable administration costs*. See *accountant's fees, recovery of; attorney's fees, recovery of; position of the United States; prevailing party; reasonable administrative costs; Taxpayer's Bill of Rights.*

reasonable moving expenses a limitation on the allowance of a *deduction* for certain *moving expenses* under §217. The *regulations* deny moving expense deductions to the extent they are unreasonable. For example, extra costs attributable to taking scenic routes or enjoying lavish meals or lodging are *disallowed*. The regulations, instead, require the *taxpayer* to take the shortest and most direct route from the old *principal residence* to the new principal residence, using conventional modes of transportation and to move with appropriate speed in order to qualify for full deductibility of expenses. Reg. §1.217-2(b)(2)(i).

reasonable needs of the business, accumulated earnings tax accumulations of *earnings and profits* that are reasonable in purpose and amount, hence, available. A minimum amount of $250,000 ($150,000 for personal service companies in the fields of health, law, accounting, etc.) may be accumulated by all corporations, including holding and investment companies. §535(c). The corporation is subject to the accumulated earnings tax if there is an intent to avoid the tax on the shareholders. §535(c). In order to justify an accumulation of income, there must be a reasonable need and a definite plan for use. Reasonable needs *include business and plant expansion.* Unacceptable grounds are *loans to stockholders and investments not related to the business.* See *accumulated earnings credit; excess business holdings redemption needs; section 303 redemption needs.*

reasonableness, accumulated earnings tax   see *reasonable needs of the business, accumulated earnings tax.*

reasonableness, compensation   see *reasonable compensation.*

reasonable prospect of recovery   a factual conclusion that the chances of a recovery are better than a remote possibility. The standard is virtually impossible to express. The *judicial opinion holds* that a 40 percent or better prospect of recovery was reasonable. To the extent that there is a reasonable prospect of recovery of a claim for reimbursement, Reg. §1.165-1(d)(2)(i) bars a *casualty loss deduction.*

reasonable salvage value   a *salvage value* (i.e., anticipated value at the expiration of the *taxpayer's* anticipated use of the property) that is reasonable in light of the facts at the time the *depreciation* method with respect to the property was selected. §1.167(a)-1(c)(1). Except where the *class life asset depreciation range system* was selected, *net salvage values* may be used. Section 167(f) allows an additional 10 percent reduction in salvage value for *personal property* with a useful life of at least three years. Reasonable salvage values sets the limit on allowable *depreciation.* Salvage values may be changed in extraordinary circumstances. The *accelerated cost recovery system* (ACRS) assumes no salvage values at the end of an asset's *recovery period.* §168(b)(4).

reasonably segregable materials   materials that, after the exempt portions are deleted, still convey meaningful information that does not mislead the reader. Reg. §601.701(b)(4). Such portions must be disclosed under the *Freedom of Information Act* where the record is otherwise subject to disclosure but for its being intertwined with exempt material.

reattribution   the *attribution* of ownership of *stock* from one *taxpayer* to another taxpayer, thence from that taxpayer to a third taxpayer, etc. For example, if a son owns stock, his mother is deemed to own it under §318(a)(1). His mother's derivative ownership is in turn reattributed to a *partnership* in which she is a partner under §318(a)(3). See *attribution rules.*

rebate, accuracy-related penalty   see *underpayment of tax, accuracy-related penalty.*

rebate, deficiency   an *abatement, refund, credit,* or other repayment that the *IRS* made to a *taxpayer* because the tax shown on the *return,* as increased by previous *assessments* or collected without *assessment* and reduced by previous rebates, exceeded what the

IRS determined to be the *correct tax* for the year. §6211(g)(2); Reg. §301.6211-1(f). A rebate is one element of a *deficiency.* §6211(a); Reg. §301.6211-1(a). For example, a *quickie refund* is a rebate which can be recovered via a *deficiency* procedure.

rebate, negligence penalty   the portion of an *abatement, credit, refund,* or other repayment made because the tax imposed was less than the excess of timely paid or reported taxes over previous rebates. Former §6653(c)(2); Former Reg. §301.6653-1(c)(2). For an important current definition, see *underpayment of tax, accuracy-related penalty.*

rebuttable presumption   a factual assumption that can be reversed upon a showing of sufficient contradictory evidence. See *presumption.*

rebuttable presumption of collapsibility   a rule of administrative convenience that creates a *rebuttable presumption* that a *corporation* is a *collapsible corporation* if the *fair market value* of its *section 341 assets* is at least 50 percent of the fair market value of its total assets (excluding cash, stock, and obligations, if the obligations are *capital assets* in its hands) and at least 120 percent of the *adjusted basis* of its *section 341 assets.* §341(c)(1).

recapitalization   an adjustment of a *corporation's* capital structure. For details, see *Type E reorganization.*

recapture   a sort of revenge the *Code* imposes on *taxpayers* for what turns out to be, with the benefit of hindsight, claims to undue *tax benefits.* Recapture imposes current tax burdens, rather than adjustments to prior years, usually in the form of either (1) increased *ordinary income* to offset claims for undue previous *deductions;* or (2) direct tax liabilities as a result of what, in retrospect, were excessive claims for previous tax *credits.* Probably the most common case involves recharacterizing *capital gains* as *ordinary income* on the *disposition* of property to the extent the taxpayer is statutorily deemed to have claimed excessive *depreciation* or cost recovery deductions. Recapture can also arise as a result of indirect *dispositions.* See, e.g., §751 *(collapsible partnership rules).*

recapture, alimony   a reference to the operation of §71(f) under which rapidly declining *alimony or separate maintenance payments* are partially taxed in later years to the payor, and partially *deductible* by the payee. The calculations are complex. The overall purpose of alimony recapture is to limit *taxpayer's* abilities to convert property payments into deductible payments. See *frontloading of alimony.*

recapture, at-risk rules   the context of §456(e), the gist of which is that to the extent amounts *at risk* become negative, the excess is treated as *ordinary income* in that year, with a *carryover* of the disallowed loss to a future year. For example, assume a *taxpayer* invests $10 in cash and borrows $90 with personal liability to undertake an activity subject to the *at-risk rules*. She writes off $20 of losses in the next year, and in year three, when there is no income or loss, the *debt* becomes *nonrecourse debt*. In year three, §465(e) compels recapture (i.e., reporting as income) of the $10 as income, the extent to which the at-risk amount, as reduced by prior losses, is negative. However, the $10 becomes a *deduction* to be carried over to future years, subject to the at-risk rules in those later years. §465(e)(1)(B).

recapture, controlled foreign corporation stock   a *recapture* provision that has the effect of taxing as *dividends* what would otherwise be *capital gains* on the *sale, exchange, redemption*, or *liquidation* of a *controlled foreign corporation* (CFC) to the extent of the CFC's post-1962 *earnings and profits* while the *stock* was held by the *United States person* holding at least 10 percent of its voting power. §1248. Note that the corporation does not need to be a CFC nor does the United States person need to be a 10 percent shareholder in the year of the transaction that triggers recapture. §1248(a)(2).

recapture, cost recovery   see *recapture, depreciation.*

recapture, depletion   see *recapture, mining exploration expenditures.*

recapture, depreciation   the practice, imposed by §§1245 and 1250, of recharacterizing all or a portion of a *taxpayer's capital gains* on the *disposition* of property as *ordinary income*, if the taxpayer or a predecessor claimed *depreciation, amortization*, or *cost recovery* on the property. The details of the *recapture* provisions diverge considerably in the treatment of *real property* as opposed to personal property, a statement that is confused by the fact that the *accelerated cost recovery system* (ACRS) treats some classes of *real estate* (domestic nonresidential *real estate* written off with the accelerated rates determined under §168) as if they were *personal property*. Generally speaking, dispositions of *personal property* result in all *gains* attributable to depreciation, *amortization*, or *cost recovery* being treated as *ordinary income*, whereas only the accelerated (additional depreciation) portion of the write-off with respect to *realty* is treated as *ordinary income*.

recapture, farm land development costs   see *farm-land recapture.*

recapture, farm losses   see *excess deduction award.*

recapture, foreign extraction losses   the contents of §907(c)(4), the gist of which is that for *taxable years* beginning after 1982, if a *taxpayer* has an overall *foreign oil extraction loss* in a year, which reduces nonextraction income, then the loss is subject to recapture as

ordinary income from foreign sources in a later year in which the taxpayer has overall foreign oil and gas extraction income. The rule is designed to prevent a taxpayer from using an extraction loss in one year to reduce taxable *United States* source income, and in the following year using the full net extraction income as the basis for a *foreign tax credit*. The result is a reduction of oil companies' *foreign tax credits*.

recapture, foreign losses   a *recapture* system built into §904(f) under which *losses* from sources without the *United States* in a prior *taxable* year in which there was an *overall foreign loss* have the effect of converting taxable income from sources without the United States in later years into income from sources within the United States, thereby reducing the numerator of the limitation on *foreign tax credits* and reducing *creditable foreign taxes*. The system also applies to *credits* associated with *taxes* attributable to income from *possessions* (§936). See *recapture, foreign extraction losses; separate basket loss recapture provision.*

recapture income, charitable contributions   income that would ordinarily be treated as *long-term capital gain*, but is treated instead as *ordinary income*, e.g., because of one of the following *recapture* rules: (1) *depreciation* or *cost recovery* of *personal* or *real property*; (2) farm losses on *disposition* of *farm recapture property*; (3) *development expenditures deducted* under §617; or (4) *intangible drilling and development costs*. While *charitable contributions* do not trigger recapture, the amount of the *taxpayer's* contribution is reduced to the extent of this phantom recapture. §170(e)(1)(A).

recapture income, installment sales   the dollar amount which would be reported as *ordinary income* as a result of *section 1245* or *section 1250 recapture* for the year of the *installment sale* if all payments were received in the year of the *installment sale*. §453(i)(1). Such amounts are *ordinary income* in the year of an *installment sale*, (and added to *basis*) with only the balance treated as being received reported on the *installment method. Id.* The effect is often instant recapture in an *installment sale* with no corresponding cash.

recapture, intangible drilling and development costs   the *recapture* as *ordinary income* of *gains* attributable to the *disposition* (including the *sale, exchange, involuntary conversion*, or *other disposition*) of an oil, gas, or geothermal *property* which was the subject of currently deducted *intangible drilling and development costs* (IDCs). §1254. The amount subject to recapture is the amount of the IDCs deducted under §263(c) which, but for the *deduction*, would be reflected in the *adjusted basis* of the *property*, less the amount by which *depletion* would be increased if they had been *capitalized* rather than currently deducted.

recapture, investment credit the effect of a *disposition* or cessation of qualifying use of *section 38 property* prior to the expiration of the *useful life* or *recovery period* on which the *investment tax* credit was based. §50. In such cases, the *taxpayer* incurs a debt to the United States equal to the portion of the credit claimed, which, with the benefit of hindsight, turned out to be excessive. For example, if *five-year recovery property* that costs $10,000 was the subject of a full claim (generating a $1,000 credit), but was disposed of after three years of use, then 40 percent of the credit ($400) must be recaptured (i.e., repaid to the Treasury).

recapture, leaseback or long-term agreement a reference to §467(c), which may cause *recapture* of *gain* on the *disposition* of *property* subject to a leaseback or long-term lease as *ordinary income*. It arises where the prior transfer was not a *disqualified leaseback or long-term agreement* because it was not designed to avoid taxes. The details are complex, but the basic idea is to punish *taxpayers* by forcing them to recapture would-be *capital gains as ordinary income* on the lessor's dispositions of leased property with increasing future rents. The system applies to so-called *section 467 rental agreements*. Such recapture occurs and to the extent that taxpayers eluded the *rent-leveling provisions* and instead accrued rents on a *discounted present value* basis, the difference between the methods being called the *prior unstated inclusion*. §467(c)(2), (3). For example, assume property subject to a long-term lease has a basis of $4 million and is sold for $5 million; therefore, *gain* realized is $1 million. Assume a $700,000 excess for the amount that would have been accrued under constant rental accrual over the amount that was actually reported as income, and that *ACRS* recapture is $200,000. The amount recaptured as ordinary income (called the recapture amount) is $700,000, which is the lesser of the *gain realized,* reduced by other recapture ($1 million minus $200,000), or the prior unstated inclusion of $700,000.

recapture, LIFO inventories various provisions that force *recapture* of the tax benefits of use of the *last-in, first-out* (LIFO) inventory method. Section 336(f)(1) forced *corporations* that made *liquidating distributions* of assets reported on the LIFO method to treat the additional *inventory amount* resulting from use of LIFO as opposed to the *first-in, first-out* (FIFO) method (the LIFO *recapture amount*) as a *gain*. See also §1363(d)(4) (five-year recapture of LIFO method on conversion to *S corporation*. The term is also referred to as involving the recapture of LIFO reserves.

recapture, mining development expenditures the operation of §1254(a), which has the effect of taxing as *ordinary income* the portion of the *gain* on the *disposition* of a mineral property with respect to prior *deductions* that would otherwise have had to have been *capitalized.* Only post-1986 properties are affected. See *section 1254 recapture.*

recapture, mining exploration expenditures one of several *recapture* provisions by which certain *expenditures* for exploring for minerals, other than oil and gas, which were optionally *deducted* under §617(a), are recaptured as *ordinary income* when the mine reaches the *producing stage* or is sold. §617(b) through (d). The mechanics of the provision compel the miner either (1) to elect to include in income the *adjusted exploration expenditures* chargeable to the mine, which were previously *deducted,* simultaneously increasing the *basis* of the property by the amount so reported as income, and later recovering the recaptured amount through *depletion deductions*; or (2) to forgo *depletion* until deductions so forgone are equal to the adjusted exploration expenditures previously deducted. To the extent that expenditures are not recaptured by either of these methods, they are recaptured on the *sale* or *other disposition* of the mining property. Such alternate recapture is similar to the recapture system applicable to recapture of *depreciation* deductions under §§1245 and 1250. In addition, §1254 forces recapture of *gains* as *ordinary income* to the extent they would have been part of basis if not deducted. See *section 1254 recapture.*

recapture, soil, water conservation, and land clearing expenditures a technique imposed by §1252, the effect of which is to tax *sales* of certain farm land as *ordinary income*. It arises where land is sold before 10 years have elapsed since the year in which *deductible soil and water conservation expenditures* (§175) and *land clearing expense* (former §182) was claimed. Recapture in interim years declines annually.

recapture year the *taxable year* in which *section 38 property*, the *basis* or cost of which was taken into account when a *taxpayer's qualified investment* was computed, is *disposed of* or otherwise ceases to be §38 property. Reg. §1.47-1(1)(ii)(B). The term relates to *recapture* of the *investment tax credit*. See *recapture, investment tax credit.*

receding of the face doctrine a tax law doctrine to the effect that *expenditures* for equipment that would ordinarily have to be *capitalized* may be currently *deducted,* if incurred to maintain the normal output of a mine, solely by virtue of the recession of the working face of the mine. Such expenditures are currently *deductible,* only if they cannot (1) increase the value of the mine; (2) decrease the cost of producing mineral units; or (3) represent amounts expended in restoring property for which earlier allowance is or has been made. Reg. §1.612-2(a). The rationale is that if such costs were *capitalized,* mining costs would rise as the face of the mine receded, resulting in a *distortion of income.*

recently purchased stock   *stock* of a *target company* bought within the 12-month *acquisition period* to which §338 relates. §338(b)(6)(A). Such stock is used to "gross up" the value of assets (in the typical case) of the target in the hands of the acquiring company as a result of a deemed *purchase* of the target's assets. See §338(a)(2) and (b). *"Nonrecently purchased stock"* (stock not acquired in the 12-month acquisition period) is excluded from the gross-up calculation (but is instead added dollar-for-dollar in determination of asset basis) unless the acquiring *corporation* makes a special election. See §338(b)(2) and (5) and Reg. §1.338-4T. Note that target company liabilities are included in the gross-up. See *section 338(b)(3) election.*

recipient, employee leasing   someone who receives services from another *individual* who is leased to the recipient. §414(n)(1). It includes all members of a *controlled group of corporations,* using a 50 percent standard for control, and people who are considered related under §267 or §707(b), as well as persons who must be aggregated under §414(b)-(c), (m), and (o). §414(n)(6)(B). See *employee leasing.*

reciprocal exemption, transportation   see *transportation income.*

recognition   taking into account for the purposes of federal *income tax* reporting. §1001(c). Compare *recognition* with *realization,* which involves economically incurred *gains* and *losses* of which *recognized gains* and losses are a subset. For example, *tax-free exchanges* of *like-kind property* frequently involve substantial realized *gains,* none of which are currently recognized.

recognition period, neutrality principle   the five-year period beginning on the *change date.* §382(h)(7)(A). If the *old loss corporation* has *net unrealized built-in loss,* any such *loss which is recognized* within the *recognition period* is treated as a *pre-change loss* and, as such, is subject to the *section 382 limitation,* but if a loss corporation has *net unrealized built-in gain,* the section 382 limitation is increased by any such *gain recognized* within the recognition period (i.e., in any so-called *recognition period taxable year*). This same term is used for purposes of the *preacquisition loss limits* of §384, except that it uses the term "*acquisition date,*" not change date. See §384(c)(4).

recognition period, S corporation   the 10-year period following conversion from *C corporation* to *S corporation* status. See *built-in gain tax, S corporation; recognized built-in gain, S corporation.*

recognition period taxable year, neutrality principle   any *taxable year* or portion thereof which falls in the five-year *recognition period.* §382(h)(7)(B). A variant of this term is also used in §384 in connection with the *preacquisition loss limits.*

recognition property   any *property* as to which a *corporation* would have *recognized gain* if it had transferred the property in a *current* or *liquidating distribution* or if it had disposed of the property in a liquidating *sale* governed by §337. Former §336(c). It includes property covered by a statutory exception to these *nonrecognition provisions* of *subchapter C* (e.g., *recapture*) or by an overriding judicial doctrine such as the *tax benefit rule.* A *current* or *liquidating distribution* or a liquidating *sale* of a *partnership interest* is treated as a direct distribution (or *sale*) by the corporation, of its proportionate share of the "recognition property" of the partnership, thereby closing a loophole under which partnership interests could be distributed without attracting the *collapsible partnership rules* of §751. See §§311(a), (b)(3) and 336.

recognize   see *recognition.*

recognized built-in gain, neutrality principle   any *gain recognized* on the *disposition* of an asset during the five-year *recognition period,* if the *new loss corporation* establishes that the asset was held by the *old loss corporation* immediately before the *change date,* to the extent the *gain* does not exceed the excess of the *fair market value* of such asset on the change date over the *adjusted basis* of the asset on that date. §382(h)(2)(A). It includes items of income (e.g., preacquisition *accounts receivable*) economically accrued prior to the change date. §382(h)(6)(A). Recognized built-in gains are included in the *section 382 limitation*—a pro-*taxpayer* result—in determination of the amount of post-*ownership change losses* that the *loss corporation* can report during the recognition period. §382(h)(1)(A). The *anti-stuffing rule* prevents loading up the loss corporation with gain assets so as to avoid the section 382 limitation. See *neutrality principle; preacquisition loss limits.*

recognized built-in gain, preacquisition loss limits   any *gain recognized,* in the five-year *recognition period* that follows acquisition of a *gain corporation* or its assets, on the *disposition* of any asset, except to the extent it is shown that (1) the asset was not held by the gain corporation on the *acquisition* date; or (2) the gain is greater than the asset's built-in gain on that date. §384(c)(1)(A). Other income items that have economically *accrued* before the acquisition date are swept in as well by §338(c)(1)(B). Section 338(c)(1)(C) goes on to provide that built-in gains for any *recognition period taxable year* cannot exceed the *net unrealized built-in gain,* less the recognized built-in gains for earlier years in the recognition period that would otherwise have been offset by *preacquisition losses.* The core idea of §384 is to prevent a corporation from using its preacquisition losses to shelter the built-in gains of a *gain corporation* (usually the target) which are recognized in the five-year period following the acquisition or the gain corporation's stock or assets from offsetting the acquiror's preacquisition losses. §384(a). See *net unrealized built-in gain, preacquisition loss limits.*

recognized built-in gain, S corporation all *gain* that is *recognized* on the *disposition* of any asset during the 10-year *recognition period* following the making of an *S election,* except to the extent the corporation establishes that it did not own the asset at the time of the election, or that the recognized gain exceeds the built-in gain at the time of the election. §1374(d)(2). It includes income (such as collection of *accounts receivable* by *cash method taxpayers*) arising on the relinquishment or disposal of claims or rights that arose before the recognition period. This is the base on which the potentially onerous *built-in gains tax* falls. It can be avoided if the corporation patiently waits out the post-election decade. See *built-in gain tax, S corporation.*

recognized built-in loss, neutrality principle any *loss recognized* on the *disposition* of an asset during the *recognition period,* if the *taxpayer* establishes that the asset was held by the *old loss corporation* immediately before the *change date,* or that the loss exceeds the excess of the asset's *adjusted basis* on the change date over its *fair market value* on that date. §338(h)(2)(B). It includes *deductions* economically *accrued* before the change dates as well as *depreciation, depletion,* and *amortization* allowable in the recognition period with respect to built-in loss property. These losses are treated as losses subject to the *section 382 limitation* under the *neutrality principle,* to the extent the corporation had net unrealized built-in losses. See §338(h)(2)(B)(i). This same term is used for purposes of the *preacquisition loss limits* of §384, except that it uses the term *acquisition date,* not *change date.* See §384(c)(4). See *neutrality principle.*

recognized built-in loss, S corporation the converse of the concept *recognized built-in gain, S corporation.* See §1374(d)(4).

recognized gains and losses *gains* and *losses* that are *realized* and are not shielded from having an immediate tax impact as a result of some exception. §1001(c). Examples of statutory exceptions that bar current *recognition* are §§1031 (tax-deferred *like-kind exchanges*) and 354 (tax-deferred *corporate reorganizations*). All realized gains and losses are presumptively subject to immediate recognition. §1001(c).

recomputed basis for purposes of determining the amount of *gain* on the *disposition* of an asset that is subject to *recapture* as *ordinary income,* the term means the *adjusted basis* of the asset, adding back *depreciation, cost recovery,* or *amortization,* which was *allowed or allowable* since 1961, unless §1245(a)(3) specifies a different date. §1245(a)(1). If the *taxpayer* can show that the amounts allowed were less than the

amounts allowable, then the only amounts actually allowed reduce *basis*; this rule avoids confiscatory application of §1245. Section 1245 applies to *personal property,* as well as to certain *real estate.* To take a simple example, if a taxpayer bought a car for business use in 1992 at a price of $10,000 and wrote it off to zero over three years, the recomputed basis is $10,000. All *sales* proceeds up to $10,000 would, in such a case, be recaptured and therefore treated as ordinary income rather than as *capital gains.*

reconstruction of income the determination of a *taxpayer's* income in the absence of adequate *books and records.* The *IRS* uses various means to reach such inferences, such as the *bank deposit method,* the *net worth method,* and the *cash flow method.* Reconstruction of income issues are especially prevalent in *civil* and *criminal fraud* cases.

records, foreign corporate reporting books, papers, or other data. §§6038A(c); 6038C(e).

recoupment, equitable see *equitable recoupment.*

recourse debt synonymous with *recourse liability.*

recourse liabilities, partnership taxation in general, *liabilities* as to which a *partner* is personally liable. They are discerned by one's assuming that the partnership's assets are worthless, all debts are due and payable, and the partnership dumps all its assets in a taxable transaction for no consideration and to search for liabilities for which partners have responsibility. See Reg. 1.704-1T(a)(1). See *liability, partnership taxation.*

recourse liability *debt* for which the borrower or owner of property securing the debt is personally liable. For the *allocation* of *partnership* liabilities to particular *partners,* see Reg. §1.752-5. For the antonym, see *nonrecourse liabilities.*

recoverable units generally, the number of units (e.g., tons, pounds, ounces, or barrels) of minerals, oil, or gas in the ground and economically worth extracting, estimated according to the best available information and industry standards. Reg. §1.611-2(c). *Cost depletion* turns on estimating recoverable units. Revisions are allowed. §611(a); Reg. §1.611-2(c)(2).

recovery the return to, or recoupment by, a *taxpayer* of amounts previously *deducted.* Generally, such amounts are taxable to *taxpayers,* subject to the *exclusion* provided by §111. The absence of an actual recovery no longer bars application of the *tax benefit rule.* See *recovery exclusion; tax benefit rule.*

recovery exclusion an element of §111, which assures that *taxpayers* will not be treated as being in receipt of income to the extent that a prior expenditure did not reduce *gross income* or taxable income. For example, assume that in 1992 a couple had a medical deduction of $100 because medical expenses exceeded $7\frac{1}{2}$ percent of AGI. If the couple itemized in 1992 and received a $300 medical reimbursement in 1993, only $100 would be includible in AGI since they benefitted in 1992 by obtaining a $100 deduction. If the couple had taken a standard deduction in 1992, none of the $300 reimbursement would have been taxable in 1993.

recovery of capital   a far-reaching concept, the gist of which is that a *taxpayer* should not be viewed as having *gross income* until the original investment is recovered, using the taxpayer's *basis of property* as the investment, and *amounts realized* as the measure of the repayment. Regulation §1.1001-1(a) suggests the generality. In fact, the tax law takes highly varied positions on this issue. For example, under the general tax rules concerning *annuities, gain* is taxed well before capital is recovered. §453. The *open transaction* doctrine clearly reflects the concept, as does the repayment of *debt,* subject, however, to §§483 (*unstated interest*) and 1232 (*original issue discount*).

recovery period   an element of the *accelerated cost recovery system (ACRS).* The ACRS allows recovery of capital costs for most tangible depreciable property through use of accelerated methods of cost recovery over predetermined periods. It applies to property placed in service after 1980 but before 1987. Generally, property placed in service after 1986 must use the modified accelerated cost recovery system (MACRS). The ACRS system allows repaid recovery of an asset's cost through use of fixed recovery schedules over prescribed statutory periods. §168. The MACRS rules retain many of the original ACRS rules. There are, however, differences between the recovery periods under ACRS and MACRS. Assets that qualify for the ACRS and MACRS are called "*recovery property*" and include most *tangible depreciable property.* See *recovery property.*

recovery property   *tangible property* acquired after 1980 from unrelated persons that is of a *character subject to depreciation* and either used in a *trade or business* or *held for the production of income.* §168(a),(f). Such property is classed into one of eight categories and attributed fixed *recovery periods* over which it can be written off (i.e., the cost can be recovered) without regard to *salvage values.* Certain property is excluded, especially property written off on a method not involving the passage of time (e.g., mileage), certain *public utility property,* and property received in *tax-free exchanges* as well as from certain related parties. Most films and videotapes are not recovery property, but *qualified films* and videotapes could formerly earn an *investment tax credit* and qualify for *ACRS* treatment. *Sound recordings* could qualify electively. §48(r). See *accelerated cost recovery system (ACRS); anti-churning rules; recovery period.*

recreational clubs   see *social club.*

recurring item exception   an exception to the *economic performance requirement* which permits *taxpayers* other than most *tax shelters* to accrue a *deduction* before economic performance where four basic requirements are met: (1) the *all events test* with respect to an item is met during the *taxable year*; (2) economic performance occurs with respect to the item within the shorter of a reasonable period following the close of the *taxable year* or eight and one-half months after the close of the taxable year; (3) the item is recurring in nature and the taxpayer has to consistently treat items of the kind as incurred in the taxable year in which the events test is met; and, (4) either the item is not material or the *accrual* of the item in the taxable year in which the all events test is met must more properly match the item against the income that it generated than would accrual of the item in the taxable year in which economic performance takes place. §461(c)(3). Materiality of the *expense* is determined by taking into account the size of the item, in absolute terms and relative to the taxpayer's income and other expenses. When the propriety of the matching of income to expenses is considered, generally accepted accounting principles are important but noncontrolling. When one determines whether an item is recurring in nature and treated consistently by the taxpayer, the frequency with which the item occurs and the way which it is reported for tax purposes should be considered. See *matching concept, accounting.*

redeem   the act of engaging in a *redemption.*

redeemable ground rents   a state law characterization of a *real estate* practice used in Maryland, Virginia, and Pennsylvania, which in substance amounts to a mortgage. §1055; Reg. §1.1055-1 through -4. In this analysis, the *real property* subject to the ground rent is viewed as held subject to a *mortgage.* Reg. §1.163-1(b) renders ground rent payments *deductible* as *interest* and amounts paid to redeem a ground rent as nondeductible *capitalized* cost of acquiring title to a property.

redemption   the process by which an *entity* purchases an owner's interest. See *liquidation, partnership interest; stock redemption.*

redemption by affiliated corporations   a *shareholder's sale* or *exchange* of one *corporation* to another corporation, which is analyzed as a *stock redemption* under §§302, 303, 304. The *exchange* can involve either *brother-sister corporations* (when one or more shareholders are in control of each of the corporations and a parent-subsidiary relationship is not present) (§304(a)(1)), or a *parent* corporation and its *subsidiary* corporation (§304(a)(2)). *Example 1:* Zee owns all 100 shares of stock of X and Y Corporations. Zee sells 40 shares of X's stock to Y Corporation for $10,000. The net result of this transaction is that Zee has received a

$10,000 cash distribution from Y Corporation and Zee still has control of both corporations. *Example 2:* Caroline owns all 100 shares of the Parent Corporation. Caroline sells 40 shares of Parent Corporation to Subsidiary Corporation for $10,000. The net result of this transaction is that Zee has received a $10,000 cash distribution from Y Corporation and Zee still has control of both corporations. Section 304 requires that a sale of stock of one controlled corporation to a second controlled corporation be treated as a *stock redemption*. Where §§304 and 351 (transfers to *controlled corporations*) overlap, §351 controls only as to the stock-for-stock element of the transaction, plus debt incurred to acquire stock of the contributed company and transferred to the transferee corporation. This closed a popular loophole under which taxpayers "contributed" stock and took back cash. §§304(b)(3), 351(f)(5). Also, the tax-free corporate reorganization rules preempt the redemption rules of §304 where they overlap. §304(b)(3)(A), as amended. See *stock redemption; acquisition indebtedness exception.*

redemption costs, qualified discount coupons   with respect to any coupon: (1) the lesser of the amount of the discount provided by the terms of the coupon, or the amount incurred by the *taxpayer* for paying such discount; plus (2) the amount incurred by the taxpayer for a payment to the retailer (or other person redeeming the coupon from the person receiving the price discount), but only if the amount so payable is stated on the coupon. §466(c)(1). Section 466(a) grants *accrual method* taxpayers a favorable *deduction* for redemption costs associated with *qualified discount coupons.*

redemption in complete termination of shareholder's interest   a *complete stock redemption* which eliminates the *shareholder's* proprietary interest in a *corporation*; it is treated for tax purposes as a *sale* of *stock* rather than a *distribution* of money or property. §302(b)(3). It may occur in stages. PLR 8204159 (Oct. 20, 1981). In determining whether all the shareholder's stock has been completely redeemed, the *attribution rules* of §318(a) apply, but the attribution rules relating to stock owned by family members may be waived under the complex rules of §302(c)(2). See *stock redemption; waiver of family attribution rules.*

redemption not essentially equivalent to a dividend   a *stock redemption* that is treated as an exchange rather than a *distribution* of money or property. §302(b)(1). The same standard is applied under §356 (*boot* in acquisitive *corporate reorganizations*) by analogizing the *boot* received in such transactions to amounts received in a redemption. Whether a redemption is not essentially equivalent to a distribution depends on *all facts and circumstances* of such redemption. Although a redemption can be classified as not essentially equivalent to a dividend as a result of various distinct transac-

tions, the underlying principle is that the redemption must result in a meaningful reduction of the *shareholder's* proportionate interest in the corporation.

redemption of stock to pay death taxes   a caption describing §303. Section 303 provides that when a portion of the *stock* held in the *gross estate* of a *decedent* (or stock included in the decedent's estate but held by other persons) in a *corporation* is redeemed, *distribution* treatment is avoided (i.e., the *redemption* is treated as an *exchange,* not a distribution) if the value of decedent's stock equals at least 35 percent of the decedent's *adjusted gross estate.* However, only the amount of the redemption proceeds payable to the decedent's estate up to the amount of the estate's *inheritance,* succession, and *estate taxes* (which includes the *federal estate tax* and *interest* on death taxes), *funeral expenses,* and *administration expenses* are given automatic *exchange* treatment. For purposes of meeting the 35 percent test, business interests can be aggregated if the decedent alone or the decedent and the decedent's *spouse,* as *community property* or in *joint tenancy, tenancy in common,* or a *tenancy by the entirety* owned 20 percent or more of two or more *corporations.* Because §1014 gives the stock a *basis* equal to its *fair market value* at death, the redemption should be tax-free to the redeemed estate or other *taxpayer.* See *adjusted gross estate; stock redemption.*

redemption period, qualified discount coupons   generally, the six-month period immediately following the close of the *taxable* year, unless the *taxpayer* selects a shorter period. Any change in the redemption period is treated as a *change of accounting method.* §466(c)(2). Costs associated with *qualified discount coupons* outstanding at year-end and redeemed within the redemption period may be *deducted* by *accrual method* taxpayers. §446(a). See *redemption costs, qualified discount coupons; redemption reserves.*

redemption premium   a payment for the redemption of *stock* (usually preferred stock) in excess of the issue price of the stock. Redemption premiums may result in taxable *distributions* to redeeming *shareholders* under §305(c). See especially §305(c)(3), which affects unreasonable redemption premiums by permitting the issuance of *regulations* which use *original issue discount* principles over the period that the stock is outstanding.

redemption reserves   obligations to make payments to satisfy their trading stamp and premium coupons. *Accrual method* taxpayers who sell such stamps and coupons to merchants, as well as the merchants and manufacturers themselves, may deduct the cost of merchandise, cash, and property they use to redeem stamps and coupons, along with an addition to the reserve for future expenses associated with coming redemptions. Reg. §1.451-4(a). See *trading stamp company.*

redetermination the activity of the *Tax Court* in increasing or decreasing a *deficiency* assessed against a *taxpayer*.

redevelopment purposes the application of *net proceeds* of a *qualified redevelopment* bond used to finance improvements in *designated blighted areas*. The purposes are (1) acquisition of realty in a designated blighted area by a government with a power of eminent domain; (2) land clearing in such areas for redevelopment; (3) rehabilitation of such acquired property or property otherwise owned by the government unit; and (4) relocation of occupants. However, the proceeds cannot be used to build new buildings or to enlarge or improve existing ones. §144(c)(3). If the proceeds are properly used for redevelopment purposes, then a bond may be a *qualified redevelopment* bond whose *interest* is not taxable to the holder, despite the fact that the bond is otherwise a *private activity bond*. See *qualified bond; tax-exempt bond*.

reduced normal retirement benefits the benefit to which a *participant* would have been entitled under the plan at *normal retirement age*, reduced in accordance with reasonable actuarial standards. Reg. §1.401 (a)-14(c)(2).

reduced to practice a term used in connection with §1235, referring to the time when a patented item begins its *holding period*. It occurs when the invention has been tested and operated successfully under operating conditions, but not later than when commercial exploitation begins. The benefit of §1235 is that it makes it possible to generate *long-term capital gains* from broad royalty arrangements. See *all substantial rights to a patent*.

reduction for estate tax a reference to both (1) *deductions* from *gross income* for federal *estate taxes* attributable to the inclusion in the *gross estate* of an item of *income in respect of a decedent* (taxable as income of the person reporting the income); and (2) a deduction for the *generation-skipping transfer tax* (and associated state taxes). §691(c). Not to allow this deduction would result in inordinate multiple taxation.

reduction in purchase price, income see *purchase price adjustment*.

reduction of salvage value, election a reference to §167(f), which allows *taxpayers* to elect to reduce the *salvage value* of *personal property* with an estimated *useful life* of three years or more by 10 percent of the *basis* of the property. The election is irrelevant to §168 (*cost recovery*), under which no salvage value is used.

re-employment commencement date, qualified plans the first day after a *one-year break in service,* an *employee* is entitled to be credited with an *hour of service* for duties performed after the first *eligibility* computation period following an eligibility computation period in which he or she is credited with more than 500 hours of service (or a shorter period in the case of the maritime industry). Labor Reg. §2530.200b-4(b)(1)(ii). The date is used for purposes of determining eligibility to participate in *qualified plans*.

reference price in general, the average per-*barrel* wellhead price for domestic crude oil during a *calendar year* as determined by the *IRS*. The term is used for purposes of the *enhanced oil recovery credit* and *percentage depletion* rate for *marginal production* and for purposes of the *credit for producing fuels from nonconventional sources*. §§613A(c)(6)(C), 29(d)(2)(C), and 43(b)(2).

reference written determination one of two types of *written determinations* that the *IRS* may issue in the form of a *ruling, determination letter,* or *technical advice memorandum*. §6110(b)(1). The IRS considers such determinations, unlike *general written determinations,* to be valuable references and may be the basis for a published *revenue ruling*. If such a determination is used as the basis for a revenue ruling, it will remain as a reference written determination until the revenue ruling becomes ineffective. Although the IRS must keep all reference written determinations and related materials, it may reclassify them as general written determinations if they do not become the basis of a revenue ruling, which are subject to being discarded earlier than reference written determination materials. Reg. §301.6110-2.

referral report a report prepared by a *revenue agent* on Form 2797 ("Referral Report for Potential Fraud Cases") which refers a case to the *Criminal Investigation Division* of the *IRS* for possible treatment as a *criminal fraud* case.

refinancing the practice of borrowing against encumbered property. Refinancing generally does not create *gross income*. Refinancing can increase the interest to principal ratio of loan payments or permit the extraction of cash with no taxable *gain*.

refiner, depletion a *person* whose refinery, on any day during the *taxable year,* exceeds 50,000 *barrels*. §614A(d)(4). The exemption accorded to *independent producers and royalty owners* by §614(c) is inapplicable to refiners; hence, they cannot benefit from *percentage depletion* of oil and gas. See *percentage depletion; small producers' exemption*.

reforestation credit a reforestation credit of 10 percent of the amortizable basis of qualified timber property acquired during the year. §48(b)(1). This basis has to be reduced by the reforestation expenditure deduction under Section 192. §§48(b), 194. See *reforestation expenditures*.

reforestation expenditures direct costs of planting or seeding for reforestation or forestation purposes, including site preparation, costs of seeds or seedlings, hand tools, and *depreciation* on reforestation equipment. §194(c)(3)(A). Such expenditures incurred in connection with *qualified timber property* create a so-called amortizable *basis,* which can be written off for 84 months under §194(a). Expenditures incurred in connection with *qualified timber property* can be the basis for a *reforestation credit.* If such costs are reimbursed by the government, then they may be *amortized* only if the *taxpayer* included such reimbursements in *gross income.* §194(c)(3)(B). See *reforestation credit.*

refund a remittance of overpaid taxes to the *taxpayer.* They are commonly triggered by a *claim for refund or credit* filed within the time limits imposed by §6511(a).

refundable credit a *credit* that can reduce tax liabilities to a negative amount. The effect is to render the refunded negative amount into an outright subsidy, not merely an elimination of the tax liabilities (namely, the *credit for withholding on wages, the earned income credit,* the *credit for withholding of tax at source,* the *credit for certain uses of gasoline and special fuels,* and *credit for overpayment of tax*).

refund annuities *annuities* containing a feature that assures that the annuitant will recover at least the *investment in the contract,* either to the annuitant during his or her lifetime, or in part to the annuitant during life, with the balance to some other identified person after death. Such refunds may be treated as recovery of the investment in the contract under §101 or §72(e), but the tax burden is a reduced *exclusion ratio,* based on actuarial analyses. Reg. §§1.72-5 and -11.

refund bond a bond that is issued to pay off an outstanding bond. *State and local bonds* that are refund bonds are subject to special limitations. See, *qualified small issue bond*; *refunding issue.*

refund feature see *refund annuities.*

refunding bond a bond that is part of a *refunding issue.*

refunding issue obligations issued to refund prior obligations. Section 146(i) generally provides that, for purposes of the *state volume cap,* a *private activity bond* does not include a refunding issue which is not larger than the refunded issue. That favorable generalization is not available for advance refunding (i.e., refunding in advance of need) and is subject to maturity restrictions in the case of *student loan bonds* and *qualified mortgage bonds.* §146(i)(2)-(4). See *state volume cap.* A *private activity bond* does not include a bond that refunds another (refunded) bond. This does not apply to *advance refunding issues.*

refund or credit devices by which *taxpayers* may recover overpaid taxes. A *refund* is a repayment (cash);

a *credit* is used as a reduction of future tax liabilities. See *claim for refund or credit.*

refund suits see *suit for refund.*

Regional Appeals Officer see *Appeals Office.*

Regional Counsel an intermediate layer of attorneys sandwiched between the Office of the *Chief Counsel* of the *IRS* in Washington D.C., and the local *District Counsels,* in particular *District Offices* of the IRS. The Regional Counsel supervises District Counsels and has staffs engaged in criminal tax litigation, general litigation, and tax litigation.

Regional Counsel conference a conference between the *taxpayer* (or *taxpayer representative*) and a representative of the *Regional Counsel* at which there is an opportunity to review the case prior its being handed on to the *Department of Justice.* The conference does not occur if the case has been assigned to the United States Attorney. See Reg. §601.107(c). See *Justice conference.*

Regional Director of Appeals an *IRS* officer who is in charge of the administration of tax appeals for the office's IRS Region. See *Regional Office.*

Regional Inspector see *Office of Regional Inspector.*

Regional Office one of seven *IRS* field organizations (Southeast, North Atlantic, Midwest, Central, Southwest, Mid-Atlantic, and Western), headed by a Regional Commissioner who exercises authority over numerous *District Offices.* The function of the office is to implement national revenue programs and policies, to coordinate and direct the District Offices, and to administer tax appeals arising in the region.

regional pollution control authorities a *political subdivision,* created by state law to control air or water pollution, that operates air or water *pollution control facilities* and contains within its jurisdictional boundaries all or part of at least two counties or equivalent political subdivisions. Former §103(b)(11)(C). Interest on *industrial development bonds* was tax-exempt if substantially all the proceeds of the issue were used by such authorities to acquire pollution control facilities. See generally *industrial development bond.*

regional prototype plan a *defined benefit plan* or a *defined contribution plan* that is made available by a regional sponsor (professional firm) for adoption by *employers.* It is part of a system outlined in Rev. Proc. 89-13, 1989-7 I.R.B. 25 that the *IRS* has designed to accelerate approval of cookie-cutter-style *qualified plans.* The plan consists of an adoption agreement containing elective provisions that the employer does or does not accept in adopting the plan, a basic plan document (containing the nonelective provisions), and (absent a *trust* or *custodial account* in the plan document), a trust or custodial account agreement. See Form 4461.

registered form bond   generally, a bond that states on its face that the debtor is obligated only to the person duly registered on its books as creditor, and that any unregistered transfer is invalid. The *Code* does not contain a definition of the term "*registered form*"; presumably, the *Gerard* meaning applies. Authorities cited in RIA Fed. See also Reg. §1.453-3(a) for the requirements in connection with *installment sales* under prior law. *TEFRA* added various registration requirements. See, e.g., §163(f)(2)(B). For purposes of mandatory registration, something is in registered form if (1) its transfer can be effected by surrender of the old instrument to the issuer followed by either a new issuance or a reissuance; or (2) rights to principal and interest can be transferred only through a book-entry system used to record ownership. See *registration-required obligation.*

registered historic district   any district (1) located in the National Register of Historic Places; or (2) designated under a statute of the appropriate state or local government if the statute is certified by the Secretary of the Interior as containing criteria that will substantially achieve the purpose of preserving and rehabilitating buildings of historic significance to the district, and which is certified by the Secretary of the Interior as meeting substantially all the requirements for listing districts in the National Register. §47(c)(3)(B). Structures located in such districts can qualify for the most generous form of *rehabilitation credit.*

registration of tax shelters   a reference to the requirements of §6111(a) that *tax shelter organizers* register *tax shelters* by notification to the *IRS* where the *tax shelter ratio* is 2:1 or greater and certain other conditions are met. Section 6707 imposes substantial penalties for noncompliance. The IRS in turn assigns an identification (registration) number which is turned over to investors for use in reporting the results of the shelter. See *tax shelter, registration.*

registration-required bond   any bond other than one which is not of a type offered to the public, has a maturity of over a year, or a *registration-required obligation.* §149(a). Any such bond will not be tax-exempt under §103(a) or any other provision of law unless it is in *registered form. Id.* There is a limited exception for federally guaranteed bonds. §143(b). See *registered form bond; tax-exempt bond; state or local bond.*

registration-required obligation   any obligation, including one issued by a governmental *entity,* which is of a type offered to the public, with a maturity at the date of issue of more than one year. The term excludes any obligation issued by an *individual.* The term also excludes any obligation reasonably designed to ensure

sale (or resale in connection with the original issue) only to a person who is not a *United States person,* and which, if not in registered form (1) yields *interest* payable only outside the United States and its *possessions*; and (2) bears a statement on its face that any United States person who holds it will be subject to limitations under United States income tax laws. §163(f)(2)(A) and (B). The *Treasury Department* may include, by *regulations,* other obligations of a type used frequently in avoiding federal taxes. §163(f)(2)(C). See *registered form bond; targeted offshore offering.*

regular corporation   a term often used informally to describe *corporations* that are neither *S corporations* nor *closely held corporations.*

regular interest, REMIC   an interest in a *real estate mortgage investment conduit (REMIC).* The interest must be issued on the *start-up day*; must entitle the investor to receive unconditionally a specified principal amount and *interest* payments, if any, at a fixed rate (or a variable rate as provided in regulations) or shares in certain mortgages whose rate does not fluctuate during the period under scrutiny; and must be designated as a regular interest. §860G(a)(1). Regular interests are taxed as if they were *debt* instruments, with interest on the underlying obligations *accrued* daily. §860B.

regularly traded, branch profits tax   a reference to *stock* that trades on an established securities market in specified volume (i.e., at least 30 percent of the outstanding securities trade during the year) and with specified frequency (i.e., the securities regularly traded) if they trade on an established securities market in specified volume (i.e., at least 30 percent of the outstanding securities trade during the year) and with specified frequency (i.e., the securities trade on at least 60 days during the year). Reg. §1.884-5T(d)(4). The term is used in connection with determining if the publicly traded corporation is a *qualified resident* of the *foreign* country. The term is valuable because it is a rare case of when "regularly traded"—a term that recurs throughout the Code—is actually defined.

regular net tax liability   *regular tax liability* less *nonrefundable credits.* §38(c)(2). The term is used as part of a computation of the limitation on *general business credits.* The general business credit may not exceed net income tax less the greater of (a) the tentative minimum tax or (b) 25 percent of net regular tax liability above $25,000. §38(c)(1). Net income tax is the sum of the regular tax and the alternative minimum tax (AMT). §§26, 55.

regular tax, alternative minimum tax   the *regular tax liability* (§26(b))—not including *interest* on *deferred* taxes—reduced by the *alternative minimum tax foreign tax credit,* and excluding the tax on *lump-sum distributions* (§402(e)), *recapture* of the *investment* *tax credit,* recapture of the *low-income housing credit,* and disregarding the *possession tax credit.* §55(c)(1). The term is crucial in the setting of the alternative minimum tax (AMT) because only if the *tentative minimum tax* exceeds regular tax is there any AMT liability. See *alternative minimum tax; regular tax liability.*

regular tax liability the *taxpayer's income tax* liability, less the following taxes: (1) the *alternative minimum tax;* (2) the *environmental tax;* (3) certain penalty taxes on *premature distributions* from certain *qualified plans* (§72(m)(5)(B) or (q)), and from *modified endowment contracts* (§72(v)) and the additional tax on income from early distributions from certain *qualified retirement plans* (§72(t)); (4) the tax on *nonqualified withdrawals* from the *capital construction fund;* (5) the *accumulated earnings tax;* (6)the *personal holding company tax;* (7) the tax on certain recoveries of *foreign expropriation losses;* (8) *built-in gain tax* of *S corporations;* (9) the tax on *excess net passive income* of an S corporation; (10) the 30 percent tax on United States source income earned by *nonresident aliens* and *foreign corporations* that is not *effectively connected income;* (11) taxes on transfers of certain *residual interests* in *REMICs;* (12) the *branch profits tax;* (13) *interest,* paid as additional income tax, imposed on the tax deferred by the *installment sales* of *timeshares* and residential lots, and certain installment sales of non*dealer property* in excess of $150,000 (§453A(c)); (14) *recapture tax* on the federal subsidy from use of *qualified mortgage bonds* and *mortgage credit certificates.* §26(b). Regular tax liability less the *tentative minimum tax* (the *alternative minimum tax foreign tax credit* is ignored) sets the limit on the availability of personal *nonrefundable credits* for the taxable year. §26(a). It is also used as a reference in various places, including §383 (restrictions on *tax credits* of acquired *corporations*), *passive loss rules,* and in a modified form for purposes of the *alternative minimum tax.*

regular tax liability, alternative minimum tax the regular *tax liability* that is used for determining the limitation on various *nonrefundable credits* (§26(b), reduced by (1) the regular *foreign tax credit* and the *possession tax credit,* (2) not including (a) the averaging taxes on *lump-sum distributions* from *qualified retirement plans* and (b) any *recapture* of *investment credit.* §55(c). One subtracts regular tax from potential *alternative minimum taxes* by §55(a)(2) to determine the extent to which that tax applies. See *regular tax liability.*

regular tax liability, passive loss rules same as *regular tax liability* under §26(b). §469(j)(3).

regular time hours, qualified plans hours worked in a *bona fide* standard workday, work week, or maximum work week under the Fair Labor Standards Act of 1938, §7(a). Labor Reg. §2530.200b-3(d)(3)(ii). Plans using

this method of counting *hours of service* must treat 750 regular-time hours as 1,000 hours of service and 375 such hours as 500 hours of service. The term is used to determine an *employee's* eligibility to participate in a *qualified plan.*

regular way sale see *trade date.*

regulated futures contract basically, a *commodity futures contract* traded on a commodities exchange, which is subject to being deemed sold at year-end in order to limit tax avoidance. Section 1256(b) defines it as a contract (1) with respect to which the amount required to be deposited and the amount that may be withdrawn depends on a *mark-to-market* system; and (2) that is traded on or subject to the rules of a *domestic* board of trade designated as a contract market by the Commodities Trading Commission or the body which the *IRS* designates under §1256. Such contracts, whether open or closed, are marked-to-market at year-end and are considered *sold* and are treated as being 60 percent *long-term capital gain* or *loss* and 40 percent *short-term capital gain or loss,* as the case may be. Cash delivery contracts are treated as regulated futures contracts, as are *foreign currency contracts. Losses* on these contracts may be *carried back* three years (but not before 1981) and forward indefinitely. §1212.

regulated investment company a *domestic corporation* registered with the SEC under the Investment Company Act of 1940 and some venture companies. §851; Reg. §1.851-1. The basic feature of the elective status is that such companies are taxed only on *undistributed* income. To qualify, the *entity* must derive at least 90 percent of its *gross income* from *dividends, interest,* currency transactions, *capital gains,* and related income from options and futures contracts. Less than 30 percent of its income can be from short-term (less than three months) stock and securities, currency or commodities trading, including commodities futures and forward contracts, as well as unrelated foreign currency gains. §851(b)(2) and (3). In order for the company to be classified as a regulated investment company, an election, which is binding for later years, is required. §851; Reg. §§1.851–11.851-7. See *designated hedge; excise tax; venture capital companies.*

regulated public utility an *entity* categorized in one or more of the following classifications: (1) a *corporation* engaged in furnishing or selling electric energy, gas, water, or sewage disposal services; (2) a corporation engaged as a common carrier in furnishing or selling transportation of gas by pipeline, if subject to the jurisdiction of the Federal Power Commission; (3) a corporation engaged as a common carrier in furnishing or selling transportation by railroad, if subject to the jurisdiction of the Interstate Commerce Commission; (4) a corporation engaged in furnishing or selling telephone or telegraph service, if the rates for such furnishing or selling meet the requirements of (1) above; (5) a corporation engaged in furnishing or selling transportation as a common carrier by air, subject to the jurisdiction of the Civil Aeronautics Board; (6) a corporation engaged in furnishing or selling transportation by common carrier by water, subject to the jurisdiction of the Interstate Commerce Commission, or subject to the jurisdiction of the Federal Maritime Board; (7) a *railroad corporation* subject to part I of the Interstate Commerce Act; and (8) a common *parent corporation* which is a common carrier by railroad subject to part I of the Interstate Commerce Act, if at least 80 percent of its gross income (disregarding capital gains or losses) is derived directly or indirectly from sources described in (1) through (6) herein. There are other detailed requirements. See §§118 (*contributions in aid of construction*), 1503 (affiliated groups).

regulated transportation corporation a *corporation,* 80 percent or more of whose *gross income* is derived from furnishing or selling transportation described in §7701(a)(33)(A) (electric railroads, trackless trolleys, or buses), (C)(i) (ICC-regulated railroad), (E) (CAB-regulated common carriers by air), or (F) (certain ICC-regulated water carriers); or a corporation that is described in §7701(a)(33)(G) (certain railroads) or (H) (certain other railroads); or a corporation that is a member of a regulated transportation system. §172(g)(1). A corporation is a member of a regulated transportation system if it is a member of an *affiliated group* of *corporations* making a *consolidated return,* provided that 80 percent or more of the aggregate gross income of the members of the group is derived from furnishing or selling transportation described in §7701(a)(33)(A), (C)(i), (E), or (F). §172(g)(2).

regulated transportation system see *regulated transportation corporation.*

regulations see *regulations, Treasury administrative and procedural,* for which this is a common shorthand term.

regulations, Treasury administrative and procedural regulations issued by the *Commissioner* of the *IRS,* with the approval of the *Secretary of the Treasury,* pursuant to §7805(b), which authorizes needful *interpretative* and *procedural regulations,* or by a direct grant of quasi-legislative power under some special *Code* section such as §§1501–1502, authorizing the issuance of regulations governing *consolidated returns.* The latter, *legislative regulations,* are virtually unassailable, whereas interpretative regulations are fairly often rejected by the courts, despite the common assertion that they are presumptively correct. Interpretative regulations are not subject to the Administrative Procedure Act, although they are frequently made the subject of comments and hearings, including an opportunity for the SBA to comment. See *interpretative regulations; legislative regulations; procedural regulations.*

rehabilitation credits tax *credits* of (1) 10 percent of *qualified rehabilitation expenditures* for buildings *placed in service* before 1936, and (2) 20 percent for *certified historic structures* regardless of age. §47(a). The building itself must be a *qualified rehabilitated building* as defined in §47(c)(1). Miscellaneous features of the credits are that (1) they cannot be combined with the *energy* or *investment tax credits*; (2) the *straight-line* cost *recovery* election must be made as to the remaining property; (3) only in the case of historic structures can the property be residential; (4) the credit reduces the *basis* in the property; and (5) no credits are allowed for enlargement or acquisition. See *external walls requirement.*

rehabilitation investment credit see *rehabilitation credits.*

rehabilitation percentage the portion of the *investment credit* defined in §46 that arises from rehabilitating *historic property* and certain improved nonresidential realty. See §47. It is part of the *general business credit.*

reimbursed moving expenses a shorthand term for the more cumbersome language of §82. The effect of §82 is to force the inclusion of all *moving expenses* (including those not *deductible* under §217) in the *gross income* of *employees* and *independent contractors* to the extent they were defrayed (directly or by reimbursement) by others. Reg. §1.82-1(a)(5). Because amounts *deductible* under §217(a) must be *included* in the reimbursed person's *gross income,* tax parity arises as between reimbursed and unreimbursed moving expenses, since under prior law such reimbursements were not considered gross income. *Taxpayers* must also include the value of services furnished in kind. Reg. §1.82-1(a)(5).

reimbursement bond another name for a potentially *tax-exempt bond* used to reimburse previously paid expenditures. See Notice 91-28, 1991-36 I.R.B. 52.

reincorporation a transaction in which operating assets of a *putatively liquidated corporation* find their way into the hands of another corporation, with the result that the putative liquidation is disregarded and the overall transaction is treated as some type of *reorganization.* This recharacterization is designed to foil *taxpayers'* attempts to withdraw cash from what are, realistically, ongoing enterprises at *capital gains* rates and also wiping out the *earnings and profits* account achieving a *stepped-up basis* for the assets retained in the business. The *IRS's* approach in attempting to characterize these transactions as *Type D reorganizations* or, under prior law, *Type F reorganizations,* has met with occasional success, although not without the courts being induced to strain those interpretations greatly.

reinvestment element   the portion of the improvements to *real property* purchased, constructed, or reconstructed during the *reinvestment period,* the cost of which does not exceed the net *amount realized* on the *disposition* of a *qualified housing project,* less *gain* recognized. The concept is used in connection with *rollover* of *low-income housing.* See Reg. §1.250-3(h)(2), example 1 (illustration). Amounts invested in excess of this amount are classified as additional cost elements.

reinvestment period, involuntary conversion   a period during which the proceeds of property which was the subject of an *involuntary conversion* can be reinvested in property that is *similar or related in service or use* (or certain other qualified replacement property). The period begins on the earlier of disposition, or the earliest date when condemnation or requisition was threatened, and ends two years after the first *taxable year* in which any part of the *gain* was realized, unless extended by the *IRS.* §1033(a)(2)(B). Accordingly, the reinvestment period is flexible and can be extensive. Furthermore, the two-year term is three years for involuntarily converted realty that meets the *like-kind* test of §1033(g)(1). §1033(g)(4).

related and subsidiary services, DISC   basically, services ancillary to the *domestic international sales corporation's* (DISC's) activities. The *domestic international sales corporation* (DISC) generally has been replaced by a system of foreign sales corporations (FSCs). See §§921–927 and *domestic international sales corporation.*

related entity, tax-exempt entity   for purposes of limiting *accelerated cost recovery deductions* for *tax-exempt use property,* the term means any one of four relationships. §168(h)(4). First, each governmental unit and agency or instrumentality of a governmental unit is related to each other unit, agency, or instrumentality which directly or indirectly serves its powers, rights, and duties in whole or in part from the same sovereign authority. §168(h)(4)(A)(i). The United States, each *state,* and each *possession* is treated as a separate sovereign authority. §168(h)(4)(A)(ii). Second, an *entity,* other than a governmental unit or an agency or instrumentality of such a unit is related to any other entity if the two have significant common purposes and substantial common membership or if they have directly or indirectly substantial common direction or control. §168(h)(4)(B). For example, a local chapter of a national fraternity or of the Red Cross is related to its national organization. Third, an entity is related to another entity if either owns at least a one-half interest in the capital or profits of the other, directly or through one or more entities. See §48(d) (*limitations on the investment tax credit* for certain *taxpayers*), §48(e) (denial of the credit for property used by *tax-exempt entities*), §48(a)(5) (denial of the former credit for property used by gov-

ernmental units), or §48(g)(2)(B)(v) (*limits on qualified rehabilitation expenditures*).

related foreign export corporations, DISC   a *foreign corporation* that is a *foreign international sales corporation,* a *foreign real property holding company,* or an *associated foreign corporation.* Investments in these *corporations* qualify as *export assets,* enhancing the likelihood of finding *domestic international sales corporation* (DISC) status. §993. The DISC provisions were largely replaced by the *FSC* rules in the *Tax Reform Act of 1984.*

related party avoided cost debt   see *deferred asset method.*

related party avoided cost rules   a feature of the *uniform capitalization rules* relating to *interest expenses* in the context of related parties. Parties are considered related if they are members of the same *parent-subsidiary controlled group* of *corporations.* Notice 88-99, 1988-36 I.R.B. 29, §VIII(B). Such persons can use the *deferred asset method* or the *substitute cost method,* which is elective.

related party, DISC taxation   a party that meets any one of three possible definitions: (1) a *related taxpayer* under §267 (relating to the disallowance of *losses,* etc., between related taxpayers); (2) a related party under §707(b) (relating to the disallowance of losses between *partners* and *controlled partnerships,* and between commonly controlled partnerships); and (3) a member of the same *controlled group* as the *domestic international sales corporation* (DISC), as defined by §1563(a), as modified. Reg. §1.993-1(a)(6). The *Domestic International Sales Corporation* (DISC) generally has been replaced by a system of foreign sales corporations (FSCs). See §§921–927 and *domestic international sales corporation.*

related party, foreign corporate reporting   a 25 percent *foreign shareholder* and any person treated as related to either the reporting corporation or a 25 percent foreign shareholder under §§482, 267(b), and 707(b)(1). For purposes of determining if a party is related, modified *constructive ownership* rules apply. §§6038A(c); 6038C(e).

related party insurance income   *insurance income* attributable to any insurance or reinsurance policy as to which the direct or indirect insured is a *United States shareholder* (modified to include shareholders holding any stock) in a *foreign insurer* or is a *related person* as to that shareholder. The term "related person" is modified to make *partners* related to their own *partnerships* and to make corporate officers, *employees,* and directors related to their corporations. §953(c)(6). For purposes of making the insurance corporation a *controlled foreign corporation* (CFC) the minimum level of ownership by United States shareholders' drops to at least 25 percent by vote or value, rather than the usual standard of over 50 percent. §953(c)(1)(B). Related person insurance income is a kind of *subpart F income,* which is generally taxable to the corporation's United States shareholders even though distributions are not distributed. See *related person, controlled foreign corporation; subpart F income; United States shareholder, CFC.*

related peripheral equipment see *qualified technological equipment.*

related person defined in various divergent fashions throughout the *Code.* The function of the term is typically to treat related persons as a single person so as to disallow *tax benefits* associated with transactions among such *taxpayers* on an underlying theory that no real change occurred.

related person, controlled foreign corporation (1) an *individual, partnership, trust, or estate* that controls the *controlled foreign corporation (CFC);* (2) a corporation that controls, or is controlled by, the CFC (parent-subsidiary relationship); or (3) a *corporation* that is controlled by the same person or persons who control the CFC (brother-sister relationship). Control means over 50 percent of voting power or value of a corporation's *stock,* or over 50 percent of the value of the *beneficial interests* in the case of a partnership, trust, or estate. §954(d)(3). The term is used to determine if a (CFC) is dealing with a related person for purposes of finding *foreign company sales income.* It is also used for purposes of (1) defining certain income that is not *foreign personal holding company income* (§953(c)(3)); (2) excluding certain *interest* from being *passive income* (§904(d)(2)(H)), using a modified definition); and (3) excluding certain *dividends* and interest from being *subpart F income,* along with *rents* and *royalties* earned in an active *trade or business* (§954(c)(2)(A)). See also §861(c)(2)(B) and 881(c)(4).

related person dividend or interest *dividends* or *interest* received from a *related person* that is not a *foreign personal holding company (FPHC).* The dividends or interest must be described in §954(c)(3)(A); that grouping consists of items that are not FPHC income for *subpart F income* purposes, specifically income in the form of dividends or interest from a payor organized in the same country, and with a substantial share of its *trade or business* assets in that country. Related person dividends and interest are added back to the denominator of the fraction used for determining if the company is a FPHC. Related person dividends and interest are treated as *foreign personal holding company income* to the extent attributable to FPHC income of a related person. §552(c) See *foreign personal holding company; related person, controlled foreign corporation.*

related person factoring the sale of receivables to a related party, usually at a discount. The practice was abused to shift income to overseas *tax havens,* but was curtailed by the *Tax Reform Act of 1984.* See §864(d)(1), (2). The pattern involves isolating *trade or service receivables* and treating them as loans to the obligor under the receivable. See *foreign personal holding company income: foreign personal holding company income, subpart F.*

related person, installment sales of depreciable property same as *related person, sales of depreciable property,* but including two *partnerships* in which the same persons directly or indirectly own over half the *profits interest* or *capital interests* in each partnership. §453(g)(3).

related person, sales of depreciable property a *taxpayer* and any *trust* in which the taxpayer (or his or her *spouse*) has an interest other than as a *remote contingent beneficiary,* as well as the taxpayer and any so-called *controlled entity.* §1239(b). A controlled entity arises where a *person* directly or indirectly owns over half of a *corporation's* outstanding stock or over half of a *partnership's profit interest* or *capital interest.* It also includes *related parties* under §267(b)(3), (10)-(12), meaning two corporations in the same *controlled group,* a corporation and a *partnership* if the same person owns over half of the stock and the partnership's *profits* or *capital interest,* and two *S corporations,* or an S and a *C corporation,* if the same person owns over half the value of each, applying a limited form of the *attribution rules* of §267. Finally, it includes an *employer* and a person related to the employer under §1239(b) along with *welfare benefit funds* controlled by such persons. §1239(c). Erstwhile *capital gains* on *sales* of *depreciable property* to a related person (where the transferee can claim *depreciation*) become *ordinary income.* §1239(a). The same definition is used for purposes of *installment sales* to related persons, as to which §453 is denied if *tax avoidance* is a principal purpose of the sale. Also, the related buyer does not get *basis* in the property until the seller reports income. For this purpose, related persons include *partnerships* in which the same persons own over 50 percent of the *capital* or *profits interests.* §453(g).

related taxpayer, mitigation of effect of statutes of limitations and other provisions *spouses; grantors* and *fiduciaries*; grantors and *beneficiaries*; fiduciaries and beneficiaries, *legatees,* or *heirs; decedents* and their *estates; partners*; and *members of affiliated groups* of *corporations,* as defined (in §1504) for *consolidated return* purposes. §1313(c). The relationship is tested in the year the error occurred. Reg. §1.1313(c)-1.

related taxpayers, loss and deduction denial *persons* between whom *losses* on *sales* or *exchanges* (technically undefined except to exclude complete *corporate liquidations*) are disallowed by §267(a)(1), namely: (1) members of a family (defined below); (2) an *individual* and a *corporation*, more than 50 percent of the outstanding *stock* of which (by value) is owned directly or indirectly by or for such individual; (3) two corporations which are members of a controlled group (similar to a *controlled group of corporations*, but one which uses a 50 percent test with certain other minor changes); (4) two corporations, more than 50 percent of the outstanding stock of each of which (by value) is owned directly or indirectly by or for the same individual, if either such corporation in its *taxable year* preceding the date of the sale or exchange was a *personal holding company* or a *foreign personal holding company*; (5) a *grantor* and a *fiduciary* of any *trust*; (6) a fiduciary of a trust and a fiduciary of another trust, where the same person is a grantor of both trusts; (7) a fiduciary of a *trust* and a *beneficiary* of the trust; (8) a fiduciary of a trust and a beneficiary of another trust, if the same person is a grantor of both trusts; (9) a fiduciary of a trust and a corporation, more than 50 percent in value of the outstanding stock of which is owned directly or indirectly by or for the trust or by or for a person who is a grantor of the trust; (10) a person and an *exempt organization* under §501 and controlled directly or indirectly by such person or, if the person is an individual, by members of his or her family; (11) a *C corporation* and a *partnership*, both of which are more than 50 percent owned by the same person; (12) two *S corporations* both which have more than 50 percent common ownership; or (13) an *S corporation* and a C corporation if the same persons own over 50 percent of the value of the stock of each. §267(b). For these purposes, family members are siblings (by the whole or half blood), *spouses*, ancestors, and lineal descendants. Section 267(c) contains fairly extensive stock *attribution rules* and §267(e) contains powerful indirect ownership rules for partnerships and S corporations (referred to as "pass-through entities"). The purpose of these rules is to disallow manufactured losses and manufactured *deductions* for unpaid services and interest. §267(a)(1) and (2). This definition of related *taxpayers* is commonly adopted for other purposes as well.

related terminal income the income of a *terminal railroad corporation* derived from (1) services or facilities of a character ordinarily and regularly provided by terminal railroad corporations for railroad corporations or for the *employees*, passengers, or shippers of railroad corporations; (2) the use by *persons* other than railroad corporations of portions of a facility or a service that is used primarily for railroad purposes; (3) any railroad corporation for services or facilities provided by such terminal railroad corporation in connection with railroad operations; and (4) the *United States* in payments for facilities or services in

connection with mail handling. For purposes of (2) above, a substantial addition to a facility is treated as a separate facility. §281(d)(2). Such income is not taxed to a *terminal railroad corporation* if used to reduce charges to its *shareholder* railroad corporations for use of its terminal facilities. §281(a). See *terminal railroad corporation.*

related terminal services services or use of facilities included in the computation of *related terminal income* (e.g., switching, bridges, and ferry services for railroads). §281(d)(3). See *terminal railroad corporation.*

release of levy an *IRS* practice of releasing seized property back to the *taxpayer* under various circumstances, including posting a bond, assignment of wages, etc., with expedited procedures for *tangible personal property* used in a *trade or business.*

release of tax lien complete extinction of a *federal tax lien*, in contradistinction to a "discharge," which frees certain specific property from the lien, but leaves the lien intact, or "subordination" of a lien, which merely changes the priority of the lien. See §6325(a), (b), and (d).

relevance the utility of an item of evidence in advancing an inquiry. The issue is especially important in determining the *IRS*'s power to compel the production of records and persons (i.e., to enforce an IRS *summons* issued under §7602); the general view is that the government must show that the materials sought are relevant and material to the inquiry, in the sense that there is a reasonable expectation that the summons may yield useful information or that the materials sought might shed light upon the tax issue which is the subject of the inquiry (e.g., correctness of a return).

relevant or material records see *relevance.*

religious or apostolic organizations, exempt organizations having a common treasury, engaging in an internally operated business for the common benefit of their members, provided that the members include in their own *gross incomes* their pro rata share of the group income for the *taxable year*, regardless of whether it is distributed. §509(d). See Rev. Rul. 78-100, 1978-1 C.B. 162. Such organizations are tax-exempt, but contributions to them do not qualify as *deductible charitable contributions.*

religious order the general characteristics of a religious order are the following: (1) the organization is described in §501(c)(3); (2) the members of the organization vow to live under a strict set of rules requiring moral and spiritual self-sacrifice: (3) the organization is, directly or indirectly, under the control and supervision of a church or convention or association of churches; (4) the members of the organization normally live together as part of a community and are held to a significantly stricter level of moral and religious discipline than that required of lay church members. There are other detailed definitions. Members of religious orders are generally except from self-employment tax, FUTA, FICA, and federal income tax withholding. §§1402(c)(4), 3121(b)(3); Reg.§§31.1321(b)(3) and 3401(a)(9). See *religious organization.*

religious organization   for purposes of §501(c)(3), which relates to the most common group of *exempt organizations,* the term includes any organization dedicated to religious purposes, including such disparate purposes as preparing food consistently with religious dietary laws (Rev. Rul. 74-575, 1974-2 C.B. 161) and operating a religious broadcasting station (Rev. Rul. 68-563, 1968-2 C.B. 212), provided they are operated exclusively for religious purposes. No inquiry is made into the tenets of the belief or their merits, a matter of First Amendment right, but it does appear that there must be a genuine conviction in some principle or principles of ultimate concern. See *church.*

remaining life plan   a way of calculating the *sum-of-the-years'-digits method* of *depreciation* using a conversion to decimal equivalents. See Reg. §1.167(b)-3(a) (table using this technique).

remedial amendment period   a period for which prior defects in *qualified pension, profit-sharing, stock bonus,* and *annuity plans* can be retroactively cured. The period may be extended by the *IRS* in its discretion. Reg. §1.401(b)-1(c).

remote area, overseas camps   an overseas area where satisfactory housing is unavailable within a reasonable commute of the job site. See *camp.*

remote job site   a nontechnical term for a place of work far from home. *Meals* and *lodging* provided at such sites can be considered on the premises of the *employer,* hence, *excludable* from *gross income* by the *employee.* See Reg. §1.119-1(d), example 7.

renegotiation   any transaction that is a renegotiation within the meaning of the Renegotiation Act of 1951, ch. 15, 65 Stat. 7 (codified as amended at 50 U.S.C.A. 1211 et seq. (1976)), any modification of one or more contracts with the United States or any agency thereof, and any agreement with the United States or any of its agencies with respect to one or more contracts or subcontracts thereunder. §1481(a)(1)(A). See *renegotiation of government contracts.*

renegotiation credit   see *renegotiation of government contracts.*

renegotiation of government contracts   the negotiation of a private contract (or a subcontract, under the Renegotiation Act of 1951) with the federal government

or any of its agencies to eliminate an *excessive profit.* Section 1481, in effect, treats the tax imposed in a prior year, which is attributed to the excessive portion of the profit, as a down payment (i.e., a credit) on the amount to be repaid to the United States as a result of the *renegotiation.* §1481(a).

renewal commissions   commissions paid to life insurance agents upon the renewal of life insurance contracts. Such amounts can be deferred.

rent   generally, amounts paid in money or property for the use or possession of property. In order to claim a *trade or business deduction* for rent, the *taxpayer* must not take title to property and must not have equity in the property. §162(a)(3). While the latter requirement appears to be directed at obvious cases in which the taxpayer seeks to deduct a payment of principal on a debt or part of a purchase price, the *IRS* reads equity in a way that denies a deduction to a lessor to whom the property will revert. Rev. Rul. 57-315, 1957-2 C.B. 624. Putative rental arrangements are subject to reclassification if they are in fact purchases or financing arrangements. See §7701(e)(1), Reg. §1.162-11. Tenants' improvements are rent only if intended as such by the parties. See *lease; lessee improvements; sale and leaseback.*

rental activity   an *activity* is a rental activity during the *taxable year* if during that year *tangible property* held in connection with the activity is used by customers or held for use by customers, and *gross income* attributable to the conduct of the activity during the year represents amounts paid principally for the use of *tangible property.* The use can be under a lease, service contract, or other arrangement, no matter what the parties call it. Reg. §1.469-1T(e)(3)(i). Various tests prevent what is otherwise a rental activity from being so classified: (1) *average period of customer use* is seven days or less; (2) average period of customer use is under 30 days and *significant personal services* are provided by the owner, or on the owner's behalf, in connection with making the property available for use by customers; (3) the owner, or someone acting on behalf of the owner, provides *extraordinary personal services* in connection with making the property available for use by customers; (4) rental of the property is *incidental to a nonrental activity*; (5) the property is customarily made available during defined business hours for the nonexclusive use of customers; and (6) the *taxpayer* provides property for use in an activity conducted by a *partnership* or *S corporation* in which he or she owns an interest, and the activity is not a rental activity. Reg. §1.469-1T(e)(3)(ii). See *activity, passive loss rules; extraordinary personal services; passive loss rules; significant personal services.*

rental expense deduction   a *deduction* allowed by §162(a)(3) for payments for the use of another's property for *trade or business purposes*. Section 212 authorizes rental expense deductions in connection with *gain-seeking activities* other than in a *trade or business*.

rental pool an arrangement for the sharing of multiple properties, whereby the owners share the rental income, usually without regard to the extent particular units were actually rented out. The *regulations* issued under the *vacation home rules* of §280A define the term at Reg. §1.280A-3(e)(2) and impose sharp restrictions on *deductions* associated with rental pools.

rent-leveling rules a set of remedial rules under §467, that require a special *accrual method* be used to account for certain payments for the use of property or services, regardless of the *taxpayer's* regular accounting method, under which unallocated rents or stepped (increasing) rents are leveled out and *deducted* and reported as *gross income* symmetrically by payor and payee. Also, §467(e) forces *taxpayers* who engage in a *disqualified leaseback or long-term agreement* to fix a uniform rental in connection with the *lease* for its entire term using *discounted present value* concepts. The pattern entails determining a *constant rental amount* which is *allocated* to each lease period. This remedial system can also apply if there is no rent allocation (e.g., because there is merely a duty to pay a fixed sum at the end of a five-year lease). See *constant rental amount; disqualified leaseback or long-term agreement; prior unstated inclusion.*

rent-restricted unit, low-income housing credit a *residential unit* (other than under §8 of the Housing Act of 1937 and a federal utility allowance) as to which the tenant's *gross rent* does not exceed 30 percent of the *imputed income limitation* applicable to the unit. §42(g)(2). Such units can qualify a project for the *low-income housing credit*. For this purpose, gross rent excludes federal, state, or local rent subsidies (a big advantage). Also, gross rent can exceed 30 percent of the tenant's income if federal payments decline because the tenant's income increases and certain other conditions are met. §42(g)(2)(D) and (E). See *gross rent, low-income housing credit*. The low-income housing credit expired on June 30, 1992.

rents, depletion payments for the use of natural resource property that depend on production; such rents are subject to *depletion deductions*. Reg. §1.612-3(c). This definition is not consistently followed. The term is used in connection with defining *gross income from the property*. A *delay rental* is not considered rent for this purpose by the *IRS*. See Rev. Rul. 72-165, 1972-1 C.B. 177.

rents, personal holding company income compensation, however expressed, for the use of, or right to use, property, as well as *interest* on *debts* owed the *corporation* to the extent the debts represent the price for

which realty held as *dealer property* (e.g., a tract home) was *sold* or *exchanged* by the *corporation*. §543(b)(3). Gross income from rents is reduced by depreciation, amortization, property taxes, interest, and rent to arrive at *adjusted income from rents. Adjusted gross income from rents* is included in personal holding company income unless the special exception applies for corporations earning predominantly rental income. Personal holding company income does not include rents if (1) adjusted gross income from rents is at least 50 percent of adjusted ordinary gross income and (2) the dividends-paid deduction equals or exceeds the amount by which nonrental personal holding company income exceeds 10 percent of ordinary gross income. §543(a)(2). It excludes amounts received that are characterized as *personal holding company income* under another provision of §543(a), such as *produced film rents* as defined in §543(a)(5). A corporation with substantial rental activities can declassify its rental income from being treated as personal holding company income if it either has almost no other personal holding company income or distributes enough dividends, an advantage unique to the real estate industry. §543(a)(2).

rents, S corporations see *passive investment income, S corporations.*

renunciation see *corporate reorganization.*

reorganization for *federal income tax* purposes, one of a confined number of specific types of transactions defined in §368(a)(1), pursuant to which corporate structures may be rearranged, on a tax-deferred basis, ranging from simple *recapitalizations* and changes of state of incorporation to complex asset acquisitions, *mergers*, and *consolidations*. See *Type A reorganization; Type B reorganization; Type C reorganization; Type D reorganization; Type E reorganization; Type F reorganization; Type G reorganization.*

reorganization distribution see *distribution in reorganization.*

reorganization exchange a colloquial term for an *exchange* of *stock, securities,* or other property in connection with a *corporate reorganization*, such as an exchange of all the stock of a target company in exchange for voting stock of the acquiring corporation in a *Type B reorganization*. In general, if an acquired company is to avoid being taxed in connection with a reorganization, it must distribute all its assets, other than stock or securities, pursuant to the *plan of reorganization*. §361.

repair a restoration of property in the nature of mending, as opposed to materially prolonging its life, replacing it, adding materially to its value, improving it, or adapting it to a new use. Reg. §§1.162-4, 1.263(a)-1(b). Generally, repairs to *business* or *investment* property are currently *deductible*. §§162, 212. Note that the *class life* *asset depreciation range system* eliminated disputes over *capitalization* versus *deduction* by providing a system of *repair allowances*. Reg. §1.167(a)-11(d)(3)(ii). Under this elective system, only amounts in excess of a specified annual maximum were *capitalized*. For the antonym, see *improvements*.

repair allowance an element of the *class life, asset depreciation range system*, which allows *taxpayers* to elect to characterize a fixed amount of annual *expenses* as unqualifiedly being treated as *deductible repairs*. Reg. §1.167(a)-11(d)(2)(ii). Annual expenses in excess of this amount are *capitalized*. Reg. §1.167(a)-11(d)(2)(iv)(a). The effect is to eliminate disputes over whether an expenditure is a deductible *repair* or an improvement that has to be capitalized. See Rev. Proc. 72-10, 1972-1 C.B. 721.

replacement leg a *commodity futures contract* purchased to replace a portion of a *straddle* previously sold. Acquiring a replacement leg in the form of a new commodity futures contract can result in denial of *losses* on the previous *sale* as a result of the application of the *wash sales* rule. §1091.

replacement period, inventory interruptions three *taxable years* following the *liquidation year*, unless a shorter period is specified by the *Secretary* in a notice published in the Federal Register regarding that particular *qualified inventory interruption*. §473(d)(3). See *qualified inventory interruption*.

replacement period, involuntary conversions see *reinvestment period, involuntary conversion*.

replacements major structural substitutions, such as adding a new roof or new sewers and drains. The *regulations* contrast incidental *repairs* and repairs in the nature of replacements, which indicates that the distinction is a matter of degree. Reg. §1.162-4. As a result, a regular program of annual repairs that result in every wire in a building being replaced over the course of, say, five years is likely to be treated as a series of *deductible* annual *repairs*, whereas if all the work were done in one year, the result would be a replacement which would have to be *capitalized*, as dictated by §263. Where the line is drawn between these extremes is difficult to say. The regulations and the courts concentrate on whether the replacement appreciably prolongs the life of the property or involves the substitution of major structural components. See *repair*.

replacement year any *taxable* year in the *replacement period* during which goods are replaced. §473(d)(2). See *qualified inventory interruption; qualified liquidation*.

replevin an action brought to recover goods unlawfully taken. *Taxpayers* can bring actions in replevin if the IRS unlawfully takes their property. §7426(b).

reportable real estate any present of future *ownership* interest in (1) improved and unimproved land, including air space; (2) inherently permanent structures, including any residential, commercial, or industrial building; (3) any condominium unit and its *appurtenant* fixtures and common elements (including land); or (4) *stock* in a *cooperative housing corporation*. Reg. §1.6045-4. An "*ownership interest*" is defined to include a fee simple interest; a life estate, reversion and remainder interests; a perpetual easement; or any previously created rights to possess or use for all or a portion of any year, provided such rights have a remaining term, as of the closing date, of at least 30 years. It excludes an *option* to require otherwise reportable real estate. A *real estate transaction* involving reportable real estate requires the *real estate reporting person* to make a *broker's return*. §6045. The return called for is an *information return* only. See *real estate reporting person*.

reportable transaction, foreign corporations a transaction involving *foreign related parties* that is subject to mandatory retention of *records* and reporting under §6038A. The following transactions between the *reporting corporation* and the foreign related parties are reportable transactions: (1) *sales* and purchases of *stock in trade*; (2) sales and purchases of *tangible property* other than stock in trade; (3) *rents* and *royalties* paid and received (but not amounts reported under (4) *infra*); (4) sales, purchases, and amounts paid and received as consideration for the use of *intangible property* such as *copyrights*, designs, formulas, inventions, models, *patents*, processes, *trademarks*, and other similar property rights; (5) consideration paid and received for rendering technical, managerial, engineering, construction, scientific, or like services; (6) commissions paid and received; (7) amounts loaned and borrowed (except open accounts resulting from sales and purchases otherwise reported which arise and are collected in full in the ordinary course of *business*) (see Form 5472 for further requirements); (8) *interest* paid and received; (9) *premiums* paid and received for *insurance* and reinsurance. Reg. §1.6038-2. Importers are subject to additional reporting requirements. Reportable transactions are reported on Form 5472.

Reporting Agents Authorization a writing prepared by a *taxpayer* authorizing someone else to act as an agent empowered to sign and prepare *employment tax returns*. Form 8655 is available for the purpose. The authorization is part of a program to get federal tax data on magnetic tapes.

Reporting Agents File an *IRS* file consisting of *Reporting Agents Authorizations*.

reporting corporation a *domestic corporation* that is a *twenty-five percent foreign-owned corporation*, and any *foreign corporation* that is engaged in a *United States business* if it is a *twenty-five percent foreign-*

owned corporation. Such corporations are subject to mandatory retention of records and reporting under §6038A (and further *regulations*) on their *reportable transactions* with *foreign related parties.* §§6038A(a) and 6038A(c). It must make a separate annual *information return* on Form 5472 with respect to each related party with which it has had any specified transactions during the *taxable year.* §6038A(a); Reg. §1.6038A-1(a)(1). See *noncompliance rule.*

repos a general term for financial arrangements under which a holder of securities in form sells securities to a lender, subject to an obligation to repurchase the securities at a future date. In reality, the arrangement is a lending transaction, using securities (usually United States Treasury securities) as collateral. See, e.g., Rev. Rul. 74-27, 1974-1 C.B. 24; Rev. Rul. 77-59, 1977-1 C.B. 196; Rev. Rul. 79-195, 1979-1 C.B. 177. Repos are also used as the foundation for complex *tax shelter* activities, with a view to insuring *interest expense deductions* and *long-term capital gains* on the *disposition* of the underlying securities. See *reverse repos.*

repossession of property generally, the creditor's act of taking back encumbered property on the buyer's default. Section 1038 grants substantial relief from current taxation of seller-creditors who repossess real estate subject to purchase money mortgages or similar liens, by limiting *gain* or repossessions to money and the value of other property, other than the repossessed property, received by the seller to the extent not already reported in income.

representative see *taxpayer representative.*

representative market or field price when oil and gas are spoken of, the term refers to prices representative of those for which oil and gas can be sold in the *taxpayer's* competitive area. If representative market prices cannot be established, then some other fair approximation has to be used. When minerals are spoken of, the term refers to comparable competitive prices of minerals of a *like-kind and grade* to those of the taxpayer. The term is important for the determination of *gross income from the property* for *percentage depletion* purposes. §613; Reg. §1.613-3.

representative payees persons who, having received Social Security benefits for the benefit of children and incompetent adults, hold or invest the unneeded funds. Rev. Rul. 63-140, 1963-2 C.B. 609. The funds and the interest are the property of (and therefore are taxed to) the *beneficiary* and not the representative payee.

request for administrative adjustment a complicated *partnership* analog of a *claim for refund or credit* or an *amended return* in connection with a *TEFRA audit.* §6227. Such a claim must be filed within three years of the later of the filing date or the actual due date (without extensions) of the original *return* but before the *tax matters partner* (TMP) has been issued a notice of *final partnership administrative adjustment.* If it is filed by the TMP as an amended partnership return, then it may be treated as the correction of *mathematical or clerical error,* open to a triggering of additional *assessments* against the partners without *notice of deficiency.* §§6227(b)(1), 6230. If not, it may result in allowance of the claim for refund or credit, a further proceeding, or no action. §6227(b)(2) and (3).

request for prompt assessment a request for *assessment* submitted by a *taxpayer* (dissolving *corporation* or *person* filing a *decedent's* last return) to the *IRS,* the effect of which is to give the IRS only 18 months to assess a *deficiency.* §6501(d); Reg. §301.6501(d)-1.

request for ruling a *taxpayer's* request, submitted to the *National Office* of the *IRS,* for a *ruling.*

required accrual period the period beginning with the first *taxable year* for which a *pass-through entity* (e.g., *trust*) meets the ownership test (below) and ending with the first *taxable year* the test is not met, and with respect to which the *IRS* consents to the termination of the required accrual period. The ownership test is met for any taxable year if, on at least 90 days in the year, at least 20 percent of the value of the interests in the entity is owned by certain *persons* subject to rules forcing the current inclusion of *acquisition discount* on *short-term government obligations.* §1281(b)(2). *Gross income* arises in the hands of pass-through entities which own short-term government obligations on any day during the required accrual period when the entities are forced to report such income as to obligations acquired on or after the first day of the entities' taxable years. §1281(b)(2)(A) and (D).

required annual payment the *lesser* of 93 percent (for 1992, an increase from prior years) of a *corporate taxpayer's federal income taxes* for the year or 100 percent of the *last year's tax.* §6654(d)(1). Different estimated payments rules are used for large corporations. In a revenue raising measure, the minimum estimated tax payments for all corporations were temporarily increased, starting for tax years 1992 (93 percent) through 1996. The new increased minimums for years after 1992 are 94 percent for 1993 and 1994, and 95 percent for 1995 and 1996. The minimum is slated to return to 90 percent for 1997. Individual taxpayers must also meet specific minimum requirements. §6655(d)(1)(B). The term is used to determine the extent to which taxpayers have fallen short of their duty to pay *estimated taxes.* See *exceptions to estimated tax, corporate; exceptions to estimated tax, individual.*

required beginning date not later than April 1 of the *calendar year* following the calendar year in which the employee attains age 70½, or in the case of a *governmental plan* or *church plan,* April 1 of the calendar year following the year in which the *employee* retires. §401(a)(9). If the employee was a *five-percent* owner, the required beginning date was April 1 of the calendar year following the calendar year in which the employee attained age $70\frac{1}{2}$, prior law, effective until 1989. These required beginning date rules apply to post-1988 years, and are a required element of a *qualified deferred compensation plan, IRA, section 457 plan*, and *tax-sheltered annuity*.

required deposit a reference to *deposits* of tax payments with government depositories of various taxes. See §6656, imposing penalties for delays in payment. See *penalty, failure to make timely deposits*.

required distribution, elective deferrals see *elective deferrals*.

required distribution, real estate investment trust see *excise tax, undistributed income of a real estate investment trust*.

required distribution, regulated investment company see *excise tax, undistributed income of an RIC*.

required expenditure schedule a schedule according to which funds raised by the issuance of a *tax-exempt* construction bond must be disbursed for construction, on pain of paying *civil tax penalties* (the *unspent proceeds penalty*) for delaying. The schedule is generally 10 percent within six months, 45 percent in one year, 75 percent in 18 months, and 100 percent in two years. §148(f)(4)(C). This is part of the *arbitrage bond* rules.

required installment a mandatory minimum payment of *estimated taxes*. For individuals, payments are due on a quarterly basis, generally April 15, June 15, September 15, and January 15. §6654(c). The amount is determined under §6654(d) as to noncorporate *taxpayers* and §6655(d) for *corporations*. Such payments produce *refundable credits*. See §53. See *required annual payment*.

required payments if a *partnership* or *S corporation* qualifies to make a *section 444 election* and wants to make the election, it must file Form 8716 in accordance with Reg. §1.444-3T and must comply with the requirements of §7519. The payments are calculated on Form 8752 and are designed to eliminate the fiscal benefit of the election.

required percentage see *at-risk rules, investment tax credit*.

required rebate a payment to the *United States* government to pay back the benefits of issuing *tax-exempt bonds* and applying the proceeds at a higher yield in what would be other taxable investments. §148(f). Failure to pay the required rebate, or to pay a penalty in lieu of the rebate, results in loss of *tax exemption* for the *interest* payments. See *arbitrage bond; state or local bond*.

required records doctrine a doctrine that supports the maintenance of governmentally prescribed business records of an essentially regulatory nature and the obligation to disclose them on demand, despite self-incrimination issues that might be raised. Whether the doctrine applies to federal tax laws is unclear. The doctrine arose from the Emergency Price Control Act of 1942 (50 U.S.C.A. §901 et seq.).

required taxable year the *taxable year* forced on *partnerships* by §706(b), *S corporations*, by §1378, or *personal service corporations* by §441(i). §444(e). Such entities may make the so-called *section 444(i) election* and retain a *fiscal year*. See *personal service corporation, taxable year*.

required year, specified foreign corporation see *specified foreign corporation*.

requirements contracts contracts under which a manufacturer promises to meet a buyer's requirements for a product.

res another word for the *corpus* of a *trust*.

resale DISC a term used to describe a *domestic international sales corporation* (DISC) that buys for resale as a principal. The *domestic international sales corporation* (DISC) generally has been replaced by a system of foreign sales corporations (FSCs). See §§921–927 and *domestic international sales corporation*.

resale price method a standard for determining whether *sales* prices between related *businesses* are proper or should be adjusted under §482. With use of this standard, the *arm's length* price of a controlled sale is determined by comparing the controlled sale to a later sale to an unrelated party. Thus, if subsidiary A sells a product to subsidiary B for $10, and if B sells it to the public for $30, this standard begins by one looking at the last ($30) sale, then subtracting an appropriate mark-up and making some other appropriate modifications to adjust the $10 controlled sale price. Reg. §1.482-2(e)(3)(i). See *reallocation of income and deductions by Commissioner*.

rescission, notice of deficiency setting aside a *notice of deficiency*. It can be done by mutual consent between the *IRS* and the *taxpayer*. Once rescinded, it is deemed never to have existed, but it does not affect the suspension of the *statute of limitation*. §6212(d).

rescission, statutory notice of deficiency when the *taxpayer* and *IRS* both agree, the *statutory notice of deficiency* may be canceled. This cancellation voids limitations with respect to *assessments,* refunds, and *credit*. The *taxpayer* will have no right to *petition* a *Tax Court* based on a rescinded notice. However, the *Senate Finance Committee* has indicated that after the notice has been rescinded, the *IRS* would be authorized to issue another notice of deficiency of an amount greater than or lesser than the original amount. The IRS sets procedures for implementing the notice withdrawal so it can be certain the taxpayer is aware of all possible consequences arising from the rescission and has, nevertheless, consented. §6212(d).

research and development see *research and experimental expenditures.*

research and experimental expenditures expenditures for research and development activities in the experimental or laboratory sense, and not for literary, historical, or similar research projects. Reg. §1.174-2(a)(1); Rev. Rul. 80-245, 1980-2 C.B. 72. The *regulations* expressly exclude costs incident to the development of an experimental or pilot model, a plant process, a product, a formula, an invention, or similar property, and the improvement of already existing property. It also includes the cost of testing products or materials for quality control, efficiency surveys, management studies, consumer surveys, advertising, or promotional activities. Reg. §1.174-2(a)(1). Expenditures to acquire or to improve land or *depreciable* or *depletable property,* even if used in connection with research or experimentation, are disqualified, although depreciation allowances are considered research or experimental expenditures. Payments to outside contractors for research or experimental services also qualify. Reg. §1.174-2(a)(2).

research and experimentation credit see *credit for increasing research activities.*

reserved oil payment an *oil payment* reserved in a transfer of an interest in oil and gas. The sale of a mineral interest, which is subject to a reserved oil payment, is now considered a *sale* subject to a *purchase money mortgage.* §636(b).

reserve plan a form of *qualified foreign plan* under which *employers* establish *reserves* for future liabilities. §404A(c)(1) and (f). Such a plan is not subject to the usual funding rules.

reserve ratio test a test applicable to assets *placed in service* before 1971 and written in accordance with Rev. Proc. 62-21, 1962-2 C.B. 418. The test was designed to determine whether the *taxpayer's* practices with respect to retiring and replacing assets were consistent. The provision is largely antique, except that Rev. Proc. 62-21 apparently still has utility for setting *useful lives* of property not covered by *ADR* or *ACRS.*

reserves for bad debts accounts once used by certain business *taxpayers* on the *cash method* (as to monies lent) or *accrual method* of accounting to reflect anticipated *bad debts.* Such taxpayers could claim current *deductions* for reasonable additions to such *reserves.* Former §166(c); Rev. Rul. 74-604, 1974-2

C.B. 60. Later, when debts were actually shown to be *worthless,* the reserve was reduced, but, later, recoveries were likewise added to the reserve, thereby reducing allowable additions to the bad debt reserve for the year of the recovery. Former Reg. §1.166-4(b)(2). For years beginning *after 1986,* taxpayers, (other than certain financial institutions) may only use the *specific charge-off* method in accounting for bad debts. Certain financial institutions are allowed to use the *reserve method* for computing deductions for bad debts. §§166(a) and 1.166. See *experience method, reserves for bad debts; percentage of taxable income method, reserves for bad debts.*

reserves for estimated expenses amounts established for financial reporting purposes by *accrual method taxpayers* as a *deduction* against current *income,* designed to reflect future *expenses.* The effect is a current reduction in net income but a later reversal of the account (and correspondingly increased income in later years), and a rational matching of income and expenses. The repeal of this provision allowing general reserve accounting (§462 was repealed in 1955) was influential in denying the practice for *federal income tax* purposes, and the passage of §461(h) (*economic performance requirement*) put an end to reserves for estimated expenses other than those specifically allowed by the *Code.*

residence, estate tax *domicile,* meaning where the *taxpayer* resides and intends to stay indefinitely. Reg. §20.01(b)(1). Such residence in the *United States* by an *alien* attracts the federal *estate tax.* §2001(a).

residence, generally a place where a *taxpayer* lives, regardless of his or her intention to stay. See *domicile.*

residence, moving expenses former residence means the *taxpayer's principal residence* before his departure for a new *principal place of work.* New residence means the taxpayer's principal residence within the general location of a new principal place of work. Neither term includes other residences owned or maintained by the taxpayer or members of his or her family or seasonal residences such as a summer beach cottage. Whether property is used as the principal residence depends upon *all facts and circumstances.* Property used as the principal residence may include a houseboat, a house trailer, or similar dwelling. The term "new place of residence" generally includes the area within which the taxpayer might reasonably be expected to commute to a new principal place of work. Paraphrased from Reg. §1.217-2(b)(8).

resident alien an alien is considered to be a United States resident for income tax purposes if he or she (1) is a lawful permanent resident of the United States at any time during the calendar year, (2) meets the "*substantial presence*" *test,* or (3) makes the first-year election. §§7701(b)(1)(A)(i), 7701(b)(1)(A)(ii) and (b)(3), 7701(b)(4). A alien who does not qualify under any of these tests is treated as a *nonresident alien*. §7701(b)(1)(B). Resident aliens are generally taxed on their worldwide incomes as if they were United States citizens. See *election to be treated as resident; green-card test; substantial presence test*.

residential construction contract   contracts, other than *home construction contracts,* for which 80 percent or more of the total estimated *costs* are reasonably expected to be for the building, construction, reconstruction, or rehabilitation of, or improvements to, *real property* directly related to and located on the site of *dwelling units.* Adding a structural component such as an air conditioning system is to be considered a qualifying cost for purposes of the definition of a residential construction contract. A dwelling unit is a house or apartment that provides living accommodations, but not a hotel, motel, inn, or other establishment where over one-half of the units are *used on a transient basis.* Residential construction contracts which are not home construction contracts are subject to the *percentage of completion—capitalized cost method* using a 70/30 (as opposed to 90/10) proration. §460(e)5). See *dwelling unit, low or moderate-income rental housing rehabilitation.*

residential real estate management association   an *organization* whose purpose is to acquire, construct, manage, maintain, and care for *association property* with respect to a development, subdivision, or an area where substantially all of the lots or buildings are *individual* residences. §528(c)(3). See *homeowners' association.*

residential real property   generally, real estate used for human habitation. The term is defined for purposes of the *capitalization* of *construction period interest and taxes* as to *residential rental property* (as defined in §167(j)(2)(B)), *dwelling units* (as defined in §§167(k)(3)(c), 1250(a)(1)(B)) held for sale as *dealer property,* or *inventory.* Former §189(e)(4).

residential rental property   a building or structure with respect to which at least 80 percent of the gross rental income for the *taxable year* is from dwelling units, other than units in a building in which more than one-half of the units are *used on a transient basis* (e.g., a motel). If any portion of such building or structure is occupied by the *taxpayer,* gross rental income includes the rental value of the portion so occupied. §§167(j)(2)(B) *(depreciation* generally), 168(e)(2)(A) *(cost recovery),* 167(k)(3)(C) (low-income housing). The term is important in the determination of *depreciation deductions* and *recapture* of depreciation. §1250(a)(2)(B)(iii). See *dwelling unit, low or moderate income rental housing rehabilitation.*

resident, tax treaties   generally, an *individual* or *entity* with significant contacts in a particular country. The concept is generally defined in the *tax treaty,* but if not, the *tax* considers residence to be defined by the tax laws of the country of the person claiming to be a resident of the treaty country.

residual group   *boot* and property transferred that is not of a like kind or *like class* with any property received, and property received that is not of a like kind or like class with any property transferred. Money or property allocated to the residual group equals the difference between the aggregate *fair market value* of the properties transferred in all of the exchange groups and the aggregate fair market value of the properties received in all of the exchange groups, with liabilities taken into account. Note that the residual group will consist of either money or property transferred in the exchange or money or property received in the exchange, not both. The money and properties allocated to the residual group are deemed to come from the specified assets in a certain order, namely, from *Class I Assets,* then from *Class II Assets,* then from *Class III Assets,* and then from *Class IV Assets.* Reg §1.1031(f)-1.

residual interest, REMIC   an interest in a *real estate mortgage investment corporation (REMIC)* which is not a *regular interest,* which is issued on the *start-up day,* and which is so designated. §860G(a)(2). A *REMIC* may have only one class of residual interests. The holders are the equity owners. §860D(a)(3). The *net income* or *loss* of the *REMIC* is passed through to the residual interest holders to be taxed under §§860C and 860E.

residual method   a method for determining *goodwill* and *going concern value,* calculated by subtracting the value of the *tangible* and *intangible* assets from the total purchase price. It is required in connection with purchases of business. §1060. *Taxpayers* are expected to use Reg. §1.338(b)-2T, which allocates the price first to cash and similar items, then to marketable securities, etc., then to other assets, then finally to *goodwill* and *going concern value.* See *applicable asset acquisition; Class I assets; Class II assets, Class III assets; Class IV assets.*

residual value   the value of an asset at the end of some particular period.

resourcing rules   another term for tax rules that change the sources of income. The *Code* provides, for example, that the source of *interest* income on bank deposits in the *United States* is generally not the United States. §861(a)(1)(B).

responsible person   the *person* responsible for collecting and paying over *federal withholding taxes* on *wages,* meaning any person connected or associated with an *employer* so as to have the power to see that such taxes are paid. The term is read broadly and has been used to sweep in *partners,* corporate officers, *shareholders* with practical control, and even outsiders such as banks, if they have practical control of the employer's finances. See *penalty, failure to collect and pay overtax, or attempt to evade or defeat tax.*

restoration the repayment of an amount previously included in *gross income*. Section 1341 provides statutory relief in such cases, granting *taxpayers* whose restoration payment exceeds $3,000 the better of a *deduction* in the present year or a present *credit* equal to the tax burden created by the prior inclusion. The deduction or credit for restorations provided by §1341 is designed to mitigate the *claim of right doctrine* under which equivocal receipts are nonetheless taxed.

restoration, depletion see *depletion, restoration.*

restoration rights, qualified plans provisions that grant the *employee* a right to recover forfeited *accrued benefits* from *employers,* if the employee repays the full withdrawal to the plan. §411(a)(3)(D)(ii).

restricted class see *early termination limitations.*

restricted consent a *consent to extend statute of limitations,* confined to particular issues, leaving other issues open to being barred by the running of the *statute of limitations.* Rev. Proc. 79-22, 1979-1 C.B. 563 and I.R.M. 4541.71(2), M.T. 4500-401 (June 12, 1984). See *subtle alteration rule.* See *waiver of statute of limitations.*

restricted group see *early termination limitations.*

restricted interest cases cases in which a *taxpayer* does not receive the benefit of *interest* on *overpayments.* A common example is the overpayment of *estimated taxes.* See Rev. Rul. 60-17, 1960-2 C.B. 942.

restricted property property which is *transferred* in exchange for services, but which is either not transferable or subject to a *substantial risk of forfeiture.* Section 83 contains elaborate rules dealing with such property. See *property, restricted property rules; restricted property rules; transfer, restricted property rules.*

restricted property rules a complex network of *federal income tax* provisions dealing with the *recognition* and timing of *gross income* paid in *property* in *exchange* for the performance of services by an *employee* or *independent contractor.* The focal point is a payment in property such as the employer's stock as to which there is a *risk* of *forfeiture* in the recipient's hands, and a significant restriction on transferability. §83. Generally, the payee includes the *fair market value* of restricted property in *gross income* only when transferability arises or when risk of forfeiture lapses. At that time, the property is said to be substantially *vested.* Only then, if at all, can the payor claim a *deduction.* §83(h). Payees may use the *section 83(b) election* to include the *fair market value* of restricted property, less the amount paid for such property, in the year it is received, such that subsequent

increases in value may be treated as *capital gains.* Reg. §1.83-1(a). These rules do not apply to *employee stock purchase plans; incentive stock options; restricted stock options*; options lacking ascertainable values; *qualified pension, profit-sharing,* or *stock bonus plans*; *employee annuity* plans; or transfers of property under the exercise of an option that has a readily ascertainable value when granted. Reg. §1.83-6(a)(3). See *property, restricted property rules; restricted property; transfer, restricted property rules.*

restricted stock options a form of *statutory stock option* applicable to options granted before 1964, or pursuant to a contract to grant such options, which was entered into before 1964 and exercised before May 21, 1981. The benefit of the stock options was to create no *gross income* to the *employee* at the time of the grant or exercise if the stock was held for a sufficient period, and substantial opportunities for *long-term capital gains.* The *section 83(b) election* may be used.

restricted stock plans *nonqualified deferral compensation* plans pursuant to which *stock* of the *employer,* which cannot be sold and is subject to *substantial risks of forfeiture,* is transferred to the *taxpayer.* The notion is to cause the stock to become the *employee's* in lots as the period of employment grows. As the restrictions lapse, the employee is taxed, and the employer is entitled to a tax *deduction.* §§83, 404.

restricted waiver same as a *restricted consent.*

restructured transaction a real-world transaction that is reclassified for tax purposes, e.g., a *triangular dividend* or an alleged *sale and leaseback* which is reclassified as a *mortgage.*

retail commission salesman an *employee* engaged in soliciting orders from ultimate consumers for merchandise offered for sale by the *employer.* The term excludes people who solicit orders from wholesalers, retailers, or others for merchandise for resale. Reg. §31.3402(j)-1(b). *Income tax withholding* is not required from non-cash remuneration paid to retail commission salesmen, provided the salesmen are ordinarily compensated solely by way of cash commissions. §3402(j).

retailer, depletion a *taxpayer* who sells (directly or through a related person) oil, natural gas, or petroleum products through a retail outlet that the taxpayer owns or to any *person* allowed to operate one of the taxpayer's retail outlets. It is intended that retailers not enjoy the benefits of *percentage depletion* if they have substantial retail operations, unless their retail operations are nominal compared to their production operations. To insure only this intended result: (1) bulk sales of oil and natural gas to commercial or industrial users are not considered retail sales; (2) the retailer exclusion does not apply to small retailers, i.e., to taxpayers whose combined gross receipts from the sale of oil, gas, or related products at the taxpayer's (or a related person's) retail outlet do not exceed $5 million for the *taxable year*; and (3) retail sales do not include sales of oil, gas, and related products sold outside the *United States* if none of the taxpayer's *domestic* production was exported during the taxable year or the immediately preceding taxable year. §613A(d)(2). The exemptions accorded to *independent producers* and *royalty owners* do not apply to retailers; hence, they cannot benefit from percentage depletion of oil and gas. See *small producers' exemption.*

retail inventory method a specialized method for retailers to compute the value of *inventory* for a *last-in, first-out* (LIFO) inventory system. This is an addition to the *dollar-value method* and uses retail prices instead of costs to compute inventory values. Rev. Proc. 72-21, 1972-1 C.B. 745. The technique involves determining selling prices and then reducing them by a formula set forth in Reg. §1.471-8.

retail sale for purposes of *percentage depletion* of oil and gas, a term excluding sales to industrial accounts, to distributors for resale, or to *political subdivisions.* Such sales, if in sufficient volume, prevent the use of percentage depletion. §613A(d)(2)-(4). See *small producers' exemption.*

retain certificates see *per-unit retain certificate.*

retained earnings—appropriated a *reserve* against retained earnings designed to reflect restrictions (e.g., *sinking funds* for repayment of debt) on *dividend*-paying ability. Schedule M-2 of Form 1120, the corporate *income tax return,* requires this information. See *retained earnings—unappropriated.*

retained earnings—unappropriated retained earnings that are not subject to restrictions (other than management policy) on the payment of dividends. Schedule M-2 of Form 1120, the corporate *income tax return,* requires this information. See *retained earnings—appropriated.*

retained interest, contract with economic interest see *disposal with a retained economic interest.*

retained interest, depletion an interest held back by a transferor and subject to *depletion.* Examples include a landowner who grants a *working interest* to an oil company but retains a right to a landowner's *royalty.* The oil company or other *lessee* may in turn transfer its working interest to another party, retaining an *overriding royalty.* So long as the transfers involve retentions of *economic interests* in the resource, as opposed to outright *sales* of the mineral in place, the holder of the interest can properly claim *depletion deductions.* §611. For what appears to be an identical concept of a retained interest, used in connection with transfers of timber, coal, and domestic iron ore, see *disposal with a retained economic interest.*

retained production payment a *production payment* which is held back by the transferor of a *mineral estate.* For tax treatment, see *carved-out production payment.*

retirement accounting a system of *depreciation* under which *deductions* are claimed only when an asset is retired from use.

retirement, ADR depreciation an asset is considered retired from a *class life asset depreciation range system* (ADR) *vintage account* when it is permanently withdrawn from use in a *trade or business* or is no longer *held for the production of income* by the *taxpayer.* It can arise by *sale, exchange,* conversion for scrap, or any other permanent *disposition.* Reg. §1.167-11(d)(3)(C).

retirement bonds certain *federal* bonds that could be used as the funding medium for *individual retirement arrangements, Keogh plans,* and certain *pension* and *profit-sharing plans* established by *employers.* The principal features of these bonds are that they are nontransferable, pay interest at maturity, can be bought in limited amounts, and cease to generate any yield when the owner reaches age $70\frac{1}{2}$ or five years after death (but not later than the date the deceased owner would have attained age $70\frac{1}{2}$), whichever occurs earlier. §§405, 409. Their features tend to assure compliance with the tax law rules and are simple to understand. Sales of such bonds have ceased. See *qualified bond purchase plan.*

Retirement Equity Act of 1984 P.L. 98-397, 98th Cong., 2d Sess. (1984). Its principal features are that it provides a maternity leave exception to *break in service* rules, requires automatic *joint and survivor* pension plan benefits (with spousal consent needed for waiver), and gives exceptions to *ERISA's* anti-alienation provisions for *qualified domestic relations orders.*

retirement income credit see *credit for the elderly and disabled.*

retirement income endowment contract an *endowment policy* that pays an *annuity* at retirement. Such contracts can qualify as annuities for purposes of tax rules relating to *tax-deferred annuities for exempt and educational organization employees.* Rev. Rul. 70-581, 1970-2 C.B. 94 (provided death benefits not greater than 100 times each dollar of monthly annuity). See *tax-deferred annuities for exempt and educational organization employees.*

retirement of property a permanent withdrawal of *depreciable property* from its use in a *trade or business* or from its being *held for the production of income.* Regulation §1.167(a)-8(a) provides that a retirement may arise from a *sale, exchange,* abandonment, transfer to scrap, or other *disposition.* Retirements may result in the *realization* of *gains* or *losses.* See *retirement, ADR depreciation.*

retirement plan a *qualified pension, profit-sharing,* or *stock bonus plan* or *trust,* a *qualified annuity plan,* or a *qualified bond purchase plan.* §7476(c) (relating to permissible *declaratory judgments* in the *Tax Court*). The term is not otherwise defined. See *pension plan, Internal Revenue Code.*

retirement plan bonds see *retirement bonds.*

retirement, securities calls and redemptions of securities pursuant to the terms of the obligation, involuntary surrender for less than face value forced by the debtor's financial difficulties, whether paid at once or over time and whether or not the obligation is canceled. Retirements of certain securities qualify as *exchanges.* §1232(a).

retirement test, Social Security benefits a test that limits the amount of personal service income a person receiving OASDI (Social Security retirement income, principally) benefits can earn without suffering reduced OASDI benefits. See 42 U.S.C. §§402, 403(b) (1976). Both retirees who are *wage* earners and those who are self-employed are affected; persons are self-employed if they render *substantial services* in the year or month in question. See 42 U.S.C. §403(f)(4)(A), supp. III 1979 (criteria used to evaluate whether services are substantial).

retiring partner a *partner* who ceases to be a partner under local law. Reg. §1.736-1(a)(1)(ii). Section 736 dictates the tax results to a deceased or retiring partner in a continuing *partnership,* whereas §708 determines whether there is a *termination* and §§731 and 751 control the impact of a termination of the partnership. See *section 736 payments; termination, partnership.*

retroactive allocations *allocations* to a *partner* of *profits* or *losses* arising prior to the admission of the partner to the *partnership.* Such allocations are barred by §706(c)(2)(B).

retroactive amendments, partnerships modifications to *partnership agreements* made before the *partnership's filing* date, not including extensions. Section 761(c) generally permits such amendments to be effective for such purposes as ordinary *partnership* provisions allocating *gains* and *losses* for the *taxable year* to which the *return* relates. See Reg. §1.761-1(c). If, for example, the *partners* of a *calendar-year* partnership amend their agreement on February 10, 1993, then the amendment can affect allocations of 1992 income and loss, but such amendments may not be used to create *retroactive allocations.*

return a document filed with the *IRS,* often to accompany a tax payment (e.g., an *individual's* annual *income tax* return on *Form 1040*) or merely to provide information to the IRS and others (e.g., *Form 1099Div* is used to report corporate *dividend* payments). A return is not considered to have been made unless the *taxpayer* substantially complies with the reporting requirements; as a result, *civil tax penalties* may apply and *statutes of limitations* may not start to run. The demand for substantial compliance evidently means that the taxpayer must provide enough information to enable the IRS to determine whether tax can be computed and *assessed* against the taxpayer. In addition, the return must be final. See *valid return.*

return information data included on a *tax return,* including the *taxpayer's* identity, address, and identifying number, the nature, source, or amount of *gross income,* payments, receipts, *deductions, exemptions, credits,* assets, liabilities, net worth, tax liability, tax withheld, *deficiencies, overassessments,* and tax payments (whether the return is, was, or will be examined or investigated), or any other data concerning the determination of the existence of the liability of any *person* for any tax, penalty, *interest,* fine, forfeiture, or other imposition or offense. Such data are supplied to the *IRS* by a *taxpayer representative* in connection with an *audit* of the return or under *summons* issued in connection with an investigation (information not shown on the return, but held by the IRS in connection with the taxpayer's return or *federal income tax* liability, is known as off-return information). §6103(b)(2). Such information is subject to limitations on disclosure. See *Privacy Act; return, Privacy Act.*

return of capital a payment, or a portion of a payment, that is viewed as resulting in the recovery of the *taxpayer's* investment, rather than as a *gain* or *loss*-producing transaction. The leading illustrations are the repayment of principal to a creditor, the *open transactions doctrine,* and *distributions* from *partnerships* and *corporations* to *partners* and *shareholders* that are not considered to reflect profits. See *open transactions.*

return of tax withheld a report filed by *persons* required to *withhold* tax from amounts payable to others. Persons filing such *returns* are considered to act as the government's *agent* for the collection of taxes imposed on the payees.

return preparer injunction bond a bond (basically cash) posted pursuant to §7407(c) which permitted *tax return preparers* to stay *injunctions* by the government against prohibited conduct.

return preparer penalties various *civil tax penalties* imposed on *tax return preparers* for bad acts of various sorts. In addition, there are *criminal tax penalties* (not described in the following list, most notably for *tax return information disclosure*). See *penalty, failure of employers of tax return preparers to file correct information report; failure of tax return preparer to furnish copy of return to taxpayer; penalty, failure of tax return* *preparer to furnish identification number; penalty, failure of tax return preparer to retain copies of tax returns; penalty, failure of tax return preparer to sign return; penalty, negotiation of refund check by preparer; penalty, negligence by tax return preparer; penalty, unrealistic position by tax return preparer.*

return, Privacy Act   any *tax return, information return, declaration of estimated tax,* or *claim for refund or credit* contemplated by the *Code,* as well as supporting materials. §6103(b)(1). Returns are subject to strict limitations on disclosure. See *Privacy Act.*

return test, net lease   see *interest on investment indebtedness limitation.*

revenue   governmental receipts. The term does not appear in the *Code.*

Revenue Act and Pension Protection Act of 1987   a fairly minor but complex act designed to raise a modest amount of revenue by cutting back on various tax benefits (such as the availability of *estate freezes*) and to protect *employees'* interests in pension plans. See H.R. 100-495, 100th Cong., 1st Sess., Conference Report on the Omnibus Reconciliation Act of 1987, accompanying H.R. 3545 (Dec. 21, 1987).

Revenue Act of 1987   Title X of HR 3545, the first amendment to the *Internal Revenue Code of 1986.* It contains a variety of minor revenue-raising measures.

revenue agent   an *individual employee* of the *IRS* whose function is to *audit taxpayers' returns* and submit reports of proposed changes in their tax liabilities. They operate out of *District Offices* of the IRS. See *Revenue Agent's Report.*

Revenue Agent's Report   a two-part examination report prepared by *revenue agents* and finalized by the *District Office* as the result of an *audit* of a *taxpayer.* The first part of the report consists of identifying information, an explanation of the examination, findings, and recommendations with attached worksheets and schedules. The second part is retained by the *IRS;* it contains impressions and opinions of the agent. Unless the taxpayer and the agent agree to the contents, the portion of the report containing findings and recommendations is mailed to the taxpayer along with a *thirty-day letter.*

Revenue District   an Internal Revenue District. See *District.*

revenue neutral   neither increasing nor decreasing federal *revenues.* It is politically popular to back such a bill. For example, the *Tax Reform Act of 1986* was allegedly revenue neutral.

revenue officer   an *employee* of the *IRS* whose function is to collect taxes due. Revenue officers have no interest in the merits of whether a tax is due or not, in contrast to *revenue agents.*

revenue procedure   a published official statement of the *IRS* regarding a matter of federal tax procedure, published by the *National Office* of the IRS, first in *Internal Revenue Bulletins,* then in permanent form in *Cumulative Bulletins.* Appears as *Rev. Proc.*

Revenue Recognition Act of 1990   part of the larger *Omnibus Budget Reconciliation Act of 1990 (OBRA 90).* Among the many changes is the elimination of the "tax rate bubble," the application of a flat maximum tax rate of 31 percent to persons with taxable income above certain amounts, a limit on itemized deductions, and an increase in the Medicare hospital insurance tax.

revenue ruling   a published official interpretation of the tax law by the *National Office* of the *IRS* which first appears in the *Internal Revenue Bulletin.* Rulings are often based on replies to *requests for rulings* made by *taxpayers.* Such interpretations are prepared by the National Office of the IRS for the guidance of the public as well as for IRS officials and other persons, first in the *Internal Revenue Bulletins,* then in permanent form in the *Cumulative Bulletins.* They have modest authoritative weight. Rev. Proc. 78-24, 1978-2 C.B. 503. However, they do bind the IRS unless and until revoked. Statement of [IRS] Procedural Rules §601.201(a)(6). The private (unpublished) counterpart is the *private letter ruling.* Appears as *Rev. Rul.* See *ruling.*

reverse acquisition   if a transaction qualifies as a reverse acquisition, whether or not intended, the results can have adverse consequences to the surviving members. A *reverse acquisition* occurs (1) when a common parent ("first corporation"), or subsidiary of the first corporation, acquires, in exchange for the stock of the first corporation, either another corporation (second corporation) or a group of corporation (second group); and (2) the second corporation's (second group's) shareholders own more than 50 percent of the fair market value of the outstanding stock of the first corporation. For example, assume that Able Corporation and its two wholly owned subsidiaries, Tango and Foxtrot, have filed consolidated tax returns for the last six years, showing large consolidated profits each tax year. Able Corporation is owned equally by three individuals, Xerxes, Yugo, and Zen. Baxter Corporation and its two wholly owned subsidiaries, Dex and Eden, are 100 percent owned by Frank, an individual. Baxter Corporation and its two subsidiaries have experienced consolidated losses from the time of its formation five years ago. On January 1, 1993, the Able group merges into the Baxter group. As a result of the merger, the Able group receives 90 percent of the fair market value of the outstanding stock of Baxter. Because Baxter Corporation ("first corporation") and the Able shareholders (second corporation's shareholders) own more than 50 percent of the outstanding stock of Baxter, a *reverse acquisition* *has taken place*. Baxter survives, and Able's former shareholders control Baxter. If the requirements for a reverse acquisition are met, the Regulations provide the following: (1) the first corporation's group terminates at the date of acquisition, in this case Baxter; (2) the second corporation's group (Able) is treated as remaining in existence; and (3) the first corporation (Baxter) becomes the parent of the continuing group. §§1.1502-75(d)(3)(i)(b), Reg. 1.1502-75(d)(1).

reverse branch rule a doctrine found in the *regulations* in connection with *subpart F*. To explain by illustration, consider an overseas branch that, rather than doing the selling, does the manufacturing, with the parent doing the selling. In such cases, Reg. §1.954-3(b)(1)(ii) asserts that the sales income is *foreign base company income*. This is questionable, since the statute speaks of a branch having sales income. See *foreign base company sales income*.

reverse freeze recapitalization a corporate *recapitalization* in which senior shareholders get common *stock* and junior members get preferred *stock*. See Rev. Rul. 82-191 1982-1 C.B. 78 (senior shareholder's preferred treated as *section 306 stock* where the shareholder retained preferred and got common and preferred stocks). See *Type E reorganization*.

reverse merger see *reverse triangular merger*.

reverse mortgage loan a loan pursuant to which the lender makes *installment payments* of the loan to the borrower, with accrued *interest* added to the balance of the loan. See Rev. Rul. 80-248, 1980-2 C.B. 164 for tax impact on *cash method taxpayers*.

reverse repos another name for securities repurchase agreements (*repos*) under which securities investors buy government obligations on credit. The obligations ordinarily have substantial *accrued interest* at the time of purchase. Some time after the purchase, the investor enters into a repurchase agreement, usually through the brokerage firm (which in turn lays off the risk). Accrued interest is treated as a *return of capital* when received, and before maturity there are significant *interest expenses*. At maturity there can be a *long-term capital gain*. The term "reverse" refers to the fact that the transaction is viewed from the security owner's perspective; the creditor will be viewed as having engaged in a repos.

reverse Starker exchange a transaction in which the *taxpayer* receives the replacement property before transferring away the present property. This does not fit the mold of a deferred *like-kind exchange* contemplated by the statute.

reverse triangular merger a three-party *Type A reorganization* involving the *merger* of a *subsidiary* of the controlling *corporation* (*parent*) into another corpora-

tion (surviving corporation) whereby (1) the surviving corporation holds *substantially all of the properties* of both corporations (i.e., merged subsidiary and surviving corporation) after the transaction; and (2) in the transaction, former *shareholders* of the surviving corporation *exchange stock* constituting *control* for *voting stock* of the controlling corporation (parent of the merged subsidiary). §368(a)(2)(E). See Reg. §1.368-2(j) and -6(c); see also Rev. Ruls. 78-397, 1978-2 C.B. 150; 77-428, 1977-2 C.B. 117; 77-307, 1977-2 C.B. 117; 75-464, 1975-2 C.B. 474, 74-564, 1974-2 C.B. 124; 74-565, 1974-2 C.B. 125; Rev. Proc. 77-37, 1977-2 C.B. 568. Section 368(a)(3)(E) allows reverse triangular merger treatment to apply to *Type G reorganizations* if the former shareholders of the surviving corporation (i.e., the debtor) receive no consideration for their stock and if former creditors of the debtor corporation receive voting stock of the controlling corporation (parent) equal to 80 percent of the total value of the debt. See *corporate reorganization; Type A reorganization*.

reversionary interest transaction a term used to describe an arrangement common in the oil and gas industry under which an operator/sponsor invests cash, which is recovered only after the investors recover their investments.

revised issue price the *issue price* and the aggregate amount of *original issue discount* includible in *gross income* for all holders for the period previous to the taxpayer's acquisition of the *bond*. §1278(a)(4). If the bond has original issue discount, then *market discount* will exist if and to the extent the revised issue price exceeds the *taxpayer's basis* in the bond immediately after its acquisition, subject to a *de minimis rule*. §1278(a)(2)(B). This terminology is used for purposes of *stripped bonds*.

Revised Uniform Gifts to Minors Act a 1965 uniform act drafted by the National Conference of Commissioners on Uniform State Laws. It streamlines the *Uniform Gifts to Minors Act*.

Revised Uniform Limited Partnership Act a uniform act adopted in many states that updates the older *Uniform Limited Partnership Act* (ULPA). The *regulations* treat it like the ULPA. Reg. §301.7701-2(a)(5).

Revised Uniform Partnership Act an updated version of the *Uniform Partnership Act* currently under consideration by the National Conference of Commissioners on Uniform State Laws.

revoked terminated. The term is often used in reference to administrative positions to refer to the *IRS's* repudiation of a *revenue ruling* or a *revenue procedure*.

revolving charge accounts see *revolving credit plan*.

revolving credit plan cycle budget accounts, flexible budget accounts, continuous budget accounts, and other similar plans or arrangements for the sale of *personal property* by a dealer under which the customer agrees to pay each *billing month* a part of the outstanding balance of his or her account. The *installment method of accounting may not be used* for sales of personal property under a revolving credit plan, sales of stock or securities that are traded on an established exchange, and, to the extent provided by regulations, sales of other property of a kind regularly traded on an established market. All payments received are to be treated as received in the year of disposition. §453(k). See *dealer disposition; nondealer real property installment obligations.*

revolving credit sales   sales of *personal property* under a *revolving credit plan.*

rights, stock   the privilege attaching to a share of *stock* to subscribe to other securities in a fixed ratio. Rights are transferable *property* interests. They can be either sold, exercised, or allowed to expire. The rules for determining if a stock right is taxable to the shareholder are the same as those for stock dividends. §§305, Reg. §1.305-1. Thus, receipt of nontaxable stock rights has *no effect* on the shareholder's income in the year received. See *stock dividend.*

Right to Financial Privacy Act of 1978   a federal statute controlling the *IRS*'s and others' access to institutional creditors' records of their customers by restricting the creditors' rights to supply the IRS with information. 12 U.S.C. §3401 et seq. (1981 Supp. V). It forces the IRS to use the *third-party summons* procedures of §7609.

roll-out   another name for a transaction in which a *corporation* transfers its assets to a *master limited partnership* (MLP) in exchange for MLP interests, often in connection with a public offering of further MLP interests in order to fund the new MLP. It is a means of disincorporation of assets. See *publicly traded partnership.*

rollover   a *tax-deferred* transaction in which cash or other consideration is received, followed (or sometimes even preceded) by reinvestments of comparable amounts, with tax-deferred results. Examples include cash transferred from one *individual retirement arrangement* to another, reinvestments in new *principal residences,* and certain investments of insurance proceeds from *involuntary conversions.* Rollovers are distinct from *exchanges,* in that the party engaging in the rollover first receives a distribution of cash or property and then reinvests those proceeds.

rollover contributions   a nontechnical reference to potentially taxable transfers of retirement funds into *qualified plans* in a fashion designed to avoid current taxation of the amounts rolled over. The most common case involves the *employee* who separates from service with the *employer* and is paid *vested benefits* by the employer and who then transfers the distribution to an *individual retirement plan* within 60 days. See

§§402(a)(5)(A), 403(a)(4)(A). See *rollover distribution, qualifying.*

rollover distribution, qualifying   one or more distributions from a *qualified trust,* within an *employee's taxable year,* on account of termination of the *qualified retirement plan,* or with respect to a complete discontinuance of *contributions* to a *profit-sharing* or *stock bonus plan,* or as a *lump-sum distribution* (as modified), or which constitute a distribution of *accumulated deductible employee contributions.* Such amounts can generally be rolled over on a *tax-deferred* basis. See §402(a)(5)(D)(1). See *eligible retirement plan; partial distribution.*

rollover, individual retirement arrangements   a reference to *taxpayers'* rights arising under §408(d)(3) to engage in tax-free reinvestments of *distributions* from *individual retirement accounts* and *annuities.* Such amounts may be promptly transferred to *IRAs* or *qualified plans.*

rollover of principal residence   another term for transactions that meet the requirements of §1034, which can result in *deferral* of *gain* on the *sale* or *exchange* of a *principal residence* (house, condominium, trailer, etc., and related land not used for profit). The principal requirements of §1034 are that the *taxpayer* buy or construct a new principal residence within 24 months before or after the sale of the old residence, and that the taxpayer occupy the replacement property within the applicable 24-month period. Also, the residence must not lose its character, e.g., via excessive rental efforts. If the conditions of §1034 are met, the taxpayers *recognize gain* on sale or *exchange* of their principal residences only to the extent the *adjusted sales price* of the former principal residence is less than the cost of the new principal residence (including improvements made to the replacement property within the statutory period). §§1001, 1034(a). To the extent gain is deferred as a result of §1034, *basis* in the new principal residence is reduced. §1034(e). Section 1034 is mandatory and can be combined with the elective $125,000 exclusion from *gross income* provided by §121.

rollover, proceeds of involuntary conversion   a colloquial reference for the use of proceeds of an *involuntary conversion* of *property* to acquire other property that is sufficiently similar to the former property to justify deferring the *recognition* of *gains* under §1033. In the typical case, the proceeds are from casualty insurance policies, and the *taxpayer* must acquire property that is *similar or related in service or use* within a two-year *reinvestment period.* The details of this *deferral* provision are ornate, providing special rules for *real estate,* acquisition of certain *corporations* holding qualified property, livestock, billboards, and certain other special situations. See *threat or imminence of condemnation, involuntary conversions.*

roll up see *exchange offer.*

royalties, generally amounts received or accrued for the right to use *intangible property* such as a *patent, copyright, trademark,* secret process, or secret formula, or for the right to exploit natural resources such as gas, oil, coal, timber, sand, or gravel payable over the life of the contract, without dollar limitation. When the property is a patent, secret formula, or secret process, the agreement is often called a *license,* in which case the parties are classified licensor and licensee. Rev. Rul. 78-328, 1978-2 C.B. 215. Natural resource royalties are distinguished from *production payments* in that the former involves the right to a specified percentage of production over the life of the *lease* without limitation to a particular sum. Reg. §1.636-3(a)(1). There is an extensive body of judge-made law as to whether a transaction creates a sale, a royalty, or a license.

royalties paid or incurred, depletion amounts *paid or incurred* as *royalties* in connection with natural resource extraction. Payments of the *lessor's* taxes can be treated like royalties. Rev. Rul. 72-165, 1972-1 C.B. 177. A royalty owner has a *nonoperating interest* in the property, as opposed to an *operating interest.* A royalty interest is an *economic interest* that entitles the payee to *depletion deductions.* Royalties paid or incurred are *excluded* from *gross income* when *percentage depletion* is calculated. §613(a); Reg. §1.613-2(c)(5)(i). But for this rule, *percentage depletion* could be improperly duplicated. See *economic interest, depletion allowance.*

royalties, personal holding company income amounts received for the privilege of using *patents, copyrights,* secret processes and formulas, *goodwill, trademarks,* trade brands, franchises, and other similar *intangible personal property.* As used in this context, the term royalties does not include (1) *rents* (§543(a)(2)); (2) mineral, oil, and gas royalties (§543(a)(3)); (3) *copyright royalties* (§543(a)(4)); or (4) *produced film rents* (§543(a)(5)). Reg. §1.543-1(b)(3); see, e.g., Rev. Rul. 70-153, 1970-1 C.B. 139; Rev. Rul. 54-284, 1954-2 C.B. 275. Royalties are viewed as passive income and form part of the *personal holding company income* base. §543(a)(1).

royalties, section 1244 stock under section 1244, losses on "section 1244 stock" generally treated as ordinary income rather than capital losses. If section 1244 stock is sold at a loss, the single taxpayer may deduct up to $50,000 annually against ordinary income. Taxpayers who file jointly may deduct up to $100,000. Section 1244 treatment applies if the corporation is an "operating company" when the shareholder's loss is sustained. §1244(c). A corporation is treated as an operating company if at least 50 percent of its gross receipts for the five most recent taxable years ending before the date of the loss are derived from sources *other than* royalties, rents, dividends, interest, annuities, and gains

from sales or exchanges of stocks or securities. §1244(e)(1)(C). *Royalties* include mineral, oil, and gas royalties (as defined in Reg. §1.543-11(b)(ii) and (iii)) and amounts received for the privilege of using intellectual property.

royalty trusts *trusts* established by oil and gas companies to which *royalty* interests are transferred. The trust's *beneficiaries* are the shareholders of the *corporation,* who benefit from *depletion deductions.* The trust interests are typically transferable *certificates of beneficial interest.* The primary benefit of such trusts is avoidance of the *corporate income tax.*

rule of 45 an alternate *vesting* rule for *qualified deferred compensation plans* under which the plan must provide that *employer contributions* for an unterminated *employee* with at least five years of service must vest when the sum of his or her age and *years of service* equals or exceeds 45. It is being phased out.

rule of parity, qualified plans a provision that allows a *qualified plan* to disregard a non*vested participant's* service before a *one-year break in service* if the number of consecutive one-year breaks in service is at least equal to his or her aggregate pre-break service. §411(a)(6)(D). Aggregate pre-break service does not include any years of service disregarded under this rule because of any previous break in service. The effect can be to sharply limit the *employee's* ability to participate in the plan after re-employment. *Nonqualified plans* also are permitted to use this rule. *ERISA,* Pub. L. No. 93-406, §203(b)(3)(D), 88 Stat. 829.

rule of seventy-eights a procedure that allows *accrual* of *interest* on *debt* in each month to be computed as the product of the entire amount of interest payable over the term of the debt times a fraction, the numerator of which is the remaining number of months of the debt and the denominator of which is the sum of the numbers from 1 to the number of months in the term of the debt. If the procedure can be applied properly to *accrual method taxpayers,* annual payments on the debt commonly are substantially less than the interest *deductions* in the first several years of the debt. Rev. Rul. 72-100, 1972-2 C.B. 122 (*cash method* taxpayers are allowed to use the rule of seventy-eights with respect to the installment obligations issued at a discount). The *IRS* accepts the formula for consumer loans for up to five years. Rev. Rul. 83-84, 1983-23 I.R.B. 12; Rev. Proc. 83-40, 1983-23 I.R.B. 22.

ruling a writing issued in response to a *taxpayer,* or *taxpayer representative* by personnel of the *IRS National Office* pursuant to authority granted the Assistant Commissioner (Technical), and redelegated to branches of the National Office. Reg. §601.201(a)(2). Such rulings, generally, may be issued before or after a transaction and take the form of written statements which interpret the law and apply it to the taxpayer's circumstances. Taxpayers are generally entitled to rely on such rulings, absent misrepresentation in the taxpayers' inquiry. Rulings are in the public domain, and related *background file documents* may be requested after appropriate deletions of factual matters are made to both the ruling and the background file documents. See Rev. Proc. 79-45, 1979-2 C.B. 508. Rulings have no formal protective value for different taxpayers. For *no ruling* areas, see Rev. Procs. 77-27, 1977-2 C.B. 537; 76-19, 1976-1 C.B. 500; 76-1, 1976-1 C.B. 542; 74-17, 1974-1 C.B. 438; 72-9, 1972-1 C.B. 718. The term "ruling" is synonymous with letter rulings and private letter rulings. They are distinct from *revenue rulings,* which are public and may be relied on.

ruling amount   the amount for any year, that the *IRS* rules necessary (1) to fund future *nuclear power plant decommissioning costs,* and (2) to prevent excess funding or funding at a more rapid than level funding. §468A(d)(2). Such amounts are a limit on permissible *accruals* of future *expenses* for such decommissionings. §468A(b).

ruling request   see *request for ruling.*

runaway spouse rule   another nickname for §7703(b), which defines marital status, the gist of which is that a *taxpayer* may file a special *separate return* if his or her *spouse* was not a *member of the household* during the last half of the *taxable year,* and if he or she provided more than one-half the cost of maintaining a household at home, which was the *principal place of abode* of a son, daughter, stepson, or stepdaughter who qualifies as a *dependent,* for more than one-half of the year. A special exception eliminates the dependency requirement in divorce cases where the *noncustodial parent* gets the exemption and for certain custody cases affected by prior law. The effect of the rule is to allow the spouse who meets these tests to file as a *head of household,* thereby enjoying more favorable tax rates than if filing a *separate return* as a *married person* and a large *standard deduction.* §§2(b), (c), and 152(e).

Runzheimer-type plan   a plan under which *employees* who are drivers are paid a fixed dollar amount each month plus a cents-per-mile reimbursement. The *IRS* is expected to apply §62(c) to such plans. See *accountable plan.*

rural electric cooperatives, eligible state deferred compensation plans   (1) any *exempt organizations* engaged primarily in providing electric service on a mutual or cooperative basis; and (2) any exempt *civic leagues* or *organizations* or *business leagues* (§501(c)(4) and (6)), at least 80 percent of whose members are described in (1) above. §457(d)(9)(B). *Eligible state deferred compensation plans* can cover rural electric cooperatives. §457(d)(9). See also §401(k)(7) (certain *cash or deferred plans*).

S

S corporation   a *corporation* treated for federal *income tax* purposes in a manner somewhat similar to a *partnership* if it and its *stockholders* so elect and consent, respectively. To be able to make the election, a corporation must be *domestic,* not a member of an *affiliated group* (determined without regard to whether the corporation is an *includible corporation* under §1504(b)) and may own only *inactive subsidiaries.* The corporation must not have (1) more than 35 *stockholders*; (2) any stockholder, other than an *estate* and certain *trusts,* who is not an *individual*; (3) a *nonresident alien* as a stockholder; and (4) more than one class of stock, although voting right variations are tolerated. §1361(a). In addition to not being a member of an affiliated group, it must not otherwise be an *ineligible corporation* (e.g., a *DISC* or small *bank* that can use *reserves for bad debts*). §1361(b)(1). Tax benefits to the corporation's stockholders include the stockholders' *deducting* their share of the corporation's *net operating losses* on their personal *tax returns* (§§1366 and 1374) and the stockholders' including their share of the corporation's *net capital gain* on their personal tax returns (§1366), in exchange for not applying the *corporate income tax.* See *small business corporation, S corporations; straight debt.*

S period   the most recent continuous period during which a *corporation* has been an *S corporation,* excluding any *taxable year* beginning before January 1, 1983. §1368(e)(2).

S short year   see *S termination year.*

S termination year   a year in which an *S corporation* terminates its status (e.g., because *stock* was sold to a *nonresident alien*). A termination creates two *short* periods, one of which is an *S short year* and the other a *C short year.* §1362(e).

SAR   an acronym for a *stock appreciation right (SAR)* or *special agent's report.*

SBIC   an acronym for a *small business investment company.*

SCIN   an acronym for a *self-canceling installment note.*

SEC   an acronym for *Securities and Exchange Commission.*

SECA   an acronym for Self-Employment Contributions Act of 1954, 26 U.S.C. §1401 et seq. (1976). See *self-employment tax.*

Sen. Rep.   Senate Report.

SEP   an acronym for *simplified employee pension plan (SEP).*

SEP-CODA plan   an acronym for a hybrid consisting of a *simplified employee pension plan* and a *salary reduction plan.* §408(k)(6). See *salary reduction SEP.*

SIC   an acronym for *standard industrial classification codes.*

SIGNID   an acronym for a *significant new issuance of debt.*

SLOB   an acronym for a *separate line of business* under §414(r).

S.R.   Senate Report.

SRLY   an acronym for *separate return limitation year.*

SRLY fragmentation rule   a reference to Reg. §1.1502-21A(g)(2), which is now threatened with extinction.

SSI recipient   any *individual* who is certified by the *designated local agency* as receiving supplemental security income benefits under Title XVI of the Social Security Act (including supplemental security income benefits of the type described in §1616 of that Act or §212 of Pub. L. No. 93-66) for any month ending in the preemployment period. §51(d)(5). See *SUTAB trust; targeted jobs credit.*

SUTAB trust   a *supplemental unemployment benefit trusts.*

safe harbor   a provision in the *Code* or *regulations,* the effect of which is to assure a particular tax result if objective conditions are met. Typically, safe harbor provisions are found with respect to murky areas of tax law, such as the determination of whether a *stock redemption* should be treated as a *sale* of corporate *stock* or a *distribution.* Thus, for example, §302(b)(2) and (3) provide safe haven provisions for closely defined partial and complete redemptions of a *shareholder's* interest. The benefit of such provisions is administrative efficiency for *taxpayers* and the government.

safe harbor rule   a provision which assures a result, usually in a precarious area of the law. See *safe harbor.*

safety achievement award   an item of *tangible personal property* awarded to an *employee* for a safety achievement. (The term "*safety achievement*" is undefined.) However, an award is deemed not for safety achievement if, during the *taxable year,* employee achievement awards (other than awards *excludable* as *de minimis fringe benefits*) for safety achievement have previously been awarded by the *employer* to more than

10 percent of the employees of the employer (excluding employees described below), or if the item is awarded to a manager, administrator, clerical employee, or other professional employee. §274(j)(4)(c). The award is exempt from the $25 limit on *business gift deductions,* provided it is *tangible personal property* that (1) costs $400 or less, or (2) is a *qualified plan award.* §274(j)(4)(C). Such awards may be *deductible* by the payor up to $400 or $1,600, depending on whether they are *qualified plan awards,* and may be equally *excluded* from *gross income by* the recipient. §274(j) and (c). See *employee achievement award; excess deduction award; qualified plan award.*

safety zones a term often used to describe the various relaxations of the rules relating to *required installments* or of *estimated taxes.*

sailing permit a reference to a certificate of compliance with *federal income tax* laws required of most *aliens* who depart the *United States.* The requirement does not apply to a number of classes of persons, including diplomats and like officials, vacationers, temporary business travelers, and Mexican and Canadian guest workers. §6851(d)(1).

salary reduction, cash or deferred arrangement a form of *cash or deferred* plan applied by reducing the *employee's* basic compensation.

salary reduction plans adjuncts to *qualified profit-sharing, stock bonus, pre-ERISA money purchase,* or *rural electric cooperatives plans,* relatively obscure until the recent rediscovery of §401(k), which permits *elective deferrals* by *employees* up to $8,728 (in 1992), and adjusted for inflation annually) of their *wages* or salaries, with the *employer* placing such amounts in its *qualified trust.* Excess *contributions* attract an *excise tax.* In order to qualify for favorable tax treatment, it must be a *qualified cash or deferred arrangement.* If, in addition to meeting the general requirements for all qualified profit-sharing or stock bonus plans, certain further requirements are met, then employees are not taxed on current *deferrals* and such amounts are freed of *federal employment taxes* and *withholding taxes,* and accumulate tax-free until distributed. §402(a)(8). These plans are also commonly referred to as *cash* or *deferred* plans. See *highly compensated employee, cash or deferred plans; qualified plan.*

salary reduction SEP a *simplified employee pension plan (SEP)* which operates on the basis of salary reductions. The *deferred compensation* is contributed to an *IRA,* thereby saving administrative burdens for the *employer.* §408(k)(6). Deferred income is not taxable to the *employee* until payout from the SEP, but it is subject to federal *employment taxes.* §402(h) and 3121(a)(5). Only employers with 25 or less eligible employees at any time during the year can qualify. §408(k)(6)(B).

Deferrals are capped at $7,000 per year for each employee. §§408(k)(6), 401(a)(30), and 402(g). At least one-half of the employees must choose to defer some compensation into the SEP. §408(k)(6)(A). There are further tests geared toward not discriminating in favor of *highly compensated employees.* §414(s). See *compensation, qualified plans.*

sale a transfer of *property* in exchange for money or a promise of money. Section 1001(a) is the principal authority for defining *gains* or *losses* from *sales.* A sale is considered a basis for finding a *realization* of gain or loss, such that those gains or losses must be reported for *federal income tax* purposes, absent a *nonrecognition provision.* A sale may be *constructive* as well as actual; see, for example, §165(g) relating to *worthless securities.* An actual or constructive sale or *exchange* is required in order for a *capital transaction* to be found. §1222. See *amount realized; exchange.*

sale and leaseback a transaction in which, in form, *a taxpayer sells* property to another *person* and then *rents* it back from the buyer, usually in order to raise cash. Such transactions are often entered into in order for the taxpayer to shift income from rents, to create rental *deductions,* to realize a *loss,* to create *stepped-up basis,* or some combination of purposes. The loss may be disallowed as a *like-kind exchange* if a 30-year (or longer) *lease* is involved, since a 30-year lease is viewed as *real estate* under §1031, or the overall arrangements may be recharacterized as a *mortgage,* especially if the real economic interest in the property remains with the seller-lessee.

sale and purchase inventory method an *inventory accounting* method under which returnable containers are included in inventory until sold along with their contents.

sale for contingent payments a *sale* whose price terms are determined after the year of closing, such as a sale of mineral property, the price of which varies with mineral extraction. Before enactment of the *Installment Sales Revision Act of 1980,* such sales were disqualified from *installment sales* reporting and were on occasion treated as *open transactions.* Now, however, they qualify for installment sales reporting, even under extreme circumstances (e.g., if the contract contains neither the maximum sales price nor a stated number of years, then *basis* is generally recovered over 15 years). See Reg. §15a.453-1(c)(2). The *income forecast method* may be available to mitigate hardships in such cases. Reg. §15a.453-1(c)(6).

sale on the installment plan a *sale* of *personal property* by the *taxpayer* under any plan for the sale or other *disposition* of personal property, which plan, by its term and conditions, contemplates that each sale under the plan will be in two or more payments. It may be on a *traditional installment plan* or sales on a *revolving credit plan*. Reg. §1.453-2(b). See PLR 8746077 (Aug. 20, 1987). Dealers generally can no longer (but previously could) use the *installment method*. See *installment method*.

sale or other disposition   a *sale* or other *disposition* of *property*. §1001(a). While other dispositions create *realized gains* or *losses*, only *sales* or *exchanges* are considered to create *capital transactions*. §1222. See *disposition; property*.

sales price, unstated interest rule   the price at which *property* changes hands, in which *interest* stated in the contract is ignored. Reg. §1.483-1(b)(1). The term is a needed part of the mechanism used to impute the existence of *unstated interest*. See *imputed interest*.

sales, revolving credit plans   *sales* of services, such as a charge for watch repair, as well as sales of property; finance or service charges are not included. Reg. §1.453-2(d)(6)(i). They cannot use the *installment method*. §453(k). See *revolving credit plan*.

sales taxes   see *compensating use tax*.

salvage value   the value of an asset, reduced by removal costs, at the end of the asset's *useful life*, for purposes of establishing *depreciation* and *amortization deductions* under §167.

same business enterprise   see *change of business*.

same-country exception   a rule originally expressed in Rev. Proc. 68-23, 1968-1 C.B. 821, §3.02(1)-(a)(iii)(B) to the effect that where at least 80 percent of the *stock* of a *foreign* subsidiary is transferred to another *foreign corporation* in the same country and controlled by the same parent, no *section 367 ruling* is required. See PLR 8313099 (Dec. 29, 1982) for an alternate route to avoiding a *toll charge* where there was a good *business purpose* for a transfer that does not qualify under this exception. Since then, it has been codified in §367 by the *legislative history* to the *Tax Reform Act of 1984*.

sandwich lease   another name for *lease* transactions under which a *tax-exempt entity* is interposed between two taxable parties as a lessee-sublessor to achieve *deferral* of income to the ultimate *lessor* without sacrificing the *deductions* of the *lessee*. Section 467 was designed to thwart such transactions.

saving plan, qualified plan   any *qualified plan* that allows voluntary *employee* contributions. See *voluntary employee savings plan*.

savings clauses   treaty clauses designed to prevent *citizens* or *residents* of a treaty country (e.g., American *citizens*) from using a *tax treaty* (e.g., Canada–United States Treaty) to minimize local (e.g., United States) taxes. Basically, such clauses provide that the

United States may tax *resident aliens, citizens of the United States,* and *corporations* as if a treaty had not come into effect.

savings plan   see *voluntary employee savings plan*.

schedule C-EZ for self-employed persons   starting in 1992, self-employed taxpayers can use a streamlined Schedule C-EZ, "Net Profit from Business." Most cash method sole proprietors who have only one business, and gross receipts of $25,000 or less, and who do not have more than $2,000 in expenses, are eligible to use this form. IR 92-79, July 15, 1992.

schedule K-1 forms   issued to *partnerships (1065 K-1), S corporations (1120 K-1),* and trusts *(1041 K-1),* respectively, to report the recipient's tax results for the *entity's taxable year*.

scholarship   an amount paid to an undergraduate or graduate student who is a candidate for a degree at a qualified educational organization that is *excludable* from income. The amount to be excluded by a degree candidate covers tuition, books, supplies, and equipment. §117. No exclusion is allowed payments covering room and board. In addition, the exclusion will *not* apply to amounts representing payments for teaching, research, or other services performed by the student that are a condition for receiving the scholarship. §117(c). Non-degree candidates must include scholarships and fellowships in income. See *educational assistance plan*.

scientific organization   a type of potentially *exempt organization* which can also receive *charitable contributions* which are *deductible* to the *donor*. It must perform basic or applied research in the public interest. Scientific research is considered to be performed in the public interest if the results, including any patents, copyrights, processes, or formulas, are made available to the public on a nondiscriminatory basis, or if the research is performed for the *United States*, its agencies or instrumentalities, or a state or its *political subdivisions*, or if the research is directed toward benefiting the public. §501(c)(3); Reg. §1.501(c)(3)-1(d)(5); Rev. Rul. 78-426, 1978-2 C.B. 175.

scrip dividends   a general term referring to *distributions* that entitle the *shareholder* to money, securities, or some other form of property at a future date. Such distributions result in immediate taxation, even though all that is being distributed is a promise. Generally, scrip dividends are only taxable as *dividends* if cash in lieu of scrip were distributed. Rev. Rul. 69-202, 1969-1 C.B. 95.

second disposition rule, installment sales   a *disposition* by an installment purchaser that has the effect of accelerating the *recognition* of *gains* by a related installment seller under §453(e). The measure is designed to prevent installment sellers from *recognizing* income slowly while related installment purchasers promptly dispose of their acquisitions. A precondition, therefore, is a first disposition to a *related taxpayer* as defined in §267(b). §453(f). In turn, there must be a second disposition of the property within two years of the first disposition, except for *marketable securities* for which the second disposition rules apply any time before full pay-down on the first sale. See *related taxpayers, loss and deduction denial*.

second examination   an additional inspection of a *taxpayer* and his or her books of account for the same *taxable year*. §7605(b); Reg. §301.7605-1(b). The definition is closely confined. It excludes records held by the taxpayer's attorney or other third persons for years that have neither been accepted by the *IRS* nor been closed by a written notice from the IRS (PLR 8030014 (Apr. 18, 1980)). There are various further restrictions. The courts will deny the IRS the right to a second inspection unless the IRS provides a proper written notice that a second inspection is necessary. §7605(b). This is distinct from the more general obligation on the part of the government not to engage in *unnecessary examinations*.

second level withholding tax   an informal term for a *withholding tax* imposed on *distributions* and *interest* from *domestic corporations* to *nonresident aliens* and *foreign corporations*. §§1441–1442.

second-tier corporation, foreign tax credit   a *foreign corporation* of which a *first-tier corporation* owns at least 10 percent of the voting *stock*. §902(b). As long as a *domestic corporation* has at least a five-percent indirect ownership interest in the second-tier corporation, the *deemed paid foreign tax credit* provisions consider the first-tier corporation to have received a *distribution* (along with any actual *dividends*) equal to its ratable share of the second-tier corporation's foreign *taxes*. See *first-tier corporation, foreign tax credit; foreign tax credit*.

second-tier excise tax   an informal term for any of the *excise taxes* imposed on *private foundations* under §§4941–4945 as a result of failure to correct the abuse that attracted the so-called *first-tier excise tax*. See *excise taxes, private foundations*.

second-tier partnership   a *partnership*, at least some of the interests of which are owned by another *(first-tier) partnership*.

second-tier subsidiary   a subsidiary of a subsidiary. Likewise, a third-tier subsidiary is a subsidiary of a second-tier subsidiary. The control requirements to find a second, third, etc., subsidiary vary with the particular *Code* section.

second-tier withholding tax   a *withholding tax* on *dividends* paid by *foreign corporations*. The second-tier

tax does not apply if the *branch profits tax* does apply. §884(e)(3)(A).

Secretarial list   a term used in §6662(d)(2)(D) to describe a list of tax reporting positions that will be periodically issued by the *IRS* that the government states to be unauthoritative. Positions on the list (*list positions*) will have no credibility with the government, even though they were disclosed on the return. Thus, *adequate disclosure* of the positions will not dispel the penalties. See *penalty, substantial understatement of income tax*.

Secretary   when used in the *Code*, the term refers to the *Secretary of the Treasury* or his or her *delegate*, unless otherwise distinctly expressed or manifestly incompatible with the intent of the provision in which it appears. §7701 (a)(11)(B). See *Treasury Department*.

Secretary of the Treasury   when used in the *Code*, the term refers to the Secretary of the Treasury personally, and it does not include any *delegate* thereof, unless otherwise distinctly expressed or manifestly incompatible with the intent of the provision in which it appears. §7701(a)(11)(A). See *Treasury Department*.

section 38 property   *property* that qualified for the former *investment tax credit*, as defined in §48. Generally, it consists of *tangible personal property* which is *held for the production of income* or *used in a trade or business*. Certain other tangible property which would generally be *real estate* (other than *buildings* and their *structural components*) also qualifies, if used for certain industrial or extractive purposes, as do *elevators and escalators, single-purpose agricultural and horticultural structures, qualified rehabilitated buildings*, research facilities, certain bulk *storage facilities*, and timber *reforestation*. Property used overseas is largely excluded.

section 79 life insurance   see *group-term life insurance*.

section 125 plan   same as a *cafeteria plan*.

section 171(c) election to amortize taxable bonds   investors in taxable bonds may *elect* to amortize the bond premium, but the bond premium on tax-exempt bonds must be amortized. The amount of the amortized premium on taxable bonds is permitted as an interest deduction.

section 170(b)(1)(A) organizations   organizations with respect to which *individual taxpayers* may make *charitable contributions* that qualify for the favorable 50 percent limitation on the currently *deductible* amount of such gifts. These organizations consist of (1) *churches, conventions, or associations of churches*; (2) exempt *educational institutions*; (3) *exempt hospital or medical research* organizations; (4)

public or government-supported organizations holding and investing property for a state college or university; (5) a *state, federal,* or local governmental unit; (6) an organization that normally receives a substantial part of its support from the public or a governmental unit; (7) a *private operating foundation*; (8) other *private foundations* that distribute all their contributions to public charities (or otherwise make qualifying distributions) within two and one-half months after the end of their *taxable years*; (9) organizations that normally receive (a) more than one-third of their support from the public in the form of contributions, membership fees, and the like, and (b) not more than one-third from gross *investment* income; and (10) community foundations (often called *community trusts*) that pool taxable contributions into a common fund and permit the contributor to designate a recipient charity. §170(b)(1)(A); Reg. §1.170A-9.

section 170(b)(1)(C)(iii) election   an election that permits a *taxpayer* to reduce the *basis* of property as to which there is a *capital gain* in order to qualify for the 50 percent limit on *charitable contributions*. It is irrevocable, under the *doctrine of election*.

section 179 election to expense certain depreciable business assets   permits an election to write off up to $10,000 of the acquisition cost of tangible personal property used in a trade or business. Amounts that are expensed may not be capitalized and depreciated.

section 195 election to amortize start-up expenses if a taxpayer is in a business that is not the same as the one being investigated, and if the investigation effort actually leads to the acquisition of a new business, the business investigation expenses must be capitalized. The taxpayer may then elect to amortize the costs over a period of 60 months or more.

section 243(d) dividend   a *dividend* paid by a *foreign corporation* out of *earnings and profits* that were accumulated while it was subject to federal *income taxes*. Such dividends are treated as if paid by taxable *domestic corporations*. §243(d). They can qualify for the *dividends-received deduction* of §243(a). As such, they may be so-called *qualifying dividends*. See *qualifying dividends, dividends-received deduction*.

section 248 election to amortize organizational expenditures   under Section 248, a corporation may elect to amortize organizational expenses over a period of *60 months or more*. Organizational expenditures consist of legal services incident to organization (e.g., drafting the corporate charter), necessary accounting services, expenses of temporary directors, and fees paid to the state of incorporation. If the election is not made on a timely basis, the expenditures cannot be deducted until the business ceases operations and liquidates.

section 269 acquisitions   see *acquisition to evade or avoid taxes*.

section 303 redemption needs   if corporate stock represents a substantial portion of a decedent's estate, a redemption of the stock from the estate or its beneficiaries may be eligible under §303. The intent of this Code provision is to help those shareholders who inherit stock in a closely held corporation and who are required to sell their stock to pay estate taxes, inheritance taxes, and funeral and administrative expenses. If the stock cannot be readily sold on the open market, a stock redemption may provide the estate and the beneficiaries with sufficient liquidity to meet their cash requirements. Section 303 *redemption* needs are considered a valid reason for accumulating earnings. §537(a)(2). See *accumulated earnings tax; reasonable needs of the business, accumulated earnings tax*.

section 306 stock   *stock* that, when redeemed or *sold*, will generally result in the *shareholder* realizing *ordinary income*. Section 306 is designed to bar *"bailout"* of *earnings and profits* through the issuance and later the sale or *redemption* (or both) of preferred stock. Section 306 stock is stock other than common stock that (1) is received as a nontaxable stock dividend; (2) is received tax-free in a corporate reorganization or separation to the extent that either the effect of the transaction was substantially the same as the receipt of a stock dividend or the stock was received in exchange for section 306 stock; or (3) has a basis determined by reference to the basis of section 306 stock. If section 306 stock is redeemed, the shareholder simply treats the proceeds as a current *distribution,* unless the *redemption* is in complete termination of the shareholder's interest under §302(b)(3). §306(a)(2). The amount realized in a redemption of section 306 stock is a *dividend to the extent of earnings and profits* in the year of redemption. Unlike a sale of Section 306 stock, earnings and profits are reduced as a result of the redemption. See *common stock, section 306 stock; holding company bailouts; tax avoidance*.

section 331 liquidation   another name for a straightforward *corporate liquidation* other than of an 80-percent-owned subsidiary. Section 331(a) generally treats the *shareholder* as having *exchanged* his or her *stock* for the proceeds of the liquidation. The amount of the shareholder's gain or loss equals the difference between the amount realized and his basis for the stock. If a shareholder assumes or acquires liabilities of the liquidating corporation, the amount of these liabilities reduces the amount realized by the shareholder. See *Form 966*.

section 332 liquidation   a complete *liquidation* of a controlled subsidiary *corporation* into its parent corporation, the so-called *80 percent distributee*. The transaction can be accomplished *free of current taxes* to the parent if the various conditions of §332 are met, but at the price of taking a *basis* in the subsidiary's assets equal to their basis in the subsidiary's hands (i.e., *tax deferral* only, except that if and to the extent the subsidiary has *recognized gains or losses*). §334(b). The transaction is also largely tax-free to the subsidiary. *Control* is defined under the 80 percent standard applicable to *affiliated groups*. §332(b)(1). See *Form 966.*

section 333 liquidation   a pre-1986 law construct involving an elective form of *complete liquidation* available to *domestic corporations* that could result in a substantial portion of the *gain realized* from the transfer of property by the liquidating corporation being deferred. To qualify for this preferential tax treatment, which was available only to *qualified electing shareholders,* the liquidation had to be made in pursuance of a plan of liquidation and all the corporate property had to be distributed in some particular calendar month period in complete cancellation or *redemption* of all its *stock.* Section 333 was most commonly used to liquidate corporations holding appreciated property only, the result of which is deferral of income at the price of a basis in the property equal to the shareholders' basis in the stock of the liquidated company. Former §334(c). Such liquidations were often referred to as *one-month liquidations.* See *qualified electing shareholder.*

section 336(e) election   an election to treat the *sale, exchange,* or *distribution* of all the *stock* of a subsidiary as if the transaction were a *disposition* of all the assets of the subsidiary. No gain or loss is recognized on the sale, exchange, or distribution of the stock. The tax implications of §336(e) are favorable, but they have not been fully worked out. See *triple tax, corporate.*

section 337   (prior law) a pre-1986 law construct involving the *complete liquidation* of a *corporation,* pursuant to which all the assets (except minor retentions to meet claims), including proceeds from *dispositions* of the assets formerly owned by the liquidating corporation, or both, could be distributed within one year of the shareholders' adoption of a plan of complete liquidation. Former §337. *Sales* or *exchanges* of *property* in connection with such liquidations could be largely or entirely tax-free under former §337, although *losses* were not *recognized.* The *Tax Reform Act of 1986* repealed the 12-month liquidation provisions of §337 and replaced them with a new §337 that provides an exception to the general rule requiring recognition of *gain* or loss; however, no gain or *loss* is *recognized* when a controlled subsidiary corporation is liquidated into its parent corporation. §332(a). See *liquidating distribution; section 332 liquidation.*

section 338 acquisition   a corporate liquidation under which a purchasing and target corporation elect an indirect acquisition of the assets by first having the target corporation's shareholders sell their stock to the acquiring corporation and then having the acquiring corporation make a deemed liquidation election with respect to the target corporation. The section 338 election permits the basis of the target corporation's assets to be increased by the amount paid by the acquiring corporation for the target corporation's stock. The provisions of §338 are very complex. See *affirmative action carryover basis election; consistency period, section 338 acquisitions; consistency requirements, section 338 acquisitions; deemed election, section 338 acquisitions; grossed-up basis; protective carryover basis election; section 338 election; target affiliate, section 338 acquisitions.*

section 338 election treating certain stock purchases as asset purchases   an election pursuant to which *purchases* of *stock* of a *target company* may be treated as being followed by an imaginary *liquidation* of the target, followed by the repurchase of those assets by the target on the following day. The election is made on *Form 8023.* The practical effect is to adjust the *basis* of the target company's assets to *fair market value* at the price of a current tax that falls on the target as an unconsolidated *corporation.* (This is subject to an exception allowing the filing of a *consolidated deemed sale return* if a group of target corporations was bought on the same *acquisition date.*) §338(a), (h)(9), and (h)(15). The election may also arise involuntarily. The *Tax Reform Act of 1984* clarified §338(a)(1) to provide that the target is deemed to sell its assets at *fair market value.* The gross-up procedure to determine the deemed purchase price was amended to allow the acquirer to elect, at the price of a likely *capital gain,* to step up the basis of *nonrecently purchased stock* (stock acquired before the *12-month acquisition period*). §338(b)(3). These are further refinements. See *deemed election, section 338 acquisitions.*

section 338(b)(3) election to step up basis of targets—non-recently purchased stock—earlier than 12 months before acquisition date   an election that allows acquiring *corporations* to elect to step up the *basis* of *nonrecently purchased stock* at the price of a tax so as to increase the basis of assets of the *target corporation.* The tax assumes that nonrecently purchased stock was sold at a price reflecting the cost of the *recently purchased stock.* §338(b)(3)(B).

section 338(g) election   same as a *section 338 election.*

section 338(h)(10) elective recognition of gain or loss by target corporation, together with nonrecognition by selling consolidated group   an election that permits a target corporation (e.g., a subsidiary) to recognize gain or loss as if it had sold the assets in a single transaction while still a member of the selling group. The asset sale is then treated as a taxable transaction. The election is to be made jointly by purchasing and selling consolidated groups in a statement on *Form 8023*. The statement must contain (1) the name, address, and identification numbers of each member of the purchasing group, target corporation, and selling group; (2) location where the selling group filed its consolidated return for the period that includes the acquisition date or last taxable period for which the return was filed; and (3) signatures of an authorized representative of the purchasing group and a person from the common parent of the selling group. Reg. §1.338(h)(10)-1T. See *section 338 acquisition*.

section 1.338-6T shareholder   a *target corporation* that directly owns *stock* in an *affected target* that meets the requirements for filing a *consolidated return* under §1504(a)(2). A target *recognizes* no *gain* or *loss* on the deemed *sale* of stock of an affected target that is a section 1.338-6T shareholder if a section 338(g) election is made with respect to the affected target. This prevents multiple taxation under §338. See *section 338 election*.

section 341 assets   certain properties held by a potentially *collapsible corporation* less than three years, specifically: (1) *stock in trade*; (2) *dealer property*; (3) *section 1231 assets,* regardless of their *holding period,* but not property used in connection with the manufacture, construction, production, or *sale* of property set forth in (1) or (2) above; and (4) *unrealized receivables or fees* except those relating to items (1) through (3) above. §341(b)(3). *Holding periods* of such assets are *tacked* in the case of *tax-free exchanges,* but the three-year period does not begin to run until manufacture, construction, etc., is completed *Id*. The importance of the definition is that a corporation *formed or availed of* principally to purchase property cannot be a collapsible corporation unless the purchased property consists of section 341 assets. §341(b)(1). For these purposes, "*unrealized receivables or fees*" means any rights to payment for goods *deducted* or to be deducted, which sales give rise to *ordinary income* or *losses,* or services rendered or to be rendered, provided, in both cases, the income from such transactions has not yet been reported. §341(b)(4). See *collapsible corporation; unrealized receivables or fees, collapsible corporations*.

section 341(f) election   a relief provision whereby a *United States corporation,* whether or not in fact a *collapsible corporation,* may allow its *shareholders* to sell their *stock* at *long-term capital gains* rates without the burdens of collapsible corporation stock status, if the corporation consents to *recognize gain* on the eventual *disposition* of its *subsection (f) assets* as *ordinary income*. §341(f). (Reg. §1.341-7(a)(2) includes exchanges as well as sales.) *Foreign corporations'* right to the election will be limited by future *regulations*. See *collapsible corporation; subsection (f) assets, collapsible corporations*.

section 351 transactions   a shorthand term for transfers of *property* to *corporations* solely in *exchange* for

stock (or, under prior law, *securities* if transfer was made before October 3, 1989) if the person (transferor) transferring the property is in control of the corporation immediately after the exchange. For purposes of §351, control is defined in Section 368(c). Further, the transferors must possess at least 80 percent of the total combined voting power of all classes of stock entitled to vote and at least 80 percent of the total number of shares of all other classes of stock of the corporation. Section 351 can overlap §368; it is not clear which section controls in such cases. See *control, corporate reorganizations, divisions, and transfers to controlled corporations; holding company bailouts*.

section 367 notice   a statement filed by a *taxpayer* with a United States *tax return* which discloses participation in a foreign transaction described in §367. Failure to give notice may result in major penalties and extensions of the *statute of limitations* against taxpayers. See *section 367 rulings*.

section 367 rulings   *rulings* formerly required as a condition of nontaxability of various transactions involving *inbound* and *outbound transfers* of property to, from, and between *foreign corporations*. Such rulings are no longer required as a condition of nontaxability of various transactions involving *inbound* and *outbound transfers* of property to, from, and between foreign corporations. They are *now discretionary only*.

section 382 limitation   a core feature of the *neutrality principle,* under which a *corporation's* annual *net operating loss carryovers* are confined to a mechanically determined limit. See §382(b)(1). The limit is an objective rate of return (the *long-term tax-exempt rate*) times the *old loss corporation's* equity value.
  Illustration: Corporations X and Y have net operating loss carryforwards. X and Y merge into corporation W under I.R.C. §386. The former shareholders of X and Y receive 10 percent and 30 percent, respectively, of the *stock* of W. Thus, an *ownership change* occurs that causes I.R.C. §382(a) to apply to both X and Y. Before the *ownership change,* the value of X's stock was $3,000. The value of Y's stock was $9,000. On the date of the merger, the *long-term tax-exempt rate* is 10 percent. Thus, the annual limit on the use of X's losses is $300. The separate annual limit on the use of Y's losses is $900. (In both cases, these ceiling amounts for the year of the merger would be proportionately reduced if and to the extent the ownership change did not occur at the beginning of their *taxable years*.)
  The section 382 limitation does not apply with respect to assets of the target (as opposed to its *NOLS*) unless the built-in gain or built-in loss exceeds the lesser of 15 percent of the *fair market value* of the corporation's assets or $10 million. See *neutrality principle*.

section 384 limitation   vernacular for the operation of §384, which limits the acquiring or surviving corporation from offsetting its *NOLs* or other potential losses by using gains on property owned by an acquired *corporation* after the acquisition. See *preacquisition loss limits.*

section 401(h) account tax slang for an *individual medical benefit account.* It is a reference to a feature of *qualified pension plans* to provide the payment of sickness, accident, hospitalization, and medical expenses for retired employees, their *spouses,* and their *dependents* by establishing health benefit accounts.

section 401(k) plan another term for a plan of *deferred compensation* that meets the requirements of §401(k). See *qualified cash or deferred arrangement.*

section 403(b) annuities see *tax-deferred annuities for exempt and educational organization employees.*

section 444 election of fiscal tax year by partnership, S corporation, or personal service corporation (PSC) section 444 permits a partnership to adopt or change to a fiscal year so long as the deferral period is no greater than the shorter of the deferral period now in use or three months. For an S corporation, the fiscal year elected must have a deferral period of three months or loss. A professional service corporation (PSC) may elect under §444 to use a fiscal year that does not satisfy the normal purpose requirement. Under this election, a new corporation may elect to use a September 30, October 30, or November 30 year-end. If a PSC elects a physical year under §444, it must meet minimum distribution requirements to employee-owners during the deferral period. The election is made on *Form 8716* with the appropriate Internal Revenue Service Center.

section 446(b) power a power granted to the *IRS* to force *taxpayers* to change or adopt *methods of accounting* either in cases where the IRS finds that the present method does not result in a *clear reflection of income* or where none has been adopted. The IRS's power is especially broad in this area.

section 457 plan a reference to an *eligible deferred compensation plan,* i.e., a specialized plan for *employees* of state and local governments.

section 457(f) plan a *deferred compensation plan* which permits unlimited deferrals for *state* and local government *employees.* The benefits are taxable when the risk of forfeiture expires.

section 481 adjustment an adjustment to income imposed upon *taxpayers* who change *methods of accounting.* It is designed to phase in the impact of the change by spreading it over the current year and a limited number of future years. Rev. Proc. 84-74, 1984-2 C.B. 736 controls voluntary changes undertaken with *IRS* consent. Section 481 is designed to cause orderly transitions. See *change of accounting method; net adjustment; six-year spread forward.*

section 482 reallocations see *reallocations of income and deductions by Commissioner.*

section 483 shelter a type of *tax shelter* transaction under which the investors purchase *depreciable property* (usually *real estate*) with long-term zero interest notes. The notes are subject to the rules of §483 (*imputed interest*), the effect of which is to mandatorily recharacterize a major portion of each installment of the note as interest, *deductible* by the payor. The *regulations* under §483 are exploited by these deals in that they tend to overstate interest charges in the early years. At least some of these transactions involve sales to the investors of turnkey contracts, not *tangible property*; hence, §483 may not apply in such cases. The *Tax Reform Act of 1984* amendments to the *OID* rules should have rendered such shelters unattractive.

section 501(c)(3) organizations a term used to describe the most common variety of *exempt organizations* (e.g., schools, *churches,* hospitals, and charities). They are described in §501(c)(3) of the *Code* and consist of corporations and any community chest, fund, or foundation organized and operated exclusively for religious, charitable, scientific, testing for public safety, literary, or educational purposes; to foster national or international amateur sports competition (provided no part of its activities involve the provision of athletic facilities or equipment, unless it was organized to conduct or support amateur athletes for national or international sports competition); or for the prevention of cruelty to children or animals. No part of the *net earnings* of such organizations can *inure* to the benefit of any *private shareholder or individual*; no substantial part of such organization's activities can involve carrying on propaganda or otherwise attempting to influence legislation (except as otherwise provided); and such organizations cannot participate or intervene in (including the publishing or distributing of statements) any political campaign on behalf of any candidate for public office. §170(c). Section 501(c)(3) organizations are exempt from *federal income taxes,* and *charitable contributions* to them are generally tax-*deductible.* Also, *private foundations* are a subset of these organizations. §509(a). The term now includes certain day care organizations.

section 509(a)(2) organizations see *public charities.*

section 534 statement a writing, prepared by *taxpayers* in *IRS audits* concerning the *accumulated earnings tax,* that explains the taxpayer's factual grounds for contested accumulations. If the statement is properly prepared, the *burden of proof* on the issue shifts to the IRS in *Tax Court* cases as to the factual grounds presented in the statement. §534(a)(2).

section 709 election to amortize organization and syndication fees over a period of not less than 60 months an election made by attaching a statement to the partnership return for the taxable year in which the partnership begins business.

section 732(d) elective adjustment to have partner's adjusted basis in partnership property distributed to him, adjusted to reflect his purchase price, if such distribution was within two years of partner's acquisition of partnership interest   a special elective adjustment available to *partners.* Specifically, if a partner receives an interest by *sale* or *exchange,* or through death of a partner, and the *partnership* has not made an *optional basis election,* then if *property* (other than money) is distributed to him within two years of receiving the interest, the partner may elect to make a *section 743 adjustment* to such property as if an optional basis election had been made. §732(d). See *optional basis election; section 743 adjustment.*

section 734 adjustment   an elective adjustment to the *basis* of *partnership* assets, designed to bring asset bases into relation with their relative *fair market values* at the time of the adjustment. A partnership, which so elects under §754, is required to increase or decrease the basis of retained partnership assets in certain instances when partnership *distributions* are made. §734(a). The basis of partnership assets are increased either when *gain* is *recognized* on a partnership *distribution,* or to the extent the *adjusted basis* of an asset distributed is greater in the hands of the partnership than in the hands of the distributee-partner immediately after the transfer. §734(b)(1). The partnership makes corresponding reductions of basis in its property in the reverse circumstances. §§734(b)(2), 755.

section 736 payments   payments to buy out a retired *partner.* A *partnership* can continue indefinitely with only one owner if a stream of section 736 payments is being made. This fact can be important with respect to *first user* status of property and avoidance of *recapture* of the *investment tax credit.* Such payments are broken down in section 736(b) payments (for property) and section 736(a) payments (for *unstated goodwill* or *unrealized receivables*). The latter produces *ordinary income* as *guaranteed payments* or *distributions* of profits.

section 743 adjustment   an adjustment to the *basis* of *partnership* property on a change in membership to reflect the difference between the new member's *basis in the partnership interest* and her proportionate share of the partnership's *basis* in its assets. Specifically, if a partnership so elects under §754, the *basis* of partnership property must thereafter be adjusted upon each transfer of an interest in the partnership by *sale* or *exchange,* or upon the death of a partner. §743(a). The *adjusted basis* of partnership property is either increased to the extent the incoming partner's basis in her partnership interest is greater than her proportionate share of the adjusted basis of all partnership assets, or

decreased to the extent the incoming partner's basis in the partnership interest is less than her proportionate share of the adjusted basis of all partnership assets. §743(b). Note that the above adjustment in the basis of partnership property is made only with respect to the incoming partner. See *optional basis election.*

section 751 assets   another term for a series of assets that create ratable *ordinary income* on the *sale* or *exchange* of a *partnership* interest, or on certain disproportionate *distributions* by the partnership. Such assets include *unrealized receivables,* meaning any rights to income that have not been included in *gross income* under the partnership's *method of accounting.* Apparently the term also includes *installment obligations* held by partnership that are not yet due, provided the property sold was not a *capital asset.* Unrealized receivables also include a long list of *recapture* items. Section 751 assets also include *substantially appreciated inventory items,* a term which includes other assets which would not be capital assets or *section 1231 assets* if sold by the partnership or by the *partner,* had he or she held them. They are deemed substantially appreciated if their *fair market value* is more than 120 percent of their *adjusted basis* to the partnership and more than 10 percent of the fair market value of all partnership property other than money. The 120 percent test applies to all partnership inventory items, not to specific items or groups. The provision is at the heart of the *collapsible partnership rules* and operates as a loophole-plug. See *collapsible partnership rules; inventory items; unrealized receivables, partnerships.*

section 754 election   a misnomer for a *section 734 adjustment* or a *section 743 adjustment.* The election shall be made in a written statement filed with the partnership return for the taxable year during which the distribution (under Section 734(b)) or transfer (under Section 753(b)) occurs. The election must be filed with the partnership return not later than the return's due date, including any extensions.

section 761 election   an election not to be subject to federal *partnership* tax law provisions. Unincorporated organizations may be excluded from some or all of *subchapter K* if (1) the partnership is considered either an *investment partnership,* a partnership availed of for the joint production, extraction, or use of property (but not for the purpose of selling services or property produced or extracted), or a temporary underwriting syndicate; and (2) the income of the partners may be adequately determined without the computation of *partnership income.* §761. The election may be made no later than the time for filing the partnership *return* (including extensions) for the first *taxable year* the exclusion is desired. Reg. §1.761-2(b)(2). Opting out of the partnership provision may be desirable to avoid restrictions on *taxable years* and *allocation* of *gains* and *losses* on contributed property, or to allow each partner to make a separate election with respect to *depletion, depreciation,* or *cost recovery* methods.

section 897(i) election   an irrevocable election by a *foreign corporation* entitled to nondiscrimination benefits under a *tax treaty* to be treated as a *domestic corporation.* It enables such a corporation to avoid the complexities of §897 when it disposes of *United States real property interests.* Such corporations remain foreign for *FIRPTA withholding* purposes, however.

section 898(c)(1)(B) election   an election that permits certain *foreign corporations* which are *controlled foreign corporations* to elect a *taxable year* that begins a month earlier than the taxable year of the majority *United States shareholder.* See Rev. Proc. 90-26, 1990-17 I.R.B. 16. See *United States shareholder, CFC.*

section 902 credit   a synonym for *foreign tax credit.*

section 904(d)(1) "basket"   the nine categories of *foreign source income* that are subject to separate application of the *foreign tax credit limitation.* See §904(d)(1). The categories are (I) *passive income,* (II) *high withholding tax income,* (III) *financial services income,* (IV) *shipping income,* (V) *dividends* from each *noncontrolled section 902 corporation,* (VI) dividends from a *DISC* or former DISC (as defined in §992(a)) to the extent such dividends are treated as income from sources without the *United States,* (VII) *taxable income* attributable to *foreign trade income* of a *foreign sales corporation* (FSC) (within the meaning of §923(b)), (VIII) distributions from a *foreign sales corporation* (or former FSC) out of *earnings and profits* attributable to *foreign trade income* or qualified interest and carrying charges (as defined in §§245(c) and 927(d)(1)), and (IX) income other than income described in any of the preceding subparagraphs. The purpose for distinguishing between each group is to prohibit cross-crediting of excess *foreign tax credits* from the high-taxed income to the low-taxed income, which would result in avoidance of United States tax and the *Treasury* in effect having to subsidize the high-tax nations, or from another point of view, allow foreign nations to tax United States income.

section 936 credit   see *possession tax credit; section 936 election.*

section 936 election   an election under which *domestic corporations* that derive income from a *trade or business* in a *possession* or Puerto Rico, other than the United States Virgin Islands, (so-called *possessions corporations*) can elect the *possessions tax credit* against regular *federal income taxes* for income derived from a possession. See *possessions corporations; possession tax credit.*

section 988 hedging transaction   a transaction entered into primarily to reduce the risk of loss due to currency fluctuations with respect to property held, or obligations made, by the *taxpayer.* §988(d)(2)(A). To qualify, the taxpayer must identify the transaction as a *section 988 hedging transaction* by the close of the business day on which it was entered into, or the *Secretary* may designate it as such at a later time. §988(d)(2)(B). Any *section 988 transaction* that is a part of a *section 988 hedging transaction* is included in the hedging transaction, and the transactions are treated as a whole. §988(d)(1). Since hedging transactions reduce the likelihood of *foreign currency gain or loss,* §988 treats such transactions more favorably than other *section 988 transactions.* Section 988 contains a variety of elections (e.g., to treat certain *regulated futures contracts* and *nonequity options* (§988(c)(1)(D)) as *section 988 transactions*). See Notice 88-124 for temporary rules regarding such election.

section 988 transaction   a transaction in which the amount to be paid or entitled to be received is denominated in a *nonfunctional currency,* or is determined by reference to the value of one or more nonfunctional currencies. §988(c). It includes entering into forward contracts, futures contracts, and the like even if subject to the *mark-to-market* rules. §988(c)(1)(B)(iii). Even if a regulated futures contract is not affected by the mark-to-market rules, the *taxpayer* can elect to treat it as a *section 988 transaction,* unless the taxpayer is a partnership that has elected *qualified fund* status. *Section 988 transactions* generally include trade receivables or payables. The term is integral to the taxation of foreign currency transactions. See *foreign currency gain or loss; functional currency; qualified fund, foreign currency gain or loss.*

section 1017 adjustments   another term for adjustments (reductions) to *basis* of *depreciable property* (as specially defined) that are made when a debtor elects to *exclude gross income* from the *discharge of indebtedness* (reported on *Form 1072*). The advantages of doing so include the avoidance of *ordinary income* and the preservation of certain favorable *tax attributes* (e.g., *net operating loss carryovers*). §1017. The adjustments are made in tandem with §108.

section 1231 assets   the following property (including leaseholds), provided it is held for more than a year: (1) *depreciable property* used in a *trade or business*; (2) realty used in a trade or business; and (3) *capital assets* that were the subjects of an *involuntary conversion.* §1231(a) (the so-called *hotchpot*). Transactions in such properties are netted and, if they yield a *gain,* that gain is a *long-term capital gain,* although *recapture* of *depreciation* must first be extracted. If they yield a loss, that loss is *ordinary,* rather than capital, in character. Overall losses from *thefts* and *casualties* of property used in a trade or business or from any capital asset held for more than a year are, however, excluded from §1231(a), whereas overall gains from such transactions are included in the overall netting process. The latter rule regarding casualties and thefts is imposed by the last sentence of §1231(a), formerly referred to as the *subhotchpot.* Section 1231(b)(1) defines assets used in the trade or business to exclude *inventory, dealer property,* intellectual property of the types defined in §1221(3), and certain United States government publications, but to include (1) certain timber, coal, and domestic iron ore subject to a *disposal with a retained economic interest* under §631; (2) livestock, other than poultry, held for specified *holding periods* for draft, breeding, dairy, or sporting purposes; and (3) unharvested crops held for more than one year and disposed of with the land to the same person in one transaction.

section 1231 gain   a term sometimes used to describe overall *gains* from dealing in *section 1231 assets* and from certain compulsory or *involuntary conversions* computed under §1231(a)(3)(A). See *section 1231 assets.*

section 1231 loss   the reverse of a *section 1231 gain.*

section 1244 stock   see *small business corporation stock.*

section 1245 property   property that is or has been subject to *cost recovery, depreciation,* or *amortization,* and which includes depreciable personal property and other depreciable property (other than buildings or their structural components) used in manufacturing, production, or extraction, or in furnishing transportation, communications, electrical energy, gas, water, or sewage disposal services. When *section 1245 property* is disposed of, any gain is treated as ordinary income to the extent of depreciation deducted. §1245(a)(1).

section 1245 recapture   recapture of *depreciation* or *cost recovery* with respect to *personal property* (as modified) as *ordinary income.* See *recapture, depreciation; section 1245 property.*

section 1248 amount   *earnings and profits* that would have been attributable to the *stock* of a *foreign corporation* under §1248 if the stock had been *sold* and subjected to §1248, where the stock was in fact *exchanged.* Reg. §7.367(b)-2(b). The terminology is important in the determination of the taxability of the *inbound transfers* involving controlled foreign corporations under §367, especially *liquidations* of foreign subsidiaries, certain *reorganizations* involving foreign mutual funds, certain *spin-offs,* and so forth.

section 1250 class property   *depreciable property,* other than *section 1245 property* and *elevators and escalators.* Former §168(g)(4). The term is significant for former purposes of classifying *recovery property* under the *accelerated cost recovery system* (ACRS)

provisions of §168 prior to amendment.

section 1250 property   generally, *real property* that is or was of a *character subject to depreciation* and is not *section 1245 property,* and not §1245. §1250(c). *Elevators and escalators* are disqualified, but *leaseholds* of land or tangible *section 1250 class property* generally may qualify. Reg. §1.1250-1(e)(3). It implicitly includes *buildings* and their *structural components,* and all *tangible real property* except *section 1245 property.* §1250(c). See *building, investment tax credit; structural components.*

section 1250 recapture   *recapture* of *depreciation* or *cost recovery* with respect to *real property.* See *recapture, depreciation; section 1250 property.*

section 1252 recapture   see *recapture, soil, water conservation, and land clearing expenditures.*

section 1254 recapture   a provision that recharacterizes as *ordinary income* a part of the *gain* on *disposition* of oil, gas, and mineral *property.* §1254(a)(3). One form of *recapture* arises when *depletion deductions* in the past reduced the *adjusted basis* of such property. §1254(a)(1)(A)(ii). Another form arises where *intangible drilling and development expenses,* mineral *exploration expenditures* (§617), and mineral *development expenditures* (§616), were previously claimed as *current deductions,* such deductions are recharacterized as *ordinary income* when the property is disposed of to the extent of the gain. §1254(a)(1)(A)(i). Section 617 also has its own internal recapture provisions, but §1254(a)(4) prevents duplication.

section 1255 recapture   *recapture* as *ordinary income* of nontaxable *cost-sharing payments* for timber properties, if the timber property benefited from *excludable* payments within 10 years of the grant. The recapture phases down between the tenth and twentieth years. §1255(a)(3). See *cost-sharing payments, conservation.*

section 1256 contract   any *regulated futures contract, foreign currency contract, nonequity option,* or *dealer equity option.* The term is used in connection with the tax rules applicable to the *mark-to-market system* and the *sixty-forty rule* to which these contracts are now subject.

section 1362 election to be classified as an S corporation   the election must be filed at any time during the taxable year that immediately precedes the first taxable year in which the election is to be effective. To be effective for the current year, the election must be made on or before the fifteenth day of the third month of that year. The election is made on *Form 2553.*

section 1377(a)(2) election to terminate S year upon termination of a shareholder's interest in the corporation   the corporation files a statement that elects under §1377(a)(2) to have the rules of §1377(a)(1) apply. If the shareholders' interest is completely terminated during the tax year, all shareholders may elect to treat the S taxable year as two taxable years, with the first year ending on the date of the termination. Under this election, an interim closing of the books is undertaken, and the owners report their shares of the S corporation items as they occurred during the year.

section 1491 excise tax see *excise tax, transfers to foreign corporations, trusts, estates, and partnerships.*

section 1501 election to file a consolidated tax return this election is filed by each corporation which has been a member during any part of the consolidated group's first taxable year. The consent is made by filing *Form 1122.*

section 1504(a)(4) stock a formal description for *preferred stock* issued by a corporation that files a *consolidated return.* Such stock is not considered for purposes of determining if there is control for purposes of the right to file a *consolidated return.* See *applicable preferred stock; preferred stock.*

section 6038A agreement an agreement enabling reporting *corporations* to enter into individual agreements with the *IRS* which modify their obligations to report under §§6038A and 6038C. Such corporations are either *domestic corporations* that are 25 percent or more owned by a *foreign stockholder* or *foreign corporations* that conduct a *trade or business* in the *United States.* See Rev. Proc. 9-38, 1991-30 I.R.B. Reg. §1.6038A-3C.

section 6045 return see *broker's return.*

secured, deferred compensation evidenced by notes or otherwise transferable. Such *deferred compensation* is immediately taxable to a *cash method taxpayer* under the *cash equivalents* or *economic benefit doctrines.* Rev. Rul. 60-31, 1960-1 C.B. 174. The term has received little attention.

secured indebtedness a *debt* due to the seller if the seller has the right to take title or possession of the *property,* or both, if there is a default with respect to such indebtedness. A sale of real property may give rise to an indebtedness to the seller, although the seller's recourse is limited to the property for payment of the indebtedness in the case of default. Reg. §1.1038-1(a)(2)(ii). Such debt is required in order for one to benefit from the §1038 *deferral* of *gain* on certain repossessions of *real estate.*

secured obligations, installment sales *debt* secured by a *nondealer real property installment obligation.* §453A(d)(1). The result is that if the *taxpayer* (seller) secures the obligation, the proceeds of the loan are treated as payments received and can cause immediate *recognition* of *gains.* Indebtedness is secured (either under the terms of the debt or any other arrangement) to the extent its principal or *interest* is directly secured by any interest in the installment obligation. §453A(d)(4). See *payment, installment method.*

securities see *security, corporate taxation.*

securities acquisition loan a loan to a *corporation* or to an *ESOP* for a term of not over 15 years to acquire or refinance the acquisition of *employer securities,* or a loan to a corporation promptly followed by a transfer to the ESOP of employer securities in an amount equal to the loan, but in all cases only if the ESOP got over 50 percent of the employer's *stock* (defined as not preferred stock in §1504(a) as well as certain *rights*) and the *participants* can direct how the stock is voted. §133(b). There are further details. One-half of the *interest* on such loans is *excludable* from *gross income* if earned by a *bank, life insurance company,* a corporation actively engaged in the *business* of lending money, or a *regulated investment company.* This is an indirect boost for ESOPs. See *excise tax, premature disposition by ESOP of employer securities acquired with securities acquisition loan.*

Securities and Exchange Commission (SEC) a federal agency charged with regulating the issuance and distribution of securities, capital markets, investment companies and their advisers, and certain holding companies.

security agreement an agreement entered into between a *foreign corporation* directly or indirectly holding United States *real estate* and the *IRS* that ensures the payment of any tax due with regard to the future *disposition* of the *real estate*; it also prevents disclosure of the identity of the *shareholders* of that corporation under §6039C.

security, corporate taxation an obligation issued by a *corporation* that represents a continuing interest in the company. Generally, *debt* with a maturity of at least 10 years is clearly a security. Rev. Proc. 79-14, 1979-1 C.B. 496. The term has the same meaning for purposes of §351 (incorporations and expansions under prior law) as for §§354(a)(1) and 361(a) (*corporate reorganizations*). Generally, short-term debt creates a cash *sale* result as to the recipient (whether the recipient tenders such debt or takes it back) rather than a continuing interest in the corporation. See §354(a).

security, identification of securities held for investment by dealers and floor specialists any share of *stock* in any *corporation,* certificate of stock or interest in any corporation, note, bond, debenture, or evidence of indebtedness, or any evidence of an interest in or right to subscribe to or purchase any of the foregoing. §1236(c). *Dealers* have until the close of business for the day to identify securities as held for *investment* (hence, capable of generating *capital gains*). §1236(a)(1). As to securities in which *floor specialists* specialize, such *taxpayers* have until the end of the seventh business day following the acquisition to identify such securities, provided they acquired their securities in connection with their duties on the exchange. §1236(d).

security, worthlessness   a share of *stock, right,* bond, note, certificate, or other evidence of indebtedness issued by a *corporation,* government, or political subdivision of a government, with an *interest* coupon or in *registered form.* §165(g)(2). The *worthlessness* of a security is treated as if the security had been *sold* or *exchanged,* except in the case of a security in an *affiliated corporation.* §165(g)(1).

seedstock   genetically superior animals used for breeding. The creation of these improved animals is frequently the object of *cattle breeding shelters.*

segregation rules   a system of rules under §382 relating to limitations on carryovers of *tax attributes,* especially *net operating losses,* the effect of which is to break down groups of *persons* who own under 5 percent of a *loss corporation's* stock into separate owners. See Reg. §1.382-2T(j)(2). See Rev. Rul. 90-15, 1990-7 I.R.B. 17 (role of options). See *neutrality principle.*

segregation transactions, neutrality principle   a series of transactions that have the effect of breaking down public *shareholders* into separate groups. See Reg. §1.382-2T(j)(2). The transactions consist of (1) certain *equity structure shifts* and transactions under §1032 (basically, *stock* issued as consideration); (2) "*redemption* type transactions" by the loss *corporation* in *exchange* for its own stock; (3) certain deemed acquisitions of stock via *rights* offerings and convertible *debt*; and (4) certain other transactions to be announced. In general, these provisions are complex and tend to show that the *neutrality principle* is difficult to implement.

seizure   see *levy.*

selection bonus, natural resources   oil and gas terminology for an amount paid by a *lessee* in exchange for exercising options to lease selected properties within a larger overall area that the lessee wants to explore. They may be treated as *delay rentals* or *bonuses* for federal *income tax* purposes, with sharply different consequences.

self-cancelling installment note   an *installment obligation* that expires on the death of the seller; an alternative to the *private annuity.* From a *federal income tax* vantage, such obligations may arguably be preferable to *private annuities.* See §453B(f) for major restrictions.

self-dealing, black lung benefits trust   any direct or indirect (1) tax *sale, exchange,* or leasing of *real* or *personal property* between a *black lung benefit trust* (§501(c)(21)) and a *disqualified person*; (2) lending of

money or other extension of credit between such a trust and a disqualified person; (3) furnishing of goods, services, or facilities between such a trust and a disqualified person; (4) payment of compensation or reimbursement of expenses by such a trust to a disqualified person; and (5) transfer to, use by, or benefit for a disqualified person of the income or assets of such a trust. An *excise tax* of 10 percent is imposed on the amount involved in each act of self-dealing. §4951(a)(1) and (d)(1).

self-dealing tax, private foundations   an *excise tax* imposed on *disqualified persons* at the rate of 5 percent ($2\frac{1}{2}$ percent on *foundation managers* who knowingly participate) in which the dollar value involved in the self-dealing transaction is used with the *private foundation* as the base. The transactions are (1) *sales* and *exchange* of property; (2) *leases*; (3) loans of money; (4) furnishing of goods, services, or facilities; (5) excessive compensation or expense reimbursements; (6) use of the foundation's property or income; and (7) contributions involving assumptions of property mortgaged by disqualified persons. The 5 percent or $2\frac{1}{2}$ percent taxes are imposed annually, but in the event of failure to correct the transactions 90 days after the deficiency, the *Code* imposes a further 200 percent tax on the disqualified person and a 50 percent on the foundation manager. §4941.

self-employed individual, Keogh plan   generally, an *individual* who is not a *common law employee* and who has *net earnings from self-employment.* See §401(c)(3). Reg. §1.401-10(b) extends the term to include people running *losses.*

self-employed individual, moving expenses   an *individual* who performs services as a *partner* or *sole proprietor* of a *trade or business.* §217(f)(1). When such a person moves, he or she is considered still self-employed when he or she makes substantial arrangements to begin work. §217(f)(2). Self-employed individuals' rights to claim *moving expense deductions* are slightly different than those for *employees.*

self-employed person   see *independent contractor.*

self-employed retirement plan or fund   see *Keogh plan.*

self-employment income   the base on which the *self-employment tax* (SECA) falls. It is based on *net earnings from self-employment* but is limited by *wages* with respect to which *Social Security taxes* (FICA) have already been levied. If the taxpayer has met his old-age and survivors and disability (OASDI) portion ($57,600 for 1993 and rising thereafter), as well as his hospital insurance portion ($135,000 for 1993 and rising thereafter) through the receipt of salary, then he or she is not subject to the self-employment tax. The self-employment tax can also be met by a combination of salary and self-employment income. (See *Form 1040SE*). Earnings subject to the self-employment tax include the following: (1) net earnings from a sole proprietorship; (2) directors fees; (3) taxable research grants; and (4) distributive share of partnership income plus guaranteed payments from the partnership. §6017; Rev. Rul. 57-246, 1975-1 C.B. 338. If net earnings are under $400, there is no self-employment tax.

self-employment tax a two-part tax imposed on *individuals* (other than *nonresident aliens*) in *business* or professions for themselves, and on certain *partners* on their *net earnings from self-employment* on amounts up to the *contribution and benefit base. Farmers* and share-farmers are subject to a simplified optional farm method. See *farm optional method, self-employment tax.*

self-incrimination, privilege against a privilege to remain silent, granted to *individuals* in the Fifth Amendment to the United States Constitution. The scope of the privilege in respect to documents is complex. Generally, only personal records are protected.

self-insured Medical Malpractice insurance pool see *physicians and surgeons mutual protection association.*

self-insured medical reimbursement plan an *employer's* plan that provides for *employees* to be reimbursed for *medical care* expenses that are not covered by a health or accident insurance policy. §105(h)(6). Such plans can result in benefits for employees, which are excluded from *gross income,* and *current deductions* for employers.

selling consolidated group any group of *corporations* that, for the taxable period including the transaction (purchase of control of another corporation), files a *consolidated return* and includes the corporation (the *target corporation*) whose *stock* was acquired by another corporation in a *qualified stock purchase* under §338. §338(h)(10)(B). An election may be made under which no *gain* or *loss* will be *recognized* on stock *sold* or *exchanged* in the transaction by members of the selling consolidated group (including the target corporation), provided that the target corporation (1) was a member of the group before the transaction, and (2) recognizes gain or loss with respect to the transaction as if it sold all of its assets in a single transaction. §338(h)(10)(A). The *section 338(h)(10) election* effectively frees the group from taxation of *gains* on the *sale* of *stock* in exchange for the group's being forced to *recognize gains* on the target company's deemed asset sale. See *section 338 acquisition.*

selling expenses, percentage depletion *expenditures* with respect to sales of unprocessed natural resources as well as a reasonable portion of expenditures attributable to sales of processed goods. Reg. §1.613-5(c)(4). Such expenses are subtracted for purposes of determining *taxable income from the property* for purposes of the 100 percent limit on *percentage depletion.*

selling price, installment sales the total consideration received by a seller of property, with no reduction for *debt* encumbering the property, *interest,* or selling expenses. Temp. Reg. §15a.453-1(b)(2)(ii). See *gross profit ratio, installment sales; installment method.*

Senate Finance Committee the committee of the United States Senate responsible for revenue laws.

separate accounting, employment and excise taxes a burden imposed on *employers* or collectors of *excise taxes* who fail to comply with the tax laws by delaying, failing to pay over, and so forth, the onus of which is to compel the miscreant to designate a separate account at a *bank,* as *trustee* for the United States, to which deposits must promptly be made or the miscreant may be subjected to criminal penalties. §7512.

separate and identifiable operations exception a tax relief provision, designed to permit *taxpayers* to escape the presumption that participation in an *international boycott* as to any operation meant participation as to all of the taxpayer's operations. If a *taxpayer* shows that different operations within the same country, or operations in different countries, are clearly separate and identifiable, then only the demonstrably tainted activities are adversely affected by the antiboycott rules. §999(b)(2). See *international boycott activity, participation and cooperation.*

separate basket limitation a feature of the *foreign tax credit limitation* which calls for breaking down income from overseas sources into eight different types plus a residual category and applying the limitation to each of the nine *baskets.* See *section 904(d)(i) basket.*

separate basket loss recapture provision a provision to the effect that where a *basket* (i.e., overseas income of one of nine types defined in §904(d)(1)) previously showed a *separate limitation loss* which was *allocated* against income in other baskets, subsequent income in the loss basket is recharacterized as income of the type that it previously offset, in proportion to the prior loss *allocation* not previously taken into account under the recharacterization provision. §904(f)(5). See *foreign income, war profits and excess profits taxes; foreign tax credit; foreign tax credit limitation; recapture, foreign losses; section 904(d)(1) "basket".*

separate charge, foreign tax credit a levy imposed by a foreign government which (1) is imposed at a separate rate; (2) is paid by *persons* engaged in a particular industry (or industries) pursuant to provisions of foreign law; (3) is imposed pursuant to contractual modifications of foreign law entered into with the person on whom the charge is imposed (e.g., country X agrees to impose its generally applicable tax on patent royalties only if creditable in the United States); (4) is imposed at a flat rate on several separate bases, such as *interest, dividends,* or *wages.* Temp. Reg. §4.903-1(a). The foreign tax credit rules of §§901 and 903 are applied independently in each separate charge, and each such charge is considered eligible for credit in its entirety for all persons subject to that charge. Temp. Reg. §§4.901-2(a) and 4.903-1(e)(4).

separate currency pools method   an elective method by which *foreign* banks apportion *interest expense deductions* to the United States branch. See Reg. §1.882-5(b)(3)(ii)(A)-(C). The method determines the deduction on the basis of each currency in which the branch borrowed funds, calculating the total *interest expense deduction* as the total interest expense deduction in each currency. See Reg. §1.882-5(c), ex. (2). For the alternative method, see *branch book/dollar pool method.*

separate five-percent public group   a *public group* of the *loss corporation* or a *first-tier entity* or *higher-tier entity* that is identified as a *five-percent shareholder* under *segregation rules* that apply to *equity structure shifts* and certain other kinds of transactions. Reg. §1.382-2T(f)(4). The term is important for purposes of determining if an *ownership change* has taken place, which may in turn attract the *section 382 limitation* under the *neutrality principle.*

separate foreign levy   an element of a *creditable foreign tax,* requiring an analysis of each separate levy. Reg. §1.902-2(a). For example, if a foreign income tax system, taken as a whole, falls short of being creditable against *federal income taxes,* but it can be broken into separate levies, some of which are creditable, the *taxpayer* stands to benefit. In general, one finds a separate levy if the base on which the levy is imposed on *one class of taxpayers differs in kind, and not merely degree, from the base for another class.* Reg. §1.902-2(d)(1). Levies of one taxing authority are always separate from the levies of another taxing authority in the same country. See *foreign tax credit.*

separate improvement   each *capitalized* improvement to *real estate* made within 36 months of the close of any *taxable year,* provided the capitalized amounts exceed the greatest of (1) 25 percent of the property's *adjusted basis*; (2) 10 percent of its adjusted basis, with *amortization* and *depreciation* ignored; and (3) $5,000. §1250(f)(4)(A). Once this sorting has occurred, the effect is to isolate only relatively major *capitalized* improvements. Aggregate *gain* on the *disposition* of property is apportioned among the separate elements, with separate *holding periods* for purposes of *recapture* of *depreciation.* See Reg. §1.1250-5. The provision is designed to avoid inadvertent overuse of the beneficial *applicable percentage* system by attribution of excessive holding periods to post-acquisition improvements.

separate income   income of a *spouse* in a *community property* jurisdiction arising from *property* that is the *separate property* of one spouse under local law. If the couple files *separate returns,* each must report all of his or her separate income. For the antonym, see *community income.*

separate interests doctrine   a doctrine developing under Rev. Rul. 77-214, 1997-1 C.B. 408 whose effect is that corporate attributes of *free transferability of interests* and *continuity of life* are deemed to exist where all the interests in an *entity* are owned by the same ultimate owner; as long as the entity has one of the two remaining corporate attributes, it is a *corporation* under United States tax law.

separate limitation income   with respect to any income category (each of the nine separate "*baskets*"), the *taxable income* from sources outside the *United States,* separately computed for that category. §904(f)(5)(E)(ii). The term is used in connection with the *recapture* of *foreign losses* for purposes of the *foreign tax credit.* See *recapture, foreign losses; separate basket limitation.*

separate limitation interest   net *interest* income from various sources which were subjected to a separate calculation for purposes of the *foreign tax credit limitation.* See §904(d). The rules were complicated but seemingly child's play compared to the successor provisions found in the *separate section 904(d) basket* provisions imposed by the 1986 Act. For a special application of the rule to *tax-avoidance* efforts, see *designated payor corporation.*

separate limitation loss   with respect to any income category (each of the nine separate *baskets*), the *loss* from sources outside the *United States,* separately computed for that category. §904(f)(5)(E)(iii). The term is used in connection with the *recapture* of *foreign losses* for purposes of the *foreign tax credit.* See *recapture, foreign losses*

separate line of business   *bona fide* distinct product or service lines, based on an evaluation of all the *facts and circumstances,* including: (1) differences and similarities among the products and services; (2) the manner in which the *employer* is organized; and (3) comparative benefits under plans for different alleged lines of business, especially if there is any tendency to favor *highly compensated employees.* §414(r)(1). Separate lines of business are treated as separate employers for purposes of *minimum coverage rules* (§410) and for including excess benefits in income in the case of *discriminatory welfare benefit plans.*

separately computed items   another term for items of *income, deduction, credit,* and the like from an *S corporation,* the effect of which could be to have a special federal tax impact on any *shareholder.* §1366(a)(1)(A).

Such items must be reported separately. The same concept is found in §§702(a) and 703(a)(1) as to *partnerships*. See *separately stated items, partnership taxation*.

separately stated items, partnership taxation   items that a *partnership* must segregate and disclose in its *tax return* (Form 1065), consisting of various items of *gain, loss*, and the like in order that each *partner* can separate the items for appropriate treatment. They include *gains* and *losses* on *section 1231 assets, capital gains* and *losses, charitable contributions*, and so forth, segregated because they have independent significance for the partners. §§702(a), 703(a).

separate maintenance   a circumstance resulting from a decree of separate maintenance, that is, a decree preceding divorce which calls for the legal (but seemingly not physical) separation of *spouses*, and a duty of one spouse to pay living expenses of the other. It appears that the determination as to whether there has been a legal separation is a matter of state law. Separate maintenance can be an important element in the determination of whether a payment is *deductible* as an *alimony or separate maintenance payment*. §71(a)(1). See *alimony or separate maintenance payments; legally separated*.

separate property   property that is demonstrably the property of one *spouse* or another. *Prenuptial contracts* in *community property states* may provide that property acquired by a spouse separately will not be *community property* (the property of both spouses). Also, *gifts* and *inheritances* of one spouse during the marriage will generally be the separate property of the inheritor or *donee*.

separate return   a *return* filed by *married persons* that shows separate income tax information and liabilities, as contrasted with the unified *joint return*. It may also apply to a return of a *corporation* that might otherwise file as a member of a group filing a *consolidated return*. Such returns are generally required for couples when one *spouse* is a *nonresident alien*, unless both make a special election under §6013(g), pursuant to which the nonresident alien is taxed on worldwide income. §6013(h) has a comparable rule for the year in which the nonresident becomes a *resident alien*. Section 1(d) prescribes higher rates for separate returns than for joint returns. §§63(b)(6) and 151(b) restrict claims to *standard deductions* and an additional *personal exemption*, respectively, in such cases. Such returns are permissible if the *taxpayers* are *legally separated* under a decree. §7703(a). See *separate return year*. For the antonym, see *joint return*.

separate return limitation year   a year in which a company now a member of an *affiliated group* of *corporations* filing a *consolidated return* was not a member of the group. Reg. §1.1502-1(f). Reg. §1.1502-21

(c) limits *net operating losses* from such years to absorption by later income from the recently absorbed member company alone. Other comparable limitations are imposed by Reg. §§1.1502-22(c) (*capital loss carryovers*), 1.1502-4(f) (*foreign tax credit carryovers*), and 1.1502-3(c) (*investment tax credit carryovers*). See Reg. §1.1502-75(d)(3) as to *consolidated return changes of ownership*.

separate return tax liability   the tax liability of a *member of an affiliated group* of *corporations* filing a *consolidated income tax return*, calculated as if the member had filed a *separate return*. Reg. §1.1552-1(a)(2)(ii). Certain items must, however, be reported on a consolidated basis, such as *intercompany transactions, inventory* adjustments, *excess losses, recapture* of the *investment tax credit*, and intercompany *dividends*. Reg. §1.1552-1(a)(2). The computation of separate return tax liability is necessary in order to *apportion* the consolidated tax liability to *individual* members of the affiliated group under the method described in Reg. §1.1552-1(a)(2). See *excess loss account; separate taxable income*.

separate return year   a year during which a *corporation* did not file as a member of the *affiliated group* being considered, or filed as a member of another group. Reg. §1.1502-1(d). The definition focuses on the corporation that is presently a member of an affiliated group. See *separate return limitation year*.

separate taxable income   the *taxable income* of a *corporation* filing a *consolidated return*, disregarding *gains* or *losses* from transactions with respect to *stock*, bonds, or *debt* obligations between *members of an affiliated group*, built-in deductions denied under Reg. §1.1502-15, *mining exploration expenditures* limited under Reg. §1.1502-16, adjustments made due to *changes of accounting methods, inventory* adjustments, income realized due to a *sale* of a subsidiary with *excess losses, net operating loss deductions, capital gains* and *losses, section 1231 gains* and losses, *charitable contribution deductions, western hemisphere trade corporation* deductions (now defunct), and *dividends-received deductions*. Reg. §1.1502-12(a) through (p). The computation of separate taxable income of each of the affiliated members is the first step in computing *consolidated taxable income*. See *excess loss account*.

separation from service, lump-sum distributions   an *employee's* death, retirement, resignation, or discharge unless the employee continues on the job with a different *employer*, or as a result of a liquidation, merger, or consolidation of the former employer. Rev. Rul. 79-336, 1979-2 C.B. 187. See also Rev. Rul. 81-141, 1981-1 C.B. 204 (continued employment by *target company* in an acquisition does not give rise to separation from service) and PLR 8327033 (Apr. 6, 1983) (discharge of employee creates separation from service despite later rehiring when the acquiring company reemployed laid-off employees). A *lump-sum distribution* from a *qualified plan* on a separation from service can result in favorable taxation to the recipient employee under §402(e). See *lump-sum distribution, qualified plans.*

series E bonds   the predecessor of *series EE bonds.*

series EE bonds   a class of saving bonds sold by the United States government at a deep discount that permits *cash method* holders to elect to report discount *interest* thereon currently or at maturity. §454(a).

series fund   a kind of *regulated investment company* (mutual fund) that consists of several classes of *stock,* each with different underlying portfolios (e.g., a bond portfolio underlying class A and a portfolio of growth stock underlying class B). The 1986 Act treats each fund as a separate *corporation,* making tax-free *exchanges* impossible for investors.

series H bonds   the predecessor of *series HH bonds.*

series HH bonds   a class of savings bonds issued by the United States government into which *series EE bonds, series E bonds,* or United States savings notes can be converted tax-free, with *interest* income on converted bonds deferred until maturity or *disposition* of the series HH bonds. §1037(a); Reg. §§1.454-1(c)(1)(iii); 1.1037-1(a)(3). Income on series HH bonds is paid and must be reported semiannually.

Service   a word often used in lieu of the term *Internal Revenue Service.* In its lowercase form, the term refers to work for an *employer* to create *accrued benefits* for *pension plan* purposes. See especially Labor Reg. §2530.204.

service, benefit accrual   any method of calculating periods of *service* for an *employee* for purposes of determining *accrued benefits* for *pension plan* purposes, provided the method complies with Labor Reg. §2530.204-3(a). The plan need not use hours of service or the methods (*elapsed time,* career compensation, and credited hours) exemplified in Labor Reg. §2530.204-3(b).

Service Centers   administrative offices of the *IRS.* The centers primarily carry out relatively routine affairs such as receiving *tax returns,* notifying *taxpayers* of apparent filing errors, and the like.

service contracts   see *personal service contract.*

service costs, uniform capitalization rules   the total direct and indirect *costs* of administrative, service, or support functions or departments (*service departments*) that directly benefit a production or resale activity. These costs are a type of *allocable cost* which are subject to the *uniform capitalization rules.* Service costs that benefit production or resale activities as well as other functions (*mixed service costs*) are also subject to

specified allocations. Reg. §1.263A-1T(b)(4)(ii). See *allocable costs, uniform capitalization rule; allocation methods, uniform capitalization rules; indirect production costs; mixed service costs, uniform capitalization rules; step-allocation method.*

service department, uniform capitalization rules   administrative, service, or support functions or departments. If they benefit a particular production or resale activity, they are directly allocated to such activity; if service costs directly benefit several production or resale activities, then such costs are allocated to particular activities under specialized rules found in Reg. §1.263-1T(b)(2). See *mixed service costs, uniform capitalization rules.*

service mark   see *trademark.*

service organization   any *corporation, partnership,* or other *organization,* the principal *business* of which is the performance of services. §414(m)(3). The *employees* of such enterprises are aggregated for certain *qualified plan* purposes; e.g., violation of the *minimum participation standards* of §401(a)(26) can disqualify the plan.

service partner   a *partner* who provides services but little or no capital. The term is especially relevant in the case of *partnerships* in which capital is a *material income-producing factor,* but the partner does not in fact provide capital. Such persons are recognized as partners only if there is a genuine intent to be a partner.

service recipient   see *service returns.*

service returns   *information returns* required of any *service recipient* (a *person* for whom a service is performed) engaged in a *trade or business* who, in the course of the trade or business, pays remuneration to any *person* for services performed by that person. The information in such filings is to be compiled on a *calendar year* basis for payments made after December 31, 1982, and must include the name, address, and aggregate amount paid to each person for whom that amount is $600 or more. §6041A(a). In the case of any payments by any governmental unit, or any agency or instrumentality thereof (included for these purposes in the term "person"), the trade or business requirement is dropped. §6041A(d). A service return is not required if a statement with respect to the services is required under §§6051 (receipts for *employees*), 6052 (returns regarding payment of *wages* in the form of *group-term life insurance*), or 6053 (reporting of tips). §6041A(c).

set-aside requirements, low-income housing   see *qualified low-income housing project, low-income housing credit.*

set off   a term often used in connection with the collection of taxes to refer to the *Collection Division's* power to apply *refunds* and other amounts due the *tax-*

payer to reduce tax liabilities, sometimes to the disadvantage of people who acquired the taxpayer's claim against the government. §6402.

settlement date   the day on which payment for a securities transaction is made. *Cash method* sellers report *gains* in the year in which the settlement date falls, but they report *losses* in the year of the *trade date.* Rev. Rul. 70-344, 1970-2 C.B. 50.

settlement options   options provided in *life insurance policies* that allow the *beneficiary* to select the form of payout.

seven-year property   includes *tangible property* within a *class life* of 10 years or more but less than 16 years, as well as any railroad tracks, *single-purpose agricultural or horticultural structures,* and property that does not have a class life and is not otherwise classified. §168(e)(3)(C).

seventy-percent PCM   another name for the *percentage of completion—capitalized cost method.*

several liability   *individual* liability of several codebtors that extends to the whole debt without need for the holder to seek recovery against other codebtors. See *joint and several liability.* One significance is that, where the *taxpayer* is severally liable for taxes, the person making the payment is entitled to the *deduction,* if any, for the payment. Rev. Rul. 72-79, 1972-9 I.R.B. 9.

severance from service date   the earlier of (1) quitting, retiring, discharge, or death; or (2) the anniversary date of the first date of a period in which the *employee* is absent for any other reason (e.g., sickness or layoff). Labor Reg. §2530.200b-9(b)(2). The term is used to measure periods of service in the determination of *employee participation* in *qualified plans* under the *elapsed time method.* See *accrued benefits.*

severe hardship, extension of time for filing return   the showing required of the *taxpayer* for the granting of a non*automatic extension* of time for filing a *tax return,* statement, or other document, when the taxpayer did not first avail him- or herself of an automatic extension under Reg. §1.6081-4. Few taxpayers can meet the severe hardship test, evidently because of the urgency with which the *IRS* apparently wants taxpayers to use the automatic extension provisions, since in such cases it is typically quite liberal in granting additional extensions. Although no standard is set forth in the Code or *regulations,* the IRS provides its personnel with the following examples: (1) death or serious illness of the tax practitioner, a key member of his or her staff, the taxpayer, or a member of his or her immediate family; (2) destruction of the taxpayer's records by fire or other casualty; and (3) interference due to a civil disturbance.

sewage disposal facility   any property used for the collection, storage, treatment, utilization, processing, or final disposal of sewage. Reg. §1.103-8(f)(2)(i). *Interest* on obligations issued to provide such facilities could be tax-exempt even though the obligation might otherwise be an *industrial development bond.* Former §103(b)(4)(E). Section 142(a)(5) (current law) states that a *private activity bond,* 95 percent of whose *net proceeds* are used for a "sewage facility," can be an *exempt facility bond (producing tax-exempt interest),* but it does not define the term. The first definition ("sewage disposal facility") presumably applies under current law and can prevent a *private activity bond* from losing its character as a *state or local bond.*

sewage facility   see *sewage disposal facility.*

shadow stock   stock used as a measure of *deferred compensation* plan obligations, but which is not actually purchased. The use of shadow stock is a popular *nonqualified deferred compensation* practice.

sham transactions   a tax law doctrine applied to misrepresented transactions that can properly be disregarded. For example, if X purports to sell a house to Y for $10,000 but has an option to acquire it for $1, the transaction will doubtless be disregarded as a sham.

shared equity financing agreement   an agreement under which two or more *persons* acquire a *dwelling unit* and one or more of such persons is entitled to occupy the dwelling unit as a *principal residence* and is required to pay rent to the nonoccupant co-owners. Each of the co-owners must acquire an undivided interest for more than 50 years in the entire dwelling unit and any *appurtenant* land acquired in the transaction to which the shared equity financing agreement relates (i.e., hold a *qualified ownership interest*). §280A(d)(3)(C). In the case of *fair market value rentals* to a person who has an interest in the dwelling unit, §280A(d)(3)(B) provides that such use is not considered *personal use* by the lessor if the rental is under a shared equity financing agreement. Such arrangements permit relatives to advance capital for the acquisition of a residential property for use by their relatives, but have also been used as the basis for *tax shelter* activities. But for the special relief provision of §280A(d)(3), the absentee investor would be greatly circumscribed in his or her ability to *deduct* current *losses* with respect to the property because use by the co-owner would be considered use by the investor. See *vacation home rules.*

shared FSC   any *corporation* if (1) it maintains a separate account for transactions with each *shareholder* (or person related to a shareholder); (2) *distributions* to each shareholder are based on the amounts in such account; and (3) it meets such other tests as *regulations* may impose. §927(g)(3). Shared *foreign sales corporations* (FSCs) are generally treated as separate corporations, and various standards applied to FSCs are tested at the shared FSC level, thereby allowing smaller companies to join forces. §927(g)(1). See *foreign sales corporation.*

shareholder a *person,* also known as a *shareholder,* who owns corporate *stock,* preferred or common. The term is not defined, but it implicitly depends on a showing that the person's interests genuinely constitute *stock* under the *debt-equity rules* of §385. For purposes of *distributions* of *stock dividends* and the like under §305, the term includes holders of convertible securities and *rights.* §305(d)(2). This book often uses the term in italics, even though the *Code* may in fact use the term "shareholder."

shareholder-employee, S corporation, fringe benefits in the application of the fringe benefit provisions of the Code, an S corporation is treated as a partnership and an employee-shareholder who owns *more than 2 percent of its stock* is treated as a partner. §1372. Thus, the value of the fringe benefits provided to a 2 percent or more shareholder must be included in the shareholder's gross income unless the Code permits an exclusion from income. See *two-percent shareholder.*

shareholders' liquidating trust see *liquidating trust.*

shareholder, stock dividends a traditional *shareholder* as well as a holder of stock *rights* and convertible securities. §305(d)(2). See *rights, stock.*

sharing agreement, extractive industries a contract by which a party receives an interest in oil and gas or mineral property in exchange for contributing to the acquisition, exploration, or development of such property; a *carried interest* is one form of sharing arrangement. G.C.M. 22730, 1941-1 C.B. 214.

sheltered workshop a school providing special instruction or training designed to alleviate the disability of the *individual,* which is operated either by an exempt *charitable organization,* a state or *possession* or one of its subdivisions, the United States, or the District of Columbia. §151(c)(5)(B). Income received by a permanently and totally disabled individual for services performed at such a workshop need not be counted for purposes of determining whether the *dependent* has *gross income,* if the availability of *medical care* is the principal reason for the individual's presence at the workshop and the income arises solely from activities of the workshop which are incidental to the medical care. §151(c)(5)(A). As a result, the person can be someone else's *dependent,* despite earning income from the workshop.

shelters see *tax shelter.*

shifting allocation a type of *allocation* of *partner's distributive shares* which fails the requirement that allocations be *substantial.* It occurs if, when the allocation is agreed to, there is a strong likelihood that the net increases and decreases in the partner's *capital accounts* for the *taxable year* will not differ substantially from the net changes in the capital accounts that would arise absent of the allocation, and the allocation would reduce the total tax liability of all the partners. Reg. §1.704-1(b)(2)(iii)(b). Such an allocation is defective because it is not "substantial." See *substantial economic effect test.*

shifting of income the practice of changing the flow of taxable income from one person to another to *minimize aggregate income taxes.* For example, parents should consider giving a younger child assets that defer taxable income until the child reaches age 14. Uniform Gifts to Minors Act also facilitates the shifting of income by allowing the donor to make a gift of intangibles (e.g., bank accounts, stocks, bonds) to a minor but with an adult serving as custodian. Such planning is limited by the tax liability calculation provision for a child under the age of 14 (the *kiddie tax rules*).

shipowners' protection and indemnity associations *associations* organized on a nonprofit basis, none of the *net earnings* of which *inure* to any private shareholder, that provide mutual protection and indemnity for their participants. §526. Section 526 exempts such associations from federal *income taxes* except as to their income from *interest, dividends,* and *rent.*

ship passengers international departure tax a tax of $3 per passenger on a covered voyage. §4471(a). It is paid by the person providing the covered voyage, either at the time of first embarkation or disembarkation in the *United States.*

shipping income a category of *foreign source income* to which the *foreign tax credit limitation* applies separately. §904(d)(1). This category consists of income of any *person* which would be *foreign base shipping income.* §904(d)(2)(D). The use of the term "*any person*" sweeps in *United States persons* and income of *controlled foreign corporations.* Since income of this character is often not taxed by foreign countries, the *Code* segregates it to avoid having businesses apply unrelated excess credits to it and escape taxation altogether. Where they overlap, *dividends* from a *noncontrolled foreign corporation* take precedence over the shipping basket, and when CFC income is taxed abroad at over 90 percent of the top United States rate, the CFC's dividends paid out of its shipping income go into a separate *basket.* See *section 904(d)(1) "basket."*

short form, Form 1040A or Form 1040EZ filed by *individuals* who do not *itemize* their *deductions.* Form 1040A is only permitted when taxable income is less than $50,000. Form 1040EZ can only be used by single taxpayers with no dependents.

short-form merger see *practical merger.*

short period an *accounting period* shorter than one year (and not a *fifty-two-, fifty-three-week taxable year*).

Short periods commonly call for *annualization of income*. §443(b). Such periods arise for reasons such as creation or dissolution of an *entity,* birth, death, or voluntary changes of *accounting periods.*

short sale   a transaction in which a party (the short seller) contracts to sell shares (or sometimes other property) not then owned to another at a fixed price in the expectation of a decline in price, with delivery to be made at a time when, under the rules of the exchange, delivery must be made. Ordinarily, such a transaction is undertaken by securities investors, who borrow stock through a broker, later to be replaced by the delivery of securities acquired in the marketplace in the future (one hopes at a lower price), thereby closing the position. Short sale contracts result in taxation at the closing (delivery) only. The *character* of the *gain* or *loss* depends on the character of the securities held by the short seller who closes the transaction, and the *holding period* determines whether the gain is *long-term* or *short-term.* §1233(a). If, at the time of entering into the short sale (or thereafter), the *taxpayer* owns *substantially identical property,* the rules become considerably more complex, generally resulting in *tax deferrals.* See *extraordinary dividend, short sale; short sale against the box.*

short sale against the box   a *short sale* entered into when the *taxpayer* owns securities *substantially identical* to those that are the subject of the short sale. The tax planning purpose of such transactions is to defer *gains* and *losses,* and to freeze the associated *holding periods,* to a future year when the short sale closes. Sections 1233(b) and (d) are the operative provisions, and they apply only to short sales of *stock,* securities, and commodities futures that are *capital assets,* and only to the extent the taxpayer holds or acquires substantially identical assets. For example, suppose X holds 100 shares, worth $1,000, of ABC Corporation that cost $100 and are now (11 months later) capital assets in X's hands. Taxpayer X enters into a short sale against the box by selling short an equal number of shares. When the transaction closes next year, the long and short positions will offset each other. Pursuant to §1233, X will have a $900 *short-term capital gain* in that later year. Reg. §1.1233-1(c). See *substantially identical stock or securities.*

short-term capital gains   *gains* from the actual or *constructive sale* or *exchange* of *capital assets* held for not more than a year. A 24-month rule applies to cattle and horses where §1231 applies under §1231(b)(3)(A). §1222(1). See *holding period.*

short-term capital losses   *losses* from *sales* or *exchanges* of *capital assets* held for not more than a year. §1222(2). A 24-month rule applies to cattle and horses where §1231 applies. Such sales or exchanges may be actual or *constructive.* For example, a loan not made in the ordinary course of business is classified as a nonbusiness receivable. If the receivable becomes completely worthless during the year, it is a *nonbusiness bad debt,* to be treated as a *short-term capital loss.* §166(d). See *holding period.*

short-term government obligation   a taxable obligation of the United States or any of its *possessions,* or of a *state* or a *political subdivision* thereof, or of the District of Columbia, which is issued on a discounted basis and is payable without interest at a fixed maturity date not exceeding a year from the date of issue. §1271(a)(3)(B). *Acquisition discount* on such obligations is not currently included in the *gross income* of certain *taxpayers.* §§1281(a) and 1283(c). However, when the debt is *sold, gain* not in excess of the ratable share of *acquisition discount* is taxed as *ordinary income.* §1271(a)(3).

short-term holding period   a *holding period* of *property* of a year or less, except in the case of cattle or horses held for draft, breeding, dairy, or sport purposes (two years or less for purposes of defining *section 1231 assets* only). The term is vital to determine whether a *gain* or *loss* is a *long-* or *short-term capital gain* or *loss.*

short-term nongovernmental obligation   an obligation which has a fixed maturity date of not over a year from the date of issue and is not a *short-term governmental obligation.* §1271(a)(4)(B). *Acquisition discount* on such obligation is treated as *interest,* either on *sale* or *exchange,* less any *ratable share of acquisition discount* (or comparable elective accrual of *interest* on a *constant interest rate amortization method*).

short-term obligation   noninclusively defined to include a bond, debenture, note, certificate, or other evidence of indebtedness (other than a *tax-exempt obligation*) having a fixed maturity date not more than one year from the date of issue. §1231(a)(1). Such obligations are subject to particularized tax rules. For example, they are treated as *unrealized receivables* of a *partnership.* §751(c).

short-term obligation, acquisition discount   any *debt* due on a fixed maturity date not more than one year after issuance (other than tax-exempt state and local government debt), if the holder uses the *accrual method,* holds the obligation as a *dealer,* is a *bank, mutual fund,* or *common trust fund,* or holds the obligation as part of a hedging transaction. The *daily portion* of acquisition discount must be included in *gross income* as it is earned. §1281.

short year   see *short period.*

shut-in royalty   payments in lieu of production-based *royalties* as a result of a decision not to extract minerals, oil, or gas from a proven site. They are used extensively in the natural gas extraction industry.

sick and accident benefits, voluntary employees' beneficiary associations   amounts furnished to or on behalf of a member or a member's *dependents* in the event of illness or personal injury. The term includes payments in lieu of income when the member is unable to work due to sickness or accidental injury. See Reg. §1.501(e)(9)-3(c). See *voluntary employees' beneficiary associations.*

sick pay, income tax withholding amounts paid to *employees,* under plans to which the *employer* is a party, in lieu of remuneration while the *employees* are temporarily absent due to sickness or personal injury. §3402(o)(2)(C). Such amounts are subject to *income tax withholding* if they constitute *wages* or if the employee requests withholding.

significant business presence, possessions corporations a condition to an *island affiliate's* eligibility to elect *cost-sharing* for a product or type of service, designed to assure that the affiliate is engaged in real and significant *business.* §936(h)(5)(B). An island affiliate satisfies the requirement, with respect to a product or service, if (1) more than 25 percent of the value added by the affiliated group to the product is added by the island affiliate in a *possession* (which includes Puerto Rico but not the United States Virgin Islands), or (2) at least 65 percent of the direct labor costs of the affiliated group for the product or service, or in connection with the purchase and sale of goods not produced by the affiliated group, are incurred by the island affiliate and are compensation for services rendered in a possession or Puerto Rico. §936(h)(5)(B)(ii). If the significant business presence test is failed for a product or type of service within the *product area* covered by the cost-sharing election, then the cost-sharing payment is not reduced by the product area research expenditures *paid or accrued* by the *possessions corporation*; the general rule allocating *intangible property* income to United States shareholders will then apply to that particular product or service. The test is also used for purposes of the so-called *fifty-fifty split* election.

significant new issuance of debt a term used in the reporting requirements of §6043(c) in connection with determining if there has been a substantial change in a *corporation's* capital structure, especially value-enhancing *distributions* and leveraged restructuring.

significant OID a concept used to help identify an *applicable high-yield discount obligation.* An obligation has significant OID (*original issue discount*) if the aggregate amount that would be includible in *gross income* with respect to the instrument before the close of any accrual period ending more than five years after the date of issue exceeds the sum of (1) the aggregate amount of *interest* to be paid before the close of such accrual period; and (2) the product of the *issue price* of the instrument and its *yield to maturity.* For this purpose, amounts required to be paid on the last day of the accrual period are deemed required to be paid before the close of the accrual period. §163(i)(2). See *applicable high-yield discount obligation.*

significant participation activity a *trade or business* in which the *taxpayer* participates significantly, but not to the point of *material participation* under the other six tests found in Reg. §1.469-5T(a). It calls for participation in an *activity* for over 100 hours per year. Reg. §1.469-5T(c). If the *individual's* participation in all his or her significant participation activities for the year exceeds 500 hours, he or she is deemed to materially participate in each significant participation activity. Reg. §1.469-5T(a). This represents one of the primary objective methods for determining how much participation is enough to avoid the *passive loss rules.* The disadvantage for taxpayers is that, if such activities produce *net income* but the taxpayer did not materially participate under any other standard, that net income is *portfolio income* and cannot offset other passive losses. Reg. §1.469-2T(f)(10). See *material participation, passive loss rules; passive loss rules.*

significant personal services services performed by *individuals* which in light of *all the facts and circumstances* are significant. See Reg. §1.469-1T(e)(3)(iv). Certain activities cannot count, namely, services needed to make the use of the property lawful, repairs and improvements, or services provided to users of the property that are typical of a long-term high-grade lease arrangement such as garbage collection, elevator service, repairs, etc. If a *taxpayer* provides significant personal services in connection with renting of property for periods of not over 30 days on the average, then the income from the activity is not income from a *rental activity.* That means that if the taxpayer is otherwise active enough, the income may be classified as not income from a *passive activity.* See *passive loss rules.*

significant power, right or continuing interest any power, right, or interest retained by a transferor of a *franchise, trademark,* or *trade name* sufficient to deny *capital gain* or *loss* results on the transfer of such *property.* Section 1253(b)(2) provides that the term includes, but is not limited to, six specific rights, namely, the right (1) to disapprove further assignments; (2) to terminate at will; (3) to prescribe standards of quality; (4) to limit the products sold or advertised to those of the transferor; (5) to require that the transferee purchase supplies and equipment from the transferor; and (6) to contingent payments.

significant purpose rule, subpart F a relief provision to the effect that the burdens of *subpart F* will not fall on *foreign base company* transactions that do not have substantial tax reduction as a significant purpose. §954(b)(3)(B).

Silver Queen Motel doctrine an *IRS*-accepted judicial doctrine permitting a *taxpayer,* whose attempt to use an erroneous method of *depreciation* was disallowed by the *IRS,* to adopt, without the Commissioner's consent, the *straight-line* method or any other method of depreciation that would have been permissible had it been adopted initially. Rev. Rul. 72-491, 1972-2 C.B. 104. This doctrine may also be applied for *open years* even when the *statute of limitations* prevents correction of the error for other years when the erroneous method was used.

similar or related in service or use   a use of *property* that is substantially similar to the use of property that was the subject of an *involuntary conversion*. By way of illustration, the following uses have been said to satisfy the standard: (1) a truck and cattle farm replaced with apricot, prune, and walnut orchards; and (2) a seafood processor on land for a seafood processor used at sea (Rev. Rul. 77-192, 1977-1 C.B. 249). The following do not meet the standard: (1) a billiard center for a bowling center (Rev. Rul. 76-319, 1976-2 C.B. 242); and (2) art in different mediums (Letter Rul. 8127089 (Apr. 10, 1981). Involuntary conversions of realty and billboards and certain other exceptional cases need only satisfy a *like-kind property* standard. §1033(g)(1). Also, §1033 allows purchases of 80 percent control of a *corporation* holding property similar or related in service or use to qualify. §1033(a)(2)(A). For cases involving lessors of personal property, see *functional use test, involuntary conversions*. For cases involving lessors of personal property, see *functional use test, involuntary conversions*.

similar property, copyright, etc.   *property* of the same type as the other items described in §1221(3). Reg. §1.1221-1(c) states that similar property includes, for example, such property as a theatrical production, a radio program, a newspaper cartoon strip, or any other property eligible for copyright protection (whether under statute or common law), but it does not include a *patent* or an invention, or a design which may be protected only under the patent law and not under the *copyright* law. Such property cannot be a *capital asset* in the hands of the creator or persons who got the property on a tax-deferred basis.

simplified depreciation election   a taxpayer may elect to combine depreciable assets having the same asset class, recovery period, depreciation method, and placed-in-service year into one or more homogeneous groups. This would eliminate the need to calculate depreciation on an asset by asset basis. Each asset group would be depreciated as one asset. Prop. Reg. §1.168(i)-1.

simplified dollar-value LIFO method   a method of pricing *inventories* under which the *taxpayer* maintains a separate *inventory pool* for each *major category* in the *applicable government price index*; the change in each pool is based on the change from the prior *taxable year*

in the component of the index for the major category. §474(b)(1). The applicable government price index is the Producer Price published by the Bureau of Labor Statistics, except that, for retailers using the *retail inventory method,* it is the Consumer Price Index. §474(b)(2). The major category is the standard two-digit industrial classification number used in the Producer Price Index or any general expenditure category in the Consumer Price Index, as the case may be. §474(b)(3). So-called *eligible small businesses* can use this method. The last term refers to a *taxpayer* whose average annual gross receipts for the past three years do not exceed $5 million.

simplified employee pension plan (SEP)   a plan pursuant to which *individual retirement annuities* or *accounts* (IRAs) are established for *employees* (including *independent contractors*), to which *employers* (including a *partner* or *sole proprietor*) can contribute (and *deduct*) the lesser of $30,000 or 15 percent of the employees' taxable compensation. §408(j). In this type of plan, the corporation must make a contribution for *each employee* who has reached age 21, has performed service for the employer during the calendar year and at least three of the five preceding calendar years, and has received at least $374 (for 1992) in compensation from the employer for the year, §408(k)(2). See *integration, Social Security; salary reduction SEP*.

simplified look-back method   a way of applying the *look-back* provision applicable to *partnerships, S corporations* and *trusts* using the *percentage of completion method* applicable to *long-term contracts* under which *federal income taxes* over- or underpaid are determined by multiplying the amount of contract income over- or underreported for the *taxable year* by the top tax rate for the year. The calculation is made at the *entity* level and the entity pays or receives the *interest* due or receivable. If the entity is primarily owned by *individuals,* one uses the top individual *federal income* rate. This method does not apply to contracts, much of whose income is from overseas, or if the entity is a *closely held pass-through entity,* meaning a *partnership, S corporation,* or *trust,* at least 50 percent of whose *beneficial interests* by value are held by five or fewer *persons,* applying *constructive ownership rules*. §460(b)(5). See *look-back method, long-term contracts*.

simplified production method   an alternative application of the *uniform capitalization rules* used to sort inventoriable costs from amounts currently deducted as *costs of goods sold*. It applies to self-produced *inventory* and *dealer property* of a high-turnover, repetitive type. See Reg. §1.263A-1T(b)(5)(i). The method allocates costs to *inventory* in the same proportion as the ratio that additional costs bear to the *taxpayer's* total production costs (aside from additional section 263A costs) incurred during the year. It is complicated in its details. The taxpayer is free to generate its own *allocation method* instead. Reg. §1.263-1T(b)(3)(iii). See *allocation methods, uniform capitalization rules.*

simplified resale method, uniform capitalization rules a method available to *taxpayers* who acquire *property* for resale to determine what portion of purchasing, off-site storage, handling, and *mixed service costs* are allocable to *inventory*. In the case of purchasing, handling, and off-site storage costs, the allocable portion is determined by applying the *allocation ratio* to the amount of current purchases in *closing inventory*. In the case of *mixed service costs,* the allocable portion is determined by multiplying the total of such costs by the ratio of labor costs incurred by purchasing, handling, and off-site storage activities to the taxpayer's total labor costs. Reg. §1.263A-1T(d)(4)(ii)-(iii). See *mixed service costs, uniform capitalization rules; allocation methods, uniform capitalization rules.*

simplified service cost method, uniform capitalization rules a method of determining what portion of *mixed service costs* must be *capitalized* in *inventory*. A *taxpayer,* holding *stock* or *property* primarily for resale, may determine the portion of mixed service costs that must be allocated to inventory by multiplying the total of such costs by the ratio of total production costs to total operating costs. Reg. §1.263A-1T(b)(6)(ii)-(iii). See *mixed service costs, uniform capitalization rules; allocable costs, uniform capitalization rules.*

simultaneous examination programs programs of the *IRS* to simultaneously examine multinational *taxpayers* to establish *arm's length* pricing, done under *tax treaty* authority. 1981 I.R.M. 42(10)(10).

single category method, securities identification see *average basis method election.*

single inventory pool election, small business see *inventory pool election, small business.*

single life annuity an *annuity* payable until the death of a named *annuitant.*

single person (or taxpayer) unmarried. Marital status is generally tested at year-end except in cases of death of a *spouse*. See *married person.* The term means someone who under *state* law does not maintain a legally recognized marital relationship with a *spouse*. Such persons include (1) those who have never married; (2) those who are *legally* separated from their spouses under a decree of divorce or *separate maintenance*; and (3) certain *individuals* who are legally married and who live apart for the entire year, but only as to the spouse who maintains a household for a *dependent child*. §7703. See *married person; runaway spouse rule.*

single plan, qualified plans a standard used to determine whether a merger or consolidation of *qualified plans* has occurred. Generally, a plan is a single plan

only if, on an ongoing basis, all its assets are available to pay benefits to covered *employees* and their *beneficiaries*. Reg. §1.414(1)-11(b). If a single plan results from a merger, consolidation, or transfer of assets, then the plan must provide that *participants* will receive plan termination benefits at least equal to the termination benefits before the transaction. §401(a)(12).

single purpose agricultural or horticultural structure a structure (e.g., barn or poultry coop) or enclosure (including for housing the necessary equipment and replacements) designed, constructed, and used exclusively for housing, raising, and feeding a particular class of livestock and their produce, or a greenhouse designed, constructed, and used for the commercial production of plants, and a structure designed, constructed, and used for the commercial production of mushrooms. The *Code* defines the terms "single purpose lifestock structure" and "single purpose horticultural structure" separately, but they are combined under this heading. Such structures have a 10-year *recovery period*. §163(e)(3)(D)(i), (i)(13).

sinking fund depreciation a little-used method of *depreciation* that modifies depreciation *deductions* to take the *time value of money* into account; it is modeled on the assumption that the depreciation *reserve* earns *interest* in the manner of a savings account, resulting in rising depreciation deductions over the years. Reg. §1.167(b)-4(a).

six-month temporary investment exception a limit on the *arbitrage bond* provisions. The exception generally provides that the arbitrage rebate and penalty rules do not apply if the gross proceeds of the issue are spent within six months. Even then, there can be *bona fide* debt service funds, *four R funds,* and reserves for unanticipated proceeds. §148(f)(4)(B).

Sixteenth Amendment the 1913 amendment to the United States Constitution sanctioned both the federal individual and corporate income taxes. Various revenue acts were passed between 1913 and 1954. The current law is entitled the Internal Revenue Code of 1986, which carried over substantial portions of the 1954 Code. There have been several amendments to the Code since 1986.

sixty-five percent of taxable income ceiling a cap on *percentage depletion* of oil and gas, under which *depletion* that is otherwise allowable is limited to 65 percent of the *taxpayer's taxable income* from all sources, computed without percentage depletion, *net operating losses, capital loss carrybacks,* and, for *individuals,* the *standard deduction*. §613A(d)(1). See *percentage depletion.*

sixty-five years of age age 65 not later than January 1 of the next year. §151(c); Reg. §1.151-1(c)(2) (for purposes of claiming an additional limited *standard deduction* on account of age). A taxpayer is considered to be age 65 on the day before his or her sixty-fifth birthday. Reaching age 65 enables the taxpayer to take an increased standard deduction.

sixty-forty rule another name for the generality that *gains* or *losses* from *regulated commodity futures contracts* and other *section 1256 contracts* must be reported annually on the *mark-to-market system,* with 60 percent of gains or losses on such contracts treated as *long-term capital gain* or *loss* and 40 percent treated as *short-term capital gain* or *loss* (except as to *limited partners* and *limited entrepreneurs*). §1256(a)(3).

six-year graded vesting an alternative *vesting schedule* that a *top-heavy plan* may satisfy. It satisfies the schedule if an *employee* has a nonforfeitable right to 20 percent of the *accrued benefit* after two years of service, 40 percent after three, 60 percent after four, 80 percent after five, and 100 percent after six or more years of service. §416(b)(1)(B).

six-year spread forward a reference to a feature of Rev. Proc. 84-74, 1984-2 C.B. 736 under which adjustments arising out of *changes of accounting methods* are spread into the following six years. It is the general rule and applies whether the result is to spread positive or negative amounts of income. The formal term for the amount to be spread is the "*net adjustment.*"

skeleton protest a *protest* that only outlines the *taxpayer's* position without dwelling on the facts or law.

sleep or rest rule a requirement that a *taxpayer* who has left the area of his or her *tax home* must reasonably be expected to need to sleep or rest during free time. The standard provides a rough and ready test to determine whether one-day trips can qualify as *travel* such that meals and lodging on the trip can be *deducted.* Unless there is a need for sleep or rest, the associated *deductions* may still be available, but only as *entertainment* or *transportation expenses.*

slush fund see *questionable payments.*

slush fund questionnaire a list of five questions designed to uncover corporate *tax evasion* schemes involving loans, kickbacks, bribes, secret accounts, political expenditures, or other *questionable payments.* The list was revised and condensed from an earlier 11-question version and is set forth in I.R. 1943 (Jan. 20, 1978). The questionnaire, administered under penalty of perjury at least once to selected officials, key *employees,* and other specified parties of all large *corporations* (financial institutions and utilities with gross assets exceeding $1 billion, or other corporations with gross assets exceeding $250 million), requires disclosure of any transactions, lawful or otherwise, that fit into the designated categories. I.R. 1590 (Apr. 17, 1976). The questionnaire may also be used for any corporation if the facts and circumstances warrant, but not as a general

rule. I.R. 1615 (May 13, 1976). Additional questions may be asked if warranted by the answers given, and any evidence of fraud or false statement will be turned over to the *Criminal Investigation Division.* The questionnaire is administered under §7602 as a part of a regular *IRS examination* for the purpose of determining compliance with the tax laws (primarily to monitor the propriety of §162 *trade or business deductions*) and the inquiry is apparently limited to matters relevant to corporate tax liability.

small business corporation a *corporation* whose *stock* qualifies for the special *deduction* available for *losses* on stock of such corporations. See *small business corporation stock.*

small business corporation, S corporations part of the definition of an *S corporation* concerning the company's ownership and capital structure. It means a *domestic corporation* that does not have (1) over 35 *shareholders*; (2) a shareholder who is not an *individual* (except for certain *trusts*; (3) a *nonresident alien* shareholder); (4) or more than one class of *stock.* There is no actual size requirement. §1361(b)(1). As to the one class of stock rule, see *straight debt.*

small business corporation stock corporate *stock* (common or preferred) qualifying under §1244 of the *Code.* The significance of such stock is that its *sale, exchange,* or *worthlessness* can create *net operating losses* (rather than *capital losses* under §165(g)) for *individual shareholders* in amounts up to $50,000 per year ($100,000 for *joint returns*). §1244(a) and (b). A corporation qualifies as a small business corporation if the amount of money and other property it receives as a contribution to capital does not exceed $1 million. This determination is made at the time the stock is issued, but it also includes amounts received for such stock and for all stock issued.

small business, inventories see *inventory pool election, small business.*

small business investment company a company operating as a licensee under the Small Business Investment Company Act of 1958 (13 C.F.R. Part 107 contains pertinent regulations). At the shareholder level, losses on the sale or exchange of *worthless* stock in such companies (if otherwise capital in nature) are classified as ordinary in nature and qualify as *operating losses.* §1242. At the company level, losses on convertible debentures acquired pursuant to §304 of the Small Business Act of 1958 qualify as *ordinary losses.* §1243. The real advantage of SBICs is that they can borrow large amounts of money for investment on a *nonrecourse* basis from the government. The result is great leverage. The *entity* does not need to be a *corporation.*

Small Business Investment Company Act of 1958 see *small business investment company.*

Small Claims Division in most cases, the taxpayer has a choice of four trial courts: a Federal District Court, the U.S. Claims Court (recently renamed the U.S. Court of Federal Claims), the U.S. Tax Court, or the Small Claims Division of the U.S. Tax Court. The jurisdiction of the Small Claims Division is $10,000 or less and its decisions are not reviewable by any higher court.

small contractor exception an informal term for an exception provided for certain construction contracts made by *taxpayers* with no more than $10 million in average gross receipts for the preceding three tax years. In general, the requirement that the *percentage of completion method* or the *percentage of completion capitalized cost method* be used does not apply to any construction contract made by such a taxpayer who estimates completion within two years. Gross receipts include those of any predecessor of the taxpayer or of any predecessor of any of commonly controlled trades or businesses or controlled group members referred to in the preceding paragraph. §460(e)(2).

small ethanol producer credit a *credit* given to an eligible small ethanol producer (one whose productive capacity for alcohol is not over 30 million gallons per day) may claim the small ethanol producer credit of 10 cents per gallon on production of up to 15 million gallons per year of ethanol. The credit is recaptured through the imposition of a tax of 10 cents per gallon if the producer fails to use the ethanol or ethanol mixture as fuel. §40.

small FSC a *foreign sales corporation (FSC)* which has made a timely election to be treated as a small FSC and is not a member of a controlled corporate group which includes an FSC (unless the other FSC has also made such an election). §922(b). A small FSC is exempt from certain of the *foreign management* and *economic process* requirements, but its *exempt income* cannot exceed an amount based on a ceiling of $5 million of *foreign trading gross receipts*. §924(b)(2). This provision helps small *DISCs* that were adversely affected by the repeal of the DISC provisions by the *Tax Reform Act of 1984*.

small hand tools exception a rule to the effect that tools that are relatively simple and have a short *useful life* are *deductible* in the year when purchased. Although such tools may have a useful life in excess of one year, for *federal income tax* purposes, the *taxpayer* is not required to *depreciate* them. Other more complex tools must be written off over their useful lives. In order to claim this *deduction,* the taxpayer should be able to substantiate the cost, number, and type of tools to be deducted. Farmers and professionals receive comparable benefits under Reg. §1.162-12 and -6, respectively. The rule is often applied to items other than tools.

small insurance company alternative tax an election granted to every *insurance company,* other than a *life insurance company,* that has net written premiums for the *taxable year* between $350,000 and $1,200,000 permitting it to apply the section 831 alternative tax which is computed by multiplying the company's *taxable investment income* by the corporate *income tax* rates imposed by §11(b). §831(b).

small issue exemption, beneficiary limitations certain overall limitations that any *beneficiary* can receive from a small issue of *industrial development bonds (IDBs).* In general, *interest* on such bonds is taxable if a beneficiary (owner or principal user of a financed facility) received an aggregate amount of IDB financing in excess of $40 million over a three-year period beginning the later of the date of the small issue IDB, or the date the financed facility is *placed in service.* §103(b)(15)(D).

small life insurance company generally, a *life insurance company* with less than $500 million of assets. See *small life insurance company deduction.* See *special deductions, life insurance companies.*

small partnerships *partnerships* having 10 or fewer *partners* each of whom is an *individual* (but not a *nonresident alien*) or an *estate,* and each of whom, or which, shares equally in each partnership item; *spouses* count as one *taxpayer.* §6231(a)(1)(B)(i). Small partnerships are excluded from the rules governing *TEFRA audits* of partnership under §§6221–6231, unless they elect to be covered. §6231(a)(1)(B). See *unified proceedings.*

small producers' exemption a shorthand term for "exemption for independent producers and royalty owners," appearing in the heading of §613A(c). In essence, it grants the *percentage depletion* method to small oil and gas producers and royalty owners and for several types of mineral properties such as coal and iron. §613A(c). Percentage depletion for oil and gas properties is 15 percent times the gross income from the property. However, it may not exceed 100 percent of taxable income before the depletion is deducted. The percentage limitation was 50 percent before 1991. It is also known as the *independent producers and royalty owners exemption.* Other minerals are subject to percentage depletion at rates between 22 percent and 5 percent. See *percentage depletion.*

small S corporation an *S corporation* with five or fewer *shareholders,* each of whom is an *individual* or an *estate.* Temp. Reg. §301.6241-1T(c)(2). Such corporations are exempt from the *unified proceedings* under which *TEFRA audits* occur at the corporate level unless they elect to the contrary. See *unified proceedings.*

small SEP an *SEP* of an *employer* having less than 25 *employees.* See *SEP-CODA.*

small tax cases   cases in the *Tax Court* involving not more than $10,000 (*deficiency,* including *additions to tax,* or claimed *overpayment*) for any single *taxable year.* Such cases can be subjected to simplified procedures at the *taxpayer's* election, but only if the Tax Court agrees. §7463. Such decisions cannot be reviewed or used as precedents for other cases. §7463(b). The procedure includes *income, estate,* and *gift taxes,* as well as *excise taxes* relating to *private foundations, qualified plans,* and the former *crude oil windfall profits tax.* See F. Burnett & G. Kafka, *Litigation of Federal Tax Controversies* §§9.10-9.12 (1990).

Smith-Jacobson rule   *short-term losses* resulting from closing out either a long or short position in commodities trading are not allowed under §165(c)(2) if the *taxpayer* replaces the closed-out position with an equivalent one for a different month while maintaining a corresponding short or long position in the same commodity. The rule is a backstop to the complex *Code* provisions relating to *straddles.*

soak-up tax   a *foreign tax* imposed only with relation to the availability of a *foreign tax credit* for the tax in the *taxpayer's* home country. Such charges are not *creditable foreign taxes* to that extent. See Reg. §1.901-2(c). See *foreign tax credit.*

social club   clubs organized and operated exclusively for pleasure, recreation, and other nonprofitable purposes, no part of the *net earnings* of which *inures* to the benefit of any *private shareholder.* §501(c)(7). Exempt income of social clubs includes only *exempt function income,* which generally means gross income from dues, fees, and charges that members pay for goods and services that are the basis of the exemption. Social commingling among members is required. Rev. Rul. 70-32, 1970-1 C.B. 132. Recreation is broadly defined (e.g., it can include gambling). Rev. Rul. 69-68, 1969-1 C.B. 153. Discrimination on the basis of race, color, or religion is prohibited by §501(i). Rev. Rul. 74-168, 1974-1 C.B. 139; Rev. Rul. 74-489, 1974-2 C.B. 1969; Rev. Rul. 67-428, 1967-2 C.B. 204. Not all the club's activities need to serve its *exempt purposes.* Examples include college alumni groups, country clubs, hobby clubs, fraternities, and the like. *IRS* Pub. No. 557 (1976) (further illustrations and guidance). See §501(c)(7) (requirements in order for a club to qualify as an *exempt organization*). *Gifts* to clubs do not qualify for a *charitable contribution deduction.* Nonexempt function income (basically income derived from nonmembers) is taxed as *unrelated business taxable income* whether or not the activity is regularly carried on. §512. See *exempt function income, social clubs and voluntary employee beneficiary associations.*

Social Security beneficiaries, limitation on earnings
Social Security beneficiaries aged 65 through 69 can earn a maximum of $10,560 in 1993 without losing any Social Security benefits. For those under the age of 65, the earnings limit will rise to $7,680.

Social Security benefits   a broad term that includes monthly Social Security benefits, Railroad Retirement Act benefits, and worker's compensation benefits paid in lieu of Social Security benefits. §86(d)(1). Social Security benefits are subject to *federal income taxes* in an amount equal to the lesser of (1) one-half the annual benefits, or (2) one-half of *modified adjusted gross income* (basically *adjusted gross income* plus *tax-exempt interest,* certain being excluded foreign source income, and income from United States possessions and Puerto Rico being excluded) less a base amount varying from $32,000 (for *married* persons filing jointly) to $0 (for married persons filing separately and who are not permanently separated from their *spouses* all year) and $25,000 (for all other taxpayers). §86. See *modified adjusted gross income; Social Security benefits; base amount, Social Security.*

Social Security integration   see *integration, Social Security.*

Social Security number   a number used, among other things, to identify *individuals* and *decedents' estates* for *federal income tax* purposes. Reg. §301.6109-1(a).

Social Security retirement age   the age used as the retirement age under §216(1) of the Social Security Act, except that for purposes of reducing the dollar limit, the age increase factor is ignored and the early retirement age under §216(1) is deemed 62. §415(b)(2)(C) and (D). Social Security retirement age is age 65 through the year 2002. The adjustment to the dollar limit for a *participant* in a *defined benefit plan* generally declines for benefits beginning before the participant's Social Security retirement age and increases as to benefits beginning after the participant's Social Security retirement age. Among other variations, there are exceptions for *government plans, exempt organization plans,* and merchant marine plans. Social Security retirement age is determined by birth date. For *participants* born before 1938, it is 65; it is 66 for people born after 1938 but before 1955; it is 67 for others. See *defined benefit plan, Code.*

Social Security self-employment tax   see *self-employment tax.*

Social Security supplement, qualified plan   a benefit that begins and ends before the age when *participants* are entitled to old-age insurance benefits by virtue of their age under the Social Security Act, §202(a) and (g), and which is not greater than the old-age benefit. §411(a)(9); Reg. §1.411(a)-7(c)(4). The determination of early retirement benefits for *vesting* purposes with respect to *qualified plans* is determined without regard to Social Security supplements. §411(a)(9).

Social Security tax   a term often used for the tax imposed on both *employers* by §3111 and *employees* by §3101 to provide funds for the Social Security benefits of employees. If an individual is classified as an employee, a Social Security tax is imposed on the employee at a 7.65 percent rate on wages up to $57,600 (for 1993) with an equal tax imposed on the employer. The 1.45 percent medicare hospital portion of the Social Security tax continues to apply to both the employee and employer until a $135,000 ceiling (for 1993) is reached. A matching tax is also imposed on the employer. If an individual is self-employed, a self-employment tax is imposed at a rate of 15.3 percent on the individual's income, with a ceiling base of $57,600 (for 1993). Self-employed individuals are also subject to an additional Medicare hospital insurance premium up to $135,000 (for 1993). Self-employed individuals receive an income tax deduction equal to 50 percent of taxes paid on their self-employment tax in the computation of adjusted gross income. See also *self-employment tax* for the parallel provisions for *independent contractors.*

Social Security wage base   a reference to the *contribution and benefit base* (statutorily determined dollar amounts set forth in §230 of the Social Security Act) in effect for the *calendar year* in which the *taxable year* begins (e.g., $57,600 for 1993). The 1.45 percent Medicare hospital portion of the Social Security tax continues to apply to both the employee and employer until a $135,000 ceiling (for 1993) is reached. Self-employed individuals are also subject to similar earnings base limitations. See *Social Security tax.*

social welfare organization   a term describing a class of *exempt organizations* described in §501(c)(4) that "are not operated for profit but operated exclusively for the promotion of social welfare." Such organizations are required to engage primarily in activities that offer a common good, operating for the general welfare of the people of a fairly broad community. Contributions to such organizations do not qualify for *deductions* under §170 (but may under §162 or §212); on the other hand, these organizations can engage in lobbying without loss of tax exemption, whereas Reg. §1.501(c)(3)-1(c)(3)(v) explicitly disallows §501(c)(3) status for *action organizations.*

soil and water conservation expenditures   *expenditures* by persons *engaged in the business of farming* in order to conserve soil or water or to prevent erosion with respect to land used for farming. Such expenditures include those for earth moving, grading, building and improving ditches, dikes, dams and ponds, etc. Reg. §1.175-2(a); Rev. Rul. 70-255, 1970-1 C.B. 51. Such expenditures, which would otherwise have to be *capitalized,* may be currently *deducted,* within limits and subject to *carryovers* under §175. Public assessments for these benefits also qualify. §175(c)(1).

solar energy property, energy investment credit   equipment, materials, and parts solely related to the functioning of such equipment that uses solar energy directly to (1) generate electricity; (2) heat or cool a building or structure; (3) provide hot water for use within a building or structure; or (4) provide solar process heat. §48(1)(4). Qualified solar energy property was *energy property* for purposes of the *energy investment credit* under former §48(l)(2). The current law definition, discussed under *energy investment credit,* seems to incorporate these meanings.

Sol Diamond rule   a judicial decision that taxes a *partner* who receives a *profits interest* in a *partnership* in consideration for prior services, where there is a clear measure of the value of the profits interest. The Sol Diamond rule seems contrary to Reg. §1.721-1(b)(l), which implies that, while an exchange of a *capital interest* for past services should be currently taxed, a similar *exchange* for a profits interest should not. The rule has also been subject to criticism because a profits interest in a partnership is a mere expectancy of income and, therefore, is not readily subject to current valuation. Nonetheless, the rule seems well embedded and is colorably supported by the *restricted property rules* of §83 (subsequent legislation).

solely for voting stock   a requirement of a *Type B reorganization,* the gist of which is that no consideration other than *voting stock* of the acquiring *corporation* or its parent can be used to acquire stock of the target company. However, other consideration may be used to acquire assets other than stock, and the acquiring company may pay certain reorganization expenses (transfer taxes, legal and accounting fees, etc.) that are directly related to the transaction. Rev. Rul. 70-269, 1970-1 C.B. 82. Also, stock held by target shareholders may be redeemed for cash, provided it clearly comes from the target company. Rev. Rul. 55-440, 1955-2 C.B. 226. See *voting stock, corporate reorganizations.*

sole proprietorship   an unincorporated *business* owned by a single *individual* (the *sole proprietor*). The financial results of such businesses are taxed directly to the proprietor, who reports the results on Schedule C of *Form 1040.*

Solicitor General of the United States   generally, the lawyer who represents the United States government. Among other things, the Solicitor General determines, with the help of the *Chief Counsel's* office, whether to appeal a tax decision and argue cases before the Supreme Court.

solid waste energy producing facility   any solid waste disposal facility and any facility for the production of steam and electric energy provided: (1) substantially all the fuel for the steam and electric energy facility is derived from solid waste processed in the solid waste disposal facility; (2) both the solid waste disposal facility and the steam and electric energy facility are owned and operated by the authority which issues the obligations; and (3) the steam and electric energy produced at the facility (and not used by the facility) is sold for purposes other than for resale to an agency or instrumentality of the United States government. §141(b)(2), P.L. 96-223 (1980). Such a facility enjoys special tax-exempt financing benefits. §241(b). See *exempt facility bond.*

solvency the excess of the *fair market value* of asset over the face amount of liabilities, immediately before *debt* is discharged. §108(d)(3). It is not clear whether assets exempt from bankruptcy court are included. To the extent a *taxpayer* is *solvent* after *discharge of indebtedness,* there may be *gross income.* See §108(a)(1)(B). See *insolvent debtor.*

son of mirror another name for a variant of a *mirror subsidiary transaction.* It involves an acquisition of a target *corporation,* followed by *sales* at a *gain* of unwanted assets (increasing the target's *earnings and profits*) and a distribution of appreciated assets to the acquiring corporation, followed by a *loss* sale of the subsidiary where the loss on the sub's stock sale offsets the gains. The *loss disallowance rule* of Reg. §1.1502-20T is designed to thwart this transaction.

sound recording a work that results from the fixation of a series of musical, spoken, or other sounds, regardless of the nature of the material object, such as a disc, tape, or other phonographic recording, in which such sounds are embodied. §168(f). The term was used for purposes of special treatment for *investment tax credit* purposes under §48(r) as *three-year property* and for purposes of allowing the *deduction* of expenses for the production of sound recordings over their income-producing period under former §280. Sound recordings do not qualify for *ACRS* treatment. §168(f)(4) (same definition).

source and application of funds method see *cash flow method.*

source rules a term often applied to §§861–863, the function of which is to classify income as being from *United States* sources, *foreign* sources, or a combination of the two. For example, most *inventory sales produce income attributed to the place of sale, whereas other sales of personal property* are generally attributed to the seller's residence. Thus, a *United States resident's* sales of *stock* will generally be income from sources within the United States. The source rules are of great importance for purposes of determining income subject to tax and classifying it, and also for purposes of determining the *taxpayer's* right to claim a *foreign tax credit.* There are also specialized source rules for specialized purposes, e.g., §904(g) (*United States–owned foreign corporations*).

special agent an *IRS* agent whose functions relate to penalties, frauds, and criminal cases. Agents who work with the *Criminal Investigation Division* of the Internal Revenue Service examine possible cases of tax fraud. Such agents are empowered to execute and serve search and arrest warrants, make arrests for acts violating the internal revenue laws that occur in the agent's presence, or seize property subject to forfeiture pursuant to the revenue laws. §7608.

special agent's report a report prepared by a *special agent* after he or she completes a criminal tax investigation. It is forwarded to his or her superiors for review to determine if the case should be prosecuted.

special allocations *allocations* of one or more particular items of *income, gains, losses, deductions,* or *credits* to a *partner* that depart from the *partner's bottom-line allocation* of *profits* and losses. For example, if a partnership allocates 50 percent of a partnership's profits and losses to partner A, but also allocates 65 percent of the *depreciation* deductions to A, there has been a special allocation of such deductions. Whether the special allocation will stand depends on whether it has *substantial economic effect,* a potentially difficult question. §704(b). See Reg. §1.704-2. See *substantial economic effect test.*

special assessments see *local benefit assessments.*

special call price for purposes of *amortizable bond premium,* the term refers to an alternate call price at which bond trustees call bonds for *redemption* using identified funds. For purposes of establishing the *earlier call date* in order for the bond premium to be calculated, the Supreme Court has held that the special call price may be used at the owner's election, thereby reversing Rev. Rul. 60-230, 1960-1 C.B. 688.

special enforcement area cases involving *jeopardy assessments, termination assessments,* criminal investigations of income, *foreign partnerships,* or other subjects that are identified by *regulations* yet to be issued as being in need of special enforcement. §6231(c). Such areas will be treated as *nonpartnership items.* §6231(b)(1)(D).

special enrollment examination an annual exam given at *IRS District Offices* over two days. Passage permits applicants to *practice before the* IRS. 31 C.F.R. §10.4(a). *Form 2587* is used to apply to sit for the exam.

special estate tax lien a *lien* that comes into existence at the date of the death of a *decedent* and continues for a decade, unless the *estate tax* is fully paid or slips behind the *statute of limitations.* §6324(a). It attaches to property in the *gross estate.*

special gift tax lien a *lien* that comes into existence when gifts are made and which lasts a decade, unless the *gift tax* is paid or the *statute of limitations* intervenes. The *donee* is personally liable for unpaid taxes, up to the value of the gift. §6324(a) and (b). See *shifting lien.*

special procedure staff a segment of the *Collection Division* that handles bankruptcy and receivership proceedings and provides technical advisory services to that Division. See I.R.M. 5912, M.T. 5-133 (Apr. 14, 1978).

special reliance procedure a special procedure granted after the passage of *ERISA* and effective until 1978 under which *employee* plans could phase in their adaptation to ERISA. Rev. Proc. 76-31, 1976-2 C.B. 649.

special school a school attended by a physically or mentally *handicapped individual* if the principal reason for the individual's attendance is that the school's facilities help to alleviate the handicap. Reg. §1.213-1(e)(1)(v)(a). Tuition costs of such a school may be claimed as a *deductible medical expense* under §213. That portion of the tuition covering meals and lodging may also be included in the *deduction.* Reg. §1.213-1(e)(1)(v)(a). Tuition paid to regular schools by a *taxpayer* whose child is mentally retarded may also be deductible where a program to the educable mentally handicapped is offered. Rev. Rul. 70-285, 1970-1 C.B. 52.

special subsidiary preferred stock *stock* issued by a subsidiary of a parent corporation with large *net operating losses.* The sub's assets are invested in high-yield securities. The interest is sheltered by the parent's losses. The parent enjoys the spread between the interest earned and the dividend paid, at the price of using its losses to offset the interest income. Such stock raises a variety of tax issues, including whether acquisition of the stock was done for *tax avoidance* reasons. For the legislative reaction, see *applicable preferred stock.*

specific debts requirement, partial worthlessness deductions a requirement that claims for *bad debt losses* based on partial *worthlessness* be justified debt-by-debt. Reg. §1.166-3(a).

specific goods method one of two basic methods of computing *inventory* values in a *last-in, first-out* (LIFO) inventory method, the other being the *dollar-value method,* which seems to be more widely used. The specific goods method measures quantities in terms of physical units, and each type of inventory item is treated separately. Reg. §1.472-1(d), (e), and (f), and -3(a). It is the simpler method and is used for large homogeneous inventories.

specific item adjustment method a method of proving concealment of income by showing the omission of a particular item (such as the sale of an item of property at a gain).

specific penalties a synonym for *criminal tax penalties.*

specific refund claim a *claim for refund or credit* filed by a *taxpayer* that specifically states the grounds and the facts upon which the alleged overpayment is based. Such claims may be amended after the *refund claim* period but before final determination, in certain circumstances. Amendments have been allowed in the following situations: (1) when they increase the refund amount but rely on the same facts; or (2) when they supplement the facts of the original claim.

specific shareholder test a standard used in connection with *collapsible corporations* in order to determine whether a *shareholder* can avoid the burdens of §341(a). Reg. §1.341-6(a)(5). Even if the *general corporate test* is met, the standard is used on a shareholder-by-shareholder basis to test the availability of the relief granted by §341(e)(1) and (e)(2). The test is highly intricate, but, generally speaking, the more the shareholder's interest in the corporation exceeds 5 percent, the more assets are investigated for *net unrealized appreciation,* and the more likely it is that the burden of §341(a) will apply to the *taxpayer.* See *section 341(e) assets.*

specified foreign corporation a *controlled foreign corporation* (CFC) in which a *United States shareholder* (modified definition) owns on each testing day (generally, the first day of the *taxable year*) over 50 percent (by vote or value) of the stock in the CFC. §898(b)(2)(A). This large shareholder is referred to as a *majority United States shareholder* and its tax year is known as the *majority United States shareholder year.* The *subpart F attribution rules* are used to determine stock ownership. §898(b)(2)(B). A *foreign personal holding company* as defined for subpart F purposes can also be a specified foreign corporation. §898(b)(1)(A)(ii). The *taxable year* of a *controlled foreign corporation* (CFC) that is also a specified foreign corporation must be a *required year,* meaning either (1) the *majority United States shareholder year,* or (2) a taxable year starting one month before the majority United States shareholder year. §898(a), (c)(1)(B). If there is no majority United States shareholder year, the taxable year of the specified foreign corporation will be set by *regulation.* §898(c)(1)(A)(ii). The election to a change in the taxable year of the CFC is referred to as a *section 898(c)(1)(B) election.* See Rev. Proc. 90-26, §3.04, 1990-17 I.R.B. 16. A specified foreign corporation's *taxable year* is treated as its annual *accounting period.* §6038.

specified fringe benefit plan a *group-term life insurance plan, an accident or health plan, a dependent care assistance plan, a qualified group legal services plan, cafeteria plan,* and an *educational assistance plan.* In this connection, each *Code* section authorizing the *exclusion* is known as the *applicable exclusion*. Such plans must engage in reporting of benefits and associated record-keeping. §6039D(2).

specified information reporting requirements   a term used in connection with a *civil tax penalty* for failure to provide certain information in a timely manner. The requirements are listed in §6723(d)(3). The primary examples are the inclusion of correct *taxpayer identification numbers* on a *return* or statement and any requirement to provide a correct identification number to another party.

specified liability loss   the sum of the *taxpayer's deductions* and *losses* from products liability (including investigations, defending claims, and so forth), *deductible federal* or *state* tort claims, and certain nuclear decommissioning costs. §172(f). Such losses can qualify for a 10-year *carryback*. §172(b)(1)(C).

specified possession   Guam, American Samoa, and the Northern Mariana Islands. §931(c). Income earned in specified possessions is generally exempt from United States taxes if earned by a *bona fide* resident. §931(a).

specified private activity bond   a *private activity bond* issued after August 7, 1988, subject to an exception for certain bonds covered under a congressional statement of March 14, 1986. See §57(a)(5) and *Tax Reform Act of 1986, §701*. The term also excludes *qualified 501(c)(3) bonds* and certain refundings of pre–August 8, 1988 bonds. Income on such a bond is part of an *individual's alternative minimum tax* base (and generates *deductible interest* for debt used to buy or continue such debt). §57(a)(5). Also, interest on such a bond is treated as income for the limited purpose of calculating the limit on *investment interest expense deductions* (§163(d)) under the *alternative minimum tax* in the case of *individuals*. §56(b)(1)(C)(iii). Likewise, interest expenses for carrying such bonds are *deductible* for this limited purpose. Id.

speculative indebtedness   alleged *debt,* the extent of which cannot be ascertained. Such debt cannot be added to the *basis* of property.

speculative investments excise tax, private foundations   an *excise tax* imposed on a *private foundation* at a rate of 5 percent of the amount of any *speculative investments*. The *foundation manager* is also subject to a 5 percent tax (up to $5,000) if the manager knowingly participated. The tax is imposed annually until the expenditure is corrected or a *notice of deficiency* is mailed, and an additional 25 percent tax on the foundation and 5 percent on the manager may be imposed if the investment is not promptly corrected. §4944. See *excise taxes, private foundations.*

speculative investments, private foundations imprudent investments by a *private foundation* or its

foundation manager. Such investments can attract an annual *excise tax* of 5 percent, based on the amount of the investment. Such investments may include options, warrants, commodities futures, and margin purchases of stock. §4944. See *speculative investments excise tax, private foundations.*

Spending Reduction Act of 1984   the second part (called a Division in the text) of the *Deficit Reduction Act of 1984.*

spin-off   a method used to effectuate a tax-free *corporate division* pursuant to §355. The parent *corporation* distributes *stock* representing a *control* (defined in §368(c) to mean at least 80 percent of the total combined voting power of all classes of *stock* entitled to vote and at least 80 percent of the total number of shares of all other classes of stock of the corporation) in its subsidiary corporation to one or more of the parent corporation's *shareholders* in a *distribution* in which they surrender none of their stock of the parent corporation. The subsidiary may be newly created for the purpose. See *corporate division.*

spin-off, qualified plans   see *plan spin-off.*

split-dollar life insurance   insurance on the life of an *employee,* pursuant to which the *employer* pays for the portion of the policy equal to the increase in *cash surrender values,* while the employee pays for the life insurance risk element. At death, the employer receives the *cash surrender value* and the decedent's *beneficiaries* receive the balance. According to Rev. Rul. 64-328, 1964-2 C.B. 11, the employee is taxed annually on the difference between the annual cost of one year's *term insurance* coverage and the employee's portion of the premium. The split of the policy is accomplished either by *endorsement* or *collateral assignment*. The employer often pays all the premiums.

split gifts   elective *gifts* of property of one *spouse* to a particular *donee,* the effect of which is to permit a doubling (to $20,000 per donee) of the *annual gift tax exclusion.* To illustrate: Mrs. G gives her car, worth $20,000, to her son. If Mr. and Mrs. G elect, they can treat the car as half Mr. G's. As a result, they can take full advantage of the $20,000 exclusion as to the gift of the car. §2513. See *joint gifts.*

split-off   a method used to effectuate a *corporate division* pursuant to §355. The parent *corporation* distributes *stock* representing a *control* (defined in §368(c) as at least 80 percent of the total combined voting power of all classes of stock entitled to vote and at least 80 percent of the total number of shares of all other classes of stock of the corporation) in its subsidiary corporation to one or more of the *shareholders* of the parent corporation. The shareholders, in exchange for receiving a distribution of the subsidiary corporation's stock, surrender some or all of their stock in the parent corporation. It bears an obvious resemblance to a *stock redemption*. Split-offs can be tax-free to shareholders if the conditions of §355 are met. See *corporate division*.

split-up one method used to effectuate a *corporate division* pursuant to §355. The parent *corporation distributes* to its *shareholders*, in *complete liquidation*, the *stock* owned by the parent in two or more subsidiary corporations, and the existence of the parent corporation is terminated. Split-ups can be tax-free to shareholders if the conditions of §355 are met. See *corporate division*.

spot contract a contract to buy or sell a *nonfunctional currency* within two business days after the contract is formed. Such contracts are not subject to specialized forward transaction currency accounting rules. Reg §1.988-1T(B), and -2T(d)(1)(ii).

spot rate convention a currency translation convention for *accounts receivable* and *accounts payable* in *nonfunctional currencies,* under which one uses the same exchange rate for all such transactions in a short period (not over a month). See Reg. §1.988-1T(d)(3).

spousal individual retirement account (IRA) an *IRA* established for a nonworking *spouse,* or one with compensation of under $250 for the year. If such an IRA is established, up to a total of $2,250 per year can be contributed and *deducted* annually. §219(c).

spouse a husband or wife. This status is generally determined at year-end, or as of the date of death if earlier. §7703. See *married person*.

spread period a five-year period over which *taxpayers* must make rather complicated adjustments to their income in consideration for being allowed to report *acquisition discount* in *income* on a current basis. The period begins with the year the election is made and permits taxpayers to claim associated *interest expense deductions* on a current basis. See §1281. The term is also used in connection with *changes of accounting method*. See, e.g., *six-year spread forward*.

standard cost method a method for attributing *indirect production costs* to *closing inventory,* under which a *taxpayer* allocates to the goods in *closing inventory* a ratable portion of any net negative or net positive overhead variances and any net negative or net positive direct production cost variances, ignoring insignificant variances unless they are allocated in the financial reports. A net positive overhead variance is the excess of total standard, or anticipated, indirect production costs over total actual indirect production costs, while a net negative overhead variance is the reverse. See Reg. §1.471-11(d)(3). The same concepts apply for purposes of the *uniform capitalization rules*. Reg. §1.263A-1T.

standard deduction an allowance granted to most *individuals* by §63(c). It consists of a *basic standard*

deduction (§63(c)(2)), depending on the *taxpayer's* filing status, and an *additional standard deduction* for being *blind* or over age 65 (§63(f)). The amounts are adjusted for inflation each year. The amounts are as follows:

Filing Status	1992	1993
Married individuals filing joint returns and surviving spouses	$6,000	$6,200
Heads of households	5,250	5,450
Unmarried individuals (other than surviving spouses and heads of households)	3,600	3,700
Married individuals filing separate return	3,000	3,100
Additional standard deductions for aged and blind		
Individual who is married and surviving spouses	700	700
Individual who is unmarried and not a surviving spouse	900	900

A taxpayer will use either the standard deduction or one's *itemized deductions,* whichever is larger. Various individuals, such as *nonresident aliens,* do not qualify for the standard deduction. §63(a)(6).

standard industrial classification (SIC) codes a series of numerical codes used to identify *taxpayers* and their *trades* or *businesses* activities by type. The information is called for on various *tax returns.*

standard meal allowance a concept found in, e.g., Rev. Proc. 83-71, 1983-39 I.R.B. 19, under which *taxpayers* may elect to *deduct* specified daily amounts for meals while traveling *away from home* in lieu of substantiating the actual cost of each meal. Time, purpose, and place of the trip must still be substantiated.

standby letter of credit a *letter of credit* issued by a bank or other financial institution that serves as a guarantee of the evidence of indebtedness secured by the letter of credit, nonnegotiable and nontransferable, except together with the evidence of indebtedness that it secures. It will be treated as nonnegotiable and nontransferable, if applicable local law so provides, whether or not the letter of credit explicitly states it is nonnegotiable and nontransferable. A letter of credit is not a standby letter of credit if it may be drawn upon in the absence of default in payment of the underlying evidence of indebtedness. Reg. §15a.453-1(b)(3)(iii). Standby letters of credit are not considered *payments* for *installment sale* purposes. Reg. §15a.453-1(b)(3)(i).

stapled entities any group of two or more *entities,* if over 50 percent by value of the *beneficial ownership* in each of such entities consists of *stapled interests.* §269B(c)(2). Two or more interests are stapled "interests" if, due to forms of ownership, restriction on transfer, or other terms or conditions in connection with the transfer of one interest, the other interests also are transferred or required to be transferred. §269B(c)(3). This rule does not apply to any *entity* that was a stapled entity as of June 30, 1983, which was entitled to a *tax treaty* benefit as of that date, but conflicting treaty provisions are otherwise generally overridden. Section 269B does not apply to *domestic* and certain Puerto Rican *corporations* that meet the activity test of §957(c)(2), which were stapled entities on June 30, 1983. For these purposes, an entity is a corporation, *trust, estate, association,* or other form if it is carrying on *business.* §269B(c)(1). Section 269B provides that, when a *domestic* and a *foreign corporation* are stapled entities, the foreign corporation is deemed a domestic corporation taxable on its worldwide income. For §1563 purposes, *stock* in a second corporation that is a stapled interest as to stock of the first corporation is deemed owned by the first corporation; thus stapled entities are denied multiple *graduated taxes* and multiple *accumulated earnings tax credits.* All stapled entities are treated as one *entity* for purposes of determining whether a stapled entity is a *regulated investment company* or a *real estate investment trust.* §269B(a). See *stapled interests.*

stapled interests   two or more interests if, by reason of form of ownership, restrictions on transfer, or other terms or conditions in connection with the transfer of one of such interest, the other such interests would also be transferred or would have to be transferred. §269B(c)(3). See *stapled entities.*

stapled stock   see *stapled entities.*

Starker trust   a *trust* used to hold funds in connection with a *deferred like-kind exchange.*

start-up day, REMIC   any day selected by a *real estate mortgage investment conduit* (REMIC), which is on or before the day the interests are issued. §860G(a)(9). *Regulations* may extend the *day* up to 10 days. The startup day is used to determine if the REMIC qualifies as such.

start-up expenditures   advertising, *employee* training expenses, professional consulting fees, and the like, attributable to the starting of a new *trade or business,* provided they would be currently *deductible ordinary and necessary* expansion costs if incurred in an existing business undergoing expansion. §195(b). The term *start-up expenses* also includes investigatory expenses, meaning the costs of investigating the creation or acquisition of an active trade or business before the final decision to enter into or buy the new trade or business, such as expenses incurred in analyzing potential markets, products, labor, and transportation facilities. §195(b)(1)(A). If the business is acquired or begun, then §195(a) lets *taxpayers* elect to *amortize* such expenditures over a *period* not shorter than 60 months, starting when the taxpayer actually

enters the new trade or business. The *deduction* is tricky; if the expenditures are actually *deductible,* then they do not fall under §195. If later denied §195 treatment, they may offer no tax benefit. But for §195, such expenses are generally *nondeductible capital expenditures.* See *begins business, amortization of corporate organizational expenditures; pre-opening expenses.*

state   generally, the 50 states and, where appropriate, the District of Columbia. *Indian tribal governments* are deemed states for many purposes. §7871. For purposes of *withholding* of *federal income taxes,* the term includes Puerto Rico, the United States, Virgin Islands, Guam, and American Samoa. §3121(e)(1). For purposes of return disclosure under the *Privacy Act,* it further includes the Northern Mariana Islands and the Trust Territory of the Pacific Islands. §6103(b)(5).

state and local government deferred compensation plans   see *eligible deferred compensation plan.*

state and local income taxes   *taxes* imposed by a *state,* a *possession of the United States,* or a *political subdivision* of the foregoing, or one of the foregoing. Such taxes are generally *deductible* under §164. See *taxes.*

state and local personal property taxes   see *personal property taxes.*

state death tax credit   see *credit for state death taxes.*

stated goodwill   in a *partnership* context, the reference is to the amount of *goodwill* which has been established by the *partnership agreement* as payable to a deceased or retiring *partner* on *liquidation* of his or her *partnership interest.* Amounts paid for such goodwill fall under §736(b) and are taxable as *capital gains.*

stated interest   *interest* expressly set forth in a deferred payment sale of *property.* Unless stated interest is at least a minimum amount (a figure which varies with *regulations*), *unstated interest* may be found in certain cases, especially under §483, and taxable to the seller (and *deductible* to the buyer) as such. See *imputed interest.*

stated redemption price at maturity, market discount   usually the price at which a bond is redeemed at maturity, but if there is *original issue discount* (*OID*), then the *revised issue price* is substituted. §1278(a)(2). The latter term means the issue price plus OID included by prior holders, with reductions in OID where later holders pay an acquisition premium ignored. §1278(a)(4). The stated redemption price is used to fix *market discount* on a *market discount bond.* Both the revised issue price and the stated redemption price at maturity are subject to being adjusted in the case of principal payments made in installments. §1278(c).

stated redemption price at maturity, original issue discount   the amount fixed by the last modification of the purchase agreement relating to the *debt instruments,* including *principal* and *interest,* and any other amounts, however designated, payable at that time other than interest payable unconditionally, at a fixed rate and at least annually. §1273(a)(2). This tricky rule can create inadvertent *OID.* If the obligation is issued as part of an *investment unit* that includes an option, security, or other property, the stated redemption price would be the amount payable on maturity for the debt instrument alone. §1273(c). The term is critical to the definition of *original issue discount.* See *daily portion, original issue discount; issue price.*

state historic preservation officer   the *individual* in charge of a state's historic preservation activities. The Congress intends that such officials cooperate in the administration of the *rehabilitation credit* for upgrading *certified historic structures.* See 36 C.F.R. §1208 (1981).

state or local bond   a bond issued by a *state,* a *political subdivision,* the District of Columbia, or any *possession of the United States* (collectively called a *"state"* in §103(c)(2)). §103(c)(1). *Interest* on such a bond is generally *tax-exempt.* Id. However, the exemption does not extend to such a bond if it is a *private activity bond,* unless it is a *qualified bond,* nor to a *hedge bond,* nor to an *arbitrage bond,* nor to a bond that is not registered if it is a *registration-required bond.* Id. and §149. There are numerous other requirements for tax-exempt status found in §149 (no federal guarantees, registration, exemption found in the *Code,* reporting rule for some bonds, and general prohibition on *advance refunding*). See *tax-exempt bond.*

state or local tax   a tax imposed by a *state* or *possession of the United States,* or any *political subdivision* of the foregoing, or the District of Columbia. §164(b)(3). Such tax is *deductible* if it is (1) a *real property tax*; (2) a *personal property tax*; (3) an income, war profit, and *excess profit tax*; or (4) (under prior law) a *general sales tax.* §164(a). If such a tax or any other taxes, are incurred in a *trade or business* or for the production of income, then they are generally *deductible* without regard to these special classifications. See *state and local income taxes; tax.*

state pick-up plan   a governmental plan under which the government *employer* pays for (i.e., picks up) contributions that are designated as *employee* contributions. Such payments are treated as *employer contributions.* §414(h)(2) (contradicting the general rule of §414(h)(1)(B) that the declared character of a contribution is controlling).

state volume cap   see *volume cap.*

statistical area, qualified mortgage issue   the area in and around a city of at least 50,000 inhabitants (or equiva-lent area) as defined by the Secretary of Commerce (metropolitan statistical area), and any county (or the portion thereof) that is not within a standard metropolitan statistical area. §143A(k)(2). In the case of any portion of a state that is not within a county, an area designated by the *Secretary* as the equivalent of a county is used. §143(k)(2)(D). If there is insufficient recent statistical information with respect to a county (or portion or equivalent), then the Secretary may substitute another area for which there is sufficient recent statistical information. §143(k)(2)(C). The statistical information is used to limit the types of residences eligible for financing with proceeds from a *qualified mortgage issue.* See *average area purchase price, qualified mortgage issue; targeted area residences.*

stat notice   a shorthand term for a *statutory notice of deficiency.*

statute of limitations   a statutory provision that places time limits on a person's legal power to initiate judicial or administrative proceedings. In the tax arena, there are a variety of statutes of limitations that operate both against the government and against *taxpayers.* Although roughly stated, a few major statutes of limitations follow: (1) two years—suit to protest denial of *refund claim* (§6532(a)); (2) three years from the date of filing or two years from the date of payment, whichever is earlier—*assessments* of run-of-the-mill *deficiencies,* or litigation absent *assessment,* against taxpayers (§6501), and *claims for refunds or credits* submitted by taxpayers (§6511); (3) six years—assessment of deficiency or suit in the event of a 25 percent or more omission from *gross income* stated on return (§6501(e)), most *criminal fraud* prosecutions (§6531), and collection of taxes after assessment, or longer if amount is still collectible (§6502); and (4) no limit–no return, *civil fraud* (§6501(c)), or return prepared by *IRS* for the taxpayer (§6501(b)(3)). Generally, taxpayers are free to extend statutes of limitations in their disfavor, before the statutes have run. The doctrines of *estoppel* and *recoupment, duty of consistency,* as well as the provisions of §§1311–1314 *(mitigation of effect of limitations and other provisions),* can disturb generalities about statutes of limitations. See also §7502 (the *timely mailing rule).* See *waiver of statute of limitations.* See also §7502 (the *timely mailing rule).*

statutory employee benefit plan   a term for purposes of specialized *nondiscrimination rules* relating to certain fringe benefits for the *employee.* It encompasses *group-term life insurance plans* and *accident and health plans,* and at the *employer's* election, *qualified group legal services plans, educational assistance plans,* and *dependent care assistance plans.* §89(i).

statutory notice of deficiency   the formal terminology for a *notice of deficiency.*

statutory notice of disallowance of claim for refund or credit   see *notice of disallowance of claim for refund or credit.*

statutory recovery period   see *disqualified leaseback or long-term leaseback.* For the precise definition, see §467(e)(3).

statutory sales   another name for transactions treated as if they were *sales* or *exchanges.* Examples include *retirement* of corporate and government bonds (§1232), *worthless securities* (§165(g), *patent* transfers that might otherwise be viewed as *royalty* transactions (§1235), and disproportionate *distributions* of *property* by a *partnership* (§751). The effect of such provisions is often to confer *capital gain* or *loss* results on transactions that would otherwise yield *ordinary income* or *losses* because of a lack of a sale or exchange.

statutory stock options   a term used to describe *stock option* arrangements with particular *tax benefits* made available under specialized tax provisions (e.g., *incentive stock options* and *qualified stock options*). See *nonstatutory options.*

step-allocation method   an *allocation* method applicable to *service costs* under the *uniform capitalization rules.* Reg. §1.263A-1T(b)(4)(iii)(B). Under this method, a sequence of allocations is made, starting with the allocation of the mixed *service department* which provides benefits to the most other service departments. Reg. §1.263A-1T(b)(4)(iii)(B). Service department costs are allocated to (1) manufacturing operations; (2) other service departments; and (3) nonservice departments (e.g., financial planning or tax department) that benefit only nonproduction activities. As a result, the cost of a service department includes its *direct costs* and costs allocated to the department from other service departments. Costs allocated to nonservice departments are not reallocated to any other service department.

stepped rents   generally, rents that rise over the years.

stepped-up basis   see *step-up in basis.*

step transaction doctrine   a judicial doctrine that applies to the entire field of federal taxation, under which separate steps of an overall transaction will be treated as part of a single transaction if the steps can fairly be integrated. The three common variants follow: (1) under the *end result test,* the steps will be collapsed if the *taxpayer* intended the result from the steps; (2) under the *mutual interdependence test,* the steps are collapsed if each step is so dependent on the others that they would be futile unless completed collectively; and (3) under the *binding commitment test,* the steps are collapsed only if there is a binding commitment to take the subsequent steps.

step-up in basis   a phrase used to describe increased *basis* in property. Achieving a step-up in basis commonly means enhanced *depreciation deductions* and *tax credits* or reduced *gains* on later *dispositions,* hence, much tax planning is dedicated to the goal of increasing basis with a minimum tax cost. Perhaps the leading example arises under §1014, which grants the property of a *decedent's estate* a basis equal to its *fair market value* at the decedent's date of death.

stipulations   agreements between litigants that settle areas in which there is no disagreement. See, e.g., Tax Ct. Rule 91(a).

stock   an *equity* interest in a *corporation,* whether common or preferred, voting or nonvoting. See §385 and its deferred *regulations* for an effort to distinguish *debt* from equity. *Warrants* and stock *rights* are generally not stock or *securities.* The §385 definition applies throughout the Code. See *debt-equity rules.*

stock, affiliated group   somewhat circular. For purposes of testing for *affiliated group* status to file a *consolidated return,* the term excludes any *stock* that (1) is not entitled to vote; (2) is limited and preferred as to dividends and does not participate in corporate growth to any significant extent (e.g., preferred with a big dividend rate can, therefore, be stock); (3) has redemption and liquidation rights that do not exceed the paid-in capital or par value represented by the stock, except for a reasonable redemption premium in excess of that paid-in capital or par value; and (4) is not convertible into another class of stock. §1504(a)(4). The definition is incorporated by reference in a number of unrelated *Code* sections.

stock appreciation right (SAR)   a *nonqualified deferred compensation* technique under which service providers (usually executives) can elect to either exercise a *stock option* or take a bonus equal to the value of the *stock's* appreciation. When the income is received, the *employee* reports *ordinary income* and the payor claims a compensation *expense deduction.* §§83, 404. See also PLR 8104119 (Oct. 30, 1980) and 8120103 (Feb. 20, 1981).

stock bonus plan   a *plan* established and maintained by an *employer* to provide benefits similar to those of a *profit-sharing plan,* except that the contributions by the employer are not necessarily dependent upon profits, and the benefits are distributable only in *stock* of the employer company (or stock of its parent or subsidiary) at retirement, death, or termination of employment. For purposes of *allocating* and distributing the stock of the employer that is to be shared among the *employees* or their *beneficiaries,* such a plan is subject to the same requirements as a profit-sharing plan. Reg. §1.401-1(b)(1)(ii). See *profit-sharing plan, Code; qualified deferred compensation plan.*

stock distribution   a transfer of *stock* by a *corporation* to its *shareholders.* See §305 for the taxability of shareholders. See *stock dividend.*

stock dividend generally, an actual or *constructive distribution* of *stock* to a corporation's shareholders qua shareholders. Stock dividends are subject to complex *regulations* under §305, which defines stock to include *rights*, and shareholders as *persons* holding rights and convertible securities. §305(d). Generally, only *pro rata* stock-on-stock distributions, *section 306 stock*, and *recapitalizations* are exempt from taxation under §305(a). Constructive distributions can arise under §305(c) through such features as call premiums. Note that the term is imprecise because a taxable "stock dividend" is a true *dividend* only to the extent of the distributing *corporation's earnings and profits*. §301. See *constructive disproportionate distribution; isolated redemption.*

stock for debt discharges cases in which a *corporation* issues its stock in exchange for its debt. See *stock for debt exception; workout.*

stock for debt exception on redeeming or repurchasing its own stock, a corporation recognizes no gain, even if the amount paid is less than the stock's par or stated value. In contrast, the retirement of debt for less than its face amount ordinarily generates *cancellation of indebtedness income* under general tax principles. However, under §108, *three types of exclusions* are provided in the following priority order: (1) a debt discharged in a bankruptcy action under title 11 of the United States Code and the discharge is either granted by or under a plan approved by the court; (2) a discharge when the taxpayer is insolvent outside bankruptcy; and (3) a discharge of qualified farm indebtedness. The term "insolvent" means that liabilities are in excess of the fair market value of the assets immediately prior to discharge. In addition, while bankrupt and insolvent debtors do not realize current income on the cancellation of debt, their tax attributes (i.e., the net operating loss and capital loss carryovers) are correspondingly reduced. §§108(a)(1) and 108(e)(10)(B). Thus, §108 remains a powerful tool for avoiding cancellation of indebtedness income in a bankruptcy or insolvency setting. Also, §108(e)(10)(C) formerly relaxed the rule in certain *workouts* with creditors. That provision called for a *qualified workout*. See *cancellation of indebtedness income; nominal or token shares; workout.*

stock-for-stock exchange see *Type B reorganization.*

stock in trade a synonym for *inventory*. It is undefined, evidently because the word "inventory" has engulfed it. For evidence of its redundancy, see §§311(b)(2)(A) and 312(b)(2)(A)(i).

stock life insurance company a *life insurance company* organized and owned by *shareholders* for their benefit. The company may issue participating policies in which the policyholder shares in the savings or profits of the company. However, the predominant type of

policy issued by stock companies is nonparticipating. For tax purposes, the surplus of a stock life insurance company was divided into a *shareholders' surplus account*, a *policyholders' surplus account*, and other accounts. The other accounts include such items as pre-1958 accumulated earnings and profits, paid-in capital, contributions of capital, realized capital *gains* relating to pre-1959 appreciation, and so forth. To the extent that a distribution is made from these other accounts, no tax is imposed on the company. The shareholders' and policyholders' surplus accounts apply only to stock life insurance companies and have no relationship to the accumulated profits of the company for other *federal income tax* purposes; they cease to enjoy further accumulation after 1983. The tax incidents of these insurers was radically changed by the *Tax Reform Act of 1984*. See *life insurance company taxable income; Phase III tax.* See *life insurance company taxable income.*

stock, neutrality principle *stock*, other than preferred stock as indirectly defined in §1504(a)(4). §382(k)(6)(A). Section 1504(a)(4) defines preferred stock as largely nonparticipating nonvoting stock, limited and preferred as to dividends, redeemable and liquidatable at no more than a reasonable premium, and not convertible into another class of stock. Future *regulations* may substantially modify the definition. §368(v)(6)(B). See *debt-equity rules; neutrality principle; preferred stock.*

stock options *options* to purchase *stock*. See *incentive stock option; restricted stock options.*

stock or securities generally, common or preferred *stock*, or corporate indebtedness other than short-term notes. The term is of critical importance in connection with transfers to controlled *corporations* (*section 351 transactions*) as well as *corporate reorganizations* and *corporate divisions*. It seems reasonably clear that the term has the same meaning for purposes of all three areas, since the concept of *boot* in such transactions is uniform. The important notion is that a person who receives stock or securities may have engaged in a transaction that involves a continuing interest in the corporation, as opposed to a mere *sale* of *property*. Unfortunately, the term "securities" is used with no clear definition in many *Code* sections, and it is not clear that Congress intended a uniform definition of the term. See *security corporate taxation; stock.*

stock property and liability insurer an *insurance company*, other than a *life insurance company*, that is not a mutual insurer. Such companies, along with mutual marine insurers and *factory mutuals*, are taxed under §§831 and 832, that is, as *corporations* generally, but with major modifications that reflect the contents of their *annual statements* imposed by the National Association of Insurance Commissioners. Perhaps most importantly, net premiums are taxable as earned, estimates are allowed as to casualties already sustained but not paid off, and dividends to policyholders are *deductible*.

stock redemption   a transaction in which a *corporation* acquires its *stock* from a *shareholder* in *exchange* for *property* other than the corporation's stock, or *rights* to acquire such stock. Once the corporation acquires the stock, it may cancel or retire the stock or hold it as Treasury stock. §317(b). A corporate *distribution* in redemption of its stock is treated as a §301 *distribution* of property if the distribution does not fit into any one of four specific categories. If a distribution does fall within a special category, the distribution is treated as an exchange, hence potentially taxable as a *long-term capital gain*. §302(a) and (d). The four categories in which a redemption is treated as a sale of stock are (1) a *redemption not essentially equivalent to a dividend* (§302(b)(1)); (2) a *substantially disproportionate redemption* of stock (§302(b)(2)); (3) a *redemption in complete termination of the shareholder's interest* (§302(b)(3)); and (4) a redemption in *partial liquidation* of the corporation (§302(b)(4), a rule applicable only to noncorporate shareholders). The first category is determined under *all facts and circumstances*. The latter three categories are mechanical. The redemption model for determining whether to cast a payment to a shareholder as a distribution or a sale applies to (1) acquisitions of stock by related corporations or subsidiaries (§304), and (2) to *boot* received in *corporate reorganizations*. The stock redemption model of §302, which sorts distributions from sales, recurs frequently through *subchapter C* (corporations) of the *Code*. See *property, corporate distributions*.

stock redemption payments   generally, any amounts *paid* or *accrued* by a *corporation* in connection with *redeeming* its *stock* (other than *interest expenses,* the *dividends-paid deduction* under §651, and mutual fund redemptions). §162(k). Such amounts are *nondeductible*. This rule is designed to limit the making of *greenmail* payments.

stock rights   see *rights, stock*.

stock, survival of tax attributes (prior law)   any *stock* (seemingly under the usual *debt-equity rules'* definition) except nonconvertible stock that does not vote, is fixed and preferred as to dividends, does not participate in corporate growth to any significant extent, and is limited as to its claims in redemption or *liquidation*. §382(c)(1). The term is important for purposes of determining the survival of *tax attributes* in various corporate transactions such as acquisitions and mergers under the stillborn 1976 amendments to §382. The term "attribution" is designed to assure that the rules regarding adverse effects of major changes in stock ownership are not eluded. Such stock is further subdivided into *participating stock* (stock with nonlimited interest in earnings

and assets) and nonparticipating stock; diminutions in either can cause a loss of tax attributes. (1991). See *survival of tax attributes*. For current law, see *stock, neutrality principle*.

storage facility   a facility used for bulk storage of fungible goods. Examples include corn cribs and grain bins. Storage facilities could be deemed *personal property* so as to qualify for the former *investment tax credit*. If, instead, they are real property because of their permanently affixed natures, then they may still qualify when used as part of certain essentially industrial-affiliated research activities (former §48(a)(1)(B)) or if they are used in connection with the distribution of any *primary product of petroleum* (former §48(a)(1)(G)). They are also deemed personal property for *depreciation recapture* purposes under §1245(a)(3)(B)(iii).

straddle, generally   the acquisition of an equal number of *puts* or other contracts to sell and offsetting *calls* or other arrangements to buy and sell underlying property in a manner that causes movements in the prices of the offsetting positions to neutralize each other.

straddle, loss deferral rule in unregulated futures contracts   see *loss deferral rule, straddles*.

straddler   a *taxpayer* who regularly purchases a spot commodity and enters into a sale contract for future delivery. Such taxpayers are required to maintain *inventory* records. Rev. Rul. 74-226, 1974-1 C.B. 119. See *mark-to-market system; regulated futures contracts; straddle, unregulated futures contract*.

straddle sale   another name for a *sale* of *property* at a *loss* by a *corporation* before the corporation adopts a plan of *liquidation,* followed by sale of property at a *gain* after the corporation adopts a plan of liquidation and elects former §337 liquidation treatment. The losses were used to offset corporate income and gains realized after the plan of liquidation was adopted; such losses were tax-free if the corporation met the one-year, tax-free liquidation tests of former §337. The term still makes sense in connection with sale of loss-producing assets prior to a liquidation. But see §336(d)(2)(A) which hampers *dispositions* of property contributed within two years of adopting the plan of liquidation.

straddle, unregulated futures contracts   an *offsetting position* in *personal property* (other than most *stock*), that is, transactions in which, and to the extent, risk of *loss* is neutralized by a reverse position. §1092(c)(1). Section 1092 denies *losses* with respect to *straddles* that are not *regulated futures contract* straddles, and it applies the *short sales* and *wash sales* rules to such straddles. Under the general *loss deferral rule* of §1092(a)(1)(A), losses on the *disposition* of one leg of these straddles can be recognized only to the extent that such losses are greater than the unrealized *gain* on the other leg, subject, however, to a carryover rule and a special rule relating to *identified straddles* or these purposes, personal property means any personal property that is actively traded; presumably that excludes such items as artworks. *Stock* and *stock options* are generally exempt from §1092. §1092(d)(2)(A). *Qualified covered call options* are exempted from §1092 and §263(g) (loss deferral rule and *capitalization* of *expenses*). §1092(c)(4)(A)(ii). See *personal property, straddles.*

straight debt a form of *debt* of an *S corporation* that is assured of not being classified as *stock,* hence, cannot create a prohibited second class of stock. §1361(c)(5)(B). To qualify, there must be a written unconditional promise to pay on demand or on a specified date, a certain sum, the *interest* rate of which is not contingent on profitability or discretion of the borrower, provided the instrument is not convertible into stock and the creditor would otherwise qualify as a *shareholder* of an S corporation. This provision was added by *TEFRA* as a *safe harbor* rule. It does not entirely dispel the existence of §385, which provides a more general system of *debt-equity rules,* and the failure to pay *interest* may create a fatal contingency.

straight-line amortization *amortization* of *intangible property* (and sometimes of *tangible property* by fiat; for example, under former §167(k)) in equal amounts each year.

straight-line depreciation *depreciation* of *tangible property* in equal amounts each year; this is the presumed choice, absent a specific selection of some other method. The straight-line method is permitted for property placed into service before January 1, 1981, and for certain property placed in service after December 31, 1980.

straight-line recovery of intangibles either equal monthly *amortization* of *intangible drilling and development costs* (IDCs) over 120 months beginning in the month production from the well begins or any method of *cost depletion* of the well that the *taxpayer* selects. §57(b). Straight-line recovery of intangibles serves as a base for determining whether the taxpayer's actual practice of currently *deducting* IDCs gives rise to an *item of tax preference.* Taxpayers can avoid this preference by electing straight-line amortization for all purposes. Note that the CNEPA of 1992 (Pub. L. 102-486) repeals the alternative minimum tax preference for excess intangible drilling costs. §1915. See *alternative minimum tax.*

strap a stock option arrangement consisting of two *calls* and one *put.*

straw man a euphemism for a *person* who is drawn into a transaction for purely technical reasons, usually in order to temporarily hold *property* for another person.

straw man mortgage a *mortgage* involving a mortgagor acting as a convenient intermediary, for example, where a judgment-proof *individual* takes title to property on behalf of a solvent *corporation,* or where a corporate straw executes mortgage notes to avoid usury laws.

streamlined district one of 12 relatively small *Internal Revenue Districts* lacking certain intermediate levels of management common to other districts. In such a district, the *District Director,* of necessity, exercises more direct supervision of the front-line activities. The administrative structure in such a division is modified to accommodate the smaller staff; multiple functions are designated to certain officials. Administrative support services and certain functions (such as the examination review function) may be performed for any of these 12 districts by one of seven nearby, and larger, *prime districts.* I.R.M. 1118.3(2).

street name a colloquial term for the name of a brokerage firm as the record owner of stocks or securities that are beneficially owned by customers. Tax information filings (e.g., *Forms 1099*) are sent to such holders in the first instance, since there is no way to identify the *beneficial* owner.

strike and lockout benefits amounts paid striking union members by the union in connection with a strike by workers or a lockout by the *employer.* Such amounts are generally *excludable* from gross income as gifts if based on the worker's need, rather than an interest in extending the strike.

strike price generally, the price at which a *stock option* is exercisable. See, e.g., §1092(c)(4)(F) (certain covered call options).

strip a *stock option* arrangement consisting of two *puts* and one *call.*

strip-off dispositions of unwanted assets in connection with anticipated mergers or acquisitions.

stripped bond a *bond* issued with interest coupons where there is a separation in ownership between the bond and any coupon that has not yet become payable. §1286(e)(2). The term can include mortgages sold by the lender, to be serviced by the seller out of interest proceeds. Rev. Rul. 91-46, 1991-33 I.R.B. 8. See Reg. §1.1287-1T. See *anti-coupon stripping rules; bond, market discount, original issue discount and coupon stripping; coupon stripping.*

stripped coupon any coupon relating to a *stripped bond.* §1286(e)(3).

stripper well property a *property* which for any *calendar year,* from which the average daily production, divided by the number of producing wells on the property, is 15 or less barrel equivalents of oil and gas. §613A(c)(6)(E). A "barrel equivalent" is a *bar-*

rel of oil or 6,000 cubic feet of natural gas. See *marginal production*.

structural components   those parts of a *building* or other structure necessary to make it complete, such as walls, partitions, doors, windows, central air conditioning, plumbing, and electrical wiring. Reg. §§1.48-1(e)(2), 1.1245-3(c)(2), 1.1250-1(e)(3)(i). Note, machinery whose sole justification is maintenance of temperature or humidity to sustain other machinery or processing is not treated as a structural component for *investment tax credit* purposes, but may be included as part of the real property under the *accelerated cost recovery system* (ACRS). Structural components were denied the benefit of the former *investment tax credit* and are treated as *section 1250 property* (i.e., real estate). The degree of attachment and the damage caused by removal are the principal determinants of whether an item is a structural component for this purpose. Rev. Rul. 75-178, 1975-1 C.B. 9. See *inherently permanent structure; rehabilitation credits; substantial improvement*.

structure, certified historic structure   see *certified historic structure*.

structured settlement   a nontechnical term for settlement arrangements to pay a plaintiff damages over time. They are commonly funded by *annuity contracts*. Section 130 contains favorable rules concerning so-called *qualified assignments* involving *qualified funding assets* tailored to personal injury cases.

student, dependency deduction, and child and dependent care credit   an *individual* who, during each of five calendar months during the *calendar year* in which the *taxable year* of the *taxpayer* begins, is a full-time student at an educational organization described in §170(b)(1)(A)(ii) or is pursuing a full-time course of institutional, on-farm training under the supervision of an accredited agent of an educational institution, or of a *state* or *political subdivision* of a state. A full-time student is one who is enrolled for some part of five calendar months for the number of hours or courses that is considered to be full-time attendance. The five calendar months need not be consecutive. School attendance exclusively at night does not constitute full-time attendance. However, full-time attendance at an educational institution may include some attendance at night in connection with a full-time course of study. §151(c)(4). Reg. §1.151-2(b). Students under age 24 can have more than an amount equal to the *exemption amount* of *gross income* and still be considered *dependents*. §151(c)(1). The regulations interpreting the *child and dependent care credit* construe the statutory terms "student" and "full-time student" used in §21(f)(7) in the same manner, but exclude "institutional, on-farm training." Reg. §1.44A-2(b)(3)(iii).

student loans   a class of loans made to medical persons. The cancellation of such loans, pursuant to their terms, in exchange for working in certain rural and low-income areas can be tax-free. See §108(f).

student, nonresident aliens   a class of *individuals* who do not become *resident aliens* by virtue of time spent (the *substantial presence test*) in the *United States*. The term refers to any individual who is temporarily present in the United States under §101(15)(F) of the Immigration and Nationality Act (INA) or as a student under §101(15)(J) of the INA and who substantially complies with the requirements for being so present. §7701(b)(4)(D). After the fifth calendar year for which he or she was a teacher, trainee, or student, an individual is not treated as a student, unless the individual establishes to the *IRS's* satisfaction that he or she does not intend to permanently reside in the United States and that he or she substantially complies with the requirements for being temporarily present as a student. §7701(b)(4)(E)(ii).

subchapter A   the subchapter of the *income tax* provisions of the *Code* dealing with the determination of tax liability.

subchapter B   the subchapter of the *income tax* provisions of the *Code* dealing with the computation of *taxable income*.

subchapter C   the subchapter of the *income tax* provisions of the *Code* dealing with the corporate *distributions* and adjustments.

subchapter C corporation   a *corporation* other than an *S corporation*.

subchapter C earnings and profits   *earnings and profits* attributable to previous tax years during which an *S corporation* was a *C corporation* (i.e., not an S corporation). §1362(d)(3)(B). (Note, earnings and profits can nominally arise in an S year; if so, they are not subchapter C earnings and profits.) If an S corporation has *passive investment income* of more than 25 percent of its *gross receipts* for each of its three prior years and has subchapter C earnings and profits, then its *subchapter S election* is automatically terminated. §1362(d)(3)(A). Also, even if the election is not lost, the presence of such earnings and profits can attract a tax on *excess net passive income*. §1375.

subchapter D   the subchapter of the *income tax* provisions of the *Code* dealing with the *deferred compensation*.

subchapter E   the subchapter of the *income tax* provisions of the *Code* dealing with the *accounting periods* and *methods of accounting*.

subchapter F   the subchapter of the *income tax* provisions of the *Code* dealing with the *exempt organizations*.

subchapter G   the subchapter of the *income tax* provisions of the *Code* dealing with the *corporations* used to avoid income tax on shareholders.

subchapter H   the subchapter of the *income tax* provisions of the *Code* dealing with the banking institutions.

subchapter I   the subchapter of the *income tax* provisions of the *Code* dealing with the natural resources.

subchapter J   the subchapter of the *income tax* provisions of the *Code* dealing with the *estates, trusts, beneficiaries,* and *decedents.*

subchapter K   the subchapter of the *income tax* provisions of the *Code* dealing with the *partners* and *partnerships.*

subchapter L   the subchapter of the *income tax* provisions of the *Code* dealing with the insurance companies.

subchapter M   the subchapter of the *income tax* provisions of the *Code* dealing with the *regulated investment companies* and *real estate investment trusts.*

subchapter N   the subchapter of the *income tax* provisions of the *Code* dealing with the taxes based on income from sources within or without the United States.

subchapter O   the subchapter of the *income tax* provisions of the *Code* dealing with the *gain* or *loss* on *dispositions* of property.

subchapter P   the subchapter of the *income tax* provisions of the *Code* dealing with the *capital gains* and *losses.*

subchapter Q   the subchapter of the *income tax* provisions of the *Code* dealing with the adjustment of tax between years and special limitations.

subchapter S   the subchapter of the *income tax* provisions of the *Code* dealing with the tax treatment of *S corporation* and their *shareholders.*

subchapter S corporation   see *S corporation.*

subchapter S election   an election to be taxed as an *S corporation.* See *Form 2553.*

subchapter S item   any item the *Treasury Department* determines by regulations to be more appropriately determined at the *S corporation,* rather than *shareholder,* level. §6245. Such items are subject to *unified proceedings* in the interest of effective and consistent audit results. These include pro rata shares of items reported to shareholders, and contributions to and *distributions* from the corporation. See Reg. §301.6245-1T.

Subchapter S Revision Act of 1982   an act that substantially liberalized the taxation of *S corporations* largely by drawing such *corporations* much closer to a *partnership* tax model. Pub. L. No. 97-354, 96 Stat.

1669. The principal features were liberalizing the one class of stock requirement by providing for *straight debt,* expanding from 25 to 35 the maximum number of permissible *shareholders,* relaxing the limits on *passive investment income,* allowing unlimited foreign source income, and barring new shareholders from being able to jeopardize subchapter S status by affirmatively refusing to assent to the election.

subchapter S trust   see *qualified subchapter S trusts.*

subchapter T   the subchapter of the *income tax* provisions of the *Code* dealing with the *cooperatives* and their *patrons.*

subchapter V   the subchapter of the *income tax* provisions of the *Code* dealing with the *bankruptcy* cases.

subdivided real estate   see *subdivision, real estate.*

subdivider   a nontechnical term for someone who divides unimproved land into lots for sale to others. For tax relief for subdividers, see *subdivision, real estate.*

subdivision, real estate   generally, the process of dividing a tract of land into lesser lots for *sale* to the public. Ordinarily, such activities result in *ordinary income* or *loss* because such land constitutes *dealer property.* §1221(1). However §1237 provides substantial relief (i.e., possible *capital gains*) for noncorporate *taxpayers* if (1) the taxpayer did not previously hold any part of the same land as *dealer property,* nor in the year of sale hold any other real estate for sale to customers; (2) the taxpayer did not make *substantial improvements,* while holding the land, that considerably increased the value of the lot sold, except for special instances when the land had been held for 10 years or more; and (3) the taxpayer held the land sold for five years or more, unless it was acquired by *inheritance* or *devise.* See *substantial improvement, subdivision.*

subgroup method   a method used by the *consolidated return regulations* with respect to the filing of such returns by *life insurance companies* and their members. The pattern involves creating two subgroups (including insurance companies taxed under §821 as nonlife companies), with losses of each subgroup carried back against prior subgroup income. Reg. §1.1502-47(a)(2).

subhotchpot   the last sentence of former §1231(a), relating to *losses* from *thefts* and *casualties.* It now appears in §1231(a)(4)(C). See *section 1231 assets.*

sublease   a transfer by a tenant (*lessee*) of an *estate* less than the entire estate, either temporally, spatially, or both, held by the tenant. It is a state law concept. An assignment of a lease is distinct in that the assigning tenant transfers the entire estate. A sublease in the tenant's hands constitutes *property* for purposes of §1221 relating to *capital assets.*

subnormal goods   goods in *inventory* that cannot be sold at normal prices or used in the normal way because of damage, imperfections, shop wear, style changes, odd or broken lots, or other similar causes, including secondhand goods taken in exchange. Reg. §1.471-2(c). Such goods may be written down below the usual *lower of cost or market inventory valuation* ordinarily used for determining *closing inventories.* But see *Thor Power Tool v. United States,* 439 U.S. 522 (1979) (actual sales required to substantiate such pricing).

subordinate benefit rule   a requirement (also sometimes referred to as the *incidental benefit rule*) a *qualified deferred compensation plan* must meet in order for associated medical benefits for retired *employees* or *life insurance* benefits to be *tax-exempt.* Basically, the *contributions* for such amounts must not exceed fixed percentages of all contributions. See Reg. §1.401-14. See *incidental life insurance; individual medical benefit account.*

subordination of lien   see *release of tax lien.*

subpart F   a portion of the *Code* containing §§951–964, designed to thwart the manipulative use by *United States persons* of *foreign corporations* to minimize *federal income taxes.* The thrust of the subpart is to compel United States persons who hold significant blocks of *stock* to report numerous classes of earnings generated overseas through *controlled foreign corporations* as if their ratable shares of such earnings had been *distributed* to them as current *dividends.* Because it is designed to close loopholes in the law, its provisions are unusually ornate. See *subpart F income.*

subpart F deemed paid credit   a *foreign tax credit* available under §960 to *domestic corporations* when they are taxed on *subpart F income* of 10 percent or more owned *foreign corporations.* The inclusions are deemed to include an element consisting of foreign taxes borne by the foreign corporation. See *deemed paid foreign tax credit.*

subpart F foreign personal holding company income   *personal holding company income* of a *controlled foreign corporation.* See *foreign personal holding company income, subpart F.*

subpart F income   income taxed to *United States shareholders* of a *controlled foreign corporation,* including *insurance income; foreign base company income*; illegal *bribes, kickbacks, and other payments*; and *international boycott income.* §952. Foreign base company income, the most important element, is the sum of five types of gross income, reported in the pertinent *functional currency*: (1) *foreign personal holding company income* (with the subpart F modifications); (2) *foreign base company sales income*; (3) *foreign base company services income*; (4) *foreign base company shipping income*; and (5) *foreign base company oil-related income.* Foreign base company gross income, however, is reduced by *deductions* properly allocable to the income, including taxes. Likewise, income from insuring United States risks and boycott-related income are by definition incomes reduced by allocable expenses. There are extensive limitations and exceptions to these rules. Subpart F income cannot exceed modified *earnings and profits* for the year. §952(c). See *qualified chain member.*

subsection (e) assets, collapsible corporation   generally, property held by a *collapsible corporation* that would result in *ordinary income* if sold by the *entity* or certain major *shareholders.* §341(e)(5). More specifically, the reference is to (1) *property* not used in the *trade or business,* if the *gain* on a *sale* generates ordinary income (property held by the corporation is included in this class if, in the hands of any shareholder directly or constructively owning more than 20 percent of the value of the corporation's *stock,* it would not be a *capital asset* or *section 1231 property,* such as a car owned by the company as an investment where an auto dealer is a 25 percent shareholder); (2) property used in the trade or business with respect to which there is a *net unrealized depreciation*; (3) property used in the trade or business with respect to which there is a *net unrealized appreciation,* if it would neither be a capital asset nor §1231 property in the hands of a more than 20 percent shareholder; and (4) *copyrights,* literary compositions, letters, memoranda, or similar property, if created in whole or in part by the personal efforts of an *individual* owning more than 5 percent (directly or constructively) of the corporation's stock (or in the case of letters and memoranda, was produced for a five-percent individual shareholder). See *collapsible corporation; specific shareholder test.*

subsection (f) assets, collapsible corporations   *noncapital assets* that a potentially *collapsible corporation* holds or has an *option* over on the date of any *sale* of *stock* by a *shareholder* (subject to a special consent), including any interest in *realty,* other than a *mortgage* or other security interest, and *unrealized receivables or fees* (§341(b)(4)), regardless of whether they are *noncapital assets.* Also, if assets of the foregoing types are being manufactured when the stock is sold, the property produced from the manufacturing process, after the sale, is included, as are improvements to realty resulting from construction that begins within two years after the date the stock is sold. §341(f)(4); Reg. §1.341-7(h). If consents are obtained, then sales of stock of a *domestic corporation* can occur without the burdens of §341(a), at the price of the corporation's *recognition* of *ordinary income* when it disposes of these assets. §341(f)(1) and (2). See *section 341(f) election.*

subsidiary   a term used to describe a *corporation* entirely or principally owned by another corporation.

The term has various meanings, distinguished on the basis of *stock* ownership levels, throughout the *Code*.

subsidiary, consolidated returns   any *member* of the *affiliated group* other than the common parent. Reg. §1.1502-1(c).

subsidiary liquidation   see *liquidation of a subsidiary.*

subsidiary tracking stock   *stock* issued by a parent *corporation,* which has a divided rate that depends on the performance of the subsidiary. Sections 305, 311, and 1032 bear some relationship as to whether issuance is part of a *triangular reorganization.* It is often used for corporate acquisitions.

subsidized energy financing, energy credit   financing under any federal, state, or local program, a principal purpose of which is to provide subsidized financing for projects designed to conserve or produce energy. §48C(a)(4)(C). See also former §44A(c)(10).

substance over form doctrine   a tax law doctrine to the effect that the substance of a transaction will prevail over the form it is cast in. For example, if a corporation purports to pay an inflated purchase price for some particular piece of property sold by an officer of the company, the doctrine may be applied to recharacterize part of the price paid as salary in substance.

substance versus form   see *substance over form doctrine.*

substantial and bona fide business discussion   a situation in which the *taxpayer* actively engages in a *business* discussion, meeting, negotiation, or other transaction to obtain income or some other business benefit. For an *associated entertainment expense* to be *deductible,* the business activity must be substantial in relation to the entertainment, a requirement which will be satisfied if the principal aspect of the business/entertainment activity was the active conduct of business. Reg. §1.274-2(d)(3)(i)(a). Certain meetings presumptively meet the test (e.g., certain business conventions). Reg. §1.274-2(d)(3)(i)(b).

substantial authority   a defense to the substantial understatement of income tax penalty of §6662(d). Moreover, even a showing of substantial authority for a tax treatment of an item will not reduce the penalty unless the taxpayer reasonably believes that the tax treatment was more likely than not the proper treatment. §6662(d)(2(C). The Internal Revenue Service is required to publish an annual list of positions for which it believes there is no "substantial authority" if a significant number of taxpayers would be affected. §6662(d)(2)(D). The reliable authority includes the Code provisions and other statutory provisions, regulations, court decisions, and *administrative pronouncements* (*including revenue rulings* and *revenue proce-*

dures), *treatises, and expressions of congressional intent, proposed regulations; private letter rulings; technical advice memoranda; actions on decisions; General Counsel's Memoranda; information releases; notices; announcements*; and other similar documents published by the *IRS* in the *Internal Revenue Bulletin* and *blue book*. Conclusions in treaties, legal periodicals, legal opinions, or opinions of other tax professionals do not quality. In such cases, it is up to the courts to evaluate the authorities that underlie such expressions of opinion. Reg. §1.6661-3(b)(2). See also Notice 90-20, 1990-10 I.R.B. See *penalty, substantial understatement of income tax.*

substantial change in capital structure   includes a recapitalization (whether or not taxable) or other transaction in which a substantial portion of a *corporation's* equity is replaced with *debt.* Such transactions could include leveraged *distributions,* leveraged *redemptions,* or the issuance of debt to *shareholders.* §6043(c). There are major *civil tax penalties* as well as possible *criminal liabilities* for failure to notify the IRS of major changes in capital structure. §6043.

substantial contributor   any *person* who contributed or bequeathed an aggregate amount of more than $5,000 to the *private foundation,* if such amount is more than 2 percent of the total contributions and *bequests* received by the foundation before the close of the *taxable year* of the foundation in which the contribution or *bequest* is received by the foundation by such person. (§507(d)(2)(A)). It includes a creator of a *trust.* Reg. §1.507-6(a)(1). Once activated, the status is almost inescapable. §507(d)(2)(B)(iv). But see §501(d)(2)(C). The term is used in connection with termination of private foundation status and certain *excise taxes* arising from *prohibited transactions* by such foundations with persons who have influence over the foundation. The term appears elsewhere in the *Code* as well, e.g., §§170(b)(1)(E)(iii), 508(d)(1)(B), 4940, 4943, 4946 (substantial contributor as a *disqualified person* for *excise tax* purposes), and 6033(b)(5). See *disqualified person, private foundations.*

substantial economic effect test   a standard for determining whether a *partnership allocation* (overall or of a particular partnership item) is valid for federal *income tax* purposes or is instead subject to appropriate reallocation. It also applied under §514(c)(9) to determine the extent to which there is *acquisition indebtedness* that can affect an *exempt organization* and whether *cost recovery* must be on the *alternative depreciation method* because of *tax-exempt use property.* Controversial regulations under §704(b)(2) contain a complex set of principles to determine whether an allocation has "*substantial*" economic effect so as to get within a *safe harbor.* Allocations are not substantial if they are *offsetting allocations, shifting allocations,* or *transitory allocations.* Failing the substantial economic effect test means that allocations to partners may be redetermined on the basis of the *partner's interest in the partnership* (i.e., all the facts and circumstances).

substantial gainful employment, disability income exclusion   amounts received by employees under employer-financed accident and health plans may be *excluded from income.* §§105, Reg. 1.105-1. A self-employed person is not an employee for purposes of this exclusion. The exclusion applies to both individuals employed by a private employer as well as to individuals covered by a state government plan. Amounts received by employees as reimbursement for medical care and payments for permanent injury or loss of bodily function under an employer-financed accident or health plan are also excludible from income.

substantial improvement   an improvement to *real property* that results in an increase (over a two-year period) of at least 25 percent (unreduced by *depreciation* and *amortization* adjustments) of the *adjusted basis* of the property as of the first day of that period and that is made not less than three years after the building was *placed in service.* Former §168(f)(1)(C). Such an improvement is treated as separate property and can be the subject of separate *recovery periods* and methods. For current law, see §168(i)(6), which simply treats each addition or improvement as a new asset.

substantial improvement, subdivision   generally, an improvement that increases the value of the lot by more than 10 percent and, when all relevant factors are considered, is substantial. Reg. §1.1237-1(c)(3)(ii). If the subdivided property was held for 10 years or more before a *sale,* the seller's improvements, otherwise considered substantial, are not considered substantial if (1) improvements consist of installation of water, sewer, or drainage facilities, roads (including hard-surface roads), curbs, and gutters when they are necessary to make the lot or parcel marketable at the prevailing local price for similar building sites; and (2) the seller elects neither to add the cost of the improvements to the *basis* of the lots sold or to the basis of any other property nor to *deduct* the *cost* as an *expense.* Sales of subdivided lots do not automatically qualify for *capital gains* benefits under §1237 if such lots were substantially enhanced in value as a result of substantial improvements made anywhere on the tract by the *taxpayer* or anyone else pursuant to a sales contract between the taxpayer and buyer. An improvement is made by the taxpayer if it was made by a member of the taxpayer's family, a *corporation* in which the taxpayer owns directly or indirectly more than 50 percent of the voting *stock,* or a *partnership* in which the taxpayer is a *partner.* §1237(a)(2).

substantial investor in United States real property   any *foreign person* who, at any time during the *calendar year* held an interest in an *entity,* other than a *domestic*

corporation, the *fair market value* of whose ratable share of such entity's *United States real property interests* exceeded $50,000. Rather elaborate attribution and indirect ownership rules apply. §6039C(b)(4)(B) and (C), and (e)(1). *Foreign corporations,* domestic, or *foreign partnerships, trusts,* or *estates* having a substantial investor in United States real property must file annual *returns* disclosing the names and addresses of such persons and certain other information. §6039C(b)(1) and (4).

substantially all of the properties, forward triangular mergers and reverse triangular mergers   see *substantially all of the properties, Type C reorganizations.* These mergers, described in §368(a)(2)(D) and (E), are treated much the same as *Type C reorganizations.* In fact, however, there are subtle disparities.

substantially all of the properties, Type C reorganizations   practically all of a target *corporation's* operating assets. For ruling purposes, the *IRS* generally considers 90 percent of net assets and 70 percent of gross assets satisfactory. In fact, such matters as the nature of the properties and the reason for retaining assets must also be taken into account. Rev. Rul. 57-518, 1957-2 C.B. 253. See §368(a)(2)(C) (general duty to disgorge all assets).

substantially all of the properties, Type D reorganizations   see *substantially all of the properties, Type C reorganizations.* Note, however, that because of the courts' willingness to find a *Type D reorganization* in a *reincorporation* setting, the term has often been defined more loosely.

substantially appreciated inventory items   *inventory items* held by a *partnership* that are worth more than 120 percent of their *adjusted bases* and more than 10 percent of the *fair market value* of all partnership property other than money. §751(d)(2). One momentarily includes *unrealized receivables* as well in order to apply the percentage tests. See *inventory items.*

substantially disproportionate redemption   a *stock redemption* that will be treated for *income tax* purposes as an *exchange* of *stock for property* rather than a §301 *distribution* of property. §302(b)(2). Three mechanical requirements must be met for a substantially disproportionate redemption to be found as to a particular *shareholder*: (1) immediately after the redemption, the shareholder must own, actually or constructively, less than 50 percent of the total combined voting power of all classes of stock entitled to vote; (2) the shareholder's interest in the voting stock of the corporation must be reduced by over 20 percent after the redemption; and (3) the shareholder's interest in the voting and nonvoting common stock of the corporation must be reduced by over 20 percent after the redemption. The constructive ownership rules of §318(a) must be applied to the three requirements. For those purposes, voting stock means stock with current, not contingent, voting rights. Reg. §1.302-3(c)(3). If these requirements are met, non-voting preferred stock may be redeemed along with common stock with an *exchange* result, unless it is *section 306 stock*. Reg. §1.302- 3(a). A redemption of voting preferred from a shareholder with no common stock may qualify under §302(b)(2), even if the shareholder cannot satisfy the 80 percent test relating to common stock. Rev. Rul. 81-41, 1981-1 C.B. 121. A plan to engage in a series of redemptions that will not result in a substantially disproportionate redemption can disqualify the *redemption* from *sale* status. §302(b)(2)(D); Rev. Rul. 85-14, 1985-1 C.B. 83. See *stock redemption*.

substantially identical commodities, regulated futures contracts and short sales   a key term in §1256 for which a definition is not yet available. Parallel §1233(e)(2)(B), relating to *short sales,* provides that contracts calling for delivery in different months are not substantially identical. Reg. §1.1233-1(d)(2) says that futures in different commodities, such as corn and wheat that are not generally through custom of the trade used as cross-hedges are not considered substantially identical, but that if futures contracts are otherwise substantially identical, it is irrelevant that they were purchased through different brokers or that the contracts trade on different markets, with their propensity to change price in tandem as the principal factor to be considered. The *short sale rule* of §1233 now applies to *commodities futures contract* transactions involving *straddles.* §1092(b). See *straddles, unregulated futures contracts.*

substantially identical property, short sales   see *substantially identical stock or securities.* The meaning is the same. Reg. §1.1233-1(d).

substantially identical stock or securities   recently acquired *stock* or *securities* that are not different in any material or essential way from the stock or securities disposed of. Characteristics such as *interest* rates, *dividend* rights, liquidating preferences, conditions of retirement, and maturity dates are all considered. Generally, rather minor variations suffice to find a lack of substantially identical natures. Taxpayers who sell stock or securities at a *loss* and, during the *61 days* surrounding the *sale,* purchase substantially identical stock or securities of the same *issuer* are disallowed the *loss* (but defer it) under the *wash sales* rules of §1091.

substantially rehabilitated   for purposes of the *tax credit* for *qualified rehabilitations* granted by §47, the term refers to rehabilitation expenditures with respect to a *qualified rehabilitated building* in excess of the greater of $5,000 or the *adjusted basis* of the building. §47(c)(1)(C). Land costs are not included in adjusted basis. See *rehabilitation credits.*

substantially similar or related property, straddles in stocks   unclear. It includes *stock* and convertible debentures of the same *corporation* where the price movements of the two positions are related and a short position in a stock index, *regulated futures contract (RFC)* or an option on such an RFC or an *option* on the stock index, and stock in an investment company whose principal holdings parallel the performance of the stocks included in the index, or a portfolio of stocks whose performance parallel the performance of the stocks included in the index. The same result will be applicable under the provision suspending the running of the *holding period* of stock held by a corporation for purposes of the *dividends received deduction,* where the *taxpayer* has reduced his or her risk of loss by holding another position in substantially similar or related property; however, stock offset by another nonoption position in substantially similar or related stock, which may result in a reduction in a corporate taxpayer's holding period for purposes of the *dividends received deduction,* is not a straddle. See *offsetting position, stock.*

substantial nonbusiness assets   basically portfolio assets of *investment*-oriented *corporations.* Specifically, if at least one-third of the value of a *new loss corporation's* assets consists *of nonbusiness assets,* the value of the *old loss corporation,* which is crucial in the determination of the *section 382 limitation,* is reduced, thus decreasing the section 382 limitation for such a corporation. The reduction in value of the old loss corporation is the excess of the *fair market value* of the old loss corporation's *nonbusiness assets* basically over the nonbusiness asset share of *debt* for which the corporation is liable. *Nonbusiness assets* basically means assets held for *investment.* §382(1)(4)(c). Nonbusiness assets share of *debt* is the amount of corporate debt bearing the same ratio to the corporation's total debt as the value of the nonbusiness assets bears to the value of total assets. §382(1)(4)(D). (The effect is to shear away a proportionate share of debt along with investment assets.) *Stock* and *securities* in a subsidiary are ignored and a parent corporation is deemed to own a ratable share of the subsidiary's assets. A subsidiary is any company in which the parent owns 50 percent by voting power or stock value; §382(1)(4)(E). *Regulated investment companies, real estate investment trusts,* and *real estate mortgage investment conduits* are exempt from this rule. §382(1)(4)(B)(ii). See *neutrality principle.*

substantial, partnership allocations   one element of the *substantial economic effect test* which is used to determine whether a *partnership allocation* will be validated for federal *income tax* purposes. The test will generally be met if there is a reasonable possibility that the allocation will substantially affect the dollar amount to be received by the *partners* from the partnership independent of tax consequences. Reg. §1.704-1(b)(2)(iii)(a). If allocations are *offsetting, shifting,* or *transitory allocations,* they are not substantial. There are further complex applications of this concept in the regulations. The other requirement is that there be an *economic effect.*

substantial presence test   a test used to determine whether an *alien individual* is a *resident alien* in the United States. It is based on measuring days spent in the *United States.* §7701(b)(3)(A). See *property, restricted property rules; resident alien.*

substantial risk of forfeiture   a standard applied by §83 to determine whether *funded deferred compensation* should be taxed to the payee. Reg. §1.83-3(c)(1) provides in general that substantiality of a risk of forfeiture is determined case by case, but that a substantial risk exists where rights in property that are transferred are conditioned, directly or indirectly, on the future performance (or refraining from performance) of substantial services by any person, or the occurrence of a condition related to a purpose of the transfer, and the possibility of forfeiture is substantial if the condition is not satisfied. Reg. §1.83-3(c)(2) gives, as an example of a substantial risk, the case of an underwriter who is issued stock on the condition that there be a successful underwriting of stock. On the other hand, other illustrations indicate a careful and realistic analysis of conditions, such as forfeitures based on taking a job with a competitor, and it is clear that (1) the history of enforcement of forfeiture provisions should be reviewed, and (2) the payee's influence over the payor must be scrutinized. See *restricted property.*

substantial services   generally, 45 hours or more per month worked by an *independent contractor* after retirement but before age 70. Soc. Sec. Reg. §404.446. In the case of particularly valuable services, however, a much smaller number of hours may be substantial. Rendition of substantial services in any month can result in a reduction of Social Security benefits for that month. 42 U.S.C. §403(f)(3) (1981 Supp. V).

substantial shareholder   any person who on July 1, 1982, owns more than 40 percent by value of the *stock* of the *corporation.* Subchapter S Revision Act of 1982, Pub. L. No. 97-354 §6(c)(3)(D), 96 Stat. 1669. See *qualified oil corporation.*

substantial transformation test   a standard used to distinguish selling from manufacturing activities, for the purpose of treating a *controlled foreign corporation* (CFC) as not engaged in *foreign base company sales income.* See Reg. §1.954-3(a)(4). The *regulations* provide that a CFC can escape the web of *subpart F* by showing, on the basis of *all facts and circumstances,* either that it engages in substantial transformation of goods or that at least 20 percent of the total *cost of goods sold* arises from the CFC's cost of transforming the property. Reg. §1.954-3(a)(4)(iii). For example, if foreign subsidiary A is formed in and sells goods in country X for delivery in country Z, after buying them

from an affiliate in country Y, the subpart F problem erupts, but not if the sales are preceded by a substantial transformation (or substantial manufacture) of the goods in country X.

substantial understatement   see *penalty, substantial understatement.*

substantial user   generally, a *person* (or a broad array of related persons) who regularly uses a part of a facility financed by *private activity bonds* in his or her trade or business. §147(a); Reg. §1.103-11(b). The presence of such a user generally renders the *interest* on a *state or local bond* taxable. A nonexempt person, including various related persons, is considered a substantial user if all or part of a facility is constructed, reconstructed, or acquired specifically for that person, or if (1) the gross revenue derived by the user with respect to the facility is more than 5 percent of the total revenue derived by all users of such facility; or (2) the amount of area of the facility occupied by such user is more than 5 percent of the entire usable area of the facility. Former Reg. §1.103-11(b)(presumably still effective).

substantiation   generally, the preparation and submission of appropriate evidence to support an asserted fact. Substantiation is especially important with respect to claims for *deductions* for *travel, entertainment,* and *business* gifts. Under §274(d), no deduction is allowable for *travel expenses* while *away from home, entertainment expenses,* or *business gifts* unless the *taxpayer* substantiates all of the following for each such expenditure: (1) amount; (2) time and place of travel or entertainment (or use of a facility with respect to entertainment), or date and description of a gift; (3) *business purpose*; and (4) business relationship to the *taxpayer* of each person being entertained, using an *entertainment facility,* or receiving a *gift.* The term *"business"* contemplates *investment* and, presumably, tax-related activities as well.

substitute cost method   an elective system, under which a producing *taxpayer capitalizes* otherwise *deductible* current costs (known as *substitute costs*), rather than having the related party capitalize *interest* on its *related party avoided cost debt.* The amount of substitute costs to be capitalized by the producing taxpayer equals the additional interest expense that the producing taxpayer would have capitalized if the producing taxpayer's *eligible debt* had been equal to the average balance of its accumulated production expenditures during the production period. Notice 88-99, 1988-366 I.R.B. 29, §IX(B)(2). See *uniform capitalization rules.*

substituted basis   *basis* of *property,* which depends on the *taxpayer's* basis or *adjusted basis* in previously owned property. For example, in a tax-free *corporate reorganization,* shareholders who *exchange stock* in their corporation for stock in an acquiring corporation take, as their basis in their newly received stock, the basis they had in their former shares. §358. The term is also used sometimes to refer to *carryover basis,* that is, basis in property the transferee determines by reference to its basis in the transferor's hands. See §1016(b). The typical case of the second type is a simple *gift.* §1015. Section 1223(2) causes tacking to the transferor's holding period in such cases.

substitute for ordinary income a phrase used to describe a payment received in *exchange* for what is concluded not to be *property* for *capital gain or loss* purposes, but rather for a stream of *ordinary income.* Because the standard is so potentially destructive of *capital transactions* (e.g., is the sale of a bond partly an anticipation of future years of interest income?), it is generally confined to cases where the *taxpayer* retains the underlying property (e.g., sells the coupon and retains the body of the bond) and sales in anticipation of receiving ordinary income (e.g., sale of an *endowment policy* that is about to mature, creating ordinary income to the insured).

substitute payments payments in lieu of *dividends, tax-exempt interest,* or other items to be specified by the *IRS.* §6045(d)(2). Brokers who receive payments in lieu of such in connection must report them to the government. §6045(a). See *broker's return.*

successor corporation a distributee or transferee *corporation* that succeeds to or takes into account the *tax attributes* of a *loss corporation* affected by the *neutrality principle.* See Reg. §1.382-2T(f)(4). (The *regulation's* definition is more technical. The term is used in connection with determining whether the *section 382 limitation* applies.)

suit for refund a lawsuit in the federal courts, other than the *Tax Court,* following the denial of a *claim for refund or credit,* the sole means of obtaining jurisdiction. Federal courts do not have jurisdiction over a refund suit if the *taxpayer* has not paid the entire *assessment* for the year, unless the suit is for a refund of *divisible taxes.* See *full payment rule, refund suit; notice of disallowance of claim for refund or credit.*

suit on account stated see *account stated.*

summary plan description a description of a *qualified retirement plan,* calculated to be understood by the average plan *participant.* Such descriptions must be provided to participants and their *beneficiaries* within 120 days after the plan's adoption, with a copy filed with the Department of Labor during that 120-day period. Summary descriptions of material modifications must be furnished to participants and their beneficiaries within 210 days after the end of the *plan year* in which such modifications take place. The summary plan description must be provided to new *employees* within 90 days of their becoming participants. See Labor Reg.

§2520.102-3 for contents. But see Labor Reg. §2520.104(b)-2 which relaxes reporting requirements. Plans with less than 100 participants must file a Form 5500-R in two out of every three years in the form of a brief registration statement giving the *IRS,* the Department of Labor, and the *Pension Benefit Guaranty Corporation* an overview of the plan. Periodic filings on Form 5500-C are also required.

summons an administrative demand for relevant records from the *taxpayer* or others (*third-party recordkeepers*), issued by the *IRS,* usually by a *revenue agent,* under the authority of §§7602, 7609, and 7610. Such summonses are not self-executing, but rather must be enforced in *district courts.* The court issues an order on the taxpayer to show cause why the summons should not be enforced. The parties then dispute the propriety of the summons, after which the court grants or denies enforcement of the summons, which may be appealed. The summons power extends to summonses served on third persons, subject to the taxpayer's power to enjoin such demands. The summons power is restricted in numerous ways, including rules against *second examinations,* Constitutional limits, demands for IRS good faith, and *proper purpose.* See *third-party recordkeeper.*

sum-of-the-dollars method, cost depletion another name for a method of calculating *cost depletion* with respect to a *production payment* fixed in terms of dollars. It is applied by multiplying the *taxpayer's predepletion* year-end adjusted cost for the production payment times production payment received during the year (A) *divided by* A plus money expected to be received in the future. See *decline in principal method, cost depletion; unit of production method, cost depletion* production.

sum-of-the-months-digits method see *rule of seventy-eights.*

sum-of-the-years-digits method of depreciation a method under which changing fractions are applied each year to the original cost or other *basis,* less *salvage value.* The numerator of the fraction in each year represents the remaining *useful life* of the asset, and the denominator (which is constant) is the sum of the numerals representing each of the years of the *estimated useful life.* For example, if the asset has a useful life of four years, the denominator is 10 (i.e., $1 + 2 + 3 + 4$). The numerator in the first year would be 4, in the second year 3, and so forth. Thus, in the first year, 40 (4/10) percent of the potential depreciation would be claimed.

Superfund another name for the Comprehensive Environmental Response Compensation and Liability Act (CERCLA). It is geared to cleaning up old waste sites and is funded in part by an *excise tax* on various feedstocks.

Superfund taxes a triad of taxes designed to fund hazardous waste site clean-ups. They are the *environmental tax,* the *petroleum tax,* and the *chemical feedstock tax.*

superpriorities, tax liens a series of security interests created after a federal *tax lien* is filed that, nonetheless, take priority over the federal lien, such as attorneys' liens and passbook loans. §6323(b) and (c).

super royalty a reference to an element of §482 that primarily forces a proper attribution of income from royalties. For example, if a *domestic corporation* developed a valuable patent which it transferred for a low price to a *foreign subsidiary,* the super royalty provision would force the foreign corporation to, in effect, pay a significant royalty to the parent, commensurate (and likely fluctuating) with the income the patent generated. The provision applies to *intangible personal property.*

superseded *ruling* or *revenue procedure* merely restates the substance and situation of a prior revenue ruling or revenue procedure. If a new ruling does more than restate the substance of a prior portion, a combination of terms is used. For example, *modified and superseded* describes a situation where the substance of a previously published ruling is being changed in part and continued without change in part and it is desired to restate the valid portion of the previously published ruling in a new ruling that is self-contained. In this case, the previously published ruling is first modified and then, as modified, is superseded.

supervisory test, domestic building and loan association one of three tests used to determine if a *domestic building and loan association* qualifies for special tax treatment. The supervisory test looks to see if the domestic building and loan association is either an insured institution within the meaning of the National Housing Act or supervised and examined by *state* or federal authority. §7701(a)(19); Reg. §301.7701-13A(a) and (b). See *domestic building and loan association.*

supper money money paid to *employees* to provide them with dinners. Employees may exclude from *gross income* supper money paid them by their *employers* in order that they can work late. O.D. 514, 2 C.B. 90 (1920). This rule was apparently absorbed into the new rules on *fringe benefits as a de minimis fringe benefit.*

supplemental Social Security income recipient, targeted jobs credit see *SSI recipient; targeted jobs credit.*

supplemental unemployment benefit trusts *trusts* forming part of a plan to pay *supplemental unemployment compensation benefits,* provided they are incapable of diversion of assets and are nondiscriminatory with respect to *highly compensated employees.* §501(c)(17). The definition is intricate in terms of the implications of benefit payments from other sources on discrimination. The contemplated benefits are from work force reductions, plant closings, and the like and can include subordinate sickness and accident benefits. Such organizations are tax-exempt, but payments to them are not *charitable contributions.*

supplemental unemployment compensation benefits benefits paid to an *employee* because of involuntary separation from the employment of the *employer* (whether or not temporary) resulting directly from a reduction in force, the discontinuance of a plant or operation, or other similar conditions, and sick and accident benefits subordinate to the benefits just described. §501(c)(17)(D). See *supplemental unemployment benefit trusts.*

supplemental wages such miscellaneous direct payments as bonuses, overtime pay, commissions, and the like paid to *employees.* Reg. §31.3402(g)-1(a)(2). Such amounts are subject to *income tax withholding* at a flat 20-percent rate. Rev. Rul. 82-200, 1982-2 C.B. 239. See *wages.*

supplemental young child credit a 5-percent *credit* that accompanies the *low-income credit.* §32(b)(1)(D).

supplementary contract a contract that evolves at the termination of an original benefit policy, in full or partial settlement of the amount payable thereunder. Supplementary contracts are generally in the form of interest options, fixed period options, or fixed amount options. The term is peculiar to the taxation of *life insurance companies.*

supplemented an *IRS* term used in situations in which a list, such as a list of the names of countries, is published in a *ruling* and that list is expanded by adding further names in subsequent rulings. After the original ruling has been supplemented several times, a new ruling may be published that includes the original list as well as the additions and *supersedes* all prior rulings in the series. I.R.B. 1982-40, 21.

supplies, credit for increased research activities see *in-house research expenses.*

support, charities gifts, grants, contributions, membership fees, gross receipts from nonbusiness activities, net income from *unrelated trade or business* activities, *gross investment income,* tax revenues of certain types, and the value of certain facilities or services provided by government units, but not *capital gains.* §509(d). Support percentages are especially important in determining whether an *exempt organization* is a *private foundation.* See Reg. §1.170A-9(e)(9) for details.

support, dependency exemptions amounts provided in cash or in kind to provide *necessities* (e.g., food, clothing, shelter, medical and dental care, and so on) determined in accordance with federal standards. Rev.

Rul. 76-344, 1976-2 C.B. 82. The support test to claim a *dependency exemption* requires that the *taxpayer* furnish more than one-half the total support for a *dependent* during the *taxable year.* §152(a). Total support is based on comparing the amount spent by the taxpayer with that spent by the *dependent* and by any other persons who furnished support items. Contributions to the support of an *individual* may include income ordinarily excluded from *gross income,* such as Social Security benefits, subsistence allowances under the GI Bill of Rights, savings account withdrawals, aid to families with dependent children, and child support payments. Scholarships are not taken into account in determining whether a parent or step-parent has provided more than one-half the support of a child. §152(d). If the item of support furnished to an individual is in the form of property or lodging, it is necessary to measure the amount of such item of support in terms of its *fair market value.* Reg. §1.152-1(a)(2)(i). See *necessities.*

supporting organization   an *exempt organization* deemed not to be a *private foundation* which, although not publicly supported, is organized and operated exclusively for the benefit of one or more *public charities,* such that it is deemed to be publicly supported. See §509(a)(3). The supporting organization must, at all times, operate exclusively for the benefit of, perform the functions of, or carry out the *exempt purpose* of at least one public charity. §509(a)(3)(A).

support test   one of three alternative tests used by the *Code* as part of its definition of an *operating foundation.* A *private foundation* satisfies the support test if: (1) at least one-half of its support is other than *gross investment income* (§509(d) and (e)); (2) at least 85 percent of its *support* other than gross *investment* income is normally received from the public and from at least five *exempt organizations*; and (3) not more than 25 percent of its support other than gross investment income is normally received from any one such *exempt organization.* §4942(j)(3)(B)(iii); Reg. §53.4942(b)-2(c). See *assets test, operating foundation; endowment test; operating foundation.*

survival of tax attributes   a reference to the continuation of a *corporation's tax attributes* (e.g., *accounting method, taxable year, basis of property, net operating losses*) following a *corporate reorganization* or certain *liquidations* of *subsidiaries* into their *parent* corporations. Section 381 provides noninclusive rules granting survival of attributes, while §§382 and 383 provide certain explicit limits. See *reincorporation; neutrality principle.*

surviving spouse   a *spouse* who outlives the spouse to whom he or she was married. For purposes of §l(a), concerning the privilege of filing *joint returns,* §2(a) defines the term as meaning a *taxpayer* whose spouse died in either of the two preceding *taxable years* and

who *maintains a household* (i.e., pays more than one-half the cost of maintaining the household) that is the *principal place of abode* of a child, stepchild, or foster child who is a *dependent.* People who remarry cease to be surviving spouses. In any case, one is not a surviving spouse for these purposes unless one could have filed a *joint return* with the *decedent,* had the decedent lived. §2(a); Reg. §1.2-2. See §2(a)(3) and Rev. Rul. 76-468, 1976-2 C.B. 202, for spouses of persons missing in action. See *married person.*

survivorship annuity   an *annuity* payable first to one *annuitant,* then to another annuitant for his or her life.

suspended   a term used by the *IRS* in rare situations to show that the previous published *revenue ruling* or *revenue procedure* will not be applied, pending some future action such as the issuance of new or amended *regulations,* the outcome of cases in litigation, or the outcome of an IRS study.

suspense account   "an account in the general ledger used to hold over unposted items so that the business day can be closed in a state of balance." As applied to federal *income taxes,* it refers to accounts held open pending future events. For example, the *loss* deferral rules of §704(d) may limit a *partner's* losses to his or her *basis in the partnership interest*; losses so limited are placed in a suspense account, pending the earnings of future income or contributions. The *at-risk rules* of §465 operate similarly. See §166(f)(4) for the explicit use of the term in connection with *dealers' reserves,* allowing *dealers* who go out of business a *deduction* for *bad debt reserves* established in prior years with no *tax benefit.*

suspension of assessment period   the suspension of the running of the *statute of limitations* on *assessments.* Examples of events that will suspend the period are *deficiency notices* and filing a *petition* in the *Tax Court.* §6503(a)(1).

swap fund   a device that permitted groups of *taxpayers* to transfer *appreciated* securities to a newly-formed *investment company* in a tax-free organization under §351. Such *diversifications* are now prohibited by §351(e) and Reg. §1.351-1(c)(1). *Partnership swap funds* are also proscribed by §721(b). See also §368(a)(2)(F) (limiting *investment company* reorganizations). Absent these limits, taxpayers could achieve diversification of risk without recognizing *gains.* See *section 351 transactions.*

sweep-out dividend   a *distribution* by a *regulated investment company* pursuant to §855, which provides that a regulated investment company may *deduct,* on its federal corporate *income tax return* for the *taxable year,* a *dividend* paid after the close of the taxable year if such a dividend is declared within the time prescribed by law for filing the company's *tax return* (including authorized extensions) as long as the dividend is paid no later than the company's first regular dividend and, in all events, within 12 months of the close of the company's taxable year. The same term is used in connection with an *S corporation's* election to eliminate its *earnings and profits* under §1369(e)(3) by making a major actual distribution.

syndicate an underwriting arrangement under which investment bankers agree to purchase, then immediately resell, stock or securities to the public, but is sometimes used to refer to buying groups generally. Perhaps it is best defined as a *joint venture* of a financial type. Syndicates are generally deemed *partnerships*. §761(a).

syndicate, hedging exception a *partnership, S corporation,* or other *entity,* other than a *C corporation,* more than 35 percent of the *losses of which are allocable to limited partners* or *limited entrepreneurs* (within the *farming syndicate* rules' definition in §464(e)(2)). §1256(e)(3). The purpose is to keep *tax shelter syndications from exploiting the hedging exception* to the *mark-to-market* rule for *commodity straddles.*

syndication fees, corporate see *capital structure expenditures.*

syndication fees, partnerships *expenditures* for promoting the sales of, or of selling, an interest in a *partnership.* Such expenses must be *capitalized,* although the identity of the account so capitalized is unclear, but is evidently the *partner's basis in the partnership interest.* §709(a).

synthetic put a transaction in which a *taxpayer* sells *stock* at a *loss* and immediately writes a naked *in the money put,* such that the *taxpayer* can virtually be assured that the put will be exercised.

systematic direct or indirect borrowing of part or all of the increases in cash value a pattern of borrowing against the *cash surrender value* of a *life insurance, endowment,* or *annuity policy* pursuant to a plan of purchase. §264(a)(3). If the *taxpayer* subjectively intended such a plan, then *interest expenses* on *debt* incurred or continued to purchase or carry the policy are rendered *nondeductible.* Because of the problems of proof in this area, Reg. §1.264-4(c)(1) rebuttably presumes the existence of such a plan if borrowings are used in connection with premiums for more than three years.

system group one or more chains of *corporations* connected through *stock* ownership with a common parent corporation, if at least 90 percent of each class of stock (other than: (1) stock that is preferred as to both dividends and assets; and (2) stock that is limited and preferred as to dividends but not preferred as to assets, only if the total value of such stock is less than one percent of the aggregate value of all classes of stock not preferred as to both dividends and assets) of each of the corporations (except the common parent corporation) is owned directly by one or more of the other corporations, and if the common parent corporation directly owns at least 90 percent of each class of stock (other than stock preferred as to both dividends and assets) of at least one of the other corporations. §1082(d). No corporation is a member of a system group unless it is either a *registered holding company* or a *majority-owned subsidiary company.* As a general rule, both types of ownership tests must be met under §1083(d), since a corporation, in order to be a member of a system group, must also be a registered holding company or a majority-owned subsidiary company. §1083(d); Reg. §1.1083-1(d). Section 1081(a) allows tax-free transfers of stock within a system group pursuant to *SEC* orders.

T

TAM an acronym for *Technical Advice Memorandum.*

TAMRA an acronym for the *Technical and Miscellaneous Revenue Act of 1988.*

TBT an acronym for *tax benefit transfer.*

TC an acronym for *Tax Court.*

TCE program an acronym for the Tax Counselling to the Elderly program. See Ann. 89-106, 1989-35 I.R.B.22.

TCM an acronym for *Tax Court Memorandum,* a reference to a routine decision of the Tax Court.

TCMP an acronym for Taxpayer Compliance Measurement Program, an *IRS* program designed to sample particular tax topics (e.g., *tax shelter partnerships*) to determine the degree of noncompliance with tax law and administrative positions, for the purpose of determining whether IRS resources are being well allocated, usually by forcing close *audits* of *returns* on a line-by-line basis.

TD an acronym for *Treasury Decision.*

TEFRA an acronym for *Tax Equity and Fiscal Responsibility Act* of 1982, Pub. L. No. 97-248, 96 Stat. 324, a law designed to roll back some of the excesses of *ERTA,* raise revenues, and coordinate *qualified plans,* as between corporate and noncorporate *employers.*

TEFRA audit same as a *unified proceeding.*

Temp. Reg. a *temporary regulation.*

TIN an acronym for a *taxpayer identification number.*

TIR an acronym for *Technical Information Release.*

TLC an acronym for *Tax Legislative Counsel.*

TM an acronym for *Technical Memorandum* or *Tax Management,* a Bureau of National Affairs multivolume publication, each of which is referred to as a portfolio. Each portfolio contains concentrated information on a narrow topic of tax law.

TMM an acronym for Tax Management Memorandum, a publication of the Bureau of National Affairs (a private publishing company), which provides commentary on current tax topics.

TMP an acronym for *tax matters partner.*

TRAC an acronym for *terminal rental adjustment clause.*

TRAN an acronym for *tax and revenue anticipation notes.*

TRASOP an acronym for *tax credit employee stock ownership plan.*

TSA an acronym for a *tax-sheltered annuity.* See *tax-deferred annuities for exempt and educational organization employees.*

tacit consent rule, joint return a principle that allows the *IRS* to presume that a nonsigning *spouse* on a *joint return* signed only by one spouse has given tacit consent to have the return filed. The rule is applicable where it can be shown that the nonsigning spouse was aware a joint return was being filed and did not file a *separate return.* This rule is generally used by the IRS where it intends to hold the nonsigning spouse liable for taxes. See *innocent spouse rule.*

tacking of holding periods the effect of provisions found in §1223 (extending *holding periods* of *property* by reference to the holding period of other property or holders). The principal rules are that (1) where property is received in an *exchange* with no or limited *recognition* of *realized gain* or *loss,* the holding period of the property received in the exchange starts on the date of the acquisition of the property surrendered in the exchange; (2) the holding period of property acquired by transfer in *trust* or by *gift* includes the time the property was held by the *donor* and the *donee,* if the donee is required to use the donor's *basis* as his or her own (if, however, the value at the time of the gift is used to determine a *loss,* the donor's holding period may not be used); (3) property acquired from a *decedent* is given an automatic *long-term holding period*; and (4) property received in a *wash sale,* an *involuntary conversion* with a *carryover basis,* a nontaxable *stock dividend,* or a tax-free *corporate division* acquires a holding period that includes the holding period of the *stock* sold, the converted property, stock with respect to which the dividend was distributed, and stock held before the corporate division, respectively. See also §735(b) (property received in a distribution from a *partnership*).

tainted assets, outbound transfers an informal term used to describe a class of assets that result in taxability when made part of an *outbound transfer* (i.e., overseas transfer) even though they may be used in the *active conduct of a trade or business* outside the *United States.* The assets consist of *stock in trade, inventory* or *dealer property; installment obligations, accounts receivable,* or similar property; foreign currency or other property denominated in foreign currency; property leased by the *United States person* to a person other than the transferee at the time of the transfer; and *intangible property* (e.g., *patents* and *copyrights*). A transfer of a *partnership interest* by a *United States person* to a *foreign corporation* is treated as a transfer of the United States person's pro rata share of the partnership's assets, except as provided in *regulations* to be issued. §367(a)(3)(B).

tainted stock a term often used to describe stock classified as *section 306 stock.*

tandem stock option a *stock option* pursuant to which two options are issued together and the exercise of one eliminates the right to exercise the other. The *IRS* asserts that such plans cannot be used to evade the limits on *incentive stock option.* Temp. Reg. §14a.422-1, Q&A 39.

target affiliate, section 338 acquisitions a *corporation* that, during any portion of the *consistency period* ending on the *acquisition date,* was affiliated with the *target corporation* within the meaning of §1504 (*affiliated group* of corporations). The term excludes *foreign corporations, domestic international sales corporations, possessions corporations* that make the *section 936 election,* and corporations doing business in the United States Virgin Islands. §338(h)(6). See *section 338 acquisition.*

target benefit plans qualified *money purchase pension plans* under which target benefits begin at *normal retirement age,* stated in the plan, with *employer contributions* under the *individual* level premium funding method, actuarially determined, with *forfeitures* and contributions separately accounted for as to each *participant,* and with benefits provided exclusively from such separate accounts. The method ignores investment performance and calls for recalculations each time *compensation* changes. Rev. Rul. 74-464, 1974-2 C.B. 115. Actual benefits will vary with the performance of amounts invested in the *pension trust.*

target corporation, section 338 acquisitions a *corporation* whose *stock* is acquired by another corporation in a *qualified stock purchase.* §338(d)(1). See *section 338 acquisition.*

targeted area projects basically, low- or moderate-income housing projects that can be financed with *tax-exempt bonds* without one running afoul of the rules against *private activity bonds.* §143(j) and former §103(b)(4) and (12). The term is defined as a project located in a *qualified census tract* or an area of chronic economic distress (defined in §143(j)(3) and former §103A(k)(3) as a HUD-approved, state-designated area in economic difficulty, ascertained by one applying factors listed in §143(j)(3)(B) and former §103A(k)(3)(B)).

targeted area residences residences located in a *qualified census tract* or in an *area of chronic economic distress.* §143(j) and former §103A(k)(1). See *average area purchase price, qualified mortgage issue.*

targeted jobs credit an elective *credit* for hiring unrelated *individuals* (as defined in §51(d)) who are *members of targeted groups.* The credit equals 40 per-

cent of the first $6,000 of *qualified wages* paid for the first year of employment to a member of a targeted group. Such wages consist of total *qualified first-year wages* (i.e., amounts paid to members of target groups in their first 12 months of employment). The targeted jobs credit expired for employees who start work after June 30, 1992.

targeted offshore offering an offering of obligations that is targeted to the domestic capital markets of a single *foreign* country in accordance with customary local practices and documentation; that is neither listed nor the subject of an application for listing on a securities exchange outside the targeted foreign country; and that consists solely of obligations denominated in the local currency of the targeted foreign country, provided the issuer or any "distributor" (see below) knows or has reason to believe that a substantial portion of the offering will be sold or resold outside of the domestic markets of the targeted foreign country in connection with the original issuance. Regulation §1.163-5 (c)(2)(i)(D)(7)(iii) eliminates the certificate requirements related to *registration required obligations* for targeted offshore offerings if the obligations are sold during a restricted period in a targeted offshore offering. See also 54 CFR 35200. See *registration-required obligation.*

tariff a duty imposed on the importation of goods across international boundaries. The term also refers to rates, such as those imposed by a shipper or telephone company.

tax "an enforced contribution, exacted pursuant to legislative authority . . . for the purpose of raising revenue to be used for public or governmental purposes, and not as a payment for some special privilege or service rendered," regardless of its label, and not a "charge primarily imposed for the purpose of regulation." Rev. Rul. 57-345, 1957-2 C.B. 132. Although Rev. Rul. 57-345 was revoked by Rev. Rul. 60-366, 1960-2 C.B. 63, it is still considered the standard for determining whether a tax qualifies as an *expense* which is *deductible* under §164. See also Reg. §1.164-4(a). See also *personal property taxes; state and local income taxes; state or local tax.*

tax accounting *methods of accounting* properly used for tax purposes (e.g., *installment sales*) as opposed to *financial accounting* for commercial or personal purposes. Such methods need not be consistent with nontax financial reporting, and it is clear that to the extent the two methods depart, tax accounting rules take precedence for purposes of reporting *income* and *loss* to the *IRS.* See *methods of accounting.*

tax accrual workpapers workpapers, including memoranda, generated by accountants to evaluate a *taxpayer's* (usually a corporation) contingent tax liability. Naturally, the *IRS* has a great interest in having access to such papers; its right of access to such papers is not limited by *accountant-client privilege*. See *United States v. Arthur Andersen & Co.,* 104 S.Ct. 1495 (extensive discussion). See *accountant-client privilege.*

tax adjustment account a financial account which reflects cumulative timing differences between financial and *tax return* information.

tax allocation method any one of four basic methods of charging all or a portion of the *consolidated tax liability* of an *affiliated group* to particular members of that group. §1552. It is necessary to choose a proper tax allocation method in order that a member can be charged with its share of *federal income taxes* for purposes of computing *earnings and profits* and so that intercompany payments can be made to correct any overpayments of tax made by a member.

tax and revenue anticipation notes (TRANs) notes issued to bridge periods between revenue flows. Such obligations enjoy a *safe harbor* exemption from the *required rebate* provisions relating to *arbitrage bonds* if they are promptly applied to governmental uses. §148(f)(4)(B)(iii). See *arbitrage bond; required rebate.*

Tax Appeals, Board of the predecessor of the present *Tax Court.* See *Tax Court.*

tax assessment see *assessment.*

tax attributes tax characteristics of a *taxpayer,* such as *accounting method, earnings and profits* accounts, *capital loss carryovers,* and the like. The subject is of particular significance to *corporate reorganizations* (other than the B, F, and G varieties), *tax-free liquidations* of *subsidiaries,* and *cancellation of indebtedness income.* Section 381 provides a nonexclusive list of corporate attributes that carry over to the surviving corporation in such transactions and provides for their continuance. Sections 382 and 383 in turn limit the transferability of certain attributes, especially *net operating losses* and various *tax credits.* See *neutrality principle.*

tax attributes, Bankruptcy Tax Act a series of tax characteristics that may be reduced in bankruptcy or outside of bankruptcy as a result of the bankrupt entity not *recognizing discharge of indebtedness* income. These characteristics include (1) *net operating losses* and their *carryovers;* (2) carryovers of *general business credits;* (3) *capital losses* and their carryovers; (4) the *basis* of the *taxpayer's* assets (both *depreciable* and *nondepreciable);* and (5) carryovers of the *foreign tax credit.* §108(b)(2). The provisions calling for application of the reductions are intricate.

tax auditor see *office auditor.*

tax avoidance a term commonly used to describe tax minimization practices that fall short of *tax evasion.* Tax avoidance is generally viewed as legitimate. The term has little analytical value.

tax avoidance or evasion see *tax avoidance; tax evasion.*

tax base the base on which *taxes* are imposed. For example, the *federal income tax* is imposed on *taxable income.* §1. The tax base times the rate produces the tax liability.

tax benefit generally, any diminution in *tax* liability. The term appears to have no formal definition, but it usually concerns such matters as *deductions, losses,* and *credits* specifically allowed by the Code as opposed to reductions in tax liability by virtue of one's simply having diminished income.

tax benefit rule a pervasive concept that primarily attempts to overcome inequities to the *taxpayer* or to the government that result from the preference for closing *taxable years.* In its statutory form, among other things, it compels the *recapture* of *depreciation* as *ordinary income* rather than *capital gains* (in order to limit the tax benefit of ordinary *deductions* that reduce *ordinary income* by imposing comparable tax burdens); treats *recoveries* of previously deducted items as creating a tax liability, but not beyond the prior tax base's reduction (e.g., where a previously *deducted charitable contribution* is returned to the *donor*); and grants deductions or *credits* for the repayment of amounts previously included in income. §§1245, 1250, 111, 1341.

tax book method a method of apportionment of *interest expenses* on the basis of the historical values of assets shown on the *taxpayer's* books rather than on the *fair market values* of the taxpayer's assets. It uses the *adjusted bases* of assets, not the historical cost adjusted by *depreciation* used for financial reporting purposes. When this method is applied, §864(e)(4) provides, allocates, and apportions expenses on the basis of assets when the assets are *stock* in one of certain *corporations.* Section 864(e)(4) also provides rules relating to the *basis* of stock in certain corporations which is adjusted for earnings and profit changes. Importantly, the adjusted basis of any asset which is stock in a corporation which is not included in the affiliated group must be increased by the amount of the *earnings and profits* of that corporation attributable to such stock and accumulated during the period the taxpayer held such stock, or reduced (but not below zero) by deficits in that period. There are also stock ownership requirements.

tax bracket generally, the *marginal income tax rate* applicable to a particular range of *taxable income.* See §§1, 11. The marginal tax rate concept is useful for planning because it measures the tax effect of a proposed transaction. *Corporations* and *trusts,* as well as *individuals,* are generally taxed at *progressive* tax rates according to an income bracket system. The concept is generally applicable to federal *estate* and *gift taxes* but is somewhat less commonly used in that context.

tax certificate a document, issued by the Federal Communications Commission to a *taxpayer,* which certifies that the sale of *stock* or property is necessary or appropriate to effect FCC policies regarding ownership of radio broadcasting stations. §1071(a). Such a certificate can result in qualification of the transaction for *involuntary conversion* treatment under §1033. See Rev. Rul. 82-70, 1982-1 C.B. 114 (complex application of these provisions). The advantage of §1033 is that *gains* arising from *involuntary conversions* can be deferred through *rollovers* of such amounts into property that is *similar or related in service or use* to the former property.

tax claim in bankruptcy a claim for taxes by the *IRS* or lesser authority for unpaid taxes in a bankruptcy proceeding. The IRS participates in bankruptcy proceedings to assure that its claims are satisfied. The Federal Bankruptcy Code grants tax claims a specified priority in bankruptcy.

tax collection waiver Form 900, used (by agreement) to extend the period for collection of taxes.

tax cost basis a term used to describe the *basis of property* that was not received in *exchange* for property or money but reported as *gross income.* Reg. §1.61-2(d)(2) is the leading authority and treats property received as compensation for services as having a *fair market value* basis. In such cases, the *taxpayer* reports the value as income. The amount of such income becomes the property's so-called tax cost basis.

Tax Counseling for the Elderly see *TCE program.*

Tax Court a trial court of original jurisdiction (as opposed to an appellate court) headquartered in Washington, D.C., but which hears cases on a traveling basis and decides federal *income, estate,* and *gift* (but not *employment*) *tax* disputes and, to a very limited extent, *excise tax* disputes. It can also restrain premature *assessments* and certain collections, order *tax refunds,* and review certain sizures, among other miscellaneous powers. §§6213(a), 6512(b), 6863(b)(3), and 7441–7487. It is unique because the *taxpayer* need not first pay the *deficiency* that the *IRS assesses* in order to have a day in court. *Tax Court* jurisdiction arises after the IRS issues a *statutory notice of deficiency* (i.e., *ninety-day letter*) to the taxpayer and the taxpayer files a *petition* for a hearing within the prescribed time. Another significant Tax Court power is its ability to issue *declaratory judgments* with respect to the status of certain *exempt organizations,* charitable donees, *private foundations, private operating foundations, qualified retirement plans,* and adverse *rulings* regarding foreign transfers. §§7428, 7476, 7477. It also has certain disclosure powers over the IRS. §6110. Appeals from the Tax Court are heard in the federal courts of appeal. The Tax Court also has a small claims procedure. See *ancillary refund jurisdiction; small tax cases.*

Tax Court Memorandum decision see *TCM.*

tax credit a *credit* against taxes. See *credit.*

tax credit employee stock ownership plan a qualified *defined contribution plan* (i.e., a *stock bonus* or combined *money purchase pension* and *stock bonus plan*) that primarily invests in *employer securities.* The advantage of the TRASOP is that contributions of stock by the *employer* entitled the *employer* to an extra 1 percent *investment tax credit* (ITC) plus an additional .05 percent to the extent matched by *employee* contributions of cash, which credits are available if the employer is otherwise entitled to claim the ITC. Such plans had to meet the requirements of §401(a), relating to *qualified plans,* as well as the requirements of §409(b) through (h) and (o), which call for such provisions as immediate *vesting,* certain voting rights, allocation of employer securities to employees in accordance with compensation levels, limitations on *distribution* of employer securities, and employee's rights to demand stock and to require the employer to repurchase such stock. The credit was replaced when the PAYSOP system took hold.

tax credit for increasing research activities see *credit for increasing research activities.*

tax credit for the elderly see *credit for the elderly and disabled.*

tax deferral a tax result or strategy under which reportable income is *deferred* until a future *taxable year.* There are a great number of tax deferral patterns, including (1) *rollovers of principal residences* under §1034; (2) *like-kind exchanges* under §1031; (3) qualified and nonqualified *deferred compensation* for services; (4) *installment sale* reporting under §453; (5) rewriting contracts to extend payments or due dates; and (6) such securities transactions as *short sales against the box* and perhaps certain *straddles.* Deferral can also be done by accelerating *deductions* into the current year.

tax-deferred annuities a nontechnical term often used for *deferred annuities.*

tax-deferred annuities for exempt and educational organization employees a reference to *annuities* bought for *employees* that qualify for *tax deferral,* indexed for inflation (namely, $8,728 in 1992) or up to $9,500 per year of elective deferrals for *qualified employees* of *qualified organizations*) if bought by *employers* that are *section 501(c)(3) organizations* (which includes many schools), or state or local government agencies operating a school or university with a regular faculty and student body. §403(b). The vital feature of these annuities is that they can be funded directly or by salary reduction agreements, with the employer passively purchasing an annuity for the employee. Such annuities must be nonforfeitable. Payouts to the employee are taxable under the annuity rules, but contributions by the employer which were excludable under the *exclusion allowance* provision are not part of the employee's *investment in the contract* and are, therefore, fully taxable. See *catch-up provision, tax-deferred annuities for exempt and educational organization employees; contribution not made under a salary reduction agreement; elective deferrals; exclusion allowance; mutual fund custodial accounts; qualified employee, catch-up election; qualified organization, catch-up election.*

tax deficiency see *deficiency.*

tax determination see *expenses in connection with the determination, collection, or refund of any tax.*

Tax Division a division of the *Justice Department* responsible for federal tax litigation not in the *Tax Court.* 28 U.S.C. §507(a) (1976).

taxes see *tax.*

tax evasion a term commonly used to describe *tax planning* activities of an illegitimate variety. Section 7201 defines criminal tax evasion as a *willful* attempt to evade or defeat any tax due and owing and provides for a maximum sentence of five years imprisonment for each separate attempt, plus a substantial fine. See *penalty, civil fraud; willful attempt to evade tax.*

tax-exempt bond a *bond* issued by or on behalf of a state or local government (including D.C. and *possessions*), the *interest* on which is excluded from the holder's *gross income.* §103(a). See also §150(a)(6). They are formally called *state or local bonds.* Tax-exempt status is denied in numerous cases, including that for state and local *private activity bonds* that are not *qualified bonds, arbitrage bonds,* certain *pooled financing bond issues,* and *registration required bonds* which are not in registered form. §§103(b), 150(a)(6). For several requirements for the exemption, see *state or local bond.*

tax-exempt bond financed property any *recovery property* to the extent such property is financed (directly or indirectly) by an obligation, the *interest* on which is *exempt* from *income tax* under §103(a). It does not include *qualified residential rental property.* §168(g)(5)(A) and (C). See *tax-exempt use property.*

tax-exempt bonds and securities a term used to describe obligations that generate *tax-exempt interest.* See *state or local bond.*

tax-exempt controlled entity a taxable *corporation,* at least 50 percent of the value of whose *stock* is owned by one or more *non-foreign tax-exempt entities*; only five-percent *shareholders* are considered if the company is publicly traded, and the *attribution rules* of §318 are applied. If such an *entity* is owned by a *partnership*

or other pass-through entity, it is treated as a *tax-exempt entity* for purposes of limiting *deductions* for *cost recovery* in connection with leasing property to tax-exempt enterprises. §168(h)(6)(F)(iii). See PLR 9040039 (July 9, 1990). See *tax-exempt entity.*

tax-exempt entity for purposes of §168(h) relating to leases of *tax-exempt use property,* the term includes the United States, any *state* or *political subdivision* thereof, any *possession of the United States,* or any agency or instrumentality of any of the foregoing; an organization (other than an *exempt farmers' cooperative* which is *exempt* from federal *income taxes*; and any *foreign person* or *entity.* For this purpose, a foreign person or entity means foreign government, any international organization, or any agency or instrumentality of any of the foregoing, and any person who is not a *United States person,* but not any foreign *partnership* or other foreign pass-through entity. §168(h)(2)(C). §168(h)(2)(A). *Disqualified leases* of property to such entities can force the property onto the relatively slow *alternative depreciation system.* §168(g). There is a special exception for certain property subject to United States tax and used by a *foreign person.* §168(g)(2)(B). See *tax-exempt use property.*

tax-exempt farmers' cooperatives see *exempt farmers' cooperatives.*

tax-exempt income items that could be, but are not, included in *gross income* under §61. Examples include *gifts* and *inheritances* (§102), *life insurance proceeds* (§101), interest on certain state or local bonds (§103), and within limits, *Social Security benefits.* Tax-exempt income is distinct from the *deferral* of *realized gains* in circumstances such as incorporations (§351) and *exchanges* of certain *like-kind property* (§1031). See *exclusion from gross income; exempt income.*

tax-exempt interest a nontechnical term for *interest* that is excluded from *gross income* by §103 and is, therefore, not subject to federal *income taxes.* See *state or local bond.*

tax-exempt obligation an obligation, the *interest* on which is *excluded* from *gross income* by §103 or exempt from tax regardless of the holder's identity. Holders of discounted tax-exempt obligations must accrue *original issue discount* for purposes of determining their bases. §1288(a)(2). This closes a loophole based on generation of artificial losses. The key exemption is for interest on a *state or local bond.* See *state or local bond.*

tax-exempt organizations any one of 21 types of organizations that has been or can be granted partial or complete exemption from *federal income taxes.* See *exempt organizations.*

tax-exempt pension trust see *qualified trust.*

tax-exempt portion the *market discount* on a *tax-exempt bond* that has been stripped of its coupons, or the bundle of stripped coupons, that arises because the yield on the stripped bond when it is bought is higher than the yield when it was originally issued. Such discount is taxed as *original issue discount* and included in *gross income*. The term is formally defined as the amount by which the *stated redemption price at maturity*, or the amount payable on due date of a coupon, exceeds an issue price that would produce a *yield to maturity* as of the purchase date of the stripped coupon or stripped bond equal to the lower of (1) the coupon rate on the tax-exempt obligation from which the coupons were stripped, or (2) the yield to maturity based on the purchase price of the stripped bond. This rule applies to post–June 10, 1987 purchases or sale of stripped bonds or coupons. Note that, in general, OID on tax-exempt obligations is tax-exempt.

tax-exempt trust a term often used to describe a *trust* used as the funding vehicle for a *qualified pension, profit-sharing,* or *stock bonus plan.* See §§401(a), 501(a). A variety of other trusts are rendered entirely or partially *tax-exempt* by §501 and other *Code* sections (e.g., trusts operating *charitable organizations* and *black lung benefit trusts*).

tax-exempt use personal property generally, the portion of personal property leased to a *tax-exempt entity.* See *tax-exempt use property.*

tax-exempt use property that portion of any *tangible recovery property* (other than *nonresidential real property*) leased to a *tax-exempt entity* in a *disqualified lease.* §168(h)(1). For this purpose, such property is forced on to the relatively slow *alternative depreciation system* of §168(g). §168(g)(3). For this purpose, nonresidential real property includes *residential rental property.* §168(h)(1)(E). A foreign government or entity is considered a tax-exempt entity. §168(h)(2)(A)(iii). See *disqualified lease.*

tax expenditures diminutions in government tax revenues that result from tax benefits granted for policy reasons and that diminish a *comprehensive tax base* (e.g., *deductions* for *interest expenses* on home mortgages).

tax fraud see *fraud.*

tax-free covenant bonds obligations containing a provision to the effect that the issuer would pay the holder's taxes on income from the obligation. See §1451 (requiring withholding, generally at a 2 percent rate, on such bonds issued before 1934).

tax-free exchanges a reference to various provisions under which properties can be *exchanged* free of immediate *federal income taxes.* Examples include *corporate reorganizations* in which *shareholders* tender old *stock*

for stock of a different *corporation* (§354), exchanges of certain *life insurance* and *annuity* products (§1035), and *like-kind exchanges* of business or investment property (§1031). The term is a misnomer in that the exchanges generally result only in *deferrals,* not permanent exemptions.

tax-free incorporations formations of *corporations* that benefit from §351, the gist of which is that if *property* is transferred to a corporation by one or more *persons* (acting under a collective agreement in the latter instance) in exchange for its *stock* or *securities,* then no *gains* or *losses* will be *recognized* to the transferor(s), provided they wind up in *control* of the corporation. Section 351(a), however, is subordinate to numerous doctrines and limitations, including the *assignment of income doctrine,* the *IRS*'s power to force a *clear reflection of income* (§§446(b) and 482), the *tax benefit rule,* and probably the demand for a *business purpose* (Rev. Rul. 60-331, 1960-2 C.B. 189). See *section 351 transactions.*

tax-free liquidations *corporate liquidations* undertaken pursuant to §§332 (liquidations of controlled subsidiaries into parent corporations) and formerly 333 (so-called *one-month liquidations*). Such liquidations can be free of immediate *federal income taxes.* Alternatively, the reference is to former §337, which allowed corporations that distribute all their assets within one year of adopting a plan of liquidation to sell most of their properties tax-free. See *section 332 liquidation; section 333 liquidation.*

tax-free reorganization exchanges see *corporate reorganization.*

tax-free repossessions a reference to §1038, the gist of which is that a seller-*mortgagee* of realty who reacquires the property in full or partial satisfaction of the defaulted *mortgage* debt, whether by voluntary conveyance or foreclosure, can generally avoid current *recognition* of *gain* or *loss,* with further relief for prompt dispositions of the property in the case of repossessions of *principal residences.*

tax-free rollovers a reference to transactions in which cash or property is received by the *taxpayer,* then reinvested in another form free of current federal *income taxes.* For example, under §1033 proceeds of governmental takings are tax-free if reinvested in property that is *similar or related in service or use.* Another common example is the right to avoid taxation of *distributions* from *qualified plans* if they are promptly invested in an *individual retirement arrangement.*

tax-free termination, private foundation a device by which a *private foundation* can end its status on a tax-free basis. Basically, the foundation can change its activities to behave more like a *public charity* or transfer its assets to *public charities.* The former method involves operating as one of three types of charities for 60 months and notifying the *IRS* of its plan to qualify. The three types of charities are (1) a *fifty-percent charity*; (2) a type of *publicly supported organization* (§509(a)(2) variety); and (3) a *supporting organization* (§509(a)(3) type). §507(b)(1)(B). The second method involves a transfer of net assets to one or several organizations that qualify as so-called fifty-percent charities for at least 60 consecutive months before the transfer. §507(b)(1)(A). These relief provisions are not generally available to scofflaws. See *taxable termination, private foundations.*

tax-freedom day a humorous term for the day of the year when workers can be viewed as no longer working for governments but instead beginning work for themselves.

tax gap a euphemism for the shortfall in federal taxes attributable to noncompliance with federal tax laws.

tax haven a country with low (or no) internal taxes. Tax havens are often used, and abused, by overseas affiliates or other entities that concentrate earnings under the laws of the tax havens (e.g., by establishing a Bahamian sales subsidiary of a United States corporation) with a view to deferring repatriation of those overseas earnings. The *controlled foreign corporation* rules of §951 et seq. (*Subpart F*) are the principal weapons to combat the use of tax havens.

tax home the *taxpayer's* principal *business* headquarters or, absent such headquarters, the taxpayer's regular place of abode. See, e.g., Rev. Rul. 60-189, 1960-1 C.B. 60 (Treasury's view). Numerous federal courts of appeal have instead defined the term in its natural sense of the taxpayer's principal place of abode. The term *tax home* has the same meaning for purposes of the *foreign earned income exclusion.* §911(d)(3). See *tax home, foreign earned income, and foreign housing exclusions; travel expenses.*

tax home, foreign earned income, and foreign housing exclusions same as *tax home* for purposes of *travel expense deductions.* §911(d)(3). *Taxpayers* are not treated as having a foreign tax home while they have a United States abode. As a result, a United States tax home means neither a *foreign earned income exclusion* under §911(a)(1), nor a *foreign housing cost exclusion* under §911(a)(2), nor a *foreign housing cost deduction* under §911(c)(3)(A). §911(d)(1).

tax information authorization an authorization signed by a *taxpayer,* submitted to the *IRS* in order to allow a designated *representative* to inspect or receive tax information of a confidential nature in an identified tax case. Form 2848-D is most commonly used. The authorization permits further powers on the part of the representative (e.g., to discuss ruling requests with IRS personnel) but is more limited in scope than *a power of*

attorney, though practitioners commonly speak of the 2848-D as a "power of attorney." Reg. §601.502(c)(2).

Tax Legislative Counsel a branch of the *Treasury Department* involved in joining *federal* tax policy.

tax lien see *federal tax lien.*

Tax Management Memorandum see *TMM.*

tax matters partner a *general partner* designated by the *partnership agreement* or, if no *partner* is designated, the general partner having the largest *profit interest* at the close of the *taxable year* involved. If the partner is not identified under either standard, the *IRS* makes the selection. §6231(a)(7). The tax matters partner acts on behalf of the partnership when a partnership is under *TEFRA audit* by the IRS in a *unified proceeding.* Some of his or her duties include receiving notice of the proceedings, keeping partners informed, seeking the judicial review, and binding certain partners with a *settlement agreement.* §§6223, 6224, 6226.

tax matters shareholder the analog of a *tax matter partner* in a *TEFRA audit* applied to an *S corporation.* See §6244. See *unified proceedings.*

tax on excess business holdings an *excise tax* imposed by §4943(a)(1), at the rate of 5 percent, on *excess business holdings* of a *private foundation.* See *excess business holdings, private foundations.*

tax on lobbying expenditures an *excise tax* imposed on certain *public charities* (not available to *churches*) at the rate of 25 percent of the *excess lobbying expenditures.* §4911. This is an elective tax under which certain organizations can engage in limited lobbying activities (i.e., make expenditures for the purpose of influencing legislation) without forfeiting their *exempt organization* status. §501(h) (not available to churches). "Excess lobbying expenditures" are the greater of (1) the excess of expenditures to influence the opinions of the general public or any segment thereof (*grass roots expenditures*) over 25 percent of the "lobbying nontaxable amount" (*the grass roots nontaxable amount*); or (2) the excess of all lobbying expenditures over the entire *lobbying nontaxable amount.* The lobbying nontaxable amount is an amount, not greater than $1 million, computed by adding 20 percent of the first $500,000 of *exempt purpose expenditure* to 15 percent of the next $500,000 to 10 percent of the next $500,000 to 5 percent of the rest. §4911(c)(2) and (b). Exempt purpose expenditures include amounts expended to accomplish the organization's *charitable purposes,* under §170(c)(2)(B), administrative expenses paid or incurred for those purposes, and lobbying expenditures, but they do not include amounts paid or incurred for fund raising. §§4911(e)(1), 170(c)(2)(B). See *excise tax, political expenditures.*

tax on unrelated trades or businesses an *income tax* imposed by §511 on *trade or business* activities of otherwise *exempt organizations*. The pattern is to segregate such activities and tax them as if they were earned by a *corporation*. See *unrelated business taxable income; unrelated trade or business*.

tax option corporation   a synonym for an *S corporation*.

tax partnership   an arrangement among co-owners which is only colorably a *partnership* for *federal income tax* purposes, but not for state law purposes. Such arrangements are common in the oil and gas industry, and are commonly used to avoid the *fractional interest rule* and problems imposed by Rev. Rul. 77-176, 1977-1 C.B. 77. See *fractional interest rule, natural resources*.

tax practitioners' mailing list   a list maintained by a *District Director* upon which attorneys, CPAs, *enrolled agents,* or *tax return preparers* can be placed, entitling them to receive releases regarding tax information, forms, and the like. See Rev. Proc. 67-36, 1967-2 C.B. 666.

tax preferences   a shorthand form for *items of tax preference*.

Tax Reduction Act stock ownership plan   see *tax credit employee stock ownership plan*.

Tax Reform Act of 1984   the first part (Division) of the *Deficit Reduction Act of 1984*, Pub. L. No. 88-369 (1984). It contains the vast bulk of the revenue provisions of that act and is often thought of as the *1984 Act* because of the virtually trivial quantity of tax-related provisions in the second Division.

Tax Reform Act of 1986   an exceptionally complex and weighty tax law (Pub. L. No. 99-514) passed by the 99th Congress. Its primary features are the introduction of the *passive loss rules* and reduction of top income tax rates for *individuals* to 28 percent, subject to a 5 percent surcharge to take back the benefits of *personal exemptions,* and lower tax brackets for lower levels of *taxable income*.

tax refund   a cash payment to a *taxpayer* to repay overpaid taxes. See *claim for refund or credit*.

tax refund intercept program   a federal program to enforce payment of *past due support*. See *past due support*.

tax return   see *return; valid return*.

tax return information disclosure penalty   a criminal sanction against the unauthorized disclosure of the contents of a return or the return itself by government *employees* and others. A violation is a felony, punishable by a fine of not more than $5,000 and imprisonment of not more than five years, or both. §7213(a). See *return information; unauthorized use of tax information*.

tax return information disclosure penalty, preparer   a criminal sanction against the unauthorized disclosure or use of information on or for a *tax return* by *tax return preparers*. A violation is a misdemeanor, punishable by a fine of not more than $1,000 or imprisonment for not more than one year, or both. In addition, the preparer may be required to pay the costs of prosecution. §7216(a).

tax return preparer   the Code imposes technical standards via its civil and criminal penalty provisions. Several of these provisions apply to tax return preparers as defined in §7701(a)(36). In general, anyone who prepares an initial tax return or a later amended return or claim for refund may be classified as a return preparer. Regulations explaining the Code definition also stress that an individual can be a preparer "*without regard to educational qualifications and professional status requirements.*" Reg. §301.7701-15(a)(3). The significance of being a preparer is considerable exposure to penalties. Section 7216 imposes criminal sanctions for *tax return information disclosure*; §6694(a) imposes a $250 *unrealistic position civil tax penalty*; §6694(b) imposes a $1,000 fraud or reckless disregard civil tax penalty; and §7407 authorizes civil actions to enjoin wrongful preparation activities. See §§6060, 6107, 6695 (associated penalties). There is also a $25 penalty for a preparer's failure to obtain the taxpayer's written confirmation of compliance with the recordkeeping requirements for *listed property* and a 5 percent negligence penalty where an underpayment results from failure to substantiate under the rules forcing contemporaneous records. See *penalty, unrealistic position by tax return preparer; return preparer penalties; return preparer injunction bond*.

tax sharing payments   payments among commonly controlled *corporations* designed to compensate other affiliates for tax benefits gained by the payor as a result of filing a *consolidated return*. Such payments are generally treated as *nondeductible contributions to capital* of the payee. See §1552(a) and Rev. Rul. 73-605, 1973-2 C.B. 109. See *tax allocation method*.

tax shelter   a general term that usually refers to publicly or privately distributed offerings of *limited partnership* interests, or sometimes direct ownership interests, which offer significant tax benefits that can reduce taxes on income from other sources. Popular examples, at least in the past, included oil and gas drilling programs, real estate syndications, and equipment leasing (e.g., railroad boxcar) partnerships. Alternatively, the term refers to any device designed to minimize federal *income tax* burdens. Tax shelters typically have the characteristics of *deferral* of income, converting the *character* of income (e.g., offering current *deductions* in exchange for later *capital gains*), and leverage.

tax shelter, accuracy-related penalty a *partnership* or other *entity,* any investment plan or arrangement, or any other plan or arrangement whose principal purpose is tax *avoidance* or *evasion* of *federal income taxes.* §6662(d)(2)(C)(ii). *Taxpayers* who invest in tax shelters and attempt to avoid the penalty on substantial underpayment must show a high level of *substantial authority* for their positions. This definition is used elsewhere in the *Code,* e.g., §461(i)(3). See *accuracy-related penalty; penalty, substantial understatement of income tax.*

tax shelter, cash method disallowance rules generally, the same as *tax shelter, economic performance.* §§448(d)(3) and §461(i). In the determination of whether an activity constitutes a tax shelter, consideration should be given to whether there is a reasonable and significant expectation that either *deductions* exceeding income from the activity will be available to reduce income from other sources or *credit* exceeding the tax attributable to the activity will be available to offset taxes on income from other sources. *S corporations* that merely seek exemption from state registration are not inherently tax shelters. §448(d)(3). Section 448 generally prevents tax shelters (other than certain oil and gas ventures (section 461(i)) from using the *cash-method* of accounting and generally prevents investors in tax shelter partnerships from deducting expenses based borrowed amounts. See *tax shelter, economic performance.*

tax shelter, economic performance (1) any enterprise (aside from a *C corporation*), interests in which have ever been offered for sale through an offering required to be registered with a *federal* or *state* agency; or (2) any *partnerships* or other *entity* (other than a *C corporation*), if over 35 percent of its *losses* are allocable to *limited partners* or *limited entrepreneurs* (persons who do not actively participate in the management of an enterprise, a family syndicate, or a partnership or other entity, any investment plan or arrangement; or (3) any other plan or arrangement, the principal purpose of which is to avoid or evade *federal income tax.* §461(i)(3). The last element of the definition arises by cross-reference to §6662(d), which contains its own definition of a tax shelter for purposes of the *penalty* for *substantial underpayments.* In the case of a farm *business,* a tax shelter is defined differently; one uses definitions (1) or (2) above and substitutes the term "*syndicate*" as used for purposes of the *hedging exception.* §461(i)(4). The *recurring item exception* to the economic performance standard does not apply to tax shelters, and there is a special relaxation of the economic performance requirement for *IDC deductions* that are modestly *prepaid.*

tax-sheltered annuities see *tax-deferred annuities for exempt and educational organization employees; tax-sheltered annuities for schoolteachers.*

tax-sheltered annuities for schoolteachers a nontechnical term used to describe programs, often quite informal, whereby public school systems or *exempt organizations* (which include religious, scientific, etc., organizations) purchase nonforfeitable *deferred annuities* for their *employees,* usually as a result of salary reduction agreements. §403(b). See *tax-deferred annuities for exempt and educational organization employees.*

tax shelter farm activity, alternative minimum tax (1) a *farming syndicate;* and (2) any other *passive activity* consisting of farming. A *taxpayer* is treated as materially participating in the activity under the *material participation* standard set forth for regular tax purposes in §469 (relating to *passive losses rules*), if a member of the taxpayer's family (within the meaning of §2032A(e)(2)) so participates, or if the taxpayer meets the requirements of paragraph (4) or (5) of §2032A(b) (relating to certain retired or disabled *individuals* and *surviving spouses.*) §58(a)(2). This provision applies to *personal service corporations* as well as all other noncorporate taxpayers. For purposes of computing alternative minimum taxable income, one excludes *tax shelter farm losses.* §58(a). In calculating a farm loss, one applies the preferences and adjustments called for under the alternative minimum tax. §58(a)(4). See *alternative minimum taxable income; personal service corporation, passive loss rules.*

tax shelter identification number see *registration of tax shelters.*

tax shelter, IRS view an investment which has a significant and intended tax purpose feature, with either of the following attributes: (1) *deductions* in excess of *income* from the investment being available in any year to reduce income from other sources in that year; or (2) *credits* in excess of the tax attributable to the income from the investment being available in any year to offset taxes on income from other sources in that year. Excluded from the term are *municipal bonds, annuities,* certain family *trusts, qualified retirement plans, individual retirement accounts, stock option plans, securities* issued in a *corporate reorganization,* mineral development ventures (if the only tax benefit would be *percentage depletion*), and *real estate* where anticipated annual deductions will not exceed *gross income* from the investment or tax credits will not exceed the tax attributable to *gross income* from the investment. Whether an investment is intended to have tax shelter features depends on the objective facts and circumstances of each case; significant weight is given to the features described in the offering materials. Reg. §10.33(c).

tax shelter opinion, IRS view advice by a practitioner directed to persons other than a client concerning the tax aspects of a *tax shelter* which appears in or is referred to in either the offering materials or in connection with sales promotion efforts. It includes all discussion (usually including financial forecasts and projections) of the tax aspects of the tax risks portion of the offering materials prepared by the practitioner or used in connection with sales promotion efforts. It does not include advice rendered solely for the offeror or reviewing offering materials so long as neither the nature of the practitioner nor the fact that a practitioner has rendered advice concerning tax aspects is either referred to in the offering materials or in connection with sales promotion efforts. Reg. §10.33(c).

tax shelter organizer for purposes of §6111 relating to mandatory *registration of tax shelters,* the term refers to the *person* principally responsible for organizing the *tax shelter* (typically the promoter or *general partner*). §6111(d)(1)(A). If that person fails to register the shelter as required, then any person who participates in the organization of the shelter is deemed the organizer. §6111(d)(1)(B). Failing that, §6111(d)(1)(C) states that anyone participating in the sale or management of the investment at a time when the shelter was not registered is declared an organizer. Tax shelter organizers are responsible for registering the shelter with the *IRS* before sales begin. See *tax shelter, registration.*

tax shelter, penalty for substantial understatement of income tax same as *tax shelter, accuracy-related penalty.*

tax shelter ratio see *tax shelter, registration.*

tax shelter, registration any investment (including service and leasing contracts) with respect to which a *person* could reasonably infer from the representations made or to be made in connection with any offer for sale of any interest in that, as of the close of any of the first five years, the ratio with respect to any investor of *A* (the aggregate of *deductions* and twice the *credits* potentially allowable thereto) and *B* (the aggregate of the cash invested and the *adjusted basis* of other *property* contributed by the investor, reduced by any liability to which that property is subject) is greater than two-to-one. The *A*/*B* ratio is called the *tax shelter ratio.* For purposes of computing this ratio, amounts borrowed from a participant in the organization, sale, or management of the shelter or a person related to a participant are not considered cash invested. *Regulations* will include or exclude amounts in the aggregate of cash invested and the *adjusted basis* of *contributed* property. The B portion of the investment ratio is called the *investment base.* For registration with the *IRS* to be required, a tax shelter must also be (1) required to register under a federal or state law regulating the offering or sale of securities; (2) offered for sale pursuant to an exemption from registration requiring the filing of a notice with a *federal* or *state* agency regulating securities; or (3) a substantial investment, meaning that the aggregate nominal amount that may be offered for sale to all investors exceeds $250,000 and that five or more

investors are expected. The aggregate nominal amount offered for sale includes all cash, all contributions of property, and all loans, whether *recourse* or *nonrecourse.* The aggregate nominal amount offered for sale is not the same as the investment amount used to compute the tax shelter ratio. §6111(c)(1). Form 8264 is used for registration. See *potentially abusive shelter.*

tax shelter registration number see *registration of tax shelters.*

tax straddles another term for matched commodities transactions in which the *taxpayer* simultaneously enters into a contract to deliver a commodity at a future date and a sale of a contract for delivery of the same commodity in a different month. The notion is that the contracts will inevitably move in opposite directions such that the taxpayer can close out the losing *leg* at will. If the taxpayer wishes (assuming no tax law impediments), he or she could then enter into another transaction to offset the *unrealized gain* in the appreciated leg. These transactions were popular devices for deferring income and for converting *ordinary income* into *capital gain* and *short-term capital gains* into *long-term capital gains.* They have been greatly curtailed by the *mark-to-market* rules for *regulated futures contracts* (RFCs) and the *loss deferral rules* applicable to non-RFC transactions, as well as by the *Smith Jacobsen rule.*

tax swaps another term for year-end sales of *stock or securities,* followed by purchases of comparable property in a fashion that avoids the *wash sale* rules. For example, a *taxpayer* might sell 100 shares of depreciated Ford stock and use the proceeds to purchase 100 shares of GM stock. The loss cannot be disallowed under the *wash sales* rules because different issuers are involved, yet if the investments are comparable, the taxpayer's investment in the automobile industry continues unabated. See *wash sales.*

tax table method the calculation of *individual federal income taxes* on the basis of tables provided in instructions to *Form 1040* (individual *income tax returns*), which permit federal income tax liabilities to be conveniently determined once the *taxpayer* has determined his or her *taxable income, filing status,* and number of *dependents.*

tax tables tables of *federal income tax* rates, broken down by *filing status* (single, joint return, etc.) and *taxable income.* The tables must be used by *taxpayers* who meet the tables' specifications. For 1991 and prior years, the tax tables were based on taxable income of less than $50,000. For tax years beginning in 1992, the tax tables apply to taxable income up to $100,000. See §3.

tax treaty a *treaty* negotiated between foreign governments relating to taxation. Such treaties are negotiated on behalf of the United States by the *Treasury Department.*

tax wash lease   see *wash lease*.

tax year   see *taxable year*.

taxable estate   the *gross estate* of a *decedent*, less the *deductions* provided in §§2052–2057. §2051. The taxable estate is part of the base on which the *unified gift and estate tax* is levied at death. The deductions fall into two basic classes, those that reduce wealth and those granted because they pass to preferred recipients. See *estate tax charitable contribution; estate tax deductions; marital deduction*.

taxable event   a transaction involving *property* considered sufficiently significant to justify finding that a *gain* or *loss* on the transaction can be said to be *realized*. The term is synonymous with the phrase "*sale or other disposition*" used in §1001(a), the provision that defines gains and losses. Examples of transactions that are not taxable events include leases and divisions of property between co-owners. Examples of taxable events include, among others, abandonments of encumbered property and, of course, outright *sales* and *exchanges*. See *disposition*.

taxable exchange   an *exchange* of *property* that is not subject to a *nonrecognition provision*. See *recognition*.

taxable expenditures excise tax, private foundations an *excise tax* imposed on a *private foundation* at the rate of 10 percent of any *taxable expenditures*. A $2\frac{1}{2}$ percent tax is also imposed on a *foundation manager* who knowingly agrees to an improper expenditure. An additional tax may be imposed on the foundation at a rate of 100 percent of the taxable expenditures (50 percent on the manager) if the expenditures are not corrected by the date on which the *notice of deficiency* is mailed or the tax is *assessed*, whichever is earlier. §4945. The tax is intended to discourage the use of private foundation funds for lobbying and other political activities.

taxable expenditures, private foundations   certain expenditures that attract an *excise tax* of 10 percent imposed on the *private foundation* and $2\frac{1}{2}$ percent on its management (with up to 150 percent taxes for failures to correct), but not more than $15,000 per expenditure, on amounts paid or incurred by a private foundation attempting (1) to influence some or all of the public or government personnel as to legislation; (2) to influence the result of a specific public election or to directly or indirectly carry on a voter registration drive; (3) to provide grants to an *individual* for travel, study, or similar purposes, unless made on an objective, nondiscriminatory basis; (4) to provide grants to other organizations, except if the private foundation exercises *expenditure responsibility*; or (5) to perform any non-charitable function. §4945. Section 4945(i) provides a correction period, after which a stiffer penalty is imposed if the expenditures have not been corrected. See *expenditure responsibility*.

taxable foreign source income, FSC   that portion of an FSC's *foreign trade income* which is treated as *effectively connected income* from the conduct of a *United States trade or business* through a *permanent establishment* within the United States. §921(d). It is generally taxed currently and treated as United States source income for purposes of the *foreign tax credit limitation*.

taxable gifts   the total amount of *gifts* made during the *calendar year*, less the *deductions* for *marital gifts* and *charitable contributions*. §2503(a). For this purpose, the total amount of gifts equals the aggregate value of all gifts *of present interests* made in the calendar year less any applicable $10,000 *annual gift tax exclusions*. Reg. §25.2503-1. *Qualified transfers* for tuition and *medical care* are exempted, as are *waivers* of certain pension benefits (§2503(e)-(f)) and loans of *qualified works of art* to *public charities* and *private operating foundations*. Taxable gifts are the base on which the federal *gift tax* rates apply. §2502(a). See *unified transfer tax*.

taxable income   the base on which the *federal income tax* falls. In the case of *individuals*, the term means *gross income*, less *adjustments to gross income*, *deductions* for *personal exemptions* and *dependents*, and either *itemized deductions* or the *standard deduction*, whichever is higher. §63. Section 1 imposes the tax on *estates, trusts*, and individuals. See §641 et seq. for the determination of their *tax bases*. Section 11 taxes the taxable incomes of *corporations*. In the case of corporations, taxable income means gross income less allowable deductions. §63(a). For income taxation of estates and trusts, see *subchapter J*, which treats these entities much like individuals, but with a major deduction for *distributions* of income. *Credits* against taxes are applied after pre-credit tax liabilities (determined by applying pertinent tax rates to taxable income) are calculated.

taxable income for the taxable year attributable to base period export receipts, DISC   a portion of the *adjusted taxable income* of a *domestic international sales corporation* (DISC).

Such amount is derived according to the following formula (§ 995(b)(1)(E)):

$$\text{Adjusted taxable income} \times \frac{\text{67 percent of base period average export gross receipts}}{\text{export gross receipts for the taxable year}}$$

The amount computed is taxed to the shareholders as a *deemed distribution*. Former §995(b)(1)(E). The DISC has been displaced by the *FSC*. The continuing rules pertaining to DISCs are concerned with taxing their previous accumulations.

taxable income from military property, DISC   gross income of a *domestic international sales corporation*

(DISC) for the *taxable year* attributable to *military property,* less allocable costs. §995(b)(3). One-half of this amount is a *deemed distribution.* §995(b)(1)(D). The DISC provisions were largely replaced by the *FSC* provisions in the *Tax Reform Act of 1984.*

taxable income from sources within the United States *gross income from sources within the United States,* less allocable *expenses, losses,* and other *deductions.* §861(b). The rules governing the *allocations* of *expenses, losses,* and other deductions are complex. Reg. §1.861-8. See *source rules.*

taxable income from sources without the United States *gross income from sources without the United States,* less allocable *expenses, losses,* and other *deductions.* §862(b).

taxable income from the property, depletion allowance *gross income* from a natural resource *property,* less allowable *deductions* (excluding *depletion* deductions) attributable to the extraction of minerals, oil, gas, or geothermal energy processes. Such deductions include *mining transportation,* operating *expenses,* selling expenses, administrative and financial overhead, *depreciation* and *cost recovery, taxes, intangible drilling and development costs,* and *exploration* and *development expenditures,* reduced by *recapture* of *gains* as *ordinary income* under §1245. §613(a); Reg. §1.613-5(a). Allowable deductions would exclude, for example, personal expenses or penalties for violations of law; the *regulations* require *apportionment* of expenses if they are attributable to several activities. Reg. §1.613-5(a). The significance is that *percentage depletion* deductions cannot exceed 50 percent of taxable income from the property. §§613, 613A. See *property, depletion.*

taxable income, S corporation *taxable income* computed as if an *individual taxpayer,* except that certain *deductions* are not allowable: (1) *personal exemptions;* (2) deductions for *foreign taxes;* (3) *charitable contribution deductions;* (4) *net operating loss deductions;* (5) additional *itemized deductions* (§§211–222, e.g., *medical expenses, moving expenses,* and other deductions peculiar to individuals); and (6) *depletion* deductions under §611. Also, *organizational expenditures* must be *capitalized.* §1363(b). The definition has no immediate impact, except to indicate that its tax computations are guided by rules applicable to individuals.

taxable mortgage pool any *entity,* other than a *real estate mortgage investment conduit,* whose assets are substantially all *debt* obligations, which obligations are primarily *real estate mortgages.* The entity must be the obligor under debt obligations with two or more maturities. §7701(i)(2). The payments from the underlying mortgages determine payments to the investors. This entity is treated as a *corporation* for federal *income tax* purposes. §7701(i)(1).

taxable period qualified plan the period during which a *prohibited transaction* can be reversed so as to eliminate a second tier of heavier penalties. See Reg. §1.4975-13, which relies on terminology and definitions under the *private foundation* rules. See *correction period.*

taxable stock dividend a *stock dividend* (e.g., a two-for-one stock split) that is taxable under §305(b) (e.g., because shareholders can elect cash in lieu of *stock*). Stock dividends are generally tax-free under §305(a), but §305(b) contains a variety of provisions that can render them taxable. The term "taxable stock dividend" is explicitly used in §643 in connection with the taxation of *trusts* and *estates,* but without any definition, although the controlling influence of §305 seems obvious.

taxable substance any substance that the *IRS* lists as such when sold or used by the importer. §4672(a)(1). The IRS must include substances which meet either a weight or value test. §4672(a)(2)(B). It can eliminate substances that meet neither such test. The list of items includes, among many items, acetic acid, acetone, acrylic resins, nickel oxide, nickel powders, nickel waste and scrap, polystyrene resins, and wrought nickel rods and wire. The tax is imposed on any taxable substance sold or used by its importer, at the rate which would have applied on taxable chemicals if they had been sold in the United States for use in manufacture or production of the taxable substance. See *chemical feedstock tax.*

taxable termination, private foundations two ways for a *private foundation* to end its status at the price of a *termination tax,* one voluntary and the other involuntary. Under the voluntary method, the foundation notifies the *IRS* of its intent to terminate, pays the tax, and is generally treated as a taxable *corporation* the next day. §507(a)(1). Under the involuntary method, the IRS compels termination, asserting the foundation's willful or flagrant acts, willful and repeated acts, or failures to act, which create liability for *excise taxes* on wrongdoing listed in Chapter 42 of the *Code.* §507(a)(2). In both cases, the termination tax is subject to *abatement.* §507(a) and (g).

taxable wage base, FICA a monetary base on which *employers* pay *Social Security taxes* on *wages* paid to their *employees.* The FICA tax is comprised of two components: *Social Security tax* (old-age, survivors, and disability insurance) and *Medicare tax* (hospital insurance). Starting in 1991, the top base amount differs for the Social Security portion ($57,600 for 1993) and the Medicare portion ($135,000 for 1993). See *contribution and benefit base.*

taxable year the annual *accounting period* during which *taxable income* or loss is determined on the *taxpayer's books and records.* §441. For most *individuals,* it is simply the *calendar year. Partnerships, trusts, estates,* and *corporations* can, to varying extents, select other opening and closing points such as *fiscal years* (e.g., June 30 to July 1) and *fifty-two, fifty-three week taxable years.*

taxicab fuels exemption   an exemption from the 4-cent-per-gallon partial motor fuels tax for qualifying taxicabs, as defined in §6427(e)(2).

taxpayer   generally, any *person* subject to any internal revenue tax. §7701(a)(14).

Taxpayer Assistance Order   an order issued by the *Ombudsman,* after determination that the *taxpayer* is suffering or is about to suffer significant hardship as a result of the way the internal revenue laws are being administered. It is part of the *Taxpayer Bill of Rights.*

taxpayer assistance order   an internal administrative order issued by the *Taxpayer Ombudsman* to help a distressed *taxpayer.* See *Taxpayer Ombudsman.*

Taxpayer Compliance Measurement Program   see *TCMP.*

taxpayer identification number   a nine-digit, *IRS*-issued number used to identify *taxpayers* other than *individuals* and *decedent's estates.* Reg. §301.6109-(1)(a). *Sole proprietors* engaged in a *trade or business* or individuals who are *employers* are also required to have such a number. Individuals and decedent's estates use their Social Security numbers. §6109(a).

taxpayer, mitigation of statute of limitations   any *person* subject to tax under the applicable revenue laws. §1313(b).

Taxpayer Ombudsman   the head officer of the *IRS's Problems Resolution Office.* He or she, or a designee, can issue *taxpayer assistance orders* on a showing of actual or imminent harm to a *taxayer,* which orders can be requested by taxpayers or their representatives. See §7811.

taxpayer representation letter   a letter typically entered into between an accounting firm and a *taxpayer* laying out the terms of their agreement as to the financial audit of the taxpayer. The IRS likes to obtain such letters in examining the taxpayer's return.

taxpayer representative   someone representing a *taxpayer* before the *IRS.* Generally, attorneys, CPAs, and *enrolled agents* are entitled to represent taxpayers after obtaining written *powers of attorney* or *tax information authorization* (Forms 2848 or 2848-D). See *practice before the IRS.*

taxpayer return information, Privacy Act   *return information* submitted to the *IRS* by or for the *taxpayer.* §6103(b)(3). Improper disclosure of such information by *government employees* attracts criminal penalties under §7213(a). See *Privacy Act.*

taxpayer rights statement   an informal term for a mandatory statement of *taxpayer* rights given to the taxpayer in connection with any *IRS* contact about the determination or collection of taxes. §7521(b). It is part of the so-called *Taxpayer's Bill of Rights.*

Taxpayer's Bill of Rights   an element of *TAMRA* that significantly improved the position of *taxpayers* vis-à-vis the *IRS* in *audit* and with respect to *collection of taxes.* The principal features, all of which are embodied in the *Internal Revenue Code,* are (1) a duty to inform taxpayers of their procedural rights (the *taxpayer rights statement*); (2) improved interviews, including a right to a *reasonable time and place;* (3) the right to make a recording; (4) a greater chance to recover attorney's and accountant's fees, even in administrative proceedings; (5) a right to rely on official written IRS advice; (6) *taxpayer assistance orders* from the *Taxpayer Ombudsman;* (7) clearer contents of *deficiency notices;* and (8) damages in *district court* to redress IRS abuses.

Taxpayer Service Division   an administrative unit of a *District Office* that manages its disclosures, public affairs, and *taxpayer* service activities. It helps taxpayers to prepare *returns* and respond to communications from the *IRS.* It also houses the *Disclosure Officer,* who administers disclosure matters, the Resources Management Division, and, in certain cases, an Employee Plans and Exempt Organizations Division.

teacher or trainee   a class of *individuals* who do not become *resident aliens* by virtue of time spent (the *substantial presence test*) in the *United States.* The term refers to any individual who is temporarily present in the United States under §101(15)(J) of the Immigration and Nationality Act (other than a student) and who substantially complies with the requirements for being so present. §7701(b)(5)(C). An individual is not treated as a teacher or trainee for the current year if, for two *calendar years* during the six preceding calendar years, he or she was a teacher, trainee, or student. §7701(b)(5)(E)(i).

team audits   *audits* undertaken by a group of *revenue agents* in cases where there are multiple related *taxpayers* or related transactions (e.g., conglomerate corporations or large *tax shelter partnerships*).

technical advice   advice or guidance as to the interpretation and proper application of the *federal* tax law to a specific set of facts relating to a substantive or procedural matter, furnished by the *National Office* upon request of a *District Office* in connection with an *audit* of a *tax return* or a *claim for refund or credit.* Reg. §601.105(b)(5)(i)(a). Technical advice is furnished as a means of assisting District Office personnel in closing cases and establishing and maintaining consistent holdings, but such advice does not include memoranda or matters of general technical application not furnished in connection with the examination of a specific *taxpay-*

er's return. Although it is the responsibility of the District Office to determine whether to request technical advice, the *taxpayer* may request that an issue be submitted and may appeal to the Chief, Examination Division, if the request is denied. Reg. §601.105(b)(5). See *Technical Advice Memorandum.*

Technical Advice Memorandum a memorandum issued in two parts by the *National Office* of the *IRS* which embodies its reply to a request for *technical advice* by *taxpayers* and *IRS* administrative personnel involved in an *audit*. The first part contains the facts, precedents, reasoning, and conclusions with respect to the request. This document is intended to give direct answers and detailed discussions regarding the specific request. A copy of this part is ordinarily furnished to the taxpayer, but there are some exceptions such as advice relating to cases involving *criminal* or *civil fraud* investigations. The second part of the National Office's reply consists of a transmittal memorandum, which usually provides the *District office* with administrative or other information that may not be discussed with the taxpayer. The technical advice binds audit personnel below the level of the regional *Appeals Officer*. See Rev. Proc. 82-38, 1982-1 C.B. 505, as updated.

Technical and Miscellaneous Revenue Act of 1988 a fairly short change in the laws, primarily of a technical nature, but containing some important changes as well, including a so-called *Taxpayer's Bill of Rights.*

Technical Memoranda government documents explaining reasons for promulgation of *Treasury* decisions that might accompany final *regulations*. Such memoranda are publicly disclosed.

telephone companies, exempt a class of *exempt organizations* operating small-scale telephone companies. See *mutual or cooperative telephone companies.*

telescoping analyzing a series of transactions and collapsing them; a synonym for "applying the *step transactions doctrine*."

temporary life annuity an *annuity* that expires at the earlier of the death of the *annuitant* or a fixed number of years. See Reg. §1.72-5(a)(3) for modifications in the *exclusion ratio* computation called for by this feature.

temporary living expenses, moving expenses a term loosely used to describe the meals and lodging (but not personal living expenses such as personal grooming) while one occupies temporary quarters in the general location of the new *principal place of work* during any consecutive 30-day period after obtaining new employment. §217(b)(1)(D). Such *expenses* are considered *moving expenses*. See *moving expense deduction.*

temporary living expenses, travel living expenses (e.g., meals, lodging, and dry cleaning) incurred while traveling *away from home*. §162(a)(2); Reg. §1.162-2.

temporary regulation a *Treasury Department regulation* issued as an interim measure and considered generally equivalent to a final regulation, except for the expectation of future amendment or formalization.

temporary trust see *short-term trust.*

tenant-shareholder a *person* who owns stock in a *cooperative housing corporation* whose stock is fully paid-up at what the local *District Director* considers an appropriate price. §216(b)(5)(6). Tenant shareholders may generally claim their proportional shares of *real property taxes* and mortgage *interest*. §216(a)(1) and (2); Reg. §1.216-1(e). Such shareholders can include owners of professional apartments. Rev. Rul. 90-35, 1990-17 I.R.B. 5.

1040PC program an alternative filing method for practitioners who do not choose to participate in the IRS's electronic filing program. Using IRS-approved software, the preparer generates one or two sheets containing all information from Form 1040 and accompanying forms and schedules. The shortened form is then filed by mail in place of the usual Form 1040.

tentative carryback adjustment a provision under which *taxpayers* with a *net operating loss carryback*, a *capital loss carryback*, certain *unused credits*, or a *claim of right* adjustment can apply for a tentative adjustment or *refund* of taxes for a year affected by the carryback of such loss, credits, or adjustment. §6411 (using Forms 1045 for *individuals* and 1139 for *corporations*). The application is not a *claim for refund or credit* as such, and its entire or partial rejection cannot be the basis of a *suit for refund*, but, if rejected, taxpayers may still file a regular *claim for refund or credit*; likewise, an *IRS* grant of a refund can later be reversed. §6213. Refund claims based on tentative carryback adjustments force the IRS to allow or disallow the claim within 90 days of the earliest of the date the application was filed or the last day of the month in which the *return* for the loss or unused credit year is due, including extensions, or the date of overpayment in the claim of right adjustment cases. §6411(b).

tentative minimum tax a building block for calculating the *alternative minimum tax*. In the case of *individuals* it is (1) 24 percent × (*alternative minimum taxable income* less an *exemption amount*); (2) minus the *foreign tax credit*. See §55(b). *Corporations* are subject to a 20 percent rate. To the extent the tentative minimum tax exceeds the *regular tax*, (even if that tax is not based on *taxable income*) there is an alternative minimum tax bill. See *alternative minimum tax.*

tentative refund claim see *tentative carryback adjustment.*

tentative return not defined. Generally, a *return* that does not disclose a *taxpayer's* tax liability is no return in the sense that it does not cause the *statute of limitations* to run, whereas a return in need of only modest corrections does.

tentative tax a preliminary tax liability resulting from an intermediate calculation. The concept arises frequently throughout the *Code*. See, e.g., §2(a)(1) (phase-in of certain tax rate changes). See *tentative tax, foreign tax credit*.

tentative tax, foreign tax credit a step in the *foreign tax credit* calculation, referring to a *domestic taxpayer's* United States tax liability before application of the credit. See *overall limitation, foreign tax credit*.

ten-day letter another name for a demand from the *IRS* for payment of taxes due, nonpayment of which can result in collection activities in 10 days (30 days for a *levy*). The threat appears on Forms 3967-C, 4839, and 4840, each of which is a more powerful letter than the last, so it is unclear just what a practitioner might mean when referring to a ten-day letter.

ten-employee rule see *group-term life insurance*.

ten-fifty baskets *dividends* received from each *foreign subsidiary* in which the taxpayer owns a voting interest between 10 and 50 percent, unless the subsidiary is controlled by United States owners, in which case a look-through rule applies. See *section 901(d)(1) "basket."*

ten-fifty corporation same as a *noncontrolled section 902 corporation*.

ten-percent corporate shareholder, gain on sale or exchanges of stock in certain any *domestic corporation* which, as of the day before the *exchange* (see below), owns directly, indirectly, and *constructively* (under the rules of §958(b) relating to *controlled foreign corporations*) at least 10 percent by vote of all classes of voting *stock* at any time in the five-year period ending on the date of the exchange when the foreign corporation was a controlled foreign corporation. §1248(i)(2). If *shareholders* of a domestic corporation exchange their stock for stock of the ten-percent-owned foreign corporation, the transaction is recast with the foreign corporation viewed as having first issued stock to the domestic corporation, with the domestic corporation viewed as having distributed the stock to its shareholders. §1248(i)(1). The result may be a *dividend* to the domestic corporation equal to the value of the stock received by the shareholders and the domestic corporation's *basis* in the stock of the foreign corporation.

ten-percent-owned foreign corporation, section 988 transaction any *foreign corporation,* 10 percent or more of which is directly or indirectly owned by a *United States person.* §988(a)(3)(D).

ten-percent threshold test, percentage of completion method an election which provides that, for purposes of the *percentage of completion method* of accounting for *long-term contracts,* a *taxpayer* may choose not to *recognize gross income* under the contract and not to take into account any costs allocable to the long-term contract for any *taxable year if,* as of the end of that taxable year, less than 10 percent of the estimated total contract costs have been incurred. For the first taxable year in which the 10 percent threshold is met, all costs that have been incurred as of the end of the taxable year are to be taken into account in the determination of the percentage of the contract that has been completed and in the determination of the amount of allowable *deductions* under the contract. §460(b)(5)(A) and (B). This is subject to the application of a *look-back method,* which may require payment of *interest* to the *IRS* on the deferred tax attributable to an overestimation of expected total contract costs. The election affects all long-term contracts of a taxpayer that are entered into during the taxable year that the election is made and any subsequent taxable year that the election is in effect. §460(b)(5)(C)). See *look-back method, long-term contracts.*

ten-year forward averaging a prior law relief provision that permitted payees of *lump-sum distributions* from *qualified plans* (but not *IRAs*) to treat the share of the distribution attributable to post-1973 *employer contributions* (the *ordinary income* portion) as being earned in 10 years by someone who presumably had no income other than a base amount. §402(e)(4). Pre-1973 amounts generally qualified for *long-term capital gains* treatment. The computational rules were complex and were made more so by §402(e)(4)(L), which allowed *employees* with at least five years of participation to combine pre-1974 and post-1973 amounts, and to subject both to the forward averaging rule. Nonetheless, application of the 10-year forward averaging rule resulted in extraordinary tax savings. Employee contributions and *net unrealized appreciation* on *employer securities* are not considered. §402(e)(4)(D). It has been replaced by *five-year forward averaging.*

ten-year property generally, *taxable property* with a *class life* of 16 years or more and less than 20 years. §168(e)(3)(D). It includes a *single-purpose agricultural or horticultural structure* and any tree or vine-borne fruits or nuts. §168(e)(3)(D). This class of *recovery property* is the product of the *Tax Reform Act of 1986.*

ten-year vesting a *vesting* alternative provided by §411(a)(2)(C) pursuant to which an *employee* with 10 *years of service* is 100 percent vested in *employer contributions.* Vesting can be as small as zero percent before 10 years of service elapse, which represents the extreme case of so-called *cliff vesting.*

term certain annuity an *annuity* payable over a fixed period of time (e.g., seven years). If the *annuitant* dies early (e.g., in five years), the balance is payable to another designated payee.

terminal railroad corporation   a *domestic* railroad *corporation* that is not a *member* (other than as a common parent corporation) *of an affiliated group* and has the following characteristics: (1) all of the *shareholders* are domestic railroad corporations providing transportation subject to subchapter I of chapter 105 of Title 49; (2) the primary *business* is providing railroad terminal and switching facilities and services to domestic railroad corporations that provide transportation subject to subchapter I of chapter 105 of Title 49, and to the shippers and passengers of such railroad corporations; (3) a substantial part of the services for the *taxable year* is rendered to one or more of its shareholders; and (4) each shareholder computes *taxable income* on the basis of a *taxable year* beginning or ending on the same day that the taxable year of the terminal railroad corporation begins or ends. These corporations can reduce their *federal income tax* base to the extent they reduce their charges (by crediting *related terminal income*) to their shareholder railroad corporations that use their terminal facilities. §281(a). The shareholder is not taxed as a result of the *credit*, but also receives no *deduction*.

terminal rental adjustment clause   a clause in a lease that, in effect, forces the user to bear loss in value of the leased property. While such so-called TRAC clauses may be found to create a mere *conditional sales agreement* under traditional tax analysis, *TEFRA* §210 generally bars the *IRS* from denying lease status to pre-TEFRA motor vehicle (and trailer) lease agreements governing business vehicles (so-called qualified motor vehicle agreements).

termination assessment   an immediate *assessment* for the current *taxable year* or immediately preceding taxable year, or both, permitted in cases where collection of a tax may be jeopardized because of the likelihood of the *taxpayer's* fleeing the country, taking property from the country, concealing property or him- or herself, impending *insolvency,* ignoring the tax, or otherwise frustrating collection. In these circumstances, the tax becomes immediately due and payable. After assessment, the *IRS* must mail a *notice of deficiency* and make demand for payment of the tax, *interest,* and penalties within prescribed time limits. §6851. The termination assessment is somewhat more extreme than a *jeopardy assessment,* in that the latter is used after the end of the year to which it relates; the termination assessment can occur earlier. See §7429 for administration and judicial review.

termination insurance, ERISA   certain insurance paid by *employees* to underwrite risks associated with their withdrawal from certain *qualified plans.* See *pension benefit guaranty corporation.*

termination, partnership   the end of a *partnership* as a *federal income tax* reporting *entity,* a question determined by the *federal* tax law, not *state* law (which is concerned with legal *dissolutions*). §708(b)(1). Termination may result from a complete cessation of *business,* or a *sale* or *exchange* of 50 percent or more of the total partnership *capital* and *profits interests* in a 12-month period (with consecutive sales of the same interest ignored.) A termination also occurs if only one *partner* remains, unless the disappearing partner's interest passes to his or her *estate* or successor in interest. Reg. §1.708-1(b)(1)(i)(a). A termination resulting from sales of more than 50 percent of the interests is considered for tax purposes to result in a *distribution* of assets to the partners, followed by their immediate contribution of those assets to a new partnership. Reg. §1.708-1(b)(1)(iv). Withdrawals, admissions, and deaths of partners generally do not result in a closing of the partnership's *taxable year.* Reg. §1.706-1(c)(1). A division of a partnership's business among its partners may or may not result in a termination. §708(b)(2)(B). Finally, a termination closes the partnership's *taxable year.* A corporation's or partnership's distribution of a *partnership interest* is treated as an *exchange* for this purpose. §761(e). See *section 736 payments.*

termination, private foundation status   a series of four ways that a *private foundation* can lose its status, two taxable and two nontaxable. §507. See *tax-free termination, private foundations; taxable termination, private foundations.*

termination tax, private foundations   an *excise tax* imposed on *private foundations* equal to the lesser of (1) total *income, estate,* and *gift tax* benefits that accrued to its *substantial contributors,* and *income taxes* not paid by the *private foundation,* with interest, or (2) the foundation's net asset value. §507(c). The purpose is to *recapture* the *tax benefits* of *section 501(c)(3) organization* status at the time of a *taxable termination* of the private foundation.

term insurance   a form of *life insurance* protection for a particular number of years that expires without *cash surrender value* if the insured survives the period of coverage. For purposes of §79, which grants an *exemption* from taxation for *group-term life insurance* premiums for up to $50,000 worth of group-term life insurance coverage for *employees* and retirees, the *regulations* acknowledge that a *whole life insurance* policy can have a portion of its costs allocated to a deemed death benefit (i.e., term coverage) and other benefits, thereby permitting a portion of the premiums attributable to the constructive term coverage to be *excluded* from *gross income.* Reg. §1.79-1(d). See *current life insurance; protection, qualified plans; group-term life insurance.*

term loan   a loan for a fixed period. See *below-market loan.*

term loan, below-market loan   see *below-market loan.*

tertiary recovery method, deduction of injectants any method described in subparagraphs (1) through (9) of §212.78 of the June 1979 energy regulations (10 C.F.R. §212.78, as defined by §4996(b)(8)(C)), and any other method to provide tertiary enhanced recovery approved by the Secretary for purposes of the deductibility of tertiary injectants under §193. §193(b)(3). They are generally expensive, last-ditch efforts. They include, among other costs, miscible fluid displacement, steam-drive injection, various types of flooding techniques, or any other *IRS*-approved method.

testamentary   by will, as opposed to during life.

testamentary disposition   a transfer of property by will at death.

testamentary power of appointment   a *power of appointment* over property that can be exercised only through the will (i.e., on the death) of the holder.

testamentary trust   a *trust* established pursuant to a *decedent's* will.

testator   someone who makes a will.

testing date   each date on which the *loss corporation* is required to make a determination as to whether an *ownership change* has taken place. All computations of increases in percentage ownership are made as of this date, and any transactions that occur on that date are considered to occur at the same time. Reg. §1.382-2T(a)(2)(i)(B). See *neutrality principle.*

testing period, discriminatory employee benefit plan either the *plan year* or, at the election of an *employer* with numerous plans, a common 12-month period used to test for prohibited discrimination. The common year can also be used to identify *highly compensated employees.* §89(g)(2).

testing period, ownership change   the time period in which to determine that an *ownership change* has occurred and to determine whether a *person* is a *five-percent shareholder.* See §§382(g)(1) and (k)(7). It is the three-year period ending on the day of the *owner shift* involving a *five-percent shareholder* or the *equity structure shift.* §382(i)(1). The *Code* shortens the testing period under the following conditions: (1) when an ownership change occurs, a new testing period cannot begin before the next day; (2) the testing period may not start before the first day of the first *taxable year* from which the *corporation* has a *net operating loss* or *tax credit carryforward* to the first *post-change year*; (3) nor can the testing period begin before May 6, 1986, §382(i) and *Tax Reform Act of 1986* §621(f)(3). The testing period does not begin before the earlier of the first day of the first taxable year from which there is a carryforward of a loss or *excess credit,* or the first day of the taxable year in which the tested transaction occurs. §382(c)(3). A change in ownership or equity structure shift of a corporation can cause the *section 382 limitation* to apply to *net operating loss carryover* as well as other limits on the carryover of certain *tax attributes.* See *neutrality principle.*

theft   the unlawful taking and removal of the property of another person with the intention of keeping it. IRS Pub. No. 547, at 1 (1980). Such amounts are *deductible* in a *nonbusiness* or *noninvestment* context under §165(c)(3), are subject to favorable treatment under §§1231 and 1033(a), and have been interpreted to include more indirect takings such as blackmail, kidnapping, larceny, cheating by false pretenses, extortion, and embezzlement. The vital element is that the taking is an illegal taking under local law with the requisite criminal intent. Reg. §1.165-8(d); Rev. Rul. 72-112, 1972-1 C.B. 60. See *involuntary conversion; section 1231 assets.*

thin capitalization   see *thin incorporation.*

thin incorporation   the formation of a *corporation* whose capital structure is extremely debt-laden. As a result, a portion of the *debt* may be characterized as *stock.* §385. See *debt-equity rules.*

third-party contacts   a term used in the caption of §6110(d)(1) in reference to communications before the *IRS*'s issuance of a *written determination* from parties other than the IRS, the Chief of Staff of the *Joint Committee on Taxation,* or the party seeking the determination (or the *taxpayer representative*). The category of such persons must be publicly disclosed when the written determination is publicized; §6110(d)(3) provides a judicial channel to force disclosure of the identity of the third-party contact.

third-party recordkeeper   one of an exclusive list of parties likely to hold records of tax significance to another person. §7609. The list, in abbreviated form, consists of *banks, barter exchanges,* savings and loan associations, credit unions, consumer reporting agencies, *RICs,* persons extending credit with credit cards, brokers, lawyers, and accountants. It has been read to include general customers of telephone companies. Section 7609 grants *taxpayers* who are the subjects of the inquiry (noticees) a limited right to notice of *summonses* served on such recordkeepers (third-party recordkeepers) regardless of the recordkeeper's willingness to provide evidence. Section 7609 has exceptions to its coverage, especially for *John Doe summonses.* §7609(a)(4), (c)(2), and (g). Any person who is entitled to notice of a summons has the right to begin proceedings to quash the summons. §7609(b)(1), (2). See *summons.*

third-party sick pay   *sick pay* (defined in §3402(o)(2)(C)) that is not considered *wages* for *income tax withholding* purposes and is paid on behalf of the *employer* by a third party (e.g., an insurer). Such payors must submit *information returns* to the employer not later than January 15 of the next year and may have to engage in withholding on such pay at the payee's request. §§6051(f), 3401(o).

third-party summons an *IRS summons* issued on a *third-party recordkeeper*, pursuant to the authority of §7602, the general summons power. The power is confined by §7609. See *third-party recordkeeper*.

third-party taxes another name for taxes that are collected or withheld for payment to the Treasury Department. See §7202.

third-tier corporation, foreign tax credit a *foreign corporation* in which a *second-tier corporation* owns at least 10 percent of the voting *stock*. §902(b). As long as a *domestic corporation* has at least a five-percent indirect ownership interest in the third-tier corporation, the *deemed paid foreign tax credit* provisions consider the second-tier corporation to have received a *distribution* (along with any actual *dividends*) equal to its ratable share of the third-tier corporation's *creditable foreign taxes*. See *foreign tax credit.*

thirty-day letter a form letter issued by the *IRS* following an IRS *audit* that sets forth *proposed adjustments* of *federal* tax liability and explains the *taxpayer's* rights. The letter, which accompanies the *Revenue Agent's Report,* carries a statement that failure to respond within 30 days will result in a *statutory notice of deficiency* or other action such as denial of a *claim for refund or credit* or a notice of adjustment. Taxpayers may (1) do nothing and await a *ninety-day letter (statutory notice of deficiency)*, which operates as a ticket to the *Tax Court*; (2) pay the asserted liability and perhaps file a *claim for refund or credit*; or (3) inform the *District Director* of disagreement and request an *Appeals Conference,* in which case if the amount in controversy resulting from a *field examination* exceeds $2,500, a written *protest* is required. Reg. §601.105. Such letters come in various forms, but their principal function is to notify the taxpayer of the conclusion of the audit and of the proposed adjustments.

thirty-one-point five-year nonresidential real property tangible *section 1250 property* (basically *real estate*) other than *residential rental property* (§167(j)) or property with a *class life* of less than 27.5 years. §168(e)(2)(B). This class of *recovery property* is the product of the *Tax Reform Act of 1986.*

thirty-percent charity the successor of the *twenty-percent charity*, except for certain contributions of *capital gain* property under §170(b)(1)(D) and gifts to *nonoperating foundations* under §170(b)(1)(B)(i). See *twenty-percent charity.*

thirty-percent PCM another name for the *percentage of completion, capitalized cost method* after 1987.

thirty-percent tax a flat rate tax that, in the absence of an applicable *tax treaty,* is imposed on *interest, rents,* and an extensive list of *fixed or determinable annual or periodical gains, profits, and income* from *United States* sources paid to *nonresident aliens* and *foreign corporations* on nonbusiness income. The tax is imposed by §§871 and 881 and is *withheld* at the source under the rules of §§1441 and 1442. The tax is prospectively repealed for certain new interest-bearing obligations, apparently to help finance vast federal deficits. See §§1441(c)(9), 1442(a). See *portfolio interest.*

thirty-three and one-third percent of support test, exempt organizations a standard used to determine whether an *exempt organization* is publicly supported. That is, if at least one-third of its total *support* normally comes from government units and the public, then the test is met. Reg. §1.170A-9(e)(2). *Charitable contributions* to such organizations qualify for generous limits on amounts *deductible* by contributors in any one year. A similar test is used as part of a two-pronged test that can free an organization from *private foundation* status. §509(a)(2)(A). See *fifty-percent charities.*

Thor Power rule a doctrine from the Supreme Court's decision in *Thor Power Tool v. United States,* 439 U.S. 522 (1979), the gist of which is that the value of excess *inventory* cannot be written down to a net realizable value unless it has been scrapped, sold, or offered for sale at a reduced price. The rule is important for *taxpayers* using *inventory accounting.*

threat or imminence of condemnation, involuntary conversions a status generally considered to exist when a property owner is informed, either orally or in writing, by a representative of a governmental body or public official authorized to acquire property for public use, that such body or official has decided to acquire the owner's property and the property owner has reasonable grounds to believe, from the information conveyed by such representative, that the necessary steps to condemn the property will be instituted if a voluntary sale is not arranged. The same general rule applies where a *taxpayer* obtains information through a news medium as to a decision to acquire the owner's property for public use, provided the owner obtains confirmation from a representative of the governmental body or public official involved as to the correctness of the published report and has reasonable grounds to believe from the published report and its confirmation that the necessary steps to condemn the property will be instituted if a voluntary sale is not arranged. Rev. Rul. 63-221, 1963-2 C.B. 332. *Gains* on property *disposed* of under such circumstances (including transfers other than to the condemning authority and transfers of economically interrelated property) may qualify for *tax deferral* under §1033. See *condemnation; involuntary conversion; rollover, proceeds of involuntary conversion.*

three-cornered exchange   a multiple-party *exchange* of *trade, business,* or *investment* property designed to qualify as a *like-kind exchange* under §1031. For example (of its simplest form) A, owner of Blackacre (an investment property that has greatly appreciated), agrees with B that B will acquire Whiteacre from C. At the closing, A and B will exchange Whiteacre and Blackacre. A receives the benefits of *tax deferral* under §1031 if A meets the other requirements of §1031. These exchanges need not be simultaneous; however, the nonsimultaneous three-cornered exchange was controversial, especially where the property to be exchanged (Whiteacre in the illustration) had not been identified when the other property was transferred. The deferral period is now limited. See §1031(a)(3).

three-family corporation   see *family corporation.*

three-percent rule, accrued benefits   a rule relating to *defined benefit plans* which generally provides that a *participant* must annually accrue at least 3 percent of the benefit which would be payable to someone who begins *participation* at the earliest entry date and continues to be *employed* until age 65 or normal retirement age, whichever is earlier. §411(b)(1)(A). The rule is one of three alternate minimums, only one of which needs to be satisfied in order for the plan not to be disqualified on this ground.

three-seven vesting   an alternative minimum *vesting schedule* under which a *participant* must be fully vested after seven years and have 20 percent vesting on attaining three *years of service.* §411(a)(2)(B). Such a vesting schedule can satisfy the requirements relating to vesting of benefits under *qualifed plans* or *trusts.* See *vesting schedules.*

three-year average test   a test used to determine if a *personal service corporation* satisfies a minimum distribution requirement in order to permit its payments to owner-employees to be fully deductible despite having made a *section 444 election.* The amount determined under the three-year average test is the applicable percentage multiplied by the *adjusted taxable income* for the deferral period of the applicable election year. The "applicable percentage" is the percentage (not over 95 percent) determined by dividing (a) the *applicable amounts* during the three taxable years of the corporation (or, if fewer, the *taxable year* the corporation has been in existence) immediately preceding the applicable election year; by (b) the adjusted taxable income of such corporation for such three taxable years (or, if fewer, the taxable years of existence). See *personal service corporation; taxable year; preceding-year test; tiered structure; tiered structures.*

three-year property   *tangible personal property* with a *class life* of four years or less. §168(c), (e). It is one of the eight classes of *recovery property* in effect after 1986 and includes two-year-old race horses and older horses, but excludes autos and light trucks. See *accelerated cost recovery system (ACRS).*

three-year rule, collapsible corporations   a shorthand term for the content of §341(b)(3), which provides that *section 341 assets* exclude property held at least three years. As a result, patient corporate *taxpayers* can often avoid the *collapsible corporation* rules by aging the property.

three-year vesting   a permissible *vesting schedule* of the *cliff vesting* variety, under which a *participant's accrued benefit* is fully nonforfeitable after three years. Such schedules allow the plan to demand that the *employee* be at least age 21 or complete two *years of service* (whichever occurs later) in order to participate. §401(a)(1)(B)(i); Reg. §1.410(a)-3(a)(2). More relaxed rules apply to educational organizations. §410(a)(1)(B)(i). This form of vesting is also an alternate vesting schedule that a *top-heavy plan* may use. §§416(b)(1)(A), 410(c)(1).

threshold underpayment   see *large corporate underpayment.*

thrift plan   a type of elective *profit-sharing plan* that, if chosen by an *employee,* provides for mandatory employee *contributions,* usually through *withholding,* of a uniform specified percentage of salary. The *employer* then matches the contributions, either dollar for dollar, or by some specified proportion, but only from profits.

thrift savings fund   an *employee benefit plan* for federal *employers* as defined in 5 U.S.C. §84 to which an *employee* may contribute up to 10 percent of his or her base pay. Amounts contributed to the plan are not includible in *gross income* for the year of contribution, but they are taxable when distributed from the plan. §7701(j).

throwback credit, trust beneficiary   a tax *credit* for *federal income taxes* paid by a *trust,* available to a *beneficiary* of a trust who is subject to taxation under the *throwback rules.* §667. See *throwback rules; throwback tax.*

throwback rules   an anti-*tax avoidance* arrangement built into §§665–668, the effect of which is to tax *beneficiaries* of *complex trusts* on delayed *distributions* of earnings, other than *capital gains,* roughly as if the beneficiary had received the earnings on a current basis. In order to avoid double taxation, however, beneficiaries are entitled to a *throwback credit* to reflect the tax burden previously imposed on the trust. The general pattern is first to determine *undistributed net income* (UNI), roughly meaning accumulations of *ordinary income* in prior years, less *federal income taxes* imposed on the trust for such years. §665(a). Second, one determines the extent to which there has been an *accumulation distribution* in the present year, basically meaning distributions in excess of current *income*. §665(b). The next step is to presume that accumulation distributions are attributable to the earliest years in which there was an accumulation (i.e., "throw them back"), to the extent of UNI in that throwback year. The amount thrown back is imaginarily increased by allocable taxes imposed on the trust's *ordinary income* (but not by more than what the *beneficiary* would have paid if the beneficiary had been paid all current income in the throwback year). The foregoing is a sketch only. The throwback rules contain numerous exceptions and complexities. Because of the compression of the tax rate schedules for fiduciary taxpayers beginning in 1987, there is little incentive for trustees to accumulate income in order to reduce income taxes.

throwback tax   a tax imposed on *beneficiaries* of *complex trusts* who receive *distributions* of *ordinary income* accumulated in prior years. See *throwback rules*. See *throwback rules*.

throwback year   a year to which *accumulation distributions* of complex trusts are attributed. See *throwback rules*.

tiered structure   a *partnership, S corporation,* or *personal service corporation* (PSC) is considered a member of a tiered structure if (1) the partnership, S corporation, or PSC directly owns any portion of a "*deferral entity,*" or (2) a deferral entity directly owns any portion of the partnership, S corporation, or PSC. A "deferral entity" is a partnership, S corporation, PSC, or trust. In the case of an *affiliated group of corporations* filing a *consolidated return* that is treated as a personal service corporation pursuant to Reg. §1.441-4T (i), the affiliated group is considered to be a single deferral entity. A *grantor trust* is not a deferral entity. Under an anti-abuse rule, a partnership, S corporation, or PSC is considered a member of a tiered structure if the entity or related taxpayers have organized or reorganized their ownership structure or operations for the principal purpose of obtaining a significant unintended tax benefit from making or continuing a *section 444 election.* An affiliated group of personal service corporations filing a consolidated income tax return is a single entity for purposes of determining whether a taxpayer is part of a tiered structure. Reg. §1.444-2T(b)(2)(i). If an entity is a member of a tiered structure, the entity cannot make or continue a section 444 election unless the *same taxable year exception* provided in Reg. §1.444-2T(e) applies. Whether an entity is a member of a tiered structure for a particular taxable year depends on whether the partnership, S corporation, or PSC is a member of a tiered structure on the last day of the required taxable year ending within that year. If a particular taxable year does not include the last day of the required taxable

year for that year, the entity is not considered a member of a tiered structure for the year. See *downstream de minimis rule; upstream de minimis rule.*

tiered structures   generally undefined, but clearly implying multilevel ownership, for example, a *partnership* which is a *partner* in another partnership. The term is defined in the regulations under §444 as a situation in which a partnership, *S corporation,* or *personal service corporation* which directly owns any part of, or is directly owned in whole or in part by, a *deferral entity* (same three entities plus *grantor trusts*) at the end of the deferral entity's *required taxable year.* See *section 444 election.*

tier partnerships   *partnerships* that contain partnerships as *partners.* Where there is only one layer of partnership partners, the partnership is often referred to as a two-tier partnership. Because both partnerships are conduits for tax purposes, the structure assures that the character of the earnings and debt of the bottom-tier partnership will be reflected in the top tier.

tier system   a construct built into the *Code* that classifies amounts received by *beneficiaries* of *estates* and *complex trusts* as *gross income* or *capital,* through the creation of an arbitrary system of priorities. The first tier consists of *income for the taxable year required to be distributed currently* (so-called *first-tier distributions*); those amounts are the first to offset the *distributable net income* (DNI) of the *entity* and are taxable to the so-called *first-tier beneficiaries* (those entitled to such amounts). If DNI exceeds such mandatory distributions, then the balance is taxed to *second-tier beneficiaries* (those persons receiving other distributions). For example, assume A and B are beneficiaries of a complex trust who are always entitled to $5,000 of current income annually. The trust distributes $6,000 to A, $5,000 to B, and $1,000 to C, a *beneficiary* who may receive only discretionary amounts. If the trust has DNI of $10,000; the extra $2,000 is equally shared by A and C. The result will be $5,000 each of *taxable income* to A and B. The $2,000 balance goes untaxed. On the other hand, if DNI had been $12,000, then A would be taxed on $6,000, B on $5,000, and C on $1,000. §662. B is in the first tier only, A is in both, and C is in the second only. The alternative systems could be proportional sharing of the taxable income, or the prior, and even more complex, three-tier system.

timber   generally undefined. The subject can arise with respect to (1) *depletion,* where the focal point is standing trees more than one year old; (2) *disposal* of timber *with a retained economic interest,* for which there is a fragmentary definition; and (3) the *hypothetical sale election,* where the focus is again on standing trees more than one year old. The lack of a definition is likely attributable to the fairly obvious meaning of the term. The term generally applies to trees usable for producing lumber, pulp, or other wood products, and evergreen trees over six years old when severed at the roots (i.e., most Christmas trees), but not forest products such as tops, limbs, and trees used for landscaping (i.e., those pulled up by the roots). Reg §1.613-2(e)(3) (depletion); Rev. Rul. 56-434, 1956-2 C.B. 334 (tops and limbs remain timber if attached to a standing tree). See *disposal with a retained economic interest.*

timber account   an account established for the purpose of *depletion* of *timber.* Generally, each account contains all the merchantable timber in a particular *block,* describing the number of units (cords, board feet, etc.) and their values and bases, periodically adjusted over time by additions, growth, and other changes. Reg. §1.611-3(d) and (e).

timber cruise   a timber owner's investigation of timber property to determine the logical cutting areas, the trees that should be cut, the growth rates, and the like. Such cruises are considered a currently *deductible business expense* under §162 and should presumably qualify for current deductibility under §212 if the timber is held for *gain*-seeking activities that fall short of being a *business.*

timber, disposal with retained economic interest see *disposal with a retained economic interest.*

timely mailing rule   a rule to the effect that timely mailing is timely *filing.* Specifically, §7502 provides that if a claim, *return,* statement, or document must be filed with the *IRS* or *Tax Court,* or if any payment must be made on or by a specified date, then, if the envelope containing the document, etc., is delivered by mail, with a United States postmark (including a private frank, according to some authority), registration, or certification date not later than the due date, the document, etc., is deemed timely filed or paid, provided it is accurately addressed. Private mail carriers do not qualify. Foreign postmarks are entitled to the same respect if they are the official foreign postmark. Tax deposits to Federal Reserve banks do not enjoy this benefit unless they are postmarked at least two days before the deadline. §7502(e). See *filing, return.*

time of participation, qualified retirement plans the time when an *employee* who has met the *minimum age and service requirements* of §410(a)(1) must commence *participation* in the *retirement plan.* The employee must begin participation in the plan upon the earlier of (1) the first day of the *first plan* year following the date that the employee satisfied the *minimum age and service requirements* (i.e., on the plan's anniversary date), or (2) six months following the date the employee satisfied the minimum age and service requirements. §410(a)(4). Note that since the commencement of participation must be the earlier of the two above-stated time periods, the best way to meet this

requirement is to have two participation dates, for example, January 1 and July 1.

timeshare   for purposes of *installment method,* a timeshare right to use or a timeshare ownership interest in residential *real property* for not more than six weeks per year, or a right to use specified campgrounds for recreational purposes. It includes timeshare rights to use, or timeshare ownership interests in, property held by the spouse, children, grandchildren, or parents of on an *individual.* §453(l)(2)(B). Such interests are not subject to the special *interest* charge rules for *nondealer real property installment obligations.* §453A(b)(4).

time-sharing   a system for dividing the *occupancy* of property, usually resort property, among a number of owners, giving each a specific time of occupancy in each year for a number of years. The legal forms by which a time-sharing arrangement is created can vary. According to the *regulations,* for purposes of the *vacation home rules,* it does not matter whether each owner owns the property outright during the rental period or instead owns an individual interest throughout the year. See Reg. §1.280A-3(f)(2). Such arrangements are easily subjected to the vacation home rule's limitation on *losses* because use by a co-owner is considered *personal use* by each owner. Reg. §1.280A-3(f)(3).

time value of money   a reference to the fact that money paid or received in the future is worth less than money paid or received today. The concept is of growing importance in drafting the *Code.*

tips, allocation of employee   if tipped *employees* in *large food or beverage establishments* do not report tips in an amount equaling at least 8 percent of the establishment's gross receipts, the *employer* is to allocate the difference between 8 percent and the amount actually reported. *Employers* may allocate in one of two ways: (1) according to an agreement with the employee; or (2) in accordance with Reg. §31.6053-3(f)(1)(iv). The employer may allocate tips based upon the gross receipts attributable to the employee in a payroll period if the establishment employs less than 25 full-time employees or their equivalent during a *payroll period.*

Title 11 case   a proceeding under the bankruptcy provisions of the United States Code, 11 U.S.C. §101 et seq. (1981 Supp. V). §108(d)(2). Provided the court has jurisdiction over the *taxpayer* and the taxpayer is released from indebtedness under a court-approved plan or by a grant by the court, *the discharge of indebtedness income* is *excluded* from *gross income* in such cases, even if the debtor is rendered *solvent.* §108(a)(1)(A). The price exacted is a reduction of *tax attributes.*

Title 11 or similar case   a case under *Title 11* of the United States Code, of a receivership, foreclosure, or similar proceeding in a *federal* or *state* court. §268(a)(3)(A). The term is used for purposes of §108(e)(8) relating to certain *workouts* and to a *Type G reorganization*. In the case of Type G reorganizations, a transfer of assets is treated as made in a Title 11 or similar case only if the *corporation* is under the court's jurisdiction and only if the transfer is pursuant to a court-approved plan or reorganization. §368(a)(3)(B). See also §312(b)(2) (*earnings and profits*—same definition), 351(e)(2) (same definition for *section 351 transactions*), 382(l)(5) (*neutrality principle*—same definition), 542(c)(9) (*personal holding companies*—same definition), and 815 (*insurance companies*, certain transitional rules regarding certain *distributions*—same definition). See *Title 11 case*.

title-holding companies *corporations* or *trusts* organized exclusively to take direct title (e.g., not as a tenant) to *real property* and related *personal property*, collect income therefrom, and to remit such income (less any *expenses*) to one or more exempt *section 501(c)(3) organizations; qualified pension, profit-sharing, and stock bonus trusts*; or governments. Such entities are treated as *exempt organizations*, provided they have not more than 35 owners or one class of *stock* or *beneficial interests*. Title-holding companies can hold the stock of a *qualified subsidiary*. The title-holding companies' *disqualified owners* are taxed on *unrelated trade or business* income passed up from the title-holding company. §501(c)(25). It is distinct from a pure *nominee*. See *acquisition indebtedness*.

title passage test a standard used to determine whether income from the sale of goods is *United States* or *foreign source income*, focusing on the place where rights, title, and interest (realistically meaning *beneficial ownership*) was transferred. §861(a)(6); Reg. §1.861-7(c).

tobacco tax an *excise tax* on tobacco products of all sorts, including paper and cigarette tubes. §5701.

toll to suspend, used in reference to the running of *statutes of limitations*.

tools see *small hand tools exception*.

top-hat plan another name for a *deferred compensation plan* maintained primarily for a select group of management and highly compensated *employees*. See *ERISA* §§201(2), 301(a)(3), and 401 (a)(1) for exemptions for such plans.

top-heavy group a group of otherwise *qualified plans* that is combined for testing standards (an aggregation group) with respect to which, as of the *determination date*, the sum of the present value of the accumulated *accrued benefits* for the *key employees* under all the *defined benefit plans* in the group and the sum of the account balances of the key employees under all the *defined contribution plans* in the group exceed 60 percent of the aggregate accumulated accrued benefits and account balances for the group. §416(g)(2). See *top-heavy plan*.

top-heavy plan one of two types of *qualified plans* that are skewed in favor of elite *participants*. The first is a *defined benefit plan*, if either the *present value* of accumulated *accrued benefits* for *key employees* exceeds 60 percent of the present value of all accumulated accrued benefits for all *employees* under the plan, or if the plan is part of a *top-heavy group*. §416(g)(1)(A). The second type of plan is a *defined contribution plan*, if either the total account balances of key employees exceed 60 percent of the total account balances of all employees under the plan, or if the plan is part of a top-heavy group of plans. In both cases, the tests are applied annually as of the *determination date*. Top-heavy plans must meet stricter requirements as to *vesting*, minimum benefits, includible *compensation*, and *distributions* in order to be *qualified plans*.

top paid group someone who, for the year, was in the top 20 percent of *employees*, by *participant's compensation* (§415(c)(3) meaning) paid for the year. §414(q)(4). The term is used for purposes of determining whether someone is a *highly compensated employee*. One disregards so-called *excluded employees*, meaning employees (1) who have not completed six months of service; (2) who normally work under $17\frac{1}{2}$ hours per week; (3) who normally work six months or less during any year; (4) under age 21; (5) included in a unit of employees covered under a collective bargaining agreement; and (6) *nonresident aliens* who receive no United States source earned income. See *participant's compensation; highly compensated employee*.

total contract price the *selling price* reduced by any *qualifying indebtedness* assumed by or taken subject to the buyer, which is not greater than the seller's *basis* in the property. Reg. §15a.453-1(b)(2)(iii). The total contract price excludes the value of *like-kind property* received in a *like-kind exchange*. §453(f)(6)(A). Dealers in personal property can very rarely use the installment method. The total contract price is used to calculate the *gross profit ratio* in connection with an installment sale. See *installment sale method; sale on the installment plan*.

total taxable amount a term used to describe the portion of a *lump-sum distribution* from a *qualified plan* that qualifies for favorable tax treatment. It is derived by subtracting *employee* contributions and net *unrealized appreciation on employer securities*. §§72(b) and (c), 402(e)(4)(D) and (J). See *five-year forward averaging*.

total unstated interest the excess of payments due under a deferred payment contract (except *interest*) over the *discounted present value* of future payments under the contract, using the *Treasury Department's* discounting figures then in effect (9 percent simple interest; 6 percent simple interest for certain intrafamily land sales). §483(b). The excess is spread over the life of the contract as payments are made. §483(a). For details, see *imputed interest.*

Totten trust a *trust* formed under New York law, whereby the *grantor* deposits his or her own funds in a bank account in his or her own name as *trustee* for a *beneficiary.* The grantor retains control and ownership of the funds until death, or completes the gift by some unequivocal act during his or her lifetime. Such trusts are revocable at will by the grantor until completion of the gift and may be revoked in the grantor's will. Where the grantor does not complete the gift during lifetime, he or she is treated as the owner of the trust, and any income it derives must be included in the grantor's *gross income* for *federal income tax* purposes. It is typically used to avoid probate. See, generally, §§676(a), 671; Rev. Rul. 62-148, 1962-2 C.B. 153. Most states recognize the Totten trust.

traced debt *debt* directly attributable to particular *production expenditures.* Traced debt takes priority under the *uniform capitalization rules.* §263A(f)(2)(A)(i); Reg. §1.263A-1T(b)(2)(iv)(B). One uses the rules of Reg. §1.163-8T to do the tracing. If it is not traced debt, one uses the *avoided cost method.* Only *eligible debt,* as defined under §163(h), is subject to the tracing approach.

tract of real property a single piece of *real property.* Two or more contiguous pieces of real property are considered a single tract, even though they may be divided by a road, street, or stream. The *taxpayer* may have acquired them over a period of time and own them separately, jointly, as a *partner,* or in any combination of such forms of ownership. Reg. §1.1237-1(g). See *subdivision, real estate.*

tract or parcel of land, depletion a term that describes the physical scope of the land to which the *taxpayer's* interest relates, as opposed to the nature of his or her rights or interests in the land. All contiguous areas (even though separately described) included in a single conveyance or grant or in separate conveyances or grants at the same time from the same owner constitute a single separate tract or parcel of land. Areas included in separate conveyances or grants (whether or not at the same time) from separate owners are separate tracts or parcels of land, even though the areas described may be contiguous. Reg. §1.614-1(a)(3). Taxpayers' claims to *depletion deductions* are determined in part by reference to tracts or parcels of land in defining the term "*property.*" See *property, depletion.*

trade an activity carried on by a *taxpayer* with a reasonable degree of regularity, continuity, and profit motivation so as to qualify the activity for various tax benefits such as *expense deductions* under §162, *depreciation* deductions under §167, or *cost recovery* under §168. The *Code* uses the term "*trade or business,*" but the courts and the *IRS* are not concerned with distinguishing one from the other. Generally, the term "*trade*" suggests a professional's or artisan's activity, such as practicing medicine as opposed to a capital intensive activity, e.g., manufacturing goods. A taxpayer need not hold him- or herself out as engaged in selling goods or services to the public in order to be engaged in a *trade or business.*

trade associations see *business leagues.*

trade date the date on which a customer's order to *buy* or sell securities on an organized securities exchange is executed. The customer's *holding period* begins one day after the trade date and ends on the day the sale order is executed. Rev. Rul. 70-598, 1970-2 C.B. 168. This pattern involves settlement the "regular way," that is, with actual payment deferred usually for five days. *Cash method taxpayers* may instead order the transaction to be a cash or next-day sale, i.e., with settlement the next day such that, in the case of sales near year-end, the transaction can be reported in the present year. Cash method taxpayers who sell at a *loss* recognize their losses on the trade date. Rev. Rul. 70-344, 1970-2 C.B. 50.

trademark any word, name, symbol, device, or combination thereof adopted and used by a manufacturer or merchant to identify his or her goods and distinguish them from those goods manufactured or sold by others. Reg. §1.1253-2(b). Section 1253 provides clarity as to the tax consequences of transfers of trademarks. It is not clear whether §1253 applies to other types of marks that are dealt with in the Lanham Act, such as service marks (marks used to identify and distinguish services rather than goods), certification marks, or collective marks. The mark need not be registered or registerable.

trademark, trade name, and franchise expenditures a transfer of a franchise, trademark, or trade name is generally not a sale or exchange of a capital asset. §1253. A business expense deduction can be taken for amounts paid or incurred on selling or transferring a trademark, trade name, or franchise that is contingent on its productivity, use, or disposition. §1253, Prop. Reg. 1.1253-(1)(c)(1). However, the timing of the deduction will depend upon the form of payment. The grant of a trademark or trade name results in a deduction for payments made as a business expense. A noncontingent lump-sum payment of up to $100,000 is capitalized and may be amortized over the shorter of the agreement period or 10 years. Noncontingent lump-sum payments exceeding $100,000 must be capitalized and may be amortized over 25 years.

trade name any name used by a manufacturer or merchant to identify or designate a particular *trade or business,* or the name or title lawfully adopted and used by a person or organization engaged in a trade or business.

Reg. §1.1253-2(c). See Lanham Act, 15 U.S.C. §1127 (1976). Section 1253 provides clarity as to the tax consequences of transfers of trade names.

trade or business   generally any activity regularly and continuously undertaken for a *bona fide* profit (even if unreasonable, such as trying to invent an antigravity machine), other than the activities of an investor trading in securities. The *Code* expressly includes performance of the functions of a public office. §7701(a)(26). It does not call for dealing with more than one other person. Sometimes the tax law requires that the enterprise contain every economic element, including such items as a billings and disbursement function. See, e.g., Reg §1.989(a)-1(c) (part of definition of *qualified business unit*). See *trade; business.*

trade or business expenses   *expenses* associated with a *trade or business.* See *business expense.*

trade or business, self-employment tax   same as for purposes of the *business expense deduction* of §162, but excluding the performance of service by an *individual* as an *employee,* with exceptions discussed below. The following are not a *trade or business:* (1) the performance of service by an individual as an employee or employee representative covered under the Railroad Retirement System; (2) the performance of the functions of a public office, with certain exceptions; (3) the performance of service by an *individual* during the period when an exemption from self-employment tax for members of certain *religious orders* who have taken a vow of poverty is effective; (4) service by a duly ordained, commissioned, or licensed minister of a church in the exercise of his or her ministry or by a member of a religious order in the exercise of duties required by the order; (5) service by an individual in the exercise of his or her profession as a Christian Science practitioner. §1402(c). It includes part-time work. IRS Pub. No. 533 (1989), p. 1. Certain employees are deemed engaged in a trade or business for this purpose, namely: (1) newspaper sellers under age 18; (2) sharecroppers; (3) *citizens of the United States* in their capacities as representatives of foreign governments, certain foreign instrumentalities, and *international organizations*; (4) services described in (4) above; (5) certain *fishing crew members* (persons working small fishing boats for a share of the catch); and (6) people who perform religious work for a church or qualified church-controlled organization which has elected out of coverage on the grounds of opposition to insurance. §1402(c)(2). Income is not taxable as self-employment income unless it is derived from a trade or business.

trade or business within the United States   generally, any personal service performed in the *United States* or any other activity within the United States that is regular and continuous enough to constitute the conduct of a *trade or business* in the United States under general Code

standards, whether performed directly or through resident *agents* or *employees.* Foreign persons are also considered engaged in a United States trade or business through *partnerships* so engaged. §875(1). Although the concept takes several expressions (e.g., engaged in business in the United States, conduct of a trade or business in the United States), its meaning seems constant. See *effectively connected income; partnership withholding tax.*

trade or service receivable   any *account receivable* or evidence of indebtedness from the disposition by a related *person* (i.e., a *related taxpayer* under §267, and a *United States shareholder* under §915(b) and any *related taxpayer*) of *inventory* or the performance of services by a related person. §864(d)(3). For its significance, see *related person factoring.*

trader   one who purchases and sells property through brokers, regardless of volume, with the result that *gains* and *losses* are *capital* in nature. §1221(1).

trade show   see *qualified convention and trade show activity.*

trade union   see *business leagues.*

trading stamp company   an *accrual method taxpayer* that is principally engaged in the *business* of selling trading stamps or premium coupons redeemable for at least one year from the date of sale, provided the taxpayer fulfills certain requirements described in Reg. §1.451-4(a)(2). If these requirements are met, then the taxpayer subtracts from gross receipts the *cost* of merchandise, cash, and other property used for redemptions in the *taxable year* plus any additions to a *reserve* for future redemptions during the taxable years. Reg. §1.451-4(a)(1).

trafficking in loss corporations   a disparaging characterization of entering into transactions to garner *tax benefits* associated with acquisitions and mergers involving *corporations* with histories of business *losses.* The area is principally controlled by §§269 *(acquisition to evade or avoid taxes),* 382, and 383 (limitations on *carryovers* of *tax attributes*). See *neutrality principle; section 382 limitation.*

transaction entered into for a profit   the acquisition or change in use of property with a sincere view to a subsequent profit from use or resale. It is the basis upon which *individuals, partners, estates,* and *trusts* can claim *losses* with respect to property other than *casualty, theft,* and *trade or business-related losses.* §165(b) and (c)(2). The usual inquiry is whether the *taxpayer* subjectively intended to earn a profit as a result of a later *disposition* of purchased property (e.g., a purchase of artworks for *investment*). Also, converting property to rental use can qualify as a transaction (leasing) entered into for a profit, so as to qualify post-conversion losses (e.g., conversion of a home into a rental property). Reg. §1.165-9(b) (conversion; *basis* adjustment). Property acquired by *gift* or *inheritance* can also qualify, if the recipient did not use it for personal purposes.

transaction method, foreign currency transactions a method for reporting currency *gains* and *losses* under which each transaction is reported on the basis of currency exchange rates prevailing at the time of each transaction.

transferable, restricted property capable of being *transferred* to someone other than the original transferor (the *employer* in most cases), provided the transferee's rights are not subject to a *substantial risk of forfeiture*. §83(c)(2); Reg. §1.83-3(d). If the holder who provided the services can sell, assign, or pledge his or her interest in the property to someone other than the original transferor (e.g., employer), and if the transferee is not required to give up the property or its value if the event triggering forfeiture occurs, then the property is transferable. Reg. §1.83-3(d). Once property given for services is transferable, it is taxable to the payee (holder) and *deductible* (if at all) to the payor. §83(a) and (h). See *transfer, restricted property rules.*

transferability, restricted property rules see *transfer, restricted property rules.*

transferee, broker's return see *real estate reporting person.*

transferee liability the liability of a *transferee* of a *taxpayer* who incurred an *income, gift,* or *estate tax* liability. Section 6901 provides a procedure whereby the *IRS* may be able to assert the transferor's liabilities against the transferee (including *interest* and penalties), but it does not in itself cause liability; rather, actual liability must result from substantive law, which may include a contractual agreement between the parties under which the transferee makes him- or herself personally liable for the transferor's tax liabilities; a *state* statute; or a transfer in which the transferor was rendered *insolvent*. Section 6901 generally requires the IRS to use the same *assessment* and collection techniques against the transferee as it would have used against the transferor. Transfers that are fraudulent or result in insolvency according to state law are common bases for imposing transferee liability. Fiduciaries who distribute income or property without paying applicable taxes are also subject to §6901. Second transferees may also be reached. Section 6901(c) grants the IRS an extra year to *assess deficiencies* against transferees and an additional year in the case of retransfers. The list of transferees is extensive. §6901(h); Reg. §301.6901-1(b). Buyers who pay full value are generally not included. The concept is altogether distinct from *fiduciary liability*. See *fraudulent conveyances.*

transferee's broker see *real estate reporting person.*

transfer for less than adequate consideration the basis on which *gift taxes* are imposed. See *full and adequate consideration in money or money's worth; gift, gift taxes.*

transfer for value rule a limit on the general rule of §101 permitting *life insurance proceeds* to be excluded from *gross* income, the gist of which is that if a *life insurance policy* is disposed of, in whole or in part, for valuable consideration, then the transferee may *exclude* from *gross income* only consideration paid for the policy, plus *net premiums* later paid by the transferee. The limitation is, in turn, confined by exceptions for transfers in which the transferee takes the transferor's *basis* in whole or in part and transfers to the insured, a *partner* of the insured, or a *corporation* in which the insured is an officer or shareholder. See Reg. §1.101-1(b).

transfer incident to divorce a transfer of cash or *property* between former *spouses* which is *incident to divorce*. Such transfers have much the same *federal income tax* status as *gifts*. §1041. See *incident to divorce.*

transfer pricing methodology a taxpayer-proposed method for determining appropriate prices in transactions between related organizations, *trades,* or *businesses* under §482. Such methodologies should following the principles of §482. Provision of an appropriate transfer pricing methodology is required in connection with getting an *advance pricing agreement* from the *IRS* that will protect the pricing system from IRS examination under §482. See Rev. Procs. 91-22, 1991 I.R.B.; 91-23, 1991 I.R.B.; and 91-24, 1991 I.R.B. See *advance pricing agreement; reallocation of income and deductions by Commissioner.*

transferred basis *basis* of *property* determined by reference to the basis of property in the hands of the transferor. For example, under §1015 a *donee's* basis in property received by *gift* is the *donor's* (the transferor's) basis, with an adjustment for gift taxes paid. Section 1223(2) tacks the transferor's *holding period* to the transferee's where the transferee takes the transferor's *basis* in the property, other than by death, in which case §1223(11) gives the transferee an automatic *long-term holding period*. The term is descriptive rather than analytical. It is synonymous with *carryover basis*. See *tacking of holding periods.*

transferred basis property *property* received in a transaction in which the transferee's *basis* in *property* received is determined at least in part by the *grantor's, donor's,* or other transferor's basis. §7701(a)(43). This recent term is used in connection with calculating *market discount* or *original issue discount*. Such property can, among others, arise in corporate liquidations under former §333 and in *nonliquidating distributions* of *partnership* property. §1276(c)(3). See also *exchanged basis property.*

transfer, restricted property rules   a change in the *beneficial interest* in *property* (taking into account *nonlapse restrictions*), other than grants of *options* transfers of property that will be returned, or transfer solely for *nonrecourse liabilities* (at least until payments are made). The *regulations* observe several factors to evaluate the realism of a putative transfer. Reg. §1.83-3(a)(1)-(6). The ability to freely pledge or otherwise dispose of an interest in the property to someone other than the transferor results in *transferability,* unless the transferee is subject to a *substantial risk of forfeiture.* See *restricted property rules.*

transfer taking effect at death   any transfer of an interest in *property* from the *decedent*, in *trust* or otherwise (except to the extent for *full and adequate consideration in money or money's worth*), if three conditions are met: (1) possession or enjoyment of the property could have been obtained only by surviving the decedent; (2) the decedent had retained a *reversionary interest* in the event the *donee* predeceased the transferor; and (3) the value of the reversionary interest immediately before the decedent's death exceeded five percent, actuarially determined, of the value of the entire property. Reg. §20.2037-1. Property so transferred is includible in a decedent's *gross estate.*

transfer tax   a term often used to describe the *federal estate* or *gift tax,* both of which can be viewed as *excise taxes* on the transfer of *property*. It is also used with the more obvious meaning of any tax imposed on a transfer of property, such as the New York stock transfer tax.

transfer to avoid income tax   see *excise tax, transfers to foreign corporations, trusts, estates, and partnerships.*

transfers to controlled corporations   generally, transactions in which *corporations* are created or infused with further property in exchange for *stock* or *securities*. If the requirements of §351 are met, the transfers can be tax-free to the *shareholders* and the *corporation*. See *section 351 transactions.*

transition rules   generally, interim rules that apply while a law is being phased in.

transitory allocation   a type of *allocation* of a *partner's distributive share* which fails the requirement that allocations be *substantial*. Reg. §1.704-1(b)(2)(c). It arises where a *partnership agreement* provides for the possibility that one or more allocations (the "original allocation(s)") will be largely offset by one or more other allocations (the "offsetting allocation(s)"). It applies to such offsetting allocations only if two conditions are met, the first of which is satisfied if when the allocation agreement is agreed on, there is a strong likelihood that the net increases and decreases in the *partner's capital accounts* for the years in which the allocations apply will not differ substantially from the net increases and decreases in their absence. The second condition is met if the total tax liability of the partners will be less than it would have been had the allocations not been made. See *substantial economic effect test.*

Transmittal Memorandum   see *Technical Advice Memorandum.*

transportation benefits   employees may exclude up to $60 per month in employer-provided transportation benefits (e.g., transit passes and van pooling) for years after 1992. CNEPA of 1992 (Pub. L. 102-486), §1911.

transportation expenses   expenses of transporting the *taxpayer,* directly attributable to the conduct of a *trade or business* or *investment* activity, while she or he is not *away from home overnight*. Such expenses include the cost of going by air, rail, bus, or taxi and the cost of operating and maintaining an automobile. The cost of *meals* and *lodging* is not considered a transportation expense. Under §162, a *taxpayer* can *deduct* transportation *expenses as ordinary and necessary* expenses incurred in a *trade or business*. For example, a grocery store owner who uses a delivery truck may deduct the expenses attributable to operating the truck as transportation expenses under §162, as may the businessperson who interrupts his or her working day by taking a cab across town to attend a brief business meeting. Transportation expenses may also be *deductible* tax-related expenses under §212. Under the CNEPA of 1992 (Pub. L. 102-486), effective for amounts paid after 1992, employment away from home at a single location will be treated as *indefinite* if it lasts for one year or more. As a result, travel expenses in connection with such employment will not be deductible. §1938.

transportation income   for purposes of determining the source (*domestic* or *foreign*) of certain income of a *United States person,* the term means income derived from, or in connection with, the use (or hiring or leasing for use) of a vessel or aircraft or the performance of services directly related to its use. The term *vessel or aircraft* includes any container used in connection with a vessel or aircraft. §863(c)(3). All income from transportation that begins and ends in the United States is United States source income. If the transportation is between the United States and an overseas country or a *possession,* then only 50 percent of the income is United States source income. Section 887 imposes a 4 percent tax on annual *United States source gross transportation income* of *nonresident aliens* and foreign corporations, referring to *gross income from transportation* that is treated as 50 percent from United States sources but not *effectively connected income*. That tax uses the §863(c)(3) definition of transportation income, with minor adjustments.

travel expenses   expenses incurred while *away from home overnight* in the pursuit of a *trade or business,* or *employment-related activity.* §162(a)(2). Travel expenses generally include *transportation* expenses, as well as such specific travel expenses as *meals* and *lodging* en route. To qualify as a travel expense deduction, the following requirements must be met: (1) the purpose of the trip must be connected with a trade or business, and (2) the taxpayer must be away from home overnight or for a sufficient duration to require resting before returning home. The position of the IRS is that a person's tax home is the location of his or her *principal place of employment,* regardless of where the family residence is maintained. Travel expenses incurred in the production or collection of income are also deductible even though the travel is not connected with employment or with a trade or business. §212(1), Rev. Rul. 84-113, 1984-2 C.B. 60. Under the CNEPA of 1992 (Pub. L. 102-486), effective for amounts paid after 1992, employment away from home at a single location will be treated as indefinite if it lasts for one year or more. As a result, travel expenses in connection with such employment will not be deductible. §1938. See *sleep or rest rule; tax home; temporary living expenses, travel.*

treasure trove found wealth. Treasure trove is includible in *gross income* when reduced to *undisputed possession* under local law. Reg.§1.61-14(a); Rev. Rul. 61, 1953-1 C.B. 17.

Treasury administrative and procedural regulations see *regulations, Treasury, administrative and procedural.*

Treasury decision the *IRS's* vehicle for officially releasing final *regulations.* Treasury decisions are published upon release in the *Federal Register.*

Treasury Department the federal department with responsibility for administering and enforcing the federal tax laws. The *Secretary* of the Treasury, its chief official, has largely delegated that authority to the *Commissioner* of the *Internal Revenue Service,* an *employee* of the Treasury Department, under §7802(a).

treaty an agreement between nations (if between *states,* then the term "*compact*" is generally used). International treaties are supreme law of the land, unless superseded by later *federal* law or a later treaty between the parties to the treaty. See *tax treaty.*

treaty-based return position a position taken on a *tax return* that is based on the authority of a *tax treaty.* A *taxpayer* who asserts that a treaty modifies the internal revenue laws must disclose that position to the IRS. §6114; Reg. §301.6114-1T.

treaty disclosure penalty see *penalty, treaty disclosure.*

treaty-shopping the practice of using a third-country *tax treaty* in order to *gain* advantages not otherwise available. A typical case might be an Arab *individual* who plans to invest in the *United States,* forming a Netherlands Antilles *corporation* to take advantage of the benefits of a United States–Netherlands Antilles treaty.

treaty trader an informal term for an *alien individual* who comes to the *United States* to trade under a *treaty* between the United States and his or her country. Such an *individual* is presumed to be a *nonresident alien* if he or she is present in the United States for less than one full *taxable year,* but that individual is presumed *resident* if he or she is present for one full *taxable year* and the facts show that person is not a transient. Rev. Rul. 64-285, 1964-2 C.B. 184. The viability of this rule seems doubtful now. See *resident alien.*

treble damages the two-thirds of a recovery under the Clayton Anti-Trust Act, which is punitive in nature. Section 162(g) denies *deductions* for such payments.

trial court the court with original jurisdiction of a lawsuit. Federal tax cases begin in either the *Tax Court,* the United States *District Court,* or the *Claims Court.*

triangular dividend another name for a *dividend* which is hypothesized when *corporations* under a shareholder's common control do business with each other in a manner designed to benefit one or more shareholders. The area is a difficult one. See, e.g., G.C.M. 38676 (Apr. 6, 1981), which states that a triangular dividend may also be found as a result of an *IRS*-imposed adjustment under §482.

triangular merger a merger of a target company and a subsidiary of the acquiring *corporation.* Such a merger may be tax-free and is made possible by §368(a). See *triangular reorganization.*

triangular reorganization any *corporate reorganization* in which *stock* of a parent or higher-tier *corporation* is used as consideration for the reorganization. Section 368(a)(1)(B) and (C) (parentheticals) and (2)(D) (*Type A reorganization*). See *forward triangular merger; reverse triangular merger.*

tribal corporation a *corporation* organized pursuant to §17 of the Indian Reorganization Act of 1934 to organize an American Indian tribe. Such corporation should be tax-exempt.

triple A account a synonym for *accumulated adjustments account.*

triple tax, corporate a possible result of the virtual repeal of the *General Utilities doctrine.* It can occur if an acquiring company buys *stock* of a *subsidiary* from a holding company, followed by a *liquidation* of the target company and the holding company, because the target company may be taxed on its liquidation, as may the holding company and its *shareholder.* Section 336(e) may alleviate this problem.

troubled thrift institutions see *financially troubled thrift institutions*.

true taxable income a standard used in §482 (authorizing *IRS* reallocation of *gross income* and *expenses*, etc., among related *business taxpayers*) to determine what a controlled taxpayer's income (or lesser included item such as a particular *deduction*, etc.) would have been had it been independent of its affiliates. Reg. §1.482-1(a)(6). True taxable income is used both to defeat distortions and as a standard for modifying a taxpayer's accounts so as to impose economic reality for *income tax* purposes. Reg. §1.482-1(b)(1). See *reallocation of income and deductions by Commissioner*.

trust a legally recognized and enforceable arrangement, established by will or *inter vivos*, whereby one or more *persons (trustees)* take title to property in order to protect or conserve it for one or more *beneficiaries* of the *entity*. The beneficiaries and *grantor(s)* may overlap. Reg. §301.7701-4(a). Trusts may be classified as *associations taxable as corporations* if they have a *business* purpose, even if the *grantor*, rather than the *beneficiaries*, supplied the *corpus* of the trust. Reg. §301.7701-4(b). Noncharitable trusts are taxable much like *individuals*, subject to a key *deduction* for *distributable net income* that renders them quasi-*conduits*. See *business trust*.

trustee a *person* who holds *legal title* to property for the purpose of protecting or conserving it for the benefit of others (*beneficiaries*) under the rules of courts of *equity* or chancery. Trustees are held to particularly high standards of *fiduciary* duties. See Reg. §301.7701-4(a). See *trust*.

trusteed plans, qualified plans a term used to describe *qualified plans* for *employees*, the assets of which are held by a *trust* that meets the standards of §401(a). Trusteeship is generally required, except for special cases such as funding pension benefits though retirement *annuities* purchased from *insurance companies*.

trustee, real estate investment trust a *person* who holds *legal title* to the property of the *real estate investment trust* (REIT) and has rights and powers that satisfy the requirement of *centralized management* under Reg. §301.7701-2(c). To qualify as a REIT, the *entity* must be managed by one or more *trustees* or directors. §856(a)(1); Reg. §1.856-1(b)(1) and (d)(1).

trust fund taxes the *employee's* share of *Social Security taxes held by an employer* for *deposit* with the *IRS*. The employer's share of Social Security and federal unemployment tax are non–trust fund taxes. The holding of such monies is viewed as being a holding in *trust* and creates major liabilities for such holders.

trustor a person who transfers property to a *trustee*; a *grantor*, a *settlor*.

tuition or medical payments, gifts see *medical and tuition expenses, gift tax exclusion*.

twelve-month acquisition period, section 338 acquisitions any 12-month period, beginning when an acquiring *corporation* first *purchases stock* included in a *qualified stock purchase* (or engaged in a *constructive* purchase). §338(h)(1). This period operates as the point in time core which is bracketed by the longer *consistency period* and for determining whether stock is *recently purchased stock* for *basis* adjustment purposes when there is a deemed *liquidation*. §§338(h)(4) and 338(b)(6)(A). If stock acquired from a related person qualifies as a purchase, then the 12-month acquisition period begins on the date the acquirer is first treated, under the *attribution rules* of §318, as owning stock actually owned by the related corporation. §338(h)(1). This means that the acquisition period begins no later than when the acquirer is first deemed the constructive owner of the stock later acquired from the related corporation. See *purchase, section 338 acquisition*.

twenty-five percent foreign-owned corporation a *corporation* as to which any one *foreign person* owns at any time during the taxable year at least 25 percent of (1) the total voting power of all classes of *stock* entitled to vote; or (2) the total value of all classes of stock. Such a person is a "25 percent foreign shareholder." §6038A(c)(1)(A), (b), (c)(1). In evaluating whether one foreign person owns 25 percent by vote or value, *proposed regulations* say consideration would be given to *all facts and circumstances* as per Reg. §1.957-1(b)(2) (arrangements to shift formal voting power). Reg. §1.6038A-1(c)(3)(ii). The *attribution rules* of §318 apply to determine 25 percent foreign shareholder and related party. §6038A(c)(5). Transactions by a *domestic* or *foreign partnership* are attributed to any reporting corporation whose direct or indirect interest in the capital or profits of the partnership (when combined with the interests of all related parties to the reporting corporation partner) equals 25 percent or more of the total partnership interests, but only to the extent of the partnership interest held by the reporting corporation partner. See Reg. §1.6038A-1(e)(2). See *reporting corporation*.

twenty-five percent omission a *taxpayer's* (or couple's) failure to report over 25 percent of *gross income* (before deducting *costs of goods sold* or services) shown on the *return*. The effect of such omissions is a six-year *statute of limitations* on *assessments* or suits against the taxpayer, unless the taxpayer made an *adequate disclosure* on the return (or attachment) notifying the *IRS* of the omitted item. §6501(e)(1). There are comparable rules for *estate, gift,* and *excise taxes*. §6501(e)(2) and (3). See *innocent spouse rule; adequate disclosure rule*.

twenty-four-month construction issue exception a limit on the *arbitrage bond* provisions. The exception generally provides that the arbitrage rebate and penalty rules do not apply if the proceeds of a construction bond financing ("available construction proceeds") are spent on construction within 24 months of the issuance. §148(f)(4)(C). The details are complex.

twenty-pay contracts   a contract that demands at least 20 nondecreasing annual premiums and was issued under a plan of insurance filed before September 28, 1983. §7702(i)(2)(A), (B) and (3). Certain *transition rules* can allow such contracts to continue to qualify as *life insurance contracts* for purposes of §101 *excluding death benefits from gross income.*

twenty-percent charity   any *exempt organization* described in §170(c) and not found under §170(b)(1)(A). The *deduction* for the *contribution* to or for the use of such a charity may not exceed 20 percent of the *taxpayer's contribution base.* See former §170(b)(1)(B); Reg. §§1.170A-8(c), 1.170-2(b)(1). Examples include *fraternal benefit societies, veterans' organizations, cemetery companies,* and certain *private foundations* as well as gifts for the use of *fifty-percent charities.* The 30 percent limit is actually the lesser of 30 percent of the contribution base or the excess of 50 percent of the contribution base for the *taxable year* over the contributions qualifying for the 50 percent cap, including carryovers. The 20 percent cap remains for gifts of cash or *ordinary income property* as to *private nonoperating foundations* (and all contributions outside §170(b)(1)(A)) and gifts of *capital gain property* to nonoperating foundation. §170(b)(1)(B)(i) and (1)(D).

twenty-percent corporate shareholder   any *corporation* that owns (including under the *attribution rules* of §318) 20 percent or more of (1) the total combined voting power of all classes of voting *stock,* or (2) total stock value (with nonvoting preferred stock ignored), provided the corporation would be entitled to a *dividends-received deduction* under §§243–45. §301(e)(2). Such corporations calculate the distributing corporation's *earnings and profits (E&P)* as if there were no §312(k) or (n). §301(e)(1). Section 312(k) forces the distributing company to use *straight-line depreciation* for E&P purposes. Section 312(n) generally modifies E&P to conform it more to economic reality (e.g., by forcing slower *IDC* deductions). The net result is to limit corporations' exploitation of the *dividends-received deduction* by their selling stock soon after payment of a dividend.

twenty-seven-point five-year residential rental property   includes *buildings* or structures with respect to which 80 percent or more of the gross rental income is from dwelling units. The definition of *residential rental property* (§167(j)) is used for this purpose. If any part of the building or structure is occupied by the *taxpayer,* gross rental income from the property includes the rental value of the unit occupied by the taxpayer. A

dwelling unit means a house or apartment used to provide living accommodations, but not a unit in a hotel, motel, inn, or other establishment in which more than 50 percent of the units are *used on a transient basis.* §168(e)(2)(A).

twenty-year property   includes *tangible property* with a *class life* of 20 years or more, as well as municipal sewers. §168(e)(3)(F).

two-and-one-half month rule, deduction denial   a former rule embodied in §267(b) to the effect that where an *accrual method taxpayer* is obligated to pay *expenses* (e.g., a year-end bonus) or *interest* to a *related taxpayer* (e.g., major *shareholder-employee*) who is on the *cash method,* the payment has to be made within $2\frac{1}{2}$ months of the close of the payor's year or be lost forever. The rule has been replaced with a *deferral* provision. See *related taxpayers, loss and deduction denial.*

two-family corporation   see *family corporation.*

two hundred percent declining-balance method   see *declining-balance depreciation.*

two-in-three rule, back-up withholding   tax slang for a provision under which a payor who receives two notices within three *calendar years* from the *IRS* that a payee has furnished an incorrect *taxpayer identification number* must begin *back-up withholding* within 30 days of receiving the notice. Reg. §35a.3406-1(f) to -(h)

two or more trades or businesses under common control   a group of *trades or businesses* that is either a *parent-subsidiary group under common control,* a *brother-sister group under common control,* or a *combined group* of trades or businesses under common control. Reg. §11.414(c)-2(a). For these purposes, trades or businesses explicitly include *sole proprietorships, trusts, estates, partnerships, or corporations.* Trades or businesses under common control are subject to aggregation for purposes of testing their *qualified plans'* compliance with *coverage, participation, accrual of benefit, vesting,* and limitations on benefit requirements for qualification. §414(c).

two- or three-family corporation   see *family corporation.*

two-payment rule   a provision of §453(e), prior to amendment, the gist of which was that *installment sale* reporting was impermissible unless there were at least two payments in two different *taxable years.* That limitation has been repealed; hence, for example, one can sell property in 1993, with the sole payment in 1993, and still qualify for installment sales reporting.

two-percent floor on itemized deductions   a *nondeductible* floor of 2 percent of adjusted gross income (AGI) applies to most types of unreimbursed employee expenses. The 2 percent disallowance applies before the 3 percent scale down of total itemized deductions is considered for upper-income individuals with AGI in excess of $100,000. §68. *Unreimbursed employee expenses* are combined with *investment counseling fees, safe deposit rentals for income-producing properties, tax preparation fees, certain education courses required for the job, the purchase and maintenance of special clothing, job-hunting expenses for seeking employment, professional journals, professional dues, union dues, and small tools and supplies* when the amount subject to the two-percent floor is calculated. §67. Thus, for example, if an *individual* who itemizes his or her *deductions* with AGI of $30,000 incurs miscellaneous itemized deductions totaling $757, the allowable amount of such deductions is $157. ($757 − $600 ($30,000 × 2 percent)). Use *Form 2106* for unreimbursed employee business expenses. See *uniforms.*

two-percent shareholder any *person* who, on any day of an *S corporation's taxable year,* owns more than 2 percent of the outstanding *stock* or the voting power of all of the *corporation's* stock, with the *attribution rules* of §318 used to determine stock ownership. Section 1372(b). §1372(a) treats S corporations as *partnerships* (and, therefore, certain *shareholders* as *partners*) for *fringe benefit* purposes, effectively preventing *exclusion* of these benefits from *gross income* for lack of an *employer.* Rev. Rul. 91-26, 1991-15 I.R.B. 23.

two-tier partnerships see *tier partnerships.*

two-trust estate plan an *estate planning* device under which each *spouse* forms a separate *revocable trust* during life, which a *pour over will* to transfer any assets not placed in the trust to the trust at death, and on the death of the first spouse, the spouse's revocable living trust converts to a *credit equivalent trust.* The idea is to decrease the survivor's *estate* by $600,000 so as to take advantage of the *unified estate and gift tax credit.*

two-year rule, installment sales another term for the content of §453(e), the gist of which is that if *property* is sold to a related party on the *installment method* and resold within two years, then the original seller's *gain* will be accelerated by the second disposition. The two-year period is *tolled* while risk of loss is diminished, and there is no time limitation if the subject matter of the sale is *marketable securities.* See *second disposition rule, installment sales.*

Type A reorganization a *merger* or *consolidation,* pursuant to a *plan of reorganization,* of two or more *corporations* pursuant to the laws of the District of Columbia, the United States, or of any *state.* §368(a)(1)(A). In general, the only restriction is that at least 50 percent of the total consideration employed be the acquiring corporation's stock. In addition, the judicial requirements that there be a *business purpose* for

the transaction, *continuity of proprietary interest,* and *continuity of business enterprise* must be satisfied. If all these definitional tests are met, these transactions can qualify for tax-free treatment. Such reorganization includes *forward triangular mergers* and *reverse triangular mergers.*

Type B reorganization the acquisition, pursuant to a *plan of reorganization,* by one *corporation,* in *exchange solely for* all or a part of its or its parent's *voting stock,* of *stock* of another corporation if, immediately after the acquisition, the acquiring corporation has *control* of the other corporation (whether or not it had control before the acquisition). §368(a)(1)(B). Cash can be issued for fractional shares or as part of a pre-reorganization *stock redemption* and these acquisitions can be done over time as long as control is acquired in a 12-month period or some longer period determined under the *step transaction doctrine.* The public stock-for-stock tender offer is the traditional example of Type B organization. In addition, the judicial requirements that there be a *business purpose* for the transaction, *continuity of proprietary interest,* and, at least colorably, *continuity of business enterprise* must be satisfied. If all these definitional requirements are satisfied, these transactions can qualify for tax-free treatment, with the target company winding up as a *subsidiary* of the acquiring company. For this purpose, voting stock may include contractual rights to acquire extra voting stock.

Type C reorganization the acquisition, pursuant to a *plan of reorganization,* by one *corporation,* in *exchange* solely for all or a part of its own or its parent's *voting stock* (but not both), of *substantially all the properties* of another corporation, after which the target company distributes all its assets unless the *IRS* waives that duty. Assumption of liabilities is permitted in a limited manner, as is the use of consideration other than *stock* under the so-called *boot relaxation rule.* The Type C reorganization is defined in §368(a)(1)(C) and (2)(G), while the boot relaxation rule is found in §368(a)(2)(B). In addition, the judicial requirements that there be a *business purpose* for the transaction and *continuity of business enterprise* must be satisfied. If all these definitional requirements are satisfied, these transactions can qualify for tax-free treatment.

Type D reorganization one *corporation's* transfer of some or all of its operating assets to another corporation if, immediately after the transfer, the transferor or one or more of its *shareholders* (including shareholders immediately before the transfer), or both, are in *control* (basically, 80 percent voting power for *corporate divisions* and 50 percent for acquisitions) of the transferee corporation, provided that, pursuant to the *plan of reorganization, stock* or *securities* of the transferee corporation are *distributed* to its shareholders in a specified manner. The kinds of distributions that are acceptable are those described in §355 *(corporate divisions)* or §354 (acquisitive *reorganizations*). An example of a divisive Type D reorganization is the formation of a new subsidiary (New Co.) which receives half the parent's (Old Co.) assets, with New Co.'s stock distributed to Old Co.'s shareholders under §355 (a *spin-off*). In typical acquisitive Type D reorganization, New Co. gets *substantially all of the properties* of Old Co. (a mandatory element) and Old Co. distributes all the New Co. stock to its shareholders, as called for by §354(b), and then liquidates. In addition, the judicial requirements that there be a *business purpose* for the transaction, *continuity of proprietary interest,* and *continuity of business enterprise* must be satisfied. If these various tests, and certain others found in §§354 and 355, are met, then the transaction can qualify for tax-free treatment. In a divisive Type D reorganization, however, the continuity of proprietary interest doctrine is relaxed. Reg. §1.368-1(b). See *acquisitive D reorganization; corporate division; reincorporation; spin-off; split-off; split-up; substantially all of the properties, Type C reorganization.*

Type E reorganization   a recapitalization, that is, a reshuffling of the capital structure of one *corporation* in which, pursuant to a *plan of reorganization,* some or all the *shareholders* exchange some or all of their *stock* or *securities.* §368(a)(1)(E). In addition, the judicial requirement that there be a *business purpose* for the transactions must be satisfied. If *these* various definitional tests are met, the transaction may qualify for tax-free treatment. However, an exchange of outstanding stock for cash, notes, or bonds is taxable (§§354(a)(2)(A), 356(a)), and the entire transaction may be disallowed *reorganization* treatment in extreme cases.

Type F reorganization   a mere change in the identity, form, or place of organization, however effected. §368(a)(1)(F). The extent to which the Type F reorganization is applicable to the fusion of *corporations* was controversial, but the possibility of fusing two operating corporations has been eliminated by *TEFRA,* which amended §368(a)(1)(F) to limit the Type F reorganization to one operating corporation cases as to post–August 31, 1982 transactions. By inference, Type F reorganizations can involve several corporations but only one active corporation, whatever that term may mean; note that the limitation superficially at least makes it impossible for a holding company to change *states* of incorporation, probably an unintended effect. In addition, it seems that all of the judicial requirements (i.e., a *business purpose* for the transaction and *continuity of business enterprise*) must be satisfied. If these definitional requirements are satisfied, the reorganization can be free of current *federal income taxes.*

Type G reorganization   a transfer, pursuant to a *plan of reorganization,* by a *corporation* of some or all of its operating assets to another corporation in a *Title 11 or similar case,* provided the transferee corporation distributes its *stock* or *securities* to its *shareholders* tax-free or partially tax-free. §368(a)(1)(G). Transfers to a troubled corporation as well as from such a corporation can qualify. Because of the mandatory cross-reference to §354(b)(1), substantially all of the assets of the transferor must be transferred; failing that, the transaction must instead meet the requirements of §355 relating to tax-free *corporate divisions.* This new reorganization type is designed to be relatively flexible; e.g., creditors' interests may count as equity interests for *continuity of proprietary interest* as well as certain control requirements, and the *substantially all the properties* test is relaxed. The judicial requirements of continuity of proprietary interest, *continuity of business enterprise,* and *business purpose* evidently apply to these reorganizations, albeit in modified forms. If the judicial and statutory criteria, as modified, are all satisfied, then a Type G reorganization can be tax-free to all the parties to the plan of reorganization. See *financially troubled thrift institutions.*

U

UBIT an acronym for *unrelated business income tax.*

UCC an acronym for Uniform Commercial Code.

UNI an acronym for *undistributed net income.*

UNICAP rules an acronym for the *uniform capitalization rules.*

U.S. individual retirement bonds the *Treasury Department's* label for *retirement bonds.* §405; 31 C.F.R. §346 (1979).

U.S. net equity basically, the portion of the earnings of the *United States branch* of the *foreign corporation* not remitted to the foreign parent company but, instead, reinvested in branch operations, used for the purpose of determining adjustments to a corporation's *dividend equivalent amount.* It becomes part of the *tax base* on which the *branch profits tax* falls by forming part of the *dividend equivalent amount* on which the tax falls. See §884(b). See *branch profits tax; dividend equivalent amount, branch profits tax..*

U.S. ratio method a method of *allocating costs* under the *uniform capitalization rules* applicable to *foreign persons.* It does not cover allocation of *interest.* The method involves allocating such costs to property produced by foreign persons in proportion to the way additional costs that must be allocated in the *applicable United States trade or business* of a related *taxpayer.* The applicable United States trade or business basically means the *trade or business* conducted in the *United States* by a foreign *branch* of a *United States person* or a related person that is the same as or most similar to the trade or business conducted by the foreign person. See Notice 88-104, 1988-38 I.R.B. 20. See *foreign person, UNICAP.*

USC an acronym for *United States Code.*

USCA an acronym for *United States Code Annotated.*

USRPHC an acronym for *United States real property holding corporation.*

ultimate 25 percent stockholder a 25 percent *foreign stockholder* whose ownership of *stock* in the *reporting corporation* is not attributed (under 958 principles) to any other such shareholder, except one wholly or partially owned or participated in by such shareholder that also has an ownership interest in such shareholder. Rev. Proc. 91-55, 1991-23 I.R.B. 5. One can limit reporting under §6038A to direct and ultimate 25 percent shareholders, ignoring others in the chain.

unadjusted basis, ADR generally, the *cost* or other *basis* of an asset in a *vintage account* established under the *class life asset depreciation range system (ADR),* less *bonus depreciation,* and after all adjustments other than *depreciation* or *amortization.* Reg. §1.167(a)-11(c)(1)(v)(a).

unagreed case an *audit* of a *taxpayer* as to which the *taxpayer* does not agree. In such a situation, a copy of the *Revenue Agent's Report* is not sent to the taxpayer, but instead the taxpayer gets a summary report plus Form 4549-A ("Income Tax Audit Changes"). The *District Office* sends a so-called *30-day letter* as well, kicking off the tax appeal process.

unallowable items program an *IRS* program used at *Service Centers* which picks up obviously impermissible items for rejection.

unauthorized use of tax information disclosure or use by federal *employees* of information contained in a tax *return* (return information) or a copy thereof without the consent of the *taxpayer.* §7213. Such conduct may result in imposition of a fine, imprisonment, and discharge from employment. §7213(a)(1). *State* employees are also subject to such penalties, as well as those preparing the taxpayer's return; however, in such a case the offending activity is considered a misdemeanor. §§7213(a)(5), 7216. In some instances, however, disclosure of information in a tax return may be permitted. Reg. §301.7216-2(a). Generally, where the taxpayer has granted written permission to have the return information disclosed, no penalty will result. Reg. §301.7216-3(a)(2) and (3); see also Reg. §301.7216-2(c) and (n). See *penalty, improper use of information; Privacy Act; return, Privacy Act; return information.*

uncontrolled sales *sales* in which buyer and seller are not members of the same commonly controlled group of *trades* or *businesses.* Reg. §1.482-2(e)(2)(ii). See *comparable uncontrolled price method; reallocation of income and deductions by Commissioner.*

under a divorce or separation instrument see *incident to divorce.*

undercapitalization see *debt-equity rules.*

underfunding excise tax a 5 percent *excise tax* (rising to 100 percent if not timely cured) imposed on *employers* who fail to fund a *qualified plan* at minimum required levels. §4971. The base of the tax is the so-called *accumulated funding deficiency.*

underpayment of estimated income taxes a failure to pay 90 percent (66⅔ percent for fishermen and *farmers*) of the amount of *income taxes* (as reduced by *credits*) due for a taxable quarter, minus amounts actually paid for the quarter out of income tax *withholdings* and payments of *estimated taxes.* §6654(b) (individuals). If lower, one-fourth of last year's taxes is used instead of 90 percent of this year's tax. The standard is entirely objective. Two statutory provisions (also known as safety zones) allow an *individual taxpayer* to avoid the *penalty for underpayment of estimated tax.* §6654(d). The exceptions are generally referred to as "*last year's tax*" (meaning 100 percent of the tax shown on the prior year's initial *return*) and the "tax on annualized current-year's income," which can protect *taxpayers* whose incomes balloon late in the year. §6654(d)(1). If neither of these exceptions apply and there is an underpayment, then the taxpayer will be subject to a penalty for the period of underpayment. §6654(a). There is also no penalty if (1) there was no tax in the prior year; (2) net tax liability after *wage* withholding *credits* is under $500; or (3) the *IRS* determines it would be unfair because the underpayment was caused by a casualty or disaster, recent retirement at age 62 or older, or recent disability. §6654(e)(1) and (3). To avoid an underpayment penalty where there is a substantial increase in a taxpayer's AGI, taxpayers whose adjusted gross income increases by more than $40,000 from a prior year and whose adjusted gross income is more than $75,000 must make estimated tax payments at least equal to 90 percent of the current year's tax liability rather than 100 percent of the prior year's tax liability. The Internal Revenue Service is also authorized to abate any underpayment in 1992 caused by the underwithholding due to the issuance of revised withholding tables (effective March 1992). Section 6654(d) provides a similar pattern for *corporations,* with no 90 percent buffer for *large corporations* (those with taxable income of at least $1 million in any one of the three immediately preceding tax years). For years beginning in 1992, the required annual payment, which includes a corporation's alternative minimum tax liability, is the lesser of (a) 93 percent (94 percent for 1993 and 1994, and 95 percent for 1995 and 1996) of the corporation's final tax, or (b) 100 percent of the tax for the preceding year if that was a 12-month tax year. The minimum tax is slated to return to 90 percent for 1997. §6655(d) and (e) as amended by the Tax Extension Act of 1991. See *estimated tax, corporations; estimated tax due dates; estimated tax, individuals; estimation year; exceptions to estimated tax, corporate; exceptions to estimated tax, individual.*

underpayment of tax, accuracy-related penalty   the amount by which any tax imposed exceeds the amounts shown as the tax by the *taxpayer* on his or her *return,* plus amounts shown on the return but previously *assessed* or collected, over the amount of *rebates* made. For this purpose, the term "rebate" means that so much of the *abatement, credit, refund,* or other payment was made on the ground that the tax imposed was less than the excess of the tax shown on the return, assessed, or collected over the rebates previously made. §6663(d)(2). The amount of underpayment is reduced

by disclosure on the return or in situations where there is or was *substantial authority* for the position taken or if the issue involved a *tax shelter.* See *accuracy-related penalty; tax shelter, accuracy-related penalty.*

undertaking, passive loss rules   generally, the smallest unit of operations that can constitute an *activity* under the *passive loss rules.* It consists of all the *business* and rental operations the same person (an *individual* or *entity,* including an *S corporation* or a *partnership*) conducts at the same "*location*" (generally, a fixed place of *business* where operations are conducted), regardless of their similarity or diversity. Where the basic undertaking consists of both *rental* and *nonrental* operations, there must be a further inquiry into the number of undertakings, but in general they are separated. Oil and gas wells that qualify for the special exception for *working interests* are always separate undertakings. Reg. §1.469-4T. See *activity, passive loss rules.*

undisputed possession   dominion over property against all the world other than the true owner of the property. At the moment found property (*treasure trove*) is reduced to undisputed possession, the property is included in the *taxpayer's gross income.* Reg. §1.61-14(a).

undistributed capital gains, regulated investment company   the amount designated by a *regulated investment company* as undistributed *gains* in accordance with Reg. §1.852-9, and proportionately *includable* in a *shareholder's gross income* and subject to taxation at the company level. Reg. §1.852-4(b)(2). Such amounts can be *deemed distributed* and taxed to shareholders as *long-term capital gains* or can be retained and taxed to the company. §852(b)(3).

undistributed foreign personal holding company income   *taxable income* of a *foreign personal holding company,* subject to numerous adjustments, less the *dividends-paid deductions* described in §561. §556(a). The adjustments to taxable income are primarily designed to reflect dividend-paying ability; hence, there is an allowance for *income taxes* and *charitable contributions* (which use a modified *contribution base*), but *dividends-received deductions, net operating loss carryover* deductions, certain *losses* on corporate-owned rental properties, special deductions for *shareholder* taxes paid by the corporation, deductions for *qualified deferred compensation contributions,* and certain other minor deductions are disallowed. §556(b). Undistributed foreign personal holding company income is taxed to *United States shareholders,* thereby increasing *basis* in their *stock* through the *constructive dividend.* §551.

undistributed income excise tax, private foundation   a 15 percent *excise tax* designed to force *private foundations* to disgorge their accumulations; imposed on private foundations, other than *operating foundations,* and pre–May 27, 1979, foundations required to accumulate income, based on *undistributed income*. §4942. See *undistributed income, private foundation*.

undistributed income, private foundation the amount by which the *distributable amount* for the *taxable year* exceeds the *qualifying distributions* theretofore made from the distributable amount. §4942(c). A 15 percent *excise tax* is imposed on the undistributed income of a *private foundation*. §4942(a). See *undistributed income excise tax, private foundation*.

undistributed net income the basis on which the *throwback tax* is imposed on *distributions* of prior accumulations of *trust* income. The term is defined on a cumulative year-by-year basis as *distributable net income* (DNI), minus various taxes imposed on the trust with respect to the undistributed DNI and required and discretionary (*first-* and *second-tier*) distributions for the year. §665(a). All or a portion of the taxes (other than the *alternative minimum tax*) imposed on the trust for the throwback year attributable to an *accumulation distribution* are deemed distributed along with the accumulation distribution, a beneficial provision. §665(d); Reg. §1.665(d)-1. Once undistributed net income (UNI) for prior years is determined, the *beneficiary's* tax is determined on the basis of deemed distributions of UNI from prior years. §§666, 667. See *throwback tax*.

undistributed personal holding company income in addition to the regular tax on corporate income, a special 28 percent tax is imposed on the "*undistributed personal holding company income*" of a personal holding company. §541. The tax applies only to undistributed income, which basically is the corporation's taxable income less the amount of its federal income tax and the dividends paid by it.

undistributed subpart F income another term used to describe the amount of a *controlled foreign corporation's subpart F income* that is not actually distributed but is, nonetheless, subject to current inclusion in the hands of *United States shareholders*. See *subpart F*.

undistributed taxable income a term formerly used in connection with the taxation of *S corporations* and their *shareholders*, the effect of which was to tax shareholders as such amounts were earned. The provision antedates the Subchapter S Revision Act of 1982. The same concept is embedded in current law, §1366. See AAA, which is an acronym for *accumulated adjustments account*, which is a corporate account associated with an *S corporation*. Essentially, the AAA is a cumulative total of undistributed net income items for S corporation taxable years beginning after 1982. See *taxable income, S corporation*.

undivided interest in an entire interest a fractional or proportional interest (e.g., 10 percent) of each substantial interest or right (e.g., use, power to rent) owned by a *taxpayer*. Reg. §1.170A-7(b)(1). *Charitable contributions* of such interests, even though *partial interests*, are *deductible*. §170(f)(3)(B)(ii).

undocketed case a case that is not docketed (i.e., the *taxpayer* has not filed a *petition*) in the *Tax Court*. Such cases can be freely settled by the *Appeals Office*. In the ordinary course of a tax *audit*, the *taxpayer* will file a timely *protest*, thereby eliminating the possibility that a *statutory notice of deficiency* will be issued, cutting off Tax Court jurisdiction. See *docketed case*.

undue hardship, extension of time for paying tax or deficiency the showing required by a *taxpayer* for the granting of an extension of time under §6161 for payment of any tax or deficiency. A general statement of hardship will not suffice; rather, the taxpayer must provide evidence showing that payment by the due date would result in substantial financial loss to the taxpayer. The *regulations* state that an example of undue hardship in which substantial financial loss would result is the sale of property at a sacrifice price, but also assert that if a market exists, the sale of property at the current market price is not ordinarily considered to result in undue hardship. Taxpayers' showings of undue hardship that would result if the extension were refused must be accompanied by a statement of the assets and liabilities of the taxpayer and an itemized statement showing all receipts and disbursements for each of the three months immediately preceding the due date of the amount to which the application relates, presumably to show inability to pay. Reg. §1.6161-1(b). See *extension of time to pay tax*.

unearned income generally, income from investments.

unemployment benefit trust see *supplemental unemployment benefit trust*.

unemployment compensation any amount received under *federal* or *state* law in the nature of unemployment compensation. §85(b). Such amounts are fully taxable. §85(a). Private unemployment compensation has always been fully taxed. See, e.g., Rev. Rul. 59-5, 1959-1 C.B. 12.

unexpected or unusual event, casualty loss an occurrence that is either unanticipated or extraordinary in relation to the everyday life of the *taxpayer*. Rev. Rul. 72-592, 1972-2 C.B. 101. Such occurrences, if also sudden, are generally regarded as *other casualties* for purposes of claiming a *casualty loss*. A casualty may be either unexpected or unusual; it need not be unexpected and unusual. Rev. Rul. 76-134, 1976-1 C.B. 54. See *casualty loss*.

unfunded deferred compensation *deferred compensation* arrangements that involve mere promises to pay in the future, leaving the promisee in the position of being a *general creditor* of the promisor. Provided such agreements are made before payment is due and are not evidenced by a note or otherwise *secured, cash method taxpayers* are not taxed on such deferrals until actually paid. See Rev. Rul. 60-31, 1960-1 C.B. 174. See *secured, deferred compensation.*

unfunded past service liabilities unfunded liabilities for pension benefits for services rendered in prior years. Such liabilities are most acute when an *employer* establishes a new *pension plan* that takes account of services rendered in pre-plan years. Section 412 generally requires that funding deficiencies be corrected within fixed periods (e.g., 40 years in the case of existing unfunded past service). See *accumulated funding deficiency; minimum funding standards.*

unified audit see *unified proceedings.*

unified credit see *unified gift and estate tax credit.*

unified gift and estate tax credit a reference to a feature of the present *unified transfer tax* system under which a limited amount of combined *inter vivos* and *testamentary* transfers may be made free of *estate* and *gift taxes.* Specifically, §§2010(a) and 2505(a) provide a mandatory *credit* against combined federal gift and estate taxes of $192,800. The unified gift and estate tax credit can exempt a taxable estate of less than $600,000 from tax. Inter vivos use of a portion of the gift tax credit reduces the available credit against federal estate taxes. §2505(a) and (b).

unified proceedings an informal reference to *audits* of *partnerships* and *S corporations* under which the members are investigated and their tax liabilities are disposed of as a group. The partnership rules are contained in §§6221–6232, but the S corporation rules are only incorporated by reference in §6244. The unified procedures do not apply to S corporations with five or fewer *shareholders* unless the corporation elects to have them apply. Similarly, partnerships with 10 or fewer *partners* are exempted. §§6231(a)(1)(B), 6244; Reg. §301.6241-1T. They are also known as *TEFRA audits.*

unified transfer tax the combined *federal estate* and *gift tax* system applicable to gratuitous transfers of an *individual's* wealth by *gift* and at death. §2001(c). The underlying concept is to tax transfers of wealth as well as create neutrality as to whether the transfers are made during the transferor's lifetime, at death, or both combined, but to offset taxable transfers with a major *credit,* the so-called *unified gift and estate tax credit.* For estates of decedents dying, and gifts made, after 1987 and before 1993, the tax is levied on amounts transferred in excess of $10,000,000 but not exceeding $21,040,000, in order to recapture the benefit of any tax rate *below the maximum rate of 55 percent* as well as the unified credit. In the case of decedents dying, and gifts made, after 1992, the additional tax is levied on

amounts transferred in excess of $10,000,000 but not exceeding $18,340,000, which recaptures the benefit of any transfer tax below 50 percent. See *unified gift and estate tax credit.*

unified transfer tax credit see *unified gift and estate tax credit.*

uniform capitalization rules comprehensive rules requiring *capitalization* of all otherwise *deductible allocable costs* associated with *realty* and *tangible personal property "produced by the taxpayer"* or *tangible* and *intangible property* acquired for resale by a *taxpayer* engaged in a *trade or business* or in an activity conducted for profit. §263A. The rules supersede the *full absorption accounting* rules formerly applicable to *inventories* under Reg. §1.471-11. Property is "produced by the taxpayer" if it is constructed, built, installed, manufactured, developed, improved, created, or grown (property produced for the taxpayer is produced *by* the taxpayer to the extent the taxpayer pays for it). Reg. §1.263A-1T(a)(5)(ii). In the case of property held as *inventory,* allocable costs must be included in inventory. In the case of all other property, allocable costs must be capitalized. Tangible personal property produced by the taxpayer includes films, sound recordings, videotapes, books, and other similar property containing words, ideas, concepts, images, or sounds. Reg. §1.263A-1T(a)(5)(iii). Certain types of property are exempt: *IDCs* for oil and gas wells, mineral *exploration* or *development,* costs associated with the production of property pursuant to a *long-term contract,* extended *long-term contract, deductible research and experimental expenditures,* costs associated with *cushion gas* acquired for resale, costs associated with the raising, growing, or harvesting trees other than crop-producing or ornamental trees. §263A(c) and Reg. §1.263A-1T(a)(6). There are further exemptions. The uniform capitalization rules do not apply to interest costs associated with real or personal property acquired for resale. §263A(f). See *allocable costs, uniform capitalization rules; allocation methods, uniform capitalization rules; burden rate method, uniform capitalization rules; direct labor costs, uniform capitalization rules; direct material costs, uniform capitalization rules; direct reallocation method; farming business, uniform capitalization rules; indirect costs, uniform capitalization rules; linear algebra method; production expenditures; service costs, uniform capitalization rules; service department, uniform capitalization rules; standard cost method; standard cost method; traced debt.*

uniformed services the Army, Navy, Air Force, Marine Corps, Coast Guard, National Oceanic and Atmospheric Administration (formerly the Environmental Science Services Administration), and Public Health Service. 37 U.S.C. §101(3) (1976). This definition applies for purposes of §§122 (reduced uniformed services retirement pay) and 6013(f) *(joint return* for *spouse* of individual in *missing status)*. §6013(f)(3)(A); Reg. §1.122-1(a). For the definition of uniformed service for purposes of the *FICA* tax, see *member of a uniformed service, federal insurance contribution act (FICA)*.

Uniform Gift of Securities Act   a uniform act passed by a number of *states* under which securities can be irrevocably transferred to a *custodian* (an adult, bank, or trust company) for a minor, with the result that income from the securities is taxed to the minor.

Uniform Gifts to Minors Act   a set of roughly uniform *state* laws that authorizes the transfer of *property* to a *custodian* who holds the property for a minor, distributing all property and income when the minor reaches adulthood under local law. Income earned on the property is taxed to the minor, except to the extent the income is used to discharge a duty of *support* owed to the minor by another. Rev. Rul. 59-357, 1959-2 C.B. 212. The act is designed to be easily applied. Although the kinds of property that can be accepted are fairly confined, establishing a custodial arrangement is easy; custodians can be parents and do not need to have special skills. The custodial funds can be spent for the benefit of the minor or can be retained in the custodian's discretion until majority. See G. Turner, *Irrevocable Trusts* §5.06 (1985).

uniform inventory capitalization rules   another name for §263A to the extent applicable to *inventory*.

uniformity clause   Article I, §8, Clause 1 of the United States Constitution, which requires "all Duties, Imposts and Excises" to be "uniform throughout the United States." The term has been read to refer to geographical uniformity.

Uniform Limited Partnership Act   a uniform *state* law, widely adopted by state legislatures, that provides the legal framework for *limited partnerships*. Such acts are necessary because limited partnerships are not recognized by the *common law*. See *Revised Uniform Limited Partnership Act*.

uniform minimum distribution rules   a set of rules applied generically to *qualified plans,* including *governmental plans* and plans of *exempt organizations,* relating to the minimum rate at which *distributions* from the plan to its *participants* or *beneficiaries* must be made. See §§401(a)(9), 402(a)(5), 408(d)(3), and 4974. Noncompliance can cause disqualification of the plan. Amounts that must be distributed under these rules do not qualify for tax-deferred *rollovers*. §§402(a)(5)(b), 403(a)(4)(B), and 401(a)(g)(G). See *excise tax, failure to make minimum distributions*.

Uniform Partnership Act   a uniform *state* law, widely adopted by state legislatures, that provides a legal framework for *general partnerships*. Unlike limited partnerships, *general partnerships* are also recognized by the *common law*.

uniforms   clothing required by the *employer* and not readily adaptable for general purposes (i.e., not usable in place of regular clothing). Rev. Rul. 70-474, 1970-2 C.B. 35. The costs of requiring and maintaining a uniform are *itemized deductions* subject to a reduction of 2 percent of AGI.

Uniform Transfers to Minors Act (UTMA)   an act adopted in a few *states* which replaces the *Uniform Gift to Minors Act*. It generally defers the date of mandatory payout and allows the holding of *realty, intangible property* generally, *partnership interests* (limited and general), *patents,* and *royalties,* among others. The *custodian* has broad reinvestment powers, but the *property* cannot be recovered by the *donor*.

unimproved real estate   land in its raw or undeveloped state.

union IRA   an *individual retirement arrangement* (IRA) established for an association of *employees* or of *independent contractors*. Reg. §1.408-2(c)(1). Each *participant* in such IRAs must have a separate account, in addition to the usual qualification rules. Reg. §1.408-2(c)(4)(i).

unions, credit   see *credit unions, exempt*.

unions, labor   see *labor union*.

union-sponsored IRA   a synonym for *union IRA*.

unitary assets   see *mass assets*.

unit benefit plans   *defined benefit plans* that ordinarily define the pension to be received by the *participant* on the basis of some kind of increasing formula that takes account of both *years of service* and *compensation*. Two particularly common forms are the *career average* and *final average* pay unit benefit plans.

United States   when used in a geographical sense, only the 50 *states* and the District of Columbia. §7701(a)(9). *Possessions,* therefore, are excluded. The sea bed and subsoil of those submarine areas (i.e., the continental shelf) that are adjacent to the territorial waters of the United States, over which the United States has exclusive rights in accordance with international law with respect to the exploration and exploitation of natural resources, are included with respect to mines, oil and gas wells, and other natural deposits. §638(1). See also *continental United States*.

United States bond purchase plan   see *qualified bond purchase plan*.

United States business office or other fixed place of business   generally, a fixed facility such as a place, site, or structure where a *nonresident alien, foreign cor-*

poration, or *dependent agent* of the foregoing engages in a *trade or business.* §864(c)(4)(B); Reg. §1.864-7. Where management authority rests is inconclusive. Reg. §1.864-7(c). In order for income earned from foreign sources to be *effectively connected* with a *United States* trade or business, the nonresident alien individual and foreign corporation must both engage in a United States trade or business and maintain a United States office or other fixed place of business, and then only income attributable to the office, site, etc., is subject to *graduated federal income taxes* as opposed to the generally less desirable flat tax rates on *gross income* from the activity. A *facts and circumstances test* is applied to determine the presence of a business office or other fixed place of business.

United States Code the official compilation of United States statutes. The bulk of the *federal* tax laws appear in Title 26.

United States Code Annotated the *United States Code,* including interpretative cases and some *legislative history.*

United States corporation see *domestic corporation.*

United States Court of Appeals for the Federal Circuit the successor of the *Court of Claims* in its tax functions. It has other (nontax) functions as well. See *Federal Circuit.*

United States dollar approximate separate transactions method a currency translation method usable in inflationary overseas economies, under which historical costs are translated to dollars when incurred, and other transactions are generally accelerated. It requires a *hyperinflationary currency.*

United States group, foreign personal holding company see *foreign personal holding company.*

United States–owned foreign corporation any *foreign corporation* in which at least half the *stock,* by vote or value, is held directly or indirectly by *United States persons.* Indirect ownership, for purposes of this definition, is ownership through the chain-of-ownership attribution rule applicable with respect to *controlled foreign corporations.* §§904 (g)(6), 958(a)(2). For this purpose, "stock" includes any certificate entitling the holder to voting power, in the case of a foreign *mutual insurance company* (under §958(a)(3)). Indirect ownership also includes the ownership of *options* to acquire the corporation's stock. A United States person, for these purposes, is a *citizen of the United States* or *resident alien,* a *domestic partnership,* a *domestic corporation,* or an *estate* or *trust* whose foreign income is subject to United States tax. *Distributions* from such corporations are subject to being reclassified as income from United States sources for purposes of the *foreign tax credit limitation.*

United States person a *United States citizen* or *resident,* a *domestic partnership,* a *domestic corporation,* or an *estate* or *trust* whose foreign income is subject to United States tax. See separate headings for definitions of the various *foreign taxpayers;* namely, *foreign corporations, foreign partnership, foreign trust, foreign estates,* and *nonresident aliens* taxation. §7701(a)(30).

United States property, subpart F *tangible property* located in the *United States, stock* of a *domestic corporation,* an obligation of a *United States person,* or any right to a *copyright, patent,* invention, model, design, formula, process, or similar property right acquired or developed by the *controlled foreign corporation* (CFC) for use in the United States. §§951(a)(1)(B), 956(a).

United States real property holding corporation a *domestic corporation,* the gross *fair market value* of whose direct and indirect *interests* in *United States real property* is at least 50 percent of the combined gross fair market value of its worldwide real property and business assets at any time over a five-year period before the sale date (or shorter period, beginning June 19, 1980, if applicable). §897(c)(1)(A)(ii) and (c)(2). For exceptions, see §897(c)(1)(B) and (c)(3). *Sales* or *exchanges* of *stock* in such corporations by *nonresident aliens* and *foreign corporations* are subject to *federal income tax.*

United States real property interest an interest in *United States* or United States Virgin Islands *real property,* which includes fee ownership, co-ownership, leaseholds of land, and options to acquire land, mines, wells, natural deposits, and leaseholds of land, or any improvements thereon, including related *personal property* and interests in *domestic corporations* that are or were *United States real property holding corporations* or their controlled corporations during particular periods. For these purposes, real property includes, among other things, *buildings* and *inherently permanent structures* and their components. Reg. §1.897-1(b)(4). Sales of such properties by foreigners are now largely subject to withholding. See *FIRPTA withholding.*

United States retirement bonds plan see *qualified bond purchase plan.*

United States resident the simple meaning is a synonym of a *resident alien.* There is a complex definition for purposes of the *source rules* under which the term means a *citizen of the United States* or a *resident alien* without a *tax home* abroad. Nonresident aliens are treated as United States residents if they have a tax home in the *United States,* and are treated *corporations, trusts,* or *estates* are treated as United States residents if they are *United States persons.* A United States citizen or resident alien with an overseas tax home is considered a nonresident, and *partnerships* are evaluated for residency status at the *partner* level. United States citizens and resident aliens with foreign tax homes are United States residents if income from a *sale* is not subject to an effective tax of 10 percent or more, subject to exceptions for Puerto Rico and certain Pacific islands. §865(g)(1). The second meaning is important in determining whether *income* or *loss* arose within or without the United States. See *source rules; tax home, foreign earned income and foreign housing exclusions.*

United States risks insurance or reinsurance risks under *insurance* or *annuity contracts* properly identified as being within the *United States.* Section 953 defines such risks in terms of the location of the property, life, or business activity or under an arrangement whereby another *corporation* receives a substantially identical amount for insuring such risks. §953(a)(1). The concept is important in defining *insurance income* under subpart F.

United States savings bonds see *series E bonds; series EE bonds; series HH bonds.* There are other less significant savings bonds as well. These bonds can offer substantial *tax deferral.*

United States shareholder, CFC a *United States person* who owns, directly, indirectly, or *constructively,* at least 10 percent of the total combined voting power of all classes of voting *stock* of a *foreign corporation.* §951(b). Certain *shareholders* of limited classes of corporations organized in Puerto Rico, the United States Virgin Islands, and certain United States *possessions* are exempted by §957(d). The term has dual significance. First, more than half the voting stock of a foreign corporation must be owned by United States shareholders in order for a finding of a *controlled foreign corporation* (CFC) to be made. §957(a). Second, only such shareholders owning stock at year-end are forced to include their pro rata share of the corporation's *subpart F income.* §951(a).

United States shareholders, foreign personal holding companies *citizens* or *residents* of the United States, *domestic corporations,* and *domestic trusts* and *estates,* unless the estate or trust has no income from sources within the United States. Reg. §1.551-1. United States shareholders of *foreign personal holding companies* are subject to having their ratable shares of *undistributed foreign personal holding company income* imputed to them under §551, as if those funds had been distributed to them.

United States source gross transportation income *transportation income* from *United States* sources. §887(b)(1). The 4 percent tax on gross transportation income applicable to *foreign corporations* and *nonresident aliens* is imposed on United States source gross transportation income. §887(a).

United States tentative tax see *tentative tax, foreign tax credit.*

unit investment trust a *trust* registered under the Investment Company Act of 1940. §851(a)(1). Such

trusts fall into two groupings. The first are trusts authorized to invest in a fixed type of *investment* (e.g., a single series of New York City tax-exempt bonds) with no power to vary their investments; therefore they are treated as trusts rather than *associations taxable as corporations.* Reg. §301.7701-4(c). Such trusts are commonly used to raise capital in public offerings and are often referred to as *fixed investment trusts.* The second type are trusts formed to engage in periodic payments to bank *custodians* in order to invest in designated mutual funds. Reg. §1.851-7(c).

unitization, oil and gas properties a practice whereby two or more *taxpayers* who own individual *property interests* in oil and gas and land agree to operate their property jointly on a voluntary basis or because they are required to do so. Reg. §1.614-8(b)(6). Such an agreement may also arise where owners of several mineral leases agree to pay *royalties* based on *individual* shares of the oil and gas from all the leases. Reg. §1.614-8(b)(6).

unit livestock price method a method of *inventory valuation* used by *farmers* under which livestock raised, or purchased before maturity to be raised to maturity, are grouped by age and class and then valued at normal cost for such groups. Reg. §1.471-6(e). If the farmer bought the animal, it is valued at *cost,* unless it was immature when purchased, in which case its value must be increased annually and consistently with similar animals the farmer raised. Reg. §1.471-6(g). The effect of the system is to *capitalize expenses* for raising animals but to roughly offset the amount realized on their disposition with such capitalized expenditures. If the method is adopted, it must be applied to all raised livestock held for draft, breeding, dairy, or sport purposes. Reg. §1.471-6(f).

unit of production method a *depreciation* method that measures the *useful life* of an asset in terms of its production capacity and allocates *depreciation* according to the units it is responsible for producing. For example, if a business *taxpayer* buys a machine for $10,000, which is estimated to be capable of producing 1,000 widgets during its useful life, and in 1993 it produces 20 widgets, then, assuming no *salvage value,* the depreciation deduction for 1993 under this method is $200 (i.e., $10,000 × 20/1,000).

unit of production method, cost depletion a general method of calculating *cost depletion* under which the *taxpayer's* share of annual sales is multiplied by a fraction:

Predepletion *adjusted basis* in the mineral property

Unsold reserves at end of period
plus sales for the period

The method is also used to deplete *production payments*

which are denominated in volume, rather than money. See Reg. §1.611-2(a)(2)(ii). See *decline in principal method, cost depletion; sum-of-the-dollars method, cost depletion.*

unit of production method, depreciation a method of claiming *depreciation deductions* in proportion to the units produced by the property. For example, if a machine cost $1,000 and could be used in the manufacture of 1,000 widgets, the owner of the machine can claim a depreciation of $1/widget. Such depreciation is outside the *ACRS* system. §168(f)(1)(B). See *depreciation.*

unit of property, repair allowance deduction a portion of a machine or piece of equipment used in a *trade or business* that is a separate unit performing distinct functions. Reg. §1.167(a)-11(d)(2)(vi). The *individual* piece of equipment must be such that it is of the kind the *taxpayer* usually obtains for original installation and ceases to use as a unit. Reg. §1.167(a)-11(d)(2)(iv). Expenditures made on the replacement or repair of such property are considered to be *excluded additions* for purposes of the *repair allowance deduction* under the *class life asset depreciation range system.*

unlimited consent Form 872-A, which indefinitely extends the period for *assessment of deficiencies.* See *waiver of statute of limitations.*

unlimited marital deduction a reference to the present law that the *marital deduction* for both *estate* and *gift taxes* has no monetary or percentage limit as long as the *donee* is a *citizen of the United States.* The rule extends to interspousal transfers of such items as *community property* and certain *terminable interests.* §§2040(b), 2044, 2053, 2056, 2207, 2519. See *marital deduction.*

unmarried head of household see *head of household.*

unnecessary examinations and investigations term used in §7605(b), which provides a limitation on *IRS* discretion, the gist of which is that *taxpayers* shall not be subjected to unnecessary examinations and investigations. The language has force only in cases of oppressive or arbitrary examinations and is rarely of help to the taxpayer. It has developed into a mild *one-examination rule.* See *closed year; second examination.*

unpublished rulings see *rulings.*

unrealistic position by tax return preparer a position for which there is no realistic possibility of being sustained on the merits. See *penalty, unrealistic position by tax return preparer.*

unrealized appreciation an increase in the value of property that the *taxpayer* has not yet realized by *sale* or *other disposition.* See *realization; subsection (e) assets, collapsible corporation.*

unrealized gain appreciation in the market value of *property* that has not yet been *realized.* The *Code* does not tax such *gains.* §61, 1001; Reg. §§1.616(a), 1.1001-1(a). See *realization.*

unrealized gain, loss deferral rule for straddles in the case of any *position* the *taxpayer* held at year-end, the *gain* that would be taken into account as to the position if it were sold at its *fair market value* at year-end. §1092(a)(3). Such *gains* are used to defer *losses* in *straddle* positions. §1092(a)(1)(A). See *loss deferral rule, straddles.*

unrealized loss a *loss* which has not yet been *realized.* For the antonym, see *unrealized gains.*

unrealized receivables or fees, collapsible corporations a class of *section 341 assets,* defined as any contractual or noncontractual right to payment for goods delivered or to be delivered to the extent that the proceeds therefrom would be treated as amounts received from the *sale* or *exchange* of property, other than a *capital asset* or services rendered or to be rendered, to the extent the right was not previously includible in *gross income* under the *corporation's method of accounting.* §341(b)(4). The existence of such assets can contribute to the existence of a *collapsible corporation.* §341(b)(3). The provision, among other things, is clearly designed to prevent sales of goods by *cash method* corporations, followed by immediate *sale* of the *stock* before the company reports the income.

unrealized receivables, partnerships for purposes of the *collapsible partnership rules,* the effect of which is to characterize a portion of the proceeds of a *sale* or *exchange* of a *partnership interest,* or certain disproportionate *distributions* to a *partner,* as being in exchange for non-*capital assets.* The term "unrealized receivables" also includes certain property to the extent of the amount of gain that would have been realized and treated as ordinary income under Code §§617 (*recapture, mining exploration expenditures*); 1245 (*recapture of depreciation* or *cost recovery* on personal property); 1250 (recapture of depreciation or cost recovery on real property); 1248 (certain *foreign corporation stock*); former 1251 (farm loss recapture; *excess deduction account*); 1252 (*farm land recapture*); 1253 (*gains* from *dispositions* of *franchises, trademarks,* and *trade names*); and 1254 (mining, oil, gas, or geothermal recapture), had the partnership sold such property. §751(c). It also refers to amounts not yet included in partnership income from rights to payments relating to sales of goods other than *capital assets* and from services rendered or to be rendered (defined broadly by the courts). §751(c), last paragraph. See Reg. §1.751-1(g). See *collapsible partnership rules; inventory items; section 751 assets.*

unreasonable accumulations tax see *accumulated earnings tax.*

unreasonable compensation an unjustifiably high level of compensation for services. Only reasonable compensation for services actually rendered is *deductible* under §162(a) as a *trade or business* expense (although the nondeductible portion is nonetheless taxable to the payee). The unreasonable portion may be recast as a corporate *distribution* under §301, if paid to a *shareholder*. Reg. §1.162-8. Factors influential in determining whether compensation is unreasonable are (1) industry standards; (2) the skill of the payee; (3) the production of the *employee*; and (4) whether the payment (although seemingly too large) arises from a contingent compensation agreement that was the result of an arm's length *free bargain* between negotiating equals that was reasonable when struck, in which case it will be treated more liberally. In the determination of whether a putative compensation is excessive, bonuses and *fringe benefits* are considered as well. Reg. §1.162-9; Rev. Rul. 56-400, 1956-2 C.B. 116. See, generally, Reg. §1.162-7. See *free bargain concept; golden parachute agreement.*

unrecaptured net section 1231 losses aggregate *net section 1231 losses* (i.e., *section 1231 losses* over *section 1231 gains*) for the last preceding five years beginning after December 31, 1984, over the amount of such losses that were theretofore converted into *ordinary income* by the *recapture* provision of §1231(c)(1). The *net section 1231 gain* is treated as *ordinary income* to the extent that it does not exceed unrecaptured net §1231 loss. See *section 1231 assets.*

unrecognized gain a *gain* which is *realized* but not *recognized.*

unrecognized loss a *loss* which is *realized* but not *recognized.*

unrecovered inventory amount the lesser of the *intercompany profit amount* (the profit inherent in intercompany sales of inventory) in a *consolidated return year* or the *initial inventory amount*. Reg. §1.1502-18(e)(1). To the extent the unrecovered inventory amount of a *corporation* for the current year is less than in the preceding year, the decrease is treated as a *loss* from the *sale* of a *noncapital asset*. Reg. §1.1502-18(c)(2). To the extent the unrecovered inventory amount of a corporation for the current year is greater than for the preceding year, the increase is treated as a *gain* from the sale of a *noncapital asset*. See *initial inventory amount; intercompany profit amount.*

unrecovered losses briefly, *losses* arising from breaches of contract, fiduciary duty, or antitrust violations to the extent they did not create a *tax benefit* to the *taxpayer*. §186(d). The formal definition is cumbersome; it speaks of *net operating losses* (NOLs) for each *taxable year* within the *injury period* to the extent the losses are attributable to a *compensable injury,* reduced by the NOLs that were allowed as offsets against income in earlier years. *Id*. Such NOLs are further reduced by any recovery of a compensatory amount in any other years against which such losses were offset. §186(d)(1)(B). If an *NOL carryover* to the year of receipt of a compensatory amount is attributable to the injury for which the recovery is received, then the *carryover* is reduced by the *deduction* allowed under §186(a) for that recovery. §186(e). If the NOL carryover period has expired with respect to any part of the unrecovered losses sustained because of the injury, then the deduction allowed under §186(a) is correspondingly reduced. §186(e)(1). Recoveries with respect to such losses can, in effect, be received tax-free. §186(a).

unregulated futures contract a *futures contract* that is not a *regulated futures contract.*

unrelated business income tax a tax imposed by §511 on *exempt organizations* as if they were *business corporations*. §511. The *base tax* is *unrelated business taxable income* and *unrelated debt-financed income*. §§512 and 514. There is also a specific exemption for the *first $1,000* of unrelated business income. §512(b)(12).

unrelated business taxable income *unrelated trade or business income* of an *exempt organization,* less directly related *deductions* typical of any *trade or business* (e.g., *expenses, depreciation, losses*), with various modifications. There is also a specific exemption for the *first $1,000* of unrelated business income. §512(b)(12). Otherwise *exempt organizations* are taxed on such income. §511(a). See also §6031(d) (reporting of such information to nontaxable *partners*).

unrelated debt-financed income the same percentage (up to 100 percent) of the *gross income* derived from *debt-financed property* of an *exempt organization,* however characterized (*rents, interest, capital gains,* etc.), as the *average acquisition indebtedness* bears to the average *adjusted basis* of such property. Reg. §1.514(a)-1(a)(1). Average acquisition indebtedness means the average of the amount of outstanding *acquisition indebtedness* at the beginning of each month of the *taxable year* during which an *exempt organization* held the encumbered property. *Average adjusted basis* means the average of the *adjusted basis* for the same period. Reg. §1.514(a)-1(a)(2) and (3). For example, if for two months of the year an exempt organization held debt-financed property with a constant adjusted basis of $200,000 subject to constant acquisition indebtedness of $100,000 at the beginning of each month, and, if the property generated monthly rents of $1,000, then $500 per month is unrelated debt-financed income, subject to taxation as *unrelated business taxable income* at corporate *income tax* rates by §§511(a) and 514(a). Likewise, *recognized capital gains* on the *disposition* of such property are subject to federal income taxes in the same proportion, subject to minor modifications.

unrelated or disproportionate use proceeds the proceeds of a *state or local bond* issue that are applied to a private *business* use that is not related to a government use (i.e., "unrelated") as well as the proceeds that are disproportionately applied to a related government use (i.e.,"disproportionate"), plus any payments, property, or borrowed money with respect to the foregoing. §141(b)(3)(A)(i). Any state or local bond issue is deemed to satisfy the *private security or payment test* if over 5 percent of its proceeds are unrelated or disproportionate use proceeds and the debt service is privately secured or derived. §141(b)(3)(A)(i). As a result of stacking the use of the proceeds in favor of the private sector, the bonds are more likely to be taxable *private activity bonds*. See *private activity bond; private security or payment test*.

unrelated trade or business when *exempt organizations* (other than *federal corporations*) are spoken of, the term means any regularly conducted *trade or business,* even if absorbed within a larger *exempt purpose* (e.g., advertising revenues of a *church*), the conduct of which is not substantially related (aside from the organization's need for income or funds or the use it makes of the profits) to the exercise or performance of the organization's *exempt purpose*. §513(a). Net income from such a business is taxed as if earned by a *corporation*. Only if the trade or business significantly advances the purposes of the organization will it be exempt from tax. Thus, for example, vending machine and laundromat income from students, provided for their convenience and necessary for their daily living, or sales of drugs to patients of staff doctors by a hospital do not generate taxable income to the university or hospital.

unrestricted option see *nonstatutory options.*

unsecured deferred compensation *deferred compensation* that is not evidenced by notes. Rev. Rule. 60-31, 1960-1 C.B. 174. There is little classification of this term.

unspent proceeds penalty a *civil tax penalty* of 1.5 percent imposed on unspent proceeds of a *tax-exempt* construction *bond*. §148(f)(4)(C). There are further sanctions for failure to pay the penalties. The problem arises if the bond proceeds are not spent fast enough to meet the *required expenditure schedule*. This is part of the *arbitrage bond* rules.

unstated goodwill *goodwill,* payments for which are not provided for in the *partnership agreement*. Section 736(a) causes such goodwill, when paid for in connection with the *liquidation* of a *partner's interest in the partnership,* as either a distributive share of partnership income or a *guaranteed payment*. They are one form of *premium payment,* i.e., a payment to a partner which exceeds the *fair market value* of the partner's share of partnership property. See Reg. §1.736-1(a)(2).

unstated interest interest conclusively presumed to exist in certain deferred payment contracts. §483. See *imputed interest; original issue discount.*

unused credit the excess of the *available tax credit* earned for the *taxable year,* over the limitation based on the amount of tax for that year. §46(b)(1).

unused foreign tax otherwise *creditable foreign taxes* that cannot be the subject of a *foreign tax credit* because of the limitations of §904. Reg. §1.904-2(b)(2)(ii). Such amounts generally can be *carried forward* or *carried back* under §904(c).

unused housing credit carryover the excess (if any) of the *unused state housing credit ceiling* for that year, over the excess (if any) of (a) the aggregate *low-income housing credit* dollar amount allocated for the year, over (b) the sum of $1.25 multiplied by the state population, plus the amount of state housing credit ceiling returned in the *calendar year*. §43(h)(3)(D)(ii)(II).

unused state housing credit ceiling the excess (if any) of the sum of [the $ 1.25 multiplied by the population of the *state* and the state housing credit ceiling returned in the *calendar year* for the preceding year] over [the aggregate *low-income housing credit* dollar amount *allocated* by the state for the preceding year]. §42(h)(3)(C). This means that returned credits, like unused credits, may be carried over for one year.

upstream de minimis rule a rule providing that if an entity is directly owned by one or more *deferral entities,* such ownership is disregarded if deferral entities directly own, in the aggregate, 5 percent or less of the entity desiring to make or continue a *section 444 election*. See *tiered structure.*

upstream merger a merger of a *subsidiary* into its *parent corporation.*

usage leases *lease* agreements that provide for rent based upon the time, mileage, production, or other such measures of use of property. Such agreements are regarded as *leases* and, therefore, rental payments may be *deductible.*

use as a residence *personal use* (as defined in §280A(d)(2)) of rented property for more than 14 days and more than 10 percent of the number of days for which the property was rented at *fair market rates* to unrelated *persons*. §280A(d)(1). The effect of use as a residence is to deny *losses* based on *depreciation, cost recovery, insurance, utilities,* or *maintenance expenses*. §280A(c)(5). See *vacation home rules.*

used in the trade or business dedicated to *trade or business* use, even if idle on standby status, but not held as *inventory, stock in trade, dealer property,* or for demonstration (Rev. Rul. 75-538, 1975-2 C.B. 34). See Reg. §1.167(a)-2 (*depreciation*); §§1221(2) (*capital* *asset* status), 1231(b)(1) (*hotchpot* treatment, subject to various further exclusions and inclusions), 165(c) (*loss deductions* for *individuals*), 167(a)(1), and 168(a) (*depreciation* and *cost recovery*).

used property, ADR   property, the *original use* of which does not begin with the *taxpayer*. Reg. §1.167(a)-11(b)(6) (*class life asset depreciation range system*).

used property, depreciation   *realty* or *personal property,* the *original use* of which did not begin with the *taxpayer*. §167(j)(2)(A)(ii) and (j)(4). Such property is confined to slower rates of *depreciation* (but not *cost recovery*) than new property.

useful life   the time during which an asset is reasonably estimated to be used in a *taxpayer's* hands, applied to determine *depreciation* or *amortization deductions* under §167. It is not the same as the physical life of an asset. Except for *ACRS* purposes, *salvage values* are set as of the end of the asset's estimated useful life. It is vital that the useful life of an asset be *ascertainable*; if not, it is not subject to depreciation, amortization, or *cost recovery*. For example, a painting by a Dutch Master has no estimated useful life.

useful life agreement   an agreement between the *IRS* and a *taxpayer* in which they agree in advance to the *useful life* of property for purposes of *depreciation* under §167. See §167(d).

use it or lose it rule   an *IRS*-imposed limit, announced in 1984, on a *flexible spending account* which requires the person having funds in the account to use them up by year-end or forfeit them.

user fee   a fee charged for a government service. For example, the *IRS* charges user fees for *requests for rulings.*

use taxes   see *compensating use tax.*

usurious debt   debt that violates local *usury* laws. Such debt can create *interest expense deductions* and cannot create a *bad debt* deduction if local law renders the debt unenforceable. Reg. §1.166-1(c).

usury   the charging of interest in excess of lawful rates. Usurious interest is generally *deductible,* unless viewed as a gratuitous payment, because it is unenforceable. As to *bad debt losses,* see *usurious debt.*

utility customer rebates   any subsidy paid by a public utility for the purchase of an energy conservation measure. For years after 1992, customers may *exclude* the rebate from gross income. "*Energy conservation measure*" means any installation or modification designed to reduce the consumption of electricity or natural gas or to improve the management of energy demand. The CNEPA of 1992 (Pub. L. 102-486) §1912.

V

VAT   an acronym for *value-added tax*.

VEBA   an acronym for *voluntary employees' beneficiary association*.

VITA   an acronym for *voluntary income tax assistance (VITA)*.

vacation home rules   complex rules embodied in §280A. The following *three tax treatments* are permitted by the Code: (1) If the residence is rented for less than 15 days per year, it is treated as a personal residence and the rent income is excluded from income. Mortgage interest and real estate taxes paid by the taxpayer are allowed as itemized deductions. (2) If the residence is not used for personal purposes for more than the greater of (a) 14 days or (b) 10 percent of the total number of days rented, the residence is treated as rental property. §280A(d). Expenses are allocated between personal and rental days, and any excess loss may be deductible under passive income rules. (3) If the residence is rented for 15 days or more *and* is used for personal purposes for the *greater* of (a) 14 days or (b) 10 percent of the total days rented, its use is treated as partly personal and partly as a residence, and expenses (e.g., maintenance, insurance) are allowed only to the extent of rental income. See *home office deductions; qualified rental period; shared equity financing agreement; use as a residence*.

vaccine excise tax   an *excise tax* on the sale of DPT, DT, MMR, and polio vaccine to compensate for the occasional freak injury those benign, common vaccines may cause. §4131-(b)(1). The money goes to the Vaccine Injury Compensation Trust Fund. §4131-(c)(1).

Vaccine Injury Compensation Trust Fund tax   an *excise tax* fixed at the rate of a fixed dollar amount per dose on a selective list of human vaccines. §4131.

valid return   another term for a signed filing with the *IRS* that contains enough information to enable the IRS to compute and assess a tax liability. §6061. A valid return is commonly required to begin the running of the *statute of limitations* or to avoid penalties. Striking out the penalty of perjury declaration evidently invalidates a return. §6065. See *return*.

valuation basis   a nontechnical term for *basis of property*, determined according to the value of the property as of a certain date. For example, basis in property acquired from a *decedent* acquires a valuation basis (*fair market value* at date of death or six months later). §1014.

valuation, estate and gift taxes   the process of determining the *fair market value* of transferred property, that is, the price at which the property would change hands between a willing buyer and a willing seller, neither being under any compulsion to buy or to sell, both having reasonable knowledge of the relevant facts. Reg. §§20.2031-1(b) (valuation of a *gross estate*), 25.2512-1 (valuation of *gift* property). A gift is valued on the date the gift is made. An estate is valued immediately after the *decedent's* death or, if an *alternate valuation date* election is made, six months after the date of decedent's death, if the result is a tax reduction and a reduction in the estate. §§2032, 2032A, 2512. See *estate tax; gross estate*.

valuation overstatement   see *gross valuation overstatement*.

variable annuity   a form of *annuity* under which the payout, or the premiums paid in, vary with the performance of the investment medium in which the net premiums are invested. Such annuities are taxed like regular annuities, with necessary modifications to account for their peculiarities. See Reg. §§1.72-2(b)(3), -4(d)(3), -7(d), and -11(d); see also §801(g)(1)(A) (tax treatment of the *life insurance company*). See *annuity, generally*.

variable effect items   a shorthand term for items of *partnership income* or *loss* that could have different tax consequences to the *partners*. See §702(a)(1)-(6). These items are broken out separately at the partnership level for tax reporting purposes.

varying interests rule   a shorthand term for §706(c)(2)(B), which requires *partnerships* to compute their *distributive shares* allocable to particular *partners* in accordance with the interest they have over the course of the year. This makes it possible to adjust for such matters on *sales* of *partnership interests* and additions of new partners. It also prevents *retroactive allocations*.

venture capital companies   a nontechnical term for *corporations* that benefit from liberalized diversification standards in the determination of whether they qualify as *regulated investment companies* for federal *income tax* purposes because of their activities in connection with developing innovative businesses. §851(e). For a company to qualify, the SEC must certify that the company is principally engaged in furnishing capital to other corporations that are principally engaged in the development or exploitation of inventions, technological improvements, new processes, or products not previously generally available. §851(e)(1); Reg. §1.851-6(b).

venture capital limited partnership   executives, in this type of *deferred compensation* scheme, invest as *limited partners* in an investment *partnership* furnished with bargain rate loans from the *employer,* hoping for *long-term capital gains* or *appreciation* in the value of the partnership. The *limited* partnership interests may perhaps be subject to the *restricted property* rules of §83, especially the *section 83(b) election.*

verification of returns an affirmation of the truthfulness of the facts upon which a *tax return* is based. *IRS* forms characteristically contain a recitation that the preparer believes the return to be "true, correct, and complete." See §6065.

vessel or aircraft see *transportation income.*

vested accrued benefit that portion of a *participant's* (i.e., a participant in a *qualified retirement plan*) *accrued benefit* that is *nonforfeitable* upon the termination of his or her *participation* in the plan. §411. See *accrued benefits; vesting.*

vesting a concept designed to ensure that a participating *employee* in a *qualified retirement plan* will receive a percentage of his or her *accrued benefit*; it does so by rendering some or all of the accrued benefit *nonforfeitable.* Satisfaction of the *minimum vesting rules* is required if a plan or *trust* is to be qualified under §401(a). §§401(a)(7), 411. To the extent that a participating *employee* in a qualified retirement plan is vested (expressed as a percentage of his or her accrued benefit), then there may be no *forfeiture* of that employee's accrued benefit. For example, if an employee is 50 percent vested and has an accrued benefit of $1,000, then the employee is unqualifiedly entitled to $500. The remaining $500 is accrued, but not vested. Note the distinction for purposes of vesting between the two sources of *contributions* which make up the accrued benefit; that is, *employee* contributions to which the employee must be 100 percent vested at all times (§411(a)(1)), and *employer contributions* that may allow for delayed vesting (§411(a)(2)). As to the latter, see *delayed vesting; normal retirement age; top-heavy plan; vesting schedules.*

vesting schedules various mathematical rates at which *vesting of accrued benefits* occurs. Section 411(a)(2) generally demands that vesting after 1988 not fall short of at least one of two schedules: (1) full vesting after five *years of service (cliff vesting);* (2) "*graded vesting*", ranging from 20 percent after three years to 100 percent after 7 years (known as *three-seven vesting*). Nonvested accrued benefits must be vested at *normal retirement age* (§411(a)) and on certain plan terminations or discontinuations of *contributions* (§411(d)(3)). There must not be discrimination in favor of *highly compensated employees.* §411(d)(1)(A) and (B). *Top-heavy plans* are subject to mandatory accelerated vesting schedules. In addition, the *IRS* has occasionally imposed its own internal views of minimum vesting schedules.

veteran a person who served in the active military, naval, or air service, and was not dishonorably discharged or released. 38 U.S.C. §101(2) (1976). This is the standard the *IRS* uses for purposes of the *qualified veterans mortgage bond* requirements. Reg. §6a.103A-3(c). For a different standard for purposes of qualifying a *veterans' organization* as an *exempt organization* under §501(c)(19), see *veterans' organization; war veteran.*

veterans mortgage bond see *qualified veterans' mortgage bonds.*

veterans' organization a post or organization of past or present members of the *armed forces* of the United States or a related auxiliary, society, *trust,* or foundation, treated as an *exempt organization* if it is organized in the *United States* or its *possessions.* At least 75 percent of the membership must consist of past or present members of the Armed Forces of the United States and substantially all other members must, after August 1982, either be cadets, or their *spouses,* widows, or widowers, and no part of its *net earnings* may *inure* to the benefit of any *private shareholder or individual.* §501(c)(19). A *charitable contribution deduction* is allowed for transfers to such organizations to the extent proceeds are used for certain charitable purposes. §170(c)(3).

vintage account an account containing eligible assets *placed in service* during the *taxable year,* and no others. *Taxpayers* were compelled to use vintage accounts for the purpose of *depreciation* of property under the former *class life asset depreciation range system.* Reg. §1.167(a)-11(b)(3) defines vintage accounts as annual accounts containing property, whether an item or a group, of the same *guideline class,* established for the year property is first *placed in service.* Not all like assets needed to be placed in the same vintage account, and certain items (e.g., new and used) had to be segregated. Reg. §1.167(a)-11(b)(5)(iv)-(vii). The accounts had to carry depreciation *reserves,* which had to be modified by various asset retirements, but the account remained open until all assets in the account were retired. The term is synonymous with a *closed-end* or year-of-acquisition account.

volume cap the heading of §146, which imposes limits on the dollar volume of *private activity bonds* that a *state* can issue (or is deemed to issue) in any *calendar year.* The limits now extend to bonds to finance multifamily housing, *qualified mortgage bonds,* bonds for government-owned facilities such as docks, wharves and airports, as well as *qualified bonds* issued by *exempt organizations.*

volume submitter program an *IRS* program that enables the *Key District* Offices to expedite the issuance of *determination letters* in response to applications for approval of individually designed *retirement plans.* The program is administered locally by each Key District Office. Under the program, a practitioner who qualifies may request the IRS to issue an advisory letter regarding a volume submitter specimen plan. See Ann. 89-107, 1989-36 I.R.B. 25

voluntary compliance resolution program (VCR) a plan announced by the *IRS* in September 1992, designed to encourage pension plan sponsors to approach the *IRS* to help bring their plans into compliance. The *VCR* program will allow eligible plan sponsors to *voluntarily disclose their operational plan defects, pay a fixed compliance fee, agree to make "full correction," and, in appropriate cases, implement appropriate procedures.* Specifics of the program are to be issued at the end of 1992.

voluntary employee contributions *contributions* to *qualified retirement plans* made by *employees* in their discretion. For *deductible* voluntary contributions, see *qualified voluntary employee contribution; voluntary employee savings plan.*

voluntary employee savings plan an otherwise *qualified pension, profit-sharing,* or *stock bonus plan* that provides for completely voluntary *contributions* by covered *employees,* not in excess of a stated annual amount. Rev. Rul. 80-350, 1980-2 C.B. 133. Plans may be qualified even if funded solely with such contributions. Rev. Rul. 80-306, 1980-2 C.B. 131. See also *thrift plans.* For *deductible* contributions, see *qualified voluntary employee contribution.*

voluntary employees' beneficiary associations organizations that provide life, sickness, accident, or other benefits to members or their *dependents* or *beneficiaries,* provided none of their *net earnings inure* to the benefit of any *private shareholder or individual,* except, of course, through benefit payments. §501(c)(9). The organization must consist of *employees,* and membership must be voluntary. Reg. §1.501(c)(9)-1. Such associations are *exempt organizations,* but gifts to them are not *deductible* as *charitable contributions.* §§501(c)(9), 170(c)(2)(B). They are popular devices for avoiding various limitations on employee benefits.

voluntary expenditures *expenditures* that are not required and, therefore, may be denied *deductibility* under §162. The issue arises where an *employee* makes payments on behalf of his or her *employer* (e.g., the cost of picking up business associates at the airport in a private car) when the employment agreement does not require such expenditures.

voluntary income tax assistance (VITA) an *IRS* program that accepts and trains volunteers to help elderly, low-income, and foreign-language-speaking *individuals* with *federal income tax* issues. Volunteers' out-of-pocket expenses are *deductible.* Rev. Rul. 80-45, 1980-1 C.B. 54.

voluntary nondeductible contributions, qualified plans *contributions* to *qualified plans* established by *employers* or to *Keogh plans,* which are not *deductible* by

the payor, but which accumulate tax-free until paid out. Restraints on such contributions, if there were *owner-employees* and regular employees, have been repealed. *TEFRA* §237(c). See *qualified voluntary employee contribution; voluntary employee savings plan.*

voluntary unemployment contributions discretionary *employer* contributions to *state* unemployment insurance funds in excess of the state law requirements. They may be partially or fully *deductible* as *business expenses,* but federal tax treatment varies somewhat according to state law.

volunteer fire department an organization that is organized and operated to fight fires and provide emergency medical help within an area of a *political subdivision* which is not provided with other fire fighting services (subject to limited grandfathering) and required, by written agreement, by the political subdivision to provide fire fighting services in the area. §50(e)(2); Reg. §1.103-16. Obligations of these organizations (referred to as qualified volunteer fire departments) are considered issued by a *political subdivision* and their interest can be tax-exempt, provided that substantially all the proceeds of the issue are used to acquire or improve firehouses or fire trucks. §150(e)(1). In the same vein, volunteer firefighters qualify for special *IRA* deductions on a limited basis. §219(g)(6)(B).

voting securities, regulated investment companies any securities presently carrying the right to vote for the election of directors, but not including shareholders' voting agreements, stock *warrants, stock options,* stock *rights,* convertible debentures, or similar rights acquired in connection with its loan agreements. Rev. Rul. 66-339, 1966-2 C.B. 274. In addition to other restrictions, *regulated investment companies* may lose their status if they hold more than 10 percent of the voting securities of any one issuer. §851(b)(4) (a test applied to half the company's portfolio). See *regulated investment company.*

voting stock, consolidated returns *stock* entitling its holder to participate in electing directors, even if it cannot participate in electing all of the directors. It does not include preferred stock that carries voting rights only for incidental questions, nonvoting preferred stock that is convertible into voting common stock, or nonvoting preferred stock that will acquire voting rights upon the *corporation's* failure to pay *dividends.* In the latter instance, the stock will become voting stock if the corporation defaults and the stock gets its voting rights. Rev. Rul. 71-83, 1971-1 C.B. 268; Rev. Rul. 69-126, 1969-1 C.B. 218. The term is important in determining whether there is sufficient control under §1504(a)(2) to include a corporation in the *affiliated group* in order to file a *consolidated return.* §1504(a).

voting stock, corporate reorganizations *stock* that presently carries the right to significant participation in the management of the affairs of the *corporation*. Rev. Rul. 63-234, 1963-2 C.B. 148. This term does not include stock with contingent voting rights unless and until the contingency occurs.

voting stock, foreign tax credit   common or preferred *stock* with present voting rights. See I.T. 3896, 1948-1 C.B. 72, declared obsolete in Rev. Rul. 68-100, 1968-1 C.B. 572. The *deemed paid foreign tax credit* depends on the recipient's holding at least 10 percent of the *foreign corporation's* voting stock. §902(a); Reg. §1.902-1(a)(8).

voting stock, redemptions   common or preferred *stock* that currently has voting rights. It does not include stock with contingent voting rights unless and until the contingency occurs. Reg. §1.302-3(a). Section 302(b)(2) treats *stock redemptions* which materially reduce the shareholder's interest in voting *stock* as sales rather than *distributions*.

voting stock, regulated investment companies   see *voting securities, regulated investment companies*.

voting trust   a *trust* that holds voting *stock* of a *corporation*. Such trusts are commonly used to concentrate the voting power of *shareholders* over a *corporation*. Such trusts are permissible *shareholders* of *S corporation* stock. §1361.

voting trust certificates   certificates evidencing ownership of an interest in a *voting trust*.

W

wage bracket method   a method of withholding *federal income taxes,* from *wages* authorized by §3402(c). The *IRS* issues annual tables (wage bracket tables) to determine for each period (e.g., a biweekly *payroll period*) the amount of federal income taxes to be withheld, depending on graduated levels of periodic income. The tables sort the *taxpayer* by *filing status* (i.e., single, married, or *head of household*). *Employers* use *employees'* statements printed on *Forms W-4* to determine the employees' *filing status* and number of exemptions. See *income tax withholding.*

wage bracket tables   see *wage bracket method.*

wage continuation plan   a plan whereby salaries are continued during an *employee's* illness or disability. These *wages* are deemed *gross income,* unless specifically exempted under rules for sickness and accident payments (i.e., §§104, 105). See *disability income exclusion.*

wagering   engaging in games of chance, as opposed to making speculative investments. Section 165(d) allows *deductions* for *losses* from wagering transactions only to the extent of any *gains* from such transactions.

wages   remuneration for services performed by an *employee* for his or her *employer,* ostensibly including the cash value of all remuneration paid in any medium other than cash, including retroactive wages, overtime, and back pay awards, salaries, fees, insurance sales commissions, bonuses, pensions, and retirement pay (except if payable as an annuity). Reg. §31.3401(a)-1. Such amounts are subject to *employment taxes.* §§3121(a) (*FICA* taxes), 3306(b) (*FUTA* taxes), 3401(a) (*income tax withholding*). That an item is excluded from *gross income* does not assure freedom from FICA and FUTA taxes (except as to *meals and lodging*). See *wages, Federal Insurance Contributions Act (FICA); wages, Federal Unemployment Tax Act (FUTA).*

wages, Federal Insurance Contributions Act (FICA) remuneration for *employment,* supposedly including the cash value of remuneration paid in any medium other than cash. §3121(a). The name by which the remuneration is designated and the basis upon which the remuneration is paid are immaterial. Reg. §31.3121(a)-1. Various types of remuneration are expressly excluded. Among the exclusions are the amount of remuneration that exceeds the *contribution and benefit base,* pension and retirement pay, *state pick-up plan contributions* by *employers, group-term life insurance premiums* for

retirees, and payments on account of sickness or accidental disability and medical or hospital expenses. Reg. §31.3121(a)(1)-1, (3)-1, and (4)-1. See *employment, FICA taxes; wages.*

wages, Federal Unemployment Tax Act (FUTA) remuneration paid an *employee* by his or her *employer* for employment, including the cash value of all remuneration paid in any medium other than cash, including tips. §3306(b)(s). The name by which the remuneration is designated and the basis upon which the remuneration is paid is immaterial. Reg. §31.3306(b)-1. Various types of remuneration are excluded. Among the exclusions are the amount of remuneration that exceeds $6,000 (§3306(b)(1)), pension and retirement pay (Reg. §31.3306(b)(3)-1), and payments on account of sickness or accident disability, and medical or hospital expenses (Reg. §31.3306(b)(4)-1). See Reg. §31.3306(b)-1 through (b)(10)-1. That an item is excluded from *gross income* does not assure freedom from FUTA taxes (except as to *meals and lodging*). See *wages.*

wages, income tax withholding   remuneration for services performed by an *employee* for his or her *employer,* including the cash value of remuneration paid in any medium other than cash. §3401(a). Wages do not include compensation to 20 categories of persons, principally various public officials, members of the armed forces engaged in combat, persons engaged in agricultural labor, domestic servants, employees of foreign governments or *international organizations,* ministers and certain other religious officials, people under age 18 who deliver newspapers, and Peace Corps Volunteers. §3401(a)(1). The name by which the remuneration is designated and the basis upon which the remuneration is paid is immaterial. Reg. §31.3401(a)-1(a). Various miscellaneous payments are also excluded, such as *group-term life insurance* premiums, distributions from various *qualified pension plans,* and contributions to *IRAs* if deductible by the employee, other miscellaneous fringe benefits, medical care reimbursements under a *self-insured medical reimbursement plan,* and minor tips. See *wages.*

wages under the control of the employer   the formal term for subject matter of *withholding* taxes on income (i.e., *wages*), other than noncash consideration and tips, less *FUTA* taxes, withholding taxes, and *state* or local taxes on imposed and *withheld* remuneration (other than state and local taxes on tips). Reg. §31.3402(k)-1(a)(1).

waiver   generally, the intentional abandonment of a known right or claim. *Taxpayers* commonly waive their right (1) to have the *IRS* delay *assessment* of a *deficiency* for at least 90 days, and (2) to the protection of the *statute of limitations* so as to extend the period during which the IRS can *assess* a *deficiency.* See *waiver of restrictions on assessment and collection; waiver of statute of limitations.*

waiver of dividend a *shareholder's* disclaimer of his or her right to receive *dividends* from the *corporation* whose stock he or she holds, while the remaining shareholders continue to receive dividends. If such a waiver is effective, the waiving shareholder does not have to include any amount of dividends so waived in *gross income*. A waiver will generally be effective if there is no family or direct business relationship between the majority shareholder who waives his or her right to receive dividends and the minority shareholders who continue to receive dividends. There must also be a *bona fide* business reason for the waiver. Rev. Rul. 53-45, 1953-1 C.B. 178. A waiver will generally not be effective if a majority shareholder waives the right to his or her pro rata share of dividends and the pro rata share of dividends is paid, in the form of increased dividends, to his or her relatives and *employees* as minority shareholders. Rev. Rul. 56-431, 1956-2 C.B. 171.

waiver of family attribution rules a method by which an *individual shareholder* can terminate his or her actual proprietary interest in a *corporation* under a §302(b)(3) *redemption in complete termination of shareholder's interest* and, thus, receive the preferential tax treatment that flows from an *exchange* rather than a *distribution,* by virtue of the *family attribution rules* of §318(a)(1) not being applied. But for this relief provision, ownership of stock by a family member would render a complete redemption unachievable. See *prohibited interest.*

waiver of restrictions on assessment and collection a *taxpayer's waiver* of the *IRS's* duty to *assess* an agreed *deficiency* and collect taxes only after issuing a *statutory notice of deficiency.* §6213(d). *Form 870* is used. The result is to eliminate the *Tax Court* (unless the *statutory notice of deficiency* has been issued) and to force the use of a *claim for refund or credit* (and later a court action if the claim is rejected) if the taxpayer has a change of heart. In most cases, signing the form represents the end of a tax controversy. See Statement of IRS Procedural Rules §601.105(b)(4). It is used at the *District Office* level. Compare the *offer of waiver of restrictions on assessment and collection* (Form 870-AD) used at the *Appeals Office* level in *nondocketed cases,* which is a true offer.

waiver of statute of limitations action by *taxpayers* voluntarily extending the period during which the *IRS* may *assess deficiencies* or bring actions against taxpayers. §6501(c)(4). Provided they are submitted before the *statute of limitations* has run and not under duress, they are valid. *Form 872* is generally used to extend the *assessment period* to a specific date and may be renewed. *Form 872-A,* generally for *Appeals Division,* revocable by Form 872-T, is used to extend the assessment period to a date 90 days after either one of the following: (1) the IRS's mailing of a written notice of ter-

mination of consideration; (2) receipt by the IRS of the taxpayer's election to terminate the agreement; or (3) mailing by the IRS of a *notice of deficiency* (but the time for making assessment will expire 60 days after the period in which an assessment is prohibited). Such waivers may be restricted as to specific issues, limited in time, or relatively unlimited (a so-called unlimited consent). See Rev. Proc. 79-22, 1979-1 C.B. 563.

war veteran an *individual* who has served in the *armed forces* of the United States during a period of war. To qualify for a tax exemption as a *veterans' organization,* such an organization is required to have at least 75 percent of its members be war veterans. §501(c)(19). This requirement has since been amended to replace "war veteran" with "past or present member of the armed forces of the United States." See *veterans' organization.*

war veterans' organization see *veterans' organization.*

wash lease a *sale and leaseback* arrangement under which *rents* exactly match debt service requirements.

wash sales transactions in *stock* (including *options*) or securities or certain *straddles, losses* on which are *deferred* under §1091. The purpose of §1091 is to bar *taxpayers* other than *corporations* from selling stock or securities and promptly repurchasing substantially identical property. The rule applies to *sales* where, within 30 days before or 30 days after the sale, the taxpayer acquires (or contracts to acquire) identical or *substantially identical stock or securities* in a taxable transaction. For example, if a taxpayer sells a block of 100 shares of General Motors on June 30 at a loss and buys 50 shares on July 8, the losses on 50 of the shares will be disallowed. The taxpayer's *basis* in the new 50 shares will be equal to his or her basis in the 50 shares sold, plus any premium paid for the new block, or minus any discount. §1091(d). The rule is logical. For example, if the 100 shares had a basis of $50 each but were sold for $40 and the new block of 50 shares was repurchased for $45, then the basis of the new block would be $55 each. For purposes of the wash sales rule, repurchases are defined to include indirect acquisitions through exercise of rights, warrants, contracts to purchase, or acquisition of options to purchase substantially identical stock or securities. Reg. §1.1091-1(a); Rev. Rul. 77-201, 1977-1 C.B. 250; Rev. Rul. 71-520, 1971-2 C.B. 311.

Ways and Means Committee see *House Committee on Ways and Means.*

wear and tear the physical deterioration of an asset over its useful life. Sections 167 and 168 grant *deductions* for *depreciation* and *cost recovery,* respectively, to restore losses through wear and tear, as well as *obsolescence.*

weighted average exchange rate   the average of the spot exchange rates for each day over a given period of time. See Notice 88-102, 1988-2 C.B. 442. For the purpose of the *appropriate exchange rate,* the weighted average exchange rate is used to translate *nonfunctional currency* distributions from *controlled foreign corporations, foreign personal holding companies, qualified electing funds,* and *qualified business units* into a *taxpayer's functional currency.* See *appropriate exchange rate.*

welfare benefit fund   a fund (defined below) which forms part of an *employer's* plan which provides welfare benefits to *employees* or their beneficiaries. §419(e)(1). A "fund" is primarily (1) any exempt *social club, VEBA, SUTAB trust, group legal services organization*; (2) a *corporation, trust,* or other *entity* that is not tax-exempt (including a *retired lives reserve* held by an insurance company); (3) an account held by any employer for any one, to the extent allowed by regulations; (4) amounts held under an insurance contract covering certain business-related insureds; and (5) amounts held by an insurer under certain *qualified nonguaranteed contracts.* §419(e)(4). "Welfare benefit" means for these purposes any benefit other than (1) one affected by the *restricted property rules*; (2) most *deferred compensation* arrangements whose *deductions* are controlled by §404; (3) *foreign deferred compensation plans*; and (4) (formerly) a *vacation plan* for which accruals are claimed under §463. §419(e(2). While contributions to such funds are generally nontaxable, their *deduction* is generally *deferred* until payment takes place. The principal purpose of §419(e) is to stop employers from taking premature deductions for *expenses* which have not yet been incurred, through interposing intermediary organizations which hold assets used to provide benefits to employees. Nonexempt income of such funds is taxed to employers. §419A(g). See *deferred benefit.*

welfare benefit plan   any one of several plans described in Reg. §1.162-10, established to provide miscellaneous benefits for *employees,* such as dismissal wages, vacations, hospitalization, recreation, or similar benefits. *Contributions* to such plans generally have the attraction of being currently *deductible,* even though payouts may to some extent be delayed.

welfare payments   see *general welfare fund payments.*

western hemisphere trade corporation   a *domestic corporation* all of whose business, other than incidental purchases, was conducted in any country or countries in North, Central, or South America or the West Indies and satisfied certain conditions. *Repealed for taxable years beginning after December 31, 1979.*

willful   generally, deliberate. The word "willfully" in the criminal provisions of the *Code* (§§7201–7207)

connotes a voluntary, intentional violation of a known legal duty.

willful attempt to evade tax   the principal tax crime, described in §7201, providing that "any person who willfully attempts in any manner to evade or defeat any tax" is guilty of a felony, which is punishable by a fine of not more than $10,000 or imprisonment for not more than five years, or both, and the costs of prosecution and any other penalties provided by the law (of which there are many). §7201. The focus is on a voluntary, intentional violation of a known legal duty, something that can be inferred from other facts and circumstances. The second element is uncertain. The statute suggests an attempt is enough, whereas numerous courts call for an actual understatement of tax liability. Finally, there must be a so-called affirmative act of *tax evasion* or attempted tax evasion, not merely nonfiling, but virtually any other evasionary tactic counts. Examples include destroying records or concealing assets. Because §7201 entails a crime, guilt must be shown beyond a reasonable doubt. See *willful.*

windfall   a *gain* that requires no investment or effort. Examples are found money (so-called *treasure trove*) and the punitive two-thirds of a treble damages award under the antitrust laws. Such amounts are clearly taxable. Reg. §1.61-14(a).

withdrawal liability   see *employer withdrawal liability.*

withdrawals of previously excluded subpart F income   the caption of §955, which has the effect of causing previously deferred *subpart F income* (i.e., such income that, but for certain special relief provisions, would have been currently taxed to *United States shareholders*) to be taxed to United States shareholders as withdrawals of certain favored foreign investments occur. The favored investments are those in *less developed countries* and *qualified investments in foreign base company shipping operations.* The less developed country deferral privilege was repealed in 1976, but prior investments remain deferred until withdrawn.

withholding   the process of reducing a payment to another party in order to remit it to the government as a prepaid tax. The most common example entails *employment taxes.*

withholding agent   a person who is required to *deduct* and *withhold* certain *federal income taxes* in accordance with the provisions of §§1441, 1442, 1443, 1446, and 1451 of the *Code,* which provide for withholding of taxes on *nonresident aliens,* withholding of tax on *foreign corporations,* foreign *tax-exempt organizations, foreign partners' effectively connected income,* and *tax-free covenant bonds,* respectively. §7701(a)(16). Such agents are often *employers.* Withholding agents are liable for the taxes that they are required to collect. §1461. Moreover, they are liable for *civil fraud penalties* and *additions to tax,* even if the payee pays its tax liabilities in full. §1463. See *withholding of tax at source.*

withholding allowances units of *personal exemption* (called exemption amounts), used by *individual taxpayers* to reduce current *withholdings* as an offset against the base on which her current *income tax withholdings* are calculated. The claim to such allowances is made on *Form W-4.*

withholding certificate a certificate issued by the *IRS* at the request of either a transferor or transferee of a *United States real property interest* to reduce or eliminate *FIRPTA withholding.* See Reg.§1.1445-3 and Rev. Proc. 88-23, 1988-19 I.R.B. 32. It can be issued on the basis of an exemption from *FIRPTA,* a showing that the seller's *maximum tax* liability is less than the amount otherwise required to be withheld, or an agreement to pay tax. Reg. §1.1445-3. Certificates can be issued to cover multiple sales of real estate within a 12-month period (*blanket withholding certificates*). See *FIRPTA withholding.*

withholding exemption same as *withholding allowance.*

withholding from wages see *income tax withholding.*

withholding of tax at source a term often used to describe the effects of sections such as §§1441 (*foreign* noncorporate payees), 1442 (foreign corporate payees), and 1446 (*foreign partners*) under which United States payors are required to act as *withholding agents* as to 30 percent (or lower *tax treaty* rate) of *dividends, rents, royalties, interest,* and other *fixed or determinable annual or periodical income* paid from sources within the *United States,* unless *effectively connected* with the conduct of a United States *trade or business.* Certain *portfolio interest* is exempt. Foreign partners are taxed at top corporate rates on *effectively connected income.* Intermediaries, e.g., a *domestic trust,* perform the withholding in lieu of the original payor. §§1441(a), 1442(a). For *employer's* withholding of *employee's* income tax, see *income tax withholding.* See *active foreign business income; credit for withholding of tax at source; partnership withholding.* For employer's withholding of employee's income tax, see *income tax withholding.*

withholding return see *return of tax withheld.*

withholding tax a *tax* which is collected by *withholding.* The most common example is an *employer's* withholding of *employment taxes.*

without recourse an indication of no personal liability on a *debt* or other obligation. From a tax perspective, its significance concerns a *taxpayer's* ability to create *basis in property,* hence, *depreciation* and cost recovery *deductions* and *investment tax credits,* even though the debt used to finance the acquisition is merely secured by the property, such that the borrower has no personal liability to the lender. See *at-risk rules, generally; at-risk rules, investment tax credit; substantial economic effect test.*

work clothes see *uniforms.*

working capital the excess of current assets over current liabilities, identifying the relatively liquid portion of total enterprise capital, which constitutes a margin or buffer for meeting obligations within the ordinary working cycle of the business. Accounting Research Bull. No. 43, ch. 3, §A, paragraph 2 of the AICPA. The need for working capital is one justification for retaining earnings and can be used as a defense to the imposition of the *accumulated earnings tax.* Reg. §1.537-2(b)(4). See *Bardahl formula.*

worker's compensation payments received by workers for sickness or accidents arising out of, and in the course of, their employment under a *worker's compensation act.* Such compensation is *excluded* from *gross income* except to the extent the amount received reimburses the taxpayer for previously *deducted medical expenses.* §104(a)(1). The exclusion is applicable to payments received under federal acts and statutes that provide compensation for personal injuries and sickness, state worker's compensation laws, and in the case of death, amounts received as worker's compensation by an *employee's* survivors. Reg. §1.104-1(b); Rev. Rul. 72-400, 1972-2 C.B. 75.

work of art, estate tax contributions any federally copyrighted *tangible personal property.* §2055(e)(4)(B). *Qualified contributions* of a work of art to *qualified organizations* can be segregated into the copyright and the *tangible property* itself for purposes of *charitable contribution deductions* for *estate tax* purposes. §2055(e)(4). For a comparable rule relating to *gift taxes,* see §2522(c).

workout generally, an arrangement between a debtor and a creditor whereby a *debt* is rearranged. For purposes of §108(e)(8), the term includes an *insolvent* corporate debtor or one in a *Title 11 or similar case,* as defined in §368(a)(3) (which includes receiverships, foreclosures, and the like) and, under prior law, a *qualified workout* which restructures the distressed *corporation's* debt. Section 108(e)(8) provides that, even in insolvency or Title 11 situations, unsecured creditors who get relatively small amounts of stock in exchange for debt may cause the debtor corporation to be taxed. It is an exception to the general rule of nontaxability. See *nominal or token shares; qualified workout; stock for debt exception.*

work-product doctrine a judicial doctrine, codified in Rule 26(b)(3) of the Federal Rules of Civil Procedure, which generally prevents the unauthorized disclosure of materials collected or prepared by an attorney in anticipation of litigation, especially conclusions and theories concerning the litigation. The doctrine also applies to an *IRS* tax enforcement *summons,* Fed. R. Civ. P. 26(b)(3), 81(a)(3). Sufficient cause to overcome the privilege may be established in the case of documents and other tangible materials by showing substantial need or that the information could not be obtained elsewhere. However, a higher degree of necessity and hardship must be established where the materials sought reflect the mental processes of an attorney, such as notes prepared by an attorney concerning oral statements obtained from witnesses.

worthless debt   *debt* that becomes *worthless* during the *taxable year.* The worthlessness may be partial or entire, thereby allowing *deductions* for partially (if *business bad debts*) or entirely worthless debts under §166(a). For these purposes, a *debt* generally means a bona fide enforceable obligation, whether or not (1) the debtor is personally liable, or (2) the obligation is presently payable. Reg. §1.166-1(c). Worthlessness arises if the facts indicate that a legal action to enforce payment would in all probability not result in the satisfaction of execution or a judgment. Reg. §1.166-2(b). Bankruptcy of the debtor is inconclusive. Reg. §1.166-2(c). See *debt; identifiable event; partially worthless bad debt; reserves for bad debts.*

worthlessness   being without value as a result of some *identifiable event* occurring in the *taxable year* in which the *loss* resulting from the worthlessness is claimed; the identifiable event limitation is in fact questionable. The standard is virtually impossible to express, but it clearly calls for a rational judgment rather than undue optimism or pessimism. The term is used in connection with *bad debts* and *worthless securities.* §§165, 166. Note that partial worthlessness of a *business bad debt* may be *deductible.* See *worthless debt.*

worthless security   a security, including stock, that has become worthless during the *taxable year.* If a security that is a *capital asset* becomes worthless during the taxable year, the loss is treated as a *capital loss.* §165(g)(1). See also §582(a), (b). For the applicable definitions of the terms "worthless" and "security," see *security, worthlessness; worthlessness.*

worthless stock   see *worthless security.*

wraparound annuities   *annuity* contracts that allow the *annuitant* to select the medium in which the net annuity premiums are invested, such as stocks, bonds, or mutual funds. The *IRS* is hostile to these arrangements but agrees that they may be properly treated as annuities such that the annuitant reports no income or *loss* until payments are made under the contract if the investment is in shares of a mutual fund that is not publicly traded. Rev. Rul. 81-225, 1981-2 C.B. 13.

wraparound loan   a loan in an amount greater than the underlying wrapped loan that it includes. See *wraparound mortgage.*

wraparound mortgage   a *mortgage debt* issued by a buyer in a greater amount than an underlying mortgage that continues to encumber the transferred property. For example, Smith owns an apartment building worth $200,000, subject to a $50,000 mortgage. Jones buys the building for $200,000, of which $50,000 is a cash down payment, providing a mortgage of $150,000 for the balance, and Smith undertakes to continue payments on the first mortgage of $50,000. The $150,000 is a wraparound mortgage. In its pure form, Jones has no liability on the first mortgage and Smith pays the first mortgage holder directly on his own account and not as Jones's agent. With respect to transactions not on the *installment method,* the *IRS* takes the view that if Smith is not personally and principally liable on the first mortgage, then Smith pays as Jones's agent, with the result that there are two mortgages, both of which Jones pays, a first mortgage of $50,000 and a second of $100,000. The result of the IRS's analysis is that Jones's claim for *interest expense deductions* is reduced. See Rev. Rul. 75-99, 1975-1 C.B. 197 (*interest* reclassified as principal on the facts).

written determination   for purposes of a *taxpayer's* right to inspect other taxpayers' submissions to the *IRS,* the term means *rulings, determination letters,* and *Technical Advice Memoranda* issued to a taxpayer or to an *IRS employee* in the course of an *audit* or collection matter. §6110(b)(l); Reg. §301.6110-2(a).

written election of allocation method   an elective method of *allocating interest expenses* under Reg. §1.891-9T(f)(3). It is part of a complex system applicable to determining the *foreign tax credit.* See Notice 89-91, 1989-33 I.R.B. 18.

written notice of allocation   any capital stock, revolving fund certificate, *retain certificate,* certificate of indebtedness, letter of advice, or other written notice that discloses to the recipient, *patron* of a *cooperative,* the stated dollar amount allocated to him or her by the cooperative and the portion, if any, which constitutes a *patronage dividend.* §1388(b).

written separation agreement   a written agreement, signed by husband and wife (or presumably their representatives), prepared in connection with the separation of the parties, whether or not legally enforceable. The term is not defined in the *Code* or *regulations.* Rev. Rul. 73-409, 1973-2 C.B. 19. Payments made after, and pursuant to, a written separation agreement could qualify as *periodic payments* so as to be taxable to the recipient under former §71(a)(2) and *deductible* to the payor under §215. The term is now used in connection with revamped §71(b)(2) as part of the definition of a *divorce or separation agreement.* This is a pre-1984 Act term, whose meaning survived amendment of §71. See §71(b)(2)(B).

wrongful death action an action for damages by survivors of a deceased tort victim. *Damages* received for wrongful death have been ruled *excludable* from *gross income,* whether awarded in a suit or by agreement in lieu of a suit by such survivors for their losses. §104(a)(2); Reg. §1.104-1(c); Rev. Rul. 54-19, 1954-1 C.B. 179. However, to the extent the damages reimburse the *taxpayer* for *medical expenses* previously *deducted,* the amount is included in gross income. Rev. Rul. 75-230, 1975-1 C.B. 93. See *damages.*

wrongful levy a *levy* on exempt property, property in which the *taxpayer* had no interest at or after the time the *lien* arose, a levy pursuant to an invalid lien or in circumstances where the levy would irreparably injure property rights superior to the government's lien. Wrongful levies may also arise because the levy destroys other parties' ability to recover from the debtor despite the fact that in form they hold creditor positions superior to the government's. Reg. §301.7426-1(b)(1). Such levies give the claimant various judicial rights under §7426 and under the Tucker Act (28 U.S.C.A. §1346(a)(2) (1976)). See *property exempt from levy.*

Y

year of acquisition account   a *vintage account,* also known as a *closed-end account,* a type of *multiple asset account.*

year of participation, qualified plans   a period of service during which a *participant* in a *defined benefit plan* enjoys *accrual of benefits.* There are a number of alternate methods of measuring such a period (e.g., *elapsed time method,* actual or implicit *hours of service*), but the overall notion is to measure from the earliest date on which the *employee* became a participant, and (usually) to apply an accrual computation period or periods designated by the plan, unless the elapsed time method is used. Generally, any 12-consecutive-month period can be used as the computation period; the usual choice is to establish one or two entry dates for the plan and to use the anniversary date of the applicable entry date as the computation period. §411(b); Labor Reg. §2530.204-2, -3, and -4. Years of service exclude *breaks in service.*

year of service   generally, a 12-month period during which an *employee* has 1,000 or more *hours of service,* or the equivalent. §410(a)(3)(A). However, in the case of any seasonal industry where the customary period of employment is less than 1,000 hours during a *calendar year,* the Secretary of Labor may prescribe regulations defining the duration of time necessary for a year of service. §410(a)(3)(B). This term is important under the *minimum participation standards* of §410, as well as the minimum *vesting* standards under §411(a).

yield to maturity   in financial parlance, a constant rate of increase over a fixed number of periods, compounded at the end of each of those periods that results in the initial amount (e.g., the *issue price*) increasing to some other amount (e.g., the *stated redemption price at maturity*) at the end of the final of those periods. It is stated as a percent per year, regardless of the actual period. It is also defined as the interest rate at which the *present value* of all payments required to be made under a debt instrument is equal to the *issue price* of the debt. Reg. §1.1272-1(f)(1). It is a common concept in the *original issue discount* area.

Z

ZEBRA an acronym for a *zero balance reimbursement account.*

zero balance reimbursement account a feature of a *cafeteria plan* which provided for reimbursement of uninsured medical and dental expenses or dependent care expenses without establishing an actual account from which payment was made. Under these plans, reimbursements were typically made on payday, with an equal reduction in the *employee's* paycheck for that day. This was often referred to as a "zero balance reimbursement account" or "ZEBRA," which did not qualify under §125. See *flexible spending account.* For more information, see the definition of the companion *benefit bank flexible spending arrangement.*

zero coupon bonds long-term bonds payable without current *interest* with payment of interest at maturity date. The excess of the *stated redemption price at maturity* over *issue price* creates *original issue discount,* thereby creating large *deductible* discount expenses for the issuer. Such *amortization* was financially unrealistic and resulted in major tax savings for the issuer. Obligations issued after July 1, 1982, are subject to calculations that somewhat reduce the tax benefits of zero coupon bonds. They are popular investments for pension plans. See *original issue discount.*